Managers and the Legal Environment

2010 Custom Edition

Constance E. Bagley | Diane Savage

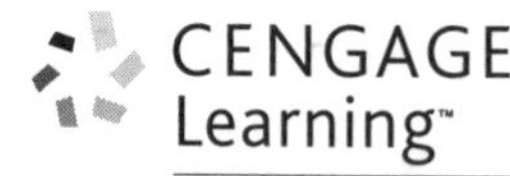

CENGAGE Learning™

Australia • Brazil • Japan • Korea • Mexico • Singapore • Spain • United Kingdom • United States

Managers and the Legal Environment
2010 Custom Edition

Constance E. Bagley | Diane Savage

Executive Editor:
Maureen Staudt
Michael Stranz

Senior Project Development Manager:
Linda de Stefano

Marketing Specialist:
Sara Mercurio
Lindsay Shapiro

Production/Manufacturing Manager:
Donna M. Brown

PreMedia Supervisor:
Joel Brennecke

Rights & Permissions Specialist:
Kalina Hintz
Todd Osborne

Cover Image:
Getty Images*

Source: Managers and the Legal Environment: Strategies for the 21st Century, Bagley/Savage, 2008 South-Western

ISBN-13: 978-1-111-06402-0

ISBN-10: 1-111-06402-4

Cengage Learning
5191 Natorp Boulevard
Mason, Ohio 45040
USA

Cengage Learning is a leading provider of customized learning solutions with office locations around the globe, including Singapore, the United Kingdom, Australia, Mexico, Brazil, and Japan. Locate your local office at: **international.cengage.com/region**

Cengage Learning products are represented in Canada by Nelson Education, Ltd.

For your lifelong learning solutions, visit **www.cengage.com/custom**

Visit our corporate website at **www.cengage.com**

Printed in the United States of America
3 4 5 6 7 12 11 10

CUSTOM TABLE OF CONTENTS

1

LAW, VALUE CREATION, AND RISK MANAGEMENT

INTRODUCTION

Winning Legally[1]

Governments immerse modern organizations "in a sea of law."[2] Public law provides the rules of the game[3] within which firms compete to create and capture value. Law does more than regulate and constrain, however. It also enables and facilitates.[4] Indeed, multiple-country studies reveal that the efficiency of a country's capital markets is directly related to the country's legal environment.[5] Researchers found a statistically significant relationship between a country's economic prosperity, as measured by the per capita gross domestic product, and each of the following:

- Judicial independence.
- Adequacy of legal recourse.
- Police protection of business.
- Demanding product standards.
- Stringent environmental regulations.
- Quality laws relating to information technology.
- Extent of intellectual property protection.
- Effectiveness of antitrust laws.[6]

For example, adequate protection of minority rights increases investment in new ventures.[7] Conversely, excessive regulation, including burdensome licensing requirements and filing fees, can hamper new venture formation.[8]

"Legally astute" managers who understand and proactively manage the legal aspects of business can use the law and the legal system to increase both the total value created and the share of that value captured by the firm.[9] As Tom Hinthorne remarked, "[L]awyers and corporate leaders who understand the law and the structures of power in the U.S.A. have a unique capacity to protect and enhance shareowner wealth."[10] For example, companies can use patents, copyrights, trademarks, and trade secrets to differentiate their products, command premium prices, erect barriers to entry, sustain first-mover advantage, and reduce costs. Managers can also make their own "private law" by entering

1. *See generally* CONSTANCE E. BAGLEY, WINNING LEGALLY: HOW TO USE THE LAW TO CREATE VALUE, MARSHAL RESOURCES, AND MANAGE RISK (2005).
2. L.B. Edelman & M.C. Suchman, *The Legal Environments of Organizations,* 23 ANN. REV. SOC. 479 (1997).
3. DOUGLASS C. NORTH, INSTITUTIONS, INSTITUTIONAL CHANGE AND ECONOMIC PERFORMANCE 3–4 (1990).
4. M.C. Suchman, D.J. Steward & C.A. Westfall, *The Legal Environment of Entrepreneurship: Observations on the Legitimization of Venture Finance in Silicon Valley, in* THE ENTREPRENEURSHIP DYNAMIC: ORIGINS OF ENTREPRENEURSHIP AND THE EVOLUTION OF INDUSTRIES (C.B. Schoonhoven & E. Romanell eds., 2001).
5. R. La Porta, F. Lopez-de-Silanes, A. Shleifer & R.W. Vishny, *Legal Determinants of External Finance*, 52 J. FIN. 1131 (1997).
6. M.E. Porter, *Enhancing the Microeconomic Foundations of Prosperity: The Current Competitiveness Index*, *in* WORLD ECONOMIC FORUM, THE GLOBAL COMPETITIVENESS REPORT 2001–2002 (2002).
7. S. Johnson, R. La Porta, F. Lopez-de-Silanes & A. Shleifer, *Tunneling,* 90 AM. ECON. REV. 22 (2000).
8. S. Djankov, R. La Porta, F. Lopez-de-Silanes & A. Shleifer, *The Regulation of Entry,* 117 Q.J. ECON. 1 (2002).
9. *See* Constance E. Bagley, *Winning Legally: The Value of Legal Astuteness,* 33 ACAD. MGMT. REV. 378 (2008).
10. Tom Hinthorne, *Predatory Capitalism, Pragmatism, and Legal Positivism in the Airlines Industry,* 18 STRATEGIC MGMT. J. 509 (1996). *See also* George J. Siedel, *Six Forces and the Legal Environment of Business: The Relative Value of Business Law Among Business School Core Courses,* 37 AM. BUS. L.J. 37 (2000).

into contracts and crafting certain governance structures. A variety of legal tools, ranging from insurance policies to contractual indemnification provisions and limitations on liability, can help firms allocate and manage risk.

CHAPTER OVERVIEW

The purpose of this chapter is to provide a framework for analyzing the intersection of law and management. It introduces the systems approach to business and society, *a descriptive framework that integrates legal and societal considerations with mainstream theories of competitive advantage and social responsibility. We then outline the four primary public policies furthered by business regulation in the United States. The chapter concludes with a discussion of how legally astute managers can enhance realizable firm value.*

EXHIBIT 1.1 Systems Approach to Business and Society

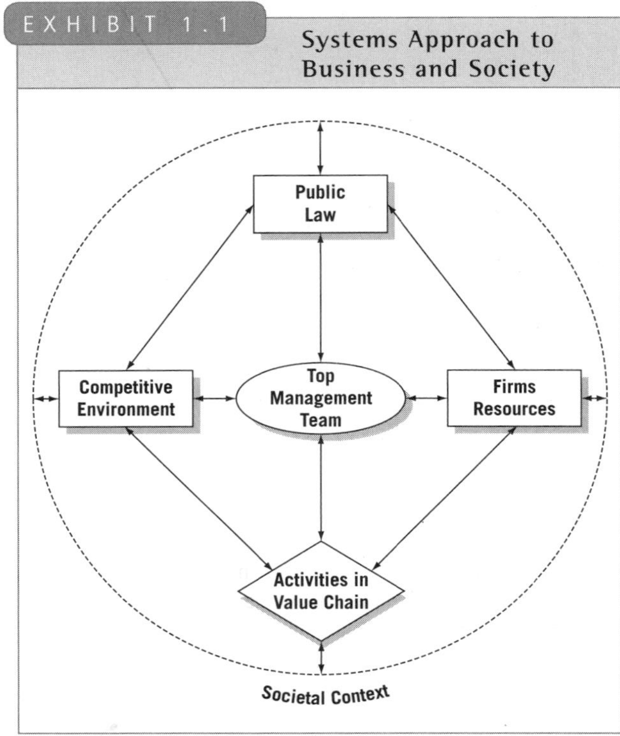

A SYSTEMS APPROACH TO BUSINESS AND SOCIETY

Society grants rights and powers to business, but society can revoke those rights and powers if firms do not act responsibly.[11] As Tom Stephens, CEO of Manville Corporation, put it when he decided to add labels to Manville's fiberglass products warning of possible carcinogenic risks, "The laws of society are more powerful than any law that Congress can put on the books. Woe to any businessman who doesn't read the laws of society and understand them."[12] As a result, "the task of anticipating, understanding, evaluating, and responding to public policy developments within the host environment is itself a critical managerial task."[13] Exhibit 1.1 shows how law and business are part of a broader societal context.

At the center is the top management team (TMT), which evaluates and pursues opportunities for value creation and capture while managing the attendant risks. Given the characteristics of the members of the TMT and their values, the parameters set by the public law, the firm's position within the competitive environment, and the nature and uniqueness of the firm's resources, the TMT defines the value proposition and selects and performs the activities in the value chain.

"THE MORAL ASPECTS OF CHOICE"

The systems approach recognizes that "business decisions consist of continuous, interrelated economic and moral components"[14] and that "the moral aspects of choice" are the "final component of strategy."[15] It also builds on

11. D.J. Wood, *Corporate Social Performance Revisited,* 16 ACAD. MGMT. REV. 691 (1991).

12. W. Glaberson, *Of Manville, Morals and Mortality,* N.Y. TIMES, Oct. 9, 1988. Unfortunately, enlightened self-interest is not always a substitute for government regulation. Paul Krugman criticized former Federal Reserve Board Chair Alan Greenspan and other banking regulators for ignoring warnings about the predatory lending practices that contributed to the $700 billion subprime mortgage crisis in 2007–2008. Paul Krugman, *Disastrous De-Regulation: For Greenspan and Bush, Ideology Trumps Oversight,* PITTSBURGH POST-GAZETTE, Dec. 22, 2007, at B7. Krugman quoted a 1963 essay in which Greenspan dismissed the idea that business leaders would, left to their own devices, "attempt to sell unsafe food and drugs, fraudulent securities and shoddy buildings" as a "collectivist myth" and instead asserted that "it is in the self-interest of every businessman to have a reputation for honest dealings and a quality product." *Id.* Krugman faulted Greenspan for putting "ideology above public protection." *Id.*

13. L.E. PRESTON & J.E. POST, PRIVATE MANAGEMENT AND PUBLIC POLICY: THE PRINCIPLE OF PUBLIC RESPONSIBILITY 4 (1975).

14. D.L. Swanson, *Addressing a Theoretical Problem by Reorienting the Corporate Social Performance Model*, 20 ACAD. MGMT. REV. 43 (1995).

15. E.P. LEARNED, C.R. CHRISTENSEN, K.R. ANDREWS & W.D. GUTH, BUSINESS POLICY: TEXT AND CASES 578 (1969).

stakeholder theory's insight that firms have relationships with many constituent groups, which both affect and are affected by the actions of the firm.[16]

EFFECT OF LAW ON THE COMPETITIVE ENVIRONMENT AND THE FIRM'S RESOURCES

Law helps shape the competitive environment and affects each of the *five forces* that determine the attractiveness of an industry: buyer power, supplier power, the competitive threat posed by current rivals, the availability of substitutes, and the threat of new entrants.[17] Law also affects the allocation, marshaling, value, and distinctiveness of the firm's resources. Under the *resource-based view (RBV)* of the firm, a firm's resources can be a source of sustained competitive advantage if they are valuable, rare, and imperfectly imitable by competitors and have no strategically equivalent substitutes.[18] Conversely, failure to integrate law into the development of strategy and of action plans can place a firm at a competitive disadvantage and imperil its economic viability.[19]

Consider the demise of investment bank Drexel Burnham in the wake of the insider trading scandals of the 1980s; the collapse of the savings and loan industry as a result of massive fraud; the implosion of Barings, England's oldest merchant bank, after illegal trades by Nick Leeson; and the disintegration of the once venerable accounting powerhouse Arthur Andersen. Violation of the criminal laws can also land an executive in prison, as happened to Jeffrey Skilling, former CEO of Enron, who was convicted of fraud and sentenced to more than twenty-four years in prison.

Even if the firm survives, noncompliance destroys value. Illegal conduct can put a firm at a competitive disadvantage by diverting funds from strategic investments, tarnishing the firm's image with customers and other stakeholders, raising capital costs, and reducing sales volume.[20] Researchers found that *Fortune* 500 firms convicted of illegal conduct earned significantly lower returns on assets than unconvicted firms. In 2000, Cendant paid $3.19 billion to settle securities fraud cases against it arising out of its fraudulent financial reporting. The market capitalization of the firm had dropped $14 billion in one day after the fraud came to light. In the case of WorldCom, $200 billion of shareholder value was lost in fewer than twelve months, making it the largest corporate fraud in history.[21]

In contrast, at least under certain circumstances, the ability to proactively go beyond the letter of the law can result in competitive advantage.[22] Legally astute management teams practice *strategic compliance management*.[23] They view the cost of complying with government regulations as an investment, not an expense. Instead of just complying with the letter of the law, they seek out and embrace operational changes that will enable them to convert regulatory constraints into innovation opportunities.[24]

Proactive strategies for dealing with the interface between a firm's business and the natural environment that went beyond environmental regulatory compliance have been associated with improved financial performance.[25] Yet firms' ability to reduce pollution became a source of competitive advantage only after managers replaced the mindset of reducing pollution to meet government end-pipe restrictions with a search for ways to use environment-friendly processes to create value.[26]

LAW AND THE VALUE CHAIN

As seen in Exhibit 1.2, each activity in the value chain has legal aspects. From a firm's choice of business entity to the warranties it offers and the contracts it negotiates, law pervades the activities of the firm, affecting both its internal

16. T. Donaldson & L.E. Preston, *The Stakeholder Theory of the Corporation: Concepts, Evidence, and Implications,* 20 ACAD. MGMT. REV. 65 (1995).

17. Michael E. Porter, *How Competitive Forces Shape Strategy, in* ON COMPETITION 21–22 (1996). *See also* RICHARD G. SHELL, MAKE THE RULES OR YOUR RIVALS WILL (2004).

18. M.A. Peteraf & J.B. Barney, *Unraveling the Resource-Based Tangle*, 24 MANAGERIAL & DECISION ECON. 309 (2003). *See also* GEORGE J. SIEDEL, USING LAW FOR COMPETITIVE ADVANTAGE (2002).

19. Bagley, *supra* note 9.

20. M.S. Baucus & D.A. Baucus, *Paying the Piper: An Empirical Examination of Long-Term Financial Consequences of Illegal Corporate Behavior,* 40 ACAD. MGMT. J. 129 (1997).

21. *See* Richard Breeden, *Restoring Trust,* filed with the WorldCom bankruptcy court on August 26, 2003.

22. Bagley, *supra* note 9.

23. *Id.*

24. Regulation may prompt firms to innovate, making them more competitive. B.M. Mitnick, *The Strategic Uses of Regulation—and Deregulation, in* CORPORATE POLITICAL AGENCY: THE CONSTRUCTION OF COMPETITION IN PUBLIC AFFAIRS (B.M. Mitnick ed., 1993); M.E. Porter & C. van der Linde, *Green and Competitive*, HARV. BUS. REV., May 1995, at 120.

25. *See* W.Q. Judge & T.J. Douglas, *Performance Implications of Incorporating Natural Environmental Issues into the Strategic Planning Process: An Empirical Assessment*, 35 J. MGMT. STUDIES 241 (1998); R.D. Klassen & D.C. Whybark, *The Impact of Environmental Technologies in Manufacturing Performance*, 42 ACAD. MGMT. J. 599 (1999).

26. C. Nehrt, *Maintainability of First Mover Advantages When Environmental Regulations Differ Between Countries*, 23 ACAD. MGMT. REV. 77 (1998).

EXHIBIT 1.2

Law's Role in the Value Chain

Support Activities		
	Firm infrastructure	*Limited liability, corporate governance, choice of business entity, tax planning & securities regulation*
	Human resource management	*Employment contracts, at-will employment, wrongful termination, bans on discrimination, equity compensation, Fair Labor Practices Act, National Labor Relations Act, workers' compensation & Employment Retirement Income Security Act*
	Technology development	*Intellectual property protection, nondisclosure agreements, assignments of inventions, covenants not to compete, licensing agreements & product liability*
	Procurement	*Contracts, Uniform Commercial Code, Convention on the International Sale of Goods, bankruptcy laws, securities regulation & Foreign Corrupt Practices Act*

Inbound logistics	**Operations**	**Outbound logistics**	**Marketing and sales**	**Service**
Contracts *Antitrust limits on exclusive dealing contracts* *Environmental compliance*	*Workplace safety & labor relations* *Environmental compliance* *Process patents and trade secrets*	*Contracts* *Environmental compliance*	*Contracts* *Uniform Commercial Code* *Convention on the International Sale of Goods* *Consumer protection laws, including privacy protection* *Bans on deceptive or misleading advertising or sales practices* *Antitrust limits on vertical and horizontal market division, tying & predatory pricing* *Import/export controls* *World Trade Organization*	*Strict product liability* *Warranties* *Waivers & limitations of liability* *Doctrine of unconscionability* *Customer privacy*

Primary Activities

Margin

Sources: Diagram and text in roman type from MICHAEL E. PORTER, COMPETITIVE ADVANTAGE: CREATING AND SUSTAINING SUPERIOR PERFORMANCE (1985); text in italic type adapted from BAGLEY, *supra* note 1, and M.E. Porter & M.R. Kramer, *Strategy and Society: The Link Between Competitive Advantage and Corporate Social Responsibility,* HARV. BUS. REV., Dec. 2006, at 78.

organization and its external relationships with customers, suppliers, and competitors.

LAW IS DYNAMIC

The systems approach recognizes the dynamic nature of law. Law affects the market and market players, but market players also affect the law and how it is interpreted, applied, and changed over time. Thus, law is not just a static external force acting upon managers and their firms. Instead, law and organizations are "endogenously coevolutionary."[27] By lobbying legislators and members of the executive branch, forming coalitions, and working directly with regulatory bodies, managers can help shape the environment in which they do business.[28] Conversely, laws enacted in response to corporate misdeeds often impose greater restrictions and costs on business than would have been imposed had firms acted more responsibly at the outset.

LAW AND PUBLIC POLICY

Public law—the formal rules embodied in constitutions, statutes enacted by legislatures, judicial decisions rendered by courts, and regulations promulgated by administrative agencies—both reflects and helps shape social expectations. The laws and regulations applicable to U.S. business in the early twenty-first century further four primary public policy objectives: promoting economic growth, protecting workers, promoting consumer welfare, and promoting public welfare. This typology is depicted in Exhibit 1.3.

Other major economic powers tend to have laws that further these same objectives, albeit with varying degrees of emphasis on the different objectives and varying ways of furthering them.[29] Indeed, much of the current debate on what constitutes good corporate governance turns on how much weight each country gives to the interests of shareholders, debtholders, employees, customers, and suppliers and to the protection of the environment.

27. Edelman & Suchman, *supra* note 2, at 501.

28. As with any other activity, managers engaged in lobbying and other political activities must be mindful of the ethical aspects of their actions. *See* L.G. Weber, *Citizenship and Democracy: The Ethics of Corporate Lobbying*, 6 Bus. Ethics Q. 253 (1996).

29. For example, Germany seeks to promote economic growth by facilitating the capital markets, but its goal of protecting workers has led to the system of codetermination whereby half of the members of the supervisory boards of large German corporations are elected by the workers and unions, and half are elected by the shareholders.

PROMOTING ECONOMIC GROWTH

Various laws and regulations promote economic growth. As Exhibit 1.4 shows, this is done by protecting private property rights; enforcing private agreements; allocating risks;[30] facilitating the raising of capital; creating incentives to innovate; promoting liquid and skilled labor markets; providing subsidies, tax incentives, and infrastructure; and promoting free trade in the global markets.

PROTECTING WORKERS

Worker protection constitutes a second major public policy underlying U.S. business law. As depicted in Exhibit 1.5, this is accomplished by regulating certain terms and conditions of employment, requiring the employer to provide certain benefits, and protecting workers' civil rights. Complying with these requirements imposes costs on employers that society, acting through the legislature and the courts, has deemed it appropriate for employers to bear.

PROMOTING CONSUMER WELFARE

As shown in Exhibit 1.6, business regulation is designed to promote consumer welfare by encouraging the sale of safe and innovative products and services at a fair price, preventing deceptive practices, and protecting consumer privacy.

PROMOTING PUBLIC WELFARE

As depicted in Exhibit 1.7, business regulation promotes public welfare by ensuring the effective administration of justice, collecting taxes and spending money, protecting fundamental rights, and protecting the environment.

POLICY CONFLICTS

Sometimes there is a conflict among these various policies, as seen in the following case, in which the court sought to reconcile the exclusionary rights granted patent holders with the Sherman Act's ban on monopolistic behavior.[31]

30. For an excellent discussion of government's role in allocating risk, see David A. Moss, When All Else Fails: Government as the Ultimate Risk Manager (2001).

31. For further discussion of this conflict, *see* Constance E. Bagley & Gavin Clarkson, *Adverse Possession for Intellectual Property: Adapting an Ancient Concept to Resolve Conflicts Between Antitrust and Intellectual Property Laws in the Information Age,* 16 Harv. J.L. & Tech. 327 (2003).

EXHIBIT 1.3 Underlying Public Policy Rationales of U.S. Laws

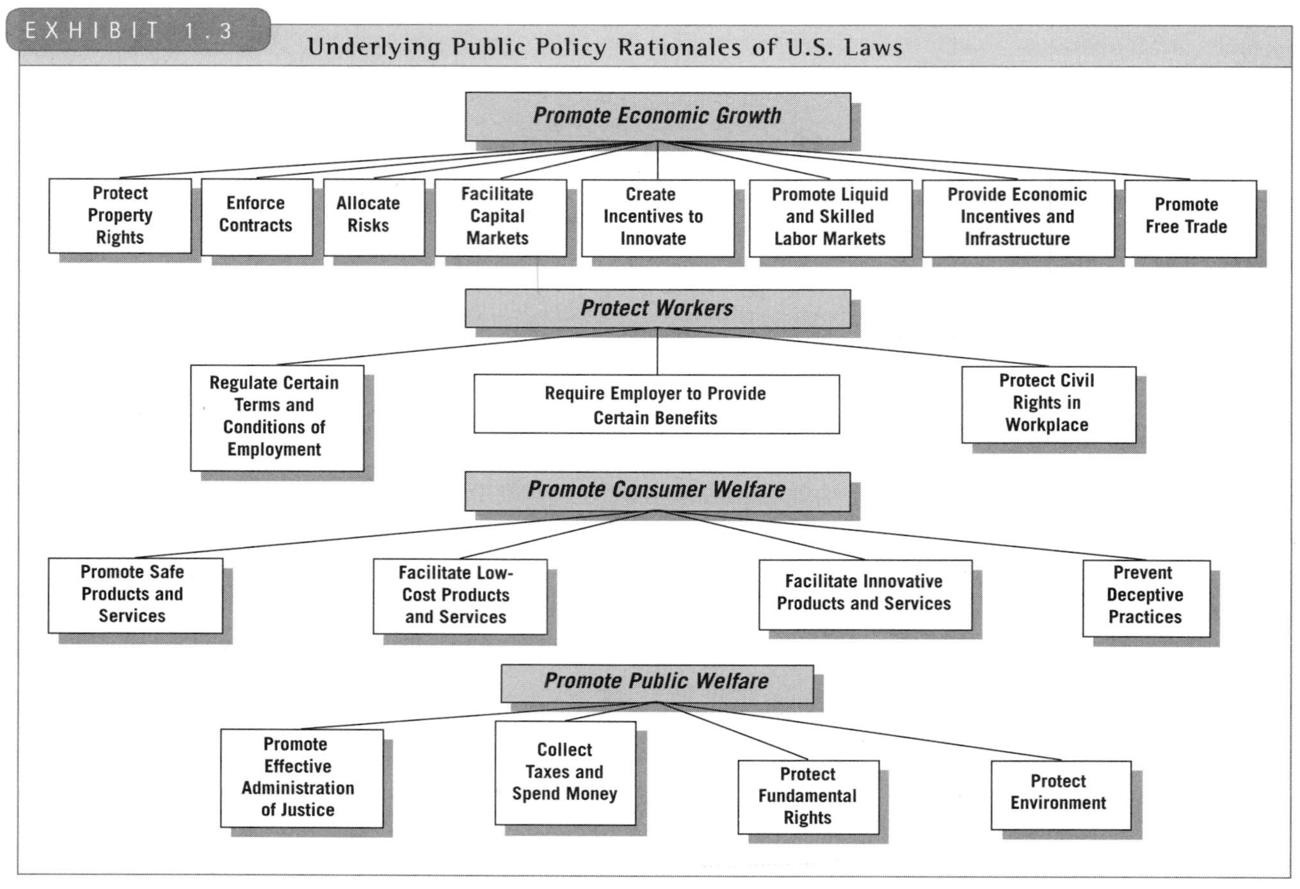

A CASE IN POINT

CASE 1.1

IMAGE TECHNICAL SERVICES V. EASTMAN KODAK CO.

UNITED STATES COURT OF APPEALS FOR THE NINTH CIRCUIT
125 F.3D 1195 (9TH CIR. 1997).

SUMMARY

FACTS Eastman Kodak manufactured, sold, and serviced photocopiers and micrographic equipment. It also made specialized replacement parts for its machines. Kodak originally made the parts available to all buyers, but, as Kodak encountered more competition in the servicing of its machines, it stopped selling parts to independent service organizations (ISOs). Without access to the parts, the ISOs could not compete in the service market. The ISOs sued Kodak, claiming the company had violated antitrust laws under the Sherman Act. After the U.S. Supreme Court ruled that the relevant product market was replacement parts for Kodak photocopying equipment, the case was remanded to the district court for trial.

The jury found in favor of the ISOs and awarded damages totaling $71.8 million, after determining that Kodak had monopolized or attempted to monopolize the sale of service for Kodak machines in violation of Section 2 of the Sherman Act. The district court also imposed a ten-year injunction requiring Kodak to sell all parts to ISOs on reasonable and nondiscriminatory terms and prices. Kodak appealed.

CONTINUED

ISSUE PRESENTED Do Kodak's intellectual property rights in sixty-five patented parts establish a legitimate business justification defense for refusing to sell those specialized parts to the ISOs?

SUMMARY OF OPINION The U.S. Court of Appeals for the Ninth Circuit first explained that in order to prevail on their monopoly claim the ISOs had to prove that Kodak possessed monopoly power in the relevant product market and willfully acquired or maintained that power. Kodak had a 95 percent share of the Kodak high-volume photocopier service market and an 88 percent share of the Kodak micrographic service market. Kodak equipment customers experienced "lock-in," and the ISOs presented evidence that Kodak earned supracompetitive profits in service and overall. As a result, Kodak held a monopoly in the markets for the parts and service of its photocopier and micrographic machines.

The court then addressed whether Kodak had a defense that would protect it from antitrust liability, noting:

> Our conclusion that the ISOs have shown that Kodak has both attained monopoly power and exercised exclusionary conduct does not end our inquiry. Kodak's conduct may not be actionable if supported by a legitimate business justification. . . . A plaintiff may rebut an asserted business justification by demonstrating either that the justification does not legitimately promote competition or that the justification is pretextual.

Kodak asserted that the protection of its patented parts and copyrighted works was a valid business justification for its refusal to sell parts.

The court analyzed the interplay of the competing public policy interests furthered by the antitrust and intellectual property laws:

> While antitrust regulations loathe a monopoly and the dangers it poses to competition, intellectual property statutes create monopolies to stoke the fires of creativity and innovation. Intellectual property law requires that some weight be given to the intellectual property rights of the monopolist. Accordingly, courts generally do not view a monopolist's unilateral refusal to license a patent as impermissible exclusionary conduct.

Although a monopolist's unilateral refusal to license a patent or copyright, or to sell its patented or copyrighted work, may constitute exclusionary conduct, the court held that a monopolist's "desire to exclude others from its [protected] work is a presumptively valid business justification for any immediate harm to consumers."

Nonetheless, in this case the evidence suggested that Kodak's refusal to sell parts to the ISOs was not motivated by the desire to protect its intellectual property rights: "Kodak's parts manager testified that patents 'did not cross [his] mind' at the time Kodak began the parts policy." In other words, the legitimate business justification presumption had been rebutted and shown to be pretextual. To find otherwise would obstruct the ultimate aim of both areas of law: furthering the public interest. In the words of the court, "Neither the aims of intellectual property law, nor the antitrust laws justify allowing a monopolist to rely upon a pretextual business justification to mask anticompetitive conduct."

RESULT The trial jury's verdict in favor of the ISOs was affirmed, but the appeals court reversed the damages award after finding that certain losses were not caused by Kodak's actions. The court remanded the case to the lower court with instructions to amend the terms of the injunction to allow Kodak to charge any nondiscriminatory price the market would bear.

EXHIBIT 1.4 How U.S. Law Promotes Economic Growth

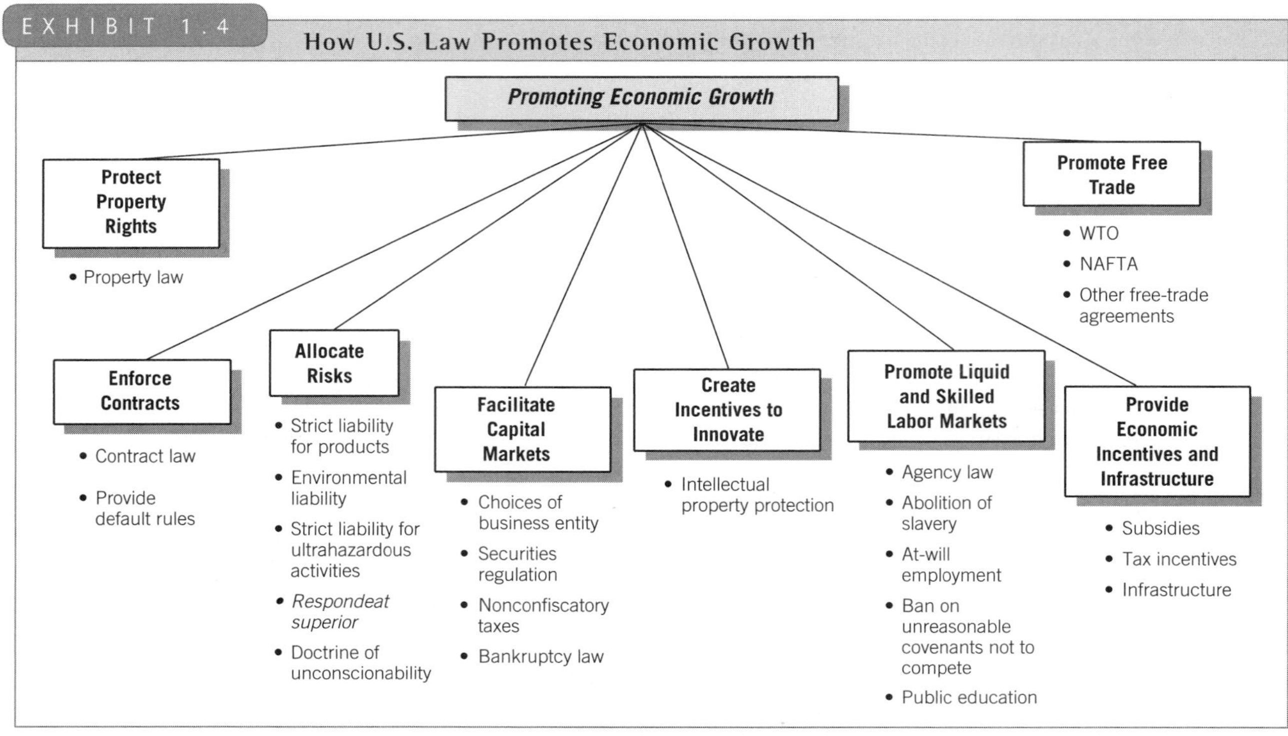
Promoting Economic Growth
Protect Property Rights
• Property law
Promote Free Trade
• WTO
• NAFTA
• Other free-trade agreements
Enforce Contracts
• Contract law
• Provide default rules
Allocate Risks
• Strict liability for products
• Environmental liability
• Strict liability for ultrahazardous activities
• *Respondeat superior*
• Doctrine of unconscionability
Facilitate Capital Markets
• Choices of business entity
• Securities regulation
• Nonconfiscatory taxes
• Bankruptcy law
Create Incentives to Innovate
• Intellectual property protection
Promote Liquid and Skilled Labor Markets
• Agency law
• Abolition of slavery
• At-will employment
• Ban on unreasonable covenants not to compete
• Public education
Provide Economic Incentives and Infrastructure
• Subsidies
• Tax incentives
• Infrastructure

EXHIBIT 1.5 How U.S. Law Protects Workers

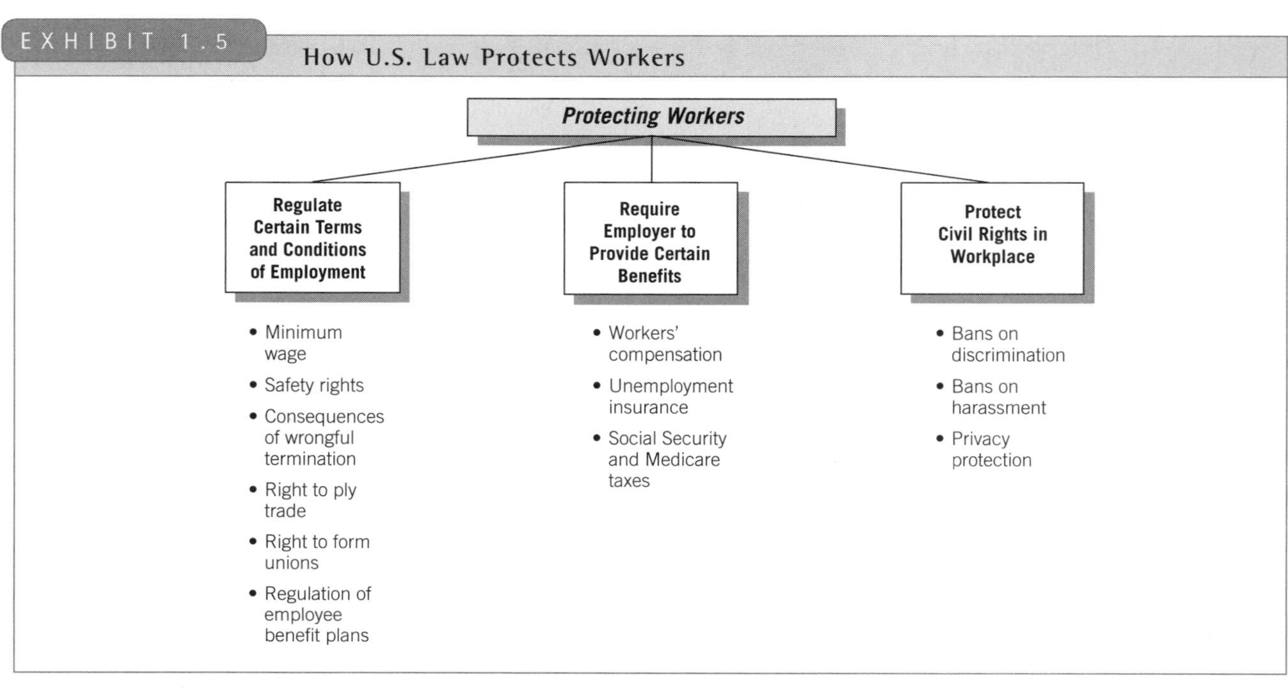
Protecting Workers
Regulate Certain Terms and Conditions of Employment
• Minimum wage
• Safety rights
• Consequences of wrongful termination
• Right to ply trade
• Right to form unions
• Regulation of employee benefit plans
Require Employer to Provide Certain Benefits
• Workers' compensation
• Unemployment insurance
• Social Security and Medicare taxes
Protect Civil Rights in Workplace
• Bans on discrimination
• Bans on harassment
• Privacy protection

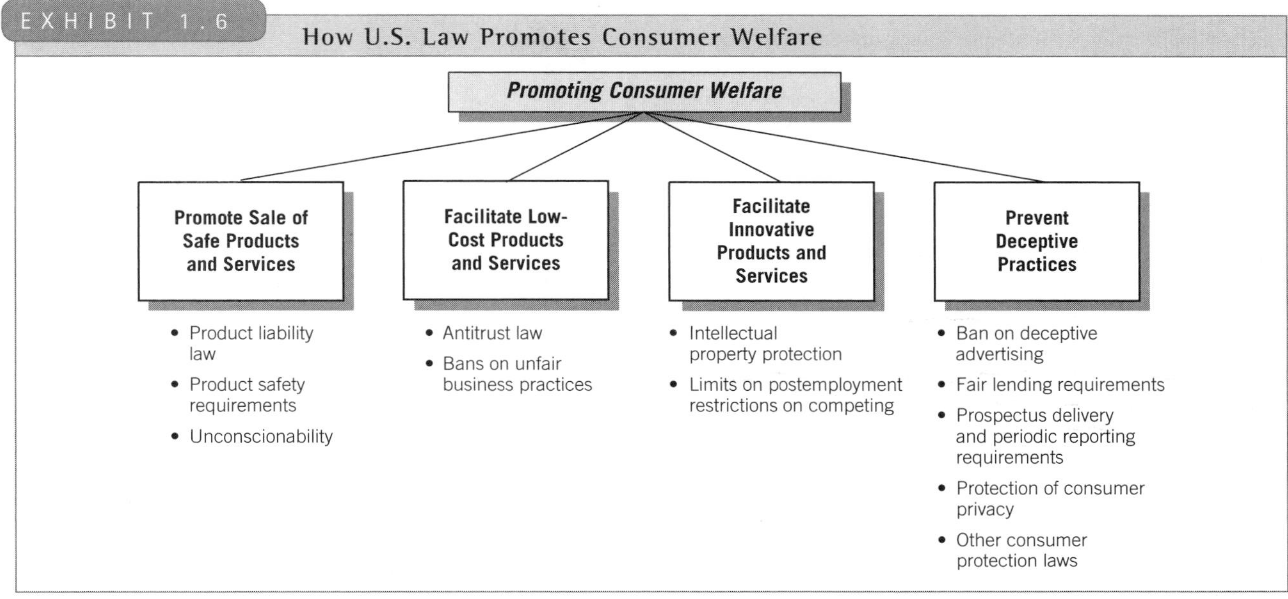
EXHIBIT 1.6
How U.S. Law Promotes Consumer Welfare
Promoting Consumer Welfare
Promote Sale of Safe Products and Services
• Product liability law
• Product safety requirements
• Unconscionability
Facilitate Low-Cost Products and Services
• Antitrust law
• Bans on unfair business practices
Facilitate Innovative Products and Services
• Intellectual property protection
• Limits on postemployment restrictions on competing
Prevent Deceptive Practices
• Ban on deceptive advertising
• Fair lending requirements
• Prospectus delivery and periodic reporting requirements
• Protection of consumer privacy
• Other consumer protection laws

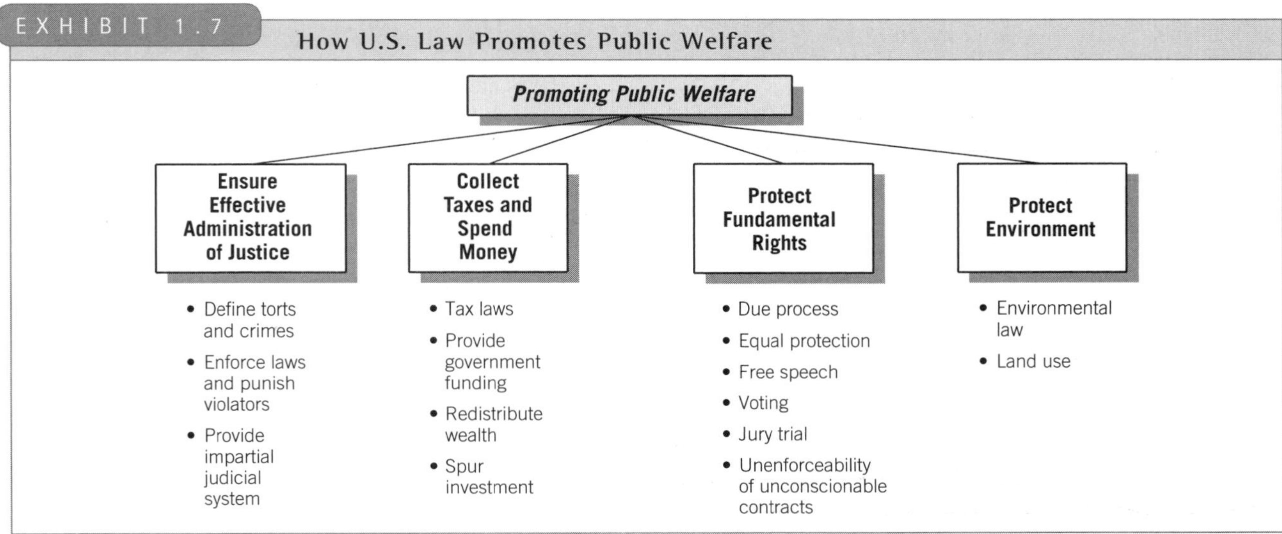
EXHIBIT 1.7
How U.S. Law Promotes Public Welfare
Promoting Public Welfare
Ensure Effective Administration of Justice
• Define torts and crimes
• Enforce laws and punish violators
• Provide impartial judicial system
Collect Taxes and Spend Money
• Tax laws
• Provide government funding
• Redistribute wealth
• Spur investment
Protect Fundamental Rights
• Due process
• Equal protection
• Free speech
• Voting
• Jury trial
• Unenforceability of unconscionable contracts
Protect Environment
• Environmental law
• Land use

THE LEGALLY ASTUTE MANAGER

At its core, *legal astuteness* is the ability of a manager to communicate effectively with counsel and to work together to solve complex problems.[32] For example, legally astute managers can (1) negotiate contracts as complements to trust building and other relational governance techniques to define and strengthen relationships and reduce transaction costs, (2) protect and enhance the realizable value of the firm's resources, (3) create options through contracts and other legal tools, and (4) convert regulatory constraints into opportunities.[33]

32. Bagley, *supra* note 9.

33. *Id.*

Legal astuteness has four components: (1) a set of value-laden attitudes about the importance of law to the firm's success, (2) a proactive approach to regulation, (3) the ability to exercise informed judgment when managing the legal aspects of business, and (4) context-specific knowledge of the law and the appropriate use of legal tools.[34]

VALUE-LADEN ATTITUDES

Legal astuteness begins with respect for the law. Legally astute management teams appreciate the importance of meeting society's expectations of appropriate behavior and of treating stakeholders fairly.

They accept responsibility for managing the legal dimensions of business and recognize that it is the job of the general manager, not the lawyer, to decide which allocation of resources and rewards makes the most business sense. At the end of the day, as long as counsel has not advised that a particular course of action is illegal, it is up to the management team to determine whether a particular risk is worth taking or a particular opportunity is worth pursuing.

PROACTIVE APPROACH

Legally astute managers include legal considerations at each stage of strategy development and implementation. They bring counsel in early and do not wait until a deal has been struck or a problem has arisen to seek legal advice. They demand legal advice that is business oriented and expect their lawyers to help them address business opportunities and threats in ways that are legally permissible, effective, and efficient.

EXERCISING INFORMED JUDGMENT

Legally astute managers understand that legal analysis is often ambiguous and that managing the legal aspects of business requires the exercise of informed judgment. Even the most skilled and experienced advisers, including lawyers, get it wrong sometimes. A lawyer's judgment can be clouded by personal interests, such as increasing billable hours or angling for more power within the firm, or by oversensitivity to risk or overconfidence bias.[35] Legally astute managers take this into account when factoring in legal advice.

34. *Id.*

35. D.C. Langevoort & R.K. Rasmussen, *Skewing the Results: The Role of Lawyers in Transmitting Legal Rules*, 5 So. Cal. L. Rev. 375 (1997).

CORPORATE LEADERS GATHER IN A FIELD OUTSIDE DARIEN, CONNECTICUT, WHERE ONE OF THEM CLAIMS TO HAVE SEEN THE INVISIBLE HAND OF THE MARKETPLACE.

Every legal dispute is a business problem requiring a business solution.[36] Legally astute managers take responsibility for managing their disputes and do not hand them off to their lawyers with a "you-take-care-of-it" approach.

CONTEXTUAL KNOWLEDGE OF THE LAW AND LEGAL TOOLS

Legally astute managers have content-specific knowledge of the law and the application of legal tools. Managers who can harness the creative power of legal language are more adept at seeing and shaping the legal structure of their world. They are also better equipped to communicate effectively with their lawyers.

The law offers a variety of tools that legally astute management teams can use to increase realizable value and to manage risks. For example, the choice of business entity (e.g., corporation, partnership, or limited liability company) will determine the investors' liability for the debts of the business, the rights and responsibilities of the managers and equity holders, and the level at which tax is levied. The legal tools of greatest relevance to managers will vary with the firm's overall strategy, its external environment, and the stage of development of the business. Certain tools, such as contracts, have broad application.

Exhibit 1.8 shows how managers can use law to create and capture value and to manage risk during the five stages of business development:

- Evaluating the opportunity and defining the value proposition, which includes developing the business concept for exploiting the opportunity.

36. Constance E. Bagley, *Legal Problems Showing a Way to Do Business,* Fin. Times, Nov. 27, 2000, at 2.

- Assembling the team.
- Raising capital.
- Developing, producing, and marketing the product or service.
- Harvesting the opportunity, through sale of the venture, an initial public offering of stock, or reinvestment and renewal.[37]

Exhibit 1.8 does not purport to be an all-inclusive list of techniques for using the law to increase realizable value while managing risk. Rather, it is intended to suggest both the variety and the pervasive nature of the tools available.

37. Professors Stevenson, Roberts, and Grousbeck break down the entrepreneurial process into five steps: (1) evaluating the opportunity, (2) developing the business concept, (3) assessing required resources both human and capital, (4) acquiring needed resources, and (5) managing and harvesting the venture. HOWARD H. STEVENSON, MICHAEL J. ROBERTS & H. IRVING GROUSBECK, NEW BUSINESS VENTURES AND THE ENTREPRENEUR 17–21 (2d ed. 1985). The five steps in Exhibit 1.8 are based on this model with modifications to reflect the fact that very different but significant legal issues arise in the course of marshaling human resources and raising money and in the course of managing the development, production, marketing, and sale of the product or service and in harvesting the venture.

EXHIBIT 1.8 Legal Tools for Increasing Realizable Value While Managing Risk

Stages of Business Development

Managerial Objectives		Evaluating Opportunity and Defining Value Proposition	Assembling Team	Raising Capital	Development, Production, Marketing, and Sale of Product or Service	Harvest
	Create and Capture Value	• Ask whether idea is patentable or otherwise protectable. • Examine branding possibilities.	• Choose appropriate form of business entity and issue equity to founders early. • Structure appropriate equity incentives for employees. • Enter into nondisclosure agreements and assignments of inventions. • Secure intellectual property protection.	• Be prepared to negotiate downside and sideways protection and upside rights for preferred stock. • Be prepared to subject at least some founder stock to vesting. • Sell stock in exempt transaction.	• Implement trade secret policy. • Consider patent protection for new business processes and other inventions. Select a strong trademark and protect it. Register copyrights. • Enter into licensing agreements. • Create options to buy and sell. • Secure distribution rights. • Decide whether to buy or build, then enter into contracts.	• If investor, exercise demand registration rights or board control to force initial public offering or sale of company. Rely on exemptions for sale of restricted stock. Ask whether employee vesting accelerates on an IPO or sale. • Negotiate and document arrangements with underwriter or investment banker.
	Manage Risk	• Ask whether anyone else has rights to opportunity.	• Document founder arrangements and subject founders' shares to vesting. • Analyze any covenants not to compete or trade secret issues. • Require arbitration or mediation of disputes. • Comply with antidiscrimination laws in hiring and firing. Institute harassment policy. • Avoid wrongful termination by documenting performance issues. • Caution employees on discoverability of e-mail. • Provide whistleblower protection.	• Be prepared to make representations and warranties in stock-purchase agreement with or without knowledge qualifiers. • Choose business entity wtih limited liability. • Respect corporate form to avoid piercing of corporate veil.	• Enter into purchase and sale contracts. • Impose limitations on liability and use releases. Buy insurance for product liabilities. Recall unsafe products. • Create safe workplace. • Install compliance system. • Do due diligence before buying or leasing property to avoid environmental problems. No tying or horizontal price-fixing. Integrate products; no bolting. • Be active in finding business solutions to legal disputes. • Avoid misleading advertising. • File tax returns on time and pay taxes when due. Do tax planning.	• Be mindful of difference between letter of intent and contract of sale. • Consider entering into no-shop agreements if buyer. Negotiate fiduciary out if seller. • Disclose fully in prospectus or acquisition agreement. Secure indemnity rights. • Perform due diligence. • Allocate risk of unknown. • Make sure board of directors is informed and disinterested. • Ban insider trading and police trades.

GLOBAL VIEW

Lobbying in the European Union

"This shows you are never too old to get surprised."[38] That was the reaction of sixty-six-year-old Jack Welch, CEO of General Electric, after the European Commission rejected GE's proposed $40 billion merger with Honeywell International on the grounds that the vertical combination would have anticompetitive effects in the European Union (EU).[39] The deal would have vertically integrated two aerospace industry leaders. GE builds engines and leases aircraft, while Honeywell makes avionics components. The decision marked the first time a merger of two U.S.-based corporations was derailed by EU officials.[40] Welch remarked, "In this case, the European regulators' demands exceeded anything I or our European advisers imagined, and differed sharply from antitrust counterparts in the U.S. and Canada."[41]

GE's experience is illustrative of the new reality facing U.S.-based corporations wishing to gain access to the 500 million consumers[42] in the EU's twenty-seven members: finalizing a deal will require spending significant time in Brussels, Belgium, the EU's center of operations. "Every company of a certain size has a Washington representative. Increasingly the same is true of Brussels," commented Hogan & Hartson LLP partner Raymond S. Calamaro.[43] An estimated 15,000 lobbyists now are pursuing their clients' interests before the EU.[44]

GE hired Finsbury International Political and Regulatory Advisers to present its position to regulators in individual nations,[45] but the company apparently underestimated the level of resistance it faced in Europe. GE did not make concerted efforts to influence the outcome until after the competition commission, a branch of the European Commission, released a preliminary draft opinion opposing the combination.[46] The competition commission makes recommendations to the EU regarding issues that affect economic competition within the member states.[47] After the adverse preliminary opinion was released, GE representatives met with competition regulators and official members of the European Commission,[48] but by then the die was already cast.

One angle GE did not pursue was asking for public support from U.S. politicians.[49] That instinct was probably correct. Experts believe that public comments by President Bush and Treasury Secretary Paul O'Neill in the weeks leading up to the European Commission's decision on the GE–Honeywell merger, which were calculated to put pressure on regulators, served only to stiffen the EU's position.[50] In another example, Homeland Security Secretary Tom Ridge attempted to negotiate with individual European countries the right to station U.S. Customs officers in their ports to inspect cargo containers.[51] EU representatives informed him that he needed to pursue the matter through the collective government, not on a nation-by-nation basis. Once he conformed to their protocol, the EU consented to Ridge's plan in its entirety.

GE's U.S. competitors, including United Technologies and Rockwell International,[52] and foreign rivals, such as Rolls Royce, lobbied aggressively against the deal.[53] European antitrust regulators are often more sympathetic to competitors than U.S. authorities are. "The European Union's process offers a lot more credence to competitors," commented a Washington-based management consultant.[54] He added, "In the U.S., they listen to competitors but don't

CONTINUED

38. *GE Pessimistic on Merger,* CNNMoney.com, June 14, 2001, http://money.cnn.com/2001/06/14/europe/ge/.
39. Edmund Andrews & Paul Meller, *Europe Ends Bid by G.E. For Honeywell*, N.Y. Times, July 4, 2001, at 1.
40. *Id.*
41. *GE Pessimistic on Merger, supra* note 38.
42. *European Imperialism*, Wall St. J., Oct. 31, 2007, at A20.
43. Nicholas Kulish, *Euro Brash,* Wash. Monthly, Apr. 1, 2004, at 24.
44. Carol Matlack, *Why Brussels Is Abuzz with Lobbyists*, Bus. Wk., Oct. 29, 2007, at 81.
45. Boris Grondahl & James Ledbetter, *Cutting Europe's Red Tape*, Industry Standard, July 9, 2001, *available at* http://findarticles.com/p/articles/mi_m0HWW/is_27_4/ai_76964767.
46. Andrew Ross Sorkin, *G.E.-Honeywell: If at First . . .* , N.Y. Times, June 27, 2001, at 1.
47. Andrew Ross Sorkin, *U.S. Businesses Turn to Europe to Bar Mergers*, N.Y. Times, June 19, 2001, at 1.
48. *Id.*
49. *Id.*
50. Andrews & Meller, *supra* note 39.
51. Kulish, *supra* note 43.
52. Sorkin, *supra* note 47.
53. Paul Meller, *Another Step in Killing Deal For Honeywell*, N.Y. Times, June 26, 2001, at 1.
54. Andrews & Meller, *supra* note 39.

give them as much weight."[55] An attorney who has brought several antitrust complaints before the EU explained, "If you are a competitor, you want to go where you will get a sympathetic hearing."[56]

According to Mario Monti, the EU Commissioner in charge of competition from 1999 to 2004,[57] objectivity was not an issue. Three months before the GE–Honeywell merger was rejected, he commented: "We are sufficiently non-naive as to be able to discount the elements provided by competitors for their vested interests. Competitors are a rather powerful source of overall assessment of mergers and potentially for the identification of remedies."[58] Ultimately, GE unsuccessfully appealed the European Commission's decision and was ordered to pay the legal costs of the EU and its allies, including Rolls Royce.[59]

GE and Honeywell are not the only companies to run afoul of European competition officials. EU regulators blocked WorldCom's proposed $130 billion purchase of Sprint in 2000. As discussed further in the "Inside Story" in Chapter 17, the European Court of First Instance upheld a $689 million fine against Microsoft for antitrust violations in September 2007. In total, the court levied $3.6 billion in antitrust fines during the first three quarters of 2007.[60]

European companies are not exempt from European antitrust scrutiny. In 2000, Volvo and Scania, the two Swedish truck manufacturers, scuttled a proposed $7 billion merger due to antitrust concerns.[61]

Nor are the issues limited to antitrust law. EU environmental laws applicable to the preparation of poultry meat have effectively kept U.S. producers out of Europe even though the concerns expressed are related to the disposal of chemical cleaners, not the healthfulness of the meat itself.[62] Sales in Romania of chicken from the United States dropped from $63 million to zero after Romania joined the EU in 2007.[63]

As Europe continues to consolidate its economic power, its impact on corporate planning and strategy will become even more evident. Consumer privacy, emissions standards, chemical usage, and accounting standards are just a few areas where EU and U.S. law differ.[64] Companies doing business globally may find themselves having to conform to EU regulations when they impose higher standards than the United States. Managers hoping to participate in creating the rules governing their business would be wise to start booking flights to Brussels.

55. *Id.*
56. Sorkin, *supra* note 47.
57. Mario Monti biographical information on Bruegel website, http://www.bruegel.org/Public/Scholars.php?ID=1167&contactID=2041.
58. Sorkin, *supra* note 47.
59. Paul Meller, *GE and Honeywell Lose Merger Appeal*, INT'L HERALD TRIB., Dec. 14, 2005, *available at* http://www.iht.com/articles/2005/12/14/yourmoney/merger.php.
60. Matlack, *supra* note 44.
61. Sorkin, *supra* note 47.
62. *European Imperialism, supra* note 42.
63. *Id.*
64. Kulish, *supra* note 43; *European Imperialism, supra* note 42.

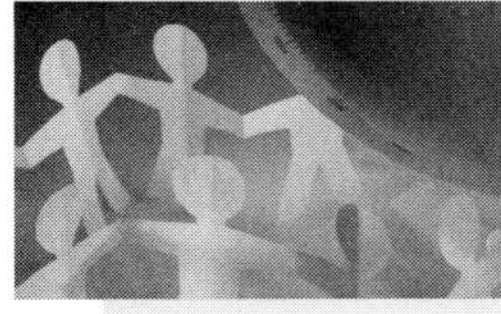

THE RESPONSIBLE MANAGER

DEALING WITH POSSIBLE CORPORATE WRONGDOING

Managers who hear rumors of wrongdoing may be tempted to dismiss them in hopes they are not true. At the other extreme, sometimes managers respond by immediately launching a full-fledged internal investigation. Given the spate of corporate scandals and attendant bad publicity in recent years, the impulse to be aggressive is understandable. No firm wants to be seen as even tacitly condoning illegal behavior. In most circumstances, however, neither extreme is the optimal first step.

Managers disregard rumors of unlawful behavior at their peril. According to Harry Brandon, a business intelligence specialist with Smith Brandon International, 75 percent of investigations uncover proof of a violation.[65] If the rumors are true, not only is the company in trouble, but managers with knowledge, or a reasonable suspicion, of

CONTINUED

65. Joseph Finder, *The CEO's Private Investigation,* HARV. BUS. REV., Oct. 2007, at 54.

the offending activities may face civil claims and perhaps criminal charges.

It is difficult to investigate quietly, however. Employees must be questioned, and documents and files reviewed; meanwhile, expenses begin to add up.[66] The more people who know about the investigation, the less likely the news can be contained. At the very least, the people with whom the company does business—up and down the value chain—as well as competitors often will learn of an investigation and may assume that where there's smoke, there's fire. Although the investigation may turn up nothing, bad publicity can hurt even a company without broad name recognition.

Unfortunately, there is no strict formula for determining when an investigation is necessary. The facts of each particular situation will drive the ultimate decision. Managers should evaluate the information on hand and remember the advice of Eric Klein, a partner at Katten Muchin Rosenman LLP, "[M]anage the process, not the crisis."[67]

If managers are dealing only with loose talk, the first step is to make preliminary inquiries. As noted by Lockheed Martin's chief financial officer Christopher Kubasik and its general counsel James Comey, "Even the FBI, when it conducts criminal investigations, does not go from zero to 60 right out of the gate."[68] Depending on the issue and the corporate structure, this can mean contacting the executive responsible for ethics or the person in charge of internal auditing.[69]

If additional information seems to substantiate the rumors, even partially, the manager should report that information either to the appropriate superior or through the corporate ethics program. At this point, the CEO should inform the board. Doing so protects the CEO from personal liability; it also promotes good corporate governance practice within the firm, positions the CEO to participate in designing the inquiry, and reinforces the CEO's position as someone concerned with the company's interests.[70] The board will likely be helpful in assessing the situation and deciding which steps to take next.[71]

Documents will be a primary source of information in any investigation.[72] Whenever an investigation appears likely, managers should remind all employees to retain physical and electronic documents, including e-mails. Disposing of documents in anticipation of a government investigation can result in significant penalties, including charges of obstruction of justice, and future juries may draw negative inferences about the purpose behind the document destruction. If no investigation is commenced, the retained documents can be discarded pursuant to an appropriate preexisting document retention and deletion policy. Chapter 3 outlines the essential elements of an effective document retention policy.

Employee statements are the other primary investigatory source. Michael N. Levy, Michael L Spafford, and Lothlorien S. Redmond of Washington law firm McKee Nelson LLP stress the importance of trying to minimize the impact of an investigation on the day-to-day workings of the company. This may include providing employees with legal representation:

> [I]t is frequently in the best interests of the corporation to pay legal fees for counsel to represent employees—whether or not those employees are alleged to have participated in any alleged wrongdoing. Contrary to what some might assume, providing counsel for employees usually increases the efficiency and completeness of an investigation. An internal investigation is a stressful, anxious time for employees. Talking to an investigator can seem intimidating, and even the most well-intentioned employees who have done nothing wrong do not always know how best to respond.
>
> Providing counsel to represent the interests of these employees often makes them more comfortable speaking with investigators and allows them to focus on their work while their lawyers focus on the investigation. Providing counsel also may be an important incentive for employees to stay with the company during a critical time.[73]

One way managers can keep from being preoccupied with an investigation is to remember that internal investigations are best made independently.[74] This means bringing in outside experts to conduct the inquiry. Unlike in-house counsel, third-party investigators are free from the appearance of potential biases and lend an air of objectivity. Their reports may be important defense tools if the government becomes involved.[75] Once outside examiners have been brought in, managers should cease digging around on their own.[76] Managers should keep abreast of the investigators' progress but remember that undue management snooping can compromise the independence of the official probe[77] and divert managers' attention from the business of creating and capturing value.

66. *Id.*

67. *Id.* at 58.

68. *Id.* at 56.

69. *Id.*

70. *Id.* at 58.

71. *Id.* at 60.

72. Michael N. Levy, Michael L. Spafford & Lothlorien S. Redmond, *The Changing Nature of Internal Probes,* Fin. Exec., Jan. 1, 2007, at 51.

73. *Id.*

74. *Id.*

75. *Id.;* Finder, *supra* note 65, at 54.

76. Finder, *supra* note 65, at 60.

77. Levy, Spafford & Redmond, *supra* note 72.

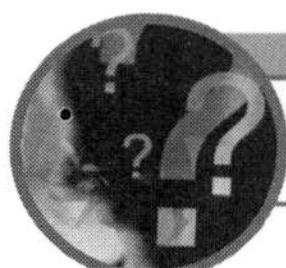

A Manager's Dilemma

Putting It into Practice

Guanxi: Networking or Bribery?

Johanna Lu is the new head of international business development for Dexter Motors, a leading manufacturer of heavy truck engines. Dexter has recently entered into a joint venture with the Chinese state automotive company to produce fuel-efficient, low-emission engines. From conversations with business school classmates working in China, Lu knows that companies in China engage in a variety of political activities. These range from providing questionable gifts or money, inviting government officials to banquets, hiring the children of government officials, and electing executives as national or local congresspersons, to engaging in *guanxi* (relationship-based) lobbying,[78] making charitable contributions, and reporting important issues to the government.

Only two laws apply to corporate political activities in China.[79] The Election Act of China gives businesspeople the right to be elected as congresspersons. The Criminal Law of China prohibits businesses from paying bribes to government officials, but a payment of money is not considered a bribe unless the amount is significant.

A recent survey of 195 executives attending the Huazhong University of Science and Technology (HUST) revealed a consensus that it was unethical to give money or gifts to government officials or to provide paid travel.[80] Even though paying honoraria for speaking, inviting government officials to banquets, and hiring the offspring of officials are ethically questionable in the West, most of the HUST respondents considered such activities to be ethically acceptable.[81]

Lu knows that her success will depend in part on her ability to work cooperatively with a variety of Chinese government officials. A friend has suggested that she encourage Dexter's local manager to seek election as a congressperson as part of a broader political action initiative. Should Lu encourage the manager to run for office? Engage in *guanxi* lobbying to encourage the district leaders to impose stiffer emissions and mileage requirements for heavy trucks? Hire the son of a prominent local official?

78. For a discussion of *guanxi,* see Xiao-Ping Chen and Chao C. Chen, *On the Intricacies of the Chinese* Guanxi *Development*, 21 Asia Pac. J. Mgmt. 305, 306 (2004) (defining *guanxi* as "an informal, particularist personal connection between two individuals who are bounded by an implicit psychological contract to follow the social norm of *guanxi,* such as maintaining a long-term relationship, mutual commitment, loyalty, and obligation").

79. Yongqiang Gao & Wenchuan Wei, *Are Corporate Political Actions Ethical? An Investigation of Executives in Chinese Enterprises,* 1 Int'l J. Bus. Innovation & Res. 464 (2007).

80. *Id.*

81. *Id.*

Inside Story

MICKEY MOUSE, FAST FOOD, AND CHILDHOOD OBESITY

Advertisers, including Coca-Cola, Hershey, and Kellogg, spend $900 million each year on television ads pitched to children under twelve.[82] Advocacy groups, such as Action for Children's Television (ACT) and Center for Science in the Public Interest (CSPI), and government actors from Congress to the Federal Trade Commission (FTC) to state legislatures have increased the pressure on "family-oriented" companies to consider the impact of their advertising on children's health issues, specifically childhood obesity.[83]

The McDonald's Corporation's Happy Meal fast food-plus-toy children's meal is "arguably the most successful marketing

CONTINUED

82. Brooks Barnes, *Limiting Ads of Junk Food to Children,* N.Y. Times, July 19, 2007.

83. Jess Alderman, Jason Smith, Ellen Fried & Richard Daynard, *Prevention and Treatment: Solutions Beyond the Individual: Application of Law to the Childhood Obesity Epidemic,* 35 J.L. Med. & Ethics 90, 94 (Spring 2007).

strategy in human history . . . turning a visit to a fast food restaurant into a favored activity for children."[84] A Happy Meal consisting of a cheeseburger, small fries, and 1 percent milk has almost as many total grams of fat 27.5 as a Big Mac.[85] This includes four grams of artery-clogging trans fats. The same Happy Meal contains 650 calories.

McDonald's president and chief operating officer Michael Roberts called the Happy Meals promotions with Walt Disney Company's film tie-ins among the company's most successful marketing strategies.[86] Notwithstanding its ability to market films ranging from *Toy Story 2* to *Aladdin* directly to parents and children grabbing a quick bite to eat at McDonald's, Disney announced in 2006 that it was not renewing its co-marketing agreement with McDonald's.

The Childhood Obesity Problem and the Advertising Link

A 2007 symposium article summed up the extent of the childhood obesity problem:

> Childhood obesity is a national public health problem. Regardless of gender, race, socioeconomic status, or geographic location, children are "gaining weight to a dangerous degree and at an alarming rate." Since 1980, the number of overweight children has doubled; among adolescents the number has almost tripled. Today, among children who are more than six years old, about nine million are obese. Many of the factors that contribute to obesity occur at a societal level, prompting the Surgeon General to conclude that preventing obesity is a "community responsibility."[87]

Numerous studies have tied childhood obesity to marketing strategies of food companies.[88] An Institute of Medicine review of 123 empirical studies on the topic concluded that "television advertising 'influences children to prefer and request high-calorie and low-nutrient foods and beverages,' and 'influences the short term consumption of children ages 2–12.'"[89]

Historically, food advertisers have successfully fought off enhanced government oversight. In 1974, in an attempt to halt governmental regulation aimed at stopping marketing that preyed on children's vulnerability, the industry created the Children's Advertising Review Unit (CARU).[90] Industry leaders claimed the CARU would use a strict standard of review in assessing the fairness of children's advertising.[91] Nonetheless, the FTC found that television commercials for unhealthy foods violated the FTC Act. Following a protracted battle, during which members of Congress were lobbied hard by advertising representatives over proposed regulations to curb marketing that targets children, Congress rescinded the FTC's jurisdiction over advertising to children in 1980.[92] Since then, oversight of children's advertising has been left to the CARU.[93]

As the public has become more concerned with childhood obesity, Congress has begun to reconsider its decision to take away the FTC's jurisdiction over the fairness of children's advertising.[94] The Federal Communications Commission is considering a ban on certain types of children's advertising, including interactive commercials.[95] State legislatures in more than thirty states have proposed requiring fast-food labels or limiting the availability of junk food in schools, or both.[96]

Disney Takes a Stand

In May 2006, Disney announced that it would discontinue its marketing relationship with McDonald's when their contract expired at the end of the following year.[97] Anonymous Disney officials were cited as saying that the company wanted to distance itself from the childhood obesity problem, but spokespeople for both companies denied that health concerns played any role in the decision.[98] Yet five months later, in announcing

CONTINUED

84. Juliet B. Schor & Margaret Ford, *Perspectives on the Problem: From Tastes Great to Cool: Children's Food Marketing and the Rise of the Symbolic*, 35 J.L. MED. & ETHICS 10, 12 (Spring 2007) (citations omitted).
85. Nutritional information as disclosed on McDonald's Corp.'s website (last visited May 5, 2008). Popular food items nutritional data are available at http://www.mcdonalds.com/app_controller.nutrition.index1.html. Happy Meals nutritional data are available at http://www.mcdonalds.com/app_controller.nutrition.categories.happymeals.index.html.
86. Melanie Warner, *McDonald's Reaches Deal with Studio,* N.Y. TIMES, July 28, 2005, at 7.
87. Alderman *et al., supra* note 83 (citations omitted).
88. Schor & Ford, *supra* note 84.
89. *Id.*
90. Alderman et al., *supra* note 83.
91. *Id.*
92. *Id.*
93. *Id.*
94. *Id.*
95. *Id.* at 99.
96. Schor & Ford, *supra* note 84.
97. Rachel Abramowitz, *Disney Loses Its Appetite for Happy Meal Tie-Ins*, L.A. TIMES, May 8, 2006, at A1.
98. Eric Noe, *Did Childhood-Obesity Worries Kill Disney-McDonald's Pact?*, May 8, 2006, http://abcnews.go.com/Business/story?id=1937651&page=1.

the health guidelines that now govern the use of Disney characters in advertising, Disney CEO Robert Iger said, "A company such as ours, with the reach we have, has a responsibility because of how much we can influence people's opinions and behavior." He noted the strategic implications of the new guidelines: "There's also a business opportunity here."[99]

If opportunities are gauged by what consumers think, then Iger was correct. A *Wall Street Journal*/Harris Interactive poll conducted just one month after his statement found that 84 percent of American adults believed childhood obesity was a "major problem."[100] Sixty-five percent believed that food advertising was a major factor contributing to the increase in obesity among children.[101] As part of the initiative announced by Iger, Disney will permit its characters to pitch children's foods only if they meet these guidelines:

- Appropriate kid-sized portions do not exceed a cap on calories.
- Total fat does not exceed 30 percent of calories for main and side dishes and 35 percent of calories for snacks.
- Saturated fat does not exceed 10 percent of calories for main dishes, side dishes, and snacks.
- Added sugar does not exceed 10 percent of calories for main dishes and side dishes and 25 percent of calories for snacks.
- Disney will continue to license special-occasion sweets such as birthday cakes and seasonal candy as part of its product range but will limit the number of indulgence items in its licensed portfolio to 15 percent by 2010. In addition, most special-occasion sweets will be available in single-serving packets.[102]

In addition, Disney altered the default makeup of the kids' meals in its theme parks.[103] Milk, juice, or water replaced soft drinks, and a healthier side dish, such as applesauce or carrots, replaced French fries. In the fall of 2007, Disney also began marketing an agricultural line branded as Disney Garden. The line includes teriyaki sugar snap peas, honey orange carrot coins, and an assortment of miniature fruits.[104]

The Center for Science in the Public Interest, an advocacy group that has lobbied against marketing to children, commended Disney's dietary and character use guidelines, saying the move put Disney "head, shoulders, and ears" above other children's entertainment companies, such as Nickelodeon's parent company Viacom, Inc. whose "programming is filled with junk-food ads and whose characters grace all kinds of junk-food packaging."[105]

Critics assert that Disney is not sincere in its efforts to link itself to healthier food choices. They cite continued junk food ads on the company's websites and on its ABC television network, as well as the continued presence of McDonald's vending carts in Disney theme parks.[106] That may be so, but the company's investment in building a health-conscious image could well protect it from onerous future regulations as the laws governing food and advertising continue to evolve.

99. Merissa Marr & Janet Adamy, *Disney Pulls Its Characters from Junk Food*, WALL ST. J., Oct. 17, 2006, at D1.

100. Beckey Bright, *More Americans See Childhood Obesity as Major Problem in U.S., Poll Finds*, WALL ST. J. ONLINE, http://online.wsj.com/article/SB115190208989196887.html.

101. *Id.*

102. Press Release, Walt Disney Company, The Walt Disney Company Introduces New Food Guidelines to Promote Healthier Kids' Diets (Oct. 16, 2006), *available at* http://corporate.disney.go.com/news/corporate/2006/2006_1016_food_guidelines.html.

103. *Id.*

104. *Disney Characters to Push Produce,* CNNMoney.com, Oct. 12, 2007, http://money.cnn.com/2007/10/12/news/companies/disney_characters.ap/index.htm?postversion=2007101212.

105. Marr & Adamy, *supra* note 99.

106. Drew McLellan, *Does Disney Really Care If Your Kids Are Fat?*, The Marketing Minute Blog, Oct. 30, 2007, http://www.drewsmarketingminute.com/2007/10/does-disney-rea.html?referer=sphere_related_content.

KEY WORDS AND PHRASES

five forces 4

legal astuteness 10

resource-based view (RBV) 4

strategic compliance management 4

systems approach to business and society 3

QUESTIONS AND CASE PROBLEMS

This chapter introduced important conceptual frameworks to be used while reading the cases and text and analyzing the Questions and Case Problems in each of the chapters that follow. Questions to consider include:

1. What are the "moral aspects of choice" implicated by the conduct at issue?
2. What effect does this body of law or legal tool have on the competitive environment and the firm's resources?
3. Where does this body of law or legal tool fit in the value chain?
4. What public policies are furthered by this law? To what extent are there conflicts among the policies served and how will they affect the way the law in this area is interpreted, applied, and changed?
5. Does this conduct meet societal expectations? If not, what new laws would be likely to result if a substantial number of firms acted this way?
6. How can managers responsibly help shape the legal environment in which they do business?
7. Did the manager in this situation exemplify the four components of legal astuteness? If not, what could the manager have done differently?
8. How could the managers in this case have avoided the litigation that ensued?

ETHICS AND THE LAW

INTRODUCTION

Ethics Matter

When asked which qualities were most important for successful leaders, legendary investor Warren Buffett responded, "Integrity, intelligence and energy. Without the first, the other two will kill you."[1]

Compliance with the law is just the baseline for effective and responsible managerial action. Legally astute managers consider not only what the firm *can* do but also what it *should* do.[2] Greatness in the global marketplace requires attention to ethics and social responsibility as well as to the financial return to shareholders.[3] Conversely, failure to meet the firm's responsibilities to employees, customers, the community, and the environment "puts at risk the company's ability to operate, grow, and deliver future value to shareholders."[4]

Good ethics are simply good business. As the Business Roundtable, the leading association of CEOs in the United States, proclaimed, "[Long-term] shareholder value is enhanced when a corporation treats its employees well, serves its customers well, fosters good relationships with suppliers, maintains an effective compliance program and strong corporate governance practices, and has a reputation for civic responsibility."[5]

Maintaining a reputation for integrity and honesty is more important than ever as customers vote with their feet and boycott clothing made in sweatshops in Mauritius or gasoline made from oil transported in pipelines built with slave labor in Myanmar. Current and prospective employees also care. Through postings on websites and Internet message boards, questions in job interviews, and contacts between present and past employees, job hunters search for clues to a firm's ethical values when evaluating a potential employer. The mere existence of a code of conduct or a toothless ethics program is not enough to attract individuals who are not just looking for employment, but also want to protect their personal integrity, retirement savings, and future employability by working only for upstanding organizations. For many of the same reasons, the ethical reputation of an employer makes a difference to its current employees as well.

Jurors, as members of the public and arbiters of guilt and damages, also care about a corporation's ethical reputation. In a study conducted partially by the Los Angeles jury consulting firm DecisionQuest, even support from white males—the category of jurors that has historically been most supportive of large corporations—has eroded dramatically in light of recent scandals.[6] According to Arthur

1. Ibolya Balog, *Ethics on Their Shoulders: Boards Bear the Burden,* 20 ACCT. TODAY 12, at 14 (Nov. 27, 2006).
2. C. ROLAND CHRISTENSEN ET AL., BUSINESS POLICY 121 (6th ed. 1987). On legal astuteness, see Constance E. Bagley, *Winning Legally: The Value of Legal Astuteness,* 33 ACAD. MGMT. REV. 378 (2008).
3. LYNN SHARP PAINE, VALUE SHIFT: WHY COMPANIES MUST MERGE SOCIAL AND FINANCIAL IMPERATIVES TO ACHIEVE SUPERIOR PERFORMANCE (2003). *See also* Constance E. Bagley & Karen L. Page, *The Devil Made Me Do It: Replacing Corporate Director's Veil of Secrecy with the Mantle of Stewardship,* 33 SAN DIEGO L. REV. 897 (1999).
4. ROBERT S. KAPLAN & DAVID P. NORTON, STRATEGY MAPS: CONVERTING INTANGIBLE ASSETS INTO TANGIBLE OUTCOMES 165 (2004).
5. THE BUSINESS ROUNDTABLE, PRINCIPLES OF CORPORATE GOVERNANCE 31 (2005).
6. Tamara Loomis, *Business Scandals Rock Juror Attitudes,* 228 N.Y.L.J. 1, 1 (2002).

Patterson, a psychologist with DecisionQuest, "For years, our jury research has shown an increasing distrust of corporate America. Now jurors have validation for their distrust."[7]

Finally, as demonstrated graphically by the passage of the Sarbanes-Oxley Act of 2002, corporate conduct that violates society's expectations can also result in "[n]ew forms of regulation or effective enforcement . . . without regard for feasibility or cost."[8] This insight prompted Professor Christensen and his business policy colleagues to caution students of management fifteen years before the passage of Sarbanes-Oxley that "government regulation is not a good substitute for knowledgeable self-restraint."[9]

CHAPTER OVERVIEW

The purpose of this chapter is to provide a framework for analyzing how ethics, business, and law interact. It explains the business leader's role in setting the ethical tone of the firm and provides several examples of executives who failed to fill that role. The chapter then presents the Ethical Business Leader's Decision Tree, a tool managers can use to evaluate the legal and ethical aspects of their strategy and its implementation.[10]

7. *Id.*
8. CHRISTENSEN ET AL., *supra* note 2, at 461.
9. *Id.*
10. Adapted from Constance E. Bagley, *The Ethical Leader's Decision Tree,* HARV. BUS. REV., Feb. 2003, at 18.

We conclude by providing several positive examples of responsible behavior and suggesting steps managers can take to promote ethical behavior.

THE RELATIONSHIP BETWEEN LAW AND ETHICS

The law does not prohibit all "bad" behavior. An action that is unethical may nonetheless be legal. In finding that former executives of General Development Corporation had not violated a criminal law even though they had "behaved badly," the U.S. Court of Appeals for the Eleventh Circuit explained:

> [I]t is true that these men behaved badly. We live in a fallen world. But "bad men, like good men, are entitled to be tried and sentenced in accordance with law." And, the fraud statutes do not cover all behavior which strays from the ideal; Congress has not yet criminalized all sharp conduct, manipulative acts, or unethical transactions. We might prefer that [the defendants] would have told these customers to shop around before buying. But, "there are . . . things . . . which we wish that people should do, which we like or admire them for doing, perhaps dislike or despise them for not doing, but yet admit that they are not bound to do."[11]

The following case exemplifies the failure of the law to address all unethical conduct.

11. United States v. Brown, 79 F.3d 1550 (11th Cir. 1996).

A CASE IN POINT

CASE 2.1

BAMMERT V. DON'S SUPER VALU, INC.

SUPREME COURT OF WISCONSIN 646 N.W.2D 365 (WIS. 2002).

SUMMARY

FACTS For some twenty-six years, Karen Bammert worked at Don's Super Valu, Inc. in Menomonie, Wisconsin. Her husband was a sergeant in the Menomonie police department. On one occasion, Bammert's husband administered a breathalyzer test to Nona Williams, the wife of Don Williams, owner of Don's Super Valu. Nona failed the test and was arrested for drunk driving. Don's Super Valu then fired Karen Bammert, allegedly in retaliation for her husband's participation in the arrest.

Karen Bammert was an at-will employee. Although at-will employees can generally be fired for any reason or for no reason at all without risk of judicial action, there is a public policy exception to this rule in Wisconsin. An at-will employee can recover for wrongful termination "when the discharge is contrary to a fundamental and well-defined public policy as evidenced by existing law."[12] Bammert sued Don's Super Valu for wrongful discharge, claiming that her firing was contrary to

CONTINUED

12. Brockmeyer v. Dun & Bradstreet, 335 N.W.2d 834, 834 (Wis. 1983).

both the public policy against drunk driving and the public policy promoting marriage, both of which were reflected in existing Wisconsin law.

The trial court rejected Bammert's argument and dismissed the complaint for failure to state a claim. The court of appeals affirmed, and the Supreme Court of Wisconsin accepted review.

ISSUE PRESENTED Does the public policy exception to the employment-at-will doctrine apply when an at-will employee is fired in retaliation for the lawful actions of her nonemployee spouse?

SUMMARY OF OPINION The Supreme Court of Wisconsin began by pointing out that the public policy exception was intended to be a narrow one. For purposes of this exception, a public policy must be clearly articulated, fundamental, and well defined. The court went on to stress the value and importance of the employment-at-will doctrine and advised that employment contracts are the best way to protect against unjust firings.

After acknowledging that the policies implicated in this case were clearly articulated, fundamental, and well defined, the court noted that previous cases had not addressed the vindication of a public policy by a third party: "Bammert was not fired for her participation in the enforcement of the laws against drunk driving; she was fired for her husband's participation." Previous cases had dealt with behavior only within the context of employment.

The Wisconsin Supreme Court concluded that "[e]xtending [the public policy exception] to discharges for fulfillment of an affirmative obligation which the law places on a relative would go too far, and have no logical stopping point." The court feared that the exception, once expanded to include "police officers' spouses fired in retaliation for the officers' conduct in the line of duty," might expand to "spouses of prosecutors, judges, . . . or IRS agents." The court questioned whether "discharges in retaliation for the conduct of nonemployee parents, children, and siblings" would be included in such an exception. The court concluded that the public policy exception to the employment-at-will doctrine should not be expanded to protect an at-will employee from firing in retaliation for the actions of his or her nonemployee spouse.

RESULT The Supreme Court of Wisconsin declined to expand the public policy exception to the employment-at-will doctrine and affirmed the dismissal of Bammert's complaint, leaving her with no legal recourse.

COMMENTS The Wisconsin Supreme Court acknowledged that Bammert's firing was retaliatory and "reprehensible." The dissenting judge lamented that "society owes its police officers a duty not to put them in the no-win position that Bammert's husband was placed in." Some would argue that courts and lawmakers should expand the law to punish all unethical behavior. But, even though courts can and do retroactively expand or contract the law when they elect to interpret it broadly or narrowly, such judicial alteration of the law can lead to inconsistent outcomes when today's case becomes tomorrow's precedent.

Ethics and law are related, however. First, a judge or jury's assessment of the ethical character of an action may determine how the law is interpreted and applied in a given case.[13] Second, law often reflects society's consensus about what constitutes appropriate behavior. Third, law can help define the roles managers play, how they play those roles, and whether they have played them well.[14] Fourth, patterns of unethical behavior tend to result in illegal behavior over time. Therefore, creating an organization that encompasses exemplary conduct may be the best way to prevent damaging misconduct.[15] Finally, as noted earlier, unethical conduct tends, over time, to lead to more onerous business

13. Model Rules of Prof'l Conduct R. 2.1 cmt. at 70 (2002) ("moral and ethical considerations impinge upon most legal questions and may decisively influence how the law will be applied").

14. J. Nesteruk, *A New Role for Legal Scholarship in Business Ethics,* 36 Am. Bus. L.J. 515 (1999).

15. Lynn Sharp Paine, *Managing for Organizational Integrity,* Harv. Bus. Rev., Mar.–Apr. 1994, at 106, 117.

regulation. Passage of the Sarbanes–Oxley Act of 2002 in the wake of widespread accounting fraud and of the Foreign Corrupt Practices Act of 1977 in response to the payment of government bribes by Gulf Oil, Lockheed Aircraft, and other major U.S. corporations are but two examples of this phenomenon.

The Ethical Tone Is Set at the Top

The chief executive officer plays the most significant role in instilling a sense of ethics throughout the organization. As William F. May, chair of the Trinity Center for Ethics and Corporate Policy, explained: "The CEO has a unique responsibility; he's a role model. What he does, how he lives, and the principles under which he operates become pretty much those the rest of the corporation emulate."[16] Ben Heineman, Jr., former general counsel at General Electric, expanded this leadership responsibility to include all corporate executives and noted how even small quips or gestures can hinder company ethics objectives:

> Companies are preternaturally attuned to leadership hypocrisy. The stirring call for performance with integrity at the large company meeting can be eroded by the cynical comment an executive makes at a smaller meeting, by the winks and nods that implicitly sanction improprieties, by personal actions (dishonesty, lack of candor) that contradict company values. It is fundamental: A culture of high standards for employees requires high standards from the CEO and the senior operating and staff officers.[17]

This is not to downplay the role of middle management. An employee's immediate supervisor often has the most direct effect on the employee's choices. Nevertheless, direction from the top signals to middle management that the CEO has a serious commitment to ethics.

A corporation cannot establish an ethical culture overnight but can achieve it through strong leadership and support from the CEO and the board of directors. Conversely, failure to create an ethical culture that enables employees to do what is right can have catastrophic effects.

16. Alden Lank, *The Ethical Criterion in Business Decision Making: Operational or Imperative?*, in Touche Ross & Co., Ethics in American Business: A Special Report 28 (1998) (hereinafter Touche Report).

17. Ben W. Heineman, Jr., *Avoiding Integrity Land Mines*, Harv. Bus. Rev., Apr. 2007, at 100. Reproduced by permission.

THE IMPERIAL CEO

In 2005, the average CEO took home $11.6 million in pay or more than 400 times more than the average worker.[18] The multiple was less than 150 in 1990.[19] Critics of overly generous executive compensation packages argue that putting CEOs on a compensatory pedestal can often lead to greedy and unethical behavior and reinforces narcissistic tendencies. Indeed, some even argue that narcissistic personality disorder (recognized and classified by the American Psychiatric Association) is prevalent within the corporate world for exactly this reason.[20] Sam Vaknin, former director of an Israeli investment firm, who was himself diagnosed with narcissistic personality disorder while imprisoned for engaging in stock manipulation, described the disorder: "The narcissist lacks empathy—the ability to put himself in other people's shoes. . . . He does not recognize boundaries—personal, corporate or legal."[21] Consider Vaknin's description while reading the following examples of executives on trial.

Dennis Kozlowski

Leo Dennis Kozlowski took over as CEO of Tyco International in 1992 and became chair in 1993. In May 2001, at the pinnacle of his career, Kozlowski appeared on the cover of *BusinessWeek*. Less than two years later, Kozlowski was forced to resign when he was charged with tax evasion after allegedly having art he had bought in New York shipped out of state to avoid paying $1 million in New York sales tax. Soon thereafter, Kozlowski and Mark H. Swartz, Tyco's former chief financial officer (CFO), were charged with stealing $600 million from the company. During Kozlowski's reign, Tyco's stock price dropped from a high of $63.21 in 2001 to a low of $6.98 in 2002.[22]

At trial, uncontested testimony revealed that Kozlowski had had sexual affairs with at least two Tyco employees and spent tens of millions of Tyco's money to purchase and outfit apartments in New York.[23] Kozlowski allegedly spent $2 million on his wife's birthday party and billed half of the cost to Tyco. Among other items paid for as corporate

18. Phred Dvorak, *Theory and Practice: Limits on Executive Pay: Easy to Set, Hard to Keep,* Wall St. J., Apr. 9, 2007, at B1.

19. *Id.*

20. Tim Race, *Like Narcissus, Executives Are Smitten, and Undone, by Their Own Images,* N.Y. Times, July 29, 2002, at C4.

21. *Id.*

22. Floyd Norris, *Tyco to Pay $3 Billion In Settlement,* N.Y. Times, May 16, 2007, at 1.

23. Alex Berenson, *Tyco Chief and His Deputy Avoid Convictions, but Not Tattered Reputations*, N.Y. Times, Apr. 3, 2004, at C5. Reproduced by permission.

expenses were a $6,000 shower curtain, a $15,000 poodle-shaped umbrella stand, a $6,300 sewing basket, two sets of sheets for $5,960, a $2,200 wastebasket, coat hangers totaling $2,900, and a $445 pincushion.[24]

Ironically, about a month before prosecutors announced the tax evasion charges, Kozlowski had cautioned graduating students at St. Anselm's College:

> As you go forward in life, you will become leaders of families, communities and even companies. . . . You will be confronted with questions every day that test your morals. The questions will get tougher and the consequences will become more severe. Think carefully, and for your sake, do the right thing, not the easy thing.[25]

In 2005, a jury convicted Kozlowski of grand larceny, conspiracy, and fraud. He was sentenced to eight and a third to twenty-five years in prison.[26] He will not be eligible for parole until January 17, 2014.[27] In addition, Kozlowski must repay $97 million to Tyco and is responsible for another $70 million in fines.[28] He was incarcerated in the Mid-State Correctional Facility in Marcy, New York, pending appeal.[29]

The Rigas Family

John J. Rigas, founder and former CEO of Adelphia Communications Corporation, and his son, Timothy, the company's former CFO, were convicted in 2004 of defrauding investors out of billions of dollars by looting Adelphia, the nation's fifth-largest cable company. Eighty-year-old John received a fifteen-year sentence; Timothy received twenty years.[30] Appeals failed, and the men were ordered to surrender to the Federal Bureau of Prisons in mid-2007.[31] Another son, Michael, the former chief operating officer, pled guilty to falsifying records and was sentenced to ten months of home confinement.[32]

The family had used the company as their personal piggy bank and engaged in extensive, undisclosed self-dealing. They misappropriated Adelphia money to cover margin calls on their personal portfolios, purchase timber rights to land in Pennsylvania, construct a golf course on private land, pay off personal loans and family debts, and purchase luxury condominiums for the family in Colorado, Mexico, and New York City.[33] Financial data were fabricated through what James R. Brown, Adelphia's former vice president of finance and the prosecution's star witness, called "aggressive accounting."[34] After Adelphia revealed in March 2002 that it had understated its debt and overstated the number of subscribers to its services, its market capitalization dropped from $4.6 billion to $3.4 billion in two days of trading.[35] By June 2002, when Adelphia filed for bankruptcy protection, its capitalization had plummeted to just $31.5 million.[36]

Jacob Alexander

Within three months, Jacob "Kobi" Alexander went from being the CEO of Comverse Technology, Inc., a leading voicemail software and hardware producer, to a fugitive from justice. In 2006, Alexander was charged with fraud, conspiracy, and money laundering stemming from an employee stock option backdating scheme. According to the Securities and Exchange Commission, on at least twenty-six occasions since 1991, Alexander falsified stock option grant dates. Instead of pricing the options at the stock price on the date of grant, he allegedly determined Comverse's lowest share price in the previous period and then had forms prepared, sometimes months later, that made it look as if the options had actually been granted on that day. Looking at eight suspicious grants during that time period, the *Wall Street Journal* calculated the odds of Alexander actually selecting all of those advantageous dates in advance at one in six billion.[37] Had Alexander correctly reported the option

24. Linda Hales, *The Curtain That Just Won't Wash,* WASH. POST, Apr. 3, 2004, at C1.
25. Berenson, *supra* note 23.
26. Mark Maremont, *Tyco Figures Will Be Jailed at Least Seven Years,* WALL ST. J., Sept. 20, 2005, at C1.
27. N.Y. State Department of Correctional Services' "Inmate Lookup" website, http://nysdocslookup.docs.state.ny.us/GCA00P00/WIQ3/WINQ130 (last visited July 24, 2007).
28. Maremont, *supra* note 26.
29. *60 Minutes* interview (CBS television broadcast July 29, 2007).
30. Roben Farzad, *Jail Terms for 2 at Top of Adelphia*, N.Y. TIMES, June 21, 2005, at 1.
31. *Rigases Told to Report to Prison*, N.Y. TIMES, June 28, 2007, at 13.
32. Chad Bray, *Adelphia Ex-Executive Avoids Jail for False Report,* WALL ST. J., Mar. 4, 2006, at B4.
33. SEC v. Adelphia Commc'ns Corp., Litigation Release No. 17627, *available at* http://www.sec.gov/litigation/litreleases/lr17627.htm.
34. Christine Nuzum, *Star Witness in Adelphia Case Felt "Relief" When Fraud Got By,* WALL ST. J., May 18, 2004, at C6.
35. Floyd Norris, *Loans Backed by Company Helped Family to Buy Shares,* N.Y. TIMES, March 28, 2002, at 1; Jared Sandberg & Joann Lublin, *Questioning the Books: Adelphia Draws Market Criticism over Debt, Loans,* WALL ST. J., Mar. 29, 2002, at A4; Floyd Norris, *Adelphia May Redo Results to Show $2.3 Billion Debt,* N.Y. TIMES, Apr. 17, 2002, at 4.
36. Peter J. Howe, *Trying Too Hard to Please Wall Street: Pressure to Keep Stock Price High Led to Telecom's Fall,* BOSTON GLOBE, June 30, 2002, at G1.
37. Charles Forelle & James Bandler, *The Perfect Payday—Some CEOs Reap Millions by Landing Stock Options When They Are Most Valuable; Luck—or Something Else?,* WALL ST. J., Mar. 18, 2006, at A1.

grant dates, Comverse would have been required to take a charge against earnings for granting "in the money" options, that is, options with a strike price less than the underlying stock's fair market value on the date of grant; the employee-recipients might also have had adverse tax consequences. (Option backdating is discussed further in Chapter 14.)

The ensuing investigation revealed that Alexander had done more than tinker with grant dates. In 1999, he allegedly created a slush fund and instructed subordinates to invent fake employees, whose names were interspersed with those of real employees on option approval documents submitted to the board.[38] After the board signed off on the grants, the options designated for the phony employees were dumped into the fund.[39] Over the years, hundreds of thousands of options were stashed in the fund and then given to employees as rewards or incentives to remain with the company. As part of at least one such "bonus," Alexander also had the vesting period of 48,000 options altered so that the recipient could sell the underlying shares immediately to reap a $2 million windfall. When the company's auditor, Deloitte & Touche LLP, asked for documentation related to option grants, Alexander directed an employee to remove the report page containing information about the slush fund options. Confronted with the backdating allegations, Alexander justified his actions by stating that it was a common business practice.

Instead of fighting the charges, Alexander fled to Namibia.[40] He had wired $57 million to Israeli bank accounts earlier in the month.[41] Even though Alexander was arrested in Namibia in September 2006 and recent changes to Namibia's extradition laws permitted his delivery to the United States, he was set free on a $1.4 million bond. He was, however, prohibited from leaving Windhoek, the country's capital, and required to report to an Interpol office twice a week.[42]

Conrad Black

Conrad Black, the former chair and CEO of media conglomerate Hollinger International, along with three other Hollinger executives, was convicted in 2007 of fraud and obstruction of justice. Black, also known as Lord Black of Crossharbour after he gave up Canadian citizenship to become a British lord, diverted millions of dollars of non-compete payments to himself that belonged to Hollinger.[43] Although Black claimed that the purchasers wanted the agreements structured that way, the purchasers denied this at trial.[44] Black charged that corporate governance "terrorists" were trying to steal his company, but he was caught by a security camera attempting to derail the government's investigation by removing boxes of documents from his Toronto office.[45]

The Ethical Business Leader's Decision Tree

The *Ethical Business Leader's Decision Tree* in Exhibit 2.1 provides a tool business leaders and their counsel can use to evaluate the legal and ethical aspects of their strategy and its implementation.

IS THE ACTION LEGAL?

Managers should first ask themselves whether the proposed action is legal. Legality is addressed first to reinforce the notion that legal compliance is the baseline standard. If an action is not in accordance with the letter and the spirit of the law, then, regardless of the likely effect on shareholder value, the action should not be taken. Although the spirit of a law is more vague than its letter, managers must attend to both components because "[w]hen you try to keep to the letter of the law while undermining the spirit, you are likely to violate the letter in the end."[46]

WOULD IT MAXIMIZE SHAREHOLDER VALUE?

The filter for shareholder value is intended to require managers to consider early on whether the interests of the shareholders—the group given the ultimate legal authority to change management—are being served by the proposed action. Yet the inquiry need not stop there.

Contrary to popular belief, maximization of shareholder value, so-called *shareholder primacy,* is not legally mandated,

38. Charles Forelle & James Bandler, *Dating Game—Stock-Options Criminal Charge: Slush Fund and Fake Employees,* Wall St. J., Aug. 10, 2006, at A1.

39. *Id.*

40. John Grobler, *Extradition of Former Comverse Chief Delayed in Namibia,* N.Y. Times, Apr. 26, 2007, at 2.

41. James Bandler & Steve Stecklow, *Ex-Comverse CEO Is Fugitive in Options Case,* Wall St. J., Aug. 15, 2006, at A3.

42. Grobler, *supra* note 40.

43. *Black and Blue,* Wall St. J., July 16, 2007, at A12.

44. Emily Steel, Ashby Jones & Douglas Belkin, *Press Baron Black Guilty in Fraud Case,* Wall St. J., July 14, 2007, at A3.

45. *Id.*

46. Mark Gimein, *The Skilling Trap,* Bus. Wk., June 26, 2006, at 31.

EXHIBIT 2.1 The Ethical Business Leader's Decision Tree

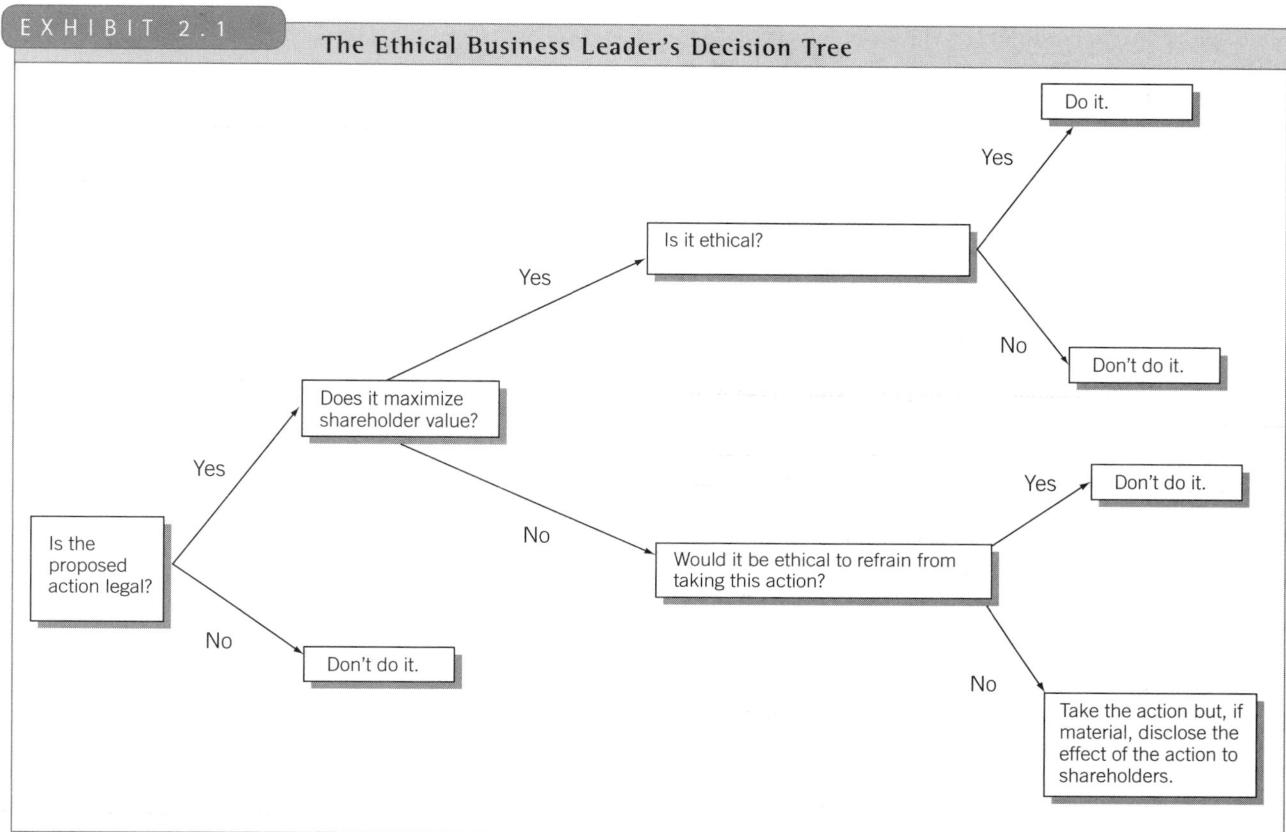

except in very narrow circumstances.[47] The courts and many state legislatures have made it abundantly clear that the directors' obligation is to manage the corporation "for the best interest of the corporation." In deciding what is in the best interest of the corporation, the board may legitimately consider not only the effect a decision might have on the shareholders, but also the effect it might have on employees, customers, suppliers, and the community where the corporation does business.[48] Legislatures in a majority of the states have enacted so-called constituency statutes, which expressly authorize the boards of corporations incorporated there to take into account all stakeholders and constituencies even when a change in control or breakup of the corporation has become inevitable.[49]

Although Delaware, where a majority of the *Fortune* 500 companies are incorporated, does not have a constituency statute, the Delaware Supreme Court has made it clear that the role of the director shifts from "being a protector of the corporate bastion" to being an "auctioneer" charged with obtaining the highest realizable short-term value for the shareholders only when the breakup of the corporation or a change of control has become inevitable.[50] As explained more fully in Chapter 21, the Delaware Supreme Court defines change of control narrowly. For example, it ruled that there was no change of control when two publicly traded companies combined because control was vested in a large disaggregated group of public shareholders before and after the transaction.[51] As a result, the Time, Inc. board could legally rebuff an any-or-all cash bid by Paramount favored by Time's

47. *See* Bagley & Page, *supra* note 3.

48. Unocal Corp. v. Mesa Petroleum Co., 493 A.2d 946 (Del. 1985).

49. *See, e.g.,* Steven M.H. Wallman, *The Proper Interpretation of Corporate Constituency Statutes and Formulations of Director Duties,* 21 Stetson L. Rev. 1 (1991). *See also* Julian Velasco, *The Fundamental Rights of the Shareholder*, 40 U.C. Davis L. Rev. 407, 463 (2006) (twenty-nine states have enacted constituency statutes).

50. Revlon, Inc. v. MacAndrews & Forbes Holdings, Inc., 506 A.2d 173 (Del. 1986).

51. Paramount Commc'ns, Inc. v. QVC Network, Inc., 637 A.2d 34 (Del. 1994).

shareholders to pursue a merger with Warner Communications even though a majority of the Time shareholders, if asked, would have voted against the merger with Warner. The Time board justified its decision by asserting that a merger with Paramount would impair Time's journalistic integrity and imperil the Time culture.

Thus, the CEO who asserts, "I have a duty to maximize value for my shareholders. I can't let my own sense of right and wrong get in the way," is just plain wrong as a matter of law. CEOs or board members may *choose* to do things in the name of the corporation that they would feel wrong doing in their personal lives, but they are not legally *required* to do so. In the same way that medical ethics do not compel a physician to do something that violates his or her own personal ethics, corporate law does not require managers to check their sense of right and wrong outside the executive suite.

Notwithstanding the lack of a legal duty to maximize shareholder value, Milton Friedman, a Nobel Prize winner in economics, and his followers would have the inquiry stop here. In his seminal article, *The Social Responsibility of Business Is to Increase Its Profits,*[52] he asserted that the only guiding criterion for the corporation should be profitability within the confines of the law. He argued that it is not the role of business to promote social ends in and of themselves. Friedman asserted that a corporation is an "artificial person" with no true responsibilities to any constituencies other than its owners, the shareholders. When a company makes a decision to spend money for a social cause, it is in essence making the decision for someone else and spending someone else's money for a general social interest.

Friedman argued that spending money in ways that are not consistent with shareholder wishes is tantamount to imposing a tax and unilaterally deciding where the money will be spent. Because taxation is a governmental function and only the government has sufficient legislative and judicial protections to ensure that taxation and expenditures fairly reflect the desires of the public, a corporation making taxation decisions on its own would render the executive "simultaneously legislator, executive and jurist."

Friedman concluded his landmark article by asserting that "social responsibility" is an inherently collectivist attitude and a "fundamentally subversive doctrine." In a free society, "there is one and only one social responsibility of business—to use its resources and engage in activities designed to increase its profits so long as it stays within the rules of the game, which is to say, engages in open and free competition without deception or fraud."

52. Milton Friedman, An Economist's Protest 177–84 (1972).

"Your Honor, my client pleads guilty to an overzealous but well-intentioned pursuit of the profit motive."

Professors Henry Mintzberg, Robert Simons, and Kunal Basu characterized the assertion that corporations exist solely to maximize shareholder value as a "half-truth" that contributed significantly to the "syndrome of selfishness" that took hold of corporations and society in the late twentieth and early twenty-first century.[53] They argued that focusing on shareholder value without taking account of other stakeholders' interests "reflects a fallacious separation of the economic and social consequences of decisionmaking."[54]

Even economist Michael C. Jensen, a staunch believer in shareholder primacy, acknowledged in a 2001 article the importance of focusing on long-term, not short-term, shareholder value: "Short-term profit maximization at the expense of long-term value creation is a sure way to destroy value."[55] Jensen explained, "In order to maximize value, corporate managers must not only satisfy, but enlist the support of, all corporate stakeholders—customers, employees, managers, suppliers, local communities."[56] He cautioned that "we cannot maximize the long-term market value of an organization if we ignore or mistreat any important constituency."[57]

53. Henry Mintzberg et al., *Beyond Selfishness,* Sloan Mgmt. Rev., Fall 2002, at 67.

54. *Id.* at 69.

55. Michael C. Jensen, *Value Maximization, Stakeholder Theory, and the Corporate Objective Function,* 14 (1) J. Applied Corp. Fin. 8, 16 (2001).

56. *Id.* at 8, 9.

57. *Id.*

Thus, a myopic focus on shareholder value can result not only in unfair treatment of nonshareholder constituencies, but also in harm to the shareholders.[58] In the age of the Internet and 24/7 cable news networks, misdeeds in faraway places are often featured on the evening news at home the same day. Nongovernment organizations (NGOs) and other interest groups track and report on the working conditions in overseas factories, the dumping of hazardous waste and spoliation of forests and rivers, the exploitation of indigenous peoples, and the sale of shoddy and dangerous products. As former General Electric general counsel Heineman noted, "The changes in laws, regulations, stakeholder expectations, and media scrutiny that have taken place over the past decade can now make a major lapse in integrity catastrophic."[59]

Edward Simon, president of Herman Miller, goes even further and encourages managers to focus not just on avoiding harm but on doing good: "Why can't we do good works at work? . . . Business is the only institution that has a chance, as far as I can see, to fundamentally improve the injustice that exists in the world."[60]

Finding the "Sweet Spot"

Ethical behavior need not be a drag on corporate performance, nor merely incidental. Ideal courses of action are ethically sound and maximize shareholder value. Great managers reframe issues and work hard to create such solutions. Ralph Larsen, CEO of Johnson & Johnson, rejected what he termed the "tyranny of the 'or'" and refused to treat social responsibility and profit maximization as mutually exclusive. When asked whether he would rather be a good corporate citizen or maximize profits, Larsen replied, "Yes."[61]

While recognizing that "[t]he most important thing a corporation can do for society . . . is to contribute to a prosperous economy," Michael E. Porter, the renowned strategy professor, and Mark Kramer, a corporate social responsibility specialist, also acknowledge that successful corporations need a healthy society.[62] They contend that social responsibility "can be much more than a cost, a constraint, or a charitable deed—it can be a source of opportunity, innovation, and competitive advantage."[63]

Rather than trying to take on all the ills of the world, companies should, according to Porter and Kramer, focus on social issues that intersect with their particular business and value proposition. Managers should first eliminate as many negative value-chain impacts, such as emissions and waste and depletion of scarce natural resources, as possible. Then, they should identify areas of the social context where they can create "shared value" for the firm and society through a small number of initiatives that both generate competitive advantage for the firm and benefit society.[64] Examples include Toyota's Prius, a hybrid gasoline-electric vehicle that both reduced emissions and gave Toyota a distinct position with customers, and Whole Foods Market's ability to charge premium prices for healthful food products that are (1) sourced from local farmers, (2) sold in stores constructed with a minimum of virgin raw materials and utilizing electricity that is offset by renewable wind energy credits, and (3) increasingly delivered in trucks powered by biofuels.[65]

Third-generation Timberland CEO Jeffrey Swartz described the integral role of social good in Timberland's strategy:

> The company has the belief that each individual can and must make a difference in the way we experience life on this planet.... As a company we have both a responsibility and an interest in engaging the world around us. By doing so, we deliver value to our four constituencies: consumers, shareholders, employees and the community. We offer the consumer a company to believe in and get involved with; we offer our employees a set of beliefs that transcend the workplace; we offer the community an active and supportive corporate neighbor; and we offer shareholders a company people want to both buy from and work for.[66]

IS THE ACTION ETHICAL? WHAT IS ETHICAL?

The next question to consider is whether the proposed action would be ethical. But how does one define what constitutes good ethical behavior? This is sometimes difficult, in part

58. Bagley & Page, *supra* note 3.
59. Heineman, *supra* note 17.
60. Quoted in PETER M. SENGE, THE FIFTH DISCIPLINE: THE ART AND PRACTICE OF THE LEARNING ORGANIZATION 5 (1990).
61. Quoted in Ira M. Millstein, *The Responsible Board,* 52 BUS. LAW. 407, 408–09 (1997).
62. Michael E. Porter & Mark R. Kramer, STRATEGY AND SOCIETY: THE LINK BETWEEN COMPETITIVE ADVANTAGE AND CORPORATE SOCIAL RESPONSIBILITY, HARV. BUS. REV., Dec. 2006, at 78.
63. *Id.*
64. *Id.* at 88.
65. *Id.* at 88–91.
66. James Austin, *Timberland and Community Involvement* (Harvard Bus. Sch. Case No. 796-156, 2001).

because there are numerous and diverse ethical theories. People, consciously or not, employ ethical theories when making their decisions. The important thing for a manager to remember is that there may be different "ethically correct" ways of looking at a decision. As a result, a manager's constituencies may not always reach a similar decision and hence may not be as willing to accept the implications and consequences of the manager's decision.

Teleological and Deontological Schools

The two main schools of ethical thought are teleological and deontological. *Teleological theory* is concerned with consequences. The ethical good of an action is to be judged by the effect of the action on others. *Deontological theory* focuses more on the motivation and principle behind an action than on the consequences.

For example, suppose that a construction company donates materials to build shelters for the homeless. In judging this action within the teleological framework, the fact that some homeless people are given housing is the important issue. Within a deontological framework, one would want to know why the company was motivated to supply the materials for the shelters. As another example, suppose that an employer promises to throw a party if the firm reaches profitability and then breaks the promise. Under teleological theory, as long as the consequences of breaking the promise are insignificant, the action of breaking the promise is not in and of itself bad. Deontological theory, however, would suggest that there is something intrinsically wrong with breaking a promise, no matter what the consequences. Thus, a particular action can be evaluated differently, depending on the system under which it is examined.

A brief examination of several theories within these two schools further illustrates their differences. *Utilitarianism* is a major teleological system that operates under the proposition that the ideal is to maximize the total benefit for everyone involved. Under a utilitarian theory, no one person's particular interest is given more weight than another's, but rather the utility of everyone as a group is maximized.

For example, suppose that a $10,000 bonus pool is to be divided among three project managers and that their marginal benefits from receiving a portion of the money can be quantified. Imagine that the money can be allocated in either of two ways: Under Distribution 1, the three persons benefit 6, 12, and 24 units, respectively. Under Distribution 2, the three persons benefit 8, 12, and 16 units, respectively. A utilitarian would want Distribution 1 because the total benefit (6 ⊠ 12 ⊠ 24 ⊠ 42) is greater than under Distribution 2 (8 ⊠ 12 ⊠ 16 ⊠ 36). The utilitarian would not be concerned that the other distribution seems more equal and fair or that under the benefit-maximizing utility distribution, the worst-off person has considerably less than the worst-off person in Distribution 2.

In contrast, *Rawlsian moral theory,* a deontological theory, aims to maximize the plight of the worst-off person in society by developing principles behind a "veil of ignorance." Each person in society is to imagine that he or she does not know what his or her allotment of society's resources will be and then to decide which principles should govern society's interactions. John Rawls believed that behind the veil of ignorance individuals would create a system that benefited the least-well-off people most. According to this theory, Distribution 2 should be favored because it is the one that would be preferred by the person who faced the possibility of getting the worst share.

Kantian theory is another important deontological line of thought. Immanuel Kant's categorical imperative looks to the form of an action, rather than the intended result, in examining the ethical worth. The form of an action can be delineated into universalizability and reversibility. *Universalizability* asks whether one would want everyone to act in this manner; *reversibility* looks to whether one would want such a rule applied to oneself.

For example, suppose that a manager is deciding how long a break to give the workers on an assembly line. In choosing between a system allowing a ten-minute break every three hours with bathroom breaks whenever necessary versus a longer lunch break, the manager might ask—under universalizability—whether he or she would like a world in which all companies applied a similar system. Under reversibility, the manager would decide whether he or she would want to be subjected to a particular break system as an employee.

Some proponents of the deontological school would argue that courses of action that confer incidental benefits on stakeholders are not truly ethical if they were motivated primarily by the desire to maximize shareholder value. This appears to elevate form over function. An action that confers a benefit (incidentally or otherwise) on stakeholders in addition to maximizing shareholder value is clearly more ethical than two alternatives: maximizing shareholder value without conferring any benefit on other stakeholders or maximizing shareholder value while harming other stakeholders.

Comparative Justice

The consequences of an action motivated by a certain ethical system can also be evaluated within a comparative justice framework. This framework allows the rights-based moral theories of Kant or Rawls to be compared to, for example, a utilitarian framework. Distributive, compensatory, and retributive theories of justice are the three main categories within this framework.

Distributive justice focuses on how the burden and benefits of a particular system are distributed. An ideal system maximizes the overall pie by dividing it such that incentives are enough to entice persons to produce more. The system also concerns itself with a fair distribution of these goods—compensating those who contributed while still upholding a certain minimum standard. For example, the use of progressively higher income tax rates for those with more income and earned income tax credits for those earning the least can be understood within a distributive justice framework.

Compensatory justice aims at compensating people for the harm done by others. For example, if someone is found to be responsible for making another person miss five days of work, a compensatory system of justice would demand that the victim be somehow compensated for the lost wages.

Retributive justice is also concerned with the harm people do to others, but here the focus is more on how to deter them from inflicting further harm. For example, suppose that *X* steals an idea from *Y* and makes $10,000. If the idea had not been stolen, *Y* would have made $5,000. Under a compensatory framework, *X* would compensate *Y* for the thievery by paying *Y* $5,000. Under a retributive framework, *X* should be taught that stealing an idea is wrong. Thus, *X* would be required to give up any benefit and pay *Y* $10,000.

How Do Business Leaders Define Ethics?

Many business leaders associate ethics with such concepts as integrity, fairness, and honesty. For more than seventy-five years, the J.C. Penney Company has considered ethical business behavior to be that which conforms to the Golden Rule: Do unto others as you would have them do unto you. Carly Fiorina, former CEO of Hewlett-Packard, remarked, "Good leadership means doing the right thing when no one's watching."[67]

The CEO of a highly successful Scandinavian multinational tells his managers to conjure up the following scenario: Assume that the decision you are about to make in Timbuktu becomes public knowledge in our home country, the host country, and significant developing countries where our company is operating. Assume further that you, as the decision maker, are called upon to defend the decision on television both at home and abroad. If you think you can defend it successfully in these public forums, the probability is high that your decision is ethical.[68]

ACTIONS THAT MIGHT MAXIMIZE SHAREHOLDER VALUE BUT WOULD BE UNETHICAL

Some actions might be legal and maximize at least short-term shareholder value but are nonetheless unethical. Evidence suggests that, if asked, most shareholders would not want managers to act unethically even if doing so would boost the financial return. Seventy-five percent of investors polled in a 2007 Pepperdine University survey indicated that they would likely withdraw their investment—even if that meant sacrificing a high return—if they learned that a company was engaged in unethical but legal behavior.[69] In 2005, shareholders introduced 360 separate resolutions aimed at improving corporations' social responsibility.[70]

Ethical business leaders will not sacrifice their ethics to secure a short-term gain. Joseph Neubauer, CEO of Aramark Worldwide Corporation, walked away from two well-priced and fully negotiated overseas acquisitions that were perfectly suited to Aramark's goal of international expansion after a closer look at their operations and books revealed unsavory business practices. He justified the loss of time and money, stating, "It takes a lifetime to build a reputation, and only a short time to lose it all."[71]

ACTIONS THAT NEITHER MAXIMIZE SHAREHOLDER VALUE NOR ARE ETHICALLY MANDATED

If an action does not maximize shareholder value and the firm has no ethical reason to act, the action should not be taken. Indeed, taking actions that will not maximize shareholder value without any other justification might result in liability for waste of corporate assets.

ACTIONS THAT DO NOT MAXIMIZE SHAREHOLDER VALUE BUT ARE ETHICALLY REQUIRED

Sometimes, firms will have an ethical reason to act, even though acting will not maximize shareholder value (at least not in the short term). These situations can present the most

67. Stephen Overell, *Blowing Your Own Credibility,* PERSONNEL TODAY, May 27, 2003, at 13.

68. TOUCHE REPORT, *supra* note 16, at 48.

69. Press Release, Pepperdine Univ., Study: Investors Likely to Move Investments if Board Engages in Legal but Unethical Behavior (June 26, 2007).

70. Porter & Kramer, *supra* note 62.

71. Nannette Byrnes et al., *The Good CEO,* BUS. WK., Sept. 23, 2002, at 80.

Historical PERSPECTIVE

Aquinas on Law and Ethics

Saint Thomas Aquinas (1225?–1274), a theologian and philosopher, believed that an unjust law could not properly be considered a law at all. The only true laws were those that followed eternal law—as far as eternal law could be discovered by the use of human reason and revelation. Eternal law is the orderly governance of the acts and movements of all creatures by God as the divine governor of the universe. Because not every individual follows a natural inclination to do good—that is, to act virtuously in order to achieve happiness and to avoid evil—human laws are framed to train, and sometimes compel, a person to do what is right, as well as to restrain the person from doing harm to others. According to Aquinas, for human law to be considered law, that is, binding on human conscience, it must be just. To be just, a human law must be (1) consonant with a reasoned determination of the universal good; (2) within the power of individuals to fulfill; (3) clearly expressed by legitimate authority; (4) approved by custom, that is, the declaration of right reason by a community; and (5) widely promulgated. To the extent that human law is just, it is in concert with eternal law, as discerned through human reason, and it is binding on individuals. Human laws that promote private benefit over the common good are unjust, and individuals are bound not to obey them. Instead, individuals should "disregard them, oppose them, and do what [they] can to revoke them."[a]

Most modern legal theorists separate the question of a law's status as law from the question of its inherent morality. They argue that a law may help to resolve moral issues, punish immoral action, and serve a moral purpose (as, for example, when laws permit participation in government); but a law need not be inherently moral to be a real law. In this so-called positive-law view, any law counts as a real law if it has been created according to recognized procedures by someone with the recognized authority to do so—for instance, a king in a monarchy or, in the U.S. system, a legislature, judge, or administrative agency. A properly created law may, of course, be criticized as immoral. Some people may even wish to disobey it. But they do so in the full knowledge that they are disobeying a valid law.

In the United States, the split between legal and moral debate has always been less clear than positive-law theorists might wish. Americans have always given their moral debates a peculiarly legal flavor, mainly because certain important but ambiguous phrases in the U.S. and state constitutions invite a person to "constitutionalize" moral questions. Moral questions are readily translatable into questions about the meaning and scope of the constitutional doctrines of due process of law, liberty, equal protection under the laws, or cruel and unusual punishment. For example, in upholding a woman's right to have an abortion, the U.S. Supreme Court stated: "At the heart of liberty is the right to define one's own concept of existence, of meaning, of the universe, and of the mystery of human life."[b]

It has become a national trait of Americans to expect their constitutions to support their moral convictions. Just as Aquinas believed that unjust laws could not accord with eternal law, many Americans believe that unjust laws cannot be constitutional. Perhaps it is for this reason that many of the most controversial American moral debates, such as those on slavery, segregation, affirmative action, same-sex marriage, abortion, student-led prayer in public school, capital punishment, and the right to die, have focused on the interpretation of constitutions or have been framed in terms of possible constitutional amendments. In some ways, the tendency in the United States to look to constitutions for substantiation of the just quality of law is akin to the use by theologians of the Judeo-Christian scriptures as supernatural revelation of knowledge of the universal good that is eternal law.

As this comparison of present-day constitutional analysis to thirteenth-century theology indicates, the past is often a valuable pointer to the future. At the same time, one must be able to distinguish differences between doctrines that prevailed in the past and those that should prevail in the future. In this regard, it is important to recall the positivists' distinction between law and morals. If people confuse what's "allowed" with what's "right," they risk cutting their ethical discussions short and missing opportunities both for the encouragement of morality by law and for the reform of law in the light of society's morals.

a. P. GLENN, A TOUR OF THE SUMMA 170 (1978).

b. Planned Parenthood of Southeastern Pennsylvania v. Casey, 505 U.S. 833 (1992).

difficult issues for ethical business decision making. Even when shareholder value and ethics appear to be at odds, managers should follow the ethical high road. Failure to meet societal expectations of ethical behavior can tarnish a firm's reputation, erode employee morale, and result in more onerous business regulation. Nonetheless, when managers take actions that could have a material adverse effect on today's shareholders, they should disclose the actions and the reasons for taking them to the shareholders.[72] Disclosure is important to prevent managers from using social responsibility as a fig leaf to cover up mediocre performance or self-dealing.

Consider a company establishing a manufacturing facility overseas in a country that has much less stringent environmental laws than the United States. The managers legally may and should consider not only the possibility that those laws might later be tightened and applied retroactively to require costly cleanups that will adversely affect shareholder value, but also the cost of installing pollution-control equipment and the potential harm that would result if the equipment were not installed. Thus, top management might feel ethically compelled to install $5 million worth of pollution-control equipment in a country that does not require such equipment if a failure to do so would cause $100 million worth of damage or certain loss of life or serious physical injury. Spending that money may even provide a source of competitive advantage over firms that wait until more costly "tail-pipe" regulations are put into effect. If the company elects to spend a material amount of the shareholders' money to install such equipment, the board should disclose its decision and the reasons for it in its periodic reports to shareholders.

Conoco (one of the largest U.S. oil companies) took the high road in the wake of the environmental disaster created in 1989 when the *Exxon Valdez* ran aground, spilling 10.1 million gallons of crude oil into the waters of Prince William Sound in Alaska. Experts believe double-hulled tankers can prevent or limit spills, but they were not required even after the *Valdez* spill. Notwithstanding the lack of a legal requirement to install double hulls, Conoco announced in April 1990 that it was ordering two new oil tankers with double hulls. Conoco president and CEO Constantine S. Nicandros explained the decision to incur the extra cost: "We are in the business by the public's consent. We are sincere in our concern for the air, water and land of our planet as a matter of enlightened self-interest."[73]

72. Bagley & Page, *supra* note 3.

73. *Conoco Says It Will Order Oil Tankers with Double Hulls,* L.A. TIMES, Apr. 11, 1990, at D1.

THE TENSION BETWEEN LONG-TERM AND SHORT-TERM RETURNS

This is not to suggest that ethics always pay. Sometimes good guys do come in last. Moreover, the reality is that, at least in the short term, there can be tension between behaving ethically and maximizing economic returns. Although Costco Wholesale Corporation, one of the nation's top warehouse retailers, is well known for having the best employee benefits in retail, it has come under attack from investors for that very reason.[74] In early 2004, Costco employees started at $10 an hour; within three and a half years, a full-time hourly worker could make $40,000 per year. In early 2004, Costco paid 92 percent of its employees' health-care premiums, compared to Wal-Mart's 66.6 percent; further, 82 percent of Costco employees were covered by company health insurance, compared to 48 percent of Wal-Mart employees.

But Costco's employee benefits came at a cost. In early 2004, Costco's shares traded at around twenty times projected per-share earnings, while Wal-Mart's traded at around twenty-four. Bill Dreher, a retailing analyst with Deutsche Bank Securities, Inc., said, "From the perspective of investors, Costco's benefits are overly generous." He continued, "Public companies need to care for shareholders first. Costco runs its business like it is a private company." On a previous occasion, Dreher criticized Costco's strict markup ceiling because it "place[d] club member interests too far ahead of shareholder interests."[75] Costco's CEO James Sinegal disagreed and reiterated his belief "that in order to reward the shareholder in the long term, you have to please your customers and workers."[76] Subsequent criticism of Wal-Mart's stingy employee benefits may prove Sinegal correct.

PLANT CLOSINGS, OUTSOURCING, AND USING CONTINGENT WORKERS

This tension also arises when companies consider closing plants, outsourcing, or using contingent workers. In 1993, Stride Rite, renowned for its focus on social responsibility, announced that it was closing its plant in New Bedford, Massachusetts. Facing an unemployment rate of about 14 percent, residents of New Bedford criticized the firm's decision; two suspicious fires caused damage estimated

74. Ann Zimmerman, *Costco's Dilemma: Be Kind to Its Workers, or Wall Street?*, WALL ST. J., Mar. 26, 2004, at B1.

75. Byrnes et al., *supra* note 71, at 82–83.

76. Zimmerman, *supra* note 74, at B1.

at $750,000. Chair Ervin Shames defended the shoe company's seemingly split personality: "Putting jobs into places where it doesn't make economic sense is a dilution of corporate and community wealth. . . . It was a difficult decision. Our hearts said, 'Stay,' but our heads said 'Move.' "[77] A former chair of the company, Arnold Hiatt, acknowledged the inherent difficulty in this situation: "To the extent that you can stay in the city, I think you have to, [but] if it's at the expense of your business, I think you can't forget that your primary responsibility is to your stockholders."[78]

Many corporations stand to save large amounts of money by outsourcing upscale jobs. Accenture, Microsoft, Conseco, Delta Air Lines, General Electric, Intel, Oracle, and Boeing are among the firms that have expanded their overseas employment in recent years in an effort to utilize inexpensive, but well-educated, workforces in other countries.[79] Aerospace engineering work that would cost $6,000 a month in the United States costs $650 a month in Russia; chip design work that would cost $7,000 a month in the United States costs $1,000 a month in India and China; architectural work, $3,000 a month in the United States versus $250 in the Philippines; equity research and industry reports prepared by finance specialists, $7,000 in the United States versus $1,000 in India; and bookkeeping, taxes, and financial reports, $5,000 a month in the United States versus $300 in the Philippines.[80]

Critics of outsourcing claim that these companies are shipping valuable jobs overseas and often simultaneously laying off loyal, white-collar American workers. Proponents of the practice maintain that better jobs will be created in the United States with the money saved by the outsourcing. At a minimum, companies should be honest about what they are doing. After an employee leaked a memo that called on IBM's managers to hide the decision to outsource more programming jobs to India, IBM came under fire and subsequently reduced the number of planned layoffs.[81]

In addition to substantially reducing their full-time domestic workforce, many large companies have also hired "nonstandard" or "alternative arrangement" workers, such as part-time, temporary, and contract workers, for many of the jobs that remained. According to the Bureau of Labor Statistics (BLS), more than 12.3 million workers, or 8.9 percent of the American workforce, were employed in temporary or contract jobs or as independent contractors in 2005.[82] If other types of nonpermanent positions (another 8.2 million workers) are included, the percentage increases to 14.7 percent.[83] In an analysis funded by the U.S. Department of Labor, the Iowa Policy Project, a nonprofit research group, estimated that nonstandard workers actually made up about one-quarter of the U.S. workforce in 2005.[84] The same study found that only 21 percent of nonstandard workers received health-care insurance benefits from their employer and only 23 percent had employment-based retirement plans.[85]

Supporters of the trend to use temporary workers argue that it is necessary to give U.S. companies the flexibility to adjust the workforce to reflect changing and seasonal needs for labor. Critics claim that the practice saps worker morale and ultimately adversely affects worker productivity.[86] Edward Hennessy, Jr., former chair and CEO of Allied-Signal, Inc., cautioned:

> If we choose to deny the larger human and social impact of the corporation, if we try to reduce the company to the bare essentials of a commercial transaction, we will end up with a work force that is less capable and less dedicated over the long run. We will also cause society to be indifferent—if not completely hostile—to the interests of corporations and their shareholders.[87]

APPROACHES TO RESOLVING THE TENSION

Managers can take affirmative steps to help resolve the tension between short-term results and long-term value.

Soften the Edges

To avoid or reduce layoffs, many companies soften the edges of difficult economic times by cutting personnel costs through other means. Less draconian measures include hiring freezes, shortening the workweek, reducing pay and

77. Joseph Pereira, *Social Responsibility and Need for Low Cost Clash at Stride Rite,* WALL ST. J., May 28, 1993, at A1.

78. *Id.*

79. Pete Engardio et al., *The New Global Job Shift,* BUS. WK., Feb. 3, 2003, at 50.

80. *Id.*

81. William M. Bulkeley, *IBM Now Plans Fewer Layoffs from Offshoring,* WALL ST. J., July 29, 2004, at B1.

82. *See* Press Release, Bureau of Labor Statistics, Contingent and Alternative Employment Arrangements, February 2005 (July 27, 2005), *available at* http://www.bls.gov/news.release/pdf/conemp.pdf.

83. *Id.*

84. The Iowa Policy Project, *Nonstandard Jobs, Substandard Benefits: A 2005 Update* (September 2006), *available at* http://www.iowapolicyproject.org/2006docs/060929-nonstd_full.pdf.

85. *Id.*

86. *See* JEFFREY PFEFFER, THE HUMAN EQUATION: BUILDING PROFITS BY PUTTING PEOPLE FIRST 161–94 (1998).

87. TOUCHE REPORT, *supra* note 16, at 44.

bonuses, eliminating bonuses altogether, reducing salary increases, reassignments, and offering buyout packages to employees who might be considering leaving anyway.[88]

When declining demand for its goods caused Levi Strauss & Co. to close eleven U.S. plants, lay off 5,900 employees, and move more of its manufacturing offshore, the company committed to providing a $245 million employee package. Levi gave employees eight months' notice, as much as three weeks of severance pay for every year of service, up to eighteen months of medical coverage, an enhanced early retirement program, and a flexible allowance of up to $6,000 for training and start-up expenses.[89]

Lobby for Changes in the Law or the Enactment of Codes of Conduct

In many instances, corporations or coalitions of corporations have the economic and political power to lobby for changes in applicable law. By encouraging the passage and enforcement of laws prohibiting unethical conduct, such as the dumping of hazardous waste or the use of child labor, managers can ensure that they compete on a level playing field.

In 1976, the Organisation of Economic Co-operation and Development (OECD) promulgated a generalized code of business conduct for multinationals reflecting the views of government, business, labor, and consumer groups. The OECD comprises thirty nations from North America, Europe, and Asia–Pacific representing more than half of the goods and services produced worldwide. Its members are committed to an open-market economy, pluralistic democracy, and respect for human rights.

The OECD code of business conduct requires multinational corporations to (1) act in accordance with the economic, commercial, and social goals and priorities of the host country; (2) abstain from bribery and other corrupt practices seeking favorable treatment from the host government; (3) abstain from political intervention in the host country; (4) make a positive contribution to the balance of payments of the host country; (5) abstain from borrowing from local financial institutions so that they can reserve their capital for local enterprises; (6) monitor the multinational's impact on employment, wages, labor standards, working conditions, and industrial relations; (7) protect the environment of the host country; and (8) disclose information on the multinational's activities so that the home country and the host country can formulate government policy. A 1999 OECD convention criminalized bribes to government officials and recommended a prohibition on the tax deductibility of bribes.[90] The U.S. government and U.S. firms had lobbied for such agreements since the Foreign Corrupt Practices Act (FCPA) was enacted in 1977. As discussed further in Chapter 25, the FCPA prohibits U.S. companies from paying bribes to government officials.

Several other international bodies have also taken a role in combating corruption. In 2005, the United Nations Convention Against Corruption (UNCAC) entered into force. Aimed at coordinating anticorruption efforts, strategies, and policies, the UNCAC requires its sovereign parties to legislate against bribery and influence peddling, and to participate in asset reclamation efforts. As of 2007, 103 countries had ratified the convention.[91] In 2007, the World Bank and the United Nations (UN) announced a joint program designed to help countries recover money stolen by corrupt officials and ensure that the repatriated capital actually goes to its designated public project.[92]

It is particularly important for developing countries to curtail corruption because it is correlated with lower annual capital inflows and lower productivity.[93] In his speech before the General Assembly following the adoption of the UNCAC, UN Secretary General Koffi Annan stated, "Corruption hurts the poor disproportionately by diverting funds intended for development, undermining a government's ability to provide basic services, feeding inequality and injustice, and discouraging foreign investment and aid."[94] The African Union has estimated that corruption siphons more money from the continent than it receives in foreign aid.[95]

Unfortunately, the UNCAC and OECD conventions taken alone have proved inadequate to stop corruption. Transparency International's 2006 Bribe Payers Index ranks the thirty leading export countries by their companies' inclination to

88. Karen F. Lehr, *Smart Companies Use Alternatives Instead of Layoffs*, WASH. BUS. J., Nov. 9. 2001, *available at* http://www.bizjournals.com/washington/stories/2001/11/12/editorial4.html.

89. Miles Socha, *Bad Day at Levi's! 11 Plants to Close, Costing 5,900 Jobs*, WOMEN'S WEAR DAILY, Feb. 23, 1999, at 1.

90. G. Pascal Zachary, *Industrialized Countries Agree to Adopt Rules to Curb Bribery*, WALL ST. J., Feb. 16, 1999, at A18.

91. United Nations Office on Drugs and Crime website, http://www.unodc.org/unodc/en/treaties/CAC/signatories.html (last visited Nov. 10, 2007).

92. Warren Hoge, *World Bank and U.N. to Help Poor Nations Recover Stolen Assets*, N.Y. TIMES, Sept. 18, 2007, at 5.

93. Transparency International, *2003 Transparency International Corruption Perceptions Index, available at* www.transparency.org/content/download/3222/19543/file/cpi2003.pressrelease.en.pdf (last visited Oct. 8, 2008).

94. United Nations Office on Drugs and Crime website, *supra* note 91.

95. Opening Statement of Huguette Labelle, Chair, Transparency International, *2007 Transparency International Corruption Perceptions Index, available at* http://www.transparency.org/policy_research/surveys_indices/cpi/2007/statements (last visited Nov. 10, 2007).

bribe abroad. Companies based in Turkey, Russia, and China continued to be among the most likely to pay bribes even though all three countries have ratified either the UN or the OECD anticorruption convention.[96] India, the worst offender on the 2006 list, is not a party to either agreement, however.

Adopt an Ethics Program

Managers can help make ethics a priority within the firm by enacting a code of conduct, establishing an ethics training program, arranging a formal system for reporting misconduct, and setting up an ethics advice line or office. Employees are more likely to report misconduct when they know that management will take appropriate corrective action and protect those who report unethical conduct.[97] In fact, the more elements an organization's ethics program has, the more likely employees are to report misconduct.[98] The reasons employees cite most often for not reporting misconduct are a lack of confidence that corrective action will be taken and a lack of trust that the report will be kept confidential.[99] Perhaps most important, employees who work for organizations with more comprehensive ethics programs are more satisfied with their organizations than those with less comprehensive programs.[100]

Walk the Walk

Managers should resist the temptation to settle for "the appearance of a compliant reputation."[101] As Richard S. Gruner warned, "Compliance programs that are treated by management as a sham tend to encourage cynicism by employees. Such cynicism, in turn, tends to cause employees to pay less attention to legal requirements and to be more willing to commit offenses."[102] It takes discipline for managers to maintain this kind of commitment to ethical standards, but many firms are already exemplifying that discipline.

The decision to terminate employees who themselves act unethically can be relatively easy. Even though the business consequences may be painful, the connection between the behavior and the dismissal is clear. On at least two occasions, General Electric faced a more difficult scenario: whether to hold business unit leaders responsible for ethical lapses by their subordinates.[103] One case involved procurement fraud and the other falsification of regulatory documents. Even though neither unit leader had participated in or known of the transgressions, both had failed to create an ethical culture within their respective units. At GE, this shortcoming was deemed equivalent to commercial failure, and both individuals were asked to leave the company.

INDIVIDUAL RESPONSIBILITY

Individual employees, particularly those without substantial authority, are faced with a daunting task when they see their company acting in an unethical manner or are asked to engage in unethical behavior themselves. The individual should first determine whether the activity is illegal. Supervisors and managers cannot legally require subordinates to engage in illegal behavior. As discussed further in Chapter 12, even at-will employees are generally protected from discharge in retaliation for refusing to commit an illegal act. Furthermore, if an employee chooses to follow orders (and breaks the law), the fact that the employee was ordered to do so by a superior is no defense in a criminal trial. Thus, if asked to engage in illegal behavior, an employee is fully justified in "just saying 'no' " and is well advised to do so.

If an employee is asked to engage in legal, but unethical, behavior, the course of action is often less clear. First, the employee should review the company's code of conduct for guidance. Often consulting an ombudsperson or calling an ethics hotline, if available, is a good idea. Sometimes, it may be worthwhile to make others (coworkers, managers, supervisors, or even the board of directors) aware of the ethical implications of the situation because those implications may not be apparent to persons who are not intimately involved in the specific case. If no one else takes interest, a careful appraisal of one's own personal beliefs, an assessment of the social, environmental, or other ethical consequences of the action, and a realistic understanding of the consequences of refusing to take the action are all essential to deciding how to proceed.

Sometimes, managers have conflicting responsibilities and must decide "[w]hat to do when one clear right thing must be left undone in order to do another or when doing the right thing requires doing something wrong."[104] When trying to resolve problems that raise questions of personal integrity and moral identity, Professor Joe Badaracco calls on managers to ask, "Who am I?" and "What is my moral center?"[105] When managers with power over others

96. Transparency International, *2006 Transparency International Bribe Payers Index, available at* http://www.transparency.org/policy_research/surveys_indices/bpi/bpi_2006 (last visited Nov. 10, 2007), and *2002 Transparency International Bribe Payers Index, available at* http://www.transparency.org/policy_research/surveys_indices/bpi/bpi_2002 (last visited Nov. 10, 2007).

97. Ethics Resource Center, National Business Ethics Survey 42 (2003).

98. *Id.*

99. *Id.* at 43.

100. *Id.* at 58.

101. Quoted in William S. Laufer, *Corporate Liability, Risk Shifting, and the Paradox of Compliance,* 52 Vand. L. Rev. 1343, 1372 n.127 (1999).

102. *Id.*

103. Heineman, *supra* note 17.

104. Joseph Badaracco, Jr., Defining Moments: When Managers Must Choose Between Right and Right 6 (1997).

105. *Id.* at 13.

are faced with organizational challenges, they should ask, "Who are we? What do we stand for? What norms and values guide how we work together and treat each other? How do we define ourselves as a human institution?"[106]

Jim Metcalf, the president and chief operating officer of USG Corporation, the largest manufacturer of building materials in the United States (including Sheetrock brand wallboard), remarked when describing USG's approach to the multitude of asbestos cases it faced in 2001:

> We were committed to doing what was best for the shareholders and all stakeholders. Before joining USG as a trainee, I worked in a steel mill during the summer while attending college at The Ohio State University. It's important to remember who you are and where you're from. Then you fight like hell to be good stewards.[107]

Social Responsibility

Companies have suffered severe financial setbacks as a result of decisions that, in hindsight, were perceived by the public as unethical. Consumer products companies are particularly sensitive to public perception, given their reliance on individual retail sales. As William D. Smithburg, chair and CEO of the Quaker Oats Company, wrote: "[I] know ethical behavior is sound business practice because every day at the Quaker Oats Company I am reminded that we succeed or fail according to the trust consumers have in us."[108] Senior executives must negotiate with stakeholders to define the firm's role in society and its relationship with its customers, employees, and investors.[109]

CUSTOMERS AND CLIENTS

Issues of social responsibility arise in many areas, including product safety, advertising campaigns, client conflicts of interest, anticompetitive practices, and customer service.

Product Safety

Socially responsible businesses place a heavy emphasis on the safety of their products. Huge costs have been associated with failure to meet the public's perception of what is safe. Mattel's massive recall of lead-tainted toys made in China, the subject of the "Inside Story" in Chapter 18, is just the latest example of the perils of failing to ensure the safety of consumer products.

Bridgestone/Firestone, Ford, and Tire Failures In 2000 and 2001, Firestone spent $450 million to replace more than 6.5 million tires, many of which were installed on Ford Explorers.[110] More than 270 people had died and another 700 were injured when the tread on their Firestone tires separated from the rest of the tire.[111] Investigators discovered that Firestone had test results dating to 1996 showing that 10 percent of the company's tires had tread separation defects. The company had faced similar tread separation issues in Saudi Arabia but had dealt with them in such a way as to avoid having to inform U.S. officials of the problem.[112]

The Firestone unit of Bridgestone/Firestone, which had previously accounted for 40 percent of the parent company's revenue, posted a net loss of $510 million for the fiscal year ending December 2000, after taking a $750 million one-time charge for legal expenses.[113] In 2001, Bridgestone/Firestone took another $570 million charge, including $210 million to close the Decatur, Illinois, plant, which employed 1,380 workers and had produced most of the recalled tires.[114]

In May 2001, Ford CEO Jacques Nasser announced that Ford would replace all 13 million Firestone tires installed on Ford's sport utility vehicles, including the 1.5 million replaced by Firestone. "We simply do not have enough confidence in the future performance of these tires' keeping our customers safe," he stated.[115] In all, the replacement program cost Ford $3 billion.[116] Nasser testified before Congress, "This is a tire issue and only a tire issue."[117]

106. *Id.* at 18.

107. Constance E. Bagley & Eliot Sherman, *USG Corporation (C)* (Harvard Bus. Sch. Case No. 807-121, 2007).

108. Touche Report, *supra* note 16, at 45.

109. *Id.* at 22–23.

110. Todd Zaun, Jospeph White & Timothy Appel, *Firestone Parent Will Set Aside Cash for Claims—Bridgestone Says Lawsuits Won't Force U.S. Unit into Bankruptcy Court,* Wall St. J., Dec. 6, 2000, at A6.

111. Caroline E. Mayer & Carrie Johnson, *Firestone to Recall More Tires; Agreement Ends U.S. Probe of Accidents,* Wash. Post, Oct. 5, 2001, at E1.

112. Keith Bradsher & Matthew L. Wald, *More Indications Hazards of Tires Were Long Known*, N.Y. Times, Sept. 7, 2000, at 1.

113. Todd Zaun, *Tire Recall Hits Bridgestone's Bottom Line*, Wall St. J., Feb. 23, 2001, at A12.

114. Timothy Appel & Todd Zaun, *Firestone Plans to Close Troubled Decatur Factory,* Wall St. J., June 28, 2001, at A3.

115. Keith Bradsher, *Ford Intends to Replace 13 Million Firestone Wilderness Tires,* N.Y. Times, May 23, 2001, at 1.

116. *Id.*

117. Frank Swoboda & Caroline E. Mayer, *Firestone, Ford CEOs Duel at Hearing; Safety Agency Says It Will Test Tires,* Wash. Post, June 20, 2001, at A1.

John Lampe, Firestone's CEO, dubbed Ford's call for the replacement of the additional 13 million Firestone tires "an attempt to scapegoat our tires by falsely alarming consumers about some very real safety problems of [Ford's] vehicle which should be addressed honestly and seriously."[118] Ultimately, Lampe said:

> I've always believed that for any relationship to be solid, to go forward, to prosper, you have to have mutual respect for one another. With Ford not willing to share its information on Explorers, with its continued insistence to divert all attention to the tire and not address the vehicle aspect of the problem, it was very concerning.[119]

The companies' inability to reach a mutually acceptable solution to the problem and continued infighting cost them a business relationship that had stood for ninety-five years.[120]

General Motors and the Chevrolet Malibu's Exploding Fuel Tank In 1999, General Motors Corporation was ordered to pay $4.8 billion in punitive damages and $107.89 million in compensatory damages to six people who were burned when their 1979 Chevrolet Malibu exploded after its fuel tank was ruptured in a crash.[121] Internal GM memos introduced during the trial suggested that GM executives had decided that redesigning the fuel system to reduce fire risk at a cost of $8.59 per car would impose a greater cost than paying claims for fuel-fire deaths. A key memo written by a GM engineer estimated that each death from burns from a fuel-related fire would cost the company $200,000. Based on that amount, the memo calculated that such deaths would cost $2.40 for every one of the potentially dangerous vehicles that had been sold. The memo cautioned, however, that "a human fatality is really beyond value, subjectively."[122] Subsequent to the case, the GM lawyer stated that the company had no plans to notify owners of cars with the same fuel system as the Malibu that the system was dangerous.

The GM case is reminiscent of Ford Motor Company's ultimately very costly decision to produce the Ford Pinto without safety modifications to keep the gas tank from rupturing when rear-ended at low speeds. Ford managers relied on a classic cost-benefit analysis, which compared the $4 to $8 cost of the alterations with the cost of defending the lawsuits stemming from injuries or deaths caused by the exploding gas tanks.[123]

Advertising: Marketing Tobacco and Beer to Children

Targeted advertising raises a variety of ethical issues. Parents and public health officials sharply criticized RJR Nabisco, the maker of Camel cigarettes, for its advertisements featuring a cartoon figure, Old Joe Camel. Ads showing this sharply dressed camel, who frequents pool halls and pickup bars, were tremendously successful in targeting children. In a study involving 229 children ages three to six, more than half were familiar with the figure and associated him with cigarettes. Six-year-olds were nearly as familiar with Joe Camel as they were with the Mickey Mouse logo for the Disney Channel.[124]

Faced with a threat by the Food and Drug Administration (FDA) to regulate nicotine as a drug[125] and increasingly hostile public opinion, RJR voluntarily agreed in 1997 to abandon the Joe Camel ad campaign in the United States. Nevertheless, Joe Camel continued to thrive outside the United States. He started showing up in other countries in 1996. Argentinian antismoking activists became incensed when Joe Camel and friends began appearing in smoking advertisements and promotional gimmicks primarily targeted at teenagers and young adults in that country.[126]

After surveying advertising by the eight largest alcoholic beverage companies in the United States (including Anheuser-Busch, Bacardi-Martini U.S.A., Miller Brewing Company, and Joseph E. Seagram & Sons), the Federal Trade Commission (FTC) concluded that they were targeting children.[127] The companies placed products on eight of the fifteen TV programs most popular with teenagers and in movies targeted at young audiences, including PG and PG-13 movies. The FTC recommended that companies impose stricter voluntary rules and establish a third-party review to ensure that

118. *Id.* at 120.

119. *Id.*

120. Frank Swoboda & Caroline E. Mayer, *Firestone Cuts Ties to Ford in Recall Fight,* WASH. POST, May 22, 2001, at A1.

121. Subsequent to the decision in this case, the U.S. Supreme Court ruled that "few awards exceeding a single-digit ratio between punitive damages and compensatory damages, to a significant degree, will satisfy due process." Mutual Auto. Ins. Co. v. Campbell, 538 U.S. 408 (2003).

122. Jeffrey Ball & Milo Geyelin, *GM Ordered by Jury to Pay $4.9 Billion—Auto Maker Plans to Appeal Huge California Verdict in Fuel-Tank-Fire Case*, WALL ST. J., July 12, 1999, at A3.

123. *See* Grimshaw v. Ford Motor Co., 174 Cal. Rptr. 348, 361–62 (Cal. Ct. App. 1981).

124. Kathleen Deveny, *Joe Camel Is Also Pied Piper, Research Finds,* WALL ST. J., Dec. 11, 1991, at B1, B6.

125. The FDA subsequently adopted regulations regarding tobacco, but the Supreme Court ruled that because Congress had consistently acted to regulate tobacco on its own, this implied that it had not granted the FDA the authority to do so. FDA v. Brown & Williamson Tobacco Corp., 529 U.S. 120 (2000).

126. Jonathan Friedland, *Under Siege in the U.S., Joe Camel Pops Up Alive, Well in Argentina,* WALL ST. J., Sept. 10, 1996, at B1.

127. Denise Gellene, *Leave Alcohol Ad Curbs to Industry, FTC Report Says,* L.A. TIMES, Sept. 11, 1999, at C1.

they are following these codes, but it stopped short of recommending government regulation of the $1 billion alcohol advertising market.

Conflicts of Interest: Merrill Lynch and Other Brokerage Firms

Undisclosed conflicts of interest erode client confidence. In 2001, a pediatrician named Debases Kanjilal filed an arbitration claim alleging that Henry Blodgett, a broker at Merrill Lynch & Co., had urged him not to sell his Infospace, Inc. stock when it was trading at $60 a share. Kanjilal took the advice and lost $500,000 when he later sold the stock for $11 a share. The complaint alleged that Blodgett fraudulently promoted low-quality stocks to curry favor with Merrill's investment banking clients. In the wake of this lawsuit, New York State Attorney General Eliot Spitzer launched an investigation that ultimately unearthed and made public hundreds of documents, including analyst-written e-mails that privately disparaged the same stocks the analysts were publicly promoting, calling them "crap" and "junk."[128] On May 21, 2002, Merrill agreed to pay $100 million to New York and other states and to substantially change the way it paid analysts. Merrill apologized for the behavior of its analysts but did not admit to any wrongdoing. Nevertheless, Spitzer commented, "You don't pay a $100 million fine if you didn't do anything wrong."[129]

In the fall of 2003, a group of brokerage firms agreed to pay $1.3 billion to settle similar state and federal charges of analyst conflicts of interest. Citigroup's Salomon Smith Barney paid the largest fine—$324 million.

In February 2003, the Securities and Exchange Commission (SEC) adopted Regulation Analyst Certification (Regulation AC). Regulation AC requires analysts to certify that their reports "accurately reflect their personal views" and to indicate if any of their compensation is tied to the report.[130] Regulation AC was a direct consequence of the failure of Merrill and other investment banks to protect their clients from analyst conflicts of interest and is yet another example of increased regulation being prompted by unethical behavior.

Anticompetitive Tactics: Boeing

In June 2003, Boeing Company alerted the U.S. Air Force and Boeing competitor Lockheed Martin Corporation that Boeing employee Richard Hora, a former Lockheed Martin official, had "retained several [Lockheed Martin] proprietary or competition sensitive documents."[131] Boeing later acknowledged that data produced by Hora were utilized in the pricing calculations for a successful bid on an Air Force rocket in 1999. Matt Jew, the mid-level Boeing manager responsible for preparing computer models for costs, voluntarily walked into the U.S. attorney's office and began cooperating with investigators. Jew resigned in April 2004 and recanted previous statements that the Lockheed Martin documents had had no impact on Boeing's bids. The Pentagon suspended Boeing from bidding on rocket contracts indefinitely, costing it billions of dollars of business. The investigation was subsequently expanded to determine whether another former Lockheed Martin employee brought other sensitive documents to Boeing from Lockheed Martin and whether Boeing made use of those data in decisions concerning rocket-launch contracts with NASA.

Boeing also held illegal employment talks with Darlene Druyun, an Air Force procurement officer, while she was responsible for billions of dollars of business on which Boeing was bidding. She admitted giving Boeing preferential treatment for years and steering several contracts its way.[132] In one instance, she attempted to help Boeing avoid procurement steps in its effort to secure an Air Force contract for 100 refueling tankers. Druyun and Boeing's chief financial officer, Michael Sears, were sent to federal prison. Ultimately, the scandals cost Boeing CEO Phil Condit his job and cost Boeing not only lost business but also more than half a billion dollars in fines.

Discriminatory Customer Service: Denny's

When the Civil Rights Act of 1964 was promulgated, the laws prohibiting discrimination in public accommodations, such as restaurants, were designed with the lunch counters of Birmingham, Alabama, in mind. Some thirty years later, in the largest settlement under the federal public accommodation laws, Denny's Restaurants agreed to pay more than $54 million to settle two class-action lawsuits filed by African American customers. The customers received $46 million, and another $8.7 million was paid to their attorneys.[133]

African American customers of Denny's had filed more than 4,300 claims of discrimination, which included not being served, having to pay a cover charge, and having to prepay for meals. Among the claims were those of six

128. Marcia Vickers et al., *How Corrupt Is Wall Street?,* Bus. Wk., May 13, 2002, at 37.

129. Patrick McGeehan, *$100 Million Fine for Merrill Lynch,* N.Y. Times, May 22, 2002, at A1.

130. Andrew Countryman, *SEC Adopts New Rule on Analyst Assurance,* Chi. Trib., Feb. 7, 2003, at N3.

131. Andy Pasztor & Jonathan Karp, *As Boeing Tries to Put Scandals to Rest, Prosecutors Widen Probe,* Wall St. J., Apr. 27, 2004, at A1.

132. Andy Pasztor, *Boeing to Settle Federal Probes for $615 Million,* Wall St. J., May 15, 2006, at A1.

133. Stephen Labaton, *Denny's Restaurants to Pay $54 Million in Race Bias Suit,* N.Y. Times, May 25, 1994, at A1.

African American Secret Service agents assigned to President Bill Clinton's detail. In 1994, fifteen white Secret Service agents were seated and served in a Denny's in Annapolis, Maryland, while the African American agents were refused a table. In another incident, an African American federal judge from Houston and his wife, who had been traveling for eighteen hours, were forced to wait for almost an hour at a Denny's in California, while white teenagers taunted them, calling them "niggers."[134]

Rachel Thomas, the thirty-three-year-old vice president of a skin-care company, recalled how she, her husband, and their three children waited for an hour and twenty minutes after a waitress took their order and never returned. Referring to her children, she remarked, "Those babies don't have anything to do with this racism, and they were the ones put out by it. . . . You can't explain it to them; they don't understand."[135] Denny's denied that it had a policy of discrimination.

John Relman, a lawyer for the Washington Lawyers' Committee for Civil Rights, blamed management for failing to lead by example:

> We believe that there was, at the company, an attitude that went into the management level, but we don't know exactly how high. This attitude at the company, at the management level and working its way down, had the effect of causing discriminatory attitudes going down to the lowest levels of the company.[136]

In 1999, Denny's corporate parent, Advantica Restaurant Group, spent millions of dollars on a publicity campaign designed to persuade minorities that Denny's had changed its ways. The corporation published statistics showing that it did $125 million worth of business (approximately 18 percent of its business) with minority-owned companies and that one-half of Denny's workforce and one-third of Advantica's management team were African American. In 1993, only one Denny's franchise was owned by African Americans; in 1999, more than a dozen African Americans and other minorities owned 36 percent of Denny's franchise restaurants. In 2000, in a dramatic demonstration of how a company can radically alter its culture, the Council on Economic Priorities (a New York–based nonprofit promoting corporate social responsibility) named Denny's the winner of its diversity award and declared it "one of the most successfully diverse places to work in America."[137]

134. Timothy Ziegler, *Denny's Victims Discuss Harassment,* S.F. CHRON., May 25, 1994, at A3.

135. *Id.*

136. Labaton, *supra* note 133.

137. *Business Bulletin,* WALL ST. J., Apr. 27, 2000, at A1.

EMPLOYEES

Companies face issues relating to sweatshops and child labor, jobs and pensions, and employment discrimination.

Sweatshops and Child Labor

A number of firms have lost business in the wake of allegations of questionable workplace practices.

Nike In 1996, critics claimed that Nike was exploiting workers in developing countries in Asia by working with subcontractors that used child labor, paid substandard wages, and provided hazardous working conditions.[138] One factory producing Nike shoes had only seven toilets available for 10,000 employees. Other factories were cited for having blocked fire exits and permitting only one bathroom break and two water breaks in an eight-hour day. Reports of abuse, both physical and verbal, were common, as were accounts of sexual harassment and corporal punishment. At one Vietnamese factory, fifty-six women were made to run laps around the building because they had not worn regulation shoes to work. They were forced to continue running even after women started to collapse; eventually, twelve of the women had to be hospitalized. Activists also reported that Nike's subcontractors paid their workers a regular average wage well below the livable wage in Indonesia and that Nike forced its employees to work overtime. Nike denied the allegations.

Nike and others initially maintained that the company had done more good than harm in Indonesia and other Asian countries by improving working conditions, raising the standard of living, and moving people from farming jobs to factory jobs (purportedly a key step in industrialization). Nike's CEO Phil Knight eventually recognized that the buying public expected Nike to do more to ensure fair treatment of its contract workers and the payment of a living wage. Nike enlisted third parties to inspect its contract factories and publicly report their findings, and it hired more than eighty employees to focus exclusively on compliance issues in the supply chain.

Child Labor at Wal-Mart In 1992, the press revealed that some of the products Wal-Mart labeled "Made in the U.S.A." were actually made in Bangladesh by child laborers working for pennies a day. Rosalene Costa, a human rights worker in Bangladesh interviewed by *NBC Dateline,* said the children working at the factory were about twelve years old. The children told her their real ages when the supervisor was

138. Keith Richburg & Anne Swardson, *US Industry Overseas: Sweatshop or Job Source?,* WASH. Post, July 28, 1996, at A1.

not around.[139] The head of Wal-Mart's Bangladesh operation denied that they were children, saying, "The workers just look young because they are malnourished adults."[140] In September 2005, Wal-Mart refused to allow independent inspections of its suppliers' factories, stating, "We are a global leader in monitoring supplier factory conditions and if we find that any of our suppliers' factories are unwilling to correct problems, we end our relationship with them."[141]

Jobs and Pensions: Enron

Once the nation's seventh-largest company by revenue, Enron Corporation filed for Chapter 11 bankruptcy in late 2001 in the wake of an accounting scandal described in the "Inside Story" for this chapter. While encouraging employees to hold on to or purchase more Enron stock, former CEO Jeffrey Skilling netted $89 million in profit from selling around $200 million worth of Enron stock and options between 1998 and 2001.[142] Former chair Kenneth L. Lay collected more than $209 million from selling the stock over the same period.[143] In 2006, the two were convicted of fraud and conspiracy.

The accounting fraud that eventually resulted in the energy giant's collapse also led predictably to the layoffs of some 6,000 employees[144] and the decimation of employees' pensions. Almost 21,000 Enron employees held $2.1 billion of securities in the company's 401(k) plans at the end of 2000; the value of the Enron stock (which represented 63 percent of the assets in the plans) was wiped out when Enron filed for bankruptcy. Another 7,600 employees held an additional $1 billion worth of stock in the employee stock ownership plan.[145] Former directors of Enron agreed to pay up to $86.5 million to settle part of the $3 billion in employee pension-fund claims related to the company's collapse.[146] As of July 2007, only $265 million had been recovered on behalf of the former employee participants in Enron's retirement plans.[147]

139. *Id.*

140. *NBC Questions Wal-Mart's "Buy America" Campaign*, United Press Int'l, Dec. 22, 1992.

141. Steve Greenhouse, *Wal-Mart Questions Motives of Lawsuit by Labor Group*, N.Y. Times, Sept. 16, 2005, at 6.

142. Kurt Eichenwald, *Enron's Skilling Is Indicted by U.S. in Fraud Inquiry*, N.Y. Times, Feb. 20, 2004, at A1.

143. Carrie Johnson, *Prosecutors to Seek Charges Against Lay,* Wash. Post, June 20, 2004, at A8.

144. David Streitfeld & Dana Calvo, *Ex-CEO Arraigned in Fraud at Enron,* L.A. Times, Feb. 20, 2004, at A1.

145. Jo Thomas, *Enron's Collapse: Fading Nest Eggs,* N.Y. Times, Jan. 24, 2002, at C6.

146. *Deal Reached on Enron Pensions,* N.Y. Times, May 13, 2004, at C4.

147. Kristen Hays, *Do the Math*, Hous. Chron., July 3, 2007, at 1.

Discrimination

Racial and other forms of discrimination deprive companies of qualified workers and can cost hundreds of millions of dollars in damages.

Texaco In 1996, Texaco lost $1 billion in market capitalization in one day after a group of its African American employees filed a Title VII class-action suit alleging racial discrimination in hiring and promotion. The complaint included racist comments made by a member of top management who had been secretly recorded by a disgruntled employee. After the Reverend Jesse Jackson organized a consumer boycott, Texaco agreed to pay more than $100 million to settle the charges of racial discrimination and to implement a comprehensive diversity program.

Discrimination costs more than money. It also saps employee morale. After the lawsuit, employee morale hit lows not seen since the $10.5 billion verdict rendered against Texaco when it was sued by Pennzoil over the acquisition of Getty Oil (discussed in the "Inside Story" in Chapter 7). One executive, who had suffered through the Pennzoil ordeal, said that friends called and asked how she could work at a "place like that." She commented, "It's one thing to be called stupid; it's another to be called a bigot."[148]

Texaco's newly elected CEO, Peter Bijur, responded to the lawsuit by summoning his top management team and instructing them to get the word out to all managers that there would be zero tolerance of racial epithets, taunts, and joking on the job. When one officer asked whether Bijur thought this was realistic, given the somewhat rowdy atmosphere on oil rigs and the like, Bijur responded, "Tell the local managers that if they can't enforce this policy, then you will replace them." He went on to say, "And if you can't find managers who can enforce this policy, I'll replace you."[149] Although Bijur's predecessor, Al deCrane, had circulated memos about Texaco's policies against discrimination, Bijur went a step further and instituted a policy requiring an African American and a woman to be present at each human resources meeting to ensure that there would be no repeat of the odious comments that had triggered the lawsuit.[150]

Coca-Cola In 2000, the Coca-Cola Company paid $192.5 million to settle charges of racial bias. Allegedly, African American workers at Coke made an average of $26,000 less per year than white workers—the black employees

148. Constance E. Bagley, Winning Legally: How to Use the Law to Create Value, Marshal Resources, and Manage Risk (2005).

149. Peter Bijur, Keynote Address at the Stanford Law School General Counsel Institute, Palo Alto, Cal. (Jan. 14, 1998).

150. Bagley, *supra* note 148.

sometimes made even less than the white subordinates they trained or supervised.[151] The plaintiffs also charged that African American employees were routinely denied promotions. Under the settlement, more than 2,000 former and current black employees of the company were made eligible to receive around $40,000 each.

INVESTORS: MANAGED EARNINGS

In an effort to meet securities analysts' earnings expectations and thereby avoid the punishing drop in stock price that usually follows a company's announcement that its earnings were below Wall Street's estimates, a number of public companies managed earnings.[152] They used what Arthur Leavitt, former chair of the SEC, called "accounting hocus-pocus" to recognize revenue improperly, take unjustified restructuring charges, and create "cookie-jar reserves" that could be used to smooth out earnings by making up earnings shortfalls in later periods.[153] The disclosure of improper inflation of operating income and other accounting irregularities at Cendant caused the company's stock to drop by more than $14 billion in a single day.

Rite Aid

In 1999, Martin L. Grass was ousted from his position as CEO of Rite Aid, the corporation that his father had cofounded. Following his departure, he orchestrated a two-year conspiracy to cover up his fraudulent inflation of financial results and self-dealing. In 2000, Rite Aid restated its earnings downward by $1.6 billion. Grass was prosecuted and sentenced to eight years in prison—longer than the seven years recommended by prosecutors. The judge also fined him $500,000 and gave him three years' probation. Prior to his sentencing, Grass addressed the judge, saying, "In early 1999, when things started to go wrong financially, I did some things to try to hide that fact. Those things were wrong. They were illegal. I did not do it to line my own pockets."[154]

Strong Financial

Richard S. Strong founded Strong Financial Corporation in 1974. The mutual fund manager had warned investors since 1997 against market timing, also known as rapid trading, whereby investors buy and sell fund shares in the course of days or even hours. Rapid trading is not illegal, but it is discouraged because it can hurt the performance of the fund. Beginning in 1999, the firm repeatedly told its own employees that its funds were not to be used as short-term trading vehicles.

While Strong Financial was publicly advocating this stance, Richard Strong was doing the opposite.[155] According to the SEC, Strong traded rapidly in and out of the company's funds and allowed one hedge fund, Canary Capital Partners LLC, both to engage in market timing and to make illegal trades after the market had closed. The SEC alleged that over the course of one year, Strong made over 500 trades in the company's funds, with the value of one of his short-term trades exceeding $1 million. Strong agreed to pay $60 million and issued a written apology to settle state and federal claims against him. He was banned from the investment industry for life. Strong Financial agreed to pay another $80 million and to reduce its fees by at least $35 million over five years. In his apology, Strong admitted:

> Throughout my career, I have considered it to be my sacred duty to protect my investors; and yet in a particular and persistent way I let them down. In previous years, I frequently traded the shares of the Strong funds, at the same time that the advice which we gave our investors was to do the opposite and to hold their shares for the long term. My personal behavior in this regard was wrong and at odds with the obligations I owed my shareholders, and for this I am deeply sorry.[156]

Strong Financial was just one of a number of mutual fund operators implicated in the largest scandal to rock the $3 trillion mutual fund industry. Putnam Investors paid a $100 million fine and suffered a 9 percent decline in funds under management after being investigated for market timing and illegal after-hours trading.

THE ENVIRONMENT

Failure to meet societal expectations concerning the protection of the environment can tarnish a firm's reputation and hurt innocent people.

Shell Oil

In 1995, Royal Dutch/Shell announced its plan to dispose of its Brent Spar oil platform by towing it from the North Sea and sinking it in the North Atlantic. Shell represented that

151. Greg Winter, *Coca-Cola Still Faces Suits in Race Discrimination Case,* N.Y. Times, July 7, 2001, at C3.

152. *See* Carol J. Loomis, *Lies, Damned Lies, and Managed Earnings,* Fortune, Aug. 2, 1999, at 74.

153. Arthur Leavitt, Taking on the Street (2003).

154. Mark Maremont, *Rite Aid's Ex-CEO Sentenced to 8 Years for Accounting Fraud,* Wall St. J., May 28, 2004, at A3.

155. Christopher Oster, *A Fund Mogul's Costly Apology,* Wall St. J., May 21, 2004, at C1.

156. *A Statement of Apology,* N.Y. Times, May 21, 2004, at C2. Reproduced by permission.

it had complied with environmental regulations and that dumping was the "best practicable environmental option."[157] In April 1995, Greenpeace activists boarded the platform in protest and began a publicity campaign that resulted in consumer boycotts throughout Europe. Two months later, Shell backed down and agreed to spend as much as $42 million to salvage the oil rig—more than twice what the company had planned to spend to dump the rig at sea.[158]

As a result of the media backlash from the Brent Spar incident and Shell's failure to try to stop the hanging of the Ogoni activists in Nigeria (where Shell has a major presence), Shell released a new operating charter in 1997 reflecting a commitment to the environment, health, safety, and human rights. Shell executives reasoned that the company's investment in sustainable development would give it a competitive edge over other companies facing similar challenges. Mark Wade, a manager on Shell's sustainable development team, said, "Brent Spar was our wake-up call telling us that there are heightened expectations towards corporate behavior that we hadn't recognized."[159]

Shell has voluntarily reported on environmental and social issues since 1998, in accordance with the Global Reporting Initiative and the United Nations Global Compact principles. Parts of each report are supported by reports from external auditors.

Disposal of Electronics

According to environmental groups, high-tech garbage is causing substantial health and safety risks in China, India, Pakistan, Nigeria, and other developing countries. Businesses in the United States that offer to recycle retired electronics are often not recycling them responsibly, perhaps because dismantling and reusing the waste in America is substantially more expensive than the alternatives. For instance, it costs ten times more to dismantle and reuse the materials in a computer monitor in the United States than to ship it to China for recycling.[160] Up to 80 percent of electronics waste collected in America for recycling ends up in developing countries where laborers tear the waste apart, often by hand, to extract traces of copper, small amounts of gold, and other valuable minerals.[161]

The health and environmental risks are substantial because the waste contains many toxic materials. An average fourteen-inch monitor contains five to eight pounds of lead, which can seep into groundwater or disperse into the air if the monitor is crushed and burned. Semiconductor chips contain cadmium; computer exteriors contain chromium; batteries and switches contain mercury; and circuit boards contain brominated flame retardants.[162] As workers pick apart the waste and its toxic ingredients disperse into the soil and air, people in China are suffering high incidences of birth defects, infant mortality, tuberculosis, blood diseases, and severe respiratory problems.[163] Recently, several U.S. computer companies, including Dell and Hewlett-Packard, started offering more responsible recycling services.

COMMUNITIES

A number of firms have wrestled with issues related to their responsibilities to the communities in which they do business.

Union Carbide and Bhopal

On December 3, 1984, in the most lethal industrial accident ever, forty tons of methyl isocyanate gas were emitted from a Union Carbide Corporation pesticide factory outside Bhopal, India. More than 3,000 people died at the time of the accident; nearly 11,000 more died later from related illnesses.[164] Estimates of the number of individuals who were injured and still suffer from damage to their lungs and immune system vary, but at least 120,000 remained chronically ill.

Prior to the accident, a team of experts had warned Union Carbide that the plant had "serious potential for sizable releases of toxic materials."[165] In addition, six serious accidents had occurred at the Bhopal facility during the six years that preceded the disaster. Union Carbide has long claimed the leak was a result of sabotage.

In a settlement with the Indian government, Union Carbide—which had $5 billion in equity at the time—agreed to pay $470 million to settle all present and future

157. Rubin Grove-White, *Brent Spar Rewrote the Rules (Shell Oil Co.'s Decision to Dispose of the Brent Spar Oil Platform in the North Sea)*, NEW STATESMAN, June 20, 1997, at 17.

158. *Shell Makes Move to End Dispute over Oil Platform—Plan to Cut Up Brent Spar to Make a Pier in Norway Pleases Environmentalists*, WALL ST. J., Jan. 30, 1998, at B7E.

159. Konstantin Richter, *Managers & Managing: Sustainable Development Teases Consultants—Potential Looks Big, but Field Has Taken Off Slowly,* WALL ST. J., Dec. 14, 1999, at 4.

160. Peter S. Goodman, *China Serves as Dump Site for Computers,* WASH. POST, Feb. 24, 2003, at A1.

161. *Id.*

162. *Id.;* P.J. Huffstutter, *Recycled Electronics Pose a Health Hazard in Asia,* L.A. TIMES, Feb. 26, 2002, pt. 3, at 1.

163. Goodman, *supra* note 160.

164. *Faulty Design Blamed for Union Carbide Plant '84 Gas Leak*, DOW JONES BUS. NEWS, Jan. 12, 2000.

165. Robert Sherrill, *Corporate Crime and Violence: Big Business Power and the Abuse of the Public Trust*, NATION, Nov. 28, 1988, at 568.

claims. This amounted to approximately $500 per victim, a sum that Kathy Hunt, PR Head at Dow Chemical (which acquired Union Carbide in 2001), characterized as "pretty good for an Indian."[166] These amounts were low even by Indian standards.[167]

In late 1999, individual survivors and victims' organizations sued Union Carbide and its former CEO, Warren Anderson, in the U.S. District Court for the Southern District of New York for violating international law and the fundamental human rights of the victims and survivors.[168] Union Carbide argued that it was not required to provide further compensation after the 1988 settlement. Anderson disappeared and could not be served with a summons to appear in the New York federal court, but the company accepted it on his behalf. Union Carbide and Anderson were also put on trial as criminal defendants in India, but Anderson and other company officials refused to subject themselves to the jurisdiction of the Bhopal district court. The Indian government issued an arrest warrant for Anderson in 1992 and finally asked the United States for extradition in 2003.[169] The U.S. government denied the request, and all claims filed under U.S. law were effectively dismissed by separate decisions.[170]

Doing Business with Repressive Regimes

Besides expressing concern about product and environmental safety, the public has put pressure on corporations and institutional investors to invest responsibly, that is, in a way that does not lend support to unjust, oppressive regimes. For instance, many companies with direct or indirect economic ties to South Africa were the subject of consumer boycotts and shareholder resolutions prohibiting investment in South Africa. South Africa's policy of racial segregation (called *apartheid*) relegated its black citizens to second-class status in employment, housing, and opportunity. The boycotts and shareholder resolutions were critical in helping end apartheid in South Africa, a result for which Nelson Mandela and F.W. de Klerk won the Nobel Peace Prize in 1993.

Energy giant Chevron Corporation, which purchased rival Unocal in 2005, has been sharply criticized for its continuous involvement with the $1.2 billion Yadana pipeline in the country of Myanmar, formerly known as Burma.[171] Rather than ceding power after a free election won by an opposing party, Myanmar's military leaders took control in 1990. The government has since established a reputation as one of the most oppressive in the world.

Chevron is the largest U.S. investor remaining in Myanmar. Myanmar's state-owned oil company, Unocal's partner on the pipeline, has allegedly been involved in rapes, murders, and slavery.[172] President Clinton banned any new American investments in Myanmar in April 1997,[173] but Unocal's existing investment was grandfathered.[174] In May 2004, President George W. Bush labeled the military government an "extraordinary threat" to U.S. interests and renewed an import ban against the country.[175] In 2007, the U.S. government imposed additional sanctions prohibiting American banks and companies from doing business with fourteen Myanmar officials, including the country's military ruler, General Than Shwe, and froze any assets held in the United States by those individuals.[176]

Between 1996 and 2004, various parties filed numerous lawsuits in the United States against Unocal with no real success, although the company did settle claims brought by Myanmar exiles for an undisclosed amount.[177] In 2004, Charles Williamson, Unocal's chair and CEO, defended the company's involvement in Myanmar, calling it "good for stockholders . . . and the country."[178] Several years later, Chevron vice chair Peter Robertson pointed out that Chevron has paid for teachers and doctors in affected communities and stated: "I'm convinced that hundreds of thousands of people in Burma have benefited. . . . They benefit from us being there."[179]

166. *Dow "Help" Announcement Is Elaborate Hoax,* http://www.dowethics.com/r/about/corp/bbc.htm (last visited May 5, 2008); Anthony Spaeth, *Court Settlement Stuns Bhopal Survivors,* WALL ST. J., Feb. 22, 1989, at A12.

167. Chris Hedges, *A Key Figure Proves Elusive in a U.S. Suit over Bhopal*, N.Y. TIMES, Mar. 5, 2000, at 4.

168. Frederick Noronha, *Union Carbide Sued in U.S. for 1984 Bhopal Gas Release*, ENV'T NEWS SERVICE, Nov. 16, 1999.

169. Saritha Rai, *Bhopal Extradition Sought,* N.Y. TIMES, July 3, 2003, at W3.

170. *See* Bano v. Union Carbide Corp., 361 F.3d 696 (2d Cir. 2004), and Sahu v. Union Carbide, 2006 U.S. Dist. LEXIS 84475 (S.D.N.Y. 2006), *aff'd*, Bano v. Union Carbide, 198 Fed. App'x 32 (2d Cir. 2006).

171. David R. Baker, *Rights Groups Press Chevron to Leave Burma,* S.F. CHRON., Oct. 4, 2007, at A1.

172. Steven Erlanger, *Clinton Approves New U.S. Sanctions Against Burmese,* N.Y. TIMES, Apr. 22, 1997, at A1.

173. The U.S. Supreme Court struck down a Massachusetts statute barring state entities from buying goods or services from companies doing business with Myanmar in *Cosby v. Nat'l Foreign Trade Council,* 530 U.S. 363 (2000).

174. Jay Solomon & James Hookway, *U.S. Sanctions on Myanmar May Affect Firms in West*, WALL ST. J., Sept. 28, 2007, at A3.

175. *Shareholders Reject Bid for Dissidents' Access to Board,* L.A. TIMES, May 25, 2004, at C2.

176. Solomon & Hookway, *supra* note 174.

177. Baker, *supra* note 171.

178. *Shareholders Reject Bid, supra* note 175.

179. Baker, *supra* note 171.

Positive Action

Although examples of corporate misdeeds abound, there are also encouraging instances of responsible corporate behavior.

CUSTOMERS AND PRODUCT SAFETY: JOHNSON & JOHNSON AND TYLENOL

Johnson & Johnson's Tylenol success story is a classic illustration of socially responsible behavior. In September 1982, several Tylenol capsules were tampered with and laced with cyanide poison. As soon as the first deaths were reported, the company recalled 31 million bottles of Tylenol at a cost of approximately $100 million.

James Burke, chair of Johnson & Johnson during the Tylenol scare, credited Johnson & Johnson's code of ethics with helping the company deal with the crisis.[180] Johnson & Johnson's code begins: "We believe that our first responsibility is to the doctors, nurses and patients, to mothers and fathers, and all others who use our products and services. In meeting their need, everything we do must be of high quality."[181] Burke recalled, "Dozens of people had to make hundreds of decisions on the fly. There was no doubt in their minds that the public was going to come first in this issue because we had spelled it out [in our credo] as their responsibility."[182]

Although the short-term economic costs of the Tylenol recall were enormous, within a matter of months Johnson & Johnson was able to regain the market share it had lost. By living up to its reputation for integrity and social responsibility, Johnson & Johnson enhanced both its public image and its long-term profitability. That image was later tarnished, however, by claims that Johnson & Johnson had been slow to warn consumers that Tylenol can cause liver damage—a demonstration of the importance of being ever vigilant to protect a firm's reputation.[183]

EMPLOYEES: AUDITING OF SUPPLIER WORK CONDITIONS

For many years, American companies claimed that their foreign factories were not stereotypical sweatshops, but they stubbornly refused to release the reports detailing the audits they used to substantiate those claims. Some companies now go public with the audit reports. Adidas-Salomon, Nike,[184] and other companies post the results of their factory audits on the Fair Labor Association (FLA) website, http://www.fairlabor.org. This has put pressure on other companies, particularly those with less than stellar human rights reputations, to publicize their audits as well. Some critics maintain, however, that the posted audit reports do not evaluate whether the factories pay a living wage and claim that the inspection regime is "watered down."[185] Nonetheless, some accountability is better than none at all.

THE ENVIRONMENT

Most automakers are members of the Alliance of Automobile Manufacturers, the trade group leading the fight against tougher fuel and emissions standards. Honda Motor Company stands out as a notable exception. In 2002, Honda shocked other automakers by telling regulators that most sport utility vehicles, pickup trucks, and minivans should meet the same fuel standards as passenger cars.[186]

Honda released America's first gasoline-electric hybrid vehicle, the Insight, in 1999. Three years later, Honda released a hybrid version of its popular Civic. Honda also opened a "green" facility in 2002. The warehouse was designed, constructed, and will continue to operate using environmentally friendly products and practices. James Olson, the top lobbyist for Toyota, commented, "Honda is a superb technical company, they have very strong principles, and they're very honest."[187] Toyota released its popular Prius hybrid sedan in Japan in 1997, making it the first mass-produced hybrid vehicle. The 2008 Prius is the most fuel-efficient car sold in the United States (48 miles per gallon in the city and 45 on the highway).[188]

---

180. Richard Tedlow, *James Burke: A Career in American Business* (Harvard Bus. Sch. Case No. 389-177, 2005).

181. Quoted in PATRICK E. MURPHY, EIGHTY EXEMPLARY ETHICS STATEMENTS 123 (1998).

182. Stanley J. Modic, *Corporate Ethics: From Commandments to Commitment,* INDUSTRY WK., Dec. 14, 1987, at 33.

183. See Thomas Easton, *Medicine, J&J's Dirty Little Secret: Despite Bad Publicity and Costly Legal Settlements, Johnson & Johnson Refuses to Put Ample Warnings on Its Tylenol Labels,* FORBES, Jan. 12, 1998, at 42.

184. In addition, Nike has an in-house staff of ninety-seven that inspected 600 factories in the two-year period ending in 2004 and graded them. Maria S. Eitel, the Nike vice president for corporate responsibility, commented, "You haven't heard about us recently because we had our head down doing it the hard way. Now we have a system to deal with the labor issue, not a crisis mentality." Quoted in Stanley Holmes, *The New Nike,* BUS. WK., Sept. 20, 2004, at 78, 84.

185. Aaron Bernstein, *Sweatshops: Finally, Airing the Dirty Linen,* BUS. WK., June 23, 2003, at 100.

186. Danny Hakim, *Honda Takes Up Case in U.S. for Green Energy*, N.Y. TIMES, June 12, 2002.

187. *Id.*

188. Environmental Protection Agency, *2008 Most and Least Fuel Efficient Vehicles*, *available at* http://www.fueleconomy.gov/feg/best/bestworstNF.shtml (last visited Jan. 4, 2008).

In 2004, Ford released the first gasoline-electric hybrid sport utility vehicle, the Escape Hybrid.[189] The 2008 Escape Hybrid gets 34 miles per gallon in the city and around 30 on the highway, or more than 400 miles on one 15-gallon tank of gas.[190] Other car manufacturers have followed suit. Toyota offers several of its sport utility vehicles in a hybrid version. General Motors, Chrysler, Mercedes Benz, and BMW each plan to release at least one hybrid SUV for the 2009 model year, including the first full-size hybrid SUV, the Cadillac Escalade Hybrid.[191]

General Electric launched a major "green" initiative in 2005, dubbed "Ecomagination." CEO Jeff Immelt announced that GE would double its annual spending on research and development of "clean technology," including lower-emission turbines and other products designed to produce fewer greenhouse gases, to $1.5 billion a year by 2010.[192] Employing the motto "green is green," Immelt remarked, "My environmental agenda is not about being trendy or moral. It's about accelerating economic growth."[193]

COMMUNITIES: POULTRY AND ANTIBIOTICS

For years, poultry farmers have used chicken feed containing antibiotics to stimulate growth, a practice that critics claim contributes to the spread of antibiotic-resistant strains of bacteria. Four major poultry companies—Tyson Foods, Foster Farms, Gold Kist, and Perdue Farms—have voluntarily changed their ways. Tyson and Foster used antibiotics in just 1 percent of their flocks in 2004, primarily to treat sick birds. Perdue Farms had instituted a similar protocol in 2001.[194] These four companies produced 38 percent of all chicken consumed in the United States in 2005.[195]

SOCIALLY RESPONSIBLE INVESTMENT

Individual and institutional investors continue to promote more environmentally responsible behavior. In 1989, the Coalition for Environmentally Responsible Economies (CERES) promulgated investor guidelines that focus on environmental awareness and corporate activities, such as using and preserving natural resources, safely disposing of pollutants, marketing safe products, and reducing environmental risks. CERES is a diverse network of more than eighty investors, environmentalists, labor unions, and community advocates, collectively representing more than $400 billion in invested capital. As of 2007, more than fifty companies (including General Motors, American Airlines, Coca-Cola, and Sunoco) had endorsed the CERES principles.[196]

CERES launched the Investor Network on Climate Risk (INCR) in 2003 with ten institutional investors controlling $600 billion in assets. By 2007, the group included fifty investors managing nearly $4 trillion.[197]

Many large mutual fund companies, 401(k) retirement plans, and college saving plans offer socially responsible options,[198] and American investors are investing in responsible funds and companies in increasing numbers.[199] Assets in "green" funds grew almost 700 percent from 2001 to 2007.[200] Private and venture capitalists invested $1.1 billion in clean energy projects in 2006, an increase of more than 50 percent over 2005.[201] Vanguard's Social Index fund grew from $77 million in 2001 to $650 million in 2007, while assets in Neuberger Berman's SRI fund increased from $100 million in 2002 to $1.5 billion in 2007.

Europe has seen a similar growth in socially responsible funds.[202] In 2007, the European Social Investment Forum estimated that 15 percent of all invested European capital was in some form of vehicle that screens for ethical

189. Bill Griffith, *Miles of Versatility in Escape Hybrid,* Boston Globe, Sept. 30, 2007, at J1.

190. *Id.*

191. Patrick Danner, *The Call of the Hybrid*, Miami Herald, Nov. 9, 2007; David Kiley, *Is GM's Green Tech Better Than Toyota's?*, Bus. Wk. Online, Nov. 15, 2007, http://www.businessweek.com/autos/content/nov2007/bw20071113_975898.htm?chan=top+news_top+news+index_businessweek+exclusives (last visited Nov. 11, 2007).

192. Amanda Griscom Little, *G.E.'s Green Gamble*, Vanity Fair, July 10, 2006.

193. *Id. See also* the "Inside Story" in Chapter 16.

194. Elizabeth Weise, *"Natural" Chickens Take Flight*, USA Today, Jan. 24, 2006, at D5.

195. *Id.*

196. CERES Coalition and companies, *available at* http://www.ceres.org/page.aspx?pid=553 (last visited Oct. 8, 2008).

197. CERES Investor Programs, *available at* http://www.ceres.org/page.aspx?pid=554 (last visited Oct. 8, 2008).

198. Jilian Mincer, *Socially Responsible Funds Grow,* Wall St. J., May 29, 2007, at D2.

199. This is not to suggest, however, that capital does not continue to flow to companies engaged in more venal pursuits. The ViceFund, which invests solely in companies engaged in the sale of alcoholic beverages, tobacco, casinos and gaming machines and facilities, and aerospace and defense, had $177 million under management in 2007. It has averaged an annual return of 19.5 percent since inception in 2002. The ViceFund prospectus is available at http://vicefund.com/docs/vicex_web.pdf (last visited Dec. 11, 2007).

200. Jane Bryant Quinn, *How to Make a Buck Green*, Newswk., Apr. 23, 2007, at 63.

201. *$1.5 Billion to Help Westmont Firm Make Green Turbines,* Chi. Sun-Times, Nov. 16, 2007, at 59.

202. Sara Calian & Tamzin Booth, *Ethical-Investment Practices Expand in U.K. in Response to New Legislation,* Wall St. J., June 19, 2000, at A15B.

considerations.[203] Moreover, pursuant to a regulation that went into effect in July 2000, pension-fund trustees in the United Kingdom must disclose in their statement of investment principles the extent, if any, to which they consider social, environmental, or ethical factors when deciding in which companies to invest. Although the regulation does not require trustees to have a policy on these issues, they must disclose the lack of one. Experts have called for the SEC to adopt similar requirements in the United States.[204]

Promoting Ethical Behavior

In addition to leading by example, CEOs and other managers use a variety of techniques to promote ethical behavior.

CRAFT A MISSION STATEMENT

Corporations sometimes include ethical language in their corporate mission statements. Even if there is no express reference to ethics, companies may stress their responsibilities to employees, customers, and society at large. For example, Toyo Glass Company, a Japanese supplier of glass products, includes the following statement:

1. Our objective is to contribute our share of work towards the happiness of the public at large.
2. Profit is not our first aim to attain, it is a natural outgrowth of successful business activities.
3. Everybody is expected to do his duty as a service to the public, individually and collectively, and thus to benefit the property of his own as well as others.[205]

ADOPT A CODE OF ETHICS

Business leaders consider a code of ethics to be one of the most effective measures for encouraging ethical business behavior. A code of ethics is a written set of rules or standards that states the company's principles and clarifies its expectations of employee conduct in various situations. Although these codes vary from company to company, they govern such areas as selling and marketing practices, conflicts of interest, political activities, and product safety and quality.

The 2003 *National Business Ethics Survey* published by the Ethics Resource Center reported that approximately 87 percent of large for-profit organizations surveyed had adopted a code of conduct or other written standard of ethical conduct.[206] Having a code in place before a crisis strikes is essential. Bowen H. "Buzz" McCoy, one of *National Real Estate Investor Magazine*'s 100 real estate "icons" of the twentieth century, observed that "if a common sense of values has not been discussed and articulated before an ethical issue intrudes unexpectedly, it is too late."[207]

A company code of ethics is ineffective without proper implementation. Enron had a great policy on paper. It is not enough simply to state general rules; the code must show employees how the principles apply to particular decisions. The code should be a living document that is reviewed periodically to meet new circumstances. Managers should go over the code with personnel to ensure that they understand the company's values. The company should also pay increased attention to ethical standards in recruiting and hiring.

PROVIDE ETHICS TRAINING

Employers should supplement the written code with ethics education programs. Seventy-five percent of employers surveyed in 2007 reported that their company provided some form of ethics training.[208] Companies cite two primary goals of ethics training: (1) developing a general awareness of ethics in business and (2) drawing attention to practical ethical issues. Sixty percent of the companies that provide ethics training do so during the orientation process for new employees.

Several companies have developed innovative methods for educating their employees in ethics. Aircraft manufacturer Boeing offers an online quiz (with answers) to try to guide its staff through the whole gamut of moral quandaries from how to deal with employees who fiddle with their expenses to suppliers who ask for kickbacks.[209] In the wake

203. Ruth Sullivan, *SRI "Safe Haven in Times of Turmoil,"* Fin. Times, Sept. 24, 2007, at 11.

204. Bagley & Page, *supra* note 3.

205. Robert E. Allinson, Global Disasters: Inquiries into Management Ethics (1997).

206. Ethics Resource Center, *supra* note 97, at 7.

207. Bowen H. McCoy, *Real Estate Ethics,* 4 Real Est. Rev. 27, 31 (2000).

208. Ethics Resource Center, 2007 National Business Ethics Survey 5 (2007).

209. Boeing Frontiers Online, *Ethics Training Module Online,* Sept. 2003, http://www.boeing.com/news/frontiers/archive/2003/september/i_nan2.html; Boeing Education and Awareness, *available at* http://www.boeing.com/companyoffices/aboutus/ethics/education.htm.

of repeated scandals, Citigroup instituted mandatory online ethics training for all Citigroup employees worldwide.[210]

Ethics training may be particularly important for business managers. Research indicates that students planning a career in business are more likely to cheat than students planning to pursue other disciplines (76 percent of business students admitted that they had cheated on at least one test).[211] Other research supports the assertion that business students are more tolerant of unethical behavior than other students.[212] Moreover, courses in classic economics may enhance students' tendencies to act in a selfish manner.[213] Nonetheless, business schools are trying to increase the scope and quality of their ethics coverage.

To preserve the reputation of tomorrow's business leaders and to prevent unethical behavior in the future, there must be a renewed focus on trustworthiness and personal responsibility in business schools.[214] Many business schools offer stand-alone courses in ethics or corporate responsibility and business law, and most try to integrate such topics into strategy and accounting courses, among others. The Yale School of Management has developed an integrated core curriculum that trains students to analyze business decisions from a variety of perspectives, including investors, employees, customers, competitors, and state and society.[215]

PROVIDE OVERSIGHT

In an effort to enforce ethical standards, some companies have set up oversight committees, and many large firms employ at least one full-time ethics officer. The Ethics Officer Association has grown from a dozen members in 1992 to more than 1,000 members in 2007. The association's member companies include more than half of the *Fortune* 100. As of 2007, defense and engineering giant United Technologies had an international network of more than 270 "business practice officers," who were responsible for distributing and reinforcing a code of ethics in more than twenty-eight languages to its employees around the world.[216]

In general, ethics committees are responsible for setting standards and policy and for handling employee complaints or infractions. Executive officers or directors of the company are often members. Ombudspersons investigate employee complaints. Judiciary boards usually decide cases of ethics code violations.

Another method of oversight is the social audit. Increasingly, companies have been performing social audits of their activities in sensitive or controversial areas. For example, a semiconductor company might conduct an internal audit of its disposal of chemical waste, or a bank might audit the reporting practices of its securities trading division. The Body Shop retained ethics expert Kirk Hanson to audit the effect of its activities on the environment and the communities where it operates.

A 2000 study of social auditing revealed that corporate financial performance typically improves with increased social responsibility. The companies studied increased their efficiency and productivity, lowered legal exposure and risk to the company's reputation, and reduced direct and overhead costs as a result of adopting socially responsible practices.[217] The financial payback to the company was between six and twenty times the audit cost over periods of six months to three years.[218]

MAKE IT EASIER TO BLOW THE WHISTLE

Many employees are reluctant to "blow the whistle"—to report illegal or unethical conduct that they observe at work—for fear of being considered a troublemaker or of being fired. A number of federal, state, and local laws prohibit reprisals against employees who report activities that they believe violate a law, rule, or regulation. The Sarbanes–Oxley Act made it illegal to fire, demote, or harass employees of publicly traded companies who provide information concerning federal securities fraud, accounting violations, and other financial crimes.[219] Aggrieved employees can sue for reinstatement and damages.[220] The Act also made it a

210. Hamilton Nolan, *Citigroup Kicks Off Internal Efforts to Clarify Standards,* PR Wk., April 4, 2005, at 3. On more than one occasion, CEO and lawyer Charles O. Prince commented, "My goal for Citi is to be the most respected global financial services company." Prince resigned in late 2007 as the company faced upwards of $4 billion in losses related to the collapse of the subprime mortgage market.

211. Donald L. McCabe & Linda Klebe Trevino, *Cheating Among Business Students,* 19 J. Mgmt. Educ. 205 (1995).

212. M. Lynette Smyth & James R. Davis, *An Examination of Student Cheating in the Two-Year College,* 31 Community C. Rev. 17 (2003).

213. F. Ferraro, J. Pfeffer & R.I. Sutton, *Economics Language and Assumptions: How Theories Can Become Self-Fulfilling,* 30 Acad. Mgmt. Rev. 8 (2005).

214. Carolyn Y. Woo, *Personally Responsible,* BizEd, May/June 2003, at 22.

215. A description is available at http://www.mba.yale.edu.

216. This information was gleaned from the United Technologies website, http://www.utc.com/responsibility/ethics/index.htm (last visited Nov. 17, 2007).

217. Sandra Waddock & Neil Smith, *Corporate Responsibility Audits: Doing Well by Doing Good,* Sloan Mgmt. Rev., Winter 2000, at 75.

218. *Id.* at 82.

219. Sarbanes–Oxley Act of 2002, Pub. L. No. 107-204, § 806, 116 Stat. 745.

220. *Id.* at § 806.

federal crime for public or private companies to retaliate against individuals who provide truthful information to the government about possible violations of any federal law.[221] Further, the law requires companies to provide a mechanism for employees to confidentially inform directors of problematic accounting. Whistleblowing is discussed further in Chapter 12.

Even with legislative and judicial protections, whistleblowers still suffer. Edna Ottney, a quality assurance engineer who has investigated employee concerns in the nuclear power industry since 1985, reported that 90 percent of the 1,700 whistleblowers she interviewed had experienced negative reactions. A person who reported violations at the Comanche Peak nuclear plant in Glen Rose, Texas, warns: "Be prepared for old friends to suddenly become distant. Be prepared to change your type of job and lifestyle. Be prepared to wait years for blind justice to prevail."[222]

For example, on the eve of the space shuttle *Challenger*'s takeoff in January 1986, two senior engineers from Morton Thiokol warned that the shuttle's O-ring gaskets manufactured by Morton Thiokol might be affected by the forecasted cold weather. The launch was not canceled, and seven astronauts died when the shuttle exploded in a ball of flame. According to the *Economist,* even though the two Morton Thiokol employees were praised for their actions, their careers suffered.[223]

A study published in the September 1993 issue of the *British Medical Journal* shows that this problem transcends national borders. Of thirty-five Australian whistleblowers surveyed, eight lost their jobs as a result of whistleblowing, ten were demoted, ten resigned or retired early because of ill health related to victimization, fifteen were taking prescribed medication to deal with stress, and seventeen had considered suicide.[224]

A manager can make it easier for employees to blow the whistle by protecting them from retaliation by their immediate supervisor and coworkers. A manager provides moral and psychological support by emphasizing to coworkers the courage shown by the whistleblower and by providing free counseling to deal with any victimization by coworkers.

Honor or the Morals of the Marketplace?

In the case of partners and certain other relationships of confidence and trust, the law imposes a *fiduciary duty* to act in the best interest of the other party. In the oft-quoted words of Chief Judge Cardozo:

> Many forms of conduct permissible in a workaday world for those acting at arm's length are forbidden to those bound by fiduciary ties. A trustee is held to something stricter than the morals of the market place. Not honesty alone, but the punctilio of an honor the most sensitive, is then the standard of behavior.[225]

In the following case, the judges on the New York Court of Appeals (the highest court in New York) wrestled with the extent of the duties a finder owes its client.

221. *Id.* at § 1107.

222. Quoted in Joel Chineson, *Bureaucrats with Conscience,* Legal Times, Apr. 17, 1989, at 50.

223. *Good Takes on Greed,* Economist, Feb. 17, 1990, at 72.

224. Marcy Mason, *The Curse of Whistle-Blowing,* Wall St. J., Mar. 14, 1994, at A14.

225. Meinhard v. Salmon, 164 N.E. 545 (N.Y. 1928) (Case 5.1).

A CASE IN POINT | **IN THE LANGUAGE OF THE COURT**

CASE 2.2

Northeast General Corp. v. Wellington Advertising, Inc.

Court of Appeals of New York
624 N.E.2d 129 (N.Y. 1993).

FACTS In 1988, Northeast General Corporation entered into an agreement with Wellington Advertising, Inc. whereby Northeast agreed to act "as a non-exclusive independent investment banker and business consultant for the purposes of finding and presenting candidates for purchase, sale, merger or other business combination." The agreement further provided that Northeast General would be entitled to a finder's fee, based on the size of the transaction, if a transaction was completed within three years of Wellington's introduction to the "found" buying party. In the course of his discussion with Northeast's new president, Dunton, Wellington's president, Arpadi, had confided that he was "terrified" he "would lose everything" in a bad merger.

Margolis, one of Northeast General's agents, consulted with Dunton and then introduced Sternau to Arpadi as a potential purchaser of Wellington. Ultimately, Sternau and Wellington entered into an acquisition agreement.

CONTINUED

Before introducing Sternau to Wellington, Dunton was informed by an unidentified investment banker that Sternau had a reputation for buying companies, removing assets, rendering the companies borderline insolvent, and leaving minority investors unprotected. Dunton did not disclose this information to Wellington prior to the closing of the Wellington–Sternau deal.

After Northeast introduced Sternau to Wellington, but prior to the signing of the acquisition agreement, Dunton called Arpadi and offered further help with the transaction. Arpadi declined that help and discouraged Dunton from any further involvement. After the acquisition agreement was signed, companies controlled by Sternau purchased the controlling stock of Wellington, leaving Wellington's principals, including Arpadi, as minority investors. Ultimately, Wellington was rendered insolvent, and Arpadi and other minority investors suffered financial losses. Wellington delivered a check to Northeast for its finder services but stopped payment before the check could be negotiated.

Northeast sued Wellington to recover its finder's fee. After a trial, the jury found in favor of Northeast and awarded it the agreed finder's fee. The trial court judge set aside the jury's verdict. The judge's decision, which rested on arguments of public policy, imposed a fiduciary-like duty on finders to disclose adverse information to their clients. The appellate division court upheld the trial court judge's action, and Northeast appealed.

ISSUE PRESENTED Does a finder–seller agreement create a relationship of trust with a "fiduciary-like" obligation on the finder to share information with the seller regarding the potential buyer's bad reputation?

OPINION BELLACOSA, J., writing on behalf of the New York Court of Appeals:

Before courts can infer and superimpose a duty of the finest loyalty, the contract and relationship of the parties must be plumbed. We recognize that "[m]any forms of conduct, permissible in a workaday world for those acting at arm's length, are forbidden to those bound by fiduciary ties" (*Meinhard v. Salmon,* 249 N.Y. 458, 464 (1928)). Chief Judge Cardozo's oft-quoted maxim is a timeless reminder that "[a] trustee is held to something stricter than the morals of the market place. Not honesty alone, but the punctilio of an honor the most sensitive" (*id.*). If the parties find themselves or place themselves in the milieu of the "workaday" mundane market place, and if they do not create their own relationship of higher trust, courts should not ordinarily transport them to the higher realm of relationship and fashion the stricter duty for them.

The Northeast–Wellington agreement contains no cognizable fiduciary terms or relationship. The dissent ascribes inordinate weight to the titles non-exclusive "independent investment banker and business consultant." These terms in the context of this agreement are not controlling, since Dunton did not perform the services of an investment banker or consultant. Instead, Dunton's sole function was "for purposes of finding and presenting candidates." That drives the analysis of this case because he was a traditional finder functioning under a finder's agreement, and his role ceased when he found and presented someone. The finder was not described or given the function of an agent, partner or co-venturer.

Probing our precedents and equitable principles unearths no supportable justification for such a judicial interposition, however highly motivated and idealistic. Indeed, responding to this fine instinct would inappropriately propel the courts into reformation of service agreements between commercially knowledgeable parties in this and perhaps countless other situations and transactions as well.

This Court may sense a sympathetic impulse to balance what it may view as the equities of a situation such as this. The hard judicial obligation, however, is to be intellectually disciplined against that tug. Instead, courts must focus on the precise law function reposed in them in such

CONTINUED

circumstances, which is to construe and enforce the meaning and thrust of the contract of the parties, not to purify their efforts.

The character of the Northeast–Wellington agreement was not one of trust importing duties beyond finding a prospect. The fact that Wellington did not employ its own independent, traditional methods to check out the reputation of the prospect and accepted what turned out to be a bad prospect does not warrant this Court rescuing it from its soured deal by any post-agreement fiduciary lifeline.

The commonplace mores of the market place suffice and are appropriate to govern relationships established by a contract of the type involved here, which contemplates and asks nothing more of the parties than performance of a simple service. In sum, defendants' financial losses from their market mishap with Sternau is not reason enough to propel a sweeping new fiduciary-like doctrine into finders' agreements.

DISSENT HANCOCK, J., dissenting from the majority opinion:

A fiduciary relationship is one founded on trust or confidence reposed by one person in the integrity and fidelity of another. The term is a very broad one. It is said that the relation exists, and that relief is granted, in all cases in which influence has been acquired and abused, in which confidence has been reposed and betrayed. The origin of the confidence and the source of the influence are immaterial. The rule embraces both technical fiduciary relations and those informal relations which exist whenever one man trusts in and relies upon another. Out of such a relation, the law raises the rules that neither party may exert influence or pressure upon the other.

The narrow question applying the above rules is whether Arpadi's and Dunton's relationship exhibits sufficient trust and de facto control upon which to ground Dunton's duty to disclose negative information regarding the very deal he was promoting. The record reveals more than enough evidence to demonstrate both elements. By imparting confidential business details as well as his personal plans and intentions, Arpadi reposed trust in Dunton as a business counselor to find candidates likely to conform to Arpadi's investment goals. Arpadi expected Dunton to perform as a finder with Arpadi's interests at heart, i.e., not to remain silent as Wellington was being circled by a corporate predator. Dunton exerted de facto control and influence over Arpadi by fostering Arpadi's false belief that there was no reason not to accept Sternau as a suitable candidate. Dunton's review of the intimate details of Arpadi's business marked Dunton's acceptance of that trust. There is no doubt that as regards the proposed merger with [Sternau's company], Dunton and Arpadi stood in a fiduciary relation to each other.

There is a final point. Even if only the agreement between Northeast and Arpadi were to be considered, the law would, I submit, imply a duty on the part of Dunton to disclose critical adverse information in these circumstances. Indeed, I believe that many would agree that even the "morals of the market place" would require it. Surely [Dunton] should not be rewarded for his failure.

RESULT The judgment for Wellington was reversed by the New York Court of Appeals, and Wellington was ordered to pay the finder's fee to Northeast General.

CRITICAL THINKING QUESTIONS

1. What language could Wellington have added to its contract with Northeast to ensure that it was apprised of the reputation of any proposed buyer?
2. The court stated that a broker, who helps negotiate a deal and thereby brings the parties to an agreement, has a fiduciary duty to act in the best interests of the person who hired him or her. Should a finder, who merely introduces the parties, be governed by a lesser ethical standard?

GLOBAL VIEW

"When Ethics Travel"[226]

With the rapid globalization of the marketplace, many corporations face complex ethical challenges abroad. Sometimes, actions regarded as ethically unacceptable in the United States are common practice in foreign countries. How should managers deal with such differences? Corporations take diverse approaches. One method is simply to conform to host-country customs; another is to apply home-country customs uniformly and ignore host-country customs. Both of these extreme approaches present problems. Universally conforming to host-country customs places no limits on the potential abuses that take place in developing countries. The opposite approach, however, amounts to ethical imperialism and leaves no room for legitimate local norms.

Professors Dunfee and Donaldson, of the Wharton School at the University of Pennsylvania, argue that the better option is to balance the opportunity for local identity with the acknowledgment that certain values transcend individual communities. They call these transcendent values "hypernorms." One such hypernorm, known as the efficiency hypernorm, requires that economic agents efficiently utilize resources when their society has a stake. Another hypernorm, at least in democratic or quasi-democratic states, values citizen participation in political affairs. Both of these hypernorms relate to the controversial international business ethics issue of bribery.

Although bribery is prevalent in many countries, it is overwhelmingly regarded as ethically (and legally) wrong, even in those countries where it is widespread. Thus, for that reason alone, bribery should not be viewed as an acceptable norm, even where it is common. But bribery often also interferes with the two hypernorms described above. The efficiency hypernorm frequently proscribes bribery in business dealings because bribe recipients make decisions based on bribes rather than price and quality. Business decisions based on bribery, therefore, undermine the market mechanism. Bribery of high-level government officials in democratic and quasi-democratic states violates the hypernorm that values citizen participation in political affairs. This is because such bribery undercuts accountability to the citizenry in favor of an official's personal gain.

Managers must make other, far more subtle, ethical judgments in international management. Although many legitimate cultural norms that are not proscribed by hypernorms are consistent from culture to culture, others fall into an area known as moral free space. Consider the following value matrix shown to 567 managers in twelve nations:

1. Clean, obedient, polite, responsible, and self-controlled.
2. Forgiving, helpful, loving, and cheerful.
3. Broad-minded, capable, and courageous.
4. Imaginative, independent, and intellectual.

Japanese managers assigned a significantly high priority to the first value dimension (i.e., clean, obedient, polite, responsible, and self-controlled). In contrast, Swedish and Brazilian managers assigned a significantly high priority to the third (i.e., broad-minded, capable, and courageous). Thus, managers in different countries value different characteristics. Many managers in Hong Kong, for instance, view taking credit for the work of another as more unethical than bribery or gaining competitor information.

A global manager would be well advised to understand and respect such cultural differences, rather than trample them with moral imperialism. In the end, a manager unprepared to balance moral tensions is unprepared for the international business realm where subtle, and not so subtle, cultural differences abound.

226. This discussion is based on Thomas Donaldson & Thomas W. Dunfee, *When Ethics Travel: The Promise and Peril of Global Business Ethics*, 41 CAL. MGMT. REV. 45 (1999).

THE RESPONSIBLE MANAGER

ENSURING ETHICAL CONDUCT

Ethical behavior is reinforced when (1) top management exemplifies the company's values and takes a leadership role in programs to promote ethics, (2) managers work to create "shared value" for both the corporation and society, (3) the company creates an atmosphere of openness and trust in which employees feel comfortable reporting violations, and (4) managers engage in activities to enhance and reward ethical behavior at every operational level of the company.

High ethical standards and business success go hand in hand. Although ethics alone may not ensure long-term success, unethical behavior often leads to illegal activity and can result in business failure. Members of top management cannot just pay lip service to this notion. Rather, they should show a dedication and commitment to ethics.

The manager should recognize the critical importance of self-esteem at both the individual and the organizational levels. In the same way that a woman cannot be a little bit pregnant, a manager cannot be a little bit unethical. Once a person starts breaking the little rules, he or she is destined to fall into bigger ethical lapses, often culminating in illegal behavior. If a manager will cheat on the little stuff, imagine what he or she will do when the stakes really matter.

Sometimes, even the best managers fail to be true to their ethical resolutions. But it is critical not to let such lapses go unnoticed. Instead, ethical managers pick themselves up from the ground and reorient their sights to the high ground. Managers who set their sights on the stars are far more likely to reach the top of the mountain than those who aim for the foothills.

Managers should strive to strike a proper balance between economic performance and ethics and look for opportunities to create shared value for the firm and society. A strong ethical culture is a prerequisite to long-term profitability, and social responsibility may be a source of competitive advantage. Managers should look at the firm honestly and objectively, then ask themselves what factors, including industry pressure or internal corporate structure, inhibit employees from being ethical.

A corporation needs a clearly written policy, such as a code of ethics. This policy must be legitimized and reinforced through formal and informal interaction with the entire management, beginning with the board of directors and the CEO. It should include procedural steps for reporting violations of the code of ethics and enforcing the code. The company should include a reference to the code of ethics in its employment agreements.

A company should institute ethics training, including setting up a forum to discuss ethical dilemmas. In deciding whether a course of action is ethically right, managers should ask whether it is fair or unfair to the firm's personnel, customers, and suppliers and to the communities where it does business. Managers should consider the direct and indirect results of a particular decision, including the impact on public image. They should ask themselves how much short-term benefit they are willing to forgo for long-term gain.

Ethics are related to laws, but they are not identical. The legal thing to do is usually the right thing to do—but managers often have to go beyond their legal obligations to act ethically.

The law acknowledges that in a business deal, misunderstandings may arise, unforeseen events may occur, expected gains may disappear, or dislikes may develop that tempt one party to act in bad faith. By requiring each party to act in good faith, the law significantly reduces the risk of a party breaking faith.[227] When reading the chapters that follow, consider whether the courts, in applying the law, are doing anything more than requiring businesspersons to do what they knew or suspected they really should have been doing all along.

227. *See* Robert S. Summers, *"Good Faith," in General Contract Law and the Sales Provisions of the Uniform Commercial Code*, 54 VA. L. REV. 195 (1968).

A Manager's Dilemma

Putting It into Practice

Quantifying the Value of Life

André Gastaux is the CEO of Euro Air, a large international airline with an excellent safety record, having had only two fatal crashes in its fifty years of operations. Unfortunately, a flight from New York to Paris with 350 passengers crashed off the coast of Canada, killing everyone on board.

Gastaux has tentatively decided to compensate all of the victims' families immediately by giving each of them a $150,000 check. Euro Air's insurers have complained that these payments would be overly generous and premature, and they have advised Euro Air not to make any payments until the claims are litigated in court, a process that could take several years. Euro Air's lawyers and its insurers have also advised Gastaux to offer the families of non-American passengers a smaller sum than he offers American families because the non-American passengers earned substantially less than the American passengers and only U.S. courts award large damages to the families of airplane crash victims. Should Gastaux delay making payments to the families of the victims? Should he offer every family the same amount of money even though he knows that the courts in many of the countries with citizens on the doomed plane would award far less if the cases were litigated? What factors should Gastaux consider in making these decisions?

Inside Story

ENRON IMPLODES

Enron Corporation began as a modest gas pipeline company but evolved over the course of the 1990s into an energy giant and a Wall Street favorite. At its pinnacle, the corporation was the nation's seventh-largest public company by revenue, with 32,000 employees worldwide. But the company's increasingly aggressive accounting, which began as clever tricks and grew into complex and illegal schemes, led to the energy giant's demise in 2001.[228]

Largely due to the brilliance and foresight of Harvard MBA Jeffrey K. Skilling, Enron was among the vanguard corporations in the field of energy trading. Skilling was the de facto leader of Enron—insiders say that Kenneth Lay was largely a figurehead even before Skilling was named CEO. By all accounts, Skilling was a genius, but he was reportedly also shrewd and hypercompetitive. Enron was a dog-eat-dog world where short-term shareholder value was paramount, and the "deal" was everything.

Upon joining Enron to lead the gas trading business, Skilling insisted that the business use mark-to-market accounting. In *mark-to-market accounting,* a business books the entire value of a contract on the day it is signed, rather than as cash is collected. Enron estimated the value of natural gas a decade in advance and booked the profits of a ten-year contract at once. This system led to a tremendous drive for growth at Enron, and a huge difference between its reported profits and its cash flow.

Even when Enron was trading profitably, Skilling and Lay avoided calling Enron a trading corporation because Wall Streeters understood the extraordinary volatility of energy trading. Instead, Skilling and Lay dubbed Enron a logistics company. After the corporation reaped a sizable windfall through speculative (and perhaps illegal) trading during the energy crisis in California, the profits were moved into reserve accounts and saved for subsequent quarters. This was but one of many dubious accounting strategies that Enron utilized to manipulate its books.

Andrew S. Fastow, former CFO at Enron, was long touted as a wunderkind. He employed a number of structured finance tools, such as special-purpose entities to hide debt, manufacture profits, and fabricate capital. He personally profited by millions of dollars from some of the transactions.

According to the felony charges filed against Richard A. Causey, the company's former chief accounting officer, the reported value of one Enron asset known as Mariner Energy

CONTINUED

228. The discussion that follows is based on Bethany McLean & Peter Elkind, The Smartest Guys in the Room: The Amazing Rise and Scandalous Fall of Enron (2003) and other public sources.

was arbitrarily increased by $100 million in 2000 so that Enron could meet its projected earnings for the quarter—the same quarter in which Enron had collected, but not reported, profits from the California energy crisis. Enron reported profits from sham sales of assets to an investment partnership called LJM2, which Fastow controlled. The profits were not legitimate because Enron had agreed to bear any losses after the sales. To make matters worse, Enron used its own stock to hedge and secure its obligations.

LJM2 also acted as a nominally independent investor in Enron's off-the-books partnerships. The law required such partnerships to have at least 3 percent of their capital from an independent investor. This requirement was intended to ensure the legitimacy of off-the-books deals. At least one set of off-the-books partnerships, called the Raptors, received the 3 percent from LJM2. Fastow went so far as to arrange for LJM2 to retrieve its 3 percent (plus a substantial profit) before the Raptors engaged in any hedging. This guaranteed Enron compensation if one of its assets lost value. Thus, LJM2, the "independent" investor, did not have any true interest in the Raptors or the legitimacy of their dealings.

Because Enron had used its own stock to hedge its obligations, the scheme depended on the maintenance of Enron's high stock price to achieve its purpose. After the stock price began to fall, a few of Enron's faults surfaced, causing the stock to fall farther, exposing more problems. Enron's myopic focus on short-term shareholder value blinded those with the power to prevent this inevitable and foreseeable cycle. Fastow and other decision makers at Enron apparently believed that as long as an action maximized short-term shareholder value and was even arguably legal, it should be taken. The pressure to meet earnings projections and hide volatile results increased as time went on until desperate measures were required to meet those pressures. At some point, executives at Enron began taking illegal actions to avoid exposing the corporation's frail state.

Burdened by $67 billion of debt, Enron filed for Chapter 11 bankruptcy in late 2001. Many of Enron's assets were sold to pay creditors. The company's original natural-gas pipeline business was sold in November 2004, and an investment bank bought the energy trading business. In September 2006, Enron sold its last remaining significant business asset, a company holding power plants and pipelines in eleven countries.[229] Portland General Electric withdrew from its partnership with Enron and went public independently. By June 2007, Enron had only 300 employees. It had renamed itself Enron Creditors Recovery Corporation and paid out $11.5 billion to creditors.[230]

The Enron Task Force, formed by the Department of Justice to prosecute the illegal conduct that destroyed the company, had mixed success. In May 2006, Lay and Skilling were found guilty of fraud and conspiracy. Lay's conviction was vacated after he died of a heart attack two months before his appeal could be heard. Skilling was sentenced to twenty-four years in prison and began serving his sentence on December 13, 2006; his appeal was pending in 2008. Arthur Andersen LLP, the accounting firm responsible for auditing Enron's financial statements, saw its criminal conviction for obstruction of justice overturned by the U.S. Supreme Court,[231] but not before the company had collapsed. Once 28,000 employees strong, Andersen had just 200 employees at the time of the reversal. They were working out the last details for closing the firm, not providing accounting advice.[232] By 2008, eighteen individuals, including three British bankers, had pleaded guilty to crimes related to the collapse; three people, including Skilling, had been convicted of fraud-related activity; five fraud convictions had been overturned, but three of those individuals may yet be retried and another remained jailed on obstruction of justice and perjury charges; three others were awaiting trial.[233]

The collapse also spawned a host of civil litigation. A lawsuit filed on behalf of former Enron employees who lost their investments in Enron's retirement accounts ultimately netted $265 million.[234] Former Enron shareholders recovered $7.2 billion in settlements through a lawsuit that named former Enron executives and directors as well as Enron's investment banking partners as defendants.[235] Citigroup alone agreed to pay $2.56 billion to settle claims that it had misrepresented Enron's financial condition to secure Enron's investment banking business. Only $89 million of the settlement proceeds payable to Enron's former workers had been paid as of early 2008.[236]

In March 2007, the U.S. Court of Appeals for the Fifth Circuit ruled that the shareholders' class-action suit against the remaining bank defendants, Merrill Lynch, Barclays, and Credit Suisse First Boston, could not proceed because the plaintiffs could not show that they had relied on public

CONTINUED

229. Kristen Hays, *Enron Takes a New Name*, HOUS. CHRON., Apr. 3, 2007, at 1.

230. *Id.*

231. Arthur Andersen v. United States, 544 U.S. 696 (2005) (jury instructions erroneously stated that Arthur Andersen could be found guilty even if the jury did not find that Andersen employees acted with knowledge and intent to commit a crime).

232. Linda Greenhouse, *Justices Reject Auditor Verdict in Enron Scandal*, N.Y. TIMES, June 1, 2005, at 1.

233. *Prosecution Scorecard,* Chron.com, http://www.chron.com/news/specials/enron/ (last visited Nov. 7, 2007).

234. Hays, *supra* note 147.

235. Kristen Hays, *Possible Enron Settlement Emerges*, HOUS. CHRON., July 28, 2007, at 1.

236. Associated Press, *Error Shorts Enron Settlement Fund,* Jan. 24, 2008.

statements made by the defendants.[237] In January 2008, the U.S. Supreme Court denied the shareholders' petition for *certiorari,* all but eradicating the investors' hopes of making additional recoveries. That same month, the Supreme Court held in a case not involving Enron that shareholders have no private right of action to sue third parties—such as suppliers, accountants, and lawyers—for securities fraud committed by the companies with which they did business unless the shareholders can show that they relied on public statements by those third parties in making the decision to invest.[238]

237. Regents of the Univ. of Cal. v. Credit Suisse First Boston (USA), Inc., 482 F.3d 372 (5th Cir. 2007), *cert. denied*, Regents of the Univ. of Cal. v. Merrill Lynch, Pierce, Fenner & Smith, 2008 U.S. LEXIS 1120 (U.S. Jan. 22, 2008).

238. Stoneridge Inv. Partners v. Scientific-Atlanta, Inc., 128 S. Ct. 761 (2008) ("[T]he implied [private] right of action does not reach customer/supplier companies because the investors did not rely upon their statements or representations.") (Case 23.1).

Key Words and Phrases

apartheid 44
compensatory justice 31
deontological theory of ethics 30
distributive justice 31
Ethical Business Leader's Decision Tree 26
fiduciary duty 49
Kantian theory 30
mark-to-market accounting 54
Rawlsian moral theory 30
retributive justice 31
reversibility 30
shareholder primacy 26
teleological theory of ethics 30
universalizability 30
utilitarianism 30

Questions and Case Problems

1. Christine Bancroft is a twenty-five-year-old blonde with a face and a figure that some of her male colleagues thought seemed better suited to the cover of the *Sports Illustrated* swimsuit issue than *Advertising Age.* After spending her first three months as an analyst at the privately held advertising boutique Scot Wayne More, sitting in her cubicle doing research on the Hispanic market, she looked forward to the day she would have a chance to wow clients with the finely honed marketing skills she had acquired while pursuing her MBA at Northwestern University.

   Christine knew that Allen Scot and Bart Wayne had a reputation for entertaining clients from out of town at San Francisco's all-male Pacific Union Club, so she was pleasantly surprised when Allen asked her to join him and Bart for lunch with Andrew Wise at the World Trade Club. Wise was an account executive from the Cincinnati headquarters of Quinn & Inder, the second-largest consumer products firm in the United States. At first, Christine thought that she'd been invited to discuss their plans to extend their reach into the Hispanic youth market. But when she asked Bart how she might best prepare for the meeting, he just smiled and said, "Just wear that little black dress you wore at the firm's holiday party and leave the talking to Allen and me. Andrew asked for California, so we're giving him California."

   What should Christine do? What would you do if you were head of human resources for Scot Wayne More and overheard the conversation between Bart and Christine while waiting in Allen's office to go over an offer letter for a new hire? [Inspired in part by Joseph L. Badaracco, Jr., Defining Moments: When Managers Must Choose Between Right and Right (1997).]

2. In August 1969, followers of Charles Manson killed seven persons, including actress Sharon Tate, in two Los Angeles homes. Manson has been denied parole repeatedly and remains in prison for the gruesome murders that he and members of his cult committed. Now shops have

begun selling a line of clothes depicting Manson, and the rock band Guns 'N' Roses has included a song written and sung by Manson in one of its albums.

Cesar Turner is in charge of ordering policies for Mammoth Records, a large national retail chain of stores selling compact discs, DVDs, and T-shirts. He has received a flood of letters and e-mails from angry parent groups, church leaders, politicians, and others demanding that Mammoth pull the Guns 'N' Roses CD and stop selling the Manson T-shirts. Turner knows that these are very popular items at the retail stores. If Mammoth stops selling them, its competitors will pick up the extra business, thereby reducing Mammoth's profits. What should Turner do?

Mammoth has also come under fire from local right-to-life groups because it sells directories of physicians and clinics that will perform abortions. Should Turner stop selling the directories? Does it matter whether Turner personally views abortion as legalized murder or as a choice every woman should have?

Finally, local police and Broad Based Apprehension Suppression Treatment and Alternatives (an antigang coalition) are pressuring record stores to stop carrying the CD "G.U.N. Generations of United Norteños . . . XIV Till Eternity," which includes songs exhorting members of the Norteños (a Northern California gang) to kill members of the Southern California gang Sureños. Lyrics include the lines, "It's up to Norteños to kill the beast. All Sureños must cease." In what ways, if any, should Turner's analysis of this request differ from his analysis of the controversies over the Guns 'N' Roses CD, the Manson T-shirts, and the abortion directories?

3. Zandra Quartney is a manager/buyer in charge of purchasing children's shoes for a large retail store chain. She is also a die-hard football fan. This year, the Super Bowl will be played in the Georgia Dome in Atlanta, Georgia, her hometown. Quartney's favorite team, the Steelers, is expected to reach the Super Bowl.

   Currently, the store chain carries four brands of children's rain boots. In an effort to streamline its product line, the CEO has decided to cut back to three brands of rain boots, leaving to Quartney the decision of which brand to cut. Assume that all four brands are equally profitable. If the makers of Brand One send Quartney a pair of Super Bowl tickets, should she accept them? Does it matter whether the maker of Brand One is also a close friend of hers?

4. Assume the same facts as in Question 3, except that Brand One underperforms the other three brands. How, if at all, should that affect Quartney's decision? What if it is mid-January and the Steelers are definitely in the Super Bowl? Quartney has waited her entire life to watch the Steelers play in the Super Bowl. Even if she would not accept the tickets before, should she accept them now? Can she get out of her dilemma by offering to pay the face value of the tickets? Should she accept the tickets if she has already decided to discontinue Brand One?

5. Ginny Pocock, a recent graduate of New York University, is a first-year associate with the McBain Consulting Group. The partner in charge of a major strategy study for an important new client in the shipping business has asked Pocock to call low-level employees in competing shipping companies to gather competitive data to be used to devise a winning strategy for the client. She was instructed not to identify the client but to introduce herself as a consultant doing an analysis of the shipping industry.

   Assume that Pocock knows that senior managers in the competing firms would consider the data she is collecting proprietary and would not talk with her at all if they knew that she worked for a direct competitor. Is it ethical for Pocock to question the lower-level employees without revealing that she is working for a direct competitor? What should she do if after telling the partner that she considers it unethical to make the calls, she is told that consultants do this all the time and that refusal to do it would be a career-limiting move?

6. Indra Wu, a sales rep at Rite Engineering, attended a trade show and conference at company expense. Many exhibitors donated prizes, which were awarded to attendees based on a drawing of free tickets given to all attendees upon registration. Wu won a $12,000 plasma television in one of the drawings. The winner's certificate included the winner's name with no mention of the company.

   What should Wu do? What should Wu's supervisor do if she learns of the prize from someone other than Wu?

7. Jody Hunter and Jim Boling, two managers at Georgia-Pacific Corporation, a paper manufacturer, disagree about continuing the company's membership in Business for Affordable Medicine (BAM), a coalition of state governors and corporations supporting a U.S. Senate bill that would bring generic versions of brand-name drugs to market more quickly. Experts predict that the bill, if adopted by Congress, will reduce total spending on prescription drugs by $60 billion over the next ten years. Hunter, Georgia-Pacific's director of health and welfare, strongly supports the bill. Georgia-Pacific's prescription drug costs for employees increased by 21 percent in the last year alone. If the bill becomes law, the resultant drop in health-care costs will save Georgia-Pacific large amounts of money (in addition to saving money for other people across the country who need prescriptions).

Eli Lilly & Co., a large, name-brand pharmaceutical firm for which Georgia-Pacific is the leading supplier of paper goods and packaging, has been pressuring the paper company to withdraw from BAM. Boling, a Georgia-Pacific sales manager, fears that "we may lose our business position if this is not managed correctly." Boling points out that Lilly plans to launch six new compounds next year, "which could mean millions of dollars in paper business for us." In one e-mail, Boling mentioned that a three-year agreement with Lilly "is sitting on the Procurement Managers [sic] desk now to be signed." Should Georgia-Pacific withdraw from BAM? Is it ethical for Lilly to use its business relationship to try to force Georgia-Pacific to withdraw? [This question is drawn largely from Laurie McGinley, *Georgia-Pacific Curbs Push to Speed Generic Drugs,* WALL ST. J., Sept. 4, 2002, at 2.]

8. In April 1999, Tim Rudolph left the Stanford Graduate School of Business to become the founder and CEO of IPO.com, a securities brokerage firm specializing in helping young companies use the Internet to raise money from the public. IPO.com went public on March 2, 2000. On September 5, 2000, Rudolph personally sold one million shares of stock for $75 million. He used $10 million of the proceeds to buy a large house in Atherton, California, an easy commute to the company's Silicon Valley offices. Rudolph still owns another four million shares.

   IPO.com employs thirty senior computer programmers who are paid a starting salary of $125,000 and given stock options potentially worth millions. The company also employs five janitors who empty the trash, clean the latrines, and vacuum the senior programmers' work areas. These janitors are paid approximately $15,000 a year. Due to the astronomical cost of living in Silicon Valley, several janitors with children have second jobs and rent out space in their one-bedroom apartments to make additional money to support their families. Four of the company's janitors are non-English-speaking immigrants from Mexico who are desperate for employment and, as a result, are willing to work for the low salary.

   Although there is a large pool of unskilled workers willing to work as janitors for $15,000 a year, the market for skilled programmers is so tight that IPO.com has had to institute special incentives to keep the programmers happy. Most recently, the senior programmer was given a Hummer, the civilian version of the U.S. Army's Humvee vehicle, to celebrate the completion of an important piece of code.

   What ethical and business considerations should a corporation and its CEO consider when setting the salaries for the different types of workers it employs?

3

COURTS, SOURCES OF LAW, AND DISPUTE RESOLUTION

INTRODUCTION

Equal Justice Under the Law

"Equal justice under the law" is the inscription on the front of the U.S. Supreme Court building in Washington, D.C. It is a reminder that the judicial system is intended to protect the legal rights of those who come before a court. In 1790, President George Washington underscored the importance of the judiciary when he told the U.S. Supreme Court: "I have always been persuaded that the stability and success of the National Government, and consequently the happiness of the American people, would depend in a considerable degree on the interpretation and execution of its laws."

In a litigation-prone society, it is important for managers to understand the judicial system and be prepared to use it, when appropriate, to protect their rights and the rights of their companies. By the same token, managers should recognize when pursuing litigation is not in the company's best interest. Appreciating the pros and cons of the common alternatives to litigation permits managers to find the right resolution mechanism for the particular problem at hand.

CHAPTER OVERVIEW

This chapter begins with a discussion of the federal and state court systems, including standing to sue and jurisdiction. We then identify sources of law, including constitutions, statutes, regulations, and common law. The chapter discusses factors managers should consider when selecting a dispute resolution mechanism and when deciding whether to settle. We then suggest litigation strategies for both plaintiffs and defendants and outline the litigation process. The chapter describes various alternative dispute resolution techniques, such as mediation and arbitration. We conclude with a discussion of discovery, attorney–client privilege, and document retention and deletion policies.

HOW TO READ A CASE CITATION

When an appellate court decides a case, the court writes an opinion, which is usually published in one or more *reporters*—collections of court opinions. Some trial courts also publish opinions. The citation of a case (the *cite*) includes the following information:

1. The plaintiff's name.
2. The defendant's name.
3. The volume number and title of the reporter in which the case is reported.
4. The page number at which the case report begins.
5. The court that decided the case (if the court is not indicated, it is understood to be the state supreme court or the U.S. Supreme Court, depending on the reporter in which the case appears).
6. The year in which the case was decided.

When a lawsuit is originally filed, the case name appears as *plaintiff v. defendant.* If the case is appealed, the case name usually appears as *appellant* or *petitioner* (the person who is appealing the case or seeking a writ of certiorari) *v. appellee* or *respondent* (the other party). So, if the defendant loses at the trial level and appeals the decision to a higher court, the name of the defendant (now the appellant) will appear first in the case citation.

For example, *Hershenow v. Enterprise Rent-A-Car of Boston,* 840 N.E.2d 526 (Mass. 2007), indicates that in 2007 the Massachusetts Supreme Judicial Court issued an opinion in a case involving Hershenow as the petitioner and Enterprise Rent-A-Car of Boston as the respondent. The case is reported in volume 840 of the second series of the North Eastern Reporter, beginning on page 526. *In re Delta Air Lines, Inc.,* 370 B.R. 552 (Bankr. S.D.N.Y. 2007), refers to the bankruptcy proceedings of Delta Air Lines, the international carrier offering flights worldwide. The case is reported in volume 370 of the Bankruptcy Reporter, beginning on page 552.[1] The parenthetical information indicates that this is a U.S. Bankruptcy Court sitting in the Southern District of New York.

Some cases are reported in more than one reporter. For example, the famous New York taxicab case discussed in Chapter 20, *Walkovszky v. Carlton,* is cited as 18 N.Y.2d 414, 223 N.E.2d 6, 276 N.Y.S.2d 585 (1966). One may locate this case in volume 18 of the second series of New York Reports, in volume 223 of the second series of the North Eastern Reporter, or in volume 276 of the second series of the New York Supplement.

Opinions are also available online from Westlaw at Westlaw.com and from LexisNexis. An opinion that has not yet been placed into a printed reporter receives an alphanumeric designation until it is given a published cite of the type described above. For example, *Triad Consultants, Inc. v. Wiggins,* WL 2733687 (10th Cir. Sept. 17, 2007), is available online at Westlaw.com; WL 2733687 is its temporary number until it is published in the third edition of the Federal Reporter. The same case in the LexisNexis database has the cite U.S. App. LEXIS 22226 (10th Cir. Sept. 17, 2007). Once the case is in print, the citation will change from WL 2733687 or U.S. App. LEXIS 22226 to a citation with the volume and page number in "F.3d."

THE U.S. AND STATE COURT SYSTEMS

The United States has two judicial systems: federal and state. Federal and state courts have different *subject matter jurisdiction,* meaning that they have the power to hear different kinds of cases. In general, federal courts are courts of limited subject matter jurisdiction, meaning they can adjudicate only certain types of cases. As is discussed further in Chapter 4, the jurisdiction of the federal courts arises from the U.S. Constitution and statutes enacted by Congress. By contrast, state constitutions and statutes give state courts general subject matter jurisdiction, so they can hear any type of dispute. The two coexisting judicial systems are a result of the federalism created by the U.S. Constitution, which gives certain powers to the federal government while reserving other powers to the states.

The basic structure of the federal and state court systems is diagrammed in Exhibit 3.1. In practice, this structure is more complex than the diagram indicates. For example, an applicant may appeal an adverse decision from the U.S. Patent and Trademark Office to the Board of Patent Appeals and Interferences. The person may then appeal an unfavorable ruling from this court to the Court of Appeals for the Federal Circuit. Alternatively, the applicant may appeal the unfavorable ruling of the Board of Patent Appeals and Interferences by filing a civil action, in the U.S. District Court for the District of Columbia, against the Commissioner of the U.S. Patent and Trademark Office.

FEDERAL JURISDICTION

Federal courts derive their legal power to hear civil cases from three sources: federal question jurisdiction, diversity jurisdiction, and jurisdiction when the United States is a party. The Eleventh Amendment to the U.S. Constitution generally protects a state (or an agency thereof) from being sued without its consent in a federal court. Congress can abrogate this immunity only if it unequivocally expresses its intention to do so and acts pursuant to a constitutional grant of authority, such as Section 5 of the Fourteenth Amendment. Chapter 4 addresses this shield in more detail.

FEDERAL QUESTION JURISDICTION

Federal courts have nonexclusive jurisdiction over cases involving a federal question. A *federal question* exists when the dispute concerns federal law, that is, a legal right arising under the U.S. Constitution, a federal statute, federal common law, a treaty of the United States, or an administrative regulation issued by a federal government agency. Cases involving a federal question may also be brought in state court, but the defendant has the right to remove such a case to federal court if the defendant so chooses. There is

1. When quoting a particular passage from an opinion, one should include the page number on which the quotation is found after the first page number of the case in the reporter. A comma should separate the two numbers.

EXHIBIT 3.1 Structure of the Federal and State Court Systems in the United States

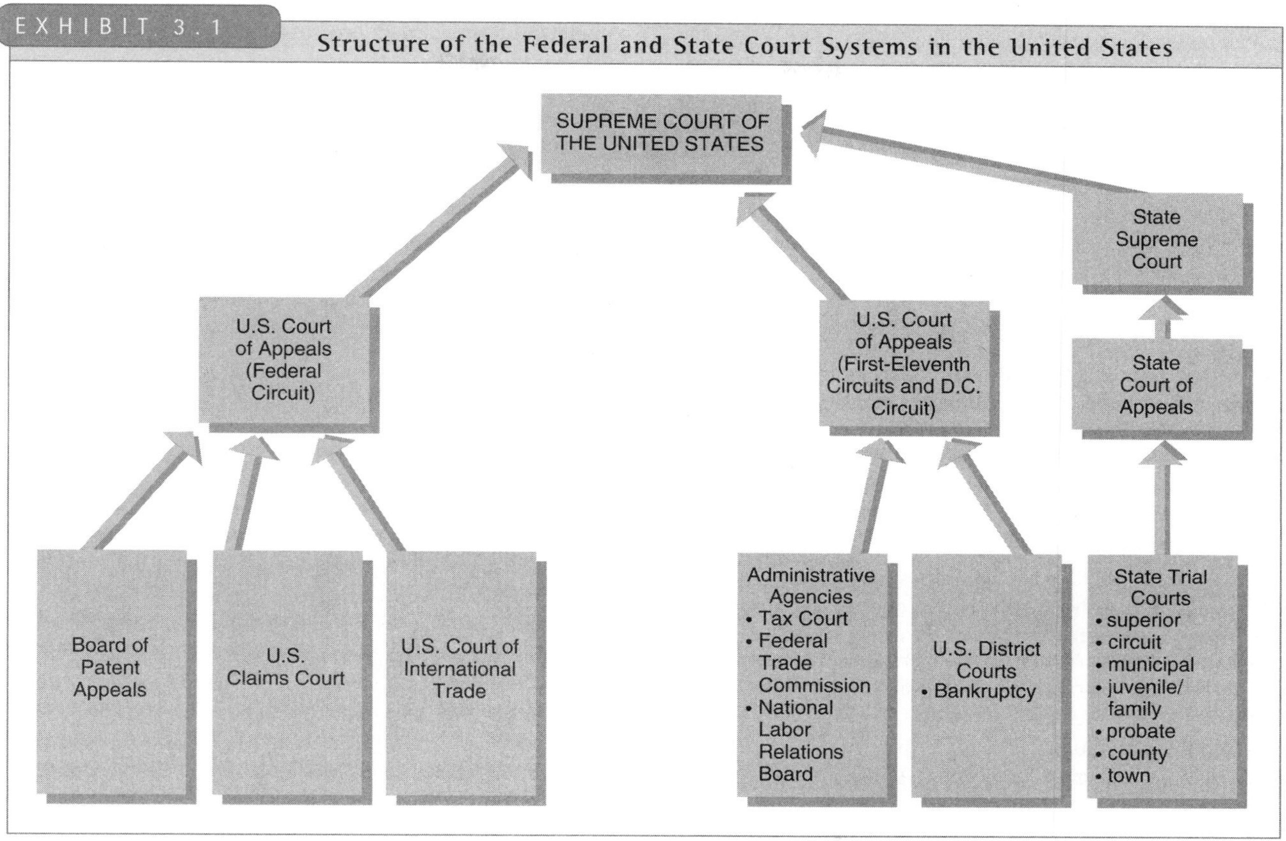

no minimum monetary requirement for lawsuits involving a federal question.

DIVERSITY JURISDICTION

Diversity jurisdiction exists when a lawsuit is between citizens of two different states, or between a citizen of a state and a citizen of a foreign country, and the amount in controversy, exclusive of interest and all costs, exceeds $75,000. The purpose of the monetary requirement is to prevent trivial cases from overwhelming the federal judicial system. Diversity cases may also be brought in state court. The defendant may remove the case to federal court as long as the amount in controversy exceeds $75,000.

Diversity jurisdiction was traditionally justified by the fear that state courts might be biased against the out-of-state party. In federal district court, all litigants are in a neutral forum, and there should be no local prejudice for the home team.

Most diversity cases do not involve federal statutes or the U.S. Constitution and thus could also be resolved pursuant to state law in state court. In a landmark case, *Erie Railroad Co. v. Tompkins,*[2] the U.S. Supreme Court held that a federal court exercising its diversity jurisdiction must apply state law to the dispute unless the lawsuit concerns the U.S. Constitution or a federal statute. The *Erie doctrine,* as the holding of this case is known, ensures that the outcome of a diversity case in federal court will be similar to the outcome in a state court because the same state law will govern either adjudication. This prevents litigants (the parties to a lawsuit) from *forum shopping* between federal and state courts in an attempt to have the more favorable law govern their dispute.

A federal court hearing a diversity case will apply the *conflict-of-law rules* promulgated by the state in which it is sitting to determine which state's law should govern the dispute. For example, if a New York state court would apply the law of the state where an accident occurred to a lawsuit alleging negligent operation of a motor vehicle, then a federal court sitting in New York City hearing a case involving an automobile accident in Connecticut would apply Connecticut law to determine whether the driver was negligent.

2. 304 U.S. 64 (1938).

Determining Citizenship

An individual is a citizen of the state where that person has his or her legal residence or domicile. An individual may have a house in more than one state but is a citizen only of the state he or she considers home.

A corporation, in contrast, may have dual citizenship. A corporation is deemed a citizen of both (1) the state in which it has been incorporated and (2) the state where it has its principal place of business. Federal courts usually apply one of three tests to determine where a company engaged in multistate operations has its principal place of business. The first is the *nerve-center test*. To find the corporation's nerve center, courts consider where (1) the executive and administrative offices are located, (2) the income tax return is filed, and (3) the directors and shareholders meet. The second test focuses on the location of the majority of the corporation's physical operations, such as its manufacturing facilities or offices. The *total-activity test,* a combination of the first two tests, considers all aspects of the corporate entity, including the nature and scope of the company's activities. The total-activity test is gaining popularity among the courts.

JURISDICTION IN CASES IN WHICH THE UNITED STATES IS A PARTY

Federal courts have exclusive jurisdiction over all lawsuits in which the U.S. government, or an officer or agency thereof, is the plaintiff or the defendant. As with federal question jurisdiction, there is no minimum monetary requirement for lawsuits in which the United States is a party.

FEDERAL COURTS

The main function of the federal courts is to interpret the U.S. Constitution and laws of the United States. Congress's first piece of legislation, "An Act to Establish the Judicial Courts of the United States," created the federal district courts. Two years later, Congress created the federal courts of appeals. The three-tiered system of district courts, courts of appeals, and the U.S. Supreme Court remains today.

The president of the United States nominates each judge who serves on a federal court. The U.S. Senate, pursuant to its "advice and consent" power, then votes to approve or reject the judicial nominees. The Constitution does not impose any age or citizenship requirements on judicial candidates. Once confirmed by the Senate, federal judges have a lifetime appointment to the bench. They may be removed from office only by legislative impeachment if they violate the law. Lifetime tenure protects federal judges from public reprisal for making unpopular or difficult decisions. As a result, the federal judiciary is more independent than either the executive or the legislative branch.

U.S. DISTRICT COURTS

The U.S. district courts are the trial courts of the federal system. Currently, the country is divided into ninety-four judicial districts. Each state has at least one district; the more populous states have as many as four. Exhibit 3.2 shows the various districts.

Many districts have two or more divisions. For example, the main location for the U.S. District Court for the Southern District of Florida is Miami, but that district also has courts in Key West, Fort Lauderdale, West Palm Beach, and Fort Pierce. Thus, a plaintiff may file its lawsuit with the nearest federal district court, provided, of course, that the court has jurisdiction over the particular controversy.

U.S. COURTS OF APPEALS

The primary functions of a court of appeals are (1) to review decisions of the trial courts within its territory; (2) to review decisions of certain administrative agencies and commissions; and (3) to issue *writs,* or orders, to lower courts or to litigants. Only final decisions of lower courts are appealable. A decision is final if it conclusively resolves a discrete issue in a dispute or the entire controversy. The court of appeals can affirm or reverse the decision of the lower court. It may also *vacate,* or nullify, the previous court's ruling and *remand* the case—send it back to the lower court for reconsideration in light of the appellate court's opinion.

Cases before the courts of appeals are usually presented to a panel of three judges. Occasionally, all the judges of a court of appeals will sit together to hear and decide a particularly important or close case. This is called an *en banc* (or *in banc*) *hearing.* Frequently, the panel of judges will decide an appeal based upon the legal briefs, or written memoranda, submitted to the court, rather than hearing oral arguments presented by the lawyers.

There are thirteen courts of appeals, one for each of the twelve regional circuits in the United States and one for the Federal Circuit. The Ninth Circuit, encompassing nine states and Guam, is the largest circuit, with twenty-six active judges and two with inactive status. The Court of Appeals for the First Circuit has only six active judges. Exhibit 3.2 shows the geographic boundaries of the circuits.

The Court of Appeals for the Federal Circuit, created in 1982, does not have jurisdiction over a specific geographic region but rather hears appeals from various specialized

EXHIBIT 3.2 **Map of Federal Judicial Districts and Circuits**

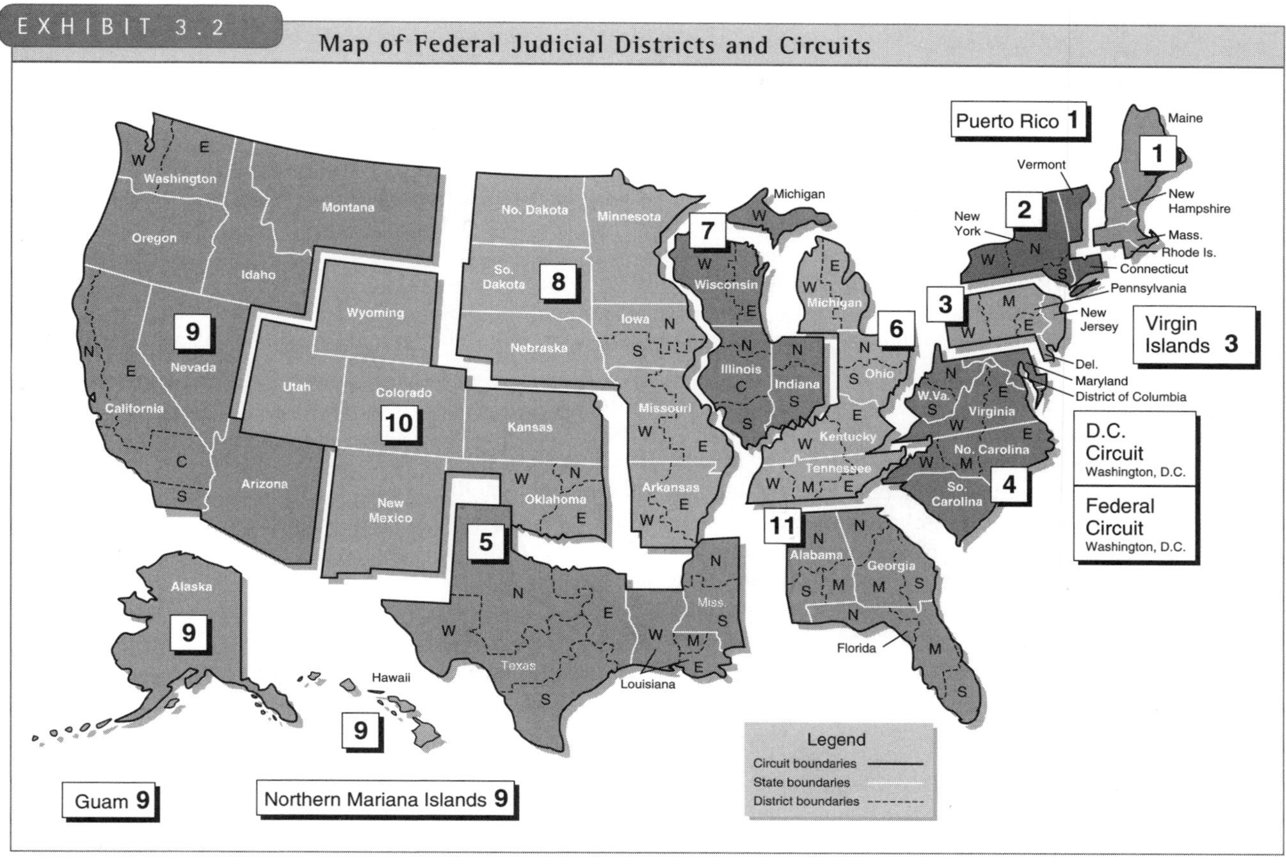

federal courts, including the Court of Federal Claims, the Court of International Trade, and the International Trade Commission, which handles disputes involving unfair practices in import trade. The Federal Circuit also hears all cases involving patents. Exhibit 3.3 lists the states and territories included within each circuit.

EXHIBIT 3.3 **Geographic Regions of the U.S. Courts of Appeals**

Circuit	Region
District of Columbia	District of Columbia
First	Maine, Massachusetts, New Hampshire, Puerto Rico, and Rhode Island
Second	Connecticut, New York, and Vermont
Third	Delaware, New Jersey, Pennsylvania, and Virgin Islands
Fourth	Maryland, North Carolina, South Carolina, Virginia, and West Virginia
Fifth	Canal Zone, Louisiana, Mississippi, and Texas
Sixth	Kentucky, Michigan, Ohio, and Tennessee
Seventh	Illinois, Indiana, and Wisconsin
Eighth	Arkansas, Iowa, Minnesota, Missouri, Nebraska, North Dakota, and South Dakota
Ninth	Alaska, Arizona, California, Guam, Hawaii, Idaho, Montana, Nevada, Oregon, and Washington
Tenth	Colorado, Kansas, New Mexico, Oklahoma, Utah, and Wyoming
Eleventh	Alabama, Florida, and Georgia
Federal	Based in Washington D.C., but hears cases dealing with patents and certain other matters from all regions

Political PERSPECTIVE

Splitting up the Ninth Circuit

The Ninth Circuit is the largest circuit in the country, with twenty-eight statutorily authorized judgeships.[a] Republicans in the U.S. Senate, known historically to favor less activist judges, have proposed splitting the Ninth Circuit into several circuits. They point to several factors to support their argument for breaking up the Ninth Circuit. First, the Ninth Circuit has a significant backlog of cases. Even judges sitting on the circuit admit that it has too many cases and too few judges. Secondly, its sheer size dwarfs all the other circuits. Due to its size, the judges rarely sit for en banc review. Instead, eleven judges, who may not include the three judges who originally heard the case, are randomly selected to hear a "limited en banc." Finally, and most controversially, Republicans argue that the Ninth Circuit is particularly liberal and activist compared with other circuits. They point out that the Ninth Circuit has been overturned by the U.S. Supreme Court more than any other circuit and that seventeen of the twenty-eight judges were appointed by Democrats.

Democrats counter that five of the judges appointed by Democrats are solidly conservative, leaving sixteen conservative judges as a counterweight to their more activist colleagues. In response, Republicans point to controversial decisions that were subsequently overturned by the U.S. Supreme Court. These include *Newdow v. U.S. Congress*,[b] in which the Ninth Circuit ruled that teacher-led recitations in school of the Pledge of Allegiance, which contains the phrase "under God," violated the U.S. Consitutions's Establishment Clause, and *Planned Parenthood Federation of America v. Gonzales*,[c] in which the Ninth Circuit struck down the Partial-Birth Abortion Ban Act of 2003 as an impermissible inference with a woman's right to privacy. (*Planned Parenthood Federation of America v. Gonzales* is discussed in Chapter 4.) Democrats insist that the Ninth Circuit's perceived "liberal bias" is illusory and that its size is manageable. As for the number of overturned verdicts, the Democrats assert that this is simply a function of the number of cases decided by the Ninth Circuit. The number of overturned verdicts, as a percentage of all verdicts rendered, is, in fact, not much higher than that of other circuits.

a. Press Release, Dave Madden, Public Information Office, United States Courts for the Ninth Circuit, Idaho to Celebrate Investiture of Ninth Circuit Judge N. Randy Smith (June 30, 2007), *available at* http://www.ca9.uscourts.gov/ (last visited Sept. 10, 2007).
b. 328 F.3d 466 (9th Cir. 2003), *rev'd sub nom.* Elk Grove Unified Sch. Dist. v. Newdow, 542 U.S. 1 (2004) (parent had no standing to challenge Pledge of Allegiance on behalf of minor child).
c. 435 F.3d 1163 (9th Cir. 2006), *rev'd*, 127 S. Ct. 1610 (2007).

SPECIALIZED FEDERAL COURTS

The federal system has several specialized courts that resolve legal disputes within particular subject areas.

The bankruptcy courts are units of the federal district courts that hear proceedings involving the bankruptcy laws and regulations of the United States. When Fruit of the Loom (clothing manufacturer), Enron Corporation (energy company), and United Airlines filed for protection from their creditors under Chapter 11 of the bankruptcy laws, they did so in federal bankruptcy court. (The law of bankruptcy is discussed in Chapter 24.)

The tax courts hear taxpayer petitions or appeals regarding federal income, estate, and gift taxes. The Court of International Trade has jurisdiction over disputes involving tariffs, or import taxes, and trade laws. This court also hears cases on appeal from the U.S. International Trade Commission. The U.S. Court of Appeals for the Armed Forces hears cases from the lower courts and tribunals within the armed services. Military veterans and their families may petition the U.S. Court of Appeals for Veterans Claims to review administrative decisions regarding their entitlement to veterans' benefits.

U.S. SUPREME COURT

The U.S. Supreme Court comprises one chief justice and eight associate justices. At least six justices must be present to hear a case. A majority of the cases heard by the Supreme Court are on appeal from the U.S. courts of appeals. A decision by a state supreme court is also appealable to the U.S. Supreme Court, but only when the case concerns the U.S.

Constitution or some other federal law. The Supreme Court may also hear direct appeals from a federal district court decision declaring an act of the U.S. Congress unconstitutional. For example, the Supreme Court directly reviewed the invalidation by the U.S. District Court for the District of Columbia of portions of the Bipartisan Campaign Reform Act of 2002.[3]

The Supreme Court has *discretionary review*, meaning that it decides which cases within its jurisdiction it will adjudicate. When it agrees to hear a case, the Supreme Court issues a *writ of certiorari* ordering the lower court to certify the record of proceedings below and send it up to the Supreme Court. Four justices must vote to hear a case before a writ can be issued. If a writ was sought but denied by the Supreme Court, the citation for the case will indicate *"cert. denied."*

The Supreme Court will not decide cases that involve a political question. A *political question* is a dispute that is more appropriately decided by democratically elected officials in the executive or the legislative branch of government. Nonetheless, the Court effectively determined the outcome of the 2000 U.S. presidential election when it prohibited Florida from doing a manual recount of the ballots in *Bush v. Gore*.[4] Courts have also recognized a privilege for "state secrets."[5]

STATE COURTS

State courts handle the bulk of litigated disputes in the United States. Each state's constitution creates the judicial branch of government for that state. For example, the Constitution of Texas provides:

> [T]he judicial power of this State shall be vested in one Supreme Court, in one Court of Criminal Appeals, in Courts of Appeals, in District Courts, in County Courts, in Commissioners Courts, in Courts of Justices of the Peace, and in such other courts as may be provided by law.[6]

The state constitution then provides the details of the state judicial system. These include the number of justices sitting on the state's supreme court, the jurisdiction of the state courts, the geographic districts of the various appellate courts, the way in which justices and judges are selected or appointed, and the tenure of justices and judges.

STATE TRIAL COURTS

At the lowest level of the state trial court system are several courts of limited jurisdiction. These courts decide minor criminal matters, small civil suits, and other specialized legal disputes. Examples include traffic courts, small claims courts, juvenile courts, and family courts. In these courts, the procedures are often informal. Parties may appear without lawyers, the court may not keep a complete transcript or recording of the proceedings, and the technical rules of evidence and formal courtroom procedures may not apply. The jurisdiction of a small claims court is usually limited to disputes involving less than, for example, $5,000. Any dispute involving more than this amount must be heard by a higher-level trial court.

The second level of state trial courts consists of courts of general or unlimited jurisdiction. These courts have formal courtroom procedures, apply the standard rules of evidence, and record all proceedings.

State court actions cover a broad spectrum of business activities. For example, the family of an eight-year-old girl sued a toy store in New York state court after she was severely bitten by the business owner's dog while shopping.[7] A Louisiana state court ruled that a former group home worker fired for sleeping on the job was not disqualified from receiving unemployment benefits.[8] A jury in Texas awarded Pennzoil Company more than $10 billion in damages from Texaco, Inc. for intentionally interfering with Pennzoil's contract to buy Getty Oil.[9]

In 2002, the State of Michigan created the first "cybercourt" to hear business-related litigation. Circuit court judges preside over the court, which uses videoconferencing, digital record keeping, and other online tools. All filings and briefs are filed online. The court's goal is to expedite business litigation involving more than $25,000 and significantly lower its cost. The success of the Michigan cybercourt has prompted several other states to consider starting their own cybercourts.

STATE APPELLATE COURTS

A state appellate court is similar to its counterpart in the federal system. It usually consists of a panel of three judges who review lower court rulings for errors in the application of the law or the procedures followed. An appellate court may affirm, reverse, or vacate and remand any final decision of a lower

3. McConnell v. Fed. Election Comm'n, 540 U.S. 93 (2003).
4. 531 U.S. 98 (2000).
5. Tenet v. Doe, 544 U.S. 1 (2005).
6. Tex. Const. art. V, § 1.
7. Bernstein v. Penny Whistle Toys, Inc., 834 N.Y.S.2d 173 (N.Y. App. Div. 2007).
8. Delta Am. Healthcare, Inc. v. Burgess, 930 So. 2d 1108 (La. Ct. App. 2006).
9. The case, which is the subject of the "Inside Story" in Chapter 7, ultimately settled for $3 billion.

court. The appellate court usually accepts the trial judge's or jury's findings of fact, unless a particular finding is clearly unsupported by the evidence presented at trial. The appellate court is not required to accept the lower court's conclusions of law, however; it may consider legal issues *de novo,* or anew, as if the trial court had not resolved any questions of law.

STATE SUPREME COURT

Each state has one court that acts as the highest judicial authority in that state. Most states call that court the supreme court. (In New York, however, the highest state court is called the New York Court of Appeals; the intermediate appellate court is called the Supreme Court, Appellate Division; and the state trial courts are called Supreme Courts.) The number of justices on a state supreme court varies from three to nine.

A state supreme court usually has discretionary jurisdiction over all decisions of a court of appeals. A state supreme court may also have jurisdiction over cases where a statute of the state or the United States has been ruled unconstitutional in whole or in part. In addition, the state supreme court will decide all appeals in criminal cases in which a sentence of death has been imposed.

STANDING

Courts will not hear a case unless a real and substantial controversy is involved and resolving the lawsuit will provide actual relief to one party.[10] Further, the party pursuing the litigation must have standing to sue. *Standing* means that the party seeking relief (1) is the proper party to advance the litigation, (2) has a personal interest in the outcome of the suit, and (3) will benefit from a favorable ruling.[11] A party challenging an administrative agency's interpretation of a statute must be arguably "within the zone of interests" to be regulated or protected under the statute in question.[12] In the following case, the National Security Agency questioned whether the American Civil Liberties Union and other plaintiffs had standing to challenge the constitutionality of warrantless wiretaps pursuant to the Terrorist Surveillance Program.

10. United States v. Hays, 515 U.S. 737 (1995).

11. Stated more technically by the U.S. Supreme Court, to establish standing, "First, the plaintiff must have suffered an 'injury in fact'—an invasion of a legally protected interest which is (a) concrete and particularized and (b) 'actual or imminent, not 'conjectural' or 'hypothetical.' Second, there must be a causal connection between the injury and the conduct complained of—the injury has to be 'fairly . . . trace[able] to the challenged action of the defendant, and not . . . the result [of] the independent action of some third party not before the court.' Third, it must be 'likely,' as opposed to merely 'speculative,' that the injury will be 'redressed by a favorable decision.'" Lujan v. Defenders of Wildlife, 504 U.S. 555, 560–61 (1992).

12. Nat'l Credit Union Admin. v. First Nat'l Bank & Trust Co., 522 U.S. 479 (1998) (commercial banks had standing to challenge the National Credit Union Administration's determination that the Federal Credit Union Act permitted federal credit unions comprising unrelated employer groups). Congress responded to this litigation by passing legislation that expressly adopted the NCUA's intepretation.

A CASE IN POINT

CASE 3.1

AMERICAN CIVIL LIBERTIES UNION v. NATIONAL SECURITY AGENCY

UNITED STATES COURT OF APPEALS FOR THE SIXTH CIRCUIT
493 F.3D 644 (6TH CIR. 2007).

SUMMARY

FACTS A group of plaintiffs, including the American Civil Liberties Union, journalists, scholars, and lawyers, filed a lawsuit challenging the U.S. government's warrantless international Terrorist Surveillance Program (TSP) as a violation of their constitutional rights and the Foreign Intelligence Surveillance Act of 1978 (FISA). In the wake of the September 11, 2001 terrorist attacks, President George W. Bush instituted the TSP and instructed the National Security Agency (NSA) to intercept without a warrant telephone and e-mail communications involving at least one party located outside the United States who the NSA has "a reasonable basis to conclude . . . is a member of al Qaeda, affiliated with al Qaeda, or a member of an organization affiliated with al Qaeda, or working in support of al Qaeda." The plaintiffs asserted that they communicated with persons living overseas who were the types of people targeted by the TSP and were therefore likely to have been subjected to the NSA's eavesdropping. The district court granted summary judgment in the plaintiffs' favor and enjoined the NSA from utilizing the TSP. The court concluded that "three publicly acknowledged facts about the TSP—(1) it eavesdrops, (2) without warrants, (3) on international

CONTINUED

telephone and e-mail communications in which at least one of the parties is a suspected al Qaeda affiliate—were sufficient to establish standing" and constituted a violation of the Fourth Amendment to the U.S. Constitution. The NSA appealed on the grounds that the plaintiffs lacked standing because they could not prove that they personally had been injured by the program.

Issue Presented Do individuals have standing to challenge a warrantless international wiretapping program when they cannot prove that their conversations were intercepted?

Summary of Opinion Although the Fourth Amendment prohibits unreasonable search and seizure without a warrant, the U.S. Court of Appeals for the Sixth Circuit explained that the plaintiffs could not challenge the warrantless wiretaps unless they could demonstrate that their conversations had been intercepted. In this case, the plaintiffs were unable to present evidence that they themselves had been subjected to warrantless wiretaps, in part because the state secrets doctrine prevented them from obtaining such evidence through discovery. The *state secrets doctrine* bars the discovery or admission of evidence that would "expose [confidential] matters which, in the interest of national security, should not be divulged."[13] The court ruled that even if the plaintiffs could obtain a list of the conversations intercepted, the state secrets doctrine would preclude the introduction of that evidence.

Result The case was dismissed for lack of jurisdiction. The plaintiffs had no standing to challenge the warrantless wiretap program, so the court never reached the question of whether the warrantless wiretaps violated the Fourth Amendment.

Comments The district court noted that if it were to deny standing, the President's actions would be immunized from judicial scrutiny. It then stated (or in the words of the Sixth Circuit, "editorialized"), "It was never the intent of the Framers to give the President such unfettered control. . . ." In response, the Sixth Circuit cited *Schlesinger v. Reservists Committee to Stop the War,*[14] in which the U.S. Supreme Court stated, "The assumption that if respondents have no standing to sue, no one would have standing, is not a reason to find standing." The Sixth Circuit also quoted another decision in which the Supreme Court noted that the Founding Fathers did not intend "to set up something in the nature of an Athenian democracy or New England town meetings to oversee the conduct of the National Government by means of lawsuits in federal courts."[15] Instead, the Court explained, the Constitution created a representative government, and citizens are free to assert their views in the political forum or at the polls.[16] "Slow, cumbersome, and unresponsive though the traditional electoral process may be thought at times, our system provides for changing members of the political branches when dissatisfied citizens convince a sufficient number of their fellow electors that elected representatives are delinquent in performing duties committed to them."[17]

13. United States v. Reynolds, 345 U.S. 1, 10 (1953).
14. 418 U.S. 208. 277 (1974).
15. United States v. Richarson, 418 U.S. 166, 179 (1974).
16. *Id.*
17. *Id.*

Personal Jurisdiction

For a court to hear a case, the court must have personal jurisdiction over the defendant. *Personal jurisdiction* means that the court has legal authority over the parties to the lawsuit. Personal jurisdiction may be based upon the residence or activities of the person being sued (called *in personam jurisdiction*) or upon the location of the property at issue in the lawsuit (called *in rem jurisdiction*). For example, if an individual does any business in a state, then he or she is properly within the jurisdiction of that state's courts. Owning property in a state, causing a personal injury or property damage within the state, or even paying alimony or child support to someone living within the state might justify the exercise of personal jurisdiction by that state's courts.[18]

18. The Anticybersquatting Consumer Protection Act gave trademark owners the ability to bring an *in rem* suit to invalidate an Internet domain name registration by a cybersquatter, a person who wrongfully registers a domain name to extract money from the trademark owner. 15 U.S.C. § 1125(d) (2006). *In rem* jurisdiction is available only in situations where the plaintiff has "disproved" the existence of personal jurisdiction. Heathmount A.E. v. Technodome.com, 106 F. Supp. 2d 860 (E.D. Va. 2000). Cybersquatting is discussed further in Chapter 11.

INTERNATIONAL SNAPSHOT

In 2002, the European Union (EU) adopted the Brussels Conventions to standardize the rules for determining where suits involving e-commerce may be brought. A person may bring suit (1) in the EU state where he or she is domiciled; (2) in the EU state where the defendant is domiciled; (3) in the place of performance when the case involves a contract dispute; or (4) in the place the harmful act occurred in the event of a tortious (that is, wrongful) act. The Brussels Conventions are designed to ensure that courts in the EU use the same jurisdiction standards for e-commerce as for commerce not involving the Internet.

EU members are considering jurisdictional rules for noncontractual disputes, such as tort litigation. Called "Rome II" because they build upon the 1980 Rome Convention agreements, the regulations would clarify the tangle of regional choice-of-law rules with which EU citizens must contend when litigating a lawsuit. As of 2008, the language of the proposed regulation had not been finalized.

Most states have *long-arm statutes,* which can subject an out-of-state defendant to jurisdiction in the state, as long as constitutional due process requirements are satisfied. The Due Process Clause exists, in part, to give "a degree of predictability to the legal system that allows potential defendants to structure their primary conduct with some minimum assurance as to where that conduct will and will not render them liable to suit."[19] The critical test is whether the defendant has certain *minimum contacts* with the state "such that the maintenance of the suit does not offend 'traditional notions of fair play and substantial justice.'"[20]

The courts generally require that the nonresident defendant (1) have done some act or consummated some transaction in the jurisdiction in which it is being sued or (2) have purposefully availed itself of the privilege of conducting activities in that state, thereby invoking the benefits and protections of the forum. Courts have held that negotiating business contracts by means of telephone calls, the mail, or even a fax machine is sufficient to give a court personal jurisdiction over an individual or corporation. Personal jurisdiction may also be proper over a nonresident defendant who committed an intentional tort outside the forum when the tortious conduct was aimed at the forum and the brunt of the harm was felt by the plaintiff in the forum.[21]

Service of process, which notifies the defendant of the filing of a lawsuit, has traditionally been accomplished either by mail or by personally handing a prospective defendant a copy of the complaint. If a party is physically present in the forum, personal service will always be considered proper regardless of the party's contact with the forum. The Supreme Court has gone as far as to allow someone merely vacationing in a state to be served and then forced to answer to charges in that state.[22] Service via alternative means, such as fax or e-mail, may also be acceptable if the plaintiff obtains prior approval from the court.[23]

19. World-Wide Volkswagen Corp. v. Woodson, 444 U.S. 286 (1980).
20. International Shoe Co. v. Washington, 326 U.S. 310, 316 (1945) (quoting Milliken v. Meyer, 311 U.S. 457, 463 (1940)).
21. Price v. Socialist People's Libyan Arab Jamahiriya, 294 F.3d 82 (D.C. Cir. 2002).
22. Burnham v. Superior Court of Cal., 495 U.S. 604 (1990).
23. *See* Brockmeyer v. May, 383 F.3d 798, 805–806 (9th Cir. 2004).

SOURCES OF LAW

Federal and state courts look to the U.S. and state constitutions, statutes, regulations, and common (or case) law to ascertain the applicable law.

CONSTITUTIONS

Courts may be called upon to interpret the U.S. or state constitutions. For example, lawsuits concerning random drug testing of employees have centered on whether this testing violates the Fourth Amendment ban on unreasonable searches and other constitutional provisions guaranteeing the right to privacy. The following case considered whether it was constitutional to require random drug testing of student athletes.

A CASE IN POINT

IN THE LANGUAGE OF THE COURT

CASE 3.2

BOARD OF EDUCATION OF INDEPENDENT SCHOOL DISTRICT NO. 92 OF POTTAWATOMIE COUNTY V. EARLS

SUPREME COURT OF THE UNITED STATES
536 U.S. 822 (2002).

FACTS The Tecumseh, Oklahoma school district adopted a policy requiring all student-athletes to consent to urinalysis drug testing as a condition of participating in extracurricular activities. In effect, this gave schools the right to test athletes without any suspicion of drug use. Earls, along with another student and their parents, claimed that this policy violated the Fourth Amendment to the U.S. Constitution's ban on unreasonable searches.

ISSUE PRESENTED Does requiring student-athletes to take a drug test without any suspicion of drug use violate the Fourth Amendment?

OPINION THOMAS, J., writing for the U.S. Supreme Court:

The Fourth Amendment to the United States Constitution protects "[t]he right of the people to be secure in their persons, houses, papers, and effects, against unreasonable searches and seizures." Searches by public school officials, such as the collection of urine samples, implicate Fourth Amendment interests. . . . We must therefore review the School District's Policy for "reasonableness," which is the touchstone of the constitutionality of a governmental search.

Respondents argue that drug testing must be based at least on some level of individualized suspicion. It is true that we generally determine the reasonableness of a search by balancing the nature of the intrusion on the individual's privacy against the promotion of legitimate governmental interests. But we have long held that "the Fourth Amendment imposes no irreducible requirement of [individualized] suspicion.". . . "[I]n certain limited circumstances, the Government's need to discover such latent or hidden conditions, or to prevent their development, is sufficiently compelling to justify the intrusion on privacy entailed by conducting such searches without any measure of individualized suspicion." Therefore, in the context of safety and administrative regulations, a search unsupported by probable cause may be reasonable "when 'special needs, beyond the normal need for law enforcement, make the warrant and probable-cause requirement impracticable.' "

In *Vernonia*,[24] this Court held that the suspicionless drug testing of athletes was constitutional. The Court, however, did not simply authorize all school drug testing, but rather conducted a fact-specific balancing of the intrusion on the children's Fourth Amendment rights against the promotion of legitimate governmental interests. Applying the principles of *Vernonia* to the somewhat different facts of this case, we conclude that Tecumseh's Policy is also constitutional.

[*Editor's note:* Justice Thomas went on to identify and examine several factors influencing the Court's decision, including the nature of the students' privacy being compromised by the drug testing, the degree to which a urinalysis is intrusive to the students, and the urgency of a school's need to obtain results quickly. After discussing and weighing these factors, the Court ruled that the policy was appropriately tailored to further the school district's goal of lower drug use among its student-athletes.]

RESULT In a five-to-four decision, the Supreme Court ruled that the random drug testing of student-athletes was constitutional.

DISSENT GINSBURG, J., joined by O'CONNOR, STEVENS, and SOUTER , JJ., dissenting:

"[T]he legality of a search of a student," this Court has instructed, "should depend simply on the reasonableness, under all the circumstances, of the search.". . . The particular testing program upheld today is not reasonable; it is capricious, even perverse: [Tecumseh's] policy targets for testing a student population least likely to be at risk from illicit drugs and their damaging effects. I therefore dissent. . . .

Concern for student health and safety is basic to the school's caretaking, and it is undeniable that "drug use carries a variety of health risks for children, including death from overdose."

CONTINUED

Those risks, however, are present for all schoolchildren. *Vernonia* cannot be read to endorse invasive and suspicionless drug testing of all students upon any evidence of drug use, solely on the ground that drugs jeopardize the life and health of those who use them.

CRITICAL THINKING QUESTIONS

1. Do you find the argument of the majority or the dissent more persuasive?
2. Several famous American professional athletes, including Major League Baseball (MLB) players and Olympic medalists, have admitted using both "designer steroids" and human growth hormone (HGH) to enhance physical performance and using masking agents to keep the substances from showing up in drug tests.[25] Although possession of these drugs without a prescription is illegal, the substances themselves were not banned by state or federal law. MLB and the players' union agreed to ban use of steroids and HGH in 2005. The World Anti-Doping Agency, which helps oversee Olympic drug testing, recently developed a blood test for HGH that could be ready for use during the 2008 MLB season.[26] MLB executives have indicated that the league would like to include this test in its drug detection program, but any change to the current system would need to be negotiated with the MLB Players' Association. To date, the players' representatives have been less than enthusiastic. What, if any, impact do you think the Supreme Court's decision in *Board of Education v. Earls* might have on the negotiations between the parties?

24. Vernonia Sch. Dist. 47J v. Acton, 515 U.S. 646 (1995).
25. MARK FAINARU-WADA & LANCE WILLIAMS, GAME OF SHADOWS (2006).
26. ESPN.com news services, *Report: MLB Would Push to Implement Blood Test for HGH* (Sept. 13, 2007), http://sports.espn.go.com/mlb/news/story?id=3017042 (last visited Sept. 13, 2007).

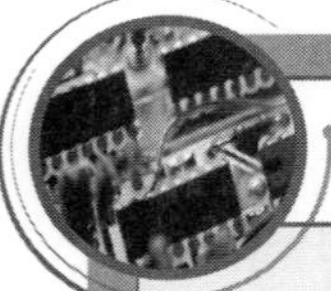

VIEW FROM CYBERSPACE

Personal Jurisdiction and the Web

The global reach of the Internet has raised complicated issues about the permissible scope of personal jurisdiction based on use of the Internet. In general, "the likelihood that personal jurisdiction can be constitutionally exercised is directly proportionate to the nature and quality of commercial activity that an entity conducts over the Internet."[a] The U.S. District Court for the Western District of Pennsylvania adopted a sliding scale, stating:

> At one end of the spectrum are situations where a defendant clearly does business over the Internet. If the defendant enters into contracts with residents of a foreign jurisdiction that involved the knowing and repeated transmission of computer files over the Internet, personal jurisdiction is proper. At the opposite end are situations where a defendant has simply posted information on an Internet Web site that is accessible to users in foreign jurisdictions. A passive Web site that does little more than make information available to those who are interested in it is not grounds for the exercise of personal jurisdiction. The middle ground is occupied by interactive Web sites where a user can exchange information with the host computer. In these cases, the exercise of jurisdiction is determined by examining the level of interactivity and commercial nature of the exchange of information that occurs on the Web site.[b]

On one end of that spectrum lies *Pavlovich v. Superior Court*,[c] the first case involving jurisdiction based on Internet postings to reach the California Supreme Court. In this case, Pavlovich, a Texas resident, was sued in California for posting on the Internet decryption codes that could be used to decode and copy DVDs. The plaintiff, DVD Copy Control Association, Inc., claimed that Pavlovich, the president of Media Driver, LLC, facilitated the illegal copying of DVDs and thereby reduced sales

CONTINUED

of authorized DVDs by motion picture companies based in California. The California Supreme Court ruled that posting the codes merely provided information that was accessible to users in foreign jurisdictions. It did not subject the defendants to personal jurisdiction in California because the website did not, in itself, have any particular contact with California.

At the other end of the spectrum lies *Aitken v. Communications Workers of America*.[d] Two agents of the Communications Workers of America labor union, posing as Verizon managers, sent spam e-mails to Verizon employees touting the benefits of union membership and disparaging Verizon's employment practices. Verizon and the managers whose identities had been stolen asserted a variety of claims in a Virginia federal court, including violations of federal and state anti-spam laws, defamation, invasion of privacy, and conspiracy. The district court ruled that the agents' spamming activities subjected them to personal jurisdiction in Virginia because they had "intentionally [sent] scores of emails to '@verizonbusiness.com' email addresses, the servers for which are located in Virginia, and transmitt[ed] the emails to the targeted Verizon employees, including some employees located in Virginia."

To date, most U.S. courts have been unwilling to extend personal jurisdiction to out-of-state defendants who post defamatory articles about an in-state resident on a passive website. In *Best Van Lines, Inc. v. Walker*,[e] an Iowa resident had posted free assessments of moving companies, including a negative review of Best Van Lines, which was located in New York. Best filed a suit for defamation in the U.S. District Court for the Southern District of New York. The U.S. Court of Appeals for the Second Circuit examined Walker's activities to determine whether he had "purposefully availed himself of the privilege of conducting business activities within New York." Requiring "something more" than just universal accessibility of the information to establish personal jurisdiction, the court concluded that "the nature of Walker's comments did not suggest that they were purposefully directed to New Yorkers rather than a nationwide audience." Although Walker accepted donations through his website, the court concluded that that act was insufficiently tied to the comments in question. Other jurisdictions have reached a similar result.[f]

In contrast, the High Court of Australia exercised personal jurisdiction over Dow Jones & Co. after it published allegedly defamatory statements about an Australian citizen on the Internet.[g] The Court based jurisdiction solely on the accessibility of the company's website in Australia. The English Court of Appeals extended jurisdiction even further when it permitted one U.S. citizen to bring a defamation suit in England against another U.S. citizen based on statements posted on a website.[h] The English court reasoned that granting jurisdiction was proper because the offending article could be downloaded in England and the plaintiff possessed a reputation in England that he was entitled to defend. Jurisdiction in defamation suits is such a divisive issue in the European Union that the European Commission dropped it from the proposed jurisdictional guidelines under consideration by the European Parliament.[i]

a. Zippo Mfg. Co. v. Zippo Dot Com, 952 F. Supp. 1119, 1124 (W.D. Pa. 1997).
b. *Id.*
c. 58 P.3d 2, 31 (Cal. 2002).
d. 496 F. Supp. 2d 653 (E.D.Va. 2007).
e. 490 F.3d 239 (2d Cir. 2007).
f. *See, e.g.*, Revell v. Lidov, 317 F.3d 467 (5th Cir. 2002) (Texas had no jurisdiction over the out-of-state author of an online article about a former FBI agent living in Texas); Young v. New Haven Advocate, 315 F.3d 256 (4th Cir. 2002), *cert. denied*, 538 U.S. 1035 (2003) (Virginia had no jurisdiction over a Connecticut newspaper that had posted an article about a Virginia resident on the Internet).
g. Dow Jones & Co. v. Gutnick (2002) HCA 56, 194 A.L.R. 433.
h. Lewis v. King, [2004] EWHC (Q.B.) 168, *aff'd*, [2004] EWCA (Civ.) 1329.
i. Diana Wallis MEP, EU *Needs to Find Coherent Cross-Border Legislation*, LAW., Jan. 15, 2007, at 8.

STATUTES

Congress enacts statutes in such areas as antitrust, food and drugs, patents and copyrights, labor relations, and civil rights. For example, Title 42 of the United States Code, Section 2000(a), provides that "all persons shall be entitled to the full and equal enjoyment of the goods, services, facilities, privileges, advantages, and accommodations of any place of public accommodation . . . without discrimination or segregation on the grounds of race, color, religion or national origin." State legislatures also adopt statutes covering a broad range of topics, from requirements for a will to the formation and governance of corporations to rights of employers. For example, Section 16600[27] of the California Business and Professions Code generally invalidates employee covenants not to compete except in connection with the sale of an employee's stock in a transaction involving the sale of the corporation as a going concern.

27. CAL. BUS. & PROF. CODE § 16600 (2006).

REGULATIONS

Courts sometimes hear cases arising under federal and state regulations. *Regulations* are provisions issued by federal and state administrative agencies and executive departments to interpret and implement statutes enacted by the legislature. For example, the Securities and Exchange Commission issues regulations governing the sale of securities, and the Bureau of Citizenship and Immigration Services in the Department of Homeland Security issues regulations governing immigration and naturalization as a U.S. citizen. Federal regulations and rules are printed in the multivolume *Code of Federal Regulations (CFR),* which is revised and updated every year. Administrative rules and regulations are discussed in Chapter 6.

COMMON LAW

Common law is case law—the legal rules made by judges when they decide a case where no constitution, statute, or regulation exists to resolve the dispute. Common law originated in England. U.S. common law includes all of the case law of England and the American colonies before the American Revolution, as well as American case law decided since the colonial period.

Stare Decisis

Common law is developed through the doctrine of *stare decisis,* which means "to abide by decided cases." Once a court resolves a particular issue, other courts in the same jurisdiction addressing a similar legal problem will generally follow that court's decision.

A legal rule established by a court's decision may be either persuasive or authoritative. A decision is *persuasive* if it reasonably and fairly resolves the dispute. Another court confronting a similar dispute will probably choose to apply the same reasoning. An *authoritative decision,* by contrast, is one that must be followed, regardless of its persuasive power. As the U.S. Court of Appeals for the Seventh Circuit explained:

> Whether a decision is authoritative depends on a variety of factors, of which the most important is the relationship between the court that decided it and the court to which it is cited later as a precedent. The simplest relationship is hierarchical: the decisions of a superior court in a unitary system bind the inferior courts. The most complex relationship is between a court and its own previous decisions.
>
> A court must give considerable weight to its own decisions unless and until they have been overruled or undermined by the decisions of a higher court, or other supervening developments, such as a statutory overruling. But [a court] is not absolutely bound by [its previous rulings], and must give fair consideration to any substantial argument that a litigant makes for overruling a previous decision.[28]

Every court must follow a decision of the U.S. Supreme Court, unless powerfully convinced that the Supreme Court itself would change its decision at the first possible opportunity.

Reversing U.S. Supreme Court Precedent The U.S. Supreme Court rarely overrules its previous decisions, but it does do so on occasion. In *Planned Parenthood of Southeastern Pennsylvania v. Casey,*[29] the Court articulated four primary questions to be considered when deciding whether an earlier decision should be overruled:

1. Has the prior decision's central rule proved unworkable?
2. Can the rule be changed without serious inequity to those who have relied upon it, or would such a change significantly damage the stability of the society governed by the rule in question?
3. Has the law's growth in the intervening years left the prior decision's central rule a doctrinal anachronism discounted by society?
4. Have the prior decision's premises of fact so greatly changed since the decision was issued as to render its central holding somehow irrelevant or unjustifiable in dealing with the issue it addressed?

Courts apply *stare decisis* more "rigidly" in statutory cases than in constitutional cases.[30] In addition, the fact that a case involves property or contract rights giving rise to reliance interests argues against overruling precedent.[31]

Consider the Supreme Court's explanation in *Casey* of why the "separate but equal" rule for applying the Fourteenth Amendment's equal protection guarantee test, first adopted in *Plessy v. Ferguson,*[32] was appropriately overruled in *Brown v. Board of Education,*[33] the 1954 school-desegregation case:

> In *Plessy v. Ferguson* the Court held that legislatively mandated racial segregation in public transportation was no denial of equal protection and rejected the argument that racial separation enforced by the legal machinery of American society treats the black race as inferior. The *Plessy* Court considered "the underlying fallacy of the

28. Colby v. J.C. Penney Co., 811 F.2d 1119, 1123 (7th Cir. 1987).
29. 505 U.S. 833 (1992).
30. Fed. Election Comm'n v. Wisconsin Right to Life, 127 S. Ct. 2652 (2007).
31. Payne v. Tennessee, 501 U.S. 808 (1991).
32. 163 U.S. 537 (1896).
33. 347 U.S. 483 (1954).

plaintiff's argument to consist in the assumption that the enforced separation of the two races stamps the colored race with a badge of inferiority. If this be so, it is not by reason of anything found in the act, but solely because the colored race chooses to put that construction upon it." Whether, as a matter of historical fact, the Justices in the *Plessy* majority believed this or not, this understanding of the implication of segregation was the stated justification for the Court's opinion. But this understanding of the facts and the rule it was stated to justify were repudiated in *Brown v. Board of Education*. . . .

The Court in *Brown* addressed these facts of life by observing that whatever may have been the understanding in *Plessy's* time of the power of segregation to stigmatize those who were segregated with a "badge of inferiority," it was clear by 1954 that legally sanctioned segregation had just such an effect, to the point that racially separate public educational facilities were deemed inherently unequal. Society's understanding of the facts upon which a constitutional ruling was sought in 1954 was thus fundamentally different from the basis claimed for the decision in 1896. While we think *Plessy* was wrong the day it was decided, . . . we must also recognize that the *Plessy* Court's explanation for its decision was so clearly at odds with the facts apparent to the Court in 1954 that the decision to reexamine *Plessy* was on this ground alone not only justified but required.

In *Casey,* the Supreme Court declined the invitation by right-to-life groups to overrule its decision in *Roe v. Wade*[34] upholding the right of a woman to have an abortion before the fetus becomes viable.

In *Lawrence v. Texas,*[35] the Supreme Court struck down the ban on sodomy that it had upheld seventeen years earlier in *Bowers v. Hardwick.*[36] The *Lawrence* Court concluded that "*Bowers* was not correct when it was decided, and it is not correct today." Among other authorities, the Court cited the case of *Dudgeon v. United Kingdom,*[37] in which the European Court of Human Rights held that laws proscribing consensual homosexual conduct were invalid under the European Convention on Human Rights. The Court reasoned that this decision was at odds with the premise in *Bowers* that the liberty claim put forward by homosexuals was "insubstantial in our Western civilization."

In a biting dissent, Justice Scalia questioned "the Court's surprising readiness to reconsider a decision rendered a mere 17 years ago in *Bowers v. Hardwick,*" stating:

> [A]n "emerging awareness" is by definition not "deeply rooted in this Nation's history and tradition[s]," as we have said "fundamental right" status requires. Constitutional entitlements do not spring into existence because some States choose to lessen or eliminate criminal sanctions on certain behavior. Much less do they spring into existence, as the Court seems to believe, because *foreign nations* decriminalize conduct.

The majority responded that its reference to decisions by European and Canadian courts did not imply deference to foreign courts, but rather evidenced changing societal norms that warranted a departure from *stare decisis.*

Justice Scalia predicted that the Court's determination that the state had no compelling interest in preserving the morals of its citizens would lead to same-sex marriage as well as the legalization of prostitution, pornography, and polygamy. In 2003, relying in part on the decision in *Lawrence v. Texas,* the Massachusetts Supreme Judicial Court struck down the Massachusetts statute that permitted a man and a woman but not a same-sex couple to marry.[38]

In the majority opinion in *Leegin Creative Leather Products, Inc. v. PSKS, Inc.,*[39] written by Chief Justice Roberts in which Justice Scalia joined, the Supreme Court overruled the *per se* ban on minimum resale price maintenance established in 1911 in *Dr. Miles Medical Co. v. John D. Park & Sons Co.*[40] and reaffirmed just ten years earlier in *State Oil Co. v. Khan.*[41] Even though *Casey* is widely recognized as the Supreme Court's most definitive statement on *stare decisis,* Chief Justice Roberts did not even cite *Casey* when explaining why the Court was overruling almost 100 years of precedent.[42] In a dissent joined by Justices Ginsburg, Souter, and Stevens, Justice Breyer asserted that "every stare decisis concern this Court has ever mentioned counsels against overruling" the *per se* ban on minimum prices established in *Dr. Miles Medical.*

Splits in the Circuits Just as one trial court does not have to follow another trial court, the court of appeals

34. 410 U.S. 113 (1973).
35. 539 U.S. 558 (2003). *See also* Constance E. Bagley, Lawrence v. Texas *and the Role of* Stare Decisis, (Harvard Bus. Sch. Case No. 804–016, 2003).
36. 478 U.S. 186 (1986).
37. 45 Eur. Ct. H.R. P52 (1981).
38. Goodridge v. Dep't of Pub. Health, 798 N.E.2d 941 (Mass. 2003).
39. 127 S. Ct. 2705 (2007).
40. 220 U.S. 373 (1911).
41. 522 U.S. 3 (1997).
42. Leegin Creative Leather Prods., Inc. v. PSKS, Inc., 127 S. Ct. 2705 (2007). It would be easier for the Roberts Court to overturn *Roe v. Wade* using the lax standard applied in *Leegin Products* than the stricter standard articulated in *Casey.*

above the trial court need not follow other appellate courts. A court of appeals in one circuit does not have to follow a decision by a court of appeals in another circuit. When different courts of appeals disagree on a legal issue, there is said to be a *split in the circuits*. Thus, if the U.S. Court of Appeals for the Tenth Circuit (based in Denver) interprets a federal air pollution regulation in a certain way, the U.S. Court of Appeals for the Sixth Circuit (based in Cincinnati) may follow that interpretation, but it is not compelled to do so. The authority of the Tenth Circuit does not reach beyond its own geographic boundaries. However, a federal district court in Tulsa, which is within the Tenth Circuit, would be compelled to interpret the regulation in accordance with the decision of the Court of Appeals for the Tenth Circuit.

RESTATEMENTS

Today, many rules that originated as common law have been collected into *restatements* compiled after careful study by the American Law Institute, a prestigious group of legal scholars, practicing attorneys, and judges. There are restatements of various areas of the law, such as torts, contracts, property, and trusts. The restatements are persuasive rather than authoritative. They do not compel a judge to make a particular decision unless the rule has been adopted by the state's legislature or its highest court.

CHOICE OF FORUM, WAIVER OF RIGHT TO TRIAL BY JURY, AND CHOICE OF LAW

Parties to a contract may specify in advance where any disputes will be litigated. This is done by including a *choice-of-forum clause*. A contract may also include a waiver of the right to a jury trial or, as discussed more fully later in this chapter, provide that disputes will be decided by a method other than litigation, such as arbitration. They may also agree in advance which law will govern any future dispute. This section is often entitled "Governing Law" or "Choice of Law." A court will usually uphold the contracting parties' choice of forum and law.

CHOICE OF FORUM

Courts in the United States will honor clauses in a valid contract requiring disputes to be resolved in another forum under its laws unless (1) the clause was fraudulently included in the contract, (2) enforcement would deprive a party "of his day in court," or (3) enforcement would contravene a strong public policy of the forum in which suit is brought.[43] Parties should take care in how they word such provisions, however. Even when a clause appears at first blush to require all disputes to be litigated in a particular forum, a court may read the clause narrowly and apply it to only those disputes clearly specified in the clause.

INTERNATIONAL SNAPSHOT

Although issues of choice of forum and choice of law often arise in cases involving parties from different jurisdictions within the United States, similar issues arise when parties are from different countries. In either context, the court adjudicating the dispute must balance the competing interests of different sovereignties and resolve the conflict according to one jurisdiction's conflict-of-laws rules. To avoid confusion, it is customary for a contract involving parties from different jurisdictions to specify where the dispute will be tried and which country's laws will govern.

For example, a U.S. citizen filed suit in New York against the English companies involved in recording and producing his albums.[44] The parties' agreement stipulated that any dispute "that may arise out of the [contract]" would be resolved by English law in an English court. The Second Circuit ruled that the artist could not bring his breach-of-contract claim for unpaid royalties in a U.S. court because the contract clearly laid out the defendant's payment obligations.

The court also ruled, however, that the artist could assert his causes of action for federal copyright infringement, as well as unfair competition and unjust enrichment under state law, in a U.S. court because they did not "arise out of" the contract. The court reasoned that the term "arise out of" did not encompass all claims that "have some possible relationship with the contract, including claims that may only 'relate to,' be 'associated with,' or 'arise in connection with' the contract." To be covered by the choice-of-forum clause, the claim had to originate from the recording contract. Because the plaintiff's ownership of the music was based on authorship, not on the contract, the clause did not apply to those claims. As a result, the U.S. courts were free to assert jurisdiction over the copyright infringement, unfair competition, and unjust enrichment claims.

43. The Bremen v. Zapata Off Shore Co., 407 U.S. 1 (1972).

44. Phillips v. Audio Active, Ltd., 494 F.3d 378 (2d Cir. 2007).

Doctrine of *Forum Non Conveniens*

The doctrine of *forum non conveniens* may be invoked by a defendant to require a change of forum when there is no applicable choice-of-forum clause to enforce[45] and the forum chosen by the plaintiff is inconvenient for the defendant. The following case highlights several of the factors a court will consider in determining whether it is the proper forum.

45. Abbott Labs. v. Takeda Pharm. Co., 476 F.3d 421, 426 (7th Cir. 2007) (holding that a forum selection clause is a "substitute" for the doctrine of *forum non conveniens*, not another name for it).

A CASE IN POINT

SUMMARY

CASE 3.3

RADELJAK V. DAIMLER-CHRYSLER CORP.

SUPREME COURT OF MICHIGAN
719 N.W.2D 40 (MICH. 2006).

FACTS An automobile accident in Croatia involving a Jeep Grand Cherokee manufactured by DaimlerChrysler resulted in the death of one passenger and injuries to the driver and other passengers. The families of the victims, all Croatian residents and citizens, sued in Wayne County, Michigan, where DaimlerChrysler had automotive plants. They alleged that the transmission of the Jeep Grand Cherokee had slipped from park into reverse, causing the vehicle to roll into a ravine.

The trial court in Michigan granted DaimlerChrysler's motion to dismiss on the basis of *forum non conveniens*. The court concluded that Croatia would be a more convenient forum because the accident occurred in Croatia, the victims were Croatian, Croatian law would most likely apply, and the transmission—the allegedly defective product—had been designed and manufactured outside the United States. On appeal, the Michigan appellate court held that the lower court had abused its discretion because Wayne County was not a "seriously inconvenient" forum. DaimlerChrysler appealed.

ISSUE PRESENTED May a Michigan court dismiss a case under the *forum non conveniens* doctrine in favor of another more appropriate forum even though litigation in Michigan would not be "seriously inconvenient" for the defendant?

SUMMARY OF OPINION The Michigan Supreme Court acknowledged that trial court judges are generally within the bounds of their discretionary powers in applying the *forum non conveniens* doctrine. The court explained, however, that the dispositive issue in deciding whether to apply the doctrine is not the residency of either party, but the determination of which forum best serves the convenience of the parties and the interests of justice. The Michigan Supreme Court ruled that there was no requirement that a forum be "seriously inconvenient" for a *forum non conveniens* dismissal.

The court then reviewed the factors the trial court had used in analyzing the motion to dismiss based on *forum non conveniens* to determine whether it had abused its discretion in granting the defendant's motion. Four of the seven private factors considered by the trial court favored neither forum over the other, but three favored Croatia: (1) "ease of access to sources of proof," because it would be easier for the plaintiffs in Croatia to obtain documents related to the choice of transmissions from Michigan than it would be for the defendant in Michigan to obtain documents from Croatia related to the accident; (2) "other practical problems which contribute to the ease, expense, and expedition of the trial," because a Michigan trial would not allow the defendant to include third-party Croatians who could be responsible for the plaintiffs' injuries; and (3) "possibility of viewing the premises," because it would be almost impossible for a Michigan jury to visit the crash site. The three public factors considered by the trial court also weighed in favor of trying the case in Croatia: (1) the goal of avoiding court congestion, (2) the fact that many of the people concerned about the proceeding lived in Croatia, and (3) the burden of jury duty on a community with little relationship to the incident.

RESULT The Michigan Supreme Court ruled that the trial court had not abused its discretion when it granted the defendant's motion to dismiss. The plaintiffs could not force DaimlerChrysler

CONTINUED

to defend the case in Michigan even though the automobile manufacturer had extensive operations there.

COMMENTS In her dissent, Justice Kelly argued that the plaintiffs' choice of forum should be given deference unless the balance of *forum non conveniens* factors strongly favored the defendant. Because the plaintiffs in this case had not filed suit in Michigan merely to "vex," "harass," or "oppress" the defendant, she argued, its choice of forum should have been respected.

WAIVER OF RIGHT TO JURY TRIAL

As discussed more fully in Chapter 4, the U.S. and state constitutions guarantee the right to trial by jury in all criminal cases and most civil cases. Increasingly, employers, residential lessors, banks, lenders, and other firms are requiring employees and customers to agree in advance to waive their right to a jury trial.[46] The dispute is still litigated, but it is decided by a judge, not a jury. Studies suggest that judges find in favor of employees in roughly the same proportion of cases as juries, but judges tend to award substantially lower damages than juries. Although courts in New York, Massachusetts, and Florida have generally upheld these prelitigation waivers, courts in California and Georgia have refused to enforce them.

CHOICE OF LAW

Even if a court sitting in a particular jurisdiction agrees to hear a case, it still may not apply the law of that state to the dispute. The question of which jurisdiction's law to apply comes up not only in the context of diversity cases heard in federal court but also in state court actions involving the citizens of more than one state. This question is governed by a complicated set of conflict-of-laws rules. In general, the jurisdiction that has the greatest governmental interest in the dispute will provide the governing law. Put another way, the selection of the governing law is guided by a grouping of contacts: the state with the strongest contacts with the litigants and the subject matter of the litigation has the greatest interest in the application of its law.[47]

46. Jane Spencer, *Waiving Your Right to a Jury Trial,* WALL ST. J., Aug. 17, 2003, at D1.

47. When more than one state or country has an interest in the outcome of a case, the court is permitted to apply the laws of different places to different issues, under the doctrine of *depeçage. See, e.g.,* Berg Chilling Sys., Inc. v. Hull Corp. 435 F.3d 455 (3d Cir. 2006) (court applied Pennsylvania law to determine whether the puchase of a Pennsylvania corporation had successor liability for defective products sold by the acquired firm and New Jersey law to determine whether the purchaser's disclaimer of successor liability in the purchase contract violated New Jersey public policy).

Sometimes a state will use formalistic rules, however. For example, some states look only to where a contract was entered into to decide which state's contract law should govern a dispute. For example, because Pennzoil and Getty Oil Company entered into their acquisition agreement in New York, the trial court in Texas applied New York's contract law to determine whether the preliminary negotioations had ripened into a binding contract.

LAWS FAVORING SETTLEMENT OR ALTERNATIVE DISPUTE RESOLUTION OVER LITIGATION

Like other business decisions, choosing a dispute resolution mechanism involves many trade-offs. Litigation is expensive and takes a toll on management and employees. In addition to generating legal fees, lawsuits distract management from the company's business, risk damaging the firm's public image, and jeopardize relationships with the opposing party. Instead of automatically taking legal conflicts to the courthouse, more firms than ever are using *alternative dispute resolution (ADR)* techniques, such as negotiation, mediation, arbitration, med-arb, arb-med, minitrials, and summary jury trials, to resolve disputes. They are discussed in detail later in this chapter. The use of ADR techniques in international disputes is discussed in Chapter 25.

The government promotes settlement and other alternatives to litigation in a variety of ways, including requiring courts to refer appropriate cases to ADR programs, such as mediation, minitrials, and summary jury trials;[48] mandating pretrial settlement conferences; penalizing plaintiffs who reject favorable settlement offers; limiting the ability of a party to introduce willingness to negotiate as evidence

48. *See, e.g.,* Alternative Dispute Resolution Act of 1998, 28 U.S.C. § 652.

EXHIBIT 3.4 **Resolution of Cases in Federal Courts**

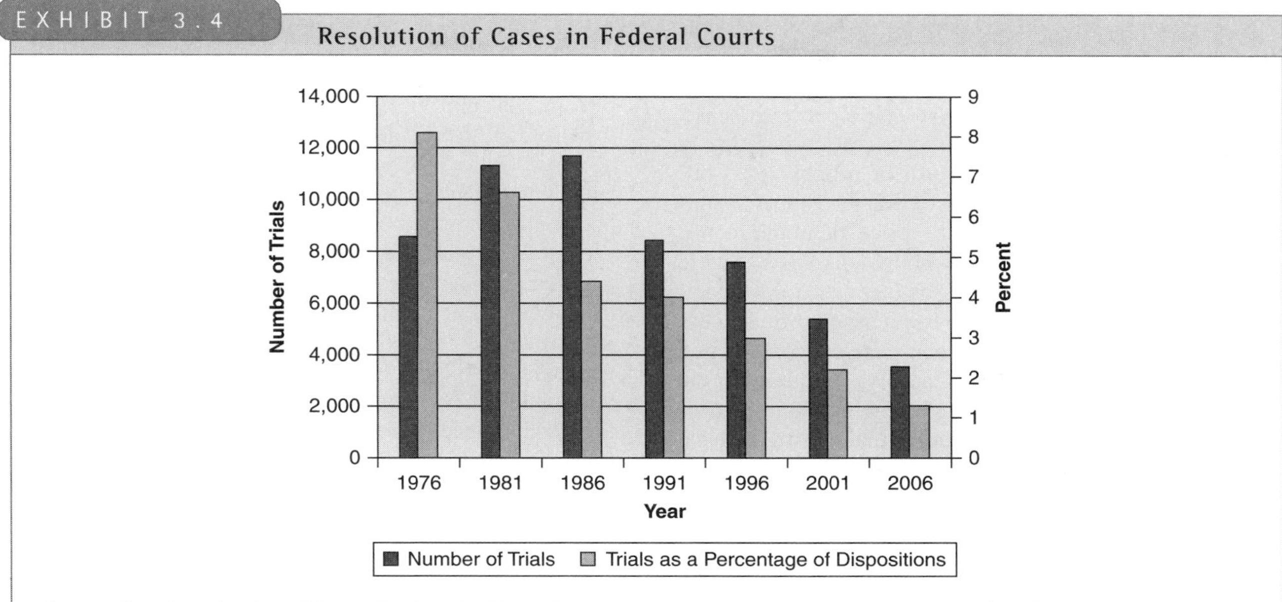

Sources: Data drawn from Marc Galanter, *The Vanishing Trial: An Examination of Trials and Related Matters in Federal and State Courts,* 1 J. EMPIRICAL LEGAL STUDIES 459, 533–34 (Nov. 2004) (Table A-2: Percentage of Civil Terminations During/After Trial in U.S. District Courts, 1962–2002); ADMINISTRATIVE OFFICE OF THE U.S. COURTS, 2006 JUDICIAL BUSINESS OF THE UNITED STATES COURTS: ANNUAL REPORT OF THE DIRECTOR 186 (2006) (Table C-4: U.S. District Courts—Civil Cases Terminated, by Nature of Suit and Action Taken, During the 12-Month Period Ending September 30, 2006).

of fault; providing liberal discovery; and generally enforcing agreements to arbitrate. In addition, federal legislation requires federal agencies to use ADR to resolve administrative cases.[49] The Equal Employment Opportunity Commission has successfully used mediation to reduce its case backlog.[50]

The states have also supported efforts to use ADR rather than courts to resolve disputes. The court systems in more than half of the states now either require or encourage resolving cases through ADR in order to reduce case backlogs and provide a quicker resolution of disputes.[51]

These efforts appear to be working. Although Americans are filing cases in court at a record pace, partly due to the growing population in the United States, the percentage of cases that actually go to trial before a jury or the bench (in a *bench trial,* a judge, not a jury, decides all issues) has seen a steady decrease in the last thirty years. This trend is evident in Exhibit 3.4.

PRETRIAL CONFERENCES

The *Federal Rules of Civil Procedure (FRCP),* which govern trial practices in the federal system, and their counterparts in the state systems allow judges to require disputants to meet and explore settlement before beginning a trial. Indeed:

> Empirical studies reveal that when a trial judge intervenes personally at an early stage to assume judicial control over a case and to schedule dates for completion by the parties of the principal pretrial steps, the case is disposed of by settlement or trial more efficiently and with less cost and delay than when the parties are left to their own devices.[52]

49. For example, the Administrative Dispute Resolution Act of 1996 requires federal agencies to look at their mission to see where ADR might be effective. 5 U.S.C. §§ 571–585.

50. Aurora Mackey, *Close Calls,* CAL. LAW., June 1999, at 36.

51. Legal Information Institute, *Alternative Dispute Resolution: An Overview, available at* http://www.law.cornell.edu/topics/adr.html. For actual state statutes governing ADR, see http://www.law.cornell.edu/topics/state_statutes.html#alternate_dispute_resolution.

52. 28 U.S.C. § 471.

For example, the judge assigned to ten of the suits brought by twenty-seven utility companies against Westinghouse Corporation in 1975 forced the chief executives concerned to meet in his office to try to settle the case. Westinghouse, then the thirty-sixth largest corporation in the United States with a net worth of roughly $2.3 billion, had breached its contracts to deliver about 70 million pounds of uranium after the price of uranium had more than doubled. The plaintiffs sought damages of up to $2.6 billion. If the court forced Westinghouse to pay damages, Westinghouse would have been crippled financially and might not have been able to complete the construction of certain nuclear power plants that it was building for the same utility companies. The judge concluded that a business solution to the lawsuits, rather than a strictly legal one, was needed:

> I am tired of pussyfooting and, more than that, I am tired of talking to lawyers when other, more powerful men, who have the ultimate power of decision, have not been here. . . . Any decision I hand down will hurt someone and, because of the potential damage, I want to make it clear that it will happen only because certain captains of industry could not together work out their problems so that the hurt might have been held to a minimum.[53]

Inventive and mutually beneficial settlements were reached in many of the cases.[54]

REJECTED-OFFER SANCTIONS

The rules of civil procedure provide a stick for plaintiffs unwilling to seriously entertain reasonable settlement offers. Rule 68 of the Federal Rules of Civil Procedure allows a defendant to offer to accept judgment against it for a specific amount of money no fewer than ten days before the trial begins. If the plaintiff accepts the offer, the case concludes, and the court enters judgment in accordance with the agreement. If the plaintiff refuses, the case goes to trial. If the final judgment is not more favorable than the rejected offer, then the plaintiff must pay the defendant's legal expenses incurred subsequent to the offer. This possibility gives defendants an added incentive to make serious settlement offers as early as possible and encourages plaintiffs to consider those offers seriously.

53. William Eagan, *The Westinghouse Uranium Contracts: Commercial Impracticality and Related Matters,* 18 Am. Bus. L.J. 291 (1980). Reproduced by permission.

54. *Id.*

NEGOTIATION AS EVIDENCE OF FAULT

A defendant may be reluctant to make a realistic settlement offer if the plaintiff can introduce the offer into evidence at trial to help establish the defendant's liability. For example, a manager faced with a highly dubious claim of product defect might be willing to replace the item to preserve customer goodwill, but be unwilling to reimburse the customer for the profits it lost because of the alleged defect. At a trial, the customer might try to introduce the manager's offer to replace the product as evidence of the defect: "After all, ladies and gentlemen of the jury, why would a company give my client a new product if there was nothing wrong with the old one?" Looking ahead to such a possibility, the manager may be reluctant to negotiate at all for fear that sincere efforts to preserve goodwill could appear later as admissions of fault. At a minimum, the manager will use exceedingly circumspect language. Either result makes settlement more difficult and less likely.

To avoid this chilling effect on negotiations, Rule 408 of the *Federal Rules of Evidence*, which govern the introduction of evidence in federal courts, prohibits the use of settlement offers in federal court as evidence of liability. The protection extends to conduct and statements made in such negotiations, as well as formal offers of settlement. The goal is to insulate the entire negotiation process from the threat of exposure at trial. As Congress observed when enacting the restriction, "The purpose of [the] rule is to encourage settlements which would be discouraged if such evidence were admissible."[55]

Managers should not take too much comfort in Rule 408, however. Often damaging revelations made in negotiations are otherwise discoverable and therefore admissible. Similarly, although offers to settle may not be used as evidence of liability, such offers may be used to show witness bias or obstruction of criminal investigation or to disprove a suggestion of undue delay. In short, a clever lawyer can often find a way to introduce some evidence concerning negotiations.

LIBERAL DISCOVERY

Discovery, the pretrial process through which the parties obtain documents from the other side and ask both written and oral questions, is designed to promote settlement and more efficient trials by reducing the *asymmetric information* problem, which arises because each party has information not possessed by the other party. If both the plaintiff and the defendant have similar information, there is less uncertainty to resolve through a lengthy and expensive trial. Discovery is discussed in more detail later in this chapter.

55. Fed. R. Civ. P. 16, Notes of Advisory Committee on Rules.

ENFORCING AGREEMENTS TO ARBITRATE

Federal law also promotes an alternative to litigation by requiring courts to honor most agreements to arbitrate disputes. The enforcement of arbitration clauses will be discussed in detail later in the chapter.

TORTIOUS DISPUTE RESOLUTION

Although the law supports settlements and alternative dispute resolution, managers are not immune from the law simply because they pursue alternative mechanisms to resolve their disputes. The applicability of tort and criminal law is a good example.

As discussed in Chapter 9, a *tort* is a civil wrong causing injury to a person, his or her property, or certain economic relationships. A party who intentionally misleads another by making a material misrepresentation of fact upon which the plaintiff reasonably relied to his or her detriment may be liable for fradulent misrepresentation. This may not only result in the obligation to pay damages for the harm caused by the misrepresentation but also invalidate any agreement to settle the dispute. Furthermore, an overly aggressive attempt to "resolve" a dispute by force or threats—"making an offer he can't refuse," as Don Corlene put it in *The Godfather*—may constitute criminal extortion or assault and expose the manager to liability for damages for civil assault, intentional infliction of emotional distress, defamation, invasion of privacy, disparagement, injurious falsehood, interference with contractual obligations, or interference with prospective business advantage. Attempting to settle a conflict outside of court does not exempt managers from the law.

LITIGATION STRATEGY

Once a party has concluded that a dispute cannot be resolved without litigation, the litigation strategy must be developed. Experts recommend that companies construct a prelitigation "decision tree," which determines at each step of the proceeding the chances of prevailing or losing, the costs of going forward, and the potential amount of recovery.[56] Developing a decision tree forces a company to conduct a substantial factual and legal analysis of its claim.

LITIGATION STRATEGIES FOR PLAINTIFFS

When planning to file a lawsuit, the plaintiff must decide which legal claim is most likely to succeed. Courts can impose monetary penalties or "sanctions" on companies, individuals, and attorneys who file lawsuits without sufficient facts or the legal basis to support their claims.

The attorney and client should then select a court in which to file the lawsuit. State courts are usually skilled in handling a variety of business disputes ranging from contract matters to personal-injury cases. Federal courts are often more accustomed to handling complex business litigation, such as that involving federal securities law or employment-discrimination laws. Other considerations about where to file include (1) the convenience and location of necessary witnesses and documents, (2) the location of trial counsel, (3) the reputation and size of the company and its opponent in a particular area, and (4) the possibility of favorable or unfavorable publicity.

Texas plaintiffs' lawyer Anthony Buzbee came under fire after he told a small gathering of maritime defense lawyers that filing lawsuits in Starr County on the western edge of the Rio Grande Valley in Texas on behalf of workers hurt at sea "probably adds about seventy-five percent to the value of the case."[57] He claimed that when he has an injured Hispanic client before a completely Hispanic jury and a Hispanic judge in Starr County, "you need to just show that the guy was working, and that he was hurt."[58] According to the American Tort Reform Association, the five venues most hostile to defendants are, in order:

1. West Virginia.
2. South Florida.
3. Rio Grande Valley and Gulf Coast, Texas.
4. Cook County, Illinois.
5. Madison County, Illinois.[59]

Pretrial Preparation

Having decided to file a lawsuit, the company should carefully select the personnel who will act as contacts with the attorneys. These individuals should have substantial authority in the company and ensure that the necessary information and documents are gathered for the attorneys.

56. See Roger Fisher, *He Who Pays the* Piper, HARV. BUS. REV., Mar.–Apr. 1985, at 150. *See also* Joseph A. Grundfest & Peter H. Huang, *The Unexpected Value of Litigation: A Real Options Perspective*, 58 STAN. L. REV. 1267 (2005).

57. Nathan Koppel, *A Lawyer's Speech Opens a New Venue in Ongoing Battle*, WALL ST. J. Feb. 27, 2007, at B1.

58. *Id.*

59. *Id.* at B2.

Executives or senior management who will be involved in the lawsuit or with the corporate attorneys should not handle public relations. This could lead to disputes regarding waiver of the attorney–client privilege (discussed later in this chapter).

The company should also tell all employees not to destroy any documents that may be relevant to the lawsuit. Destruction of these documents, particularly after the claim is filed, can be harmful and even illegal. Document-retention policies are discussed in greater detail later in this chapter.

Top management should tell employees not to discuss the lawsuit with anyone, including family or close friends. Casual comments about bankrupting the opposing party or teaching an opponent a lesson may turn up as testimony at trial, with undesirable consequences.

The company and its attorney should develop a budget for the lawsuit. Then, at each step of the case, strategic options can be discussed on the basis of cost-benefit analysis. The budget should include not only the attorneys' fees but also (1) the cost of employee time, (2) damage to company morale, (3) disruption of business, and (4) other hidden expenses. A budget will help the company manager and lawyer decide whether to pursue the lawsuit or attempt to settle.

As mentioned earlier, all courts urge the parties to confer and settle the case if possible. The judge will act as a settlement mediator and objectively assist counsel in recognizing the strengths and weaknesses of their cases. Many state courts require a settlement conference before a specially designated settlement judge. The parties may also hire retired judges, professional mediators, law school professors, or mediators who are part of a bar association settlement program to facilitate settlement.

LITIGATION STRATEGIES FOR DEFENDANTS

A defendant receiving a complaint and summons notifying it that a lawsuit has been filed should never let the lawsuit go unattended. The defendant should plan a defense strategy and follow it step by step. Factual and legal preparation should be done promptly so that important evidence—such as the memory of key witnesses—is not lost.

When a company is served with a complaint, it should try to determine why the plaintiff felt it necessary to sue. Some of the factors may include (1) whether prior bargaining or negotiations with the plaintiff broke down, and why; (2) whether the company's negotiator was pursuing the wrong tactics or following an agenda inconsistent with the company's best interests; and (3) whether the lawsuit resulted from bad personnel practices that the company still needs to correct.

The defendant should always promptly consider the possibility of a settlement and review the ways in which amicable negotiations could be commenced or resumed. Senior executives should get together and decide whether it would be beneficial to discuss the lawsuit with the plaintiff. With reference to Texaco's failure to negotiate a settlement with Pennzoil (subject of the "Inside Story" in Chapter 7), then Texaco Deputy Chair James Kinnear remarked, "The case should have and could have been settled."[60] The defendant may also want to consider mediation or arbitration as alternatives to an expensive trial. Sometimes an apology can be more important than a vigorous defense in a case where the plaintiff feels unjustly wronged.

If the lawsuit cannot be settled, then the defendant should proceed with the same steps required of the plaintiff—plan a strategy, prepare a budget for the action, and so on. If the suit was filed in a state court, the defendant must decide whether it is possible and desirable to move the action to federal court.

If the plaintiff has sued in a place that is inconvenient for the defendant and its witnesses, the defendant may file a motion for a change of *venue,* that is, location, under the doctrine of *forum non conveniens*. A federal district court in one state may transfer the case to a federal district court in another state. A state court can only transfer the case to another location within that state, however.

CLASS ACTIONS

If the conduct of the defendant affected numerous persons in a common way, the case may be brought as a *class action* by a representative of the class of persons affected. This was done in the silicone-breast-implant cases involving Dow Corning and others, and the smoking cases brought against the tobacco companies. Class actions are the norm in actions alleging securities fraud.

Written notice of the formation of the class must be mailed to all potential class members. Until recently, it was difficult to do this effectively. As a result, many potential class members never received notice of the suit. Now, however, the Internet and websites, such as Findlaw.com, Classactiononline.com, Classactionamerica.com, and numerous small sites, have made finding and joining these suits much easier.[61]

Anyone who wants to litigate separately can opt out of the class. If a person does not opt out, he or she is a member

60. CONSTANCE E. BAGLEY, WINNING LEGALLY: USING THE LAW TO CREATE VALUE, MARSHAL RESOURCES, AND MANAGE RISK 205 (2005).

61. Dina Temple-Raston, *Class-Action Lawsuits Gain Strength on the Web,* N.Y. TIMES, July 28, 2002, at 10.

of the class and will be bound by any decision or settlement reached in the class action.

Although corporate defendants have historically condemned class actions as an easy way for an eager plaintiff and his or her lawyer to get to court, this is changing. Some companies view class actions as a "strategic management tool" that can end litigation nightmares and work to their advantage by avoiding potentially devastating jury awards, reducing litigation costs, and limiting long-term liability.[62] A product liability class action can have the following advantages: (1) the settlement can bind not only present class members but also future claimants; (2) standardized payment schedules can avoid the risk of widely divergent jury awards; (3) some claimants who suffered less harm than others can be excluded from the settlement; and (4) the filing of suits and the settlement can occur on the same day.[63]

Any settlement of a class action requires approval by the court hearing the case. Until recently, courts were hesitant to reject a mutually agreed upon settlement. In *Amchem Products, Inc. v. Windsor,*[64] however, the U.S. Supreme Court tightened the requirements for class certification, making settlement more difficult. The named plaintiffs, nine individuals who were exposed to asbestos, filed a class-action complaint, answer, and settlement proposal with the defendants, including Amchem Products, Inc. They purported to represent the class of individuals who had not previously sued asbestos manufacturers and either (1) had been exposed to asbestos attributable to the defendants through their occupations or the occupations of a household member or (2) had a spouse or family member who had been exposed to asbestos. The size of the class was indeterminate but was estimated to include hundreds of thousands, perhaps millions, of individuals. Only half of the named plaintiffs currently manifested medical conditions as a result of exposure; others had allegedly been exposed to asbestos but had not yet developed any asbestos-related medical condition.

The Supreme Court held that the proposed class did not satisfy two Federal Rules of Civil Procedure. First, it did not satisfy Rule 23(b)(3)'s requirement that common questions "predominate over any question affecting only individual members." The "sprawling" differences between the class members were greater than their commonalties.

Second, the class failed to satisfy Rule 23(a)(4)'s requirement that the representatives of a class have the same interests as the class members. There was an inherent conflict between those already suffering from an asbestos-related disease and those who had been expsoed to asbestos but were currently asymptomatic: those currently injured would seek immediate payment whereas exposure-only plaintiffs would seek a generous, protected fund for future compensation. Thus, it was impossible to ensure that the class representatives could adequately represent the interests of all members of the class.

62. Richard B. Schmitt, *The Deal Makers: Some Firms Embrace the Widely Dreaded Class-Action Lawsuit*, WALL ST. J., July 18, 1996, at A1.

63. Catherine Yan, *Look Who's Talking Settlement,* BUS. WK., July 18, 1994, at 72.

64. 521 U.S. 591 (1997).

CIVIL PROCEDURE: LITIGATION STEPS

Civil procedure refers to the methods, procedures, and practices that govern the processing of a civil lawsuit from start to finish. Each court system has its own rules or guidelines to ensure the orderly processing of litigation. As mentioned earlier, the Federal Rules of Civil Procedure (FRCP) control the trial practices in all of the U.S. district courts. Each federal district court may also adopt its own local rules, which apply only within that district, to supplement the federal rules. Individual judges may even have their own particular rules for certain procedures in their courts.

Each state has a set of rules governing the procedures in the state trial court system. Often, the state rules are similar to the federal rules. Separate sets of rules govern practice before the various appellate courts and supreme courts. These rules address every requirement, from the time deadline for filing an appeal, to the contents of the notice of appeal, to the paper size, line spacing, and type style for briefs filed with the court.

FILING, PROSECUTING, AND DEFENDING AGAINST A CLAIM

The plaintiff's complaint, the defendant's answer (including any counterclaim), and any reply to the answer filed by the plaintiff are referred to as the *pleadings.* Exhibit 3.5 provides a typical timeline for a suit filed in federal court.

Complaint

The *complaint* briefly states a grievance and alleges (1) the particular facts giving rise to the dispute; (2) the legal reason why the plaintiff is entitled to a remedy; and (3) the *prayer,* or request for relief. The complaint should also explain why this particular court has jurisdiction over the alleged dispute and indicate whether the plaintiff requests a jury trial. If the plaintiff does not request a jury trial within the time limit, that right is deemed to be waived.

EXHIBIT 3.5 Typical Timeline for a Suit Filed in Federal Court

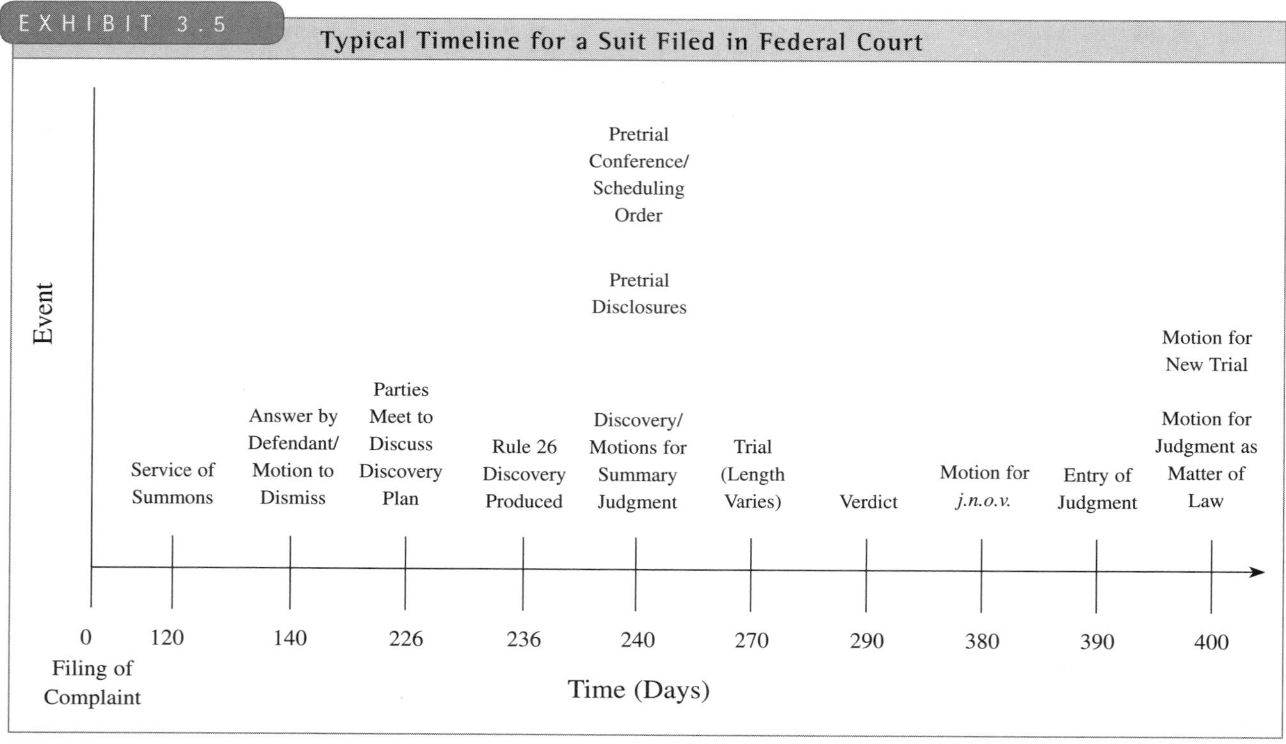

Summons

After the plaintiff files the complaint, the clerk of the court prepares a summons. The *summons* officially notifies the defendant that a lawsuit is pending against it in a particular court and that it must file a response to the complaint within a certain number of days. The clerk then stamps the official seal of the court on the summons. Next, the plaintiff or the clerk serves the official summons and complaint on the defendant. Service is usually completed by sending the documents to the defendant by mail.

Answer and Counterclaim

The defendant's *answer* may admit or deny the various allegations in the complaint. If the defendant believes that it lacks sufficient information to assess the truth of an allegation, it should state this. Such a statement has the effect of a denial. The answer may also deny that the law provides relief for the plaintiff's claim regardless of whether the plaintiff's factual allegations are true.

The answer may put forth affirmative defenses to the allegations in the complaint. An *affirmative defense* admits that the defendant has acted in a certain way but claims either (1) that the defendant's conduct was not the real or legal cause of harm to the plaintiff or (2) that the defendant's conduct is excused for some reason. An example of an affirmative defense in a contract case is the requirement under the statute of frauds (discussed in Chapter 7) that certain agreements must be in writing to be enforceable.

An answer may also include a *counterclaim,* a legal claim by the defendant against the plaintiff. The counterclaim need not be related to the plaintiff's claim.

Default Judgment

If the defendant does not file an answer within the time required, a *default judgment* may be entered in favor of the plaintiff. The defendant may, however, ask the court to set aside the default judgment if there were extenuating circumstances for not filing an answer to the complaint on time.

PRETRIAL ACTIVITY

Before the trial begins, the parties conduct discovery (discussed later in this chapter) and the attorneys for each party and the judge usually meet to discuss certain issues.

Pretrial Motions

A lawsuit may be resolved by the judge before trial pursuant to either a motion to dismiss or a motion for summary judgment. A *motion* formally requests the court to take some action.

Motion to Dismiss A *motion to dismiss* seeks to terminate the lawsuit on the ground that the plaintiff's claim is technically inadequate. A judge will grant a motion to dismiss if (1) the court lacks jurisdiction over the subject matter or the parties involved, (2) the plaintiff failed to properly serve the complaint on the defendant, or (3) the plaintiff has failed to state a claim on which relief can be granted. If a case is *dismissed with prejudice,* the plaintiff is precluded from asserting the same claims in another case. If a case is *dismissed without prejudice,* however, the plaintiff is permitted to refile the complaint (or an amended version thereof) and recommence litigation of the same claims.

A party may file a motion to dismiss immediately after the complaint and answer have been filed. This is known as a *motion for judgment on the pleadings.* One party, usually the defendant, argues that the complaint alone demonstrates that the action is futile.

The moving party may file *affidavits,* that is, sworn statements, or other written evidence in an attempt to show that the cause of action is without merit. When information or documents other than the pleadings are involved, the motion becomes a *motion for summary judgment.*

Summary Judgment Judges normally decide all questions of law, and juries resolve all disputes over factual matters. A judge will grant *summary judgment* when (1) all of the written evidence before the court clearly establishes that there are no disputed issues of material fact and (2) a party is entitled to judgment in its favor as a matter of law. If there is even a scintilla, that is, even the slightest bit, of evidence that casts doubt on an important fact in the lawsuit, the judge will not grant summary judgment. A judge may, however, grant summary judgment on some issues of the case and let the other issues proceed to trial. This is called a *partial summary judgment.*

Pretrial and Status Conferences

During pretrial and status conferences, the attorneys for the litigants meet with the judge to discuss the progress of their case. Such conferences may be held either in open court or in the judge's chambers. Topics addressed typically include:

- Prospects for settlement of the dispute.
- Issues raised by the pleadings.
- Any amendments to the pleadings.
- Scheduling of future discovery and a plan for the timely completion of discovery.
- The status of pending motions or prospective motions that a party may file.
- The schedule for the disclosure of production of exhibits.

As noted earlier, the judge will often hold a *settlement conference* to give each side a candid assessment of the strengths and weaknesses of its case and the likely outcome if the case goes to trial. If a settlement clearly is not feasible, then the pretrial conference will focus on formulating an efficient plan for the trial.

Under recently revised FRCP Rule 16, parties are required to alert the court early on about potential issues related to the discovery of electronically stored information, such as e-mails. Electronic document-retention policies are discussed in more depth later in this chapter.

TRIAL

A trial usually goes through the following stages:

1. Selection of the jury (if the trial is before a jury). The judge or attorneys may question the potential jurors.
2. Opening statements, first by the plaintiff's attorney and then by the defendant's attorney.
3. Presentation of evidence and witnesses by the plaintiff's attorney. This consists of:
   a. Direct examination of witnesses by the plaintiff's attorney.
   b. Cross-examination of witnesses by the defendant's attorney.
   c. Redirect examination by the plaintiff's attorney.
   d. Recross-examination by the defendant's attorney.
   e. Redirect and recross-examination until both sides have no further questions to ask.
4. Presentation of evidence and witnesses by the defendant's attorney. This consists of:
   a. Direct examination of witnesses by the defendant's attorney.
   b. Cross-examination of witnesses by the plaintiff's attorney.
   c. Redirect and recross-examination until both sides have no further questions to ask.
5. Motion for a directed verdict by either attorney.
6. Closing arguments, first by the plaintiff's attorney, then by the defendant's attorney, and then rebuttal by the plaintiff's attorney.
7. The judge's instructions to the jury.

8. Jury deliberations.
9. Announcement of the jury verdict.

Selection of Jury

Each side may challenge any number of jurors for cause during the questioning of potential jurors, which is called *voir dire.* Cause includes any relationship between the potential juror and any of the parties or their counsel. Most jurisdictions also permit a limited number of preemptory challenges. These can be used by counsel to remove potential jurors who counsel thinks might be inclined to decide for the other side. It is unconstitutional to use a preemptory challenge to remove a potential juror due to race or gender, however.[65]

65. *See* Batson v. Kentucky, 476 U.S. 79 (1986) and Rice v. Collins, 546 U.S. 333 (2006) (race); J.E.B. v. Alabama, 511 U.S. 127 (1994) (gender).

› ETHICAL CONSIDERATION

You are a manager of Dow Chemical Company, overseeing the silicone-breast-implant litigation across the United States. Your market research tells you that most individuals distrust Big Business and that most consumers cannot identify many products of your company, except those involved in the litigation. With an upcoming trial in Louisiana, you are considering conducting a full-scale advertising campaign to boost Dow Chemical's public image. The goal is to influence public opinion in the jurisdiction of the suit, thereby creating a positive image in the minds of potential jurors. You have several options for the campaign:

1. Emphasize Dow Chemical's citizenship: employee volunteers, donations to charities, and the improvement of society as a result of Dow's products.
2. Describe the benefits of silicone products. Without mentioning the breast-implant issue, tell numerous heart-wrenching tales about how silicone products have saved the lives of children.
3. Begin the final campaign the week before jury selection. Highlight the greed of attorneys who represent plaintiffs in such cases and lament the growing litigiousness of our society. The final slogan: "You can stop the greedy lawyers!"
4. Same as option 3, but also argue that silicone breast implants do no harm.

What should you do? If you were the plaintiff, how would you respond to these tactics?

Source: *See* Richard B. Schmitt, *Can Corporate Advertising Sway Juries?,* WALL ST. J., Mar. 3, 1997, at B1.

Motion for a Directed Verdict

After all the evidence has been presented, either attorney may ask the judge to grant a motion for a *directed verdict.* The moving party asserts that the other side has not produced enough evidence to support the legal claim or defense alleged. The motion requests that the judge take the case away from the jury and direct that a verdict be entered in favor of the party making the motion. If the judge agrees that there is not even an iota of evidence to support one party's claim or defense, then he or she will issue a directed verdict in favor of the other party. This does not happen very frequently.

Jury Verdict

After both sides have presented their closing arguments, the judge instructs the jury on applicable rules of law. After deliberating in private, the jury delivers its verdict, specifying both the prevailing party and the relief to which that party is entitled. In federal court, the six-person jury verdict must be unanimous. In state courts, a unanimous jury verdict is not always required. Frequently, nine out of twelve votes is sufficient.

POSTTRIAL MOTIONS

The announcement of the jury verdict does not necessarily conclude the case. Either party may make a motion to set aside the verdict or to have the case retried.

Judgment Notwithstanding the Verdict

Immediately after the jury has rendered its verdict and the jury has been excused from the courtroom, the attorney for the losing party may make a motion for a *judgment notwithstanding the verdict.* Such a judgment, also known as a *judgment n.o.v.,* from the Latin *non obstante veredicto,* or *j.n.o.v.,* reverses the jury verdict on the ground that the evidence of the prevailing party was so weak that no reasonable jury could have resolved the dispute in that party's favor. The judge will deny the motion if there is any reasonable possibility that the evidence could support the jury verdict.

New Trial

The judge may order a new trial if there were serious errors in the trial process. Examples include misconduct on the part of the attorneys or the jurors and the improper admission of evidence that severely prejudiced one party's chances for a fair trial.

APPEALS

If the trial judge does not grant the motion for a *j.n.o.v.* or a new trial, the losing party can appeal the decision. The appellate court will review the manner in which the trial judge applied the law to the case and conducted the trial. The appeals court can review the presentation of evidence at trial, the denial of a motion for a directed verdict, the jury instructions, and even the jury award of damages. The appellate court will not review the facts *de novo* and will reverse a judge's findings of fact only if they are clearly erroneous.

If the appellant loses before the court of appeals, it may want to have the supreme court consider the decision. Appeals are expensive, however, so the losing party should seriously consider the likelihood of success at the higher court before pursuing an appeal.

ALTERNATIVE DISPUTE RESOLUTION

In many cases, negotiation, mediation, and other alternative dispute resolution (ADR) procedures can help the company maintain a relationship with the opposing party, reduce legal expenses, dispose of issues relatively quickly, and allow for flexible business-oriented solutions. Certain forms of ADR, such as mediation, are usually accepted readily by the opposing party—the proceeding is informal and can be terminated at any time, and a mediator can also protect the confidentiality of sensitive data that might be made public during litigation. Others, such as arbitration, usually have to be agreed to in advance.

There are three basic varieties of ADR: negotiation, mediation, and arbitration. By mixing these with each other and the formal judicial system, a manager has four more options: minitrials, med-arb, arb-med, and summary jury trials. Some companies negotiate ADR clauses into all of their standard business contracts. Other companies leave it to their attorneys to decide which disputes are better resolved by ADR than by litigation.

NEGOTIATION

Negotiation is the give-and-take people engage in when coming to terms with each other. One can view negotiation along several different dimensions. First, negotiation can be either forward looking with concern for desired relationships—*transactional negotiation*—or backward looking to address past events that have caused disagreement—*dispute negotiation.* For example, two firms involved in a joint venture might engage in a transactional negotiation, whereas a steel manufacturer that failed to deliver I-beams and the construction company that has already paid for them would engage in a dispute negotiation. In the former, both parties are looking to the future with positive expectations; in the latter, the parties are looking to the past and apportioning blame. Conflicts need not be simply one or the other. Labor negotiations often have elements of both transactions and disputes. The parties must work together in the future but may also feel the need to apportion blame for the event that precipitated the crisis.

Second, negotiation can be viewed as involving a fixed or a growing pie. In *distributive* or *zero-sum negotiations,* the only issue is the distribution of a fixed pie. In contrast, in *integrative* or *variable-sum negotiations,* mutual gains are possible as parties trade lower-valued resources for higher-valued ones.

Distributive negotiations can easily become adversarial and strain even the closest relationships. With nothing to do but fight over the same pie, the parties inevitably do fight. Integrating other issues into the discussion creates the possibility of trade-offs that allow both parties to gain relative to their distributive starting point.

For example, consider a dispute between the manufacturer of a telecommunications device and the supplier of one of the device's critical components. The supplier delivered the component as scheduled, but the component failed to work properly in the device, causing significant friction between the manufacturer and the supplier. It is unclear which party caused the problem. In distributive negotiations, the parties would merely battle over who should absorb the resulting loss, a process that could irreversibly injure the manufacturer–supplier relationship and lead to litigation. By looking beyond the boundaries of the original transaction and dispute, however, the parties may be able to create value between them. For instance, the supplier may have the capacity to expedite delivery of a modified component at very little cost in a short period of time. The manufacturer, in turn, might highly value the ability to secure this modified component. Thus, the parties could strike a deal whereby the manufacturer agrees to pay the original amount owed plus a small premium for replacement in exchange for the supplier's agreement to expedite a modified component. Both parties receive more than was originally due and preserve their relationship.

While CEO of Texaco, James Kinnear successfully employed this strategy to resolve a $300 million dispute with a major customer that had sued Texaco for a variety of business torts. Texaco had agreed to supply oil at a fixed price to an aging plant that the customer had kept open only to preserve the value of the nontransferable fixed price contract. The two CEOs first met to hear evidence from lawyers from both sides. After it became clear that no speedy resolution of the legal claims was likely, Kinnear negotiated a deal whereby Texaco agreed to let the customer transfer the fixed-price contract to a more efficient plant in exchange for the customer's agreement to drop the lawsuit.[66]

66. BAGLEY, *supra* note 60, at 203–204.

INTERNATIONAL SNAPSHOT

In negotiating across cultures or in international settings, cultural myopia is a serious barrier to success. For instance, eye contact implies dramatically different attitudes in Japan and the United States. In the United States, a negotiator who avoids eye contact will be perceived as being intimidated or shifty. In Japan, that same behavior is taken as a sign of respect. When signals are misinterpreted, complex negotiations become even more difficult. Consider the Tokyo conference room where respectful officials of Mitsubishi avoid eye contact as they begin discussions with the aggressive owners of a Texas car dealership who rarely avert their eyes. What of teetotalling in Moscow? Bare heads in Jerusalem? Shoed feet in Beijing?[a]

The following excerpt from an essay written by an anonymous Japanese negotiator provides insight into how the Japanese view the American style of negotiation:

> Often they [the Americans] argue among themselves in public, so it is safe to assume that they argue even more in private. This is part of their idea of adversary proceedings and they seem to feel no shame about such embarrassing behavior. . . .
>
> Americans like to concentrate on one problem at a time. They seem not to understand that the whole picture is more important, and they spend little time on developing a general understanding of the views and interests of both sides. Since their habit of focusing on one issue often forces a direct disagreement, they often propose setting the issue aside, but they come back to it later with the same attitude and concentration. A negotiation with them may therefore become a series of small conflicts and we must always make a special effort to give proper attention to the large areas of agreement and common interest.[b]

a. For discussions of issues in cross-cultural negotiation, see Frank E. A. Sader & Jeffrey Z. Rubin, *Culture, Negotiation, and Eye of the Beholder,* 7 NEGOTIATION J. 249 (1991); Stephen E. Weiss, *Negotiating with "Romans"—Part 1,* SLOAN MGMT. REV. 51 (Winter 1994); John L. Graham, *The Japanese Negotiation Style: Characteristics of a Distinct Approach,* 9 NEGOTIATION J. 123 (1993).

b. YUKO YANAGIDA ET AL., LAW AND INVESTMENT IN JAPAN 219–20 (1994).

Liability for Failed Negotiations

In the United States, it is difficult to establish legal liability on the grounds that a party did not finalize a contract after a series of negotiations. As explained more fully in Chapter 7, a party negotiating in the United States is generally free to terminate negotiations for any or no reason at any time prior to contract formation. For example, in *Apothekernes Laboratorium for Special Praeparater v. IMC Chemical Group, Inc.,*[67] IMC's board of directors rejected a negotiated deal with Apothekernes after a letter of intent had been signed and IMC's negotiator had assured Apothekernes that the board would approve the deal. Even though the negotiators had a meeting of the minds, the U.S. appeals court held that there was no contract because the letter of intent expressly stated that the terms were "subject to our concluding an Agreement of Sale which shall be acceptable to the Boards of Directors of our respective corporations, whose discretion shall in no way be limited by this letter." In some jurisdictions, however, a covenant of good faith and trust applies to negotiations even if they do not ripen into a contract.[68]

MEDIATION

Mediation is another less hostile and less costly alternative to a lawsuit. In *mediation,* the parties agree to try to reach a solution with the assistance of a neutral third party who helps them find a mutually satisfactory resolution. This third party is the *mediator.* Unlike a judge, a mediator cannot dictate a solution; the parties must come to a resolution themselves and then agree to abide by it.

Mediation can offer resolutions that are speedy, inexpensive, and logistically simple when compared to litigation. Like negotiation, mediation can lead to joint gains and help preserve relationships that might otherwise break under the strain of conflict. In a survey of 1,000 large U.S. corporations, 81 percent of the respondents indicated that they used mediation because it provided "a more satisfactory process" than litigation; 66 percent said it provided more "satisfactory settlements"; and 59 percent asserted that it "preserves good relationships."[69]

67. 873 F.2d 155 (7th Cir. 1989).

68. *See, e.g.,* the Tokyo High Court's decision in *D. James Wan Kim Min v. Mitsui Bussan K.K.* (1987), excerpted in YUKO YANAGIDA ET AL., LAW AND INVESTMENT IN JAPAN 223–29 (1994) ("In the event that preparation between two parties progresses towards conclusion of an agreement and the first party comes to expect that the agreement will surely be concluded, the second party becomes obligated under the principles of good faith and trust to try to conclude the agreement, in order not to injure the expectation of the first party.").

69. DAVID LIPSKY & RONALD SEEBER, THE APPROPRIATE RESOLUTION OF CORPORATE DISPUTES: A REPORT ON THE GROWING USE OF ADR BY U.S. CORPORATIONS (1998).

Companies in a variety of industries have saved money, time, and other resources by mediating. Chubb & Son, Inc. has resolved nearly a dozen disputes under mediation pacts with other insurance companies and saved between $150,000 and $200,000 per case. The Travelers Insurance Company found that more than 85 percent of the cases it submitted to mediation were settled. Even when a settlement could not be reached, the mediation process helped the litigants focus on the most important issues, which allowed for a quicker resolution at trial.[70]

The Mediation Process

By definition, mediation is a flexible process that allows for many different structures, rules, and procedures. Because parties are less likely to agree to anything once a dispute has arisen, mediation organizations have evolved sets of default rules to which disputants can subscribe in advance of a specific conflict or to which they can defer once a conflict has arisen. Disputants are also free to establish alternative ground rules that are specifically tailored to their particular conflict and needs.

In many ways, mediation is an extension of the negotiation process. A mediator's role is to guide the parties through a structured set of discussions about the issues and alternatives and to suggest ways to resolve the dispute fairly. He or she confers with both parties, together and in private, and points out the elements in dispute and the areas of agreement. Because mediators can allow parties to vent their feelings and encourage them to at least acknowledge each other's perspectives, mediation can diffuse difficult interpersonal tensions. If the parties can reach an agreement, they often formalize the arrangement with contracts, public statements, or letters of understanding.

Although not pronouncing final judgment, a mediator can powerfully affect the outcome of the dispute. Unlike the parties, a mediator can offer compromises without fear of appearing weak or too eager to settle. By asking some questions but not others, the mediator can move the discussion toward or away from an issue. By suggesting solutions and reacting to proposals, the mediator can influence both parties' attitudes toward fairness, risk aversion, and trust. A skilled mediator knows how to bring disputing parties to genuine settlement; an unskilled mediator can push parties into agreements they later regret or, worse, can inflame the situation.

70. Margaret A. Jacobs, *Industry Giants Join Movement to Mediate,* WALL ST. J., July 21, 1997, at B1.

When to Use Mediation

Mediation is an appropriate option only when the parties sincerely desire to settle their dispute. If they are unwilling to compromise or seek to harm their opponents, mediation will be a frustrating waste of time. Conversely, parties who wish to preserve their relationship may find that mediation is their best option. Litigation and arbitration frequently leave the parties feeling negative about each other.

The more uncertain a party's legal claims are, the more attractive mediation often is. If the law is clear and one party's rights are clearly being violated, compromise may appear unnecessary. When the law is uncertain, mediation allows parties to resolve their differences without being subjected to undeveloped, ill-formed, or uncertain legal doctrine.

The need for privacy may also make some disputes more appropriate for mediation. Lawsuits require the filing of public documents and can alert the media to sensitive areas of business. A company may wish to keep trade secrets, controversial research, organizational structures, and internal training documents from the front pages of newspapers. Suppliers and customers may also become nervous if problems that could have been kept confidential are reported in the press. "Keeping it between ourselves" is much more realistic if few outsiders are involved.

Dangers Critics of mediation point to the lack of procedural protections. Some parties may be surprised to find that legal rights that would be protected in litigation are not protected in mediation. Parties with equal bargaining power may wisely agree to trade such rights for expediency. When one party has superior bargaining power, however, it may unfairly take advantage of the other side. For example, in a mediation of a conflict between a landlord and rent-controlled tenants over a rat infestation, the tenants might accept the placing of rat traps instead of the full-scale extermination that the housing code and a court would mandate.

Mediation may also effect changes in the distribution of power in a relationship. For example, introducing mediation into a nonunion plant may effectively defuse tensions and hinder efforts to unionize the plant.[71] Before agreeing to mediation, parties should consider the possibility of such consequences, including possible effects on continued adjudication of the dispute, future dealings with the opponent, and the firm's reputation with internal and external constituencies.

71. WILLIAM L. URY ET AL., GETTING DISPUTES RESOLVED 52 (1988).

Preserving Confidentiality

Ensuring confidentiality is central to negotiation and mediation. If parties do not feel comfortable revealing important, sensitive information, they are less likely to identify opportunities for mutual gain. Unlike negotiation, mediation allows disputants to confide in a third party without fear of being exploited. Whether the mediation process involves caucusing or shuttle diplomacy, confiding in a mediator can allow the mediator to identify potential gains and point them out to the parties. If that confidentiality is doubted, the parties will withhold useful but potentially damaging information. Even worse, if the promise of confidentiality is not honored, the parties will come to regret their decision to mediate.

To protect such confidences, many states extend legal privileges to mediators; others do so only if the parties have agreed to keep communications with the mediator confidential. Although federal law does not directly address the question, federal courts have shown a willingness to recognize a mediation privilege, even if doing so deprives a party of truthful probative evidence.[72]

Selecting a Mediator

Mediation agreements may or may not specify how a mediator will be selected. According to the Society of Professionals in Dispute Resolution (SPDR), qualified mediators (1) understand the negotiating process and the role of advocacy, (2) earn trust and maintain acceptability, (3) convert the parties' positions into needs and interests, (4) screen out nonmediable issues, (5) help the parties invent creative options, (6) help the parties identify principles and criteria that will guide their decision making, (7) help the parties assess their nonsettlement alternatives, (8) help the parties make their own informed choices, and (9) help the parties assess whether their agreement can be implemented.[73]

The CPR International Institute for Conflict Prevention and Resolution (CPR), a nonprofit alliance of 500 major corporations and law firms, offers a standard mediation clause for parties to incorporate into their contracts: "The parties shall endeavor to resolve any dispute arising out of or relating to this Agreement by mediation under the CPR Mediation Procedure. Unless otherwise agreed, the parties will select a mediator from the CPR Panels of Distinguished Neutrals." The Panels of Distinguished Neutrals are the CPR's rosters of 700 attorneys, former judges, legally trained executives, and academics who can mediate disputes. The CPR is a strong proponent of self-administered ADR, in which the parties and the mediator manage the process themselves. Self-administered ADR provides the parties with optimum control over the dispute resolution process and is cheaper and more efficient.

72. *See, e.g.,* Dell v. Dep't of Commerce, 618 F.2d 51 (9th Cir. 1980).

› ETHICAL CONSIDERATION

During a dispute with a competitor over copyrighted software that is similar to the competitor's products, you ask a mediator friend about his work in ADR. In the course of a few nameless anecdotes about his recent clients, you are shocked to learn how much sensitive information a skilled mediator can induce parties to share. At the same time, your attorneys tell you that without more evidence against your competitor, a lawsuit is not justified or economically prudent at this time. Should you propose mediation to the other company in the hope of learning enough information to justify legal action? If such a proposal is accepted, should you send as your representative a new employee who has no sensitive information to reveal? Should you hire a professional investigator as your representative to elicit as much damaging information as possible from your competitor?

ARBITRATION

Arbitration is the resolution of a dispute by a neutral third party, called an *arbitrator.* The process is consensual and created by a contract.

Although *nonbinding arbitration* is certainly an option, most parties enter *binding arbitration* whereby they agree to be bound by the arbitrator's decision. In *final-offer arbitration,* used most notably in baseball salary disputes, each side submits its "best and final" offer to the arbitrator, who then chooses one of the two proposals. Such a structure strongly encourages the parties to submit fair and reasonable offers. Otherwise, the less reasonable party is likely to lose with no chance for further concessions. Without its binding nature, such an exercise would be pointless. Nonetheless, the result of nonbinding arbitration can serve as a guide to what is fair. If a neutral third party has heard the strongest evidence and best arguments of both sides in a dispute, his or her opinion can serve as a baseline for what a court might decide.

Arbitration Process

Arbitration is the most formal of the ADR methods. It differs from both negotiation, in which there is no structure unless the parties first negotiate one, and mediation, in which the

73. NAT'L INST. OF DISPUTE RESOLUTION, DISPUTE RESOLUTION FORUM (May 9, 1989).

mediator focuses more on creating dialogue than on enforcing a technical format. Arbitration is more like a trial. The first stage is usually a *prehearing,* in which the parties may submit trial-like briefs, supporting documents, and other written statements making their case. Because neither federal nor state statutes grant arbitrators the authority to use discovery devices at this stage, prehearing discovery is usually limited to what the parties voluntarily disclose unless the parties agreed to greater discovery when they agreed to arbitrate the dispute.

The *hearing* is more structured than the prehearing and is often adversarial. The precise structure varies from arbitration to arbitration, but Rule 32 of the Commercial Arbitration Rules, Conduct of Proceedings, promulgated by the American Arbitration Association (AAA), provides an illustration:

> The claimant shall present evidence to support its claim. The respondent shall then present evidence to support its defense. Witnesses for each party shall also submit to questions from the arbitrator and the adverse party. The arbitrator has the discretion to vary this procedure, provided that the parties are treated with equality and that each party has the right to be heard and is given a fair opportunity to present its case.

Although arbitrators, unlike judges, are not required to apply detailed rules of evidence or procedure, many arbitrators believe that compliance with some of these rules is useful and necessary. Arbitrators may also subpoena documents and witnesses for the hearing.

After considering all the evidence presented in the prehearing and the hearing, the arbitrator makes his or her award in the final, *posthearing* phase. Often the award is not accompanied by any discussion or explanation of the decision. "Written opinions can be dangerous because they identify targets for the losing party to attack," warns one arbitration scholar.[74] In a profession neither subject to appeal nor constrained by precedent, arbitrators may be reluctant to give extra grist to the loser's mill. The U.S. Supreme Court, however, has noted that "a well reasoned opinion tends to engender confidence in the integrity of the process and aids in clarifying the underlying agreement."[75] In some settings, such as federal labor arbitrations under the auspices of the National Labor Relations Board (NLRB), arbitrators are required to write an opinion. Similarly, the California courts have taken the position that arbitration clauses in employment agreements must require a written opinion to be enforceable. Also, parties can insist on an opinion as part of their contract with the arbitrator.

Choice of Arbitrator

The choice of an arbitrator is crucial. Unlike a judge's decision, which can be set aside if erroneous, an arbitrator's ruling is generally binding and not subject to appeal.

74. R. Coulson, Business Arbitration—What You Need to Know 29 (3d ed. 1986).

75. United Steelworkers of Am. v. Enter. Wheel & Car Corp., 363 U.S. 593, 598 (1960).

Historical PERSPECTIVE

Early Binding Arbitration

In one of the earliest examples of ADR, two women brought their dispute over the maternity of an infant boy to a leading official:

> Then the king [Solomon] said, "The one says, 'This is my son, who is living, and your son is the dead one'; and the other says, 'No! For your son is the dead one, and my son is the living one.'"
>
> And the king said, "Get me a sword." So they brought a sword before the king. And the king said, "Divide the living child in two, and give half to the one and half to the other."
>
> Then the woman whose child was the living one spoke to the king for she was deeply stirred over her son and said, "Oh my lord, give her the living child and by no means kill him."
>
> But the other said, "He shall be neither mine nor yours; divide him!"
>
> Then the king answered and said, "Give the first woman the living child and by no means kill him. She is his mother."
>
> When all Israel heard of the judgment which the king had handed down, they feared the king; for they saw that the wisdom of God was in him to administer justice.[a]

a. 1 *Kings* 3:23–28.

An arbitration clause may list the names of potential arbitrators. If so, the parties should check the availability of these candidates before enlisting them. Like judges and their courts, particular arbitrators may be too busy to provide speedy resolution. Alternatively, the arbitration clause may defer the selection of an arbitrator to the American Arbitration Association, which represents 18,000 arbitrators, or another dispute resolution organization. Arbitrators from the AAA are skilled, and the association makes special efforts to identify arbitrators experienced in handling particular types of disputes. The AAA decides how many arbitrators to appoint (usually from one to three) and may include arbitrators from different professions, unless the arbitration clause specifies the number and kind of arbitrators desired. Arbitration clauses often provide that each party will choose its own arbitrator and that these two will pick a third. In some states, the government itself is willing to intervene. In New York, for instance, a court may name the arbitrator upon application by either party.[76] The Federal Arbitration Act has a similar provision.[77]

The ability to select an arbitrator familiar with the industry or form of dispute further distinguishes arbitration from much of the judicial system. Judges tend to be experts in judicial procedure. Consequently, they hear cases touching on many substantive areas of the law. A federal district judge, for instance, could in a single day preside over cases ranging from felony narcotic sales to toxic tort class actions; the judge's docket might include price-fixing cases, contract disputes between financial institutions, and racially motivated employment discrimination. Arbitrators tend to focus on business sectors or conflict types, such as labor relations or landlord–tenant disputes. To the extent one is more concerned with substance than procedure, arbitration can be an attractive alternative to litigation.

76. N.Y. C.P.L.R. 7504 (1999).

77. 9 U.S.C. § 5.

› Ethical Consideration

In many businesses, volume discounts are standard practice, and large customers reasonably expect to receive favorable treatment. How should a large, international corporation with a steady stream of disputes screen prospective arbitrators or mediators? Statistics have shown that companies using a particular arbitration service more than once are five times more likely to win in a repeat use than a first-time user. Even when repeat users do lose, they pay only 20 percent of the usual award.[a] Is it appropriate for a manager to point out to prospective arbitrators or mediators the potential for future lucrative business "if this one goes well"?

a. Panelists Say Ethics, Neutrality Challenges Create Vulnerability for Arbitration Providers, 70 U.S.L.W. 2616 (2002).

Arbitration Clauses

Parties typically agree to arbitrate their disputes by including an *arbitration clause* in their contract. Most arbitration clauses simply state that the parties will arbitrate all disputes relating to or arising out of their contract—leaving the parties to fight over the specifics of arbitration after a dispute arises. Instead, parties should specify in the agreement the types of issues and disputes to be resolved through arbitration as well as the procedure and rules to be used at the arbitration. It is far easier for parties to negotiate these terms at the beginning of their relationship than later after a dispute has arisen. The agreement should expressly state whether the arbitration will be binding or nonbinding. Parties should also stipulate the scope of discovery available, the types of permissible damages awards (including whether punitive damages will be available),[78] the location of the hearings, a reasonable timetable for resolving the dispute, and any other procedural matters on which they can agree.

To minimize conflict over such specifics, parties often designate that arbitrations will be conducted according to the rules of a third-party organization, such as the American Arbitration Association. Such organizations have evolved certain rules and procedures that may serve as defaults for disputing parties. Unfortunately, these rules rarely include provisions concerning the scope of discovery and limits on punitive damages. Parties are better served by including specific provisions concerning these matters.

When drafting a contract, managers should consider the scope of any arbitration clause. In *mandatory arbitration,* one party will not do business with the other unless he or she agrees to arbitrate any future claims. Usually, the parties to the contract are the parties to the arbitration. Sometimes, however, a dispute may arise between parties to several different contracts. For example, there may be a dispute between a construction subcontractor and an architect. The parties should ensure that each contract contains an arbitration clause and that each party agrees to a consolidated arbitration with other parties on related issues.

The more standard and reasonable an arbitration clause, the less likely it is to spawn derivative litigation questioning

78. In some states, such as Illinois, an arbitrator cannot award punitive damages unless the parties expressly authorize such an award.

the obligation to arbitrate. When there is a challenge to the entire contract, however, a claimant may be able to bring suit in a court of law.[79]

Judicial Enforcement of Arbitration Clauses: Federal Arbitration Act

In 1920, New York enacted the first arbitration statute in the United States, giving parties the right to settle current disputes and resolve future ones through private arbitration. The New York act served as a model for the Uniform Arbitration Act enacted thirty-five years later. Today, most states have amended their laws to conform to the Uniform Arbitration Act, making agreements to arbitrate and arbitration awards judicially enforceable.

Five years after New York blazed the trail, Congress passed what is now known as the *Federal Arbitration Act (FAA)*. Many years later, the Supreme Court proclaimed that in enacting the law, "Congress declared a national policy favoring arbitration and withdrew the power of the states to require a judicial forum for the resolution of claims which the contracting parties agreed to resolve by arbitration."[80]

Recent decisions have given arbitrators increasing power to make determinations that are not directly related to the issue the parties agreed to arbitrate. For example, the U.S. Supreme Court held that it was the responsibility of the arbitrator, not a court, to decide whether a group of borrowers could pursue a class arbitration on behalf of themselves and others similarly situated against Green Tree Financial for failure to inform them of their right to name their own lawyers and insurance agents.[81] The arbitration clause was silent on the availability of class arbitration.

Section 2 of the FAA provides that arbitration agreements in contracts concerning interstate commerce are "valid, irrevocable, and enforceable, save upon such grounds as exist at law or in equity for the revocation of any contract." By placing arbitration agreements on the same footing as other contracts, Congress precluded the states from "singling out arbitration agreements for suspect status."[82] For example, the Supreme Court struck down a Montana law that rendered an arbitration clause unenforceable unless "[n]otice that [the] contract is subject to arbitration" was "typed in underlined capital letters on the first page of the contract."[83] Montana's first-page notice requirement conflicted with the FAA because it applied only to arbitration agreements and not to all contracts.

› ETHICAL CONSIDERATION

A common premise underlying advocacy of ADR is that the parties have consented to the dispute resolution mechanism as opposed to the judicial system. Should the manager of a local appliance store whose sales contracts call for binding arbitration—in barely legible typeface buried in the middle of five pages of legalese—be able to enforce those arbitration clauses? Does it matter that this is the only refrigerator distributor for miles in a poor urban area? If the store serves a neighborhood where most residents speak only Chinese, should the agreement be in Chinese?

Parties seeking to invalidate an arbitration clause sometimes claim that the contract itself (including its arbitration clause) is void due to force, fraud, or the like. As with other unconscionable contracts, courts will not enforce an agreement, including its arbitration clause, if it operates in a harsh and one-sided manner without any justification.

Arbitration of Statutory Rights The U.S. Supreme Court has enforced arbitration clauses, even when the rights at issue were protected by federal law. For example, in *Rodriguez de Quijas v. Shearson/American Express, Inc.*,[84] the Supreme Court held that a predispute agreement to submit any controversy relating to a securities investment to compulsory arbitration was enforceable even though the plaintiff alleged claims under the Securities Act of 1933. The Court has upheld agreements to arbitrate claims under the Securities Exchange Act of 1934,[85] the Racketeer Influenced and Corrupt Organizations Act (RICO),[86] and the antitrust laws.[87] By agreeing to arbitrate a statutory claim, the Court reasoned, a party does not forgo the substantive rights afforded by the statute. The agreement means only that the resolution of the dispute will be in an arbitral, rather than judicial, forum.

Employment Disputes Employees are increasingly being required to sign applications or employment agreements that require mandatory arbitration of all future claims, including discrimination claims arising out of Title VII of the Civil Rights Act of 1964.

79. Spahr v. Secco, 330 F.3d 1266 (10th Cir. 2003).
80. Southland Corp. v. Keating, 465 U.S. 1, 2 (1984).
81. Green Tree Fin. Corp. v. Bazzle, 539 U.S. 444 (2003).
82. Doctor's Assoc., Inc. v. Casarotto, 517 U.S. 681, 687 (1996).
83. *Id.*
84. 490 U.S. 477 (1989).
85. Shearson/Am. Express v. McMahon, 482 U.S. 220 (1987), *reh'g denied,* 483 U.S. 1056 (1987).
86. *Id.*
87. Mitsubishi Motors Corp. v. Soler Chrysler-Plymouth, Inc., 473 U.S. 614 (1985).

An employee's agreement to arbitrate is clear when the employee signs an application form or agreement requiring arbitration, receives something of value from the employer, and is given a copy of the relevant arbitration rules. Some jurisdictions will infer an employee's agreement to arbitrate if the employee continues to work for the firm after receiving notice of the company's policy requiring all employees to arbitrate their claims. In *Howard v. Oakwood Homes Corp.*,[88] a North Carolina court found that an employee's continued employment with the company after she received a written notice of the employer's required program of dispute resolution reflected her assent to the terms of the agreement. As a result, she was compelled to arbitrate her claims of wrongful termination pursuant to the terms of the dispute resolution program.

In contrast, in *Rosenberg v. Merrill Lynch, Pierce, Fenner & Smith, Inc.*,[89] the First Circuit ruled that Merrill Lynch could not compel Rosenberg, a financial consultant who filed a suit against the company alleging age and gender discrimination, to arbitrate these claims because the company had not provided her with proper notice of its policy regarding arbitration. Although Rosenberg had signed a standard securities industry form agreeing to arbitrate certain claims, Merrill Lynch never provided her with a copy of the relevant arbitration rules. To ensure that an agreement to arbitrate will be enforceable, employers should make sure both that the agreement is supported by consideration (something of value from the employer) and that conspicuous notice of the obligation to arbitrate, including relevant arbitration rules, is given to the employee or applicant.

Even though the FAA by its terms does not apply to "contracts of employment of seamen, railroad engineers, or any other class of workers engaged in foreign or interstate commerce,"[90] the U.S. Supreme Court in *Circuit City Stores v. Adams*[91] read that exclusion narrowly to apply only to contracts involving employees in the transportation industries. All other employment contracts are subject to the FAA, meaning that courts must enforce agreements to arbitrate even where the employee is asserting Title VII claims. Employees who have signed individual agreements to arbitrate can also be required to arbitrate age discrimination claims under the Age Discrimination in Employment Act[92] and statutory claims under the Employment Retirement Income Security Act (ERISA), which governs pensions and other benefits.[93]

Even though the U.S. Supreme Court held in *Circuit City v. Adams* that employees could be required to arbitrate Title VII claims, on remand, the Ninth Circuit still refused to require arbitration.[94] The Ninth Circuit characterized Circuit City's arbitration policy as "a thumb on Circuit City's side of the scale should an employment dispute ever arise between the company and one of its employees." Citing language in the Supreme Court decision to the effect that arbitration clauses could be invalidated on grounds applicable to contracts generally, the Ninth Circuit held that the entire contract was voidable under California law because it was an unconscionable contract of adhesion. A *contract of adhesion* is a standard form that is drafted by the party with superior bargaining power and leaves the other party with only two options—sign the contract as is or reject it entirely.

Today, most major collective bargaining agreements include arbitration clauses. The Supreme Court has upheld provisions for mandatory arbitration of claims arising under a collective bargaining agreement,[95] but in 1974 it struck down a collective bargaining agreement's provisions for mandatory arbitration of statutory Title VII claims.[96] This decision may not stand in the face of the Supreme Court's decision in *Circuit City* upholding mandatory arbitration of Title VII claims.

The employee's agreement to arbitrate in no way limits the relief, including damages, that the Equal Employment Opportunity Commission (EEOC) is entitled to recover on the employee's behalf in a court of law, however.[97] The EEOC may file a claim in court on its own behalf against an employer, even if the employee involved had entered into an enforceable arbitration agreement, if the EEOC is either (1) seeking a permanent injunction enjoining an employer from engaging in discriminatory practices or (2) enforcing the individual rights of the employee.

In the following case, New York's highest state court refused to enforce an arbitration clause in a collective bargaining agreement negotiated with a public-sector employer on the grounds that it violated public policy.

88. 516 S.E.2d 879 (N.C. App. 1999), *cert. denied,* 528 U.S. 1155 (2000).
89. 170 F.3d 1 (1st Cir. 1999).
90. 9 U.S.C. § 1.
91. 532 U.S. 105 (2001). In a dissenting opinion by Justice Stevens, in which Justices Ginsburg and Breyer joined, he asserted that the legislative history of Section 1 of the FAA made it clear that the act "was not intended to apply to employment contracts at all."
92. Gilmer v. Interstate/Johnson Lane Corp., 500 U.S. 20 (1991).
93. Shearson Lehman/Am. Express v. Bird, 493 U.S. 884 (1989).
94. Circuit City Stores, Inc. v. Adams, 279 F.3d 889 (9th Cir. 2002), *cert denied*, 535 U.S. 1112 (2002).
95. AT&T Tech., Inc. v. Commu'n Workers of Am., 475 U.S. 643 (1986).
96. Alexander v. Gardner-Denver Co., 415 U.S. 36 (1974).
97. EEOC v. Waffle House, Inc., 534 U.S. 279 (2002).

A CASE IN POINT

CASE 3.4

County of Chautauqua v. Civil Service Employees Association

New York Court of Appeals
869 N.E.2d 1 (N.Y. 2007).

SUMMARY

FACTS The County of Chautauqua concluded that layoffs were necessary for budgeting reasons. In carrying out those layoffs, the county disregarded two provisions of its collective bargaining agreement (CBA) with the Civil Service Employees Association (CSEA), believing that they were incompatible with state law. One provision required the county to use seniority to determine which employees to lay off without first considering other factors, such as title or the importance of the position. The other allowed employees facing layoff to displace or "bump" less senior employees outside their own department. The union pursued grievances on behalf of the affected workers. It alleged that by ignoring those terms, the county had violated the CBA. When the grievances failed, the CSEA sought to arbitrate the dispute. The county filed suit seeking a permanent stay of arbitration. After lower court rulings in the county's favor on one issue and the union's on the other, the parties sought review from New York's highest court.

ISSUE PRESENTED Should the county be granted permanent stays of arbitration regarding the two CBA provisions at issue?

SUMMARY OF OPINION In New York, courts apply a two-part test to determine whether an issue is arbitrable or a stay of arbitration should be imposed. The first step is to determine whether the agreement conflicts with a law or public policy. If there is no conflict, the court then determines whether the parties actually agreed to arbitrate the particular dispute.

The New York Court of Appeals ruled that only one of the grievance issues was arbitrable. The court concluded that the first CBA provision at issue, which required the county to administer layoffs by applying only seniority principles, conflicted with a state regulation governing civil service. The law requires municipalities engaging in layoffs to first decide which positions are essential to providing services and then to protect the senior people in those positions. In contrast, the CBA provided seniority protection without regard for the municipality's determination about the essentialness of the position. The court ruled that complying with the CBA language would require the county to ignore its statutory obligation to assess staffing and budget needs. Calling the clash of terms "plainly irreconcilable," the court held that an arbitrator could not be asked to interpret that provision of the CBA.

The court ruled that the second issue—whether laid-off employees should have been permitted to bump junior workers in other departments—could proceed to arbitration. Although an arbitrator might fashion an award that conflicted with the state rules about displacement rights, such a conflict was not a foregone conclusion. State law limited interdepartmental bumping, but an arbitral determination in the union's favor would not necessarily exceed those limitations.

RESULT The court granted the county's petition for a permanent stay of arbitration as to the issue of how the county determined which employees to lay off, but granted the union's motion to compel arbitration of the bumping issue.

COMMENTS In *City of Long Beach v. Civil Service Employees Association,*[98] the New York Court of Appeals refused to enforce a collective bargaining agreement that purported to grant certain employment rights to provisional employees that went beyond those permitted by New York law. The New York intermediate appellate court subsequently applied the public policy rationale in a private setting and refused to enforce an arbitration agreement to resolve a dispute between a tenant and landlord about a leaky window and roof.[99] That court decided that the disagreement over roof and window issues was "more than a private dispute" and that it "transcend[ed] an

CONTINUED

98. 867 N.E.2d 389 (N.Y. 2007).

99. D'Agostino v. Forty-Three East Equities Corp., 842 N.Y.S.2d 122 (N.Y. App. Div. 2007).

individual landlord–tenant dispute." According to the court, allowing an arbitrator to hear the matter would exclude the government entities with ultimate responsibility for public interests, namely, the courts and the New York Department of Housing Preservation and Development. These rulings by the New York courts may have interpreted the public policy exception to arbitrability too broadly and will likely face challenges on that issue.

Judicial Review of Awards

The FAA lists only four circumstances in which an arbitration award may be set aside by a court: (1) the award was procured by corruption, fraud, or undue means; (2) the arbitrator was demonstrably impartial or corrupt; (3) the arbitrator engaged in misconduct by refusing to postpone the hearing when given sufficient reason or by refusing to hear pertinent evidence; and (4) the arbitrator exceeded his or her powers or executed them so badly that a final award on the issue put to arbitration was not made. Although parties to arbitration generally have the right to tailor their own procedural rules, the Ninth Circuit held that the parties could not by contract give a court broader review power than is granted by the FAA.[100] The parties in that case had agreed to permit a judge to overturn an arbitration award if he concluded that it was not supported by substantial evidence. The Ninth Circuit ruled that the parties had no authority to supplant congressional determinations of judicial limits.

100. Kyocera Corp. v. Prudential-Bache T Servs., 341 F.3d 987 (9th Cir. 2003), *cert. dismissed*, 540 U.S. 1098 (2004).

International Snapshot

The United Nations Convention on the Recognition and Enforcement of Foreign Arbitral Awards, Article III, implemented in the United States by Chapter 2 of the Federal Arbitration Act, provides: "Each Contracting State shall recognize arbitral awards as binding and enforce them in accordance with the rules of procedure of the territory where the award is relied upon, under the conditions laid down in the following articles."[a] As of 2007, 141 nations and the Vatican were signatories to the Convention.[b] International arbitration is discussed more fully in Chapter 25.

a. 9 U.S.C. § 201 (2006).

b. For the full text of the Convention and a list of signatories, see the dedicated section of the United Nations Commission on International Trade Law website at http://www.uncitral.org/uncitral/en/uncitral_texts/arbitration/NYConvention.html.

Although courts tend to look favorably on arbitration and favor its results, case law suggests that awards may be reversed for reasons beyond those enumerated in the FAA. A court may strike down an arbitration award if it would "violate some explicit public policy that is well defined and dominant."[101] This has been construed narrowly, however. The Supreme Court held that an arbitration award reinstating an employee who had been fired for drug use could not be set aside by a court for public policy reasons even though the employee was involved in the "safety sensitive" job of operating heavy machinery.[102]

Similarly, the Connecticut Supreme Court upheld an arbitration award that reinstated an employee who was fired after pleading nolo contendere to embezzling his employer's money.[103] A defendant making such a plea does not deny or admit guilt but agrees not to contest the charges. The collective bargaining agreement required termination of any employee convicted of an offense involving job duties but was silent on the effect of a nolo contendere plea. After the arbitrator decided that the employee should not have been terminated and ordered the town to reinstate him, the town went to court to try to vacate the arbitrator's decision on the grounds that it violated public policy. The Supreme Court of Connecticut upheld the award after concluding that it could not use the employee's nolo contendere plea as an admission of guilt. In a dissent, Chief Justice McDonald stated, "Under the majority's reasoning, a dishonest employee very simply avoids the application of the personnel rule [requiring termination for conviction of an offense involving job duties] by pleading nolo contendere."

A court can also set aside an arbitrator's decision if it was "arbitrary and capricious,"[104] or if the arbitrator

101. United Paperworkers Int'l Union v. Misco, Inc., 484 U.S. 29 (1987).

102. Eastern Associated Coal Corp. v. United Mine Workers, 531 U.S. 57 (2000).

103. Town of Groton v. United Steelworkers of Ame., 757 A.2d 501 (Conn. 2000).

104. Wilko v. Swan, 346 U.S. 427 (1953), *overturned by* Rodriquez de Quijas v. Shearson/Am. Express, Inc., 490 U.S. 477 (1989), on other grounds.

manifestly disregarded the law.[105] Courts tend to act only in egregious cases, however. As New York's highest court stated three decades ago, "An arbitrator's paramount responsibility is to reach an equitable result, and the courts will not assume the role of overseers to mold the award to conform to their sense of justice. Thus, an arbitrator's award will not be vacated for errors of law and fact committed by the arbitrator."[106]

In fact, courts have consistently ruled that once arbitrators are chosen, their rulings are final even if they lack professional training or are actually incompetent. Thus, it is very much in the interest of the parties to learn as much as they can about potential arbitrators because all parties involved will be bound regardless of "however bad [the arbitrators'] choices appear to be."[107]

HYBRIDS

Various hybrid forms of ADR are available, including med-arb, arb-med, minitrials, summary jury trials, and collaborative law.

Med-Arb

In *med-arb* the parties to a dispute enter mediation with the commitment to submit to binding arbitration if mediation fails to resolve the conflict. A danger of med-arb is that honesty in mediation could become damaging revelation in arbitration, especially if the mediator then acts as arbitrator. Looking ahead to such a possibility, parties in the "med" stage of med-arb may be reluctant to participate openly and in good faith, thus ensuring the final "arb" stage from the beginning. To avoid this, it is usually preferable to specify that a different person will act as arbitrator if mediation fails to resolve the conflict.

Arb-Med

Parties using arbitration/mediation *(arb-med)* present their case to an arbitrator who makes an award but keeps it secret while the parties try to resolve the dispute through mediation. If the mediation fails, then the arbitrator's award is unsealed and becomes binding on the parties.

105. Greenberg v. Bear, Stearns & Co., 220 F.3d 22 (2d Cir. 2000), *cert. denied,* 531 U.S. 1075 (2001).

106. Sprinzen v. Nomberg, 389 N.E.2d 456, 458 (N.Y. 1979).

107. IDS Ins. Co. v. Royal Alliance Assocs., 266 F.3d 645 (7th Cir. 2001). American Express accused the arbitrators of incompetence and not addressing the issues, but the court found that to be immaterial because all parties agreed to be bound by the arbitrator's decision.

Minitrial

In a *minitrial,* lawyers conduct discovery for a limited period, usually a few weeks. They then exchange legal briefs or memoranda of law. At this point, the top managers of the two businesses hear the lawyers from each side present their case in a trial format. The presentations are moderated by a neutral third party, often an attorney or a judge.

After the minitrial, the managers of the two businesses meet to settle the case. If they are unable to reach a settlement, the presiding third party can issue a nonbinding opinion. The managers can then meet again to try to settle on the basis of the third-party opinion.

Minitrials have several advantages. Like litigation, they allow a thorough investigation and presentation of the parties' claims. But, unlike in litigation, they give the managers the opportunity to work out their differences directly rather than through their attorneys. By shortening the time for discovery and presentation of the case, minitrials can reduce the possibility of the two sides becoming locked into opposing positions. The presence of a neutral third party gives the process an added element of discipline. Should the managers come to an impasse in their discussions, the third party can offer suggestions about a settlement. Finally, minitrials can be relatively private.

Because minitrials involve discovery, the production of briefs, oral argument, and the hiring of a third party, they can still be fairly expensive. Only when disputes are expected to involve large damages awards or protracted litigation do minitrials make economic sense.

Summary Jury Trial

In a *summary jury trial (SJT),* parties to a dispute put their cases before a real jury, which renders a nonbinding decision. Like nonbinding arbitration, this allows the parties to assess how a decision maker might decide the case in a real trial. The result is often the basis for a negotiated settlement. Like minitrials, SJTs offer disputants the opportunity to present their best case in a trial-like setting. Because the SJT makes use of abbreviated procedures, the result is achieved more quickly and with less expense.

A unique feature of SJTs is that they can be used like focus groups. Disputants often debrief jurors after the trial to find out how and why they reached their decision. Like discovery, this helps align the parties' information and expectations, so there is less reason to go through the expense of a formal trial. For example, a car accident victim suing for $5 million may balk at the insurance company's offer of $50,000 to settle the claim. If the jury in an SJT renders an award of only $75,000, the plaintiff will be more willing to consider settlement. If the jury awards $3 million,

"I'll tell you, mock jury duty beats cancer testing."

however, the defendant insurance company will be forced to reconsider its settlement offer. Either way, the parties' expectations will be brought closer together, making settlement more likely.

Collaborative Law and Other Techniques

Collaborative law attempts to combine mediation and negotiation into a more efficient, cheaper, more satisfying, and ultimately more successful form of dispute resolution. Attorneys who practice collaborative law attempt to work out both business and family disputes without going to court. The typical courtroom divorce takes about twenty months and costs from $10,000 to $25,000 per spouse. The typical collaborative law divorce takes about three months and costs about $3,000 per spouse.

Usually, collaborative law negotiations are four-way meetings with attorneys and clients present. The lawyers enter into contracts with their clients requiring them to seek other attorneys to represent them if the negotiations break down and the dispute goes to court. This removes any incentive the attorneys might otherwise have to go to trial.[108] Collaborative law is practiced in more than twenty states by about 3,000 attorneys and is used widely in Canada.[109]

Ombudspersons can also help parties resolve conflict. Such a person hears complaints, engages in fact-finding, and generally promotes dispute resolution through information methods such as counseling or mediation. An ombudsperson allows aggrieved parties to vent their concerns and alert *related* parties to problems before they become *opposing* parties.

The "In Brief" on the next page summarizes the most common ADR techniques in use today.

Discovery

Before a trial is held and sometimes before an arbitration hearing or minitrial is conducted, the parties collect evidence to support their claims through the process of discovery. In general, parties may obtain discovery regarding any matter relevant to the dispute. Exceptions include certain information protected by the attorney–client privilege, the attorney–client work-product doctrine, and other privileges discussed later in this chapter.

Discovery includes *depositions,* which are written or oral questions asked of any person who may have helpful information about the facts of the case; *interrogatories,* which are written questions to the parties in the case and their attorneys; and *requests for production of documents,* such as medical records and personnel files. In addition, personal notes and computer files, including e-mail correspondence, are also subject to discovery and are often the source of crucial evidence.

The basic purpose of discovery is to eliminate the "game" elements in a trial. By revealing the strengths and weaknesses of the various claims, discovery frequently allows the lawsuit to be resolved by agreement without a trial. At the least, discovery helps prevent any major surprises from occurring at trial because each side has already learned about the other's case.

Discovery serves other useful functions. First, it can preserve evidence. For example, depositions preserve the testimony of important witnesses who may otherwise be unavailable at trial. Second, discovery reduces the number

108. Steven Keeva, *Working It Out Amicably,* 89 A.B.A. J. 66–67 (June 2003).

109. Bette A. Winik, *Breakthrough in Law Practice,* NEWTON MAG., Sept. 4, 2002, at 21–22. The American Bar Association ethics committee concluded that collaborative law practice does not violate the Model Rules of Professional Conduct as long as the lawyer engaging in the practice first obtains informed consent from the client. ABA Standing Comm. on Ethics and Prof'l Responsibility, Formal Op. 07–447 (Aug. 9, 2007).

IN BRIEF

Models of Alternative Dispute Resolution

	Negotiation	Mediation	Arbitration	Med-Arb/ Arb-Med	Minitrial	Summary Jury Trial
How are the disputants represented?	Disputants represent themselves or legal counsel negotiates on their behalf	By themselves	By legal counsel	By legal counsel	By legal counsel	By legal counsel
Who makes the final decision?	Disputants mutually decide	Disputants mutually decide	If binding arbitration, arbitrator(s) decides	Arbitrator(s) if parties can't agree	Disputants mutually decide	Jury
How are the facts found and standards of judgment set?	Parties decide ad hoc	Parties decide ad hoc	Arbitrator(s) decides based on preset rules, e.g., those of the AAA	Parties and arbitrator(s) decide	Parties decide ad hoc	Rules of court
What is the source for the standard of resolution?	Mutual agreement	Mutual agreement	Arbitrator's sense of fairness	Arbitrator's sense of fairness	Mutual agreement	Jury's sense of fairness
How will the resolution by enforced?	Agreement usually turned into a contract that is enforceable by the courts	Agreement usually turned into a contract that is enforceable by the courts	By courts, according to the agreement to arbitrate the dispute	By courts, according to the agreement to arbitrate the dispute	Agreement usually turned into a contract that is enforceable by the courts	By courts
Who will pay the dispute resolution fees?	Parties decide ad hoc	Parties decide ad hoc	Parties decide before entering arbitration, often in arbitration clause	Parties decide in advance	Parties decide ad hoc	Parties decide ad hoc

of legal issues to be presented at trial because the parties can see beforehand which claims they have evidence to support and which ones are not worth pursuing.

Discovery has its drawbacks, however. The process is labor-intensive and therefore very expensive. Frequently, hours and days of depositions and hundreds of interrogatories will be undertaken. The strategy behind such a plan can be twofold: to wear down the opposing party by making the lawsuit more expensive than a victory would be worth, or to keep the papers flowing at such a rate that the other side cannot discern what all the documents really state. Such tactics often lead to discovery disputes that end up before the court. Taken too far, these strategies can lead to discovery abuse, which reduces the already slow pace of litigation,

> **ETHICAL CONSIDERATION**
>
> You are a top manager at a major corporation. The company has recently been sued in federal district court by an individual who was injured by one of its products. Your in-house counsel tells you that the plaintiff's counsel is competent but a sole practitioner specializing in family law. You discuss litigation strategy with your attorney. One possible tactic is to overwhelm opposing counsel through the discovery process. Your counsel provides several options: (1) delivering forty boxes of corporate documents a day for four days, of which perhaps sixty pages are relevant to the suit, then moving for dismissal on the fifth day; (2) actively mislabeling or hiding documents in the above "document dump"; (3) not providing any relevant information to opposing counsel but sending box after box of useless material; (4) stalling and delaying document requests because the corporation "is unable to locate them"; (5) accurately labeling the relevant material, but including it in a "document dump"; (6) declaring that only through extensive travel would opposing counsel be able to access the relevant information (sending individuals likely to be deposed all over the world on "important projects"); (7) continuously delaying and extending the number of depositions, interrogatories, and other materials needed in order to "effectively prepare for trial"; (8) promptly providing only the relevant information in a way the opposing counsel may easily access it; and (9) lying and destroying all relevant documents. Which option should you select and why?

significantly increases costs, and can anger judges. Congress has responded by limiting discovery in some circumstances, such as securities fraud cases subject to the Private Securities Litigation Reform Act, which is discussed further in Chapter 23.

Rule 26 of the Federal Rules of Civil Procedure imposes certain mandatory disclosure requirements on parties. Prior to a discovery request, parties must produce (1) the names of individuals likely to have discoverable information relevant to disputed facts at issue in the case, (2) documents relating to the facts alleged in the complaint, (3) documents relating to the calculation of damages, (4) insurance agreements that may cover the claims at issue in the case, and (5) the names of expert witnesses who may testify at trial. Recent amendments to Rule 26 have clarified the parties' obligations for making electronically stored information, such as e-mail, accessible to discovery efforts. The amendments also include steps for protecting electronic data that are accidentally provided during discovery.

Courts may penalize companies and their counsel for discovery abuses. In 2005, Qualcomm, a leading wireless technology company, filed a patent infringement suit against Broadcom, another microchip maker. Toward the end of the trial, a Qualcomm engineer testified that company attorneys had not turned over twenty-one of her e-mails to Broadcom as required under discovery rules.[110] That revelation led to the unearthing of more than 200,000 pages of e-mails and other electronic documents that Qualcomm had failed to produce before trial. Although a Qualcomm attorney called the failure a "mistake" that was "inadvertent," the judge overseeing the case concluded that "Qualcomm had engaged in 'widespread and undeniable misconduct,' and its lawyers in 'an organized program of litigation misconduct and concealment' throughout the litigation."[111] The judge ordered Qualcomm to pay Broadcom's $8.5 million legal bill and referred the case to a U.S. magistrate to determine whether additional penalties should be imposed on Qualcomm and its attorneys. With its litigation conduct facing increased scrutiny, Qualcomm chose to dismiss two pending patent litigation cases and may have greater difficulty enforcing its intellectual property rights around the globe.[112]

If a party has legitimately lost e-mails, FRCP Rule 37 may offer some relief. It provides a safe harbor for companies that lose electronic data due to routine operation of computer systems, as long as that operation was in good faith. If the party knows it is facing a suit, yet allows automated e-mail destruction to continue, however, then it will most likely not be protected by the rule.

ATTORNEY–CLIENT PRIVILEGE, ATTORNEY WORK-PRODUCT DOCTRINE, AND OTHER PRIVILEGES

Although generally any person with knowledge of facts relevant to a case can be required to testify in depositions or at trial, the attorney–client privilege and other privileges

110. Elliot Spagat, *Lawyers Face Sanctions in Qualcomm Suit*, AP NEWSWIRES, Oct. 12, 2007, *available at* http://www.factiva.com (last visited Oct. 15, 2007).

111. Gina Keating, *Qualcomm Evidence Failure Could Haunt It Legally*, REUTERS NEWS, Oct. 10, 2007, *available at* http://www.factiva.com (last visited Oct. 15, 2007).

112. *Id.*

designed to protect certain relationships limit the introduction of certain types of evidence.

ATTORNEY–CLIENT PRIVILEGE

Perhaps the most important limitation on discovery and testimony at trial is the *attorney–client privilege.* It dates back to the sixteenth century and provides that a court cannot force the disclosure of confidential communications between a client and his or her attorney. The privilege survives after the client is no longer represented by the attorney and even after the client's death.

The attorney–client privilege is intended to promote the administration of justice. An attorney is better able to advise and represent a client if the client discloses the complete facts. Clients are more likely to make a full and frank disclosure of the facts if they know that the attorney cannot be compelled to pass the information on to adverse parties. The privilege may also help to prevent unnecessary litigation because an attorney who knows all the facts should be better able to assess whether litigation is justified.

To be protected by the privilege, a communication must occur between the attorney and the client. The communication must also be intended to be confidential. If the client plans to relay the information to others or makes the communication in the presence of other individuals not involved in the lawsuit, there is no confidentiality.

The attorney–client privilege belongs to the client alone. The attorney, however, has an obligation to alert the client to the existence of the privilege and, if necessary, to invoke it on the client's behalf. The client can waive the privilege over the attorney's objection if the client so desires.

Corporate Clients

A corporation is unable to communicate with the attorney except through its officers, directors, employees, and agents. Although communications between a corporate client and an attorney can be protected by attorney–client privilege, it can be difficult to determine which element of the corporation is the client. In *Upjohn Co. v. United States,*[113] the Supreme Court ruled that, in cases brought in federal court, the privilege protects the communications or discussions of any company employee with counsel as long as the subject matter of the communication relates to that employee's duties and the communication is made at the direction of a corporate superior (the *subject matter test*). Thus, communications between a corporation's attorneys and any of its employees, not just a small, upper-level group, are protected under the federal attorney–client privilege as long as those communications pass the subject matter test. The Court also ruled that the attorney–client privilege extends to communications made to both in-house and outside counsel as long as the attorneys are acting in a legal capacity. In contrast, most European countries do not extend the privilege to in-house attorneys.[114]

A number of state courts and the British House of Lords do not apply *Upjohn*'s subject matter test. Instead, they apply the *control group test* and extend the privilege only to communications between counsel and upper-echelon employees who are in a position to control, or at least take a substantial role in making, the decision about the action the corporation might take based on the corporate attorney's advice.[115]

The attorney–client privilege may also extend to communications between a consultant hired by a corporation and an attorney, although courts will examine the specific facts of each situation to determine whether the privilege applies. In *In re Bieter Co.,*[116] the U.S. Court of Appeals for the Eighth Circuit held that the attorney–client privilege extended to communications between a partnership's attorney and a consultant to the partnership who was the functional equivalent of an employee. Even though the consultant was an independent contractor, not an employee, he was still a representative of the client partnership. He had daily contact with the partnership's principals, had acted as the partnership's sole representative in critical meetings, and had worked with the partnership's attorneys on the lawsuit.

The decision in *Upjohn* did not resolve all of the uncertainties regarding the application of attorney–client privilege to corporations. The Supreme Court did not decide whether the attorney–client privilege applies to communications with former employees. Nor did it specify what constitutes a voluntary waiver of the attorney–client privilege

113. 449 U.S. 383 (1981).

114. Thomas E. Spahn, *Business Lawyers: Listen Up!,* BUS. L. TODAY, May–June 2005.

115. *Id.*

116. 16 F.3d 929 (8th Cir. 1994). *But see* Cavallaro v. United States, 284 F.3d 236 (1st Cir. 2002) (privilege did not extend to accounting firm rendering accounting advice to attorneys representing parties to a merger).

by a corporation. Finally, there is still uncertainty about the protection the privilege gives corporations in suits brought against them by shareholders.

Guidelines Following the Supreme Court's decision in *Upjohn,* experts have suggested several techniques to keep communications within the scope of the federal attorney–client privilege.[117]

1. Because communication between an attorney and a corporation is protected only when a client is seeking or receiving legal advice, not business advice, corporations should request legal advice in writing and assign communication with the attorney to a specific employee who has responsibility over the subject matter at issue. How the interactions of an attorney and client are characterized can determine whether a court will find them to be protected. In *Satcom International Group PLC v. Orbcomm International Partners LP,*[118] the district court held that Virginia's attorney–client privilege protected discussions between corporate executives and the company's lawyer at a meeting called for the purpose of making a legal decision, even though this decision had commercial ramifications, as long as the corporation's counsel was present to provide legal advice and all discussion concerned the legal decision. Even documents that appear to be business in nature may fall under the privilege if they are created in connection with threatened or pending litigation.
2. Corporations should make sure that all communication between employees and corporate counsel is directed by senior management and that the employees know they must keep all communications confidential. Sharing communications too widely within the corporation—beyond the employees with a need-to-know—can waive the privilege.[119] Forwarding an e-mail from counsel to a third party, such as the corporation's public relations firm, will also destroy the privilege. For example, a large bank forfeited its privilege when it shared the attorney communication with its investment advisers.[120]
3. Employees should deal directly with counsel (not through intermediaries) and maintain confidential files and documentation.
4. When a corporation gives a government agency access to its communications or files, the corporation should negotiate a written agreement of confidentiality with the agency. Even with such an agreement, however, documents disclosed to the government lose the protection of the attorney–client privilege and therefore are discoverable in civil and class-action suits brought by private parties.[121]

Limitations

The attorney to whom the communication is made must be a practicing attorney at the time of the communication, and the person making the communication must be a current or prospective client seeking legal advice. A conversation between the client and the attorney about nonlegal matters is not protected. In *United States v. Frederick,*[122] the U.S. Court of Appeals for the Seventh Circuit held that neither the attorney–client privilege nor the work-product doctrine (discussed below) protected documents created by or communications with a lawyer who was acting as both an attorney and a tax preparer in preparing a client's tax returns. The court reasoned that a taxpayer "must not be allowed, by hiring a lawyer to do the work that an accountant, or other tax preparer, or the taxpayer himself, normally would do, to obtain greater protection from government investigations than a taxpayer who did not use a lawyer as his tax preparer." Similarly, in *Cavallaro v. United States,*[123] the U.S. Court of Appeals for the First Circuit ruled that the attorney–client privilege did not protect documents produced by an accounting firm helping the lawyers for two companies arrange a merger. The accounting company had not been retained to facilitate legal representation; it was merely providing accounting advice.

The attorney–client privilege does not protect client communications that are made to further a crime or other illegal act. Thus, if an executive asks his or her attorney the best way to embezzle money without being caught, that conversation is not privileged.

117. This discussion is based in large part on Block & Remz, *After "Upjohn": The Uncertain Confidentiality of Corporate Internal Investigative Files,* A.B.A. Sec. Litig.: Recent Developments in Attorney–Client Privilege, Work-Product Doctrine and Confidentiality of Communications Between Counsel and Client (1983).

118. 1999 WL 76847 (S.D.N.Y. Feb. 16, 1999).

119. Verschoth v. Time Warner, Inc., 2001 U.S. Dist. LEXIS 3174 (S.D.N.Y. Mar. 22, 2001).

120. Stenovich v. Wachtell, Lipton, Rosen & Katz, 756 N.Y.S.2d 367 (N.Y. App. Div. 2003).

121. McKesson HBOC, Inc. v. Superior Court of San Francisco County, 9 Cal. Rptr. 3d 812 (Cal. Ct. App. 2004).

122. 182 F.3d 496 (7th Cir. 1999), *cert. denied,* 528 U.S. 1154 (2000).

123. 284 F.3d 236 (1st Cir. 2002).

In July 1997, the Florida Court of Appeal rejected the tobacco companies' claim of attorney–client privilege for eight confidential documents, including attorneys' notes from in-house meetings on legal strategy.[124] Because the documents contained evidence that the tobacco attorneys had participated in an industry-wide conspiracy to defraud the public about the danger of smoking, the documents came within the exception for communications to further commission of fraud or a crime. This ruling was instrumental in the tobacco industry's decision to enter into a multibillion dollar settlement of claims related to the dangers of smoking.

Attorney–Client Privilege Under Siege?

The attorney–client privilege has come under attack on four fronts. First, Section 307 of the Sarbanes–Oxley Act of 2002 greatly expanded the responsibility of corporate attorneys to report "up the ladder" evidence of material violations of securities laws, breaches of fiduciary duty, and "similar" violations of Securities and Exchange Commission (SEC) rules. The goal is to promote better corporate responsibility by requiring lower-level lawyers to report wrongdoing to the supervising attorney. If nothing is done to remedy the situation, then the supervising attorney must report to the CEO. If the situation remains unresolved, then the supervising attorney must report the violation to the board of directors.

Second, in an effort to implement Section 307 of Sarbanes–Oxley, the SEC has submitted two versions of a proposed regulation governing lawyers who withdraw from representation because the board has failed to remedy the wrongdoing after becoming aware of it. The initial proposal called for a "noisy withdrawal," which would have required the lawyer both to withdraw and to inform the SEC of the withdrawal.[125] After receiving sharp criticism from a number of commenters, the SEC proposed that the issuer, rather than its attorney, be required to notify the SEC of the attorney's withdrawal in much the same way as the issuer must give notice of withdrawal by its auditors.[126]

Third, recent changes to Rule 1.13 of the American Bar Association's (ABA's) Model Rules of Professional Conduct, which have been adopted by several states, direct an attorney representing a corporation to "report up the ladder" any actions by employees that the attorney feels will significantly injure the corporation.[127] Attorneys face possible disbarment if their conduct is inconsistent with the state rules of professional conduct, which are usually patterned after the ABA's model rules. Rule 1.13 gives attorneys the right (but not the obligation) to reveal client confidences to third parties if doing so is necessary to prevent serious financial harm.[128]

Fourth, as discussed further in Chapter 15, prosecutors have pressured companies under government investigation to waive attorney–client privilege and disclose any reports of internal investigations in exchange for leniency in prosecution or sentencing.

ATTORNEY WORK PRODUCT

The attorney *work-product doctrine* protects information that an attorney prepares in the course of his or her work. This information includes the private memoranda created by the attorney and his or her personal thoughts while preparing a case for trial. The rationale behind the work-product rule is that lawyers, while performing their duties, must "work with a certain degree of privacy, free from unnecessary intrusion by opposing parties and their counsel."[129] Work-product materials may be obtained only with a showing of extreme necessity, such that the failure to obtain the materials would unduly prejudice an attorney's case or create hardship and injustice. The work-product doctrine is broader than the attorney–client privilege and may thus protect materials that are not protected by the privilege. For example, even though a court concluded that a corporation had waived the attorney–client privilege regarding notes summarizing its counsel's legal advice at board meetings by permitting an assistant to one of the directors to attend the meetings, the assistant's notes were protected by the work-product doctrine

124. 66 U.S.L.W. 1112 (Aug. 19, 1997).

125. SEC Proposes Rules to Implement Sarbanes-Oxley Act Provisions Concerning Standards of Professional Conduct for Attorneys, Release No. 220–158, *available at* http://www.sec.gov/news/press/2002–158.htm; *see also* Final Rule: Disclosure Required by Sections 406 and 407 of the Sarbanes-Oxley Act of 2002, Release No. 33–8177 (Jan. 24, 2003), *available at* http://www.sec.gov/rules/final/33–8177.htm.

126. SEC Adopts Attorney Conduct Rule Under Sarbanes-Oxley, Release No. 2003–13, Jan. 23, 2003, *available at* http://www.sec.gov/news/press/2003–13.htm.

127. MODEL RULES OF PROF'L CONDUCT R. 1.13 (2002).

128. *Id.*

129. Hickman v. Taylor, 329 U.S. 495, 510 (1947).

because they summarized the lawyer's advice regarding litigation against the corporation.[130]

OTHER PRIVILEGES

A party may also assert several other privileges to protect information the opposing party seeks to discover. Discussions between a physician and patient are privileged unless the patient has made his or her medical condition an issue at trial. For example, a person claiming damages for a back injury resulting from a workplace accident will be deemed to have waived the privilege at least as to any medical history relating to his or her back. The U.S. Supreme Court has recognized a privilege protecting discussions between a psychologist or licensed social worker and a patient as well.[131] The priest–penitent privilege protects disclosures made to a priest or other minister during confession. The Fifth Amendment to the U.S. Constitution gives any person the right to refuse to testify if it would tend to incriminate him or her.

Several courts have recognized a privilege for corporate "self-critical analysis," on the grounds that the forced disclosure of such potentially negative information could deter socially beneficial investigation and evaluation. For instance, in *Tice v. American Airlines, Inc.,*[132] the plaintiffs sought to obtain American Airlines' "top-to-bottom" safety reports in connection with their claim that the forced retirement of airline pilots over the age of sixty constituted age discrimination. The court upheld American Airlines' claim of privilege, emphasizing that "the public has a strong interest in preserving the free flow of airline safety [monitoring- and improvement-] related information."

DOCUMENT RETENTION AND DELETION

When a company is a defendant in a lawsuit or the subject of a governmental investigation, company documents, including computer files, may be used to prove liability. Nearly any corporate document can become a powerful weapon in the hands of opposing counsel. Electronic mail has become crucial evidence in corporate litigation, with parties routinely demanding access to company e-mail dating back ten to twenty years.[133]

Federal and state regulations require companies to retain certain records. The Code of Federal Regulations contains more than 2,400 regulations requiring that certain types of business records be maintained for specific periods of time. Many regulatory agencies have increased their retention requirements, forcing some companies to increase their file capacities by more than 15 percent a year.

In general, documents that a company is not required to retain for any business or legal purpose should be eliminated from company files. If the documents to be destroyed contain sensitive personal information, such as Social Security numbers, financial data, and medical records, then they should be shredded, erased, or otherwise modified to make the personal information undecipherable.[134] Consumer privacy is discussed further in Chapter 9.

Many companies do not have effective policies regarding document retention and deletion. They practice what some professionals call the "search and destroy" technique of file management: arbitrarily cleaning out file cabinets when storage space is running low. Yet, as former "Big Five" accounting firm Arthur Andersen learned the hard way when it was convicted of obstruction of justice after shredding a "significant" amount of correspondence and papers relating to its audit of Enron Corporation, it is illegal to destroy potentially relevant documents in the face of a threatened or pending lawsuit or government investigation. The "smoking gun" was an e-mail in which Nancy Temple, one of Andersen's top attorneys, encouraged auditors in the Houston office to abide by Andersen's document-retention policy. The prosecution contended that the e-mail directed employees to destroy evidence in the face of a pending government investigation. Even though Anderson's conviction for obstructing justice was eventually overturned by the U.S. Supreme Court,[135] the firm never recovered from the ensuing government investigation and criminal indictment.[136]

130. Nat'l Educ. Training Group, Inc. v. SkillSoft Corp., 1999 WL 378337 (S.D.N.Y. June 9, 1999).

131. Jaffee v. Redmond, 518 U.S. 1 (1996).

132. 192 F.R.D. 270 (N.D. Ill. 2000).

133. David S. Bennahum, *Old E-mail Never Dies,* WIRED, May 1999, at 100.

134. Section 1798.81 of the California Civil Code requires businesses having custody of personal information about California residents to take all reasonable steps to destroy personal customer data in this fashion.

135. Jima Anne Kato, *The Brave New World of Electronic Discovery and Document Management*, 49 ORANGE COUNTY LAW. 6, 13 (2007).

136. *Managing E-mail Risk: An Executive Leadership Guide*, TG GROUP AMERICAS, Apr. 28, 2003, at 4 ("Arthur Andersen's deleting of e-mail was a cornerstone in the investigation that later damaged the firm's reputation and led many clients to take their business elsewhere").

Largely in response to Andersen's behavior, the Sarbanes–Oxley Act made it a felony punishable by up to twenty years in prison to alter or destroy documents with intent to impair their use in an official proceeding.[137] Moreover, accountants who knowingly and willfully fail to keep audit documents and work papers for at least five years are subject to up to ten years of imprisonment.[138]

A well-designed and well-executed document-management program can (1) reduce corporate liability; (2) protect trade secrets and other confidential firm information; (3) protect employee privacy, especially as it relates to medical information; and (4) save on litigation costs.[139] Time and money are wasted when corporate staff and lawyers are forced to search for documents during discovery. With an organized document-management program, a company knows exactly what documents are in its possession and where these documents are located. It is critical to remember, however, that the duty to preserve any document, including electronic files, either by law or court order will always override a document-management program, no matter how well planned.

An employee's private diaries, calendars, and notebooks are also subject to discovery. Opposing counsel can glean from them a great deal about a company's operations. Even if a company has been careful to destroy unnecessary records, duplicates may exist in an employee's personal files, where they are still subject to discovery. For example, in the mid-1970s, the Weyerhaeuser Company paid $200 million in a case after company documents were found in personal files in the home of a retired company administrative assistant. Companies should therefore include this type of record in their document-management programs.

NECESSARY ELEMENTS OF A DOCUMENT-RETENTION PROGRAM

To stand up in court, a document-retention program must satisfy several requirements.

- *Well planned and systematic.* The program must be well planned and systematic. Companies should appoint a single person (perhaps the compliance officer) or department to be responsible for supervising, auditing, and enforcing the document-management program.[140] Policies should be established as to the types of documents to be destroyed, including documents stored on computer or word-processing disks and portable digital devices. As long as no lawsuit or government investigation is threatened or pending, documents not otherwise required to be retained should be systematically destroyed according to an established time frame (for example, when they reach a certain age).
- *No destruction in the face of a potential lawsuit or government investigation.* It is illegal to destroy documents when the company has notice of a potential lawsuit or government investigation. A company cannot wait until a suit is formally filed against it to stop destroying relevant documents. It must halt destruction as soon as it has good reason to believe that a suit is likely to be filed or an investigation started. Companies that did not halt destruction of documents have been forced to pay damages even when they acted accidentally. For example, in *Carlucci v. Piper Aircraft Corp.*,[141] flight data essential to the case were missing. The judge did not believe Piper Aircraft's claim that it had not deliberately destroyed the relevant document. The judge issued a directed verdict for the plaintiff and rendered a $10 million judgment against Piper.
- *No selective destruction.* The importance of a systematic document-management program cannot be emphasized enough. The court will scrutinize whether document destruction was done in the ordinary course of business. Any hint of selective destruction jeopardizes the defensibility of a document-management program. If a court does determine that document destruction was improper, the court may remedy the situation by instructing the jury that it may infer that whatever documents were destroyed would have had a negative impact on the party that destroyed them. This is known as a *spoliation inference.*

137. 18 U.S.C. §§ 1501–1520.

138. 18 U.S.C. § 1520.

139. Much of the discussion of document retention that follows is based on the work of John Ruhnka, Bard Family Term Professor of Entrepreneurship at the University of Colorado at Denver Business School, and Robert B. Austin, CRM, CSP, of Austin Associates, Denver. *See* John Ruhnka & Robert Austin, *Design Considerations for Document Retention/Destruction Programs,* 1 CORP. CONFIDENTIALITY & DISCLOSURE LETTER 2 (1988).

140. *Id.*

141. 102 F.R.D. 472 (S.D. Fla. 1984).

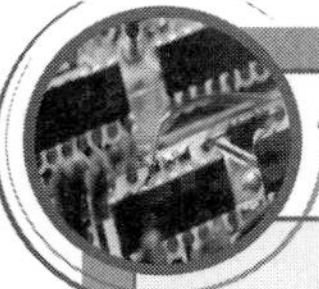

VIEW FROM CYBERSPACE

E-Discovery

With the proliferation of electronic documents, e-mails, text messaging, and instant messaging (IM), electronic communications are quickly becoming the most voluminous files that must be dealt with by a document-management system. By late 2003, office workers were exchanging an estimated 2.8 billion e-mails a day, and 99.997 percent of all documents were created and stored electronically.[a] Hence, managing electronic files is a primary concern for any document-management system.[b] Electronic discovery and document-retention requirements now extend to wireless devices, such as BlackBerry or Treo devices, USB portable drives, digital cards, and even the Subscriber Identity Module (SIM) card in cellular phones.[c]

Unlike official documents that employees are likely to treat as formal communications, electronic communications, such as e-mail and instant text messaging, are often far less formal. As demonstrated by the embarrassment and government scrutiny resulting from careless e-mails written by Whole Foods Market's CEO John Mackey (the subject of this chapter's "Inside Story"), managers should never put anything in an e-mail or instant message that they would not put in a written memo to the file. Parties are frequently able to recover "deleted" e-mail messages from backup tapes and hard drives. In fact, computer specialists can restore e-mail messages from magnetic tapes even if they have been overwritten several times.[d] In addition, virtually all IM programs automatically save all communications in log files, making these files discoverable.[e]

Moreover, failure to implement an effective policy for the retention and deletion of electronic documents can have disastrous effects. If an e-mail retention policy calls for e-mail destruction without regard to content or the existence of a threatened lawsuit or government investigation, the company risks violating federal obstruction of justice statutes and discovery rules and encouraging judicial sanctions.[f]

Failing to produce all electronic documents, such as e-mails and their attachments, in an organized manner can damage a company's case. Courts have punished parties for incomplete production and for jumbled production.[g] For example, a former employee sued UBS Warburg for employment discrimination and requested the recovery and production of a number of e-mails and other records. The court required UBS Warburg to bear the $106,000 cost of producing the e-mails. When it could not produce some of these e-mails, the judge instructed the jury that it could assume that the e-mails not produced were damaging to UBS Warburg's case.[h]

---

a. Ronald Raether, *E-mail Maelstrom: Electronic Documents Must Be Managed,* BUS. L. TODAY, Sept.–Oct. 2003, at 57–59.
b. Tom Ingram, *Help Your Clients Deal with Document Retention and Deletion,* J. INTERNET L., Apr. 2004, at 3.
c. Derek Hill, *Wireless Technology: A Minefield for Litigation,* L. TIMES, May 14, 2007, at 11.
d. David S. Bennahum, *Old E-mail Never Dies,* WIRED, May 1999, at 109.
e. Deborah H. Juhnke & David P. Stenhouse, *Instant Messaging: What You Can't See Can Hurt You (In Court), available at* http://www.discoveryresources.org/pdfFiles/TL_InstantMessaging.pdf.
f. Jima Anne Kato, *The Brave New World of Electronic Discovery and Document Management,* 49 ORANGE COUNTY LAW. 6, 13 (2007).
g. *Id.* at 6, 11.
h. Zubulake v. UBS Warburg LLC, 216 F.R.D. 280 (S.D.N.Y. 2004).

GLOBAL VIEW

Resolving Disputes Outside the United States

Managers engaged in resolving disputes outside the United States need to be mindful of important differences between U.S. practices and those elsewhere. Key differences include (1) greater willingness in some countries, such as Japan, to submit important business cases to arbitration and mediation; (2) limited or no opportunity for discovery; and (3) a requirement in the United Kingdom and many other countries that the loser pay the winner's attorneys' fees.

CONTINUED

Use of ADR

When parties to a contract are from different nations, a dispute between the parties can lead to a collision between at least one party's expectations and a foreign legal regime. To avoid such difficulties, it is often helpful to include arbitration clauses in these contracts. After all, few managers appreciate being hauled into a foreign-language court 5,000 miles from their home office and being held to unfamiliar legal standards. Many European and Asian business leaders, for example, are uncomfortable with the U.S. legal system's discovery procedures for obtaining evidence prior to trial through depositions, written interrogatories, and document production. Often the parties can draft an arbitration clause to their mutual satisfaction, but once litigation has begun, the parties cannot "negotiate around" many rules of a legal system, even if both are willing to do so.

In 1985, IBM Corporation set a precedent when it turned to international arbitration to resolve a major dispute with Fujitsu, Ltd., a Japanese electronics firm that was trying to gain access to IBM's mainframe programming materials. IBM claimed that Fujitsu had violated its copyrights by copying IBM software to develop its own operating system software. The arbitrators ultimately ruled that Fujitsu was entitled to obtain access to IBM's programs to develop and market imitations of IBM's mainframe software products in exchange for license fees of approximately $800 million.

In 2000, Toshiba America Information Systems, Inc. used mediation to settle a class action involving allegations that the company had manufactured and distributed faulty floppy-diskette controllers.[142] Toshiba agreed to pay approximately $2.1 billion in cash and to provide hardware replacement and coupons to repair the allegedly defective equipment.

Limited Discovery

Discovery rules in foreign countries are not as liberal as U.S. rules and frequently allow the parties to obtain relatively little information or none at all. As a result, if litigation in an American court concerns either an American corporation's foreign subsidiary or one of its offices located in a foreign country, it may prove difficult to obtain documents or take depositions of the employees located in the foreign country. Although litigants can obtain an order from a U.S. court that permits them to petition the court of the foreign country to obtain discovery to be used in the United States, the process is lengthy, and many countries will allow only very limited discovery or none at all. Even the United Kingdom, which has a legal system similar to the U.S. system, permits only limited discovery.

In addition, the process for taking discovery in foreign countries is frequently different from the U.S. practice. For example, countries often require a judge to be present at depositions, making the procedure more formal and controlled than it is in the United States where only lawyers and witnesses are present.

Recovery of Attorneys' Fees

Virtually every Western European country uses the "British rule"—also known as the "loser pays" rule—which requires the losing party at trial to pay the legal costs, including attorneys' fees, of the winner. The American system, by contrast, requires each litigant to bear its own attorneys' fees regardless of the trial's outcome, unless there is a contract providing that the loser must pay the winner's attorneys' fees. Efforts by the Republican majority in Congress in the mid-1990s to adopt the British rule as part of the "Contract With America" failed.[143]

The British rule is intended to compel potential litigants to evaluate the merits of their case carefully before involving the justice system. It can deter plaintiffs from filing frivolous claims to extort a settlement and defendants from adopting outlandish positions.[144] At the same time, the threat of being saddled with their opponents' costs can discourage potential litigants, particularly the poor, from asserting justifiable claims.[145] The fee-shifting rule can also inhibit the development of the law, as the financial risk of asserting novel or untested legal theories becomes too great.

142. Shaw v. Toshiba Am. Info. Sys., Inc., 91 F. Supp. 2d 942 (E.D. Tex. 2000).

143. This part of the "Contract With America" was proposed by Jim Ramstad (R-Minn.) in the 104th Congress in a bill entitled "The Common Sense Legal Reforms Act" (H.R. 956). It failed to pass the House of Representatives.

144. *Less Litigation, More Justice,* WALL ST. J., Aug. 14, 1991.

145. AGENDA FOR CIVIL JUSTICE REFORM IN AMERICA 24 (1991).

THE RESPONSIBLE MANAGER

ACCEPTING RESPONSIBILITY FOR MANAGING DISPUTES

Legal disputes often arise in business, and an amicable solution to them is not always possible. Some form of dispute resolution then becomes the next step. Legally astute managers treat legal disputes like any other business problem that requires a business solution.[146] Businesspeople usually need legal advice to make an informed decision but should resist the temptation to just "leave it to the lawyers." Law firms often wrongly assume that they call the shots and may spend more time and money on a case than the client intended.[147] Companies can reduce litigation costs by maintaining frequent contact with counsel.

To Sue or Not to Sue

Members of upper management and, in some cases, the full board of directors should be involved in deciding when to sue or use ADR, when to settle or dismiss, and how vigorously to defend. Sometimes the managers and employees intimately involved in a dispute lack the perspective and objectivity to evaluate the merits of a particular dispute resolution decision.

Frequently, parties file a lawsuit without giving sufficient thought to the various consequences. Before filing a lawsuit, managers should consider the following:

- Are the likelihood of recovery and the amount of recovery enough to justify the cost and disruption of litigation?
- Will the defendant be able to satisfy a judgment against it?
- Is the defendant likely to raise a counterclaim?
- Does the company need to preserve its relationship with the other party, or is this conflict the last interaction with that party?
- Will mutual resolution of the conflict make the company a desirable business partner, or will potential disputants seek conflict because the company appears weak and unwilling to defend itself vigorously?
- Will suing cause any ill will among customers, suppliers, or sources of corporate financing?
- Is the right decision more important than a quick resolution, or is time of the essence?
- Will public attention help in resolving the conflict, or does the matter require confidentiality?

The win-lose nature of lawsuits usually makes it impossible for both parties to claim satisfaction, save face, or forgive-and-forget. After a lawsuit, at best one party feels vindicated and the other feels wronged. Even the ostensible winner often feels angry about the time and money spent getting what it felt was its due to begin with. Or, as Jay Walker, founder of Priceline.com, put it, "It's not a matter of who wins. It's a matter of who loses less."[148]

Sometimes a lawsuit is worth pursuing simply to establish a company's credibility as one that will fight to support a legitimate business position. Notwithstanding Walker's distaste for litigation, he concluded that Priceline had to sue Microsoft Corporation and Expedia after Expedia began using reverse auctions to sell hotel rooms in violation of Priceline's patent: "[W]e concluded that the IP [intellectual property] was at the core of our ability to differentiate ourselves in an environment of low barriers to entry and the ease of imitation."[149]

If applied too rigidly, however, a philosophy favoring litigation can be expensive and may do more harm than good. Often communication, or the lack thereof, can make the difference between a minor disagreement and protracted litigation. Sometimes what the other party really wants is just an apology, a strategy Mike France of *BusinessWeek* dubbed the "mea culpa defense."[150] He called on executives to acknowledge their mistakes and apologize instead of stonewalling. As Andrew Meyer, a prominent Boston plaintiff's lawyer who represents victims of malpractice, further explained: "The hardest case for me to bring is the case where the defense has admitted error [and apologized to the injured patient]. If you have no conflict, you have no story, no debate. And it doesn't play well."[151]

CONTINUED

146. BAGLEY, *supra* note 60.
147. Ann Davis, *Businesses' Poor Communications with Law Firms Is Found Costly*, WALL ST. J., July 17, 1997, at B5.
148. Michael J. Roberts & Constance E. Bagley, *Priceline.com and Microsoft (B)* (Harvard Busi. Sch. Case No. 802–082, 2001), at 1–3.
149. *Id.*
150. Mike France, *Mea Culpa Defense,* BUS. WK., Aug. 26, 2002, at 77.
151. Quoted in Rachel Zimmerman, *Doctors' New Tool to Fight Lawsuits: Saying "I'm Sorry,"* WALL ST. J., May 18, 2004.

Deciding Whether to Settle

Parties should always consider settling the suit. Recent figures show that more than 90 percent of cases settle out of court, saving all parties the time, cost, and ill will of a trial. Filing a lawsuit can be a tactic to encourage settlement of a dispute that neither party really wishes to bring to trial.

Settlement is more likely when pursuing the lawsuit all the way to trial is not cost-efficient. For example, if a plaintiff alleges that a product is defective and caused her a loss of $4,500, the legal expenses will far exceed the original loss. Discovery alone is likely to cost more than $4,500. In such a case, it is usually in both parties' interest to settle the dispute if at all possible. If the plaintiff's claim is similar to many other identical claims that may be brought against the company, however, settling the first claim could appear to commit the defendant to paying all the other claims, too. Other lawsuits unlikely to settle include (1) cases presenting legal questions—such as the meaning of an ambiguous term in a contract—that the court should clarify to avoid future disputes between the same parties, (2) cases that could bring a large recovery if the plaintiff wins and no great harm if it loses, and (3) cases where one side has acted so unreasonably that settlement is impossible.

Establishing an ADR Program

To promote more efficient methods of resolving disputes, companies often institute an ADR program. To be successful, ADR programs require support from the managers, not just the lawyers.[152] The program should involve (1) in-house counsel; (2) the executives and corporate managers; (3) outside counsel; (4) the company's adversaries; and (5) certain field personnel, such as insurance industry claims personnel. Training of these various players is also essential.

The general counsel or another appropriate person should explain the benefits of an ADR program to company officers and executives. High-level management should demonstrate a commitment to the program. The company also needs to make clear that management's early and personal involvement in addressing disputes entering the ADR program is crucial to effectively resolving the matter.

Continuous feedback from all participants is essential to monitor, refine, and improve the program. Frequently, corporate managers are in a position to discover a weakness in a particular ADR procedure that could harm the company. The company may wish to designate one employee as the ADR "point person" who monitors the program to ensure that flaws are corrected and strengths are further enhanced.

152. This discussion is based in part on CENTER FOR PUBLIC RESOURCES, MAINSTREAMING: CORPORATE STRATEGIES FOR SYSTEMATIC ADR USE (1989).

A MANAGER'S DILEMMA

PUTTING IT INTO PRACTICE

The Propriety of Confidential Settlements

One way to avoid future claims is to settle a case pursuant to a *confidentiality agreement,* whereby the parties agree not to disclose the terms of the settlement. Such settlements may delay future lawsuits or even save the company from liability because the public may never hear about the settled claim. Also, in the event that future claims are filed, the plaintiffs will not know the economic particulars associated with the settlement, so they may settle for less than the original claim. Such settlements are a mainstay in conflict resolution and litigation in America, but in 2002, ten federal judges in South Carolina voted to ban all secret settlements on the ground that they often hide information that could be valuable to the public.[153] The judges cited the Ford–Firestone tire tread separation cases in which secret settlements deprived the public of the knowledge that some Firestone tires were dangerously defective. Had they been aware, lives might have been saved. Change seems to be in the wind, and that wind is blowing against confidential settlements. Nevertheless, for now they remain an indispensable tool in minimizing exposure for companies. If you were a manager responsible for major litigation, what factors would you take into account in deciding whether to insist on a confidentiality clause in an agreement? What factors might lead you to *not* insist on confidentiality?

153. *See* Adam Liptak; *South Carolina Judges Seek to Ban Secret Settlements*, N.Y. TIMES, Sept. 2, 2002, at A1.

INSIDE STORY

WHOLE FOODS MARKET'S CEO SOWS WILD OATS

The Federal Trade Commission's (FTC's) opposition to the merger of natural foods supermarket Whole Foods Market with competitor Wild Oats was based in part, if not largely, on e-mail statements made by Whole Foods CEO John Mackey. In correspondence with the company's board, Mackey wrote that the proposed merger would "eliminate a competitor" and "avoid nasty price wars."[154] FTC regulators seized on those statements as evidence of an intent to improperly destroy competition. Stanford Law School professor Joseph Grundfest, a former member of the Securities and Exchange Commission, commented: "It's remarkable how many corporate executives don't understand that the 'e' in email stands for both evidence and eternal."[155] He continued, "My only surprise here is that Mr. Mackey is surprised that the government got his email, read his email, and used his email against him."[156]

Electronic statements posted anonymously to an online message board were also connected to Mackey through discovery in the case. One 2005 posting criticized Wild Oats' CEO Perry Odak: "While Odak was trying to figure out the business and conducting expensive 'research studies,' to help him figure things out, Whole Foods was signing and opening large stores in OATS territories . . . Odak drove off most of the long-term OATS natural foods managers."[157] Another touted Whole Foods' prospects: in 2006, when Whole Foods projected it would reach $12 billion in sales by 2010, Mackey wrote, "[It] won't surprise me if the number ends up close to $14 billion."[158] Former SEC chair Harvey Pitt questioned Mackey's judgment in choosing to make the anonymous posts. "[It] isn't per se unlawful, but it's dicey. It's clear that he is trying to influence people's views and the stock price, and if anything is inaccurate or selectively disclosed he would indeed be violating the law . . . at a minimum, it's bizarre and ill-advised, even if it isn't illegal."[159]

Even though a court subsequently ruled that Whole Foods could proceed with its acquisition of Wild Oats,[160] Mackey's statements gave life to a weak case, embarrassed both himself and the company, and prompted investigations by the Whole Foods board and the SEC.[161] Corporate executives who would never write damaging statements in official company correspondence are often indiscreet or impolitic in e-mail, forgetting that e-mails are subject to discovery in a lawsuit. As one commentator remarked, "E-mail is a truth serum."[162]

154. Holman W. Jenkins, Jr., *Lessons from a Food Fight*, WALL ST. J., Aug. 29, 2007, at A14.

155. Scott Thurm, *Whole Foods CEO Serves Up Heated Words for FTC*, WALL ST. J., June 27, 2007, at A2.

156. *Id.*

157. David Kesmodel & John R. Wilke, *Whole Foods Is Hot, Wild Oats a Dud*, WALL ST. J., July 12, 2007, at A1.

158. Kara Scannell, *SEC Opens Informal Inquiry of Whole Foods CEO Postings*, WALL ST. J., July 14, 2007, at A2.

159. Kesmodel & Wilke, *supra* note 157, at A1.

160. FTC v. Whole Foods Mkt., Inc., 2007 U.S. App. LEXIS 20539 (D.C. Cir., Aug. 23, 2007).

161. Scannell, *supra* note 158 at A2; David Kesmodel, *Whole Foods Ends Probe of CEO Postings*, WALL ST. J., Oct. 6, 2007, at A18.

162. Bennahum, *supra* note 133, at 102.

KEY WORDS AND PHRASES

affidavit 83

affirmative defense 82

alternative dispute resolution (ADR) 76

answer 82

appellant 59

appellee 59

arbitration 88

arbitration clause 90

arbitrator 88

arb-med 95

asymmetric information 78

attorney–client privilege 99

authoritative decision 72

bench trial 77

QUESTIONS AND CASE PROBLEMS

1. Answer the following questions with regard to the case *Bush v. Gore,* 531 U.S. 98 (2000):
   a. In what year was the case decided?
   b. Which court decided the case?
   c. Can you tell from the cite which party originally brought the lawsuit or which party brought the appeal?
   d. Suppose that you want to cite the following passage that appeared on page 111:

      None are more conscious of the vital limits on judicial authority than are the members of this Court, and none stand more in admiration of the Constitution's design to leave the selection of the President to the people, through their legislatures, and to the political sphere. When contending parties invoke the process of the courts, however, it becomes our unsought responsibility to resolve the federal and constitutional issues the judicial system has been forced to confront.

   Where would the page designation go?

2. FC Schaffer & Associates, Inc. is an engineering firm based in Louisiana that did business with ODA Trading Agency, an Ethiopian entity that represents businesses wanting to do business in Ethiopia. Endrias, the founder and owner of ODA, employs Mesfin Gebreyes and an independent contractor, Kifle Gebre. Endrias left Ethiopia to live in the United States for five years. Shortly after Endrias's departure, Kifle learned that the Ethiopian Sugar Corporation was going to build a sugar mill and ethanol plant in Ethiopia. Kifle then contacted Schaffer about bidding for the project. Schaffer was interested and entered into a contract with ODA that provided that Schaffer would pay a commission to ODA if it was the successful bidder on the project. Schaffer was the low bidder and was chosen to build the mill and plant.

   Two months after Schaffer was awarded the contract, Endrias returned to Ethiopia and contacted Schaffer to introduce himself as the owner of ODA. Schaffer had never worked with or heard of Endrias and decided to enter into a new agreement with Mesfin and Kifle. This agreement purported to supersede the prior agreement between Schaffer and ODA. Schaffer refused to pay any commission to ODA under the first agreement, and Endrias sued Schaffer for breach of contract in the U.S. District Court for the Middle District of Louisiana. Can Endrias sue Schaffer in federal court? What law will apply to the breach-of-contract claim—federal law, the state law of Louisiana, or the law of Ethiopia? [*ODA v. FC Schaffer & Associates, Inc.,* 204 F.3d 639 (5th Cir. 2000).]

3. Spalding Sports Worldwide, Inc. sued Wilson Sporting Goods Company for infringement of U.S. Patent 5,310,178 pertaining to its basketball with a polyurethane cover. During discovery, Wilson asked Spalding to produce its invention record. Invention records are standard forms used by corporations as a means for inventors to disclose to the corporation's patent attorneys that an invention has been made and to initiate patent action. They usually contain such information as the names of the inventors, descriptions and scope of the invention, closest prior art, first date of conception, and disclosure to others and dates of publications. Spalding refused to produce its invention record, asserting that the record was protected by the attorney–client privilege because it was prepared for the purpose of securing legal advice concerning the patentability of the invention and served as an aid in completing the patent application. Wilson argues that even if the invention record was submitted to Spalding's patent committee, there was no evidence that the committee "acted as a lawyer" by rendering legal advice, as opposed to making business decisions. Wilson also contends that even if a portion of the invention record was submitted for the purpose of obtaining legal advice, the portion that contains technical information and does not ask for legal advice is not protected by the attorney–client privilege and should be produced.
   a. Should Spalding be forced to produce the invention record or part of it? Explain your reasoning. Would your answer be different if the invention record was the only record that contained the technical information at issue in the case?
   b. Wilson also argues that Spalding committed "fraud on the patent office" by making a material misrepresentation to the office and that, as a result, the attorney–client privilege was abrogated by the crime-fraud exception. Under the crime-fraud exception, the attorney–client privilege will be waived if the party made a communication "in furtherance of" a crime or fraud. Wilson has alleged that Spalding made a material misrepresentation but has submitted no evidence in support of this claim. Should the court find that the crime-fraud exception applies here and that Spalding has waived the attorney–client privilege? If not, what evidence would Wilson have to present to substantiate its claim that the

crime-fraud exception applies in this case? [*In re Spalding Sports Worldwide, Inc.*, 203 F.3d 800 (Fed. Cir. 2000).]

4. In a securities case, the plaintiff sought to compel documents regarding a merger between EdgeMark Financial Corporation and Old Kent Financial Corporation. EdgeMark retained David Olson of Donaldson, Lufkin & Jenrette (DLJ) to act as its investment banker in connection with the merger. EdgeMark sent a number of documents to Olson that it claims are protected by the attorney–client privilege. The plaintiff argues that these documents are no longer protected by the privilege because disclosure to Olson resulted in waiver of the privilege. EdgeMark argues that after the plaintiff's counsel threatened to sue it, EdgeMark's and DLJ's interests became "inextricably linked" because the litigation jeopardized the merger. As a result, EdgeMark argues, the documents are protected under the "common interest" rule, which is an exception to the general rule under the attorney–client privilege that the privilege is waived when a document is disclosed to a third party. The common interest rule protects from disclosure communications between one party and an attorney for another party where the parties are engaged in a joint defense effort. DLJ is not a party to the lawsuit and has not been asked to assist in the defense. Has the attorney–client privilege been waived, or does the common interest rule preserve the privilege? [*Blanchard v. EdgeMark Financial Corp.*, 192 F.R.D. 233 (N.D. Ill. 2000).]

5. Frank Boomer received a contract in the mail from his long-distance carrier, AT&T, that stated in unambiguous language that his rates were changing and that he should contact AT&T immediately if this was not acceptable. The agreement also contained a clause stating that any dispute concerning the contract would be settled by binding arbitration. Boomer did nothing initially and continued to make long-distance calls. Later, he decided to file a class-action suit against AT&T for overcharging him and other customers. Will Boomer be successful in getting his case heard by a court instead of an arbitrator? [*Boomer v. AT&T Corp.*, 309 F.3d 404 (7th Cir. 2002).]

6. Delfina Montes went to work for Shearson Lehman Brothers and signed an agreement to arbitrate any disputes arising from her employment. After the termination of her employment, Montes filed suit for allegedly unpaid overtime under the Fair Labor Standards Act (FLSA), which mandates overtime pay for certain workers. Honoring the arbitration agreement, the trial court referred the dispute to arbitration. The arbitration panel ruled that Shearson did not owe Montes any overtime pay. Montes petitioned the trial court to vacate the arbitration panel's ruling as arbitrary and capricious because the panel heeded Shearson's urging that it disregard the FLSA. In support of her claims, Montes has highlights from the transcript of arbitration in which Shearson's attorneys try to persuade the arbitrator not to follow the black letter statute. Can a plea to deliberately disregard the relevant law provide a basis for overturning the result of an arbitration? [*Montes v. Shearson Lehman Brothers, Inc.*, 128 F.3d 1456 (11th Cir. 1997).]

7. U.S.-based Exxon Mobil Corporation formed a joint venture with Saudi Basic Industries Corporation (Saudi), a company based in Saudi Arabia. Twenty years later, a dispute arose over license royalties Saudi had charged the joint venture. Saudi filed a lawsuit in Delaware state court seeking a declaratory order that the royalties were calculated in accordance with the terms of the joint venture agreement. Two weeks later and before trial commenced in state court, Exxon filed suit in federal district court. Saudi sought dismissal of the federal suit, but its motion was denied. Saudi then filed an interlocutory appeal of the district court's refusal to dismiss. Before the federal court of appeals rendered a decision on that issue, a Delaware state jury found in Exxon's favor and awarded it $400 million. Eight months later, the federal court of appeals held that although the federal district court had subject matter jurisdiction when Exxon filed its suit, that jurisdiction was terminated when the state court verdict was rendered. The appeals court applied a doctrine that prevents federal district courts from serving as appellate courts for parties that lose in state court, because only the U.S. Supreme Court has the power to review state court decisions. How should the U.S. Supreme Court rule on appeal? [*Exxon Mobil Corp. v. Saudi Basic Industries Corp.*, 544 U.S. 280 (2005).]

8. The Al-Haramain Islamic Foundation is a Muslim charity that operates in more than fifty countries. In connection with a proceeding to determine whether the foundation had ties to al Qaeda, the U.S. Department of Treasury inadvertently included a classified document among the information turned over to the foundation. The document revealed that foundation communications had been monitored under a federal warrantless surveillance program established in the wake of the September 11, 2001 terrorist attacks. Based on the contents of the classified document, the foundation filed suit in federal court against the U.S. government alleging several violations of federal law. The U.S. government claimed that the document was

protected by the state secrets doctrine. The courts agreed and prohibited the foundation from using both the document and its contents as part of its case absent a showing that other federal law preempts the state secret privilege protection. (The issue of whether the Foreign Intelligence Surveillance Act preempted the state secrets doctrine was remanded to district court.) If the document and the information it contained are off limits, and without any other evidence that the foundation was an actual subject of the federal surveillance program, does the foundation have standing to sue? [*Al-Haramain Islamic Foundation v. Bush*, 507 F.3d 1190 (9th Cir. 2007).]

Constitutional Bases for Business Regulation

INTRODUCTION

Effect of the U.S. Constitution on Business

The U.S. Constitution gives the federal and state governments the power to regulate many business activities, but it also provides that certain rights cannot be taken away from individuals and organizations. Responsibility for regulating business at the federal level is allocated to the three branches of government: the legislative (the Congress, which consists of the House of Representatives and the Senate), the executive (which includes the president), and the judicial (which includes the U.S. Supreme Court).

The Constitution became effective in 1789. The first ten amendments, called the Bill of Rights, were added in 1791. Since then seventeen other amendments have been added.

Although this chapter focuses on the U.S. Constitution, many of the legal and policy issues discussed have analogues in the constitutions of states and other countries. For example, many jurisdictions afford a certain degree of protection for commercial speech and prescribe the procedures that must be followed before a person can be deprived of life, liberty, or property.

CHAPTER OVERVIEW

This chapter first discusses the structure of the U.S. government as established by the Constitution and the allocation of different responsibilities to the three branches of government. The scope of the powers of the federal courts and the concept of judicial review are outlined, as is the Supremacy Clause. The chapter also describes the scope of executive and legislative power. This is followed by an analysis of conflicts that can arise among the three branches.

We then discuss the doctrine of federalism, which serves to allocate power between the federal government and the various state governments. The central importance of the Constitution's Commerce Clause to this doctrine is explored. Finally, the chapter outlines the individual rights established by the Constitution and the various methods of protecting those rights. Among the various constitutional issues addressed in this chapter are the rights to free speech, freedom of association and religion, and due process guaranteed under the Bill of Rights, and the concepts of substantive due process, eminent domain, and equal protection.

Structure of Government

The Constitution divides governmental power between the federal government and the state governments, giving the federal government only the powers specified therein. Without a constitutional grant of power, the federal government cannot act. All powers not expressly given to the federal government in the Constitution rest with either the states or the people.

Both the states and the federal government often regulate the same business activity. For example, there are both federal and state laws governing environmental protection, antitrust, and retail banking. If a state law conflicts with federal law, however, the federal law takes precedence, or *preempts*, the state law.

Separation of Powers

Within the federal government, power is divided among the judicial branch (the courts), the executive branch (the president and cabinet departments), and the legislative branch (the Congress). This division of power among the three branches is typically referred to as the *separation of powers*.

THE JUDICIAL POWER

The power of the judiciary is established in Articles I and III of the Constitution, which give Congress the authority to establish federal courts, and in Article III, which provides the basis for the judicial power of the federal courts.

Article III

Article III of the Constitution vests judicial power in the Supreme Court of the United States and such other lower courts as Congress may establish. Federal judicial power extends to all cases or controversies:

- Arising under the Constitution, laws, or treaties of the United States.
- Of admiralty and maritime jurisdiction.
- In which the United States is a party.
- Between two or more states.
- Between a state and citizens of another state.
- Between citizens of different states.
- Between citizens of the same state claiming lands under grants of different states.
- Between a state or citizens thereof and foreign states, citizens, or subjects.

In other words, the federal courts have *subject matter jurisdiction* to decide such cases.

Article III gives the Supreme Court *appellate jurisdiction* in all such cases, that is, the power to hear appeals from a lower court's decision. The Supreme Court also has *original jurisdiction* over cases affecting ambassadors and cases in which a state is a party. These cases are actually tried in the Supreme Court, not in a lower court. Today, the Supreme Court's original jurisdiction is used mainly to decide controversies between states.

Congress has used its authority under Article III to establish federal district courts and courts of appeals. (The structure of the federal court system was discussed in Chapter 3.) All cases that fall under one of the categories listed above, except those in which the Supreme Court has original jurisdiction, are tried in federal district courts or, in some instances, in state courts with a right to remove them to federal court.

Article I

Article I allows Congress to establish special courts other than the federal district courts and courts of appeals established under Article III. These specialized courts are often granted administrative as well as judicial powers. Examples include the U.S. Tax Court, the U.S. Bankruptcy Court, and the courts of the District of Columbia.

Judicial Review

Federal courts also have the power to review acts of the other two branches of the federal government to determine whether they violate the Constitution. This power of *judicial review* makes the federal judiciary a watchdog over the government.

Even though the Constitution did not explicitly grant the federal courts this power, the U.S. Supreme Court established its power of judicial review in 1803 in the landmark decision *Marbury v. Madison*.[1] The Supreme Court reasoned that one of its functions is to determine what the law is. Because the written Constitution is the fundamental and paramount law of the land, any law enacted by Congress that conflicts with the Constitution must be void.

THE EXECUTIVE POWER

The executive power of the president is defined in Article II, Section 1, of the Constitution. Various executive functions may be delegated within the executive branch by the president or by Congress.

Article II, Section 2, enables the president, with the advice and consent of the Senate, to appoint the justices of the U.S. Supreme Court. (The politics involved in such appointments are discussed in the "Inside Story" in this chapter.) It also gives the president the authority to appoint all ambassadors and consuls and all other officers of the United States whose appointments are not provided for elsewhere in the Constitution.

Article II, Section 2, also empowers the president to grant reprieves and pardons for offenses against the United States, except in cases of impeachment. President Gerald Ford invoked this section when he pardoned Richard Nixon after Nixon resigned from the presidency following the scandal arising out of the 1972 burglary of the Democratic National Headquarters in the Watergate Hotel in Washington, D.C. President George W. Bush used this power to commute the thirty-month prison sentence that Lewis Libby received

1. 5 U.S. (1 Cranch) 137 (1803).

for leaking the names of undercover Central Intelligence Agency operatives; only the portion of his sentence involving probation and a fine was left intact.[2]

Article I, Section 7, grants the president the power either to approve or to disapprove acts of Congress before they take effect. The president thus has *veto power* over laws that do not meet his or her approval. Congress can *override* a president's veto by a two-thirds vote of both the House of Representatives and the Senate. For example, Congress overrode President Bill Clinton's veto of the Private Securities Litigation Reform Act in 1996 and thereby helped shield public companies from frivolous shareholder lawsuits. (The Act is discussed further in Chapter 23.)

The president has extensive power over foreign affairs. Although only Congress can formally declare war, the president may take other military action through the president's power as commander in chief of the armed forces under Article II, Section 2. President George W. Bush used this power in 2003 to invade Iraq during Operation Iraqi Freedom.

The president also has the power to make treaties with the advice and consent of the Senate—that is, with two-thirds of the senators voting to ratify the treaty. The president may also make executive agreements, which do not require the advice and consent of the Senate. These agreements are superior to state law but not to federal law. (Treaties and executive agreements are discussed further in Chapter 25.)

THE LEGISLATIVE POWER

Article I, Section 8, of the Constitution enumerates the powers of the Congress, which consists of the House of Representatives and the Senate. Among other things, Congress has the power to:

- Regulate commerce with foreign nations and among the states.
- Spend to provide for the common defense and general welfare.
- Coin money.
- Establish post offices.
- Levy and collect taxes.
- Issue patents and copyrights.
- Declare war.
- Raise and support armies.

Congress also has the power to make such laws as are "necessary and proper" to carry out any power vested in the U.S. government.

CONFLICTS BETWEEN THE BRANCHES

Inherent in this system of checks and balances is the potential for conflict between the branches of government. At times, the power of one branch of the government must be curbed to ensure the integrity of another branch.

For example, it has been inferred from the extensive impeachment proceedings outlined in the Constitution that the president is immune from criminal prosecution prior to impeachment. The president also has a type of immunity known as *executive privilege*, which protects against the forced disclosure of presidential communications made in the exercise of executive power. Sometimes, however, executive privilege must give way to the judicial branch's need to obtain evidence in a criminal trial. In *United States v. Nixon*,[3] the U.S. Supreme Court held that President Nixon was required to produce tape recordings and documents relating to confidential conversations with his advisers in a criminal case involving seven advisers charged with obstruction of justice and other offenses related to the Watergate burglary.

More recently, however, the Supreme Court overturned a district court order directing Vice President Dick Cheney and other senior officials in the executive branch to produce information about the National Energy Task Policy Development Group that Cheney chaired.[4] The vice president had sought a writ of mandamus in the U.S. Court of Appeals for the District of Columbia to vacate the discovery order, but the court dismissed his petition, citing *United States v. Nixon*. The Supreme Court chided the court of appeals for reading the *Nixon* case too broadly. Although the Court acknowledged that an intrusion on internal White House deliberations was justified to produce information for a criminal case during Watergate, it cautioned that "[t]he observation in *Nixon* that production of confidential information would not disrupt the functioning of the Executive Branch cannot be applied in a mechanistic fashion to civil litigation."

Executive privilege also provides the president "absolute immunity from damages liability predicated on his official acts."[5] Such immunity does not, however, protect the president during his or her term of office from civil litigation over events that occurred before he or she took office.[6]

2. Sheryl Gay Stolberg, *Bush Spares Libby 30-Month Jail Term*, N.Y. Times, July 2, 2007, *available at* http://www.nytimes.com/2007/07/02/washington/02cnd-libby.html?hp=&pagewanted=all.

3. 418 U.S. 683 (1974).

4. Cheney v. U.S. Dist. Court for D.C., 542 U.S. 367 (2004).

5. Nixon v. Fitzgerald, 457 U.S. 731 (1982).

6. Clinton v. Jones, 520 U.S. 681 (1997).

The principle of separation of powers has been successfully invoked to invalidate certain legislation. In *Clinton v. City of New York*,[7] the Supreme Court struck down the *line item veto* given to the president by Congress in the Line Item Veto Act of 1996. The line item veto allowed the president to sign a bill into law, then cancel any dollar amounts that he or she believed to be fiscally irresponsible.[8] Because the veto gave the president the power to strike specific provisions from tax and spending bills, which usually include thousands of separate, discrete provisions, the president could shape budgetary policy without having to make the stark choice to accept or to reject an entire package of provisions. Congress could effectively override any particular line item veto by adopting a disapproval bill by a two-thirds vote of both houses.

The U.S. Supreme Court, by a vote of six to three, declared the Line Item Veto Act unconstitutional.[9] The Court ruled that the veto impermissibly altered the "single, finely wrought and exhaustively considered, procedure" in Article I, Section 7, of the U.S. Constitution, which requires that laws be approved by both houses of Congress (*bicameralism*) and then be presented to the president. The Court stated that the president must approve all parts of a bill or reject it *in toto*. The amendment and repeal of statutes must meet these same requirements. If the Act were valid, it would authorize the president to create a different law—one whose text was not voted on by either house of Congress or presented to the president for signature. The Court concluded that if there is to be a new procedure in which the president will play a different role in determining the final text of what may become a law, "such change must come not by legislation but through the amendment procedures set forth in Article V of the Constitution."

Supremacy Clause and Preemption

The Supremacy Clause of Article VI states that the Constitution, laws, and treaties of the United States take precedence over state laws and that the judges of the state courts must follow federal law. Any federal or state laws enacted in violation of the Constitution or ratified treaties are void. State law is preempted when it directly conflicts with federal law or when Congress has manifested an intent to regulate the entire area without state participation. Ultimately, preemption depends on the specificity of federal regulation, any statutory language addressing preemption, and the nature of the conflict between the federal and state approaches.

For example, the federal Clean Air Act provides that the federal government may set federal emissions standards, but it specifically allows California to set stricter standards, subject to the approval of the Environmental Protection Agency (EPA).[10] California adopted the first state law requiring auto manufacturers to begin reducing emissions of carbon dioxide and other heat-trapping gases in 2002, set standards for emissions in 2004, and petitioned the EPA for its approval of such regulation in 2005. At least sixteen other states, representing nearly half the nation's population, have adopted or were considering adopting California's emission limits. The California law was challenged by automobile manufacturers on a number of grounds, including preemption, but two federal courts rejected the challenges.[11] On December 20, 2007, however, the EPA rejected California's petition, noting that an energy bill signed by President Bush that day preempted the California law. "The Bush administration is moving forward with a clear national solution, not a confusing patchwork of state rules," EPA administrator Stephen L. Johnson stated in announcing the decision. In response, California filed a lawsuit against the federal government over its refusal to allow California to set its own tougher greenhouse gas limits on cars, trucks, and sport utility vehicles. California is asking the EPA to review its decision to deny the state a waiver that would allow it and sixteen other states to regulate vehicle emissions.[12]

In *Geier v. American Honda Motor Co.*,[13] the U.S. Supreme Court held that the National Traffic and Motor Vehicle Safety Act of 1996 (the Safety Act) preempted state product liability claims based upon a manufacturer's failure to equip a vehicle with air bags. Whereas the Safety Act deliberately provided the manufacturers of cars with a range of choices among different passive restraint devices and sought a gradual phase-in of passive restraints to allow more time for manufacturers to develop better systems, the state law imposed a duty to install an air bag. This presented an obstacle to the variety and mix of devices contemplated by the federal statute.

The U.S. Supreme Court subsequently considered whether state product liability claims arising out of the use

7. 524 U.S. 417 (1998).
8. 2 U.S.C. § 691 *et seq.* (Supp. 1997).
9. Clinton v. City of New York, 524 U.S. 417 (1998).
10. In 2007 the U.S. Supreme Court held that greenhouse gas regulation fell within the purview of the Clean Air Act. Massachusetts v. EPA, 127 S. Ct. 1438 (2007).
11. Green Mountain Chrysler Plymouth Dodge Jeep v. Crombie, 508 F. Supp. 2d 295 (D. Vt. 2007); Central Valley Chrysler-Jeep, Inc. v. Goldstone, 2007 WL 4372878 (E.D. Cal. 2007). These cases are discussed in more detail in Chapter 16.
12. Keith B. Richburg, *California Sues EPA over Emissions Rules*, *available at* http://www.washingtonpost.com/wp-dyn/content/article/2008/01/02/AR2008010202833.html.
13. 529 U.S. 861 (2000).

of Dow's herbicide by twenty-nine Texas peanut farmers were preempted by the Federal Insecticide, Fungicide, and Rodenticide Act (FIFRA).[14] The farmers alleged that the herbicide damaged their peanut crop and that Dow knew, or should have known, that the herbicide would not work on their farms because their soils had a pH level of 7.2 or higher. Dow argued that the farmers' state tort claims were preempted by Section 136v(b) of FIFRA, which prohibits states from imposing "any requirements for labeling or packaging in addition to or different from those required" under FIFRA. The U.S. Supreme Court found that each of the peanut farmers' tort claims was either not subject to preemption, or might not be, subject to further inquiry by the trial court. The Court focused on the meaning of the term "requirements," noting that FIFRA preempts only requirements for labeling or packaging in addition to or different from those required under the Act. The Court concluded:

> Rules that require manufacturers to design reasonably safe products, to use due care in conducting appropriate testing of their products, to market products free of manufacturing defects, and to honor their express warranties or other contractual commitments plainly do not qualify as requirements for "labeling or packaging." None of these common-law rules requires that manufacturers label or package their products in any particular way.

Notwithstanding its decision in *Geier,* the Court failed to address Dow's contention that the farmers' claims were impliedly preempted, stating only that "[i]n areas of traditional state regulation, we assume that a federal statute has not supplanted state law unless Congress has made such an intention 'clear and manifest.'" As discussed further in Chapter 10, subsequent Supreme Court cases have shown less deference to state product liability law.

FEDERALISM

Not only are the federal government's powers limited to those expressly granted in the Constitution, they are also subject to specific restrictions, such as those in the Bill of Rights. State governments, on the other hand, have general powers not specified in the Constitution. These general powers, sometimes termed the *police power*, include the power to protect the health, safety, welfare, and morals of state residents.

Some powers are exclusively federal because the Constitution expressly limits the states' exercise of those powers. Exclusive federal powers include the power to make treaties, to coin money, and to impose duties on imports. Other powers are inherently in the states' domain, such as the power to structure state and local governments.

THE ELEVENTH AMENDMENT

The Eleventh Amendment was added to the Constitution in 1798 to further protect the division of power between the federal and state governments. It immunizes states from lawsuits in federal court brought by citizens of another state or nation. Although on its face the Eleventh Amendment prohibits only suits by individuals of another state, it has been interpreted to bar suits against a state by citizens of that same state.[15] The Supreme Court has also held that the Eleventh Amendment precludes states from being sued in state court, even though the literal wording refers only to cases against states brought in federal court.[16] A state may waive its sovereign immunity, but it must do so voluntarily, explicitly, and in accordance with its own law.

Congress has enacted numerous laws that purport to *abrogate*, or annul, the states' Eleventh Amendment immunity. In reviewing the constitutionality of such legislation, the Supreme Court has held that a state cannot be required to litigate in federal court unless Congress both unequivocally (1) expressed its intent to abrogate that immunity and (2) acted pursuant to a valid grant of constitutional authority.

In many cases involving the Eleventh Amendment, Congress has acted pursuant to Section 5 of the Fourteenth Amendment, which gives Congress the power to bar states from denying any person due process or equal protection under the law. To invoke Section 5, Congress must identify conduct that violates the Fourteenth Amendment and tailor its legislation to remedy or prevent that conduct. The Supreme Court surprised many in 1999 when it ruled that states could not be sued in federal court for patent infringement under the Patent Remedy Act, even though Article I of the Constitution gives Congress the power to issue patents.[17] The Court ruled that Congress had not enacted the Patent Remedy Act pursuant to the valid exercise of power under Section 5 because Congress had not identified either a pattern of unremedied patent infringement by the states or a pattern of constitutional violations. In addition, the Court found that Congress had barely considered the availability of state remedies for patent infringement even though, under the Fourteenth Amendment's Due Process Clause,

14. Bates v. Dow AgroSciences LLC, 544 U.S. 431 (2005).

15. Hans v. Louisiana, 134 U.S. 1 (1890).

16. Alden v. Maine, 527 U.S. 706 (1999).

17. Fla. Prepaid Postsecondary Educ. Expense Bd. v. Coll. Sav. Bank & United States, 527 U.S. 627 (1999).

a state's infringement of a patent violates the Constitution only when the state provides no adequate remedy to injured patent owners.

In *Board of Trustees of University of Alabama v. Garrett*[18] and *Kimel v. Florida Board of Regents,*[19] the Supreme Court again ruled that Congress had exceeded its constitutional authority when it sought to abrogate the states' immunity in the Americans with Disabilities Act (ADA) and the Age Discrimination in Employment Act (ADEA), respectively. The Court noted that the Section 5 legislation under review in these cases related to a purported tendency of state officials to make disability- or age-based distinctions. Under federal equal protection law, discrimination on the basis of either disability or age is not judged under a heightened review standard and therefore is permissible as long as there is a rational basis for discriminating at a "class-based level." Accordingly, to impugn the constitutionality of state discrimination against the disabled or elderly, Congress was required not only to identify the existence of disability- or age-related discrimination, but also to establish a "widespread pattern" of irrational reliance on such criteria. The Court struck down the federal government's purported abrogation of state immunity in the ADA and the ADEA after concluding that no such showing had been made.

The Court subsequently ruled that a state employer could be sued in federal court for violating the Family and Medical Leave Act (FMLA) because gender discrimination is subject to a heightened level of scrutiny.[20] The Court began by reaffirming *City of Boerne v. Flores,*[21] which was the first case to set out the "congruence-and-proportionality test" for laws enacted under Section 5 of the Fourteenth Amendment. Under the *congruence-and-proportionality test*, federal laws enacted pursuant to Section 5 will be upheld only if they are congruent with the injury to be prevented or remedied by the Fourteenth Amendment and proportionate to the wrong they are intended to prevent or remedy. The Court then distinguished *Garrett* and *Kimel.* First, these two cases involved laws that Congress had passed to combat disability and age discrimination, neither of which is subjected to heightened scrutiny under the Constitution. Second, the laws invalidated in these cases bore little congruence and proportionality to the wrongs they sought to remedy because they prohibited almost all such discrimination. In contrast, the FMLA was enacted to combat gender-based discrimination, which is subjected to intermediate scrutiny under the Constitution. As a result, the Court found "it was easier for Congress to show a pattern of state constitutional violations." In addition, the Court concluded that the FMLA's private remedies, which place certain limits on employees' rights to take leave and limit the damages they can recover, were "congruent-and-proportional to the remedial object."

In the following case, the Court considered whether the State of Tennessee could be sued for failure to provide handicap access to its courthouses in violation of Title II of the Americans with Disabilities Act of 1990.

18. 531 U.S. 356 (2001).
19. 528 U.S. 62 (2000).
20. Nev. Dep't of Human Res. v. Hibbs, 538 U.S. 721 (2003).
21. 521 U.S. 507 (1982) (held that the Federal Religious Freedom Restoration Act of 1993 (RFRA) was unconstitutional as applied to the states). The Supreme Court subsequently upheld the application of the RFRA to the federal government in *Gonzales v. O Centro Espirita,* 546 U.S. 418 (2006).

A CASE IN POINT

SUMMARY

CASE 4.1

TENNESSEE V. LANE

SUPREME COURT OF THE UNITED STATES
541 U.S. 509 (2004).

FACTS Plaintiffs George Lane and Beverly Jones, individuals with paraplegia who use wheelchairs for mobility, sued the State of Tennessee and a number of Tennessee counties under Title II of the Americans with Disabilities Act of 1990 (ADA).[22] Title II provides that "no qualified individual with a disability shall, by reason of such disability, be excluded from participation in or be denied the benefits of services, programs or activities of a public entity, or be subjected to discrimination by any such entity." The plaintiffs sought damages because they were denied access to, and denied the services of, state courthouses due to their disabilities.

In particular, Lane alleged that he was compelled to crawl up two flights of stairs to answer criminal charges on the second floor of a courthouse because there was no elevator. When he refused to crawl again on his second appearance, he was arrested and jailed for failure to appear. Jones, a certified court reporter, alleged that she lost opportunities to work and participate in the judicial process as a result of difficulties she encountered when accessing county courthouses.

CONTINUED

22. 42 U.S.C. §§ 12131–12165.

After the district court denied Tennessee's motion to dismiss on Eleventh Amendment immunity grounds, the U.S. Court of Appeals for the Sixth Circuit affirmed the district court's denial of Tennessee's motion. The Sixth Circuit reasoned that the plaintiffs' claims were not barred by the Eleventh Amendment because they were based on due process principles. The U.S. Supreme Court granted certiorari.

ISSUE PRESENTED Does Title II of the ADA validly abrogate a state's Eleventh Amendment immunity from suits in federal court?

SUMMARY OF OPINION The U.S. Supreme Court began by noting that Congress may abrogate the states' Eleventh Amendment immunity only when Congress (1) unequivocally has expressed its intent to abrogate immunity and (2) has acted pursuant to a valid grant of constitutional authority. The Court concluded that the first requirement was easily met, because Title II of the ADA specifically provides that "[a] State shall not be immune under the Eleventh Amendment to the Constitution of the United States from an action in [a] Federal or State court of competent jurisdiction for a violation of this chapter." The remainder of the opinion focused on whether Congress had acted pursuant to a valid grant under Section 5 of the Fourteenth Amendment.

The Court observed that Congress may use its Section 5 power to enact "prophylactic legislation" that "prohibit[s] a somewhat broader swath of conduct, including that which is not itself forbidden by the [Fourteenth] Amendment's text."[23] Nonetheless, Congress may not use Section 5 to "substantively redefine" the meaning of the states' legal obligations under the Fourteenth Amendment. Accordingly, valid Section 5 legislation must exhibit "congruence and proportionality between the injury to be prevented or remedied and the means adopted to that end."

The Court noted that when it had applied the congruence-and-proportionality test in *Garrett*, it had concluded that Title I of the ADA was not a valid exercise of Congress's Section 5 power to enforce the Fourteenth Amendment prohibition on unconstitutional disability discrimination in public employment. First, the Court found that Congress's exercise of its Section 5 prophylactic power was unsupported by a relevant history and pattern of constitutional violations. Second, neither the ADA's legislative findings nor its legislative history reflected a concern that the states had been engaging in a pattern of unconstitutional employment discrimination. Finally, Title I's broad remedial scheme was insufficiently targeted to remedy or prevent unconstitutional discrimination in public employment.

Applying the same test to this case, the Court reached a different result. First, it noted that, unlike Title I of the ADA, Title II applies to courtroom access rights and therefore "seeks to enforce a variety of . . . basic constitutional guarantees, infringements of which are subject to more searching judicial review." The courtroom access rights meriting heightened scrutiny include due process rights guaranteed by the Fourteenth Amendment, a criminal defendant's rights under the Sixth Amendment's Confrontation Clause, jury rights under the Sixth Amendment's "fair cross section" jurisprudence, and public access rights to criminal proceedings under the First Amendment.

Second, the Court observed that there was a history and pattern of violations of fundamental rights of disabled persons that constituted a "backdrop of pervasive unequal treatment in the administration of state services and programs." Disabled persons had been unequally deprived of fundamental rights in a number of contexts, including voting, marriage, service on juries, unjustified commitment, abuse and neglect, zoning decisions, the penal system, and public education. Further, the Court determined that the history and pattern of violations were adequately supported by congressional findings: a 1983 U.S. Civil Rights Commission report showed that "76% of public services and programs housed in state-owned buildings were inaccessible"; witnesses testified before a House subcommittee about the inaccessibility of courthouses; and a congressional ADA task force gave "numerous examples of the exclusion of persons with disabilities from state judicial services and programs."

CONTINUED

23. *Hibbs*, 538 U.S. at 727–28.

The Court concluded that Title II was an appropriate response to this history and pattern of unequal treatment and that the remedy that Congress adopted in Title II—to "take reasonable measures to remove architectural and other barriers to accessibility"—was a "reasonably prophylactic measure, reasonably targeted to a legitimate end."

Although the State of Tennessee argued that Title II was overbroad and therefore unconstitutional because it applied not only to public education and voting-booth access, but also to seating at state-owned hockey rinks, the Court concluded:

> Whatever might be said about Title II's other applications, the question presented in this case is not whether Congress can validly subject the States to private suits for money damages for failing to provide reasonable access to hockey rinks, or even to voting booths, but whether Congress had the power under Section 5 to enforce the constitutional right of access to the Courts.

RESULT The Court affirmed the judgment of the court of appeals. Title II of the ADA, as applied to the fundamental right of courtroom access, was a valid exercise of Congress's Section 5 authority to enforce Fourteenth Amendment guarantees.

COMMENTS *Tennessee v. Lane* was a split decision, with Chief Justice Rehnquist and Justices Kennedy, Scalia, and Thomas dissenting. In his dissent, Chief Justice Rehnquist argued that the majority opinion was irreconcilable with *Garrett*. According to Chief Justice Rehnquist, Title II of the ADA authorized

> private damages suits against a State for merely maintaining a courthouse that is not readily accessible to the disabled, without regard to whether a disabled person's due process rights are ever violated. Accordingly, even as applied to the "access to the courts" context, Title II's "indiscriminate scope offends [the congruence-and-proportionality] principle," particularly in light of the lack of record evidence showing that inaccessible courthouses cause actual Due Process violations.

DUAL SOVEREIGNTY

The Supreme Court reaffirmed the system of dual federal and state sovereignty when it struck down provisions of the Brady Handgun Violence Prevention Act that required state law enforcement officers to receive reports from gun dealers regarding prospective handgun sales and to conduct background checks on prospective handgun purchasers.[24] The Court stated that "[t]he Federal Government's power would be augmented immeasurably and impermissibly if it were able to impress into its service—and at no cost to itself—the police officers of the 50 States."

In *Reno v. Condon,*[25] however, the Supreme Court upheld the Driver's Privacy Protection Act of 1994, which restricts a state's ability to disclose personal information contained in the records of the state department of motor vehicles without the driver's consent. The Court rejected the contention that the Act violated the Tenth Amendment's federalism principles, holding that the Act was a proper exercise of Congress's authority to regulate interstate commerce under the Commerce Clause. The Court explained:

> The motor vehicle information, which the States have historically sold, is used by insurers, manufacturers, direct marketers, and others engaged in interstate commerce to contact drivers with customized solicitations. The information is also used in the stream of interstate commerce by various public and private entities for matters related to interstate motoring. Because drivers' personal, identifying information is, in this context, an article of commerce, its sale or release into the interstate stream of business is sufficient to support congressional regulation.

24. Printz v. United States, 521 U.S. 898 (1997).

25. 528 U.S. 141 (2000).

THE COMMERCE CLAUSE

Another boundary between federal and state powers is the Constitution's *Commerce Clause*, contained in Article I, Section 8. The Commerce Clause, which gives Congress the power to regulate commerce with other nations, with Indian tribes, and between states, is a source of federal authority and a restraint on state action. The commerce power has been interpreted to allow federal regulation of such areas as interstate travel, labor relations, and discrimination in accommodations. As explained below, over time the U.S. Supreme Court has changed its view of the scope of the Commerce Clause.

1824 TO 1887

Chief Justice John Marshall wrote the first Supreme Court decision involving the Commerce Clause in the 1824 case *Gibbons v. Ogden.*[26] A state-granted steamboat monopoly affecting navigation between New York and New Jersey violated a federal statute regulating interstate commerce. The Court held that under the Supremacy Clause, the federal statute prevailed. In the decision, Justice Marshall expressed his view that interstate commerce—which he defined as "commerce which concerns more states than one"—included every activity having any interstate impact. The Commerce Clause gave Congress the power to regulate all such activities.

1887 TO 1937

From 1887 to 1937, the Supreme Court viewed the Commerce Clause quite differently from Justice Marshall. During this period, the Court interpreted "commerce" narrowly, holding that activities such as mining and manufacturing were not commerce and could not be regulated by Congress under the Commerce Clause. The Supreme Court was not persuaded by the fact that the products of these activities would later enter interstate commerce. Toward the end of this period, the Court struck down various pieces of New Deal legislation, arguing that the Commerce Clause did not grant Congress the power to regulate such activities.

1937 TO 1995

A turning point in the Supreme Court's attitude came in 1937 in *NLRB v. Jones & Laughlin Steel Corp.*[27] The Court held that Congress could regulate labor relations in a manufacturing plant that manufactured steel that was subsequently shipped across state lines. From 1937 until 1995, virtually all federal regulation of commerce was upheld under the Commerce Clause. As long as the legislation had a "substantial economic effect" on interstate commerce, it was upheld as a valid exercise of the commerce power.

For example, in *Heart of Atlanta Motel, Inc. v. United States,*[28] the Supreme Court upheld Title II of the Civil Rights Act of 1964, which prohibits discrimination or segregation on the grounds of race, color, religion, or national origin in any inn, hotel, motel, or other establishment of more than five rooms that provides lodging to transient guests. The party challenging the Act—the Heart of Atlanta Motel—had followed a practice of refusing to rent rooms to African Americans, and it stated its intention to continue to do so. The operator of the motel solicited patronage from both inside and outside the state of Georgia through billboards, signs, and various national advertising media, including magazines of national circulation. Approximately 75 percent of its registered guests were from out of state.

The Court noted that the population had become increasingly mobile, with millions of people of all races traveling from state to state. Because African Americans in particular were subjected to discrimination in transient accommodations, they were forced to travel great distances to secure lodging, and this impaired their ability to travel to other states.

In *Katzenbach v. McClung,*[29] the Supreme Court upheld the application of the Civil Rights Act to a restaurant because a substantial portion of the food that it served had previously moved in interstate commerce. The Court reasoned that the restaurant's discrimination against African Americans, who were potential customers, resulted in its selling less food that had traveled in interstate commerce. Thus, the discrimination had a substantial effect on interstate commerce.

1995 TO THE PRESENT

In 1995, in *United States v. Lopez,*[30] the Supreme Court again changed course when it struck down the Federal Gun-Free School Zone Act provision banning guns near schools as being beyond Congress's power under the Commerce Clause. The Court found that the statute was not a regulation of the use of the channels of interstate commerce, an attempt to prohibit the interstate transportation of a commodity through the channels of interstate commerce, or an attempt to protect an instrumentality of interstate commerce

26. 22 U.S. (1 Wheat.) 1 (1824).

27. 301 U.S. 1 (1937).

28. 379 U.S. 241 (1964).

29. 379 U.S. 294 (1964).

30. 514 U.S. 549 (1995).

or a thing in interstate commerce. The Court ruled that the law was not sustainable as a regulation of an activity that substantially affects interstate commerce because its terms had nothing to do with commerce or any sort of economic enterprise.

The Court rejected the government's argument that the statute was constitutional because possession of a firearm at school might result in violent crime, which in turn would (1) affect the functioning of the national economy by increasing costs and reducing people's willingness to travel to parts of the country deemed unsafe and (2) reduce national productivity by threatening the learning environment. The Court reasoned that the "cost of crime" argument would give Congress the power to regulate not only all violent crime, but also all activities that might lead to violent crime, and the "national productivity" argument would empower Congress to regulate any activity related to the economic productivity of individual citizens, including family laws governing marriage, child support, and divorce. As a result, there would be virtually no limitation on federal power, even in areas such as criminal law and education where the states historically have been sovereign, a result unacceptable to five members of the Court. The Court also noted that Congress had failed to state any factual findings justifying the adoption of the Gun-Free School Zone Act.

In *United States v. Morrison,*[31] the Court struck down the Violent Crimes Against Women Act, even though the Act was supported by numerous congressional findings regarding the serious impact that gender-motivated violence has on victims and their families. Christy Brzonkala, a student at Virginia Polytechnic Institute, sued Virginia Tech and two fellow students who allegedly assaulted and repeatedly raped her, under Section 13981 of the Act, which states that "persons within the United States have the right to be free from crimes of violence motivated by gender."[32] Chief Justice Rehnquist, writing for the majority, found that the existence of congressional findings is not sufficient, by itself, to sustain the constitutionality of Commerce Clause legislation. The Court also rejected the argument that Congress may regulate noneconomic violent criminal conduct based solely on that conduct's aggregate effect in interstate commerce, noting that

> the concern that we expressed in *Lopez* that Congress might use the Commerce Clause to completely obliterate the Constitution's distribution between national and local authority seems well founded. . . . If accepted, petitioners' reasoning would allow Congress to regulate any crime as long as the nationwide, aggregated impact of that crime has substantial effects on employment, production, transit, or consumption.

In 2000, the Supreme Court also ruled that Congress could not apply the federal arson statute to the burning of a private home.[33] The statute made it a crime for any person to damage or destroy "by means of fire or an explosive, any . . . property used in interstate or foreign commerce or in any activity affecting interstate or foreign commerce." The government argued that the burned Indiana home was used in at least three activities affecting commerce: (1) the homeowner used the house as collateral to obtain a mortgage from an Oklahoma lender, (2) the house was used to obtain an insurance policy from a Wisconsin insurer, and (3) the house received natural gas from outside Indiana. The Court rejected these arguments, noting that under this reasoning

> hardly a building in the land would fall outside the federal statute's domain. Practically every building in our cities, towns, and rural areas is constructed with supplies that have moved in interstate commerce, served by utilities that have an interstate connection, financed or insured by enterprises that do business across state lines, or bears some other trace of interstate commerce.[34]

Because the private residence was used for everyday family living, not commerce or any activity affecting commerce, the federal arson law did not apply. Unlike *Morrison,* where the Court struck down the Violent Crimes Against Women Act in its entirety, the Court in *Jones* did not strike down the arson statute as unconstitutional on its face. Because Congress could legitimately regulate damage or destruction to property that was in fact used in interstate or foreign commerce or in activities affecting such commerce, the Court ruled that the statute was valid as applied to such conduct.

LIMITS ON STATE POWERS

Federal powers enumerated in the Constitution impose many limits on state action. This chapter discusses only the limits on state power resulting from the commerce power, but the principles apply to other federal powers as well.

As mentioned earlier, when Congress has indicated a policy by acting, its action preempts state action because the Supremacy Clause makes federal laws supreme over state laws. Even when Congress has not taken action, the *"dormant"* or *"negative" Commerce Clause* may impose restrictions on state action.

31. 529 U.S. 598 (2000).

32. 42 U.S.C. § 13981.

33. Jones v. United States, 529 U.S. 848 (2000).

34. *Id.* at 857.

Dormant or Negative Commerce Clause

The idea behind the dormant Commerce Clause is that the grant of power to Congress under the Commerce Clause implies a negative converse that restricts states from passing laws that improperly discriminate against interstate commerce. Since the mid-1930s, the U.S. Supreme Court has tried to clarify when state regulation affecting interstate commerce is valid in the absence of preempting federal regulation. When it evaluates a dormant Commerce Clause challenge, the Court first looks at whether the statute is discriminatory or neutral on its face. If the statute is facially discriminatory, it is presumed to be unconstitutional. For example, in *City of Philadelphia v. New Jersey,*[35] the Court held that a New Jersey statute prohibiting the importation of most "solid or liquid waste which originated or was collected outside the territorial limits of the State" violated the Commerce Clause because it imposed on out-of-state commercial interests "the full burden of conserving the State's remaining landfill."

Even if a state statute is facially neutral, it is presumed to be unconstitutional if it has a discriminatory purpose or effect. For example, the Supreme Court invalidated a North Carolina statute that prohibited the sale of apples that bore a grade other than the applicable U.S. grade.[36] Although neutral on its face, the statute's effect was to discriminate against Washington apples, which bore their own state's grade on the container, a grade that was equal to or more stringent than the U.S. grade.

The presumption of unconstitutionality can be rebutted if the state can demonstrate under a strict scrutiny standard that the law is necessary (i.e., that no other nondiscriminatory means were available) to serve a compelling state objective or a legitimate local interest.[37] For example, the Court upheld a Minnesota statute banning plastic, nonreturnable milk containers in the face of claims that it discriminated against interstate commerce.[38] The statute was not "simple protectionism"; it regulated evenhandedly by prohibiting all milk retailers from selling their products in plastic containers, and it applied regardless of whether the milk, the containers, or the sellers were from inside or outside the state.

If the Court finds that the purpose and effect of the state statute are not discriminatory, but that it has some impact on interstate commerce, the Court will then balance the burden on interstate commerce against the local state interest and its putative benefit. If the interstate impacts are infrequent or insubstantial in relation to the benefits to the state, then the Court will uphold the state law.[39]

35. 437 U.S. 617 (1978).

36. Hunt v. Wash. State Apple Adver. Comm'n, 432 U.S. 333 (1977).

37. This presumption is particularly hard to rebut where the state statute is discriminatory on its face. The Supreme Court has upheld only one facially discriminatory state law. *See* Maine v. Taylor, 477 U.S. 131 (1986).

38. Minnesota v. Clover Leaf Creamery Co., 449 U.S. 456 (1981).

Federal Fiscal Powers

Two other federal powers, the taxing and spending powers, have been invoked to regulate traditionally local "police problems" as well as purely economic problems.

The Constitution grants the federal government a broad taxing power. The only specific limitations are that (1) direct taxes on anything but income and capitation (per head) taxes must be allocated among the states in proportion to population, and (2) all custom duties and excise taxes must be uniform throughout the United States. In addition, no duty may be levied upon exports from any state. The Fifth Amendment's Due Process Clause is also a general limitation on Congress's taxing power.

Taxes have an economic impact on business.[40] The federal government has imposed taxes in order to affect the behavior of business as well as to raise revenues. The Supreme Court has upheld both types of taxes under the government's power to tax without regard to the purpose behind the tax.

Congress has the power to spend in order to provide for the common defense and general welfare. An exercise of the spending power will be upheld as long as it does not violate a specific check on the federal power.

Protection of Individual Liberties

The Constitution and the Bill of Rights guarantee certain individual rights, including freedom of speech, association, and religion; due process; compensation for takings; equal protection; and the right to a jury trial.

THE CONSTITUTION

Although most explicit guarantees of individual liberty are found in the amendments to the Constitution, the original Constitution contains three specific guarantees of individual rights: (1) the Contracts Clause, (2) a ban on *ex post facto* laws, and (3) a prohibition against bills of attainder. In addition, the Constitution guarantees the privileges and immunities associated with being a U.S. citizen.

39. Pike v. Bruce Church, Inc., 397 U.S. 137 (1970).

40. For a discussion of how to integrate tax considerations into business strategy, *see* Mark A. Wolfson & Myron S. Scholes, Taxes and Business Strategy: A Planning Approach (1992).

The Contracts Clause

Article I, Section 10, of the Constitution specifically prohibits a state legislature from impairing the obligation of existing contracts. The Fifth Amendment imposes a similar bar on federal legislation that would retroactively impair the obligations of a contract. In *Calfarm Insurance Co. v. Deukmejian*,[41] insurance companies raised issues under the federal and state Contracts Clause in connection with insurance law changes mandated by California Proposition 103, a voter initiative that made fundamental changes to the regulation of automobile and other types of insurance and imposed new restrictions on an insurance company's ability to refuse to renew an automobile insurance policy entered into prior to enactment of the initiative. Seven insurers and the Association of California Insurance Companies sued to invalidate the initiative as an unconstitutional law impairing the obligations of contracts because the restrictions on renewal applied to policies issued before enactment of Proposition 103.

The California Supreme Court upheld the nonrenewal restrictions. The decision rested in part on the fact that insurance is a highly regulated industry in which further regulation can reasonably be anticipated. In addition, the court found that the public interest in making insurance available to all Californians and the fear that insurance companies would refuse to renew in California, leaving drivers without the car insurance required by law, was sufficient, when measured against the relatively low degree of impairment of contract rights involved, to justify the nonrenewal restrictions. The court explained:

> Although the language of the Contracts Clause is facially absolute, its prohibition must be accommodated to the inherent police power of the State "to safeguard the vital interests of its people." This Court has long recognized that a statute does not violate the Contracts Clause simply because it has the effect of restricting, or even barring altogether, the performance of duties created by contracts entered into prior to its enactment. Thus, a state prohibition law may be applied to contracts for the sale of beer that were valid when entered into, a law barring lotteries may be applied to lottery tickets that were valid when issued, and a workmen's compensation law may be applied to employers and employees operating under pre-existing contracts of employment that made no provision for work-related injuries.

Ex Post Facto Laws

Article I, Section 9, and Article I, Section 10, prohibit laws that punish actions that were not illegal when performed, also known as *ex post facto laws*. *Ex post facto* laws are discussed in greater detail in Chapter 15.

Bills of Attainder

Article I, Section 9, prohibits the federal government from enacting laws to punish specific individuals. Such laws are termed *bills of attainder.*

Privileges and Immunities

Article IV, Section 2, of the Constitution guarantees the privileges and immunities of citizens of the United States, that is, the rights that go with being a citizen of the federal government, such as the right to vote in a federal election and the right to travel. Article IV provides that citizens of each state shall receive all the privileges and immunities of citizens of other states. These provisions prohibit any unreasonable discrimination between the citizens of different states. Any such discrimination must reasonably relate to legitimate state or local purposes.

THE BILL OF RIGHTS

The first ten amendments of the Constitution constitute the *Bill of Rights*. The first eight amendments contain specific guarantees of individual liberties that limit the power of the federal government. Importantly, the last two make clear that the federal government's powers are limited and enumerated, whereas the rights of the people go beyond those listed in the Constitution.

The First Amendment guarantees freedom of religion, speech, press, and assembly and prohibits laws establishing religion. The Second Amendment grants persons the right to bear arms. The Third Amendment provides that no soldier shall be quartered in any house. The Fourth Amendment prohibits unreasonable searches and seizures and provides that warrants shall be issued only upon probable cause. The Fifth Amendment (1) contains the grand jury requirements; (2) forbids *double jeopardy* (that is, being tried twice for the same crime); (3) prohibits forcing a person to be a witness against himself or herself; (4) prohibits the deprivation of life, liberty, or property without due process of law; and (5) requires just compensation when private property is taken for public use. The Sixth Amendment guarantees a speedy and public jury trial in all criminal prosecutions. The Seventh Amendment gives the right to a jury trial in almost all civil (that is, noncriminal) cases when the value in dispute is greater than $20. The Eighth Amendment prohibits excessive bails and fines as well as cruel and unusual punishment. Aspects of the Fourth, Fifth, and Sixth Amendments relevant to criminal cases are discussed in Chapter 15.

41. 771 P.2d 1247 (Cal. 1989).

IN BRIEF

1:59

Outline of the Bill of Rights

Amendment I
No law establishing religion
Freedom of religion
Freedom of speech
Freedom of press
Right to assembly and petition

Amendment II
Well-regulated militia and right to keep and bear arms

Amendment III
Restrictions on quartering soldiers in homes

Amendment IV
No unreasonable search and seizure
Requirements for warrants

Amendment V
Presentment or indictment of a grand jury required for capital or otherwise infamous crime
Prohibition on double jeopardy
Prohibition on compulsory self-incrimination
Due process required before taking life, liberty, or property
Just compensation for taking private property

Amendment VI
In criminal prosecutions:
Right to a speedy and public trial
Right to a jury trial
Right to confront witnesses
Right to counsel

Amendment VII
Right to a jury trial in most civil cases

Amendment VIII
No excessive bail
No excessive fines
No cruel and unusual punishment

Amendment IX
Rights of the people not limited to those listed in the Constitution

Amendment X
Powers not delegated to the United States in the Constitution are reserved to the states or the people, except for those powers prohibited to the states by the Constitution, which are reserved to the people

Applicability to the States

The Fourteenth Amendment provides that no state shall "deprive any person of life, liberty, or property, without due process of law" (the *Due Process Clause*) and that "[n]o State shall make or enforce any law which shall abridge the privileges or immunities of citizens of the United States" (the *Privileges and Immunities Clause*).

After the Fourteenth Amendment was passed, it was argued that the Due Process Clause and the Privileges and Immunities Clause made the entire Bill of Rights applicable to state governments. The Supreme Court rejected this theory. It held that provisions of the Bill of Rights are incorporated into the Fourteenth Amendment only if they are fundamental to the American system of law or are safeguards "essential to liberty in the American scheme of justice."[42] These include freedom of speech and religion. As a result, if a state government were to abridge the freedom of speech, for example, it would violate the First Amendment as applied to state governments through the Fourteenth Amendment.

Provisions held not to apply to the states include the Second Amendment right to bear arms, the Fifth Amendment requirement of a grand jury indictment before any criminal prosecution, and the Seventh Amendment guarantee of a jury trial in civil cases. Although the Eighth Amendment's prohibition against the imposition of excessive bail has not been explicitly applied to the states, the Supreme Court has assumed

42. Duncan v. Louisiana, 391 U.S. 145 (1968). In *District of Columbia v. Heller*, 128 S.Ct. 2783 (2008), the U.S. Supreme Court invalidated the District of Columbia's total ban on handguns and its requirement that licensed firearms kept in the home be disassembled or bound by a trigger lock. The Court ruled: "Under any of the standards of scrutiny that we have applied to enumerated constitutional rights, banning from the home 'the most preferred firearm in the nation to keep and use for protection of one's home and family,' would fail constitutional muster" under the Second Amendment. Although the Court upheld an individual's right to possess a firearm unconnected with service in a militia and to use it for traditionally lawful purposes, such as self-defense within the home, the Court left undisturbed cases upholding laws barring felons and mentally ill persons from bearing arms and laws prohibiting the carrying of "dangerous and unusual weapons," such as M-16 rifles and sawed-off shotguns. The *Heller* decision did not have to reach the issue of whether the Second Amendment applies to the states because the District of Columbia is a federal district.

that it applied in a number of state cases. The Fifth Amendment's prohibition against the taking of property without just compensation has not been incorporated into the Fourteenth Amendment, but the due process guarantee in the Fourteenth Amendment has been interpreted to provide the same protection. The Supreme Court has not yet determined whether the Third Amendment, which prohibits the quartering of soldiers in private houses, and the excessive-fine provision of the Eighth Amendment are applicable to state governments.

Freedom of Speech and Press

Although the First Amendment states that "Congress shall make no law . . . abridging the freedom of speech, or of the press," the U.S. Supreme Court has not applied the First Amendment to protect all speech to the same degree. The type of speech most clearly protected is political speech, including speech critical of governmental policies and officials. Some types of expression—bribery, perjury, and obscenity—are not protected by the First Amendment at all.

A government may violate the right to free speech not only by forbidding speech, but by commanding it as well. For example, the U.S. Supreme Court ruled that Massachusetts had violated the First Amendment when it ordered organizers of South Boston's St. Patrick's Day Parade to include a group of gay and lesbian Bostonians of Irish ancestry.[43] Such compulsory inclusion of a group imparting a message the organizers did not wish to convey was forbidden by the Free Speech Clause.

Determining whether a type of speech is protected by the First Amendment is only the first step of the analysis. Even if a certain expression is protected, under certain circumstances the expression may still be regulated without violating the First Amendment. For example, public school students have First Amendment rights, but the Supreme Court has upheld certain limits on such rights. In *Tinker v. Des Moines Independent Community School District*,[44] a group of high school students decided to wear black armbands to protest the Vietnam War. School officials who learned of the plan adopted a policy that prohibited students from wearing armbands. After several students wore the black armbands, they were suspended. The students then filed a lawsuit claiming that their First Amendment rights had been violated. The U.S. Supreme Court agreed, holding that student expression cannot be suppressed unless school officials reasonably conclude that it will "materially and substantially disrupt the work and discipline of the school."

In the Court's next student speech case, a student was suspended for delivering a speech before a high school assembly in which he employed what the Court described as "an elaborate, graphic, and explicit sexual metaphor."[45] Although the Court found no basis for disciplining the student under *Tinker*, it nevertheless held that the school district "acted entirely within its permissible authority in imposing sanctions upon [the student] in response to his offensively lewd and indecent speech."

In the following case, the Supreme Court considered whether the principal of a high school could discipline a student who displayed a "Bong Hits 4 Jesus" banner.

43. Hurley v. Irish-American Gay, Lesbian & Bisexual Group of Boston, 515 U.S. 557 (1995).

44. 383 U.S. 503 (1969).

45. Bethel Sch. Dist. No. 403 v. Fraser, 478 U.S. 675 (1986).

A CASE IN POINT

In the Language of the Court

CASE 4.2

Morse v. Frederick

Supreme Court of the United States
127 S. Ct. 2618 (2007).

Facts In January 2002, the Olympic Torch Relay was scheduled to pass in front of the Juneau Douglas High School (JDHS) in Juneau, Alaska, while the school was in session. Deborah Morse, the school principal, decided to permit staff and students to observe the event as an approved class trip. As the torchbearers and camera crews passed by the school, Morse saw some of her students unfurl a fourteen-foot banner bearing the phrase "Bong Hits 4 Jesus." Consistent with school policy prohibiting messages promoting illegal drug use,[46] she directed the students to take down the banner. One student, Joseph Frederick, refused to do so. Morse then confiscated the banner and suspended Frederick for ten days.

CONTINUED

46. Juneau School Board Policy No. 5520 states: "The Board specifically prohibits any assembly or public expression that . . . advocates the use of substances that are illegal to minors." In addition, School Board Policy No. 5850 subjects "[p]upils who participate in approved social events and class trips" to the same student conduct rules that apply during the regular school program.

Frederick administratively appealed his suspension, but the superintendent of the school district upheld it. He explained that Frederick "was not disciplined because the principal of the school 'disagreed' with his message, but because his speech appeared to advocate the use of illegal drugs." Frederick then filed suit, alleging that the JDHS school board and Morse had violated his First Amendment rights. He sought declaratory and injunctive relief, as well as compensatory and punitive damages. The district court granted summary judgment for the school board and Morse, ruling that they were entitled to qualified immunity and that they had not infringed Frederick's First Amendment rights. The U.S. Court of Appeals for the Ninth Circuit reversed after concluding that Frederick's First Amendment rights had been violated because the school punished him without demonstrating that his speech gave rise to a "risk of substantial disruption."[47] The court also held that Morse was not entitled to qualified immunity because Frederick's right to display his banner was so clearly established that a reasonable principal in Morse's position would have understood her actions were unconstitutional. The school board and Morse appealed.

ISSUE PRESENTED May a public high school restrict student speech at a school event when that speech is reasonably viewed as promoting illegal drug use?

OPINION ROBERTS, C. J., writing for the U.S. Supreme Court:

Our most recent student speech case[48] . . . concerned "expressive activities that students, parents, and members of the public might reasonably perceive to bear the imprimatur of the school." Staff members of a high school newspaper sued their school when it chose not to publish two of their articles. . . . This Court . . . [held] that "educators do not offend the First Amendment by exercising editorial control over the style and content of student speech in school-sponsored expressive activities so long as their actions are reasonably related to legitimate pedagogical concerns."

. . . .

Thousands of school boards throughout the country—including JDHS—have adopted policies aimed at effectuating [the message that illegal use of drugs is wrong and harmful]. Those school boards know that peer pressure is perhaps "the single most important factor leading schoolchildren to take drugs," and that students are more likely to use drugs when the norms in school appear to tolerate such behavior. Student speech celebrating illegal drug use at a school event, in the presence of school administrators and teachers, thus poses a particular challenge for school officials working to protect those entrusted to their care from the dangers of drug abuse.

. . . .

School principals have a difficult job, and a vitally important one. When Frederick suddenly and unexpectedly unfurled his banner, Morse had to decide to act—or not to act—on the spot. It was reasonable for her to conclude that the banner promoted illegal drug use—in violation of established school policy—and that failing to act would send a powerful message to the students in her charge, including Frederick, about how serious the school was about the dangers of illegal drug use. The First Amendment does not require schools to tolerate at school events student expression that contributes to those dangers.

RESULT The Supreme Court reversed the Ninth Circuit decision and remanded the case to the district court for further proceedings consistent with its opinion. The public school did not violate Frederick's rights when it suspended him.

DISSENT STEVENS, J., joined by SOUTER and BREYER, JJ., dissenting from the majority opinion:

CONTINUED

47. Frederick v. Morse, 439 F.3d 1114, 1118, 1121–23 (9th Cir. 2006).
48. Hazelwood Sch. Dist. v. Kuhlmeier, 484 U.S. 260 (1988).

I agree with the Court that the principal should not be held liable for pulling down Frederick's banner. I would hold, however, that the school's interest in protecting its students from exposure to speech "reasonably regarded as promoting illegal drug use" cannot justify disciplining Frederick for his attempt to make an ambiguous statement to a television audience simply because it contained an oblique reference to drugs. The First Amendment demands more, indeed, much more.

. . . .

In my judgment, the First Amendment protects student speech if the message itself neither violates a permissible rule nor expressly advocates conduct that is illegal and harmful to students. This nonsense banner does neither, and the Court does serious violence to the First Amendment in upholding—indeed lauding—a school's decision to punish Frederick for expressing a view with which it disagreed.

. . . .

Even in high school, a rule that permits only one point of view to be expressed is less likely to produce correct answers than the open discussion of countervailing views. In the national debate about a serious issue, it is the expression of the minority's viewpoint that most demands the protection of the First Amendment. Whatever the better policy may be, a full and frank discussion of the costs and benefits of the attempt to prohibit the use of marijuana is far wiser than suppression of speech because it is unpopular.

COMMENTS *Morse* was a five-to-four decision that revealed major differences in opinion among the members of the Court, even between the members who formed the majority. Concurring with the majority opinion, Justice Thomas stated his belief that the standard set forth in *Tinker* is without basis in the Constitution. In his view, the history of public education suggests that the First Amendment does not protect any student speech in public schools. Justice Alito, on the other hand, speaking for himself and Justice Kennedy, joined the majority opinion based on the understanding that

> (a) it goes no further than to hold that a public school may restrict speech that a reasonable observer would interpret as advocating illegal drug use and (b) it provides no support for any restriction of speech that can plausibly be interpreted as commenting on any political or social issue, including speech on issues such as "the wisdom of the war on drugs or of legalizing marijuana for medicinal use."

CRITICAL THINKING QUESTIONS

1. Based on the majority opinion, would the Supreme Court treat a banner reading "Wine Sips 4 Jesus" as protected speech?
2. Should college students be subject to the same restrictions as high school students?

"CLEAR AND PRESENT DANGER" TEST

Throughout most of the nineteenth and early twentieth centuries, Congress followed the mandate of the First Amendment literally and made "no law" restricting freedom of speech, assembly, or the press. In response to vocal resistance to World War I, Congress passed the Espionage Act of 1917 and the Sedition Act of 1918. Charles Schenck, a dissident, was convicted under the Espionage Act for circulating to men who had been called and accepted for military service a document that stated that the draft violated the Thirteenth Amendment, which prohibits slavery or involuntary servitude. In 1919, the Supreme Court, in an opinion by Justice Oliver Wendell Holmes, first articulated the *"clear and present danger" test* and affirmed Schenck's conviction.[49]

The Supreme Court explained that many things that might be said in peacetime are not allowed in time of war:

> [T]he character of every act depends upon the circumstances in which it is done. The most stringent protection of free speech would not protect a man in falsely

49. Schenck v. United States, 249 U.S. 47 (1919).

> shouting fire in a theatre and causing a panic. . . . [The] question in every case is whether the words used are used in such circumstances and are of such a nature as to create a *clear and present danger* that they will bring about the substantive evils that Congress has a right to prevent. (Emphasis added.)

During the height of the Cold War, the clear and present danger test was applied in an expansive manner to restrict First Amendment freedoms even more severely, but the test became stricter and more protective of free speech in the 1960s. In *Brandenburg v. Ohio,* the Supreme Court held that "the constitutional guarantees of free speech and free press do not permit a State to forbid or proscribe advocacy of the use of force or of law violation except where such advocacy is directed to inciting or producing imminent lawless action and is likely to incite or produce such action."[50]

In 1997, the U.S. Court of Appeals for the Fourth Circuit ruled that the First Amendment did not bar a wrongful-death suit against the publisher of *Hit Man: A Technical Manual for Independent Contractors,* a 130-page manual of detailed factual instructions on how to become a professional killer.[51] A convicted murderer had used the book to commit a triple homicide. The publisher stipulated that it had targeted the market of murderers, would-be murderers, and other criminals and that it knew and intended that criminals would immediately use the book to solicit, plan, and commit murder. The court rejected the publisher's claim that this was abstract advocacy protected under *Brandenburg v. Ohio,* stating: "[T]his book constitutes the archetypal example of speech which, because it methodically and comprehensively prepares and steels its audience to specific criminal conduct through exhaustively detailed instructions on the planning, commission, and concealment of criminal conduct, finds no preserve in the First Amendment."

DEFAMATION OF PUBLIC FIGURES BY MEDIA

Defamatory words—words that harm a person's reputation—are protected by the First Amendment, even when they are false, if they are made by a media defendant (such as a newspaper or television network) about a public figure without knowledge they were false, that is, without actual malice. Defamation is discussed further in Chapter 9.

50. 395 U.S. 444 (1969).

51. Rice v. Paladin Enter., Inc., 128 F.3d 233 (4th Cir. 1997), *cert. denied,* 523 U.S. 1074 (1998).

OBSCENITY

Obscene material does not enjoy any protection under the First Amendment. Material is obscene if it (1) appeals to a prurient or sordid and perverted interest in sex; (2) has no serious literary, artistic, political, or scientific merit; and (3) is on the whole offensive to the average person in the community.[52] Applying this test, the U.S. Court of Appeals for the Second Circuit held that the label for Bad Frog Beer, which depicts a frog with its middle finger raised, was perhaps in bad taste, but not obscene.[53]

ACADEMIC RESEARCH

The First Amendment also protects academic research. During the U.S. government's antitrust suit against Microsoft Corporation (discussed in the "Inside Story" in Chapter 17), Microsoft sought to compel two university professors to produce notes and tape recordings of the interviews they conducted with Netscape's employees while researching their book *Competing on Internet Time: Lessons from Netscape and Its Battle with Microsoft.* The U.S. Court of Appeals for the First Circuit denied access, reasoning that the academics, in gathering and disseminating information, were acting almost as journalists. Compelling disclosure of their research materials would "infrigidate the free flow of information to the public, thus denigrating a fundamental First Amendment value."[54] In addition, Netscape nondisclosure agreements signed by the authors made the information confidential and not discoverable.

COMMERCIAL SPEECH

Unlike political speech, commercial speech, especially advertising, has always been subject to reasonable regulations regarding the time, place, and manner of such speech. In addition, the state may prohibit false commercial speech, as well as explicitly or inherently misleading commercial speech. To determine whether content-based regulation of commercial speech violates the First Amendment, the Supreme Court has formulated the following test. First, the speech must concern lawful activity and not be misleading. Even if the speech satisfies this requirement, the First Amendment still allows the government to restrict it as long as (1) the asserted governmental interest in regulating the

52. Miller v. California, 413 U.S. 15, 24 (1973).

53. Bad Frog Brewery v. New York State Liquor Auth., 134 F.3d 87 (2d Cir. 1998). The Bad Frog label can be seen at http://www.badfrog.com/about.html (last visited June 30, 2007).

54. Cusamano v. Microsoft Corp., 162 F.3d 708, 717 (1st Cir. 1998).

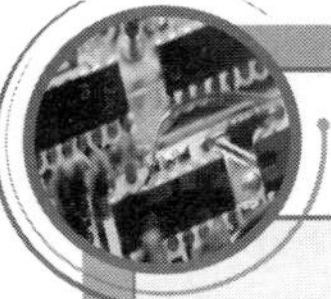

VIEW FROM CYBERSPACE

Pornography and Free Speech on the Internet

Since 1995 Congress has struggled with how to regulate pornography on the Internet. Most attempts have not withstood judicial scrutiny. In 1995, Congress enacted the Communications Decency Act (CDA), which required that material considered "indecent"—including pornography—be outlawed in public forums accessible by children, most notably the Internet.[a] The U.S. Supreme Court held that the CDA's "indecent transmission" and "patently offensive display" provisions violated the First Amendment.[b] The Court rejected the government's analogy to broadcast media, which have traditionally enjoyed less First Amendment protection, noting that the Internet, unlike other media, does not have an extensive history of government regulation, is not a scarce resource in need of monitored allocation, and is not intrusive into individuals' homes. Instead, the Court analogized the Internet to a public square, where speech is given heightened protection. Although it struck down much of the CDA, the Court left in place its prohibition of online transmission of obscene speech.

In 1996, Congress enacted the Child Pornography Prevention Act (CPPA), which criminalized the transmission of "child pornography," defined as any image that "appears to be" or "conveys the impression" of a minor engaging in sex, including computer-generated images or "virtual" child pornography.[c] In *Ashcroft v. Free Speech Coalition,* the U.S. Supreme Court struck down as unconstitutionally overbroad two subsections of the CPPA's definition of child pornography: the section that defined child pornography as any visual depiction, including a computer-generated image that "is, or appears to be, of a minor engaging in sexually explicit conduct," and the section, referred to as the "pandering" provision, that defined child pornography as any "visual depiction... [that] is advertised, promoted, presented, described, or distributed in such a manner that conveys the impression that the material is or contains a visual depiction of a minor engaging in sexually explicit conduct."[d] The Court noted that the CPPA prohibited "speech that records no crime and no victims by its production," whether or not the speech was "patently offensive." Expressing concern that certain popular works of artistic and literary value might be deemed child pornography under the CPPA, the Court concluded that the First Amendment protects images that do not involve real children unless they are obscene or the product of sexual abuse.

Congress attempted to circumvent the Supreme Court's decision in *Ashcroft v. Free Speech Coalition* by enacting the Prosecutorial Remedies and Tools Against the Exploitation of Children Today Act (PROTECT) in 2003.[e] PROTECT outlaws digitally "morphed" images made to appear as if children are having sex or being used in pornographic images if the prosecutor can prove beyond a reasonable doubt that the maker intended others to believe that the images depicted actual children. It also includes a revised pandering provision that makes it a crime to advertise, promote, or solicit through the mails or in interstate or foreign commerce any material or purported material in a manner that reflects the belief, or is intended to cause others to believe, that the material contains an obscene visual depiction of a minor engaging in sexually explicit conduct or a visual depiction of an actual minor engaging in sexually explicit conduct. In *United States v. Williams,*[f] the U.S. Court of Appeals for the Eleventh Circuit ruled that the pandering provision of PROTECT was constitutionally overbroad and therefore invalid on its face. While the court noted that the pandering provision "captured perfectly" clearly restrictable child pornography (i.e., obscene simulations of minors engaged in sexually explicit conduct and depictions of actual minors engaged in the same), it was unconstitutionally overbroad because it also criminalized noncommercial speech that promoted or solicited such materials. The Supreme Court agreed to hear the case in 2007.

In 1998, Congress passed the Child Online Protection Act (COPA).[g] To address the concerns raised by the Supreme Court when it invalidated the CDA, COPA's scope was restricted to material "deemed harmful to minors" and found on the Web rather than the Internet as a whole, and it targeted only Web communications for "commercial purposes." Under COPA, courts are instructed to consider contemporary community standards in determining whether material is "harmful to minors."

In a case challenging COPA, the U.S. Court of Appeals for the Third Circuit found that COPA's reliance on "contemporary community standards"

CONTINUED

to identify material that was harmful to minors was overbroad and would probably lead to a finding that COPA was unconstitutional.[h] The court argued that due to the "geography-free" nature of the Internet, a community standards test would require every Web communication to comply with the most restrictive community's standards. The Supreme Court vacated the Third Circuit's decision, finding that "COPA's reliance on 'community standards' to identify what material 'is harmful to minors' does not by itself render the statute substantially overbroad for First Amendment purposes," but a majority of the Court could not agree on how to measure "community standards" for the Internet.[i] The Court also did not "express any view as to whether . . . the statute is unconstitutionally vague, or whether the District Court correctly concluded that the statute likely will not survive strict scrutiny analysis once adjudication of the case is completed below."

On remand, the Third Circuit once again held that COPA was likely unconstitutional,[j] finding that the plaintiffs had established a substantial likelihood of prevailing on two claims: (1) the statute fails the strict scrutiny test because it was not narrowly tailored (and the least restrictive means) to serve a necessary state interest, and (2) the statute is unconstitutionally overbroad.

In June 2004, the Supreme Court sent the case back to the trial court, stating that the government would have to show why the voluntary use of filters would not work as well as the law's criminal penalties. Although the opinion strongly suggested that the government would not be able to meet this burden, Justice Anthony Kennedy left open the possibility that COPA might ultimately be upheld: "This opinion does not hold that Congress is incapable of enacting any regulation of the Internet designed to prevent minors from gaining access to harmful materials."[k] Notwithstanding Justice Kennedy's admonition, the district court subsequently held that COPA was unconstitutional on its face and issued a permanent injunction against its enforcement,[l] noting:

> This court, along with a broad spectrum of the population across the country yearn for a solution which would protect children from such material with 100 percent effectiveness. However, I am acutely aware of my charge under the law to uphold the principles found in our nation's Constitution and their enforcement throughout the years by the Supreme Court. I may not turn a blind eye to the law in order to attempt to satisfy my urge to protect this nation's youth by upholding a flawed statute. . . . Despite my personal regret at having to set aside yet another attempt to protect our children from harmful material, I restate today, as I stated when granting the preliminary injunction in this case, that "I without hesitation acknowledge the duty imposed on the Court . . . and the greater good such duty serves. Indeed, perhaps we do the minors of this country harm if First Amendment protections, which they will with age inherit fully, are chipped away in the name of their protection."

In 2000, Congress passed the Children's Internet Protection Act (CIPA), which requires public schools and libraries to install Internet filters on their computers so that children cannot view depictions that are harmful, obscene, or child pornography.[m] The Supreme Court upheld CIPA in a six-to-three decision in 2003.[n]

a. Pub. L. No. 104-104, 110 Stat. 133 (1996).
b. Reno v. Am. Civil Liberties Union, 521 U.S. 844 (1997).
c. Pub. L. No. 104-208, 110 Stat. 3009–26 (1996).
d. 535 U.S. 234 (2002).
e. Pub. L. No. 108-21, 117 Stat. 650 (2003).
f. 456 F.3d 1353 (11th Cir. 2006), *cert. granted*, 127 S. Ct. 1874 (2007).
g. Pub. L. No. 105-277, 112 Stat. 2681–736 (1998).
h. Am. Civil Liberties Union v. Reno, 217 F.3d 162 (3d Cir. 2000). The U.S. Court of Appeals for the Third Circuit affirmed a preliminary injunction issued by the district court to prevent enforcement of COPA. To receive a preliminary injunction, a plaintiff must show a "substantial likelihood" of prevailing on the merits of the case.
i. Ashcroft v. Am. Civil Liberties Union, 535 U.S. 564 (2002).
j. Am. Civil Liberties Union v. Ashcroft, 322 F.3d 240 (3d Cir. 2003).
k. Ashcroft v. Am. Civil Liberties Union, 542 U.S. 656 (2004).
l. Am. Civil Liberties Union v. Gonzales, 2007 WL 861120 (E.D. Pa. 2007).
m. Pub. L. No. 106-554, 114 Stat. 2763 (2000).
n. United States. v. Am. Library Ass'n, Inc., 539 U.S. 194 (2003).

speech is substantial, (2) the regulation directly advances the governmental interest asserted, and (3) the restriction is no more extensive than necessary to serve that interest.[55] Determining whether the regulation is no more extensive than necessary does not require the least restrictive means;[56] it requires only a "reasonable fit" between the government's purpose and the means chosen to achieve it.

55. Central Hudson Gas & Elec. v. Public Serv. Comm'n, 447 U.S. 557 (1980).

56. Bd. of Trustees, State Univ. of N.Y. v. Fox, 492 U.S. 469 (1989).

Liquor and Cigarette Advertising

In 1995, Coors Brewing Company successfully challenged a provision of the 1935 Federal Alcohol Administration Act that prohibited statements of alcohol content on malt beverage labels unless state law required disclosure.[57] The government's asserted goal of preventing competition based on high alcoholic strength was legitimate, but the Supreme Court found no evidence that the labeling restriction served the goal.

In 1996, the Court struck down a forty-year-old Rhode Island statute that prohibited the advertisement of liquor prices except at the point of sale.[58] Rhode Island asserted its interest in promoting temperance and argued that the law prevented retailers from competing on price and thereby encouraging alcohol consumption. The Court accepted that interest as legitimate but found the statute too restrictive to meet Free Speech Clause standards. Although commercial speech generally receives less protection than political speech under the First Amendment, the Court recognized that "where a State entirely prohibits the dissemination of truthful, nonmisleading commercial messages for reasons unrelated to the preservation of a fair bargaining process, there is far less reason to depart from the rigorous review that the First Amendment generally demands."

In 1999, more than forty-six states and the six largest tobacco companies entered into a master settlement agreement that imposed a number of restrictions on the marketing and advertising of tobacco products, including prohibitions against the use of cartoon characters, targeting youth, sponsorship of concerts or other events with significant youth audiences, and advertisements at stadiums and arenas. Notwithstanding this agreement, the Massachusetts Attorney General promulgated new regulations governing the advertising and sale of cigarettes, smokeless tobacco, and cigars that were broader than those contained in the agreement. One regulation prohibited "outdoor advertising, including advertising in enclosed stadiums and advertising from within a retail establishment that is directed toward or visible from the outside of the establishment, in any location that is within [a] 1,000 foot radius of any public playground, playground area in a public park, elementary school or secondary school." Another regulation prohibited certain point-of-sale advertising in retail stores that was visible from the outside. A group of makers and sellers of tobacco products filed suit challenging the constitutionality of the Massachusetts regulations on several bases, including that they violated their First Amendment free speech rights.

57. Rubin v. Coors Brewing Co., 514 U.S. 476 (1995).

58. 44 Liquormart, Inc. v. Rhode Island, 517 U.S. 484 (1996).

The federal district court concluded that the outdoor advertising regulations were constitutional because they directly advanced the state's substantial interest in preventing tobacco use by minors, but it invalidated the point-of-sale advertising ban on the basis that the Attorney General had not provided sufficient justification for it. The U.S. Court of Appeals for the First Circuit affirmed the district court's decision regarding the outdoor advertising, but it also upheld the point-of-sale regulations, reasoning that the Attorney General was better suited than the courts to determine what restrictions were necessary to prevent tobacco use by minors. The U.S. Supreme Court reversed the First Circuit and struck down both regulations after concluding that the regulations were more extensive than necessary to serve the state's valid interest in preventing smoking by minors.[59] The Court explained:

> A careful calculation of the costs of a speech regulation does not mean that a State must demonstrate that there is no incursion on legitimate speech interests, but a speech regulation cannot unduly impinge on the speaker's ability to propose a commercial transaction and the adult listener's opportunity to obtain information about products.

Nonspeech Business

The First Amendment also protects seemingly nonspeech business. The U.S. Court of Appeals for the Ninth Circuit affirmed a lower court's decision enjoining California's Santa Clara County from enforcing its ban on gun sales at the county's fairgrounds.[60] The county had argued that rather than regulating speech, the ban regulated the unprotected conduct of selling guns. The trial court disagreed and found that "some type of speech is necessarily involved in the sale of any gun."[61] The appeals court agreed and ruled that the offer to buy constituted protected commercial speech. Although the county asserted an interest in curtailing gun possession, the court ruled that the ban did not directly advance that interest.

Political Speech

Direct corporate expenditures to elect or defeat political candidates (so-called express advocacy) have been barred for nearly a century, a prohibition upheld long ago by the Supreme Court. Section 203 of the Bipartisan Campaign Reform Act of 2002 (also known as the McCain-Feingold

59. Lorillard Tobacco Co. v. Reilly, 533 U.S. 525 (2001).

60. Nordyke v. Santa Clara County, Cal., 110 F.3d 707 (9th Cir. 1997).

61. Nordyke v. Santa Clara County, Cal., 933 F. Supp. 903 (N.D. Cal. 1996).

Act) made it a crime for any corporation or union to give large amounts of money to party committees in the form of "soft money" and restricted such donations to organizations engaged in issues advocacy if that advocacy was a screen for backing a political candidate. In *McConnell v. Federal Election Commission*,[62] the Supreme Court ruled that the McCain-Feingold Act did not, on its face, violate the First Amendment because many groups used issues ads to target a candidate. Four years later, however, in *Federal Election Commission v. Wisconsin Right to Life, Inc.*,[63] the Court ruled that the Act, as applied to the facts of that case, violated the First Amendment. The Act provided, among other things, that radio or television ads could not mention a federally elected candidate in the jurisdiction where the candidate was running for office within thirty days of a federal primary election or sixty days of a federal general election. Wisconsin Right to Life, Inc. (WRTL), a nonprofit anti-abortion advocacy group, wanted to run several ads that clearly identified Senator Russell Feingold during the Act's blackout period; it filed an action in 2004 seeking a declaratory judgment that the restriction was an unconstitutional restriction of its free speech right. In a five-to-four decision, the U.S. Supreme Court agreed. Chief Justice Roberts, writing for the majority, noted that Section 203 of the Act was subject to strict scrutiny because it burdened political speech. This meant that the government had to prove that applying the Act to the ads furthered a compelling state interest and was narrowly tailored to achieve that interest. The Court concluded:

> [A] court should find that an ad is the functional equivalent of express advocacy only if the ad is susceptible of no reasonable interpretation other than as an appeal to vote for or against a specified candidate. Under this test, WRTL's three ads are plainly not the functional equivalent of express advocacy. . . . The ads do not mention an election, candidacy, political party, or challenger; and they do not take a position on a candidate's character, qualifications, or fitness in office.

In a vigorous dissent, Justice Souter asserted that the majority had overruled *McConnell* and questioned how the Court could reach this "unacknowledged result" less than four years after deciding *McConnell*. He concluded by observing:

> After today, the ban on contributions by corporations and unions and the limitation on their corrosive spending when they enter the political arena are open to easy circumvention. . . . The ban on contributions will mean nothing much, now that companies and unions can save candidates the expense of advertising directly simply by running "issue ads" without express advocacy, or by funneling the money through an independent corporation like WRTL.

62. 540 U.S. 93 (2003).

63. 127 S. Ct. 2652 (2007).

Encryption

In *Junger v. Daley*,[64] a professor challenged the Export Administration Regulations insofar as they attempted to restrict him from posting on his website the human readable source code of an encryption software program that he had written to demonstrate how computers work. The professor claimed that the regulations were vague, overly broad, and an impermissible prior restraint in violation of the First and Fifth Amendments to the Constitution. The U.S. Court of Appeals for the Sixth Circuit agreed: "Because computer source code is an expressive means for the exchange of information and ideas about computer programming, we hold that it is protected by the First Amendment." As such, the court determined that the regulations should be subjected to intermediate scrutiny, or the *substantially related test,* which requires the government to prove that the regulations further a governmental interest that is "important" or "substantial" and that they prevent real, not conjectural, harm "in a direct and material way." Having concluded that the First Amendment protects computer source code, the Sixth Circuit remanded the case to the district court for further consideration of the professor's constitutional claims under the substantially related test.

English-Only Laws

Freedom of speech issues also arise in connection with "English-only" laws, requiring that all government business be conducted in English. This is discussed in Chapter 13.

PRIOR RESTRAINTS

Prior restraints of speech, such as prohibiting in advance a demonstration in a public area, are considered a more drastic infringement on free speech than permitting the speech to occur but then punishing it afterwards. Restrictions concerning the time, place, and manner of speech are usually acceptable under the First Amendment, but regulations that restrict speech in traditional public forums are scrutinized closely.

For example, the city of Dallas adopted an ordinance regulating "sexually oriented businesses," defined as any "adult arcade, adult bookstore or adult video store, adult cabaret, adult motel, adult motion picture theater,

64. 209 F.3d 481 (6th Cir. 2000).

adult theater, escort agency, nude model studio, or sexual encounter center." The ordinance regulated such businesses through zoning, licensing, and inspections. It also banned motels that rented rooms for fewer than ten hours; such rooms are often used for prostitution. The Supreme Court struck down all of the ordinance, except the ban on ten-hour motels, as a prior restraint on speech that did not comply with the procedural safeguards for that type of regulation. In upholding the provision prohibiting motels from renting rooms for less than ten hours, the Court rejected the argument that the ordinance unconstitutionally interfered with the right of association. On behalf of the majority, Justice Sandra Day O'Connor stated, "Any 'personal bonds' that are formed from the use of a motel room for fewer than 10 hours are not those that have 'played a critical role in the culture and traditions of the Nation by cultivating and transmitting shared ideals and beliefs.'"[65] Similarly, the Supreme Court upheld a ban on nude dancing in 2000.[66]

Prior restraints can be particularly problematic for members of the media, who may need to publish immediately or not at all. For example, during a suit by Procter & Gamble against Bankers Trust for negligent sale of financial derivative products, *BusinessWeek* obtained confidential documents about both parties that had emerged from their court-approved secret discovery process. The trial court granted the litigants' request for a temporary restraining order (TRO) to keep *BusinessWeek* from immediately publishing the information and later enjoined the magazine from ever publishing it. The U.S. Court of Appeals for the Sixth Circuit struck down the injunction as a violation of the First Amendment.[67] Noting that "[a] prior restraint comes to a court 'with a heavy presumption against its constitutional validity,'" the Sixth Circuit concluded that the trial court's grounds for granting the TRO were insufficient to meet the high standard required for prior restraint.

Right of Association

Closely related to the right to free speech and press is the constitutional right of association. As with protection of free speech, this right is most protected when an association is formed for political ends. In 2000, the U.S. Supreme Court struck down California's law requiring political parties to hold open primaries in which any registered voter could vote to select a party's candidate for elected office.[68] The Court reasoned:

> Proposition 198 forces petitioners to adulterate their candidate-selection process—the "basic function of a political party"—by opening it up to persons wholly unaffiliated with the party. Such forced association has the likely outcome—indeed, in this case the intended outcome—of changing the parties' message. We can think of no heavier burden on a political party's associational freedom.

Similar issues arise when city or state governments enact laws banning discriminatory clubs. The courts will balance the First Amendment rights of association and free speech against the government's social policy against discrimination. To increase the likelihood that such laws will be upheld, most antidiscrimination statutes apply only to clubs of a certain size where business is conducted.

In *Warfield v. Peninsula Golf and Country Club,*[69] the California Supreme Court held that a private country club that allowed nonmembers, for a fee, to use its golf course, tennis courts, or dining areas was a "business establishment" and therefore subject to the state law prohibiting discrimination against women and minorities. It will generally be assumed that business is conducted in a private club if the member's employer pays for club dues, meals, or drinks or if it is the site of company-sponsored events.

In *Boy Scouts of America v. Dale,*[70] the U.S. Supreme Court held that applying a New Jersey law that prohibits discrimination based on sexual orientation in places of public accommodation to the Boy Scouts of America (BSA) was an unconstitutional violation of the BSA's First Amendment right of association. The Supreme Court stated that the forced inclusion of an unwanted person in a group infringes the group's freedom of expressive association if the person's presence significantly affects the group's ability to advocate public or private viewpoints. But freedom of association is not absolute. It can be overridden "by regulations adopted to serve compelling state interests, unrelated to the suppression of ideas, that cannot be achieved through means significantly less restrictive of associational freedom."

The Court noted that the BSA is an expressive association that teaches, among other values, that "homosexual conduct is not morally straight" and does "not want to promote homosexual conduct as a legitimate form of behavior." The Court concluded that the forced inclusion of a gay

65. FW/PBS, Inc. v. City of Dallas, 493 U.S. 215 (1990).
66. City of Erie v. Pap's A.M., 529 U.S. 277 (2000).
67. Procter & Gamble v. Bankers Trust, 78 F.3d 219 (6th Cir. 1996).
68. California Democratic Party v. Jones, 530 U.S. 567 (2000).
69. 896 P.2d 776 (Cal. 1995).
70. 530 U.S. 640 (2000).

man as an assistant scoutmaster would significantly affect the organization's expression and significantly burden its right to oppose homosexual conduct. The Court held that the state interests embodied in the law did not justify such a severe intrusion on the BSA's right to freedom of expressive association.

Freedom of Religion

Two clauses of the First Amendment deal with religion. The *Establishment Clause* prohibits the establishment of a religion by the federal government. The same ban applies to state governments through the Due Process Clause of the Fourteenth Amendment. The *Free Exercise Clause* prohibits certain, but not all, restrictions on the practice of religion.

Religion in government offices is a difficult issue that may bring the Establishment and Free Exercise Clauses into conflict. In 1996, the U.S. Court of Appeals for the Ninth Circuit ruled unconstitutional a near total ban on religious activity in the workplace imposed by the California Department of Education's Child Nutrition and Food Distribution Division.[71] Tensions arose in the division between computer analyst Monte Tucker and his supervisor after Tucker refused to stop signing office memos with his name and the acronym "SOTLJC," which stood for "Servant of the Lord Jesus Christ." After several warnings, the supervisor suspended Tucker and prohibited all employees from displaying religious materials outside their cubicles, engaging in any religious advocacy, and putting any acronym or other symbol on office communications. Although the state asserted its interest in avoiding workplace disruption and the appearance of religious endorsement (which would constitute a violation of the Establishment Clause), the appeals court concluded that these interests were outweighed by Tucker's constitutional right to talk about religion. Such issues also come up in the private sector, which is regulated by various statutes barring discrimination based on religion (discussed in Chapter 13).

Establishment Clause

The Establishment Clause requires the government to remain neutral in matters of religion. The U.S. Supreme Court has ruled that the Establishment Clause prohibits teacher- or student-led prayer (including benedictions at football games or graduations) in public schools.[72] It does not, however, preclude the federal government from providing secular books and other teaching materials and supplies to parochial schools on the same basis that they are given to public schools.[73] The Supreme Court also ruled that an Ohio school voucher program that allowed parents to use public money to pay for tuition at private schools, including religious schools, did not violate the Establishment Clause.[74]

A pair of five-to-four U.S. Supreme Court decisions in 2005 highlights the divisions among the members of the Supreme Court about the Establishment Clause and the government's obligation to exhibit neutrality toward religion. *Van Orden v. Perry*[75] involved a six-foot by three-and-one-half-foot stone monument engraved with the Ten Commandments that was erected by the Fraternal Order of Eagles in 1941 and displayed on the grounds of the Texas State Capitol, along with sixteen other monuments and twenty-one historical markers, which purported to commemorate the "people, ideals, and events that compose Texan identity." *McCreary County, Kentucky v. ACLU*[76] involved a large, gold-framed copy of the Ten Commandments that was prominently displayed in the courthouse in McCreary County, Kentucky. When the display was challenged by the American Civil Liberties Union (ACLU), the county authorized a second, expanded display that added eight more documents that either had a religious theme or highlighted a religious element of the document. After a district court enjoined that display, the county created a third display consisting of nine equally sized documents—the Ten Commandments and eight American "foundational documents," including the Declaration of Independence, the Bill of Rights, and the Magna Carta.

The Supreme Court upheld the display in *Van Orden* but struck down the display in *McCreary*. Justices Scalia, Thomas, Kennedy, and Rehnquist would have upheld the displays in both cases, on the basis that displays incorporating the Ten Commandments are common in many government buildings and have "an undeniable historical meaning." Justice Breyer joined with them only in *Van Orden* and for a completely different reason. He reasoned that the Establishment Clause was designed to accomplish a separation between church and state without requiring the government to purge all mention of the religious from the public sphere. He pointed out that there was no exact test that could dictate a resolution of such fact-specific cases. In *McCreary,* however, Justice Breyer sided with the majority to strike down the display, reasoning that the government violates

71. Tucker v. Cal. Dep't of Educ., 97 F.3d 1204 (9th Cir. 1996).
72. Santa Fe Independent Sch. Dist. v. Doe, 530 U.S. 290 (2000).
73. Mitchell v. Helms, 530 U.S. 1296 (2000).
74. Zelman v. Simmons-Harris, 536 U.S. 639 (2002).
75. 545 U.S. 677 (2005).
76. 545 U.S. 844 (2005).

the Establishment Clause when it acts with "the ostensible and predominant purpose of advancing religion." He concluded that the evidence of religious purpose in *McCreary* was overwhelming.

In *Hein v. Freedom From Religion Foundation,*[77] the Supreme Court restricted the right of taxpayers to challenge government expenditures that allegedly violate the Establishment Clause. It distinguished *Hein* from its 1968 decision in *Flast v. Cohen*,[78] which had given taxpayers standing to challenge congressional action alleged to be in violation of the Establishment Clause. Twenty years after that decision, the Court had applied the *Flast* principle to executive branch decisions about spending legislative appropriations for programs under the Adolescent Family Life Act.[79] The plaintiffs in *Hein* alleged that the federal offices created by the President, pursuant to executive order, to ensure that faith-based community groups were eligible to compete for federal financial support violated the Establishment Clause by organizing conferences designed to promote religious groups over secular ones. Although the U.S. Court of Appeals for the Seventh Circuit granted the plaintiffs standing to sue based on earlier Supreme Court precedent, the Supreme Court concluded that the Seventh Circuit was reading the earlier cases too broadly. The Court held that federal taxpayers have no standing to challenge spending paid for out of general executive branch appropriations, as opposed to spending mandated by congressional legislation.

FREE EXERCISE CLAUSE

In *Jimmy Swaggart Ministries v. Board of Equalization,*[80] the U.S. Supreme Court held that the imposition of general taxes on the sale of religious materials does not contravene the Free Exercise Clause of the First Amendment. The tax was only a small fraction of any sale, and it applied neutrally to all relevant sales regardless of the nature of the seller or purchaser. The Court also held that the tax did not violate the Establishment Clause. There was little evidence of administrative entanglement between religion and the government. The government was not involved in the organization's day-to-day activities, and the imposition of the tax did not require the state to inquire into the religious content of the items sold or the religious motivation behind selling or purchasing them.

The U.S. Supreme Court also upheld an Oregon statute that criminalized the use of peyote, an hallucinogenic drug, even though peyote is used in Native American religious ceremonies.[81] The Court overturned precedent that had required courts hearing Free Exercise Clause challenges to apply the compelling-state-interest test. Instead, the Court ruled that generally applicable laws that burden but do not target religion do not need to be justified by a compelling state interest to pass muster under the Free Exercise Clause. Congress responded by passing the Religious Freedom Restoration Act of 1993 (RFRA), which attempted to strengthen religious freedom by codifying the prior strict scrutiny standard. The Supreme Court subsequently struck down the RFRA as an unconstitutional encroachment by Congress on the powers of the judiciary to interpret the Constitution.[82]

Nonetheless, the Supreme Court applied the RFRA's strict scrutiny test to federal legislation in *Gonzales v. O Centro Espirita,*[83] in which Chief Justice Roberts commented in a footnote that *Flores* held that the RFRA was unconstitutional only as applied to state legislation. The Court concluded that the government had failed to demonstrate, at the preliminary injunction stage, a compelling interest in barring the sacramental use of hoasca by members of UDV, a Christian spiritualist sect. Hoasca is a tea brewed from plants that contains DMT, an hallucinogen regulated under the Federal Controlled Substance Act (FCSA). The Court rejected the government's argument that no exception to the DMT ban could be accommodated because the government had a compelling interest in the uniform application of the FCSA. It declared that under the RFRA's strict scrutiny test a challenged law must be applied to the particular claimant whose sincere exercise of religion is being substantially burdened. The Court had affirmed the feasibility of such case-by-case consideration of religious exemptions during the preceding term[84] and concluded that it was unlikely in this case that the need for uniformity outweighed the burden placed on the UDV's sacramental use of hoasca.

DUE PROCESS

The Due Process Clauses of the Fifth Amendment (which applies to the federal government) and the Fourteenth Amendment (which applies to the states) prohibit depriving any person of life, liberty, or property without due process of

77. 127 S. Ct. 2553 (2007).
78. 392 U.S. 83 (1968).
79. Bowen v. Kendrick, 487 U.S. 589 (1988).
80. 493 U.S. 378 (1990).
81. Employment Div., Ore. Dep't of Human Res. v. Smith, 494 U.S. 872 (1990).
82. City of Boerne v. Flores, 521 U.S. 507 (1997).
83. 546 U.S. 418 (2006).
84. Cutter v. Wilkinson, 544 U.S. 709 (2005).

law. *Procedural due process* focuses on the fairness of the legal proceeding. *Substantive due process* focuses on the fundamental rights protected by the Due Process Clauses.

PROCEDURAL DUE PROCESS

When a governmental action affects a person's life, liberty, or property, the due process requirement applies, and some form of notice and hearing is required. Explaining the notice requirement, the Supreme Court stated:

> [A] fundamental requirement of due process in any proceeding which is to be accorded finality is notice, reasonably calculated, under all the circumstances, to apprise interested parties of the pendency of the action and afford them an opportunity to present their objections. . . . The notice must be of such nature as reasonably to convey the required information, and it must afford a reasonable time for those interested to make their appearance.[85]

The type of hearing required varies depending on the nature of the action, but some opportunity to be heard must be provided. In general, greater procedural protections are afforded to criminal defendants because the possibility of imprisonment and even death in capital cases is at stake.

The Due Process Clause of the Fourteenth Amendment has been interpreted to make virtually all of the procedural requirements in the Bill of Rights applicable to state criminal proceedings. These rights are discussed in Chapter 15.

SUBSTANTIVE DUE PROCESS

Disputes have raged over the years as to what are the fundamental rights—the rights with which the government may not interfere—possessed by people in our society. It has been argued that such rights and liberty interests, including the right to privacy, are guaranteed by the Due Process Clauses of the Fifth and Fourteenth Amendments. This protection of fundamental rights is known as substantive due process. The notion of substantive due process was not wholeheartedly accepted by the Supreme Court until the end of the nineteenth century, mainly because substantive due process rights are not specifically listed in the Constitution.

Limit on Economic Regulation

The Supreme Court first invalidated a state law on substantive due process grounds in 1897.[86] The Court held that a Louisiana law prohibiting anyone from obtaining insurance on Louisiana property from any marine insurance company that had not complied in all respects with Louisiana law violated the fundamental right to make contracts.

Early in the twentieth century, the concept was applied to more controversial areas, such as state statutes limiting working hours. In *Lochner v. New York,*[87] the Supreme Court struck down a New York statute that prohibited the employment of bakery employees for more than ten hours a day or sixty hours a week on the basis that it interfered with the employers' and employees' fundamental right to contract with each other. From 1905 to 1937, the Supreme Court invoked the doctrine of substantive due process to invalidate a number of laws relating to regulation of prices, labor relations, and conditions for entry into business.

In 1937, the Supreme Court reversed direction. After President Franklin Delano Roosevelt threatened to "pack" the Court (discussed further in the "Inside Story"), the justices upheld a minimum-wage law for women in Washington,[88] thereby overruling an earlier decision striking down a similar statute. In 1938, the Court upheld a statute that prohibited the interstate shipment of "filled" milk (milk to which any fat or oil other than milk fat has been added).[89] The Court made it clear that if any set of facts, either known or imaginable, provided a rational basis for economic legislation, then the legislation would not be held to violate substantive due process. Under this test, economic regulation is rarely constrained by substantive due process.

Protection of Fundamental Rights

Substantive due process challenges are given more weight when fundamental rights other than the right to make contracts are at issue. Laws that limit fundamental rights violate substantive due process unless they can be shown to promote a compelling or overriding governmental interest.

Fundamental rights and liberty interests protected by the Due Process Clause include the guarantees of the Bill of Rights, the right to marry and to have children, the right to raise children, the right to travel, the right to vote, and the right to associate with other people. The fundamental rights protected by substantive due process are not limited to those specifically enumerated in the Constitution or the Bill of Rights.

Right to Privacy Substantive due process was extended to the right to privacy in *Griswold v. Connecticut.*[90] The

85. Mullane v. Cent. Hanover Bank & Trust Co., 339 U.S. 306 (1950).
86. Allegeyer v. Louisiana, 165 U.S. 578 (1897).
87. 198 U.S. 45 (1905).
88. West Coast Hotel Co. v. Parrish, 300 U.S. 379 (1937).
89. United States v. Carolene Prods. Co., 304 U.S. 144 (1938).
90. 381 U.S. 479 (1965).

executive director of the Planned Parenthood League of Connecticut and a physician who served as medical director for the league's New Haven center were charged with giving birth control advice in violation of a Connecticut statute that prohibited the use of any drug, medicinal article, or instrument to prevent conception.

Finding that the Connecticut statute was an unconstitutional invasion of individuals' right to privacy, the Supreme Court discussed the penumbra of rights surrounding each guarantee in the Bill of Rights. The Court defined *penumbra* as the peripheral rights that are implied by the specifically enumerated rights. For example, the Court noted that the First Amendment's freedom of the press necessarily includes the right to distribute, the right to receive, the right to read, freedom of inquiry, freedom of thought, freedom to teach, and freedom of association. The Fourth Amendment, which prohibits unreasonable searches and seizures, similarly includes a "right to privacy, no less important than any other right carefully and particularly reserved to the people." The Supreme Court found that the Connecticut statute encroached on the right to privacy in marriage.

The Supreme Court first held that a woman's right to have an abortion is protected by the right to privacy in *Roe v. Wade*.[91] The Court restated and reaffirmed *Roe*'s essential holding in *Planned Parenthood of Southeastern Pennsylvania v. Casey*,[92] reiterating that state regulation of access to abortion procedures must protect "the health of the woman," even after the fetus has become viable. In *Stenberg v. Carhart*,[93] the Court held that a Nebraska statute that criminalized the performance of a late-term medical procedure known as partial-birth abortion was unconstitutional because it lacked the requisite protection for the woman's health.

The U.S. Congress responded to the *Stenberg* decision in two ways when it subsequently passed the Partial-Birth Abortion Ban Act of 2003, which prohibited partial-birth abortion. First, Congress included factual findings that there was a moral, medical, and ethical consensus that partial-birth abortion is a gruesome and inhuman procedure that is not medically necessary and should be prohibited. Second, the Act prohibited only "knowingly perform[ing] a partial-birth abortion . . . that is [not] necessary to save the life of a mother."[94] In the following case, the Court considered whether the Act promoted a compelling or overriding governmental interest sufficient to justify encroachment on a woman's right to privacy.[95]

91. 410 U.S. 113 (1973).

92. 505 U.S. 833, 846 (1992).

93. 530 U.S. 914 (2000).

94. 18 U.S.C. § 1531(a). The Act defines "partial-birth abortion" as a procedure in which the doctor "(A) deliberately and intentionally vaginally delivers a living fetus until, in the case of a head-first presentation, the entire fetal head is outside the [mother's] body . . . , or, in the case of breech presentation, any part of the fetal trunk past the navel is outside the [mother's] body . . . , for the purpose of performing an overt act that the person knows will kill the partially delivered living fetus"; and "(B) performs the overt act, other than completion of delivery, that kills the fetus."

95. On appeal to the Supreme Court, *Gonzales v. Carhart* was consolidated with *Gonzales v. Planned Parenthood Federation of Am.*, 435 F.3d 1163 (9th Cir. 2006). The lower courts in both cases had invalidated the Act and granted a permanent injunction against its enforcement.

A CASE IN POINT

CASE 4.3

GONZALES V. CARHART

SUPREME COURT OF THE UNITED STATES
127 S. CT. 1610 (2007).

SUMMARY

FACTS Four physicians who perform second trimester abortions sued the U.S. Attorney General in the district court of Nebraska challenging the constitutionality of the Partial-Birth Abortion Ban Act of 2003 and seeking an injunction against its enforcement. The district court ruled the act unconstitutional, and the U.S. Court of Appeals for the Eighth Circuit affirmed. The U.S. Government appealed to the U.S. Supreme Court.

ISSUE PRESENTED Is the Partial-Birth Abortion Ban Act of 2003 constitutional? In particular, does it promote a compelling or overriding governmental interest in protecting fetal life that is sufficient to justify encroachment on a woman's right to privacy?

SUMMARY OF OPINION The U.S. Supreme Court began by construing its decision in *Planned Parenthood of Southeastern Pennsylvania v. Casey*[96] as a validation of the Government's "legitimate and substantial interest in preserving and promoting fetal life." The Court reasoned:

CONTINUED

96. 505 U.S. 883 (1992).

"A straightforward reading of the Act's text demonstrates its purpose and the scope of its provisions: It regulates and proscribes, with exceptions or qualifications to be discussed, performing the intact D&E [dilation and evacuation] procedure." Applying the *Casey* standard to the present action, the Court concluded that the Act furthered "the legitimate interest of the Government in protecting the life of the fetus that may become a child," stating:

> It is a reasonable inference that a necessary effect of the regulation and the knowledge it conveys will be to encourage some women to carry the infant to full term, thus reducing the absolute number of late-term abortions. The medical profession, furthermore, may find different and less shocking methods to abort the fetus in the second trimester, thereby accommodating legislative demand.

The Court concluded that the Act was not void for vagueness and did not impose an undue burden on a woman's right to abortion based on its overbreadth or lack of a health exception. While the Court upheld the Act against the plaintiffs' facial challenge, it also stated that it remained open to entertaining future challenges to the Act as applied in individual cases.

RESULT The Supreme Court reversed the judgments of the Eighth and Ninth Circuits and upheld the Partial-Birth Abortion Ban Act of 2003 as a constitutional exercise of Congress's power.

COMMENT Justices Ginsburg, Souter, Stevens, and Breyer dissented and called the majority opinion "alarming." They asserted that the majority had refused to take *Casey* and *Stenberg* "seriously" when it blessed a prohibition with no exception safeguarding a woman's health. The dissenting justices also claimed that moral concerns, "untethered to any ground genuinely serving the Government's interest in preserving life," had driven the majority opinion. They concluded:

> [T]he notion that the Partial-Birth Abortion Ban Act furthers any legitimate governmental interest is, quite simply, irrational. . . . In candor, the Act, and the Court's defense of it, cannot be understood as anything other than an effort to chip away at a right declared again and again by this Court—and with increasing comprehension of its centrality to women's lives. A decision so at odds with our jurisprudence should not have staying power.

CRITICAL THINKING QUESTIONS

1. In his concurring opinion, Justice Thomas noted that the question of "whether the Act constitutes a permissible exercise of Congress' power under the Commerce Clause is not before the Court."[97] Is the Partial-Birth Abortion Ban Act of 2003 a permissible exercise of Congress's power under the Commerce Clause?
2. What impact is *Carhart* likely to have on the movements in several states to ban all abortions?

97. The Act provides: "Any physician who, *in or affecting interstate or foreign commerce*, knowingly performs a partial-birth abortion and thereby kills a human fetus shall be fined under this title or imprisoned not more than 2 years, or both." (Emphasis added.)

The right to privacy is relevant in other areas as well. For example, the Supreme Court upheld a person's right to refuse life-sustaining treatment (such as lifesaving hydration and nutrition),[98] although it declined to recognize a right to physician-assisted suicide.[99] In another case,[100] a schoolteacher successfully sued a board of education, alleging that her teaching contract was not renewed because she

98. Cruzan v. Dir., Mo. Dep't of Health, 497 U.S. 261 (1990).

99. Washington v. Glucksberg, 521 U.S. 702 (1997). But the Court upheld an Oregon proposition permitting physician-assisted suicide in *United States v. Gonzales,* 546 U.S. 243 (2006).

100. Cameron v. Bd. of Educ., 795 F. Supp. 228 (S.D. Ohio 1991).

was an unwed mother and her pregnancy had been by means of artificial insemination. The district court held that a woman has a constitutional privacy right to become pregnant by means of artificial insemination. In 2003, the Supreme Court, overruling an earlier decision, held that a Texas statute criminalizing the act of sodomy performed by consenting adults in private impermissibly infringed upon their constitutionally protected right of privacy.[101] Mandatory drug testing also presents privacy issues. As will be discussed further in Chapter 13, the Supreme Court has upheld certain regulations concerning drug testing for public employees.

Limits on Punitive Damages

In certain cases involving torts, or civil wrongs, the jury is entitled to award the plaintiff not only compensatory damages equal to the plaintiff's actual loss but also *punitive* or *exemplary damages,* designed to punish and make an example of the defendant. In *BMW of North America v. Gore,*[102] the Supreme Court held that courts reviewing punitive damages awards should consider three guideposts to determine whether the award is so excessive that it violates the Fourteenth Amendment's Due Process Clause: (1) the degree of reprehensibility of the defendant's misconduct, (2) the disparity between the actual or potential harm suffered and the punitive damages award, and (3) the difference between the punitive damages awarded by the jury and the civil penalties authorized or imposed in similar cases.

Subsequent to the *Gore* decision, a Utah jury awarded Curtis Campbell $2.6 million in compensatory damages and $145 million in punitive damages (reduced to $1 million and $25 million, respectively, by the trial court) in his action against State Farm Insurance. Although investigators and witnesses had concluded that Campbell caused an automobile accident that killed one person and permanently disabled another, State Farm rejected offers by the injured parties to settle their claims within Campbell's policy limits ($25,000 per claimant) and took the case to trial. State Farm had assured the Campbells that their assets were safe, that State Farm would represent their interests, and that they did not need separate counsel. When the jury found Campbell liable for $185,849, however, State Farm refused to cover the excess liability over the policy limit of $50,000. Campbell then sued State Farm for bad faith, fraud, and intentional infliction of emotional distress. Applying the *BMW* guidelines, the Utah Supreme Court upheld the $145 million punitive damages award, noting State Farm's massive wealth and the clandestine nature of its actions. On appeal, however, the U.S. Supreme Court reversed, holding that "in practice, few awards exceeding a single-digit ratio between punitive and compensatory damages, to a significant degree, will satisfy due process."[103] The Court found that the $145 million award was neither reasonable nor proportionate to the wrong committed and that it was an irrational and arbitrary deprivation of State Farm's property. During the damages portion of the trial, the Campbells had introduced evidence showing that State Farm had a national policy of meeting fiscal goals by capping payouts on claims and describing fraudulent practices by State Farm outside Utah that bore no relationship to third-party automobile claims. The Court held that a jury must be instructed that it may not use "evidence of out-of-state conduct to punish a defendant for action that was lawful in the jurisdiction where it occurred." It also found that a jury could not use evidence of "[a] defendant's dissimilar acts, independent from the acts upon which liability was premised," as the basis for a punitive damages award. The Court left open, however, whether evidence of a defendant's similar conduct toward nonparties could be considered by a jury in awarding punitive damages.

In *Philip Morris USA v. Williams,*[104] the U.S. Supreme Court held that evidence of harm caused to third parties by similar conduct could be used to show that the conduct that harmed the plaintiff also posed a substantial risk to others and therefore was particularly reprehensible. But the Court ruled that such evidence could not be used to punish the defendant directly for harm to those nonparties. The jury found that Jesse Williams's death was caused by smoking and that defendant Philip Morris had knowingly and falsely led him to believe that smoking was safe. As a result, the jury awarded Williams's estate $321,000 in compensatory damages and $79.5 million in punitive damages. The trial court reduced the award, but it was reinstated by the Oregon Supreme Court. The Oregon Supreme Court rejected Philip Morris's argument that the trial court should have instructed the jury that it could not punish Philip Morris for injury to third parties other than the plaintiff in the instant case. The U.S. Supreme Court concluded that the Oregon Supreme Court had applied the wrong constitutional standard when considering Philip

101. Lawrence v. Texas, 539 U.S. 558 (2003).

102. 517 U.S. 559 (1996).

103. State Farm Mut. Auto. Ins. Co. v. Campbell, 538 U.S. 408 (2003).

104. 127 S. Ct. 1057 (2007). In *Exxon Shipping Co. v. Baker,* 128 S.Ct. 2605 (2008), the U.S. Supreme Court cited data that the median ratio of punitive to compensatory awards across the board is less than one-to-one and held that a one-to-one ratio was a fair upper limit in maritime cases. The *Exxon Shipping* Court made it clear that it was articulating a federal common law rule applicable only to maritime cases and was not setting a constitutional limit. Nonetheless, the Court noted the unpredictability of high punitive awards and suggested that the law should threaten violators with "a fair probability of suffering in a like degree when they wreak like damage."

Morris's appeal, and it remanded the case so that the court could apply the correct standard. The Court did not reach the issue of whether the approximately 100-to-1 ratio between the punitive and compensatory damages award rendered it constitutionally "grossly excessive."

Along with the substantive due process requirements illustrated in *State Farm* and *Philip Morris,* there is a procedural due process requirement that punitive damage awards must be subject to appellate review. In *Honda Motor Co. v. Oberg,*[105] an Oregon jury had awarded $5 million in punitive damages to a plaintiff injured in a three-wheel all-terrain vehicle accident. Honda wanted to appeal the penalty, but Oregon's constitution barred review of punitive awards unless there was no evidence to support the jury's decision. The U.S. Supreme Court concluded that the Oregon rule violated due process and was insufficient to protect Honda's constitutional rights.

COMPENSATION FOR TAKINGS

One of the first provisions of the Bill of Rights incorporated into the Fourteenth Amendment was the Fifth Amendment provision that private property may not be taken for public use without just compensation. State and federal governments have the power of *eminent domain,* which is the power to take property for public uses, such as building a school, park, or airport. If property is taken from a private owner for such a purpose, the owner is entitled to just compensation. As discussed further in Chapter 19, a more complex situation arises when the government does not physically take the property but imposes regulations that restrict its use. In a sense, all regulation takes some aspect of property away from the owner. The question is when does a regulation constitute a taking that requires compensation.

The U.S. Supreme Court held that there was a compensable taking when a homeowner was required to grant a public right-of-way through his property in order to obtain a building permit to replace his oceanfront house with a larger one.[106] Another case involved the Federal Communications Commission's regulation of the rates a utility company could charge for the attachment of television cables to the utility company's poles. The Supreme Court held that the regulation was not a taking, as long as the rates were not set so low as to be unjust and confiscatory.[107] In *Tahoe-Sierra Preservation Council, Inc. v. Tahoe Regional Planning Agency,* the Supreme Court ruled that a government-imposed moratorium on property development does not automatically constitute a taking of private property, even if it lasts for years.[108]

In *Eastern Enterprises v. Apfel,*[109] the Supreme Court invalidated the Coal Industry Retiree Health Benefits Act of 1992 under which Eastern Enterprises, a former coal mine operator that had ceased its mine operations in 1987, was required to contribute an annual premium of $5 million to a health fund for coal workers. The Act was enacted to remedy the shortfalls in the preexisting multi-employer benefits plans the coal industry had negotiated with the United Mine Workers union. It required all companies that had signed onto the union plans to contribute to a new health fund and to pay for their former employees even if the amount exceeded a company's obligation under the negotiated plan. The Supreme Court struck down the Act as an unconstitutional "taking" of private property without compensation, holding that a law violates the Fifth Amendment if "[1] it imposes severe retroactive liability [2] on a limited class of parties that could not have anticipated the liability, and [3] the extent of that liability is substantially disproportionate to the parties' experience." Chapter 16 discusses environmental cases in which the defendants argued that, in light of *Eastern Enterprises v. Apfel,* environmental statutes imposing cleanup costs could not be applied to activities that predated the statutes' enactment.

EQUAL PROTECTION

The Equal Protection Clause of the Fourteenth Amendment, which provides that no state shall "deny to any person within its jurisdiction the equal protection of the laws," places another limitation on the power of state governments to regulate. A comparable limitation is imposed on the federal government by the Due Process Clause of the Fifth Amendment. The U.S. Supreme Court's interpretation of this clause continues to be the subject of much debate.

ESTABLISHING DISCRIMINATION

To challenge a statute on equal protection grounds, it is first necessary to establish that the statute discriminates against a class of persons. Discrimination may be found on the face of the statute, in its application, or in its purpose. The statute may (1) explicitly (on its face) treat different classes of persons differently; (2) contain no classification, but government officials may apply it differently to different classes of people; or (3) be neutral on its face and in its application but have the purpose of creating different burdens for different classes of persons.

105. 512 U.S. 415 (1994).

106. Nollan v. Cal. Coastal Comm'n, 483 U.S. 825 (1987).

107. FCC v. Fla. Power Corp., 480 U.S. 245 (1987).

108. 535 U.S. 302 (2002).

109. 524 U.S. 498 (1998).

In determining whether a facially neutral law is a device to discriminate against certain classes of people, the Supreme Court looks at three things: (1) the practical or statistical impact of the statute on different classes of persons, (2) the history of the problems that the statute seeks to solve, and (3) the legislative history of the statute. Even if a government action has a disproportionate effect on a racial minority group, it will be upheld if there was no racially discriminatory purpose or intent.[110]

TESTS FOR JUDGING VALIDITY OF DISCRIMINATION

The Supreme Court uses three tests to determine the constitutionality of various types of discrimination, depending on how the statute classifies the persons concerned.

Rational Basis Test

The *rational basis test* applies to all classifications that relate to matters of economics or social welfare. Under this test, a classification will be upheld if there is any conceivable basis on which the classification might relate to a legitimate governmental interest. For example, a system of progressive taxation, in which persons with higher income are required to pay taxes at a higher marginal rate, passes muster under this test. It is a rare regulation that cannot meet this minimal standard.

Strict Scrutiny Test

A classification that determines who may exercise a fundamental right or a classification based on certain suspect traits, such as race or color, is subject to strict scrutiny. Under the *strict scrutiny test,* a classification will be held valid only if it is necessary to promote a compelling state interest and is narrowly tailored to achieve that interest. The right to privacy, the right to vote, the right to travel, and certain other guarantees in the Bill of Rights are fundamental rights. Rights such as welfare payments, housing, education, and government employment are not fundamental rights.

Substantially Related Test

The Supreme Court occasionally applies a third test, which is stricter than the rational basis test but less strict than strict scrutiny. This intermediate-level test, known as the substantially related test, applies to classifications such as gender and legitimacy of birth. Under this test, a classification will be upheld if it is substantially related to an important governmental interest.

110. Arlington Heights v. Metro. Hous. Dev. Corp., 429 U.S. 252 (1977) (upholding a largely white suburb's refusal to rezone to permit multifamily dwellings for low- and moderate-income tenants, including members of racial minorities).

"And, in a move sure to attract the attention of regulators, the private sector made a bid to acquire the public sector."

RACIAL DISCRIMINATION

Racial discrimination was the major target of the Fourteenth Amendment, so it is clear that racial classifications are suspect. Nonetheless, from 1896 to 1954, the "separate but equal" doctrine allowed governments to provide separate services for minorities as long as they were equal to the services provided for whites. For example, in *Plessy v. Ferguson,*[111] the U.S. Supreme Court upheld a law requiring all railway companies to provide separate but equal accommodations for African American and white passengers. Fifty-eight years later, the Supreme Court ruled in *Brown v. Board of Education*[112] that the separate but equal doctrine had no place in education. The justices unanimously held that "segregation of children in public schools solely on the basis of race, even though the physical facilities and other 'tangible' factors may be equal, deprives the children of the minority group of equal educational opportunities." Supreme Court rulings following *Brown* made it clear that no governmental entity may segregate people because of their race or national origin.

Complications concerning racial classifications have arisen more recently in the area of affirmative action programs intended to benefit racial or ethnic minorities. A debate raged over whether strict scrutiny should be applied only to legislation that discriminates against a minority or to any legislation that generally discriminates based on race. The Supreme Court resolved that issue in *Adarand Constructors, Inc. v. Peña,*[113] when it held that all racial classifications—whether imposed by federal, state, or local government—are

111. 163 U.S. 537 (1896).

112. 347 U.S. 483 (1954).

113. 515 U.S. 200 (1995).

subject to strict scrutiny. In *Adarand,* the white owner of a construction company successfully challenged regulations adopted by the U.S. Department of Transportation that used race-based presumptions in awarding lucrative federal highway project contracts to economically disadvantaged businesses. The Court rejected the argument it had accepted in an earlier case[114] that, because the Equal Protection Clause was adopted after the Civil War to protect African Americans, it permits "benign" (or protective) racial classifications as long as there is a rational basis for the classification.

A number of cases have raised the question of whether universities and schools can consider an applicant's race when deciding to admit the student. In *Grutter v. Bollinger,*[115] the U.S. Supreme Court considered the constitutionality of the University of Michigan Law School's admissions policy, which required admissions officials to consider diversity as one of a list of factors in evaluating potential students. Although the admissions policy did not define diversity solely in terms of race and ethnicity, and did not restrict the types of diversity eligible for consideration, the policy affirmed the school's commitment to diversity, with specific references to African American, Hispanic, and Native American students. After the law school denied admission to Ms. Grutter, a white Michigan resident with a 3.8 GPA and a high LSAT score, she filed suit alleging, among other things, that the school had discriminated against her on the basis of race in violation of the Fourteenth Amendment. The district court found that the law school's use of race as an admissions function was unlawful, but the U.S. Court of Appeals for the Sixth Circuit reversed,[116] holding that *Regents of University of California v. Bakke*[117] had established diversity as a compelling state interest and that the law school's use of race was narrowly tailored because race was merely a "'potential' plus factor" and the policy was "virtually identical" to the Harvard admissions program described by the Court and appended to the *Bakke* decision.

The Supreme Court affirmed the decision of the Sixth Circuit, holding that the Equal Protection Clause did not prohibit the law school's narrowly tailored use of race in admissions decisions to further a compelling interest in obtaining the educational benefits that flow from a diverse student body. Applying the strict scrutiny test, the Court found that the law school's use of race was justified by a compelling state interest. The Court noted that "[a] core purpose of the Fourteenth Amendment was to do away with all governmentally imposed discrimination based on race" and stated that race-conscious admissions policies should therefore be limited in time. Observing that it had been twenty-five years since Justice Powell first approved the use of race to further an interest in student body diversity, the Court stated that "[w]e expect that 25 years from now, the use of racial preferences will no longer be necessary to further the interest approved today."

Although the Supreme Court voted five to four to uphold the use of race by the University of Michigan Law School in *Grutter,* in *Gratz v. Bollinger* it struck down the University of Michigan's undergraduate admissions policy, which awarded points to African Americans, Hispanics, and Native Americans on an admissions rating scale.[118] The Court concluded that this use of race was not "narrowly tailored" to achieve the university's diversity goals.

In the following case the Supreme Court considered whether a public school district could voluntarily adopt a student assignment plan that relies upon race to determine which public schools children may attend.

114. Metro Broad., Inc. v. FCC, 497 U.S. 547 (1990) (upholding two minority-preference policies mandated by Congress to achieve broadcast diversity).

115. 539 U.S. 306 (2003).

116. Grutter v. Bollinger, 288 F.3d 732 (6th Cir. 2002).

117. 438 U.S. 265 (1978).

118. 539 U.S. 244 (2003).

A CASE IN POINT

IN THE LANGUAGE OF THE COURT

CASE 4.4

PARENTS INVOLVED IN COMMUNITY SCHOOLS V. SEATTLE SCHOOL DISTRICT NO. 1

SUPREME COURT OF THE UNITED STATES
127 S. CT. 2738 (2007).

FACTS Seattle [Washington] School District No. 1, a public school district that had never operated legally segregated schools, operated ten regular public high schools. In 1998, it adopted a student assignment plan that allowed incoming ninth graders to choose from among any of the district's high schools, ranking however many schools they wished in order of preference. Some schools were more popular than others. If too many students listed the same school as their first choice, the district employed a series of "tiebreakers" to determine who would fill the open slots at the oversubscribed school. The first tiebreaker selected students who had a sibling at the school. The next tiebreaker depended upon the racial composition of the particular school and the race of the individual student. If an oversubscribed school was not within ten percentage points of the district's overall white/nonwhite racial balance, the district selected for assignment students whose race "will serve to bring the school into balance."

CONTINUED

The Jefferson County [Kentucky] Public School District adopted a voluntary student assignment plan in 2001, a year after its court-ordered desegregation decree had been dissolved. The plan required all nonmagnet schools to maintain a minimum black enrollment of 15 percent and a maximum black enrollment of 50 percent. At the elementary school level, each student was designated a "resides" school based on his or her address. Elementary resides schools were "grouped into clusters in order to facilitate integration." Parents of kindergartners, first-graders, and new students could submit an application indicating a first and second choice within their cluster; students who did not submit an application were assigned to a school within the cluster by the district. If a school had reached the "extremes of the racial guidelines," a student whose race would contribute to the school's racial imbalance would not be assigned there. After assignment, students at all grade levels were allowed to apply for transfer between nonmagnet schools in the district. Transfers could be requested for any number of reasons and could be denied because of lack of available space or on the basis of racial guidelines.

Parents of students who were denied assignment to particular schools under these plans solely because of their race brought suit, contending that allocating the children to different public schools on the basis of race violated the Fourteenth Amendment guarantee of equal protection. The U.S. Courts of Appeals for the Ninth and Sixth Circuits upheld the plans, and the parents appealed.

ISSUE PRESENTED May a public school district that has not operated legally segregated schools and that is not the subject of court-ordered desegregation rely upon racial classifications in making school assignments?

OPINION ROBERTS, C. J., writing for the U.S. Supreme Court:

In order to satisfy [the strict scrutiny standard of review applicable to racial classifications], the school districts must demonstrate that the use of individual racial classifications in the assignment plans . . . is "narrowly tailored" to achieve a "compelling" government interest.

. . . .

[O]ur prior cases, in evaluating the use of racial classifications in the school context, have recognized two interests that qualify as compelling. The first is the compelling interest of remedying the effects of past intentional discrimination. . . .

. . . .

The second government interest we have recognized . . . is the interest in diversity in higher education upheld in *Grutter*. The specific interest found compelling in *Grutter* was student body diversity "in the context of higher education." The diversity interest was not focused on race alone but encompassed "all factors that may contribute to student body diversity." . . .

. . . .

The entire gist of the analysis in *Grutter* was that the admissions program at issue there focused on each applicant as an individual, and not simply as a member of a particular racial group. . . .

. . . .

In the present cases, by contrast, race is not considered as part of a broader effort to achieve "exposure to widely diverse people, cultures, ideas, and viewpoints"; race, for some students, is determinative standing alone. . . .

. . . .

Before *Brown* [*v. Board of Education*], schoolchildren were told where they could and could not go to school based on the color of their skin. The school districts in these cases have not carried the heavy burden of demonstrating that we should allow this once again—even for very different reasons. For schools that never segregated on the basis of race, such as Seattle, or that have removed the vestiges of past segregation, such as Jefferson County, the way "to achieve a system of determining

CONTINUED

admission to the public schools on a nonracial basis," is to stop assigning students on a racial basis. The way to stop discrimination on the basis of race is to stop discriminating on the basis of race.

RESULT The Court struck down the policies, reversed the judgments of the courts of appeals, and remanded the cases for further proceedings.

DISSENT STEVENS, J., dissenting from the majority opinion (Justice Breyer, who wrote a separate dissent, was joined by Justices Stevens, Souter, and Ginsburg).

There is a cruel irony in the Chief Justice's reliance on our decision in *Brown v. Board of Education*. The first sentence in the concluding paragraph of his opinion states: "Before *Brown*, schoolchildren were told where they could and could not go to school based on the color of their skin." This sentence reminds me of Anatole France's observation: "[T]he majestic equality of the la[w], forbid[s] rich and poor alike to sleep under bridges, to beg in the streets, and to steal their bread." The Chief Justice fails to note that it was only black schoolchildren who were so ordered; indeed, the history books do not tell stories of white children struggling to attend black schools. In this and other ways, the Chief Justice rewrites the history of one of this Court's most important decisions.

The Chief Justice rejects the conclusion that the racial classifications at issue here should be viewed differently than others, because they do not impose burdens on one race alone and do not stigmatize or exclude. The only justification for refusing to acknowledge the obvious importance of that difference is the citation of a few recent opinions—none of which even approached unanimity—grandly proclaiming that all racial classifications must be analyzed under "strict scrutiny." . . .

CRITICAL THINKING QUESTIONS

1. Is the need for a diverse student body as compelling in the case of elementary and secondary schools as it may be in law schools?
2. What implications, if any, will this decision have on affirmative action by public and private employers?

Private employers are not limited by the Equal Protection Clause, which applies only to governmental actors, such as state and local governments, schools, and police departments. However, as explained in Chapter 13, private entities are subject to the Civil Rights Act and other regulations imposed by federal and state antidiscrimination statutes.

OTHER FORMS OF DISCRIMINATION

The U.S. Supreme Court has applied the substantially related test to laws that classify on the basis of gender, illegitimacy, and alienage.

Gender

In *United States v. Virginia,*[119] the Supreme Court ruled that the Virginia Military Institute, an all-male, state-supported military college, violated the Equal Protection Clause by excluding women. The Court held that classifications based on gender must (1) serve important governmental objectives, (2) be substantially related to achieving those objectives, and (3) rest on an "exceedingly persuasive justification." Justice Ruth Bader Ginsburg's majority opinion can be read to require gender classifications to meet a standard somewhere between intermediate and strict scrutiny. In prior cases, the Court invalidated statutory provisions that gave female workers fewer benefits for their families than male workers; upheld differential treatment for women when it was compensatory for past discrimination, but not when it unreasonably denied benefits to men; upheld a statutory rape law that applied only to male offenders; upheld exempting women from the draft; and upheld disability insurance policies that excluded insurance benefits for costs relating to pregnancy, but not other disabilities. Gender discrimination is discussed further in Chapter 13.

Illegitimacy

Classifications based on the legitimacy of children will be held invalid unless substantially related to a proper state

119. 518 U.S. 515 (1996).

interest. The Supreme Court will usually look at the purpose behind the classification and will not uphold any law intended to punish children born out of wedlock.

Alienage

Aliens, that is, persons who are not citizens of the United States, do not receive the protection of all constitutional guarantees, many of which apply only to citizens. For example, in 1990, the Supreme Court held that the Fourth Amendment prohibition of search and seizure without a warrant did not apply to a drug raid of an alien's premises in Mexico.[120]

120. United States v. Verdugo-Urquidez, 494 U.S. 259 (1990).

Because of Congress's *plenary* (or absolute) power to regulate aliens and immigration, classifications imposed by the federal government based on alienage are valid as long as they are not arbitrary and unreasonable. State and local laws that classify on the basis of alienage are subject to strict scrutiny, however, except for state laws discriminating against alien participation in certain state government positions, which are evaluated under the rational basis test. Foreign organizations without property or presence in the United States also have no constitutional rights.[121]

121. People's Mojahedin Org. of Iran v. Dep't of State, 182 F.3d 17 (D.C. Cir. 1999), *cert. denied,* 529 U.S. 1104 (2000).

Historical PERSPECTIVE

The Initiative Process

In 1898, South Dakota became the first state to establish a procedure whereby citizens could initiate laws on their own without going through their elected representatives. During the next twenty years, eighteen other states adopted citizen initiative processes; by 2008, the number had grown to twenty-four states and the District of Columbia. The initiative process is also used by thousands of counties, cities, and towns across the country. Unlike representative democracy, initiatives give direct legislative power to voters by allowing them to make new laws, either by amending their state constitution or by enacting legislation. Some states, such as California, do not allow an executive veto of initiatives (unlike legislation passed by the state legislature) and forbid repeal except by subsequent voter initiative. The initiative process has been used by citizens seeking to change governmental policy on a wide range of topics including child labor, women's suffrage, gambling, alcohol, prostitution, civil rights, the death penalty, environmental protection, and property taxes.

Although it has been in existence in states for over a century, the initiative process has seen most of its use in recent years. A total of seventy-nine citizen and legislative initiatives went before voters in thirty-seven states during 2006, representing the third largest total since the initiative process was first used in 1898. Voters approved thirty-two of the seventy-nine initiatives, a 41 percent approval rate that is equal to the historical average.[a]

In recent years, a number of major public policy battles have moved out of the state capitols and into the land of initiatives. In 1994 and again in 1997, Oregon voters authorized physician-assisted suicide for competent, terminally ill adults.[b] In 1996, voters in California and Arizona legalized medical use of marijuana by ballot initiative,[c] and voters in California also approved Proposition 209, which sought to end racial preferences by state and local governments. One year later, voters in Houston turned down an initiative to end that city's affirmative action program. In 2006, Proposition 87, an initiative to tax oil extraction and use the money for the development of renewable fuels, failed in California. Promoters and opponents of this initiative had spent more than $150 million, breaking the previous record for the most money ever spent on a single ballot proposition by more than 50 percent.[d]

Voters have also used initiative-type processes to remove elected officials from office. In 2003, groups opposed to newly reelected California Governor Gray Davis gathered enough signatures to force a recall election. In October 2003, Governor Davis was recalled by California voters, who replaced him with Arnold Schwarzenegger.

CONTINUED

a. *Initiative Use, Overview of Initiative Use, 1904–2007,* Initiative and Referendum Institute, Jan. 2008, available at http://www.iandrinstitute.org/IRI%Initiative%20Use.pdf.
b. The Oregon proposition permitting physician-assisted suicide was affirmed by the Supreme Court in *United States v. Gonzales*, 546 U.S. 243 (2006).
c. Proposition 215 was overruled by the Supreme Court in *United States v. Oakland Cannabis Buyers' Cooperative*, 532 U.S. 483 (2001).
d. Ballotwatch, *supra* note a.

Sources: This discussion is based in part on K. K. DuVivier, *By Going Wrong All Things Come Right,* 63 U. CIN. L. REV. 1185 (1995); P. K. Jameson & Marsha Hosack, *Citizen Initiatives in Florida,* 23 FLA. ST. U. L. REV. 417 (1995); and David L. Callies et al., *Ballot Box Zoning,* 39 WASH. U. J. URB. & CONTEMP. L. 53 (1991).

RIGHT TO JURY TRIAL

The Seventh Amendment provides that "[i]n Suits at common law, where the value in controversy shall exceed twenty dollars, the right of trial by jury shall be preserved." The phrase "suits at common law" refers to suits in which legal rights are to be ascertained and monetary damages awarded, in contrast to suits where only equitable rights and remedies (such as injunctions) are recognized. To determine whether a particular action will resolve legal rights, a court must analyze both the nature of the issues involved and the remedy sought. In particular, a court will compare the suits to eighteenth-century actions brought before the American Revolution in the courts of England prior to the merger of the courts of law and equity and examine the remedy sought to determine whether it is legal or equitable in nature.[122] In this two-part analysis, the second inquiry is more important than the first.

As previously discussed, the Seventh Amendment has not been interpreted to apply to the states. As a result, there is no federal constitutional requirement that jury trials be held in state court civil cases. When a federal court is hearing a case involving state law, the matter becomes more complicated. In *GTFM, LLC v. TKN Sales, Inc.*,[123] the U.S. Court of Appeals for the Second Circuit ruled that when a federal court has jurisdiction in a case based solely on diversity of citizenship (that is, when no federal question is involved), the federal court should require a jury trial only if a state court in that state would require a jury trial.

122. Chauffers, Teamsters & Helpers Local No. 391 v. Terry, 494 U.S. 558 (1990).

123. 257 F.3d 235 (2d Cir. 2001).

GLOBAL VIEW

Free Speech Rights in the European Union

Freedom of speech, or expression, is the concept that individuals should be able to express themselves freely, without governmental intervention. The right to freedom of speech is guaranteed under international law through a number of human rights instruments, including Article 19 of the Universal Declaration of Human Rights, which was adopted by the General Assembly of the United Nations in 1948. Article 19 provides that "[e]veryone has the right to freedom of opinion and expression; this right includes freedom to hold opinions without interference and to seek, receive and impart information and ideas through any media and regardless of frontiers." In practice, however, there is a "free speech" spectrum along which countries may be placed, with the United States providing the most freedom, totalitarian countries providing the least, and most European Union countries falling somewhere in the middle.

The First Amendment to the U.S. Constitution provides that "Congress shall make no law . . . abridging the freedom of speech, or of the press . . . ." The U.S. concept of free speech requires the government to refrain from interfering in individual expression, subject to narrow exceptions. The European approach, set forth in Article 10 of the Convention for the Protection of Human Rights and

CONTINUED

Fundamental Freedoms, affirms that everyone has the right to freedom of expression; however, it also states that the exercise of free speech "carries with it duties and responsibilities" and "may be subject to such formalities, conditions, restrictions and penalties as are prescribed by law and are necessary in a democratic society."[124] In Europe, the concept of free speech includes the idea that the government should prevent certain types of prohibited speech through active intervention. This approach is followed in most other democratic countries, including Australia, Canada, and Japan.[125]

Racist speech provides an example of the differences between the U.S. and the European approach to regulation of expression. Racist speech in the United States is protected political speech, no matter how disgusting, dangerous or extreme it may be. As Supreme Court Justice Oliver Wendell Holmes stated: "The principle of free thought is not free thought for those who agree with us but freedom for the thought we hate."[126]

In Europe, however, laws against inciting hatred and violence exist in many countries, including France, the Netherlands, Germany, and Denmark. Such laws have led to criminal convictions and, in the case of foreigners, expulsion. In recent European speech cases:

- An Austrian court sentenced British historian David Irving to three years in prison for denying the Holocaust.
- A German court convicted a sixty-one-year-old businessman of insulting Islam by selling toilet paper printed with the word "Quran," the Muslim holy book.
- Three French intellectuals and the publisher of the nation's premier newspaper, *Le Monde*, were ordered by a French court to pay 1 euro each to Attorneys Without Borders for defaming Jews in an op-ed article.
- An Italian judge ordered the now deceased journalist Oriana Fallaci to stand trial on charges that she defamed Islam in her book, *The Force of Reason*, when she wrote that Islam "sows hatred in the place of love and slavery in the place of freedom." (Fallaci died in 2006, while on trial.)
- London Mayor Ken Livingston received a four-week suspension for comparing a Jewish journalist to a Nazi concentration camp guard.

The growth of the Internet has highlighted these differences, as countries have attempted to apply their own free speech standards to Internet communications. An early example of this occurred in the late 1990s, when La Ligue Contre Racisme et L'Antisemitisme (LICRA) and L'Union Des Etudiants Juifs de France (UEJF) filed a complaint in France against Yahoo!, asserting that the sale of Nazi memorabilia on Yahoo!'s auction site violated a French law that prohibits the sale or display of symbols that incite racism. In May 2000, a French court ruled that there were sufficient links with France to give it jurisdiction to hear the complaint. Specifically, the court found that the auctions of Nazi memorabilia were open to bidders worldwide (including France); the viewing and display of these objects in France caused a public nuisance and violated French criminal law; and Yahoo! was aware that French residents used its site. The court issued a preliminary injunction against Yahoo! pending further review.[127]

In response to Yahoo!'s arguments that it was technologically impossible to block French users from the auction sites, the judge ordered three technology experts—one American, one French, and one other European—to study the issue and present their findings to the court. Based on their conclusion that Yahoo! could achieve a significant filtering success rate, the French court issued an order for Yahoo! to prevent French Internet users from accessing auction sites with Nazi paraphernalia within three months or face a fine of 15,244.90 euros per day.

Under pressure from U.S. organizations, Yahoo! banned hate-related goods from its auction site and removed

CONTINUED

124. 213 U.N.T.S. 222, *entered into force* Sept. 3, 1953, *as amended by* Protocols Nos. 3, 5, 8, and 11, *which entered into force* Sept. 21, 1970, Dec. 20, 1971, Jan. 1, 1990, and Nov. 1, 1998, *respectively*.

125. Benoît Frydman & Isabelle Rorive, *Regulating Internet Content Through Intermediaries in Europe and the USA*, 23 Zeitschrift Fur Rechtssoziologie 41 (2002), *available at* http://www.isys.ucl.ac.be/etudes/cours/linf2202/Frydman_&_Rorive_2002.pdf (last visited July 5, 2007).

126. United States v. Schwimmer, 279 U. S. 644 (1929). The U.S. Supreme Court did, however, rule that state and local governments could permissibly draft carefully tailored statutes banning cross burning conducted with an intent to intimidate. The Court noted that the Ku Klux Klan had historically used burning crosses as "a tool of intimidation and a threat of impending violence" to African Americans. Nonetheless, the Court ruled that the government could not prohibit ritualistic cross burning conducted not to intimidate but to symbolize "shared group identity and ideology," because such ritualistic practices constituted political speech. Virginia v. Black, 538 U.S. 343 (2003).

127. Peter D. Trooboff, *Recent 'Yahoo!' Ruling*, Nat'l L.J., Mar. 6, 2006, *available at* http://www.cov.com/files/Publication/a4f2de20-f384-49fe-8957-973c20895265/Presentation/PublicationAttachment/e777c041-431f-43ec-9d35-9-e0ca1c06d65/oid6796.pdf.

numerous pro-Nazi Web pages from Geocities, although it claimed that these actions had nothing to do with the French judge's decision. At the same time, Yahoo! filed suit in a federal district court in California against LICRA and UEJF seeking a declaratory judgment that the French decision was unenforceable in the United States because it violated the First Amendment. In November 2001, the district court voided the French court's decision,[128] but the U.S. Court of Appeals for the Ninth Circuit reversed this decision in 2004 on the basis that it had no personal jurisdiction over the French plaintiffs.[129]

The case sparked a controversy in the United States where many saw it as the censoring of a U.S. publication by a foreign country. The U.S. Court of Appeals for the Ninth Circuit agreed to hear the case en banc, and on January 1, 2006, the panel issued an opinion that, like the earlier three-judge panel, reversed the judgment of the district court and remanded the case with directions to dismiss the action. The court noted that "Yahoo! is necessarily arguing that it has a First Amendment right to violate French criminal law and to facilitate the violation of French criminal law by others. . . . the extent—indeed the very existence—of such an extraterritorial right under the First Amendment is uncertain."[130]

Attempts to establish international standards for racist speech on the Internet have made some progress. In November 2002, the Council of Europe (CoE)[131] approved an Additional Protocol to the Cybercrime Convention on the Criminalization of Acts of a Racist or Xenophobic Nature Committed Through Computer Systems that would make it illegal to distribute or publish anything online that "advocates, promotes or incites hatred [or] discrimination." Although the United States is a signatory to the Cybercrime Convention,[132] which is designed to encourage other countries to enact computer crime and intellectual property laws, and participated in the drafting and negotiation of the Protocol, it has informed the CoE that it will not become a party to the Protocol because it believes that the final version of the Protocol is not consistent with the First Amendment.[133]

128. Yahoo! Inc. v. La Ligue Contre Le Racisme et L'Antisemitisme, 145 F. Supp. 2d 1168 (N.D. Cal. 2001). Under the principle of comity, courts will respect and enforce judgments of foreign tribunals. However, Judge Jeremy Fogel noted that the principle of comity is not without exceptions. Generally, U.S. courts will not enforce foreign judgments that are inconsistent with fundamental U.S. public policies. Here, the French court decision ran counter to the First Amendment's free speech protections.

129. Yahoo! Inc. v. La Ligue Contre Le Racisme et L'Antisemitisme 379 F.3d 1120 (9th Cir. 2004).

130. Yahoo! Inc. v. LICRA, 433 F.3d 1199 (9th Cir. 2006).

131. The Council of Europe consists of forty-four member states, including all of the members of the European Union, and was established in 1949 primarily as a forum to uphold and strengthen human rights and to promote democracy and the rule of law in Europe. The CoE has been the negotiating forum for a number of conventions on criminal matters in which the United States has participated.

132. Thirty-four countries signed the Convention on Cybercrime in November 2001 but, as of December 16, 2006, only six had actually ratified it and no major European country had agreed to be bound.

133. Declan McCullagh, *U.S. Won't Support Net "Hate Speech" Ban,* CNET NEWS.COM, Nov. 15, 2002, http://news.com.com/2100-1023-965983.html (last visited July 5, 2007).

THE RESPONSIBLE MANAGER

PRESERVING CONSTITUTIONAL RIGHTS

Although the Constitution is directed primarily at establishing and limiting the powers of the federal and state governments, its provisions have a profound effect on private actors in society. The costs are usually high, but at times a company may find it worthwhile to challenge a regulation on constitutional grounds. This was true for Eastern Enterprises, the former coal company that successfully challenged the $5 million assessment to fund health plans for former employees,[134] and for State Farm, the insurance company that successfully challenged the $145 million punitive damages award against it.[135]

CONTINUED

134. Eastern Enter. v. Apfel, 524 U.S. 498 (1998).

135. State Farm Mut. Auto. Ins. Co. v. Campbell, 538 U.S. 408 (2003).

Managers often have an interest in influencing legislation or other government action through direct lobbying or political action committees. When pursuing change, it is important to know the constitutional limitations placed on different government segments.

Although many provisions in the Constitution apply only to government actions, managers of private organizations should be aware of the societal values reflected in the Constitution. These include the right to fair and equal treatment and respect for the individual.

It may seem at times that constitutional law is far removed from the world of business. This is a misconception. Constitutional law is as close as the nearest private club that does not admit African Americans, Jews, women, or gays. Such clubs may be important places for conducting business and for general networking. A manager invited to become a member of such a club, or to accompany his or her boss or client as a guest, may face a tough choice between his or her personal values and the perceived need to not challenge an important business colleague.

A Manager's Dilemma

Putting It into Practice

Drawing the Line Between Personal and Corporate Fundraising

The federal election laws prohibit corporate contributions to political candidates but allow corporations to establish separate segregated funds known as political action committees (PACs). A corporation may solicit contributions to these PACs from a "restricted class" comprising its stockholders and administrative and executive personnel and their families. A member of a restricted class may contribute a maximum of $5,000 to a federal PAC, but a corporation is prohibited from giving annual bonuses to its executives with the understanding that they will contribute part of the bonus to the corporation's PAC or to a candidate. Although corporations may also solicit employees who are not in the restricted class, this solicitation is highly restricted and regulated.

The CEO of Techno Corporation, Sunil Zamba, is a friend and supporter of Senator Wood from Idaho, where Techno is headquartered. Zamba has sent memos to all of the executives and managers in the company reminding them that legislation is pending in the Senate that could negatively affect Techno's business and that Senator Wood opposes the bill. Although he has not instituted a formal company policy, Zamba has strongly suggested that all of the executives and managers attend a fundraising dinner for Senator Wood and persuade at least one other business associate outside Techno to attend. Attendance at the dinner requires a donation of $6,000 per person. Zamba has made it clear that Techno will reimburse the cost of the dinner for the Techno employees and their business associate guests, claiming that this dinner is an opportunity for Techno managers and executives to network with potential clients. Have Zamba and Techno Corporation violated the federal election laws? Have they acted ethically? Would your answer be different if the dinner cost only $500 per person? If you were a Techno executive and personally preferred Senator Wood's opponent because of her stand on oil drilling in Alaska, would you attend the event?

Inside Story

EFFECT OF POLITICS ON SUPREME COURT APPOINTMENTS

The nomination process for the U.S. Supreme Court has grown increasingly politicized and controversial over time. Nomination to the Supreme Court now brings along with it a process of public scrutiny akin to running for national political office. Politics, however, is not new to the process of selecting Supreme Court justices.

Franklin Delano Roosevelt was probably the first president to attempt explicitly and publicly to use the power of judicial

CONTINUED

appointment to change the Court's position on key political issues. Frustrated because the Supreme Court was invalidating much of his New Deal legislation, Roosevelt introduced a Court-packing bill that would have added one justice to the Court for every sitting justice who had reached the age of seventy, thereby increasing the Court's membership to fifteen. By appointing additional justices, Roosevelt hoped to gain a majority sympathetic to his programs. Although the bill was never passed by the Senate, the Court quickly capitulated and abandoned its commitment to limited government, especially regarding economic liberty.

Other presidents have made considerations of diversity and representation key to their selection of nominees. President Lyndon Johnson's appointment of Thurgood Marshall took into consideration for the first time the need for African Americans to be represented on the Court. The appointments of Justices Sandra Day O'Connor (the first female member of the Court) and Clarence Thomas by Presidents Ronald Reagan and the elder George Bush, respectively, served to expand and maintain the Court's gender and racial diversity.

Other presidents have used the appointment power to reward political allies. In 1953, President Dwight Eisenhower appointed Earl Warren, the Republican governor of California and an important supporter of Eisenhower's successful bid for the presidency, Chief Justice, despite misgivings by powerful Republicans, including Vice President Richard Nixon, about Warren's progressive stance on certain issues.

In 1987, President Ronald Reagan nominated Robert Bork, a well-known conservative constitutional scholar with an extensive "paper trail" of opinions and writings on constitutional matters. Lengthy Senate hearings in which Bork was forced to attempt to explain the reasoning behind some of his more radical statements over the years, and the resultant political uproar across the nation, led the Senate to deny his confirmation to the Court.

The 1991 nomination of Clarence Thomas to the "black seat" on the Supreme Court, vacated by Justice Thurgood Marshall's resignation, was supposed to be quiet but resulted in another Bork-like public spectacle. Thomas seemed to be a safe bet: his writings and opinions were sparse and generally without controversy. After completing an initial hearing, however, Thomas was called back before the Judiciary Committee to face allegations of sexual harassment by Anita Hill, an African American law professor and former colleague. The ensuing melee became a circus in which actors on both sides paraded before the committee, asserting their versions of the truth. Thomas, undaunted by the allegations, charged the committee with conducting a "high-tech lynching of uppity-blacks." This aggressive challenge to the senators dulled the edge of their remaining questions, and the Senate subsequently approved Thomas by a vote of fifty-two to forty-eight.

When President Bill Clinton nominated Ruth Bader Ginsburg to the Court, the politics swirled around the question of whether the Senate should apply an abortion "litmus test" to her appointment in light of the changing Supreme Court position on the pivotal issue of whether a woman has a constitutional right to an abortion. In an effort to preempt potential litmus test–type questions, Judge Ginsburg began her hearing with opening remarks that hinted at the inappropriateness of deciding a case in advance and promised to impartially hear each case before the Court "without reaching out to cover cases not yet seen." She was easily confirmed by a vote of ninety-six to three, and her hearing served as an opportunity to reduce hostility in the nomination process.

More recently, President George W. Bush had the opportunity to fill two vacancies on the Court created by the death of Chief Justice William Rehnquist and the retirement of Justice Sandra Day O'Connor. After listening to three hours of opening statements in which Democratic senators expressed fears that he would move the Court to the right on abortion, civil rights, and other issues, President Bush's nominee for Chief Justice, John Roberts, Jr., tried to allay their fears. Although he offered no specifics on his views, Judge Roberts assured the senators that justices must have "the humility to recognize that they operate within a system of precedent." [136]

Senator Dianne Feinstein (D-Cal.) questioned Judge Roberts about a memorandum that he wrote in the 1980s, in which he stated, "Some might question whether encouraging homemakers to become lawyers contributes to the common good, but I suppose that's for the judges to decide." Judge Roberts responded that he supported "equal rights for women, particularly in the workplace" and claimed that he had been joking with his boss when he wrote the memo.[137]

Notwithstanding his professed respect for precedent, Chief Justice Roberts authored the opinion overturning almost one hundred years of precedent when the Court ruled that an agreement between a manufacturer and retailer to charge a minimum price for goods (*resale price maintenance*) was no longer illegal *per se* but should be judged under the rule of reason to determine whether the benefits to consumers

CONTINUED

136. Charles Babington & Jo Becker, *"Judges Are Not Politicians," Roberts Says,* WASHINGTONPOST.COM, Sept. 13, 2005, http://www.washingtonpost.com/wp-dyn/content/article/2005/09/12/AR2005091200642.html.

137. Amy Goldstein & Charles Babington, *Roberts Avoids Specifics on Abortion Issue,* WASHINGTONPOST.COM, Sept. 14, 2005, http://www.washingtonpost.com/wp-dyn/content/article/2005/09/13/AR2005091300682.html.

outweighed the costs.[138] Chief Justice Roberts made no reference to *Casey v. Planned Parenthood*,[139] which is widely regarded as the Court's leading pronouncement on the role of precedence and the standards courts should follow when deciding whether to reverse prior holdings. In his dissent, Justice Breyer faulted the majority for overturning ninety-six years' worth of antitrust precedent without satisfying *Casey's* standards.

President Bush's first nominee for the seat vacated by Justice O'Connor was a close friend with no prior judicial experience, White House chief lawyer Harriet Miers. In the maelstrom of criticism that followed her nomination, even the President's most ardent supporters questioned his judgment. Their concern was that Miers had no record of supporting their conservative political agenda. As conservative Pat Buchanan said, "Ms. Miers' qualifications for the Supreme Court are utterly non-existent. . . . She has not only not ruled or written on any of the great controversies of our time—religion or faith, morality—she has shown no interest in them in 40 years."[140]

After Miers withdrew her name, President Bush delighted conservatives by nominating Samuel Alito, a federal appeals court judge with fifteen years' experience on the bench. Like Roberts, Judge Alito offered few specifics in his confirmation hearing to help the Senate predict his future performance. On abortion, Judge Alito simply said, "I would approach the question with an open mind." When he was pressed by Senator Feinstein on whether he agreed with Roberts's testimony that the *Roe v. Wade* precedent was "well settled," Judge Alito replied, "That depends on what one means by the term 'well settled.'"[141]

Since the confirmations of Judges Roberts and Alito, the Supreme Court has taken an undeniable turn to the right, which could become one of the enduring legacies of President George W. Bush's tenure.[142] One Court watcher at the end of the first full Term on which Justices Roberts and Alito served noted:

> [A]t the end of a course-changing, gut-wrenching Supreme Court term littered with heated 5–4 decisions, one bit of clarity is shining through: The Roberts Court, and especially its newest member, Samuel Alito, are both very conservative and very pro-business—more so than any Supreme Court in decades.[143]

During the 2007 term, the Supreme Court upheld the Partial-Birth Abortion Ban Act despite a 2000 decision that found a nearly identical law unconstitutional; allowed school officials to censor and punish student speech that could be interpreted as celebrating the use of illegal drugs; required employees to file a complaint within 180 days after their pay is set in order to sue for discrimination; held that taxpayers could not sue to block federal spending on the Office of Faith-Based and Community Initiatives; opened a broad exception to restrictions on political advertisements in the McCain-Feingold Act that it had upheld four years earlier; limited the ability of school districts to use race to assign students to schools in an effort to achieve integration; ended a ninety-six-year ban on price floors, allowing manufacturers and retailers to agree on minimum resale prices in some cases; continued to curb punitive damages awards; made it more difficult for investors to sue companies, executives, and underwriters when they suspect securities fraud or unlawful manipulation; and upheld a state law requiring unions to obtain nonmember consent before using union fees for political purposes.

As U.S. Chamber of Commerce lawyer Robin Conrad observed, "We've been representing the business community before the Supreme Court for 30 years, and this is our strongest showing since the inception" of the National Chamber Litigation Center, the Chamber's litigation arm. "There wasn't a significant case in which a business argument was made where the business side did not prevail," according to Mark Levy, head of Kilpatrick Stockton's appellate practice.[144]

---

138. Leegin Creative Leather Prods. v. PSKS, Inc., 127 S. Ct. 2705 (2007).

139. 505 U.S. 833 (1994).

140. Justin Webb, *Chorus of Disapproval over Court Pick*, BBC News, Oct. 14, 2005, *available at* http://news.bbc.co.uk/1/hi/world/americas/4342582.stm.

141. Warren Richey, *Cautious Alito Follows Roberts's Script in Quest for Supreme Court Spot*, Christian Science Monitor, Jan. 13, 2006, *available at* http://www.csmonitor.com/2006/0113/p03s02-usju.htm.

142. Linda Greenhouse, *In Steps Big and Small, Supreme Court Moved Right*, N.Y. Times, July 1, 2007, at A1.

143. Tony Mauro, *A Mind for Business*, Legal Times, July 2, 2007, *available at* http://www.law.com/jsp/article.jsp?id=1183107990440.

144. *Id.*

KEY WORDS AND PHRASES

abrogate 117
appellate jurisdiction 114
bicameralism 116
Bill of Rights 125
bills of attainder 124
clear and present danger test 128
Commerce Clause 121
congruence–and–proportionality test 118
dormant Commerce Clause 122
double jeopardy 124
Due Process Clause (Fifth and Fourteenth Amendments) 125
eminent domain 141
Establishment Clause 135
executive privilege 115
exemplary damages 140
ex post facto laws 124
federalism 113
Free Exercise Clause 135
judicial review 114
line item veto 116
negative Commerce Clause 122
original jurisdiction 114
override (of a president's veto) 115
penumbra 138
plenary 146
police power 117
preempts 113
prior restraints 133
Privileges and Immunities Clause (Fourteenth Amendment) 125
procedural due process 137
punitive damages 140
rational basis test 142
resale price maintenance 151
separation of powers 114
strict scrutiny test 142
subject matter jurisdiction 114
substantially related test 133
substantive due process 137
veto power 115

QUESTIONS AND CASE PROBLEMS

1. Most of the athletic shoes sold by Nike, Inc. are manufactured by female workers under the age of twenty-four employed by subcontractors in China, Vietnam, and Indonesia. Beginning in March 1993, Nike assumed responsibility for its subcontractors' compliance with applicable local laws and regulations regarding minimum wages, overtime, safety, health, and environmental protection. In 1996, the television program *48 Hours* reported that Nike products were made in factories where workers were paid less than the applicable minimum wage; were required to work overtime and encouraged to work more than the legal overtime limits; were subjected to physical, verbal, and sexual abuse; and were exposed to toxic chemicals, noise, heat, and dirt, in violation of applicable occupational health and safety laws. These allegations were repeated in articles published in a variety of media.

   In response, Nike issued press releases, letters to newspapers, letters to university presidents and athletic directors, and other documents (including full-page advertisements in leading newspapers) stating that the allegations were false and misleading, that its workers were paid in accordance with applicable local laws, and received free meals and medical care, and that their working conditions complied with safety and health rules. Marc Kasky sued Nike on behalf of the general public under California Business and Professions Code Sections 17204 and 17535, claiming that Nike's statements were false and misleading and were made with knowledge or reckless disregard of California laws prohibiting false and misleading statements. Nike moved to dismiss the complaint on the grounds, among others, that its statements were protected by the First Amendment to the U.S. Constitution. Can a corporation participating in a public debate be subjected to liability for factual inaccuracies? [*Kasky v. Nike, Inc.*, 45 P.3d 243 (Cal. 2002), *cert. granted,* 537 U.S. 1099 (2003), *cert. dismissed as improvidently granted,* 539 U.S. 654 (2003).]

2. The Connecticut State Employee Campaign raises funds for 900 charities through voluntary contributions by state employees; the employees can designate which of the participating organizations will receive their contributions. The Boy Scouts of America (BSA) has a policy against employing known or avowed homosexuals as commissioned, professional Scouts or in other capacities (including adult volunteer leaders or youth members) in

which such employment or position would interfere with the BSA's mission of transmitting values to youth. The BSA received about $10,000 annually from the Campaign until 2000, when the state dropped the organization from the Campaign after the state Human Rights Commission asserted that including the BSA would violate Connecticut's gay rights law, which prohibits the state from "becoming a party to any agreement, arrangement or plan which has the effect of sanctioning discrimination." The BSA sued on the basis that it was "singled out and excluded" from the Campaign based on its First Amendment right of association, a right that the U.S. Supreme Court had recognized in *Boy Scouts of America v. Dale,* 530 U.S. 640 (2000). What will each side argue? Who will win? [*Boy Scouts of America v. Wyman,* 335 F.3d 80 (2d Cir. 2003), *cert. denied,* 541 U.S. 903 (2004).]

3. Most wine in the United States is distributed through a three-tier network that developed after the repeal of Prohibition. First, the winery obtains a permit to sell wine. Next, the winery sells its wine to a licensed wholesaler, who pays excise taxes and delivers the wine to a retailer. The retailer then sells the wine to consumers. As demand for wine has increased over the last two decades, the number of wineries has grown to more than 2,000, including many small wineries. Meanwhile, the number of wholesalers has declined from several thousand to a few hundred. As a result, many small wineries are unable to find wholesalers to carry their wine and are trying to market their wine directly to consumers.

   Juanita Swedenburg runs the Swedenburg Estate Vineyard in Middleburg, Virginia. People from all over the United States visit her winery and purchase wine to take home with them. Once they get home, many call the winery or use its website to order more bottles. However, the laws in twenty-six states prohibit the direct shipment of wine to consumers across state lines. The states claim that the Twenty-first Amendment, which repealed Prohibition, gives them the authority to regulate the importation of alcohol. Their claim is based on Section 2 of the amendment, which states that "[t]he transportation or importation into any state, territory, or possession of the United States for delivery or use therein of intoxicating liquors, in violation of the laws thereof, is hereby prohibited." Swedenburg, other winery owners, and wine lovers challenged the direct-shipment laws. Are these direct-shipment laws constitutional? Explain why or why not. [*Granholm v. Heald,* 544 U.S. 460 (2005).]

4. John and Judith Rapanos were accused of destroying wetlands, without a permit, on three central Michigan sites that they hoped to develop. Regulators sought as much as $1.4 million in fines and restoration of the site. Rapanos argued that his land is far away from the nearest river tributary—twenty miles in the case of one site. The U.S. Court of Appeals for the Sixth Circuit concluded, however, that the Clean Water Act covered the property because the land had a hydrological connection to navigable waterways because it ultimately drained into either the Tittabawassee River or Lake Huron. Rapanos argued that extending the Clean Water Act's jurisdiction to every intrastate wetland with any sort of hydrological connection to navigable waters, no matter how tenuous or remote, exceeds Congress's constitutional power to regulate commerce among the states. Is the Clean Water Act, which gives permitting authority to the U.S. Army Corps of Engineers, for wetlands that are not adjacent to a river or other navigable waterway, but are hydrologically connected to these waterways because they drain into a tributary of a river or navigable waterway, a constitutional exercise of Congress's power under the Commerce Clause? Explain why or why not. [*Rapanos v. United States,* 547 U.S. 715 (2006).]

5. In 2000, the city of New London, Connecticut, approved a development plan, anchored by a $300 million Pfizer research center, that was projected to create more than 1,000 jobs, to increase tax and other revenues, and to revitalize the economically distressed city, including its downtown and waterfront areas. The city designated the NLDC, a nonprofit development corporation, as its development agent to be in charge of the development and to purchase property in the ninety-acre area or to acquire it by eminent domain in the city's name. The NLDC successfully negotiated the purchase of most of the property, but a few people refused to sell. Thereafter, the NLDC began condemnation proceedings. Several property owners brought an action in state court, claiming, among other things, that the taking of their properties would violate the Fifth Amendment provision that states that private property may only be taken for "public use" with just compensation. Is the taking of private land by a private developer as part of an economic development project a permitted "public use"? Should it be? [*Kelo v. New London,* 545 U.S. 469 (2005).]

6. The State of Washington created a new college scholarship program, pursuant to which it awarded Promise Scholarships to low- and middle-income students who had achieved an excellent academic record in high school. Joshua Davey was awarded one of the Promise Scholarships. The director of financial aid at Northwest College, however, determined that Davey did not meet the enrollment requirements for the Promise Scholarship because

he was pursuing a degree in pastoral ministries. Davey filed a lawsuit in which he alleged that the provision of the Washington law that denied Promise Scholarships to students pursuing a degree in theology is unconstitutional. What arguments can Davey make? What arguments can the state make in its defense? Who will win the lawsuit? [*Locke v. Davey,* 540 U.S. 712 (2004).]

7. The U.S. Congress enacted the Controlled Substances Act (CSA) as part of the Comprehensive Drug Abuse Prevention and Control Act of 1970. The CSA establishes that marijuana is a controlled substance and makes it unlawful to knowingly or intentionally manufacture, distribute, dispense, or possess with intent to manufacture, distribute, or dispense a controlled substance, including marijuana. The CSA was enacted pursuant to Congress's authority under the Commerce Clause and includes findings that controlled substances have a substantial detrimental effect on the health and general welfare of Americans, that controlled substances manufactured and distributed intrastate cannot be differentiated from controlled substances manufactured and distributed interstate, and that federal control of the intrastate incidents of traffic in controlled substances is essential to the effective control of the interstate incidents of such traffic.

   In 1996, California voters passed Proposition 215, codified as the Compassionate Use Act of 1996, to ensure that patients and their primary caregivers who obtain and use marijuana for medical purposes upon the recommendation of a physician are not subject to criminal prosecution. Angel McClary Raich and Diane Monson are California citizens who use marijuana as a medical treatment. Raich has been diagnosed with more than ten serious medical conditions, including an inoperable brain tumor, and Monson suffers from severe chronic back pain caused by a degenerative disease of the spine. In April 2002, deputies from the Butte County Sheriff's Department and agents from the U.S. Drug Enforcement Administration (DEA) came to Monson's home. The sheriff's deputies concluded that Monson's use of marijuana was legal under the Compassionate Use Act. Nonetheless, after a three-hour standoff involving the Butte County District Attorney and the U.S. Attorney for the Eastern District of California, the DEA agents seized and destroyed Monson's six cannabis plants. Fearing raids in the future and the prospect of being deprived of medicinal marijuana, Raich and Monson filed suit against the U.S. Attorney General and the Administrator of the DEA, alleging that the CSA is unconstitutional. Is the CSA unconstitutional? Explain why or why not. [*Gonzales v. Raich,* 545 U.S. 1 (2005).]

8. Northwest Airlines prohibited smoking on all domestic and most international flights, but it permitted smoking on most flights to and from Asia. Julie Duncan filed a class-action personal-injury suit against Northwest on behalf of nonsmoking flight attendants who served as crew on these smoking flights. Duncan claimed that by permitting smoking, Northwest breached its duty under Washington state law to provide a safe and healthy work environment for its employees. Northwest filed a motion to dismiss, asserting that Duncan's action was preempted by Section 1305(a)(1) of the Airline Deregulation Act, which provides that "no state or political subdivision thereof and no interstate agency or other political agency of two or more states shall enact or enforce any law, rule, regulation, standard, or other provision having the force and effect of law relating to the rates, routes or service of any air carrier."

   Is the state action tort claim preempted by the Airline Deregulation Act? Explain why or why not. [*Duncan v. Northwest Airlines, Inc.,* 208 F.3d 1112 (9th Cir. 2000), *cert. denied,* 531 U.S. 1058 (2000).]

5

AGENCY

INTRODUCTION

Agency and the Conduct of Business

Agency is perhaps the most pervasive legal relationship in the business world. In an *agency* relationship, one person—the *agent*—acts for or represents another person—the *principal.* The principal delegates a portion of his or her power to the agent. The agent then manages the assigned task and exercises the discretion given by the principal. The agency relationship can be created by an express or implied agreement or by law.

Businesses of all kinds require the assistance of agents in order to conduct multiple operations in various locations. Indeed, without the law of agency, corporations could not function at all. Only through its human agents can a corporation enter into any kind of binding agreement.

CHAPTER OVERVIEW

This chapter defines and discusses the central principles of agency law. First, it describes the different methods by which an agency relationship can be formed. The chapter identifies the different types of agency relationships (employer–employee and principal–independent contractor) and the consequences that flow from each. We examine the duties an agent owes to the principal and an agent's authority to enter into agreements that bind the principal. Finally, the chapter discusses the extent to which a principal may be liable for the tortious or illegal conduct of an agent.

FORMATION OF AN AGENCY RELATIONSHIP

The agency relationship is consensual in nature and is typically created by agreement of the parties, which can be either written or oral. If, however, the agent enters into an agreement of a type that must be in writing to be enforceable (such as an agreement for the sale of real property), then the agent's signature on the agreement will not bind the principal unless the agency relationship itself is evidenced by some signed writing. This is called the *equal dignities rule*.

An agency agreement can also be implied from conduct. For example, suppose that Techno Computers, Inc. agrees that its sales representative, Computers International (CI), will sell Techno's computers to retailers and end users. CI solicits sales for Techno, and Techno pays CI a commission for each sale. An agency relationship exists between Techno and CI, even if they have not entered into a formal agreement.

Agency relationships can be formed without agreement based on apparent authority. *Apparent authority,* also referred to as *agency by estoppel,* occurs when a person leads another to believe that someone else is his or her agent and is thereafter estopped (prevented) from denying it. For example, suppose that Jack causes Kendra to believe that Lori is his agent, and Kendra, relying on this, proceeds to deal with Lori. Even if Lori is not in fact Jack's agent, Kendra's reliance creates an agency by estoppel. As a result, Lori's dealings with Kendra will bind Jack.

An agency relationship can also be formed without agreement by ratification. If a principal approves or accepts the benefits of the actions of an otherwise unauthorized agent, he or she has formed an *agency by ratification.*

TYPES OF AGENCY RELATIONSHIPS

Agency relationships are present in numerous situations. Broadly defined, an "agent" is a party that effects the legal relations of another party, the principal. The agent can effect legal relations in several ways but does so primarily by entering into contracts on behalf of the principal and acting on the principal's behalf. An agent may be either an employee of the principal or an independent contractor.

EMPLOYER–EMPLOYEE

The most common form of agency relationship is the employer–employee relationship, sometimes still referred to as the master–servant relationship. The basic characteristic of this relationship is that the employer has the right to control the conduct of the employee. The employee may have the authority to bind the employer to a contract under theories of actual or apparent authority.

PRINCIPAL (CLIENT)–INDEPENDENT CONTRACTOR

An *independent contractor,* such as a lawyer working for a client or a plumber working for a house builder, is not an employee of the person paying for his or her services because the independent contractor's conduct is not fully subject to that person's control. The person hiring an independent contractor bargains only for results.

An independent contractor may or may not be an agent. Generally, an agency relationship exists when the hiring person gives the independent contractor authority to enter into contracts on his or her behalf. For example, suppose that a builder contracts to build a house for Ken for $200,000. Ken has no control over the builder's manner of doing the work because the house is one of a large group of houses that the builder is constructing in a housing subdivision. The builder is not Ken's agent. In contrast, if Ken expressly authorized the builder to buy redwood siding from a lumber company on his behalf, the independent contractor would be Ken's agent for purposes of buying the siding.

DISTINGUISHING BETWEEN EMPLOYEES AND INDEPENDENT CONTRACTORS

Determining whether a worker is an employee or an independent contractor is a legal issue with several important consequences, including the liability of the principal for the worker's wrongful misconduct, as well as the principal's duty to deduct and pay certain taxes on behalf of the worker and to permit the worker to participate in employee benefit plans.

Under the doctrine of *respondeat superior* (literally, "let the master answer"), employers are liable for the torts (and many crimes) of their employees, as long as the employee was acting within the scope of employment. In contrast, persons hiring independent contractors are generally not liable for torts committed by the independent contractor.

Employers are required to deduct or pay income, Social Security, and unemployment taxes for employees but not for independent contractors. Independent contractors are responsible for paying their own self-employment taxes. Moreover, independent contractors are generally not eligible for the same fringe benefits provided to employees, such as medical insurance, stock options, and 401(k) retirement plans. Although the distinction between employees and independent contractors is an important one, there is no bright-line test to distinguish one from the other. Significantly, the label used in a contract does not determine the status of a worker.

Whether a person is an independent contractor or an employee depends on what he or she does, not on how the relationship is characterized by the parties. Courts and regulatory agencies frequently look through the parties' characterization of their relationship to make an independent determination, based on a variety of factors, including the following:

1. How much control can the employer exercise over the details of the work?
2. Is the employed person engaged in an occupation distinct from that of the employer?
3. Is the kind of work being done usually performed under the direction of an employer or by a specialist without supervision?
4. What degree of skill does the work require?
5. Does the employer provide the worker with tools and a place of work?

6. For how long is the worker employed?
7. Is the worker paid on the basis of time or by the job?
8. Does the worker offer his or her services to the public at large?

Employee status is more likely to be found for workers who are lower paid and less skilled, lack bargaining power, and have a high degree of economic dependence on their employers.

Because an employer does not pay employment taxes and may not provide fringe benefits for independent contractors, employers may be tempted to hire temporary workers and independent contractors as a less costly alternative to hiring employees, but this decision could turn out to be an expensive mistake. During the 1980s, Microsoft employed a number of freelance workers as independent contractors to perform services as software testers, production editors, proofreaders, formatters, and indexers. The freelancers often worked on teams with regular employees, sharing the same supervisors, performing identical tasks, and working the same hours. Unlike employees, however, they were not permitted to assign their work to others, they were not invited to official company functions, and they were not paid overtime wages. In addition, the freelancers were required to submit invoices for their services, documenting their hours and the projects on which they worked, and they were paid through the accounts receivable department rather than Microsoft's payroll department.

Although the freelancers had acknowledged in their Independent Contractor Agreements that they were independent contractors and had agreed to be responsible for all federal and state taxes, tax withholding, and Social Security, the Internal Revenue Service (IRS) concluded that Microsoft had misclassified these workers and that they should have been classified as employees for withholding and employment tax purposes. Microsoft therefore was required (1) to pay overdue employer withholding taxes, (2) to issue retroactive W-2 forms to allow the freelancers to recover Microsoft's share of Social Security taxes (which they had been required to pay), and (3) to pay the freelancers retroactively for any overtime they had worked.

After learning of the IRS rulings, eight freelancers, on behalf of themselves and as representatives of the class of freelance workers, filed a lawsuit against Microsoft, seeking various employee benefits, including benefits under an employee stock purchase plan (ESPP), which allowed employees to purchase company stock at 85 percent of the fair market value on either the first or the last day of each six-month offering period, whichever was lower. Microsoft denied liability because each of these workers had signed an Independent Contractor Agreement that expressly provided that the worker was personally responsible for all of his or her own benefits. The U.S. Court of Appeals for the Ninth Circuit ruled that the approximately 10,000 current and former independent contractors and longtime "temporary" employees at Microsoft who worked at least half-time, or five months a year, had become "common-law" employees of the company and thus were entitled to compensation for their exclusion from the ESPP.[1] At the time of the decision, analysts estimated that Microsoft would have to pay approximately $100 million to the workers.

> **ETHICAL CONSIDERATION**
>
> **Is it ethical for an employer to create artificial differences between its regular employees and workers whom it characterizes as "contractors" so that it will not have to provide the "contractors" with insurance and other benefits? Should individuals who work side by side, on the same project or job, under the same supervisor, always receive the same benefits?**

Many companies responded to the *Microsoft* decision by leasing workers from temporary employment agencies instead of hiring them directly. This arrangement may not be fail-safe, however. The fact that leased workers are on the payroll of an employment agency does not preclude them from being considered employees of the company—the agency and company could be considered joint employers.

To determine whether a company is a joint employer of leased workers, a manager should consider such factors as whether the company (1) supervises the workers, (2) has the ability to hire and fire, (3) is involved in day-to-day labor relations, (4) establishes wage rates, or (5) has the power to promote or discipline the worker. As with questions surrounding the independent contractor label, the bottom line is that if leased employees are treated the same as regular employees, they may be treated as common-law employees of the company.

FIDUCIARY DUTY

In agreeing to act on behalf of the principal, the agent becomes a *fiduciary*. Loyalty, obedience, and care are the hallmarks of the fiduciary relationship. An agent has a duty to act solely for the benefit of his or her principal in all matters directly

1. Viczaino v. Microsoft, 173 F.3d 713, 723 (9th Cir. 1999), *cert. denied,* 528 U.S. 1105 (2000).

connected with the agency undertaking. This is the *duty of loyalty.* For example, if Adrienne is entrusted with the power to buy a piece of land for Pierre, she cannot buy the best piece of land for herself instead. An agent is also obligated to obey all reasonable orders of his or her principal. For example, if Adrienne refuses to follow Pierre's order to purchase a particular parcel of property, her insubordination would violate the *duty of obedience.*

The following case examines the contours of the duty of loyalty.

A CASE IN POINT

IN THE LANGUAGE OF THE COURT

CASE 5.1

MEINHARD V. SALMON

COURT OF APPEALS OF NEW YORK
164 N.E. 545 (N.Y. 1928).

FACTS In 1902, Louisa Gerry leased the Bristol Hotel in New York City to the defendant, Walter Salmon, for a term of twenty years, beginning in 1902 and ending in 1922. Salmon was to renovate the hotel building for use as shops and offices at a cost of $200,000. Salmon needed funds to complete his proposed renovations to the building, and he persuaded Morton Meinhard to act as a financial backer. Salmon and Meinhard entered into a joint venture agreement with the following terms: Meinhard agreed to pay to Salmon one-half of the money necessary to reconstruct, alter, manage, and operate the property, and Salmon agreed to pay to Meinhard 40 percent of the net profits for the first five years of the lease and 50 percent for the years thereafter. If there were losses, each party was to bear them equally. Salmon, however, was to have sole power to "manage, lease, underlet and operate" the building.

In January 1922, with less than four months of the lease to run, Elbridge Gerry, who had become the owner of the property, approached Salmon, and they agreed to enter into a new twenty-year lease for the Bristol Hotel and an entire tract of property surrounding it. The new lessee (the entity leasing the property) was the Midpoint Realty Company, which was owned and controlled by Salmon. Under the new lease, the Bristol Hotel would eventually be torn down, and new buildings would be built on the old Bristol site and adjacent lots at a cost of $3 million. Salmon did not tell Meinhard about the new lease between Gerry and the Midpoint Realty Company, which was signed and delivered on January 25, 1922, and Meinhard did not learn of the existence of the new project until February, after the new lease had been signed.

Meinhard demanded to be included in the new lease, but Salmon and Gerry refused, and Meinhard sued. A referee found in favor of Meinhard but limited his interest in (and corresponding obligations under) the lease to 25 percent. Both the plaintiff and the defendant cross-appealed to the Appellate Division of the New York Supreme Court. On appeal, Meinhard was awarded one-half of the interest in (and corresponding obligations under) the lease. Salmon appealed to the New York Court of Appeals, the highest state court in New York.

ISSUE PRESENTED Did Salmon, as Meinhard's joint venturer, have a relationship of trust (or *fiduciary duty*) to Meinhard that obligated him to give Meinhard the opportunity to be included in a new lease covering property that was originally leased by Salmon on behalf of the joint venture?

OPINION CARDOZO, C. J. (later a justice of the U.S. Supreme Court), writing for the New York Court of Appeals:

Joint adventurers, like copartners, owe to one another, while the enterprise continues, the duty of the finest loyalty. Many forms of conduct permissible in a workaday world for those acting at arm's length, are forbidden to those bound by fiduciary ties. A trustee is held to something stricter than the morals of the market place. Not honesty alone, but the punctilio of an honor the most sensitive, is then the standard of behavior. As to this there has developed a tradition that is unbending and inveterate. Uncompromising rigidity has been the attitude of courts of equity when petitioned to undermine the rule of undivided loyalty by the "disintegrating erosion" of particular exceptions. Only thus has the level of conduct for fiduciaries been kept at a level higher than that trodden by the crowd. It will not consciously be lowered by any judgment of this court.

CONTINUED

The owner of the [property], Mr. Gerry, had vainly striven to find a tenant who would favor his ambitious scheme of demolition and construction. Baffled in the search, he turned to the defendant Salmon [who was] in possession of the Bristol, the keystone of the project. . . . To the eye of an observer, Salmon held the lease as owner in his own right, for himself and no one else. In fact he held it as a fiduciary, for himself and another, sharers in a common venture. If this fact had been proclaimed, if the lease by its terms had run in favor of a partnership, Mr. Gerry, we may fairly assume, would have laid before the partners, and not merely before one of them, his plan for reconstruction. . . . The trouble about [Salmon's] conduct is that he excluded his coadventurer from any chance to compete, from any chance to enjoy the opportunity for benefit that had come to him alone by virtue of his agency. This chance, if nothing more, he was under a duty to concede.

. . . .

We have no thought to hold that Salmon was guilty of a conscious purpose to defraud. Very likely he assumed in all good faith that with the approaching end of the venture he might ignore his coadventurer and take the extension for himself. He had given to the enterprise time and labor as well as money. He had made it a success. Meinhard, who had given money, but neither time nor labor, had already been richly paid. There might seem to be something grasping in his insistence upon more. Such recriminations are not unusual when coadventurers fall out. They are not without their force if conduct is to be judged by the common standards of competitors. That is not to say that they have pertinency here. Salmon had put himself in a position in which thought of self was to be renounced, however hard the abnegation. He was much more than a coadventurer. He was a managing coadventurer. For him and for those like him the rule of undivided loyalty is relentless and supreme. . . .

RESULT The judgment for the plaintiff, Meinhard, was affirmed. He was granted one-half of the interest in (and corresponding obligations under) the new lease between Salmon and Gerry.

COMMENTS In *Meinhard v. Salmon*, the court seemed to assume without explanation that joint venturers had a fiduciary duty to one another. Judges can disagree on what types of business relations give rise to a standard that is "stricter than the morals of the marketplace," thereby giving rise to a fiduciary duty. Furthermore, there is even disagreement as to what constitutes the proper morals of the marketplace. In *Northeast General Corp. v. Wellington Advertising,* decided by the New York Court of Appeals, the same court that decided *Meinhard v. Salmon*, a majority of the judges concluded that a finder hired by the seller of a business to find a buyer of a majority interest in the business did not have a fiduciary duty to disclose to the seller the unsavory reputation of the potential buyer.[2] The dissenting judge disagreed. He argued that there was a fiduciary relationship between the parties and that, even if there were not, the morals of the marketplace would require disclosure.

2. 624 N.E.2d 129 (N.Y. 1993) (Case 2.2).

An agent also has a duty to act with due care. This *duty of care* includes a duty to avoid mistakes, whether through negligence, recklessness, or intentional misconduct. Some states require an agent to use the same level of care a person would use in the conduct of his or her own affairs. Others use a comparative approach: an agent must exercise the same level of care that a reasonable person in a like situation would use. Application of these duties to officers, directors, and controlling shareholders is discussed in Chapter 21.

Sometimes it is not clear whether an agency relationship has been established between an independent contractor and its employer, thereby imposing a fiduciary obligation on the contractor. This was the issue in the following case dealing with the lead managing underwriter of an initial public offering.

A CASE IN POINT

CASE 5.2

EBC I, INC. v. GOLDMAN, SACHS & CO.

COURT OF APPEALS OF NEW YORK
83 N.E.2D 26 (N.Y. 2005).

SUMMARY

FACTS In the late 1990s, eToys, Inc., an Internet retailer specializing in the sale of products for children, retained Goldman Sachs as lead managing underwriter for the initial public offering (IPO) of its stock. On April 19, 1999, eToys and Goldman entered into an underwriting agreement pursuant to which eToys agreed to sell 8,320,000 shares of its stock to Goldman and the other underwriters for $18.65 per share. eToys also granted Goldman an option to buy an additional 1,248,000 shares at the same price to cover overallotments. The agreement obligated Goldman to offer the shares for public sale on the terms set forth in the prospectus, which fixed the initial offering price at $20 per share, capping Goldman's maximum return from the sale of eToys' stock at $12,916,800, which represented 6.75 percent of the offering proceeds.

On the first day of trading, eToys' stock opened at $79 per share, rose as high as $85 per share, then closed at $76.56. Six months later, however, the stock fell below $20 and never rose above the IPO price again. In March 2001, eToys filed a voluntary petition for reorganization under Chapter 11 of the U.S. Bankruptcy Code, and the bankruptcy court appointed the Official Committee of Unsecured Creditors, authorizing it to bring an action alleging breach of fiduciary duty, among other things, on behalf of eToys, now known as EBC I, Inc.

The complaint alleged that eToys relied on Goldman for its expertise as to pricing the IPO and that Goldman gave advice to eToys without disclosing that it had entered into arrangements whereby its customers "were obligated to kick back to Goldman a portion of any profits that they made" from the sale of eToys securities subsequent to the IPO. Because a lower IPO price would result in higher profits to these clients on resale and a higher payment to Goldman for the allotment, the plaintiff alleged that Goldman had an incentive to advise eToys to underprice its stock. As a result of this undisclosed conflict, Goldman was allegedly paid 20 to 40 percent of its clients' profits from trading the eToys securities.

The New York trial court denied Goldman's motion to dismiss the cause of action for breach of fiduciary duty, finding that the complaint sufficiently raised an issue as to the existence of an informal fiduciary relationship. The New York Appellate Division affirmed, and Goldman appealed, to the New York Court of Appeals (New York's highest court).

ISSUE PRESENTED Does advice provided to a client by underwriters on "market conditions" give rise to a fiduciary duty?

SUMMARY OF OPINION Although the New York Court of Appeals conceded that the underwriting contract itself might not have created any fiduciary duty, it noted that the plaintiff had alleged eToys "was induced to and did repose confidence in Goldman's knowledge and expertise to advise it as to a fair IPO price and engage in honest dealings with eToys' best interest in mind." The court rejected Goldman's contention that recognition of a fiduciary duty to the limited extent of requiring disclosure of Goldman's compensation arrangements with its customers would conflict with an underwriter's general duty to investors under the Securities Act of 1933. It also rejected Goldman's argument that there could be no fiduciary duty in this case because eToys and Goldman functioned as a typical seller and buyer. Unlike a typical buyer, who purchases a seller's goods at wholesale and resells at the highest possible profit, Goldman and eToys allegedly agreed that Goldman would receive a fixed profit from the sale of the securities. As a result, eToys had a further reason to trust that Goldman would act in eToys' interest. Finally, the court rejected Goldman's warning that finding a fiduciary duty in this case would have a significant impact on the underwriting industry and concluded:

> To the extent that underwriters function, among other things, as expert advisors to their clients on market conditions, a fiduciary duty may exist. We stress, however, that the fiduciary duty we recognize is limited to the underwriter's role as advisor. We do not suggest

CONTINUED

that underwriters are fiduciaries when they are engaged in activities other than rendering expert advice.

RESULT The court affirmed the denial of Goldman's motion to dismiss the plaintiff's cause of action for breach of fiduciary duty.

COMMENTS A year later, in *HF Management Services LLC v. Pistone*,[3] HF Management sued two of its former employees for breach of nonsolicitation agreements and WellCare for having raided its sales force. WellCare moved to disqualify HF's counsel, Epstein Becker, because the same law firm had served as due diligence counsel for underwriter Morgan Stanley in connection with WellCare's initial public offering. The trial court granted the motion, holding that Morgan Stanley owed a fiduciary duty to WellCare and that Epstein Becker, as Morgan Stanley's agent in the IPO, shared the underwriter's fiduciary duty. The Appellate Division reversed the trial court, holding that "New York law . . . essentially does not recognize the existence of a fiduciary obligation that is based solely on the relationship between an underwriter and issuer." Because *EBC I* was decided by New York's highest court and *Pistone* was decided by an intermediate appellate court, *Pistone* is not binding on the court of appeals. However, the first department is the appellate court for New York County (Manhattan) and hears many of the most important business cases. As such, its interpretation may be accorded substantial weight going forward.

3. 34 A.D.3d 82 (N.Y. 2006).

AGENT'S ABILITY TO BIND THE PRINCIPAL TO CONTRACTS ENTERED INTO BY THE AGENT

An agent has the ability to bind the principal in legal relations with third parties if the agent has actual or apparent authority to do so. Even in the absence of such authority, the principal may be bound by the unauthorized acts of the agent if the principal subsequently ratifies those acts. A principal can be bound even if his or her identity is undisclosed to the third party.

ACTUAL AUTHORITY

The principal may give the agent *actual authority* to enter into agreements on his or her behalf; that is, the principal may give consent for the agent to act for and bind the principal. This consent (or authority) may be express or implied.

One reason to keep minutes of meetings of the board of directors of a corporation is to answer agency questions that may arise from corporate transactions. Board minutes, when read in conjunction with corporate bylaws, can be used to determine whether an officer had actual authority to execute an agreement or to take other actions on behalf of the corporation.

Failure to document an employee's authority can lead to unintended consequences. For example, in *Mauldin v. WorldCom, Inc.*,[4] Billy Mauldin sued WorldCom, which had acquired his employer, seeking to enforce stock option agreements that provided for accelerated vesting if he suffered diminished responsibility or pay within two years of a change of control event. The option agreements gave the compensation committee broad discretion to determine all issues arising under the plan. The agreements also provided that the committee could designate company employees to assist in the administration of the plan. When Mauldin requested that he be allowed to exercise all of his options immediately on the basis that his employment terms had been altered, Dennis Sickle, WorldCom's senior vice president, who was not a member of the compensation committee, denied his request. The U.S. Court of Appeals for the Tenth Circuit stated that "in order to have acted within its power . . . , WorldCom must show that the Committee properly delegated its authority to Sickle before he denied Mauldin's request or, if it did not adequately delegate, that the Committee at least ratified Sickle's decision after he denied the request." Unfortunately for WorldCom, the court concluded that WorldCom had neither expressly authorized nor ratified Sickle's action because the meeting in which the committee approved the delegation of its authority to

4. 263 F.3d 1205 (10th Cir. 2001).

Sickle occurred *after* he had denied Mauldin's request and the minutes contained no express ratification of Mauldin's actions prior to the meeting. The court noted that it was unable to consider whether Sickle had implied authority because WorldCom did not include this argument in its appeal.

Express Authority

Express authority may be given by the principal's actual words, for example, a request that the agent hire an architect to design a new office. Express authority may also be given by an action that indicates the principal's consent, for example, by sending the agent a check for the architect's retainer. An agent has express authority if the agent has a justifiable belief that the principal has authorized the agent to do what he or she is doing.

Implied Authority

Once an agent is given express authority, he or she also has *implied authority* to do whatever is reasonable to complete the task he or she has been instructed to undertake. To determine an agent's implied authority, courts look to the usual and customary authority of the agent. *Usual authority* is the authority that the agent has been allowed to exercise in the past. For example, if a principal has allowed its purchasing agent to enter into contracts with a dollar value of up to $50,000, the agent has implied authority to continue to enter into such transactions. *Customary authority* consists of the authority that agents of that type normally would have. For example, the vice president of purchasing for a trucking business, because of his or her position, has the implied authority to purchase trucks. There are limits to such implied authority, however. For example, the vice president of purchasing for a trucking division does not have the implied authority to buy an office building. Similarly, an officer of a corporation does not have the authority to bind the corporation to sell or grant rights to purchase shares of its stock; stock issuances must be approved by the corporation's board of directors.

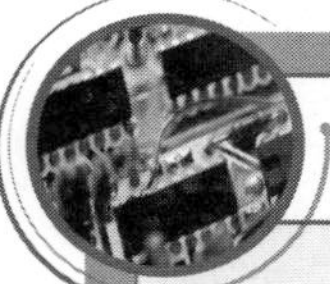

VIEW FROM CYBERSPACE

Electronic Agents and Click-Wrap Agreements

Electronic agents are autonomous computer programs that can be dispatched by the user to execute certain tasks. An important type of electronic agent can search the Internet and retrieve relevant information or serve as a "personal shopping agent" (sometimes called a "shopping bot") that makes purchases on behalf of its user.[a] A prominent feature of electronic commerce is the *click-wrap agreement* whereby users assent by clicking on an acceptance box.[b] The use of electronic agents raises an interesting legal question: What happens when an electronic agent comes across a click-wrap agreement?[c] Traditional agency law does not offer clear guidance as to whether an electronic device can bind an individual to a contract. Some experts argue that the application of agency law to electronic agents is reasonable because U.S. agency law does not require an agent to have contractual capacity in order to act as an agent, nor does it require any special formalities to create an agency relationship. Nevertheless, traditional agency law principles do not resolve many issues presented by electronic agents. For example, agency law applies only to legal persons, and electronic agents are not legal persons.

The Uniform Computer Information Transactions Act (UCITA), a proposed uniform commercial code for software licenses and other computer information transactions, provides that the user of an electronic agent will be bound by its operations. Section 107 states that a person who uses an electronic agent is bound by its operations "even if no individual was aware of or reviewed the agent's operations or the results of the operations."[d] However, UCITA has been enacted into law in only two states (Virginia and Maryland), and it appears unlikely that it will be enacted into law by any other states.

The Electronic Signatures in Global and National Commerce Act (E-Sign), enacted in 2000, and the Uniform Electronic Transactions Act[e] provide that a contract in or affecting interstate or foreign commerce may not be denied legal effect, validity, or enforceability solely because it involved the action of an electronic agent, as long as the action is "legally attributable to the person to be bound." At a minimum, E-Sign requires that a consumer will not be bound unless the consumer "consents electronically, or confirms his

CONTINUED

or her consent electronically, in a manner that reasonably demonstrates that the consumer can access information in the electronic form that will be used to provide the information that is the subject of the consent."[f] Unfortunately, however, E-Sign contains no further discussion of when the actions of an electronic agent will be attributed to the person to be bound. E-Sign recognizes that the operations of electronic agents may result in agreements that are binding on the user of the electronic agent; however, it provides little guidance regarding the circumstances under which a court will find such agreements to be binding. Courts have concluded that the operations of electronic agents can bind their users to the terms of online agreements based on the contract doctrine that a user's taking of a benefit that is offered subject to stated conditions constitutes the user's assent if the benefit is taken with knowledge of the terms of the offer.

Case law on electronic agents is also scarce since electronic commerce is a relatively new area of law, and many cases that might resolve important issues wind up being settled, rather than litigated. In the first U.S. case involving an automated system of communication, a federal district court held that the response of the seller's computer and issuance of a tracking number for a purchase order did not amount to an acceptance of the buyer's offer because the telephone computer ordering system performed automated, ministerial acts that could not constitute an acceptance.[g]

In *Register.com, Inc. v. Verio, Inc.*,[h] however, Verio used an electronic agent known as a search robot to perform multiple successive queries on Register.com's website to obtain contact information for Internet domain registrants for solicitation purposes. The terms of use published on Register.com's website home page conditioned use of its database on the user's assent to such terms and expressly prohibited solicitation.[i] The U.S. Court of Appeals for the Second Circuit rejected Verio's plea that it was never contractually bound by Register.com's terms of use and held that Verio had assented to such terms because of its repeated use of Register.com's website. The court also rejected Verio's argument that it did not form a contract with Register.com when its search robot collected information from the database, attributing the search robot's actions to Verio and holding Verio liable for breach of contract.[j] A California federal district court reached a similar result in another case involving a browse-wrap agreement.[k]

There is no published U.S. case that addresses the circumstances under which an electronic agent will be deemed to bind its user to the terms of a click-wrap agreement, and many issues remain unresolved, including whether an electronic agent's clicking on the "I agree" button without the user's actual knowledge would constitute assent by the user to the terms of the click-wrap agreement.

---

a. " 'Electronic agent' means a computer program or an electronic or other automated means used independently to initiate an action or respond to electronic records or performances in whole or in part, without review or action by an individual." UNIF. ELEC. TRANSACTIONS ACT § 2(6).

b. The term "click-wrap agreement" is derived from the term "shrink-wrap agreement." Under a "shrink-wrap license," users are deemed to have assented to a licensing agreement with a software manufacturer by their act of tearing open the shrink-wrap covering the software package. The U.S. Court of Appeals for the Seventh Circuit held that shrink-wrap licenses are generally enforceable. *See* ProCD, Inc. v. Zeidenberg, 86 F.3d 1447 (7th Cir. 1996).

c. Electronic agents may someday have the natural language abilities to parse through contract provisions and accept only those terms their users have preprogrammed. But at least for the near term, these agents will likely be able only to accept or to reject online contracts in full.

d. *The Uniform Computer Information Transactions Act (UCITA): A Firestorm of Controversy,* ONLINE LIBR. & MICROCOMPUTERS, May 1, 2000.

e. The Uniform Electronic Transactions Act (UETA) is a model law that has been adopted by forty-six states, the District of Columbia, and the U.S. Virgin Islands. Section 14 of UETA provides that a contract may be formed between (1) electronic agents, even if no individual was aware of or reviewed the electronic agents' actions or the resulting terms and agreements, and (2) an electronic agent and an individual, acting on the individual's own behalf or for another person, including interactions where the individual performs actions that the individual is free to refuse to perform and which the individual knows or has reason to know will cause the electronic agent to complete the transaction or performance. Section 5(b) of UETA, however, limits the application of UETA to transactions where the parties have agreed to conduct that transaction by electronic means.

f. 15 U.S.C. § 7001.

g. Corinthian Pharm. Sys., Inc. v. Lederle Labs., 724 F. Supp. 605 (S.D. Ind. 1989).

h. 356 F.3d 393 (2d Cir. 2004).

i. This type of agreement is known as a "browse-wrap agreement" because unlike a click-wrap, which requires the user to expressly assent to its terms, it states that the user is deemed to assent to its terms by its continued use of the website.

j. The U.S. Court of Appeals for the Second Circuit distinguished its holding in *Register.com, Inc. v. Verio, Inc.* from its earlier decision in *Specht v. Netscape Communications Corp.,* 306 F.3d 17 (2d Cir. 2002), where it ruled against Netscape and in favor of the users because the users had accessed Netscape's website only once to download the software. There was also no evidence on record to suggest that any user had seen the terms of use prior to downloading and installing the software, as the link to the terms of use was not visible except by scrolling down a user's computer screen and the user had no reason to do so.

k. Cairo, Inc. v. CrossMedia Servs., Inc., 2005 WL 756610 (N.D. Cal. 2005).

APPARENT AUTHORITY

Apparent authority is created when a third party reasonably believes that an agent has authority to act for and bind the principal. This belief may be based on the principal's words or acts or on knowledge that the principal has allowed its agent to engage in certain activities on its behalf over an extended period of time.

In *CSX Transportation, Inc. v. Recovery Express, Inc.*,[5] Len Whitehead of CSX, a seller of out-of-service railcars, was contacted by e-mail by Albert Arillotta, a partner of Interstate Demolition and Environmental Corporation (IDEC). Arillotta used albert@recoveryexpress.com as his e-mail address and represented that he was from "interstate demolition and recovery express." After several e-mail and telephone exchanges, CSX delivered railcars to a location specified by Arillotta and sent invoices totaling $115,000 to IDEC at its Boston office. When Arillotta's check bounced, CSX sued IDEC and Recovery Express, a company that shared office space with IDEC, for breach of contract. Whitehead testified that, based on Arillotta's e-mail address and his representations, he believed Arillotta was representing and authorized to act on behalf of Recovery and IDEC. Recovery denied that Arillotta ever worked for it, and stated that Arillotta acquired his Recovery e-mail address as the result of another venture between Recovery and IDEC. The court said that the case was about "CSX's attempt, having been duped by a fraudulent agent of Recovery, to shift the consequences of its own gullibility to someone else" through use of the doctrine of apparent authority. Observing that apparent authority is established not by the agent's words or conduct, but by those of the principal, the court concluded that the e-mail domain name, by itself, was not sufficient as a matter of law to cloak Arillotta with authority to act on behalf of Recovery.

In the following case, the court considered whether the president of a corporation had apparent authority to enter into a contract to redeem a terminated employee's stock.

5. 415 F. Supp. 2d 6 (D. Mass. 2006).

A CASE IN POINT — IN THE LANGUAGE OF THE COURT

CASE 5.3

POWELL V. MVE HOLDINGS, INC.

COURT OF APPEALS OF MINNESOTA
626 N.W.2D 451
(MINN. APP. 2001).

FACTS From 1993 until January 1997, R. Edwin Powell was the CEO and president of CAIRE, Inc., a Delaware company that manufactured home health-care products. Powell had worked for CAIRE, a subsidiary of MVE Holdings, Inc. (Holdings), for the preceding thirteen years as an at-will employee. Powell also held 11.9 percent of Holdings.

In 1996, a group of investors formed MVE Investors LLC (Investors) to acquire a majority interest in Holdings. In June 1996, Investors purchased the shares of three Holdings shareholders at $125.456 per share, for a total of $47 million. Declining to sell his stock to Investors and retire with the other Holdings' shareholders, Powell continued as CAIRE's president and CEO.

Subsequently, CAIRE suffered a series of financial setbacks. In early 1998, an independent company valued Powell's shares in Holdings at $5.37 per share. In response to CAIRE's financial setbacks, David O'Halleran, Holdings' CEO and president, met with Powell on January 23, 1997, to fire him. O'Halleran gave Powell the option to resign in lieu of termination, and Powell chose to resign. O'Halleran and Powell also agreed on the terms of Powell's separation agreement. After the meeting, however, a dispute arose over the terms for the purchase of Powell's stock in Holdings. Powell sued Holdings, claiming, among other things, that O'Halleran, on behalf of Holdings, had contracted to buy back Powell's shares during the January 23 meeting and that Holdings had breached that contract.

At the trial, Powell testified that O'Halleran agreed, on behalf of Holdings, to buy Powell's stock at the same price that the retiring shareholders had received in 1996. Following a nine-day bench trial, the trial court found that Holdings had breached its contract to buy Powell's stock and awarded Powell $3,456,000. Holdings appealed, claiming O'Halleran did not have authority to agree to buy Powell's stock on its behalf.

ISSUE PRESENTED Does the president and CEO of a company have apparent authority to enter into a stock-redemption agreement with a former employee?

CONTINUED

OPINION LANSING, J., writing for the Court of Appeals of Minnesota:

A principal is bound not only by an agent's actual authority, but also by authority that the principal has apparently delegated to the agent. Apparent authority is authority that a principal "holds an agent out as possessing, or knowingly permits an agent to assume." To find apparent authority, (1) "the principal must have held the agent out as having authority, or must have knowingly permitted the agent to act on its behalf," (2) third parties "must have [had] actual knowledge that the agent was held out by the principal as having such authority or been permitted by the principal to act on its behalf," and (3) "proof of the agent's apparent authority must be found in the conduct of the principal, not the agent."

Whether an agent is clothed with apparent authority is a question of fact. . . . [A] court may consider any statements, conduct, lack of ordinary care or manifestation of the principal's consent, such that a third party might be justified in concluding that the agent acted with apparent authority.

. . . Because corporate presidents usually control and supervise a corporation's business, unless there is contrary evidence, contracts made by a corporation's president in the ordinary course of business are presumed to be within the president's authority. . . . Holdings argues that the stock-redemption agreement was so extraordinary that, as a matter of law, Powell could not reasonably have believed that O'Halleran was authorized to agree to it. The evidence, however, does not support this argument.

. . . .

Because corporations are engaged in many different transactions and because the pace of corporate business is too swift to insist on express approval by a corporation's board of directors for every transaction labeled as "unusual," third parties commonly rely on the authority bestowed on corporate officials. . . .

It is significant that O'Halleran's appearance of authority resulted from Holdings' conduct. Holdings placed O'Halleran in the position to ask Powell to resign or be fired and to offer Powell a severance package. Holdings also invested authority in O'Halleran to buy shares from the retiring shareholders at the time of the recapitalization, leading to Powell's reasonable belief that O'Halleran had authority to buy Powell's stock as well.

RESULT The court of appeals affirmed the trial court's judgment for Powell, finding that O'Halleran had apparent authority to bind Holdings to the stock repurchase.

CRITICAL THINKING QUESTIONS

1. Holdings fired O'Halleran from his position as CEO and president of Holdings in August 1997. As a part of his severance agreement, O'Halleran agreed to represent that he did not make any written or oral statement that could reasonably be construed to constitute any agreement concerning the redemption or other disposition of Powell's stock. Was it ethical for Holdings to condition O'Halleran's severance package on his agreement to support Holdings' position in the litigation filed by Powell?
2. Should a third party dealing with an agent have an obligation to ascertain whether the agent has the authority to complete the proposed act? What types of actions can a third party take to determine whether the agent has such authority?

RATIFICATION

The principal can bind himself or herself to an agent's unauthorized acts through *ratification*, that is, affirmation, of the prior acts. When an act has been ratified, it is then treated as if the principal had originally authorized it.

Ratification, like authorization, can be either express or implied. *Express ratification* occurs when the principal, through words or behavior, manifests an intent to be bound by the agent's act. For example, a principal could ratify an agent's unauthorized purchase of a truck by saying "OK" or simply by paying the bill for the vehicle. *Implied ratification*

IN BRIEF

Agent's Authority to Bind the Principal

Actual Authority (express and implied)	P → A	Principal communicates authority directly to Agent either by expressly authorizing certain acts (express) or by expressly authorizing certain acts that naturally suggest the power to do related collateral acts (implied).
Apparent Authority/ Estoppel	P → TP	Principal, by words, actions, or the position it puts the Agent in, leads Third Party to reasonably believe that the Agent has authority.
Ratification	P → TP	Principal agrees to be bound by the Agent's act even though it was not authorized at the time the Agent acted (either by words or by accepting the benefits of the act).

occurs when the principal, by silence or failure to repudiate the agent's act, acquiesces in it.

UNDISCLOSED PRINCIPAL

An agent may lawfully conceal the principal's identity or even his or her existence. This may be desirable if, for instance, the principal is trying to buy up adjacent properties in an area before news of a business venture is made public, or if the principal's wealth would cause the seller to demand a higher price. If the third party does not know the agent is acting for the principal (an *undisclosed principal*), the principal will nonetheless be bound by any contract the agent enters into with actual authority. In some states, an agent who negotiates a contract with a third party can be sued for breach of the contract, unless the agent discloses both that he or she is acting on behalf of a principal and the identity of the principal. If the agent acts without authority, the principal will not be bound; however, the agent may be personally liable on such a contract.

> **ETHICAL CONSIDERATION**
>
> Is it ethical to use an agent to enter into a contract with a third party who has made it clear that he or she is unwilling to enter into a deal with the undisclosed principal?

LIABILITY FOR TORTS OF AGENTS

A principal may be liable for not only the contracts, but also the torts of its agents. According to the doctrine of *respondeat superior,* an agent's employer will be liable for any injuries or damage to the property of another that the agent causes while acting within the scope of his or her employment. If the principal is required to pay damages to a third party because of an agent's negligence, the principal has the right to demand reimbursement from the agent.

SCOPE OF EMPLOYMENT

Many cases in this area turn on whether the employee was acting within the scope of employment. (Torts of independent contractors are discussed in a later section.) What constitutes scope of employment? Some of the relevant factors include (1) whether the employee's act was authorized by

"We—your agents, successors, licensees, and assigns—would like to share a few thoughts with you."

the employer, (2) the extent to which the employer's interests were advanced by the act, (3) whether the employer furnished the instrumentality (for example, the truck or machine) that caused the injury, and (4) whether the employer had reason to know the employee would perform the act. Even an action that violates the law may be within the scope of employment if the employee performed the act to serve the employer. For example, when a salesperson lies to a customer to make a sale, the tortious conduct is within the scope of employment because it benefits the employer by increasing sales, even though it may violate the employer's policy as well as the law.

It is often not clear whether an agent is acting within the scope of employment. Courts tend to use the term "detour" to refer to a slight deviation from the employer's business and "frolic" to refer to conduct that in no way serves the interests of the employer. Detours are deemed to be within the scope of employment, but frolics are not. The following case illustrates how difficult it can be to determine whether a deviation is a detour or a frolic.

A CASE IN POINT

SUMMARY

CASE 5.4

O'SHEA v. WELCH

UNITED STATES COURT OF APPEALS FOR THE TENTH CIRCUIT
350 F.3D 1101 (10TH CIR. 2003).

FACTS Anthony Welch, an Osco store manager, was driving from his store to the Osco District Office to deliver football tickets from a vendor for distribution among Osco managers. Welch frequently made trips for Osco using his own car. During his drive, Welch remembered that he needed some routine maintenance on his car and made a spur of the moment decision to turn left into a service station for an estimate. Welch allegedly failed to yield in making the turn and struck John O'Shea's car. O'Shea, who was injured, filed a suit against Welch and Osco, claiming that Welch was negligent and that Osco was liable for damages under a theory of *respondeat superior.*

On cross-motions for summary judgment, the district court granted Osco's motion and denied O'Shea's motion, holding that no reasonable jury could conclude that Welch was acting within the scope of his employment. The district court did not specifically decide whether the trip to the district office was within Welch's scope of employment. Instead, the court held that it did not matter because, even if the trip had been within the scope of Welch's employment, the attempted stop at the service station was not. After Osco was dismissed from the case, a bench trial was held on the issue of damages. Welch did not present evidence or cross-examine witnesses. The court entered judgment against Welch in the amount of $1,014,503.70.

ISSUE PRESENTED Is an employee acting within the scope of his employment when he turns into a service station for nonemergency maintenance on his car while driving to deliver a vendor's gift to his employer's office?

SUMMARY OF OPINION The U.S. Court of Appeals for the Tenth Circuit began by observing that there were no Kansas cases directly on point to help define when an employee is acting within the scope of his or her authority, and that the plaintiff (O'Shea) had proposed that the court adopt the "slight deviation" rule, which has been adopted by approximately half of the states. Pursuant to this rule, a court determines "whether the employee was on a frolic or a detour; the latter is a deviation that is sufficiently related to the employment to fall within its scope, while the former is the pursuit of the employee's personal business as a substantial deviation from . . . the employment."

Observing that its research had not revealed a single jurisdiction that had considered and rejected slight deviation analysis in third-party liability cases, the court concluded that Kansas would apply the slight deviation rule to the instant case. Courts have considered the following factors in determining whether the employee embarked on a detour or on a frolic: (1) the employee's intent; (2) the nature, time, and place of the deviation; (3) the time consumed in the deviation; (4) the work for which the employee was hired; (5) the incidental acts reasonably expected by the employer; and (6) the freedom allowed the employee in performing his or her job responsibilities.

CONTINUED

Applying these factors to this case, the court found:

> [Welch's] stop for routine maintenance on a car used for business purposes could be considered enough of a mixed purpose by a jury to keep him within the scope of his employment with Osco.
>
> . . . At the time of the accident, he had not entered the service station. He was technically still on the road en route to the District Office. Because the accident occurred on this road, not at the service station, a jury could decide that Mr. Welch had not yet abandoned his employment for a personal errand at the time of the accident. It was unclear how long the estimate would have taken. However, we do know that if he had deviated at the time of the accident, the length of the deviation was only a few minutes or less.

RESULT The court remanded the issue of whether Welch was acting within the scope of his employment to the district court for trial. It also held that if Osco was found liable, it would have the opportunity to contest the damages award because it was not involved in the damages hearing.

CRITICAL THINKING QUESTIONS

1. In the classic case of *Riley v. Standard Oil Co. of New York,*[6] a child was hit and severely injured by Million, a truck driver employed by Standard Oil of New York. The driver had been instructed to drive a company truck from the Standard Oil mill to a nearby freight yard. Before leaving the mill, however, he drove to his sister's house, which was about four blocks in the opposite direction from the freight yard. After unloading some scrap wood at her house, and while driving to the freight yard, Million hit the child. Should Standard Oil of New York be liable for Million's accident? Would your answer be different if the accident had occurred on the way to Million's sister's house? What other factors might affect your answer?
2. What public policy considerations are involved in cases like this? Is it relevant that the employer is often in a better position to pay victims or insure against liability?

6. 132 N.E. 97 (N.Y. 1921).

LIABILITY FOR TORTS OF EMPLOYEES ACTING OUTSIDE THE SCOPE OF EMPLOYMENT

Even if an employee was acting outside the scope of employment, the employer may be liable for the employee's action if (1) the employer intended the employee's conduct or its consequences, (2) the employee's high rank in the company makes him or her the employer's alter ego, (3) the employee's action can be attributed to the employer's own negligence or recklessness, (4) the employee uses apparent authority to act or to speak on behalf of the employer and there was reliance upon apparent authority, or (5) the employee was aided in accomplishing the tort by the existence of the agency relationship (the *aided-in-the-agency relation theory*). The California Supreme Court used the aided-in-the-agency relation theory to hold a city liable for a uniformed police officer who used his badge of authority to persuade a woman to get into his car and then raped her.[7] In another case, however, the U.S. Court of Appeals for the First Circuit, applying Maine law, found that a trucking company was not liable for the actions of its driver, who attacked and stabbed a motorist in an incident of "road rage" that occurred while the driver was driving a tractor-trailer for the company, because his attack was not actuated by a purpose to serve the trucking company.[8]

In the following case, the U.S. Supreme Court considered whether an employer can be vicariously liable for sexual harassment by a supervisor that led to an employee's constructive discharge.

7. Mary M. v. City of Los Angeles, 814 P.2d 1341 (Cal. 1991).
8. Nichols v. Land Transp. Corp., 223 F.3d 21 (1st Cir. 2000).

A CASE IN POINT

IN THE LANGUAGE OF THE COURT

CASE 5.5

PENNSYLVANIA STATE POLICE V. SUDERS

SUPREME COURT OF THE UNITED STATES
542 U.S. 129 (2004).

FACTS In March 1998, the Pennsylvania State Police (PSP) hired Nancy Drew Suders as a police communications operator. Her three supervisors—Sergeant Easton, who was the Station Commander, Patrol Corporal Baker, and Corporal Eric Prendergast—subjected Suders to continuous harassment during her employment. For example, Easton told Prendergast, in front of Suders, that young girls should be given instructions on how to gratify men with oral sex. Easton, wearing spandex shorts, would also sit down near Suders and spread his legs wide apart. Baker made an obscene gesture in Suders's presence by grabbing his genitals and shouting out a vulgar comment. Prendergast told Suders that "the village idiot could do her job" and pounded on furniture to intimidate her.

In June 1998, Suders told the PSP Equal Employment Opportunity Officer, Virginia Smith-Elliott, that she "might need some help." Smith-Elliott gave Suders her phone number but never followed up on the conversation. Suders contacted Smith-Elliott again in August to tell her that she was being harassed and that she was afraid. Smith-Elliott told her how to file a complaint but did not tell her how to obtain the necessary form. Suders felt that Smith-Elliott was insensitive and unhelpful, and she never filed a formal complaint with the PSP.

Several times during her employment Suders had taken a computer-skills exam to satisfy a PSP job requirement. Each time she asked her supervisors about the results, they told her she had failed. One day she found her exams in a drawer in the women's locker room. Suspecting that her supervisors had never turned in her tests for grading, she removed them from the drawer. Suders's supervisors discovered that the exams had been removed and dusted the drawer where they had been stored with a theft-detection powder that turns hands blue when touched. As they expected, Suders attempted to return the exams to the drawer, and her hands turned blue. Her supervisors confronted her, handcuffed her, photographed her hands, and began to question her. Suders had prepared a letter of resignation, which she gave them soon after they detained her, but the supervisors initially refused to release her. Instead, they took her to an interrogation room, gave her a *Miranda* warning, and continued to question her. When Suders reiterated her desire to resign, they let her leave. The PSP never brought theft charges against her.

Suders sued the PSP, alleging that she had been subjected to sexual harassment and constructively discharged in violation of Title VII of the Civil Rights Act. At the close of discovery, the district court granted PSP's motion for summary judgment.

ISSUE PRESENTED Is an employer strictly liable for a supervisor's sexual harassment that results in the constructive discharge of the harassed employee?

OPINION GINSBURG, J., writing for the U.S. Supreme Court:

In [granting PSP's motion for summary judgment], the District Court referred to our 1998 decision in *Faragher v. Boca Raton*.[9] In *Faragher*, along with *Burlington Industries, Inc. v. Ellerth*,[10] decided the same day, the Court distinguished between supervisor harassment unaccompanied by an adverse official act and supervisor harassment attended by "a tangible employment action." Both decisions hold that an employer is strictly liable for supervisor harassment that "culminates in a tangible employment action, such as discharge, demotion, or undesirable reassignment." But when no tangible employment action is taken, both decisions also hold, the employer may raise an affirmative defense to liability, subject to proof by a preponderance of the evidence: "The defense comprises two necessary elements: (a) that the employer exercised reasonable care to prevent and correct promptly any sexually harassing behavior, and (b) that the plaintiff employee unreasonably failed to

CONTINUED

9. 524 U.S. 775 (1998).
10. 524 U.S. 742 (1998).

take advantage of any preventive or corrective opportunities provided by the employer or to avoid harm otherwise."

. . . .

This case concerns an employer's liability for one subset of Title VII constructive discharge claims: constructive discharge resulting from sexual harassment, or "hostile work environment," attributable to a supervisor. Our starting point is the framework *Ellerth* and *Faragher* established to govern employer liability for sexual harassment by supervisors. . . . With the background set out above in mind, we turn to the key issues here at stake: Into which *Ellerth/Faragher* category do hostile environment constructive discharge claims fall—and what proof burdens do the parties bear in such cases.

. . . .

The constructive discharge here at issue stems from, and can be regarded as an aggravated case of, sexual harassment or hostile work environment. For an atmosphere of sexual harassment or hostility to be actionable . . . the offending behavior "must be sufficiently severe or pervasive to alter the conditions of the victim's employment and create an abusive working environment." A hostile-environment constructive discharge claim entails something more: A plaintiff who advances such a compound claim must show working conditions so intolerable that a reasonable person would have felt compelled to resign. . . .

. . . .

To be sure, a constructive discharge is functionally the same as an actual termination in damages-enhancing respects. . . . But when an official act does not underlie the constructive discharge, the *Ellerth* and *Faragher* analysis, we here hold, calls for extension of the affirmative defense to the employer. . . . Absent "an official act of the enterprise," as the last straw, the employer ordinarily would have no particular reason to suspect that a resignation is not the typical kind daily occurring in the workforce. . . . Absent such an official act, the extent to which the supervisor's misconduct has been aided by the agency relation . . . is less certain. That uncertainty . . . justifies affording the employer the chance to establish, through the *Ellerth/Faragher* affirmative defense, that it should not be held vicariously liable.

RESULT The Supreme Court vacated the judgment of the court of appeals and remanded the case to the district court to determine whether an official act of the PSP gave rise to Suders's constructive discharge.

COMMENTS The Supreme Court acknowledged that the facts alleged by Suders, if true, created a sexually hostile environment. As a result of this decision, however, in order for an employer to be held liable for sexual harassment by its supervisors that results in a constructive discharge of the harassed employee, the trial court will also have to find that an official act resulted in the constructive discharge.

CRITICAL THINKING QUESTIONS

1. Based on the Supreme Court's decision, will Suders win her constructive discharge case now if the facts she has alleged are true? What act by the employer will satisfy the "official act" requirement?
2. Title VII, the federal antidiscrimination statute under which this case was filed, does not permit individual harassers—even if they are supervisors—to be held liable for their actions. Is it fair that employers are also not liable for sexual harassment by a supervisor that forces an employee to leave his or her job unless some "official act" underlies the decision to quit?

TORTS OF INDEPENDENT CONTRACTORS

The *respondeat superior* doctrine typically applies only to the actions of employees. Principals may be held liable for the torts of independent contractors only in extraordinary circumstances, usually involving highly dangerous acts or nondelegable duties. For instance, if a principal hires an independent contractor to blast boulders off its land, the principal will be liable for any injuries or damages resulting from the blast. In other words, a principal cannot avoid liability for damages resulting from ultrahazardous activities simply by contracting out the work. Similarly, the South Carolina Supreme Court ruled that a hospital could not escape liability for the medical care provided by hiring physicians as independent contractors.[11]

11. Simmons v. Tuomey Reg'l Med. Ctr., 533 S.E.2d 312 (S.C. 2000).

LIABILITY OF THE PRINCIPAL FOR VIOLATIONS OF LAW BY THE AGENT

Under the theory of ***vicarious liability***, a company can be held liable for violations of law by its employee even if a manager told the employee not to violate the law. As discussed further in Chapter 15, employers and sometimes supervisors may be criminally responsible for crimes committed by employees. The following case considers whether a corporation can be held vicariously liable under the Fair Credit Reporting Act (FCRA) for its employee's illegal use of credit records for an improper purpose.

A CASE IN POINT

CASE 5.6

SMITH V. SEARS, ROEBUCK & CO.

UNITED STATES DISTRICT COURT FOR THE SOUTHERN DISTRICT OF MISSISSIPPI
276 F. SUPP. 2D 603 (S.D. MISS. 2003).

SUMMARY

FACTS Rodney Smith married Ydonna Smith in 1996, and they divorced in 1998 after having one child. In 1999, Ydonna went to work for Sears in its retail-debt collections department where she collected debts from existing Sears account holders who were behind on their payments. In that capacity, and for that purpose, Ydonna had access to a computer and password that allowed her to use a Sears information system to obtain certain information on customers from their credit reports. At the same time, Ydonna was also trying to obtain child support payments from Rodney, but neither she nor the State of Mississippi could locate him. Ydonna used the Sears credit information system fourteen times to access Rodney's credit report in an effort to find his current address. When Rodney discovered these inquiries, he complained to Sears, which fired Ydonna for violating its policy by accessing Rodney's credit report. Rodney subsequently sued Sears to recover damages for alleged violation of the FCRA, based on Ydonna's inquiries, all of which were impermissible inquiries under the FCRA.

Sears moved to dismiss, or in the alternative, for summary judgment on the basis that it could not be held vicariously liable for Ydonna's violations of the FCRA.

ISSUE PRESENTED Is an employer liable under the Fair Credit Reporting Act for its employee's actions in obtaining a consumer credit report for an improper purpose in violation of the employer's policies?

SUMMARY OF OPINION The U.S. District Court for the Southern District of Mississippi observed that neither it nor the U.S. Court of Appeals for the Fifth Circuit had previously addressed the question whether and/or under what circumstances an employer may be held vicariously liable for its employee's violations of the FCRA, but that most courts have concluded that employers are vicariously liable for employee violations of the FCRA based on one or more common law agency principles, including apparent authority. After listing these cases and their holdings, the court concluded that it was not persuaded by them:

> Based on the rationale employed by the courts in these cases, despite an employer's best efforts to ensure compliance with the FCRA, that employer is subject to liability for the actions of any rogue employee who might manage to obtain a credit report for his own

CONTINUED

personal reasons—which is to say, short of implementing foolproof compliance procedures, there is nothing an employer can do to avoid liability.

The court stated that it could "fathom no reason why users such as Sears" should be vicariously liable under the FCRA, while the consumer reporting agencies that have primary responsibility for ensuring the sanctity of credit reports are liable only for negligent noncompliance.

The court also rejected the plaintiff's claim against Sears directly, rather than vicariously, for Sears's alleged negligence or recklessness in failing to prevent Ydonna's FCRA violations. The record established that Ydonna was given a user ID that allowed her to access information from credit reports that she needed to fulfill her job duties; she was provided personal training relating to permissible uses of the program and the information; she was expressly instructed that she was only authorized to retrieve information on existing Sears's customers and for proper purposes; and she was given copies of Sears's rules and guidelines that informed her that she was forbidden to pull credit information on any person other than Sears's account holders. She also signed a document acknowledging that the use of Sears's computer resources for anything other than company business was a terminable offense, and Ydonna admitted that she knew that accessing her ex-husband's credit report was contrary to her training and to company policy.

RESULT The court ordered that Sears's motion for summary judgment be granted.

CRITICAL THINKING QUESTIONS

1. Should Sears be strictly liable for Ydonna's actions?
2. Under the court's reasoning, under what circumstances would Sears be liable for Ydonna's actions?

GLOBAL VIEW

Efforts to Create International Agency Principles

Although commercial transactions are increasingly transnational in nature, the law of agency differs from country to country. The absence of a uniform law of agency can lead to misunderstandings between businesses, as the following example illustrates:

> A U.S. importer (P) instructs her agent (A) in the Netherlands to purchase goods from a manufacturer (TP) located in China. P grants A authority to enter into a contract between P and TP. A concludes the contract with TP, but A does not disclose the fact that he is acting on behalf of P because A does not want TP to bypass him and deal directly with P in future transactions.

Will the relationship between P and A be governed by U.S. or Dutch law? Which law applies to the relationship with TP? The answers to these questions are important because U.S. and Dutch agency law differ in important ways. Under Dutch law, TP has rights only against A unless it was or should have been clear to TP that A was only acting as an agent. Under U.S. law, however, the undisclosed principal doctrine allows TP to sue either A or P on the contract.

Because agency principles are deeply embedded within the common law and civil law principles of each country, most countries have been reluctant to agree to adopt new agency rules to govern transnational transactions. In 1978, the members of the Hague Convention[12] drafted a Convention on the Law Applicable to Agency.

CONTINUED

12. Formed in 1893, the Hague Conference on Private International Law is the preeminent organization in the area of private international law. It has pursued its purpose—to "work for the progressive unification of the rules of private international law"—by creating and assisting in the implementation of multilateral conventions that promote the harmonization of conflict-of-law principles in diverse subject matters within private international law. Sixty-seven countries, including the United States and all members of the European Union, are currently members of the Hague Convention.

The Convention did not provide for a set of agency rules that were detached from the national legal systems, but rather provided a set of principles to guide which country's agency laws should apply to transnational transactions. Although the Convention entered into force in 1992, only four countries (Argentina, France, the Netherlands, and Portugal) have signed it.

In 1983, the International Institute for the Unification of Private Law (UNIDROIT) adopted a Convention on Agency in the International Sale of Goods.[13] Unlike the Hague Convention, the UNIDROIT Convention adopted a uniform set of rules that apply to all covered transactions. The UNIDROIT Convention has never entered into force, however. It requires ten ratifications, but as of 2008, there were only nine (Chile, France, the Holy See, Italy, Mexico, Morocco, the Netherlands, South Africa, and Switzerland).

Unable to obtain support for legislation creating a single set of agency rules for transnational transactions, the Commission on European Contract Law, also known as the Lando-Commission, initiated a project to achieve a European Union–wide uniform legal basis for contract law, known as the Principles of European Contract Law (PECL).[14] Among other things, the PECL attempts to harmonize the laws of agency of European countries. Chapter 3 of the PECL deals with "Authority of Agents." Following the civil law model, it distinguishes between direct and indirect representation.

The PECL rules for *direct representation* apply when an agent acts in the name of a principal pursuant to express, implied, or apparent authority, whether or not the principal's identity is revealed at the time the agent acts or is to be revealed later. In such a case, the agent's acts bind the principal and the third party directly, and the agent is not bound to the third party. If the agent fails to identify the principal's identity within a reasonable time after a request by the third party, however, the agent will become bound by the contract. When an agent exceeds its authority, its acts are not binding on the principal and the third party.

The PECL rules for *indirect representation* apply when an intermediary acts on instructions and on behalf of, but not in the name of, a principal, or when the third party does not know or have reason to know that the intermediary is acting as an agent. In these cases, the intermediary's acts bind the intermediary and the third party. The principal and the third party are bound to each other only if (1) the intermediary becomes insolvent or (2) the intermediary commits, or prior to the time of performance it is clear that it will commit, a fundamental nonperformance toward the principal or the third party.[15]

The PECL is a private initiative and does not have the authority of national, supranational, or international law. Nonetheless, it is the Lando-Commission's intent that the PECL provisions will provide a basis for a European law of agency in the future. Even today, parties to a transnational agency relationship may agree that their contract is to be governed by the PECL. Courts and arbitrators will honor this choice, with the same effect they give an ordinary choice-of-law clause, as long as the law of the forum state allows the parties to choose the PECL as governing law. Alternatively, the parties may incorporate the PECL into the body of the contract. Finally, as with the American Law Institute's (ALI's) Restatements in the United States, the Lando-Commission hopes that the judiciary will begin to use the PECL when they are called to decide transnational contract cases involving agency issues.

13. UNIDROIT is an independent intergovernmental organization located in Rome. Its purpose is to study needs and methods for modernizing, harmonizing, and coordinating private, and in particular, commercial law between countries and groups of countries. It was established in 1926 as an auxiliary organ of the League of Nations. After the demise of the League, it was re-established in 1940 on the basis of a multilateral agreement, the UNIDROIT statute. It currently has sixty-one member countries from five continents.

14. The work of the Lando-Commission is similar to the American Law Institute, a private organization of lawyers, judges, and scholars that works on a systematic set of legal rules, known as Restatements, common to all states of the United States. The Lando-Commission explicitly refers to the Restatements as a model in the introduction to Part 1 of the PECL, and the PECL has been referred to as the "European Restatements."

15. PECL Article 8:103 states that a nonperformance of an obligation is fundamental if "(a) strict compliance with the obligation is of the essence of the contract, or (b) the non-performance substantially deprives the aggrieved party of what it was entitled to expect under the contract, unless the other party did not foresee and could not reasonably have foreseen the result, or (c) the non-performance is intentional and gives the aggrieved party reason to believe that it cannot rely on the other party's future performance."

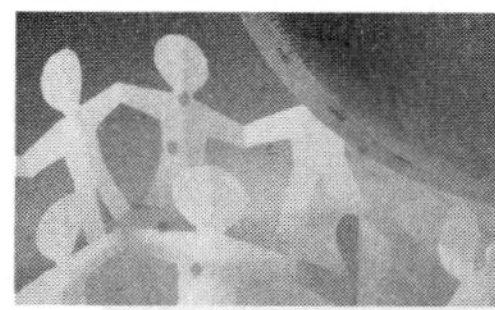

THE RESPONSIBLE MANAGER

WORKING WITH AGENTS

The relationship between a manager and his or her employer is one of trust. As an agent, a manager owes the employer fiduciary duties, which are most often summarized as the duty of care, the duty of obedience, and the duty of loyalty. The duty of care requires a manager to avoid grossly negligent, reckless, or intentional behavior that would harm the company. Rarely will an act of simple negligence be treated as a breach of fiduciary duty. The duty of obedience requires the manager to follow his or her employer's reasonable orders. The duty of loyalty imposes more complex obligations. It requires a manager to avoid self-dealing or for-profit activity that competes with the employer's business. In other words, a manager has a duty to act solely for the benefit of his or her employer in all matters related to its business. This duty includes an obligation to notify the employer of all relevant facts—all that the agent knows, the principal should know.

A manager must be concerned with the scope of authority granted to the company's workers and the company's potential liability for the actions of those workers. Perhaps the most determinable aspect of this relationship is whether the worker is deemed an employee or an independent contractor. A manager may prefer to label workers as independent contractors rather than employees for several reasons—for instance, lower tax and benefits costs or reduced exposure to liability. The manager should be aware, however, that legally the status of workers will be determined by the manner in which they are used, not by the label written into the employment agreements.

Once a manager has hired an agent, the manager must be careful to define the scope of the agent's authority. If the manager does not do this, he or she may find, for example, that a purchasing agent has inadvertently been given the apparent authority to bind the business to a large purchase of supplies, above the actual needs of the business. A manager can help avoid scope-of-authority problems by making explicit, unambiguous statements to third parties that specify the limits on an employee's ability to enter into a binding contract. When using an employee or other agent to deal with third parties, a manager must also monitor transactions to avoid conduct that might legally ratify an otherwise unauthorized agreement entered into by the agent.

The manager should ensure that the work environment and the machines and other equipment used in the business are safe. He or she should also stress to the employees the importance not only of complying with the law, but also of being concerned about safety and ethical behavior. These concerns pertain mostly to the duties owed by employers to their employees. But employers may owe similar duties even to workers properly termed independent contractors, depending on where the independent contractor works and how much control the employer exerts over that work.

Finally, an employer must be concerned about liability for the wrongdoing of its workers. Because the employer will be liable for those torts of employees that are committed within the scope of employment, a manager should attempt to decrease the risk of such vicarious liability by defining the employees' scope of employment as narrowly as possible. In light of an employer's potential liability under the aided-in-the-agency relation theory for acts outside the scope of employment, managers should exercise particular care when giving an employee authority that could be misused. Managers should ensure both that the employee is trustworthy and that any persons under the employee's control have the ability to complain to someone other than the supervisor. Because a company cannot avoid liability for injuries caused while it is engaged in an ultrahazardous activity, even if it is working through an independent contractor, managers should ensure that the company has adequate liability insurance. Finally, as discussed in Chapter 15, employers may be responsible for the criminal acts of employees. For example, if an employee violates an industry-related regulation during the normal course of employment, the employer could be held vicariously liable. In some situations, the supervising manager may be liable as well.

Although having a policy against illegal practices may not insulate the employer and its owner from civil liability for criminal acts of its lower-level employees, it reduces the chance the employees will break the law in the first place. It also reduces the likelihood that punitive damages will be asserted against the employer and its owner.

A Manager's Dilemma

Putting It into Practice

How Far Should a Company Go When It Suspects a Breach of Fiduciary Duty?

In 2000, Iron Mountain bought its chief competitor, Pierce Leahy Corporation, for $1.2 billion in stock and debt. Peter Pierce, president of Pierce Leahy, became president of Iron Mountain's main operating unit and was elected to its board of directors. Pierce also signed a noncompete agreement in which he agreed not to "own, manage, engage in, participate in, provide advice to, be employed by [or] have a financial interest in" any records storage business for five years after termination of his employment with Iron Mountain. Four months after the merger, Iron Mountain fired Pierce, but he remained on the board of directors. After Pierce's termination, Iron Mountain heard rumors that Pierce was competing; at the same time, several Pierce Leahy managers left Iron Mountain without disclosing their future plans. Iron Mountain hired a private investigator to stake out Pierce. A consultant to Iron Mountain reported that Pierce's sister and his son had provided funding for Sequedex, a competitive start-up records storage business.

At about the same time, Thomas Carr, a business partner of Pierce in Logisteq, a trucking and warehouse business, contacted Iron Mountain shortly after Pierce removed Carr as Logisteq CEO (apparently, Carr had been indicted on federal fraud charges of aiding a money-laundering scheme). Carr informed Iron Mountain that three of Logisteq's employees were secretly working at Sequedex; these employees subsequently denied in depositions that they worked for Sequedex. With Iron Mountain's knowledge, Carr began recording his conversations with Pierce to obtain documentation for his claims, and Iron Mountain's lawyers arranged to give Carr $50,000 to help him fund a lawsuit he had filed against Pierce. In March 2002, Iron Mountain sued Pierce and Sequedex, alleging that Pierce had violated his noncompete, breached his duty as an Iron Mountain director, and misappropriated trade secrets. Although Sequedex managed to sign contracts with some of Iron Mountain's customers, after Iron Mountain fought back, Sequedex received no revenue from these contracts.

In August 2002, Sequedex closed its doors. At about the same time, Logisteq filed for bankruptcy protection and loaded its records onto a truck trailer at a storage lot. Six months later, Carr's lawyer found out where the trailer was. Days later, a trucking company operator who was informally helping Carr and Iron Mountain phoned Iron Mountain's law firm to say he had the trailer. After Iron Mountain's lawyer traveled to New Jersey to inspect the trailer's contents and arrange to have them copied, the trucking company operator sent the trailer back to the lot. Although Pierce claimed at the arbitration that the trailer had been stolen and broken into, the operator said it was all a mistake.[16] Did Pierce's alleged activities subsequent to his termination constitute a breach of the fiduciary duty he owed to Iron Mountain as its director? Was Iron Mountain's alleged response to these activities legal? Was it ethical?

16. David Armstrong, *Executive Privilege: What Does a Noncompete Pact Truly Bar? Nasty Row Sorts It Out*, WALL ST. J., June 14, 2004, at A1.

Inside Story

HP DISCOVERS CORPORATE SPYING IS AN ULTRAHAZARDOUS ACTIVITY

Corporate demand for private investigative services has grown steadily since the 1980s. Several Hollywood notables had used the services of Anthony Pellicano, a private investigator (PI) who was indicted by federal prosecutors in Los Angeles in February 2007 for illegal wiretapping. In 2000, Oracle acknowledged that it had hired detectives who attempted to obtain the trash of a think tank that had defended the aggressive business practices of Oracle's archrival, Microsoft Corporation. Companies that hire PIs generally share three characteristics: (1) they are desperate to obtain sensitive information, (2) they have been unable to obtain the information through ordinary means, and (3) they often feel that the targets of their investigation have been fighting dirty.[17] Companies typically subcontract their investigative work to independent PI firms. One of

CONTINUED

17. Michael Orey, *Corporate Snoops*, BUSINESSWEEK.COM, Oct. 9, 2006, http://www.businessweek.com/magazine/content/06_41/b4004008.htm.

the benefits of subcontracting the work is that it should shield the company from liability because employers are not liable for torts committed by an independent contractor, unless the contractor engages in an ultrahazardous activity. The recent experience of Hewlett-Packard (HP) has made it clear, however, that both the companies and their management may be held liable, legally and in the court of public opinion, for the acts of independent PIs.

By 2005, HP, a $90 billion publicly held company that describes itself as demonstrating a "commitment to uncompromising integrity,"[18] had been troubled by leaks of confidential information for several years. The leaks became a subject of increased concern for Patricia Dunn, chair of the board of directors, when an unidentified person leaked the board's selection of Mark Hurd as CEO to replace Carly Fiorina. The leak caused Hurd to reconsider whether he would take the job, and last-minute negotiations were required to allay his concerns. Frustrated by these and other leaks that suggested a top-level insider was the source, Dunn hired a Boston-based PI, Ron DeLia, to find the source of the leaks. Dunn named the investigation Project Kona because she was vacationing in Hawaii at the time.

Two months later, Dunn mailed HP general counsel, Ann Baskins, a seven-page report from DeLia. The report discussed phone record searches and an investigative technique known as "pretexting," whereby a person pretends to be someone else, typically over the phone, in order to obtain information. DeLia later recalled that Baskins was curious about pretexting and concerned about its legality. When Baskins asked DeLia whether pretexting was lawful, DeLia replied that he was aware of no laws that made it illegal or of any criminal prosecutions for pretexting. E-mails showed that pretexting continued through August 2005 when Anthony Gentilucci, the manager of HP Global Security investigations, reported that the investigators still had not discovered the source of the leaks.

When confidential information about a potential HP acquisition was leaked to CNET Networks in January 2006, HP initiated a new investigation, dubbed Kona II. Kevin Hunsaker, the senior HP counsel assigned to the investigations, reported regularly to both Baskins and Dunn. On several occasions, Baskins asked Hunsaker to explore the legality of pretexting further. In response, Hunsaker had several e-mail and phone conversations with DeLia, who continued to assure him that pretexting was legal. Hunsaker also engaged in approximately one hour of online legal research himself. At separate times, DeLia and Gentilucci consulted DeLia's outside attorney, John Kiernan (with whom DeLia shared office space), who confirmed that pretexting was not a crime.

On March 10, 2006, Hunsaker sent a draft report to Dunn, Baskins, and Hurd. It identified board member and renowned physicist George Keyworth II as the source of the leaks. On March 15, Baskins and Dunn told Hurd that the investigators had concluded that Keyworth was the leaker. After consulting with Larry Sonsini, HP's outside attorney, they told the directors at the May 18 board meeting that Keyworth was the leaker. Despite strong protests about how the investigation was conducted from HP director and prominent venture capitalist Tom Perkins, the board voted six to three to ask Keyworth to resign. Keyworth refused to resign, but Perkins quit in protest. On May 22, HP filed a Form 8-K with the Securities and Exchange Commission (SEC) that announced Perkins's resignation but gave no reason for his departure.

During the summer, Perkins sent a series of e-mails and letters to the HP board, in which he challenged the legality of the investigation and informed the board that he considered the 8-K filed on May 22 to be defective.[19] Unsatisfied with HP's responses, Perkins told the California Attorney General's Office, the SEC, and others about the investigation, including the pretexting. He also notified the SEC that he objected to how HP had portrayed his resignation in its 8-K filing. Facing a storm of media criticism about its actions, HP asked its outside counsel to conduct an internal investigation of the propriety of the leak investigation. The law firm's report concluded that while the use of pretexting may not have been illegal at the time, subcontractors may have used Social Security numbers while pretexting, "which more likely than not violates federal law."[20]

After the scandal continued to build steam during September, HP hired a second outside law firm to conduct another internal investigation. The company also filed a new document with the SEC that outlined the investigation and admitted that HP had spied on at least two HP employees, seven members of the HP board, and nine reporters and their relatives.

On September 8, federal prosecutors from the U.S. Attorney's Office in San Francisco contacted the company to talk about the pretexting. Staff from the House Energy and Commerce Committee called the same day to say they were interested in talking to management about the investigation. On September 12, HP announced that Dunn would step down as chair in January 2007 but would remain on the board and that

CONTINUED

18. HP Global Citizenship Report: Ethics and Compliance, *available at* http://www.hp.com/hpinfo/globalcitizenship/gcreport/ethics.html.

19. If a director sends a letter to the board detailing his or her reasons for resigning, the company must file the letter within two business days of filing the Form 8-K announcing the resignation. HP did not file Perkins's letter or otherwise amend its 8-K. Instead, Baskins wrote back that it would be "inappropriate" to change the 8-K because it was accurate when it was filed.

20. Susan Beck, *Where Will the Troubles End for Sonsini and HP?*, AM. LAW., Dec. 6, 2006, *available at* http://www.law.com/jsp/ihc/PubArticleIHC.jsp?id=1165320502955.

Keyworth would resign from the board. Keyworth and Perkins agreed not to sue HP over what happened, and the company agreed not to sue them.

Unfortunately for HP and its executives, however, the story did not end there. As more damaging details about the investigation continued to dribble out, Dunn was forced to resign from the board. HP executives and others associated with the investigation were required to appear before congressional committees that were investigating the incident. During one congressional hearing, Baskins announced her resignation and refused to answer questions, citing her Fifth Amendment rights against self-incrimination.

In October 2006, California Attorney General Bill Lockyer brought felony criminal charges against three of the employees of the PIs (DeLia, Matthew DePante, and Bryan Wagner),[21] as well as HP board member Dunn and HP employee Hunsaker. All five defendants were charged with fraudulent wire communications, wrongful use of computer data, identity theft, and conspiracy. The first three charges carried a maximum penalty of three years in prison and a fine of $10,000. The conspiracy charge carried a maximum of one year in prison and a $25,000 fine. Attorney General Lockyer had no trouble holding the HP executives responsible for illegal activities conducted by HP's subcontractors. At the time the criminal charges were announced, he stated, "The person who orchestrated these illegal practices should be held accountable, not just those who carried them out."

On May 14, 2007, Hunsaker, DeLia, and DePante pleaded no contest to misdemeanor counts in the boardroom spying case, and the court offered to dismiss the case against them if they each completed ninety-six hours of community service and paid restitution to the victims. The court dismissed the criminal case against Dunn. It also dismissed the criminal case against Wagner because he had previously pleaded guilty to two federal felony charges. Wagner faced up to five years in prison and a fine of up to $250,000.

In exchange for the California Attorney General's agreement not to file a civil action, HP agreed to pay $14.5 million to settle civil charges related to the company's investigation. Without admitting any liability, HP agreed that for five years it would (1) employ a chief ethics and compliance officer, (2) expand the role of its chief privacy officer to review HP's investigation practices, (3) expand its employee and vendor codes to ensure they address ethical standards regarding investigations, and (4) retain an expert in the field of investigations to assist the company's chief ethics officer with regard to investigations. Of the total settlement, $13.5 million funded a new state law enforcement fund to fight violations of privacy and intellectual property rights; $650,000 represented statutory damages; and $350,000 was paid to reimburse the Attorney General's Office for the costs of its investigation.

In May 2007, HP entered into a settlement agreement with the SEC concerning its federal investigation of HP's handling of Tom Perkins's resignation from the board of directors. Under the agreement, HP agreed to a cease and desist order issued by the SEC, which stated that HP should not have limited its disclosure to the fact that Perkins had resigned. Instead, HP should also have reported that Perkins had resigned because of a disagreement with its practices, and the company should have "provided a brief description of the circumstances around the disagreement."

Even then, the story was not over. In May 2007, three journalists from CNET Networks, whose private records had been scrutinized by investigators hired by HP, announced that they intended to sue HP for invasion of privacy. Counsel for the journalists indicated that the suit would seek punitive damages against HP for its actions in connection with the spy investigation. Several other reporters who were investigated also commenced settlement negotiations with HP.

The HP incident also hastened passage of a federal law, the Telephone Records and Privacy Protection Act of 2006, that made it illegal for a person to use fraud to obtain individual customer billing records and other customer information from telephone companies. The Act also prohibited the selling of such illegally obtained records. Violators of the Act face fines and up to ten years in prison. Although some argued that passage of the Act meant that pretexting was not already a violation of federal law, that was cold comfort to HP, Dunn, and the others implicated in the spying scandal.

21. DePante was the manager of the information broker in Melbourne, Florida, that DeLia hired to conduct the pretexting activities, and Wagner was the employee who actually engaged in the pretexting.

KEY WORDS AND PHRASES

actual authority 163
agency 157
agency by estoppel 157
agency by ratification 158
agent 157

aided-in-the-agency relation theory 170
apparent authority 157
click-wrap agreement 164
customary authority 164
direct representation 175
duty of care 161
duty of loyalty 160
duty of obedience 160
electronic agents 164
equal dignities rule 157
express authority 164
express ratification 167
fiduciary 159
fiduciary duty 160
implied authority 164
implied ratification 167
independent contractor 158
indirect representation 175
principal 157
ratification 167
respondeat superior 158
undisclosed principal 168
usual authority 164
vicarious liability 173

Questions and Case Problems

1. Singer was employed by General Automotive Manufacturing Company (GAMC) as its general manager from 1953 until 1959. He had worked in the machine-shop field for more than thirty years and enjoyed a fine reputation in machine-shop circles.

   GAMC was a small concern with only five employees and a low credit rating. Singer attracted a large volume of business to GAMC and was invaluable in bolstering the company's credit rating. At times, when collections were slow, Singer paid the customer's bill to GAMC and waited for his own reimbursement until the customer remitted. Also, when work was slack, Singer would finance the manufacture of unordered parts and wait for recoupment until the stockpiled parts were sold. Some parts were never sold, and Singer personally absorbed the loss on them.

   While working for GAMC, Singer set up his own sideline operation, in which he acted as a machinist–consultant. As orders came in to GAMC through him, Singer would decide that some of them required equipment GAMC lacked or that GAMC could not do the job at a competitive price. For such orders, Singer would give the customer a price, then deal with another machine shop to do the work at a lower price, and pocket the difference. Singer conducted his operation without notifying GAMC of the orders that it (through Singer) did not accept.

   Contending that Singer's sideline business was in direct competition with its business, GAMC sued Singer for breach of fiduciary duty. What result? What were Singer's duties to GAMC as its agent? Was Singer's operation of a sideline business ethical? Would it have been ethical had he disclosed it to his GAMC superiors? [*General Automotive Manufacturing Co. v. Singer,* 120 N.W.2d 659 (Wis. 1963).]

2. NTG Telecommunications, which was interested in purchasing a computer network for its office, received a promotional letter from IBM regarding IBM's PC Server 310, Small Business Solution, a computer network server designed for and marketed to small businesses. The letter stated: "When you're ready to get down to business, give us a call. . . . We'll give you the name of the IBM business partner nearest you, as well as answer any questions you might have." The Small Business Solution was available only through an IBM business partner, which is an entity authorized to resell IBM products.

   Jud Berkowitz, president of NTG, contacted Frank Cubbage of Sun Data Services, an IBM business partner, regarding the Small Business Solution. Berkowitz decided to purchase the Small Business Solution after being informed by Cubbage that it was compatible with Windows 95, the operating system installed on each of the networked computers. After he installed the server, NTG started having serious computer problems, which were not resolved until NTG replaced PerfectOffice (which was sold as part of the Small Business Solution) with Lotus Smart Suite. Berkowitz sued IBM for fraud based in part on Cubbage's representation that the Small Business Solution was compatible with Windows 95. IBM argued that Cubbage's statement could not be attributed to it because a formal licensing or dealership agreement does not create an agency relationship. How should the court rule? [*NTG Telecommunications, Inc. v. IBM, Inc.,* 2000 U.S. Dist. LEXIS 6279 (E.D. Pa. May 8, 2000).]

3. Foley Company was the general contractor on a construction site, and All Temp was a subcontractor on the site. Foley and All Temp entered into a construction contract pursuant to which All Temp agreed to name Foley as an additional insured on its liability insurance policy with

Scottsdale Insurance Company, its carrier. At the time Foley was added to the Scottsdale policy, Scottsdale's general agent, MCI, was authorized to issue certificates of insurance with binding authority for Scottsdale, but Scottsdale prohibited MCI from delegating this authority without Scottsdale's written consent. Despite this prohibition, MCI informed its agent, CLC, that CLC could issue certificates naming general contractors, like Foley, on the All Temp policy, subject to MCI's approval, as long as doing so did not increase Scottsdale's risk. CLC subsequently issued a certificate of insurance to Foley. Scottsdale did not learn that CLC had issued the certificate until after Bryant was fatally injured at the Foley construction site. Rather than canceling All Temp's policy when it learned about the certificate, Scottsdale continued to renew the policy for three years. Subsequently, Bryant's heirs successfully recovered damages in an action against All Temp and Foley. Foley then sued Scottsdale for indemnification, and Scottsdale sought indemnification from MCI and CLC on the basis that MCI had breached the agency agreement between Scottsdale and MCI when it allowed CLC to issue a certificate of insurance to Foley. MCI and CLC moved for summary judgment against Scottsdale. Will MCI and CLC be required to indemnify Scottsdale? On what basis? [*Foley Co. v. Scottsdale Insurance Co.,* 15 P.3d 353 (Kan. App. 2000).]

4. Holabird & Root hired the Chicago law firm Sabo & Zahn to bring a collection action against a local real estate developer, Horwitz Matthews, Inc. (HM). Sabo won a $150,000 judgment against HM on behalf of Holabird and then began enforcement proceedings to collect on it. Responding to a citation to discover assets, HM provided Sabo with tax returns that were subject to a confidentiality agreement barring the attorneys from disclosing information derived from the returns to anyone outside the firm. Despite the agreement, the Sabo attorneys told about forty of HM's associates and investors by mail that HM had apportioned to itself a greater percentage of some partnership business than it was entitled to and that investors' losses had been underreported. HM sued Sabo and Holabird, claiming it was vicariously liable. Is a law firm an agent of its clients, or is it an independent contractor? Should a client be liable for torts committed by its law firm? [*Horwitz v. Holabird & Root,* 816 N.E.2d 272 (Ill. Sup. Ct. 2004), *reh'g denied,* (Oct. 4, 2004).]

5. Shortly after hiring Adams, Goodyear Tires transferred him from Houston, which was near his home, to Bryan, Texas, to work on commercial trucks. After the transfer, Adams continued to live in Houston and commuted two hours each way to work. Although Adams owned his own car, Goodyear allowed him to use a company-owned pickup truck to commute to and from work. Once or twice a week, Adams either picked up tires at the Houston shop on his way to work and delivered them to Bryan, or dropped tires from Bryan at the Houston shop on the way home. With his boss's knowledge, Adams also used the Goodyear truck during working hours to run some personal errands. After Adams left work in the company car on a Friday, he delivered tires to the Houston shop at 7 P.M., stopped for Chinese takeout, and drove to his father's house, which was about ten miles from his home, where he ate dinner, drank a few beers, and fell asleep. At 1 A.M. he woke up and drove the car to a store to buy cigarettes for his father. On the way back to his father's house, Adams fell asleep at the wheel and hit another car, severely injuring himself and the other driver. After the driver sued Adams and Goodyear, Travelers Indemnity Company (Goodyear's insurance company) refused to cover Adams or to defend or indemnify him in the lawsuit, and Adams sued Travelers and Goodyear. Travelers argued that Adams was not an "insured" under its policy with Goodyear because he did not have permission to use the truck when the accident occurred. Did Adams have implied permission to use the truck? Is Goodyear (and therefore Travelers) liable for damages arising out of the accident? If so, on what basis? [*Adams v. Travelers Indemnity of Connecticut,* 465 F.3d 156 (5th Cir. 2006).]

6. Frederick Richmond agreed to sell UForma Shelby Business Forms, Inc., a business forms printing business, to Samuel Peters pursuant to a stock-purchase agreement at a price of $3.6 million to be paid in annual installments. The amount of each installment was one-half the amount by which the profits of UForma and Miami Systems, Inc., another company owned by Peters, exceeded the 1988 and 1989 average annual profits of Miami Systems alone. The agreement stated that this formula might result in no payment being made in some years. At the time of the sale, UForma was operating at a loss. The sales agreement also stated that Peters should operate UForma according to "sound business practices." Peters paid Richmond $496,057 for 1990 and $147,368 for 1991. Because the earnings of UForma and Miami Systems were insufficient to trigger a payment under the formula in the agreement, Peters paid Richmond nothing for the years 1992 through 1995. Richmond sued Peters for breach of contract and breach of fiduciary duty, alleging that he was entitled to additional payments and that Peters had not operated UForma in accordance with sound business practices. How should the court rule? [*Richmond v. Peters,* 1998 U.S. App. LEXIS 30114 (6th Cir. 1998), *reh'g denied,* 173 F.3d 429 (6th Cir. 1999).]

7. H&R Block's tax filing service allows customers to obtain faster tax refunds in two ways: (1) the customer can pay $25 for H&R Block to file the return with the Internal Revenue Service electronically, in which case the customer will receive the refund in two weeks; or (2) if the customer wants the funds even faster, H&R Block can arrange a loan from a third-party bank in the amount of the customer's refund through its Rapid Anticipation Loan (RAL) program. H&R Block benefited financially in at least one way, and potentially in as many as three ways, from each RAL. First, H&R Block received a "license fee" of $3 to $9 for every RAL referred to a lending bank. Second, its affiliate, H&R Block Financial, purchased about one-half of the RALs from lender banks. Third, under an arrangement with Sears, Roebuck & Co., H&R Block encouraged RAL customers to cash their checks at Sears and received a fee equal to 15 percent of the check-cashing fee that Sears charged for cashing the loan checks. H&R Block did not disclose its financial participation in the RAL program to its customers. Joyce Green filed a class-action suit on behalf of all Maryland customers who obtained RAL bank loans, claiming, among other things, that H&R Block had breached its fiduciary duty by failing to disclose the benefits it received from the lending institutions to which it referred its customers. What arguments will Green make? What arguments will H&R Block make in its defense? Could H&R Block have added language to its customer contracts to ensure that it would not owe any fiduciary obligations to its customers? Even if H&R Block is found not to have a fiduciary obligation to its customers, was it ethical for H&R Block to receive fees for the RAL program and not disclose them to its customers? [*Green v. H & R Block, Inc.*, 735 A.2d 1039 (Md. Ct. App. 1999).]

8. The plaintiffs were models in a "fitness fashion show," featured as part of the Working Women's Survival Show exhibition at a convention center in St. Louis, Missouri. B.P.S., doing business as Wells Fargo Guard Service, had contracted with the city to provide guards at the center. Security arrangements at the convention center included a number of television surveillance cameras scattered around the center, which were monitored on small screens in a central control room. The direction in which each camera was pointing could be adjusted manually or automatically in the control room. The control room also had a large screen that the guards could use to view the images from the cameras or to monitor what was being taped on the VCR. The purpose of having the VCR was to enable the guards to videotape suspicious activities. The Wells Fargo guards were told to practice taping on the VCR.

   Promoters for the Working Women's Survival Show had a makeshift curtained dressing area set up near the stage for the models in the fashion show. Unbeknownst to the models, the dressing area was in a location that could be monitored by one of the surveillance cameras. That fortuity was discovered by two Wells Fargo guards, Rook and Smith. Rook had the rank of captain at Wells Fargo, denoting supervisory capacity, though there was testimony that when he worked in the control room, he had no supervisory authority. Another supervisor with disputed supervisory authority, Ramey, walked by the control room and saw the guards using the large screen to view women in a state of undress. Ramey said that he thought the guards were watching pornographic tapes that they had brought to work. (There was testimony that the guards watched their own pornographic tapes in the control room.) Either Smith or Rook (each accused the other) focused the camera on the plaintiffs and taped them as they were changing clothes for the fashion show. Is Wells Fargo Guard Service liable for the unauthorized actions of its agents, even if those actions were done for reasons of personal pleasure rather than for work? [*Does v. B.P.S. Guard Service, Inc., d/b/a Wells Fargo Guard Service,* 945 F.2d 1422 (8th Cir. 1991).]

Administrative Law

INTRODUCTION

Importance of Administrative Agencies

Administrative law concerns the powers and procedures of administrative agencies, such as the Internal Revenue Service (IRS), which collects taxes, and the Securities and Exchange Commission (SEC), which regulates the securities markets. The activities of administrative agencies affect nearly everyone, frequently on a daily basis. Administrative agencies set limits on pollution and emissions and regulate disposal of hazardous waste. They regulate radio and television, food and drugs, and health and safety. By working with administrative agencies, managers can help shape the regulatory environment in which they do business. For example, Vonage Holdings and other Voice over Internet Protocol phone companies helped their fledgling industry get off the ground when they persuaded the Federal Communications Commission not to impose the same burdensome universal access requirements applicable to intrastate landlines.[1]

Federal and state administrative agencies solve practical problems that cannot be handled effectively by the legislatures or courts. Agencies make rules to effectuate legislative enactments; they resolve conflicts by formal adjudication, a courtlike proceeding; they carry out informal discretionary actions; and they conduct investigations regarding compliance with specific laws and regulations. Although usually part of the executive branch, administrative agencies can rightly be called a fourth branch of government.

Failure to comply with applicable regulations can result in the revocation of licenses and permits and in the imposition of stiff fines. In 2007, BP Products North America agreed to pay a total of $287 million in fines to the U.S. Environmental Protection Agency, the U.S. Commodity Futures Trading Commission, and the U.S. Department of Justice for violating regulations under the Clean Air Act, the Clean Water Act, and the Commodity Exchange Act.[2] BP was also forced to pay more than $80 million in restitution to affected parties and to make more than $400 million worth of safety improvements. Even venerable humanitarian organizations are not immune from regulatory constraints. The Food and Drug Administration fined the American Red Cross a combined $9.9 million in two separate 2007 actions for failing to comply with federal blood safety laws.[3]

1. Yuki Noguchi, *FCC Asserts Role as Internet Phone Regulators,* WASH. POST, Nov. 10, 2004, at E1. FCC Chair Michael K. Powell declared, "This landmark order recognizes that a revolution las occurred. Internet voice services have cracked the 19-century mold to the great benefit of consumers." *Id. See also* Vonage Holdings Corp. v. Minn. PUC, 394 F. 3d 568 (8th Cir. 2004) (upholding an injunction prohibiting Minnesota from imposing common carrier telecommunications regulation upon Vonage).

2. Press Release, U.S. Commodity Futures Trading Comm'n, BP Agrees to Pay a Total of $303 Million in Sanctions to Settle Charges of Manipulation and Attempted Manipulation in the Propane Market (Oct. 25, 2007), *available at* http://www.cftc.gov (last visited Nov. 18, 2007); Press Release, U.S. Envtl. Protection Agency, BP to Pay Largest Criminal Fine Ever for Air Violations (Oct. 25, 2007), *available at* http://www.epa.gov.

3. *More Trouble at the Red Cross,* ST. LOUIS POST-DISPATCH, Nov. 30, 2006, at C10.

CHAPTER OVERVIEW

This chapter discusses the various ways in which administrative agencies operate and addresses the key principles of administrative law. Constitutional issues include separation of powers, delegation of authority, and the protections afforded by the Bill of Rights. Issues arising from the judicial review of agency actions include the doctrines of ripeness and exhaustion of administrative remedies. Doctrines that limit the decision-making power of agencies include the principles that agencies are bound by their own rules and that they must explain the basis for their decisions. We also explain how to find the rules of a particular agency and how to obtain documents from the government.

HOW ADMINISTRATIVE AGENCIES ACT

An administrative agency functions in four primary ways: making rules, conducting formal adjudications, taking informal discretionary actions, and conducting investigations.

MAKING RULES

Congress and the state legislatures frequently lack the time, human resources, and expertise to enact detailed regulations. Sometimes issues are so politically sensitive that elected officials lack the will to make the tough decisions. In such cases, the legislature will often pass a law setting forth general principles and guidelines and will delegate authority to an administrative agency to carry out this legislative intent. The agency will then follow a three-step procedure to promulgate appropriate rules or regulations.

Notice to the Public

First, the administrative agency gives notice to the public of its intent to propose a rule. Generally, the agency publishes the proposed rule and gives the public an opportunity to submit written comments. Comment letters are helpful to an agency and can influence the final rule. A comment letter usually (1) identifies the person that is concerned, (2) explains why that person is concerned, (3) suggests a specific change in the language of the proposed rule, and (4) provides factual information to support its position.

The Mercatus Center, an independent think tank associated with George Mason University that receives funding from many sources, has been particularly successful in promoting less rigorous business regulation. Mercatus provides formal comment letters that analyze whether the costs of a proposed rule exceed the benefits, whether the rule disadvantages consumers or small businesses, and whether there are less burdensome alternatives.[4] Of forty-four regulatory change proposals Mercatus made to the Bush administration in the months following the 2000 election, twelve were implemented.[5]

Agencies may, but are not always required to, hold a formal public hearing. They always allow people to comment on proposed rules by meeting informally with or telephoning the agency personnel. If a company is particularly concerned about a proposed rule, it should both call and meet with the proposing agency about its concerns.

Evaluation

Second, the administrative agency evaluates the comments, responds to them, and decides on the scope and extent of the final rule. If the comments prompt the agency to make substantial changes in the proposed rule, the agency may publish a revised proposed rule for public comment.

Adoption

Third, the agency will formally adopt the rule by publishing it in the *Federal Register* along with an explanation of the changes. The *Federal Register* is published daily by the U.S. Government Printing Office. Rules that are not properly published there are void. The final rule will also be *codified,* that is, added to the *Code of Federal Regulations* (CFR). The CFR contains fifty titles and includes the regulations of approximately 400 federal agencies and bureaus.

The Administrative Procedure Act (APA) requires notice to the public and an opportunity to comment before a federal agency can promulgate a rule. Rules of agency procedure and general statements of policy are exempted from this requirement. The outcome of the following case hinged on the court's categorization of National Highway Traffic Safety Administration (NHTSA) comments regarding auto manufacturer recalls as guidelines or final rules. As discussed more fully below, courts have the power to review final agency actions and binding legal rules but not mere guidelines.

4. Bob Davis, *In Washington, Tiny Think Tank Wields Big Stick on Regulation,* WALL ST. J., July 16, 2004, at A1.
5. Cindy Skrzycki, *A Paper Trail Leads to a Fight,* WASH. POST, Sept. 19, 2006, at D1.

A CASE IN POINT

IN THE LANGUAGE OF THE COURT

CASE 6.1

Center for Auto Safety and Public Citizen, Inc. v. National Highway Traffic Safety Administration

United States Court of Appeals for the District of Columbia Circuit
452 F. 3d 798 (D. C. Cir. 2006).

FACTS The NHTSA administers the National Highway Traffic Safety Administration Authorization Act of 1991 (the Safety Act) and monitors manufacturer-initiated recalls. In 1998, Kenneth N. Weinstein, NHTSA's Associate Administrator for Safety Assurance, sent letters to various motor vehicle manufacturers outlining the agency's policy guidelines for regional recalls (the 1998 guidelines). The Center for Auto Safety (CAS) and Public Citizen, Inc. filed suit claiming that the guidelines violated mandates of the Safety Act and constituted a "de facto legislative rule" that was "promulgated without public notice and comment."

ISSUE PRESENTED Are the 1998 guidelines merely guidelines, or are they tantamount to a final agency action or rule requiring public notice and an opportunity for comment?

OPINION EDWARDS, J., writing for the U.S. Court of Appeals for the District of Columbia Circuit:

In order to sustain their position, CAS and Public Citizen must show that the 1998 policy guidelines either (1) reflect "final agency action," or (2) constitute a de facto rule or binding norm that could not properly be promulgated absent the notice-and-comment rulemaking required by . . . the APA.

Agency action is generally "final" and reviewable if two conditions are satisfied: First, the action must mark the "consummation" of the agency's decisionmaking process—it must not be of a merely tentative or interlocutory nature. And second, the action must be one by which "rights or obligations have been determined," or from which "legal consequences will flow."

In determining whether an agency has issued a binding norm or merely an unreviewable statement of policy, we are guided by two lines of inquiry. One line of analysis considers the effects of an agency's action, inquiring whether the agency has "(1) impose[d] any rights and obligations, or (2) genuinely [left] the agency and its decisionmakers free to exercise discretion." The language used by an agency is an important consideration in such determinations. The second line of analysis looks to the agency's expressed intentions. This entails a consideration of three factors: "(1) the [a]gency's own characterization of the action; (2) whether the action was published in the Federal Register or the Code of Federal Regulations; and (3) whether the action has binding effects on private parties or on the agency."

As the case law reveals, it is not always easy to distinguish between those "general statements of policy" that are unreviewable and agency "rules" that establish binding norms or agency actions that occasion legal consequences that are subject to review.

Nevertheless, the distinction between "general statements of policy" and "rules" is critical. If the 1998 policy guidelines constitute a de facto rule, as appellants claim, then they would clearly meet *Bennett's*[6] test for final agency action and . . . the APA would require the agency to afford notice of a proposed rulemaking and an opportunity for public comment prior to promulgating the rule. If the guidelines are no more than "general statements of policy," as NHTSA would have it, then they would neither determine rights or obligations nor occasion legal consequences and, thus, would be exempt from the APA's notice-and-comment requirement.

On the record here, using any of the foregoing lines of analysis, NHTSA's 1998 policy guidelines do not reflect final agency action and they do not constitute binding rules. . . . As noted above, under *Bennett*, the 1998 policy guidelines cannot be viewed as "final agency action" under . . . the APA unless they "mark the consummation of the agency's decisionmaking process" and either determine "rights or obligations" or result in "legal consequences." It is possible to view the guidelines as meeting the first part of the *Bennett* test, but not the second. The guidelines are nothing more than general policy statements with no legal force. They do not determine any rights or obligations, nor do they have any legal consequences. Therefore, the guidelines cannot be taken as "final agency action," nor can they otherwise be seen to constitute a binding legal norm.

CONTINUED

6. Bennett v. Spear, 520 U.S. 154 (1997).

There is no doubt that the guidelines reflect NHTSA's views on the legality of regional recalls. But this does not change the character of the guidelines from a policy statement to a binding rule. Indeed, the case law is clear that we lack authority to review claims under the APA "where 'an agency merely expresses its view of what the law requires of a party, even if that view is adverse to the party. '"

. . . The guidelines do not purport to carry the force of law. They have not been published in the Code of Federal Regulations. They do not define "rights or obligations." They are labeled "policy guidelines," not rules. And they read as guidelines, not binding regulations [, because the language is general and conditional.]

. . . NHTSA has not commanded, required, ordered, or dictated. And there is nothing in the record to indicate that officials in NHTSA's Office of Defects Investigation are bound to apply the guidelines in an enforcement action. The agency remains free to exercise discretion in assessing proposed recalls and in enforcing the Act. There is also nothing to indicate that automakers can rely on the guidelines as "a norm or safe harbor by which to shape their actions," which might suggest that the guidelines are binding as a practical matter. And it does not matter that agency officials have encouraged automakers to comply with the guidelines.

Our conclusion that the guidelines amount to a general statement of policy, rather than a binding rule, is further fortified by the [the fact that] . . . Associate Administrator Weinstein had no authority to issue binding regulations or to make a final determination that specified regional recalls satisfy a manufacturer's duties under the Act. And his statements regarding NHTSA's regional recall policy could not change an automaker's legal obligations under the Act.

In sum, the 1998 policy guidelines do not, as appellants claim, establish new rights and obligations for automakers. We find, instead, that they set out the agency's general policy statement with respect to regional recalls, and nothing more." The effect of the [guidelines] is to inform the public of the types of [regional recalls]" that the agency is unlikely to seek to expand. But, as the concluding paragraph in the guidelines makes clear, "there is no assurance that any such plan will" go unchallenged.

RESULT The court dismissed the claims of CAS and Public Citizen, holding that the 1998 policy guidelines were merely guidelines, not a final action or rules requiring public notice and the opportunity for comment. As a result, the court had no authority to determine whether the guidelines were consistent with the Safety Act.

CRITICAL THINKING QUESTIONS

1. Why should procedural rules and policy statements be exempt from the notice-and-comment requirements?
2. What modifications might have made the NHTSA guidelines into de facto rules requiring public notice and an opportunity for comment?

The federal government has attempted to make the regulatory process less cumbersome and time-consuming, more informal, and less vulnerable to judicial review by applying the Japanese style of negotiating with the major affected groups in an effort to obtain a concensus on the substance of new regulations. Congress facilitated this process by adopting amendments to the APA entitled the Negotiated Rulemaking Act.[7] In this process, known as *regulatory negotiations* or *reg.neg.*, an agency convenes a committee representing all of the interests that will be significantly affected by the regulation to develop a proposed rule.[8] Such committees have considered a broad range of regulatory issues, from construction safety standards for cranes and derricks to the management of dogs within the Golden Gate National Recreation Area.

7. 5 U.S.C. § 561 *et seq.*

8. Notice of Intent to Negotiate Proposed Rule on All Appropriate Inquiry, 68 Fed. Reg. 10,675, 10,677 (Mar. 6, 2003).

Historical PERSPECTIVE

From Revolutionary War Vets to Homeland Security

Administrative agencies date back to the country's earliest days. The first Congress established three administrative agencies, including one for the payment of benefits to Revolutionary War veterans. The Patent Office was created in 1790, and ten other federal administrative agencies were established before the Civil War.

At three critical junctures in U.S. history, Congress has made extensive use of administrative agencies. During the Progressive Era, from 1885 until 1914, Congress turned to agencies such as the Interstate Commerce Commission, the Federal Reserve Board, the Federal Trade Commission, and the Food and Drug Administration to solve problems involving railroads and shipping, banks, trade, and food and drugs. In response to the stock market crash in 1929 and the Great Depression that followed, Congress created many agencies to deal with the crisis and delegated broad authority to them. The Securities and Exchange Commission was given broad powers to regulate the offer and sale of securities, the brokerage industry, and the securities exchanges. Finally, during the dawn of the environmental era in the 1970s, Congress turned extensively to federal administrative agencies, especially the Environmental Protection Agency, to regulate hazardous waste disposal and restrict pollution.

Following the terrorist attacks of September 11, 2001, Congress created the Department of Homeland Security to be responsible for civilian aspects of national security. In creating the department, Congress undertook a massive reorganization of the government structure. Several longstanding agencies, including the U.S. Customs Service and the Immigration and Naturalization Service, as well as newer bodies, such as the Transportation Security Administration, were transferred under Homeland Security's oversight.[a]

a. Section 402 of the Homeland Security Act (HSA) of 2002, Pub. L. No. 107-296, 116 Stat. 2135 (Nov. 25, 2002). *See also* Department of Homeland Security Organizational Chart, *available at* http://www.dhs.gov/xlibrary/assets/DHS_OrgChart.pdf.

CONDUCTING FORMAL ADJUDICATIONS

Courts do not have the time, money, or personnel to hear all cases that might arise in the course of regulating individual and corporate behavior. Consequently, legislatures frequently give administrative agencies the responsibility for solving specific types of legal disputes, such as who is entitled to government benefits or whether civil penalties should be imposed on regulated industries.

Formal agency adjudications are courtlike proceedings that can be presided over by one or more members of the agency or by an *administrative law judge (ALJ)*. The presiding official is entitled to administer oaths, issue subpoenas, rule on offers of proof and relevant evidence, authorize depositions, and decide the case at hand.

These formal adjudications typically include a prehearing discovery phase. The hearing itself is conducted like a trial. Each side presents its evidence under oath, and testimony is subject to cross-examination. The main difference between administrative adjudications and courtroom trials is that there is never a jury at the administrative level.

An administrative agency's decision in a formal adjudication can be appealed to a court. Agency actions setting rates for natural gas or providing licenses for dams are examples of the types of cases that regularly go to court. In most instances, judicial review of an agency action is based on the *record,* that is, the oral and written evidence presented at the administrative hearing. The court's review is limited to determining whether the administrative agency acted properly based on the evidence reflected in the record. In some cases, the laws governing the administrative adjudication provide for a *de novo* (i.e., new) proceeding in court, where the entire matter is litigated from the beginning.

TAKING INFORMAL DISCRETIONARY ACTIONS

The basic role of administrative agencies is to provide a practical decision-making process for repetitive, frequent actions that are inappropriate to litigate in the courts. These *informal discretionary actions* have been called the lifeblood of administrative agencies. Common examples are the awarding of governmental grants and loans, the resolution of workers' compensation claims, the administration of welfare benefits, the informal resolution of tax disputes, and the determination of Social Security claims. Informal discretionary action also governs most applications to governmental agencies for licenses, leases, and permits, such as leases of federal lands and the registration of securities offerings.

Informal discretionary actions also include contracting, planning, and negotiation. Thus, the process of negotiating a contract with a governmental agency to supply military parts or to build bridges or highways is within the realm of administrative law. In fact, most of what governmental agencies do falls within the category of informal discretionary action.

The most noteworthy aspect of these informal actions is their lack of clear procedural rules. In court, there is a strict set of rules and procedures to be followed, and a specific person (the judge) is assigned to hear the case. In informal discretionary actions, the agency frequently has no formal procedures, such as notice to the public, opportunity to file briefs, or opportunity to submit oral testimony. Informal agency actions can lead to quick and practical problem resolution, but they can also lead to seemingly endless administrative paper shuffling.

CONDUCTING INVESTIGATIONS

Many administrative agencies have the responsibility to determine whether a regulated company or person is complying with the applicable laws and regulations. They can use their subpoena power to make mandatory requests for information, conduct interviews, and perform searches. Based on these investigations, the agencies may file administrative suits seeking civil penalty assessments, or they may go to court and seek civil and criminal penalties.

Since 1970, governmental agencies have increasingly relied on their investigatory and prosecutorial powers. ChoicePoint, Inc., which collects, analyzes, and sells consumer data, faced probes by the Federal Trade Commission (FTC) and the Securities and Exchange Commission (SEC) after it sold personal information, including names and Social Security numbers, to criminals.[9] The company paid a $15 million fine to the FTC, the largest ever levied by that body, for failing to verify the identity of more than 100 dummy corporations that purchased sensitive personal information about 163,000 individuals. The SEC investigated alleged insider trading activity in the months following the company's discovery of the error and its disclosure of that issue to the public.

The investigatory powers possessed by administrative agencies can lead to fines ranging from thousands of dollars to hundreds of millions of dollars, as well as other penalties. For example, an SEC investigation led to former Qwest Communications CEO Joseph Nacchio being ordered to pay a $19 million fine, give back another $52 million in ill-gotten investment profits, and serve six years in prison for insider trading.[10]

9. Christopher Conkey & Ann Carrns, *ChoicePoint to Pay $15 Million to Settle Consumer-Privacy Case,* WALL ST. J., Jan. 27, 2006, at A2.

ADMINISTRATIVE AGENCIES AND THE CONSTITUTION

Constitutional issues raised by the creation of administrative agencies concern separation of powers, proper delegation of authority, and the limits imposed on agency actions by the Bill of Rights.

SEPARATION OF POWERS

The U.S. Constitution provides for a legislature, an executive, and a judiciary. This division of power created a system of checks and balances to preserve liberty. It does not specifically provide for administrative agencies, thus raising the question of whether the delegation of legislative and judicial powers to an administrative agency is constitutional.

The few cases addressing this issue have upheld the constitutionality of this "fourth branch" of government. In 1856, the U.S. Supreme Court upheld the authority of the Department of the Treasury to audit accounts for money owed to the United States by customs collectors and to issue a warrant for the money owed. The Court rejected the argument that only the courts of the United States were empowered to perform such activities.[11]

In 1935, in a case involving the Federal Trade Commission, the Supreme Court explained with approval that the FTC was an administrative body created by Congress to carry out legislative policies in accordance with a prescribed legislative standard and to act as a legislative or judicial aide by performing rulemaking and adjudicatory functions. It found no constitutional violation in allowing an administrative agency to perform judicial and legislative functions. The Court did not, however, provide much explanation as to why this was permissible.[12] Justice Jackson subsequently stated:

10. Carrie Johnson, *Former Qwest Chief Gets 6-Year Prison Term; Nacchio to Pay $71 Million in Insider-Trading Case,* WASH. POST, July 28, 2007, at D1.

11. Den *ex dem.* Murray v. Hoboken Land & Improvement Co., 59 U.S. 272 (1856). *See also* Noriega-Perez v. United States, 179 F.3d 1166 (9th Cir. 1999) (upholding the authority of an administrative law judge to impose a civil fine for violations of the Immigration and Nationality Act).

12. Humphrey's Ex'r v. United States, 295 U.S. 602 (1935).

> [Administrative bodies] have become a veritable fourth branch of the Government which has deranged our three-branch legal theories as much as the concept of a fourth dimension unsettles our three dimensional thinking. . . . Administrative agencies have been called quasi-legislative, quasi-executive and quasi-judicial, as the occasion required. . . . The mere retreat to the qualifying "quasi". . . is a smooth cover which we draw over our confusion as we might use a counterpane to conceal a disordered bed.[13]

The Supreme Court upheld the cross-branch nature of administrative agencies in its decision in *National Cable & Telecommunications Ass'n v. Brand X Internet Services.*[14] The majority reversed a lower court ruling, thereby permitting a Federal Communications Commission (FCC) interpretation of a statutory term to override the Ninth Circuit's existing interpretation of the same term. The Court held that the FCC's interpretation was authoritative because Congress had delegated to agencies the power to interpret ambiguous language in statutes within their jurisdiction. The Court reasoned that this delegation is not discarded merely because a court has had occasion to interpret the language before the proper agency has done so.[15] In his dissent, Justice Scalia scorned the decision as "inventing yet another breathtaking novelty: judicial decisions subject to reversal by Executive officers"[16] and raised a host of problematic consequences that could stem from permitting agencies to simultaneously ignore prior court interpretations and construct regulations.[17]

In *INS v. Chadha,*[18] the Supreme Court struck down a statute that gave either house of Congress the right to pass a resolution overturning a decision by the Immigration and Naturalization Service (INS) suspending the deportation of a deportable alien. The Supreme Court reasoned that the resolution passed by the House of Representatives revising the INS decision was essentially legislative. As such, it required passage by both houses of Congress and presentment to the president for signature or veto.

The Patriot Act

Libertarians claim that the greatest threat to the separation-of-powers doctrine in American history is embodied in the Patriot Act.[19] Passed by Congress soon after the terrorist attacks on the World Trade Center and the Pentagon on September 11, 2001, the Patriot Act gave the executive branch broad new powers in the name of fighting terrorism, while limiting traditional checks on those powers. For example, in the past if a federal agent wanted to conduct a search, he or she had to obtain a search warrant from a judge who was responsible for determining whether the reasons proffered by the government warranted the invasion of personal privacy. Now, under Section 215 of the Patriot Act, if an agent of the Federal Bureau of Investigation (FBI) investigating a terrorist threat wants to search personal belongings, then, "upon an application made pursuant to [Section 215], the judge *shall* enter [the order]." This makes judicial review of the proposed search a matter of form over substance.

Conservatives argue that this legislation does not expand any powers but merely streamlines the process to cut through bureaucratic red tape that can cause dangerous delays in the fight against terrorism. The libertarian Cato Institute has called the Act an insidious, reactionary piece of legislation capable of completely destroying the separation-of-powers doctrine that has served as one of the bedrocks of American government.[20]

The George W. Bush administration has exacerbated the separation-of-powers problem by repeatedly flouting congressional authority by attaching signing statements to amendments of the Patriot Act.[21] A *signing statement* is a document attached to a bill at its execution describing the President's interpretation of that law. In March 2006, President Bush signed a bill intended to help Congress ensure that executive branch agencies such as the FBI are not abusing their Patriot Act–based powers. Under that law, the Justice Department is required to keep records about its use of certain of those powers and to report that information to Congress. In the correlating signing statement, the President reserved the right to "withhold the information if he decided that disclosure would 'impair foreign relations, national security, the deliberative process of the executive, or the performance of the executive's constitutional duties.'" The statement continued: "The executive branch shall construe the provisions . . . that call for furnishing information to entities outside the executive branch . . . in a manner consistent with the president's constitutional authority to

13. FTC v. Ruberoid Co., 343 U.S. 470, 487–88 (1952).
14. 545 U.S. 967 (2005).
15. *Id.* at 980, 982–83.
16. *Id.* at 1016 (Scalia, J., dissenting).
17. *Id.* at 1017.
18. 462 U.S. 919 (1983).
19. Adam Cohen, *Rough Justice,* TIME, Dec. 10, 2001.
20. Timothy Lynch, Cato Institute, *More Surveillance Equals Less Liberty* (Oct. 3, 2003), *available at* http://www.cato.org/dailys/10-03-03.html.
21. Information in this paragraph is drawn from Charlie Savage, *Bush Shuns Patriot Act; In Addendum to Law, He Says Oversight Rules Are Not Binding,* BOSTON GLOBE, Mar. 24, 2006, at A1.

supervise the unitary executive branch and to withhold information." The Constitution grants Congress the authority to write laws and the executive branch the duty to "faithfully execute" them. Various members of Congress have questioned whether signing statements like this signal an intent to violate provisions of laws duly enacted by Congress.

DELEGATION OF AUTHORITY

The delegation-of-authority issue concerns the nature and degree of direction the legislature must give to administrative agencies. Because Article I of the Constitution vests all legislative powers in the Congress, "when Congress confers decisionmaking authority upon agencies, *Congress* must 'lay down by legislative act an intelligible principle to which the person or body authorized to [act] is directed to conform.'"[22] The Supreme Court has refused to uphold the delegation of power to administrative agencies in only two cases. One case concerned the delegation of power regarding shipments of oil between states in excess of government-set quotas.[23] The second case concerned the delegation of authority to the president to determine codes of fair competition for various trades and industries.[24] In both cases, the Supreme Court held that although Congress was free to allow agencies to make rules within prescribed limits, Congress itself must lay down the policies and establish the standards. Both before and after these two cases, however, the Supreme Court has upheld vague standards, such as those requiring rules to be set "in the public interest," "for the public convenience, interest or necessity," or "to prevent unfair methods of competition."

LIMITS IMPOSED BY THE BILL OF RIGHTS

There is very little limit to the investigatory powers of administrative agencies. Although agencies must comply with constitutional principles protecting freedom from self-incrimination and from unreasonable search and seizure, over time these protections have been severely eroded.

Self-Incrimination

The Fifth Amendment's protection against self-incrimination does not apply to records that the government requires to be kept. Specifically, the Fifth Amendment protections do not apply to records that are regulatory in nature, are of a kind that the party has customarily kept, and have at least some public aspect to them. In addition, the Fifth Amendment's protection against self-incrimination does not apply to corporations.

Probable Cause

In carrying out their investigatory powers, administrative agencies are not required to have probable cause—that is, reason to suspect a violation—before beginning an investigation. An agency may inquire into regulated behavior merely to satisfy itself that the law is being upheld. For example, the IRS needs no specific cause to audit a company's tax returns.

Search and Seizure

In the administrative arena, the courts have largely obliterated the protection of the Fourth Amendment against unreasonable searches and seizures. Particularly for highly regulated industries, such as liquor and firearms, government regulators can conduct full inspections of property and records almost without restriction.

Right to Jury Trial

The Seventh Amendment right to a jury trial extends only to cases for which a right to trial by jury existed in common law before the enactment of the Seventh Amendment. Because administrative agencies adjudicate statutory rights that were unknown at the time the Seventh Amendment was enacted, there is no constitutional right to a jury in a formal adjudication before an administrative agency.[25]

PRINCIPLES OF ADMINISTRATIVE LAW

General principles of administrative law include choice of approach and the need for actual authority to act.

CHOICE OF APPROACH

In some cases, Congress will require the agency to enact a regulatory program and will provide a deadline for the issuance of final regulations (for an example, see Appendix K). In the absence of congressional direction, administrative agencies have a fundamental right to decide whether

22. Whitman v. Am. Trucking Ass'ns, 531 U.S. 457 (2001) (emphasis in original).
23. Panama Ref. Co. v. Ryan, 293 U.S. 388 (1935).
24. Schechter Poultry Corp. v. United States, 295 U.S. 495 (1935).
25. *See* Wickmire v. Reinecke, 275 U.S. 101 (1927); NLRB v. Jones & Laughlin Steel Corp., 301 U.S. 1 (1937).

to promulgate regulations or to proceed on a case-by-case basis.[26] The right to proceed on a case-by-case basis is necessary because an administrative agency cannot anticipate every problem it might encounter. Problems could arise that are so specialized and varying in nature as to be impossible to capture within the boundaries of a general rule.

AUTHORITY TO ACT

Administrative agencies can be compared to large corporations in size, structure, and, to some extent, function. Agencies provide benefits, sign contracts, and produce products. In the private arena, a person acting on behalf of an organization may bind the organization in accordance with not only the person's actual authority but also his or her apparent authority (concepts discussed in Chapter 5). Under the rules for government agencies, there is only actual authority.

The Supreme Court has repeatedly upheld the fundamental principle that government employees acting beyond their authority cannot bind the government. For example, in 1917, the Supreme Court held that the United States was not bound by acts of its officials who, on behalf of the government, entered into an agreement that was not permitted by law.[27] The Court rejected the argument that the neglect of duty by officers of the government was a defense to the suit by the United States to enforce a public right to protect a public interest.

The uninitiated naturally rely on the word of a government employee as to the scope of his or her authority. This is a mistake. In fact, it is incumbent upon anyone dealing with governmental agencies to make sure that the person he or she is dealing with is authorized to act and that the proposed actions are permitted by law.

This rule is intended to prevent personal actions from circumventing congressional intent and the formal process of law. Unfortunately, the rule also takes away the incentive for the government to make sure that its officials know the law and administer it properly.

JUDICIAL REVIEW OF AGENCY ACTIONS

Congress or the appropriate state legislature sets the standards for judicial review of agency actions. If the courts control agency action with too heavy a hand, an agency can grind to a halt. If too little oversight is exercised, agencies can run roughshod over individual rights. Some agency actions are not reviewable because they are within the discretion of the agency; others are mere guidelines without the force of law.[28] Most agency actions, however, are reviewable by the courts, but the basic standard of review is highly deferential to the agency. Once it has been determined that an agency has the authority to act, its actions will be given the "highest deference possible."[29]

REVIEW OF RULEMAKING AND INFORMAL DISCRETIONARY ACTIONS

Courts will generally uphold an agency's action unless it is arbitrary and capricious. Under the *arbitrary and capricious standard,* if the agency chose from among several courses of action, the court will presume the validity of the chosen course unless it is shown to lack any rational basis.

Nonetheless, courts will invalidate any regulation that is inconsistent with the statute pursuant to which the agency was acting. In *Ragsdale v. Wolverine World Wide,*[30] the U.S. Supreme Court invalidated a regulation promulgated by the Department of Labor (DOL) that gave an employee the right to an additional twelve weeks of family or medical leave if the employer failed to notify the employee that the twelve weeks of leave provided by the Family and Medical Leave Act ran concurrently with the thirty weeks of paid disability leave provided by the employer. The Court ruled that DOL regulations could not grant entitlements that extended beyond those set forth in the statute and were inconsistent with the statute's purpose. In this case, the statute's purpose was to encourage more generous employer policies, which was exactly what this employer provided.

Courts also will not defer to an agency action when Congress has not expressly delegated rulemaking authority to the agency. In *Gonzales v. Oregon,*[31] the Supreme Court ruled that the U.S. Attorney General did not have the power to determine whether physician-assisted suicide qualified as a legitimate medical practice under the Controlled Substances Act (CSA). Analyzing the language of the CSA, the Court determined that the law was intended to fight recreational drug use, not to impose federal limitations on the way controlled substances could be utilized in the course of medical care. "[W]hen Congress wants to regulate medical practice in the given scheme," wrote the Court, "it does so by explicit language in the statute," not through an "implicit" or "oblique form." As a result, the Attorney General's Interpretive Ruling

26. SEC v. Chenery Corp. , 332 U.S. 194 (1947).
27. Utah Power & Light Co. v. United States, 243 U.S. 389 (1917).
28. *See, e.g.,* Ctr. for Auto Safety and Pub. Citizen, Inc. v. NHTSA, 452 F.3d 798 (D. C. Cir. 2006) (Case 6.1).
29. United States v. Mead Corp., 533 U.S. 218 (2001).
30. 535 U.S. 81 (2002).
31. 546 U.S. 243 (2006).

prohibiting physicians from prescribing drugs to help a patient commit suicide was invalid.

Although positive actions by agencies often grab headlines, sometimes not acting at all can have just as lasting and powerful an effect. An appeals court invalidated a Federal Communications Commission rule requiring regional telephone companies—such as Verizon Communications, BellSouth Corporation, and Qwest Communications International—to lease their local networks to national telephone companies and long-distance carriers, such as MCI and AT&T, at a discounted rate.[32] Rather than appealing that ruling to the Supreme Court, the FCC, Justice Department, and Commerce Department supported it, thereby abandoning the existing FCC rule.[33] Increased competition in the phone industry spurred by nontraditional challengers, such as wireless, cable, and voice-over-Internet companies, had diminished concern over the domination of local phone service by a small number of players.[34]

REVIEW OF FACTUAL FINDINGS

An agency's factual findings are determinations that can be made without reference to the relevant law or regulation. The arbitrary and capricious standard of judicial review is not applied to the agency's factual findings. Instead, courts use a *substantial evidence standard* to review factual findings in formal adjudications. Under this standard, courts determine whether the evidence in the record could reasonably support the agency's conclusion.[35] Courts will defer to an agency's reasonable factual determinations, even if the record would support other factual conclusions. This standard of review is similar to an appellate court's review of jury verdicts. Courts acknowledge that the agency's fact finder is generally in a better position to judge the credibility of witnesses and to evaluate evidence, especially if the evidence is highly technical or scientific.

32. U.S. Telecom Ass'n v. FCC, 359 F.3d 554 (D.C. Cir. 2004).
33. Anne Marie Squeo & Almar Latour, *U.S. Sides with Bells in Battle over Local Calling,* WALL ST. J., June 10, 2004, at A1.
34. *Id.*
35. Consol. Edison Co. v. NLRB, 305 U.S. 197 (1938).

REVIEW OF STATUTORY INTERPRETATIONS

Courts will generally defer to an agency's *construction* (i.e., interpretation) of a statute within its area of expertise. This permits those with relevant practical experience to have the greatest influence in deciding how to implement a particular law. Although the Supreme Court's position on this issue has varied somewhat, its most recent cases have reinforced the rule of deference to any "reasonable" administrative interpretation of law.[36] As noted above, the Supreme Court even granted deference to agency interpretations that conflicted with prior judicial interpretations of the statutory language at issue.[37] However, if "the agency's interpretation goes beyond the limits of what is ambiguous and contradicts [language that in the Court's] view is quite clear," then the Court will invalidate the agency's policy.[38]

In the following case, the U.S. Supreme Court considered whether the Environmental Protection Agency had properly interpreted statutory language in the Clean Air Act when it concluded that it did not have the authority to enact auto emissions regulations to combat global warming by reducing the amount of greenhouse gases in the atmosphere.

36. *See, e.g.,* Chevron U.S. A. Inc. v. Natural Res. Def. Council, Inc., 467 U.S. 837 (1984).
37. Nat'l Cable & Telecomm. Ass'n v. Brand X Internet Servs., 545 U.S. 967 (2005).
38. Whitman v. Am. Trucking Ass'ns, 531 U.S. 457 (2001) ("The EPA may not construe the statute in a way that completely nullifies textually applicable provisions meant to limit its discretion.")

A CASE IN POINT

CASE 6.2

MASSACHUSETTS V. ENVIRONMENTAL PROTECTION AGENCY

UNITED STATES SUPREME COURT
127 S. CT. 1438 (2007).

SUMMARY

FACTS In 1999, a collection of nineteen private energy and environmental groups filed a rulemaking petition with the Environmental Protection Agency (EPA). Noting that the former general counsel of the EPA had confirmed that the agency had the power to regulate carbon dioxide, the groups petitioned the EPA to combat global warming by limiting "greenhouse gas emissions from new motor vehicles," including carbon dioxide, pursuant to Section 202 of the Clear Air Act (the Act).

The EPA denied the petition for two reasons. First, despite previous contrary rulings by its own attorneys, the EPA claimed that the Act did not authorize the agency to regulate carbon dioxide. Although Congress had promulgated legislation to combat climate change, it had not specifically

CONTINUED

directed the EPA to address the issue. In particular, the agency reasoned that greenhouse gases, including carbon dioxide, could not be considered "air pollutants" as the term was used in the Act. Furthermore, the EPA argued that because the Department of Transportation (DOT) already oversaw detailed fuel economy standards, crafting the EPA's own set of emissions standards would be at best superfluous and at worst create a statutory conflict. Second, even if the Act did grant the necessary authority, the EPA reasoned that the timing was not right to enact such regulations. The agency asserted that doing so would conflict with other congressional actions aimed at remediating climate change. Moreover, the EPA claimed that the link between greenhouse gases and climate change was scientifically uncertain.

A coalition of states (including Massachusetts), local governments, and private organizations sought judicial review of the agency's decision, alleging that the EPA had "abdicated its responsibility under the [Act] to regulate [auto] emissions." After the U.S. Court of Appeals for the District of Columbia Circuit ruled in the EPA's favor, the Supreme Court granted the writ of certiorari due to "the unusual importance of the underlying issue."

ISSUES PRESENTED Does the EPA have statutory authority to regulate greenhouse gas emissions from new motor vehicles? If so, are its stated reasons for refusing to do so consistent with the Clean Air Act?

SUMMARY OF OPINION As a preliminary matter, the U.S. Supreme Court ruled that the petitioners had standing to challenge the EPA's actions in court, in part because Massachusetts owned coastal land that would be lost to rising seas caused by global warming. Although EPA action to restrict greenhouse emissions would not completely solve the climate change problem, it would be an incremental step offering the state some protection. (Standing is discussed further later in this chapter.)

The Court then examined the statutory language related to the EPA's emissions regulation powers. Section 202 of the Act calls for the EPA to regulate auto emissions if the agency judges them an "air pollutant . . . which may reasonably be anticipated to endanger public health or welfare."The Act goes on to define "air pollutant" as "any physical, chemical . . . substance or matter which . . . enters the ambient air" and to define "welfare" to include effects on weather and climate. The Court determined that this statutory language was unambiguous and therefore precluded the EPA's restrictive reading of the term "air pollutant" to exclude greenhouse gases. The Court reasoned that Congress's other efforts to fight global warming gave no guidance for interpreting the Act and, in any event, did nothing to diminish the EPA's power to regulate greenhouse gas emissions under the Act. Additionally, the Court concluded that the fact that the DOT had established fuel efficiency standards in no way absolved the EPA of its statutory regulatory responsibility. Two agencies with overlapping obligations can coordinate their efforts to avoid inconsistency.

Having determined that the EPA had the authority to regulate greenhouse gas emissions, the Court then analyzed whether the agency had properly refused to do so. Under the Act, the EPA may refuse to act only if it either (1) determines that an air pollutant poses no danger to public health and welfare or (2) provides a reasonable explanation for why it is unable or unwilling to engage in making a determination on that issue. The EPA had noted the potential policy impediments to formulating a regime for limiting the emission of greenhouse gases, but it had made no statement about whether sufficient scientific information existed to determine whether carbon dioxide and other greenhouse gases posed a danger to public health and welfare. Given the EPA's failure to articulate a rationale for not reaching a determination, the EPA's actions were "arbitrary, capricious, . . . or otherwise not in accordance with law."

RESULT The Court reversed the lower court's decision and remanded the case for further proceedings. The EPA had the power to regulate greenhouse gases, and its reasons for inaction were not consistent with its responsibilities under the Clean Air Act.

CONTINUED

> **COMMENTS** The dissent acknowledged that global warming may be the most pressing environmental problem of our time, but argued that the Court cannot use that concern to usurp the discretion Congress gave the EPA to decide whether to promulgate rules governing matters within its jurisdiction. According to the dissent, the EPA was within its congressionally granted rights when it refused to regulate greenhouse gas emissions.

LIMITED REVIEW OF PROCEDURES

Absent extremely compelling circumstances, administrative agencies are free to fashion their own rules of procedure and to pursue their own methods of inquiry when discharging their broad and varied duties. A court is not free to impose on an agency its view as to what procedures the agency must follow; the court may only require the agency to comply with its own procedural rules and to conform to the requirements of the Due Process Clause.[39]

The reason for these highly deferential review standards is evident: the role of administrative agencies is to relieve the burden on the courts by having the agencies make their own adjudications. If the courts engaged in a searching inquiry of all factual questions and exercised their own judgment on policy or procedural issues, then the effectiveness of administrative agencies would be greatly diminished.

NO RIGHT TO PROBE THE MENTAL PROCESSES OF THE AGENCY

One of the most critical points of administrative law concerns the extent to which a court can inquire into the process by which an administrative agency makes its decision. This issue was one of the first decided in the administrative law arena. It was resolved in a case involving a decision of the Secretary of Agriculture that made news headlines at the end of the New Deal era.[40]

The Packers and Stockyards Act authorized the Secretary of Agriculture to determine reasonable rates for services rendered by cattle-marketing agencies. The marketing agencies of the Kansas Stockyards challenged the ultimate price set as too low. The federal district court had allowed the marketing agents to require the Secretary to appear in person at the trial. He was questioned at length regarding the process by which he had reached his decision about the rates. The interrogation included questions as to what documents he had studied and the nature of his consultations with subordinates. The Supreme Court held that this questioning into the mental processes of the Secretary was improper.

Today, formal federal review procedures limit judicial review of agency actions to the record compiled before the agency. Thus, once an administrative process is complete, there is generally no judicial opportunity to inquire into the whys and wherefores of the decision-making process. Without this shield from judicial review, agency actions would be tied up in court.

Although a court may not inquire into the decision-making process, the legislature may probe agency officials to determine why they acted as they did. In fact, Congress regularly holds oversight hearings on how agencies are administering the law. Criticism from a key member of Congress or a congressional committee can lead to newspaper headlines and prompt changes in agency policies. Congress can also use the appropriation process to withhold funds from disfavored programs and to fund favored ones.

TIMING OF REVIEW

Two judicial doctrines are designed to prevent cases from being prematurely transferred from the administrative arena to the courts: the doctrines of exhaustion of administrative remedies and of ripeness.

Exhaustion

Exhaustion of administrative remedies concerns the timing and substance of the administrative review process. The general rule is that a court will not entertain an appeal to review the administrative process until the agency has had the chance to act and the party challenging the agency's actions has pursued all possible avenues of relief before the agency. This requirement conserves judicial resources. A party is not required to exhaust all administrative avenues when that would be futile, however.

39. Vt. Yankee Nuclear Power Corp. v. Natural Res. Def. Council, Inc., 435 U.S. 519 (1978).

40. United States v. Morgan, 313 U.S. 409 (1941).

In *Harline v. Drug Enforcement Administration,*[41] the U.S. Court of Appeals for the Tenth Circuit considered when the exhaustion of remedies requirement may properly be waived due to futility. Harline brought suit in federal district court before exhausting all remedies available before the Drug Enforcement Administration (DEA). He claimed that the DEA's use of an administrative law judge employed by the DEA violated his procedural due process rights to a fair and impartial tribunal and argued that the court should waive the exhaustion requirement. The court stated that exhaustion is waivable either by the agency or at the court's discretion when the plaintiff's interest in prompt resolution is so great that it renders the doctrine of exhaustion inappropriate. As a result, courts have discretion to waive the exhaustion requirement only when (1) the plaintiff asserts a colorable (i. e., plausible) constitutional claim collateral to the substantive issues of the administrative law proceeding, (2) exhaustion would result in irreparable harm, and (3) exhaustion would be futile. Applying this test, the court concluded that Harline's general claims of due process violations were insufficient to justify waiver of the exhaustion requirement in this case.

Statutes and agency rules often provide that courts reviewing an administrative agency's action may not rule on issues that a party failed to raise with the agency.[42] In cases where the regulatory language is silent on issue exhaustion, the court will determine whether issues not previously raised should be permitted to be brought before the court by assessing whether the administrative proceedings were sufficiently adversarial in nature to draw out all of a party's arguments.[43] For example, in *Sims v. Apfel*[44] the Supreme Court held that an individual pursuing judicial review of denial of benefits by the Social Security Administration had not waived issues she had failed to raise in administrative proceedings. Juatassa Sims had applied for disability and supplemental security income benefits under the Social Security Act. An administrative law judge denied her claim, and the Social Security Appeals Council denied her request for a review of that decision. Sims filed suit in district court, contending that the ALJ (1) made selective use of the record, (2) posed defective questions to a vocational expert, and (3) should have ordered a consultative examination. The district court rejected all of these arguments. The appeals court affirmed but held that it could not consider the second and third contentions because Sims had not raised them in her request for review by the Appeals Council.

The Supreme Court reversed on the grounds that the reasons for requiring issue exhaustion were not present in Social Security proceedings. Although many administrative proceedings are adversarial, Social Security proceedings are primarily inquisitorial. The ALJ has the duty to investigate the facts and develop the arguments both for and against granting benefits. As a result, the Court ruled, the adversarial development of issues by the parties was not essential. Therefore, a party who exhausted administrative remedies available from the Social Security Appeals Council need not also exhaust issues in order to preserve judicial review of them.

Ripeness

The *ripeness* doctrine helps ensure that courts are not forced to decide hypothetical questions. Courts will not hear cases until they are "ripe" for decision. The issue of ripeness most frequently arises in pre-enforcement review of statutes and ordinances; this occurs when review is sought after a rule is adopted but before the agency seeks to apply the rule in a particular case. The general rule is that agency action is ripe for judicial review when the impact of the action is sufficiently direct and immediate as to make review appropriate.[45]

STANDING TO SUE

To obtain judicial review of a federal agency's action, the plaintiff must have *standing* to sue. Standing involves three elements. First, the plaintiff must have suffered an injury in fact, that is, an invasion of a legally protectable interest that is (a) concrete and particularized and (b) actual or imminent, not conjectural or hypothetical. Second, the injury must be fairly traceable to the challenged action. Third, it must be "likely," as opposed to merely "speculative," that the injury will be redressed at least in part by a favorable decision.[46]

In the following case, the court considered whether an "average" U.S. citizen had standing to sue the Secretary of Agriculture for policies he felt might be exposing him and the rest of the country to added health risks.

---

41. 148 F.3d 1199 (10th Cir. 1998), *cert. denied,* 525 U.S. 1068 (1999).

42. Sims v. Apfel, 530 U.S. 103, 107–08 (2000).

43. *See e.g.*, Delta Found., Inc. v. Thompson, 303 F.3d 551 (5th Cir. 2002) (holding issue exhaustion not required by any statute or regulation governing Health and Human Services proceedings).

44. 530 U.S. 103 (2000).

45. *See* Abbott Lab. v. Gardner, 387 U.S. 136 (1967) (pre-enforcement review of FDA generic drug-labeling rule was appropriate because the issue was purely legal, the regulations represented final agency action, and the impact of the rules was direct and immediate).

46. Lujan v. Defenders of Wildlife, 504 U.S. 555 (1992). *See also* Larson v. Valente, 456 U.S. 228, 244 n.15 (1982) (holding that it is not required that the decision remedy all of the plaintiff's injuries).

A CASE IN POINT

IN THE LANGUAGE OF THE COURT

CASE 6.3

BAUR V. VENEMAN

UNITED STATES COURT OF APPEALS FOR THE SECOND CIRCUIT
352 F. 3D 625 (2D CIR. 2003).

FACTS Michael Baur is an American who eats beef and other meat. Baur became very concerned with Secretary of Agriculture Ann Veneman's policy of allowing "downed" cattle to be used for human consumption after they have passed a postmortem inspection by a veterinary officer. Downed cattle are animals that collapse for unknown reasons or are too sick to stand at the time of slaughter. Baur contended that these cattle are more likely to have a potentially lethal bovine spongiform encephalopathy (BSE), also known as mad cow disease. Humans who consume meat products from BSE-infected cattle may contract mad cow disease. There is no effective treatment or cure for the disease.

Baur sued Veneman in her capacity as Secretary of the Department of Agriculture (USDA) in an attempt to ban the use of downed livestock. Baur claimed that the British outbreak of mad cow disease had already demonstrated the very real threat of human disease through exposure to BSE—a threat made all the more serious by scientific research suggesting that downed cattle in the United States might already be infected with an unidentified variant of BSE. He also argued that preventing the human consumption of downed cattle was necessary because "current [BSE] surveillance efforts, including slaughterhouse inspection procedures," could provide only limited screening.

ISSUE PRESENTED Does mere exposure to BSE give a private citizen standing to challenge the USDA's policy on the human consumption of downed cows?

OPINION STRAUB, J., writing for the U.S. Court of Appeals for the Second Circuit:

On appeal, the parties frame a narrow question for us to consider: whether Baur's allegation that he faces an increased risk of contracting a food-borne illness from the consumption of downed livestock constitutes a cognizable injury-in-fact for Article III standing purposes. . . . To establish Article III standing, a plaintiff must . . . allege, and ultimately prove, that he has suffered an injury-in-fact that is fairly traceable to the challenged action of the defendant, and which is likely to be redressed by the requested relief.

The government does not contest causation and redressibility, and it seems clear that if the alleged risk of disease transmission from downed livestock qualifies as a cognizable injury-in-fact then Baur's injury is fairly traceable to the USDA's decision to permit the use of such livestock for human consumption and could be redressed if the court granted Baur's request for equitable relief.

In this case, only the injury-in-fact requirement of Article III standing is at issue. To qualify as a constitutionally sufficient injury-in-fact, the asserted injury must be "concrete and particularized" as well as "actual or imminent, not 'conjectural' or 'hypothetical,' [and] in evaluating whether the alleged injury is concrete and particularized, we assess whether the injury 'affect[s] the plaintiff in a personal and individual way'. . . . "

Here, the government largely concedes, at least for the purposes of this type of administrative action, that relevant injury-in-fact may be the increased risk of disease transmission caused by exposure to a potentially dangerous food product. . . . In the specific context of food and drug safety suits, however, we conclude that such injuries are cognizable for standing purposes, where the plaintiff alleges exposure to potentially harmful products.

. . . Like threatened environmental harm, the potential harm from exposure to dangerous food products or drugs "is by nature probabilistic," yet an unreasonable exposure to risk may itself cause cognizable injury. Significantly, the very purpose of the Federal Meat Inspection Act and the Federal Food, Drug and Cosmetic Act, the statutes which Baur alleges the USDA has violated, is to ensure the safety of the nation's food supply and to minimize the risk to public health from potentially dangerous food and drug products.

Baur must allege that he faces a direct risk of harm which rises above mere conjecture. While the standard for reviewing standing at the pleading stage is lenient, a plaintiff cannot rely solely on

CONTINUED

conclusory allegations of injury or ask the court to draw unwarranted inferences in order to find standing. Given the potentially expansive and nebulous nature of enhanced risk claims, we agree that plaintiffs like Baur must allege a "credible threat of harm" to establish injury-in-fact based on exposure to enhanced risk. In evaluating the degree of risk sufficient to support standing, however, we are mindful that "Supreme Court precedent teaches us that the injury in fact requirement . . . is qualitative, not quantitative, in nature." . . .

There are two critical factors that weigh in favor of concluding that standing exists in this case: (1) the fact that government studies and statements confirm several of Baur's key allegations, and (2) that Baur's alleged risk of harm arises from an established government policy. Significantly, the USDA itself as well as other government agencies have recognized that downed cattle are especially susceptible to BSE infection. . . . Based on Baur's complaint and the accompanying materials submitted by the parties, we believe that Baur has successfully alleged a credible threat of harm from downed cattle.

RESULT The court vacated the earlier judgment against Baur and remanded the case back to the lower court to be heard. Baur had standing to challenge the USDA's policy on downed cows.

COMMENTS The dissent argued that Baur did not have standing because he had asserted only a generalized grievance and could not distinguish himself from the millions of other Americans who regularly consume beef.

CRITICAL THINKING QUESTIONS

1. Should it matter that Baur could not distinguish himself from any other American who eats beef?
2. Ordinarily, a harm must have already occurred or be imminent for a court to hear a case. Baur could not demonstrate such an injury or the immediacy of an injury to him. Nonetheless, the court permitted his case to proceed. Why did the court not require Baur to demonstrate that he had contracted BSE or had almost eaten a product infected with it?

DECISION-MAKING POWER OF AGENCIES

There are a number of doctrines that limit administrative agencies' decision-making powers.

ONLY DELEGATED POWERS

The general rule is that an administrative agency may do only what Congress or the state legislature has authorized it to do. Agency action contrary to or in excess of its delegated authority is void.

OBLIGATION TO FOLLOW OWN RULES

Not only are agencies required to act within the authority delegated to them, they are also required to follow their own rules and regulations. When an administrative agency adopts a regulation, it becomes binding on the public. It also binds the agency. For example, in *Service v. Dulles,*[47] the Supreme Court held that a State Department employee could not be discharged without being provided reasons because that would be contrary to the State Department's own regulations regarding discharges under its Loyalty Security Program.

At the federal level, one of the most prominent procedural obligations is the requirement to prepare an environmental impact statement before approving major federal actions. The National Environmental Policy Act (NEPA), passed in 1969, dramatically changed the way all federal agencies conduct their business.

Before 1969, an agency could focus exclusively on its substantive legal obligations (the legal rules that define the rights and duties of the agency and of persons dealing with it) and on its own duly adopted procedural obligations (the rules that define the manner in which these rights and duties are enforced). With the NEPA's passage, each federal agency assumed a new procedural obligation to consider the environmental impacts of its proposed actions and the alternatives to those impacts. Each of the hundreds of thousands of federal actions must comply with the NEPA. As a result, each agency attempts to document its compliance as a routine part of its procedures. The agencies have not found it easy to meet these procedural requirements. Hundreds of

47. 354 U.S. 363 (1957).

cases have invalidated agency actions as a result of the failure to meet this obligation.

EXPLANATION OF DECISIONS

As discussed earlier in this chapter, courts will not inquire into the mental processes of the decision maker. The corollary to this principle is that an agency must explain the basis for its decisions and show that it has taken into account all relevant considerations as required by the statute. If an agency makes a decision and fails to provide an adequate explanation of why it acted, then the courts will invalidate the agency's action.[48] In some instances, however, the court may permit the agency to explain deficiencies in the record and to add supplementary explanations of why it acted. The judiciary's insistence that an agency make a reasoned decision, supported by an explanation of why it acted, is a major restraint on improper agency action.

FINDING AN AGENCY'S RULES AND PROCEDURES

In addition to rules and regulations set forth in officially published documents such as the *Federal Register* and the *Code of Federal Regulations,* federal agencies maintain internal guidance documents. For example, the U.S. Forest Service controls millions of acres of timber land. Its formal rules are sparse, but it publishes a manual and a handbook that contain thousands of pages of guidance on such topics as how to conduct timber sales. The Internet has made certain materials more readily accessible, and manuals and handbooks are an important source of law, agency practice, and policy. Reports of court cases provide equivalent information, but cases decided by agency adjudication usually are not reported.

Finding the rules is just a small part of the difficult task of complying with administrative rules and regulations. A small business typically must comply with more than two dozen regulatory procedures at the local, state, and federal levels in order to open.[49] This task is made even more difficult by the fact that relatively few places provide help to a small business trying to figure out the many regulations with which it must comply. Although the Small Business Administration, neighborhood economic development organizations, and banks may provide some guidance, few private small-business consultants specialize in the regulatory aspect of opening a business.

48. *See, e.g.,* Motor Vehicle Mfr. Ass'n v. State Farm Mut. Auto. Ins. Co., 463 U.S. 29 (1983).

49. Kenneth Howe, *Maze of Regulations,* S.F. CHRON., Oct. 29, 1997, at D1.

OBTAINING DOCUMENTS FROM AN AGENCY

In court proceedings and in formal agency adjudications, documents may be obtained by discovery. In other situations, individuals are entitled to obtain copies of government records pursuant to federal and state statutes. The federal statute authorizing this procedure is the Freedom of Information Act (FOIA).[50] Under the FOIA, any citizen may request records of the government on any subject of interest. Unlike discovery, a FOIA request need not show the relevance of the documents to any particular legal proceeding or that the requester has any specific interest in the documents. It is sufficient that the requester seeks the documents.

In theory, the FOIA provides an easy way to obtain documents from a government agency. The agency is required to respond to a document request within ten days. In practice, months, weeks, or even years may pass before the government responds to an FOIA request. Moreover, requesters are required to pay the cost of locating and copying the records. However, these costs are waived for public interest groups, newspaper reporters, and certain other requesters.

Not all documents in the government's possession are available for public inspection. The FOIA exempts:

1. Records required by an executive order to be kept secret in the interest of national defense or foreign policy.
2. Records related solely to the internal personnel rules and practice of an agency.
3. Records exempted from disclosure by another statute.
4. Trade secrets or confidential commercial and financial information.
5. Interagency memorandums or decisions that reflect the deliberative process.
6. Personnel files and other files that, if disclosed, would constitute a clearly unwarranted invasion of personal privacy.
7. Information compiled for law enforcement purposes.
8. Reports prepared on behalf of an agency responsible for the regulation of financial institutions.
9. Geological information concerning wells.

The government is not required to withhold information under any of these exemptions. It may do so or not at its discretion.

From the perspective of those doing business with the government, the FOIA provides an excellent opportunity to learn who is communicating with the agency and what the agency is thinking about a particular matter. The FOIA can

50. 5 U.S.C. § 552.

also be useful in obtaining government studies and learning generally about government activities.

Frequently, regulated companies are required to submit confidential information to the government. From the perspective of a company submitting such information, the FOIA presents a danger of disclosure to competitors. To protect information from disclosure, the company should mark each document as privileged and confidential so that government officials reviewing FOIA requests will not inadvertently disclose it.

Each federal agency has its own set of regulations relating to FOIA requests. These regulations must be complied with strictly, or consideration of the request may be greatly delayed.

GLOBAL VIEW

The British Financial Services Authority

In the United Kingdom, the Financial Services Authority (FSA) regulates the banking, securities, commodities futures, and insurance industries. The FSA is an independent, nongovernmental body whose board of directors is nominally appointed by the Crown. In contrast, in the United States, banks are regulated by the Federal Reserve Board, the Comptroller of the Currency, and state bank regulators; securities firms are regulated by the SEC, state securities commissions, and the National Association of Securities Dealers; commodities futures are regulated by the Commodities Futures Trading Commission; and insurance is regulated by state insurance commissions.

The FSA's self-avowed goals are to (1) maintain confidence in the British financial system, (2) promote public understanding of that system, (3) secure the right degree of protection for customers, and (4) help reduce financial crime.[51] Like its American counterparts, the FSA oversees transactions, demands ethical and legal conduct from firms, and sets standards. Unlike the American system, which utilizes government funding, the FSA charges all firms it regulates annual licensing fees and is thus privately funded. The idea is to allow the FSA to act independently by removing all subjectivity, such as governmental wishes. The concentration of power in the FSA theoretically allows it to better regulate the country's banking and trading exchanges because it does not have to coordinate with other bodies that may have diverging goals and interests.

51. For more on the FSA, see its official website at http://www.fsa.gov.uk/.

IN BRIEF

Seven Basic Steps for Working Successfully with an Administrative Agency

STEP 1
Investigate the applicable standards that will govern the agency's actions.

STEP 2
Identify and evaluate the agency's formal structure.

STEP 3
Determine what facts are before the agency.

STEP 4
Identify the interests of others who may be involved in the decision-making process.

STEP 5
Adopt a strategy to achieve the desired goal.

STEP 6
Eliminate any adverse impact on other interested parties.

STEP 7
Get involved in the administrative process early and stay involved.

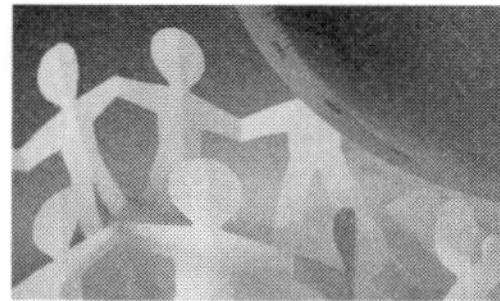

THE RESPONSIBLE MANAGER

WORKING WITH ADMINISTRATIVE AGENCIES

It is important for managers to be active, rather than reactive or passive, participants in administrative decision making and processes. Indeed, the ability to help shape the regulatory environment can be a source of competitive advantage. American Express and MCI both adopted corporate political strategies that allowed them to help shape the rules for financial services firms and telecommunications.[52] In contrast, the major U.S. automakers missed opportunities to work with the Environmental Protection Agency to create livable rules on fleet gasoline mileage requirements.[53]

Seven basic recommendations for working successfully with an administrative agency were offered in the "In Brief" on page 199. As recommended in Step 1, a manager working with an agency should first investigate the basic legal standards that will govern the agency's actions in the matter at hand. These include the agency's laws, its regulations, and its internal manuals and procedures. It is also important to investigate how the agency's administration of its laws and regulations is affected by its past history and by current political influences. Agencies, like any other bureaucracy, tend to have biases in how they carry out the applicable laws and regulations.

These investigations are important for three reasons. First, a manager needs to know what facts must be presented in order to prevail on a claim. Second, it is possible that the agency personnel may not know the applicable legal standard. Many administrative agencies have little access to legal advice and find it helpful to have a clear presentation of the law under which a person is proceeding. Third, it is important to know the law at the outset of an administrative proceeding because, under the doctrine of exhaustion of administrative remedies, issues not raised before the agency are generally deemed to be waived if the matter is later brought before a court.

The second step is for the manager to learn how the agency operates by identifying and evaluating its formal structure. Administrative agencies can have complicated structures. Because the power to make decisions may be vested in more than one official, it is important to know all of the decision maker's options before proceeding. A person can start at the top, the middle, or the bottom. The important point is to start at the right place. Finding out where that is takes some effort.

Next, the manager needs to determine what facts the agency already has (Step 3). In a judicial proceeding, the parties create the record by filing documents with the court. All parties have access to those documents and share the same factual record. The same is not true in an administrative agency proceeding. The factual record may be scattered about the agency in different files and offices. To function effectively before the agency, a manager must identify and locate this record.

Step 4 recommends that the manager identify the interests of other agencies or parties who may be involved in the decision-making process. In a court proceeding, all the parties to a case are known; in an administrative matter, the parties may not be designated formally. It helps to identify the people concerned at the outset and to determine how the proposed action will affect them.

Upon completing this background information, the manager should adopt a strategy to achieve the desired goal (Step 5). Investigation of an administrative matter could show that the agency lacks the authority to do what is proposed. In that case, the manager must persuade the agency to adopt new rules or go to the legislature to have new laws adopted. The most significant task, however, is to decide whether additional factual information should be gathered and presented to the agency. The record before the agency will normally be the record in court. The use of experts during the administrative process and the submission of key documents are important.

In reviewing a proposed action, the manager may find that the action would have undesirable impacts on other interested parties (Step 6). Elimination of those impacts is an effective way to avoid costly disputes.

Finally, as recommended in Step 7, the manager needs to participate in the administrative process at the earliest possible time and to continue participating throughout the proceedings. Once set in motion, agencies tend to stay in

CONTINUED

52. David B. Yoffie & Sigrid Bergenstein, *Creating Political Advantage: The Rise of the Corporate Political Entrepreneur,* 28 CAL. MGMT. REV. 124 (1985). *See also* David B. Yoffie, *Corporate Strategy for Political Action: A Rational Model, in* BUSINESS STRATEGY AND PUBLIC POLICY 92–111 (A. Marcus et al. eds., 1987).

53. PAUL R. LAWRENCE & NITIN NOHRIA, DRIVEN: HOW HUMAN NATURE SHAPES OUR CHOICES 234–39 (2001).

motion unless they are deflected by an outside force. The greater the momentum that has gathered, the harder it is to move the agency off the path it is pursuing. Therefore, it is important to participate early in the process in an effort to influence the agency before it makes up its mind rather than after.

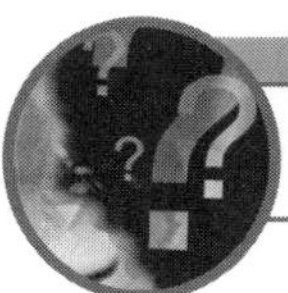

A Manager's Dilemma

Putting It into Practice

Getting into Bed with the Regulators

Dora Reilly is the executive vice president of DNA in Combat, Inc., a genetic-engineering company based in Cambridge, Massachusetts. Eighteen months ago she filed an application with the Food and Drug Administration (FDA) for approval of a promising anticancer drug, DBL. Two months ago she met Gene Splice at an après-ski party and invited him to her room at the ski lodge to listen to her MP3 collection. After that night, Splice returned to his job as a senior specialist in the division of the FDA responsible for approving new drugs based on recombinant DNA, and Reilly returned to Cambridge. Two weeks after her return, Splice wrote Reilly a letter on FDA letterhead, saying, "It was nice to see your name cross my desk on your company's petition for approval of DBL. I'd really like to see you again—why don't you fly down this weekend?"

Reilly considered requesting that the petition be referred to another specialist at the FDA. However, she is concerned that that would delay the approval process by at least eighteen months. Her chief scientist has advised her that a key competitor is expected to have a similar drug on the market in four months. What should she do? What would you advise her to do if you were head of human resources for Combat, Inc.?

Inside Story

REGULATION OF THE CABLE TELEVISION INDUSTRY

In 1984, Congress passed the Cable Communications Act (CCA). The legislation left the fledgling cable television industry largely unregulated, thereby offering cable TV the opportunity to compete with the powerful broadcast companies.[54] At the time, households receiving their programming over the airwaves far outnumbered cable customers.

As its name implies, the Federal Communications Commission (FCC) enacts most of the regulations that govern the telecommunications industry, from cable companies to national networks like Fox and NBC. There are five commissioners appointed by the President. Traditionally, three of the five seats are held by members of the President's political party.

One important feature of the CCA was the "70/70 rule." The provision stipulated that if the FCC ever concluded that at least 70 percent of American households have access to cable service and at least 70 percent of those households are cable customers, then the FCC may promulgate rules to protect and foster a "diversity of information sources."[55]

By late 2007, cable boasted between 55 million and 67 million subscribers, and the industry was fighting hard to minimize further regulation efforts.[56] The FCC had already enacted rules making it easier for telephone companies to compete with cable companies in the video service market by compelling municipalities to streamline the local approval process. The agency also invalidated thousands of agreements

CONTINUED

54. *Regulating Cable,* N.Y. Times, Nov. 27, 2007, at 30.

55. Stephen Labaton, *Cable Wins Compromise on F.C.C. Plans,* N.Y. Times, Nov. 28, 2007, at 1.

56. Amy Schatz, *FCC Cable-Regulation Plan Is at Risk amid Outside Pressure, Internal Squabbling,* Wall St. J., Nov. 27, 2007, at A3.

between cable companies and apartment complex owners that would have given the companies exclusive rights to provide service in apartment buildings.[57]

Each year, the FCC staff produces a report on the video industry that includes estimates of the factors in the 70/70 rule.[58] In 2007, the FCC staff reported for the first time that the rule had been triggered. This finding was challenged by both the cable industry and several FCC commissioners, however. Opponents charged that FCC Chair Kevin Martin had essentially rigged the report by stifling data that contradicted the conclusions in an attempt to push through new cable industry regulations.[59] Two FCC commissioners complained that they had been prevented from seeing the FCC's own information until they went looking for it themselves and charged Martin with "cooking the books."[60]

Most controversial among the proposed regulations was a limit on the percentage of cable subscribers one company could serve. Known as cable concentration caps, the proposal provided that no one company could serve more than 30 percent of U.S. cable customers.[61] Most directly affected would have been Comcast Corporation, which controlled nearly that percentage of the market.[62]

The threat of more than mere regulatory assistance for competitors stirred frantic lobbying by cable providers.[63] Cable executives meeting in Washington shortened what had been scheduled as a full-day meeting to a short breakfast so that they could spend time on Capitol Hill talking with members of Congress.[64] Cable executives and lobbyists also met with senior Bush administration officials in the White House, including chief of staff Joshua Bolten.[65] The lobbying did have some effect: the FCC commissioners failed to agree on whether the 70/70 rule terms had actually been met, thereby preventing a regulatory floodgate from opening.

Nonetheless, in a December 2007 proceeding, the commissioners voted to impose the 30 percent cable concentration cap.[66] This was not expected to end the posturing and maneuvering, however. Interested parties suggest that the courts will overturn the new caps. Comcast Executive Vice President David Cohen said that Comcast is "highly confident that the federal courts will agree that the commission's decision is not supported by the record, and that this cap is unconstitutional."[67] Robert McDowell, an FCC commissioner who voted against the limit, predicted that "the cap is sure to be struck down by the court," given a 2001 ruling overturning a comparable rule.[68] In that case,[69] the U.S. Court of Appeals for the D.C. Circuit suggested that the FCC might one day be able to justify a 60 percent cable concentration cap—double the figure approved by the FCC in 2007—but the court noted that, even then, the FCC is empowered to regulate only against "the risk of 'unfair' conduct by cable operators that might unduly impede the flow of programming." Cable companies now own only around 15 percent of the channels they provide to subscribers, compared to more than half in 1992. This, coupled with increased competition from satellite and phone companies offering television programming, seems to have further diminished the risk of restricted programming since 2001,[70] making it even harder for the FCC to justify imposing a concentration cap.

57. Stephen Labaton, *F.C.C. Reshapes Rules Limiting Media Industry,* N.Y. Times, Dec. 19, 2007, at 1.

58. Schatz, *supra* note 56.

59. Labaton, *supra* note 55.

60. Frank Ahrens, *FCC Chair Forced to Compromise on Cable Regulation,* Wash. Post, Nov. 28, 2007, at D1.

61. Stephen Labaton, *Size Limits for Cable Look Likely,* N.Y. Times, Nov. 29, 2007, at 1.

62. Amy Schatz, *Industry Seethes as FCC's Martin Sets New Curbs,* Wall St. J., Dec. 18, 2007, at A1.

63. Labaton, *supra* note 55.

64. Schatz, *supra* note 62.

65. Labaton, *supra* note 55.

66. Labaton, *supra* note 57.

67. Amy Schatz & Corey Boles, *FCC Votes to Ease Media-Ownership Rules,* Wall St. J., Dec. 19, 2007, at A3.

68. *Id.*

69. Time Warner Entm't Co. v. FCC, 240 F. 3d 1126 (D.C. Cir. 2001).

70. *Martin's Double Vision,* Wall St. J., Dec. 19, 2007, at A20.

Key Words and Phrases

administrative law judge (ALJ) 187
arbitrary and capricious standard 191
codified 184
construction 192
de novo 187
exhaustion of administrative remedies 194

Questions and Case Problems

1. A statute gives the Department of the Interior the power to allow or to curtail mining within the national forests "as the best interests of all users of the national forest shall dictate." Is this a valid delegation of legislative power to the agency, or is it too broad a delegation of power?

2. The Free Enterprise Fund and a Rwanda accounting firm filed a constitutional challenge to the creation of the Public Company Accounting Oversight Board (PCAOB), an entity created by the Sarbanes–Oxley Act (SOX) to oversee and regulate the auditors of public companies. The five members of PCAOB are appointed by the Securities and Exchange Commission (SEC) after consultation with the Chair of the Board of Governors of the Federal Reserve and the Secretary of the Treasury. No PCAOB rule becomes effective unless and until the SEC approves it after the SEC's notice-and-comment proceedings. Before approving a rule, the SEC must find that it is "consistent with the requirements of [SOX] and the securities law, or is necessary or appropriate in the public interest or for the protection of investors." (15 U.S.C. § 7217(b)(3).)

   The plaintiffs made three constitutional challenges. First, they claimed that the appointment of the PCAOB members by the SEC violates the Appointments Clause of the U.S. Constitution (art. II, § 2), which empowers the President to appoint "Officers of the United States" while giving Congress the power to vest the appointment of "inferior officers" in the President, courts of law, or heads of departments. The plaintiffs argued that because PCAOB members are neither appointed nor supervised on a day-to-day basis by principal officers directly accountable to the President, they are not inferior officers, and therefore must be appointed by the President. Second, the plaintiffs claimed that the appointment of the PCAOB members violated the separation of powers because the members were not removable at will by the President. The President can remove SEC commissioners for cause, and the SEC can remove the PCAOB members for good cause, however. Third, the plaintiffs claimed that Congress violated the nondelegation doctrine by unlawfully delegating legislative power to the PCAOB in violation of Article I, Section 1 of the Constitution, which vests all legislative powers in the Congress. How should the court rule? [*Free Enterprise Fund v. Public Company Accounting Oversight Board,* 2007 U.S. Dist. LEXIS 24310 (D.D.C., Mar. 21, 2007).]

3. After Congress decided to set stricter limits on harmful car emissions, the Environmental Protection Agency (EPA) was directed to devise a test for all automobiles to determine if they were in compliance with the stringent new emissions standard. The EPA, already stretched thin by many preexisting projects, enacted the CAP 2000 regulation, which requires all automobile manufacturers to devise their own tests for their automobiles. The EPA hopes this will do three things: cut down on the cost of producing its own test, force automobile manufacturers to share in the cost of producing cleaner cars, and result in an even more effective test for emissions.

   Ethyl Corporation produces gasoline additives. Because these tests will now be devised behind closed doors at automobile companies, Ethyl will have a more difficult time producing additives that will pass emission standards. Ethyl sued the EPA, challenging the CAP regulation. What arguments should Ethyl advance to persuade the court to strike down the EPA regulations? How else might Ethyl affect the EPA's rulemaking? [*Ethyl Corp. v. EPA,* 306 F.3d 1144 (D.C. Cir. 2002).]

4. The Food and Drug Administration (FDA), charged with implementation of the Federal Food, Drug and Cosmetic Act, refused to approve the cancer-treatment drug Laetrile on the ground that it failed to meet the statute's safety and effectiveness standards. Terminally ill cancer patients sued, claiming that the safety and effectiveness standards implemented by the FDA could have no reasonable application to drugs used by the terminally ill. The statute contained no explicit exemption for drugs used by the terminally ill. The U.S. court of appeals reviewing the case agreed with the plaintiffs and approved intravenous injections of Laetrile for terminally ill cancer patients. The United States appealed to the Supreme Court. Under what standard should the Supreme Court review the FDA's determination that an exemption from the Federal Food,

Drug and Cosmetic Act should not be implied for drugs used by the terminally ill? [*United States v. Rutherford,* 442 U.S. 544 (1979).]

5. In 1985, President Ronald Reagan signed into law the Gramm-Rudman-Hollings Act. The purpose of the Act was to reduce the federal deficit by setting a maximum deficit amount for fiscal years 1986 to 1991, progressively reducing the budget deficit to zero by 1991.

   If the federal budget deficit failed to be reduced as the Act required, an automatic budget process was to take effect. The Comptroller would calculate, on a program-by-program basis, the amount of reductions needed to meet the target. He or she would then report that amount to the President, who was required to issue a sequestration order mandating these reductions. (A *sequestration order* directs spending levels to be reduced below the levels authorized in the original budget.) Unless Congress then acted to modify the budget to reduce the deficit to the required level, the sequestrations would go into effect.

   The Comptroller, unlike the employees of the executive branch and agency officials, does not serve at the pleasure of the President. He or she can be removed from office only by Congress.

   Opponents of the Gramm-Rudman-Hollings Act argued that the Comptroller's role in the automatic budget process was an exercise of executive functions. Because the Comptroller was controlled by Congress, they argued that this role violated the constitutional requirement of separation of powers. Were they right? [*Bowsher v. Synar,* 478 U.S. 714 (1986).]

6. The Supreme Court has recognized that administrative inspections may be conducted without warrants in some situations when a company's business concerns an industry that has a history of government oversight and, as a result, has a reduced expectation of privacy. The Court held that a warrantless search would be found reasonable in the context of a pervasively regulated business if (1) there is a "substantial" government interest that underlies the regulatory scheme pursuant to which the search is made; (2) the warrantless inspection is necessary to further the regulatory scheme; and (3) the inspection program, in terms of the certainty and regularity of its application, provides a constitutionally adequate substitute for a warrant. Based on this standard, would the Court allow warrantless administrative inspections to occur in the following industries: (a) firearms, (b) mining, (c) pharmaceutical, and (d) computer software design? [In re *Subpoenas Duces Tecum,* 51 F. Supp. 2d 726 (W.D. Va. 1999).]

7. James O'Hagan was a partner in the law firm of Dorsey & Whitney in Minneapolis, Minnesota. In July 1988, the London-based company Grand Metropolitan PLC (Grand Met) retained Dorsey & Whitney as local counsel for a potential tender offer for the common stock of the Pillsbury Company, headquartered in Minneapolis. Both Grand Met and Dorsey & Whitney took precautions to protect the confidentiality of Grand Met's tender offer plans. O'Hagan, who was not working on the deal, began purchasing Pillsbury stock and call options for Pillsbury stock. When Grand Met announced its tender offer in October, the price of Pillsbury stock rose to $60 per share. O'Hagan sold his Pillsbury call options and stock, making a profit of more than $4.3 million.

   The Securities and Exchange Commission (SEC) initiated an investigation into O'Hagan's transactions that culminated in a fifty-seven-count indictment, charging O'Hagan with, among other counts, violation of Rule 14e-3(a). Rule 14e-3(a) was adopted by the SEC pursuant to Section 14(e) of the Securities Exchange Act of 1934. Section 14(e) reads in relevant part:

   > It shall be unlawful for any person . . . to engage in fraudulent, deceptive, or manipulative acts or practices, in connection with any tender offer. . . . The [SEC] shall, for the purposes of this subsection, by rules and regulations define, and prescribe means reasonably designed to prevent, such acts and practices as are fraudulent, deceptive, or manipulative.

   Relying on Section 14(e)'s rulemaking authorization, the SEC promulgated Rule 14e-3(a) in 1980. Traders violate Rule 14e-3(a) if they trade on the basis of material nonpublic information concerning a pending tender offer that they know or have reason to know has been acquired "directly or indirectly" from an insider of the offeror or the target, or someone working on their behalf. Rule 14e-3(a) requires traders who fall within its ambit to abstain from trading or to disclose the nonpublic information, without regard to whether the trader owes a preexisting fiduciary duty to respect the confidentiality of the information. In contrast, courts have interpreted Section 14(e) to apply only to situations in which the person trading violated a fiduciary duty by trading. Did the SEC exceed its rulemaking authority by adopting Rule 14e-3(a) without requiring a showing that the trading at issue entailed a breach of fiduciary duty? [*United States v. O'Hagan,* 521 U.S. 642 (1997).]

8. Section 7(a)(2) of the Endangered Species Act of 1973 (ESA) is intended to protect species of animals against threats to their continuing existence caused by humans.

The ESA instructs the Secretary of the Interior to promulgate a list of those endangered or threatened species and requires each federal agency, in consultation with the Secretary of the Interior, to ensure that any action authorized, funded, or carried out by such agency is not likely to jeopardize the continued existence of any endangered or threatened species.

In 1978, the Department of the Interior and the Department of Commerce promulgated a joint regulation stating that the obligations imposed by Section 7(a)(2) extended to actions taken in foreign nations. Thus, any actions taken by the United States would require consultation with the Department of the Interior. The Secretary of the Interior, however, reinterpreted the section to require consultation only for actions taken in the United States or on the high seas.

Almost immediately, organizations dedicated to wildlife conservation and other environmental causes sued Manuel Lujan, the Secretary of the Interior, and sought an injunction requiring the Secretary to promulgate a new regulation restoring the initial interpretation of the geographic scope. They claimed that U.S.-funded projects in Egypt and Sri Lanka would significantly reduce endangered and threatened species in the areas. Two members of Defenders of Wildlife, Joyce Kelly and Amy Skilbred, submitted affidavits indicating that they had traveled to foreign countries to observe endangered species (the Nile crocodile in Egypt, the Asian elephant and leopard in Sri Lanka) and that they planned to do so in the future. The U.S. Supreme Court ruled that Kelly and Skilbred did not have standing to challenge the new interpretation.

In *Bennett v. Spear,* however, the Court held that ranchers in irrigation districts that would be directly affected economically by a Fish and Wildlife Service finding regarding two endangered species of fish had standing to challenge it. Why did they have standing when Kelly and Skilbred did not? [*Lujan v. Defenders of Wildlife,* 504 U.S. 555 (1992); *Bennett v. Spear,* 520 U.S. 154 (1997).]

7

CONTRACTS

INTRODUCTION

Why Contract Law Is Important

Contracts are critical to the conduct of business in the United States and internationally. The principles of contract law determine which agreements will be enforced by the courts. Contract law allows a company to make plans to move its offices into a new building, knowing that the lease gives it an enforceable right to exclusive use of the space for the term of the lease at the specified rent. Similarly, an owner can rent space, knowing that the tenant will be required to pay rent and to comply with the other terms of the lease. An employee can leave his or her current employer and begin work for a start-up company, knowing that the new firm will grant the stock options it promised when it recruited the employee. All of the parties to these transactions expect that their agreements will be enforceable.

Contract law is based on case law, statutes, and tradition, subject to slight variations from state to state. Many states follow the Restatement (Second) of Contracts, which is the basis for much of the discussion in this chapter. Common law contracts include employment agreements and other contracts involving services, leases and sales of real property, loan agreements, stock purchase agreements, settlement agreements, and joint venture agreements. Commercial transactions involving the sale of goods, that is, movable personal property, are governed by Article 2 of the Uniform Commercial Code (UCC). Article 2, as well as the laws governing the sale of goods internationally and contracts for the sale and licensing of software, is discussed in Chapter 8. The "In Brief" in Chapter 8 (page 280) summarizes key differences among common law contracts, the UCC, the Convention on Contracts for the International Sale of Goods, and the Uniform Computer Information Transactions Act.

CHAPTER OVERVIEW

This chapter discusses the elements necessary for a valid contract: agreement (formed by an offer and acceptance), consideration, contractual capacity, and legality. It explains the equitable doctrine of promissory estoppel and the enforcement of an agreement to negotiate. Promissory estoppel can, in certain circumstances, result in limited relief for a party who has relied on a promise even though it lacks one or more of the elements required for a contract. The equitable doctrine of unconscionability, on the other hand, allows a court to elect not to enforce all or a portion of an otherwise enforceable contract. We discuss the need for genuine assent and the effects of fraud and duress, as well as issues concerning a misunderstanding or mistake about the meaning of a contract or the facts underlying the contract. The chapter explains the requirement that certain contracts be in writing and the rules for looking beyond the written terms of an agreement to discern the parties' intentions. It discusses damages for breach of contract and court orders for specific performance. We conclude with a brief look at acquisition agreements.

BASIC REQUIREMENTS OF A CONTRACT

A *contract* is a legally enforceable promise or set of promises. If the promise is broken, the person to whom the promise was made—the *promisee*—has certain legal rights against the person who made the promise—the *promisor*. If the promisor fails to carry out its promise, the promisee may be able to recover money damages, or it may be able to get an injunction, that is, a court order forcing the promisor to perform the promise.

Formation of a valid contract requires four basic elements: (1) there must be an agreement between the parties, formed by an offer and acceptance; (2) the parties' promises must be supported by something of value, known as consideration; (3) both parties must have the capacity to enter into a contract; and (4) the contract must have a legal purpose.

In addition, courts may invalidate contracts that do not reflect a true "meeting of the minds." For instance, if one party is induced to enter into a contract by fraud, duress, or misrepresentation, courts may refuse to enforce the contract because both parties did not genuinely assent to its terms.

AGREEMENT

A valid contract requires an offer and acceptance resulting in agreement between the two parties. Contract law has traditionally treated offer and acceptance as a rather sterile, step-by-step process. Despite its incongruity with the fluid nature of business deal making today, this narrow view continues to give the rules governing contract formation a formalistic flavor.

OFFER

An *offer* is a manifestation of willingness to enter into a bargain that justifies another person in understanding that his or her assent will conclude the bargain. An offer is effective if (1) the *offeror* (the person making the offer) has an intention to be bound by the offer, (2) the terms of the offer are reasonably definite, and (3) the offer is communicated to the *offeree* (the intended recipient).

Intention

Courts will evaluate the offeror's outward expression of intent, not his or her secret intention. Thus, if a reasonable person would consider an offeror's statement to be a serious offer, an offer has been made. Offers made in obvious jest or in the heat of anger do not meet the intention requirement, because a reasonable person would know the offer was not serious. This objective standard of contract interpretation makes it possible to plan one's business based on reasonable expectations of what the other party's words mean.

Most advertisements are treated not as offers but as invitations to negotiate. Sellers do not have an unlimited ability to provide services or an unlimited supply of goods. If advertisements were offers, then everyone who "accepted" could sue the seller for breach of contract if the seller's supply ran out. An advertisement will be treated as an offer only in the rare case where a seller makes a promise so definite that it is clearly binding itself to the conditions stated. This can arise, for example, when the advertisement calls for some performance by the offeree, such as providing information that leads to the recovery of a lost or stolen article.

Definiteness

An offer will form the basis for a contract only when the essential terms of the agreement are set forth. If essential terms (such as price, subject matter, duration of the contract, and manner of payment) are left open, then there is no contract.

Communication

The offeror must communicate the offer to the offeree. For instance, a good Samaritan who returns a lost pet cannot claim a reward offered by the owner if he or she did not know about the reward beforehand.

Termination of Offer

An offer can be terminated either by operation of law or by action of the parties.

Termination by Operation of Law An offer terminates when the time for acceptance specified by the offeror has elapsed or after a reasonable period has elapsed if the offeror did not specify a time. Death or incapacitation of either party terminates an offer, as does destruction of the subject matter.

Termination by Action of the Parties The offeror can *revoke* the offer—that is, cancel it—at any time before the offeree accepts. An offer is also terminated if the offeree rejects it or makes a new offer, which is referred to as a *counteroffer*. A counteroffer constitutes a rejection of the original offer and reverses the roles of the original offeror and offeree. If Misha responds to a job offer with a salary of $100,000 a year by saying, "That salary is too low, but I'll take the job at $120,000 per year," he is making a counteroffer, which terminates the original offer. Inquiring into the terms of an offer is not a rejection, however. Had Misha responded, "Does that include a five-week vacation?" it would have constituted an inquiry into terms, which would not terminate the original offer.

Irrevocable Offers

An *irrevocable offer* cannot be terminated by the offeror. Irrevocable offers arise (1) when an option contract has been created and (2) when an offeree has relied on an offer to his or her detriment.

Option Contracts An *option contract* is created when an offeror agrees to hold an offer open for a certain amount of time in exchange for some consideration from the other party. Under such an agreement, the offeror cannot revoke the offer until the time for acceptance has expired. For example, in exchange for a $200 payment by the offeree, a company might agree to keep the position of general manager open for ten days while the offeree decides whether to take the job.

"Your offer's a crumpled little ball in the middle of my desk."

Detrimental Reliance An irrevocable offer may also occur when an offeree has changed his or her position because of justifiable reliance on the offer. Sometimes courts will hold that such *detrimental reliance* makes the offer irrevocable.

Suppose Aunt Leila offers the use of her Maui condo to her niece Christina during spring break in exchange for Christina's promise to fix a hole in the condo roof during her stay. Under traditional contract law, Aunt Leila could revoke this offer at any time before Christina accepts. But suppose Christina relies on this offer, purchases a nonrefundable plane ticket to Maui, and passes up the opportunity to rent other condos for her stay. The modern view of this situation is quite different from traditional contract law. If Aunt Leila should reasonably have known that Christina would act to her detriment in reliance on the offer, then the doctrine of promissory estoppel would make the offer irrevocable. In other words, Aunt Leila would be estopped—or barred—from revoking her offer. The doctrine of promissory estoppel is described in more detail below.

ACCEPTANCE

Acceptance is a response by the person receiving the offer that indicates willingness to enter into the agreement proposed in the offer. For example, if Indra says to Dayle, "I'll give you $100 to install my new computer software package," and Dayle says, "OK," a contract has been formed. Indra is now legally obliged to give Dayle the money, and Dayle is obliged to install the software.

Both offer and acceptance can be oral, written, or implied by conduct. If, for example, a manager offers a consultant $5,000 to develop a business plan for her company, the consultant can accept orally or in writing, or the consultant can accept the offer by starting work on the business plan. The acceptance is implied by the consultant's action, even though he did not actually say, "I accept your offer."

Mode of Acceptance

The offeror is the "master of his offer" in that he or she can specify the means and manner of acceptance. For example, the offeror could specify that the offer can be accepted only by a facsimile (fax) sent to a stated fax number and that the acceptance is not effective until it is actually received. Absent such a provision, acceptance is effective upon dispatch of the acceptance. Thus, if a person mails a properly addressed envelope with adequate postage containing a letter accepting an offer, a contract is formed when the letter is put in the mailbox; the offeror cannot thereafter revoke the offer.

Many online service providers modify their terms of service by simply posting the updated terms of service on their websites. Joe Douglas challenged this practice on behalf of all users of Talk America after he learned that the service provider had modified its service contract to add service charges and an arbitration clause. Although Talk America posted the revised contract on its website, it did not otherwise notify users that the contract had been changed. (Although the court hearing the case did not mention it, Talk America's original service contract included language that purported to give it the right to change the terms at any time.) Talk America moved to compel arbitration based on the modified service contract, claiming that Douglas's continued use of the service after the revised terms were posted had constituted his acceptance of them.

The U.S. Court of Appeals for the Ninth Circuit disagreed, stating:

> Parties to a contract have no obligation to check the terms on a periodic basis in order to learn whether they have been changed by the other side. Indeed, a party can't unilaterally change the terms of a contract; it must obtain the other party's consent before so doing. This is because a revised contract is merely an offer and does not bind the parties until it is accepted. Even if Douglas' continued use of Talk America's service could be considered assent, such assent can only be inferred after he received proper notice of the proposed changes.[1]

Mirror Image Rule

The traditional concept of contract formation requires that what the offeree accepts must be exactly the same as what the offeror has offered. If it is not, the *mirror image rule* dictates that no contract has been formed.

Suppose Alyssa offers to rent to Roberto 6,000 square feet of office space in Houston for $60 per square foot per year. Roberto accepts the offer of 6,000 square feet of office space but says he wants ten free underground parking spaces as well. The requirements of the mirror image rule have not been met because Roberto's acceptance is not unequivocal. Accordingly, there is no contract; Roberto's request for the parking spaces is considered a counteroffer, not an acceptance.

Intent to Be Bound

Formalistic rules of contract formation often do not reflect the realities of how businesses enter into agreements. A joint venture agreement between contractors to build a hydroelectric dam, for example, can involve months of negotiations and a series of letters, memoranda, and draft contracts. As a result, it is sometimes difficult to determine precisely when the parties have entered into a legally binding contract.

At some point in the negotiations, the parties will usually manifest an intention, either orally or in writing, to enter into a contract. Such *intent to be bound* can create an enforceable contract even if nonessential terms must still be hammered out or a more definitive agreement is contemplated. Courts will look at the specific facts of each case when determining whether the parties regarded themselves as having completed a bargain.

In general, to determine the enforceability of preliminary agreements, courts examine (1) the intent of the parties to be bound and (2) the definiteness of the terms of the agreement. Most litigation concerning the enforceability of preliminary agreements with open terms has involved the issue of intent, as in the landmark case of *Pennzoil v. Texaco,* discussed in the "Inside Story" for this chapter. In that case, the court ruled that Getty Oil, the Getty Trust, and the Getty Museum intended to be bound by a four-page "memorandum of agreement" calling for the sale of Getty Oil to Pennzoil, even though the memorandum was not expressly made binding and the consummation of the multibillion dollar deal was subject to execution of a definitive agreement.

In deciding whether the parties intended to be bound, courts look to a variety of factors, including (1) the degree to which the terms of the agreement are spelled out; (2) the circumstances of the parties (e.g., the importance of the deal to them); (3) the parties' prior course of dealing with each other, if any; and (4) the parties' behavior after execution of the agreement (for example, issuing a press release announcing a deal may demonstrate intent).

The parties can make a preliminary agreement nonbinding by stating their intention not to be bound. However, courts will honor such a statement only if it is expressed in the clearest language. Titling an agreement a "letter of intent" or using the phrase "formal agreement to follow" might not be enough to prove that the parties did not intend to be bound if their other conduct suggests otherwise.

CONSIDERATION

In addition to offer and acceptance, formation of a valid contract requires that each side provide something of value, known as *consideration,* which can be money, an object, a service, a promise, or a giving up of the right to do something. For instance, an adult's promise to quit smoking for five years constitutes consideration because the promisor is giving up something he or she is legally entitled to do. A promise to take property off the market for thirty days constitutes consideration, as does a promise to conduct a midyear audit.

A promise to do something illegal, such as to pay an illegal bribe to a government official, does not constitute valid consideration, however. Likewise, a promise to fulfill a preexisting legal obligation, that is, to do something the promisor is already obligated to do—either by law or by contract—is not consideration.

Suppose Brett's Builders Corporation (BBC) has a contract to build a production facility for Hardware, Inc. for $15 million. Halfway through the project, BBC demands an additional $3 million to finish the project. Because it wants the project completed as quickly as possible, Hardware promises to pay the additional $3 million. Hardware's promise is not enforceable by BBC, because BBC's promise to "finish the project" did not constitute consideration. BBC was already contractually obligated to build the facility in its entirety for $15 million. This type of situation is explored further in the discussion of contract modification below.

1. Douglas v. U.S. Dist. Court, 495 F.3d 1062 (9th Cir. 2007).

ADEQUACY OF CONSIDERATION

Generally, courts will not scrutinize the value of the consideration or the fairness of a contract. A court will deem consideration adequate—and hold the parties to their bargain—unless it concludes that the purported consideration is a sham. Hence, the adage that even a peppercorn can be adequate consideration. The rare exception to this rule is the unconscionability doctrine discussed below.

BILATERAL AND UNILATERAL CONTRACTS

Consideration can be either a promise to do a certain act or the performance of the act itself.

A *bilateral contract* is a promise given in exchange for another promise. One party agrees to do one thing, and the other party agrees to do something in return. For example, Ibrahim promises to give Mercedes $10 if she promises to drive him to business school. The exchange of promises represents consideration and makes the promises binding.

A *unilateral contract* is a promise given in exchange for an act. For example, Ibrahim promises to give Mercedes $10 if she drives him to business school. Mercedes can accept the contract only by driving Ibrahim to business school, and no contract is formed until she does so.

Mutuality of Obligation in Bilateral Contracts

The corollary of consideration in the case of bilateral contracts is the concept of *mutuality of obligation*. To be enforceable, a bilateral contract must limit the behavior of both parties in some fashion. If one party has full freedom of action, there is no contract.

Mutuality of obligation applies only to bilateral contracts. In the case of a unilateral contract, the promisor becomes bound only after the promisee has performed the required act. Thus, in the example above, Ibrahim has no obligation to pay Mercedes $10 until she drives him to school.

Illusory Promise

A promise that neither confers any benefit on the promisee nor subjects the promisor to any detriment is an *illusory promise*. Because there is no mutuality of obligation in such a case, the resulting agreement is unenforceable. A classic case[2] involved a coal company, Wickham, that agreed to sell at a certain price all the coal that Farmers' Lumber, a lumber company, wanted to purchase from Wickham. The Iowa Supreme Court held that Farmers' Lumber's promise to purchase only what it wanted to purchase, which could be nothing at all, was illusory. Because there was no consideration flowing from Farmers' Lumber to Wickham, there was no contract. Farmers' Lumber could have avoided the finding of an illusory contract by agreeing to purchase all the coal it needed from Wickham. Such an agreement is called a requirements contract, which is discussed further below.

In the following case, the New Mexico Court of Appeals concluded that an employer's agreement to arbitrate in an employee handbook was an unenforceable illusory contract.

2. Wickham & Burton Coal Co. v. Farmers' Lumber Co., 179 N.W. 417 (Iowa 1920).

A CASE IN POINT

IN THE LANGUAGE OF THE COURT

CASE 7.1

HEYE V. AMERICAN GOLF CORP.

COURT OF APPEALS OF NEW MEXICO
80 P.3D 495 (N.M. 2003).

FACTS Melissa Heye applied, and was hired, for a position in the pro shop at Paradise Hills Golf Course, a club managed by American Golf Corporation (AGC). AGC gave her a number of documents, including the Co-Worker Alliance Handbook, which included information about AGC's arbitration policy. The Handbook included the following acknowledgment form, which Heye signed:

> My signature below indicates that I have read this AGC Co-Worker Alliance Agreement and handbook and promise and agree to abide by its terms and conditions. I further understand that the Company reserves the right to amend, supplement, rescind or revise any policy, practice, or benefit described in this handbook—other than employment at-will provisions—as it deems appropriate.
>
> I acknowledge that my employment is at-will, which means that either the Company or I have the absolute right to end the employment relationship at any time with or without notice or reason. I further understand that the president of American Golf Corporation is the only authorized

CONTINUED

> representative of the Company who can modify this at-will employment relationship and the contents of this handbook, and that any such modifications must be made in writing.
>
> I further acknowledge that I have read and agree to be bound by the arbitration policy set forth on page 20 of this handbook.

The arbitration policy referenced in the acknowledgment form included a statement that any claim of harassment, discrimination, or wrongful discharge would be resolved "exclusively by final and binding arbitration and not by court action."

Heye worked for AGC until January 2000, when she filed a charge of employment discrimination with the New Mexico Human Rights Division. She subsequently filed a lawsuit against AGC and her supervisor, George Brazil, alleging sex discrimination, among other things. The defendants moved to compel binding arbitration, and the trial court denied their motion. AGC appealed.

ISSUE PRESENTED Is an agreement to arbitrate enforceable if the employer retains the right to modify or ignore it?

OPINION CASTILLO, J., writing for the New Mexico Court of Appeals:

For a contract to be legally valid and enforceable, it must be factually supported by an offer, an acceptance, consideration, and mutual assent. Defendants assert that the arbitration agreement is supported by consideration in the form of AGC's agreement to arbitrate. . . .

"A valid contract must possess mutuality of obligation. Mutuality means both sides must provide consideration." Consideration consists of a promise to do something that a party is under no legal obligation to do or to forbear from doing something he has a legal right to do. Furthermore, a promise must be binding. When a promise puts no constraints on what a party may do in the future—in other words, when a promise, in reality, promises nothing—it is illusory, and it is not consideration.

AGC points to language . . . [in] the handbook, stating that arbitration is the "exclusive means of resolving any dispute(s)," and argues that this language does not allow AGC to modify or ignore the agreement to arbitrate. Plaintiff counters that [this] language . . . conflicts with that of the acknowledgment form . . . [which] provides "that the Company reserves the right to amend, supplement, rescind or revise any policy, practice, or benefit described in this handbook—other than employment at-will provisions—as it deems appropriate. . . ."

. . . .

. . . We disagree with AGC that it was "equally obligated to . . . arbitrate all claims." To the contrary, the agreement provided in effect that only one thing would remain unchangeable, namely Plaintiff's at-will employment status. . . . The agreement, in essence, gives AGC unfettered discretion to terminate arbitration at any time, while binding Plaintiff to arbitration. AGC remains free to selectively abide by its promise to arbitrate; the promise, therefore, is illusory. Thus, AGC's promise to arbitrate does not provide the consideration necessary to enforce the arbitration agreement.

RESULT The court of appeals affirmed the trial court's denial of the defendants' motion to compel arbitration. Heye was not required to arbitrate her claims.

CRITICAL THINKING QUESTIONS

1. Could AGC modify the Handbook to ensure that the arbitration provision would be enforced? If so, how?
2. Could an employer require an employee to arbitrate minimum-wage claims pursuant to an arbitration clause that the employer required the employee to accept as a condition to continuing to work as an at-will employee?

REQUIREMENTS AND OUTPUT CONTRACTS

In a *requirements contract,* the buyer agrees to buy all its requirements of a specified commodity, such as steel, from the seller, and the seller agrees to meet those requirements. The parties do not know how much steel the buyer will actually need, but, whatever that amount is, the buyer will buy it all from that seller. Because the buyer is precluded from buying steel from another supplier, there is a binding contract even if the buyer did not originally expect to need any steel.

In an *output contract,* the buyer promises to buy all the output that the seller produces. Again, the parties do not how know many units that will be, but the seller must sell all its output to that buyer. The seller cannot sell any of its product to another buyer.

These types of contracts are not enforceable if the requirement or output is unreasonable or out of proportion to prior requirements or outputs. The buyer cannot take advantage of the seller by increasing its requirement to triple the usual amount. The seller will not be required to sell anything over the reasonable or usual amount required by the buyer.

CONDITIONAL PROMISES

Promises conditioned on the occurrence or nonoccurrence of an event often look illusory, but they are enforceable as long as the promisor is bound by conditions beyond his or her control. On the other hand, conditional clauses will be treated as illusory promises if satisfaction of the condition is within the control of one party. For example, courts usually disallow clauses that condition an agreement on the approval of a party's own lawyer.

There are three types of *conditions*: (1) conditions precedent, (2) conditions concurrent, and (3) conditions subsequent. A *condition precedent* is an event that must occur before performance under a contract is due. For example, Lockheed Martin agreed to sell one of its operations to BTN pursuant to a contract that required BTN to demonstrate that it had "resources and assets necessary and sufficient to conduct the [transferred business] and to perform its obligations and contracts." When Lockheed demanded evidence that BTN was in compliance with the foregoing condition, BTN was unable to satisfy Lockheed. After Lockheed terminated the contract, BTN sued for breach of contract. The U.S. Court of Appeals for the Fourth Circuit concluded that Lockheed had not breached the contract because BTN had not satisfied the condition precedent.[3]

3. Bi-Tech North, Inc. v. Lockheed Martin Corp., 2005 U.S. App. LEXIS 4026 (4th Cir. Mar. 10, 2005).

A *condition concurrent* occurs when the mutual duties of performance are to take place simultaneously. For example, a buyer's obligation to pay for stock often does not become absolute until the seller tenders or delivers the stock certificates. Similarly, the seller's obligation to deliver the stock certificates does not become absolute until the buyer tenders or makes payment.

A *condition subsequent* operates to terminate an existing contractual obligation if the condition occurs. For example, if a partner agrees to sell his share of the partnership for ten times the partnership's earnings, unless an audit of the partnership's books shows earnings of less than $5 million, the partner will not be obligated to sell if the audit reveals earnings of less than $5 million (that is, if the condition subsequent occurs).

CAPACITY

A valid contract also requires that both parties possess the capacity to enter into an agreement. *Capacity* is a legal term that refers to a person's ability to understand the nature and effect of an agreement. The widely accepted rule is that minors and mentally incompetent persons lack capacity because they are unable to protect their own interests.

As a result, the law generally gives minors and incompetent persons the power to repudiate their contractual obligations. In other words, such contracts are *voidable* at the option of the person lacking capacity: that person can enforce the contract if it is advantageous for him or her to do so or disavow the contract if it is not. In some states, minors also have the right to retain any property they acquired under the voidable contract even though they have avoided their own contract obligations. In many states, though, minors cannot repudiate their contractual obligations if they misrepresented their age to the other party.

Contracts entered into by incompetent persons have the potential to be either void, voidable (at the option of the incompetent person), or valid. If the party has been legally found incompetent and a guardian has been appointed for him or her, the contract is void. If the party simply lacked the mental capacity to comprehend the subject matter, the

› ETHICAL CONSIDERATION

Should managers offer special consideration to an elderly person who is not incompetent but is less able to understand complex transactions or to protect his or her own interests than a younger person?

contract is voidable. If the incompetent person was able to understand the nature and effect of the agreement, however, then the contract is valid, even if he or she lacked capacity to engage in other activities.

These voidability rules are subject to certain limitations. Both minors and mentally incompetent persons are held to contracts for necessaries, such as food, clothing, and shelter. Otherwise, no one would be willing to provide the necessaries a minor or mentally incompetent person needs to survive. Both minors and mentally incompetent persons can *ratify* (agree to be bound by) contracts after they reach majority or gain competency.

LEGALITY

Contracts must have a legal purpose. Contracts that are contrary to a statute or to public policy are illegal and are generally considered void—that is, they are not valid contracts.

LICENSING STATUTES

Many states require licenses to conduct particular kinds of business, ranging from real estate and securities broker licenses to chauffeur and contractor licenses. Licensing statutes often provide that if a party fails to have a required license, the other party to the contract does not have to fulfill its side of the bargain, usually payment. This is true even if the unlicensed party performed the work perfectly and the other party knew beforehand that the person doing the work was unlicensed.

OTHER CONTRACTS CONTRARY TO STATUTE

Sometimes a statute will expressly make certain types of contracts illegal. For example, *usury statutes* limit the interest rate on loans and usually provide that any loan agreement in violation of the statute is unenforceable. In some jurisdictions, this means that no interest can be collected; in some states, the principal amount of the loan is also not collectible. Loans that violate the usury statutes also violate criminal law.

Other examples of *illegal contracts* include price-fixing agreements in violation of the antitrust laws, bribes, wagering contracts or bets in violation of applicable gambling laws, and unreasonable covenants not to compete. To be reasonable, a *covenant not to compete* entered into in connection with the sale of a business must be reasonable as to scope of activities, length of time, and geographic area, and must be necessary to protect trade secrets or goodwill. The enforceability of covenants not to compete in the employment context is discussed in Chapter 12.

PROMISSORY ESTOPPEL

The primary exception to the rule that only promises supported by consideration will be enforced is the doctrine of promissory estoppel. *Promissory estoppel* (sometimes referred to as detrimental reliance or *unjust enrichment*) applies only if the injured party can prove there was (1) a promise and (2) justifiable reliance on the promise (3) that was foreseeable and (4) resulted in injustice.

PROMISE

There must be a promise. A statement of future intent is not sufficient; neither is an estimate or a misstatement of fact. For example, suppose Hank asks Bart the time, and Bart mistakenly tells him that it is two o'clock when it is actually three o'clock, causing Hank to miss an important appointment. Hank relied on the information to his detriment, but there was no promise, so promissory estoppel does not apply.

JUSTIFIABLE RELIANCE

The promise must cause the promisee to take an action that he or she would not otherwise have taken. In the earlier example, when the niece Christina bought the plane ticket to Hawaii, she was relying on Aunt Leila's promise. If Christina had not bought the ticket, there would be no reliance, and breach of her aunt's promise would not entitle Christina to recover damages.

FORESEEABILITY

The action taken in reliance on the promise must be reasonably foreseeable by the promisor. It is foreseeable that the niece would buy a plane ticket as a result of her aunt's promise. It is not foreseeable that she would quit her job to take a six-month vacation in Hawaii. Therefore, under the doctrine of promissory estoppel, the aunt would probably have to pay for the plane ticket but not for the niece's lost wages.

INJUSTICE

A promise that has been reasonably relied on will give rise to relief only if the failure to provide relief would cause injustice. The exact meaning of "injustice" has been debated by legal scholars, but a good rule of thumb is to ask whether the promisee has been harmed by his or her reliance on the promise. If the niece had made a plane reservation that could be canceled without penalty, there would be no injustice in letting the aunt take back her promise; thus, promissory estoppel would not apply.

Initially, courts applied promissory estoppel only to gifts, not to bilateral exchanges. A series of cases in the mid-1960s extended the doctrine of promissory estoppel to promises made in the course of contract negotiations. The following case addresses whether a rejected tenant could seek damages from a prospective lessor that backed out of negotiations.

A CASE IN POINT

CASE 7.2

POP'S CONES, INC. v. RESORTS INTERNATIONAL HOTEL, INC.

NEW JERSEY SUPERIOR COURT
704 A.2D 1321
(N.J. SUPER. CT. 1998).

SUMMARY

FACTS Pop's Cones, a franchisee of TCBY Systems, a national franchisor of frozen yogurt products, began operating a store in Margate, New Jersey, in June 1991. In 1994, Brenda Taube, the president of Pop's, had a number of meetings with Marlon Phoenix, the executive director of business development and sales for Resorts International, a casino hotel in Atlantic City. Resorts leased retail space along prime boardwalk frontage in Atlantic City, and Taube raised with Phoenix the possibility of Pop's leasing a boardwalk property. When Taube expressed concerns about the rental fees, Phoenix assured her that Resorts was eager to have Pop's as a tenant and that "financial issues . . . could be easily resolved, such as through a percentage of gross revenue." In late July 1994, Taube drafted a written proposal to lease the location, offering Resorts "7% of net monthly sales (gross less sales tax)" for the duration of an initial six-year term with an option to renew for another six years. In mid-September, Taube asked Phoenix about the status of her lease proposal. She told Phoenix that Pop's had an option to renew its existing Margate lease and needed to notify the landlord whether it would be staying by October 1, 1994. During another conversation in late September, Taube asked Phoenix whether the proposal was "in the ballpark" of what Resorts was looking for. Phoenix responded, "[W]e are 95% there, we just need [Phoenix's boss's] signature on the deal." Phoenix told Taube that he expected his boss to follow his recommendation and approve the deal, and he advised Taube to give notice that Pop's would not extend its Margate lease.

Taube subsequently gave notice of nonrenewal and moved Pop's equipment from the Margate location into storage while she began site preparations for the new store. She sent designs to TCBY and retained an attorney to represent Pop's in finalizing the lease with Resorts. On December 1, 1994, Resorts' general counsel sent a proposed lease form to Pop's attorney whereby Resorts offered to lease the space for an initial three-year term for the greater of 7 percent of gross revenues or $50,000 in year one, $60,000 in year two, and $70,000 in year three, with a three-year option to renew after the initial term. The letter concluded:

> This letter is not intended to be binding upon Resorts. It is intended to set forth the basic terms and conditions upon which Resorts would be willing to negotiate a lease and is subject to those negotiations and the execution of a definitive agreement. . . . We think TCBY will be successful at the Boardwalk location based upon the terms we propose. We look forward to having your client as part of . . . Resorts family of customer service providers and believe TCBY will benefit greatly from some of the dynamic changes we plan. . . . We would be pleased . . . to discuss this proposal in greater detail.

Later in December, the Resorts general counsel told Taube that Resorts wanted to postpone finalizing the lease until after the first of the year because of a public announcement it intended to make about an unrelated business venture. In January 1995, the Resorts general counsel sent a letter to Pop's attorney informing Pop's that Resorts was withdrawing its offer, "This letter is to confirm our conversation of this date wherein I advised that Resorts is withdrawing its December 1, 1994 offer to lease space to your client, TCBY." Despite extensive efforts to reopen the franchise at a different location, Taube was unable to reopen until July 1996.

CONTINUED

ISSUE PRESENTED Can a party to failed lease negotiations successfully assert a claim for promissory estoppel based on precontractual negotiations and acts taken in reliance thereon?

SUMMARY OF OPINION The New Jersey Superior Court began by noting that Pop's was not seeking damages relating to a lease of the boardwalk property, but rather was seeking damages flowing from its reliance upon promises made to it prior to October 1, 1994, when it failed to renew its lease for its Margate location. Thus, the plaintiff's claim was predicated upon the concept of promissory estoppel and was not a traditional breach-of-contract claim.

The court explained that a person asserting a promissory estoppel claim has the burden of demonstrating the existence of—or for purposes of summary judgment, a dispute as to material fact with regard to—four separate elements: (1) the promisor made a clear and definite promise, (2) the promise was made with the expectation that the promisee would rely thereon, (3) the promisee must in fact have reasonably relied on the promise, and (4) the promisee incurred detriment of a definite and substantial nature in reliance on the promise. The essential justification for the promissory estoppel doctrine is to avoid the substantial hardship or injustice that would result if such a promise were not enforced.

The court found that Pop's had presented facts that clearly showed that when Taube informed Phoenix that Pop's option to renew its lease at its Margate location had to be exercised by October 1, 1994, Phoenix instructed Taube to give notice that Pop's would not be extending the lease. In reliance upon those representations, Pop's, in fact, did not renew its lease. It vacated its Margate location, placed its equipment and personalty into temporary storage, retained the services of an attorney to finalize the lease with the defendant, and engaged in planning the relocation to the defendant's property. The court implied that it was up to a jury to decide whether Taube's reliance upon Phoenix's assurances was foreseeable and reasonable.

RESULT The New Jersey Superior Court reversed the trial court's summary judgment in favor of Resorts and remanded the case for appropriate proceedings. It was up to the jury to decide whether Phoenix expected Taube to rely on his promise and whether that reliance was reasonable.

CRITICAL THINKING QUESTIONS

1. Should Taube be able to recover her opportunity costs, that is, the profits Pop's would have earned had she been able to move into the Resorts location in January 1995?
2. If Taube relocated her family to be near the new store site, should the personal moving expenses of her family be reimbursed by Resorts?

PRECONTRACTUAL LIABILITY FOR FAILURE TO NEGOTIATE IN GOOD FAITH

Under traditional contract law, the offeror is free to revoke an offer at any time before it is accepted without risk of *precontractual liability*. A party entering negotiations does so at the risk the negotiations will break off. Courts typically will impose a duty to negotiate in good faith only if a letter of intent between the two parties specifically imposes that duty. For example, Venture Associates had sent Zenith Data a letter of intent that stated, "this letter is intended to evidence the preliminary understanding which we have reached . . . and our mutual intent to negotiate in good faith to enter into a definitive Purchase Agreement." Based on the wording in the letter of intent, the U.S. district court held that the two parties had entered into an enforceable preliminary agreement to negotiate in good faith.[4]

In the following case, the court considered whether Baskin Robbins had a good faith duty to negotiate even though there was no written agreement that required the parties to negotiate in good faith.

4. Venture Associates Corp. v. Zenith Data Systems Corp., 887 F. Supp. 1014 (N.D. Ill. 1995).

A CASE IN POINT

IN THE LANGUAGE OF THE COURT

CASE 7.3

COPELAND V. BASKIN ROBBINS

COURT OF APPEAL OF CALIFORNIA
117 CAL. RPTR. 2D 875
(CAL. CT. APP. 2002).

FACTS When Baskin Robbins announced its intention to close its ice cream manufacturing plant in Vernon, California, Copeland expressed an interest in acquiring it. Copeland's offer was contingent on the execution of a co-packing agreement whereby Baskin Robbins would agree to purchase the ice cream that Copeland manufactured in the plant. In May 1999, Baskin Robbins sent Copeland a letter that stated:

> This letter details the terms which our . . . executives have approved for subletting and sale of our Vernon manufacturing facility/equipment and a product supply agreement. . . . (1) Baskin Robbins will sell [Copeland] Vernon's ice cream manufacturing equipment . . . for $1,300,000 cash. . . . (2) Baskin Robbins would agree, subject to a separate co-packaging agreement and negotiated pricing, to provide [Copeland] a three year co-packing agreement for 3,000,000 gallons in year 1, 2,000,000 gallons in year 2 and 2,000,000 in year 3. . . . If the above is acceptable please acknowledge by returning a copy of this letter with a non-refundable check for three thousand dollars. . . . We should be able to coordinate a closing [within] thirty days thereafter.

Copeland signed a statement at the bottom of the letter agreeing that "[t]he above terms are acceptable" and returned the letter to Baskin Robbins along with the $3,000 deposit.

Thereafter, the negotiations of the co-packing agreement broke down with regard to several items. In July 1999, Baskin Robbins terminated the co-packing negotiations entirely and returned Copeland's $3,000 deposit. Copeland then declined Baskin Robbins's offer to proceed with the agreement for the sale and lease of the Vernon plant assets.

Copeland filed a lawsuit for breach of contract, alleging that Baskin Robbins had breached its May 1999 letter agreement to negotiate the terms of a co-packing agreement by "unreasonably and wrongfully refusing to enter into any co-packing agreement with [him]." The trial court granted Baskin Robbins's motion for summary judgment on the ground that the letter failed as a contract because the essential terms of the co-packing deal were never agreed to and there was no reasonable basis on which to determine them.

ISSUE PRESENTED Can a party to failed contract negotiations successfully sue for breach of a contract to negotiate an agreement, or is such a "contract" merely an unenforceable "agreement to agree"?

OPINION JOHNSON, Acting P.J., writing for the California Court of Appeal:

When Baskin Robbins refused to continue negotiating the terms of the co-packing agreement, Copeland faced a dilemma. "Many millions of dollars" in anticipated profits had melted away like so much banana ripple ice cream on a hot summer day. . . . [H]e could proceed with the contract for the purchase and lease of the Vernon plant's assets and use those assets to produce ice cream for other retailers. But . . . without the Baskin Robbins co-packing agreement he could not afford to purchase the assets and pay the on-going costs of operating the plant while he searched for other business. Alternatively he could attempt to sue Baskin Robbins for breach of the co-packing agreement on the theory the terms of the agreement set out in the May 1999 letter plus additional terms supplied by the court constituted an enforceable contract. Such a suit, however, had a slim prospect of success. . . . It is still the general rule that where any of the essential elements of a promise are reserved for the future agreement of both parties, no legal obligation arises until such "future agreement is made."

Copeland chose a third course. Rather than insist the parties had formed a co-packing contract and Baskin Robbins had breached it, he claimed the May 1999 letter constituted a contract to negotiate

CONTINUED

the remaining terms of the co-packing agreement and Baskin Robbins breached this contract by refusing without excuse to continue negotiations or, alternatively, by failing to negotiate in good faith. This path too has its difficulties. No reported California case has held breach of a contract to negotiate an agreement gives rise to a cause of action for damages. . . . We believe, however, these difficulties could be overcome in an appropriate case.

Initially, we see no reason why in principle the parties could not enter into a valid, enforceable contract to negotiate the terms of the co-packing agreement. A contract, after all, is "an agreement to do or not to do a certain thing." Persons are free to contract to do just about anything that is not illegal or immoral. Conducting negotiations to buy and sell ice cream is neither.

A contract to negotiate the terms of an agreement is not, in form or substance, an "agreement to agree." If, despite their good faith efforts, the parties fail to reach ultimate agreement on the terms in issue the contract to negotiate is deemed performed and the parties are discharged from their obligations. Failure to agree is not, itself, a breach of the contract to negotiate. A party will be liable only if a failure to reach ultimate agreement results from a breach of the party's obligation to negotiate or to negotiate in good faith. . . .

. . . Baskin Robbins maintains that there are sound public policy reasons for not enforcing a contract to negotiate an agreement. In doing so, we would be injecting a covenant of good faith and fair dealing into the negotiation process whether or not the parties specifically agreed to such a term. . . . Most parties, Baskin Robbins suggests, would prefer to risk losing their out-of-pocket costs if the negotiation fails rather than risk losing perhaps millions of dollars in expectation damages if their disappointed negotiating partner can prove bad faith. Finally, Baskin Robbins argues, any precontractual wrong-doing can be adequately remedied by existing causes of action for unjust enrichment, promissory fraud and promissory estoppel. . . .

. . . [W]e believe there are sound public policy reasons for protecting parties to a business negotiation from bad faith practices by their negotiating partners. Gone are the days when our ancestors sat around a fire and bargained for the exchange of stones axes for bear hides. Today the stakes are much higher and negotiations are much more complex. Deals are rarely made in a single negotiating session. Rather, they are the product of a gradual process in which agreements are reached piecemeal on a variety of issues in a series of face-to-face meetings, telephone calls, e-mails and letters involving corporate officers, lawyers, bankers, accountants, architects, engineers and others. . . . [C]ontracts today are not formed by discrete offers, counter-offers and acceptances. Instead they result from a gradual flow of information between the parties followed by a series of compromises and tentative agreements on major points which are finally refined into contract terms. These slow contracts are not only time consuming but costly. For these reasons, the parties should have some assurance "their investments in time and money and effort will not be wiped out by the other party's footdragging or change of heart or taking advantage of a vulnerable position created by the negotiation." . . .

For obvious reasons, damages for breach of a contract to negotiate an agreement are measured by the injury the plaintiff suffered in relying on the defendant to negotiate in good faith. This measure encompasses the plaintiff's out-of-pocket costs in conducting the negotiations and may or may not include lost opportunity costs. The plaintiff cannot recover for lost expectations (profits) because there is no way of knowing what the ultimate terms of the agreement would have been or even if there would have been an ultimate agreement.

RESULT Because Copeland failed to establish any reliance damages, Baskin Robbins was entitled to summary judgment. Baskin Robbins had breached it duty to negotiate in good faith, but Copeland was unable to prove that it had suffered losses in reliance on Baskin Robbins's promise.

CONTINUED

Critical Thinking Questions

1. What other causes of action might Copeland have been able to allege against Baskin Robbins?
2. How could Baskin Robbins have structured the negotiations to avoid any potential liability when it elected to break off the negotiations related to the co-packing agreement?

In addition to imposing liability for a breach of the duty to negotiate in narrow circumstances, American courts will impose precontractual liability on theories of misrepresentation or promissory estoppel.[5] For example, the Supreme Court of Washington found misrepresentation when the owner of a warehouse told the lessee that he intended to renew the lease for three years, but in fact was negotiating the sale of the facility to someone else.[6]

Unconscionability

A contract term is *unconscionable* if it is oppressive or fundamentally unfair. This concept is applied most often to consumer contracts where the consumer may have little or no bargaining power. The seller dictates the terms of the contract, and the buyer can take it or leave it.

One state's settlement with the tobacco industry provides a vivid illustration. In August 1997, the State of Florida settled a suit against the tobacco industry for more than $11 billion. The State had hired a group of outside attorneys to represent it in the case, in exchange for a 25 percent contingency fee. The settlement agreement with the tobacco industry called for attorneys' fees to be determined by an independent arbitrator. Several of the State's outside attorneys then went to court in an effort to enforce their 25 percent contingency-fee contract.

A Florida state judge denied their claim on unconscionability grounds. The court stated that a fee of tens of millions of dollars or perhaps even hundreds of millions could be reasonable, "but a fee of 2.8 *billion* dollars simply shocks the conscience of the court." The court calculated that if the twelve principal lawyers had worked around the clock from the outset of negotiations in mid-1994 through the end of 1997, they would be paid the equivalent of $7,716 per hour if the contingency-fee agreement were upheld. The court found these figures to be "patently ridiculous" and "per se unreasonable."[7]

Courts usually refuse to enforce contract terms that they find unconscionable. Unconscionability has both a procedural and a substantive element. When the term is central to the contract, the court can either rewrite the term (for example, by substituting a fair market price) or void the entire contract.

5. For an excellent summary of the law in this area, *see* E. Allen Farnsworth, *Precontractual Liability and Preliminary Agreements: Fair Dealing and Failed Negotiations,* 87 Colum. L. Rev. 217 (1987).

6. Markov v. ABC Transfer & Storage Co., 457 P.2d 535 (Wash. 1969).

7. John McKinnon, *Florida Judge Blocks Lawyers' Bid to Collect Tobacco-Accord Fee,* Wall St. J., Nov. 13, 1997, at B3.

› Ethical Consideration

In 2002, Alliant, Inc. entered into a contract to string Rogers Communications' cable lines across thousands of utility poles in Canada's Maritime provinces for an annual fee of $9.60 per pole. The contract stated that it "shall continue in force for a period of five years from the date it is made, and thereafter for successive five year terms, unless and until terminated by one year prior notice in writing by either party." In 2005, Alliant informed Rogers that it was canceling the contract. Although Rogers argued that the intent of the agreement was to lock Alliant into a five-year obligation, the Canadian Radio-Television and Telecommunications Commission concluded, "Based on the rules of punctuation," the second comma in the provision "allows for the termination of the [contract] at any time, without cause, upon one-year's written notice." As a result, it was reported that Rogers would end up paying approximately $2.13 million more than it had expected to pay under the contract. Assuming that the parties had shared a common understanding that the contract was intended to be binding for a minimum of five years, was it ethical to rely on a grammatical error to avoid the five-year term?

Source: Grant Robertson, *Comma Quirk Irks Rogers*, Globe & Mail (Toronto), Aug. 6, 2006, *available at* http://www.theglobeandmail.com/servlet/story/RTGAM.20060806.wr-rogers07/BNStory/Business/.

Origins of the Equitable Doctrines of Promissory Estoppel and Unconscionability

Until the 1870s, the English legal system had both courts of law and courts of equity. The courts of law enforced the laws, but the range of claims that could be heard was narrow and the procedures that governed them were complicated and technical. As a result, many meritorious claimants were denied relief by the courts of law.

In such cases, a claimant could still seek relief by filing a petition with the king (or queen). Over time, the royal secretarial department, referred to as the Chancery, began to resemble a judicial body and became known as the "Court of Chancery." The Chancery courts, also referred to as equity courts, were more concerned than the courts of law with reaching a fair result, even if it did not fit within the strict letter of the law.

Although the state and federal court systems of the United States initially replicated England's dual court system, the northern states had eliminated equity courts by the late 1700s. A dual system of U.S. federal courts of law and equity continued until 1937. As equity courts were eliminated, equity powers were merged into the courts of law so that a plaintiff could seek both legal and equitable relief in the same action. Today, only four U.S. states—Arkansas, Delaware, Mississippi, and Tennessee—have completely separate Courts of Chancery. The most notable of these is the Court of Chancery in Delaware, which is renowned throughout the world as the preeminent forum for corporate matters.

There are two important equitable contract doctrines—promissory estoppel and unconscionability. The doctrine of promissory estoppel enforces some promises even though the injured party cannot establish all of the elements for a binding contract. The doctrine of unconscionability, on the other hand, allows a court to refuse to enforce an otherwise valid and enforceable contract or contract provision.

After the doctrine of promissory estoppel was developed in 1877, it fell into disfavor until 1947 when it was resurrected in *Central London Property Trust Ltd. v. High Trees House Ltd.*[a] In this case, the claimants had leased a block of apartments to the defendants at an annual rent of £2500, but agreed to accept a reduction in rent to £1250 because they could not find enough tenants during World War II. This promise to accept less rent was not supported by any consideration. When the war ended and the apartments were all leased, the claimants demanded the full rent, plus back rent for the period during the war. The court held that the claimants were entitled to full rent from the end of the war forward, but that they were estopped from going back on their promise to reduce the rent during the war because it would be inequitable to do so.

In the United States, promissory estoppel was generally confined to cases involving intrafamily transactions and donative promises to charities until the Wisconsin Supreme Court extended promissory estoppel liability to misleading precontractual representations in commercial transactions in the 1965 case of *Hoffman v. Red Owl Stores*.[b] In that case, the court gave limited relief to a plaintiff who claimed that he had sold his business and incurred other expenses in reliance on Red Owl's assurances that he had sufficient capital to purchase a Red Owl franchise. He was injured when he was unable to buy the franchise because Red Owl subsequently increased the purchase price.

By at least the mid-eighteenth century, the courts of equity in England were refusing to enforce unconscionable contracts.[c] In nineteenth-century America, the U.S. Supreme Court defined unconscionability as "behavior sufficiently outrageous to shock the conscience of the court."[d] The coming of the Industrial Revolution and the emergence of large corporations in the mid-1800s brought about fundamental changes in the mode of analysis of contract law. As goods became more complex, the seller typically knew more about them than the buyer did, and the bargaining power of large corporations often greatly exceeded that of the individuals with whom they contracted. Thus, a greater number of contracts failed to satisfy the "equal footing" condition necessary to make freedom of contract efficiency enhancing. Courts became less hesitant to intervene to protect a party to a contract who was perceived to be weaker, and the doctrine of unconscionability was expanded to cover situations where the parties were not on an equal footing. Nevertheless, courts remain reluctant to find unconscionability

CONTINUED

in negotiated contracts between two business parties because of a desire to encourage predictability in commercial transactions. As a result, most unconscionability cases involve form contracts between a business and an individual.

a. [1947] K.B. 130.
b. 133 N.W.2d 267 (Wis. 1965).
c. *See* Earl of Chesterfield v. Janssen, 2 Ves. Sen. 125, 28 Eng. Rep. 82 (Ch. 1750), in which the court defined an unconscionable contract as one that "no honest man in his senses and not under delusion would make on one hand, and as no honest and fair man would accept on the other." The doctrine of *laesio enormis,* which dates back to the Code of Justinian, barred the enforcement of contracts for the sale of land or goods for less than one half of the "just price." James Gordley, *Equality in Exchange,* 69 CAL. REV. L. 1587 (1981).
d. Eyre v. Potter, 56 U.S. 42, 60 (1853).

PROCEDURAL ELEMENT

The procedural element of unconscionability focuses on two factors: oppression and surprise. *Oppression* arises from an inequality of bargaining power that results in no real negotiation and an absence of meaningful choice for one party to the contract. *Surprise* arises when the terms of the contract are hidden in a densely printed form drafted by the party seeking to enforce these terms. Form contracts are usually drafted by the party with the superior bargaining position.

SUBSTANTIVE ELEMENT

Substantive unconscionability cannot be defined precisely. Courts have talked in terms of "overly harsh" or "one-sided" results. One commentator has pointed out that unconscionability turns not only on a "one-sided" result, but also on an absence of justification for it. The most detailed and specific commentaries observe that a contract is largely an allocation of risk between the parties; therefore, a contractual term is substantively suspect if it reallocates the risk of the bargain in an objectively unreasonable or unexpected manner. But not all unreasonable risk allocations are unconscionable. The greater the unfair surprise or the inequality of bargaining power, the less likely the courts will tolerate an unreasonable risk allocation.

LIABILITY RELEASES

The user of a facility is sometimes asked to sign a general release, especially before embarking on a dangerous activity such as skydiving or race car driving. A *general release* purports to relieve the owner of the facility of any liability, including liability for negligence that results in injuries to a person using the facility. A number of earlier cases held that the exculpatory language in a general release agreement was invalid because the agreement was unconscionable. More recently, however, releases have been enforced when (1) the language of the release evidences a clear and unambiguous intent to exonerate the would-be defendant from liability; (2) there was no vast difference in the parties' bargaining power at the time the release was executed; and (3) enforcement of the clause is not injurious to the public health, morals, or confidence in administration of the laws and does not violate public policy.[8] Courts generally will not enforce releases that purport to relieve a party from liability for an "intentional, willful or fraudulent act or gross, wanton negligence."[9]

The following case involved a release found to violate public policy.

8. *See, e.g.,* Schmidt v. United States, 912 P.2d 871 (Okla. 1996).
9. *Id.*

A CASE IN POINT | IN THE LANGUAGE OF THE COURT

CASE 7.4

ATKINS V. SWIMWEST FAMILY FITNESS CENTER

SUPREME COURT OF WISCONSIN
691 N.W.2D 334 (WIS. 2005).

FACTS Swimwest is an instructional swimming facility located in Madison, Wisconsin, with a lap pool that is open to both members and visitors. Dr. Charis Wilson, a local physician, visited Swimwest as part of a physical therapy and rehabilitation program. Because she was not a member of Swimwest, she was required to fill out a guest registration card that requested the visitor's name, address, phone number, reason for visit, and interest in membership. The following standardized "Waiver Release Statement," printed in capital letters with the same size font and color, appeared below the registration information:

CONTINUED

I AGREE TO ASSUME ALL LIABILITY FOR MYSELF WITHOUT REGARD TO FAULT, WHILE AT SWIMWEST FAMILY FITNESS CENTER. I FURTHER AGREE TO HOLD HARMLESS SWIMWEST FITNESS CENTER, OR ANY OF ITS EMPLOYEES FOR ANY CONDITIONS OR INJURY THAT MAY RESULT TO MYSELF WHILE AT THE SWIMWEST FITNESS CENTER. I HAVE READ THE FOREGOING AND UNDERSTAND ITS CONTENTS.

The card had just one signature and date line, which appeared after the "Waiver Release Statement."

Although a witness testified that she saw Wilson swimming the sidestroke up and down the length of the pool, a Swimwest employee spotted her lying motionless underwater near the bottom of the pool soon after she began swimming. Wilson died the next day, and drowning was listed as the official cause of death.

Wilson's minor child filed a wrongful death action for negligence against Swimwest through his guardian ad litem. The trial court granted Swimwest's motion for summary judgment and dismissed the action. The court of appeals certified the appeal to the Wisconsin Supreme Court to clarify Wisconsin law regarding the enforceability of exculpatory clauses in standard liability release forms.

Issue Presented Was the exculpatory provision in the Swimwest guest registration card valid and enforceable, and did it operate to bar the plaintiff's negligence claims?

Opinion CROOKS, J., writing for the Wisconsin Supreme Court:

[W]e hold that Swimwest's exculpatory clause is in violation of public policy. First, this exculpatory waiver, which uses the word "fault," is overly broad and all-inclusive. Second, the form, serving two functions and not requiring a separate signature for the exculpatory clause, thus not sufficiently highlighting that clause, does not provide the signer adequate notification of the waiver's nature and significance. Third, there was little or no opportunity to bargain or negotiate in regard to the exculpatory language in question. . . .

. . . [W]e find the waiver's broadness raises questions about its meaning and demonstrates its one-sidedness. The language chosen by Swimwest is not clear and could potentially bar any claim arising under any scenario. The waiver begins: "I AGREE TO ASSUME ALL LIABILITY FOR MYSELF WITHOUT REGARD TO FAULT. . . ." This language never makes clear what type of acts the word "fault" encompasses. Although Swimwest alleges that negligence is synonymous with fault, we find that fault is susceptible to a broader interpretation. Fault is currently defined as "[a]n error or defect of judgment or of conduct; any deviation from prudence or duty resulting from inattention, incapacity, perversity, bad faith, or mismanagement." This definition is broad enough to cover a reckless or an intentional act. A waiver of liability for an intentional act would clearly place the exculpatory clause in violation of public policy. We again emphasize that exculpatory language must be strictly construed against the party seeking to rely on it.

If Swimwest wanted to make clear that the signer is releasing it from negligent acts, it could have included the word "negligence" in the waiver. While this court has never specifically required exculpatory clauses to include the word "negligence," we have stated that "we consider that it would be very helpful for such contracts to set forth in clear and express terms that the party signing it is releasing others for their negligent acts. . . ."

Likewise, the broadness of the exculpatory language makes it difficult to ascertain exactly what was within Wilson's or Swimwest's contemplation. We have consistently held that "[o]nly if it is apparent that the parties, in light of all the circumstances, knowingly agreed to exclude the defendants from liability will the contract be enforceable.". . .

. . . Wilson likely would not have contemplated drowning in a four-foot deep pool with a lifeguard on duty, when she signed the guest registration and waiver form. The question is not whether

CONTINUED

swimming carries with it the risk of drowning, but rather whether Wilson, herself, likely contemplated that risk.

Here, the guest registration and waiver form does not provide adequate notice of the waiver's nature and significance. In this case, the form provided by Swimwest served two purposes. It was both a "Guest Registration" application and a "Waiver Release Statement." . . . The waiver in this case could have been a separate document, providing Wilson with more adequate notice of what she was signing. Also a separate signature line could have been provided, but was not. . . .

Another problem with the form was that there was nothing conspicuous about the paragraph containing the "Waiver Release Statement." . . .

. . . [T]here was no opportunity for Wilson to bargain over the exculpatory language in the guest registration and waiver form. . . . Wilson had an opportunity to read the form and ask questions. She was told that the form included a waiver, and allegedly took her time reading the card. This information alone, however, is not sufficient to demonstrate a bargaining opportunity. The form itself must provide an opportunity to bargain. . . . Wilson was without an opportunity to negotiate in regard to the standard exculpatory language used in the form. She was forced to either sign the form or not swim at Swimwest. We hold, therefore, that such an exculpatory clause, where there is no opportunity to bargain in regard to its terms, presents another significant factor in the analysis of public policy.

RESULT The court reversed the trial court's decision and remanded the case for further proceedings consistent with its opinion.

DISSENT WILCOX, J., dissenting from the majority opinion:

While I certainly do not believe that all exculpatory agreements should be upheld, the majority opinion will render it virtually impossible to enforce any exculpatory agreement in Wisconsin. The majority concludes that the agreement in this case is unenforceable as against public policy for three reasons: 1) the agreement is overly broad; 2) the agreement services two purposes; and 3) there was no opportunity for the signer to bargain or negotiate over the exculpatory language. . . . I disagree with the majority's application of factors one and two and while I am bound to accept the legitimacy of the third factor, I question the manner in which [it] is applied in this case. . . .

Individuals have a right to know what the law is so that they may conduct their affairs in an orderly fashion. . . . Because the majority fails to articulate such a test, fails to apply the first two factors in accordance with the guidelines set forth in [an earlier case], and leaves open the possibility that the lack of an "opportunity to bargain" alone is sufficient to invalidate an exculpatory agreement, I respectfully dissent.

GENUINENESS OF ASSENT

Even a contract that meets all the requirements of validity (agreement, consideration, capacity, and legality) may not be enforceable if there was no true "meeting of the minds" between the two parties. In other words, a court will refuse to enforce a contract if it feels one or both of the parties did not genuinely assent to its terms. The discussion below examines a variety of problems that could prevent a true meeting of the minds, including fraud, duress, ambiguity, and mistake.

FRAUD

A contract is voidable if it is tainted with fraud. There are two types of fraud: fraud in the factum and fraud in the inducement. *Fraud in the factum* occurs when, because of a *misrepresentation,* or untrue statement of material fact, one party does not understand that he or she is entering into a contract or does not understand one or more essential terms of the contract. For example, if a person was given a deed to sign for the transfer of real property, after being told that the document was an employment agreement, the deed could be voided by the defrauded party.

The second type of fraud, *fraud in the inducement,* occurs when a party makes a false statement to persuade the other party to enter into an agreement. If a jeweler tells a customer that the stone in a ring is a diamond when the jeweler knows it is zirconium, the purchaser would have the right to rescind, or cancel, the agreement to purchase the ring based on fraud in the inducement. A contract is not voidable due to fraudulent misrepresentation, unless the misrepresentation was material to the bargain and was reasonably relied on by the party seeking to void the contract.

Fraud in the inducement also occurs when a party has a duty to disclose information to the other party but fails to do so. The duty to disclose often arises out of a special relationship between the parties (that is, a fiduciary relationship), such as between an officer and a corporation or between a trustee and a beneficiary. For example, a partner who knows the true value of a piece of property cannot sell it to a fellow partner without disclosing the true value. Parties engaged in arm's-length transactions cannot affirmatively misrepresent a fact, but as a general rule, they do not have a duty to disclose every fact that might be material to the other party.

Promissory fraud occurs when one party makes a promise without any intention of carrying it out. This is a misrepresentation of intent, rather than a misrepresentation of fact. Because a promise to do something necessarily implies the intention to perform, when a promise is made without such an intention, there is an implied misrepresentation of fact that can give the other party the right to rescind the contract. Promissory fraud is a tort as well as a defense to a contract action, and punitive damages may be available if the injured party can prove that the other party acted with malice.

DURESS

A contract is voidable if one party was forced to enter into it through fear created by threats. Thus, inducing someone to sign a contract by physical threat, blackmail, or extortion is *duress.* Duress is present only if the threatened act is wrongful or illegal. Therefore, more subtle forms of pressure, such as an implied threat that at-will employees will lose their jobs unless they sign agreements waiving certain rights to employee benefits, do not constitute duress.

Historically, economic duress was usually not enough to invalidate a contract. Early common law provided that a contract could be voided only if the party claiming duress could show that the agreement was entered into for fear of loss of life or limb, mayhem, or imprisonment. Today, however, courts are willing to set aside contracts on the basis of economic duress when (1) the party alleging economic duress involuntarily accepted the terms of another, (2) the circumstances permitted no other alternative, and (3) the circumstances resulted from the other party's wrongful and oppressive conduct. For example, a court found economic duress when a company deliberately withheld payment of an acknowledged debt of $260,000 knowing that the other party had no choice but to accept its offer of $97,500 in settlement of the debt because of that party's own pressing debts.[10]

Under the related doctrine of *undue influence,* a court may invalidate an agreement if one party exercised improper persuasion on the other that made genuine assent impossible. Improper persuasion may result from such factors as constant pressure, a need for the victim to act quickly, unavailability of independent advice, or the weakness or infirmity of the victim. For example, if an invalid living alone, with few contacts with the outside world and dependent on a caregiver, agreed to sell her house to the caregiver at a bargain price, a court might set aside that agreement based on undue influence.

10. Totem Marine Tug & Barge, Inc. v. Alyeska Pipeline Serv. Co., 584 P.2d 15 (Alaska 1978).

› ETHICAL CONSIDERATION

When Circuit City hired Paul Mantor in 1992, it did not have an arbitration program. In 1995, Circuit City adopted its "Associate Issue Resolution Program" (AIRP). The AIRP provided that:

> . . . except as otherwise limited herein, any and all employment-related legal disputes, controversies or claims of an [employee] arising out of, or related to, an [employee's] application or candidacy for employment or cessation of employment with Circuit City . . . shall be settled exclusively by final and binding arbitration before a neutral, third-party Arbitrator selected in accordance with these Dispute Resolution Rules and Procedures. Arbitration shall apply to any and all such disputes, controversies or claims whether asserted against the Company and/or against any employee, officer, alleged agent, director or affiliate company.

The AIRP also (1) required an employee to pay a $75 filing fee to Circuit City to begin an arbitration, (2) provided that Circuit City had sole discretion to decide whether to waive the filing fee and other costs of arbitration (in a court action, an indigent plaintiff is exempt from having to pay court fees), and (3) prohibited arbitrators from hearing an arbitration as a class action.

Circuit City emphasized to its managers the importance of full participation in the AIRP, claiming that the company

CONTINUED

had been losing money because of lawsuits filed by employees. Although Circuit City circulated the forms regarding the AIRP in 1995, Mantor avoided signing them for three years. In 1998, however, Circuit City management met with him to discuss his participation in the program. When Mantor asked them what would happen if he declined to participate, they told him he would have no future with Circuit City. Soon thereafter, Mantor agreed to participate, acknowledging in writing his receipt of the program and an opt-out form by which employees could ostensibly elect not to participate in the AIRP.

Circuit City terminated Mantor's employment in 2000. When Mantor brought a civil action against Circuit City in state court, Circuit City petitioned the federal district court to compel arbitration under the Federal Arbitration Act, and the court granted the motion. The Federal Arbitration Act provides that arbitration agreements generally "shall be valid, irrevocable, and enforceable," but when grounds "exist at law or in equity for the revocation of any contract," courts may decline to enforce such agreements. On appeal, Mantor argued that the district court erred in granting the order to compel arbitration.

If you had been the manager at Circuit City who spoke with Mantor, what would you have said when he asked what would happen if he declined to participate in the AIRP? Was it ethical for Circuit City to distribute an opt-out form while informing employees orally that they would be terminated if they refused to participate in the AIRP? What arguments could Mantor make to support his position that he was not bound by the AIRP's mandatory arbitration provision?

Source: Circuit City Stores, Inc. v. Mantor, 335 F.3d 1101 (9th Cir. 2003), *cert. denied,* 540 U.S. 1160 (2004).

AMBIGUITY

Misunderstandings may arise from ambiguous language in a contract or from a mistake as to the facts. If the terms of a contract are subject to differing interpretations, some courts will construe the ambiguity against the party who drafted the agreement. More often, courts will apply the following rule: The party who would be adversely affected by a particular interpretation can void the contract when (1) both interpretations are reasonable and (2) the parties either both knew or both did not know of the different interpretations. If only one party knew or had reason to know of the other's interpretation, the court will find for the party who did not know or did not have reason to know of the difference.

In a case involving Mark Suwyn, an executive vice president of International Paper Company (the world's largest paper company), a federal court refused to enforce a noncompete agreement to prevent Suwyn from joining Louisiana-Pacific, a producer of wood products.[11] Suwyn had signed a broad covenant not to compete with International Paper after allegedly being assured by International Paper's chairman and CEO that the covenant was aimed at preventing Suwyn from going to one of the big paper companies. Suwyn had attached to the signed agreement a note indicating that it was meant to prevent him from joining a major paper company, such as Georgia-Pacific, Champion, or Weyerhaeuser. Because Louisiana-Pacific did not make paper and was not on the list, Suwyn argued that he was free to join the company. International Paper countered that the noncompete agreement included wood products, such as plywood and lumber, that both companies produced. The judge found there was no contract: Suwyn and International Paper had such different meanings in mind that there had been no real agreement on the scope of the noncompete.

MISTAKE OF FACT

Like a misunderstanding due to ambiguity, a *mistake of fact* by both parties can make a contract voidable. As a general rule, a unilateral mistake of fact by one party does not make a contract voidable. This rule has two narrow exceptions, however. A mistaken party may void a contract when either (1) the mistaken party has made an unintentional mistake in preparing its offer that makes the offer too good to be true or (2) the nonmistaken party is guilty of blameworthy conduct, such as fraud or misrepresentation.

A court's willingness to undo a contract based on a mistaken assumption of fact depends heavily on the particular circumstances. The court will look at three factors to determine if a mistake has been made: (l) the substantiality of the mistake, (2) whether the risks were allocated, and (3) timing.

Substantiality of the Mistake

A court is more likely to void the contract when the mistake has a material effect on one of the parties. For example, in the classic case *Raffles v. Wichelhaus,*[12] two parties had signed a contract in which Wichelhaus agreed to buy 125 bales of cotton to be brought by Raffles from India on a ship named *Peerless.* Unknown to both parties, there were

11. William M. Carley, *CEO Gets Hard Lesson in How Not to Keep His Top Lieutenants,* WALL ST. J., Feb. 11, 1998, at A1.

12. 159 Eng. Rep. 375 (Exch. 1864).

two ships named *Peerless,* both sailing out of Bombay during the same year. Raffles meant the *Peerless* that was sailing in December, and Wichelhaus meant the *Peerless* that was sailing in October. When the cotton arrived in the later ship, Wichelhaus refused to complete the purchase. Raffles then sued for breach of contract. The English court held that the contract was voidable due to the mutual mistake of fact. The court described the situation as one of "latent ambiguity" and declared that there was no meeting of the minds and therefore no contract.

The three-month delay had made the cotton worthless to the buyer, and thus the mistake was substantial. If the delay had been only a few days, the court would probably have enforced the contract. On the other hand, even if the delay had been only a few days, if the buyer had planned to resell the cotton on the open market and the price of cotton had dropped sharply during that period, the mistake would probably have been substantial enough to make the contract voidable.

Allocation of the Risks

If one party accepts a risk, then that party must bear the consequences even if it is doubtful that the risk will materialize. If the parties have not expressly allocated a risk, a court will sometimes place the risk on the party who had access to the most information. In other cases, the court might impose the risk on the party better able to bear it.

In the following case, in deciding whether the defendant should bear the risk of a unilateral mistake, the Hawaii Supreme Court also considered the fact that the defendant owed a fiduciary obligation to the plaintiff.

A CASE IN POINT

CASE 7.5

HONDA V. BOARD OF TRUSTEES OF THE EMPLOYEES' RETIREMENT SYSTEM OF THE STATE OF HAWAII

SUPREME COURT OF HAWAII
120 P.3D 237 (HAW. 2005).

SUMMARY

FACTS Katsumi Honda, a man with an eighth-grade education, had worked as a custodian for twenty-three years. When he reached age sixty-five in 1993, he notified the State of Hawaii Employees' Retirement System (ERS) that he intended to retire in June 1994 and asked for estimates of his retirement benefits and a retirement application. ERS sent him a letter that provided estimates of the monthly benefits for four "Modes of Retirement." The letter stated that the "Normal Option" would provide Katsumi with $239 in monthly benefits. The enclosed application required the employee to select one of four modes of retirement fund distribution: Normal, Option A, Option B, and Option C. The four modes of retirement listed on the application form were correlated with spaces for entering a beneficiary's name. In fact, employees selecting the Normal option were not entitled to survivor benefits.

On the reverse side of the application, under the heading "Modes of Retirement," the application stated, "Normal retirement allowance payable for life." Also on the reverse side of the application, under a section titled "Eligibility Requirements," were the words "Normal Retirement" again. In this instance, however, the words "Normal Retirement" referred to "eligib[ility] to receive a normal retirement allowance if you are 62 years old and have 10 years of credit service—or if you are at least 55 years old and have 30 or more years of credited service[,]" "[n]ot including any additional service for unused sick leave."

Katsumi checked off the "Normal" mode of retirement, listed his wife Helen as beneficiary, and returned the application to the ERS. In March 1994, Katsumi was diagnosed with cancer. He died on April 6, 1994, five days after his retirement from complications resulting from cancer. Helen received a letter from the ERS retirement claims examiner in May, informing her that she would not receive any benefits under her husband's plan. Helen subsequently filed a petition with the ERS Board for a declaratory order allowing her to select a new mode of retirement for Katsumi, retroactive to April 1, 1994. The ERS Board denied the request, and Helen appealed to the court. On February 7, 2001, the trial court issued a minute order in favor of Helen, and the ERS Board appealed.

ISSUE PRESENTED Was an employee who selected a retirement option based on a misleading application entitled to be released from his choice based on mistake of fact?

SUMMARY OF OPINION The Hawaii Supreme Court found that Katsumi should not have to bear the risk of the mistake because it was not allocated to him by the agreement between

CONTINUED

him and the ERS. Instead, the circumstances made it "reasonable" to allocate the risk of the mistake to the ERS, both because the ERS could have been at fault in causing the mistake and because the ERS Board had a fiduciary relationship with its members.

The court first concluded that the undifferentiated uses of the term "normal" and the dissimilar applications of the term "normal retirement" to describe a mode of retirement, and at the same time a category of eligibility for retirement, obfuscated the selection process. According to Helen's affidavit, Katsumi had "selected 'normal' retirement because he thought any other selection would result in loss of service credit, including loss of his accumulated sick leave and military service and result in less pension benefits." The ERS caused confusion when it used the same term "normal retirement" in two different ways.

Second, the court found that the application was seemingly misleading because it required the naming of a beneficiary under the normal mode of retirement even though, in effect, no survivor benefits would be distributed. Because Options A, B, and C contained identical spaces for entering a beneficiary's name, this would cause an employee to reasonably conclude that a normal retirement beneficiary would occupy a status similar to the beneficiaries indicated in Options A, B, and C.

Third, the court found that the pamphlet did not define the terms used or employ language understandable in everyday terms so as to reasonably inform the employee of the consequences of choosing the "normal" option. Even though the pamphlet contained the sentence, "The retirant receives a retirement allowance payable for life and in the event of death, there will be no further allowance payable," the court found the sentence ambiguous and seemingly inconsistent with the application form. In any event, in the overall context of what was provided to Katsumi, the court concluded that "this one sentence was plainly insufficient to reasonably convey to Katsumi the net effect of choosing a normal retirement option."

"Most significantly," the court reasoned, the ERS Board occupies a fiduciary relationship with its members and has a duty to "provide retirees sufficient information to make an informed decision in electing a retirement option." The court characterized the choice of retirement options as a "pivotal decision that may substantially affect the retiree's quality of living for the remainder of his or her life and the provision for loved ones upon the retiree's death." It ruled that legal confirmation of a fiduciary duty to the ERS members was necessary to assure that ERS members would not encounter the same or similar circumstances in future cases.

RESULT The court vacated the final judgment. The case was remanded to the ERS Board for reconsideration of Helen's request in light of the ERS's fiduciary duty to retirees and the entire record.

Timing

The party alleging a mistake of fact must give prompt notice when the mistake is discovered. If too much time passes before the other party is notified, undoing the contract might create more problems than letting it stand.

MISTAKE OF JUDGMENT

A *mistake of judgment* occurs when the parties make an erroneous assessment about some aspect of what is bargained for. For example, in a futures contract a seller agrees to sell a buyer a crop of sugar in three months at a price of fifty cents per pound. The seller is betting that the market price in three months will be less than fifty cents. The buyer is betting that the market price will be higher. One of them will be mistaken, but the futures contract will still be valid. This is a mistake of judgment. Such a mistake is not a valid defense to enforcement of the contract.

The line between judgment and fact can sometimes be unclear. In *CTA, Inc. v. United States,*[13] a company that entered into a contract to provide technical support services to the government included labor rates for its workers that

13. 44 Fed. Cl. 684 (Fed. 1999).

were substantially lower than the market rates. After realizing this discrepancy, the company argued that it had made a mistake in the numbers contained in the labor rates set forth in its bid. The court rejected this argument and found that the company had made an error in business judgment, not a mistake of fact. Had the labor rates been obviously in error, the court would probably have found a mistake of fact justifying withdrawal of the bid.

Another example is the classic case of *Sherwood v. Walker*.[14] A seller agreed to sell a barren cow for a low price, but before the sale closed, the seller discovered the cow was pregnant and therefore was worth about ten times the agreed-on price. As a result, the seller refused to proceed with the sale, and the buyer sued for breach of contract. The Michigan Supreme Court held that the contract was based on a mutual mistake of fact that made the contract unenforceable. The court reasoned:

> If there is a difference or misapprehension as to the substance of the thing bargained for; if the thing actually delivered or received is different in substance from the thing bargained for, and intended to be sold, then there is no contract . . . A barren cow is substantially a different creature than a breeding one.

A dissenting judge argued that the case involved a mistake in judgment. The buyer had believed the cow could be made to breed, in spite of the seller's statements to the contrary, and the seller disagreed. As the majority and dissenting opinions in this case demonstrate, different judges may reach different conclusions as to whether a mistake is one of fact or judgment.

Much of contract law comes down to the expectations of the parties involved. In the cow case, the seller did not believe the cow could be fertile. The buyer did not make known his secret belief that the cow could be made to breed. From the seller's point of view, the transaction was for a barren cow with no chance of breeding, but the buyer did not see the transaction that way. The case might have come out differently if the buyer had explicitly said to the seller, "I know you believe the cow is barren, but I believe she can be made to breed, and I'm willing to take the chance in buying her."

Although disclosing all expectations may make for firm contracts, it may not be the most effective negotiating technique. For example, had the buyer convinced the seller that the cow might be fertile, the seller would probably have demanded a higher price. One of the challenges of business is balancing the slim (but expensive) chances of litigation against the desire to capture value not apparent to the other party.

Statute of Frauds

Although most oral contracts are enforceable, many states have a statute, called the *statute of frauds,* which requires certain types of contracts to be evidenced by some form of written communication. If a contract covered by the statute of frauds is oral, it is still valid, but the courts will not enforce the contract if the statute of frauds is raised as a defense. Therefore, if neither party raises the issue, the contract will be enforced. Similarly, even if the party seeking to enforce the contract has not signed anything, it can still enforce the contract against a party who has signed a writing embodying the essential terms of the deal.

There are four traditional justifications for requiring certain contracts to be evidenced by writing. First, requiring a written document avoids fraudulent claims that an oral contract was made. Second, the existence of a written document avoids false claims as to the terms of the contract. Third, the statute of frauds encourages persons to put their agreements in writing, thereby reducing the risk of future misunderstandings. Fourth, the writing required by the statute has the psychological effect of reinforcing the importance of the parties' decision to enter into a contract.

Transactions Subject to the Statute of Frauds

Contracts that must be evidenced by some writing include (1) a contract for the transfer of any interest in real property (such as a deed, lease, or option to buy), (2) a promise to pay the debt of another person, (3) an agreement that by its terms cannot be performed within a year, and (4) a *prenuptial agreement* (that is, an agreement entered into before marriage that sets forth the manner in which the parties' assets will be distributed and the support to which each party will be entitled in the event of divorce).

The statute of frauds issue that arises most often in litigation is whether a contract can by its terms be performed within one year. If it cannot—that is, if the contract is longer than one year in duration—then it must be put in writing to be enforceable.

A typical "performed within one year" case involves an oral promise of "lifetime employment." For example, in *McInerney v. Charter Golf, Inc.*,[15] a golf-apparel sales representative received an offer to join a rival company, which promised to pay him an 8 percent commission. When notified of this offer, his current employer orally promised to guarantee the sales rep a 10 percent commission "for the

14. 33 N.W. 919 (Mich. 1887).

15. 680 N.E.2d 1347 (Ill. 1997).

> **ETHICAL CONSIDERATION**
>
> Is it ethical for a manager to raise the defense of failure to comply with the statute of frauds to avoid enforcement of an oral promise that the manager knows he or she made?

remainder of his life," subject to discharge only for dishonesty or disability. The sales rep accepted this offer and passed up the rival's offer. When he was fired three years later, he sued for breach of contract.

The Illinois Supreme Court ruled that a lifetime employment contract is intended to be permanent. It inherently anticipates a relationship of long duration—certainly longer than one year. Thus, the court found that the contract was subject to the statute of frauds and accordingly unenforceable because it was not in writing.

Other courts have taken a contrasting approach and construe the words "cannot be performed" to mean "not capable of being performed within one year." Because, theoretically, an employee can die at any time, these courts reason that lifetime employment contracts are *capable* of being performed within one year. As a result, they deem such contracts to be outside the scope of the statute of frauds and valid even if not in writing.

The statute of frauds does not require the agreement to be embodied in a formal, legal-looking document. An agreement can be represented by an exchange of letters that refer to each other, even if no single letter is sufficient to reflect all essential terms. Details or particulars can be omitted; only the essential terms must be stated. A writing may satisfy the statute of frauds even if the party never delivers or communicates it to the other party. What is essential depends on the agreement, its context, and the subsequent conduct of the parties. Under the *equal dignities rule,* if an agent acts on behalf of another (the principal) in signing an agreement of the type that must, under the statute of frauds, be in writing, the authority of the agent to act on behalf of the principal must also be in writing. Thus, an individual signs a written *power of attorney* to authorize a person, called an attorney-in-fact (who need not be a lawyer), to sign documents on the individual's behalf. Corporations authorize officers to sign through a combination of written authority specified in the bylaws of the corporation and the minutes of the governing body, the board of directors.

If there is clear evidence that a person made an oral promise, a court will often strain to recharacterize the nature of the agreement so that it does not come within the statute of frauds.[16] One cannot count on such leniency, however, so the prudent manager will put any agreements that might fall within the statute of frauds in writing. As the U.S. Court of Appeals for the Seventh Circuit stated:

> It is astounding in this day and age to find it necessary to repeat [the] admonition [to "get it in writing"], but no less so than to find a sophisticated party willing to leverage an agreement involving multiple years and millions of dollars solely on the enforceability of a simple handshake.[17]

THE PAROL EVIDENCE RULE

Under the *parol evidence rule,* when there is an unambiguous written contract that the parties intended would encompass their entire agreement, parol (that is, oral) evidence of prior or contemporaneous statements is inadmissible in court and cannot be used to interpret, vary, or add to the terms of the written contract. A court will usually not look beyond the "four corners" of the document to discern the intentions of the parties.

For example, in *White v. Security Pacific Financial Services, Inc.,*[18] the borrower plaintiffs tried to introduce evidence that the lender defendant had fraudulently induced them to execute a promissory note by assuring them that its sole recourse upon default would be under a deed of trust that collateralized the loan. The court found that this evidence could not be admitted because it contradicted the parties' written agreement.

CLARIFYING AMBIGUOUS LANGUAGE

The parol evidence rule does not prohibit presenting evidence to show what the contract means. Thus, courts are willing to look beyond the written agreement if its language is ambiguous. For example, if the contract stated that a party was to purchase a carload of tomatoes, it would not violate the parol evidence rule to present evidence showing that "carload" in the relevant commercial setting means a train carload, not a Chevy truckload. This evidence merely explains the ambiguous term "carload"; it does not vary the

16. *See, e.g.,* Wilson Floors Co. v. Sciota Park, Ltd., 377 N.E.2d 514 (Ohio 1978) (oral promise by construction lender to pay subcontractor if he returned to work served lender's own pecuniary interest, so the agreement did not have to be in writing to be enforceable).

17. Trustmark Ins. Co. v. Gen. & Cologne Life Re of Am., 424 F.3d 542 (7th Cir. 2005).

18. No. 5079754 (Cal. July 21, 1999), *cert. denied,* 528 U.S. 1160 (2000).

term. Parol evidence is also admissible to show mistake, fraud, or duress.

CHANGED CIRCUMSTANCES

Contracts often contain provisions for a variety of future events so that the parties involved can allocate the risks of different outcomes. It is not always possible to anticipate every occurrence, however. Three theories are used to address this situation: impossibility, impracticability, and frustration of purpose.

IMPOSSIBILITY

Suppose that Antonio signs a contract to sell Trevor computer chips of a special type manufactured only in Antonio's factory. Before he can manufacture the computer chips, however, the factory burns down through no fault of Antonio's, making it impossible for him to perform the contract. Assume that the destruction of Antonio's factory is a changed circumstance that neither party contemplated when they made the contract.

Trevor is not entitled to money damages for Antonio's nonperformance because Antonio is discharged from his obligations due to *impossibility*. If, however, the computer chips could be manufactured in another factory, Antonio would have an obligation to have them manufactured there after his factory burned down. This would be the case even if it costs Antonio more money to manufacture them at the other facility.

IMPRACTICABILITY

Closely related to impossibility is the concept of *impracticability,* where performance is possible but commercially impractical. As a rule, impracticability is difficult to prove.

Impracticability was invoked by several shipping companies in 1967 when political turmoil in the Middle East gave rise to the temporary closing of the Suez Canal. A number of merchant ships had to detour around the Cape of Good Hope at the southern tip of Africa. The detour increased shipping costs so much that the shipping companies suffered substantial losses. Several of these companies sued to nullify the contracts they had entered into before the Suez Canal was closed. They claimed performance was impractical and sought to recover the full costs of sailing the longer route around the Cape of Good Hope. In only one case did the court grant relief. The other courts found that the added costs were not so great as to make performance impracticable. (Chapter 8 addresses impracticability in contracts for the sale of goods.)

FRUSTRATION OF PURPOSE

Frustration of purpose occurs when performance is possible, but changed circumstances have made the contract useless to one or both of the parties. A famous example is the King Edward VII coronation case[19] in which Henry contracted to rent a room in London from Krell for the acknowledged purpose of viewing King Edward VII's coronation procession. Krell had advertised the room as one that would be good for viewing the coronation. When the King became ill with appendicitis and the coronation was postponed, Henry refused to pay for the apartment. Krell then sued. The English court ruled that Henry did not have to pay because the entire reason for the contract had been "frustrated."

Note that performance of the contract was not impossible: Henry could still have rented the room. The outcome of the case would have been different if the room had not been rented for the express purpose of viewing the coronation. In that case, Krell would have won because the purpose of the contract would have been for just the rental of the room, not for the viewing of the coronation.

The contract defense of frustration requires that (1) the expressed purpose in making the contract is frustrated, (2) without the defendant's fault, (3) by the occurrence of an event, the nonoccurrence of which was a basic assumption on which the contract was made. The frustration defense is unavailable if the defendant helped cause the frustrating event or if the parties were aware of the possibility of the frustrating event when they entered into the contract.

CONTRACTS WITH THE GOVERNMENT AND THE SOVEREIGN ACTS DOCTRINE

When a party's performance is made illegal or impossible because of a new law, performance of the contract is usually discharged, and damages are not awarded. But what happens when a party contracts with the government, and the government then promulgates a new law that makes its own performance impossible? If it no longer wishes to be bound by a contract, can the government discharge its obligations by changing the law to make performance illegal?

According to the *sovereign acts doctrine,* the government generally cannot be held liable for breach of contract due to legislative or executive acts. Because one Congress cannot bind a later Congress, the general rule is that subsequent acts of the government can discharge the government's preexisting contractual obligations.

This doctrine has limits, however. If Congress passes legislation deliberately targeting its existing contractual

19. Krell v. Henry, 2 K.B. 740 (C.A. 1903).

IN BRIEF

Decision Tree for Contract Analysis

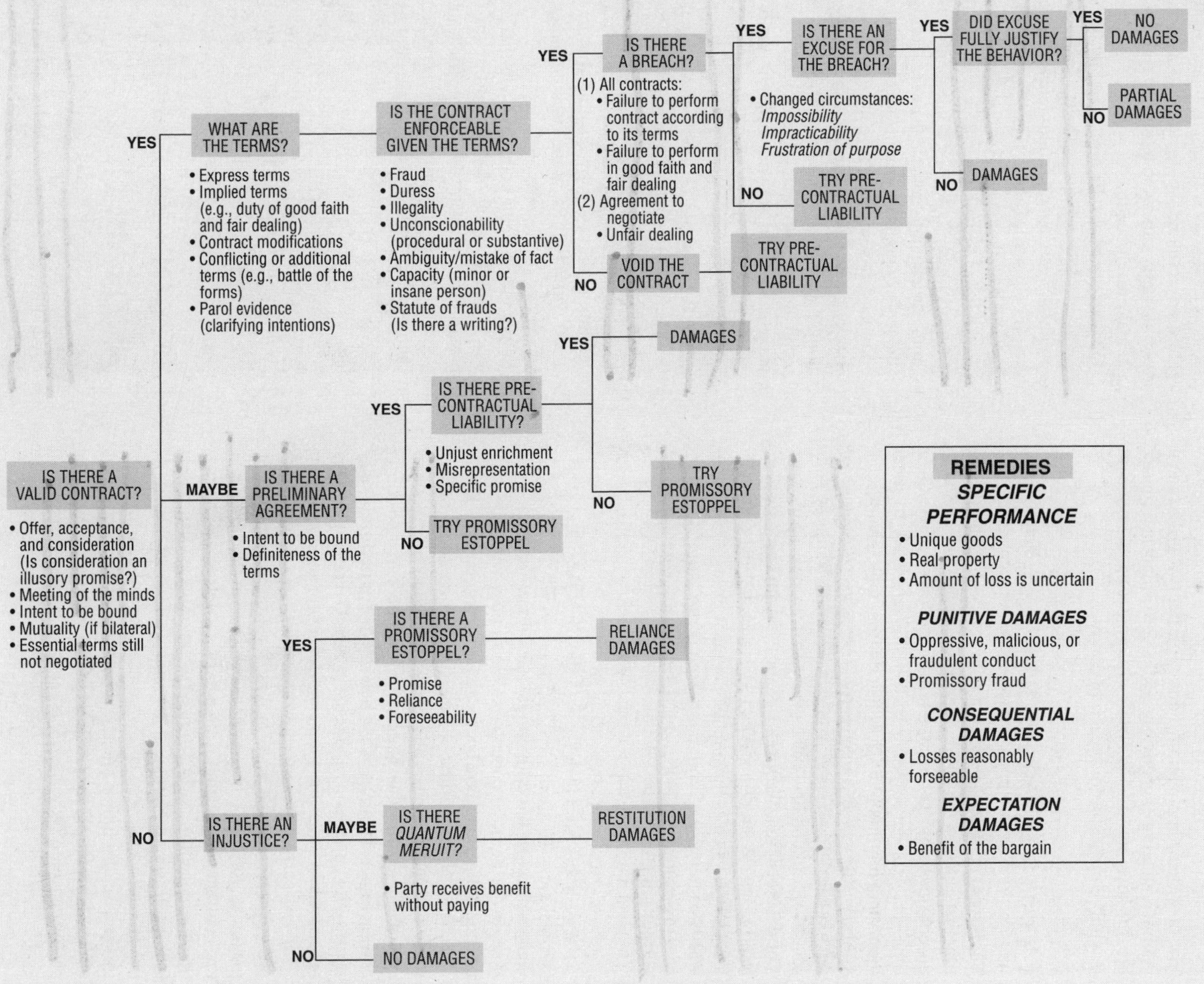

IS THERE A VALID CONTRACT?

- Offer, acceptance, and consideration (Is consideration an illusory promise?)
- Meeting of the minds
- Intent to be bound
- Mutuality (if bilateral)
- Essential terms still not negotiated

(YES) **WHAT ARE THE TERMS?**

- Express terms
- Implied terms (e.g., duty of good faith and fair dealing)
- Contract modifications
- Conflicting or additional terms (e.g., battle of the forms)
- Parol evidence (clarifying intentions)

IS THE CONTRACT ENFORCEABLE GIVEN THE TERMS?

- Fraud
- Duress
- Illegality
- Unconscionability (procedural or substantive)
- Ambiguity/mistake of fact
- Capacity (minor or insane person)
- Statute of frauds (Is there a writing?)

(YES) **IS THERE A BREACH?**

(1) All contracts:
- Failure to perform contract according to its terms
- Failure to perform in good faith and fair dealing

(2) Agreement to negotiate
- Unfair dealing

(NO) **VOID THE CONTRACT** — **TRY PRE-CONTRACTUAL LIABILITY**

(YES) **IS THERE AN EXCUSE FOR THE BREACH?**

- Changed circumstances: *Impossibility* *Impracticability* *Frustration of purpose*

(NO) **TRY PRE-CONTRACTUAL LIABILITY**

(YES) **DID EXCUSE FULLY JUSTIFY THE BEHAVIOR?**

(NO) **DAMAGES**

(YES) **NO DAMAGES**

(NO) **PARTIAL DAMAGES**

(MAYBE) **IS THERE A PRELIMINARY AGREEMENT?**

- Intent to be bound
- Definiteness of the terms

(YES) **IS THERE PRE-CONTRACTUAL LIABILITY?**

- Unjust enrichment
- Misrepresentation
- Specific promise

(YES) **DAMAGES**

(NO) **TRY PROMISSORY ESTOPPEL**

(NO) **TRY PROMISSORY ESTOPPEL**

(NO) **IS THERE AN INJUSTICE?**

(YES) **IS THERE A PROMISSORY ESTOPPEL?**

- Promise
- Reliance
- Foreseeability

RELIANCE DAMAGES

(MAYBE) **IS THERE *QUANTUM MERUIT?***

- Party receives benefit without paying

RESTITUTION DAMAGES

(NO) **NO DAMAGES**

REMEDIES

SPECIFIC PERFORMANCE

- Unique goods
- Real property
- Amount of loss is uncertain

PUNITIVE DAMAGES

- Oppressive, malicious, or fraudulent conduct
- Promissory fraud

CONSEQUENTIAL DAMAGES

- Losses reasonably forseeable

EXPECTATION DAMAGES

- Benefit of the bargain

Source: This decision tree was prepared by Sheila Bonini with information and input from Constance E. Bagley. Used by permission.

obligation, the defense otherwise provided by the sovereign acts doctrine is unavailable.[20] The government is not prevented from changing the law, but it must pay damages for its legislatively chosen breach. On the other hand, if a new law of general application indirectly affects a government contract, making the government's performance impossible, the sovereign acts doctrine will protect the government in a subsequent suit for breach of contract.

CONTRACT MODIFICATION

Traditional contract law does not allow a contract modification that changes the obligations of only one party, because no consideration has been given by the other party. Over time, lawyers developed a variety of techniques to meet the formal requirements of consideration. One technique is *novation,* by which a new party is substituted for one of the old parties, and a new contract is written (with the consent of all old and new parties) to effect the desired change. Another technique is formal change, where the consideration for the desired modification is a formal but meaningless change, such as making the payment in cash rather than with a bank check. Similarly, if both parties agree to terminate the contract and enter into a new one, the new contract will be valid.

DISCHARGE OF CONTRACT

Once a manager has entered into a legally enforceable contract, his or her next concern is determining when the contractual obligations have been satisfied or terminated, that is, *discharged.* Most commonly, discharge of contracts occurs when both parties have fully performed their obligations to one another. But what happens when one party performs and the other does not? Or when one party performs only some of its obligations under the contract? These questions are answered under the rules on discharging contracts.

If one party fails to perform a contract according to its essential terms, such as by not performing a service after receiving payment, that party has *materially breached* the contract. Any material breach of a contract discharges the nonbreaching party from its obligations and provides grounds to sue for damages. A breach is minor if the essential terms and purpose of the contract have been fulfilled. In the case of a minor breach, the nonbreaching party must still perform its contractual obligations, but it may suspend performance until the breach is cured or sue for damages.

An *anticipatory repudiation* of a contract occurs when one party knows ahead of time (before performance is due) that the other party will breach the contract. Such a repudiation is treated as a material breach of the contract. By treating an anticipatory repudiation as a breach, the nonbreaching party can avoid having to wait to take action until an actual breach occurs.

Contracts may also be discharged by the failure or occurrence of certain conditions stipulated in the contract, such as a condition precedent or a condition subsequent, as discussed above. If both parties agree, they may also terminate the contract by *mutual rescission*. A mutual rescission is itself a type of contract and, as such, requires a valid offer, acceptance, and consideration. Often the consideration is the agreement by both parties not to enforce their legal obligations.

If one party prefers to retain the original contract but wants to contract with someone else, a third party may be substituted for one of the original parties. The third party will assume the original party's rights and responsibilities. All parties must agree to the substitution. Formally, a new contract is formed, with the same terms but with different parties.

An *accord and satisfaction* is any agreement to accept performance that is different from what is called for in the contract. For example, assume a creditor believes he is owed $100,000, but the debtor believes she owes only $75,000. An *accord* is formed when the creditor accepts the debtor's offer to settle the dispute for an amount less than the creditor claims is due (say, by cashing the debtor's check for $80,000 with "Full Payment" written on it). *Satisfaction* is the discharge of the debt.

Sometimes a valid contract is discharged by operation of law. Certain types of changed circumstances, such as impossibility, impracticability, or frustration of purpose (described above), may discharge the contractual obligations of both parties. A bankruptcy proceeding by one party can also discharge its contractual obligations. Similarly, failing to file suit for breach of contract before the time specified in a statute of limitations has passed effectively discharges a contract, because the courts will no longer enforce it. In many states, an action for breach of a written contract must be filed within four years after the breach occurs.

DUTY OF GOOD FAITH AND FAIR DEALING

Every contract contains an implied covenant of good faith and fair dealing in its performance that imposes on each party a duty not to do anything that will deprive the other party of the benefits of the agreement. One court defined

20. United States v. Winstar, 518 U.S. 839 (1996).

a lack of good faith as "some type of affirmative action consisting of at least . . . a design to mislead or to deceive another."[21] The covenant has been implied and enforced in a variety of contexts, including insurance contracts, agreements to make mutual wills, agreements to sell real property, employment agreements, and leases. (Its application in the employment context is discussed in Chapter 12.)

Courts have long deemed the relationship between an insurance company and its insured a special relationship that calls for a careful examination of the faithfulness of contractual dealings. For example, suppose Reese is looking for an apartment. He comes upon Tara's apartment building and trips on a broken step, falls, and breaks his leg as he is climbing up the stairs. It is clear that the stairs had not been maintained properly. Tara has insurance of $125,000 to cover this type of liability claim. Reese's lawyer originally demands $120,000, which includes a claim for punitive damages. Tara's insurance company refuses to pay the claim and takes the case to trial. The jury awards Reese $180,000. Tara is liable for the full amount even though she was insured for only $125,000. Tara then brings an action against her insurance company for not settling the claim within the policy limits. Under the implied covenant of good faith and fair dealing, many jurisdictions will require the insurance company to pay the full $180,000 judgment. An insurance company can refuse to settle within the policy limits, but the company generally becomes contractually responsible for paying whatever amount is awarded at trial.

In addition, claims that a party has complied with the letter of the contract may not be sufficient to satisfy the duty of good faith and fair dealing. For example, Disney had entered into an agreement with Marsu B.V., pursuant to which Disney agreed to create half-hour animated films for broadcast on television and to coordinate a merchandising campaign that would provide broad exposure for "Marsupilami," a cartoon character owned by Marsu. Although Disney did some merchandising, its effort was halfhearted; among other things, it assigned junior employees to the project and failed to coordinate the campaign with the television broadcast. A memo written by Disney stated that "we have neither the time nor the resources to do Marsu right" and "we have lots of other Disney priorities, more important both financially and strategically." The U.S. Court of Appeals for the Ninth Circuit rejected Disney's argument that it had fulfilled its express obligations under the terms of the contract and affirmed the district court's determination that Disney had breached the implied covenant of good faith and fair dealing.[22]

21. Bunge Corp. v. Recker, 519 F.2d 449, 452 (8th Cir. 1975).

22. Marsu B.V. v. Walt Disney Co., 185 F.3d 932 (9th Cir. 1999).

The precise meanings of "good faith" and "fair dealing" are the subject of extended debate among legal scholars. What was considered fair dealing twenty years ago may be considered unfair today, and vice versa. Two commonly used rules of thumb offer some guidance. Managers should ask themselves whether an action would embarrass them or their company if it became public. They should also consider whether they would follow the same course of action if they were dealing with a friend or relative. Although these questions raise moral as well as legal considerations, they are useful in evaluating whether a contemplated action would meet the legal test of good faith. (Good faith in the context of negotiations is discussed more fully later in this chapter.)

Third-Party Beneficiaries

A person who is not a party to a contract can sometimes enforce the contract between the contracting parties. For example, suppose Sheila agrees to sell to Fernando a piece of real property in exchange for a $100,000 payment by Fernando to Jack. Fernando is the promisor, Sheila is the promisee, and Jack is the ***third-party beneficiary*** or intended beneficiary. A person is not a third-party beneficiary with legal rights to enforce the contract unless the contracting parties intended to benefit that party.

Creditor Beneficiary

If the promisee entered into the contract to discharge a duty he or she owed to the third party, then the third party is a *creditor beneficiary* and has the right to enforce the contract between the promisor and promisee. The third party must prove, however, that the promisee intended the contract to satisfy his or her obligation to the third party. For example, if Sheila owes Jack $100,000 and she and Fernando agree that she will sell land to Fernando to pay off that debt, Jack has enforceable rights under the contract as a creditor beneficiary. If the contract is not carried out, Jack can sue Fernando directly to compel performance. Jack also has the option of suing Sheila for the $100,000 she owes him.

Donee Beneficiary

A *donee beneficiary* is created when the promisee does not owe an obligation to the third party, but rather wishes to confer a gift. For example, if Sheila agreed to sell her property to Fernando for $100,000 in order to make a $100,000 gift to Jack, Jack would be a donee beneficiary and could enforce the contract in most jurisdictions, but only against Fernando.

Some jurisdictions, such as New York, require a family relationship between the donee beneficiary and the promisee before allowing the beneficiary to sue under the contract.

Remedies

If one party breaches a contract, the other is entitled to monetary damages or, in some instances, a court order requiring performance. The purpose of damages is to put the plaintiff in the position it would have been in had the contract been performed. A secondary purpose is to discourage breaches of contract. Because the U.S. legal system recognizes that sometimes it is economically efficient to breach a contract, courts generally will not allow punitive damages, traditionally a tort remedy, in contract cases. However, courts have developed several exceptions that allow for the award of punitive damages in cases involving (1) a breach of a promise to marry; (2) a breach of a fiduciary duty; or (3) a breach of a contract, the performance of which involves a public duty or is regulated by public authorities, such as contracts involving public utilities, common carriers, or insurance companies.

Over the years the courts have developed a variety of methods to measure appropriate monetary damages in contract cases. The three standard measures are (1) expectation, (2) reliance, and (3) restitution. The interest to be compensated determines which of these measures is most appropriate in a particular case. These measures may seem similar, but the resulting damages awards can be very different, as discussed below. In certain situations, a court may also order the equitable remedies of specific performance or injunctive relief.

EXPECTATION DAMAGES

Expectation damages give the plaintiff the benefit of its bargain, putting the plaintiff in the cash position it would have been in if the contract had been fulfilled. The general formula for expectation damages is Expectation Damages = Compensatory Damages + Consequential Damages + Incidental Damages – Avoidable Losses.

Compensatory Damages

Compensatory damages are the amount necessary to make up for the economic loss caused by the breach of contract. For example, suppose an independent contractor agrees to work for AAA Manufacturing Company for $15 per hour. When the time comes to start work, the contractor reneges. AAA can find another independent contractor elsewhere, but the market price is now $20 per hour. Instead of spending $600 for a forty-hour workweek, AAA must now pay $800. AAA's compensatory damages are the difference between the two expenditures, or $200.

Consequential Damages

In addition to damages that compensate for the breach itself, the plaintiff is entitled to *consequential damages*, that is, compensation for losses that occur as a foreseeable result of the breach. For example, suppose AAA contracts with another person at $20 per hour, but the new contractor cannot start working immediately. As a result, AAA has to use a temporary employee who charges $21 per hour for two weeks. Thus, AAA incurs an additional cost of $1 more per hour for two weeks, which results in $80 additional damages. This $80 is added to the $200 in compensatory damages. If the two-week delay causes AAA to be late in delivering its product to one of its customers, any late fees that AAA pays will also be included in the consequential damages.

Two principles operate to limit consequential damages: (1) the damages must be reasonably foreseeable and (2) they must be reasonably certain.

Foreseeability Consequential damages will be awarded only if the breaching party knew, or should have known, that the loss would result from a breach of the contract.

For example, in the classic case *Hadley v. Baxendale,*[23] the plaintiff was a mill owner who sent a broken crankshaft by carrier to be repaired. Because this was the only crankshaft the mill owned, the mill was completely shut down until the carrier returned with the repaired crankshaft. When the carrier did not deliver the shaft as quickly as promised, the mill owner sued the carrier for profits lost during the time the mill was closed. The English appellate court observed that most mills had more than one crankshaft, so the carrier had no way of knowing that nondelivery of the crankshaft would result in the closure of the mill. As a result, the court did not award damages for lost profits: they were neither reasonably foreseeable nor a natural consequence of the carrier's breach.

Uncertainty of Damages Sometimes it is not possible to know what the benefit of the bargain would have been. For example, Publisher & Sons signs a contract to publish Rachel Author's first book. Publisher later decides not to publish the book. To what damages is Rachel entitled? The benefit of her bargain would be the royalties from a

23. 156 Eng. Rep. 145 (1854).

published book, but the parties have no way to measure how much those royalties would have been. Because Rachel has the burden of proving the amount of her loss, she may collect very little in damages.

Similarly, new businesses have no record of past profits by which to estimate the loss caused by a breach. Traditionally, this prevented start-ups from collecting anything for lost profits. Today, however, with more sophisticated methods for projecting future profits, new businesses are having more success recovering damages.

Incidental Damages

Incidental damages are the lesser and relatively minor damages that a nonbreaching party incurs. Examples of incidental damages include the charges, expenses, and commissions incurred in stopping delivery; the cost of the transportation, care, and custody of goods after a buyer's default; and the expenses incurred in connection with the return or subsequent disposition of goods that are the subject of a contract.

Mitigation of Damages

The nonbreaching party has a duty to use reasonable efforts to *mitigate*, or lessen, the amount of damages that flow from the breach. As a general rule, the nonbreaching party cannot recover damages that it could have reasonably avoided. This gives the nonbreaching party an incentive to make the best of a bad situation.

For example, suppose AAA Manufacturing Company and Hazmat, a hazardous-waste collection company, enter into a contract whereby Hazmat agrees to pick up AAA's hazardous waste for a fee of $500 per pickup. If Hazmat fails to pick up the hazardous waste, AAA should *cover*—find another hazardous-waste collection company at the current market price, say, $625 per pickup, at the time of the breach. AAA will still be entitled to compensatory damages, measured by the difference between the market price at the time it learned of the breach ($625 per pickup) and the contract price ($500 per pickup), plus any consequential damages, such as extra storage fees, late fees, and incidental damages incurred in finding a substitute hazardous-waste collection company.

If AAA elects not to cover, it is limited to compensatory damages (as measured above) and cannot recover any consequential damages that could have been prevented by covering, such as late fees. If no cover is available, AAA is entitled to foreseeable consequential damages resulting from the breach.

Additionally, AAA must avoid compounding damages from the breach. If hazardous-waste collection services are available at both $625 and $650 per pickup and the quality is the same, then AAA is required to purchase at the lower price. Thus, its expectation damages are limited to $125 per pickup. Any expenses incurred by AAA in reasonably attempting to mitigate damages, such as the costs of finding another collection company, are also recoverable consequential damages, regardless of whether the efforts were successful.

From the seller's perspective, the duty to mitigate damages works similarly. For example, suppose Beta Software Company contracts to develop a customized program for Arturo Architects, LLC, a small architecture firm. Beta learns midway through the development process that Arturo plans to breach the contract. Beta should cover by finding another buyer for the software, then charge Arturo for the difference between the contract price and the resale price (compensatory damages), plus any consequential damages. If no other buyer is available, perhaps because the program is too customized, Beta should immediately stop its work and charge Arturo for expenses incurred plus the expected net profit.

RELIANCE DAMAGES

Reliance damages compensate the nonbreaching party for any expenditures it made in reliance on the contract. Reliance damages are an alternative to expectation damages when it is not possible to determine the expectation damages. Reliance damages are also awarded in promissory estoppel cases, where expectation damages are generally not allowed. Instead of giving the plaintiff the benefit of the bargain, reliance damages return it to the position it was in before the contract was formed.

For example, a seller agrees to sell a buyer a heavy drill press. The buyer tells the seller that it has invested in renovation work to strengthen the floor where the drill press will be installed. The seller then sells the drill press to someone else. Reliance damages require the seller to reimburse the buyer for the renovation expenses.

RESTITUTION AND *QUANTUM MERUIT*

Whereas reliance damages look at what the plaintiff has lost, *restitution* looks at what the other party has gained from the transaction. The usual measure of restitution is the amount it would cost the recipient of the benefit to buy that benefit elsewhere.

A court will order restitution under the doctrine of *quantum meruit* if one party has received a benefit for which it has not paid even though there was no contract between the parties. The obligation to give restitution is implied as a matter of law. For example, suppose that an entrepreneur asks an advertising agency to place an advertisement. The advertising agency contracts with an industry publication to place the advertisement but fails to pay for it. Under the doctrine of *quantum meruit,* the agency's default on payment renders the entrepreneur liable to the publication for the value of the benefit the entrepreneur received (the advertisement). The entrepreneur must pay the publication even though there was no contract between the entrepreneur and the publication.

A court may also order restitution in cases where a plaintiff seeks to rescind, or cancel, a contract that it entered into based on fraud or mutual mistake, or where the defendant has breached an executory contract (i.e., a contract under which the parties have continuing obligations to perform). Rescission terminates the parties' rights under the contract, and restitution restores the parties to the position they were in prior to entering the contract by requiring them to return any benefits they received under the contract.

In the following case, the U.S. Court of Appeals for the Federal Circuit considered whether to award Glendale Federal Bank expectation, reliance, or restitution damages as a result of the federal government's breach of contract.

A CASE IN POINT — IN THE LANGUAGE OF THE COURT

CASE 7.6

GLENDALE FEDERAL BANK, FSB v. UNITED STATES

UNITED STATES COURT OF APPEALS FOR THE FEDERAL CIRCUIT
239 F.3D 1374 (FED. CIR. 2001).

FACTS In 1981, Glendale Federal Bank, a savings and loan institution in California, entered into a supervisory merger with First Federal Savings and Loan Association of Broward County, Florida. At the time of the merger, the market value of First Federal's liabilities exceeded the market value of its assets by $734 million. Pursuant to its contract with the government, Glendale was permitted to treat First Federal's negative net worth as goodwill for regulatory capital purposes and to amortize it over a forty-year period. Otherwise, Glendale would have immediately become insolvent.

In 1989, Congress passed the Financial Institutions Reform, Recovery and Enforcement Act (FIRREA), which eliminated Glendale's ability to count goodwill as regulatory capital by requiring an accelerated amortization schedule. The FIRREA also established new capital requirements that Glendale initially failed to meet, forcing it to engineer a massive recapitalization, including the acquisition of First Federal.

The Supreme Court had previously ruled in *United States v. Winstar*[24] that banks such as Glendale had an enforceable contract with the government to treat negative net worth in supervisory mergers as goodwill and to count such goodwill toward capital requirements. Because the government breached this contract, Glendale filed suit seeking damages. After trial on damages, the U.S. Court of Federal Claims denied Glendale's claim for expectancy (expectation) damages; awarded Glendale $528 million in restitution damages, which was the amount by which First Federal's liabilities exceeded its assets on the date of the merger, less the value of the benefits Glendale received from the contract; and found that Glendale was entitled to $381,000 in nonoverlapping reliance damages, or "wounded bank damages," caused by its failure to maintain capital compliance after the breach. The U.S. Government appealed the court's award of restitution damages.

ISSUE PRESENTED Under what contract measure of relief—expectancy, reliance, or restitution—is Glendale entitled to recover damages?

OPINION PLAGER, J., writing for the U.S. Court of Appeals for the Federal Circuit:

When proof of expectancy damages fails, the law provides a fall-back position for the injured party—he can sue for restitution. The idea behind the restitution is to . . . restore the nonbreaching party to the position he would have been in had there never been a contract to breach. . . .

. . . [I]t is clear that the Government's promise that was breached had substantial value. . . .

At the same time, the action taken by [Glendale] in acquiring [First Federal] did not result in the Government . . . saving the dollar value of the net obligations of the thrift. . . .

CONTINUED

24. 518 U.S. 839 (1996).

This case, then, presents an illustration of the problem in granting restitution based on an assumption that the nonbreaching party is entitled to the supposed gains received by the breaching party, when those gains are both speculative and indeterminate. We do not see how the restitution award granted by the trial court, measured in terms of a liability that never came to pass, and based on a speculative assessment of what might have been, can be upheld; accordingly we vacate the trial court's damage award on this theory.

This does not mean that Glendale is without remedy. Glendale recognized the problems in the restitution award, and cross-appealed, arguing that, should the court reject the award, Glendale nevertheless would be entitled to damages on a reliance theory. Indeed, the trial court recognized this third category of damages, known as reliance damages, and added specified reliance damages to the total award it granted plaintiff.

RESULT The court vacated the trial court's damages award and remanded the case with instructions for further proceedings to determine the amount of Glendale's reliance damages. Glendale was entitled to recover the ascertainable prebreach and postbreach losses it suffered because it relied on the government's breached promise.

CRITICAL THINKING QUESTIONS

1. Why did Glendale not receive restitution damages?
2. Given that the plaintiff bears the burden of proving damages, why should Glendale be able to recover anything?

LIQUIDATED DAMAGES

The parties to a contract may include a clause that specifies the amount of money to be paid if one of them should later breach the agreement. Such *liquidated damages* clauses are frequently used in real estate and construction contracts. Because courts will not enforce penalties in contract cases, clauses that provide for damages that are substantially higher than the losses will not be enforced. The amount of the liquidated damages should be the parties' best estimate of what the expectation damages would be.

SPECIFIC PERFORMANCE AND INJUNCTIVE RELIEF

Instead of awarding monetary damages, a court may order the breaching party to complete the contract as promised. *Specific performance* is ordered only when (1) the goods are unique (for example, an antique car or a painting), (2) the subject of the contract is real property, or (3) the amount of the loss is so uncertain that there is no fair way to calculate damages.

Courts never force an employee to provide services under an employment contract, because that would constitute involuntary servitude in violation of the Thirteenth Amendment to the U.S. Constitution. For example, if a CEO who has agreed to work for a corporation for five years walks out after three years, the court will not force her to continue her employment. The court may, however, issue an injunction barring her from working for someone else.

CONTRACTS RELATING TO MERGERS AND ACQUISITIONS

A corporation can acquire control of another corporation (the *target*) by merger, a sale of stock by the target's shareholders, or a sale of substantially all the assets of the target.[25] A *merger agreement* is an agreement between two companies to combine into a single entity. Mergers and sales of substantially all the assets generally cannot be completed until the transaction is approved by the shareholders of both the acquiring and the target company.

25. Acquisitions are discussed in detail in CONSTANCE E. BAGLEY & CRAIG E. DAUCHY, ENTREPRENEUR'S GUIDE TO BUSINESS LAW, 595–659 (3d ed. 2008).

Mergers and acquisitions are usually highly negotiated transactions that are governed by detailed acquisition agreements containing *representations and warranties* (statements about the entity being sold and the buyer), *covenants* (promises to do or refrain from doing something), and conditions (events that must occur before either party has a duty to *close,* or consummate, the transaction, as well as events that will terminate a party's obligation to close). The seller's representations and warranties typically cover such matters as the proper organization of the entity as a corporation, the accuracy of its financial statements, title to its assets, the absence of undisclosed liabilities, the absence of undisclosed legal proceedings, and its compliance with all laws and contractual obligations by which it is bound. Seller covenants typically include promises (1) to conduct the business in the ordinary course until the closing date, (2) to refrain from entering into any new major contracts, and (3) to permit access to the business to enable the buyer to conduct due diligence.

Acquisition agreements in transactions involving private companies typically provide for indemnification by the seller for breaches of its representations, warranties, and covenants. The seller may also require the buyer to include indemnification provisions if the buyer is purchasing the target with shares of the buyer's stock. Public company acquisition agreements typically do not include indemnification clauses because collecting indemnification from numerous public shareholders would be virtually impossible. If, however, one or several shareholders own a controlling block, then they may be required to provide indemnification, at least up to the value of the consideration they receive in the sale.

The indemnification provisions often limit the seller's or buyer's exposure to some percentage of the total purchase price. In some agreements, different ceilings apply to different types of liabilities. In addition, the provisions may stipulate that breaches of representations, warranties, or covenants must be material before indemnification will be available. For example, the parties might agree that a claim must be worth at least $100,000 before the seller has an obligation to pay any damages to the buyer. If the parties decide to establish a dollar threshold, they must also decide whether the threshold should be a deductible amount or whether the indemnifying party should provide "dollar one" coverage. For example, under an agreement that uses the deductible approach, if the claim is $150,000 and the threshold is $100,000, the indemnifying party would be liable for only $50,000, the excess over $100,000. In contrast, if the agreement uses the dollar one coverage approach, the party would be liable for the full amount of $150,000.

The issue of time limits on indemnification obligations is frequently one of the most controversial negotiating points in an acquisition agreement. The indemnifying party usually wants a shorter period than the applicable statute of limitations, and many acquisition agreements will place some time limit on indemnification obligations. The seller typically argues that the buyer, as the owner and operator of the business, should discover any misstatements within a certain period of time. The buyer, however, often argues for longer time limits for tax claims, environmental claims, intellectual property claims, and capitalization matters as these problems may not surface for years.

GLOBAL VIEW

Contracting with Foreign Entities

When entering into contracts with companies in other nations, it is important to remember that most non-English-speaking countries follow the civil law tradition. This system of jurisprudence was originally used in the Roman Empire. Civil law countries rely primarily on civil codes, or statutes, rather than case-by-case common law to develop rules for behavior. In contrast, the law in the United States and England stems from a common law tradition.

Most civil law countries do not recognize certain common law contract principles. For example, many civil law countries do not recognize the doctrine of consideration, which means that no consideration is required to make a contract binding in these countries. They also do not recognize *privity of contract,* which means that third parties who are not parties to a contract may be entitled to enforce its terms. In addition, although common law countries generally treat contracts with the government in the same way as contracts with private entities, civil law countries have different rules for private and public entities.

CONTINUED

The concept of nonperformance also differs, as do the remedies for it. In the United States, expectation damages are the standard remedy for breach of contract, and specific performance or injunctive relief is left to the court's discretion. A U.S. court will enter an order for specific performance or injunctive relief only if it finds that damages would not be an adequate remedy. In civil law countries, however, specific performance is generally awarded in contract cases. Even when a civil law court is willing to award damages for breach of contract, the nonbreaching party cannot recover expectation damages. For example, a German court will attempt to put the parties in the position that they would have been in if the breach had not occurred. In France, on the other hand, a court may grant a defaulting party a grace period during which it will be allowed to perform the contract.

In general, other common law countries, such as the United Kingdom, do not recognize a common law duty to negotiate in good faith and thus do not impose liability for its breach. However, civil law countries, including France, Germany, the Netherlands, and Japan, have been more willing to impose a good faith obligation during the negotiation of a contract.[26] In 1994, the International Institute for the Unification of Private Law (Unidroit) published its Principles of International Commercial Contracts (Unidroit Principles), which set forth general rules for international commercial contracts for services. The Unidroit Principles are used primarily in international arbitration. Unidroit Article 2.1.15(2) provides that one who "breaks off negotiations in bad faith is liable for the losses caused to the other party." Like the American Law Institute's Restatements of the Law, the Unidroit Principles are not designed to be codified into statutes. As a result, in many international agreements, there may be an expectation that parties have a duty to negotiate in good faith, and they can be held liable if they fail to do so.

Since 1982, the Commission on European Contract Law, a nongovernmental body of lawyers from the European Union member states, has been working to establish Principles of European Contract Law. The main purpose of the Principles is to serve as a draft European Code of Private Law. The Principles include comments explaining the purpose of the rules as well as illustrations and notes that both explain the sources of the rules and compare them with the rules of the member states. Part I deals with the performance of contracts, nonperformance, and remedies for nonperformance. Part II contains rules on the formation of contracts, validity, interpretation, and contents.

The Commission on European Contract law, better known as the Lando-Commission, has produced a draft version of a complete code of European Contract Law. Even though the Code has not yet been enacted, the parties to an international contract may adopt the Principles. If a dispute arises, a court or arbitrator will then apply the Principles instead of national rules of law. Although the parties are free to exclude or vary most of the Principles, certain provisions are considered to be of such importance as to be mandatory. These include the provisions (1) requiring each party to act from the outset of contract negotiations in accordance with good faith and fair dealing and (2) dealing with invalidity caused by mistake, fraud, threat, undue influence, and unfair contract terms.

Because of the differences in each country's laws regarding contract interpretation, performance, and remedies, it is generally appropriate to include a provision that specifies which country's laws will govern (a *choice-of-law provision*) in every multinational contract. It may also be appropriate to include a provision that specifies which country's courts will have exclusive jurisdiction over any dispute involving the contract (a *choice-of-forum provision*). As explained in Chapter 3, courts will generally honor such provisions. Finally, many contracts involving parties located in different countries will include an agreement that any disputes will be arbitrated, rather than tried in court. Arbitration awards are enforceable in the more than 130 countries that have signed the United Nations Convention on Recognition and Enforcement of Foreign Arbitral Awards. These provisions are discussed in more detail in Chapter 25.

26. *See* D. James Wan Kim Min v. Mitsui Bussan K.K. (Tokyo High Court 1987), cited in YUKO YANAGIDA ET AL., LAW AND INVESTMENT IN JAPAN 223–29 (1994).

THE RESPONSIBLE MANAGER

ACTING IN GOOD FAITH AND DEALING FAIRLY

Legally astute managers appreciate the importance of dealing fairly in negotiations.[27] The standard of fair dealing ordinarily requires that (1) each party must actually negotiate and refrain from imposing improper conditions on the negotiation, (2) each party must disclose enough about parallel negotiations to allow the other party to make a counterproposal, and (3) each party must continue to negotiate until an impasse or an agreement has been reached.

In general, managers who are parties to a negotiation should describe as specifically as possible the duty of fair dealing to which they have agreed. Instead of simply pledging to use their "best efforts" to negotiate fairly, the parties should specify whether the negotiations are to be exclusive, how long they must continue, and what must be held in confidence. Given the uncertain state of the law on these matters, no drafter should leave these items to be filled in by a court.

Managers should avoid signing a letter of intent unless they intend to be bound by its proposed terms. Many courts will let a jury decide whether there was intent to be bound even if the letter states that it is not meant to be binding. If a letter of intent is necessary to obtain financing or to begin due diligence, then a manager who does not intend to be bound if negotiations of the definitive agreement break down should consider inserting clear language into the letter stating that it is not binding, that there is no contract unless and until the parties execute a definitive written contract, and that the letter creates no obligation to negotiate in good faith and cannot be reasonably relied upon. The manager should also label the document as a "tentative proposal" or "status letter," and should refrain from signing it.[28]

27. Constance E. Bagley, *Winning Legally: The Value of Legal Astuteness*, 33 ACAD. MGMT. REV. 385 (2008).

28. *See* William G. Schopf et al., *When a Letter of Intent Goes Wrong*, 5 BUS. L. TODAY 31 (Jan.–Feb. 1996).

It is almost always preferable to put the terms of an agreement in writing. A manager should review any contract before signing it. If the terms are unfamiliar or unclear, the manager should consult with an attorney. A manager should never sign a contract he or she does not understand.

It is rarely to a manager's advantage to try to slip a provision by the other party that the manager knows would be unacceptable if it were pointed out. It is far preferable to hash out any ambiguities at the negotiation stage, while the parties are on good terms and in the mood to make a deal. Positions tend to polarize once the agreement is signed and a dispute arises.

Similarly, it is inappropriate and often unethical to bury offensive terms in a preprinted form contract in the hope that the other party will not spot them. Courts sometimes refuse to enforce such terms, especially when they conflict with the position taken in the negotiations or are contrary to the spirit of the deal. Not only does it make both legal and ethical sense to abide by the covenant of good faith and fair dealing in negotiating a contract, it is also good business. Contract litigation is expensive and time-consuming and can destroy relationships.

Managers should also ensure that they are not tortiously interfering with the contract of another. As *Pennzoil v. Texaco*, discussed in the "Inside Story" below, demonstrates, even a very large company can be driven into bankruptcy if its executives guess wrong on whether there is a contract or whether their deal tortiously interferes with it.

It is sometimes tempting to view the drafting and review of contracts as a necessary evil. However, legally astute managers realize that contract drafting and negotiation can provide opportunities to strengthen business relationships and to protect key assets, such as trade secrets, that give a firm a competitive edge.

A Manager's Dilemma

Putting It into Practice

Trials and Tribulations

HEM Pharmaceuticals Corporation designed a new drug, Ampligen, to fight chronic fatigue syndrome. Typically, new medicines go through several phases of clinical evaluation before approval by the Food and Drug Administration (FDA) and general release onto the market. As a part of the process, HEM began a clinical trial with ninety-two patients to evaluate the effectiveness, side effects, and risks of Ampligen. The patients signed consent forms that warned them of the experimental nature of Ampligen and the possible side effects. Although the patients were free to withdraw from the trial at any time, if they remained in the study they were required to accept the risks of treatment, to forgo other drugs, to not become pregnant, and to submit to intensive and uncomfortable testing for one year. In return, after the testing ended, they would be entitled to receive Ampligen for a full year at no charge. At the end of the trial, an HEM manager considered refusing to provide the year's supply of the drug to the patients free of charge on the grounds that there was no binding contract. If you were that manager, what would you do? Why?

Source: Dahl v. HEM Pharmaceuticals Corp., 7 F.3d 1399 (9th Cir. 1993).

Inside Story

PENNZOIL v. TEXACO

In 1983, Pennzoil Company and Getty Oil Company negotiated a memorandum of agreement for a merger. While the Pennzoil lawyers were negotiating the final documents, Texaco, Inc. offered a better price for Getty. Getty accepted Texaco's offer, and Pennzoil subsequently sued Texaco for tortious interference with a contract. To win, Getty had to prove (1) the existence of a contract, (2) Texaco's knowledge of the contract, (3) Texaco's intentional inducement of a breach of the contract, and (4) damages.[29] Texaco asserted that Pennzoil never had a contract because the parties had not yet agreed on every essential term of the deal.

The Facts

It took the two parties four and a half months to present all the facts and arguments to the jury. The published opinion of the Texas Court of Appeals summarizes the events in question.[30]

29. *See, e.g.*, Kronos, Inc. v. AVX Corp., 612 N.E.2d 289 (N.Y. 1993).

30. Texaco, Inc. v. Pennzoil Co., 729 S.W.2d 768 (Tex. Ct. App. 1987), *cert. dismissed*, 485 U.S. 994 (1988).

Excerpts from the Opinion of the Court of Appeals: Facts

Pennzoil had followed with interest the well-publicized dissension between the board of directors of Getty Oil Company and Gordon Getty, who was a director of Getty Oil and also the owner, as trustee, of approximately 40.2% of the outstanding shares of Getty Oil. On December 28, 1983, Pennzoil announced an unsolicited, public tender offer for 16 million shares of Getty Oil at $100 each.

Soon afterwards, Pennzoil contacted both Gordon Getty and a representative of the J. Paul Getty Museum, which held approximately 11.8% of the shares of Getty Oil, to discuss the tender offer and the possible purchase of Getty Oil. In the first two days of January 1984, a "Memorandum of Agreement" was drafted to reflect the terms that had been reached in conversations between representatives of Pennzoil, Gordon Getty, and the Museum.

Under the . . . Memorandum of Agreement, Pennzoil and the Trust (with Gordon Getty as trustee) were to become partners on a 3/7ths to 4/7ths basis, respectively, in owning and operating Getty Oil. Gordon Getty was to become chairman of the board, and Hugh Liedtke, the chief executive officer of Pennzoil, was to become chief executive officer of the new company. The plan also provided that Pennzoil and the Trust were to try in good faith to agree upon a plan to restructure Getty Oil within a year, but if they could not reach an agreement, the assets of Getty Oil were to be divided between them, 3/7ths to Pennzoil and 4/7ths to the Trust.

CONTINUED

The Memorandum of Agreement stated that it was subject to approval of the board of Getty Oil, and it was to expire by its own terms if not approved at the board meeting that was to begin on January 2. Pennzoil's CEO, Liedtke, and Gordon Getty, for the Trust, signed the Memorandum of Agreement before the Getty Oil board meeting on January 2, and Harold Williams, the president of the Museum, signed it shortly after the board meeting began. Thus, before it was submitted to the Getty Oil board, the Memorandum of Agreement had been executed by parties who together controlled a majority of the outstanding shares of Getty Oil.

The Memorandum of Agreement was then presented to the Getty Oil board, which had previously held discussions on how the company should respond to Pennzoil's public tender offer.

The board voted to reject recommending Pennzoil's tender offer to Getty's shareholders, then later also rejected the Memorandum of Agreement price of $110 per share as too low. On the morning of January 3, Getty Oil's investment banker, Geoffrey Boisi, began calling other companies, seeking a higher bid than Pennzoil's for the Getty Oil shares.

When the board reconvened at 3 P.M. on January 3, a revised Pennzoil proposal was presented, offering $110 per share plus a $3 "stub" that was to be paid after the sale of a Getty Oil subsidiary ("ERC"), from the excess proceeds over $1 billion. Each shareholder was to receive a pro rata share of these excess proceeds, but in any case, a minimum of $3 per share at the end of five years. During the meeting, Boisi briefly informed the board of the status of his inquiries of other companies that might be interested in bidding for the company. He reported some preliminary indications of interest, but no definite bid yet.

The Museum's lawyer told the board that, based on his discussions with Pennzoil, he believed that if the board went back "firm" with an offer of $110 plus a $5 stub, Pennzoil would accept it. After a recess, the Museum's president (also a director of Getty Oil) moved that the Getty board should accept Pennzoil's proposal provided that the stub be raised to $5, and the board voted 15 to 1 to approve this counterproposal to Pennzoil. The board then voted themselves and Getty's officers and advisors indemnity for any liability arising from the events of the past few months. There was evidence that during another brief recess of the board meeting, the counter-offer of $110 plus a $5 stub was presented to and accepted by Pennzoil. After Pennzoil's acceptance was conveyed to the Getty board, the meeting was adjourned, and most board members left town for their respective homes.

That evening, the lawyers and public relations staff of Getty Oil and the Museum drafted a press release describing the transaction between Pennzoil and the Getty entities. The press release, announcing an agreement in principle on the terms of the Memorandum of Agreement, but with a price of $110 plus a $5 stub, was issued on Getty Oil letterhead the next morning, January 4, and later that day, Pennzoil issued an identical press release.

On January 4, Boisi continued to contact other companies, looking for a higher price than Pennzoil had offered. After talking briefly with Boisi, Texaco management called several meetings with its in-house financial planning group. . . .

On January 5, the *Wall Street Journal* reported on an agreement reached between Pennzoil and the Getty entities, describing essentially the terms contained in the Memorandum of Agreement. The Pennzoil board met to ratify the actions of its officers in negotiating an agreement with the Getty entities, and Pennzoil's attorneys periodically attempted to contact the other parties' advisors and attorneys to continue work on the transaction agreement.

The board of Texaco also met on January 5, authorizing its officers to make an offer for 100% of Getty Oil and to take any necessary action in connection therewith. Texaco first contacted the Museum's lawyer, Marty Lipton, and arranged a meeting to discuss the sale of the Museum's shares of Getty Oil to Texaco. Lipton instructed his associate, on her way to the meeting in progress of the lawyers drafting merger documents for the Pennzoil/Getty transaction, not to attend that meeting, because he needed her at his meeting with Texaco. At the meeting with Texaco, the Museum outlined various issues it wanted resolved in any transaction with Texaco, and then agreed to sell its 11.8% ownership in Getty Oil [for $125 per share].

At noon on January 6, Getty Oil held a telephone board meeting to discuss the Texaco offer. The board voted to withdraw its previous counterproposal to Pennzoil and unanimously voted to accept Texaco's offer. Texaco immediately issued a press release announcing that Getty Oil and Texaco would merge.

Soon after the Texaco press release appeared, Pennzoil telexed the Getty entities, demanding that they honor their agreement with Pennzoil. Later that day, prompted by the telex, Getty Oil filed a suit in Delaware for declaratory judgment that it was not bound to any contract with Pennzoil. The merger agreement between Texaco and Getty Oil was signed on January 6; the stock purchase agreement with the Museum was signed on January 6; and the stock exchange agreement with the Trust was signed on January 8, 1984.

Additional Facts and Arguments

In addition to the facts described in the excerpts from the opinion of the court of appeals, the Pennzoil lawyers emphasized several other events as evidence that both Pennzoil and Getty intended to be bound by the five-page memorandum of agreement.

At the conclusion of the January 3 Getty board meeting approving the Pennzoil merger, congratulations were exchanged, and many of the individuals present, including several Pennzoil representatives, shook hands. At trial, Pennzoil made this an issue of honor and the value of a man's word, asserting that a handshake could and often did seal a bargain.

Texaco pointed out that, handshakes notwithstanding, the Getty board of directors left the meeting without signing the memorandum of agreement. Texaco also noted that it had not made an offer until it was invited to do so by Getty. John McKinley, chairman of Texaco, repeatedly asked if Getty Oil was free to deal and was assured by Gordon Getty and by the Getty Museum that there was no contract with Pennzoil. In addition, under the law of New York, where all the deals were made, a contract does not exist until the parties have agreed on all the essential terms of the deal. Texaco argued that a five-page

CONTINUED

memorandum could not possibly cover all the essential terms in a $5 billion deal involving four parties (Pennzoil, Getty Oil Company, the Sarah Getty Trust, and the Getty Museum).

Before going further into the many legal arguments involved, it is useful to look more closely at the memorandum of agreement reproduced in Exhibit 7.1.

EXHIBIT 7.1 The Pennzoil–Getty Memorandum of Agreement

Memorandum of Agreement

January 2, 1984

The following plan (the "Plan") has been developed and approved by (i) Gordon P. Getty, as Trustee (the "Trustee") of the Sarah C. Getty Trust dated December 31, 1934 (the "Trust"), which Trustee owns 31,805,800 shares (40.2% of the total outstanding shares) of Common Stock, without par value, of Getty Oil Company (the "Company"), which shares as well as all other outstanding shares of such Common Stock are hereinafter referred to as the "Shares", (ii) The J. Paul Getty Museum (the "Museum"), which Museum owns 9,320,340 Shares (11.8% of the total outstanding Shares), and (iii) Pennzoil Company ("Pennzoil"), which owns 593,900 Shares through a subsidiary, Holdings Incorporated, a Delaware corporation (the "Purchaser"). The Plan is intended to assure that the public shareholders of the Company and the Museum will receive $110 per Share for all their Shares, a price which is approximately 40% above the price at which the Company's Shares were trading before Pennzoil's subsidiary announced its Offer (hereinafter described) and 10% more than the price which Pennzoil's subsidiary offered in its Offer for 20% of the Shares. The Trustee recommends that the Board of Directors of the Company approve the Plan. The Museum desires that the Plan be considered by the Board of Directors and has executed the Plan for that purpose.

1. **Pennzoil agreement.** Subject to the approval of the Plan by the Board of Directors of the Company as provided in paragraph 6 hereof, Pennzoil agrees to cause the Purchaser promptly to amend its Offer to Purchase dated December 28, 1983 (the "Offer") for up to 16,000,000 Shares so as:
   - **(a)** to increase the Offer price to $110 per Share, net to the Seller in cash and
   - **(b)** to increase the number of Shares subject to the Offer to 23,406,100 (being 24,000,000 Shares less 593,900 now owned by the Purchaser).
2. **Company agreement.** Subject to approval of the Plan by the Board of Directors of the Company as provided in paragraph 6 hereof, the Company agrees:
   - **(a)** to purchase forthwith all 9,320,340 Shares owned by the Museum at a purchase price of $110 per Share (subject to adjustment before or after closing in the event of any increase in the Offer price or in the event any higher price is paid by any person who hereafter acquires 10 percent or more of the outstanding Shares) payable either (at the election of the Company) in cash or by means of a promissory note of the Company, dated as of the closing date, payable to the order of the Museum, due on or before thirty days from the date of issuance, bearing interest at a rate equivalent to the prime rate as in effect at Citibank, N.A. and backed by an irrevocable letter of credit (the "Company Note")
   - **(b)** to proceed promptly upon completion of the Offer by the Purchaser with a cash merger transaction whereby all remaining holders of Shares (other than the Trustee and Pennzoil and its subsidiaries) will receive $110 per Share in cash, and
   - **(c)** in consideration of Pennzoil's agreement provided for in paragraph 1 hereof and in order to provide additional assurance that the Plan will be consummated in accordance with its terms, to grant to Pennzoil hereby the option, exercisable at Pennzoil's election at any time on or before the later of consummation of the Offer referred to in paragraph 1 and the purchase referred to in (a) of this paragraph 2, to purchase from the Company up to 8,000,000 Shares of Common Stock of the Company held in the treasury of the Company at a purchase price of $110 per share in cash.
3. **Museum agreement.** Subject to approval of the Plan by the Board of Directors of the Company as provided in paragraph 6 hereof, the Museum agrees to sell to the Company forthwith all 9,320,340 Shares owned by the Museum at a purchase price of $110 per Share (subject to adjustment before or after closing as provided in paragraph 2(a)) payable either (at the election of the Company) in cash or by means of the Company Note referred to in paragraph 2(c).
4. **Trustee and Pennzoil agreement.** The Trustee and Pennzoil hereby agree with each other as follows:
   - **(a) Ratio of Ownership of Shares.** The Trustee may increase its holdings to up to 32,000,000 Shares and Pennzoil may increase its holdings to up to 24,000,000 Shares of the approximately 79,132,000 outstanding Shares. Neither the Trustee nor Pennzoil will acquire in excess of such respective amounts without the prior written agreement of the other, it being the agreement between the Trustee and Pennzoil to maintain a relative Share ratio of 4 (for the Trustee) to 3 (for Pennzoil). In connection with the Offer in the event that more

CONTINUED

than 23,406,100 Shares are duly tendered to the Purchaser, the Purchaser may (if it chooses) purchase any excess over 23,406,000; provided, however, (i) the Purchaser agrees to sell any such excess Shares to the Company (and the company shall agree to purchase) forthwith at $110 per Share and (ii) pending consummation of such sale to the Company the Purchaser shall grant to the Trustee the irrevocable proxy to vote such excess Shares.

(b) Restructuring plan. Upon completion of the transactions provided for in paragraphs 1, 2 and 3 hereof, the Trustee and Pennzoil shall endeavor in good faith to agree upon a plan for the restructuring of the Company. In the event that for any reason the Trustee and Pennzoil are unable to agree upon a mutually acceptable plan on or before December 31, 1984, then the Trustee and Pennzoil hereby agree to cause the Company to adopt a plan of complete liquidation of the Company pursuant to which (i) any assets which are mutually agreed to be sold shall be sold and the net proceeds therefrom shall be used to reduce liabilities of the Company and (ii) individual interests in all remaining assets and liabilities shall be distributed to the shareholders pro rata in accordance with their actual ownership interest in the Company. In connection with the plan of distribution, Pennzoil agrees (if requested by the Trustee) that it will enter into customary joint operating agreements to operate any properties so distributed and otherwise to agree to provide operating management for any business and operations requested by the Trustee on customary terms and conditions.

(c) Board of Directors and Management. Upon completion of the transactions provided for in paragraphs 1, 2 and 3 hereof, the Trustee and Pennzoil agree that the Board of Directors of the Company shall be composed of approximately fourteen Directors who shall be mutually agreeable to the Trustee and Pennzoil (which Directors may include certain present Directors) and who shall be nominated by the Trustee and Pennzoil, respectively, in the ratio of 4 to 3. The Trustee and Pennzoil agree that the senior management of the Company shall include Gordon P. Getty as Chairman of the Board, J. Hugh Liedtke as President and Chief Executive Officer and Blaine P. Kerr as Chairman of the Executive Committee.

(d) Access to Information. Pennzoil, the Trustee and their representatives will have access to all information concerning the Company necessary or pertinent to accomplish the transactions contemplated by the Plan.

(e) Press releases. The Trustee and Pennzoil (and the Company upon approval of the Plan) will coordinate any press releases or public announcements concerning the Plan and any transactions contemplated hereby.

5. **Compliance with regulatory requirements.** The Plan shall be implemented in compliance with applicable regulatory requirements.
6. **Approval by the Board of Directors.** This Plan is subject to approval by the Board of Directors of the Company at the meeting of the Board being held on January 2, 1984, and will expire if not approved by the Board. Upon such approval the Company shall execute three or more counterparts of the "Joinder by the Company" attached to the Plan and deliver one such counterpart to each of the Trustee, the Museum and Pennzoil.

IN WITNESS WHEREOF, this Plan, or a counterpart hereof, has been signed by the following officials thereunto duly authorized this January 2, 1984.

/s/ GORDON P. GETTY
Gordon P. Getty as Trustee of the Sarah C. Getty Trust

The J. Paul Getty Museum
By /s/ HAROLD WILLIAMS
Harold Williams, President

PENNZOIL COMPANY
By /s/ J. Hugh Liedtke
J. Hugh Liedtke, Chairman of the Board and Chief Executive Officer

Joinder by the Company

The foregoing Plan has been approved by the Board of Directors.

GETTY OIL COMPANY
By__________

January 2, 1984

CONTINUED

Getty and Pennzoil had an agreement in principle, but did they have a contract? As soon as the board meeting adjourned on the evening of January 3, some thirty lawyers began working around the clock to draw up the merger documents and the press release to announce the deal. Both were supposed to be completed by the next morning, but only the press release was ready. Typed on Getty Oil letterhead and dated January 4, 1984, it announced that Getty Oil and Pennzoil had "agreed in principle" to a merger. It further stated: "The transaction is subject to execution of a definitive merger agreement, approval by the stockholders of Getty Oil and completion of various governmental filing and waiting period requirements."

The Texaco deal was much simpler than the Pennzoil deal. Texaco simply bought out everyone for $125 a share in cash. By 8 A.M. on January 6, a news release on Texaco letterhead had gone out. At 9 A.M., the Getty board of directors held another board meeting and approved the deal with Texaco. Texaco acquired Getty Oil, and Pennzoil was left out in the cold.

No one on Wall Street saw anything wrong with the deal, but the attitude in the Texas oil business was different. At the 1984 Pennzoil stockholder meeting, Hugh Liedtke described the decision to sue Texaco:

> It's one thing to play hardball. It's quite another thing to play foul ball. Conduct such as Texaco's is not made legal simply by protestations that the acts involved were, in fact, legal. All too often such assertions go unchallenged, and so slip into some sort of legal limbo, and become accepted as the norm by default. In this way, actions previously considered amoral somehow become clothed in respectability.[31]

TEXAS JUSTICE

On January 10, 1984, Pennzoil filed suit in Delaware against Getty Oil, Gordon Getty, the Getty Museum, and Texaco. Pennzoil wanted specific performance—that is, a court order that would give it back its deal with Getty. A few days later, on discovering that Texaco had agreed to indemnify Getty Oil from any claims arising out of its sale in Texas, Pennzoil added tortious interference with a contract to its claims against Texaco.

The Delaware case was to be tried before a judge, not a jury. Through some legal maneuvering on Pennzoil's part and Texaco's failure to file an answer in the Delaware case right away, the case against Texaco ended up in a Texas state court before a jury. (The suits against Getty, the Trust, and the Museum continued in Delaware.) For four and a half months, the two sides presented their evidence. Before the jury retired to the jury room, the judge instructed the jurors on how to apply the law to the facts they had heard. The word "contract" never appeared in the jury instructions. Instead, the judge used the word "agreement."

The Calculation of Damages

On the issue of damages, Pennzoil presented a single witness, who testified that the jury should award "replacement" damages, rather than expectation damages. He asserted that if Getty Oil had honored its deal with Pennzoil, it would have cost Pennzoil $3.4 billion, or $3.40 per barrel, to acquire the one billion barrels that it would have owned as a result of its 3/7ths ownership of Getty Oil's reserves. With the deal destroyed, Pennzoil's expert testified, Pennzoil would have to drill from scratch at a cost of $10.87 per barrel: $10.87 per barrel minus $3.40 per barrel times one billion barrels equaled $7.47 billion in replacement costs—three times the price that Pennzoil had agreed to pay to purchase its 3/7ths interest in Getty Oil. Under a benefit of the bargain analysis, Pennzoil had lost the opportunity to buy 32 million shares of Getty Oil at $112.50 each—shares that Texaco subsequently purchased for $128 each—or a total of $496 million ($15.50 per share times 32 million shares). Even though Texaco's counsel argued to the jury that the replacement damages claimed by Pennzoil were inappropriate, Texaco elected not to call an expert witness or to introduce other evidence on the issue of damages.[32]

As the jury considered the question of punitive damages during its deliberations, the jurors asked the judge, "To what extent is Texaco liable for the actions of [Gordon Getty's lawyer and Getty Oil's lawyer and investment banker]?" The Texaco lawyer thought that the jury instructions had included a charge that a party is accountable only for its own agents, so he agreed that no response to this question was required. As a result, the jury decided to award punitive damages against Texaco because it found that the actions of the indemnitees were outrageous (even though the indemnitees were not Texaco's agents and were not themselves parties to the action because the lawsuit against them was proceeding in Delaware).

The jury returned a verdict in favor of Pennzoil. For Texaco's interference with a contract, the jury awarded Pennzoil $7.53 billion compensatory damages and $3 billion punitive damages, or $1 billion for each indemnity given—$1 billion for the indemnity to Gordon Getty, $1 billion for the indemnity to Getty Oil, and $1 billion for the indemnity to the Getty Museum. (The punitive damages were eventually reduced to $1 billion. The compensatory damages were not changed.)

CONTINUED

31. THOMAS PETZINGER, JR., OIL AND HONOR: THE TEXACO–PENNZOIL WARS, 275–76 (1987).

32. Apparently, Texaco's lawyers did not want to dignify Pennzoil's claims by introducing evidence of the damages to which Pennzoil would be entitled if the jury concluded that Texaco had tortiously interfered with its contract to buy 3/7ths of Getty Oil. Bagley, *supra* note 27.

What did the judges for the Court of Appeals for the First Supreme Judicial District of Texas think of all this? In a lengthy opinion, excerpted below, they upheld the jury's verdict.

Excerpts from the Opinion of the Court of Appeals: Legal Analysis

Under New York law, if parties do not intend to be bound to an agreement until it is reduced to writing and signed by both parties, then there is no contract until that event occurs. If there is no understanding that a signed writing is necessary before the parties will be bound, and the parties have agreed upon all substantial terms, then an informal agreement can be binding, even though the parties contemplate evidencing their agreement in a formal document later.

Thus, under New York law, the parties are given the power to obligate themselves informally or only by a formal signed writing, as they wish. The emphasis in deciding when a binding contract exists is on intent rather than on form.

To determine intent, a court must examine the words and deeds of the parties, because these constitute the objective signs of such intent. Only the outward expressions of intent are considered—secret or subjective intent is immaterial to the question of whether the parties were bound.

Although the magnitude of the transaction here was such that normally a signed writing would be expected, there was sufficient evidence to support an inference by the jury that the expectation was satisfied here initially by the Memorandum of Agreement, signed by a majority of shareholders of Getty Oil and approved by the board with a higher price, and by the transaction agreement in progress that had been intended to memorialize the agreement previously reached.

Texaco claims that even if the parties intended to bind themselves before a definitive document was signed, no binding contract could result because the terms that they intended to include in their agreement were too vague and incomplete to be enforceable as a matter of law. . . . The question of whether the agreement is sufficiently definite to be enforceable is a difficult one. The facts of the individual case are decisively important. . . .

Texaco's attempts to create additional "essential" terms from the mechanics of implementing the agreement's existing provisions are unpersuasive. The terms of the agreement found by the jury are supported by the evidence, and the promises of the parties are clear enough for a court to recognize a breach and to determine the damages resulting from that breach.

The Fallout

Burdened by the largest damages award in U.S. history, Texaco filed for bankruptcy in 1987 after its appeals in the Texas courts failed. As part of its reorganization plan, Texaco agreed to settle the case with Pennzoil for $3 billion.

This case had a tremendous impact on Wall Street, which the *Wall Street Journal* dubbed "the Texaco chill." Investment banker Alan Rothenberg summarized the new attitude: "No longer can we say, 'We stole a deal fair and square.'"[33] In legal circles, the arguments still continue as to whether the Texas judges properly understood New York contract law and the jury reached the correct verdict.

Pennzoil v. Texaco is still on the books and can be cited as precedent in similar cases. Note, however, that the Texas Supreme Court's more recent decision in *Wal-Mart Stores, Inc. v. Sturges,*[34] has made it more difficult to recover damages in an action claiming interference with a prospective contractual relationship. In this case, Sturges had sued Wal-Mart, claiming that it had tortiously interfered with its prospective lease. A trial court found Wal-Mart liable and awarded Sturges $1 million in actual damages and $500,000 in punitive damages, but the Texas Supreme Court reversed the trial court's decision. The supreme court found that where a case involves a prospective business relationship as opposed to a signed contract, "aggressive but legal interference" cannot be attacked as tortious interference.

The Pennzoil-Texaco case was back in the news in October 2008 after Wachovia Corp., the fourth largest bank in the United States, purported to abandon its letter agreement to sell most of its assets to Citigroup for $1 a share in favor of an offer by Wells Fargo to acquire all of Wachovia in exchange for $7 a share in Wells Fargo stock. Citigroup, which the Federal Deposit Insurance Corporation had encouraged to buy most of Wachovia for $2.1 billion to prevent the bank's collapse, responded to the announcement of the $15.4 billion deal with Wells Fargo by stating that "a transaction with Wells Fargo is in clear breach of an exclusivity agreement between Citigroup and Wachovia. In addition, Wells Fargo's conduct constitutes tortious interference."[35] In its agreement with Citigroup, Wachovia had agreed to "continue to proceed to negotiate definitive agreements."[36] After a weekend of legal wrangling in federal and state courts in New York and North Carolina (Wachovia's state of incorporation), the Federal Reserve Board put pressure on the parties to negotiate a settlement, which might entail a higher bid by Citigroup or a break-up of Wachovia and sale of its Northeast and mid-Atlantic branches to Citigroup and its California and Southeast branches, as well as its asset management and brokerage divisions, to Wells Fargo.[37]

33. Petzinger, *supra* note 31, at 459–60.

34. 52 S.W.3d 711 (Tex. 2001).

35. Jonathan D. Glater, *Jilted in Wachovia Deal, Ponders Lawsuit*, N.Y. Times, Oct. 4, 2008, at 1.

36. *Id.*

37. Binyamin Appelbaum, *Wachovia, Suitors Agree to a Truce*, Wash. Post, Oct. 7, 2008, at D01; David Enrich, Robin Sidel & Dan Fitzpatrick, *Citigroup Is Seeking Allies in Fight to Secure Wachovia*, Wall St. J., Oct. 8, 2008.

Key Words and Phrases

acceptance 210
accord 233
accord and satisfaction 233
anticipatory repudiation 233
bilateral contract 212
capacity 214
choice-of-forum provision 240
choice-of-law provision 240
close 239
compensatory damages 235
condition 214
condition concurrent 214
condition precedent 214
condition subsequent 214
consequential damages 235
consideration 211
contract 208
counteroffer 209
covenant not to compete 215
covenants 239
cover 236
creditor beneficiary 234
detrimental reliance 210
discharged 233
donee beneficiary 234
duress 225
equal dignities rule 230
expectation damages 235
fraud in the factum 224
fraud in the inducement 225
frustration of purpose 231
general release 222
illegal contracts 215
illusory promise 212
impossibility 231
impracticability 231
incidental damages 236
intent to be bound 211
irrevocable offer 210
liquidated damages 238
materially breached 233
merger agreement 238
mirror image rule 211
misrepresentation 224
mistake of fact 226
mistake of judgment 228
mitigate 236
mutual rescission 233
mutuality of obligation 212
novation 233
offer 209
offeree 209
offeror 209
oppression 222
option contract 210
output contract 214
parol evidence rule 230
power of attorney 230
precontractual liability 217
prenuptial agreement 229
privity of contract 239
promisee 208
promisor 209
promissory estoppel 215
promissory fraud 225
quantum meruit 236
ratify 215
reliance damages 236
representations and warranties 239
requirements contract 214
restitution 236
revoke 209
satisfaction 233
sovereign acts doctrine 231
specific performance 238
statute of frauds 229
surprise 222
target 238
third-party beneficiary 234
unconscionable 220
undue influence 225
unilateral contract 212
unjust enrichment 215
usury statutes 215
voidable 214

Questions and Case Problems

1. In 1999, the plaintiff sold his New York–based public relations firm, Lobsenz Stevens, to the defendants, Publicis S.A., a French global communications company, and its American subsidiary. The sale involved two contracts: a stock purchase agreement pursuant to which the plaintiff sold all of his stock in the firm to the defendants, and an employment agreement pursuant to which the plaintiff was to continue as chairman and CEO of the new company, named Publicis-Dialog (PD), for three years. Under the stock purchase agreement, the plaintiff received an initial payment of $3,044,000 and

stood to earn "earn-out" payments of up to $4 million contingent upon PD achieving certain levels of earnings before interest and taxes during the three calendar years after the closing. The employment agreement described the plaintiff's duties as the "customary duties of a Chief Executive Officer." Within six months of the closing, signs of financial problems appeared, including the loss of PD's largest pre-acquisition client. In March 2001, the plaintiff was removed as CEO of the business and given several options, including leaving the firm, staying and working on new business, and a third option of coming up with another alternative. Thereafter, Bob Bloom, former chair and CEO of Publicis USA, and the plaintiff exchanged a series of e-mails, which culminated in a March 28 message from Bloom that set forth his understanding of the parties' terms regarding the plaintiff's new role at PD as follows:

> Thus I suggested an allocation of your time that would permit the majority of your effort to go against new business development (70%). I also suggested that the remaining time be allocated to maintaining/growing the former Lobsenz Stevens clients (20%) and involvement in management/operations of the unit (10%). This option, it would seem, is in your best interest because it offers the best opportunity for you to achieve your stated goal of a full earn-out. When I suggested this option, you seemed to have considerable enthusiasm for it and expressed your satisfaction with it so I, of course, assumed that it was an option you preferred.

The plaintiff responded with an e-mail that stated, among other things, "I accept your proposal with total enthusiasm and excitement. . . . I'm psyched again and will do everything in my power to generate business, maintain profits, work well with others and move forward." Bloom responded that he was "thrilled with [the plaintiff's] decision." Each of the e-mail transmissions bore the typed name of the sender at the foot of the message. The plaintiff subsequently filed a lawsuit based on the terms of the original employment agreement and filed a motion for summary judgment claiming that the e-mail exchanges did not constitute "signed writings" within the meaning of the statute of frauds. What arguments would you make on behalf of the defendants? Which party do you think will prevail? [*Stevens v. Publicis, S.A.*, 854 N.Y.S.2d 690 (2008).]

2. Factors, a company in the business of purchasing accounts receivable and lending money to other businesses, asked Unisearch to conduct a Uniform Commercial Code (UCC) search on its behalf for liens against The Benefit Group, Inc. Unisearch completed the search and sent Factors an invoice along with a search report showing no security interests. The invoice was identical to forty-seven others that Unisearch had previously sent to Factors. Upon receiving the report, Factors lent $100,000 to The Benefit Group, secured by its existing and future accounts receivable and other business assets. A year later, The Benefit Group defaulted, and when Factors tried to foreclose on the collateral, it discovered a prior UCC filing under the name of "The Benefits Group, Inc." Factors sued Unisearch, alleging breach of contract and negligence. Prior to trial, Unisearch brought a motion for summary judgment on damages, claiming that its liability was limited to $25 because a clause in its invoice limited liability for any action arising out of or related to the contract to that amount. The limitation of liability was printed on the front of the one-page invoice in the upper right-hand corner in a shaded box. Factors argued that the limitation of liability was unenforceable. Is the limitation of liability unenforceable? On what basis? [*Puget Sound Financial, L.L.C. v. Unisearch, Inc.*, 47 P.3d 940 (Wash. 2002).]

3. In March 1996, Harun Fountain, a minor, was shot in the back of the head at point-blank range by a playmate. As a result of his injuries, including the loss of his right eye, Fountain required extensive lifesaving medical services from a variety of medical services providers, including Yale Diagnostic Radiology. Unfortunately, Fountain did not survive the wound. Fountain's mother, Vernetta Tucker, as Fountain's guardian, sued the boy who had shot him, a settlement was reached, and funds were placed in the estate established on Fountain's behalf under the supervision of the Probate Court. Tucker was designated the fiduciary of that estate. Yale billed Tucker for $17,694 in services, but the bill went unpaid, and in 1999 Yale obtained a collection judgment against her. In January 2001, all of Tucker's debts, including the judgment in favor of Yale, were discharged pursuant to an order of the Bankruptcy Court. Following the discharge of Tucker's debts, Yale moved in the Probate Court for payment of $17,694 from Fountain's estate. What arguments will Yale make to support its application for payment? What arguments can Fountain's estate assert in its defense? Which party will prevail? [*Yale Diagnostic Radiology v. Estate of Harun Fountain*, 838 A.2d 179 (Conn. 2004).]

4. Lanci was involved in an automobile accident with an uninsured motorist. Lanci and Metropolitan Insurance Company entered settlement negotiations and ultimately agreed to settle all claims for $15,000. Lanci's correspondence accepting the settlement offer clearly indicated his belief that his policy limit was $15,000. However, Lanci did not have a copy of his policy, and, in fact, his policy limit was $250,000. When Lanci learned the correct policy limit, he refused to accept the settlement proceeds of $15,000. Should Lanci be able to void the contract? On what basis?

[*Lanci v. Metropolitan Insurance Co.,* 564 A.2d 972 (Pa. Super. Ct. 1989).]

5. Cindy Sawyer, a former friend and unpaid assistant to trial lawyer Melbourne Mills, persuaded Mills to file a class-action lawsuit on behalf of 431 fen-phen users who claimed the diet pill had damaged their hearts. According to a conversation that Sawyer had secretly recorded, Mills agreed to pay her $1 million, plus $65,000 for a new car, in a series of payments over a ten-year period, if the class-action lawsuit "obtained a big pay day." Sawyer claimed the bonus was modeled after the one received by Erin Brockovich, a California legal assistant made famous by the 2000 movie of the same name starring Julia Roberts. Mills negotiated a controversial $200 million settlement, pursuant to which he received a $23.6 million fee. Mills paid Sawyer $160,000 but refused to pay any additional amounts, and Sawyer filed a lawsuit to recover the remaining $900,000 she claimed he owed her. What arguments will Sawyer make to support her claim against Mills? What arguments can Mills make in his defense? [Ky. Courts: Sawyer v. Mills Pleadings, Statute of Frauds and JNOV, Ky. L Rev., April 27, 2006, *available at* http://www.kentuckylawblog.com/2006/04/news_fayette_ju.html.]

6. Hydrotech Systems, Ltd., a New York corporation, agreed to sell wave-pool equipment to Oasis Waterpark, an amusement park in Palm Springs, California. Although Hydrotech was not licensed to install such equipment in California, it agreed to install the wave-pool equipment after Oasis promised to arrange for a California-licensed contractor to "work with" Hydrotech on any construction.

   The contract between Hydrotech and Oasis called for Oasis to withhold a specific portion of the contract price pending satisfactory operation of the wave pool. Although the pool functioned properly after installation, Oasis continued to withhold payment for both the equipment and the installation services.

   Section 7031 of the California Business and Professions Code states that a suit may not be brought in a California court to recover compensation for any act or contract that requires a California contractor's license, unless the plaintiff alleges and proves that he or she was duly licensed at all times during the performance.

   Can Hydrotech recover its compensation due under the contract? Does Hydrotech have a valid action against Oasis for fraud? Is it ethical for Oasis to use the California law to defend itself? [*Hydrotech Systems, Ltd. v. Oasis Waterpark,* 803 P.2d 370 (Cal. 1991).]

7. Tractebel Energy Marketing, a power plant designer and builder, wanted to build a power plant. Environmental Protection Agency regulations required new power plants to offset the anticipated increase in overall emissions by purchasing emission reduction credits. Companies acquired these credits by installing better technology in existing plants or shutting down existing operations. Through a broker, DuPont entered into a contract to sell 1,000 tons of nitrogen oxides emission credits to Tractebel. Shortly thereafter, however, the New Jersey Department of Environmental Protection revoked DuPont's credits, citing new regulations. When DuPont refused to perform the contract, Tractebel sued for breach. What arguments will DuPont claim in its defense? Who will prevail in this action? [*Tractebel Energy Marketing, Inc. v. E.I. DuPont DeNemours & Co.,* 118 S.W.3d 60 (Tex. App.–Houston 2003).]

8. As lawyers assembled closing documents for a refinancing of some of the outstanding debt of United States Lines (USL), a secretary working on "Amendment No. 1 to the First Preferred Ship Mortgage" omitted three zeros from the number representing USL's outstanding indebtedness to Prudential Insurance. As a result, the document showed the amount of Prudential's first mortgage as "$92,855.00" instead of "$92,885,000.00." No one noticed the error until eight months later when USL defaulted on the notes secured by the amended mortgage and went bankrupt.

   When Prudential tried to foreclose its $92,885,000 first mortgage, USL's bankruptcy trustee objected, arguing that the mortgage should be limited to $92,885. In addition, General Electric Capital Corporation (GECC), which had lent money to USL secured by a second mortgage, brought suit for a declaration that Prudential's first mortgage was valid only to the extent of $92,855. Because GECC had lent money to USL secured by a mortgage junior to that to Prudential, GECC stood to gain by reducing the value of Prudential's first mortgage.

   GECC had been intimately involved in USL's financing for some years and knew that Prudential had a $92,885,000 first mortgage. Neither GECC nor any other creditor of USL asserted that it had relied on erroneous information about the amount of USL's outstanding debt.

   If you had been the manager of GECC in charge of the USL account, what would you have done once the typo was discovered? Is Prudential legally entitled to a $92,885,000 first mortgage? What would be the ethical thing to do? [*See* Andrew Kull, *Zero-Based Morality: The Case of the $31 Million Typo,* 1 Bus. L. Today 11 (July–Aug. 1992).]

8

SALES, LICENSING, AND E-COMMERCE

INTRODUCTION

Sales of Goods, Licensing of Software, and Electronic Commerce

Virtually all commercial enterprises engage in the purchase or sale of goods and the licensing of software. Sales of goods within the United States are governed by Article 2 of the Uniform Commercial Code (UCC); most international sales are governed by the Convention on Contracts for the International Sale of Goods. The UCC does not govern the rendering of services or the sale of land. Contracts for selling services or land are governed by common law contract principles, which are discussed in Chapter 7.

There is no comparable uniform law for software licenses. Although the National Conference of Commissioners on Uniform State Laws adopted the Uniform Computer Information Transactions Act (UCITA) as a model law in 2003, it has been enacted into law only in Virginia and Maryland, and it appears unlikely that it will be enacted by other states. Perhaps because of this lack of a uniform law, many courts have applied Article 2 of the UCC to such transactions, either directly or by analogy.

The Internet has transformed the way businesses and individuals conduct business in the United States and throughout the world. According to the Census Bureau, e-commerce transactions by manufacturers, wholesalers, service providers, and retailers amounted to $2.4 trillion in 2005 and are expected to continue to grow in coming years.[1] Due to the speed at which technology is developing and the range of novel issues it presents, state and national governments are scrambling to enact laws that protect consumers and businesses, while facilitating electronic sales transactions using the Internet. In addition, the international reach of the Internet is forcing countries throughout the world to engage in legal cooperation and collaboration.

1. Census numbers are from U.S. Census Bureau E-Stats, May 25, 2007, *available at* http://www.census.gov/eos/www/2005/2005reportfinal.pdf.

CHAPTER OVERVIEW

This chapter begins by addressing when Article 2 applies. It then discusses the application of Article 2 to software licenses, the Uniform Computer Information Transactions Act, and an issue unique to software licenses: whether parties to a software license are free to broaden the protection, or to narrow the defenses, afforded by federal intellectual property law. Next, it discusses the Uniform Electronic Transactions Act and the Electronic Signatures in Global and National Commerce Act. The chapter then deals with contract formation, including issues arising from the process of formation in the software environment and on the Internet. Major questions involve the enforcement of contract terms that become available only after assent and/or are presented in a take-it-or-leave-it standard form. It also discusses the UCC approach to the battle of the forms, which occurs when the form accepting an offer contains terms different from those on the form that constitutes the offer.

The chapter also addresses the special warranty provisions of the UCC, including express warranties and implied warranties of merchantability and fitness for a particular purpose. We explain how the risk of loss is allocated and a buyer's right to reject nonconforming goods. We then review excuses for nonperformance, including unconscionability and commercial impracticability, and remedies for unexcused nonperformance.

Finally, the chapter discusses the rules applicable to the international sale of goods and compares them with the rules applicable to domestic sales transactions governed by the UCC. The "Inside Story" addresses the increasing problem of Internet fraud and efforts by law enforcement agencies to regulate crime on the Internet where it is often difficult to identify the criminals.

ARTICLE 2 OF THE UCC

The Uniform Commercial Code deals with a broad range of commercial transactions, from the use of negotiable instruments to secured transactions. It was promulgated in the early 1940s under the joint authority of the American Law Institute (ALI) and the National Conference of Commissioners on Uniform State Laws (NCCUSL) to bring greater certainty and predictability to an increasingly national commercial system. The ALI, a national organization of lawyers, judges, and academics from all areas of the United States and some foreign countries, was organized in 1923 to address uncertainty in the law, in part by generating restatements of basic legal subjects to assist judges and lawyers in understanding the law in that area. The NCCUSL, a national organization of lawyers, judges, and academics from the fifty states, the District of Columbia, Puerto Rico, and the U.S. Virgin Islands, was organized in the late nineteenth century to provide states with nonpartisan model legislation to help bring stability and clarity to critical areas of state statutory law.

The UCC is a model law, which means that it must be enacted into law by a state legislature to become effective in that state. Because the UCC is approved by both the ALI and the NCCUSL, however, it has generally been accepted by the states more readily than model laws promulgated only by the NCCUSL.

WHAT TYPES OF CONTRACTS ARE COVERED BY ARTICLE 2?

Article 2 of the UCC deals with contracts for the sale of goods. The original version of Article 2 was first enacted in Pennsylvania in 1953 and was eventually adopted in every state except Louisiana.

Section 2-105 of the UCC defines *goods* as "all things (including specially manufactured goods) which are movable at the time of identification to the contract for sale." *Identification to the contract* means the designation—by marking, setting aside, or other means—of the particular goods that are to be supplied under the contract. Sometimes it is not clear whether an activity should be characterized as a sale of goods or a sale of services. For example, when a hospital performs a blood transfusion, is it selling blood or rendering medical services? This distinction can be critical for purposes of both the UCC warranties and product liability in tort (discussed in Chapter 10). Many states have addressed precisely this issue by passing special amendments to their versions of the UCC. These so-called blood shield statutes define blood transfusions as the provision of services, rather than the sale of goods, in order to limit hospital and blood bank liability for reasons of public policy.[2] In other states, the common law has led to the conclusion that such sales are incidental to the provision of medical services and are therefore outside the scope of the UCC.[3]

Similarly, there can be an issue as to whether something attached to land is considered goods or land. This gray area includes *fixtures,* which are items of personal property that are attached to real property and cannot be removed without substantial damage. Fixtures are not considered goods under Article 2 and, like real property, are generally subject to the common law contract principles described in Chapter 7. Courts have also struggled with whether software falls within the definition of "goods" and whether software licenses are "contracts for the sale of goods." These issues are addressed in more detail in the next section.

The UCC regulates sales of goods by both merchants and nonmerchants, but different rules may apply to them. For example, if Navrov sells a car to Jay, the UCC dictates both parties' rights and obligations under the sales contract, whether Navrov is employed as a car dealer or is simply selling his personal possessions on his own behalf. Section 2-104 of the UCC defines a *merchant* as "a person who deals in goods of the kind or otherwise by his occupation holds himself out as having knowledge or skill peculiar to the practices or goods involved in the transaction."

2. *See, e.g.,* Zichichi v. Middlesex Mem'l Hosp., 528 A.2d 805 (Conn. 1987); Garcia v. Edgewater Hosp., 613 N.E.2d 1243 (Ill. App. Ct. 1993).

3. *See, e.g.,* Lovett v. Emory Univ., Inc., 156 S.E.2d 923 (Ga. Ct. App. 1967).

SOFTWARE LICENSES

The extent to which Article 2 applies to computer software has presented a problem for the courts because computer software is usually "licensed," not "sold."

RATIONALE FOR LICENSING SOFTWARE

When the computer industry began in the mid-twentieth century, software was "bundled" with hardware by computer vendors and distributed directly to end users. In 1969, however, after a Department of Justice antitrust investigation into its practice of bundling, IBM established separate pricing policies for hardware and software. Most other computer vendors followed IBM's lead and began offering software on a stand-alone basis in order to avoid governmental scrutiny. Vendors chose to license, rather than sell, their software because it was unclear at the time whether copyright law protected computer programs.[4]

Because software is a series of instructions to a computer that can be expressed in written form or as a series of electronic impulses, it can be embodied on a disk, CD-ROM, or other tangible medium like other hard goods subject to Article 2. However, unlike hard goods, the value of the software is not the media, but the instructions themselves. As the U.S. District Court for the Northern District of California pointed out in *Adobe Systems, Inc. v. Stargate Software, Inc.*:

> The CD-ROM itself [on which the Adobe software was embedded] is worth not much more than a nominal amount, and it is the [software] code that justifies the purchase price of the [Adobe software] product. That being the case, the economic reality of [the] transaction is that a consumer is ultimately paying for the software contained on the CD-ROM, rather than the CD-ROM itself.[5]

In addition, software is unique from other goods because it can be "readily and easily copied on a mass scale in an extraordinarily short amount of time," for little or no cost.[6]

These unique attributes led vendors to continue to distribute their software products through licensing agreements even after amendments to the Copyright Act in 1976 made it clear that computer programs were copyrightable. A sales agreement generally imposes no continuing obligations on the purchaser other than an obligation to pay the purchase price. A software license, however, generally includes a number of continuing obligations, such as limitations on the right to make copies of the software, limitations on the number of computers on which the program may be installed, prohibitions against sublicensing, restrictions on the use of the software to provide services to third parties, prohibitions against modifying the software, and prohibitions against reverse engineering. By licensing, rather than selling the software, the vendor can avoid the *doctrine of first sale,* embodied in Section 109(a) of the Copyright Act, which provides, "The owner of a particular copy . . . lawfully made under this title, or any person authorized by such owner, is entitled, without the authority of the copyright owner, to sell or otherwise dispose of the possession of that copy. . . ."

LAW APPLICABLE TO SOFTWARE LICENSES

Most cases addressing the subject have held, either directly or by analogy, that Article 2 applies to most transactions involving software.[7] During the 1990s, the plan was to divide Article 2 into three sections: Article 2, which would continue to deal with the sale of goods; Article 2A, which would deal with certain lease transactions and is outside the scope of this chapter; and Article 2B, which would deal with licensing, including licensing arrangements for software. In 1999, however, the ALI rejected the final version of Article 2B. The NCCUSL elected instead to adopt it as a model state law, the Uniform Computer Information Transactions Act (UCITA).

Like the UCC, model laws such as UCITA become effective only when enacted by individual state legislatures. Although many sectors of the software industry strongly supported UCITA, it was opposed by many others, including consumer advocates, technology trade associations, law professors, the American Library Association, the Consumers Union, the Institute of Electrical and Electronics Engineers, and a long list of state attorneys general. Critics complained that UCITA provided too much protection to companies and not enough to consumers. They strongly opposed giving software vendors the right to monitor the use of their products by accessing

4. Steven A. Heath, *Contracts, Copyright and Confusion,* 5 CHI.-KENT J. INTELL. PROP. 12–14 (2005).

5. 216 F. Supp. 2d 1051 (N.D. Cal. 2002).

6. *Id.* at 1059.

7. RESTATEMENT (THIRD) OF TORTS § 19 cmt. d (1997) (stating "[u]nder the [UCC] software that is mass-marketed is considered a good" and citing numerous cases).

computers remotely, and argued that UCITA would weaken the warranty protection consumers receive under software licenses and make it more difficult to sue software vendors that sold faulty programs. Only two states (Maryland and Virginia) have adopted UCITA, while at least five states have adopted anti-UCITA laws that limit the power of their courts to apply UCITA by virtue of a choice-of-law determination. In 2003, the NCCUSL attempted to persuade the American Bar Association (ABA) to approve UCITA but withdrew its request in the face of opposition by several ABA sections. As a result, the NCCUSL decided to forgo, at least for the time being, any further efforts to convince the states to enact UCITA.[8]

Both the NCCUSL and ALI did, however, approve amendments to Article 2 in 2003, in which the NCCUSL made another attempt to address computer software by including embedded software within Article 2, but excluding "information" from the definition of "goods." This exclusion would appear to exclude electronic transfers of computer software from the scope of Article 2. As of June 1, 2008, no states have adopted the 2003 amendments, and prospects for their widespread adoption by the states are not good.[9] As a result, this chapter does not address the 2003 amendments in detail.

In 2005, the ALI decided that the statutory path for regulation of software licenses was not promising and that courts were likely to continue to make software law for the near future. As a result, the ALI decided to generate a set of Principles of the Law of Software Contracts to review the existing case law and recommend best practices for use by judges and lawyers in understanding the law in this area. The ALI Principles project is ongoing and is likely to continue several more years before completion.

LICENSE PROVISIONS AND INTELLECTUAL PROPERTY LAW

The imposition of continuing license restrictions on software has raised a number of issues regarding enforceability. License restrictions have been challenged and, in some cases, invalidated, on the basis that they conflict with applicable intellectual property law, violate public policy, or are unconscionable.

Two types of provisions have raised questions. Some provisions attempt to expand the affirmative exclusive rights that intellectual property statutes would otherwise confer; that is, they provide additional rights in protected material or create copyright or patent-like rights in unprotected material. For example, Lasercomb America, Inc. and Holiday Steel were competitors in the manufacture of steel rule dies that are used to cut and score paper and cardboard for folding into boxes and cartons. Lasercomb developed a computer-aided design/manufacturing software program, Interact, which it licensed to Holiday Steel. When Lasercomb discovered that several Holiday Steel executives had made unauthorized copies of Interact, it sued Holiday Steel and two executives for breach of contract and copyright infringement. Although the defendants did not dispute that they had made unauthorized copies of Interact, they argued that Lasercomb was barred from recovering for infringement because of copyright misuse. Their assertion was based on the following language in Lasercomb's ninety-nine-year software license agreement:

> Licensee agrees during the term of this Agreement and for one (1) year after the termination of this Agreement, that it will not write, develop, produce or sell, or assist others in writing, developing, producing or selling computer assisted die making software, directly or indirectly without Lasercomb's prior written consent. Any such activity undertaken without Lasercomb's written consent shall nullify any warranties or agreements of Lasercomb set forth herein.

Even though the defendants had not signed an agreement with Lasercomb, they proved at trial that at least one Interact licensee had entered into a Lasercomb agreement that included the above provision. The U.S. Court of Appeals for the Fourth Circuit found that this provision constituted a copyright misuse that barred Lasercomb from suing any party, including the defendants, for infringement of its copyright in the Interact program:

> Lasercomb undoubtedly has the right to protect against copying of the Interact code. Its standard licensing agreement, however, goes much further and essentially attempts to suppress any attempt by the licensee to independently implement the idea which Interact expresses. The agreement forbids the licensee to develop or assist in developing *any* kind of computer-assisted die-making software. . . . Although one or another licensee might succeed in negotiating out the noncompete provisions, this does not negate the fact that Lasercomb is attempting to use its copyright in a manner adverse to the public

8. *UCITA Update,* Com. L. Rep., Oct. 2003, at 146–48.

9. In 2004, Oklahoma enacted the exclusion of "information" from the definition of goods under Article 2, although it did not enact any other portion of the 2003 amendments. Oklahoma also excluded a "license of information" from the definition of "contract for sale." Jean Braucher, *Contracting Out of Article 2 Using a "License" Label: A Strategy That Should Not Work for Software Products,* 46 Loy. L.A. L. Rev. 261, 270 (2007).

International Snapshot

On July 1, 2003, European Union Council Directive 2002/38/EC (the E-VAT Directive) became effective.[a] The E-VAT Directive applies to sales of electronically supplied services by businesses located outside the EU to nontaxable persons located in the EU, that is, individual consumers and entities that do not carry on an economic activity (B2C or business-to-consumer commerce). *Electronically supplied services* include the electronic supply of software, music, films, and games, as well as other electronic content, web-hosting, distance maintenance of software and equipment, distance teaching, and the like.

Value-added tax (VAT) is a consumption tax that each EU member state levies on the sale of goods and services to nontaxable persons within its jurisdiction. The twenty-seven EU member states charge VAT at rates ranging from 15 to 25 percent (as of June 2008, there were different rates within the EU member states). The VAT funds about 15 percent of the EU's budget.[b]

Prior to July 1, 2003, businesses located outside the EU that sold electronically supplied services to nontaxable persons in Europe were not required to collect VAT. The EU believed that this gave such non-EU businesses an advantage over their European competitors, who were required to charge VAT for the same services delivered to locations both within and outside the EU.[c] To eliminate this competitive advantage, the E-VAT Directive treats the sale of electronically supplied services as occurring at the place where the nontaxable person resides, the "country of consumption." As a consequence, non-EU businesses are now required to charge VAT on the sale of electronically supplied services to nontaxable persons in the EU. Furthermore, EU businesses are no longer required to charge VAT on such transactions to consumers outside the EU.

The E-VAT Directive created a special registration regime that allows non-EU businesses to register with and pay VAT to the tax authorities in only one EU member state (the "country of registration"), if the non-EU business (1) registers and obtains a tax number from such country of registration, (2) distinguishes between B2C and business-to-business (B2B) sales,[d] (3) identifies the country of consumption for each transaction, (4) charges and collects VAT from each nontaxable person at the applicable rate in the country of consumption, (5) pays the VAT due for all transactions with EU nontaxable persons in a euro-denominated account in the country of registration, and (6) maintains transaction records for ten years that are sufficient to allow the tax authorities in each country of consumption to determine the VAT that was due and paid by their nontaxable persons. The authorities in the country of registration will reallocate the VAT to the EU member state where the respective nontaxable person for each transaction resides. A non-EU business that is registered in an EU member state and qualifies for this special regime is entitled to claim a credit for VAT paid, if any, on its sales of electronically supplied services and has to account for VAT on such transactions on a single quarterly electronic VAT declaration that provides details of VAT due in each EU member state.

There are also alternatives to the special registration regime. For some non-EU businesses, it might be advantageous to establish an EU subsidiary, preferably in a EU member state with a low VAT rate, but the advantages (such as a lower VAT for B2C customers and possibly a lower administrative burden in connection with tax filings) have to be weighed against the possible disadvantages (such as the costs related to setting up an EU subsidiary and other administrative efforts that would become necessary).[e] Another option for non-EU businesses might be the use of EU-based resellers.

Prior to its enactment, U.S. companies opposed the E-VAT Directive, characterizing it as "e-protectionism." The president of the U.S. Software and Information Industry Association commented: "U.S. vendors should not be tax collectors for European governments. It is also doubtful, under public international law, whether the EU has any authority to impose such a legal obligation on U.S. entities."[f]

In addition to such legal concerns, other aspects of the E-VAT Directive have also been criticized. Because the E-VAT Directive does not specify the consequences for noncompliance, these consequences are not uniform among the member states. In addition, the special registration of non-European businesses with a single EU member state is hard to enforce, and non-European businesses may therefore be able to escape taxation. (The taxation of e-commerce in the United States is discussed in the "View from Cyberspace" later in this chapter.)

---

a. Although the E-VAT Directive was scheduled to remain in force only for three years, from July 2003 until July 2006, it has been extended until the end of 2008.

b. European Commission, *Overview of the Own Resources System, available at* http://ec.europa.eu/budget/budget_detail/overview_en.htm. "Own" is defined as the revenue flowing automatically to the EU budget, pursuant to the treaties and implementing legislation, without the need for any subsequent decision by national authorities.

c. EU businesses charge nontaxable persons the VAT rate of the member state where the EU business is located, not the rate of the member state where the nontaxable person resides.

d. This is done by authentication of the business customer through its use of the unique VAT Identification Number (VAT ID).

e. Oleksandr Pastukhov, *The E-VAT Directive: Mitigating Tax Competition or Spurring It?* Int'l Com. L. & Tech. 56 (2007) (Pastukhov comes to the conclusion that the E-VAT Directive has created a misbalance in infra-EU electronic commerce by allowing such an approach).

f. Geoff Winestock, *EU Plans Rule for Web Tax; U.S. Companies Protest Proposal,* Wall St. J., June 8, 2000, at A19.

policy embodied in copyright law, and that it has succeeded in doing so with at least one licensee.[10]

Users have also challenged license provisions that narrow or exclude statutory or common law limits on exclusive rights, including terms restricting distribution of non-copyrightable factual information, prohibiting assignment, mandating grant-back licenses, and prohibiting reverse engineering. For example, in *Alcatel USA, Inc. v. DGI Technologies, Inc.*, the U.S. Court of Appeals for the Fifth Circuit found a copyright misuse when a license agreement prohibited reverse engineering necessary to test compatibility between a microprocessor card and an operating system, stressing that the copyright owner could not "indirectly seek[] to obtain patent-like protection of its hardware—its microprocessor card—through the enforcement of its software copyright."[11]

Usually, intellectual property law does not preempt enforcement of terms of private agreements, because the provisions bind only the contracting parties, but intellectual property policy may preempt certain provisions. Preemption issues are heightened, however, when software is distributed under a "take-it-or-leave-it" standard form agreement that, by virtue of state enforcement, more closely resembles state legislation competing with federal intellectual property laws. For example, although the Court of Appeals for the Federal Circuit enforced a contractual prohibition against reverse engineering in *Bowers v. Baystate Technologies, Inc.*,[12] the dissent would have invalidated the prohibition on the basis that a state cannot eliminate the fair use defense by enforcing such a provision in a nonnegotiable shrink-wrap license agreement (shrink-wraps are discussed later in the chapter).

Although Article 2 of the UCC does not answer all of the legal issues that arise in regard to software licenses, especially terms that strike at the balance between promoting public welfare by granting exclusive rights and promoting public welfare through competition fueled in part by the broad distribution of information, it has worked reasonably well for the issues that it covers, such as contract formation, battle of the forms, quality warranties, disclaimers of warranty, and remedies, and most courts have applied it, either directly or by analogy. The remainder of this chapter includes references to a number of cases involving computer software that have applied Article 2 when addressing these issues.

10. Lasercomb Am., Inc. v. Reynolds, 911 F.2d 970 (4th Cir. 1990).

11. 166 F.3d 772 (5th Cir. 1999).

12. 320 F.3d 1317 (Fed. Cir. 2003).

Electronic Contracts: The Uniform Electronic Transactions Act and the E-Sign Act

With the rise of e-commerce, more and more transactions are taking place electronically. Until recently, however, many states did not give contracts executed electronically the same legal effect as physical paper contracts. Moreover, laws governing electronic transactions varied widely from state to state.

UNIFORM ELECTRONIC TRANSACTIONS ACT

In 1999, the NCCUSL adopted the Uniform Electronic Transactions Act (UETA) to address the issue of whether electronic contracts and signatures are legal contracts. UETA serves as a model for state legislatures seeking to implement laws relating to electronic transactions. Although adoption is not mandatory, forty-eight states had enacted UETA as of 2008.

UETA sets forth four basic rules regarding contracts entered into by parties that agree to conduct business electronically:

1. A record or signature may not be denied legal effect or enforceability solely because it is in electronic form.
2. A contract may not be denied legal effect or enforceability solely because an electronic record was used in its formation.
3. An electronic record satisfies a law that requires a record to be in writing.
4. An electronic signature satisfies a law that requires a signature.[13]

Under UETA, almost any mark or process intended to sign an electronic record will constitute an electronic signature, including a typed name at the bottom of an e-mail message, a faxed signature, and a "click-through" process on a computer screen whereby a person clicks "I agree" on a web page. The essential element necessary to determine the validity of an electronic signature is whether the person intended the process or mark provided to act as a signature and whether it can be attributed to that person.

13. David Schumacher, *U.S. Addresses Legal Issues Raised by Electronic Trading,* INT'L FIN. L. REV., Apr. 1, 2000, at 19.

E-SIGN ACT

In an effort to ensure more uniform treatment of electronic transactions across the United States, Congress enacted the Electronic Signatures in Global and National Commerce Act, more commonly known as the E-Sign Act, effective October 1, 2000. Consistent with UETA, the E-Sign Act provides that a signature, contract, or other record "may not be denied legal effect, validity, or enforceability solely because it is in electronic form."[14] The provisions of the E-Sign Act are very similar to those of UETA, except that UETA, where enacted, applies to intrastate transactions, whereas the E-Sign Act governs only transactions in interstate and foreign commerce. Moreover, the provisions of the E-Sign Act are mandatory.

The E-Sign Act reconciles the inconsistency among states that have and have not enacted UETA by expressly preempting all state laws inconsistent with its provisions. The E-Sign Act does, however, demonstrate some flexibility toward those states that have adopted UETA by allowing state law "to modify, limit, or supersede" the provisions of the E-Sign Act to the extent that such variations are not inconsistent with the E-Sign Act. What variations will ultimately be considered "inconsistent" is not entirely clear and may have to be determined by the courts.

EXCLUSIONS

To protect those individuals or companies that choose not to conduct business electronically or do not have access to computers, the E-Sign Act and UETA require that the use or acceptance of electronic records or electronic signatures be voluntary. Moreover, under the E-Sign Act, if a business is legally bound to produce information to a consumer in writing, electronic records may be used only if the business first secures the consumer's informed consent.

Notwithstanding the broad scope of the E-Sign Act and UETA, several classes of documents are not covered by their provisions and thus may not be considered fully enforceable if transacted electronically. Both UETA and the E-Sign Act exclude:

- Wills, codicils, and trusts.
- Contracts or records relating to adoption, divorce, or other matters of family law.
- Contracts governed by certain provisions of the UCC in effect in each state.

Unlike UETA, the E-Sign Act also excludes:

- Court orders and notices and other official court documents.
- Notices of cancellation or termination of utility services.
- Notices regarding credit agreements secured by, or rental agreements for, a primary residence (for example, eviction notices).
- Notices of cancellation or termination of health or life insurance benefits.
- Notices of recall.
- Documents required to accompany the transport of hazardous materials, pesticides, or other toxic materials.

INTERNATIONAL COORDINATION

Of course, a national standard governing electronic transactions does not resolve inconsistencies with laws of other countries. Some form of international coordination will be necessary to ensure that electronic transactions are consistently enforced across national borders. Toward that end, an effort is under way to encourage other countries to adopt similar standards.[15] The European Electronic Signature Directive, which became effective in January 2001, requires member states to adopt laws and regulations similar to the E-Sign/UETA approach (although it also contains some special rules applicable to certification services). Some Asian countries, including Japan, have enacted digital signature laws, but to date Latin American, Middle Eastern, and African countries have generally been silent on the issue.

CONTRACT FORMATION

The UCC permits a contract to be enforced if the parties intended a binding contract, even though important terms may have been left open for later agreement. If a dispute later arises over a missing term, the court may simply use a "gap-filler" as provided by the UCC. The court will fill in missing terms, however, only if the party attempting to enforce the contract can prove that there was a genuine agreement, not a mere proposal or intention to continue negotiations. It must be apparent that an offer, acceptance, and consideration were present.

OFFER

Offer is not defined by the UCC, although it is used in several important sections. Therefore, traditional common law principles (discussed in Chapter 7) determine whether an

14. Electronic Signatures in Global and National Commerce Act, 15 U.S.C. § 7101(a)(2) (2000).

15. Office of the Press Secretary, the White House, "Statement by the President" (June 30, 2000).

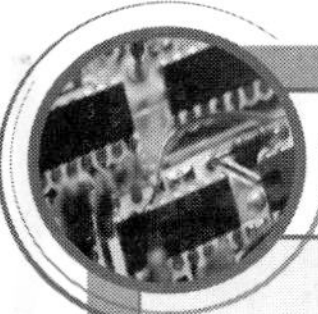

VIEW FROM CYBERSPACE

Taxing E-Commerce

The issue of whether to tax electronic commerce has generated great controversy at the state and federal level. In 1998, Congress enacted the Internet Tax Freedom Act (ITFA), which declared a moratorium on new taxes on Internet access and e-commerce (if such e-commerce taxes are "multiple or discriminatory") but allowed states to enforce existing tax laws. At the same time, Congress created the Advisory Commission on Electronic Commerce to study federal, state, local, and international taxation of transactions using the Internet. The commission included executives of America Online, AT&T, Charles Schwab, Gateway, MCI WorldCom, and Time Warner as well as representatives of government at various levels.[a]

In March 2000, the Advisory Commission narrowly approved a report to Congress on continuing the tax moratorium, but the group was too divided to reach the two-thirds majority required for any "findings and recommendations" to Congress. Under the report, activities not triggering an obligation to collect state sales and use taxes included the solicitation of orders, the presence of websites, the use of the Internet to create a website, the use of an Internet service provider, and the use of a telecommunications carrier.[b] In 2007, the ITFA was extended until November 1, 2014.[c]

Certainly, the existing maze of state sales tax regimes presents some difficulties in taxing Internet sales transactions. In *Quill v. North Dakota*,[d] the U.S. Supreme Court ruled that, given the complexity of state sales and use taxes, a business selling goods through catalogs is required to collect sales taxes only on purchases made by consumers residing within the states where the business has a physical presence. The Court acknowledged, however, that Congress could pass a law compelling the collection of sales and use tax on interstate sales.

Under the *Quill* ruling, an Internet company that sells to customers in states all over the country has no obligation to collect sales tax on sales to persons in states where it is not physically located. Forty-five states require their citizens to pay sales or use taxes on all their purchases, including those made online or in another state, but few online businesses collect these taxes, and consumers buying goods from outside their state of residence rarely pay this tax either. As a result, many Internet purchases by individuals escape sales and use tax altogether. Many online retailers have even gone so far as to locate their sale operations in the five U.S. states that do not levy a sales tax, so these retailers have no obligation to collect sales taxes from any of their customers.

States are heavily dependent on sales taxes, which on average account for one-third of state tax revenues and one-quarter of the total state and local take. In some states with no state income tax, such as Texas, the sales tax accounts for more than half of all revenues.[e] In the early years of the Internet, online transactions represented only a small percentage of retail sales. As of March 2000, for example, Internet sales amounted to less than 1 percent of all retail sales; according to Forrester Research, Inc., in 1999, states lost only $525 million, or 0.3 percent of all sales tax revenue, as a result of the Internet.[f] This situation is changing, however. Researchers at the University of Tennessee report that state and local governments lost up to $15.5 billion in sales tax revenues in 2003, and states will lose more than 6 percent of their total state tax revenue to e-commerce sales by 2011.[g]

Should the existing state tax regime be amended to address Internet sales? Regular "brick and mortar" retailers are opposed to the current system on the grounds that it gives Internet retailers an unfair advantage by allowing them to charge lower prices. As Governor John Engler of Michigan, testifying before Congress for the National Governors Association in February 2000, stated, "It is, in essence, a two-tiered system: good for clicks, bad for bricks."[h]

Opponents of taxes on Internet sales argue that the growth of Internet businesses should not be slowed down by the imposition of taxes. According to a study by an economist at the University of Chicago, Internet sales in 1998 would have been 25 to 30 percent lower if sales taxes had been charged.[i] Proponents of taxing Internet transactions point out that e-commerce has grown tremendously since 1998. Contending that it no longer needs to be protected from taxation, they cite more recent studies such as a Jupiter Research survey that found just 9 percent of consumers would buy less or stop buying from an online store if it charged sales tax.[j]

Since 2002, more than forty-four states have participated in the

CONTINUED

Streamlined Sales Tax Project (SSTP), which has developed uniform rules and improved technology to simplify the collection of sales and use tax. States that have passed some version of the SSTP also participate in the Streamlined Sales Tax Implementing States (SSTIS), which recommends legislative changes by the states. In November 2002, the SSTIS agreed on model legislation, called the Streamlined Sales and Use Tax Agreement (SSUTA), which became effective in November 2005, when member states implemented a web-based centralized point of sales tax registration (https://www.sstregister.org/sellers/Entry.aspx), with an amnesty period for sellers that have not been contacted by member states for audit, and finalized the process for certification of software to assist in sales tax collection responsibilities. Although states will not be able to require collection of sales tax on remote sales until Congress acts to enable them, more than 1,000 online companies have voluntarily agreed to begin collecting and paying sales tax to the SSTP member states in exchange for amnesty against any attempts by the states to collect back taxes.[k]

a. David Cay Johnson, *Agreement on Internet Taxes Eludes Deeply Divided Commission,* N.Y. Times, Mar. 21, 2000, at 1.
b. *Panel Passes E-Commerce Report 10-8, Administration Officials All Vote Against Plan,* 68 U.S.L.W. 2601 (2000).
c. K.C. Jones, *President Bush Signs Internet Tax Freedom Act,* InfoWorld, Nov. 1, 2007.
d. 504 U.S. 298 (1992).
e. Howard Gleckman, *The Great Internet Tax Debate: Should the States Get a Slice of Every E-Commerce Dollar or Should Cyber-Sales Be Free of Any Tax Burden?,* Bus. Wk., Mar. 27, 2000, at 228.
f. *Id.*
g. *Should States Be Allowed to Tax Internet Sales?* (Inst. on Taxation and Econ. Policy, Policy Brief No. 2, 2005), *available at* http://www.itepnet.org/pb2quill.pdf.
h. Ann Scott Tyson, *Should World Wide Web Be a Tax-Free Zone? E-Commerce Boosters Argue a Ban on Internet Taxes Is Critical for Growth, but States Worry They'll Lose Revenues,* Christian Sci. Monitor, Feb. 28, 2000, at 3.
i. *The Happy E-Shopper: How Feasible Is It to Tax Internet Spending?,* Economist, Jan. 29, 2000.
j. Bob Tedeschi, *Days of Tax-Free Sales May Be Numbered,* N.Y. Times, June 27, 2005, *available at* http://www.nytimes.com/2005/06/27/technology/27ecom.html?ei=5088&en=7027d9344094.
k. Adam Wilson, *Delivery-Based Taxes Coming* (Aug. 23, 2007), http://theolympian.com/business/v-print/story/198617.html.

offer has been made. Under the UCC, neither an invitation for bids nor a price quotation is an offer. Similarly, a proposal by a sales representative that is subject to approval by the home office is not an offer.

ACCEPTANCE

The UCC does not define *acceptance* either, except to state that an acceptance may contain terms additional to or different from those in the offer. This is different from the common law *mirror image rule,* which requires the acceptance to contain the exact same terms as the offer. Unless the offeror indicates unambiguously that his or her offer can be accepted only in a particular way, an offer may be accepted in any manner and by any medium that is reasonable in the circumstances.

The sale of software licenses in stores, by mail, and over the Internet has resulted in several specialized forms of licenses that have raised new issues about what constitutes acceptance. In *ProCD, Inc. v. Zeidenberg,*[16] the U.S. Court of Appeals for the Seventh Circuit upheld the enforceability of a software license agreement that was "encoded on the CD-ROM disks, as well as printed on the manual, and which appear[ed] on a user's screen every time the software [ran]." The court acknowledged that use of a *shrink-wrap license,* which places the license terms on the outside of the box containing the software, was not practical. The court held, though, that a notice on the box stating that the software was purchased subject to an enclosed license was sufficient, in part because the software could not be used unless and until the purchaser was shown the license and manifested his or her acceptance by using the software after having an opportunity to read the license.

A second type of license, a click-wrap, is frequently used for software that is distributed over the Internet. A *click-wrap license* presents the user with a notice on his or her computer screen that requires the user to agree to the terms of the license by clicking on an icon. The software cannot be obtained or used until the icon is clicked. The few cases that have considered click-wrap licenses have generally found them to be enforceable.[17]

Some websites use a third type of software license, a browse-wrap. A *browse-wrap license* is an online agreement that appears on a website, but does not require the user to take

16. 86 F.3d 1447 (7th Cir. 1996).

17. *See, e.g., In re* RealNetworks, Inc. Privacy Litig., 2000 WL 631341 (N.D. Ill. 2000); Hotmail Corp. v. Van$ Money Pie, Inc., 1998 WL 388389 (N.D. Cal. 1998).

any action to express his or her consent to the agreement. For example, Netscape offered its SmartDownload program free of charge on its website to all those who visited the site and indicated, by clicking their mouse in a designated box, that they wished to obtain it. The sole reference on the page to the license agreement appeared in text that was visible only if the visitor scrolled down through the page to the next screen, which included the following invitation to review the license agreement: "Please review and agree to the terms of the Netscape SmartDownload software license agreement before downloading and using the software."

Visitors were not required to indicate their assent to the license agreement, or even to view it, before proceeding to download the software. However, if a visitor chose to click on the underlined text in the invitation, a hypertext link took the visitor to a web page entitled "License and Support Agreements," which began as follows:

> The use of each Netscape software product is governed by a license agreement. You must read and agree to the license agreement terms BEFORE acquiring a product. Please click on the appropriate link below to review the current license agreement for the product of interest to you before acquisition. For products available for download, you must read and agree to the license agreement terms BEFORE you install the software. If you do not agree to the license terms, do not download, install or use the software.

In *Specht v. Netscape,*[18] the plaintiffs alleged that their use of the Smart Download software transmitted to Netscape private information about their file transfer activity on the Internet, thereby effecting an electronic surveillance of their activity in violation of the Electronic Communications Privacy Act and the Computer Fraud and Abuse Act. Netscape moved to compel arbitration and stay the proceedings, arguing that the disputes reflected in the complaint were subject to a binding arbitration clause in the license agreement for the SmartDownload software. The U.S. Court of Appeals for the Second Circuit held that the plaintiffs were not bound by the arbitration clause in the license agreement because "a reference to the existence of license terms on a submerged screen is not sufficient to place consumers on inquiry or constructive notice of those terms."

In a subsequent case, however, the U.S. Court of Appeals for the Second Circuit took a significant step toward enforcing browse-wrap agreements.[19] Register.com, an Internet registrar authorized to sell Internet domain names, accused Verio of using an automated software program to submit daily queries to Register.com to collect information about new domain name registrants from whom it would then solicit business. Register.com complained that Verio's actions violated its Terms of Use, which were provided to Verio when it received the query results. Verio argued that the Terms of Use were not binding because it never manifested its assent to the terms, but Register.com countered that Verio's conduct—repeatedly submitting queries even after it became aware of Register.com's Terms of Use—demonstrated Verio's assent to be bound by them. The court ruled in favor of Register.com, comparing the situation to a roadside fruit stand displaying a bin of apples. If a visitor, D, took an apple and bit into it before he saw a sign posted by the owner, P, that stated that the apples were for sale, D might not be obligated to pay for that apple. However, if D returned to the stand and took another apple without paying for it, the situation would be different. The court concluded, "In our view, . . . D cannot continue on a daily basis to take apples for free, knowing full well that P is offering them only in exchange for . . . compensation, merely because the sign demanding payment is so placed that on each occasion D does not see it until he has bitten into the apple."

CONSIDERATION

Contracts for the sale of goods ordinarily must have consideration to be enforceable. However, a *firm offer,* that is, a signed

› Ethical Consideration

Devon Cartagena, a dealer in antiques, sees a desk for sale for $50 at a garage sale that he recognizes as a Louis XV desk worth $15,000. Does he have a legal or ethical obligation to disclose the true value to the person holding the garage sale? Should it matter that difficult financial circumstances made it necessary for the homeowner to sell the desk? Should Cartagena get some reward for the effort he has spent in becoming an expert in antiques and for the time he has spent pawing through junk at countless garage sales?

A person recently sold a map for $3 that later turned out to be worth more than $19 million. Does the buyer have a moral duty to share the windfall with the seller? Would the seller have a moral duty to share the loss if the buyer paid $19 million for a map worth only $3?

What if a framed picture sold for $25 turns out to have an original copy of the U.S. Constitution behind the picture? Is this a mistake of judgment or of fact? (As explained in Chapter 7, a mistake of judgment is not a valid defense for enforcement of a contract, but a mistake of fact can make a contract voidable.) What, if anything, is the buyer's ethical responsibility to the seller in such a case?

18. 306 F.3d 17 (2d Cir. 2002).

19. Register.com v. Verio, 356 F.3d 393 (2d Cir. 2004).

offer by a merchant that indicates that the offer will be kept open, is not revocable for lack of consideration. The offer must be kept open during the time stated or, if none is stated, for a reasonable period of time, up to a maximum of three months. This rule is just one example of how the UCC provides more stringent standards for merchants than for nonmerchants.

Under the UCC, an agreement to modify a contract is binding even if there is no consideration for the modification as long as the modification was made in good faith. However, if the original contract was required to be in writing to satisfy the statute of frauds (discussed later in this chapter), then the agreement to modify the contract must be in writing also.

Battle of the Forms

In a *battle of the forms,* the parties negotiate the essential terms of the contract (for example, quantity, quality, and delivery date) but neglect to bargain over items that are less immediately important (for example, whether disputes will be subject to arbitration, for how long a period after delivery the buyer may assert complaints of defects, or on whom the risk of loss during shipment falls). The parties then exchange standard printed forms, each of which is filled with fine print listing all kinds of terms advantageous to the party that drew up the form. Often goods are shipped, received, and paid for before both parties have expressly accepted the same document as their contract. As a result of these exchanges, two questions arise: (1) Is there a contract? (2) If so, what are its terms?

The UCC calls a truce in the battle of the forms by effectively abolishing the mirror image rule. It is not necessary for an offer and acceptance to match exactly in order for a contract for the sale of goods to exist. Adding to or modifying terms in the offer does not make the acceptance a counteroffer, as is true under common law.

Definite Response

A definite and timely assent to an offer constitutes an acceptance. The presence of additional or different terms is not a bar to contract formation. The crucial inquiry is whether the parties intended to close a deal. Under Section 2-207, a contract exists whenever the parties act as if there is a contract between them. It is not necessary to determine which document constitutes the offer and which the acceptance. If the offeree's response manifests the intent to enter into a deal, the offer has been accepted. For example, if additional or different terms merely appear in the standard printed language of a form contract, it is likely that the offeree intended to close a deal. Once the contract is formed, the only issue to be decided is what are its terms.

If, however, the response indicates only a willingness to continue negotiations, it is not an acceptance but a counteroffer. For example, an additional or different term that directly pertains to one of the negotiated terms, such as price or quantity, is evidence that the parties are still negotiating and have not reached an agreement.

Conditional Response

If the offeree wants to make a counteroffer rather than an acceptance, he or she should state clearly that acceptance is conditioned on the offeror's agreement to the additional or different terms. The safest course is to use the language of the UCC: "This acceptance is expressly made conditional on offeror's assent to all additional or different terms contained herein. Should offeror not give assent to said terms, there is no contract between the parties." Less direct language (such as "The acceptance of your order is subject to the conditions set forth herein" or "Acceptance of this order is expressly limited to the conditions of purchase printed on the reverse side") has been held to be an acceptance rather than a counteroffer.

Acceptance with Missing Terms

What happens when the parties ship, receive, and pay for goods without first agreeing on all material terms? In that case, Section 2-207(3) provides that the terms of the contract will be those on which the writings exchanged by the parties agree, supplemented by the UCC's gap-fillers where needed.

Acceptance with Additional Terms

What is the effect of additional terms in an acceptance when the contract is not expressly made subject to the offeror's agreeing to those terms? The answer depends on whether the parties are merchants. Under Section 2-207(2), if either of the parties is not a merchant, additional terms are construed as proposals for additions to the contract that the acceptance has created. Unless the offeror expressly agrees to the added provisions, they do not become part of the contract. If all parties are merchants, on the other hand, the additional provisions in the acceptance automatically become part of the contract, unless (1) the offer expressly limits acceptance to the terms of the offer, (2) the new terms materially alter the original offer, or (3) the party making the original offer notifies the other party within a reasonable time that it objects to the new terms. If any one of these exceptions applies, the additional terms serve as proposals requiring the express consent of the offeror to become part of the contract.

ACCEPTANCE WITH DIFFERENT TERMS

What is the effect of different—as opposed to additional—terms in an acceptance when the acceptance is not expressly made subject to the offeror's agreeing to those terms? As in the case of additional terms in a response to an offer, different terms neither defeat the acceptance nor impede the formation of the contract. But do the different terms become part of the contract? Surprisingly, the language of Section 2-207 does not address this situation. Under common law, the courts usually found that an offeree's response to an offer that contained different terms was a counteroffer that the offeror accepted by continuing its performance.

The following case illustrates how most courts applying the UCC deal with the situation in which the parties have sent conflicting forms, transacted their business, and then realize that they disagree about the terms of their contract.

A CASE IN POINT

CASE 8.1

RICHARDSON V. UNION CARBIDE INDUSTRIAL GASES, INC.

SUPERIOR COURT OF NEW JERSEY, APPELLATE DIVISION
790 A.2D 962
(N.J. SUPER. CT. 2002).

SUMMARY

FACTS Prior to 1988, Hoeganaes Corporation used furnace 2S for annealing iron powders. In 1988, Hoeganaes undertook to convert furnace 2S to a distalloy furnace. As part of the conversion, Hoeganaes bought a powder transporter system from Rage Engineering, Inc. to transport iron to the input end of the furnace.

The Rage proposal included the following language, in all capital letters, at the bottom of each page:

> ANY PURCHASE ORDER ISSUED AS A RESULT OF THIS QUOTE IS MADE EXPRESSLY SUBJECT TO THE TERMS AND CONDITIONS ATTACHED HERETO IN LIEU OF ANY CONFLICTING TERMS PROPOSED BY PURCHASER.

The terms and conditions attached to the proposal were standard, boilerplate terms that were never discussed by Rage and Hoeganaes. They included the following provisions:

> LIMITATION OF ACCEPTANCE. This sale (including all services) is limited to and expressly made conditional on Purchaser's assent to these Terms and Conditions as well as all other provisions contained in any other document to which these terms or conditions are attached. . . .
>
> . . . .
>
> INDEMNITY. Purchaser shall indemnify and hold Seller harmless against and in respect of any loss, claim or damage (including costs of suit and attorneys' fees) or other expense incident to or in connection with: the goods/equipment; . . . unless such loss, claim or damage is due solely and directly to the negligence or willful misconduct of Seller.

Hoeganaes included the following language in boldface type at the bottom of its purchase order:

> THIS ORDER IS ALSO SUBJECT TO THE TERMS AND CONDITIONS ON THE REVERSE SIDE OF THIS PAGE[.]

The reverse side of the Hoeganaes purchase order included the following terms and conditions:

> 1. Compliance with Terms and Conditions of Order—The terms and conditions set forth below, along with the provisions set forth on the front page hereof, constitute the entire contract of purchase and sale between Buyer and Seller. Any provisions in the Seller's acceptance, acknowledgment or other response to this Order which are different from or in addition to any of the terms and conditions and other provisions of this Order . . . shall not become a part of Buyer's contract of purchase and sale. . . .
>
> . . . .
>
> 14. Indemnification—Seller agrees to indemnify and hold harmless Buyer, . . . from and against all losses, damages, liabilities, claims, demands (including attorneys' fees), and suits at law or equity that arise out of . . . any act of omission or commission, negligent or otherwise, of Seller, . . . or otherwise out of the performance or attempted performance by Seller of this purchase order. . . .

CONTINUED

Except as expressed in the boilerplate forms they exchanged, neither side objected to the language in the documents and the contract was performed.

Jeffrey Richardson, a Hoeganaes employee who was injured when the furnace exploded, filed suit against a number of defendants, including Hoeganaes and Rage. In its answer, Rage cross-complained against Hoeganaes for contractual indemnification. Rage filed a motion for summary judgment seeking contractual indemnification from Hoeganaes, and Hoeganaes cross-moved for summary judgment seeking dismissal of Rage's indemnification claim. The trial court granted Hoeganaes's motion and dismissed Rage's claim for indemnification. Rage appealed.

ISSUE PRESENTED If the parties have performed, but the buyer's and seller's preprinted forms contain contradictory terms, is there a contract, and if so, what are its terms?

SUMMARY OF OPINION The Appellate Division of the New Jersey Superior Court observed that when faced with conflicting terms in contracts in similar circumstances, courts have used three approaches:

> The majority view is that the conflicting terms fall out and, if necessary, are replaced by suitable UCC gap-filler provisions.
>
> The minority view is that the offeror's terms control because the offeree's different terms cannot be saved by . . . 2-207(2), because that section applies only to additional terms.
>
> The third view assimilates "different" to "additional" so that the terms of the offer prevail over the different terms in the acceptance only if the latter are materially different. This is the least adopted approach.

The court then concluded that the majority approach, the "knockout" rule, is preferable and should be adopted. The court explained that it reached this conclusion "because the other approaches are inequitable and unjust and run counter to the policy behind" Section 2-207, which jettisoned the common law "mirror image" rule by recognizing the existence of a contract even though certain terms remain in conflict or are unresolved.

The court quoted the motion judge who stated:

> The truth is, and this really is the truth, what's happening is some little person some place writing these little—trying to plan it out, trying to conflict these things out, but the business people are out there delivering and taking money. And if the people really want to really get into all of this, then they should have taken their stuff away and they should have said, ooh, you know, we—you know, this is real here and, sorry, I'm not going to be able to take your check and, sorry, you're not going to be able to keep the stuff, but they're not doing that. They're just playing a little game with forms.

As a result, the court found that even though Rage's offer had specifically limited acceptance to its terms, Rage's indemnity did not become part of the contract because the terms of the parties' writings had conflicting indemnification provisions.

RESULT The appeals court affirmed the trial court's decision to strike the contradictory indemnity provisions.

COMMENTS By formally adopting the knockout rule instead of the common law approach, the appeals court made it much harder to game the system by exchanging preprinted forms with boilerplate rejection of the other party's terms. Because conflicting terms may simply be thrown out and replaced by UCC gap-fillers, managers using such forms should be aware of which UCC provisions might replace their standard terms.

STATUTE OF FRAUDS

Section 2-201 of the UCC is a *statute of frauds.* It provides that a contract for the sale of goods for $500 or more is unenforceable unless it is at least partly in writing. It states:

1. There must be some writing evidencing the sale of goods.
2. The writing must be signed by the party against whom enforcement is sought.
3. The writing must specify the quantity of the goods sold.

"SOME WRITING"

Statutes of fraud generally require all the essential terms of the contract to be in writing, so the UCC's requirement for "some writing" is relatively lenient. The official comments to Section 2-201 state: "All that is required is that the writing afford a basis for believing that the offered oral evidence rests on a real transaction. It may be written in lead pencil on a scratch pad." The comments go on to state: "The price, time and place of payment or delivery, the general quality of the goods, or any particular warranties may all be omitted."

The only term that must appear in the writing is the quantity of goods to be sold because it is necessary to provide a basis for awarding money damages in the event of a breach. The contract is not enforceable beyond the quantity of goods shown in the writing. If no quantity is specified, the contract is unenforceable unless (1) the goods were specially manufactured for the buyer and are not suitable for sale to others in the ordinary course of the seller's business, (2) the defendant admits in a judicial proceeding that there was an agreement, or (3) payment for the goods was made and accepted or the goods were received and accepted.

SIGNATURE

The writing must be signed by the party against whom enforcement is sought, unless the sale is between merchants and (1) a confirmation of the contract has been received, (2) the party receiving it has reason to know its contents, and (3) that party has not made a written objection within ten days after the confirmation was received. For example, an invoice that a seller sent to a buyer would be a contract enforceable against the buyer if the buyer did not respond within ten days after receiving the invoice.

Historical PERSPECTIVE

From Medieval Guilds to Online Arbitration

The increased use of the Internet by businesses and individuals, combined with the lack of established legal rules, has resulted in the development of private legal institutions.[a] For example, individuals doing business on the Internet are devising ways to ensure that the information they transmit to each other will remain confidential and be used only in an authorized manner. In addition, Internet companies have established online mediation and dispute resolution sites that allow consumers to resolve their disputes without filing claims in courts. Although these private legal regimes may be revolutionary in that they are being used in connection with a new technology, private legal regimes have developed at other times in history when individuals needed to protect their rights and the existing legal regime was unable to do so.

In medieval Europe, the nation-state had not yet developed, so merchants and traders could not rely on a central government to enforce laws or contracts to protect their trading activities. As long-distance trade became more common, traders and merchants began to venture beyond the protection of a local ruler or entrusted agents to carry and deliver their goods to fairs and markets in other countries and collect payment for these goods. Because the merchants needed a mechanism to protect their interests, they developed private organizations, or guilds, and courts enforced by groups of merchants. To determine whether an unknown trader or agent was trustworthy, merchants turned to each other for information about the stranger's reputation. Merchants refused to trade with parties who breached commitments to pay or to perform services, and they organized guildwide embargoes to freeze out members of the guild who violated its rules.

CONTINUED

Similarly, in modern society, members of private organizations often agree to be governed by a legal regime created and enforced by the organization. For example, a number of trade associations have rules that govern relationships among their members and establish procedures for resolving disputes arising from breaches of these rules. Although these associations' rules are based upon public law, such as contract law, these legal regimes typically rely upon simple rules, which they interpret and apply literally.

Stock exchanges, such as the New York Stock Exchange and Nasdaq, also operate under quasi-private legal regimes. Members of an exchange must comply with its rules and are subject to its monitoring, investigation, and enforcement mechanisms. These exchanges are not subject just to a set of private rules, however. Their private rules are subject to review by the Securities and Exchange Commission and the courts, and they also incorporate public laws.

The rapid development of e-commerce is also driving the development of a private legal regime. Not only is the Internet essentially unregulated, but with its innovative technology and ability to reach billions of consumers in countries all over the world, it presents enormous challenges for legal regulation. Some early efforts to regulate the Internet reflect the introduction of privatization into this new electronic market. In addition to domain name disputes, companies are using private law regimes to deal with consumer concerns about privacy on the Internet and secure transmissions of sensitive data (such as credit card numbers) by establishing "Seal" programs. For example, TRUSTe, a nonprofit corporation founded by the Online Privacy Alliance (a group of leading Internet firms), the Electronic Frontier Foundation (a public interest group), and the Boston Consulting Group (a management consulting firm), has established a set of practices regarding user privacy to which a company wishing to display the TRUSTe seal must adhere. TRUSTe enforces its policies by several methods including a dispute resolution process.

a. This discussion is based on Gillian K. Hadfield, *Privatizing Commercial Law: Lessons from the Middle and Digital Ages* (Mar. 2000), Stanford Law and Economics Olin Working Paper No. 195, *available at* http://ssin.com/abstract=22052.

DUTY OF GOOD FAITH UNDER THE UCC

Section 1-203 of the UCC states that "every contract or duty within this Act imposes an obligation of good faith in its performance and enforcement." This section imposes on each party a duty not to do anything that will deprive the other party of the benefits of the agreement. One court defined "good faith" as "a compact reference to an implied undertaking not to take opportunistic advantage in a way that could not have been contemplated at the time of drafting, and which therefore was not resolved explicitly by the parties."[20] Good faith in the case of a merchant has been interpreted as the observance of reasonable commercial standards of fair dealing in the trade.

The UCC applies to the enforcement, performance, or modification of a contract for the sale of goods, but not to the formation or procurement of a contract. For example, the Texas Supreme Court refused to invalidate a mutual release of liabilities for violation of good faith after characterizing the mutual release as the formation, not the modification, of a contract.[21]

20. Brooklyn Bagel Boys, Inc. v. Earthgrains Refrigerated Dough Prods., Inc., 212 F.3d 373 (7th Cir. 2000).

21. El Paso Natural Gas Co. v. Minco Oil & Gas, Inc., 8 S.W.3d 309 (Tex. 1999).

WARRANTIES

Goods delivered pursuant to a contract may not live up to the buyer's expectations. In many such cases, the buyer can sue the seller for breaching an express or implied warranty that the goods sold would have certain qualities or would perform in a certain way.

The UCC's warranty provisions attempt to determine which attributes of the goods the parties have agreed on. The UCC allows a great deal of flexibility in determining which warranties apply, permitting consideration of the description of the goods, the seller's words, common uses in the trade, the price paid, and the extent to which the buyer communicated particular needs to the seller. As a result, the seller of goods may find itself bound, perhaps unintentionally, by one of the three warranties provided by the UCC: express warranty, implied warranty of merchantability, and implied warranty of fitness for a particular purpose.

EXPRESS WARRANTY

An *express warranty* is an explicit guarantee by the seller that the goods will have certain qualities. Section 2-313 of the UCC has two requirements for the creation of an express warranty. First, the seller must (1) make a statement or promise relating to the goods, (2) provide a description of the goods, or (3) furnish a sample or model of the goods. Second, this statement, promise, description, sample, or model must become a "part of the basis of the bargain" between the seller and the buyer. This second requirement is intended to ensure that the buyer actually relied on the seller's statement when making a purchasing decision. Although the UCC does not define "part of the basis of the bargain," most courts have interpreted it as requiring the buyer to prove reliance. For example, if a car dealer asserts that a car can go 130 mph and the buyer responds that she will never take it above 55, in most jurisdictions the buyer would be unable to recover for breach of warranty if the car failed to go over 75 mph because the buyer could not prove reliance on the statement.

Puffing

Section 2-313(2) provides that a warranty may be found even though the seller never used the word "warranty" or "guarantee" and had no intention of making a warranty. However, if a seller is merely *puffing*—that is, expressing an opinion about the quality of the goods—he or she has not made a warranty. For example, a car salesperson's statement that "this is a top-notch car" is puffing, whereas a factual statement such as "it will get twenty-five miles to the gallon" is an express warranty. Unfortunately, the line between opinion and fact is not always easy to draw. Much turns on the circumstances surrounding the representation, including the identities and relative knowledge of the parties involved.

A number of courts employ a two-prong test to distinguish warranty language from opinion. The first prong is whether the seller asserted a fact of which the buyer was ignorant. If so, the assertion may be a warranty. The second prong is whether the seller merely stated a view on something about which the buyer could be expected to have formed his or her own opinion and whether the buyer could judge the validity of the seller's statement. In this second instance, the seller's statement is an opinion, not an express warranty. The following case illustrates the distinction between sales talk and a warranty.

A CASE IN POINT

IN THE LANGUAGE OF THE COURT

CASE 8.2

BOUD V. SDNCO, INC.

SUPREME COURT OF UTAH
54 P.3D 1131 (UTAH 2002).

FACTS Joseph Boud visited Wasatch Marine, a Salt Lake City retailer run by SDNCO, Inc., that sells yachts manufactured by Cruisers. During the visit, Wasatch gave Boud a copy of Cruisers' sales brochure, which included a photograph of Cruisers' 3375 Esprit model apparently moving at a high rate of speed. The photograph included the following caption: "Offering the best performance and cruising accommodations in its class, the 3375 Esprit offers a choice of either stern drive or inboard power, superb handling and sleeping accommodations for six."

Based in part on the photo and caption, Boud took a test-drive and signed a contract to purchase a 3375 Esprit model yacht for more than $150,000. During the test-drive and a subsequent test-drive a week later, the yacht manifested several electrical and mechanical problems. Pursuant to a limited warranty in its sales contract, Wasatch serviced the yacht and attempted to fix the problems. After the problems persisted during a third test-drive, Boud sought to cancel the sales contract. Cruisers responded by offering to repair or replace the defective parts in accordance with its limited warranty. Boud filed a lawsuit seeking rescission on the basis that the photograph and caption were themselves an express warranty, and that Cruisers and Wasatch had breached this express warranty. The district court granted summary judgment to Cruisers on the ground that the materials in the brochure amounted to mere sales talk, or puffery, and Boud appealed.

ISSUE PRESENTED What types of statements by a seller about the capability of a yacht constitute an express warranty?

OPINION DURANT, J., writing for the Utah Supreme Court:

To qualify as an affirmation of fact, a statement must be objective in nature, i.e., verifiable or capable of being proven true or false. Similarly, to be relied upon as a promise, a statement must be highly specific or definite. The photograph and caption contained in Cruisers' brochure are not objective or specific enough to qualify as either facts or promises; the statements made in the

CONTINUED

caption are merely opinions, and the photograph makes no additional assertions with regard to the problems of which Boud has complained.

Cruisers' brochure contains language characteristic of an opinion. Specifically, its assertions that the 3375 Esprit offers the "best performance" and "superb handling" rely on inherently subjective words. While representations that a boat is "fastest in its class" or "most powerful in its class" could be objectively tested for their truth and could therefore qualify as affirmations of fact, an assertion that a boat is "best in its class" cannot. The word "best" is a description that must ultimately be measured against some opinion or other imprecise standard, and "superb" is a near synonym subject to the same qualification. Similarly, "performance" is not a single quality, but rather embodies numerous qualities a boat may possess, and different people may place different weight on each individual quality. Reasonable people could therefore disagree and legitimately argue that several different boats in a given class perform "best" based on personal preferences that would be impossible to discount or disprove. As such, it would be unreasonable as a matter of law for anyone to rely on such a statement as one of fact. Accordingly, the language contained in the caption at issue is a mere statement of opinion.

RESULT The Utah Supreme Court held that the yacht brochure lacked the specificity necessary to create an express warranty and affirmed the district court's decision granting summary judgment in favor of Cruisers.

CRITICAL THINKING QUESTIONS

1. If the seller's statements in the sales brochure had constituted an express warranty, rather than mere puffery, would the limited warranty in the contract have superseded the express warranty in the brochure?
2. If the seller's statements in the sales brochure had constituted an express warranty, would the outcome have been affected by the timing of Boud's first test-drive (i.e., whether he had test-driven the yacht before or after signing the sales contract)?

IMPLIED WARRANTY OF MERCHANTABILITY

The *implied warranty of merchantability* guarantees that the goods are reasonably fit for the general purpose for which they are sold and that they are properly packaged and labeled. The warranty applies to all goods sold by merchants in the normal course of business. It does not depend on the seller's statements or use of a sample or model. Rather, it depends on the identity of the seller as a merchant who deals in goods of a certain kind.

To be merchantable under Section 2-314(2) of the UCC, goods must (1) pass without objection in the trade under the contract description; (2) be fit for the ordinary purposes for which such goods are used; (3) be within the variations permitted by the agreement and be of even kind, quality, and quantity within each unit and among all units involved; (4) be adequately contained, packaged, and labeled as the agreement may require; and (5) conform to the promises or affirmations of fact made on the container or label, if any. Fungible goods, such as grain, must be of average quality within the contract description.

Reasonable Expectations

The key issue in determining merchantability is whether the goods do what a reasonable person would expect of them. The contract description is crucial. Goods considered merchantable under one contract may be considered not merchantable under another. A bicycle with a cracked frame and bent wheels is not fit for the ordinary purpose for which bicycles are used, but it will pass under a contract for the sale of scrap metal.

When no contract description exists, breach is most frequently based on the claim that the goods are not fit "for the ordinary purposes for which such goods are used." Proof that the goods are imperfect or flawed is often insufficient to succeed on this claim. Even imperfect goods can be fit for their ordinary purposes.

> **ETHICAL CONSIDERATION**
>
> What investigations should a seller make before putting goods on the market? Should a bookstore test every recipe in every cookbook it sells? If not, should a bookstore buy cookbooks only from well-regarded publishers that have test kitchens?

In *Lescs v. William R. Hughes, Inc.*,[22] a homeowner filed a claim against Dow Chemical Company when she became ill after moving into a house that had been sprayed with insecticide manufactured by Dow. The homeowner argued that Dow had breached the implied warranty of merchantability by marketing an unreasonably dangerous product. The U.S. Court of Appeals for the Fourth Circuit rejected her claim that the insecticide failed to meet consumer expectations because the warning label on the pesticide had been approved by the Environmental Protection Agency. The court reasoned that "it would be anomalous to hold 'that a consumer is entitled to expect a product to perform more safely than its government mandated warnings indicate.' " (In contrast, as discussed further in Chapter 9, courts have held defendants liable for the tort of negligence even when their conduct satisfied the government standards.)

IMPLIED WARRANTY OF FITNESS FOR A PARTICULAR PURPOSE

The *implied warranty of fitness for a particular purpose,* set forth in Section 2-315 of the UCC, guarantees that the goods are fit for a particular purpose beyond the scope of ordinary purposes for which the seller recommended them. Broad in scope, this warranty may apply to merchants and nonmerchants alike.

Unlike the implied warranty of merchantability, the implied warranty of fitness for a particular purpose does not arise in connection with every sale of goods. It will be implied only if four elements are present: (1) the buyer had a particular purpose for the goods, (2) the seller knew or had reason to know of that purpose, (3) the buyer relied on the seller's expertise, and (4) the seller knew or had reason to know of the buyer's reliance. Although the warranty usually arises when the seller is a merchant with some level of skill or judgment, it is not restricted to such circumstances.

A "particular purpose" differs from the ordinary purpose for which a good is used in that a particular purpose contemplates a specific use by the buyer that is peculiar to that buyer or that buyer's business. For example, a seller may know that a particular pair of shoes will be used for climbing mountains, not just walking. By contrast, the ordinary purpose is that contemplated by the concept of merchantability. For example, Jane Doe, who suffered from obsessive-compulsive disorder (OCD), bought and used the prescription medication Luvox at the suggestion of her psychiatrist. Luvox was developed and marketed to treat OCD. After the Luvox precipitated a manic episode, she sued the manufacturer for breach of the implied warranty of fitness for a particular purpose. The court granted summary judgment in favor of the manufacturer because it found that Doe had taken Luvox for its ordinary intended purpose, namely, the treatment of OCD.[23] In contrast, the court in another case upheld an apartment community's claim against its pool service company for breach of the implied warranty of fitness. The company sandblasted and repainted the apartment community's pool with a primer that it had recommended. The court found:

> Plaintiff knew, or should have known, that Defendant was reasonably relying upon Plaintiff to specify the correct preparation method (sandblasting) and the paint and primer for the indoor and outdoor pools in light of such preparation. Plaintiff breached this warranty when it recommended an incompatible primer for pools that were sandblasted and rough, like the pools at [Defendant].[24]

Disproving Reliance

To prove that the buyer did not rely on the seller's expertise, the seller may try to show that (1) the buyer's expertise was equal to or superior to the seller's, (2) the buyer relied on the skill and judgment of persons hired by the buyer, or (3) the buyer supplied the seller with detailed specifications or designs that the seller was to follow.

Identifiable patents and trademarks can play an interesting role in this area of the law. If the buyer insists on a particular brand and style, he or she cannot be relying on the seller's skill or judgment. Hence, no implied warranty results. The mere fact that a good has an identifiable patent or trademark, however, does not prove nonreliance, especially if the seller recommended the product to the buyer.

DISCLAIMING WARRANTIES AND LIMITING LIABILITY

The seller can avoid responsibility for the quality of the goods under any of these warranties. First, the seller need

22. 168 F.3d 482 (4th Cir. 1999), *cert. denied,* 528 U.S. 1119 (2000).

23. Doe v. Solvay Pharms., Inc., 350 F. Supp. 2d 257 (D. Me. 2004).

24. Horizon Chem. Co. v. OPR L.P., 55 U.C.C. Rep. Serv. 2d 667 (Minn. Dist. Ct. 2004).

not make any express warranties. This may be difficult to do, however, because even a simple description of the goods may constitute a warranty. Second, a seller may disclaim any warranties of quality if it follows specifically delineated rules in the UCC designed to ensure that the buyer is aware of, and assents to, the disclaimers. To be effective, (1) a disclaimer of the implied warranty of merchantability must mention merchantability and, if in writing, must be conspicuous; and (2) a disclaimer of the implied warranty of fitness must be in writing and conspicuous.[25] Language to exclude all implied warranties (for example, "AS IS" or "WITH ALL FAULTS") is also sufficient if it makes plain that there is no implied warranty. Third, the seller can refrain from professing expertise with respect to the goods and leave the selection to the buyer.

More commonly, the seller limits its responsibility for the quality of the goods by limiting the remedies available to the buyer in the event of a breach of warranty. A typical method is to include a provision limiting the seller's responsibility for defective goods to repair or replacement. Unless this remedy is clearly identified as exclusive, however, it will be interpreted as additional to all other remedies set forth in the UCC. In addition, a limited or exclusive remedy will not be enforced, if the remedy fails in its purpose or operates to deprive either party of the substantial value of the bargain. In that case, the remedies in the UCC will govern as if the parties had not agreed on any remedies of their own.[26] Sellers may also limit their liability by including disclaimers of liability for special or consequential damages and by capping their liability for direct damages to the amounts received under the contract. Some states limit a seller's right to limit liability, especially for personal injury.

Finally, under the UCC, a seller is not an absolute insurer of the quality of goods sold. To recover for breach of warranty, a buyer must prove that (1) the seller made an express or implied warranty under the UCC; (2) the goods were defective at the time of the sale; (3) the loss or injury was caused by the defect rather than the buyer's negligent or inappropriate use of the goods; and (4) the seller has no affirmative defenses, such as a disclaimer of warranty.

STRICT PRODUCT LIABILITY VERSUS BREACH OF WARRANTY

As an alternative (or, in some cases, in addition) to suing for breach of warranty, the plaintiff may sue in tort for strict product liability (discussed in Chapter 10.) A product liability claim may succeed where a breach-of-warranty claim would not. This may happen when there is no contractual relationship between the buyer and the seller. But the remedies available may differ. Product liability actions generally permit recovery only for bodily injury or property damage caused by a defective product. In contrast, warranty actions permit recovery of economic damage suffered by the purchaser who has purchased an inferior or defective product.

MAGNUSON-MOSS WARRANTY ACT

The Magnuson-Moss Warranty Act[27] is a federal law that protects consumers against deception in warranties. It gives a consumer purchaser of a product the right to sue a manufacturer or retailer for failing to comply with the Act or the terms of a written or implied warranty arising from the Act. The Act was adopted "to improve the adequacy of information available to consumers, to prevent deception, and to improve competition in the marketing of consumer products."[28]

Nothing in the Act requires a supplier of consumer products to give a written warranty; the Act applies only when a seller chooses to do so. If the seller does make a written promise or affirmation of fact, however, then it must also state whether the warranty is full or limited in order to inform the average consumer about the level of protection provided. A *full warranty* gives the consumer the right to free repair or replacement of a defective product. To earn the designation of "full warranty," a warranty must meet minimum standards provided in the Act. A *limited warranty* might restrict the availability of free repair or replacement. These designations inform the average consumer about the level of protection provided by the warranty. The Magnuson-Moss Warranty Act is discussed further in Chapter 18.

RIGHT TO REJECT NONCONFORMING GOODS

Generally, a buyer that has contracted to purchase goods from a seller must fulfill its obligation and pay for those goods. A buyer has the right to reject nonconforming goods, however. Under Section 2-601 of the UCC, if the goods or the tender of delivery fails to conform to the contract in any respect, the buyer may reject any or all of the goods. Section 2-602 requires that any rejection be made within a

25. *See* U.C.C. § 2-316(2).

26. U.C.C. § 2-719(2) cmt. 1 (1962).

27. 15 U.S.C. §§ 2301–12.

28. 15 U.S.C. § 2302(a).

reasonable time after the goods are delivered. After such a rejection, the buyer may not treat the goods as if it owned them. If the buyer has taken possession of the goods before rejecting them, then it must hold the goods with reasonable care for a time sufficient to allow the seller to remove them. As the following case illustrates, the right to reject can be waived inadvertently by a buyer who continues to use the goods after notifying the seller of its dissatisfaction.

A CASE IN POINT

IN THE LANGUAGE OF THE COURT

CASE 8.3

ASK TECHNOLOGIES, INC. V. CABLESCOPE, INC.

UNITED STATES DISTRICT COURT FOR THE SOUTHERN DISTRICT OF NEW YORK
2003 WL 22400201 (S.D.N.Y. 2003).

FACTS In May 1998, Cablescope, a cable supply and installation firm, entered into a contract pursuant to which ASK agreed to sell, deliver, and install new computer hardware and software. In June 1998, an ASK technician began the installation of the ASK system at Cablescope's offices. Numerous bugs in the system were discovered during the installation, and Cablescope found that the technician was either unwilling or unable to perform the work required to integrate it with Cablescope's existing system. As a result, on June 24, Cablescope informed ASK that it was dissatisfied with the technician's work and did not want him to return. On July 9, Cablescope informed ASK by letter that the installation had not been adequately performed, and on July 20, Cablescope reiterated in writing that the installation was flawed. On the basis of ASK's nonperformance, Cablescope refused to pay for the equipment and services supplied by ASK, although it continued to use the system for the next nine months.

ASK sued to recover payments plus interest for the computer system and services provided to Cablescope, alleging breach of contract.

ISSUE PRESENTED Under what circumstances will the buyer of defective goods be deemed to have accepted them?

OPINION CARTER, J., writing for the United States District Court for the Southern District of New York:

* * * *

[*Eds.:* The court first considered whether the contract, which provided for both goods (computer equipment) and services (installation and setup), was covered by the UCC. Concluding that the sale of goods represented the bulk of the value of the contract, it found that UCC Article 2 governed the transaction.] The defendant Cablescope alleges that the goods delivered were nonconforming and that the installation was defective. Under U.C.C. [Article] 2, when a buyer is not satisfied with the goods received, the buyer has three options. *See U.C.C. § 2-602, U.C.C. § 2-608, U.C.C. § 2-714.* The buyer can: (1) reject the nonconforming goods, (2) accept the goods and later revoke acceptance, or (3) accept the goods and sue for damages resulting from the nonconformity. If the buyer does none of these and fails to pay for goods received then the buyer is in breach and seller is entitled to payment.

Under the UCC § 2-607 the buyer is required to alert the seller that goods are nonconforming. In order to effectively reject or revoke, the buyer must unequivocally communicate his intent to the seller.

Through letters and phone calls defendant communicated its dissatisfaction with the quality of the work performed. Among the problems, Cablescope found dates and times that were not synchronized, printing difficulties, and a "fuzzy" monitor display. Yet, many if not most of these problems were addressed quickly, and Cablescope continued possession and use of the goods for months after its letters of dissatisfaction to ASK's president. In his testimony, Cablescope's president acknowledged that the hardware was used for nine months following installation. Such usage belies unequivocal rejection or revocation of the goods. This continued use leads the court to conclude that there was constructive acceptance of the goods.

RESULT The court ordered Cablescope to pay for the ASK system plus interest as provided in the contract.

CONTINUED

Critical Thinking Questions

1. Did Cablescope's constructive acceptance of the computer system leave it without any remedy?
2. How could Cablescope have avoided this result?

Allocation of Risk of Loss

Goods can be lost in transit due to events such as fire, earthquake, flood, and theft. In the absence of an agreement to the contrary, UCC Section 2-509 places the risk of loss on the party controlling the goods at the time loss occurs, because that party is better able to insure against loss and to take precautions to protect the goods. Section 2-319 expressly authorizes the buyer and seller to allocate risk of loss between them as they see fit and provides shorthand symbols, such as "FOB" (free on board), with defined meanings to facilitate the expression of such an agreement between the parties.

Allocation of the risk of loss can have important, and costly, consequences. In August 2007, federal contractor T.R. Systems sued IBM after a $1.4 million IBM server fell off a forklift as workers were moving it from a freight truck into T.R. Systems' warehouse. Because the risk of loss had apparently passed to T.R. Systems, IBM refused to take back the damaged server or send technicians to inspect or repair it. As a result, T.R. Systems was forced to buy a replacement server. T.R. Systems subsequently filed a lawsuit against IBM, claiming that the damages it sustained were caused by IBM's poor workmanship or defective packaging design and methods.[29]

Although Article 2 includes definitions of FOB, FAS, CIF, C&F, and Delivery Ex Ship, they are inconsistent with INCOTERMS, a set of definitions of the most important trade terms now in use, created by the international mercantile community acting through the International Chamber of Commerce. Traders of all countries are incorporating INCOTERMS into their international sales contracts. The terms are revised every ten years; the latest edition is INCOTERMS 2000.

INCOTERMS 2000 contains thirteen main trade terms, including FAS, FOB, CPT, and CIF, as well as several secondary terms. CIF, for example, requires a seller to procure, at its own cost and in a transferable form, a marine insurance policy against the risk of carriage involved in the contract.

29. Paul McDougall, *IBM Server Worth $1.4 Million Falls off Forklift*, Info. Wk., Aug. 27, 2007, *available at* http://www.informationweek.com/showArticle.jhtml;jsessionid=PNFAS5G4QBN4IQSNDLPSKH0CJUNN2JVN?articleID=201802399.

Goods Shipped by Carrier

If a sales contract requires or authorizes the seller to ship the goods by carrier, the risk of loss passes to the buyer (1) at the time the goods are properly delivered to the carrier, if the contract does not require delivery at a particular destination; or (2) at the time the carrier tenders the goods to the buyer at the specified destination, if the contract specifies one. If nothing is said about delivery, the contract is not a delivery contract and does not require delivery to the destination.

If the parties indicate that shipment is to be made "FOB seller's place of business" (or "FCA seller's place of business" if INCOTERMS are used), delivery at a particular place is not required, so the risk of loss shifts to the buyer once the goods are properly placed in the possession of the carrier. An indication in the contract that shipment is to be made "FOB buyer's place of business" (or "FCA buyer's place of business" if INCOTERMS are used) means that delivery at a particular place is required, so the risk of loss will not shift to the buyer until the goods are tendered to the buyer at its place of business. The parties' selection of an FOB (or FCA) term in a sales contract controls the allocation of the risk of loss even if contrary language exists elsewhere in the contract.

Goods Held by Independent Warehouse

When the goods are in the possession of an independent warehouse and the seller provides the buyer with a document enabling it to pick up the goods at the warehouse, the risk of loss passes to the buyer when the buyer receives the document entitling it to pick up the goods.

All Other Cases

When the goods are neither to be shipped by carrier nor held by an independent warehouse, the allocation of the risk of loss in transit depends on whether the seller is a merchant. (As mentioned earlier, a seller is a merchant if he or she possesses experience and special knowledge relating to the goods in question.) If the seller is a merchant, the risk of loss passes to the buyer only when the buyer receives physical possession of the goods. If the seller is not a merchant, the risk passes to the buyer upon *tender of delivery*, which occurs when the seller notifies the buyer that it has the goods ready for delivery.

The following case dealt with the question of when a buyer has physical possession of the goods and thus bears the risk of loss.

A CASE IN POINT

SUMMARY

CASE 8.4

LYNCH IMPORTS, LTD. V. FREY

APPELLATE COURT OF ILLINOIS
558 N.E.2D 484
(ILL. APP. CT. 1990).

FACTS On October 22, 1987, the buyers agreed to purchase a 1987 Volkswagen automobile from the seller for the price of $8,706. The agreement was set forth in a purchase order in which the following phrases were handwritten on the purchase contract: "Car to be in totally acceptable condition or money will be refunded to the customer" and "Acceptance subject to inspection."

On October 24, the buyers took possession of the vehicle and paid the seller $4,706 as partial payment of the purchase price. The balance of the purchase price was to be financed. It was understood that the car was to come with air-conditioning, but at the time of delivery it was not yet installed. One of two riders attached to the purchase contract provided that the buyer was responsible for having the vehicle fully covered under liability and collision automobile insurance from the instant the buyer took possession. The rider also stated that the buyer was not authorized to return the vehicle without the seller's authorization and that no vehicle was to be sold with the condition that the buyer might later return it.

Two to three days later, the buyers brought the vehicle to the seller to have the air conditioner installed. When they returned in the evening to pick up the vehicle, the buyers were informed that the air conditioner had been installed but that the car had sustained body damage in an accident. The buyers refused to take delivery of the automobile because of the damage and demanded that a new, undamaged car be substituted. When the seller refused, the buyers stopped payment on the check and canceled their application for financing the balance of the purchase price.

The car dealership sued the automobile purchasers for damages of $8,706 for breaching the sales contract and $4,706 for wrongfully stopping the check. The buyers filed a counterclaim for the seller's breach of contract in failing to deliver an acceptable car and sought damages of $1,330.35, representing the difference between the price paid by the buyers when they subsequently purchased a similar automobile and the contract price of the Volkswagen. The trial court granted summary judgment to the seller. The buyers appealed.

ISSUE PRESENTED When a buyer takes possession of a car, but it is understood that the buyer will return the car to have air-conditioning installed per the purchase order, has the buyer fully accepted the car and assumed complete responsibility for it?

SUMMARY OF OPINION The Illinois Appellate Court stated that there was an issue of material fact as to whether the buyers "accepted" the vehicle on October 24. The buyers argued that they did not accept the vehicle and therefore had the right to reject it, which they properly did, when it was damaged upon its return to the seller to install the air conditioner.

UCC Section 2-606 provides that acceptance is deemed to have occurred when the buyer either signifies that the vehicle is conforming or "takes or retains" the vehicle in spite of its nonconformity. It was unclear to the court what the agreement was on October 24, just before the buyers took the vehicle. This uncertainty was of particular significance because the original purchase

CONTINUED

order contained the handwritten phrases: "Car to be in totally acceptable condition or money will be refunded to customer" and "Acceptance subject to inspection."

Section 1-202 of the UCC provides that the effect of the provisions of the UCC may be varied by agreement. The court concluded that the handwritten notations in the purchase agreement were sufficient to raise an inference that the buyers did not intend to waive their right to defer acceptance until the vehicle was brought to full conformity, even though they took interim possession of the vehicle.

Under Section 2-509 of the UCC, the risk of loss does not pass to the buyer until the buyer accepts the goods, even though the buyer obtains an insurable interest under Section 2-501 after the goods are identified to the purchase contract. Thus, Rider 2, which required the buyer to obtain insurance, was not conclusive on its face to pass the risk of loss to the buyer.

RESULT Because it found that there were material issues of disputed fact, the Illinois Appellate Court reversed the lower court's grant of summary judgment for the seller and remanded the case to the trial court to determine whether the buyers had accepted the vehicle on October 24 and whether they had the right to reject it when they later discovered that it had been damaged during its return to the seller for the installation of air-conditioning.

UNCONSCIONABILITY

A party is normally bound by the terms of a contract he or she enters into. However, if the contract is so unfair as to shock the conscience of the court, the judge may decline to enforce the offending terms or the entire contract.

Section 2-302(1) of the UCC provides procedural guidelines for judicial review of unconscionable clauses in contracts for the sale of goods, but it does not define "unconscionable." The official comments, however, do provide some guidance. For example, comment 1 to Section 2-302 states:

> The basic test is whether, in the light of the general background and the commercial needs of the particular trade or case, the clauses involved are so one-sided as to be unconscionable under the circumstances existing at the time of the making of the contract. . . . The principle is one of the prevention of oppression and unfair surprise . . . and not of disturbance of allocation of risks because of superior bargaining power.

In deciding whether a contract is unconscionable, the court considers evidence in addition to the contractual language, particularly (1) whether the contractual obligation was bargained for and (2) whether the parties understood and accepted the obligation. As under common law (discussed in Chapter 7), *unconscionability* can be either procedural (relating to the bargaining process) or substantive (relating to the provisions of the contract).

PROCEDURAL UNCONSCIONABILITY

A contract is procedurally unconscionable when one party is induced to enter the contract without having any meaningful choice. For example, in highly concentrated industries with few competitors, all the sellers may offer the same unfair contracts on a "take-it-or-leave-it" basis. Such contracts are known as *adhesion contracts*. They are most prevalent in consumer transactions where bargaining power is unequal.

It is also procedurally unconscionable for a seller to tuck oppressive clauses into the fine print or for high-pressure

› ETHICAL CONSIDERATION

Merchants that sell goods on credit to low-income customers often charge a very high rate of interest. Some businesspeople suggest that because low-income persons are statistically more likely to default on loans, creditors must charge a higher interest rate to protect themselves against the increased risk of default. They argue that if sellers are not allowed to charge higher interest rates or prices, low-income buyers will not be able to buy goods on credit. How should a manager balance the need for low-income persons to have credit to buy goods with the need for businesses to make a profit? Are such higher rates and prices ethical? Should there be any limit to what a seller can charge for credit?

salespersons to mislead illiterate consumers. In commercial transactions, however, it is presumed that the parties have the sophistication to bargain knowledgeably. Hence, procedural unconscionability is more difficult to prove in a commercial setting.

SUBSTANTIVE UNCONSCIONABILITY

A contract is substantively unconscionable if its terms are unduly harsh or oppressive or unreasonably favorable to one side, such as when the price is excessive or one party's rights and remedies are unreasonably limited. The courts have not agreed on any well-defined test for determining when a price is so excessive as to be unconscionable. However, prices that were two to three times the price of similar goods sold in the same area have been held unconscionable.

In a series of recent cases, courts have invalidated portions of consumer click-wrap agreements containing forum selection or binding arbitration clauses as unconscionable. In the following case, the California Court of Appeal considered whether a class-action waiver and a choice-of-forum provision in an arbitration provision were unconscionable.

A CASE IN POINT

SUMMARY

CASE 8.5

ARAL V. EARTHLINK, INC.

CALIFORNIA COURT OF APPEAL
36 CAL. RPTR. 3D 229
(CAL. APP. 2005).

FACTS Ozgur Aral ordered DSL Internet service from EarthLink in June 2003. He received the kit containing equipment needed to operate the service approximately five weeks later. The DSL service agreement that was sent with the kit provided that the parties' agreement was governed by Georgia law and required that any dispute arising out of the contract be settled by arbitration to be held in Atlanta, Georgia. It further prohibited any class-action arbitration. Individuals who install EarthLink DSL service using EarthLink software cannot complete installation until they click on an icon indicating that they have read and agree to the DSL service agreement. Aral installed the DSL service, but filed a class-action complaint against EarthLink when he received his EarthLink bill and discovered that he had been charged based on the date that he ordered the service. EarthLink sought to compel arbitration in Georgia and to dismiss or stay the court proceedings.

ISSUE PRESENTED Are the class-action prohibition and forum selection clauses in the EarthLink service contract unconscionable and therefore unenforceable?

SUMMARY OF OPINION The California Court of Appeal began by noting that the doctrine of unconscionability has both a procedural and a substantive element. The procedural element generally takes the form of a contract of adhesion. Terms that are unconscionable substantively take various forms but are generally described as unfairly one-sided. In *Discover Bank v. Superior Court*,[30] the California Supreme Court held that a class-action waiver in a cardholder agreement in the form of a "bill stuffer" was both procedurally and substantively unconscionable. Although it did not go so far as to hold all class-action waivers unconscionable, the supreme court held:

> When the waiver is found in a consumer contract of adhesion in a setting in which disputes between the contracting parties predictably involve small amounts of damages, and when it is alleged that the party with the superior bargaining power has carried out a scheme to deliberately cheat large numbers of consumers out of individually small sums of money, then, at least to the extent the obligation at issue is governed by California law, the waiver becomes in practice the exemption of the party "from responsibility for [its] own fraud, or

CONTINUED

30. 113 P.3d 1100 (Cal. 2005).

willful injury to the person or property of another." Under these circumstances, such waivers are unconscionable under California law and should not be enforced.

In the case before it, the court of appeal found that the class-action waiver was procedurally unconscionable because it was presented on a "take-it-or-leave-it" basis either through installation of the software or through materials included in the package mailed with the software with no ability to opt out. The waiver was substantively unconscionable because it cheated numerous consumers out of small sums of money by immediately charging them for the service, even though the company knew or should have known that the service would not be available until the modem was delivered weeks later.

The court found that the forum selection clause was also unconscionable, stating:

> Although both the California Supreme Court and the United States Supreme Court place a heavy burden on the plaintiff who seeks to prove that a forum selection clause is unreasonable, particularly where the alleged unreasonableness is based on the additional expense and inconvenience of litigating far from home, the burden was not intended to be insurmountable. If it is clear that "trial in the contractual forum will be so gravely difficult and inconvenient that he will for all practical purposes be deprived of his day in court," it would be "unfair, unjust, [and] unreasonable" to enforce the forum selection provision.

RESULT The court affirmed the trial court's order denying EarthLink's petition to compel arbitration and to dismiss or stay the court proceedings. Aral was permitted to bring a class action in California.

CRITICAL THINKING QUESTIONS

1. Would the result have been different if EarthLink (a) had required users to sign the DSL service agreement and had included the following statement above the signature line in the service agreement: "By signing below, you acknowledge you have received and reviewed the EarthLink terms and conditions and agree to be bound by them, including the mandatory arbitration section contained therein," and (b) had affixed a sticker to the shipping box that stated, "By using the EarthLink service, you agree to be bound by the DSL Service Agreement, including the mandatory arbitration provision"?
2. Would the result have been different if EarthLink could have shown that at least two of its major competitors had service agreements that did not contain a class-action waiver provision?[31]

31. *See* Gatton v. J-Mobile USA, Inc., A112082 (Cal. App. June 22, 2007).

COMMERCIAL IMPRACTICABILITY UNDER THE UCC

The UCC has adopted the doctrine of *commercial impracticability* rather than the common law doctrine of strict impossibility discussed in Chapter 7. Section 2-615 states that unless the contract provides otherwise, a failure to perform is not a breach if performance is made impractical by an event unforeseen by the contract. Section 2-615, the associated official comments, and the cases that have arisen under Section 2-615 establish certain criteria that a party seeking discharge from performance must show.

FAILURE OF UNDERLYING CONDITION

First, a party must show that there was a failure of an underlying condition of the contract, that is, a condition that was not included in the parties' bargain. Contracts provide fully for certain occurrences, and the seller is assumed to have included an appropriate "insurance premium" when setting the contract price. Other risks are deemed too remote and uncertain to be included in the contract price. The function of the court in applying the doctrine of commercial impracticability is to determine which risks were, or properly should have been, allocated to the buyer and which to the seller.

UNFORESEEN CONTINGENCY

In addition to showing that a condition was not reflected in the contract price, a seller seeking discharge must prove that the contingency that prevents performance was both unforeseen and unforeseeable. To some extent every occurrence is foreseeable—there is always some probability that a fire will destroy the anticipated source of supply, that a key person will die, or that various acts of God will occur. Legally, however, a foreseeable contingency is one that the parties should have contemplated in the circumstances surrounding the contracting. If there is a standard trade custom for allocating the risk, it is assumed that a particular contract follows that custom, unless it specifies differently.

Official Comment 4 provides an illustrative, but not exhaustive, list of contingencies that are considered unforeseeable. Wars and embargoes are considered unforeseeable; market fluctuations are not.

IMPRACTICABLE PERFORMANCE

Even if a party is able to show that there was a failure of an underlying condition of the contract and that it did not implicitly assume the risk of this occurrence, the party must still prove that performance was impracticable. Increased cost alone is not sufficient reason to excuse performance unless it is a marked increase. In one case, a ten- to twelve-fold increase was considered sufficient. In another case, the court observed, "We are not aware of any cases where something less than a 100% cost increase has been held to make a seller's performance impracticable."[32] Transactions that have merely become unprofitable will not be excused. Sellers cannot rely on Section 2-615 to get them out of a bad bargain.

Some of the most famous cases dealing with the issue of impracticability involved Westinghouse Electric Corporation and its unsuccessful attempts in the mid-1970s to avoid its obligation to supply 70 million pounds of uranium pursuant to fixed-price contracts with twenty-seven utilities after a sharp increase in uranium prices.[33] Westinghouse claimed that the potential loss of $2 billion made it commercially impractical to meet its obligations. In 1976, Westinghouse brought suit against its uranium suppliers, claiming that an international cartel had caused an unforeseen and precipitous increase in the price of uranium.

As discussed in Chapter 3, the judges involved in the ensuing litigation between Westinghouse and the utilities saw the conflict as primarily a business issue and pushed for settlement. On October 27, 1978, the U.S. District Court for the Eastern District of Virginia concluded that Westinghouse had not met its burden of establishing that it was entitled to be excused from its contractual obligations under Section 2-615 of the UCC. The court did not issue its supporting findings of facts and conclusions of law at the time, however; instead, the court urged the parties to settle as it was reluctant for the case to serve as legal precedent. As noted in Chapter 3, most of the cases did, in fact, settle.

DAMAGES

The UCC generally tries to put the nonbreaching party in the same position it would have been in if the contract had been performed. This is usually done through the award of money damages.

SELLER'S REMEDIES

If a buyer wrongfully cancels a contract or refuses to accept delivery of the goods covered by the contract, the seller is entitled to damages under Section 2-708 of the UCC. The measure of direct damages is the difference between the market price at the time and place for delivery and the unpaid contract price, less expenses saved because of the buyer's breach. If this measure of damages is inadequate to put the seller in as good a position as performance would have, then the seller is entitled to recover the profit (including reasonable overhead) that it would have made from full performance by the buyer. Such a seller is called a *lost volume seller*. Under Article 2, the courts split on whether to allow sellers to recover consequential damages.

BUYER'S REMEDIES

If a seller wrongfully fails to deliver the goods or repudiates the contract, or if the buyer justifiably rejects the tendered goods, then under Section 2-711 of the UCC the buyer has several choices. The buyer may cancel the contract and recover as much of the price as has been paid and then either (1) *cover*, that is, buy the goods elsewhere and be

32. Publicker Indus., Inc. v. Union Carbide Corp., 17 U.C.C. Rep. Serv. 989 (E.D. Pa. 1975).

33. This discussion is based on William Eagan, *The Westinghouse Uranium Contracts: Commercial Impracticability and Related Matters*, 18 AM. BUS. L.J. 281 (1980).

reimbursed for the extra cost of the substitute goods, or (2) recover damages for nondelivery.

If the buyer elects to cover under Section 2-712, it must make, in good faith and without unreasonable delay, a reasonable purchase of substitute goods. The buyer may then recover from the seller the difference between the cost of cover and the contract price. If the buyer elects not to cover, then under Section 2-713 the buyer is entitled to direct damages. The measure of *direct damages* is the difference between the market price at the time the buyer learned of the breach and the contract price. Section 2-715 of the UCC also permits the buyer to recover *consequential damages* for (1) any loss resulting from general or particular requirements and needs of the buyer that the seller at the time of contracting had reason to know and that could not reasonably be prevented by cover or otherwise, and (2) injury to person or property proximately resulting from any breach of warranty.

SPECIFIC PERFORMANCE

If the promised goods are unique, then under Section 2-716 of the UCC a court may order the seller to deliver them to the buyer, that is, order *specific performance*. For example, if there is only one antique Mercedes-Benz of a certain vintage, then damages alone will not be adequate to remedy the loss suffered by the disappointed buyer. Only delivery of the promised car will suffice. On the other hand, if the car is one of thousands, monetary damages will suffice because an equivalent car can be purchased elsewhere.

GLOBAL VIEW

The Convention on Contracts for the International Sale of Goods

Article 2 of the UCC largely unified the laws of the separate states in the United States governing the domestic sale of goods. International sales of goods, however, remain outside the scope of the UCC. As international trade and the global economy grew throughout the twentieth century, the need for more uniform laws throughout the world became apparent. The Convention on Contracts for the International Sale of Goods (CISG), promulgated under the auspices of the United Nations, became effective in 1988. As of June 2008, seventy countries had ratified the Convention, including many of the world's largest economies: Canada, China, France, Germany, Russia, Singapore, and the United States.[34] Today, the signatories to CISG account for nearly two-thirds of the world's imports and exports.

Scope of the Convention

CISG sets out substantive provisions of law to govern the formation of international sales contracts between merchants and the rights and obligations of buyers and sellers engaged in such transactions.[35] Unless both parties expressly opt out of CISG, CISG automatically applies to (1) sales contracts between merchants with places of business in different countries, if those countries are bound by the Convention ("contracting states"), and (2) sales contracts between merchants with places of business in different countries, if the application of choice-of-law rules of either of these countries would apply the law of a contracting state to the transaction. In other words, sales contracts meeting these requirements will be governed by CISG even if they make no reference to it. Although parties located in contracting states may expressly elect not to have CISG govern their sales contracts, a provision that only calls for the application of the laws of a contracting state does not constitute such an opt-out.

CONTINUED

34. Several of the world's largest economies, including Brazil, Japan, South Korea, and the United Kingdom, have not yet ratified the Convention.

35. Article 4 of CISG sets forth the basic principle: "This Convention governs only the formation of the contract of sale and the rights and obligations of the seller and the buyer arising from such a contract. In particular, except as otherwise provided in this Convention, it is not concerned with: (a) the validity of the contract or of any of its provisions or of any usage; [or] (b) the effect which the contract may have on the property in the goods sold." For extensive materials relating to CISG, including international cases and commentary, see the Pace University School of Law's website on the Convention, http://www.cisg.law.pace.edu/cisg/guide.html.

CISG does not apply to sales (1) of goods bought for personal, family, or household use, unless the seller, at any time before or at the conclusion of the contract, neither knew nor ought to have known that the goods were bought for any such use; (2) by auction; (3) on execution [of a judgment] or otherwise by authority of law; (4) of stocks, shares, investment securities, negotiable instruments, or money; (5) of ships, vessels, hovercraft, or aircraft; and (6) of electricity. As for the distinction between goods and services, CISG does not apply to contracts in which goods are sold in conjunction with services unless the preponderance of the obligations of the seller consists of the supply of goods. Neither does it apply to liability of the seller for death or personal injury to any person caused by its goods.

CISG applies to oral as well as written contracts of sale. CISG contains no statute of frauds requiring certain contracts to be in writing, unless one party has its place of business in a country that has made a reservation to CISG in this regard. The United States did not make this reservation.

Legal scholars are split over the question of whether CISG is applicable to e-commerce transactions. Although the formation of contracts for the international sale of physical goods by electronic means is generally regarded as covered by CISG,[36] the question of whether the international sale of "digital (intangible) goods" would be covered by CISG is controversial.[37]

Offer and Acceptance

Under CISG, an offer becomes effective when it reaches the offeree, and it may be withdrawn if the withdrawal reaches the offeree before or at the same time as the offer. Until a contract is concluded, an offeror may revoke its offer if the revocation reaches the offeree before the offeree has dispatched its acceptance. An offer cannot be revoked, however, if the offer indicates that it is irrevocable or if the offeree reasonably relied on its irrevocability. Even if irrevocable, an offer is terminated when the offeree's rejection reaches the offeror.

A contract is concluded at the moment acceptance of an offer becomes effective; a statement made by the offeree indicating its assent constitutes such an acceptance. Conduct indicating assent is also acceptance, but silence or inactivity does not in itself amount to acceptance under CISG. An acceptance becomes effective when it reaches the offeror, although an acceptance is not effective if it fails to reach the offeror within the time the offeror has specified for such acceptance. If the offeror has specified no time, then the acceptance must reach the offeror within a reasonable time. If the offer is oral, however, it must be accepted by the offeree immediately unless circumstances indicate otherwise.

Recognizing the importance of custom and practice, CISG also provides that if the parties have established practices between themselves, the offeree may accept the offer by performing an appropriate act, such as sending the goods or paying the price, without notifying the offeror. In such a case, acceptance is effective as soon as such act is performed. Such acceptance by performance without notification differs from the UCC, which allows for acceptance by performance but requires notification.

Battle of the Forms

An important difference between the UCC and CISG is the approach to the battle of the forms. Under CISG, a reply to an offer that purports to be an acceptance but contains additional terms or other modifications that *materially* alter the terms of the offer is a rejection of the offer and constitutes a counteroffer. Thus, under CISG, there is no contract in this situation. If, however, the modifications in the reply to an offer do *not materially* alter the terms of the offer and the offeror fails to object in a timely fashion, then there is a contract under CISG. In that situation, the contract will include the terms of the offer with the modifications stated in the acceptance. CISG lists categories of differences that are presumed to alter the terms of the offer materially: price, payment, quality and quantity of the goods, place and time of delivery, extent of one party's liability to the other, and settlement of disputes. The list leaves little for the sphere of "immateriality" and largely effects the old mirror image rule. As explained earlier, under the UCC, an acceptance with additional or conflicting terms may still result in a contract unless the offeree clearly specifies that there will not be a contract unless the offeror accepts the additions or modifications.

CONTINUED

36. Siegfried Eiselen, *Electronic Commerce and the UN Convention on Contracts for the International Sale of Goods (CISG) 1980*, 6 EDI L. Rev. 21–46 (1999).

37. *See* Jacqueline Mowbray, *The Application of the United Nations Convention on Contracts for the International Sale of Goods to E-Commerce Transactions: The Implications for Asia*, 7 Vindobona J. Int'l Com. L. & Arb. 121–50 (2003).

Good Faith

CISG provides that it is to be interpreted with regard for promoting "the observance of good faith in international trade." As noted earlier, Section 1-203 of the UCC provides that "[e]very contract or duty within this Act imposes a duty of good faith in its performance or enforcement." The UCC provision at first appears to be broader than the CISG principle, which literally applies only to the interpretation of CISG rather than the conduct of merchants under it. Throughout CISG, however, there are numerous requirements of "reasonableness," such as those for giving notice, making substitutions, relying, measuring inconvenience and expense, delaying performance, examining goods, incurring expenses, and making excuses.

Certain commentators have suggested that the combination of CISG's requirements of good faith in interpretation and of reasonableness in so many areas of merchant behavior makes for a broad, albeit uncertain, duty for merchants to conduct themselves with good faith.[38] If that interpretation is correct, then, for example, if a seller requests additional time to deliver goods, a buyer would be required to act in good faith when deciding whether to grant that request. The buyer could not simply decide to enforce the letter of the contract to the seller's detriment if the delay would not, in fact, adversely affect the buyer. This would contrast with the UCC's *perfect tender rule,* which gives the buyer an absolute right to reject any goods not meeting all the contract requirements, including time of delivery.

Implied Warranties

Under CISG, the seller must deliver goods that are of the quantity, quality, and description required by the contract, and such goods must be packaged as specified by the contract. Like the UCC, the Convention holds sellers liable for implied warranties of merchantability and fitness for particular use and for any express warranties they make.[39] CISG makes clear, however, that the implied warranty of merchantability does not attach if the buyer knew that the goods were not fit for ordinary use.

Obligations of the Parties

CISG sets forth the main obligations of both the seller (in Chapter II: Delivery of goods and handing over of documents) and the buyer (in Chapter III: Payment of the price and taking delivery). CISG also deals with breach of contract of the parties and their failure to perform.

Exclusion of CISG from Agreements

U.S. lawyers tend to opt out of CISG in written agreements because of uncertainty regarding the legal consequences of its application. Because CISG differs from the UCC (and for that matter from the laws that govern the sales of goods in other jurisdictions) in several aspects, in some instances it might offer an attractive legal alternative (often only to one of the parties, depending on the role of such party and the otherwise applicable law). The parties should try to understand what their rights and obligations under CISG would be so that they can make an informed decision about its use; if the parties decide that they want to exclude CISG from an agreement, they will need to ensure that it is excluded correctly and completely.

---

38. *See, e.g.,* Phanesh Koneru, *The International Interpretation of the UN Convention on Contracts for the International Sale of Goods: An Approach Based on General Principles,* 6 MINN. J. GLOBAL TRADE 105 (1997).

39. 15 U.S.C. app. (1987), Convention on Contracts for the International Sale of Goods, art. 35: "Except where the parties have agreed otherwise, the goods do not conform with the contract unless they: (a) are fit for the purposes for which goods of the same description would ordinarily be used; (b) are fit for any particular purpose expressly or impliedly made known to the seller at the time of the conclusion of the contract, except where the circumstances show that the buyer did not rely, or that it was unreasonable for him to rely, on the seller's skill and judgment; (c) possess the qualities of goods which the seller has held out to the buyer as a sample or model; (d) are contained or packaged in the manner usual for such goods or, where there is no such manner, in a manner adequate to preserve and protect the goods."

IN BRIEF

Comparison of Article 2 of the UCC, Common Law, UCITA, and CISG

	Scope	Battle of the Forms	Warranties	Statute of Frauds
Article 2 of UCC	Sale of goods	If both parties are merchants, additional terms are generally incorporated; if not, mirror image rule applies. For different terms, "knockout" rule applies.	1. Implied warranties of merchantability and fitness for a particular purpose 2. Any express warranties made	Sale of $500 or more
Common Law	1. Provision of services 2. Contracts for sale of land or securities 3. Loan agreements	Mirror image rule	Any express warranties made	1. Transfer of real estate 2. Contract cannot be performed within one year 3. Prenuptial agreement 4. Agreement to pay debt of another
UCITA	Computer information (including software, computer games, and online access)	Contract even if acceptance has additional or different terms, unless acceptance materially alters the offer	1. Warranty of noninterference and noninfringement 2. Implied warranties of merchantability of computer program, informational content, fitness for licensee's particular purpose, and fitness for system integration 3. Any express warranties made	Contract for $5,000 or more
CISG	Sale of goods by merchants in different countries unless parties opt out	In practice, mirror image rule	1. Implied warranties of merchantability and fitness for a particular use 2. Any express warranties made	None

THE RESPONSIBLE MANAGER

OPERATING UNDER VARYING LEGAL REGIMES

Any manager who enters into contracts on behalf of a business should know which body of contract law will govern the transaction. In particular, the manager should determine whether the transaction is governed by Article 2 of the UCC, the common law rules concerning contracts, CISG, or UCITA. Article 2 applies only to the sale of goods, not services or real property.

Although some things are clearly goods, others may be more difficult to categorize. CISG will apply to most international sales of goods unless the parties affirmatively opt out of its provisions. In states that have enacted the Uniform Computer Information Transactions Act, UCITA governs contracts to license or buy software, computer programs, multimedia products, computer games, and online access. In the forty-eight states that have not enacted UCITA, courts will likely apply Article 2 to software licenses, either directly or by analogy. A manager should obtain legal advice if there is any doubt as to which body of law controls in a particular situation.

Managers should be aware of the requirements that must be met for the valid formation of a contract under the different regimes. In particular, managers should focus on one of the key elements in creating a valid contract: the process of offer and acceptance. This knowledge is crucial to ensuring that the company can enforce the contracts it has entered into and wishes to uphold. In addition, a manager may have a valid reason to attempt to avoid an agreement that was not formed in the correct manner. Only if the manager knows the rules of contract formation can he or she assess whether a contract was validly created.

The manner of making an appropriate offer is the same under the UCC as it is under common law. However, a manager should note that Article 2 allows an offeree to accept an offer, even if the offeree's acceptance contains terms additional to or different from those in the offer. In contrast, CISG in practice generally imposes the mirror image rule applied by the common law. The rules in this area and the corresponding case law are both complex and fact specific. Nonetheless, it is crucial that managers understand these rules before they engage in negotiations. Failure to develop this understanding can lead to unexpected results. A manager or company may be legally bound to a contract even when there was no intention to be bound. Or a manager may inadvertently extinguish an offer by proposing modifications that ultimately the offeree might have been willing to forgo.

Article 2 of the UCC, CISG, and UCITA establish three types of warranties that buyers may rely on when purchasing goods or computer information. Managers should be aware of how each warranty is created, how the warranties are applied, and how liability for products can be limited. These warranties also provide guidelines for managers as to what is expected from a product in terms of quality and suitability for its intended use. It is essential that managers obtain legal advice in this area because lawsuits for breach of warranty can lead to large awards of damages that are far in excess of the purchase price. Managers must provide adequate instruction and training to salespersons and agents about express and implied warranties. Aggressive salespersons willing to say what it takes to close a deal may unwittingly cause their company to be held liable under an implied warranty of fitness for a particular purpose when it never intended to make any such warranty at all.

Managers should also be familiar with the legal doctrines that allow parties legally to back out of contracts. The doctrine of impracticability can protect a party when unexpected changes in circumstances make performance commercially ruinous, though not literally impossible. The doctrine of unconscionability provides guidelines on the legal limits to one-sided contracts. Managers should keep in mind that sometimes more is less; extracting onerous concessions from a weaker party may backfire and cause a judge to declare a set of provisions invalid *in toto*, when less onerous provisions might have passed judicial muster.

Both the UCC and CISG require the parties to act in good faith and in a commercially reasonable manner. Managers should avoid acting in an arbitrary manner and try to accommodate the reasonable requests of the other side (e.g., a seller's request to delay delivery when the delay would not have an adverse effect on the buyer's business).

A Manager's Dilemma

Putting It into Practice

When Is a Seller Responsible for a Known Software Defect?

Mortenson, a nationwide construction contractor, had used Timberline's Bid Analysis software to assist with its preparation of bids for several years. In 1993, Mortenson issued a purchase order to Softworks, an authorized Timberline dealer, for eight copies of a new version of Bid Analysis. The purchase order did not include a clause stating that the order constituted the entire agreement of the parties. Softworks signed the purchase order and ordered the software from Timberline. The full text of the Timberline license agreement was set forth on the outside of each diskette pouch and in the inside cover of the instruction manuals delivered to Mortenson. The license agreement included the following warning:

> CAREFULLY READ THE FOLLOWING TERMS AND CONDITIONS BEFORE USING THE PROGRAMS. USE OF THE PROGRAMS INDICATES YOUR ACKNOWLEDGEMENT THAT YOU HAVE READ THIS LICENSE, UNDERSTAND IT, AND AGREE TO BE BOUND BY ITS TERMS AND CONDITIONS. IF YOU DO NOT AGREE TO THESE TERMS AND CONDITIONS, PROMPTLY RETURN THE PROGRAMS AND USER MANUALS TO THE PLACE OF PURCHASE AND YOUR PURCHASE PRICE WILL BE REFUNDED. YOU AGREE THAT YOUR USE OF THE PROGRAM ACKNOWLEDGES THAT YOU HAVE READ THIS LICENSE, UNDERSTAND IT, AND AGREE TO BE BOUND BY ITS TERMS AND CONDITIONS.

Mortenson's chief estimator claimed that Mortenson never saw any of the licensing information or any of the manuals because the software was installed by Softworks.

Mortenson subsequently used the Precision Bid Analysis software to prepare a bid for a project. On the day of the bid, the software allegedly malfunctioned many times and gave the following message: "Abort: Cannot find alternate." Nevertheless, Mortenson submitted a bid generated by the software. After Mortenson was awarded the project, it learned that the bid was approximately $1.95 million lower than it had intended. Mortenson sued Timberline and Softworks for breach of express and implied warranties. After the suit was filed, a Timberline internal memorandum surfaced stating that "[a] bug has been found . . . that results in two rather obscure problems." The memo explained that "[t]hese problems only happen if the following [four] conditions are met." Apparently, other Timberline customers had encountered the same problem, and a new version of the software had been sent to some of these customers. After extensive investigation, Timberline's lead programmer acknowledged that Mortenson's error message appeared when the four conditions were met.[40]

Did Timberline have an ethical obligation to notify all of its customers when it became aware of the defect in its software that could result in significant errors in the calculation of bids? Is Timberline's disclaimer of consequential damages enforceable? Is it unconscionable to allow Timberline to use the disclaimer of consequential damages to avoid liability to its customers for a known product defect?

40. Mortenson Co. v. Timberline Software Corp., 998 P.2d 305 (Wash. 2000).

Inside Story

CAUGHT IN THE WEB OF INTERNET AUCTION FRAUD

According to the National Fraud Information Center, a project of the National Consumers League, a nonprofit consumer organization, businesses and individuals lost $13,863,003 in 2005 as a result of Internet fraud of all kinds. Fraud in Internet auctions and nonauction sales in which goods were never delivered or were misrepresented constituted 42 percent and 30 percent of these losses, respectively.[41] The opportunity to defraud buyers has increased as the dollar value of U.S. online retail sales (including auctions) has grown from

CONTINUED

41. National Fraud Information Center, *Internet Scams/Fraud Trends January–December 2005: Top Ten Scams*, http://www.fraud.org/2005_Internet_Fraud_Report.pdf.

$47.8 billion in 2002[42] to approximately $190.9 billion in 2005.[43] Forrester Research forecasts that e-commerce will account for $316 billion in sales, or 13 percent of overall retail sales by 2010.[44]

As the use of e-commerce has increased, so have schemes to defraud buyers and sellers. A recent Internet sales scheme resulted in nearly $15 million in losses for buyers across the country. Mixitforme.com, a company that purported to sell iPods, Xboxes, cell phones, and other consumer electronics over the Internet, fulfilled only a small fraction of the hundreds of orders that it received. Even the filled orders were frequently late or generated billing problems for customers, who began complaining to law enforcement authorities. In March 2006, agents from the Secret Service, the FBI, the U.S. Postal Service, and state and local police raided the company's offices. One of the company's owners subsequently agreed to plead guilty to federal charges of conspiracy to commit wire fraud and money laundering in connection with the scheme, while the other owner has fled the country.[45]

The schemes have also become more sophisticated, although, at least in some instances, so have the victims. For example, a defendant who claimed that his company, Data Systems International (DSI), had just landed a large contract with the online casino industry, contacted two small firms that shared office space claiming that he needed to buy $500,000 of Cisco hardware from them immediately. The businesses' owners, Mike Kozlowski and Dana Andrews, became suspicious when the defendant insisted on using American Escrow, an Internet escrow company that neither of them had heard of. Having been victimized in an online scam that cost him $16,000 the previous year, Andrews wondered if the deal was too good to be true. As a result, Kozlowski asked a relative to visit DSI's San Francisco office. When they discovered that the address was bogus, Kozlowski checked the domain name registrations for DSI and American Escrow and discovered that they were created on the same day and registered to the same person. Because the escrow service was intended to serve as an independent third party in the transaction, the common ownership confirmed that something was awry. Kozlowski and Andrews then contacted the FBI, which arranged a simple sting in which Kozlowski sent what were supposed to be ten boxes of Cisco routers to a private postal company address in Las Vegas. When the defendant drove to Las Vegas to pick up the shipment, he was arrested.[46]

Online fraud has not been limited to the United States. For example, eBay acknowledges that Romania is the number one source of online auction fraud, and Romanian police believe that cybercrime is a multimillion dollar national industry. A classic Romanian scam is the "second chance audit," in which Romanian scammers target eBay users who have narrowly lost an auction. The scammers try to guess the user's e-mail address in order to contact the user directly to offer a second chance to buy the item, although they have no intention of delivering it. The scammers develop elaborate stories to persuade their targets to send money by unrecoverable methods—for example, by telling them not to tell Western Union the payment was for an eBay transaction because Western Union would charge them an extra 10 percent surcharge, though Western Union would not, in fact, impose a surcharge.

Although eBay claims that it is under no legal obligation to control the truth or accuracy of the items advertised or the ability of sellers to sell items, it has built its business, and its reputation, on a self-policing system that depends on buyers and sellers trusting one another.[47] "The fraudsters need to know we're coming after them," says Rob Chesnut, a former federal prosecutor who set up eBay's Trust and Safety division. "EBay doesn't have a product. We are in the trust business: making people feel comfortable doing business with someone they don't know.... If the bad guys have no fear of prosecution, they will continue to try to defraud users. So there has to be a cost to trying." Even though eBay has no website in Romania, the company has donated computers, digital cameras, and Internet connections to Romanian law enforcement authorities. In 2005, it also hired a small team of employees who have trained hundreds of Romanian prosecutors and a magistrate from each province, and now work side-by-side with them to investigate cases. These efforts have paid off. In 2006, 115 people were arrested and 831 crimes were identified by Romanian police; 28 cases were sent to the courts.[48]

CONTINUED

42. *E-Commerce Market Size and Trends*, http://www.goecart.com/ecommerce_solutions_facts.asp.

43. Richard K. Miller & Associates, The 2007 E-Commerce Market Research Handbook 9 (2006).

44. *Id.* at 10.

45. Paul Grimaldi, *Second Man to Plead Guilty in Internet Scam*, Dec. 22, 2007, http://www.projo.com/news/content/BZ_MIXIT_PLEAD_12-22-07_CE8B8AP_v18.1a1df04.html.

46. Bob Sullivan, *How the FBI Conned WebCon Artist*, Feb. 14, 2006, http://www.msnbc.msn.com/id/3078493/.

47. The eBay terms of use provide, among other things, "We have no control over and do not guarantee the quality, safety or legality of items advertised, the truth or accuracy of listings, the ability of sellers to sell items, the ability of buyers to pay for items, or that a buyer or seller will actually complete a transaction." *See* http://pages.ebay.com/help/policies/user-agreement.html.

48. Ian Wyles, *EBay Goes Far to Fight Fraud—All the Way to Romania*, Special to the [Los Angeles] Times, Dec. 26, 2007, *available at* http://allbusinessauctions.wordpress.com/2007/12/26/ebay-goes-far-to-fight-fraud-all-the-way-to-romania/.

Various agencies have set up websites where consumers can learn about cybercrime and file complaints about fraud. In February 2000, the Federal Trade Commission (FTC) launched Project Safebid, an effort to get local, state, and federal law enforcement to address the problem of auction fraud cases.[49] The agency also created the Computer Sentinel database, a database of consumer fraud and identity theft complaints, including complaints related to computers, the Internet, and online auctions. The Computer Sentinel database logged 204,881 Internet-related fraud complaints in 2006.[50] In April 2003, the FTC, in conjunction with the National Association of Attorneys General, launched Operation Bidder Beware, a law enforcement crackdown targeting Internet auction scams, which resulted in fifty-seven criminal and civil law enforcement actions; the operation included a consumer education campaign to alert consumers about Internet auction fraud and provide tips on how to avoid it.[51]

Due to the global reach of the Internet, regulation of Internet auction sites requires international cooperation. On April 27, 2000, the Council of Europe approved the final version of the *Convention on Cybercrime*, the first international treaty to address various types of criminal behavior directed against computer systems, networks, or data, including computer-related fraud and forgery. The Convention calls for countries to harmonize their laws on cybercrime, including hacking, fraud, and child pornography, and to cooperate in cross-border investigations. Thirty countries, including the United States, signed the Convention in November 2001, when it was opened for signature at a signing ceremony in Budapest, Hungary. Since that time, additional countries have signed. The Convention entered into legal force and effect on July 1, 2004, and became legally effective in the United States on January 1, 2007.[52]

Security experts complain that the U.S. government has overlooked international criminals who are stealing a fortune through the Internet. The FBI lists cybercrime as its third priority, but it is a distant third. For the 2008 fiscal year, the FBI budget includes more than 10,000 full-time FBI staffers assigned to its top two priorities—counterterrorism and counterintelligence—but only 1,151 employees (including 659 agents) assigned to cybercrime. Even within the cybercrime division, the threat of cyberterrorism—spies or terrorists breaking into government computers—is the top priority. "Federal law enforcement needs more agents to deal with [cybercrime investigations]," according to Ron Plesco, executive director of the National Cyber-Forensics and Training Alliance, a government-funded nonprofit that investigates cybercrime.[53]

49. Daniel Roth, *Fraud's Booming in Online Auctions, but Help Is Here Bidding Adieu*, FORTUNE, May 29, 2000, at 276.

50. Sentinel Complaints by Calendar Year, http://www.consumer.gov/sentinel/Sentinel_CY_2006/complaints_byCalendaryear.pdf.

51. Federal Trade Commission, *Internet Auction Fraud Targeted by Law Enforcers*, Apr. 30, 2003, *available at* http://www.ftc.gov/opa/2003/04/bidderbeware.shtm.

52. Council of Europe, Treaty Office, Convention on Cybercrime: CETS No. 185, *available at* http://conventions.coe.int/Treaty/Commun/QueVoulezVous.asp?NT=185&CM=1&DF=1/4/2008&CL=ENG.

53. Ryan Blitstein, *Experts Fail Government on Cybersecurity*, Dec. 27, 2007, *available at* http://www.ohio.com/business/12844007.html.

KEY WORDS AND PHRASES

acceptance 259
adhesion contracts 273
battle of the forms 261
browse-wrap license 259
click-wrap license 259
commercial impracticability 275
consequential damages 277
Convention on Cybercrime 284
cover 276
direct damages 277
doctrine of first sale 253
electronically supplied services 255
express warranty 265
firm offer 260
fixtures 252
full warranty 269
goods 252
identification to the contract 252
implied warranty of fitness for a particular purpose 268
implied warranty of merchantability 267
limited warranty 269
lost volume seller 276
merchant 252
mirror image rule 259
offer 257
perfect tender rule 279
puffing 266
shrink-wrap license 259
specific performance 277
statute of frauds 264
tender of delivery 272
unconscionability 273

QUESTIONS AND CASE PROBLEMS

1. James Moore was interested in purchasing a used Mack truck from Worldwide, but he was concerned about the eighteen-speed transmission. Worldwide's sales representative assured Moore that the transmission had been completely rebuilt and that the truck would suit his needs, because it had a large rear differential and a larger motor, allowing it to get up and down hills. Moore decided to purchase the truck. Mack's warranty stated:

   THIS WARRANTY IS MADE EXPRESSLY IN LIEU OF ANY OTHER WARRANTIES OR CONDITIONS, EXPRESSED OR IMPLIED, INCLUDING ANY IMPLIED WARRANTY OR CONDITION OF MERCHANTABILITY OR FITNESS FOR A PARTICULAR PURPOSE, AND OF ANY OTHER OBLIGATION OR LIABILITY ON THE PART OF THE MANUFACTURER INCLUDING, WITHOUT LIMITATION OF THE FOREGOING, CONSEQUENTIAL AND INCIDENTAL DAMAGES.

   Worldwide's sales agreement, which Moore signed, contained the following:

   SELLER MAKES NO WARRANTIES AS TO THE PROPERTY, EXPRESS, IMPLIED OR IMPLIED BY LAW EXCEPT, AS TO NEW VEHICLES ONLY, THE MANUFACTURER'S STANDARD VEHICLE WARRANTY, WHICH IS INCORPORATED HEREIN BY REFERENCE. SELLER SPECIFICALLY DISCLAIMS ANY IMPLIED WARRANTY OF MERCHANTABILITY OR FITNESS FOR A PARTICULAR PURPOSE AND ANY LIABILITY FOR CONSEQUENTIAL DAMAGES FOR ANY BREACH OF WARRANTY. ALL USED VEHICLES ARE SOLD "AS IS."

   Moore brought the truck in for repairs on two occasions, four months apart, and the truck was operational after the first repair. Worldwide repossessed it five months after the second repair, and Moore sued Mack and Worldwide for breach of express and implied warranty. He also alleged that he could claim consequential and incidental damages, because the defendants' exclusive remedy had failed of its essential purpose. How will the defendants respond? Will the court find in favor of Moore or the defendants? On what basis? [*Moore v. Mack Trucks, Inc.*, 40 S.W.3d 888 (Ky. Ct. App. 2001).]

2. Hardie-Tynes Manufacturing Company subcontracted with Hunger United States Special Hydraulic Cylinders Corporation to manufacture two hydraulic cylinders to be used in construction of the Jordanelle Dam in Utah. After Hardie-Tynes sent a request for quotations for Hunger's best price for the two cylinders, Hunger responded with a letter providing specific quantity, price, delivery, and payment terms. Both parties agreed that this constituted an offer to contract. A copy of Hunger's standard terms and conditions, which included a provision attempting to specify a mode of acceptance and limiting acceptance to Hunger's terms, accompanied the offer. None of the terms related to payment of attorneys' fees in the event of a contract dispute.

   Hardie-Tynes accepted Hunger's offer by sending a purchase order, which required payment of attorneys' fees in the event that Hardie-Tynes commenced litigation upon Hunger's default. Like Hunger, Hardie-Tynes limited the agreement to its own terms.

   The cylinders manufactured by Hunger did not comply with government standards. Hardie-Tynes sued Hunger for breach of contract and claimed that it was entitled to recover attorneys' fees. Did Hunger and Hardie-Tynes enter into a contract? If so, what were its terms? Would your answer differ if the 2003 revisions to Article 2 were enacted? What if the transaction was governed by CISG? [*Hunger United States Special Hydraulic Cylinders Corp. v. Hardie-Tynes Manufacturing Co.*, 41 U.C.C. Rep. Serv. 2d 165 (10th Cir. 2000).]

3. On February 15, 2001, Rohm & Haas Company (R&H) and Crompton Corporation entered into a contract pursuant to which Crompton agreed to satisfy all of its needs for 2-Mercaptoethanol (product) with product purchased from R&H, and R&H agreed to supply Crompton with all of the product it required during a three-year term. The contract obligated R&H to maintain a minimum of 150,000 pounds of product at its facility in Moss Point, Mississippi, and to have available to Crompton, on-site at a North American location, not less than 150,000 pounds of product from an approved source. The contract contained a *force majeure* provision that stated: "Deliveries may be reduced or suspended by either party upon the occurrence of any event beyond the reasonable control of such party."

   One month prior to execution of the contract, a U.S. district court entered a consent decree that resolved a suit brought by the federal and Mississippi governments on account of certain operational practices at the Moss Point facility. R&H alleged that it was forced to close the facility in December 2001, as a result of the dramatic costs associated with bringing it into compliance with the consent decree. R&H sought a declaratory judgment to determine whether it was relieved of its contractual duties to Crompton, and Crompton filed a counterclaim for damages. What arguments will R&H

make in support of its claim that its performance should be excused? Who will prevail? [*Rohm & Haas Co. v. Crompton Corp.*, 2002 WL 1023435 (Pa. Com. Pl. 2002).]

4. Before deciding what remedies are available under Article 2 of the UCC, one must first determine whether the transaction involved the sale of goods. Consider the following cases.
   a. Wachter, a construction company, entered into a contract to purchase an accounting and project management software package from DCI, a company that develops, markets, and supports software for construction companies. The package included "installation of the software, a full year of maintenance, and a training and consulting package." Was the contract for a sale of goods or services? [*Wachter Management Co. v. Dexter & Chaney, Inc.*, 144 P.3d 747 (Kan. 2006).]
   b. A customer sued a New York restaurant for breach of warranty after a glass of water allegedly exploded in his hand during the course of a meal. Does the claim involve the sale of goods? [*Gunning ex rel. Gunning v. Small Feast Caterers, Inc.*, 777 N.Y.S.2d 268 (Sup. 2004).]
   c. Brenda Brandt underwent an operation at the Sarah Bush Lincoln Health Center to implant a ProtoGen Sling to resolve her urinary incontinence. Instead of solving the problem, the sling resulted in serious complications and was subsequently removed. After the device was recalled by its manufacturer, Brandt sued the Health Center for breach of warranty. Does the claim involve the sale of goods or services? [*Brandt v. Boston Scientific Corp.*, 792 N.E.2d 296 (Ill. 2003).]

5. In 1991, Brian Yarusso catapulted over the handlebars of his off-road motorcycle while traveling over a series of dirt moguls at a dirt motocross track in Newark, Delaware. He landed on his head, flipped over, and came to rest face down in the dirt. As a result of the accident, Yarusso was rendered a quadriplegic. Yarusso was wearing a full complement of safety equipment, including a Bell Moto-5 helmet, a full-face motocross helmet that was designed for off-road use. The Bell Moto-5 helmet complied with the U.S. Department of Transportation standards and was also certified by the Snell Foundation, a leading worldwide helmet research and testing laboratory. The owner's manual for the helmet included the following:[54]

   Five Year Limited Warranty: Any Bell helmet found by the factory to be defective in materials or workmanship within five years from the date of purchase will be repaired or replaced at the option of the manufacturer. . . . This warranty is expressly in lieu of all other warranties, and any implied warranties of merchantability or fitness for a particular purpose created hereby, are limited in duration to the same duration of the express warranty herein. Bell shall not be liable for any incidental or consequential damages. . . .

   Introduction: Your new Moto-5 helmet is another in the long line of innovative off-road helmets from Bell. . . . [T]he primary function of a helmet is to reduce the harmful effects of a blow to the head. However, it is important to recognize that the wearing of a helmet is not an assurance of absolute protection. NO HELMET CAN PROTECT THE WEARER AGAINST ALL FORESEEABLE IMPACTS.

   Yarusso filed suit against Bell. He testified at trial that he had purchased the helmet based on Bell's assertion that the helmet's primary function was to reduce the harmful effects of a blow to the head. On what grounds could Yarusso sue Bell? What will Bell argue in its defense? Who will prevail? Is there anything Bell could have done to have avoided this lawsuit? [*Bell Sports, Inc. v. Yarusso*, 759 A.2d 582 (Del. 2000).]

6. Jordan Panel Systems Corporation is a construction subcontractor that contracted to install windows at an air cargo facility at John F. Kennedy Airport in New York. Jordan entered into a contract to purchase custom-made windows from Windows, Inc., a fabricator and seller of windows located in South Dakota. The contract specified that the windows were to be shipped properly packaged and delivered to New York. Windows, Inc. arranged to have the windows shipped to Jordan by common carrier and delivered the windows to the common carrier properly packaged. During the course of the shipment, however, much of the glass was broken, and many of the window frames were gouged and twisted. Jordan refused to pay for the damaged windows and Windows, Inc. sued to recover the full purchase price. Which company should win? Is there anything either company could have done to avoid this lawsuit? [*Windows, Inc. v. Jordan Panel Systems Corp.*, 177 F.3d 114 (2d Cir. 1999).]

7. American Brass manufactured and sold brass and copper products, primarily in coil form. This manufacturing process generated a considerable amount of waste in the form of dust that American Brass sold to Westmin Corporation for use in a trace mineral premix that it in turn sold to Nufeeds, Inc. for use in its cattle feed products. When it found dioxin in the dust, Nufeeds was forced to recall its

54. Owner's manual for Bell Moto-5 helmet. Reproduced by permission.

cattle feed products. Nufeeds then sued American Brass for breach of the warranty of merchantability. What arguments can American Brass make in its defense? Who should win? [*Nufeeds v. Westmin Corp.*, 59 U.C.C. Rep. Serv. 2d 422 (Md. 2006).]

8. Adobe Systems, Inc. is a leading software publishing company. SoftMan Products Company distributes computer software products primarily through its website http://www.buycheapsoftware.com. Adobe distributes its products, including certain collections of products (Collections), through license agreements with distributors. Each Adobe Collection is also accompanied by an End User License Agreement (EULA) that sets forth the terms of the license between Adobe and the end user for that specific product. The EULA is electronically recorded on the computer disk, and customers are asked to agree to its terms when they attempt to install the software. The EULA includes a provision that prohibits licensees from transferring or assigning any individual Adobe product that was originally distributed as part of a Collection, unless it is transferred with all the software in the original Collection. Adobe filed a lawsuit seeking a preliminary injunction against SoftMan on the ground that SoftMan had violated the terms of Adobe's EULA by breaking apart various Adobe Collection packages and distributing the individual pieces of them as single products. SoftMan defended on the ground that it was not subject to the EULA terms, because it did not install the software before reselling it to end users. Who should prevail and why? [*SoftMan Products Co., L.L.C. v. Adobe Systems, Inc.*, 171 F. Supp. 2d 1075 (C.D. Cal. 2001); contra *Adobe Systems, Inc. v. Stargate Software, Inc.*, 216 F. Supp. 2d 1051 (N.D. Cal. 2002).]

TORTS AND PRIVACY PROTECTION

INTRODUCTION

What Is a Tort?

A *tort* is a civil wrong resulting in injury to a person or property. A tort case is brought by the injured party to obtain compensation for the wrong done. A crime, by contrast, is a wrong to society that is prosecuted by the state. (Criminal law is discussed in Chapter 15.) Even though a crime may be committed against an individual, the victim is not a party to a criminal action. Criminal law generally is concerned with protecting society and punishing the criminal, not with compensating the victim.

The distinctions between tort and criminal law are not always as clear as they first appear, however. A criminal statute might call for the criminal to compensate the victim. The victim might sue the perpetrator of the crime in tort, using the violation of a criminal statute as a basis for the tort claim. In some instances, tort law, like criminal law, purports to protect society through the award of punitive damages.

CHAPTER OVERVIEW

This chapter first discusses intentional torts, which fall into three general categories: (1) torts that protect individuals from physical and mental harm, (2) torts that protect interests in property, and (3) torts that protect certain economic interests and business relationships. The chapter then addresses negligence (including an accountant's liability to third parties) and strict liability. Tortious activity by more than one individual or entity raises the issues of vicarious liability and apportioned responsibility. Finally, the chapter discusses laws dealing with the privacy and security of personal information.

ELEMENTS OF AN INTENTIONAL TORT AND DEFENSES

Intentional torts require the plaintiff to prove (1) actual or implied intent, (2) a voluntary act by the defendant, (3) causation, and (4) injury or harm. The act must be the actual and legal cause of the injury. The act required depends on the specific intentional tort. A single set of facts may give rise to claims under more than one tort.

INTENT

Intent is the subjective desire to cause the consequences of an act. *Actual intent* can be shown by evidence that the defendant intended a specific consequence to a particular individual. Intent is implied if the defendant knew that the consequences of the act were certain or substantially certain, even if he or she did not actually intend any consequence at all.

As the degree of certainty of the result decreases, the defendant's conduct loses the character of intent and becomes recklessness. As the result becomes even less certain, the act becomes negligence, which is discussed later in this chapter. For example, if Metro Corporation's custodian, Ted, dumped garbage out of Metro's third-floor office window onto a busy sidewalk and hit Alexa, the law would likely imply intent to hit Alexa. Even though Ted may have had no subjective intention of hitting Alexa with the garbage, throwing it onto a busy sidewalk was substantially certain to result in at least one pedestrian being hit. However, if late one night Ted put garbage in the middle of the sidewalk in front of the office building for morning pickup and Alexa tripped over it, the intent to cause harm is not so clear. If intent is not established,

Ted will not be liable for the intentional tort of battery, which requires intent to bring about a harmful or offensive contact. Alexa might still be able to establish negligence, however, if she can show that a reasonable person would not have left the garbage on the sidewalk.

Intent may be transferred. If the defendant intended to hit one person, but instead hit the plaintiff, the intent requirement is met as to the plaintiff.

DEFENSES

Even if a plaintiff has proved all the elements of an intentional tort, the defendant may raise a legal defense to absolve himself or herself of liability. The most frequently raised defense is consent. If the plaintiff consented to the defendant's act, there is no tort. Even if the plaintiff did not explicitly consent, the law may imply consent. For example, a professional athlete injured during practice is deemed to have consented to the physical contact attendant to practice. The defendant may also be absolved of liability by a claim of self-defense or defense of others.

INTENTIONAL TORTS TO PROTECT PERSONS

The intentional torts of battery, assault, false imprisonment, intentional infliction of emotional distress, defamation, and invasion of privacy are designed to protect individuals from physical and mental harm.

BATTERY

Tort law recognizes a right to have one's body be free from harmful or offensive contact. Battery is the violation of that right.

Battery is intentional, nonconsensual, harmful, or offensive contact with the plaintiff's body or with something in contact with it. Offensive contact, such as dousing a person with water or spitting in his or her face, may be a battery, even if the plaintiff has suffered no physical harm. The contact may be by the defendant directly or by something the defendant has set in motion. For example, putting poison in someone's food is a battery.

A company president committed battery when he spanked an employee with a carpenter's level in a hazing ritual while other employees watched.[1] The jury awarded $6,000 for pain and suffering and loss of consortium, and $1 million in punitive damages. The trial court found the punitive damages award excessive and reduced it to $130,000.

ASSAULT

The tort of assault also protects the right to have one's body left alone. Unlike battery, however, it does not require contact. *Assault* is an intentional, nonconsensual act that gives rise to the apprehension (though not necessarily the fear) that a harmful or offensive contact is imminent.

Generally, assault requires some act, such as a threatening gesture, plus the ability to follow through immediately with a battery. A punch thrown from close range that misses its target may be an assault, but a threat to punch someone out of punching range is not. For example, if a defendant makes a threatening gesture and says, "I would hit you if I weren't behind this desk," and the defendant is in fact behind the desk, there is no assault because the immediacy requirement has not been met. Similarly, the threat "I'll beat you up if you come to class next week" is not immediate enough to be an assault.

FALSE IMPRISONMENT

The tort of false imprisonment protects the right to be free from restraint of movement. *False imprisonment* is intentional, nonconsensual confinement by physical barriers, or by physical force, or threats of force. It requires that the plaintiff either knew he or she was confined or suffered harm as a result of the confinement.

False imprisonment has been found when the plaintiff's freedom of movement was restricted because of force applied to the plaintiff's valuable property. For example, it is false imprisonment if a store clerk grabs a package from a customer walking out the door, because the customer cannot be expected to abandon the package to leave the store.

Shopkeepers who detain and later release a person mistakenly suspected of shoplifting are sometimes sued for false imprisonment. Most states have legislation exempting shopkeepers from such claims, if the shopkeeper acted in good faith and the detention was made in a reasonable manner, for a reasonable time, and was based on reasonable cause.

INTENTIONAL INFLICTION OF EMOTIONAL DISTRESS

Intentional infliction of emotional distress protects the right to peace of mind. The law has been slow to provide redress for purely mental injuries and is still evolving in this area. Jurisdictions differ sharply in their acceptance of this tort. In most jurisdictions, to prove *intentional infliction*

1. Smith v. Phillips Getschow Co., 616 N.W.2d 526 (Wis. 2000).

of emotional distress, a plaintiff must show (1) outrageous conduct by the defendant; (2) intent to cause, or reckless disregard of the probability of causing, emotional distress; (3) severe emotional suffering; and (4) actual and proximate (or legal) causation of the emotional distress. The mental distress must be *foreseeable,* in other words, a condition that a reasonable person could have anticipated as a result of his or her actions. The defendant is liable only to the extent that the plaintiff's response is reasonably within the range of normal human emotions. The reluctance of courts to accept intentional infliction of emotional distress as an independent tort most likely stems from fear that plaintiffs will file false claims. Therefore, some jurisdictions also require a physical manifestation of the emotional distress.

The defendant's acts must be outrageous or intolerable. Insulting, abusive, threatening, profane, or annoying conduct is not in itself a tort. Everyone is expected to be hardened to a certain amount of abuse. In determining outrageousness, courts consider both the context of the conduct and the relationship of the parties. For example, an employee can expect to be subjected to evaluation and criticism in the workplace, and neither criticism nor discharge is in itself outrageous. On the other hand, sexual harassment by a supervisor in the workplace is less tolerated than it might be, for example, if a patron in a nightclub engaged in the same conduct.

In *Ford v. Revlon, Inc.,*[2] the Supreme Court of Arizona found Revlon liable for intentional infliction of emotional distress after its employee, Leta Fay Ford, was harassed by her supervisor, the manager for the purchasing department. In addition to making vulgar and threatening remarks to Ford, the manager held her in a chokehold and fondled her at a company picnic. Ford repeatedly complained to management, but Revlon did not confront the supervisor for nine months. Indeed, one manager to whom Ford complained told her that her complaint was too hot to handle and encouraged her to try not to think about her predicament. Ford not only suffered emotional distress, but also developed physical complications, including high blood pressure and chest pains, as a result of her stressful work environment. Revlon had a specific policy and several guidelines for handling sexual harassment claims but recklessly disregarded them.

In a more recent case involving similar circumstances, however, the Supreme Court of Texas ruled that Hoffman-La Roche was not liable for intentional infliction of emotional distress.[3] A jury found that Joan Zeltwinger's supervisor had sexually harassed her by making vulgar remarks, telling dirty jokes, making inappropriate references to his body parts, describing his sexual encounters, and prowling around her bedroom while at her house for a business-related reason. The Texas Supreme Court relied upon a prior decision in which it had held that the tort of intentional infliction of emotional distress is a "gap-filler" tort, judicially created for the limited purpose of allowing recovery in those rare instances where the victim has no other recognized theory of redress. Because Zeltwinger's intentional infliction claim was based on the same conduct as her harassment claim, the court limited her to causes of action based on, and the more limited remedies provided by, state laws prohibiting sexual harassment.

DEFAMATION

Defamation is the communication (often termed *publication*) to a third party of an untrue statement, asserted as fact, that injures the plaintiff's reputation by exposing him or her to "hatred, ridicule or contempt." *Libel* is written defamation, and *slander* is spoken defamation. The distinction between libel and slander is sometimes blurred with respect to modern communications.

Different rules apply to the requirement of injury to reputation depending on whether the defamation is spoken or written. In an action for slander, the plaintiff must prove that he or she has suffered actual harm, such as the loss of credit, a job, or customers, unless the statement is so obviously damaging that it falls into the category of slander *per se. Slander per se* means that the words are slanderous in and of themselves, for example, a statement that a person has committed a serious crime, is guilty of sexual misconduct, or is not fit to conduct business. In an action for libel, the law presumes injury; that is, no actual harm need be shown unless the statement on its face is not damaging.

An opinion is defamation only if it implies a statement of objective fact. In *Sagan v. Apple Computer, Inc.,*[4] noted astronomer Carl Sagan sued Apple Computer for libel when Apple changed its code name for a new personal computer from "Carl Sagan" to "Butt-Head Astronomer" after Sagan demanded that the company cease using his name. The court ruled that the dispositive question in determining whether a statement of opinion can form the basis of a libel action is whether a reasonable fact finder could conclude that the statement implies an assertion of fact. The court found that a reasonable fact finder would conclude that Apple Computer was not making a statement of fact about Sagan's competency as an astronomer in using the figurative term "Butt-Head" and would understand that the company was using

2. 734 P.2d 580 (Ariz. 1987).

3. Hoffman-La Roche, Inc. v. Zeltwinger, 144 S.W.3d 438 (Tex. 2004); *see also* Williams v. Worldwide Servs., Inc., 877 So. 2d 869 (Fla. Ct. App. 2004).

4. 874 F. Supp. 1072 (C.D. Cal. 1994).

> ### › Ethical Consideration
>
> The damage done to a person's reputation by defamation can be instantaneous, because the false statements frequently receive attention in electronic and print media. The public, quick to latch on to the initial defamatory statements, is less likely to notice a court decision some years later that holds that the statements were, in fact, false.
>
> Because of this phenomenon, someone determined to cast doubt on another person's reputation has a good chance of success. Once the damage is done, it is largely irreversible. Therefore, ethical restraint must sometimes take the place of legal restraint.

the figurative term to retaliate in a humorous and satirical way for Sagan's reaction to Apple's use of his name. In addition, the court found that the statement that Sagan was a "Butt-Head Astronomer" could not rest on a core of objective evidence, so it could not be proved true or false.

In contrast, the U.S. Court of Appeals for the Second Circuit found that a lawyer's libel claim against the American Association of University Women's Legal Advocacy Fund (AAUW) was based on a statement of fact, not opinion.[5] The AAUW compiles a directory of attorneys who are willing to consult with women involved in higher education who are considering bringing gender discrimination claims. The directory's entry on Mr. Flamm stated: "At least one plaintiff has described Flamm as an 'ambulance chaser' with interest only in 'slam dunk cases.'" The appeals court found that this statement contained in a "fact-laden" directory did not simply express an opinion, but could reasonably be interpreted to imply a factual statement that Flamm engaged in the unethical solicitation of clients and took only easy cases.

The requirement of publication generally means that the statement must be made in the presence of a third person. Thus, the statement "You are a thief" made in a one-on-one conversation is not defamation. However, some courts have adopted the doctrine of *self-publication* to give an employee a claim for defamation when an employer, in firing an employee, makes a false assertion that the employer could reasonably expect the employee would be required to repeat to a prospective employer.

Defenses

Defenses to defamation actions are framed in terms of privilege and may be asserted in a number of circumstances. An *absolute privilege* cannot be lost. A *qualified privilege* can be lost under certain conditions. If the defendant has an absolute privilege, he or she can publish with impunity a statement he or she knows to be false. The defendant can even do so with the most evil intention. Absolute privilege is limited to situations in which (1) the defendant has consented to the publication, (2) the statement is a political broadcast made under the federal "equal time" statute, (3) the statement is made by a government official in the performance of governmental duties, (4) the statement is made by participants in judicial proceedings, or (5) the statement is made between spouses.

Truth is also an absolute defense to a defamation claim in most jurisdictions. The law in most jurisdictions presumes that the plaintiff has a pristine reputation. The law will not protect a reputation the plaintiff does not deserve, however, and places the burden on the defendant to prove that the derogatory statements are true.

There is a qualified privilege (1) to make statements to protect one's own personal interests, including statements to a peer review committee; (2) to make statements to protect legitimate business interests, such as statements to a prospective employer; and (3) to provide information for the public interest, such as credit reports. A qualified privilege can be lost if the person making the statement abuses the privilege.

In addition to common law privileges, statutory defenses may protect speakers. For instance, the Communications Decency Act of 1996 (CDA) provides that no provider or user of an interactive computer service will be held liable for defamatory content provided by a third party.[6] Applying this statute, the U.S. Court of Appeals for the Fourth Circuit refused to hold America Online (AOL) liable for defamation when an unidentified user posted offensive (and false)

5. Flamm v. Am. Ass'n of Univ. Women, 201 F.3d 144 (2d Cir. 2000).

6. 47 U.S.C. § 230.

> ### International Snapshot
>
> The Australian High Court exercised jurisdiction over a defamation lawsuit arising out of an article published in the United States that was accessible on the Internet in Australia.[a] The Court rejected the single publication rule, which states that, regardless of accessibility, a piece of writing has a single time and place of publication and only the place of publication will have legal authority over the writing. The Internet has given publishers the ability to reach global markets and removed their ability to block access to their publications.
>
> a. Dow Jones & Co. v. Gutnick (Austl. 2002) H.C.A. 56.

messages related to the Oklahoma City bombing and attributed these messages to the plaintiff.[7]

It is not yet clear whether the immunity provided by the CDA extends to active republishers of defamatory or other tortious content. In *Barrett v. Rosenthal,*[8] the California Supreme Court held that CDA immunity extends to users who "actively" chose to republish a statement with notice of its defamatory liability. In contrast, the U.S. Court of Appeals for the Ninth Circuit subsequently held that CDA immunity does not apply to "those who actively encourage, solicit and profit from the tortious and unlawful communications of others."[9] The court provided a hypothetical example of a website http://www.harassthem.com, where the visitor would be encouraged to provide private or defamatory content for a fee. In addition, the website would encourage "posters to provide dirt on the victims." The court stated that "by providing a forum designed to publish sensitive and defamatory information, and suggesting the type of information that might be disclosed to best harass and endanger the targets, this website operator might well be held responsible for creating and developing the tortious information."

Public Figures and Media Defendants The media, such as newspapers, television, or radio, have a qualified privilege that is almost absolute when they are commenting on a public official or a public figure. The U.S. Supreme Court, in applying the First Amendment right of freedom of the press, has held that a public official or public figure cannot recover damages for defamation by a media defendant absent a showing of *actual malice*. That means the plaintiff must prove that the statement was made with the knowledge that it was false or with a reckless disregard as to whether it was false. (Other aspects of the First Amendment are discussed in Chapter 4.)

Public officials include legislators, judges, and police officers. *Public figures* are those who are injected into the public eye by reason of the notoriety of their achievements or the vigor and success with which they seek the public's attention. In *Wells v. Liddy,*[10] the U.S. Court of Appeals for the Fourth Circuit made it clear that a private individual does not automatically become a public figure simply because he or she is involved in a public event. The event at issue was the 1972 Watergate burglary scandal, which ultimately resulted in President Richard Nixon's resignation. The defendant was G. Gordon Liddy, the former self-described "political intelligence chieftain" and general counsel of the Committee to Reelect the President. Liddy publicly offered an alternative theory to explain the purpose of the Watergate break-in. He claimed that the burglars' objective was to determine whether the Democrats had information embarrassing to John Dean, former legal counsel to President Nixon. Specifically, Liddy claimed that the burglars were searching the desk of Ida Wells, secretary of the Democratic National Committee, to find a compromising photograph of Dean's fiancée among other photographs of women hired to offer prostitution services to out-of-town guests. After Liddy claimed that Wells was involved in setting up these guests with prostitutes, Wells sued for defamation. The court found that Wells was a private figure even though she had become involved in a public matter. As the court commented:

> There is a great temptation when evaluating a controversy as longstanding and significant as Watergate to allow the controversy itself to take precedence in the analysis and let it convert all individuals in its path into public figures. The Supreme Court has admonished us strongly against allowing the public event with which the individual is connected to be the determinative factor governing an individual's public figure designation.[11]

A publicly traded corporation is generally considered a public figure, however, and thus must prove actual malice to prevail in a defamation suit. Because proving actual malice can be difficult, a corporation that anticipates that the press may publish an unfavorable story about its business may take proactive steps to counteract the negative publicity, rather than try to initiate a defamation action after the fact in court. In October 1999, the diet product company Metabolife International, Inc. became concerned that ABC would broadcast an unfair report on the medical risks of a dietary supplement sold by Metabolife. The company therefore posted on the Internet a complete, unedited, videotaped interview between an ABC News correspondent and the company's chief executive. Although ABC said that Metabolife's decision to post the interview on the Internet would not affect the interview that it broadcast, television executives indicated that in the future networks might ask interviewees to agree not to make material from the interview public until after it is broadcast on television.

A plaintiff who is not a public figure does not need to prove malice to prevail in a defamation action. A private plaintiff can recover if the defendant acted with knowledge, acted in reckless disregard of the facts, or was negligent in

7. Zeran v. Am. Online, Inc., 129 F.3d 327 (4th Cir. 1997), *cert. denied,* 524 U.S. 937 (1998).

8. 146 P.3d 510 (Cal. 2006).

9. Fair Hous. Counsel of San Fernando Valley v. Roommates.com, 489 F.3d 921 (9th Cir. 2007), *order taking case en banc,* 506 F.3d 716 (9th Cir. 2007), *argued and submitted* Dec. 12, 2007.

10. 186 F.3d 505 (4th Cir. 1999), *cert. denied,* 528 U.S. 1118 (2000).

11. *Id.*

failing to ascertain the facts. If the plaintiff proceeds on a negligence theory, he or she must prove actual damages, such as loss of business or out-of-pocket costs. If the plaintiff proves malice, however, then damages are presumed, so no proof of damages is required.

INVASION OF PRIVACY

Invasion of privacy is a violation of the right to keep personal matters to oneself. It can take several forms.

Intrusion is objectionable prying, such as eavesdropping or unauthorized rifling through files. Injunctions or court orders are usually available to prevent further intrusion. There must be a reasonable expectation of privacy in the thing into which there is intrusion. For example, courts have held there is no legitimate expectation of privacy in conversations in a public restaurant. The tort of intrusion does not require publication of the information obtained.

Public disclosure of private facts requires publication, for example, by stating in a newspaper that the plaintiff does not pay debts or posting such a notice in a public place. The matter made public must not be newsworthy. The matter must be private, such that a reasonable person would find publication objectionable. Unlike in a defamation case, truth is not a defense. In *Benz v. Washington Newspaper Publishing Co.*,[12] a plaintiff sued for public disclosure of private facts when a former acquaintance posted her home and work e-mail addresses and phone numbers on a website in response to advertisements seeking sexual relations. The U.S. District Court for the District of Columbia denied the defendant's motion to dismiss the action, concluding that the plaintiff's contact information constituted private facts, even though it was already available on the Internet, because "[i]ndividuals have a privacy interest in their home addresses and phone numbers."

In the following case, the Minnesota Supreme Court considered whether employees could recover for invasion of privacy when their employer distributed their names and Social Security numbers in a manner that could allow a third party to steal and misuse the numbers.

12. 2006 WL 2844896 (D.D.C. Sept. 29, 2006).

A CASE IN POINT — SUMMARY

CASE 9.1

BODAH V. LAKEVILLE MOTOR EXPRESS, INC.

MINNESOTA SUPREME COURT
663 N.W.2D 550 (MINN. 2003).

FACTS Lakeville Motor Express, Inc. (LME) is a trucking company operating primarily in Minnesota. LME sent a facsimile containing the names and Social Security numbers of 204 LME employees to its sixteen terminals across six states with a coversheet that was addressed simply to "Terminal Managers." The purpose of the fax was to allow LME to keep better records of accidents and injuries throughout its trucking network. Four months later, after being advised of the potential for identity theft, Peter Martin, president of LME, sent a letter of apology to all employees informing them of the mistake. The letter also notified them that the information was not shared with anyone other than the terminal managers and that Martin had instructed all terminal managers to destroy or return the list. Despite the president's apology and assurances, several employees filed a class-action suit on behalf of all 204 employees alleging invasion of privacy. The trial court dismissed the case in favor of LME, but the court of appeals reversed and found for the plaintiffs. The defendants appealed this judgment.

ISSUE PRESENTED Does a company violate its employees' right to privacy by transmitting their names and Social Security numbers in an unsecured manner that could lead to identity theft?

SUMMARY OF OPINION After concluding that it had the authority to review the earlier findings of the lower courts, the Minnesota Supreme Court explained the rationale behind recognizing the tort of invasion of privacy: "The right to privacy is an integral part of our humanity; one has a public persona, exposed and active, and a private persona, guarded and reserved. The heart of our liberty is choosing which parts of our lives shall become public and which parts we shall hold close."

In order to find invasion of privacy, (1) the defendant must have publicized some aspect of the plaintiff's life, (2) that information must not be a legitimate concern of the public, and (3) disclosure must be offensive to a reasonable person. The employees' Social Security numbers qualified

CONTINUED

under the second and third prongs of the test because the public would have no reason to know the numbers and many found their distribution offensive and potentially dangerous. Therefore, the case turned on the meaning of publication in the first prong.

LME maintained that faxing numbers to its terminal managers did not constitute publication, because the general public never saw the numbers. The employees argued that it constituted publication because (1) the names and corresponding Social Security numbers were sent to sixteen terminals in six states with no warning of the confidential nature of the information; (2) no corrective action was taken for at least four months; and (3) most importantly, there was no guarantee that the numbers were ever destroyed. As a result, they could still be used maliciously.

The court ruled that "publicity" means that "the matter is made public, by communicating it to the public at large, or to so many persons that the matter must be regarded as substantially certain to become one of public knowledge."

RESULT Distribution of the facsimile did not constitute publication, so there was no invasion of privacy. The lawsuit was dismissed.

COMMENTS The court characterized the fax as a private transmission, but did not completely absolve LME of any potential liability simply because the fax was not *intended* to be made public. The court addressed the employees' fears of identity theft directly:

> [I]f an unauthorized transmission of private data actually resulted in pecuniary loss due to identity theft, a plaintiff may be able to bring a negligence action. Likewise, a plaintiff may have a cause of action for negligent infliction of emotional distress if, because private information was shared, the plaintiff suffered severe emotional distress with accompanying physical manifestations.

Technological developments, especially the Internet, have made it possible to amass large amounts of detailed personal information. Concerned that traditional tort law causes of action, such as invasion of privacy, were not sufficient to protect against identity theft and other violations of privacy, state and federal governments have enacted a plethora of laws dealing with the security and unauthorized use and disclosure of private data. Privacy legislation is addressed later in this chapter, and identity theft is the subject of the "Inside Story."

Appropriation of a person's name or likeness may be an invasion of privacy. For example, using a fictitious testimonial in an advertisement would be a tort, as would using a person's picture in an advertisement or article with which he or she has no connection. In *Brown v. Ames,*[13] a group of blues musicians, songwriters, and music producers sued a music producer and record label for distributing cassettes, CDs, posters, and other products using the names and likenesses of the performers. The U.S. Court of Appeals for the Fifth Circuit ruled in the plaintiffs' favor by applying Texas state law, which allows recovery for unauthorized appropriation of names or likenesses, if the plaintiff can prove that (1) the defendant misappropriated the plaintiff's name or likeness for the value associated with it and not in an incidental manner or for a newsworthy purpose, (2) the plaintiff can be identified from the publication, and (3) the defendant derived some advantage or benefit.

Public figures from John F. Kennedy to Nicole Kidman have required employees to sign confidentiality agreements, which prohibit them from talking about their famous employers, even after their employment has been terminated. Oprah Winfrey, who also requires employees to sign nondisclosure agreements, won her case against a former employee who had planned on writing a book about her time with Oprah. Courts enforce these agreements to protect celebrities' privacy.[14]

INTENTIONAL TORTS THAT PROTECT PROPERTY

The torts of trespass to land, nuisance, conversion, and trespass to personal property protect interests in property.

13. 201 F.3d 654 (5th Cir. 2000), *cert. denied,* 531 U.S. 925 (2000).

14. Coady v. Harpo, Inc., 719 N.E.2d 244 (N.Y. 1999); Margaret Graham Tebo, *Zipped Lips,* A.B.A. J., Sept. 2000, at 16.

TRESPASS TO LAND

The previously described torts involved interference with personal rights. *Trespass to land* is an interference with a property right. It is an invasion of real property (that is, land) without the consent of the owner. The land need not be injured by the trespass. The intent required is the intent to enter the property, not the intent to trespass. Thus, a mistake as to ownership is irrelevant.

Trespass may also occur below the surface and in the airspace above the land. Throwing something, such as trash, on the land and shooting bullets over it may be a trespass, even though the perpetrator was not standing on the plaintiff's land.

Refusing to move something that at one time the plaintiff permitted the defendant to place on the land may also be a trespass. For example, if the plaintiff gave the defendant permission to leave a forklift on the plaintiff's land for one month, and it was left for two, the defendant may be liable for trespass.

Trespass may also occur if an individual permitted access to property does a wrongful act in excess of and in abuse of the authorized entry. In *Food Lion, Inc. v. Capital Cities/ABC, Inc.,*[15] two ABC reporters used false résumés to obtain jobs at Food Lion supermarkets in order to videotape unsanitary meat-handling practices at the markets. Food Lion sued, alleging that the reporters had committed trespass by secretly videotaping while working at the supermarkets. The U.S. Court of Appeals for the Fourth Circuit found that the two reporters had breached their duty of loyalty to the company as employees by videotaping in nonpublic areas, thereby nullifying Food Lion's consent for them to enter the property. Accordingly, the court found that the reporters had committed trespass. However, the court rejected Food Lion's argument that misrepresentation on a job application nullifies the consent given to an employee to enter the employer's property and thereby turns the employee into a trespasser.

NUISANCE

Nuisance is a nontrespassory interference with the use and enjoyment of real property, for example, by an annoying odor or noise. The focus of nuisance claims is on the plaintiff's harm, not on the degree of the defendant's fault. Therefore, even innocent behavior by the defendant is actionable—that is, it may be the basis for a claim—if that behavior resulted in unreasonable and substantial interference with the use and enjoyment of the plaintiff's property. To determine whether the defendant's conduct resulted in unreasonable interference, the court will balance the utility of the activity creating the harm, and the burden of preventing it, against the nature and the gravity of the harm. For example, hammering noise during the remodeling of a house may be less likely to constitute a nuisance than playing loud music late at night purely for recreation.

Nuisance can be public or private.

Public Nuisance

Public nuisance is unreasonable and substantial interference with the public health, safety, peace, comfort, convenience, or use of land. An action for public nuisance is usually brought by the government. However, a suit for public nuisance may also be brought by a private citizen who experiences special harm different from that experienced by the general public.

Guns After an Illinois court ruled in 2001 that gun dealers, as well as gun makers, could be held responsible under a theory of public nuisance for distributing firearms in a way that would make them more accessible to juveniles and criminals,[16] a number of states brought similar public

15. 194 F.3d 505 (4th Cir. 1999).

16. Young v. Bryco Arms, 765 N.E.2d 1 (Ill. App. Ct. 2001), *rev'd,* Young v. Bryco Arms, 821 N.E.2d 1078 (Ill. 2004).

"Mr. Speaker, will the gentleman from Small Firearms yield the floor to the gentleman from Big Tobacco?"

nuisance suits with mixed results.[17] In addition, since 1998 thirty-three states have passed legislation granting gun makers immunity.[18]

Even more ominous for gun-control advocates, in 2005, Congress passed the Protection of Lawful Commerce in Arms Act.[19] The Act bans suits seeking to hold gun manufacturers and dealers liable in civil actions for damages when their weapons are used in crimes, subject to an exception that allows certain cases involving defective weapons or criminal behavior by a gun maker or dealer, such as knowingly selling a gun to a person who failed a criminal background check. Since its enactment, a number of federal and state courts have invoked the law to dismiss pending public nuisance lawsuits.[20] In contrast, the Indiana Court of Appeals ruled in 2007 that the federal law did not bar a public nuisance suit by the City of Gary against several gun manufacturers. The court reasoned that the federal law seeks to prevent lawsuits that try to use the judicial system to circumvent the legislative branch, but noted that Gary's claim rested on a state law passed by the Indiana legislature. The court also cited an exception to the immunity provisions of the federal law that allows certain cases to go forward, if plaintiffs can show that the manufacturers knowingly violated a statute applicable to the sale and marketing of firearms.[21]

Greenhouse Gases In July 2004, eight states (including California, New Jersey, and New York) and New York City sued five of the largest U.S. energy providers in the U.S. District Court for the Southern District of New York, invoking the federal common law of public nuisance to seek an order requiring reductions in carbon dioxide emissions. This case, which involved five of the worst polluters in the industry, who are collectively responsible for almost 25 percent of the U.S. utility sector's annual emissions of carbon dioxide, was the first time that government officials had sued private power companies to reduce greenhouse gases.[22] Two other cases were subsequently filed that also claimed greenhouse gases are a public nuisance.[23] The New York federal court dismissed the original lawsuit in 2005, concluding that the case presented "political questions" that should be decided by the legislative and executive branches, not the courts.[24] The other two lawsuits were also dismissed.[25] As of January 2008, all three cases were on appeal. As noted in Chapter 6, the U.S. Supreme Court ruled that the Environmental Protection Agency's decision not to regulate greenhouse gases violated its obligations under the Clean Air Act.[26]

Private Nuisance

Private nuisance is interference with an individual's use and enjoyment of his or her land. Destruction of crops by flooding, the pollution of a stream, or playing loud music late at night in a residential neighborhood can constitute a private nuisance.

For example, the Wisconsin Supreme Court held that stray voltage that reduced a dairy herd's milk production was actionable on a private nuisance theory.[27] The court noted that the common law doctrine of private nuisance was broad enough to meet a wide variety of possible invasions and flexible enough to adapt to changing social values and conditions.

17. In *Cincinnati v. Beretta USA Corp.*, 768 N.E.2d 1136 (Ohio 2002), the Ohio Supreme Court ruled that prosecutors could proceed with public nuisance claims against gun makers, but in *Grunow v. Valor,* 2003 WL 22020032 (Fla. Cir. Ct. 2003), a Florida appellate court set aside a trial court verdict in favor of the plaintiff.
18. One notable exception is California, which repealed a law that had protected gun manufacturers in the state. Fox Butterfield, *Gun Industry Is Gaining Immunity from Suits,* N.Y. TIMES, Sept. 1, 2002, at 19. The U.S. Supreme Court upheld private citizens' right to bear arms in *District of Columbia v. Heller,* 128 S. Ct. 1695 (2008) (striking down a ban on handguns as a violation of the Second Amendment).
19. 15 U.SC. § 7901 *et seq.*
20. *Ileto v. Glock, Inc.* was dismissed on remand on March 14, 2006, by the U.S. District Court for the Central District of California and, as of January 2008, was on appeal to the U.S. Court of Appeals for the Ninth Circuit. *See also District of Columbia Appellate Court Upholds Dismissal of Lawsuit Against Gun Makers,* Jan. 10, 2008, *available at* http://sev.prnewswire.com/legal/20080111/DC1135810012008-1.html; and National Shooting Sports Foundation, *at* Firearm Industry Litigation Scorecard, http://www.nssf.org/news/legal_idx.cfm?PR=scorecard/index.cfm&AoI=LL.
21. Smith & Wesson Corp. v. City of Gary, 875 N.E.2d 422 (Ind. Ct. App. 2007); *see also Gary Lawsuit Against Gun Makers, Dealers Can Proceed,* WSBT, Oct. 29, 2007, *available at* http://www.wsbt.com/news/indiana/10876566.html.
22. *Legal News—Notable New Developments in the Law,* 73 U.S.L.W. 2056 (2004).
23. *Comer v. Murphy Oil USA, Inc.,* Case No. 1:05-cv-00436-LG-RHW (S.D. Miss. 2006), was dismissed in 2006 and has been appealed in the U.S. Court of Appeals for the Fifth Circuit; *California ex.rel. Lockyer v. General Motors Corp.,* Case No. 3:06-cv-05755 (N.D. Cal. 2006) was dismissed in 2007 and has been appealed in the U.S. Court of Appeals for the Ninth Circuit. *See also* Michael B. Gerrard, *U.S. Supreme Court Decides Massachusetts v. EPA, available at* http://www.abanet.org/abapubs/globalclimate/.
24. Connecticut v. Am. Electric Power Co., 406 F. Supp. 2d 265 (S.D.N.Y. 2005).
25. Climate Change Domestic Debate, Global Warming Cases, *available at* http://www.eenews.net/special_reports/climate_change_domestic/case_chart/.
26. Massachusetts v. EPA, 127 S. Ct.1438 (2007) (Case 6.2).
27. Vogel v. Grant-LaFayette Elec. Coop., 548 N.W.2d 829 (Wis. 1996).

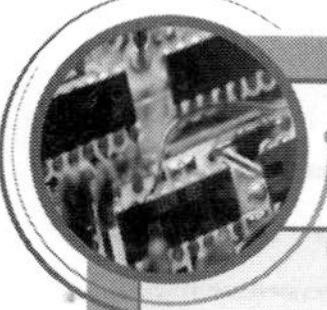

VIEW FROM CYBERSPACE

Suing to Stamp Out Spam

Statistics show that spam rates have grown exponentially. In June 2005, approximately 25 billion spam messages were sent worldwide every twenty-four hours. The number had increased to almost 100 billion by 2007. Using a spam virus, spammers are able to infect computers and turn them into "zombie computers" that can send thousands of e-mails daily without the user's knowledge. This practice was largely unknown several years ago, but more than 80 percent of spam is now sent this way.[a]

Most early spam lawsuits were filed by Internet service providers (ISPs). In an early watershed case, AOL sued a spam company named Cyber Promotions. Cyber Promotions defended on the basis that its right to free speech trumped AOL's right to restrict access to its network and customers, but the court found that the First Amendment did not apply because AOL was a private company, not a state actor.[b]

In 2004, President Bush signed the Controlling the Assault of Non-Solicited Pornography and Marketing (CAN-SPAM) Act, which preempted earlier state laws regulating spam. The CAN-SPAM Act has four main provisions: (1) it bans false and misleading header information and subject lines, (2) a response mechanism must be provided to allow the receiver to opt out of any future commercial messages from the sender, (3) the sender must clearly identify the message as an advertisement and include a valid physical mail address, and (4) any messages that contain sexually explicit material must include the warning "SEXUALLY-EXPLICIT" in the subject line. The CAN-SPAM Act is enforced by the U.S. Federal Trade Commission, and the Department of Justice also has the authority to enforce its criminal sanctions. Other federal and state agencies can enforce the law in their jurisdictions, and ISPs can also sue violators. Violation of CAN-SPAM can subject the sender to fines of up to $11,000 and imprisonment.

The number of spam lawsuits increased after passage of the CAN-SPAM Act. An ISP, Hypertouch, filed the first CAN-SPAM lawsuit in 2004, when it sued BlueStream Media and BVWebTies, LLC, the operator of home improvement guru Bob Vila's website, for BlueStream's failure to include contact information in commercial e-mails sent on behalf of BobVila.com. At the time the suit was filed, Hypertouch president Joe Wagner noted, "The CAN-SPAM Act provides only the most minimal protections to the public. But BobVila.com and BlueStream Media failed to observe even those."[c] This suit was eventually settled without any admission of guilt.

ISPs have continued to file spam suits, often combined with other charges, such as fraud, in an attempt to stem the proliferation of spam. Consumers have also banded together to file class-action suits. For example, Unspam Technologies filed a $1 billion lawsuit on behalf of people from 100 companies worldwide against those who have illegally harvested e-mail addresses for spam purposes.

Spammers have also been subject to criminal prosecution for violation of the CAN-SPAM Act, as well as other federal and state laws. In June 2007, two men who violated the CAN-SPAM Act were sentenced to more than five years in prison in one of the first criminal cases brought to trial under the CAN-SPAM Act. A federal jury convicted the defendants of a conspiracy to violate the CAN-SPAM Act and of criminal violations of its prohibitions against sending commercial e-mails with false header information and from accounts or domain names that were registered using materially false information. The defendants were also convicted of fraud, money laundering, and obscenity charges; they were fined $100,000, ordered to pay $77,500 restitution to AOL, and required to forfeit the $1.1 million in illegal proceeds from the spamming operation.[d]

Spammers are now sending text messages to consumers' cellphones. U.S. consumers received about 1.5 billion spam text messages in 2008, up from 800 million in 2006. Unlike junk e-mail, a spam text message costs the recipient between ten and twenty cents. Spam text messages also are viewed as more invasive by consumers who consider their mobile phones to be more private than their e-mail accounts. The onslaught of spam text messages has resulted in a new round of litigation by wireless carriers whose services have been inundated with these messages, and by consumers who have been hit with charges for unwanted text messages.[e]

---

a. *See* http://www.spamunit.com/spam-statistics/.
b. Cyber Promotions, Inc. v. Am. Online, Inc., 948 F. Supp. 436 (E.D. Pa. 1996).
c. Press Release, Law offices of John L. Fallat, Hypertouch Sues BobVila.com in Nation's First CAN-SPAM Case (Mar. 4, 2004), *available at* http://www.hypertouch.com/legal/bobvila.html.
d. *See generally* http://www.spamunit.com.
e. Ken Hart, *Advertising Sent to Cellphones Opens New Front in War on Spam*, WASHINGTONPOST.COM, Mar. 10, 2008, http://www.washingtonpost.com/wp-dyn/content/article/2008/03/09/AR2008030902213.html?hpid+topnews.

CONVERSION

Conversion is the exercise of dominion and control over the personal property, rather than the real property, of another. This tort protects the right to have personal property left alone. It prevents the defendant from treating the plaintiff's property as if it were his or her own. It is the tort claim a plaintiff asserts to recover the value of property that is stolen, destroyed, or substantially altered by a defendant.

The intent element for conversion does not include a wrongful motive. It merely requires the intent to exercise dominion or control over goods, inconsistent with the plaintiff's rights. The defendant does not have to know that the goods belonged to the plaintiff.

TRESPASS TO PERSONAL PROPERTY

When personal property is interfered with but not converted—that is, taken, destroyed, or substantially altered—there is a *trespass to personal property* (sometimes referred to as *trespass to chattels*). No wrongful motive must be shown. The intent required is the intent to exercise control over the plaintiff's personal property. For example, an employer who took an employee's car on a short errand without the employee's permission committed a trespass to personal property. If instead the employer damaged the car or drove it for several thousand miles, thereby lowering its value, the employer would be liable for conversion.

Trespass to chattels can include demonstrations that involve private property on private land. For example, a logging company successfully sued six members of an environmental group who climbed on and chained themselves to the company's logging equipment.[28] The members of the environmental group were required to pay punitive damages for demonstrating against government policies while on private property. The court ruled that the assessment of punitive damages did not violate the protesters' First Amendment rights.

Internet auction powerhouse eBay, Inc. successfully sued Bidder's Edge, Inc. when it discovered that Bidder's Edge had used an automated system to pull information off of eBay's website. All eBay users are required to agree to the eBay User Agreement, which specifically forbids such data mining. Bidder's Edge argued that eBay's website is public and that it had a right to use that public information. The court disagreed and ruled that Bidder's Edge's actions constituted a trespass to chattels. Even though eBay's website is public, eBay's servers are private property, and the unauthorized use of even a small portion of a server's capacity deprived eBay of its ability to use its personal property in the way it saw fit.[29]

In *Intel Corp. v. Hamidi*,[30] the California Supreme Court considered whether Intel could use the theory of trespass to chattels to prevent Hamidi, a former employee, from sending e-mails to Intel employees. Hamidi gained access to Intel e-mail addresses through a floppy disk that was sent to him anonymously. He then sent six e-mail messages to about 35,000 Intel e-mail addresses over a twenty-one-month span. Although the trial court granted Intel's motion for summary judgment and enjoined Hamidi from sending further e-mails, the California Supreme Court reversed and dismissed the lawsuit. The court distinguished this case from cases in which ISPs had successfully relied on trespass to chattels to sue spammers, noting:

> In those cases . . . the underlying complaint was that the extraordinary quantity of [unsolicited commercial e-mail] impaired the computer system's functioning. In the present case, the claimed injury is located in the disruption or distraction caused to recipients by the contents of the e-mail messages, an injury entirely separate from, and not directly affecting, the possession or value of personal property.

INTENTIONAL TORTS THAT PROTECT CERTAIN ECONOMIC INTERESTS AND BUSINESS RELATIONSHIPS

Certain economic interests and business relationships are protected by the torts of disparagement, injurious falsehood, fraudulent misrepresentation, malicious prosecution, interference with contractual relations, participation in a breach of fiduciary duty, interference with prospective business advantage, and bad faith.

DISPARAGEMENT

Disparagement is the publication of statements derogatory to the quality of the plaintiff's business, to the business in general, or even to the plaintiff's personal affairs, in order to discourage others from dealing with the plaintiff. To prove disparagement, the plaintiff must show that the defendant

28. Huffman & Wright Logging Co. v. Wade, 857 P.2d 101 (Or. 1993).

29. eBay, Inc. v. Bidder's Edge, Inc.,100 F. Supp. 2d 1058 (N.D. Cal. 2000).

30. 71 P.3d 296 (Cal. 2003).

made false statements about the quality or ownership of the plaintiff's goods or services, knowing that the statements were false or with conscious indifference as to their truth, and that the statements caused actual harm.

INJURIOUS FALSEHOOD

Knowingly making false statements may give rise to a claim for *injurious falsehood*. For example, a false statement that the plaintiff has gone out of business or does not carry certain goods is a tort if it results in economic loss to the plaintiff.

The range of damages available for injurious falsehood is more restricted than for defamation. Injurious falsehood permits recovery of only pecuniary (that is, monetary) losses related to business operations, whereas defamation permits recovery for loss of reputation, including emotional damages, as well.

Defenses

The defenses available to the defendant in a defamation action also apply to injurious falsehood. When the statement involves a comparison of goods, the privilege in an injurious falsehood case is even broader than the privilege available in defamation. For example, a defendant who favorably compares his or her own goods to those of a competitor is privileged, even though the defendant may not honestly believe in the superiority of his or her own goods.

FRAUDULENT MISREPRESENTATION

The tort of *fraudulent misrepresentation,* also called *fraud* or *deceit,* protects economic interests and the right to be treated fairly and honestly. Fraud requires proof that the defendant either (1) intentionally misled the plaintiff by making a material misrepresentation of fact upon which the plaintiff relied or (2) omitted to state a material fact when the defendant had a duty to speak because of a special relationship with the plaintiff. Intent can be constructive—in other words, a court will sometimes impute a fraudulent intent if the defendant showed reckless disregard for the truth. For example, a shareholder who relied to his or her detriment upon an intentionally misleading accountant's opinion regarding the company's financial statements might sue the accountant for fraud.

Everyone has a duty to refrain from affirmatively misrepresenting the facts, that is, lying. But, as explained in Chapter 5, as a general rule, parties dealing at arm's length are not required to disclose all facts that might be relevant to the other party's decision. If, however, one party is a fiduciary (a person entrusted to protect the interests of another), then he or she has a *fiduciary duty* to act with integrity and in the best interests of the other party. This means that the fiduciary must disclose all relevant facts to the other party even if that party has not asked any questions. For example, if an executive is negotiating to buy a piece of property from his or her corporation, the executive must volunteer all information known to him or her that might affect the terms (such as the price) on which the corporation would be willing to sell the property.

> **ETHICAL CONSIDERATION**
>
> If a person knows that his or her goods are inferior, is it ethical to claim that they are better than a competitor's?

Occasionally, a court will impose an affirmative duty to disclose even if the party required to disclose is not a fiduciary. For example, in *Brass v. American Film Technologies, Inc.,*[31] the defendant American Film Technologies (AFT) convinced Brass and other plaintiffs to buy warrants that could be used to acquire common stock, but AFT failed to reveal that the underlying stock was restricted and could not be freely traded for a period of two years. Upon discovering the omission, the plaintiffs sued for fraud. The court held that because AFT had superior knowledge about the restrictions on its securities, it had a duty to reveal those restrictions and its failure to do so was fraudulent concealment.

In contrast, the Supreme Court of Georgia held that physicians do not have a common law or statutory duty to disclose to a patient personal factors that might adversely affect their professional performance.[32] Cleveland sued his urologist for negligently performing unnecessary surgery on him and for fraudulently concealing his illegal use and abuse of cocaine. The court held that although a doctor has a common law duty to answer a patient's questions regarding medical or procedural risks, the doctor does not have the duty to disclose personal factors such as illicit drug use. The court ruled that the patient could sue the doctor for professional negligence, but could not base a claim of fraud on the physician's failure to disclose his drug use.

A mere expression of opinion generally is not a valid basis for a fraud claim. Although statements as to future

31. 987 F.2d 142 (2d Cir. 1993).

32. Albany Urology Clinic PC v. Cleveland, 528 S.E.2d 777 (Ga. 2000).

actions are generally deemed opinions and therefore not actionable, they can constitute fraud when (1) the defendant held itself out to be specially qualified and the plaintiff acted reasonably in relying upon the defendant's superior knowledge, (2) the opinion is that of a fiduciary or other trusted person, or (3) the defendant stated its opinion as an existing fact or as implying facts that justify a belief in its truth.

To state a claim of fraud, a plaintiff must establish that he or she suffered damages as a result of the fraud. In *Maio v. Aetna, Inc.*,[33] a class of persons enrolled in Aetna's health maintenance organization (HMO) plan filed a claim alleging that the company had engaged in a fraudulent scheme to induce individuals to enroll in the HMO plan by representing that Aetna's primary commitment was to maintain and improve the quality of health care given to its members. The class alleged that, in fact, Aetna was driven primarily by financial and administrative considerations. The U.S. District Court for the Eastern District of Pennsylvania ruled that the plaintiffs' vague allegation that "quality of care" might suffer in the future was too hypothetical an injury to confer standing. The court also found that Aetna's general assertions about its commitment to "quality of care" were "mere puffery" and could not serve as the basis for a fraud claim.

MALICIOUS PROSECUTION AND DEFENSE

A plaintiff can successfully sue for *malicious prosecution* by showing that a prior proceeding was instituted against him or her maliciously and without probable cause or factual basis. In addition, the earlier case must have been resolved in the plaintiff's favor. This tort originated from the tort of misuse of the criminal process, but has been adapted to redress malicious civil prosecution as well. A victorious plaintiff can recover damages for attorneys' fees paid in connection with the prior action, injury to reputation, and psychological distress.

Courts frequently state that the malicious prosecution action is disfavored under the law. Because the action has the potential to produce a chilling effect that discourages legitimate claims, courts have been reluctant to expand its reach.

Nevertheless, one state expanded the doctrine to recognize an action for *malicious defense.* In *Aronson v. Schroeder*,[34] the defendant allegedly created false material evidence while serving as defense counsel in a prior case and then gave false testimony concerning the evidence. In a ruling for the plaintiff, the New Hampshire Supreme Court stated:

> [W]hen a defense is based upon false evidence and perjury or is raised for an improper purpose, the litigant is not made whole if the only remedy is reimbursement of counsel fees. It follows that upon proving malicious defense, the aggrieved party is entitled to the same damages as are recoverable in a malicious prosecution claim.

INTERFERENCE WITH CONTRACTUAL RELATIONS AND PARTICIPATION IN A BREACH OF FIDUCIARY DUTY

The tort of *interference with contractual relations* protects the right to enjoy the benefits of legally binding agreements. It provides a remedy when the defendant intentionally induces another person to breach a contract with the plaintiff. The defendant must know of the existence of the contract between the plaintiff and the other person, or there must be sufficient facts that a reasonable person would be led to believe that such a contract existed. Interference with contractual relations requires intent to interfere. Thus, courts usually require that the defendant induce the contracting party to breach, rather than merely create the opportunity for the breach. Similarly, a defendant who knowingly participates in, or induces, a breach of fiduciary duty by another commits the tort of *participation in a breach of fiduciary duty.*

In some jurisdictions, interference with contractual relations also requires an unacceptable purpose. If good grounds exist for the interference, the defendant is not liable. For example, if a manager of a corporation is incompetent, then a stockholder of the corporation may be entitled to induce a breach of the employment agreement between the manager and the corporation. The stockholder's motive would be to protect his or her investment. On the other hand, a defendant may not interfere with another person's contract in order to attract customers or employees away from that person.

Perhaps the most famous case involving tortious interference with a contract was *Pennzoil v. Texaco,* discussed in the "Inside Story" in Chapter 7. In 1983, Pennzoil and Getty Oil Company negotiated an agreement for a merger. During the process of drafting the final merger documents, Texaco offered a better price for Getty and agreed to indemnify Getty for any claims that might be asserted by Pennzoil. After Getty accepted Texaco's offer, Pennzoil sued Texaco for tortious interference with a contract. Under New

33. 1999 WL 800315 (E.D. Pa. Sept. 29, 1999), *aff'd,* 221 F.3d 472 (3d Cir. 2000).

34. 671 A.2d 1023 (N.H. 1995).

York law, Pennzoil had to prove (1) the existence of a valid contract, (2) Texaco's knowledge of the existence of the contract, (3) Texaco's intentional inducement of a breach of that contract, and (4) damages incurred by Pennzoil as a result of the breach of contract. A jury decided against Texaco and awarded $10.5 billion to Pennzoil. The case was ultimately settled for $3 billion.

Defense

As in defamation, truth is a defense to a claim for interference with contractual relations. There is no liability if a true statement was made to induce another to break off relations with the plaintiff.

INTERFERENCE WITH PROSPECTIVE BUSINESS ADVANTAGE

Courts are less willing to award damages for interference with prospective contracts than they are to protect existing contracts. To prove *interference with prospective business advantage,* the plaintiff must prove that the defendant intentionally interfered with a relationship the plaintiff sought to develop and that the interference caused the plaintiff's loss. In rare cases, however, courts have permitted recovery when the defendant was merely negligent.

In one case,[35] Baum Research and Development Company, a manufacturer of wooden baseball bats, filed a claim of tortious interference with prospective economic advantage against several manufacturers of aluminum baseball bats, a trade association of bat manufacturers, and the National Collegiate Athletic Association. Baum claimed that the defendants had prevented it from establishing relationships with amateur baseball teams and had disrupted its sale of bats to these teams by, among other things, disseminating false information about the Baum Hitting Machine manufactured by Baum, thereby inducing baseball teams to terminate arrangements with Baum for the use of its wooden bats, and to remove and destroy Baum bats and replace them with aluminum bats. The court stated that the necessary elements of tortious interference with economic relations are (1) the existence of a valid business relationship or expectancy, (2) knowledge of the relationship or expectancy on the part of the interferor, (3) intentional interference inducing or causing a breach or termination of a relationship or expectancy, and (4) damages. Concluding that the company "had more than a mere hope for business opportunities or the innate optimism of a salesman,"[36] the court ruled that Baum had a valid claim of tortious interference with economic relations.

35. *In re* Baseball Bat Antitrust Litig., 75 F. Supp. 2d 1189 (D. Kan. 1999).

Defenses

Most jurisdictions recognize a privilege to act for one's own financial gain. In some jurisdictions, the plaintiff has the burden of showing that the defendant acted from a motive other than financial gain, such as revenge. In others, the defendant has the burden of proving that he or she acted only for financial gain. Any purpose sufficient to create a privilege to disturb existing contractual relations will also justify interference with prospective business advantage.

As in defamation and interference with contractual relations, truth is a defense. Some jurisdictions have also applied the First Amendment defenses available in defamation cases.

Interference with prospective business advantage is usually done by a competitor or at least by one who stands to benefit from the interference. Competing fairly is not a tort, however. For the purposes of competition, a defendant may attempt to increase its business by cutting prices, offering rebates, refusing to deal with the plaintiff, secretly negotiating with the plaintiff's customers, or refusing to deal with third parties unless they agree not to deal with the plaintiff.

BAD FAITH

Bad faith conduct by one party to a contract to the other party may serve as the basis for a tort claim of *bad faith.* This claim is separate and independent from a breach-of-contract claim. Typically, a claim of bad faith is brought by an insured against an insurance company for breaching its duty to act in good faith in the handling and payment of claims. The plaintiff must show that the insurer failed to exercise good faith in processing a claim and that there was no reasonable justification for the insurer's refusal to pay it.

36. *Id.*

> **ETHICAL CONSIDERATION**
>
> Is it ethical to refuse to deal with a company, to secretly negotiate with your competitor's customers, or to refuse to deal with third parties unless they agree not to deal with your competitor?

NEGLIGENCE

Intent is an essential element of every intentional tort. Negligence does not include the element of intent. Rather, the focus is on the reasonableness of the defendant's conduct. Negligence requires that all people take appropriate care in any given situation. It does not require that the defendant intended, or even knew, that his or her actions would harm the plaintiff. In fact, a defendant's conduct might still be negligent even if the defendant was full of concern for the plaintiff's safety. It is enough that the defendant acted carelessly or, in other words, that his or her conduct created an unreasonable risk of harm.

Negligence is defined as conduct that involves an unreasonably great risk of causing injury to another person or damage to property. To establish liability for negligence, the plaintiff must show that (1) the defendant owed a duty to the plaintiff to act in conformity with a certain standard of conduct, that is, to act reasonably under the circumstances; (2) the defendant breached that duty by failing to conform to the standard; (3) a reasonably close causal connection exists between the plaintiff's injury and the defendant's breach; and (4) the plaintiff suffered an actual loss or injury.

DUTY

A person with a *legal duty* to another is required to act reasonably under the circumstances to avoid harming the other person. The required standard of care is what a reasonable person of ordinary prudence would do in the circumstances. It is not graduated to include the reasonably slow person, the reasonably forgetful person, or the reasonable person of low intelligence. In determining duty, the law allows reasonable mistakes of judgment in some circumstances. In emergency situations, the duty is to act as a reasonable person would act in the circumstances. The defendant is expected to anticipate emergencies. Drivers must drive defensively. Innkeepers must anticipate fires and install smoke alarms and, in some cases, sprinkler systems, and must provide fire escapes and other fire-safety features. Owners of swimming pools in subdivisions with children must fence their property.

As explained further below, most states take a formalistic approach to duty and alter the scope of the defendant's liability depending on the court's characterization of the injured party (e.g., trespasser versus business guest). In 1993, the New Jersey Supreme Court articulated a more general framework: "Whether a person owes a duty of reasonable care toward another turns on whether the imposition of such a duty satisfies an abiding sense of basic fairness under all of the circumstances in light of considerations of public policy."[37] For that court, the analysis involves balancing many factors, including the relationship between the parties, the nature of the attendant risk, the opportunity and ability to exercise care, and the public interest in the proposed solution. As discussed further below, courts are split on whether an employer has a duty to take reasonable precautions to protect third parties from injury by employees ordered home because they are intoxicated.[38]

Duty to Rescue

The law does not impose a general duty to rescue. However, once one undertakes a rescue, the law imposes a duty to act as a reasonable person and not to abandon the rescue effort unreasonably. Thus, if Ciril Wyatt sat on a riverbank and watched Edward Donnelly drown, she would not be liable in negligence for Donnelly's death. However, if Wyatt saw Donnelly drowning, jumped in her boat, sped to him, tried to pull him into the boat and then changed her mind and let him drown, she would be liable.

A special relationship between two people may create a duty to rescue. If Donnelly were Wyatt's husband or child or parent, Wyatt would have a duty to rescue him. Other relationships that create a duty to rescue are employer and employee; innkeeper and guest; teacher and student; employee of a bus, train, or other common carrier and passenger; and possibly team members, hunting partners, and hiking partners.

There is a duty to rescue those whom one has placed in peril. For example, if Wyatt had been driving her boat in a negligent manner, thereby causing Donnelly to fall overboard, she would have a duty to rescue him.

Duty of Landowner or Tenant

A possessor of land (such as a tenant) or its owner has a legal duty to keep the property reasonably safe. Such a person may be liable for injury that occurs outside the premises

37. Hopkins v. Fox & Lazo Realtors, 625 A.2d 1110 (N.J. 1993).

38. *See* Lett v. Collis Foods, Inc., 605 S.W.3d 95 (Tenn. Ct. App. 2001) (Case 9.4) and the authorities cited therein.

INTERNATIONAL SNAPSHOT

Some countries do impose a general duty to rescue. For example, France and Brazil require bystanders to try to help those in danger, if trying to help will not put the bystanders at risk.

as well as on them. For example, a landowner may be liable for harm caused when water from a cooling tower covers the highway; when sparks from a railroad engine, which is not properly maintained, start a fire on adjacent property; or when a roof sheds snow onto the highway.

A landowner must exercise care in demolishing or constructing buildings on his or her property and in excavating his or her land. Landowners have been held liable when, after being hit by a car, a pole on a landowner's property collapsed and injured a pedestrian, and when a landowner erected a sign that obstructed the view and caused an accident.

A landowner has a general duty to inspect his or her property and keep it in repair, and he or she may be liable if a showroom window, a downspout, a screen, or a loose sign falls and injures someone. In a few jurisdictions, landowners have a duty to maintain sidewalks that abut (are right next to) their property.

Traditional Approach to Liability for Injuries on Premises Traditionally, the liability associated with injury on the premises of another has hinged on the distinctions among trespassers, licensees, and invitees. The possessor owes the least duty to a trespasser and the greatest duty to an invitee.

Duty to Trespassers In general, a possessor of property owes no duty to an undiscovered trespasser. If a substantial number of trespassers are in the habit of entering at a particular place, however, then the possessor of the property has a duty to take reasonable care to discover and to protect the trespassers from activities he or she carries on. Some courts have also established a duty to protect such trespassers from dangerous conditions, such as concealed high-tension wires, that do not result from the possessor's activities. Some jurisdictions require the possessor to exercise reasonable care once he or she knows of the trespasser's presence.

Trespassing children are owed a higher level of duty. The *attractive nuisance* doctrine imposes liability for physical injury to child trespassers caused by artificial conditions on the land if (1) the possessor knew or should have known that children were likely to trespass; (2) the condition is one the possessor would reasonably know involved an unreasonable risk of injury to such children; (3) because of their youth, the children did not discover the condition or realize the risk involved; (4) the utility to the possessor of maintaining the condition is not great; (5) the burden of eliminating the risk is slight compared with the magnitude of the risk to the children; and (6) the possessor fails to exercise reasonable care to protect the children.

Duty to Licensees A *licensee* is anyone who is on the land of another person with the possessor's express or implied consent. The licensee enters for his or her own purposes, not for those of the possessor. Social guests and uninvited sales representatives are licensees.

The possessor must exercise reasonable care for the protection of a licensee. This duty differs from that owed to a trespasser because the possessor is required to look out for licensees before they enter the land. The possessor is not required to inspect for unknown dangers, however. The duty arises only when the possessor has actual knowledge of a risk.

Duty to Invitees An *invitee*, or business visitor, is someone who enters the premises for purposes of the possessor's business. The possessor owes a higher duty to an invitee than to a licensee. The possessor must protect invitees against known dangers and also against those dangers that the possessor might discover with reasonable care.

A customer is clearly an invitee and is accordingly owed a higher duty of care than a licensee such as a social guest. Managers thus have particular reason to be concerned about invitees. Every year businesses must deal with thousands of "slip and fall" cases brought by customers who have fallen due to wet floors, icy sidewalks, or broken steps.

Invitees of a possessor of property, such as contractors, may also have a duty to other persons admitted onto the property by the owner. Contractors that create a dangerous condition while working at a construction site may be held liable for an injury caused by the dangerous condition after the contractor leaves the site and turns its work over to the property owner. In *Brent v. Unocal,*[39] ARCO Alaska, Inc. hired Unocal, Inc., as an independent contractor, to perform excavation and install sheet piling as part of a bridge construction project. After Unocal had finished its work and turned the property over to ARCO, construction worker William Brent was injured while working on the site, when he fell into a hole created by Unocal. The Supreme Court of Alaska found that Unocal was liable under Section 385 of the Restatement (Second) of Torts, which states that "a contractor is held to the standard of reasonable care for the protection of third parties who may foreseeably be endangered by his negligence, even after acceptance of the work by the contractor." Section 385 reflects the majority rule adopted by courts that have considered this issue.

39. 969 P.2d 627 (Alaska 1998).

A business's duty to invitees may even include an obligation to protect invitees from criminal conduct by third parties. States have been mixed in their application of this standard. In *Delgado v. Trax Bar & Grill,*[40] the California Supreme Court held that a bar did not have a duty to employ burdensome measures to protect patrons in its parking lot in the absence of prior similar incidents, but that did not absolve it of liability. The court adopted a "sliding scale balancing test" formulation: where there is evidence of prior similar incidents, burdensome measures like hiring guards or using security cameras are mandated, and where there is evidence of something less than prior similar acts, "minimally burdensome measures" are required. For example, in a lawsuit filed by the victim of a vicious assault against an all-night restaurant, the court noted that there was evidence of fistfights and robberies but no evidence of similar assaults. Although there was no duty for the restaurant to take burdensome measures in this case, the court concluded that it was up to a jury to decide whether the failure of the restaurant employees to take any action violated its obligation to take "minimally burdensome" measures such as calling 911.[41]

The Washington Supreme Court, on the other hand, denied a claim by an assaulted convenience store patron based on the store's failure to provide security personnel.[42] The court reasoned that imposing a requirement that businesses provide guards in all cases would unfairly shift responsibility for policing from the government to the private sector. In *dicta,* the court said that a duty to provide security guards may arise if "the construction or maintenance of the premises brings about a . . . peculiar temptation . . . for criminal misconduct" by third parties, but such facts were not present in that case.

Reasonable Care Approach The traditional approach of classifying one who enters a tenant's or landowner's property as a trespasser, licensee, or invitee has fallen into disfavor in several jurisdictions. Determining the proper classification of an injured plaintiff is often difficult and may require courts and juries to sift through hundreds of pages of testimony. Moreover, a person's status could change over the course of a day or a transaction. For example, an intruder would be deemed a trespasser, but if the landowner spotted the intruder and permitted him or her to remain, then the trespasser's status could shift to licensee. The New York Court of Appeals put it this way: "[I]t remains a curiosity of the law that the duty owed to a plaintiff on exit may have been many times greater than that owed him on his entrance, though he and the premises all the while remained the same."[43]

To eliminate this potential for confusion, some jurisdictions have abandoned the traditional "trichotomy" in favor of a reasonableness standard. Under the standard of *reasonable care under the circumstances,* courts require all landowners to act in a reasonable manner with respect to entrants on their land, with liability hinging on the foreseeability of harm. Some jurisdictions, such as New York, have collapsed all three of the old standards into a single reasonable care standard. The New York Court of Appeals explained that "this standard of reasonable care should be no different than that applied in the usual negligence action."[44] Other jurisdictions, such as North Carolina, have eliminated the distinction between licensees and invitees, but continue to treat trespassers differently because they had no right to enter the land. In determining whether the landowner has exercised reasonable care, courts will consider the identity of the person entering the property and the reasons why that person entered.

Duty of Landlord to Tenant

In general, a landlord has a duty to provide adequate security to protect tenants from foreseeable criminal acts of a third party. Relevant issues are whether (1) the property was in a high-crime area, (2) there had been earlier criminal acts, (3) there was a failure to maintain locks, and (4) the landlord had knowledge of prior criminal acts.

In *Sharon P. v. Arman, Ltd.,*[45] the plaintiff was sexually assaulted in an underground commercial parking garage below her office building. She sued the garage owner for failing to take measures to prevent criminal acts in the garage. The California Supreme Court ruled that a commercial landlord owes a duty to take reasonable steps to secure common areas against foreseeable criminal acts of third parties that are likely to occur in the absence of such precautionary measures. Under this standard, a court must balance the foreseeability of the harm against the burden imposed on the landlord if required to take precautionary measures. The court found that the garage had a ten-year history with no assaults and stated that "absent any prior similar incidents or other indications of a reasonably foreseeable risk of violent criminal assaults in that location, we cannot conclude defendants were required to secure the area against such crime."

40. 113 P.3d 1159 (Cal. 2005).

41. Morris v. De La Tore, 113 P.3d 1182 (Cal. 2005).

42. Nivens v. 7-11 Hoagy's Corner, 943 P.2d 286 (Wash. 1997).

43. Basso v. Miller, 352 N.E.2d 868 (N.Y. 1976).

44. *Id.*

45. 989 P.2d 121 (Cal. 1999), *cert. denied,* 530 U.S. 1243 (2000).

BREACH OF DUTY

Once it is determined that the defendant owed the plaintiff a duty, the next issue in a negligence case is whether the defendant breached that duty. In many cases, the required standard of conduct will be that of a reasonable person. However, a person who is specially trained to practice in a profession or trade will be held to the higher standard of care of a reasonably skilled member of that profession or trade. For example, the professional conduct of a doctor, architect, pilot, attorney, or accountant will be measured against the standard of the profession. A specialist within a profession will be held to the standard of specialists.

The court will also look to statutes and regulations to determine whether the defendant's conduct amounted to a breach of duty. Some jurisdictions merely allow the statute to be introduced into evidence to establish the standard of care. In other jurisdictions, however, once the plaintiff shows that the defendant violated a statute and the violation caused the injury, the burden shifts to the defendant to prove that he or she was not negligent. This is often an impossible burden to satisfy. This rule, sometimes referred to as *negligence per se,* applies only when the statute or regulation was designed to protect a class of persons from the type of harm suffered by the plaintiff and the plaintiff is a member of the class to be protected.

Courts will also look to the custom or practice of others under similar circumstances to determine the standard of care. Although the custom in the industry may be given great weight, it is ordinarily not dispositive or conclusive.

Res Ipsa Loquitur

The doctrine of *res ipsa loquitur*—"the thing speaks for itself"—allows the plaintiff to prove breach of duty and causation (discussed below) indirectly. *Res ipsa loquitur* applies when an accident has occurred, and it is obvious, although there is no direct proof, that the accident would not have happened without someone's negligence. For example, if a postoperative X-ray shows a surgical clamp in the plaintiff's abdomen, one can reasonably infer that the surgeon negligently left it, even if no one testifies as to how the clamp got there.

Res ipsa loquitur has three requirements. First, the plaintiff's injury must have been caused by a condition or instrumentality that was within the defendant's exclusive control. This requirement eliminates the possibility that persons not named as defendants were responsible for the condition that gave rise to the injury. Second, the accident must be of such a nature that it ordinarily would not occur in the absence of negligence by the defendant. Third, the accident must not be due to the plaintiff's own negligence.

Once *res ipsa loquitur* is established, jurisdictions vary as to its effect. In some jurisdictions, it creates a presumption of negligence, and the plaintiff is entitled to a directed verdict (whereby the judge directs the jury to find in favor of the plaintiff), unless the defendant can prove he or she was not responsible. This rule has the effect of shifting the burden of proof, normally with the plaintiff, to the defendant. Other jurisdictions leave the burden of proof with the plaintiff, requiring the jury to weigh the inference of negligence and to find the defendant negligent only if the preponderance of the evidence (including the *res ipsa* inference) favors such a finding.

CAUSAL CONNECTION

In addition to establishing duty and breach, a plaintiff claiming negligence must prove that the defendant's breach of duty caused the injury. The causation requirement has two parts: actual cause and proximate (or legal) cause.

Actual Cause

To establish *actual cause,* the plaintiff must prove that he or she would not have been harmed but for the defendant's negligence. The defendant is not liable if the plaintiff's injury would have occurred in the absence of the defendant's conduct. For example, if George Broussard put a garbage can on the sidewalk for morning pickup and Anna Chang came along and broke her ankle, Broussard's conduct would not be the actual cause of Chang's injury, if it was established that Chang had caught her heel in the sidewalk, turned her ankle, and then bumped into Broussard's garbage can.

When the plaintiff names more than one defendant, the actual-cause test may become a *substantial-factor test:* Was the defendant's conduct a substantial factor in bringing about the plaintiff's injury?

A further problem may arise if more than one individual could possibly have been the negligent party. A classic case involved two hunters shooting quail on an open range.[46] Both shot at exactly the same time, using identical shotguns. A shot from one of the guns accidentally hit another hunter. Clearly, only one of the two defendants caused the injury, but there was no way to determine which one it was. The court imposed the burden on each defendant to prove that he had not caused the injury. Because neither could do so, both were held liable for the whole injury.

Proximate Cause

Once the plaintiff has proved that the defendant's conduct is an actual cause of the plaintiff's injury, he or she must also

46. Summers v. Tice, 199 P.2d 1 (Cal. 1948).

prove that it is the *proximate cause,* that is, that the defendant had a duty to protect the particular plaintiff against the particular conduct that injured him or her. Through the requirement of proximate cause, the law places limits on the defendant's liability.

The defendant is not required to compensate the plaintiff for injuries that were unforeseeable, even if the defendant's conduct was careless. Courts apply the foreseeability requirement in two different ways. Some courts limit the defendant's liability to those consequences that were foreseeable. Others look to whether the plaintiff was a foreseeable plaintiff, that is, whether the plaintiff was within the *zone of danger* caused by the defendant's careless conduct.

A classic case involved a woman, Mrs. Palsgraf, who was injured when scales on a railroad platform fell on her.[47] Two railroad employees were helping a man carrying a bulky package climb onto a moving train. Unbeknownst to the employees, the package contained fireworks. The man dropped the package and the fireworks exploded, causing the scales, which were located many feet away, to fall on the unfortunate Mrs. Palsgraf. She sued the railroad for negligence. The New York Court of Appeals ruled that even if the employees had failed to use due care, Mrs. Palsgraf's injury was not foreseeable. As a result, the railroad was not liable for negligence because the employees' actions were not the proximate cause of her injury.

As a general rule, companies are not liable for the criminal acts of third parties, unless the company knew or should have known that their negligence might allow the crime to occur.[48] Following the 1995 Oklahoma City attack, plaintiffs alleged negligence on the part of the manufacturer of the fertilizer Terry Nichols and Timothy McVeigh used to concoct their bomb. The court dismissed the claim, finding as a matter of law that the terrorist activity was not reasonably foreseeable to the company.[49] In short, the company had no duty to protect against consumers using their product to blow up buildings because the company could not have anticipated such a use.

In a subsequent suit following the first World Trade Center attack in 1993, the court again dismissed claims against a fertilizer manufacturer on foreseeability grounds.[50] The court did, however, signal to corporate America that society would expect companies to be more wary of the potential for terrorists to misuse products and services in the future, stating that the opinion "rest[ed] largely on a slender and temporal reed."[51]

Courts revisited the issue of the foreseeability of terrorists' acts in the wake of the September 11, 2001 attacks. The plaintiffs claimed that the airlines' negligence led to the injuries and damage suffered that day.[52] While noting the novelty of the type of attack, the court rejected the position of the judges deciding the Oklahoma City and 1993 World Trade Center cases and refused to rule as a matter of law that terrorist acts were unforeseeable. The court explained: "While it may be true that terrorists had not before deliberately flown airplanes into buildings, the airlines reasonably could foresee that crashes causing death and destruction on the ground was a hazard that would arise should hijackers take control of a plane."[53]

INJURY

Finally, even if a defendant is negligent, the plaintiff cannot recover, unless he or she can show that he or she, or his or her property, was injured as a result of the defendant's conduct.

This requirement is often the controlling factor in actions for *negligent infliction of emotional distress.* The traditional rule is that a plaintiff cannot recover for negligent infliction of emotional distress, unless he or she can show some form of physical injury. In cases involving exposure to the human immunodeficiency virus (HIV), however, courts have permitted plaintiffs to recover for emotional distress (over the fear of contracting HIV) without requiring that they actually have contracted the virus. Courts have set forth objective standards that prevent someone from basing an action on an irrational fear that he or she contracted HIV. In *Bain v. Wells,*[54] the Tennessee Supreme Court ruled that a plaintiff must actually have been exposed to HIV in order to recover for emotional distress. Presumably, this means the plaintiff must demonstrate some medically sound channel of transmission. In *Williamson v. Waldman,*[55] the New Jersey Supreme Court held that a plaintiff can recover if a reasonable person would have experienced emotional distress over the prospect of contracting HIV under the circumstances. However, this hypothetical reasonable person would be presumed to have "then-current, accurate, and generally available" knowledge concerning the transmission of HIV. Again, an irrational fear of catching the virus would not be a valid basis for an emotional distress suit.

47. Palsgraf v. Long Island R.R., 162 N.E. 99 (N.Y. 1928).

48. Gaines-Tabb v. ICI Explosives, USA, Inc., 160 F.3d 613, 621 (10th Cir. 1998).

49. *Id.* at 621.

50. Port Auth. of New York & New Jersey v. Arcadian Corp., 189 F.3d 305, 315 (3d Cir. 1999).

51. *Id.* at 15.

52. *In re* Sept. 11 Litig., 280 F. Supp. 2d 279 (S.D.N.Y. 2003).

53. *Id.* at 296.

54. 936 S.W.2d 618 (Tenn. 1997).

55. 696 A.2d 14 (N.J. 1997).

Defenses to Negligence and Limits on Recoverable Damages

In some jurisdictions, the defendant may absolve itself of part or all of the liability for negligence by proving that the plaintiff was also negligent. There may also be statutory defenses and common law limits on damages.

Contributory Negligence

Under the doctrine of *contributory negligence,* if the plaintiff was also negligent in any manner, he or she cannot recover any damages from the defendant. Thus, if a plaintiff was 5 percent negligent and the defendant was 95 percent negligent, the plaintiff's injury would go unredressed. To address this inequity, most courts have replaced the doctrine of contributory negligence with that of comparative negligence.

Comparative Negligence

Under the doctrine of *comparative negligence,* the plaintiff may recover the proportion of his or her loss attributable to the defendant's negligence. For example, in *Lara v. Nevitt,*[56] plaintiff Ramon Lara was asleep in the sleeper berth of his son's big rig truck when the defendant lost control of his car and hit the truck. The jury found that Lara was 50 percent at fault because he was not wearing the seat belt or safety restraints that went across the bed in the sleeper berth. As a result, he could recover only 50 percent of his loss.

Comparative negligence may take two forms: ordinary and pure. In an *ordinary comparative negligence* jurisdiction, the plaintiff may recover only if he or she is less culpable than the defendant. Thus, if the plaintiff is found 51 percent negligent and the defendant 49 percent negligent, the plaintiff cannot recover. In a *pure comparative negligence* state, the plaintiff may recover for any amount of the defendant's negligence, even if the plaintiff was the more negligent party. For example, if the plaintiff was 80 percent negligent and the defendant was 20 percent negligent, the plaintiff may recover 20 percent of his or her loss.

Assumption of Risk

The *assumption of risk* defense requires that the plaintiff (1) knew the risk was present and understood its nature and (2) voluntarily chose to incur the risk. It applies when the plaintiff, in advance of the defendant's wrongdoing, expressly or impliedly consented to take the chance of injury from the defendant's actions. Such consent, like consent to an intentional tort, relieves the defendant of any liability. For example, the plaintiff assumes the risk if he or she, knowing that a car has faulty brakes, consents to take the chance of injury by riding in the car, or if he or she voluntarily chooses to walk where the defendant has negligently scattered broken glass.

Sometimes courts use duty to determine the viability of the assumption of risk defense. In *Mosca v. Lichtenwalter,*[57] a man who went ocean fishing and was accidentally struck in the eye by the sinker of another man's fishing pole sued the other fisherman for negligence. The California Court of Appeal found that the injury arose from a risk inherent in the activity of sport fishing and that imposing a duty on the other fisherman would alter the fundamental nature of the sport.

Similarly, a Boston court dismissed a lawsuit brought by a Red Sox baseball fan who was hit by a fly ball. There are limits, however, on the risk that plaintiffs assume. The New Jersey Supreme Court held that the general rule that baseball fans agree to assume a risk of injury from a foul ball or thrown bat applied when the injury occurs in the stands, but did not extend to other areas, including concourses or mezzanine areas. As a result, it found that a ballpark patron hit by a foul ball while buying a beer from a vending cart on the mezzanine could sue the park owner for negligence.[58] Similarly, a New York court held that a college baseball player could sue her coach and university for injuries she incurred when her coach struck her in the face with a bat while demonstrating batting techniques. The court held it was not foreseeable that a coach with years of experience would swing a bat without ensuring that the player was out of range.[59]

Statutory Defenses

In addition to common law privileges, there may also be statutory defenses. For example, the U.S. District Court for the Western District of Texas held that the immunity provision of the Communications Decency Act of 1996[60] barred a suit for negligence, gross negligence, fraud, and negligent misrepresentation brought against MySpace by the mother of a fourteen-year-old girl who was sexually assaulted by a man she met through the website.[61]

56. 19 Cal. Rptr. 3d 865 (Cal. Ct. App. 2004).

57. 68 Cal. Rptr. 2d 58 (Cal. Ct. App. 1997).

58. Maisonave v. Newark Bears Prof'l Baseball Club, 881 A.2d 700 (N.J. 2005).

59. Mark Fass, *Court Finds Exception to Assumed Risk Doctrine in Case of Student Hit by Bat-Swinging Coach,* N.Y. L.J., Jan. 11, 2008, *available at* http://www.law.com/jsp/article.jsp?id=1199786731062.

60. The Communications Decency Act of 1996, 47 U.S.C. § 230, states that "[n]o provider or user of an interactive computer service shall be treated as the publisher or speaker of any information provided by another content provider."

61. Doe v. MySpace, Inc., 474 F. Supp. 2d 843 (W.D. Tex. 2007).

ECONOMIC LOSS RULE

In many states, the *economic loss rule* bars a plaintiff who is in privity of contract with the defendant or who has entered into a commercial transaction involving the defendant from bringing a lawsuit for negligence based solely on economic losses (as distinct from damages resulting from personal injury or property damage). As explained more fully in *Banknorth NA v. BJ's Wholesale Club, Inc.* (Case 9.5), the theory is that parties who could have bargained for contractual protections, such as an express warranty, should be relegated to the remedies available under commercial law and not afforded tort remedies designed for accidents that cause property damage or personal injury.

LIABILITY OF ACCOUNTANTS AND OTHER PROFESSIONALS TO THIRD PARTIES

The liability of professionals to third parties varies depending upon the professional's degree of fault.

INTENTIONAL MISREPRESENTATION

If an accountant, attorney, or other professional commits fraud, he or she is liable not only to the client, but also to any other person whom the accountant (or other professional) reasonably should have foreseen would rely upon the intentional misrepresentation. For example, suppose that an auditor issued an audit opinion to a company's board of directors stating that its financial statements were prepared in accordance with generally accepted accounting principles, even though the auditor knew that they contained material misstatements. In this case, the auditor could be sued for fraud by not only the company but also its shareholders. If the auditor knew that the company would be giving the audited financial statements to a bank, then the auditor could also be liable to the bank, if it relied upon the audit letter when extending credit.

NEGLIGENT MISREPRESENTATION

If the claim is for professional negligence, or *malpractice*, however, rather than for fraud, the class of parties eligible to sue is more limited. Clearly, a professional owes a duty of due care to the client, and the client can sue for malpractice if the professional fails to satisfy that duty. But a professional may not have a duty to a third party with whom he or she does not have a contractual relationship.

Accountants

Courts have developed three main approaches to the duty of care owed by a public accountant to third parties who rely on the accountant's reports. New York's "near privity" approach, which several states have followed, is the most restrictive. In New York, a plaintiff claiming negligent misrepresentation against an accountant with whom the plaintiff had no contractual relationship must establish three elements: (1) the accountant must have been aware that the reports would be used for a particular purpose, (2) a known party must have been intended to rely on the reports to further that purpose, and (3) there must be some conduct by the accountant "linking" him or her to that known party. This strict limitation on the class of potential plaintiffs represents a policy determination by the New York courts that accountants will not, merely by contracting with a particular client, expose themselves to liability to an indeterminate class in an indeterminate amount for an indeterminate time.[62]

The most liberal approach, which few jurisdictions have adopted, extends an accountant's liability to all persons whom the accountant should reasonably foresee might obtain and rely on the accountant's report. States adopting the foreseeability approach compare defective audits with defective products and refuse to insulate auditors with a privity requirement, when manufacturers of defective products are strictly liable regardless of their relationship with the end user.[63]

The majority view is set forth in Section 552 of the Restatement (Second) of Torts (1977):

> [A]n accountant's duty is limited to the client and third parties whom the accountant or client intends the information to benefit. The Restatement approach recognizes that an accountant's duty should extend beyond those in privity or near-privity with the accountant, but is not so expansive as to impose liability where the accountant knows only the possibility of distribution to anyone, and their subsequent reliance.

Attorneys

In the following case, the court considered a corporate lawyer's obligation to the investors and directors of a corporation he represented.

62. *See, e.g.*, White v. Guarantee, 372 N.E.2d 315 (N.Y. 1977).

63. ML–Lee Acquisition Fund, L.P. v. Deloitte & Touche, 463 S.E.2d 618 (S.C. Ct. App. 1995).

A CASE IN POINT

IN THE LANGUAGE OF THE COURT

CASE 9.2

CHEM-AGE INDUSTRIES, INC. v. GLOVER

SUPREME COURT OF SOUTH DAKOTA
652 N.W.2D 756 (S.D. 2002).

FACTS Alan Glover represented Byron Dahl, an entrepreneur, in a number of business transactions. At some point, Glover, acting on behalf of Dahl, approached Roger Pederson and Garry Shepard about investing in a start-up company called Chem-Age Industries. Pederson and Shepard agreed to invest in the company in exchange for stock and became members of the board of directors. Soon thereafter, both investors became suspicious when the credit cards in the company's name began to accrue large balances due to charges by Dahl for what appeared to be personal items. Pederson and Shepard asked Dahl and Glover about the charges and were informed that Chem-Age Industries was in negotiations with another company to be bought out and that the charges would be paid with the proceeds from that sale. During this meeting, Glover stated that he "represented Chem-Age Industries" and that Chem-Age was owned by Dahl. Shortly after this meeting, Chem-Age failed to pay its taxes and was dissolved entirely. Pederson and Shepard sued both Dahl and Glover for negligent misrepresentation and Glover for legal malpractice.

ISSUE PRESENTED Does a company's corporate counsel have a duty to the company's investors and directors such that the counsel can be held liable to them for legal malpractice?

OPINION KONENKAMP, J., writing for the Supreme Court of South Dakota:

To prevail in a legal malpractice claim, a plaintiff must prove: (1) the existence of an attorney–client relationship giving rise to a duty; (2) the attorney, either by an act or a failure to act, breached that duty; (3) the attorney's breach of duty proximately caused injury to the client; and (4) the client sustained actual damage. Whether an attorney–client relationship existed is ordinarily a question of fact. Here, we will examine the elements for an attorney–client relationship regarding, first, the corporation and, next, the individual plaintiffs.

. . . .

Dahl hired Glover to organize the business as a corporation. By his own admission, Glover's involvement with Dahl was directly related to that incorporation, notwithstanding Dahl's earlier engagement of Glover on personal matters before and independent of the events at issue here. . . . Glover contends nonetheless that he did not represent the corporation. This is clearly a question of material fact. In the absence of some indication otherwise, Glover can be deemed the attorney for the corporation, even if he was also representing Dahl personally. An attorney may represent both a corporation and individuals in the corporation. . . . If it is shown that he represented the corporation, then it follows that Glover had a duty to the client corporation.

. . . .

South Dakota recognizes that an attorney–client relationship may arise expressly or impliedly from the parties' conduct. Such a relationship is created when: (1) a person seeks advice or assistance from an attorney; (2) the advice or assistance sought pertains to matters within the attorney's professional competence; and (3) the attorney expressly or impliedly agrees to give or indeed gives the advice or assistance. . . . Here, the individual plaintiffs sought no advice from Glover. Correspondingly, Glover never agreed to advise or assist them. . . . Glover had no personal consultation with Pederson and Shepard in creating the corporation. [Therefore, although Glover did owe a duty to the corporation, and the corporation may in turn have owed the plaintiffs a duty, Glover did not directly owe them a duty as individual shareholders or directors of the corporation.]

. . . .

We earlier found that no attorney–client relationship existed between Glover and the two investor-directors, Pederson and Shepard. We now turn to the question whether Glover may have owed a fiduciary duty to them or to the corporation, even in the absence of an attorney–client relationship.

CONTINUED

To ascertain a fiduciary duty, we must find three things: (1) plaintiffs reposed "faith, confidence and trust" in Glover; (2) plaintiffs were in a position of "inequality, dependence, weakness, or lack of knowledge" and, (3) Glover exercised "dominion, control or influence" over plaintiffs' affairs.

. . . .

Plaintiffs Pederson and Shepard have submitted no evidence to show how they were in a confidential relationship with Glover, where they depended on him specifically to protect their investment interests and, where Glover exercised dominance and influence over their business affairs. On the contrary, they never consulted with Glover during the time he is alleged to have breached a fiduciary duty to them.

. . . .

Holding attorneys liable for aiding and abetting the breach of a fiduciary duty in rendering professional services poses both a hazard and a quandary for the legal profession. On the one hand, overbroad liability might diminish the quality of legal services, since it would impose "self protective reservations" in the attorney–client relationship. Attorneys acting in a professional capacity should be free to render advice without fear of personal liability to third persons if the advice later goes awry. On the other hand, the privilege of rendering professional services not being absolute, lawyers should not be free to substantially assist their clients in committing tortious acts. To protect lawyers from meritless claims, many courts strictly interpret the common law elements of aiding and abetting the breach of a fiduciary duty.

The substantial assistance requirement carries with it a condition that the lawyer must actively participate in the breach of a fiduciary duty. Merely acting as a scrivener for a client is insufficient. A plaintiff must show that the attorney defendant rendered "substantial assistance" to the breach of duty, not merely to the person committing the breach. In *Granewich,*[64] the lawyers facilitated the squeeze-out, not just by providing legal advice and drafting documents, but by sending letters containing misrepresentations and helping to amend by-laws eliminating voting requirements that protected the minority shareholder's interest.

Another condition to finding liability for assisting in the breach of a fiduciary duty is the requirement that the assistance be "knowing." Knowing participation in a fiduciary's breach of duty requires both knowledge of the fiduciary's status as a fiduciary and knowledge that the fiduciary's conduct contravenes a fiduciary duty.

Although Glover may not have taken any active role in defrauding the investor-directors and may not have owed any direct fiduciary duty to them, Dahl did owe such a duty, and a material question of fact exists on whether Glover substantially assisted Dahl in breaching that duty. It may be that Glover, as much as Pederson and Shepard, was duped by Dahl's conniving business dealings, but that is for a jury to decide.

RESULT Although Pederson and Shepard could not sue Glover for legal malpractice or breach of fiduciary duty, they could sue him for aiding and abetting a breach of fiduciary duty by Dahl. To prevail, they had to show that Glover was aware of Dahl's breach and substantially assisted him in breaching his duty.

COMMENTS In the wake of the collapse of Enron Corporation, WorldCom, and other firms, experts have disagreed over what should be the "gatekeeper" role of lawyers and auditors.[65] The subprime mortgage crisis of 2007–2008 may well bring the issue to the fore again. As explained in Chapter 3, the Sarbanes–Oxley Act requires corporate counsel to "report up-the-ladder" ongoing material violations of securities laws or breaches of fiduciary duty to the board of directors. The

CONTINUED

64. Granewich v. Harding, 985 P.2d 788 (Or. 1999).

65. John C. Coffee, Jr., *The Attorney as Gatekeeper: An Agenda for the SEC,* 103 COLUM. L. REV. 1293 (2003).

Securities and Exchange Commission has proposed a rule that would require the "noisy withdrawal" of an attorney if a public company persists in violating the federal securities laws.[66]

Critical Thinking Questions

1. Should corporate lawyers be liable to the shareholders for malpractice? Why or why not?
2. Should a corporate attorney who discovers a breach of fiduciary duty by an officer and director be required to disclose that breach to all of the other directors?

66. Implementation of Standards of Professional Conduct for Attorneys, Release No. 34-47276, 17 C.F.R. pt. 205 (2003).

In contrast, in 1995, the New Jersey Supreme Court held a property seller's attorney liable to the buyer for providing incomplete inspection reports in the course of a sale of land.[67] Although the attorney claimed that he had no duty to the purchaser and therefore could not be liable, the court disagreed. The court ruled that when an attorney knows or should know that a nonclient buyer will rely on his or her professional capacity, then the attorney owes a duty to the third party and may be liable for breaching that duty.

Investment Bankers

The issues surrounding attorney and auditor liability to third parties closely parallel those surrounding the liability of investment bankers who issue fairness opinions in leveraged buyouts. Should shareholders be able to sue the investment bankers directly for negligent misrepresentation? Do investment bankers owe shareholders a duty? The actual client of the investment banker is the board of directors of the target company. Nevertheless, some courts have upheld negligent misrepresentation actions by shareholders against investment bankers on a foreseeability basis.[68]

Negligent Hiring and Liability for Letters of Recommendation

Employers face potential liability for negligently hiring incompetent employees and for harm caused by former employees for whom the prior employer wrote a favorable letter of recommendation.

67. Petrillo v. Bachenberg, 655 A.2d 1354 (N.J. 1995).

68. For an excellent discussion of the potential liability of investment bankers to shareholders, see Bill Shaw & Edward J. Gac, *Fairness Opinions in Leveraged Buy Outs: Should Investment Bankers Be Directly Liable to Shareholders?*, 23 Sec. Reg. L.J. 293 (1995).

Negligent Hiring

An employer may be held liable even for the negligent or tortious conduct of employees acting outside the scope of employment if the employer breached its duty to use care in hiring competent employees. (As explained in Chapter 5 and further below, employers are always liable for torts committed by employees acting within the scope of their employment.) Under the theory of *negligent hiring,* the proximate cause of the plaintiff's injury is the employer's negligence in hiring the employee, rather than the employee's wrongful act. A plaintiff must prove that (1) the employer was required to make an investigation of the employee and failed to do so, (2) an investigation would have revealed the unsuitability of the employee for the job, and (3) it was unreasonable for the employer to hire the employee in light of the information the employer knew or should have known. In addition, the plaintiff must prove that (1) the employee was "unfit" for the employment position, (2) the employer knew or should have known that the employee was unfit for the position, and (3) the employee's particular unfitness proximately caused the plaintiff's injury.

In *Van Horne v. Evergreen Media Corp.,*[69] the Supreme Court of Illinois considered whether a radio station and its owner could be held liable for negligently hiring a disc jockey who allegedly made defamatory remarks during his radio show. The plaintiff argued that the defendants knew or should have known that the disc jockey was likely to make defamatory comments because of his prior outrageous conduct. The court rejected this argument, reasoning that the fact the disc jockey had engaged in offensive and outrageous conduct did not establish that he had a propensity to make false and defamatory statements. The court cautioned that adopting the defendant's argument as its holding would have a "chilling effect on free speech," as media employers would be reluctant to hire controversial broadcasters or reporters. The court declined, however, to decide whether First Amendment concerns would preclude all attempts to

69. 705 N.E.2d 898 (Ill. 1998), *cert. denied,* 528 U.S. 811 (1999).

state a cause of action for negligent hiring of media employees based on an employee's prior defamatory statement.

DUTY OF EMPLOYERS TO THIRD PARTIES BASED ON LETTERS OF RECOMMENDATION

In recent years, many employers have backed away from providing letters of recommendation, primarily because of the fear of lawsuits.[70] Employers have instead chosen to issue "no comment" or "name, rank, and serial number" reference letters largely because writing a substantive reference may put them in a "damned if you do, damned if you don't" legal conundrum. Employers who disclose "too much" negative information may be subject to a defamation suit by the former employee. Employers who disclose "too little" negative information may be held liable to injured third parties for negligent misrepresentation.[71] In an effort to respond to the problem, more than thirty states have enacted statutes offering some protection to employers who make recommendations in good faith.[72]

STRICT LIABILITY

Strict liability is liability without fault, that is, without either intent or negligence. Strict liability is imposed in two circumstances: (1) in product liability cases (the subject of Chapter 10) and (2) in cases involving abnormally dangerous, that is, ultrahazardous activities.

ULTRAHAZARDOUS ACTIVITIES

If the defendant's activity is ultrahazardous, the defendant is strictly liable for any injuries that result. An activity is *ultrahazardous* if it (1) necessarily involves a risk of serious harm to persons or property that cannot be eliminated by the exercise of utmost care and (2) is not a matter of common usage.

Courts have found the following activities ultrahazardous: (1) storing flammable liquids in quantity in an urban area, (2) pile driving, (3) blasting, (4) crop dusting, (5) fumigating with cyanide gas, (6) constructing a roof so as to shed snow onto a highway, (7) emitting of noxious fumes by a manufacturing plant located in a settled area, (8) locating oil wells or refineries in populated communities, (9) test-firing solid-fuel rocket motors, and (10) keeping wild animals.

In contrast, courts have considered parachuting, drunk driving, maintaining power lines, and letting water escape from an irrigation ditch not to be ultrahazardous. Similarly, discharging fireworks is not ultrahazardous, because the risk of serious harm could be eliminated by proper manufacture. In most jurisdictions, liability does not attach until a court determines that the dangerous activity is inappropriate to the particular location.

Under strict liability, once the court determines that the activity is abnormally dangerous, it is irrelevant that the defendant observed a high standard of care. For example, if the defendant's blasting injured the plaintiff, it is irrelevant that the defendant took every precaution available. Although evidence of such precautions might prevent the plaintiff from recovering under a theory of negligence, it does not affect strict liability. Evidence of due care would, however, prevent an award of punitive damages. Adequate liability insurance is particularly important for companies engaged in ultrahazardous activities.

RESPONDEAT SUPERIOR AND VICARIOUS LIABILITY

Under certain circumstances, a person can be held vicariously liable for the negligent, or in some cases the intentional, conduct of another.

RESPONDEAT SUPERIOR

Under the doctrine of *respondeat superior*—"let the master answer"—a "master" or employer is vicariously liable for the torts of the "servant" or employee if the employee was acting within the scope of his or her employment. The doctrine of *respondeat superior* may also apply when the person is not paid, but acts on behalf of another out of friendship or loyalty, or as a volunteer.

Underlying the doctrine of *respondeat superior* is the policy of allocating the risk of doing business to those who stand to profit from the undertaking. Because the employer benefits from the business, it is deemed more appropriate

70. Note, *Addressing the Cloud over Employee References: A Survey of Recently Enacted State Legislation,* 39 WM. & MARY L. REV. 177 (1997).

71. *See, e.g.,* Randi W. v. Muroc Joint Unified Sch. Dist., 929 P.2d 582 (Cal. 1997) (finding liability). *But see* Richland Sch. Dist. v. Mabton Sch. Dist., 45 P.3d 580 (Wash. App. 2002) (finding that a former employer did not owe a school custodian's new employer a duty to disclose dismissal charges of child molestation, on the basis that it was not foreseeable that a person with the custodian's record of minor disciplinary problems and dismissal charges posed a foreseeable risk of physical harm).

72. For a clever way a prospective employer may be able to finesse this issue, see PIERRE MORNELL, HIRING SMART (1999). Dr. Mornell recommends that the prospective employer call the former employer at a time when the supervisor is unlikely to be in the office and leave a voice message asking the supervisor to return the call only if the supervisor considers the former employee to be an excellent candidate.

for the employer to bear the risk of loss than for the innocent customer or bystander to do so. The employer is in a better position to absorb such losses or to shift them, through liability insurance or price increases, to insurers and customers and, thus, to the community in general.

Liability for Torts Committed Within the Scope of Employment

An employer is directly liable for its own negligence in hiring or supervising an employee. In addition, the employer may be vicariously liable for an employee's wrongful acts, even though the employer had no knowledge of them and in no way directed them, if the acts were committed while the employee was acting within the scope of employment. To be within the scope of employment, activities must be closely connected to what the employee is employed to do or reasonably incidental to it. Whether an act was in the scope of employment is an issue for the jury to decide. (Scope of employment is discussed in greater detail in Chapter 5.)

Courts have held employers vicariously liable for an accident caused by an employee's negligence in driving while intoxicated, after drinking alcohol at a company function, on the grounds that the injury-producing event—the consumption of alcohol—occurred while the employee was acting within the scope of his employment by attending a company function.[73] For example, in *Dickinson v. Edwards,*[74] the Washington Supreme Court ruled that an employer hosting a banquet may be sued under *respondeat superior,* if the plaintiff establishes that (1) the employee consumed alcohol at a party hosted by the employer at which the employee's presence was requested or required by the employer, (2) the employee caused the accident while driving from the banquet, and (3) the proximate cause of the accident (the intoxication) occurred at the time the employee negligently consumed the alcohol. Because the banquet was beneficial to the employer, who required the employee's attendance, the employee negligently consumed the alcohol during the scope of his employment. The Rhode Island Supreme Court went so far as to find an employer responsible for workers' compensation benefits, when an employee got drunk at a Christmas party and fell from a third-floor window.[75]

If intentional conduct caused the plaintiff's injury, courts will look to the nexus, or connection, between the conduct and the employment. In general, an employer is liable for his or her employee's intentional torts, if the wrongful act in any way furthered the employer's purpose, however misguided the manner of furthering that purpose. Often intentional torts do not further the employer's business and are therefore outside the scope of employment. For example, one court found a security company not liable when one of its security guards raped a worker in a client's building, even though the guard used his position to create the circumstances for the rape.[76]

Employer Liability Based on the Aided-in-the-Agency Doctrine

Other courts will apply the *aided-in-the-agency doctrine* (discussed in Chapter 5) and look beyond the scope of employment to determine whether the employee exercised authority conferred by, or used assets provided by, the employer. Thus, one court held a county vicariously liable for battery, among other things, when one of its law enforcement officers stopped a woman, placed her in his patrol car, drove to an isolated place, and threatened to rape and murder her.[77]

In the following case, the Supreme Court of New Jersey considered whether an employer could be vicariously liable for intentional torts outside the scope of employment that resulted from acts within the scope of employment.

73. *See, e.g.,* Chastain v. Litton Sys., Inc., 694 F.2d 957 (4th Cir. 1982), *cert. denied,* 462 U.S. 1006 (1983); Wong-Leong v. Hawaiian Indep. Refinery, 879 P.2d 538 (Haw. 1994).

74. 716 P.2d 814 (Wash. 1986).

75. Beauchesne v. David London & Co., 375 A.2d 920 (R.I. 1977).

76. Rabon v. Guardsmark, Inc., 571 F.2d 1277 (4th Cir. 1978), *cert. denied,* 439 U.S. 866 (1978).

77. White v. County of Orange, 212 Cal. Rptr. 493 (Cal. Ct. App. 1985).

A CASE IN POINT

IN THE LANGUAGE OF THE COURT

CASE 9.3

HARDWICKE V. AMERICAN BOYCHOIR SCHOOL

SUPREME COURT OF NEW JERSEY 902 A.2D 900 (N.J. 2006).

FACTS During the 1960s and 1970s, approximately fifty young boys (grades five through eight), including John Hardwicke, attended the American Boychoir School located in a fifty-room Princeton mansion and adjacent buildings. The boys, who were full-time boarders and members of the touring choir, lived in the mansion and were supervised by faculty and staff who also resided there. The principal administrators of the School were the Headmaster and the Music Director.

From October 1970 through April 1971, Hanson, the Music Director of the School, sexually abused Hardwicke on an almost daily basis and sometimes several times a day. Many years later, Hardwicke

CONTINUED

filed claims against the School on theories of vicarious liability through application of the doctrine of *respondeat superior.* The trial court granted summary judgment in favor of the School. The court of appeals reversed in part and affirmed in part, finding that the New Jersey Charitable Immunity Act did not bar Hardwicke's claims against the School based on vicarious liability for Hanson's intentional acts. The School appealed.

ISSUE PRESENTED Can an employer be held vicariously liable for an employee's sexual assault on a minor based on the doctrine of *respondeat superior?*

OPINION PORITZ, C.J., writing for the Supreme Court of New Jersey:

The School asserts . . . that plaintiff's common-law claims against it must fail because the School cannot be held vicariously liable for the intentional acts of its employees. Plaintiff . . . responds that modern principles of agency law permit his vicarious liability claims. Under section 219 of the *Restatement* [*(Second) of Agency* (1958)], an employer is not liable for the torts of an employee acting outside the scope of the employment unless "the conduct violated a non-delegable duty of the [employer], or . . . the [employee] purported to act . . . on behalf of the [employer] and there was reliance upon apparent authority, or [the employee] was aided in accomplishing the tort by the existence of the agency relation."

In *Lehmann* [*v. Toys "R" Us, Inc.*[78]], we adopted section 219 as the framework for evaluating employer liability in hostile environment sexual harassment claims. . . . We explained that an employer could be held vicariously liable . . . even when the employee was acting outside the scope of his or her employment "if an employer [had] delegate[d] the authority to control the work environment to a supervisor and [the] supervisor abuse[d] [the] delegated authority." That inquiry, we stated, requires the fact-finder to determine that: (1) the employer gave the authority to the supervisor to control the situation about which the plaintiff complains; (2) the supervisor exercised that authority; (3) the exercise of authority resulted in a violation of the [applicable statute]; and (4) the authority delegated by the employer to the supervisor aided the supervisor in injuring the plaintiff.

. . . .

The considerations that informed our analyses in *Lehmann* . . . apply equally to claims predicated on facts indicating child abuse. . . . [T]he [New Jersey Child Sexual Abuse Act (CSAA)] recognizes the vulnerability of children and demonstrates a legislative intent to protect them from victimization. In our view, common-law claims based on child abuse are supported by the same compelling rationale. The CSAA imposes responsibility on those in the best position to know of the abuse and stop it; application of section 219 of the Restatement to plaintiff's common-law claims advances these goals.

RESULT The Supreme Court of New Jersey held that the plaintiff had stated a valid claim of vicarious liability against the School based on the aided-in-the-agency doctrine. The plaintiff was permitted to proceed with his lawsuit.

CRITICAL THINKING QUESTIONS

1. What, if anything, could the School have done to avoid liability for the Music Director's sexual assault?
2. Based on the New Jersey Supreme Court's reasoning in *Hardwicke,* would the owner of an appliance store be liable if one of its repairmen raped a customer while in her house for a service call?

78. 626 A.2d 445 (N.J. 1993).

VICARIOUS LIABILITY

Under certain circumstances, an employer may be vicariously, or indirectly, liable for harm caused by an employee even when the employee was not acting within the scope of employment and did not exercise authority conferred by, or use assets provided by, the employer. Courts are most likely to impose vicarious liability when the employer took an action (or failed to act) and thereby increased the likelihood that an employee would commit a tort.

For example, the employer may be responsible for the safe passage home of an employee who was not intoxicated, but was tired from working too many consecutive hours. In *Robertson v. LeMaster,*[79] LeMaster was an employee of the Norfolk and Western Railway Company. He was doing heavy manual labor, including lifting railroad ties and shoveling coal. After thirteen hours at work, he told his supervisor that he was tired and wanted to go home. The supervisor told him to continue working. This happened several times, until finally LeMaster said that he could no longer work because he was too tired. His supervisor told him that if he would not work, he should get his bucket and go home. LeMaster had been at work a total of twenty-seven consecutive hours. On his way home, he fell asleep at the wheel and was involved in an accident, causing injuries to Robertson. Robertson sued the railroad.

The Supreme Court of Appeals of West Virginia concluded that requiring LeMaster to work such long hours and then setting him loose on the highway in an obviously exhausted condition was sufficient to sustain a claim against the railroad. The court found that the issue in this case was not whether the railway failed to control LeMaster while he was driving on the highway, but rather whether the railroad's conduct prior to the accident created a foreseeable risk of harm. The court concluded that the railway's actions created such a foreseeable risk.

Courts are split on whether to impose liability on an employer who sends home an intoxicated employee who injures a third party en route. In *Otis Engineering Corp. v. Clark,*[80] a supervisor at Otis Engineering sent an employee home because he was drunk. The employee had a history of drinking at work and was intoxicated on the evening in question. Unfortunately, the employee was involved in a fatal automobile accident on his way home from work—the employee was killed as were two women traveling in another automobile. The husbands of the two women brought a wrongful death action against Otis. Historically, employers were not responsible for accidents caused by employees traveling to and from work. The Texas Supreme Court broke new ground and held that the corporation had a duty to prevent the intoxicated employee from causing an unreasonable risk of harm to others. The court explained that "changing social conditions [have] led constantly to the recognition of new duties. . . . [T]he courts will find a duty where, in general reasonable men would recognize it and agree that it exists."

Prior to *Otis,* no case in Texas had established a duty for employers in such a situation, making employers like Otis oblivious to the possibility that they might be held to such a standard. *Otis* proves that the law can be changed, in a sense retroactively, to hold parties to a higher standard than they might have previously expected. Because courts and lawmakers generally push the law toward higher standards, rather than lower ones, managers should make sure that they constantly reach for higher, more ethical standards.

The Arizona Court of Appeals reached a different conclusion on similar facts in *Riddle v. Arizona Oncology Services.*[81] In *Riddle,* an Arizona Oncology Services (AOS) supervisor sent an employee home because she was high on cocaine. The employee had a history of drug abuse and had consumed cocaine while at work on the date in question. On her way home, the employee drove her vehicle across the centerline and collided with Steven Riddle's vehicle, seriously injuring Riddle. Riddle brought a personal-injury action against AOS. The Arizona Court of Appeals expressly declined to follow the Texas Supreme Court's decision in *Otis* and held that AOS had no duty to protect a third party from injury allegedly caused by the employee.

Faced with these conflicting decisions, the Tennessee Court of Appeals addressed this issue in the following case.

79. 301 S.E.2d 563 (W. Va. 1983).

80. 668 S.W.2d 307 (Tex. 1983).

81. 924 P.2d 468 (Ariz. Ct. App. 1996).

A CASE IN POINT

CASE 9.4

Lett v. Collis Foods, Inc.

Tennessee Court of Appeals
605 S.W.3d 95
(Tenn. Ct. App. 2001).

SUMMARY

FACTS Lynda Mills, who was employed by Collis Foods as a Waffle House server, arrived at work intoxicated. After attempts to sober her up failed, she was ordered to clock out. She refused a ride home and attempted to drive herself. On the way home, she seriously injured JoAnne Lett in an accident. Lett filed a suit against Collis Foods. The trial court granted the defendant's motion for summary judgment, and Lett appealed.

CONTINUED

ISSUE PRESENTED Is an employer liable for negligence if an intoxicated employee ordered to leave the employer's premises causes an automobile accident en route to home?

SUMMARY OF OPINION The Tennessee Court of Appeals, citing both *Riddle* and the dissenting opinion in *Otis,* ruled that Collis Foods was not under a duty to prevent its off-duty employees from harming third parties. The court noted that Tennessee has adopted the Restatement (Second) of Torts (1965), which provides:

> There is no duty so to control the conduct of a third person as to prevent him from causing physical harm to another unless
>
> (a) *a special relation exists between the actor and the third person which imposes a duty upon the actor to control the third person's conduct, or*
>
> (b) a special relation exists between the actor and the other which gives to the other a right to protection. (Emphasis added.)

However, there is no "special relation" such as to impose liability on a defendant to control a third person's conduct, unless the defendant has the means and ability to control the third party's conduct.

Although Lett argued that the court should follow the *Otis* decision, the court was persuaded by the *Otis* dissent, which argued that there are only two situations in which an employer has a duty to exercise control over an off-duty employee: (1) when the employee is on the employer's premises or using the employer's chattel, and (2) when an employer takes control of an employee likely to cause harm. The Tennessee court concluded:

> We find that the facts of the instant case . . . do not present affirmative acts sufficient to impose a duty upon [the defendant] to control the conduct of Mills, who was off-premises and off-duty as well. She arrived at work intoxicated, and [the defendant] did not contribute to, condone, or seek to accommodate, her intoxication. It did not require her to drive home; in fact, it attempted to find her safe passage home, but she refused. In sum, the employer did not provide her mobility she otherwise did not have; it did not encourage her to drive home; and it did not contribute to the condition that made it unsafe for her to drive. In effect, the employer "did no more than acquiesce in [her] determination to drive [her] own car."

RESULT The court affirmed the trial court's summary judgment in favor of the defendant, holding that Collis Foods was not liable to the plaintiff for its employee's negligence. Her suit against Collis Foods was dismissed.

CRITICAL THINKING QUESTIONS

1. The court of appeals noted that the Waffle House assistant manager and manager disagreed on how to deal with the situation. The assistant manager wanted to keep Mills at the restaurant, but the manager instructed her to clock Mills out, saying that if she did not, "we will get sued." Faced with this situation, what would you have done?
2. Although the employer was not held liable for Mills's accident, was it ethical for the manager to allow an intoxicated employee to drive herself home?

SUCCESSOR LIABILITY

As explained further in Chapter 10, under the doctrine of *successor liability,* individuals or entities that purchase a business may be held liable for product defects and certain other tortious acts of the previous owner. For example, if a company buys the assets of a ladder manufacturer and continues in the same line of business, the acquiring company may be liable for defective ladders manufactured and sold before the acquisition.

DAMAGES

Tort damages generally attempt to restore the plaintiff to the same position he or she was in before the tort occurred. (In contrast, contract damages try to place the plaintiff in the position he or she would have been in had the contract been performed, as explained in Chapter 7.) Tort damages may include punitive as well as compensatory damages.

ACTUAL (OR COMPENSATORY) DAMAGES

Actual damages, also known as *compensatory damages,* measure the cost to repair or replace an item or the decrease in market value caused by the tortious conduct. Actual damages may also include compensation for medical expenses, lost wages, and pain and suffering.

PUNITIVE DAMAGES

Punitive damages, also known as *exemplary damages,* may be awarded to punish the defendant and deter others from engaging in similar conduct. Punitive damages are awarded only in cases of outrageous misconduct.

The amount of punitive damages may properly be based on the defendant's degree of culpability and wealth. But, as discussed in Chapter 4, the U.S. Supreme Court has indicated that, except in egregious cases, the ratio of punitive damages to actual damages should be "in the single digits."[82]

Some statutes have been held to expressly or impliedly preclude the recovery of punitive damages.[83] Several states have limited punitive damages awards to situations in which the plaintiff can prove by clear and convincing evidence that the defendant was guilty of oppression, fraud, or malice. Nevertheless, as discussed in the "Political Perspective," business leaders continue to call for legislative reform to cap or eliminate punitive damages as part of more general tort reform. Indeed, the head of the American Manufacturers Association declared, "[Trial lawyers are] the pariahs of the business community, which is more frightened by them than terrorists, China, or high energy prices."[84]

The desire to curb punitive damages seems, however, to be largely limited to product liability cases, where businesses are defendants but rarely plaintiffs. In other areas, where

82. State Farm Mut. Auto. Ins. Co. v. Campbell, 538 U.S. 408 (2003).

83. A jury awarded $507 million in compensatory and $5 billion in punitive damages to more than 32,000 fishermen and other workers whose livelihoods were damaged or destroyed by the Exxon Valdez oil spill in Alaska in 1989. The U.S. Court of Appeals for the Ninth Circuit upheld the award of punitive damages but reduced the amount to $2.5 billion. Exxon appealed to the U.S. Supreme Court, arguing that the Clean Water Act and maritime laws did not allow for punitive damages and that, even if they did, the $2.5 billion award was excessive. The Supreme Court split, four-to-four, over whether the statutes allowed for punitive damages, which had the effect of upholding the Ninth Circuit's ruling that punitive damages were available. However, the Court reduced the punitive damages award to $507 million—one-tenth of the original jury's award. Exxon Shipping Co. v. Baker, 128 S. Ct. 2408 (2008).

84. Richard A. Oppel Jr. & Glen Justice, *The 2004 Election: The Response: Kerry Gains Campaign Ace, Risking Anti-Lawyer Anger,* N.Y. TIMES, July 7, 2004, *available at* http://query.nytimes.com/gst/fullpage.html?res=9901E1D9143BF934A35754C0A9629C8B63.

Political PERSPECTIVE

The Attack on Tort Law

For years, critics and supporters of the U.S. tort system have advanced largely unchanged arguments about the perceived need for tort reform.[a] The topic became an election-year issue in 2004, when Vice President Dick Cheney called on challenger, Senator John Edwards, to defend his record as a trial lawyer and his approach to tort reform in the vice presidential debate.

Critics assert that the tort system has a random, Russian roulette flavor to it. To buttress this claim, they point to several cases where juries granted multimillion-dollar punitive damages awards to injured plaintiffs. These well-publicized horror stories include a $2.9 million award to an elderly woman, Stella Liebeck, who received third-degree burns after spilling McDonald's coffee on her lap;[b] a $4 million award against BMW for selling as new a car that had been damaged by acid rain and repainted;[c] and a $150 million award against General Motors in a case where the plaintiff who was injured in a single-car accident had admittedly consumed at least one beer and was not wearing a seat belt.[d]

The critics argue that large and unpredictable jury awards have resulted in sharply higher liability insurance

CONTINUED

rates, which in turn may (1) increase the cost of vital products and services, (2) stifle innovation in valuable but potentially dangerous products, and (3) render U.S. firms less equipped to compete with rivals abroad. Moreover, they claim that attorneys' fees and administrative costs are so extensive, that less than half of the amount awarded by verdict or settlement is paid to the injured plaintiffs.

Supporters of the present tort system respond that it is the one place where the average citizen can battle the powerful on nearly equal terms. They claim that without the threat of lawsuits and their accompanying discovery process, large corporations would have every incentive to conceal harmful information about the effects of their products. The supporters believe that if any reform of the system is necessary, judicial review and self-policing would be more effective tools than legislation at either the state or federal level.[e]

Statistical studies claim to show a connection between so-called frivolous lawsuits and the impediment of economic growth in the area. For example, in 2002, the U.S. Chamber of Commerce singled out Mississippi as the "jackpot justice" state where tort lawyers were running amok and businesses were leaving in droves.[f] The basic premise, as it has played out in Mississippi, is that jurors assume they can force big business to be more responsible by awarding large settlements against businesses in favor of the ordinary person. In 2004, Mississippi enacted comprehensive tort reform that, among other things, capped noneconomic actual damages in medical malpractice actions at $500,000; capped noneconomic actual damages in nonmedical malpractice cases at $1 million; capped punitive damages based on the defendant's net worth; abolished joint and several liability; immunized innocent sellers from strict liability for defective products; and changed premises liability to provide immunity to premises owners for death or injury to contractors or their employees, if the contractor knew or should have known of the danger.[g] Although the American Tort Reform Association claimed that these reforms were responsible for new investments in the state,[h] a 2007 study by the U.S. Chamber Institute for Legal Reform found that U.S. businesses still ranked Mississippi's tort liability system forty-ninth in terms of its reasonableness and balance.[i]

Other studies contradict claims of a "litigation explosion." A report issued by the U.S. Department of Justice's Bureau of Justice Statistics shows that the number of tort cases resolved in U.S. district courts fell 79 percent between 1985 and 2003. In the fiscal years of 2002 and 2003, 98 percent of personal-injury cases were resolved by mediation, settled out of court, or handled in some nontrial disposition. Only 2 percent of the actions filed required trials to be resolved.[j] Furthermore, according to the U.S. Department of Justice, the amount of damages awarded in tort cases is declining. The median inflation-adjusted payout in all tort (personal-injury) cases dropped 56.3 percent between 1992 and 2001, to $28,000.[k]

In addition, punitive damages awards are both extremely rare and are usually closely related to the size of compensatory damages. In 2001, juries awarded punitive damages in only 5.3 percent of the tort cases won by plaintiffs, and the median inflation-adjusted award in these cases was only $25,000.[l] Of course, fear of large punitive damages awards may cause businesses to settle cases for larger amounts than they would otherwise have agreed to pay. Large awards make headlines, but when they are reduced on appeal, as often happens, the reduction receives much less attention. Even the $2.9 million award in the notorious McDonald's coffee case, for example, was reduced to $400,000.[m] The 2003 U.S. Supreme Court decision in *State Farm Mutual Automobile Insurance Co. v. Campbell*,[n] which held that "few awards exceeding a single-digit ratio between punitive and compensatory damages . . . will satisfy due process," has also resulted in reductions in the size of punitive damages awards on appeal.

Although efforts to enact broad federal legislation to limit tort damages have been unsuccessful, President George W. Bush stunned plaintiffs' lawyers with the enactment of the Class Action Fairness Act of 2005, which moves many class actions from state courts into federal courts, thereby limiting the scope of such actions and the ability of plaintiffs to forum shop for the friendliest jurisdiction. Also during President Bush's term, federal agencies have begun inserting clauses in rules that expressly preempt tort actions under state laws against businesses that have complied with the agency's regulations or argued for implicit preemption.[o] As an example, the Food and Drug Administration (FDA), which was against implicit preemption before the Bush administration, made a historic shift and began arguing in favor of implicit preemption. As explained in Chapter 10, the U.S. Supreme Court ruled in 2008 that a medical device manufacturer that sold a device approved by the FDA after a full premarket review was immune from state-law product liability claims.[p]

In 2004, California voters approved Proposition 64, a ballot initiative that required plaintiffs to prove they were injured by an alleged violation of the state's unfair competition law in order to participate in class-action litigation. This victory triggered a movement by tort reform groups and lawyers representing some of the nation's largest corporations to enact similar legislation

CONTINUED

in other states. As part of these efforts, tort reformers have drafted model legislation that would require consumers to have suffered economic losses or injury from a company's misstatements in order to file a class action. Plaintiffs' lawyers argue that requiring reliance and actual injury will present major roadblocks to future consumer litigation. "The idea that a reliance requirement be injected into consumer protection statutes is a horrible idea," according to Todd Heyman, a partner at Shapiro Haber & Urmy who sued Philip Morris over "light" cigarettes in Massachusetts. He argues that such a requirement will, in effect, constitute a "free pass" for companies to make false statements about their products without being held accountable.[q]

More recently, the American Justice Partnership (AJP), launched in January 2005 by the National Association of Manufacturers, has been encouraging businesses to push for tort reform through the courts, by targeting rules of law they believe keep useful information from juries. The issues list may expand, but the AJP has targeted collateral source rules, which bar the jury from learning that the plaintiff received compensation from sources other than the defendant and from reducing damages awards based on that information; rules barring jurors from learning the impact of joint and several liability; rules preventing jurors from considering a plaintiff's failure to wear a seat belt in automobile accident cases and lowering damages or finding contributory negligence as a result; bans on allowing jurors to consider that a plaintiff was under the influence of drugs or alcohol, speeding, or asleep at the wheel in product defect cases; and bars on disclosing to jurors hearing toxic tort cases that the plaintiff was exposed to the hazardous materials from sources other than the defendant (including other defendants with whom the plaintiff has previously settled). As one critic of the tort reform movement, Richard W. Wright, a professor at the Chicago-Kent College of Law, noted: "[Proponents of tort reform are] frustrated that their arguments are not seen as valid by legislatures and courts. So now they're going after juries. They're asking courts to 'let juries hear this,' but they're really saying, 'Let's let juries change common law.' "[r]

a. *See, e.g.,* George Melloan, *Rule of Law or Rule of Lawyers?,* Wall St. J., Nov. 21, 2000, at A27.
b. Andrea Gerlin, *A Matter of Degree: How a Jury Decided That a Coffee Spill Is Worth $2.9 Million,* Wall St. J., Sept. 1, 1994, at A1.
c. The Alabama Supreme Court subsequently reduced this award to $2 million. BMW of North Am., Inc. v. Gore, 646 So. 2d 619 (Ala. 1994). The U.S. Supreme Court then declared the $2 million award void as "grossly excessive" and unconstitutional. BMW of North Am., Inc. v. Gore, 517 U.S. 559 (1996). On remand, the Alabama Supreme Court further reduced the award to $50,000. BMW of North Am., Inc. v. Gore, 701 So. 2d 507 (Ala. 1997).
d. Eric Peters, *Captious Spin on the Wheel of Misfortune,* Wash. Post, June 10, 1996, at A17.
e. Philip Shuchman, *It Isn't That the Tort Lawyers Are So Right, It's Just That the Tort Reformers Are So Wrong,* 49 Rutgers L. Rev. 485 (1995).
f. Todd Buchholz, *The High Cost of "Jackpot Justice,"* Wall St. J., July 8, 2002, at A23.
g. Wells Marble & Hurst, PLLC, *Mississippi Tort Reform in 2004, available at* http://www.wellsmar.com/CM/NewsandArticles/NewsandArticles33.asp.
h. American Tort Reform Ass'n, *How Tort Reform Works, available at* http://www.atra.org/wrap/files.cgi/7964_howworks.html.
i. Lawsuit Climate 2007: Rating the States, 2007 U.S. Chamber of Commerce State Liability Systems Ranking Study, *available at* http://instituteforlegalreform.com/lawsuitclimate2007/index.cfm.
j. U.S. Dep't of Justice, Federal Tort Filings Down, *available at* http://www.atla.org/pressroom/research/bjs2005.aspx.
k. Thomas H. Cohen & Steven K. Smith, *Civil Trial Cases and Verdicts in Large Counties, 2001,* Bureau of Justice Statistics, U.S. Dep't of Justice, Apr. 2004, *available at* http://www.ojp.gov/bjs/pub/pdf/ctcvlc01.pdf.
l. Ctr. for Justice and Democracy, *Mythbuster: Punitive Damages: Rare, Reasonable, Effective,* http://www.centerjd.org/MB_2007punitive.htm.
m. Gerlin, *supra* note b.
n. 538 U.S. 408 (2003).
o. Terry Carter, *Case-by-Case Tort Reform,* 92 A.B.A. J., June 2006, at 46.
p. Riegel v. Medtronic, Inc., 128 S. Ct. 999 (2008) (Case 10.5). The courts are split on the issue of whether a pharmaceutical firm that provided the warning label required by the FDA is immune from a state law failure-to-warn claim. *Compare* Wyeth v. Levine, 2006 WL 3041078 (Vt. Oct. 27, 2006), *cert. granted,* 128 S. Ct. 1118 (2008) (finding no preemption) *with* Colacicco v. Apotex, Inc., 521 F. 3d 253 (3d Cir. 2008) (finding preemption when the FDA had publicly rejected the need for the warnings the plaintiffs claimed were required by state law).
q. Amanda Bronstad, *Tort Reform's Next Big Push,* Nat'l L.J., Sept. 7, 2006, *available at* http://www.law.com/jsp/law/LawArticleFriendly.jsp?id=1157462044386.
r. Carter, *supra* note o.

businesses tend to be plaintiffs as well as defendants (such as contracts, unfair competition, and misleading advertising), reform of punitive damages appears to be less of a priority.[85]

85. Richard B. Schmitt, *Why Businesses Sometimes Like Punitive Awards,* Wall St. J., Dec. 11, 1995, at B1.

Equitable Relief

If a monetary award cannot adequately compensate for the plaintiff's loss, courts may give *equitable relief.* For example, the court may issue an *injunction,* that is, a court order, to prohibit the defendant from continuing a certain course of activity. This remedy is particularly appropriate for torts such as trespass or nuisance, when the plaintiff does not want the defendant's conduct to continue. The court may also issue an injunction ordering the defendant to take certain action. For example, a newspaper could be ordered to publish a retraction. In determining whether to grant injunctive relief, the courts will balance the hardship to the defendant against the benefit to the plaintiff.

LIABILITY OF MULTIPLE DEFENDANTS

A plaintiff may name numerous defendants. In some cases, the defendants may ask the court to join, or add, other defendants. As a result, when a court determines liability and damages, it must grapple with the problem of allocating the damages among multiple defendants.

JOINT AND SEVERAL LIABILITY

Under the doctrine of *joint and several liability*, multiple defendants are jointly (that is, collectively) liable and also severally (that is, individually) liable. This means that once the court determines that multiple defendants are at fault, the plaintiff may collect the entire judgment from any one of them, regardless of the degree of that defendant's fault. Thus, it is possible that a defendant, who played a minor role in causing the plaintiff's injury, might have to pay all the damages. This is particularly likely when only one defendant is solvent, that is, when only one has money to pay the damages.

Many states have adopted statutes to limit the doctrine of joint and several liability for tort defendants. Most states that have abolished joint and several liability have moved to a contributory regime. For example, under a joint and several liability regime, a defendant can be liable for all of a plaintiff's damages, even if the defendant was only 1 percent responsible for causing the plaintiff's injuries. This would be the result if the other defendants (those 99 percent responsible for causing the injuries) lacked funds to pay the judgment. Under contributory rules, the same defendant would under no circumstances be liable for more than 1 percent of the total damages award.

CONTRIBUTION AND INDEMNIFICATION

The doctrines of contribution and indemnification can mitigate the harsh effects of joint and several liability. *Contribution* distributes the loss among several defendants by requiring each to pay its proportionate share to one defendant; by doing so, they discharge their joint liability. *Indemnification* allows a defendant to shift its individual loss to other defendants whose relative blame is greater. The other defendants can be ordered to reimburse the one that has discharged a joint liability. It is important to keep in mind, however, that the rights to contribution and indemnification are worthless to a defendant, if all the other defendants are insolvent or lack sufficient assets to contribute their share.

PRIVACY PROTECTION

In part because private tort action lawsuits alone have not been able to stop the avalanche of privacy violations that have occurred in recent years, state and federal governments have enacted a plethora of laws regulating the collection, transmission, storing, use, and disclosure of private data. Private rights of action based upon these statutes have been largely unsuccessful, however.[86] The major obstacles have been the lack of a private right of action under most federal privacy laws and inability to plead an acceptable basis for damages. As a result, enforcement of these statutes has, in large part, been relegated to state and federal enforcement agencies. In addition, as discussed in detail in Chapter 25, strict privacy protections in the European Union and elsewhere apply to U.S. firms doing business with residents of these other countries.

STATE LEGISLATION

The states have taken the lead in formulating consumer privacy policy in the United States. In 2000 alone, more than one hundred privacy bills were introduced in forty-one states.[87] The bills fell into three general categories: (1) bills to prohibit or limit the financial industry's use of account-related information, (2) bills to regulate the use of information collected by online service providers and websites, and (3) bills to prevent state agencies from selling information about people who do business with the state, including obtaining driver's licenses.[88] As noted in Chapter 4, Congress passed federal legislation banning the sale of driver's license information.

California has been particularly active. In 1999, California passed a law that limits the information that supermarkets

86. Note, however, that as of April 2008 more than 300 class actions have been filed under the federal Fair and Accurate Credit Transaction Act (FACTA), enacted in 2006, which includes a private right of action and makes it illegal to print on a receipt more than the last five digits of a credit card number or the card's expiration date. Tresa Baldes, *Landslide of Suits over Data on Receipts,* NAT'L L.J., Apr. 7, 2008, *available at* http://www.law.com/jsp/law/lawarticlefriendly.jsp?id=1207564980737.

87. Rachel Zimmerman & Glenn R. Simpson, *Lobbyists Swarm to Stop Tough Privacy Bills in States,* WALL ST. J., Apr. 21, 2000, at A16.

88. *Id.*

can demand from customers as a condition of signing up for grocery club discount cards. Supermarkets had been selling data about their customers' purchases of items such as liquor and tobacco to insurance companies.[89] In 2000, California created the first statewide Office of Privacy Protection in the nation, with the mission of promoting the privacy rights of California consumers.[90]

In 2004, California established an information security standard requiring businesses that own or license personal information about a California resident to implement and maintain "reasonable security measures" to protect that information; health-care providers, which are already regulated under the Health Insurance Portability and Accountability Act (HIPAA), discussed below, and other entities governed by the HIPAA privacy rules issued by the federal Department of Health and Human Services were excluded.[91] The statute defines "reasonable security measures" as "procedures and practices appropriate to the nature of the information to protect the personal information from unauthorized access, destruction, use, modification, or disclosure."[92] The law applies to any business, regardless of where it is located, that owns or licenses personal information about a California resident. For example, if a company based in Maine outsources warranties to a third party in New York, then the Maine company will have to determine how that third party uses information about its California customers and ensure that it has adequate security measures in place.[93] California also requires firms to notify customers if their personal identifying information is improperly disclosed to third parties.[94]

Opponents of states' efforts to protect consumers' privacy argue that the different states are creating a patchwork of conflicting rules, undermining efforts to enact federal legislation on privacy. But some consumer privacy advocates hope that enacting strong state privacy laws will put pressure on Congress to enact stronger federal privacy legislation.

FEDERAL TRADE COMMISSION ACTIONS

For several years, the Federal Trade Commission (FTC) has taken the position that it is an unfair or deceptive trade practice under Section 5(a) of the Federal Trade Commission Act[95] for firms to fail to honor their own privacy policies. In 2006, consumer data broker ChoicePoint, Inc. agreed to pay $10 million in civil penalties (the largest civil penalty in FTC history) and $5 million in consumer redress to settle FTC charges that its security and record-handling procedures violated consumers' privacy rights and federal laws. Among other things, the agency charged that ChoicePoint had violated the FTC Act by making false and misleading statements about its privacy policies, including statements in its published privacy principles, such as "ChoicePoint does not distribute information to the general public and monitors the use of its public record information to ensure appropriate use." The settlement also required ChoicePoint to implement an information security program and to obtain third-party security audits every other year for ten years. [96]

The FTC had warned firms in 2004 that a company's failure to protect sensitive consumer information could itself be an "unfair" practice, even if the company did not promise to keep its data secure.[97] The FTC stressed that security is an ongoing process, not a static checklist. Therefore, companies must remain proactive in data protection.

The FTC subsequently brought an action against BJ's Wholesale Club, claiming that the company's failure to protect its customers' information was an unfair practice, because it caused substantial injury that was not avoidable by the customers and that was not outweighed by offsetting benefits to customers or consumers. The FTC alleged that fraudulent purchases were made using counterfeit copies of credit and debit cards used at BJ's stores. In 2005, BJ's settled the FTC charges by agreeing to implement a comprehensive security program and to obtain third-party security audits every other year for twenty years.[98]

After the fraud was discovered, banks canceled and reissued thousands of credit cards, and consumers experienced inconvenience, worry, and time loss. As a result, a number of banks filed tort lawsuits against BJ's. In the following case, the court considered whether a bank could sue BJ's for negligence based on its failure to secure and protect the cardholder information, among other things.

89. Super Market Club Card Act, CAL. CIV. CODE § 1749.60 *et. seq.*

90. CAL. CIV. CODE § 1798.81.5, *available at* http://www.leginfo.ca.gov/cgi-bin/displaycode?section=civ&group=01001-02000&file=1798.80-1798.84.

91. California Assembly Bill 1950 (2004), *available at* http://info.sen.ca.gov/pub/03-04/bill/asm/ab_1901-1950/ab_1950_bill_20040929_chaptered.pdf.

92. *Id.*

93. *In 2004, California Again Leads States in Passage of Privacy-Related Legislation,* 9 ELECTRONIC COM. & L. REP. 843 (Oct. 13, 2004).

94. CAL. CIV. CODE §§ 1798.29, 1798.82, 1798.4.

95. See Appendix F, Federal Trade Commission Act of 1914 [Excerpts].

96. *See* Press Release, Fed. Trade Comm'n, ChoicePoint Settles Data Security Breach Charges (Jan. 26, 2006), *available at* http://www.ftc.gov/opa/2006/01/choicepoint.shtm.

97. *Lax Security Could Bring FTC Enforcement Under 'Unfair' Practices Section of FTC Act,* 72 U.S.L.W. 2744 (June 8, 2004).

98. Press Release, Fed. Trade Comm'n, BJ's Wholesale Club Settles FTC Charges (June 16, 2005), *available at* http://www.ftc.gov/opa/2005/06/bjswholesale.shtm.

A CASE IN POINT

CASE 9.5

BANKNORTH NA v. BJ'S WHOLESALE CLUB, INC.

UNITED STATES DISTRICT COURT FOR THE MIDDLE DISTRICT OF PENNSYLVANIA
442 F. SUPP. 2D 206 (M.D. PA. 2006).

IN THE LANGUAGE OF THE COURT

FACTS Banknorth is a national bank that issues debit cards, including Visa debit cards, to its customers. It is an "Issuing Bank" within the Visa system. BJ's, a retailer, accepts Visa cards for payment of goods and services and is a "Merchant" within the Visa system. Fifth Third is the "Acquiring Bank" for Visa. It helps BJ's fulfill Visa card payments from customers by providing authorization for credit card transactions, crediting BJ's account, and submitting transactions to Issuing Banks for settlement. Acquiring Banks and Merchants agree to abide by Visa Operating Regulations, which, among other things, prohibit Fifth Third from allowing BJ's to "disclose Visa account information, transaction information or other cardholder information to third parties," and require it to "properly secure and protect Visa cardholder information and magnetic stripe data from unauthorized disclosure or use."

Banknorth guarantees its customers under the "Visa Zero Liability Policy" that they will not be responsible for fraudulent purchases on their credit cards. Banknorth alleged that, as a result of the BJ's security breach, unauthorized third parties obtained the magnetic stripe information from Visa debit cards owned by Banknorth customers, and used the information for fraudulent purposes. As a result, Banknorth incurred the costs of canceling and reissuing Visa debt cards to its holders.

ISSUE PRESENTED Is a retailer liable to issuing banks for its negligent failure to adequately secure cardholder information?

OPINION CALDWELL, J., writing for the U.S. District Court for the Middle District of Pennsylvania:

In this lawsuit, Plaintiff is only seeking recovery of economic damages, the cost of reissuing debit cards and of paying for the unauthorized transactions. BJ's asserts that the economic loss rule bars the negligence claim.

The economic loss rule, adopted in many states, bars recovery in a negligence claim of economic damages alone. . . .

. . . .

Our job, as a federal court sitting in diversity, is to predict how Maine's highest court would decide this issue. In performing the task, "'we must consider relevant state precedents, analogous decisions, considered dicta, scholarly works, and any other reliable date [sic] tending convincingly to show how the highest court in the state would decide the issue at hand.'" After considering the parties' arguments, including those not specifically mentioned above, we conclude that Maine's highest court would apply the economic loss rule in the circumstances here to bar the negligence claim.

. . . .

We agree that the economic loss rule can be extended to service contracts. The rationale for doing so is set forth in *Fireman's Fund Ins. Co. v. SEC Donohue, Inc.*,[99] quoted in *Fireman's Fund Ins. Co. v. Childs*,[100] in the latter court's discussion of the unsettled nature of the economic loss rule in Maine:

> A provider of services and his client have an important interest in being able to establish the terms of their relationship prior to entering into a final agreement. The policy interest supporting the ability to comprehensively define a relationship in a service contract parallels the policy interest supporting the ability to comprehensively define a relationship in a contract for the sale of goods. It is appropriate, therefore, that [the economic loss doctrine] should apply to the service industry. Just as a seller's duties are defined by his contract with

CONTINUED

99. 679 N.E.2d 1197 (Ill. 1997).
100. 52 F. Supp. 2d 139 (D. Me 1999).

a buyer, the duties of a provider of services may be defined by the contract he enters into with his client. When this is the case, the economic loss doctrine applies to prevent the recovery of purely economic loss in tort.

. . . .

Having decided that Maine would extend the economic loss rule to service contracts, we are still only partway to applying it in this case because, as Plaintiff notes, a rejection of its contract claim means there is no privity of contract between it and BJ's. However, we agree with BJ's that privity is not a requirement . . . .

As cited by BJ's, in *Miller v. U.S. Steel*,[101] the Seventh Circuit held that privity of contract was not essential for the application of the economic loss rule to a negligence claim based upon a sale of defective steel, reasoning as follows:

> The insight behind the doctrine is that commercial disputes ought to be resolved according to the principles of commercial law rather than according to tort principles designed for accidents that cause personal injury or property damage. A disputant should not be permitted to opt out of commercial law by refusing to avail himself of the opportunities which that law gives him. Back when U.S. Steel was urging Mr. Miller to specify Cor-Ten steel for the walls of his building, he could have asked U.S. Steel for an express warranty, which he could then have enforced in a suit for breach of warranty. . . . Alternatively, Miller could have extracted (again for all we know, did extract) suitable warranties from the general contractor, which might in turn have extracted a warranty from U.S. Steel.

As BJ's argues, just as the plaintiff in *Miller* could have obtained protection from the supplier of the steel or from the general contractor on the building, Banknorth could have bargained for allocating the risk of fraudulent transactions with Visa before signing its Visa contract.

RESULT The district court granted BJ's motion for summary judgment and dismissed Banknorth's negligence claim.

COMMENTS This case highlights the difficulty many plaintiffs, who have suffered only economic damages, have had in establishing actionable damages claims in suits related to theft or misuse of personal data.

CRITICAL THINKING QUESTIONS

1. Should the economic loss rule bar a negligence claim where, as here, the plaintiff has no contract with the defendant and therefore no contract claim that it can assert?
2. Could Banknorth have successfully argued that it was entitled to recover its economic damages under the promissory estoppel doctrine?

101. 902 F.2d 573 (7th Cir. 1990).

In June 2005, the Disposal Rule, promulgated by the FTC pursuant to the Fair and Accurate Credit Transaction Act of 2003,[102] became effective. The *Disposal Rule* applies to individuals and organizations of any size that obtain information from consumer reporting agencies, including resellers of consumer reports, lenders, insurers, employers, landlords, government agencies, mortgage brokers, car dealers, and individuals who obtain consumer reports on prospective domestic or home employees. The rule requires these recipients of consumer information to take "reasonable measures to protect against unauthorized access to or use of [sensitive consumer] information in connection with its disposal."[103] It calls for data destruction policies commensurate with the sensitivity of the data, the size of the business, the costs and benefits of different disposal methods, and relevant technological changes.

102. 16 C.F.R. pt. 682 (2005).

103. *Id.*

FINANCIAL INFORMATION: GRAMM-LEACH-BLILEY ACT

In 1999, Congress enacted the Gramm-Leach-Bliley Financial Modernization Act of 1999,[104] which requires financial institutions to provide privacy protections to consumers. The law applies to banks, debt collectors, credit counselors, retailers, and travel agencies. Financial institutions must give notice to their customers before sharing personal information with other entities. Financial institutions must also disclose their privacy policy annually and give customers the right to opt out of disclosures to third parties. The Gramm-Leach-Bliley Act does not preempt states from implementing stricter privacy regulations, and a number of states have enacted or introduced their own financial privacy legislation.[105]

The FTC and seven other financial regulatory agencies (including the Federal Deposit Insurance Corporation, the Federal Reserve Board, and the Securities and Exchange Commission) have issued regulations that implement the privacy protections provided by the statute. The government has attempted to force businesses to better safeguard consumers' information through the Safeguard Rule contained in the Gramm-Leach-Bliley Act.

The *Safeguard Rule* requires financial services firms to (1) promulgate a written information security plan, (2) designate at least one employee to coordinate the plan, (3) identify and assess the risks to customer financial information, and (4) evaluate the safeguards for controlling these risks. To come within the Safeguard Rule, the firm must also (1) regularly monitor and test the plan, (2) select appropriate service providers and contract with them to implement the safeguards, and (3) evaluate and adjust the plan as material circumstances change. According to the FTC, its ultimate goal is to promote awareness among companies about the importance of protecting sensitive information, while allowing the companies to tailor a plan based on their size, scope, and level of sensitive information.[106] Although some companies have called for stricter guidelines for determining whether a particular plan satisfies the rule,[107] the FTC claims that its requirements are simple and straightforward.

MEDICAL INFORMATION: HIPAA

The U.S. Department of Health and Human Services has issued regulations, under the Health Insurance Portability and Accountability Act of 1996 (HIPAA), on maintaining the privacy of personal medical information.[108] At first blush, the regulations appear to apply only to health-care providers (such as doctors, hospitals, and nurses), group health plans (such as HMOs and self-insured plans that have fifty or more participants or are administered by an entity other than the employer that established and maintained the plan), and health-care clearinghouses that process claims. Upon a closer reading, it becomes clear that, in fact, almost all employers that provide health-care coverage to their employees are affected by the privacy regulations and required to develop privacy policies and procedures to safeguard protected health information.[109]

Protected health information includes any information relating to a person's health that (1) was created by a health-care provider, health plan, employer, or health-care clearinghouse; and (2) identifies the person to whom the health information relates. For example, if, as is usually the case, the employer acts as the plan sponsor, then the employer must establish "firewalls" to ensure that private health information is used only for purposes of plan administration and not for any other employment-related decisions, such as termination of employment.

Any person who knowingly discloses individually identifiable health information to an unauthorized person can be fined up to $50,000 or imprisoned for up to one year or both.[110] If the defendant acted under false pretenses, the maximum penalty increases to not more than $100,000 and five years in prison; if the defendant acted with intent to "sell, transfer, or use individually identifiable health information for commercial advantage, personal gain, or malicious harm," the maximum penalty rises to not more than $250,000 and ten years in prison.

Although courts have consistently held that there is no private right of action under HIPAA, in recent years they have let plaintiffs use HIPAA standards to establish that defendants failed to adequately protect their sensitive medical information. For example, an appellate court allowed an invasion of privacy lawsuit to proceed, citing HIPAA standards in its determination that a doctor owed a duty of confidentiality to his patients.[111] In another case, an appellate court held that HIPAA could be used to establish the standard of care in a negligence action.[112]

104. 15 U.S.C. §§ 6801–6809.

105. Eileen Canning, *States Legislating Financial Privacy Before Federal Regulators Even Issue Draft,* 68 U.S.L.W. 2453 (2000).

106. *Id.*

107. Michael Bologna, *Attorneys Claim That FTC Safeguards Rule Has Been Greeted with Confusion, Uncertainty,* 8 U.S.L.W. 746 (2003).

108. 42 U.S.C. §§ 1320d–1320d-8; *see also* 45 C.F.R. pts. 160, 164 (Final Rules for Administrative Data Standards and for Security and Privacy of Individually Identifiable Health Information) (2000).

109. *See generally* Linda Abdel-Malek, *HIPAA Privacy Rules Impact Employers,* N.Y. L.J., May 14, 2001, at 5.

110. 42 U.S.C. § 1320d-6.

111. Sorensen v. Barbuto, 143 P.3d 295 (Utah Ct. App. 2006).

112. Acosta v. Byrum, 638 S.E.2d 246 (N.C. Ct. App. 2006).

CHILDREN'S ONLINE PRIVACY PROTECTION ACT

The Children's Online Privacy Protection Act of 1998 (COPPA)[113] prevents websites from collecting personal information from children under age thirteen without parental consent. Parental consent can be in the form of a note, credit card number, or e-mail with a password. Websites must disclose what personal information they collect from children and how they use it, including whether they share it with third parties. In 2004, the FTC fined UMG Recordings $400,000 and Bonzi Software $75,000 for violating COPPA.[114]

In 2006, Xanga.com, a popular social networking site, and its principals agreed to pay a $1 million civil penalty for allegedly violating COPPA and its implementing rule—the largest penalty ever assessed by the FTC for a COPPA violation. The FTC alleged that the defendants had actual knowledge they were collecting and disclosing personal information from children, but continued to create 1.7 million Xanga accounts for users who submitted age information indicating they were under thirteen. The consent order also contains strong conduct provisions that will be monitored by the FTC, prohibits defendants from violating any provision of the rule, and requires them to delete all personal information collected and maintained by the site in violation of the rule.[115]

In 2001, the FTC approved the self-regulatory program of the Children's Advertising Review Unit of the Council of Better Business Bureaus as the first "safe-harbor" program under COPPA. Companies that establish and comply with approved self-regulatory programs are deemed to have complied with COPPA.

113. 15 U.S.C. §§ 6501–6506. *See also* 16 C.F.R. pt. 312 (implementing regulations of Federal Trade Commission).

114. *See* Press Release, Fed. Trade Comm'n, UMG Recordings, Inc. to Pay $400,000, Bonzi Software, Inc. to Pay $75,000 to Settle COPPA Civil Penalty Charges, with links to complaints (Sept. 13, 2006), *available at* http://www.ftc.gov/opa/2004/02/bonziumg.htm.

115. *See* Press Release, Fed. Trade Comm'n, Xanga.com to pay $1 Million for Violating Children's Online Privacy Protection Rule (Sept. 7, 2006), *available at* http://www.ftc.gov/opa/2006/09/xanga.shtm.

GLOBAL VIEW

Comparing U.S. and Non-U.S. Tort Systems

U.S. tort reform advocates frequently cite comparisons of the relative liability costs in the United States versus those in other countries to confirm the horrors of a tort system that they claim has spiraled out of control. For example, a recent study by Tillinghas, a business that reports on the U.S. "tort tax," indicates that each year the United States spends $233 billion on its tort system, more than $800 per person and 2 percent of its gross domestic product (GDP), while Denmark, the United Kingdom, France, Japan, and Switzerland each spend less than 1 percent of their GDP on their respective tort systems.[116]

This type of simplistic comparison between the tort systems of the United States and other countries may be misleading. The difference in cost as a percentage of GDP may reflect the countries' very different approaches to how tort victims are compensated. For example, if a U.S. resident is injured in a railroad accident in the United States, the victim may not have health insurance and/or long-term disability insurance to cover medical expenses and lost wages until the individual is able to return to work.[117] Filing a contingency lawsuit against the likely tortfeasors may be the only avenue by which this victim can seek to recover his or her losses, including medical expenses and lost wages. Subject to any applicable tort reform laws in the jurisdiction, the victim

CONTINUED

116. Joan T. Schmit, *Court Cases or Social Programs? Comparing International Liability Systems*, UPDATE MAG., June 5, 2005, *available at* http://www.bus.wisc.edu/update/june05/tortreform.asp.

117. According to a report from Families USA, 89.6 million people under the age of sixty-five went without health insurance for some or all of the two-year period from 2006–2007. *Wrong Direction: One out of Three Americans Are Uninsured*, Sept. 20, 2007, *available at* http://www.familiesusa.org/resources/publications/reports/wrong-direction-key-findings.html.

will also be able to seek damages for pain and suffering in a jury trial.

If the same accident occurred to a resident in England, Germany, or France, the victim's medical expenses would be covered by nationalized health care, and most of that individual's wages would be paid by either the employer or the government. As a result, the accident victim is more likely to depend on the government to handle what in the United States must be handled by litigation. If the accident victim does pursue a lawsuit in one of these other countries and is unable to pay for an attorney, he or she will be able to obtain a court-appointed attorney. The case will be tried by a judge who will award damages based on a schedule of permissible awards; damages for emotional distress will be strictly limited; and punitive damages will be unavailable. If the victim loses the lawsuit, the plaintiff will be required to pay the defendant's legal costs. This loser-pay system, which is in effect in many jurisdictions outside the United States, cuts down on the number of cases filed. These differences do not necessarily make accidents less costly, however. According to Mark Geistfeld, an expert on comparative jurisprudence at New York University School of Law, "You can substitute for tort law by having more extensive social insurance and relying on regulations to a greater extent. But it's not like the cost disappears; it just becomes part of the tax base."[118]

Even as U.S. businesses are pushing for a tort system more like the European system, European businesses are expressing concern that their legislative environment is "on the verge of tipping towards a U.S.-style system of 'regulation through litigation.'"[119] Once unheard of, class-action rules have been adopted or reformed in the United Kingdom, Norway, Sweden, and the Netherlands. In the United States, any potential plaintiff is considered a class member unless he or she opts out of the class. In the United Kingdom, however, all class members are required to "opt in" and join the class before trial. Norway's Mediation and Civil Procedure Act also allows the creation of an "opt-in" plaintiff's representative to advocate for the rights of the class. Spain goes further toward permitting class actions than most other European countries, particularly in the area of consumer protection. If those who have suffered damage are easily identifiable, Spanish law allows both consumer organizations and groups of consumers to bring a claim; if those who have suffered damage cannot be easily identified, certain consumer organizations may bring the claim.[120] The Collective Settlement of Mass Claims legislation, which became effective in the Netherlands in July 2005, does not allow a class of plaintiffs to sue, but it lets them unite to negotiate an out-of-court settlement of their claims. Sweden permits class actions on an "opt-out" basis, like the United States, but as of February 2006, only one class had been certified under this law. In most European countries, a group of plaintiffs with similar claims can form an association to represent them in litigation.[121]

In the United Kingdom, plaintiffs have even found a way to work around the prohibition on contingency fees by importing a practice already used in Australia. Professional litigation funders—which can be companies or individuals other than a licensed lawyer—contract with plaintiffs to pay the costs of their lawsuit in exchange for a percentage of the award if the plaintiffs prevail.[122]

118. Mike France, Lorraine Woellert, & Michael J. Mandel, *How to Fix the Tort System*, BUS. WK., Mar. 14, 2005, *available at* http://www.businessweek.com/magazine/content/05_11/b3924601.htm.

119. http://www.europeanjusticeforum.org/. Although punitive damages are not available in France, Germany, Austria, Switzerland, and other civil law countries, they are available (albeit far less frequently than in the United States) in England, Wales, Canada, and Australia. *See* John Yukio Gotanda, *Punitive Damages: A Comparative Analysis,* 42 COLUM. J. TRANSNAT'L L. 391 (2004).

120. Contingency fee agreements are also permitted in Spain, at least in principle. *Class Actions in Europe*, Oct. 2006, *available at* http://elexica.com/depthdoc.aspx?id=306.

121. Heather Smith, *Is America Exporting Class Actions to Europe?,* AM. LAW., Feb. 28, 2008, *available at* http://www.law.com/jsp/ihc/PubArticleIHC.jsp?id=1141047298349.

122. *Id.*

THE RESPONSIBLE MANAGER

REDUCING TORT RISKS

Managers should implement ongoing programs of education and monitoring to reduce the risks of tort liability. Because torts can be committed in numerous ways, the programs should cover all possible sources of liability. For example, the management of a company that does not respond satisfactorily to an allegation of sexual harassment may be liable for intentional infliction of emotional distress. Statements made by company representatives about an individual or product can constitute defamation.

In addition to preventing intentional torts, managers should work to prevent their employees from committing acts of negligence, which can lead to large damages awards against the company. Any tort-prevention program must recognize that under the principle of *respondeat superior,* employers will be held liable for any torts their employees commit in the scope of their employment. It is crucial, therefore, to define the scope of employment clearly.

Managers should use care to avoid committing torts that are related to contractual relations and competition with other firms. For example, a company may be held liable for interference with contractual relations if a court finds that the company intentionally tried to induce a party to breach a contract. Also, although competition itself is permissible, intentionally seeking to sabotage the efforts of another firm is not. Managers may need to consult counsel when they are unsure whether their activity has crossed the line from permissible competition to tortious interference with a prospective business advantage.

Managers need to pay attention to any personal information that they are collecting. Although U.S. law does not require all businesses to establish privacy policies, certain industries, including the health-care industry and financial institutions, are regulated under federal privacy laws. In addition, the Federal Trade Commission has taken action against companies that have failed to take reasonable steps to protect the personal information of their users. Failure to comply with the various state, federal, and international laws regulating the collection, use, and storage of personal information may not only give rise to substantial liability and criminal prosecution, but may also lead to unhappy customers. International privacy laws are discussed in Chapter 25.

A program of overall risk management and reduction is essential to limit the potential of tort liability. It is often desirable to designate one person to be in charge of risk management. That person should keep track of all claims and determine which areas of the business merit special attention. The head of risk management should be free to report incidents and problems to the chief executive officer and the board of directors, in much the same way as an internal auditor reports directly to the independent directors on the audit committee. This enhances independence and reduces the fear of reprisals if the risk manager blows the whistle on high-ranking managers.

A MANAGER'S DILEMMA

PUTTING IT INTO PRACTICE

Super Size Me and Pouring Rights: Drawing the Line Between Personal and Corporate Responsibility

A number of overweight Americans brought a class-action suit for deceptive trade practices and negligence against McDonald's Corporation, the fast-food chain famous for its hamburgers, French fries, and chicken nuggets. The class claimed that McDonald's food is fatty and addictive and that the general public has no idea how bad McDonald's food is for their health. The attorneys for the class obtained copies of McDonald's food studies, which showed that the company was aware of the fat content of its food but did not look any further into the possible health consequences of eating fatty foods. Can McDonald's be

CONTINUED

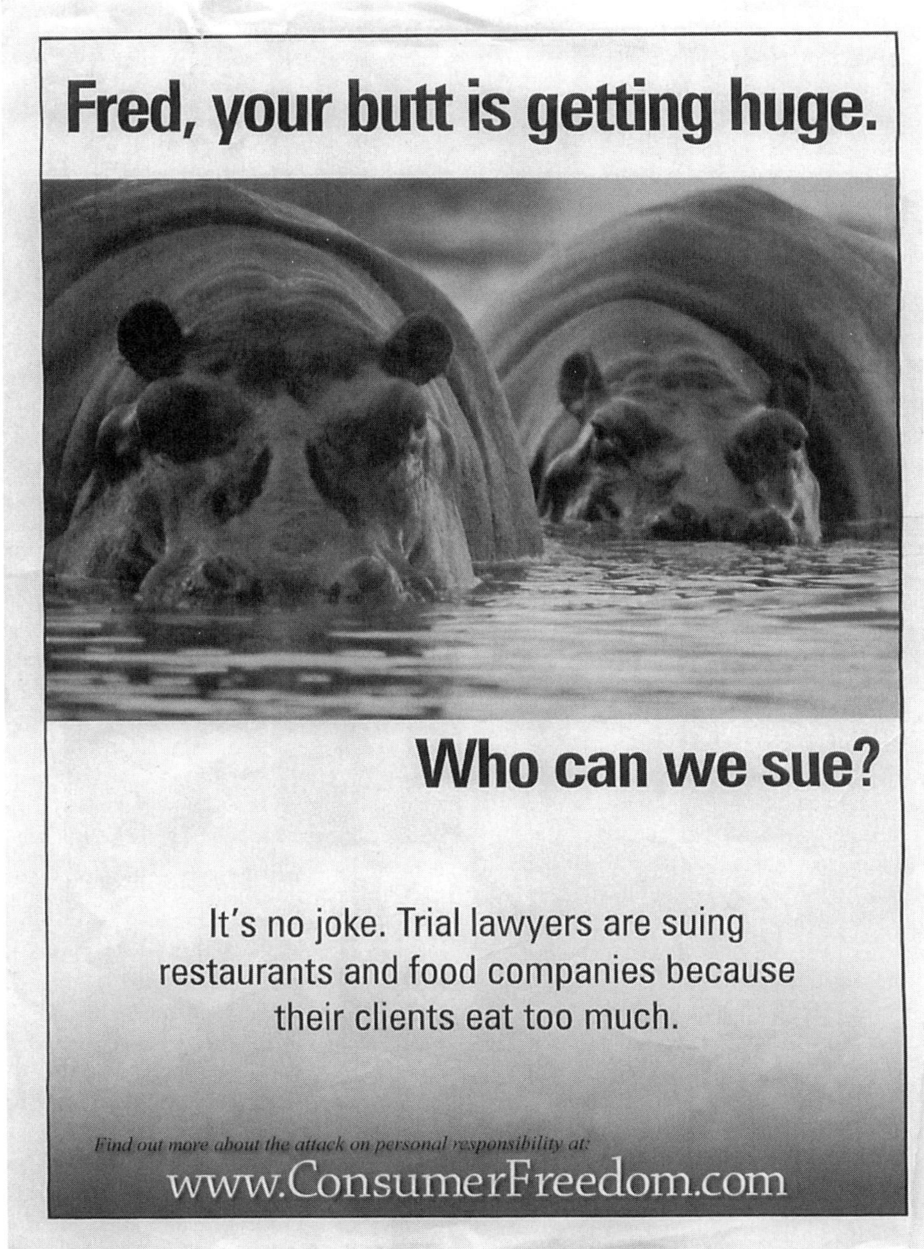

Fred, your butt is getting huge.
Who can we sue?
It's no joke. Trial lawyers are suing restaurants and food companies because their clients eat too much.
Find out more about the attack on personal responsibility at:
www.ConsumerFreedom.com

Courtesy of The Center for Consumer Freedom

held responsible for its customers' obesity?[123] Would it matter if McDonald's had added certain fats to its food after conducting another study that showed that adding those fats would make its products more addictive? What if the amount of fat needed to make the products highly addictive was so small that it would not be detected by the average consumer? If you were the CEO of McDonald's, what changes, if any, would you make in your menu and marketing strategy in response to these lawsuits?

CONTINUED

123. *See* Pelman v. McDonald's Corp., 237 F. Supp. 2d 512 (S.D.N.Y. 2003).

Nearly half of all U.S. schools had an exclusive, so-called pouring rights contract with a beverage company in the 2003–2004 school year, according to a report published by the U.S. Government Accountability Office in 2006.[124] If you were the CEO of a soft drink firm, what, if anything, would you do to secure "pouring rights" supply contracts in elementary, middle, and high schools? What beverages would you serve?

124. Chris Merces, *First Soft Drinks Obesity Lawsuit Set for Massachusetts*, Feb. 13, 2006, *available at* http://www.beveragedaily.com/news/ng.asp?n=65805-soft-drinks-obesity-aba.

INSIDE STORY

WHAT'S IN A NAME? FIGHTING IDENTITY THEFT

Identity theft is the illegal practice of gaining access to other people's credit information and then using it to the thief's advantage. In the past, getting the personal information necessary to make identity theft profitable meant going through the garbage or stealing mail, both of which could easily be combated by potential victims. Now, however, with more and more business being done online, individuals often have to disclose sensitive information on the Internet, which is far less private than the U.S. mail or even the kitchen garbage can.

With an identity theft crime occurring every seventy-nine seconds, it is the fastest-growing crime in the United States.[125] More than 8.3 million Americans had their identities stolen during 2005. The FTC reported that businesses and financial institutions lost $15.6 billion in 2005 as a result of identity theft and that victimized consumers paid more than $4 billion in out-of-pocket expenses to regain their financial identities. Identity theft costs the average victim $1,882, requires hours to deal with the problem, and results in a major blemish on the victim's credit report that remains indefinitely.[126]

The financial services companies that are the keepers of a significant amount of individual personal data have already lost billions of dollars and stand to lose billions more as identity theft victims sue the companies for allowing the theft of their information.[127] The Financial Services Technology Consortium, a coalition of leading financial services firms and technology companies, has been trying to develop technology to battle *phishing* scams, in which fraudulent websites ask for credit card numbers and other personal information.[128]

Personal credit information can be obtained on the Internet in many ways, ranging from phishing schemes to instant messages and e-mails purportedly from Internet providers or financial institutions asking for account information. Spyware makes it possible for outsiders to see everything in a computer's memory.

The growing threat has spawned new legislation. Texas and California have enacted laws prohibiting businesses from printing Social Security numbers on health plan and employer ID cards and prohibiting banks from printing Social Security numbers on bank statements and other documents sent by mail. In 2004, Governor Arnold Schwarzenegger signed S.B. 1457, which gave Californians a private right of action to sue persons who send commercial e-mail that is false or misleading.

The Fair and Accurate Credit Transactions Act of 2003 (FACT Act)[129] made identity theft a federal offense and provides specific remedies for victims. It also made it a crime to post Social Security numbers on a website with the intent to aid and abet a crime.[130] In early 2004, a computer technician became the first person to be convicted under the federal statute.

The FACT Act makes it possible for victims to work with creditors to block negative information from appearing on their reports if the problems occurred as a result of identity theft. In

CONTINUED

125. Lisa Carey, *How Serious is Identity Theft Really?* SECURITY WORLD NEWS, Jan. 2, 2008, *available at* http://www.securityworldnews.com/articles/5398/1/How-Serious-Is-Identity-Theft-Really/Page1.html.

126. Federal Trade Commission—2006 Identify Theft Survey Report, *available at* http://www.ftc.gov/os/2007/11/SynovateFinalReportIDTheft2006.pdf.

127. TRW v. Andrews, 534 U.S. 19 (2001).

128. *Financial Consortium, Technology Firms Gird for Battle Against Phishing Scams*, 9 ELECTRONIC COM. & L. REP. 842 (Oct. 13, 2004).

129. 18 U.S.C. § 10-28(A)(7).

130. Press Release, U.S. Attorney's Office, Central District of California, No. 03-052 (Apr. 16, 2004).

conjunction with the FACT Act, the FTC has instituted a number of measures that enable theft victims to place "fraud alerts" on their credit reports that tell credit-reporting agencies to contact the consumer directly, because he or she may be an identity theft victim.[131] Consumers seeking to bring suit against credit bureaus that made mistakes leading to identity theft must file these claims within two years of the actual mistake, regardless of whether the victim learned about the mistake in that time.[132]

Those who suspect they are victims of identity theft should quickly place a fraud alert on all credit accounts with a credit bureau. The United States has three main credit agencies—Experian, Equifax, and TransUnion. Alerting one will effectively alert all three. Next, victims must fill out an FTC "ID Theft Affidavit." This form is akin to a police report, and it should be sent to any company that might have had unauthorized activity with a victimized account. Finally, an actual police report should be filled out, as the credit bureaus will often take action only pursuant to an official police report.[133] Finally, victims should consult the ID Theft Data Clearinghouse, the government's database on all ID theft, which can help victims repair damage to their credit and their lives.[134]

The best way to protect against identity theft is by being proactive. Adam Cohen of *Time* recommends the following:[135]

1. Install a firewall and virus protection. A firewall acts like a gatekeeper to a network of computers so that there is one place that can deny any unauthorized access into the network (by hackers, for example) and out of the network (by employees surfing the Web, for example).
2. Do not download files from people you do not know or trust. Almost all viruses are spread by innocuous looking files, including MP3 music files.
3. Many popular Web browsers store the user's name and address in their system. Security holes can allow other websites to obtain this information and make a permanent record of it. Users should make sure the preferences for their Web browser are secure and that the browser does not disclose this information.
4. Some websites reserve the right to share whatever information they obtain with third parties. Usually, however, they must offer the option of "opting out" of this practice at the website. Users should exercise their opt-out rights.
5. Users should not accept cookies unless they are aware of their origin. *Cookies* are bits of code sent by websites that identity the user to the site at a future visit. This is how websites, such as eBay and Amazon, know a particular user has returned. Usually, cookies are harmless, but they can interact with other computer processes. Most browsers permit users to decide whether or not to accept cookies. Users should only accept cookies from websites they trust.
6. All secure, reputable websites encrypt data. The browser will tell the user when data are being encrypted. Users should not send sensitive data unless the website indicates that they are encrypted. Otherwise, anyone online can obtain this information.
7. Periodically clear the browser of cached data. A cache is a record the computer keeps of websites to allow faster access to them later. Unfortunately, this acts like a roadmap to the websites the user has visited. Even if the websites visited are safe, virus software can transmit these data back to unauthorized users who can use the information.
8. To avoid exposing sensitive company or personal information to potential Internet thieves, promulgate a thorough and well-thought-out Internet policy that limits employees to job-related Internet use.

131. *FACT Act Regulatory Plan Defines ID Theft, Requirements for Credit Report Fraud Alerts,* 72 U.S.L.W. 2652–53 (2004).

132. Amy Borrus, *To Catch an Identity Thief,* BUS. WK., Mar. 31, 2003, at 91.

133. Andrea Chipman, *Stealing You*, WALL ST. J., April 26, 2004, at R8.

134. For more information, *see* http://www.consumer.gov/idtheft.

135. Much of the following list is derived from Adam Cohen, *Internet Insecurity,* TIME, July 2, 2001, at 47–51.

KEY WORDS AND PHRASES

absolute privilege 292
actual cause 306
actual damages 318
actual intent 289
actual malice 293
aided-in-the-agency doctrine 314
appropriation of a person's name or likeness 295
assault 290
assumption of risk 308
attractive nuisance 304
bad faith 302
battery 290
comparative negligence 308
compensatory damages 318

QUESTIONS AND CASE PROBLEMS

1. The attention of a school bus driver was diverted momentarily from the road when a bee flew in the window of the bus and stung him on the neck. While the driver ducked his head and tried with his left hand to extricate the bee from under his collar, the bus veered to the left and onto the shoulder of the road, a distance of about seventy-five feet. At this point the driver raised his head and saw what had happened. He tried to turn the bus back onto the road, but was unable to do so because of the soft condition of the shoulder. The bus went down into a shallow ditch, tilting first to the left and then to the right before it could be stopped. This motion of the bus caused one of the students to be thrown from her seat and injured. The student sued for negligence. What must the student argue in order to prevail? Will the student win her case? [*Schultz v. Cheney School Dist. No. 360*, 371 P.2d 59 (Wash. 1962).]

2. A group of eBay customers successfully bid for twelve autographed baseballs at an eBay auction. When the balls arrived, the purchasers discovered that they were cheap forgeries. When the seller was nowhere to be found, the purchasers brought a lawsuit against eBay for selling forgeries. EBay never claimed to be anything other than an open marketplace. It did not hold itself out as a purveyor of collectibles. Is eBay liable for the forgeries? Even if eBay is found not liable, how should the company respond to this incident from a business point of view? What would

be the ethical thing to do? [*Gentry v. eBay, Inc.*, 121 Cal. Rptr. 2d 703 (Cal. Ct. App. 2002).]

3. Deborah Galarneau was hired as a Financial Advisor trainee by the Portland, Maine branch office of Merrill, Lynch, Pierce, Fenner & Smith (ML) in February 1989. She became a Financial Advisor (FA) in 1991. Beginning in 1998, Galarneau and her husband worked as a team called the "Galarneau Group." Amy Ford, a client of the Galarneau Group, sent ML a letter in 2003, in which she accused the Galarneaus and ML of "churning" her account. A lengthy internal investigation, as well as an investigation by Maine's Securities Division, followed. ML settled with Ford in 2003 and terminated Deborah Galarneau in January 2004. ML told her that she was being terminated because of (1) her exercise of time and price discretion; (2) her prior history, as reflected in two personnel memos and "prior warnings"; and (3) the judgment she used in trading in the Ford account. No specific reference was made to inappropriate trading, excessive trading, or churning. On February 6, 2004, ML filed a Uniform Termination Notice for Securities Industry Registration (Form U-5) with the National Association of Securities Dealers, as required by NASD rules whenever a registered stockbroker leaves a firm. In the Form U-5, ML stated the reason for terminating Galarneau as follows: "Ms. Galarneau was terminated after the firm concluded that she had (I) engaged in inappropriate bond trading in one client's account and (II) utilized time and price discretion in the accounts of three clients." This was followed by a statement disclosing that Galarneau disagreed with the firm's conclusions. After Galarneau was terminated, she tried unsuccessfully to find employment as a stockbroker at Smith Barney, Edward Jones, and Morgan Stanley. Is ML liable for defamation? [*Galarneau v. Merrill Lynch,* 504 F.3d 189 (1st Cir. 2007).]

4. CRST Van Expedited, Inc. (CRST), a trucking company, sponsors a driver training program to help its new hires become certified truck drivers. At a certain point in the training program, the driver trainer must sign a one-year employment contract with CRST if he or she wants to continue employment with the company. The employment contract provides that CRST will pay the costs associated with the training and certification, but it requires the employee to reimburse a portion of these costs, if he or she is terminated for cause or voluntarily quits. After obtaining their truck driver certifications at CRST's expense, two CRST employees were solicited for employment by Werner, a competitor. CRST claimed that Werner had a pattern of waiting for CRST to train drivers and then luring them away. Does CRST have any legal basis for suing Werner or the employees? If so, on what basis? What damages would be available? Did Werner act ethically? [*CRST Van Expedited, Inc. v. Werner Enterprises, Inc.*, 479 F.3d 1099 (9th Cir. 2007).]

5. After two years of negotiations, the four shareholders and founders of Access, Inc. sold their health-care start-up to a subsidiary of Res-Care, Inc. and agreed to stay on as employees, based on assurances from the buyer that Res-Care would not merge with VOCA of North Carolina. The Access shareholders had explained to Res-Care that they were all former employees of VOCA and had left to form Access, because of differences over the way VOCA was run. They made it clear to Res-Care that they would not sell their shares without assurances that they would never be affiliated with VOCA or their former supervisor.

   Res-Care's chief development officer told the shareholders that his company was not interested in buying VOCA, because it had poor profits and was poorly managed. Res-Care's vice president of the central region made similar assurances in a later meeting.

   A week after the Access shareholders signed the deal, Res-Care announced that it had signed a letter of intent to buy VOCA. The Access shareholders' former boss at VOCA was given the job of statewide director, thereby becoming the Access shareholders' new supervisor.

   Do the former Access shareholders have any legal basis for suing Res-Care? Assume that the acquisition agreement between the Access shareholders and Res-Care contained no representation or warranty by Res-Care regarding a possible merger with VOCA, and that it contained a standard merger clause stating that the written acquisition agreement superseded any and all prior negotiations and oral statements. What could the Access shareholders have done to avoid this dispute? [*Godfrey v. Res-Care, Inc.*, N.C. App. No. COA 03-790 (N.C. July 6, 2004).]

6. A class-action lawsuit was filed against a number of alcoholic beverage producers, asserting that the defendants target underage consumers in a manner that is "deliberate, reckless, and illegal," and that such actions constitute unfair, deceptive, and unconscionable practices in violation of state consumer protection statutes and are negligent. The plaintiffs claim that the defendants use advertisements and marketing campaigns that are likely to appeal to minors, because they employ video games and animation, attractive models, and social situations and humor that minors can identify with. Could the companies be found liable for targeting a youthful audience? Should they be? What moral responsibility, if any, do the companies have? [*Hakki v. Zima Co.,* 2006 WL 852126 (D.C. Super. 2006), aff'd, 926 A.2d 722 (D.C. App. 2007).]

7. Bruce Marecki, an employee of Crystal Rock Spring Water Company, attended a seminar sponsored by the company at a Ramada Inn. At the seminar, he drank several beers. After the seminar ended, he was planning to go to happy hour at the hotel, but at a separate location from the seminar room. Instead, he left the hotel to purchase cigarettes after discovering that the cigarette machine in the hotel was broken. While he was driving to a store to buy cigarettes, he rear-ended another car and caused injuries to the driver. The driver sued Crystal Rock Spring Water Company under the doctrine of *respondeat superior.* Should the company be liable for the injuries the driver suffered? What if Crystal Rock Spring Water Company had not supplied the liquor at the seminar, but had allowed it to be served? What if Marecki had had nothing to drink at the seminar, but then drank at the happy hour with his co-workers and had an accident when he was driving home after socializing with them? What if the seminar was optional and Marecki had no obligation to attend? [*Sheftic v. Marecki,* 1999 Conn. Super. LEXIS 2953 (Conn. Oct. 22, 1999).]

8. Harold Tod Parrot was employed as vice president of sales by Capital Corporation, a privately held investment adviser. Parrot purchased 40,500 shares of Capital stock, pursuant to a stock purchase agreement that provided that upon termination of Parrot's employment, the company would repurchase his shares at fair market value. The fair market value was to be determined by the accounting firm Coopers & Lybrand, which had been retained by Capital Corporation for that purpose. Several years after the stock purchase, Parrot was terminated. He then sought to sell his shares back to Capital Corporation at fair market value. Parrot objected to the price of the shares established by Coopers & Lybrand in the company's most recent biannual report and sued both Capital Corporation and Coopers & Lybrand. His complaint against Coopers & Lybrand alleged professional negligence and negligent misrepresentation. He argued that the accountants had changed the valuation methodology, at Capital's request, in order to reduce the price of the shares and, as a result, Parrot was induced to accept a lesser value for his stock. Does Parrot's suit against Coopers & Lybrand have merit? [*Parrot v. Coopers & Lybrand, LLP,* 702 N.Y.S.2d 40 (2000), *aff'd,* 95 N.Y.2d 479 (2000).]

PRODUCT LIABILITY

INTRODUCTION

Definition of Product Liability

Product liability is the legal liability manufacturers and sellers have for defective products that cause injury to the purchaser, a user or bystander, or their property. Liability extends to anyone in the chain of distribution: manufacturers, distributors, wholesalers, and retailers.

Today, most states in the United States have adopted strict product liability, whereby an injured person may recover damages without having to show that the defendant was negligent or otherwise at fault. No contractual relationship between the defendant and the injured person is necessary. The injured person merely needs to show that the defendant sold the product in a defective or dangerous condition and that the defect caused his or her injury.

CHAPTER OVERVIEW

This chapter discusses the evolution of the strict liability doctrine, beginning with its origin in warranty and negligence theories. It then focuses on the bases for strict liability, including manufacturing defect, design defect, and failure to warn. We examine who may be held liable for defective products and the allocation of liability among multiple defendants. The chapter discusses defenses to product liability claims, including the courts' increasing acceptance of the preemption defense to preclude state law product liability claims and legislative reforms designed to correct perceived abuses in the system. We conclude with a description of the law of product liability in the European Union.

THEORIES OF RECOVERY

The primary theories on which a product liability claim can be brought are breach of warranty, negligence, and strict liability.

BREACH OF WARRANTY

In a warranty action, the reasonableness of the manufacturer's actions is not at issue. Rather, the question is whether the quality, characteristics, and safety of the product were consistent with the implied or express representations made by the seller. A buyer may bring a warranty action whenever the product fails to meet the standards that the seller represented to the buyer at the time of purchase.

UCC Warranties

As explained in Chapter 8, a warranty under the Uniform Commercial Code (UCC) may be either express or implied. An express warranty is an affirmation made by the seller relating to the quality of the goods sold. An implied warranty is created by law and guarantees the merchantability of the goods sold and, in some circumstances, their fitness for a particular purpose.

Privity of Contract

A breach-of-warranty action is based on principles of contract law. To recover, an injured person must be in a contractual relationship with the seller, a requirement known as *privity of contract*. It necessarily precludes recovery by those persons, such as bystanders, who are not in privity with the seller.

NEGLIGENCE

MacPherson, which follows, is the landmark case in which the defendant manufacturer was found liable for negligence even though there was no contractual relationship between the manufacturer and the plaintiff. Thus, one of the obstacles posed in breach-of-warranty actions—the requirement of privity of contract—was removed. Although liability in *MacPherson* was still based on the negligence principles of reasonableness and due care, the New York Court of Appeals' abandonment of the privity requirement in this case made it an important forerunner to the doctrine of strict product liability.

A CASE IN POINT

CASE 10.1

MACPHERSON V. BUICK MOTOR CO.

COURT OF APPEALS OF NEW YORK
111 N.E. 1050 (N.Y. 1916).

SUMMARY

FACTS MacPherson purchased a new Buick car with wooden wheels from a Buick Motor Company dealer who had previously purchased the car from its manufacturer, Buick Motor Company. MacPherson was injured when the car ran into a ditch. The accident was caused by the collapse of one of the car's wheels due to defective wood used for the spokes. The wheel had been made by a manufacturer other than Buick.

MacPherson sued Buick Motor Company directly. He proved that Buick could have discovered the defect by reasonable inspection and that such an inspection had not been conducted. No claim was made that the manufacturer knew of the defect and willfully concealed it. After the trial court found in favor of MacPherson, Buick appealed.

ISSUE PRESENTED May a consumer who purchases a product from a retailer sue the manufacturer directly for negligent manufacture of the product even though there is no contract per se between the consumer and the manufacturer?

SUMMARY OF OPINION The New York Court of Appeals held that Buick could be held liable for negligence. As a manufacturer, it owed a duty to any person who could foreseeably be injured as a result of a defect in an automobile it manufactured. The court stated that a manufacturer's duty to inspect varies with the nature of the thing to be inspected. The more probable the danger, the greater the need for caution. Because the action was one in tort for negligence, no contract between the plaintiff and the defendant was required.

RESULT The court of appeals affirmed the lower court's finding that the manufacturer, Buick Motor Company, was liable for the injuries sustained by the plaintiff. Buick was found negligent for not inspecting the wheels and was responsible for the finished product sold by its dealer.

COMMENTS This case established the rule, still applicable today, that a manufacturer can be liable for failure to exercise reasonable care in the manufacture of a product when such failure involves an unreasonable risk of bodily harm to users of the product. This rule is embodied in Sections 1 and 2(a) of the Restatement (Third) of Torts: Products Liability (1997).[1]

1. This rule also appeared in the RESTATEMENT (SECOND) OF TORTS § 395 (1977).

To prove negligence in a products case, the injured party must show that the defendant did not use reasonable care in designing or manufacturing its product or in providing adequate warnings. A manufacturer can be found negligent even if the product met all regulatory requirements because, under some circumstances, a reasonably prudent manufacturer would have taken additional precautions.[2] As discussed later in this chapter, the only exception is when a federally mandated standard is deemed to have preempted state product liability law.[3]

It can be difficult to prove negligence. Moreover, injured persons have often been negligent themselves in their use or misuse of the product. This precludes recovery in a contributory negligence state and reduces recovery in a comparative negligence state.

2. *See, e.g.,* Brooks v. Beech Aircraft Corp., 902 P.2d 54 (N.M. 1995).

3. *See, e.g.,* Horn v. Thoratec Corp., 376 F.3d 163 (3d Cir. 2004).

Courts will not permit a plaintiff to prove negligence by introducing evidence of *subsequent remedial measures* taken by a defendant after an injury to improve a product. The public policy behind this rule is to encourage companies to continually strive to improve the safety of their products. If such safety measures could be used to establish negligence, companies would be deterred from improving their products.

STRICT LIABILITY IN TORT

Strict liability in tort allows a person injured by an unreasonably dangerous product to recover damages from the manufacturer or seller of the product even in the absence of a contract or negligent conduct on the part of the manufacturer or seller. Because the defect in the product is the basis for liability, the injured person may recover damages even if the seller exercised all possible care in the manufacture and sale of the product.

In 1963, in *Greenman v. Yuba Power Products, Inc.*,[4] the California Supreme Court became the first state supreme court in the United States to adopt strict product liability. The case involved a consumer who was injured while using a Shopsmith combination power tool that could be used as a saw, drill, and wood lathe. Claiming that the tool was defective and not suitable to perform the work for which it was intended, Greenman sued the manufacturer and the retailer who had sold the power tool to his wife for breach of express and implied warranties and for negligent construction of the tool. The California Supreme Court ruled that a manufacturer is strictly liable in tort when it places an article on the market, knowing that the product is to be used without inspection for defects, and it proves to have a defect that causes injury to a human being.

Rationale

The legal principle of strict product liability is grounded in considerations of public policy. The rationale has four basic parts:

1. The law should protect consumers against unsafe products. Consumers are often unable to insure against all risks. In addition, consumers should be able to rely on the marketing of manufacturers.
2. Imposing strict liability encourages manufacturers to go the extra mile to produce safer products and to improve existing products by investing in careful product design, manufacture, testing, and quality control. Manufacturers should not escape liability simply because they typically do not sign a formal contract with the end user of their product (or with nonusers who might be injured by their product). Negligence liability alone does not provide sufficient incentives to induce manufacturers to make safe products.
3. The cost of injury should be borne by the parties best able to detect, eliminate, and insure against product defects: manufacturers and others in the chain of distribution. Because the manufacturers and sellers of products can insure against the losses caused by their products and pass these costs on to all consumers in the form of higher prices, they are in the best position to bear and spread the costs of product liability.
4. The law should give sellers an incentive to deal with reputable manufacturers.

In short, the goal of strict product liability is to force companies to internalize the costs of product-caused injuries.

Elements of a Strict Liability Claim

For a defendant to be held strictly liable, the plaintiff must prove that (1) the plaintiff, or the plaintiff's property, was harmed by the product; (2) the injury was caused by a defect in the product; and (3) the defect existed at the time the product left the defendant and did not substantially change along the way. Most states have followed the formulation of Section 402A of the Restatement (Second) of Torts, which states:

1. One who sells any product in a defective condition unreasonably dangerous to the user or consumer or to his property is subject to liability for physical harm thereby caused to the ultimate user or consumer, or to his property, if
   a. the seller is engaged in the business of selling such a product, and
   b. it is expected to and does reach the user or consumer without substantial change in the condition in which it is sold.
2. The rule stated in Subsection (1) applies although
   a. the seller has exercised all possible care in the preparation and sale of his product, and the user or consumer has not bought the product from or entered into any contractual relation with the seller.

In some cases, the plaintiffs may base their suit on the anticipation of becoming ill or suffering physical injury as a result of being exposed to a toxic product, such as asbestos. In other words, parties may sue even though no actual injury or illness has yet emerged. In 2003, the U.S. Supreme Court ruled that asymptomatic plaintiffs exposed to asbestos could sue for fear of developing cancer.[5] In *Petito v.*

4. 377 P.2d 897 (Cal. 1963).

5. Norfolk & Western Ry. Co. v. Ayers, 535 U.S. 969 (2003).

A.H. Robins Co.,[6] the Florida Court of Appeal recognized a cause of action for "medical monitoring" for plaintiffs who had been prescribed the weight-loss drugs Fenfluramine and Phentermine. Although they had no physical injuries, the class members argued that taking the drugs had placed them at a substantially increased risk of developing serious cardiac and circulatory damage, including heart valve damage. The court required manufacturers and sellers to pay for a court-supervised program of medical testing, monitoring, and study of the class, reasoning, "[O]ne can hardly dispute that an individual has just as great an interest in avoiding expensive diagnostic examinations as in avoiding physical injury."[7]

The American Law Institute (ALI) promulgated the Restatement (Third) of Torts: Products Liability in 1997. Restatements provide judges and lawyers with a comprehensive view of the status of American case law (drawn from a survey of courts throughout the country) and the rationale behind it. They also reflect the drafters' vision of the way that a particular area of the law should evolve. As we explained in Chapter 3, courts are free either to follow or to ignore the restatement's formulation.

Like the Restatement (Second) of Torts, the Restatement (Third) imposes strict liability for manufacturing defects. In the case of design defects and defects based on inadequate instructions or warnings, however, it imposes a standard predicated on negligence. Because a majority of states still follow the Restatement (Second), the discussion that follows is, except as otherwise noted, based on that restatement. We will return to the Restatement (Third) standard for defects in design, instructions, and warnings later in this chapter.

Litigation Strategy and the Availability of Punitive Damages

Although negligence and breach of warranty are alleged in most product liability cases, they play a secondary role compared with strict liability. Under strict liability, the injured person does not have the burden of proving negligence and does not have to be in privity with the seller. Thus, strict liability is easier to prove than either negligence or breach of warranty.

Nonetheless, plaintiffs' attorneys usually try to prove negligence as well as strict liability. Proof of negligence will often stir the jury's emotions, leading to higher damages awards and, in some cases, to punitive damages.[8]

On the other hand, once the plaintiff has raised the issue of negligence, the defendant is permitted to introduce evidence that its products were "state of the art" and manufactured with due care. Such evidence would otherwise be inadmissible in strict liability cases governed by the Restatement (Second) and manufacturing defect cases governed by the Restatement (Third).

Prior to the U.S. Supreme Court's ruling limiting punitive damages in most cases to less than ten times the compensatory damages,[9] companies faced the possibility of astronomical punitive damages awards in product cases. For example, a jury awarded $4.9 billion in compensatory and punitive damages to six people burned after a rupture in the fuel tank of their 1979 Chevrolet Malibu caused the car to explode. The plaintiffs had introduced a damning internal memo in which a General Motors engineer calculated that fuel tank–related deaths would cost GM $2.40 for every vehicle on the road compared with an additional $8.95 to redesign the car to reduce the fire risk. Although the memo concluded that "a human fatality is really beyond value, subjectively," the jury concluded that GM should be punished for making a business decision to put people at risk rather than correct the design problem at a higher cost to the company. In August 1999, the Florida Supreme Court upheld a $31 million punitive damages award against Owens-Corning Fiberglass Corporation, the manufacturer of an asbestos-containing product, after finding that the company showed "blatant disregard for human safety."[10] The plaintiff suffered from a rare lung disease following asbestos exposure. The trial court found that Owens-Corning had intentionally and knowingly misrepresented and concealed the dangers of asbestos for more than thirty years. The company had intentionally contaminated a new product with asbestos, even though it knew that slight exposure to asbestos could cause the lung disease.

In 2006, a jury awarded $9 million in punitive damages on top of $4.5 million in compensatory damages to a plaintiff who had taken Vioxx pain medication after finding that Merck had withheld information about the drug's health risks from the Food and Drug Administration.[11] Jury foreperson Timothy Kile explained the jury's thought process: "[Merck is] responsible for people taking the medication and putting it in their bodies. To not put information out there about public safety that I feel you have a responsibility to put out there, that's willful and wanton."[12] (Statutory and court-imposed

6. 750 So. 2d 103 (Fla. App. 1999).

7. *Id.* at 105.

8. Punitive damages are discussed further in Chapters 4 and 9.

9. State Farm Mut. Auto. Ins. Co. v. Campbell, 538 U.S. 1028 (2003).

10. *$31 Million Punitive Award Upheld in Asbestos Case,* Corp. Couns. Wkly., Oct. 6, 1999, at 7.

11. Alex Berenson, *Merck Jury Adds $9 Million in Damages,* N.Y. Times, Apr. 12, 2006, at C1.

12. *Id.*

IN BRIEF

Theories of Product Liability*

	Contract—Breach of Warranty	Tort—Negligence	Tort—Strict Liability
What needs to be shown?	Express (stated in the contract) or implied (by law) warranty. Implied warranties are merchantability and sometimes fitness for a particular purpose.	**1.** The injured party (or property) was injured (damaged) by the product, resulting in an actual loss. **2.** The defendant owed a duty to the injured party. **3.** The defendant did not use reasonable care in designing the product, manufacturing the product, or providing adequate warnings. **4.** The defect caused the injury or damage. **5.** The injury was reasonably foreseeable.	**1.** The injured party (or property) was harmed by a defective product (i.e., has a design defect, a manufacturing defect, or a failure to adequately warn) that is unreasonably dangerous (i.e., the danger extends beyond that contemplated by the ordinary consumer who purchases with ordinary knowledge in the community). **2.** The product reached the consumer without substantial change in the condition in which it was sold. **3.** The seller is engaged in the business of selling the product.
Is privity of contract required?	Yes	No	No
Who is covered?	Only the parties in privity of contract	Purchasers, users, bystanders, or their property (Note: Purchasers of used property generally are not covered.)	Same as Tort—Negligence
Who is liable?	Only the parties in privity of contract	The person(s) who acted negligently	Anyone in the commercial chain of distribution: component manufacturers, manufacturers, distributors, wholesalers, and retailers (but not casual sellers and, in some jurisdictions, there are limitations on the liability of wholesalers and retailers)
Is "fault" required?	No	Yes—failure to use reasonable care in designing, manufacturing (including inspecting for defects in components), or providing adequate warnings	No
What if the injured person negligently used or misused the product?	For express warranties, the terms of the warranty generally bar or severely limit recovery. For implied warranties, especially fitness for a particular purpose, the result will be fact specific.	In contributory negligence states—no recovery. In comparative negligence states—reduced recovery. Unforeseeable misuse will generally bar recovery.	Contributory negligence does not apply. In some jurisdictions, comparative fault can reduce awards. Unforeseeable misuse will generally bar recovery.

CONTINUED

What if the product was "state of the art"? (Note: States differ as to the standard used to establish "state of the art.")	Generally no recovery	Generally precludes claims for negligent design. Manufacturing defects and failure-to-warn claims are still available.	Generally irrelevant
What if the product met all federal and state regulatory standards?	Generally irrelevant as to express warranties but may eliminate any claim under implied warranties	If the standards do not preempt state product liability law—no effect. If the standards do preempt state product liability law—recovery is limited to the preemption limitations.	Same as Tort—Negligence
What damages are recoverable?	Economic only	Economic damages, bodily injury, property damage, and pain and suffering	Same as Tort—Negligence
Are punitive damages available?	No	Yes, if the defendant's conduct was grossly negligent or reckless	No

***Key assumptions:**

1. The defendant sold a product not a service.
2. The defendant was not engaged in an ultrahazardous activity.
3. The product was not unavoidably unsafe.
4. The court will apply something similar to the Restatement (Second).
5. Variations among jurisdictions have not been noted in all possible circumstances.

limitations on punitive damages are discussed later in this chapter.)

DEFINITION OF PRODUCT

Strict liability in tort applies only to products, not services and other intangibles. What qualifies as a *product* is sometimes not clear.

PRODUCTS VERSUS SERVICES OR INFORMATION

In some cases, it is unclear whether an injury was caused by a defective product or a negligently performed service. For example, a person may be injured by a needle used by a dentist or the hair solution used by a beautician. Some courts apply strict liability in these situations. Other courts will treat the product as incidental to the service and not apply strict liability.

Courts that have addressed the definition-of-product question have required that the item giving rise to liability be tangible. But what happens when harm results from defective information contained in a book or other tangible item? Is the "product" the information or the physical characteristics of the item in which the information is embedded?

In the case of books, courts have generally taken the position that "the tangible portion of the book, the binding and printing . . . is a good[;] the thought and ideas contained therein are not."[13] For example, mushroom enthusiasts who had relied on descriptions in a book entitled *The Encyclopedia of Mushrooms* to determine which wild mushrooms were safe to eat, then become critically ill after eating a poisonous variety, could not bring a strict product liability claim based on the erroneous information.[14] The court reasoned that the allegedly defective "product" was a

13. Smith v. Linn, 563 A.2d 123, 126 (Pa. Super. 1989).

14. Winter v. G.P. Putnam's Sons, 938 F.2d 1033 (9th Cir. 1991).

> **ETHICAL CONSIDERATION**
>
> Do publishers have an ethical obligation to warn readers that information in a book may not be accurate and should not be relied on?

collection of ideas and expressions, not a tangible item. The First Amendment to the U.S. Constitution evidences the high value placed on the unfettered exchange of ideas; this could be seriously inhibited by the threat of strict liability for the contents of books. Courts have used similar reasoning to dismiss product claims based on a dieting guide,[15] an instruction guide for a floor hockey game,[16] video games,[17] and scuba diving lessons.[18]

In contrast, courts have allowed product liability claims to proceed against publishers of written materials that are akin to specialized instruments. For example, a court ruled that aeronautical charts are sufficiently tangible to qualify as products because they provide visual representations of technical information, such as headings, distances, and minimum altitudes required by pilots.[19] The charts were not merely thoughts and expressions. Similarly, if the information at issue is characterized as "an integral part of a product in a 'smart good,' such as a computerized braking system in a car," then strict product liability will apply.[20]

Software

With the evolution of the digital age, courts have also considered whether software is sufficiently tangible to be considered a product. Certain scholars argue that "the reasons for treating software differently from all other products no longer withstand close scrutiny, if they ever did," and they have called for "the extension of strict liability to defective software at the earliest opportunity."[21] But courts have reached varying results.

A federal court applying Louisiana law ruled that the software State Farm Insurance used to calculate home damage estimates was a product under the state's product liability law.[22] The homeowners had alleged that State Farm had intentionally programmed the software to underestimate the costs of repairing or replacing property damage suffered during Hurricane Katrina in 2005. In reaching its decision, the court relied on a Louisiana Supreme Court ruling on a tax code issue. In that case, Louisiana's highest court, reaching back to Roman law, had held that software is a "corporeal movable," or physical thing capable of being moved, not an "incorporeal movable," or abstract conception such a legal right.[23] (Note that Louisiana is not a common law jurisdiction.)

In another case, which examined the issue outside of the product liability context, the U.S. Court of Appeals for the Fourth Circuit came to the opposite conclusion. It characterized computer files and operating systems as "abstract ideas, logic, instructions, and information," not tangible products.[24] Accordingly, America Online's insurance policy, which covered only physical harm to tangible items, did not cover liability for claims brought by customers who alleged that AOL's update software had corrupted their electronic data and altered the operating systems in their computers.

FIXTURES AND STRUCTURAL IMPROVEMENTS

A similar issue arises when a telephone pole or other product installed in the ground is defective. Some courts take the position that fixtures of this type are structural improvements of real property and, as such, are not products for purposes of product liability actions. Other courts, such as the Alabama Supreme Court, have ruled that telephone poles maintain their product characteristics even after being attached to real property.[25] Alabama's top court has also treated the following structural improvements as products: (1) a conveyor belt installed in a grain-storage facility;[26] (2) a gas water heater in a home;[27] (3) a cylindrical rotary soybean conditioner located in a soybean extraction facility;[28] and (4) a diving board that had been installed with an in-ground, vinyl-lined swimming pool.[29] The court reasoned that the policies underlying strict

15. Gorran v. Atkins Nutritionals, Inc., 464 F. Supp. 2d 315 (S.D.N.Y. 2006).
16. Garcia v. Kusan, Inc., 655 N.E.2d 1290 (Mass. App. 1995).
17. Wilson v. Midway Games, 198 F. Supp. 2d 167 (D. Conn. 2002).
18. Isham v. Padi Worldwide Corp., 2007 WL 2460776 (D. Haw., Aug. 23, 2007).
19. Aetna Cas. & Sur. Co. v. Jeppesen & Co., 642 F.2d 339 (9th Cir. 1981).
20. Michael Traynor, *Information Liability and the Challenges for Law Reform: An Introductory Note, in* CONSUMER PROTECTION IN THE AGE OF THE INFORMATION ECONOMY 81–97 (Jane K. Winn ed., 2006).
21. Frances E. Zollers, Andrew McMullin, Sandra N. Hurd, & Peter Shears, *No More Soft Landings for Software: Liability for Defects in an Industry That Has Come of Age,* 21 SANTA CLARA COMPUTER & HIGH TECH. L.J. 745, 782 (2005).
22. Schafer v. State Farm Ins. Co., 507 F. Supp. 2d 587 (E.D. La. 2007).
23. South Cent. Bell Tel. Co. v. Bathelemy, 643 So. 2d 1240, 1244 (La. 1994).
24. Am. Online, Inc. v. St. Paul Mercury Ins. Co., 347 F.3d 89, 96 (4th Cir. 2003).
25. Bell v. T.R. Miller Mill Co., 768 So. 2d 953 (Ala. 2000).
26. Beam v. Tramco, Inc., 655 So. 2d. 979 (Ala. 1995).
27. Sears, Roebuck & Co. v. Harris, 630 So. 2d. 1018 (Ala. 1993).
28. McDaniel v. French Oil Mill Mach. Co., 623 So. 2d 1146 (Ala. 1993).
29. King v. S.R. Smith, Inc., 578 So. 2d 1285 (Ala. 1991).

product liability have little relation to the policies underlying the fixtures doctrine even though the two do intersect in some instances.[30] As a result, the application of product liability law should not be totally dependent upon the intricacies of real property law. On the other hand, Alabama considers that certain items, such as fireplaces[31] and multilayered exterior wall systems,[32] become part of the structure once installed and therefore are not products because they "will have the same useful life as the house or building itself and will not need to be replaced over the life of the building."[33]

WHAT MAKES A PRODUCT DEFECTIVE?

An essential element for recovery in strict liability is proof of a defect in the product. The injured party must show that (1) the product was defective when it left the hands of the manufacturer or seller and (2) the defect made the product unreasonably dangerous. Typically, a product is dangerous if its characteristics do not meet the consumer's expectations. For example, a consumer expects that a stepladder will not break when someone stands on the bottom step. Not all situations are so clear-cut, however.

John Wade, a noted American jurist whose articles are frequently cited by courts,[34] set forth the following factors for determining whether a product is defective:

1. The usefulness and desirability of the product—its utility to the user and to the public as a whole.
2. The safety aspects of the product—the likelihood that it will cause injury and the probable seriousness of the injury.
3. The availability of a substitute product that would meet the same need and not be as unsafe.
4. The manufacturer's ability to eliminate the unsafe character of the product without impairing its usefulness or making it too expensive to maintain its utility.
5. The user's ability to avoid danger by the exercise of care in the use of the product.
6. The user's anticipated awareness of the dangers inherent in the product and their avoidability, because of general public knowledge of the obvious condition of the product or of the existence of suitable warnings or instructions.
7. The feasibility, on the part of the manufacturer, of spreading the loss by setting the price of the product or carrying liability insurance.[35]

MANUFACTURING DEFECT

A *manufacturing defect* is a flaw in a product that occurs during production, such as a failure to meet the design specifications. A product with a manufacturing defect is not like the others rolling off the production line. For example, suppose the driver's seat in an automobile is designed to be bolted to the frame. If a worker forgets to tighten the bolts, the loose seat will be a manufacturing defect.

DESIGN DEFECT

A *design defect* occurs when a product manufactured according to specifications is, nonetheless, due to its inadequate design or a poor choice of materials, unreasonably dangerous to users. Typically, a design is defective when the product is not safe for its intended or reasonably foreseeable use. A highly publicized example was the Ford Pinto, which a jury found to be defectively designed because the car's fuel tank was too close to the rear axle, causing the tank to rupture when the car was struck from behind.

INADEQUATE WARNINGS, LABELING, OR INSTRUCTIONS

To avoid charges of *failure to warn*, a product must carry adequate warnings of the risks involved in its foreseeable use. To prevail in a failure-to-warn case, most states require the plaintiff to prove that "the defendant did not adequately warn of a particular risk that was known or knowable in

30. *Bell*, 768 So. 2d 953.
31. Wells v. Clowers Constr. Co., 476 So. 2d 105 (Ala. 1985).
32. Keck v. Dryvit Sys., 830 So. 2d 1 (Ala. 2002).
33. *Id.* at 6.
34. *See, e.g.*, Nunnally v. R.J. Reynolds Tobacco Co., 869 So. 2d 373 (Miss. 2004).
35. *Id.* at 379–80.

> **ETHICAL CONSIDERATION**

You are a manager of a major manufacturing corporation. An interview with a low-level engineer leads you to believe that the design specifications for your model PaZazz-4 are, in fact, the cause of numerous deaths. You are facing a wrongful death and product liability suit for defective design. The plaintiffs have not deposed this engineer, even though his name was provided as one of the hundreds who worked on this project. Thus, although you believe the design for PaZazz-4 was defective, it will be extremely difficult—if not impossible—for the plaintiffs to prove this. What should you do?

VIEW FROM CYBERSPACE

Jurisdictional Disputes

A local tribunal will often seek to protect the interests of those living within its jurisdiction. Consequently, any action that even remotely affects its citizens will often bring the dispute within the jurisdiction of the local court. When two tribunals' jurisdictions overlap, a battle often ensues over which one will be allowed to resolve the dispute and whose law will be applied. The inherently international character of e-commerce makes such battles more common.[a]

A fierce debate raged in the European Union (EU) as to whether and under what circumstances consumers could bring suit in their national courts against companies based in another country selling products through websites powered by computers located outside the consumer's home country.[b] Some argued that the ability to sue in the consumer's national court would promote e-commerce growth by increasing consumer confidence. Others feared that permitting suits in other countries would discourage small and medium-sized businesses from setting up websites, thereby hindering growth in e-commerce. The European Commission resolved this issue in 2000 when it approved the European Parliament's plan to grant jurisdiction in disputes between online buyers and sellers to the country of destination rather than the country of origin.[c] Although consumer activists welcomed the action, one critic complained that the ruling "means we will still have 15 [27 in 2008] separate markets in the EU rather than one unified internal market, which I thought was the aim."[d]

More generally, there is a growing consensus on the need for the international harmonization of laws regarding jurisdiction over e-commerce disputes. After conducting a yearlong study of the issue, the American Bar Assocation's Cyberspace Law Committee suggested, among other things, a global online standards association.[e] But a representative from the U.S. Undersecretary of State questioned whether an international bureaucracy was the best way to reach harmonization. Everyone seemed to agree, however, that subjecting every website to the contradictions inherent in the laws of 195 different countries could cause e-commerce to grind to a halt.[f]

a. *Industry Lobbyists Say Jurisdiction Issues Threaten E-Business if Not Addressed Soon,* 6 U.S.L.W. 215 (Feb. 2001).
b. Paul Meller, *Jurisdiction Dispute Heats Up in Europe,* STANDARD, Nov. 22, 2000.
c. Paul Meller, *Buyers Gain Online Rights in Europe; Effort Made to Lift Confidence in Web,* N.Y. TIMES, Dec. 1, 2000.
d. *Id.*
e. *Industry Lobbyists Say Jurisdiction Issues Threaten E-Business if Not Addressed Soon, supra* note a.
f. *Id.*

light of the generally recognized and prevailing best scientific and medical knowledge available at the time of manufacture and distribution."[36] For example, the manufacturer of a ladder must warn the user not to stand on the top step. A product must also be accompanied by instructions for its safe use. For example, sellers have been found liable for failing to provide adequate instructions about the proper use and capacity of a hook and the assembly and use of a telescope and sun filter.

Although a warning can shield a manufacturer from liability for a *properly* manufactured and designed product, it cannot shield the manufacturer from liability for a *defectively* manufactured or designed product. For example, an automobile manufacturer cannot escape liability for defectively designed brakes merely by warning that "under certain conditions this car's brakes may fail." As will be explained later, in cases involving certain products, such as certain types of vaccines, that are unavoidably unsafe, the adequacy of the warning determines whether a product known to be dangerous is also "defective."

Causation Requirement

To prevail on a failure-to-warn claim, the plaintiff must show both that the defendant breached a duty to warn and that the defendant's failure to warn was the *proximate cause* (or legal cause) of the plaintiff's injuries. The question of proximate cause is one for the jury to determine. As a result, the vast majority of courts will not disturb a jury's finding that a failure to warn was the proximate cause of an injury. However, in an extreme case—one in which the court believes no reasonable person could have deemed the failure to warn a proximate cause of the plaintiff's injury—the court may set aside a verdict on causation grounds.

36. Anderson v. Owens-Corning Fiberglass Corp., 810 P.2d 549, 558–59 (Cal. 1991).

Bilingual Warnings

The United States is a heterogeneous country, and diversity is one of its great strengths. With diversity can come challenges, however. Misunderstandings may arise due to differences in culture or language. Legislatures in states with substantial non-English-speaking populations have recognized the need for bilingual or multilingual documents in such areas as voting and public services. The following case addresses the need for bilingual warnings on nonprescription drugs.

A CASE IN POINT

CASE 10.2

RAMIREZ V. PLOUGH, INC.

SUPREME COURT OF CALIFORNIA
863 P.2D 167 (CAL. 1993).

SUMMARY

FACTS In March 1986, when he was less than four months old, plaintiff Jorge Ramirez exhibited symptoms of a cold or similar upper respiratory infection. To relieve these symptoms, Ramirez's mother gave him St. Joseph's Aspirin for Children (SJAC), a nonprescription drug manufactured and distributed by Plough, Inc. The product label stated that the dosage for a child under two years old was "as directed by doctor." Moreover, the package displayed this warning:

> Warning: Reye Syndrome is a rare but serious disease which can follow flu or chicken pox in children and teenagers. While the cause of Reye Syndrome is unknown, some reports claim aspirin may increase the risk of developing this disease. Consult doctor before use in children or teenagers with flu or chicken pox.

The warnings were provided only in English, although Plough was aware that non-English-speaking Hispanics purchased the product. Ramirez's mother, who could read only Spanish, did not consult a doctor before using SJAC to treat Ramirez's condition. After two days, Ramirez's mother took him to a hospital, where the doctor advised her to administer Dimetapp or Pedialyte (nonprescription medications that do not contain aspirin); she disregarded the advice and continued to treat Ramirez with SJAC. Ramirez thereafter developed the potentially fatal Reye syndrome, resulting in severe neurological damage, including cortical blindness, spastic quadriplegia, and mental retardation.

Ramirez sued Plough, alleging that he contracted Reye syndrome as a result of ingesting SJAC. He sought compensatory and punitive damages on, among other things, a theory of product liability. The complaint alleged that SJAC was defective when it left the defendant's control and that the product's reasonably foreseeable use involved a substantial and not readily apparent danger of which the defendant failed to warn adequately.

Finding no duty to warn and no causal relation between the defendant's actions and the plaintiff's illness, the trial court granted summary judgment for the defendant. On appeal, the appellate court reversed after concluding that a jury should decide whether the English warnings were adequate. The defendant appealed.

ISSUE PRESENTED May a manufacturer of nonprescription drugs that can lead to a deadly illness when taken as normally expected incur tort liability for distributing its products with warnings only in English when the manufacturer knows that there are non-English-reading users?

SUMMARY OF OPINION The California Supreme Court began by noting that a manufacturer of nonprescription drugs has a duty to warn purchasers about dangers of its products. The issue under consideration was whether the defendant's duty to warn required it to provide label or package warnings in Spanish.

The court acknowledged that although the Food and Drug Administration (FDA) encourages labeling that meets the needs of non-English speakers, it only requires manufacturers to provide full labeling in English for all nonprescription drugs except those distributed solely in Puerto Rico or another territory where the predominant language is not English.

Although the California legislature had enacted laws to protect non-English speakers in certain circumstances, California did not have a law requiring labeling in a foreign language. Because the

CONTINUED

state and federal statutes expressly required only English labeling, the court decided not to intrude upon a matter it deemed best handled by the legislature.

RESULT Because both state and federal law require warnings in English but not in any other language, the drug manufacturer was not liable in tort for failing to label the aspirin with warnings in a language other than English. Ramirez's case was dismissed.

COMMENTS The California Supreme Court was influenced by the of FDA's experience with Spanish inserts for prescription drugs. Recognizing that "the United States is too heterogeneous to enable manufacturers, at reasonable cost and with reasonable simplicity, to determine exactly where to provide alternative language inserts," the FDA for a time required manufacturers, as an alternative to multilingual or bilingual inserts, to provide Spanish-language translations of their patient package inserts on request to doctors and pharmacists. The FDA later concluded that manufacturers were having difficulty obtaining accurate translations, and eventually it abandoned the patient package insert requirement for prescription drugs altogether.

CRITICAL THINKING QUESTIONS

1. Would the result have been different if the nonprescription medicine had been for an illness particular to a certain non-English-speaking group residing in the United States?
2. Should it matter whether a drug company advertises a particular medicine in a language other than English?

UNAVOIDABLY UNSAFE PRODUCTS

If the societal value of using an *unavoidably unsafe product* outweighs the risk of harm from its use, the manufacturer may be exonerated from liability as long as it provided proper warnings. For example, certain drugs are generally beneficial, but are known to have harmful side effects in some situations. The authors of both the Restatement (Second) and the Restatement (Third) recognized that there should be a separate concept of product liability for manufacturers of prescription drugs and medical devices.

Comment b to Section 6 of the Restatement (Third) articulated the rationale behind this special treatment:

> The traditional refusal by courts to impose tort liability for defective designs of prescription drugs and medical devices is based on the fact that a prescription drug or medical device entails a unique set of risks and benefits. What may be harmful to one patient may be beneficial to another. Under Subsection (c) [of Section 6] a drug is defectively designed only when it provides no net benefit to any class of patients. . . . [M]anufacturers must have ample discretion to develop useful drugs and devices without subjecting their design decisions to the ordinary test applied to products generally.[37]

37. RESTATEMENT (THIRD) OF TORTS: PRODUCTS LIABILITY § 6 cmt. b (1997).

Nearly every jurisdiction in the United States has followed this reasoning in some form or another.[38] For example, the manufacturer of the Sabin oral polio vaccine was held not strictly liable to an individual who contracted polio from the vaccine.[39] The odds of contracting polio from the vaccine were one in a million. The drug's benefits outweighed its dangers, and the manufacturer's warning about the remote risk of harm was reasonably adequate.[40]

WHO MAY BE STRICTLY LIABLE FOR PRODUCT DEFECTS?

In theory, each party in the chain of distribution may be strictly liable for product defects: manufacturers, distributors, wholesalers, and retailers. Although disclaimers of liability are generally ineffective, parties in the chain of distribution may (and should) enter into contracts giving them a right to *indemnity* (that is, reimbursement) if they are found liable for defects caused by other members of the distribution chain.

38. *See* RESTATEMENT (SECOND) OF TORTS § 402A cmt. k (1997).

39. Johnson v. Am. Cyanamid Co., 718 P.2d 1318 (Kan. 1986).

40. *Id.* at 1324–25.

MANUFACTURERS OF PRODUCTS AND COMPONENT PARTS

A manufacturer will be held strictly liable for its defective products regardless of how remote the manufacturer is from the final user of the product. The only requirement for strict liability is that the manufacturer be in the business of selling the injury-causing product. The manufacturer may be held liable even when the distributor makes final inspections, corrections, and adjustments of the product.

Manufacturers of component parts are frequently sued as well and are generally liable for any defects in the components they produce. On the other hand, the maker of a component part is not liable for defective design specifications for the entire product as long as the component is not itself defective. For example, the maker of a car's fuel-injection system will not be liable if the automaker's specifications for the fuel-injection system turn out to be defective and the engine provides insufficient power to change lanes safely on a freeway; however, the manufacturer of the engine would be liable for a defective design. In the following case, the court considered whether a truck-seat manufacturer should be liable for injuries suffered by a driver.

A CASE IN POINT

IN THE LANGUAGE OF THE COURT

CASE 10.3

BOSTROM SEATING, INC. v. CRANE CARRIER CO.

SUPREME COURT OF TEXAS
140 S.W.3D 681 (TEX. 2004).

FACTS Dagoberto Gonzalez suffered head, collar bone, and spinal injuries when the garbage truck he was driving rolled over during an accident. He sued the truck manufacturer, Crane Carrier. Crane filed indemnification claims against two components manufacturers, including Bostrom Seating, which had produced the seat installed in the Crane-designed vehicle. After the trial court directed a verdict in Bostrom's favor, Crane appealed. The appellate court reinstated the claims against Bostrom, and Bostrom appealed, arguing that the claims against it should be dismissed because there was no evidence to establish that the seat itself was defective.

ISSUE PRESENTED Is the manufacturer of a nondefective seat component liable for injuries suffered by an end user of the truck into which the seat was installed?

OPINION SCHNEIDER, J., writing for the Texas Supreme Court:

Although this Court has never itself decided the issue, two of the State's courts of appeals have held that strict liability for component-part manufacturers is limited when the component part is integrated into a larger unit before distribution. Numerous courts outside of Texas have held likewise. We agree with these courts that if the component-part manufacturer does not participate in the integration of the component into the finished product, it is not liable for defects in the final product if the component itself is not defective. It is not proper to extend the doctrine of strict liability to the supplier of a component part used in a product according to the design of the product's manufacturer when the injuries are caused by the design of the product itself, rather than by a defect in the component. Therefore, if no evidence exists to indicate that the component part was itself defective, the component-part manufacturer should be relieved of any liability for a design or manufacturing defect in the final product, including any action for indemnification.

Thus, we turn to the question of whether the evidence presented during trial demonstrated that the seat supplied by Bostrom to Crane was itself defective. [*Eds.*: The court then reviewed the evidence related to the seat, including the following testimony by Gonzalez's expert witness John Stilson: "The bottom line is that this seat, in some other environment, may function and work perfectly safe, but in this environment it can't."]

In addition . . . Crane points to expert testimony that says there was "excessive excursion," meaning there was too much movement permitted in the vehicle's restraint system and that the Crane garbage truck as a whole was defective. [An expert] testified that there were safer alternatives that could have been used in the vehicle to prevent the kind of injuries sustained by Gonzalez. However, this evidence relates to the defectiveness of the vehicle's design and not to the specific seat in question.

CONTINUED

The parties agree that Crane designed the garbage truck and chose which seat it would use. None of the evidence cited by Crane could be used to prove that the Bostrom seat, in and of itself, was defective. Even Crane's own attorney, in his opening statement, admitted that "there isn't anything wrong with the seat." At best, the evidence supports a possible conclusion that using the seat in this specific truck created an allegedly defective restraint system design. Crane was in total control of the design of that system, and Bostrom, playing no part in the design of the truck, cannot be held liable for its possible defectiveness.

RESULT Because no evidence was presented to suggest that the Bostrom seat was itself defective, the court reversed the appeals court's decision. Crane was not entitled to indemnification from Bostrom, so the suit against Bostrom was dismissed.

COMMENTS In deciding whether to hold the component manufacturer liable for injuries suffered while using its product, the court adopted the modern view, which places explicit limitations on the imposition of tort liability on manufacturers of component parts:

> One engaged in the business of selling or otherwise distributing product components who sells or distributes a component is subject to liability for harm to persons or property caused by a product into which the component is integrated if: (a) the component is defective in itself . . . and the defect causes the harm.[41]

CRITICAL THINKING QUESTIONS

1. A supercomputer is made up of several thousand microchips. If one chip, supplied to the computer company by a third-party manufacturer, fails, destroying the whole computer, can the owner of the computer hold the third-party chip manufacturer liable?

2. At what point does a component cease to be a component and merely become part of the whole? From a public policy standpoint, should such a distinction exist?

41. *See* RESTATEMENT (THIRD) OF TORTS: PRODUCTS LIABILITY § 5 (1997).

WHOLESALERS

Wholesalers are usually held strictly liable for defects in the products they sell. In some jurisdictions, however, a wholesaler is not liable for latent or hidden defects if the wholesaler sells the products in exactly the same condition it received them.

RETAILERS

A retailer may also be held strictly liable. For example, in the automobile industry, retailers have a duty to inspect and care for the products. In several jurisdictions, however, a retailer will not be liable if it did not contribute to the defect and played no part in the manufacturing process.

SELLERS OF USED GOODS AND OCCASIONAL SELLERS

Sellers of used goods are usually not held strictly liable because they are not within the original chain of distribution of the product.[42] In addition, the custom in the used-goods market is that there are no warranties or expectations relating to the quality of the products (although some jurisdictions have adopted rules requiring warranties for used cars). A seller of used goods is, however, strictly liable for any defective repairs or replacements he or she makes. Occasional sellers, such as people who host garage sales, are not strictly liable.

SUCCESSOR, MARKET-SHARE, AND PREMISES LIABILITY

Companies may also face product liability because they acquired the firm that sold the defective product, they sold an undifferentiated product, or they operated premises tainted by defective products.

42. Allenberg v. Bentley Hedges Travel Serv., Inc., 22 P.3d 223 (Okla. 2001).

SUCCESSOR LIABILITY

Most states employ the traditional successor liability rule: a corporation purchasing or acquiring the assets of another is liable for the acquired company's debts (including product liability) only when (1) there is a consolidation or merger[43] of the two corporations, (2) the acquirer expressly or impliedly agrees to assume such obligations, or (3) the transaction was wrongfully entered into to escape liability.[44] A minority of jurisdictions have adopted one of two additional bases for succesor liability: the product-line theory and the continuity-of-enterprise aproach. Under the *product-line theory,* espoused by the California Supreme Court,[45] a successor that continues to manufacture the same product line as its predecessor, under the same name and with no outward indication of any change of ownership, may be held liable for product liability claims resulting from that product line, even if the particular item was manufactured and sold by the acquired firm prior to the acquisition. Courts applying the *continuity-of-enterprise approach* look for constancy between the buyer and seller organizations to determine whether the successor company is essentially carrying on its predecessor's enterprise. Among the factors a court will analyze are similarity of management, personnel, assets, facilities, operations, and shareholders, and whether the successor holds itself out to the public as a continuing enterprise.[46]

For example, several people injured in a boating accident caused by defects in the craft used the continuity-of-enterprise approach to successfully sue the company that succeeded the boat manufacturer.[47] Although the name of the company changed, the owners, officers, employees, address, phone number, and line of business remained the same.

MARKET-SHARE LIABILITY

When there are multiple manufacturers of identical products, the injured party may not be able to prove which of the defendant manufacturers sold the product that caused the injury. In certain cases, particularly those involving prescription drugs, the court may allocate liability on the basis of each defendant's share of the market. This doctrine of *market-share liability* was developed by the California Supreme Court in *Sindell v. Abbott Laboratories*[48] to address the specific problem of DES litigation.

Women whose mothers took the drug diethylstil-bestrol (DES) during pregnancy alleged that they were injured by the DES, which, among other things, increased their likelihood of developing cancer. Many of the plaintiffs could not pinpoint which manufacturer was directly responsible for their injuries, so they sought damages from a number of DES manufacturers.

A number of factors made it difficult to identify particular DES manufacturers. All manufacturers made DES from an identical chemical formula. Druggists typically filled prescriptions from whatever stock they had on hand. During the twenty-four years that DES was sold for use during pregnancy, more than three hundred companies entered and left the market. The harmful effects of DES were not discovered until many years after the plaintiffs' mothers had used the drug.

By the time the lawsuit was filed, memories had faded, records had been lost, and witnesses had died. Given the difficulty of identifying the defendant responsible for each plaintiff, the court held that the fairest approach was to apportion liability based on each manufacturer's national market share. The court reasoned that it was more appropriate that the loss be borne by those who produced the drug than by those who suffered injury.

Although the New York Court of Appeals applied market-share liability in DES cases,[49] it characterized the DES situation as "a singular case." The Appellate Division of the Supreme Court of New York (New York's intermediate appeals court) refused to extend the doctrine to lead-based paints because (1) 20 percent of the lead pigments could have been manufactured by defendants not named in the litigation; (2) the plaintiffs were unable to identify the years in which the house was painted, making it impossible to determine which defendants manufactured paint during the relevant period; (3) lead-based paints were not uniform, fungible products; and (4) there was no signature injury in lead poisoning cases.[50]

Many jurisdictions have rejected market-share liability outright. It has been criticized for being a simplistic response to a complex problem and for implying that manufacturers must be the insurers of all their industry's products. Market-share liability has also been challenged on the constitutional ground that it violates a defendant's right to due process of law because it denies a defendant the opportunity to prove that its individual products did not cause the plaintiff's injury.

43. The de facto merger doctrine is discussed in Chapter 20.

44. *See, e.g.,* Nissen Corp. v. Miller, 594 A.2d 564 (Md. 1991) (adopting the traditional successor liability exceptions).

45. Ray v. Alad Corp., 560 P.2d 3 (Cal. 1977). *But see, e.g.,* Semenetz v. Sherling & Walden, Inc., 851 N.E.2d 1170 (N.Y. 2006) (declining to adopt the "product-line" exception).

46. Turner v. Bituminous Cas. Co., 244 N.W.2d 873 (Mich. 1976).

47. Patin v. Thoroughbred Power Boats, 294 F.3d 640 (5th Cir. 2002).

48. 607 P.2d 924 (Cal. 1980), *cert. denied,* 449 U.S. 912 (1980).

49. Hymowitz v. Eli Lilly & Co., 539 N.E.2d 1069 (N.Y. 1989), *cert. denied,* 493 U.S. 944 (1989).

50. Brenner v. Am. Cyanamid Co., 263 A.D.2d 165 (N.Y. App. 1999).

In *Doe v. Baxter Healthcare Corp.*,[51] the U.S. Court of Appeals for the Eighth Circuit refused to apply market-share liability when a young boy became infected with HIV (human immunodeficiency virus) after using Factor VII, a drug for hemophiliacs. The parents of the boy claimed that one of several companies that produced Factor VII placed it on the market despite knowing of the risk of infection. The court determined that the plaintiffs did not present sufficient evidence to sustain the charges against any one defendant and therefore could not hold all of them responsible. In addition to finding that the plaintiffs had presented an insufficient factual case, the court generally rejected the theory of market-share liability on "broad policy grounds." Thus, market-share liability was considered an inappropriate basis for recovery.

PREMISES LIABILITY

Recently, courts have recognized liability for asbestos-related diseases on a *premises liability* theory. Under this theory, a building owner may be found liable for violating its general duty to manage the premises and warn of asbestos dangers.[52]

PRODUCT LIABILITY CLASS ACTIONS

Product liability cases are frequently resolved through class actions, a procedural device that allows a large number of plaintiffs to recover against a defendant in a single case. Lawsuits involving the tobacco industry, asbestos, silicone breast implants, and harmful diet drugs were all resolved through class actions. In contrast, as discussed in the "Inside Story" in this chapter, Merck successfully fought class certification of claims arising out of its anti-inflammatory drug Vioxx.

In *Amchem Products, Inc. v. Windsor*,[53] the U.S. Supreme Court tightened the requirements for certification of a class of plaintiffs suing asbestos manufacturers. The proposed class included both symptomatic and asymptomatic individuals who either (1) had been exposed to asbestos in products, such as roofing materials and insulation, through their occupations or the occupation of a household member, or (2) had a spouse or family member who had been exposed to asbestos. The Court denied the class certification because the class members had differing interests. For example, individuals currently suffering from mesothelioma and other asbestos-related diseases would seek immediate payment, whereas those who had been exposed but did not yet exhibit symptoms of disease and were anticipating future injury would seek to preserve a fund for future compensation for injuries manifesting themselves at a later date. The Court identified several additional differences to support its denial of class certification.

The U.S. Court of Appeals for the Eighth Circuit overturned a national class-action certification of 11,000 Americans who received allegedly faulty heart valves manufactured by St. Jude Medical, holding that each plaintiff had to show a link between any reliance on St. Jude Medical's claims about the valve and subsequent injury.[54] The court had previously rejected class certification for a health monitoring class in the case.[55] Similarly, the Ohio Supreme Court refused to certify a class of more than 4,000 workers exposed to beryllium at an Ohio job site who were seeking the creation of a medical monitoring program.[56] The members of the proposed class spanned forty-six years, multiple contractors, and multiple locations within the plant. The court concluded that "lack of cohesiveness is fatal." As a result, the individual questions outweighed the questions common to the class.

Rule 23(b)(1)(B) of the Federal Rules of Civil Procedure provides a mechanism to resolve class actions in which the total of the aggregated liquidated claims exceeds the fund available to satisfy them (*limited fund class actions*). In *Ortiz v. Fibreboard Corp.*,[57] another asbestos class action, the U.S. Supreme Court made it clear that the trial court itself must determine whether the fund is limited. Thus, it was improper for the trial court to simply accept an agreement among the lead plaintiffs, the insurance companies, and the manufacturer as to the maximum amount the insurance companies could be required to pay tort victims.

COMMON LAW DEFENSES

The defendant in a product liability case may raise the traditional common law tort defenses of assumption of risk and, in some jurisdictions, a variation of comparative negligence

51. 380 F.3d 399 (8th Cir. 2004).

52. *CA App. Ct. Reverses Exxon Nonsuit Ruling,* ASBESTOS LITIG. REP., July 16, 1999. *See, e.g.,* John Crane, Inc. v. Jones, 2004 WL 2495019 (Ga. 2004).

53. 521 U.S. 591 (1997).

54. *In re* St. Jude Med. Inc. Silzone Heart Valve Products Liability Litig., 2008 WL 942274 (8th Cir. 2008) (applying Minnesota law articulated in Group Health Plan, Inc. v. Philip Morris, Inc., 621 N.W.2d 2 (Minn. 2001)).

55. *In re* St. Jude Med. Inc. Silzone Heart Valve Products Liability Litig., 2008 WL 942274 (8th Cir. 2008).

56. Wilson v. Brush Wellman, Inc., 817 N.E.2d 59 (Ohio 2004).

57. 527 U.S. 815 (1999).

known as comparative fault. Other defenses, such as obvious risk, sophisticated user, unforeseeable misuse of the product, the government-contractor defense, and the state-of-the-art defense, may be available only in product liability cases. These defenses are sometimes codified into state statutes, and their acceptance varies from state to state. Finally, under certain circumstances, state product liability law is preempted by federal law.

ASSUMPTION OF RISK

Under the doctrine of *assumption of risk,* when a person voluntarily and unreasonably assumes the risk of a known danger, the manufacturer is not liable for any resulting injury. For example, under Ohio law, if the claimant's express or implied assumption of risk is the direct and proximate cause of harm, then recovery is completely barred.[58] Thus, if a ladder bears a conspicuous warning not to stand on the top step, but a person steps on it anyway and falls, the ladder manufacturer will not be liable for any injuries caused by the fall.

On the other hand, a Washington appellate court found no assumption of risk when a grinding disc exploded and hit a person in the eye.[59] The court reasoned that although the injured person should have been wearing goggles, he could not have anticipated that a hidden defect in the disc would cause it to explode. By not wearing goggles, the injured person assumed only the risk that dust or small particles of wood or metal would lodge in his eyes.

COMPARATIVE FAULT

Contributory negligence by the plaintiff is not a defense in a strict liability action. Nevertheless, in some states, the plaintiff's damages may be reduced by the degree to which his or her own negligence contributed to the injury. This doctrine is known as *comparative fault*.

For example, Michigan law provides that the negligence of the plaintiff does not bar recovery, but damages are reduced by his or her degree of fault—that is, the negligence attributed to the plaintiff.[60] Under Illinois law, if the jury finds that the degree of the plaintiff's fault exceeds 50 percent, then the plaintiff cannot recover damages. If the jury finds that the degree of the plaintiff's fault is less than 50 percent, the plaintiff can recover damages, but the damages will be reduced in proportion to the plaintiff's fault.[61]

> ### › ETHICAL CONSIDERATION
>
> In October 2007, medical device maker Medtronic announced that the lead connecting its electronic defibrillator to a patient's heart may fracture, causing the defibrillator to fail if the heart needs a pulse of electricity to stabilize an erratic beat. Medtronic said that five deaths had been linked to lead failures. In less dramatic cases, the broken wire caused the device to generate unnecessary shocks.
>
> Defibrillators with the faulty leads have been implanted in more than 230,000 patients, but it is expected that only 5,000 of those leads will actually fail. The cost of surgically replacing a lead is roughly $12,500. Medtronic has offered to provide a free replacement lead and contribute $800 to defray other surgical costs, but only to patients whose leads have actually broken and to others whose physicians recommend the surgery due to the patient's particular medical condition. Insurance companies are covering replacement costs only in certain cases. Some doctors are advising their patients not to have replacement surgery—which comes with its own risks—noting that the wireless monitoring technology embedded in the defibrillators allows doctors to monitor each defibrillator's status electronically. They also point out that only 80 percent of defibrillator recipients ever end up needing the device to perform.
>
> Patients are left with a disturbing choice: undergo potentially costly and unnecessary heart surgery or leave the wire in place, hoping that it does not break or, if it does, that the defibrillator is never actually needed. Those patients who opt not to have replacement surgery are clearly aware of the risk of a catastrophic heart failure posed by the flawed leads, but should they be deemed to have assumed that risk by heeding their doctor's advice? Should an implanted defibrillator be treated like a ladder or a grinding disc under the law? Is it ethical for Metronic to refuse to pay the full cost of replacing the lead? Is it good business?
>
> ***Source:*** Factual information drawn from Barnaby J. Feder, *Patients Wonder Whether to Replace a Wire That Might Fail,* N.Y. Times, Dec. 13, 2007. *See also* Larsen v. Pacesetter Sys., Inc., 837 P.2d 1273 (Haw. 1992).

OBVIOUS RISK

If the use of a product carries an *obvious risk,* the manufacturer will not be held liable for injuries that result from ignoring the risk. Although a plaintiff will argue that the manufacturer had a duty to warn of the dangers of a foreseeable use of the product, courts often apply the standard that a manufacturer need not warn of a danger that is generally known and recognized.

58. Ohio Rev. Code Ann. § 2315.42.

59. Haugen v. Minn. Mining & Mfg. Co., 550 P.2d 71 (Wash. App. 1976).

60. Mich. Comp. Laws § 600.2959 (2004).

61. 735 Ill. Comp. Stat. Ann. 5/2-1116 (2004).

For example, in *Maneely v. General Motors Corp.*,[62] two men who rode in the cargo bed of a pickup truck sued GM after sustaining serious injuries in a collision. The men argued that GM failed to warn of the dangers of riding in a cargo bed. The court rejected their claims, noting that a manufacturer should not bear the paternalistic responsibility of warning users of every possible risk that could arise from use of its product. As the public generally recognizes the dangers of riding unrestrained in the cargo bed of a moving pickup truck, GM had no duty to warn of those dangers.

SOPHISTICATED USER

The California Supreme Court articulated a *sophisticated user defense* in product liability and toxic tort actions in 2008, holding that a "manufacturer is not liable to a sophisticated user of its product for failure to warn of a risk, harm or danger, if the sophisticated user knew or *should have known* of that risk, harm, or danger."[63] The court ruled that the sophisticated user's actual knowledge was irrelevant, reasoning that "it would be nearly impossible for a manufacturer to predict or determine whether a given user or member of the sophisticated group actually has knowledge of the dangers because of the infinite number of idiosyncrasies." Rather, the duty to warn is measured by what is generally known or should have been known to the class of sophisticated users and not by the individual plaintiff's subjective knowledge. The court also made clear that the relevant time for determining user sophistication is at the time of the plaintiff's injury, rather than the date that the product was manufactured or distributed.

62. 108 F.3d 1176 (9th Cir. 1997).

63. Johnson v. Am. Standard, Inc., 179 P.3d 904 (Cal. 2008).

UNFORESEEABLE MISUSE OF THE PRODUCT

A manufacturer or seller is entitled to assume that its product will be used in a normal manner. The manufacturer or seller will not be held liable for injuries resulting from abnormal use of its product. For example, unforeseeable misuse of a product is a defense under Indiana law if it is the proximate cause of the harm and the misuse is not reasonably expected by the seller at the time the seller conveyed the product to another party.[64] On the other hand, unusual use that is reasonably foreseeable may be deemed a normal use. For example, operating a lawn mower with the grass bag removed was held to be a foreseeable use, and the manufacturer was liable to a bystander injured by an object that shot out of the unguarded mower.[65]

As a general rule, a company is not liable for the criminal acts of third parties using its products unless the company knew or should have known that its negligence might allow the crime to occur.[66] In the following case, the court considered whether a video game manufacturer was strictly liable for a teenager's shooting spree.

64. IND. CODE ANN. § 34-20-6-4.

65. LaPaglia v. Sears Roebuck & Co., 531 N.Y.S.2d 623 (N.Y. App. Div. 1988).

66. Gaines-Tabb v. ICI Explosives, USA, Inc., 160 F.3d 613, 621 (10th Cir. 1998).

A CASE IN POINT

CASE 10.4

JAMES V. MEOW MEDIA INC.

UNITED STATES COURT OF APPEALS FOR THE SIXTH CIRCUIT 300 F.3D 683 (6TH CIR. 2002), *CERT. DENIED*, 537 U.S. 1159 (2003).

SUMMARY

FACTS In 2002, a teenager in Kentucky went on a shooting spree, killing a number of his classmates at the high school he attended. The families of the victims brought this suit against Meow Media, Inc., which makes and sells video games. The families claimed that the defendant's games desensitized the shooter to violence, thereby leading to the tragedy.

ISSUE PRESENTED Is the creator of a video game, movie, or Internet site that contains violent images and themes liable under either a theory of negligence or strict product liability when children who view these images act violently?

SUMMARY OF OPINION The U.S. Court of Appeals for the Sixth Circuit first addressed the negligence claim. In order to prove negligence, the plaintiffs needed to prove three separate elements: (1) the defendant owed a duty of care to the victims, (2) it breached that duty of care, and (3) the breach was the proximate cause of the injury.

CONTINUED

To find a duty of care, the plaintiffs had to show that the shooter's actions were reasonably foreseeable by the defendant. After a lengthy discussion, the court concluded that the shooting was so aberrant as to be unforeseeable by the video game producer. Furthermore, there is a general rule, with few exceptions, that no one is responsible for the "intentional criminal acts of a third party." In this case, the shooter's intentional act of murder, regardless of the situation, made his act unforeseeable to the defendant. Since there was no duty of care, the defendant could not have breached a duty of care to the victims.

The court then considered whether the plaintiffs had proved proximate cause by establishing a direct connection between the action (in this case the shooting) and the defendant's conduct (distributing video games). The court reiterated that the shooter's actions were intentional criminal acts and found, in keeping with a century of precedent, that a third party's criminal act functions as an intervening act, rendering all actions before that act not the proximate cause of the injury.

The court also addressed the defendant's actions in light of the First Amendment guarantees of free speech and expression. Like virtually all U.S. courts, the Sixth Circuit was "loathe to attach tort liability to the dissemination of ideas."

Finally, the court characterized the plaintiffs' theory that the defendant's works were defective products as "deeply flawed." In a prior case decided more than a decade before, the court had ruled that the "words and pictures" contained in the board game *Dungeons and Dragons* were not products. In light of the changing times and rash of school shootings, the court revisited the issue rather than flatly rejecting the claim based on its earlier ruling. Nonetheless, it concluded that the same logic should apply in this case.

RESULT The plaintiffs had no valid product liability claim. Their suit was dismissed.

COMMENTS The unforeseeability of intentional criminal acts is generally a defense to liability, but if the product is intended to be used in furtherance of a criminal act, the defendant cannot avail itself of that protection. Thus, the publisher of a book entitled *Hit Man*, billed as an instruction manual for murder and actually used by a convicted killer to carry out his crime, was held liable for wrongful death.[67]

67. Rice v. Paladin Enter., Inc., 128 F.3d 233 (4th Cir. 1997), *cert. denied,* 523 U.S. 1074 (1998).

As discussed in Chapter 9, courts will impose new duties to reflect changing societal expectations. For example, certain courts have permittted plaintiffs to pursue claims against gun manufacturers[68] and drug makers[69] for contributing to a "gray market" in their respective products through faulty distribution designs. The courts ruled that the companies' sales practices made it reasonably foreseeable that their products would reach consumers who were prohibited from owning the items, in the case of gun manufacturers, or that the products would be dangerously altered, in the case of drug manufacturers. As noted in Chapter 9, other courts have dismissed such claims. Again, as discussed in Chapter 9, courts in future cases may be willing to hold manufacturers liable for the misuse of their products by terrorists.

68. Ileto v. Glock, 349 F.3d 1191 (9th Cir. 2003).

69. Fagan v. Amerisourcebergen Corp., 356 F. Supp. 2d 198 (E.D.N.Y. 2004).

GOVERNMENT-CONTRACTOR DEFENSE

Under the *government-contractor defense,* a manufacturer of products under contract to the government can avoid product liability if (1) the product was produced according to government specifications, (2) the manufacturer possessed less knowledge about the specifications than did the government agency, (3) the manufacturer exercised proper skill and care in production, and (4) the manufacturer did not deviate from the specifications. The rationale for this immunity is that the manufacturer is acting merely as an agent of the government; to hold the manufacturer liable would unfairly shift the insurance burden from the government to the manufacturer. As discussed below, the Homeland Security Act extended this defense to certain products designed to thwart terrorists.

STATE-OF-THE-ART DEFENSE

In some states, the *state-of-the-art defense* shields a manufacturer from liability for a defective design if no safer product design is generally recognized as being possible. As discussed further below, the Restatement (Third) would require all plaintiffs asserting defective design to prove the existence of an alternative design.

The contours of the state-of-the-art defense are often first laid down by judges, then codified by state legislatures. For example, an Arizona statute provides a defense "if the plans or designs for the product or the methods and techniques of manufacturing, inspecting, testing and labeling the product conformed with the state of the art at the time the product was first sold by defendant."[70]

State courts have split over two aspects of this defense. First, even states that recognize the state-of-the art defense have defined "state of the art" differently. Some states have defined state-of-the-art evidence either in terms of industry custom (e.g., Alaska and New Jersey) or in terms of compliance with existing governmental regulations (e.g., Illinois).[71] A majority of the states that accept the state-of-the-art defense, however, deem "state-of-the-art" to refer to what is technologically feasible at the time of design. Accordingly, a manufacturer may have a duty to use a safer design even if the custom of the industry is to use a less safe alternative.[72]

Second, in states that do not recognize the state-of-the-art defense, there is a split on whether to even allow the introduction of evidence of alternative designs in defective design cases. Certain courts have ruled that state-of-the-art evidence is irrelevant, and therefore inadmissible, in strict product liability cases because it improperly focuses the jury's attention on the reasonableness of the manufacturer's conduct. The overwhelming majority of states, however, hold that state-of-the-art evidence is relevant simply to determining the adequacy of the product's design.

The state-of-the art defense has also been applied in certain failure-to-warn cases. For example, a Missouri statute provides that if the defendant can prove that the dangerous nature of the product was not known and could not reasonably have been discovered at the time the product was placed in the stream of commerce, then the defendant will not be held liable for failure to warn.[73]

PREEMPTION DEFENSE

Perhaps the most significant and controversial of the defenses to product liability is the *preemption defense,* whereby certain federal laws and regulations that set minimum safety standards are held to preempt state law product liablity claims. For example, the National Traffic and Motor Vehicle Safety Act sets standards for automobiles, and the Safe Medical Devices Act sets standards for medical devices. Manufacturers that meet those standards will sometimes be granted immunity from product liability claims on the grounds of federal preemption. The rationale for deferring to the federal regulatory scheme is that allowing states to impose fifty different sets of requirements would frustrate the purpose of a uniform federal scheme. As a representative of the medical device industry put it, "What it boils down to is whether we want to have the experts at the FDA tell us what is a safe pacemaker, or do we want each jury designing its own pacemaker—one doing it one way in Brooklyn and one doing it another way in Missouri?"[74]

Manufacturing groups want preemption to serve as a "silver bullet" defense, effectively eliminating the possibility of state law product liability claims in any sphere governed by federal safety law and regulation. In practice, compliance with a regulatory scheme is not always a valid defense. Instead, the availability of the preemption defense depends largely on the language and context of the federal statute at issue. In recent years, courts have struggled to determine whether federal safety statutes preempt state product liability claims involving tobacco, outboard motors, and faulty medical devices.

In *Cipollone v. Liggett Group, Inc.* (a 1992 decision), the U.S. Supreme Court concluded that Congress intended the Public Health Cigarette Smoking Act of 1969 to have a broad preemptive effect.[75] In particular, the Court held that the Act preempted claims based on a failure to warn and the neutralization of federally mandated warnings to the extent that those claims relied on omissions or inclusions in a tobacco company's advertising or promotions. The Court ruled that the Act did not preempt claims based on express warranty, intentional fraud and misrepresentation, or conspiracy, however, which left room for lawsuits that ultimately cost the tobacco industry more than $300 billion.

Sprietsman v. Mercury Marine[76] involved state common law tort claims arising out of the death of a woman who fell off a boat and was struck by a propeller manufactured by the defendant. The Supreme Court concluded that these claims were not preempted by the Federal Boat Safety Act of 1971 (FBSA) or by the U.S. Coast Guard's decision not to issue a regulation requiring propeller guards on boat motors. The Court scrutinized the wording of the FBSA's

70. ARIZ. REV. STAT. § 12-683(1).

71. *See* Potter v. Chicago Pneumatic Tool Co., 694 A.2d 1319 (Conn. 1997).

72. *Id.* at 1347.

73. MO. REV. STAT. § 537.764 (1999).

74. Paul M. Barrett, *Lora Lohr's Pacemaker May Alter Liability Law,* WALL ST. J., Apr. 9, 1996, at B1 (quoting Victor Schwartz).

75. 505 U.S. 504 (1992).

76. 537 U.S. 51 (2002).

preemption clause, which prohibited states from enforcing "a law or regulation establishing a recreational vessel or associated equipment performance or other safety standard or imposing a requirement for associated equipment" that was not identical to a federal regulation, to discern whether the clause preempted common law claims:

> First, the article "a" before "law or regulation" implies a discreteness—which is embodied in statutes and regulations—that is not present in the common law. Second, because "a word is known by the company it keeps," the terms "law" and "regulation" used together in the pre-emption clause indicate that Congress pre-empted only positive enactments. If "law" were read broadly so as to include the common law, it might also be interpreted to include regulations, which would render the express reference to "regulation" in the pre-emption clause superfluous.

Nor did the scope of the statute indicate that Congress intended federal law to occupy the field exclusively. There was no implied conflict preemption because a private party could comply with both state and federal requirements.

Finally, the Coast Guard's decision not to adopt a regulation requiring propeller guards on motorboats was not deemed "the functional equivalent of a regulation prohibiting all States and their political subdivisions from adopting such a regulation." Even though the Coast Guard's decision "was undoubtedly intentional and carefully considered, it does not convey an 'authoritative' message of a federal policy against propeller guards."

› ETHICAL CONSIDERATION

A 1992 study by the Johns Hopkins University Injury Prevention Center and the Institute for Injury Reduction estimated that between 2,000 and 3,000 injuries and fatalities are caused by propeller strikes each year. If you were a manager of an outboard motor manufacturer, would you redesign your firm's products? At what cost?

In general, the more rigorous the federal regulatory process, the more likely that product liability claims will be preempted. *Medtronic, Inc. v. Lohr*[77] involved a pacemaker that the Food and Drug Administration (FDA) had cleared pursuant to an exemption from thorough review for medical devices "substantially equivalent" to devices already on the market.[78] Because the Medtronic pacemaker had not undergone rigorous premarket regulatory examination, the plaintiff's state law product liability claims were not preempted.[79]

In the following case involving a Medtronic catheter that *had* undergone the more thorough premarket approval process, the U.S. Supreme Court ruled that state tort liability claims of strict liability, breach of warranty, and negligent design were preempted by the federal requirements.

77. 518 U.S. 470 (1996).

78. 21 U.S.C. § 510(k).

79. This interpretation was supported by the FDA's proposal of regulations to clarify its position.

A CASE IN POINT

IN THE LANGUAGE OF THE COURT

CASE 10.5

RIEGEL V. MEDTRONIC, INC.

SUPREME COURT OF THE UNITED STATES 128 S. CT. 999 (2008).

FACTS In 1996, Charles Riegel underwent coronary angioplasty shortly after suffering a myocardial infarction. Riegel's doctor inserted the Evergreen Balloon Catheter marketed by Medtronic, Inc. into his patient's coronary artery in an attempt to dilate the diseased artery. After Riegel's doctor inflated the catheter five times, it ruptured. Riegel then developed a heart block, was placed on life support, and underwent emergency coronary bypass surgery.

The catheter was a Class III device that had received premarket approval from the FDA in 1994 pursuant to the Medical Device Amendments of 1976 (MDA);[80] changes to its label received supplemental approvals in 1995 and 1996. Riegel and his wife Donna sued, alleging that Medtronic's catheter was designed, labeled, and manufactured in a manner that violated New York common law. The trial court held that the MDA preempted Riegel's claims of strict liability; breach of implied warranty; and negligence in the design, testing, inspection, distribution, labeling, marketing, and sale of the catheter. It also held that the MDA preempted a negligent manufacturing claim insofar

CONTINUED

80. 21 U.S.C. § 360k.

as it was not premised on the theory that Medtronic violated federal law. The U.S. Court of Appeals for the Second Circuit affirmed, and the Riegels appealed.

Issue Presented Does the preemption clause in the Medical Device Amendments of 1976 bar common law claims challenging the safety and effectiveness of a medical device given premarket approval by the FDA?

Opinion SCALIA, J., writing on behalf of the U.S. Supreme Court:

I

The Federal Food, Drug, and Cosmetic Act (FDCA), as amended,[81] has long required FDA approval for the introduction of new drugs into the market. Until the statutory enactment at issue here, however, the introduction of new medical devices was left largely for the States to supervise as they saw fit.

The regulatory landscape changed in the 1960's and 1970's, as complex devices proliferated and some failed. Most notably, the Dalkon Shield intrauterine device, introduced in 1970, was linked to serious infections and several deaths, not to mention a large number of pregnancies. Thousands of tort claims followed. In the view of many, the Dalkon Shield failure and its aftermath demonstrated the inability of the common-law tort system to manage the risks associated with dangerous devices. Several States adopted regulatory measures, including California, which in 1970 enacted a law requiring premarket approval of medical devices.

Congress stepped in with passage of the Medical Device Amendments of 1976 (MDA), which swept back some state obligations and imposed a regime of detailed federal oversight. The MDA includes an express pre-emption provision that states:

> "Except as provided in subsection (b) of this section, no State or political subdivision of a State may establish or continue in effect with respect to a device intended for human use any requirement—
>
> "(1) which is different from, or in addition to, any requirement applicable under this chapter to the device, and
>
> "(2) which relates to the safety or effectiveness of the device or to any other matter included in a requirement applicable to the device under this chapter."

. . .

The new regulatory regime established various levels of oversight for medical devices, depending on the risks they present. . . .

The devices receiving the most federal oversight are those in Class III, which include replacement heart valves, implanted cerebella stimulators, and pacemaker pulse generators. In general, a device is assigned to Class III if it cannot be established that a less stringent classification would provide reasonable assurance of safety and effectiveness. . . .

Although the MDA established a rigorous regime of premarket approval for new Class III devices, it grand-fathered many that were already on the market. . . . A new device need not undergo premarket approval if the FDA finds [pursuant to MDA §510(k) that] it is "substantially equivalent" to another device exempt from premarket approval. . . .

Premarket approval is a "rigorous" process. A manufacturer must submit what is typically a multivolume application. It includes, among other things, full reports of all studies and investigations of the device's safety and effectiveness that have been published or should reasonably be known to the applicant; a "full statement" of the device's "components, ingredients, and properties and of

CONTINUED

81. 21 U.S.C. § 301 *et seq.*

the principle or principles of operation"; "a full description of the methods used in, and the facilities and controls used for, the manufacture, processing, and, when relevant, packing and installation of, such device"; samples or device components required by the FDA; and a specimen of the proposed labeling. Before deciding whether to approve the application, the agency may refer it to a panel of outside experts and may request additional data from the manufacturer.

The FDA spends an average of 1,200 hours reviewing each application, and grants premarket approval only if it finds there is a "reasonable assurance" of the device's "safety and effectiveness." The agency must "weig[h] any probable benefit to health from the use of the device against any probable risk of injury or illness from such use." It may thus approve devices that present great risks if they nonetheless offer great benefits in light of available alternatives. . . .

The premarket approval process includes review of the device's proposed labeling. The FDA evaluates safety and effectiveness under the conditions of use set forth on the label and must determine that the proposed labeling is neither false nor misleading.

After completing its review, the FDA may grant or deny premarket approval. It may also condition approval on adherence to performance standards, restrictions upon sale or distribution, or compliance with other requirements. . . .

. . . .

Once a device has received premarket approval, the MDA forbids the manufacturer to make, without FDA permission, changes in design specifications, manufacturing processes, labeling, or any other attribute, that would affect safety or effectiveness. If the applicant wishes to make such a change, it must submit, and the FDA must approve, an application for supplemental premarket approval, to be evaluated under largely the same criteria as an initial application.

After premarket approval, the devices are subject to reporting requirements. These include the obligation to inform the FDA of new clinical investigations or scientific studies concerning the device which the applicant knows of or reasonably should know of and to report incidents in which the device may have caused or contributed to death or serious injury, or malfunctioned in a manner that would likely cause or contribute to death or serious injury if it recurred. The FDA has the power to withdraw premarket approval based on newly reported data or existing information and must withdraw approval if it determines that a device is unsafe or ineffective under the conditions in its labeling.

II

Since the MDA expressly pre-empts only state requirements "different from, or in addition to, any requirement applicable . . . to the device" under federal law, we must determine whether the Federal Government has established requirements applicable to Medtronic's catheter. If so, we must then determine whether the Riegels' common-law claims are based upon New York requirements with respect to the device that are "different from, or in addition to" the federal ones, and that relate to safety and effectiveness.

. . . In *Lohr*, . . . we concluded that federal manufacturing and labeling requirements applicable across the board to almost all medical devices did not pre-empt the common-law claims of negligence and strict liability. . . .

. . . .

Premarket approval, in contrast, imposes "requirements" under the MDA. . . . Unlike general labeling duties, premarket approval is specific to individual devices. And it is in no sense an exemption from federal safety review—it *is* federal safety review. Thus, the attributes that *Lohr* found lacking . . . are present here. While §510(k) is "'focused on *equivalence,* not safety,'" premarket approval is focused on safety, not equivalence. While devices that enter the market through §510(k) have "never been formally reviewed under the MDA for safety or efficacy," the FDA may grant premarket

CONTINUED

approval only after it determines that a device offers a reasonable assurance of safety and effectiveness. And while the FDA does not "'require'" that a device allowed to enter the market as a substantial equivalent "take any particular form for any particular reason," the FDA requires a device that has received premarket approval to be made with almost no deviations from the specifications in its approval application, for the reason that the FDA has determined that the approved form provides a reasonable assurance of safety and effectiveness.

III

We turn, then, to the second question: whether the Riegels' common-law claims rely upon "any requirement" of New York law applicable to the catheter that is "different from, or in addition to" federal requirements and that "relates to the safety or effectiveness of the device or to any other matter included in a requirement applicable to the device." . . .

A

In *Lohr,* five Justices concluded that common-law causes of action for negligence and strict liability do impose "requirement[s]" and would be pre-empted by federal requirements specific to a medical device. We adhere to that view. In interpreting two other statutes [the Federal Insecticide, Fungicide, and Rodenticide Act[82] and the Public Health Cigarette Smoking Act of 1969[83]], we have likewise held that a provision preempting state "requirements" pre-empted common-law duties. . . .

. . . State tort law that requires a manufacturer's catheters to be safer, but hence less effective, than the model the FDA has approved disrupts the federal scheme no less than state regulatory law to the same effect. Indeed, one would think that tort law, applied by juries under a negligence or strict-liability standard, is less deserving of preservation. A state statute, or a regulation adopted by a state agency, could at least be expected to apply cost-benefit analysis similar to that applied by the experts at the FDA: How many more lives will be saved by a device which, along with its greater effectiveness, brings a greater risk of harm? A jury, on the other hand, sees only the cost of a more dangerous design, and is not concerned with its benefits; the patients who reaped those benefits are not represented in court.[84] . . .

B

The dissent would narrow the pre-emptive scope of the term "requirement" on the grounds that it is "difficult to believe that Congress would, without comment, remove all means of judicial recourse" for consumers injured by FDA-approved devices. But, as we have explained, this is exactly what a pre-emption clause for medical devices does by its terms. The operation of a law enacted by Congress need not be seconded by a committee report on pain of judicial nullification. It is not our job to speculate upon congressional motives. If we were to do so, however, the only indication available—the text of the statute—suggests that the solicitude for those injured by FDA-approved devices, which the dissent finds controlling, was overcome in Congress's estimation by solicitude for those who would suffer without new medical devices if juries were allowed to apply the tort law of 50 States to all innovations.

. . . .

IV

State requirements are pre-empted under the MDA only to the extent that they are "different from, or in addition to" the requirements imposed by federal law. Thus, §360k does not prevent a State

CONTINUED

82. Bates v. Dow Agrosciences LLC, 544 U.S. 431 (2005).

83. Cipollone v. Liggett Group, Inc., 505 U.S. 504 (1992).

84. The Court noted: "The Riegels . . . invoke §360h(d), which provides that compliance with certain FDA orders 'shall not relieve any person from liability under Federal or State law.' This indicates that some state-law claims are not pre-empted, as we held in *Lohr.* But it could not possibly mean that *all* state-law claims are not pre-empted, since that would deprive the MDA pre-emption clause of all content. And it provides no guidance as to which state-law claims are pre-empted and which are not."

from providing a damages remedy for claims premised on a violation of FDA regulations; the state duties in such a case "parallel," rather than add to, federal requirements.

RESULT The Court upheld the dismissal of the Riegels' claims for breach of warranty, failure to warn, and negligence.

CONCURRENCE STEVENS, J., concurring in part and concurring in the judgment:

The significance of the pre-emption provision in the Medical Device Amendments of 1976 (MDA) was not fully appreciated until many years after it was enacted. It is an example of a statute whose text and general objective cover territory not actually envisioned by its authors. In such cases we have frequently concluded that "it is ultimately the provisions of our laws rather than the principal concerns of our legislators by which we are governed." Accordingly, while I agree with Justice Ginsburg's description of the actual history and principal purpose of the pre-emption provision at issue in this case, I am persuaded that its text does preempt state law requirements that differ. I therefore write separately to add these few words about the MDA's history and the meaning of "requirements."

There is nothing in the pre-enactment history of the MDA suggesting that Congress thought state tort remedies had impeded the development of medical devices. Nor is there any evidence at all to suggest that Congress decided that the cost of injuries from Food and Drug Administration–approved medical devices was outweighed "by solicitude for those who would suffer without new medical devices if juries were allowed to apply the tort law of 50 States to all innovations." That is a policy argument advanced by the Court, not by Congress.

DISSENT GINSBURG, J., dissenting:

I dissent from today's constriction of state authority. Congress, in my view, did not intend §360k(a) to effect a radical curtailment of state common-law suits seeking compensation for injuries caused by defectively designed or labeled medical devices. . . .

I

The "purpose of Congress is the ultimate touchstone of pre-emption analysis." . . . Preemption analysis starts with the assumption that "the historic police powers of the States [a]re not to be superseded . . . unless that was the clear and manifest purpose of Congress." . . . Given the traditional "primacy of state regulation of matters of health and safety," courts assume "that state and local regulation related to [those] matters . . . can normally coexist with federal regulations."

A preemption clause tells us that Congress intended to supersede or modify state law to some extent. In the absence of legislative precision, however, courts may face the task of determining the substance and scope of Congress' displacement of state law. Where the text of a preemption clause is open to more than one plausible reading, courts ordinarily "accept the reading that disfavors pre-emption."

. . . .

A

Congress enacted the MDA "to provide for the safety and effectiveness of medical devices intended for human use." A series of high-profile medical device failures that caused extensive injuries and loss of life propelled adoption of the MDA. Conspicuous among these failures was the Dalkon Shield intrauterine device. . . . By early 1976, "more than 500 lawsuits seeking compensatory and punitive damages totaling more than $400 million" had been filed. Given the publicity attending the Dalkon Shield litigation and Congress' awareness of the suits at the time the MDA was under consideration, I find informative the absence of any sign of a legislative design to preempt state common-law tort actions.

CONTINUED

The Court recognizes that "§360k does not prevent a State from providing a damages remedy for claims premised on a violation of FDA regulations." That remedy, although important, does not help consumers injured by devices that receive FDA approval but nevertheless prove unsafe. The MDA's failure to create any federal compensatory remedy for such consumers further suggests that Congress did not intend broadly to preempt state common-law suits grounded on allegations independent of FDA requirements. It is "difficult to believe that Congress would, without comment, remove all means of judicial recourse" for large numbers of consumers injured by defective medical devices. . . .

The former chief counsel to the FDA explained:

> "FDA's view is that FDA product approval and state tort liability usually operate independently, each providing a significant, yet distinct, layer of consumer protection. FDA regulation of a device cannot anticipate and protect against all safety risks to individual consumers. Even the most thorough regulation of a product such as a critical medical device may fail to identify potential problems presented by the product. Regulation cannot protect against all possible injuries that might result from use of a device over time. Preemption of all such claims would result in the loss of a significant layer of consumer protection. . . ."

[*Eds.:* The FDA announced a new position in favor of preemption in its *amicus* brief in this case, but Justice Ginsburg concluded that the FDA's long-held view on the limited preemptive effect of §360k better comported with the presumption against preemption of state health and safety protections as well as the purpose and history of the MDA.] The Court's construction of §360k(a) has the "perverse effect" of granting broad immunity "to an entire industry that, in the judgment of Congress, needed more stringent regulation. . . ."

The MDA does grant the FDA authority to order certain remedial action if, *inter alia*, it concludes that a device "presents an unreasonable risk of substantial harm to the public health" and that notice of the defect "would not by itself be sufficient to eliminate the unreasonable risk." Thus the FDA may order the manufacturer to repair the device, replace it, refund the purchase price, cease distribution, or recall the device. The prospect of ameliorative action by the FDA, however, lends no support to the conclusion that Congress intended largely to preempt state common-law suits. Quite the opposite: Section 360h(d) states that "[c]ompliance with an order issued under this section shall not relieve any person from liability under Federal or State law." That provision anticipates "[court-awarded] damages for economic loss" from which the value of any FDA-ordered remedy would be subtracted.

B

Congress enacted the MDA after decades of regulating drugs and food and color additives under the Federal Food, Drug, and Cosmetic Act (FDCA). . . . Congress' experience regulating drugs and additives informed, and in part provided the model for, its regulation of medical devices. I therefore turn to an examination of that experience.

Starting in 1938, the FDCA required that new drugs undergo preclearance by the FDA before they could be marketed. Nothing in the FDCA's text or legislative history suggested that FDA preclearance would immunize drug manufacturers from common-law tort suits.

By the time Congress enacted the MDA in 1976, state common-law claims for drug labeling and design defects had continued unabated despite nearly four decades of FDA regulation. Congress' inclusion of a preemption clause in the MDA was not motivated by concern that similar state tort actions could be mounted regarding medical devices. Rather, Congress included §360k(a) and (b) to empower the FDA to exercise control over state premarket approval systems installed at a time when there was no preclearance at the federal level.

CONTINUED

. . . In sum, state premarket regulation of medical devices, not any design to suppress tort suits, accounts for Congress' inclusion of a preemption clause in the MDA. . . .

Congress' experience regulating drugs also casts doubt on Medtronic's policy arguments for reading §360k(a) to preempt state tort claims. . . . [T]he process for approving new drugs is at least as rigorous as the premarket approval process for medical devices. Courts that have considered the question have overwhelmingly held that FDA approval of a new drug application does not preempt state tort suits. . . .

III

Refusing to read §360k(a) as an automatic bar to state common-law tort claims would hardly render the FDA's premarket approval of Medtronic's medical device application irrelevant to the instant suit. First, a . . . medical device manufacturer may have a dispositive defense if it can identify an actual conflict between the plaintiff's theory of the case and the FDA's premarket approval of the device in question. As currently postured, this case presents no occasion to take up this issue for Medtronic relies exclusively on §360k(a) and does not argue conflict preemption. Second, a medical device manufacturer may be entitled to interpose a regulatory compliance defense based on the FDA's approval of the premarket application. Most States do not treat regulatory compliance as dispositive, but regard it as one factor to be taken into account by the jury. In those States, a manufacturer could present the FDA's approval of its medical device as evidence that it used due care in the design and labeling of the product.

Critical Thinking Questions

1. Do you find the argument of the majority or that of the dissent more persuasive?
2. Under Justice Ginsburg's reasoning, would FDA approval of a medical device ever foreclose a claim for defective design or warning?

In March 2008, an evenly split Supreme Court affirmed a New York court ruling that federal law does not preempt claims against a drug company that fraudulently gained FDA approval of the drug in question.[85] That same year, the Supreme Court agreed to review a decision by the Vermont Supreme Court upholding a $6.8 million state law judgment for insufficient warning labels against drug manufacturer Wyeth.[86] Certain experts predict that the Court will use the *Wyeth* case to extend federal preemption to shield the makers of drugs bearing FDA-approved labeling from state law liability for failure to warn.[87]

Other Legislative Limits on Liability

Legislative reforms have changed many of the common law rules discussed earlier in this chapter. For example, a number of states have enacted legislation to limit nonmanufacturers' and joint liability, cap punitive damages, deter frivolous suits, and limit the time within which a product liability suit may be brought.

85. Warner-Lambert Co. v. Kent, 128 S. Ct. 1168 (2008). The Court was evenly split, with Chief Justice Roberts recusing himself. By rule, an evenly divided Court affirms the lower court ruling, but carries no precedential weight. Linda Greenhouse, *Court Allows Suit Against Drug Maker,* N.Y. Times, Mar., 4, 2008, at 21.

86. Wyeth v. Levine, 2006 WL 3041078 (Vt. Oct. 27, 2006), *cert. granted,* 128 S. Ct. 1118 (2008).

87. Daniel Fisher, *Take as Directed,* Forbes, Mar. 10, 2008, at 44. The U.S. Court of Appeals for the Third Circuit ruled that the FDA's public rejection of calls for additional labeling to warn of the risk of suicidal behavior by adults taking the antidepressants Paxil and Zoloft preempted state law claims for failure to warn in *Colacicco v. Apotex, Inc.,* 521 F. 3d 253 (3d Cir. 2003), but the court expressly reserved the question of "whether the FDA's mere approval of drug labeling is sufficient to preempt state-law claims alleging that the labeling failed to warn of a given danger; [or] whether FDA approval of drug labeling constitutes minimum standards in the absence of the FDA's express rejection of a specific warning."

LIMITATIONS ON NONMANUFACTURERS' LIABILITY

Rather than holding all companies in the chain of distribution liable, many state legislatures have limited the liability of nonmanufacturers. For example, a Minnesota statute provides that once an injured person files a claim against the manufacturer of the product, the court must, in most cases, dismiss the strict liability claims against any other defendants. A nonmanufacturer can be held strictly liable, however, if it was involved in the design or manufacture of the product or provided instructions or warnings about the defect, or if it knew of or created the defect. The nonmanufacturer may also be held strictly liable if the manufacturer is no longer in business or if it cannot satisfy a judgment against it.[88]

An Illinois statute provides that an action against a defendant other than the manufacturer will be dismissed unless the plaintiff can show that (1) the defendant had some control over the design or manufacture of the product, or instructed or warned the manufacturer about the alleged defect; (2) the defendant actually knew of the defect; or (3) the defendant created the defect.[89]

LIMITATIONS ON JOINT LIABILITY

Traditionally, all defendants in a strict liability action were held jointly and severally liable. Each defendant was held liable not only for the injuries it severally—that is, individually—caused, but also for all of the injuries caused by the other defendants jointly. Thus, a firm such as USG Corporation, which had used asbestos in only a small subset of its products, was held jointly and severally liable for personal-injury claims asserted by workers who had been exposed to asbestos in products manufactured by other firms, such as Johns Manville and GAF, that were in bankruptcy and unable to pay their share of the liability.[90]

At least thirty-eight states have placed limits on joint and several liability, and many have abolished joint liability altogether.[91] For example, an Oregon statute limits joint and several liability as follows:

> Liability of each defendant for non-economic damages is several, not joint. Liability of a defendant who is less than 15% at fault for economic damages is several only. Liability of a defendant who is 15% or more at fault for the economic damages is joint and several, except that a defendant whose fault is less than the plaintiff's is liable only for that percentage of the recoverable economic damages.[92]

As noted earlier, "innocent" parties in the chain of distribution may, by contract, require indemnification from the co-defendants at fault for the product defect at issue. But, absent a limitation on joint liability, an indemnification provision will not relieve a member of the chain of distribution from its obligation to pay the share of any insolvent co-defendant.

88. Minn. Stat. § 544.41.

89. 735 Ill. Comp. Stat. Ann. 5/2-621.

90. *See* Constance E. Bagley & Eliot Sherman, *USG Corporation (A), (B), & (C)* (Harv. Bus. School Case Nos. 807-090, 807-120, & 807-121; 2007).

91. David Olsen, *Minnesota: Key Reform Bills Head for State Senate,* Metropolitan Corp. Couns., Feb. 2000.

92. Or. Rev. Stat. § 18.485.

Political PERSPECTIVE

Lobbying for Limitations on Product Liability

Over the last two decades, U.S. businesses have taken steps to influence both the creation and the interpretation of product liability laws. Companies can obtain legislative insulation by persuading lawmakers to incorporate protection in the core of the bill or to attach a "rider" to another piece of legislation. For example, the SAFETY Act,[a] which promotes the development of anti-terrorism tools, (1) grants exclusive federal jurisdiction over sellers of "qualified anti-terrorism technology"; (2) limits the liability of sellers of qualified anti-terrorism technologies to an amount of liability insurance coverage specified for each individual technology; (3) prohibits joint and several liability for noneconomic damages, so sellers are liable only for the percentage of noneconomic damages that is proportionate to their responsibility for the harm; (4) bars punitive damages and prejudgment interest; and (5) creates a rebuttable presumption that the seller is entitled to the "government-contractor defense," provided that its "qualified anti-terrorism technology" is certified by the Department of Homeland Security as an "Approved Product for Homeland Security."

CONTINUED

Riders are essentially add-ons and do not have to be related to the primary thrust of the bill. For example, under pressure from the White House, Congress added a rider to the Homeland Security Act of 2002[b] to protect drug companies from certain liability suits.[c]

While firms have successfully lobbied for certain congressional limits on product liability, DaimlerChrysler assistant general counsel Stephen B. Hantler claimed that "the greatest return on investment is at the state level." By 2007, business groups had procured the following victories at the state level:

- Limits on punitive damages (32 states).
- Limits on pain and suffering damages (23 states).
- Restrictions on class-action lawsuits (9 states).
- Reduction in size of bonds needed to appeal a verdict (more than 30 states).
- Bar on ability of out-of-state plaintiffs to file suit in a jurisdiction with which they have no connection (8 states).[d]

In addition, Michigan now severely restricts consumers' ability to initiate litigation against pharmaceutical companies in that state, and six states allow only a few select types of asbestos suits.[e] Statehouse lobbyists have also pushed to make it harder for affluent individuals to avoid jury duty.[f]

Business representatives have also sought to extend their influence to the state courtrooms where most product liability cases are heard. More than half of the states elect their judges, and corporate interest groups have actively supported the campaigns of those candidates seen as sympathetic to business interests.[g] For example, in 2006 candidates for the position of chief justice of the Alabama Supreme Court received more than $8 million in contributions from business and nonbusiness interests.[h]

In the 1990s, while George W. Bush was governor of Texas, his aide (and subsequent White House deputy chief of staff) Karl Rove was instrumental in shifting the makeup of the Texas Supreme Court from 100 percent Democratic to 100 percent Republican.[i] In 2004, business groups outspent plaintiffs' lawyers in the Texas State Supreme Court elections for the first time ($21.5 million in campaign contributions from the business groups versus $13.3 million from the plaintiffs' bar).[j] The Texas courts have made it increasingly difficult for plaintiffs to bring mass-injury class actions, and big jury verdicts have become more vulnerable on appeal. During its 2005–2006 term, the Texas Supreme Court ruled against consumers in 83 percent of the cases.[k] Frederick M. Baron, a Dallas plaintiffs' attorney specializing in asbestos and industrial toxin cases, remarked, "When you have a large verdict that you receive from a jury, you can't settle the case anymore because the defendants will walk in and say: 'We know we're going to win in the Supreme Court.'"[l]

Federal judges are appointed, but that does not eliminate the possibility of corporate influence. The U.S. Chamber of Commerce, which has spent an estimated $21 million lobbying influential federal policymakers—from White House staffers to members of Congress to regulating agency officials—endorses U.S. Supreme Court candidates and lobbies for their nomination.[m] The Chamber ardently supported recent Court additions Chief Justice John Roberts and Justice Samuel Alito.[n]

a. Support Antiterrorism by Fostering Effective Technologies Act, Pub. L. No. 107-296, §§ 861-865, 116 Stat. 2238. *See also* 6 C.F.R. pt. 25.3.
b. Pub. L. No. 107-296, 116 Stat. 2229.
c. Dan Morgan, *Homeland Bill Rider Aids Drugmakers; Measure Would Block Suits over Vaccines, FBI Powers Would Also Grow,* WASH. POST, Nov. 15, 2002, at A7.
d. Michael Orey, *How Business Trounced the Trial Lawyers,* BUS. WK., Jan. 8, 2007, at 44.
e. *Id.*
f. Lorraine Woellert, *Tort Reform: A Little Here, a Little There,* BUS. WK., Jan. 8, 2003, at 60.
g. Mike France & Lorraine Woellert, *The Battle over the U.S. Courts,* BUS. WK., Sept. 27, 2004, at 36.
h. Robert Barnes, *Judicial Races Now Rife with Politics,* WASH. POST, Oct. 28, 2007, at A1.
i. Orey, *supra* note d.
j. *Id.*
k. Orey, *supra* note d.
l. Quoted in *id.*, at 49–50.
m. Jeffrey Rosen, *Supreme Court, Inc.,* N.Y. TIMES, Mar. 16, 2008, at MM38.
n. *Id.*

CAPS ON PUNITIVE DAMAGES

Large awards of punitive damages by U.S. juries have been criticized for providing windfalls to injured parties far in excess of their actual losses and for motivating plaintiffs and their lawyers to engage in expensive and wasteful litigation rather than settling cases. Both legislatures and courts have sought to solve this problem by capping punitive damages.

More than thirty states have enacted legislation limiting punitive damages awards. These reforms have typically taken three basic forms. Certain states have either limited the availability of punitive damages or require a higher standard of proof (such as clear and convincing evidence rather than a mere preponderance of evidence) before punitives will be awarded; a few states have done both. For example, North Dakota requires plaintiffs to prove oppression, fraud, or actual malice before claiming punitive damages. Other states have placed outright caps on punitive damages (Georgia, for instance, caps punitives at $250,000) or have tied punitive damages to compensatory damages (in Florida, for example, punitives cannot exceed three times compensatory damages). Finally, a few states (such as New Hampshire) have banned punitive awards altogether.

In *Philip Morris v. Williams*,[93] the Supreme Court held that juries calculating the size of a punitive damages award may not take into account the harm caused to people other than the plaintiffs in the case at hand. Justice Stephen Breyer explained: "To permit punishment for injuring a non-party victim would add a near-standardless dimension to the punitive damages equation. How many other such victims are there? How seriously were they injured?"[94] Despite apparent concern about disproportional retribution, the majority opinion in *Philip Morris* explicitly permits juries to consider the impact of the defendant's conduct on others when deciding whether the conduct was "particularly reprehensible," which is a factor in determining whether any punitive damages are warranted.

As discussed in Chapter 4, the Court limited punitive damages in maritime cases to one times the compensatory damages in *Exxon Shipping Co. v. Baker*[95] Justice Alito had recused himself from the case because he owns Exxon stock.[96]

PENALTIES FOR FRIVOLOUS SUITS

Some states have enacted penalties to deter frivolous lawsuits. For example, a Wisconsin statute provides that if a claim or defense is found to be frivolous, the prevailing party can be awarded its legal costs and attorneys' fees.[97] Minnesota and South Dakota passed similar legislation in 1997.

STATUTES OF LIMITATIONS

A *statute of limitations* is a time limit, set by statute, within which a lawsuit must be brought. Ordinarily, the statute of limitations starts to run at the time a person is injured. There are exceptions, however.

Discovery-of-Injury and Revival Statutes

In many cases involving exposure to certain products, such as asbestos, the plaintiff did not become aware of the injury until after the statute of limitations had run out. This situation led to the adoption of *discovery-of-injury statutes*, which generally provide that the statute of limitations for asbestos and certain other claims does not begin to run until the person discovers the injury from exposure to asbestos.

When information about the prenatal injuries caused by the drug DES emerged, state legislatures passed *revival statutes* permitting plaintiffs to file lawsuits that had previously been barred by the running of the statute of limitations. DES manufacturers unsuccessfully argued that the revival statutes violated their rights to due process of law and to equal protection of the laws because the statutes typically apply to only a few substances, such as DES or asbestos, and not to other dangerous chemical substances. Most courts rejected these arguments and held that state revival statutes have a rational basis and that legislatures enacting such statutes are acting within their broad discretion.[98] More recently, revival statutes have been enacted to extend the time in which women may sue for injuries caused by silicone breast implants.

As injuries are increasingly being discovered long after exposure, many states have amended their statutes of limitations to define more precisely when a cause of action arises. For example, the Ohio statute provides that:

- An asbestos cause of action arises when the claimant learns or should have realized that he or she was injured by exposure to asbestos, whichever is earlier.
- An Agent Orange cause of action involving exposure of a veteran to chemical defoliants or herbicides arises when the claimant learns that he or she was injured by the exposure.
- A DES drug cause of action arises when the claimant learns from a physician that her injury might be related to her prenatal DES exposure or when she should have realized that she had such an injury, whichever is earlier.[99]

STATUTES OF REPOSE

A *statute of repose* cuts off the right to assert a cause of action after a specified period of time from the delivery of the product. A statute of repose is different from a statute of limitations, which measures the time period from the time when the injury occurred. Thus, under a ten-year statute of repose, a person injured eleven years after the product was delivered would be time-barred from suing by the statute of repose, though not by the statute of limitations.

For example, Cessna and other light airplane manufacturers lobbied Congress hard for the General Aviation Revitalization Act, which was enacted in 1994. The Act created an eighteen-year statute of repose, which limited an aircraft manufacturer's liability for performance of an aircraft after the first eighteen years of the aircraft's life. Because the average aircraft was thirty years old in 1994, the Act significantly

93. 127 S. Ct. 1057 (2007).

94. *Id.* at 1063.

95. 128 S. Ct. 2408 (2008).

96. Robert Barnes, *Justices Assess Financial Damages in Exxon Valdez Case,* Wash. Post, Feb. 28, 2008, at A2.

97. Wis. Stat. § 814.025.

98. *See, e.g.,* Hymowitz v. Eli Lilly & Co., 539 N.E.2d 1069 (N.Y. 1989), *cert. denied,* 493 U.S. 944 (1989).

99. Ohio Rev. Code Ann. § 2305.10.

limited the product liability exposure of aircraft manufacturers.[100] A fifteen-year statute of repose in Texas barred a lawsuit against the manufacturer of a Houston hospital elevator that had decapitated a physician because the elevator was more than fifteen years old at the time of the accident.[101]

Statutes of repose have usually been upheld on the ground that they serve a legitimate state purpose, such as encouraging manufacturers to upgrade their products. Absent a statute of repose, a manufacturer might not upgrade, out of fear that upgrading might be seen as an admission that the earlier version was inadequate.

USEFUL LIFE STATUTES

A small number of states have enacted useful life statutes. *Useful life statutes* are similar to statutes of limitation and repose in that they provide manufacturers and sellers some protection from liability after a particular period of time has expired, but they differ in that they define that period as the length of time a product is expected to safely provide utility to the user. Furthermore, these laws do not absolutely eliminate liability. Instead, useful life statutes establish a rebuttable presumption about how long consumers can continue safely using a product.

The details of the statutes vary significantly. For example, Idaho statutorily defines the same presumptive ten-year lifetime for all products, but Minnesota requires a multifactor analysis to determine the useful life of the product at issue. Other states combine useful life and statute of repose concepts in legislation limiting product liability.

Exhibit 10.1 summarizes the defenses available for product cases based on breach of warranty, negligance, and strict liability.

EXHIBIT 10.1 Summary of Defenses

Theory of Liability	Defenses
Breach of warranty	No privity of contract
	Statute of limitations
Negligence	Defendant used reasonable care
	Contributory or comparative negligence
	Preemption
	Statute of limitations
	Assumption of risk
Strict liability in tort	Unavoidably unsafe product
	Comparative fault (only reduces damages)
	Assumption of risk
	Obvious risk
	Sophisticated user
	Abnormal misuse
	Government contractor
	State-of-the-art
	Preemption
	Statute of repose
	Useful life statute

TOBACCO, GUNS, AND BIG FOOD

Plaintiffs' lawyers have targeted tobacco, guns, and, more recently, fatty and high calorie foods for high stakes product liability litigation.

TOBACCO

One of the most dramatic applications of product liability law has been the lawsuits against tobacco companies for illness, death, and medical expenses resulting from the use of tobacco or from secondhand smoke. In 1998, forty-six of the fifty states that had filed claims to recover billions they had spent on health-care costs related to smoking settled with the tobacco industry for $206 billion—the largest civil settlement in U.S. history.[102] The remaining four states had previously entered into settlements with tobacco companies totaling $40 billion. In 2000, the U.S. government softened its stance against tobacco. Instead of trying to recover $280 billion in profits from the tobacco companies for their alleged wrongful acts, the government sought $14 billion to pay for anti-smoking campaigns and programs to help current smokers quit. On Aug. 17, 2006, the U.S. District Court for the District of Columbia ruled that Philip Morris, Altria, and other cigarette companies violated the civil provisions of the Racketeer Influenced and Corrupt Organization Act but refused to order companies to pay the $14 billion requested by the federal government. As of mid-2008, the case was on appeal before the U.S. Court of Appeals for the District of Columbia.[103]

Individual plaintiffs have successfully pursued their cases as well. In early 2008, the Oregon Supreme Court reinstated for a third time an award of nearly $80 million in punitive

100. Allen Michel et al., *Protecting Future Product Liabil ity Claimants,* AM. BANKR. INST. J., Dec. 1999, at 3–4.

101. Michael Orey, *How Business Trounced the Trial Lawyers,* BUS.WK., Jan. 8, 2007, at 44.

102. Milo Geyelin, *States Agree to $206 Billion Tobacco Deal,* WALL ST. J., Nov. 23, 1998, at B13.

103. Altria, Department of Justice (DOJ) Tobacco Lawsuit, *at* http://www.altria.com/media/03_06_03_04_05_doj.asp (last visited 7/22/08).

damages to an Oregon widow whose husband died of lung cancer brought on by smoking.[104] The U.S. Supreme Court had twice reversed the Oregon court's rationale, ruling each time that the punitive damages levied against Philip Morris were improperly set.[105]

But in 2008 an intermediate appellate court in New York reversed a judgment of $3.4 million in compensatory damages and $17.1 million in punitive damages in favor of a 73-year-old lung cancer victim.[106] The court ruled that the plaintiff had failed to prove that Brown & Williamson Holdings and Philip Morris negligently designed cigarettes by continuing to market regular cigarettes with higher levels of tar and nicotine than so-called light cigarettes. The court rejected the plaintiff's assertion that a cigarette's function is merely "to be lit, burned, and inhaled," finding instead that individuals smoke for the taste and psychological effects of nicotine and tar. Under New York law, a manufacturer cannot be held liable for declining to "adopt an alternative product design that has not been shown to retain the 'inherent usefulness' the product offers when manufactured according to the more risky (but otherwise lawful) design that was actually used." The court concluded that the plaintiff had failed to prove that lower-tar, low-nicotine cigarettes would "have been acceptable to consumers that constitute the market for the allegedly defective product [regular cigarettes]." The dissenting judges argued that the test of consumer acceptability amounted to "nothing more than a cynical effort by the [tobacco companies] to maintain the commercial advantages of continuing to sell unreasonably dangerous addictive products to addicts."

In a set of class-action suits still pending in 2008, plaintiff smokers claimed that tobacco companies had deceptively promoted low-tar "light" cigarettes as healthier alternatives to regular cigarettes while knowing that this was not true.[107] Those litigants were seeking more than $100 billion in compensation.

The United States is not the only country where the tobacco industry faces legal problems. Litigation in India and Uganda has led to smoking bans and limits on cigarette advertising.[108] The governments of Bolivia, Guatemala, Nicaragua, and Venezuela filed claims in the federal district court in Washington, D.C., in an effort to recover health-care expenses related to smoking.[109] Similar suits have been filed in the courts of other countries. In addition, individual suits have been brought against the tobacco industry in a number of countries, including Argentina, Canada, Germany, Ireland, Israel, Japan, Sri Lanka, Thailand, and Turkey. In addition to civil proceedings, government officials in Canada and Colombia have alleged that tobacco companies committed crimes by participating in smuggling and money laundering activities.[110]

GUNS

After the enormous success of the litigation against the tobacco industry, cities and counties launched a similar attack against the gun industry. Unlike the tobacco industry, however, which has companies with deep pockets and vast assets to satisfy claims for damages, the gun industry comprises generally small, mostly privately held companies with annual sales of only $2.5 billion.[111] Nuisance suits against gun manufacturers are discussed in Chapter 9.

104. Oregon High Court Upholds $80M Award in Philip Morris Case, Dow Jones Newswires, Jan. 31, 2008.

105. Philip Morris v. Williams, 127 S. Ct. 1057 (2007).

106. Rose v. Brown & Williamson Tobacco Corp., 855 N.Y.S. 2d 119 (N.Y. App. Div. 2008).

107. Lorraine Woellert, Jane Sasseen, & Nanette Byrnes, *Tobacco May Be Partying Too Soon,* BUS.WK., July 24, 2006, at 26.

108. *Id.*

109. Richard A. Daynard et al., *Litigants Worldwide Blaming Then Branding Big Tobacco in Court,* WORLDPAPER, June 1, 2000.

110. *Id.*

111. Paul Barrett, *As Lawsuits Loom, Gun Industry Presents a Fragmented Front,* WALL ST. J., Dec. 9, 1998, at A1.

In early 2000, two Clinton administration lawyers—the deputy general counsel of Housing and Urban Development and the general counsel at the Treasury Department, which helped oversee the Bureau of Alcohol, Tobacco and Firearms—presented a list of gun-control demands to Ed Schultz, the CEO of Smith & Wesson Corporation. Smith & Wesson, a unit of Britain's Tomkins PLC, is America's largest maker of handguns. Schultz initially responded by asking one of the lawyers how old he was. When the lawyer answered that he was thirty-four years old, Schultz said, "If you live a good long life, you will not live to see this proposal happen." Two months later, however, Smith & Wesson agreed to a settlement based upon that initial proposal. In particular, Smith & Wesson agreed to make a number of changes, including the following:

- All guns would be shipped with external child safety locks.
- Within two years, all pistols would be manufactured with internal safety locks.
- Within one year, all firearms would be made child-proof.
- Handguns would have to pass a stringent performance test.
- The company would devote 2% of its gross revenues to developing a "smart" gun that can be fired only by its owner.

The company also agreed to develop a code of conduct for its dealers and distributors that would require background checks on purchases and would forbid sales to anyone who had not passed a safety exam or taken a training class.

Commentators compared Smith & Wesson's settlement with Liggett Group's decision to break ranks with the other tobacco companies and settle its tobacco cases. But whereas Liggett was a small tobacco company, Smith & Wesson was one of the most powerful companies in the gun industry. Eliot Spitzer, the New York attorney general involved in designing the Smith & Wesson settlement, commented, "The idea all along was that one responsible company would break away from the rest of the industry and that would be leverage to use against the rest."[112]

Other members of the gun industry sharply criticized Smith & Wesson. The head of the National Shooting Sports Foundation, which represents all major gun makers, stated that Smith & Wesson had "violated a trust with their consumers and with the entire domestic firearms industry." He also charged that the company had "run off and cut their own deal" in a manner that "fractures the unity we had since the first lawsuit was filed in October 1998."[113] Some claimed that Smith & Wesson's settlement amounted to an admission that guns can be made safer, thus undermining the industry's long-held position that companies have no obligation to make naturally dangerous products safer.

Commentators outside the gun industry also criticized the Smith & Wesson deal as an undemocratic way of making public policy.[114] They argued that the Clinton administration, frustrated by the partisan gridlock in Congress that prevented the enactment of gun-control legislation, had used litigation to establish new regulations for the gun industry.[115] "This is backdoor gun control through coercion and through threat of litigation," said one member of Congress.[116]

More recently, however, gun-control advocates have experienced setbacks. The City of Cincinnati dropped its four-year product liability and nuisance suit against gun makers in 2003 after concluding that the litigation was simply too expensive to continue.[117] As discussed in Chapter 9, other judicial setbacks and recently enacted federal and state laws have made it even harder for plaintiffs' lawyers to hold gun manufacturers liable for deaths and injuries caused by gun fire. Finally, the U.S. Supreme Court's decision in *District of Columbia v. Heller,* which invalidated the D.C. law prohibiting handguns and requiring trigger locks or similar devices on firearms in the home (discussed in Chapter 4), dealt another blow to gun control.

FOOD

As discussed in Chapter 2, "Big Food" has come under fire for selling fatty and high calorie foods, ranging from Big Macs and fries at McDonald's to sugar-laden sodas in schools. New York City became the first major U.S. city to ban trans fats in restaurants and to require restaurants to provide written nutritional information for each item on the menu. Although the plaintiffs lost most of the early cases alleging that fast foods caused them to gain weight and to develop diabetes and related conditions, cases based on failure to warn and misleading advertising targeted at children might ultimately have a greater likelihood of success.

112. Paul M. Barrett, Vanessa O'Connell, & Joe Mathews, *Glock May Accept Handgun Restrictions—Austrian Firm May Follow Lead of Smith & Wesson to Avoid U.S. Sanctions,* Wall St. J., Mar. 20, 2000, at A3.

113. Sharon Walsh, Gun Industry Views Pact as Threat to Its Unity, Wash. Post, Mar. 18, 2000, at A10.

114. Stuart Taylor, *Guns and Tobacco: Government by Litigation,* Nat'l L.J., Mar. 25, 2000.

115. Walter K. Olson, *Plaintiffs' Lawyers Take Aim at Democracy,* Wall St. J., Mar. 21, 2000, at A26.

116. Alan Fram, *House Kills Effort to Scuttle Safety Pact with Smith & Wesson,* Assoc. Press Newswire, June 27, 2000.

117. *Cincinnati's Council Decides to Drop Suit Against Gun Makers,* N.Y. Times, May 1, 2003, at A24.

Problems with the Product Liability System and the Restatement (Third) Approach to Design Defects and Failures to Warn

The product liability scheme that has evolved has increasingly been criticized because the financial burden it imposes on industry—in the form of huge jury awards and high insurance premiums—has been enormous. The cornerstone of the scheme is the assumption that manufacturers are in the best position to insure against loss or to spread the risk of loss among their customers. In practice, manufacturers often find it difficult to obtain an insurance policy that does not include a substantial deductible, which the manufacturer must pay. Sometimes insurance is not available at all, and companies have to pay all claims themselves. This leads to increased manufacturing costs and higher prices.

The product liability scheme also takes its toll on industry efficiency and competitiveness. Companies have become unwilling to invest in product creation or modification because this may be seen as an admission of fault. In most jurisdictions, product modification is admissible as evidence of the product's prior defective condition. Companies find themselves in a no-win situation: failing to remedy a defect may expose the company to punitive damages in a negligence case, but remedying the defect may expose the company to compensatory damages in subsequent suits.

Informed by these concerns, the American Law Institute (ALI) approved the Restatement (Third) of Torts: Products Liability in 1997. The new restatement proposed bold changes in the doctrine of product liability. As noted earlier, no court is bound by the restatement's formulation of product liability law. As of 2008, only a minority of states had adopted the Restatement (Third) approach, either in whole or in part.[118]

Design Defects and the Reasonable-Alternative-Design Requirement

Most importantly, the Restatement (Third) requires that any claim of design defect be supported by a showing of a reasonable alternative design. The effect of this change is to move away from strict liability for defectively designed products. Instead, the *reasonable-alternative-design requirement* forces plaintiffs to prove that defendants acted wrongly or negligently in choosing an unsafe design.

In many respects, those who failed in their ardent attempts to push sweeping tort and product liability reform through Congress saw their ideas embodied in the new restatement. Indeed, the most vocal critics of the Restatement (Third) charged that the effort had been captured by defense attorneys seeking to accomplish through the ALI what they could not achieve on Capitol Hill.

In the following case, the Iowa Supreme Court considered whether to accept the Restatement (Third)'s reasonable-alternative-design requirement.

118. George W. Conk, *Punctuated Equilibrium: Why Section 402A Flourished and the Third Restatement Languished,* 26 Rev. Litig. 799, 840–43 (2007).

A CASE IN POINT — **IN THE LANGUAGE OF THE COURT**

CASE 10.6

Wright v. Brooke Group Ltd.

Supreme Court of Iowa
652 N.W.2d 159 (Iowa 2002).

FACTS Robert and DeAnn Wright filed a lawsuit against all cigarette manufacturers alleging, among other things, a design defect in cigarettes that made them unreasonably dangerous. The defendants asked the Iowa Supreme Court to rule on the elements necessary to establish liability for a design defect.

ISSUE PRESENTED Should Iowa adopt the Restatement (Third) approach to design defects, which requires the plaintiff to show the existence of a reasonable alternative design before a product will be deemed unreasonably dangerous?

OPINION TERNUS, J., writing for the Iowa Supreme Court:

The Iowa Supreme Court first applied strict liability in tort for a product defect in 1970, adopting Restatement (Second) of Torts. Section 402A of the Restatement (Second) provides:

CONTINUED

Special Liability of Seller of Product for Physical Harm to User or Consumer:

(1) one who sells any product in a defective condition unreasonably dangerous to the user or consumer or to his property is subject to liability for physical harm thereby caused to the ultimate user or consumer, or to his property. . . .

Our purpose in adopting this provision was to relieve injured plaintiffs of the burden of proving the elements of warranty or negligence theories, thereby insuring that the costs of injuries resulting from defective products are borne by the manufacturers that put such products on the market.

. . . .

[The defendant] suggests this case presents an appropriate opportunity for the court to adopt the principles of law set forth in § 2 of Restatement (Third) of Torts.

In determining what test should be applied in assessing whether cigarettes are unreasonably dangerous, we are confronted with the anomaly of using a risk/benefit analysis for purposes of strict liability based on defective design that is identical to the test employed in proving negligence in product design. This incongruity has drawn our attention once again to the debate over whether the distinction between strict liability and negligence theories should be maintained when applied to a design defect case. We are convinced such a distinction is illusory. . . . Because the Products Restatement [Third] is consistent with our conclusion, we think it sets forth an intellectually sound set of legal principles for product defect cases.

The Products Restatement demonstrates a recognition that strict liability is appropriate in manufacturing defect cases, but negligence principles are more suitable for other defective product cases. . . . Accordingly, it establish[es] separate standards of liability for manufacturing defects, design defects, and defects based on inadequate instructions or warnings.

One engaged in the business of selling or otherwise distributing products who sells or distributes a defective product is subject to liability for harm to persons or property caused by the defect. . . . The "unreasonably dangerous" element of Restatement (Second) section 402A has been eliminated and has been replaced with a multi-faceted definition of defective product. This definition is set out in section 2 of the Restatement (Third):

> A product is defective when, at the time of sale or distribution, it contains a manufacturing defect, is defective in design, or is defective because of inadequate instructions or warning.

. . . .

In summary, we now adopt Restatement (Third) of Torts sections 1 and 2 for product defect cases. Under these sections, a plaintiff seeking to recover damages on the basis of a design defect must prove the foreseeable risks of harm posed by the product could have been reduced or avoided by the adoption of a reasonable alternative design by the seller or other distributor, or a predecessor in the commercial chain of distribution, and the omission of the alternative design renders the product not reasonably safe.

RESULT The court adopted Sections 1 and 2 of the Restatement (Third). To establish liability, the plaintiffs had to produce evidence of a reasonable alternative design.

COMMENTS In essence, the Restatement (Third) replaces the requirement that a product be "unreasonably dangerous" with a showing that there was a "reasonable alternative design." Considerable legal writing asserts that the alternative design and unreasonably dangerous tests are really the same test, but many lawyers concede that the alternative design test is more easily understood and applied by courts and juries.[119]

CONTINUED

119. Opinions of several large law firms are *available at* http://www.nmmlaw.com/articles/designdef.html and http://www.cliffordlaw.com/news.

Critical Thinking Questions

1. How do the approaches of the Restatement (Second) and the Restatement (Third) differ?
2. Should the plaintiff or the defendant have the burden of proving the existence of a reasonable alternative design?

FAILURE TO WARN OF FORESEEABLE RISKS OR TO PROVIDE REASONABLE INSTRUCTIONS

In failure-to-warn cases, the Restatement (Third) embodied the majority view that defendants are liable only if they failed to warn of risks that were forseeable at the time of sale.[120] It further interjected a negligence standard by providing that a product "is defective because of inadequate instructions or warnings when the foreseeable risks of harm posed by the product could have been reduced or avoided by the provision of *reasonable* instructions or warnings by the [defendant], . . . and the omission of the instructions or warnings renders the product not reasonably safe."[121]

120. *See, e.g.*, Powers v. Taser Int'l, Inc., 174 P.3d 777 (Ariz. App. 2007) (defendant is not liable for failure to warn against risks that were unforeseeable at the time of sale).

121. Restatement (Third) of Torts: Products Liability § 2(c) (1997) (emphasis added).

GLOBAL VIEW

Product Liability in the European Union

Differences among the product liability laws of the various countries within the European Union (EU) created two major problems. First, there was uncertainty as to which law would apply to cross-border disputes. This uncertainty was harmful to both consumers and manufacturers. Second, competition was distorted within the EU because liability and the severity of financial repercussions varied from one nation to another. Thus, the EU members recognized that a uniform product liability directive was needed.

In July 1985, after nearly a decade of debate, the Council of Ministers of the EU adopted a product liability directive designed to provide increased consumer protection and to harmonize competitive conditions within the EU.[122] The directive's basic purpose is to hold manufacturers strictly liable for injuries caused by defects in their products. This represented a fundamental change for manufacturers of products marketed in Europe. Traditionally, injured consumers in most of the member states had to prove both negligence and privity of contract in order to recover damages from the producer of a defective product. Only France had previously imposed strict product liability.

The directive does not apply to services, which continue to be governed solely by national law. In June 1999, following separate outbreaks of mad cow disease, *E. coli*, and salmonella, the European Commission adopted an amendment to the 1985 directive that extended product liability to cover agricultural products.[123] The European Commission decided to leave the directive unchanged in 2006, after finding that its goals were being accomplished.[124]

CONTINUED

122. 1985 O.J. (L 210) 29.

123. John R. Schmertz, Jr. & Mike Meier, *EU Amends Product Liability Directive to Include Agricultural Products,* Int'l L. Update, June 1999.

124. Report from the Commission to the Council, the European Parliament and the European Economic and Social Committee: Third report on the application of Council Directive on the approximation of laws, regulations and administrative provisions of the Member States concerning liability for defective products (85/374/EEC of 25 July 1985, amended by Directive 1999/34/EC of the European Parliament and of the Council of 10 May 1999), COM(2006) 496 final, *available at* http://ec.europa.eu/prelex/detail_dossier_real.cfm?CL=en&DosId=194649.

Comparison with U.S. Strict Liability

The liability of manufacturers under the EU product liability directive is very similar to the strict liability doctrine applied in most of the United States. To recover damages, an injured party has to prove the existence of a defect, an injury, and a causal relationship between the defect and the injury. (Plaintiffs may also sue under the traditional negligence and contract laws of the EU member states.) In determining whether a product is defective, the courts in the EU countries, like those in the United States, consider such factors as the product's foreseeable uses and the instructions and warnings provided by the manufacturer.

Unlike in the United States, a supplier or wholesaler is not strictly liable unless the injured party is unable to identify the manufacturer. In such an instance, the supplier can escape liability by informing the injured person of the manufacturer's identity. Like the Restatement (Third), the directive provides for a "development risks" or state-of-the-art defense. A producer can escape liability by proving that the state of scientific knowledge when the product went into circulation was insufficient to allow it to discover the defect.

Other available defenses are similar to those available in most jurisdictions in the United States. For example, a manufacturer will not be liable if (1) the manufacturer did not put the product into circulation, (2) the defect did not exist when the product went into circulation, (3) the product was a component that was neither manufactured nor distributed by the manufacturer of the overall product, or (4) the defect was due to compliance of the product with mandatory regulations. The manufacturer of a component part will not be liable if the defect was attributable to the overall design of the product into which the component was fitted.

The directive includes a statute of limitations and a statute of repose. An injured person must sue within three years of when he or she knew, or should have known, of the injury, the defect, and the manufacturer's identity. A manufacturer's liability will be extinguished ten years after the product was put into circulation, unless the injured party has commenced proceedings in the meantime. Thus, as in certain states in the United States, a defect that does not become manifest until eleven years after the product went into circulation may leave the injured person without a remedy. Most EU member states previously had thirty-year statutes of repose.

Importers of products into the EU are strictly liable under the directive. Thus, U.S. exporters may be required to indemnify overseas importers. It is important for U.S. exporters to carry product liability insurance that covers lawsuits in the EU and to adhere to EU safety standards.

THE RESPONSIBLE MANAGER

REDUCING PRODUCT LIABILITY RISK

Managers have a responsibility to minimize their company's exposure to liability in the design, manufacture, assembly, and use of its products. Legally astute managers will implement a product safety program to ensure that products are sold in a legally safe condition and will take appropriate steps to discover and correct any defects that may come to light after the product is sold. The goal should be to prevent accidents. If an accident does occur, evidence of a product safety program is crucial for limiting the manufacturer's liability for punitive damages and containing damage to the brand.

Managers should ensure that their products are performing as intended over the lives of the products and that the products have as little adverse effect on the environment as possible under current technology. It is helpful to establish a product safety committee and to conduct regular safety audits to identify and correct problems. The advice of experienced counsel can be helpful in this area.

Managers should have a thorough understanding of all statutes, regulations, and administrative rulings to which a product must conform. Failure of the product to comply with any of these rules will typically be deemed a product defect. Mere conformance with these rules is considered a minimum requirement, however, and does not automatically release a manufacturer from liability.

To protect against potential liabilities, managers should implement internal loss-control procedures, obtain adequate insurance protection, and seek the advice of product liability counsel from the earliest stages of product development. If

CONTINUED

a product carries risks even with normal use, warnings must be provided to consumers. Managers should make sure that contracts properly disclaim and limit product liability and, to the extent possible, include indemnification provisions, particularly if the product will be used as a component part by another manufacturer. If the firm is acquiring another company, managers should examine potential product liability exposure created by the purchase. With the variety of jurisdictional approaches to successor liability, managers should seek legal advice to help them assess and structure the acquisition.

Nonetheless, accidents and product defects will occur. One of the most difficult, and ethically challenging, decisions a manager must make is whether to undertake subsequent remedial measures. When a product is found to be inherently defective, it is in society's best interest for the manufacturer to fix the dangerous condition or to improve the design; nevertheless, manufacturers may fear that such remedies will be used as evidence against them in subsequent proceedings. For this reason, some courts refuse to allow plaintiffs to submit evidence of subsequent remedial measures as proof that the original design was defective.

Legally astute managers recall defective products and constantly strive to improve designs and processes to ensure the safety of the firm's products. Even when there is no legal obligation to recall a product, a recall can mitigate potential liability, exemplify the company's commitment to protecting consumers, and protect the brand. But once undertaken, recalls must be performed properly. Careless recalls expose the company to negligence claims.

A Manager's Dilemma

Putting It into Practice

Children's Toys—To Recall or Not to Recall?

In 2007, the U.S. Consumer Product Safety Commission (CPSC) issued recall notices on sixty-one toys totaling 25 million units.[125] A primary culprit was high levels of lead in paints used in China to finish toy surfaces. Even though immediate illness is rare, children who ingest excessive amounts of lead risk neurological damage and even death.[126] Mattel, for instance, recalled Barbie, Sesame Street, and Dora the Explorer brand items.[127] Yet, without regulations prohibiting the sale of recalled toys, these and other hazardous toys remained available for purchase; proposed federal legislation under consideration in mid-2008 would change that.[128]

Recalls are voluntary, and the CPSC must negotiate the recall terms with the company in question before the public is notified, often with frustrating results.[129] For example, in twenty-five instances in 2007, companies refused to reveal which factories built the recalled toys.[130] Instead, toy industry insiders preferred to share such information with colleagues and competitors privately.[131] Without knowing which manufacturers are using hazardous materials, other companies may unwittingly engage those suppliers, leaving consumers to discriminate by country of origin. During the 2007 holiday season, for example, many shoppers steered clear of all children's products made in China.[132]

Without a prohibition on the sale of recalled items, sellers have scant regulatory incentive to ensure that they are selling safe toys. Most retail stores simply remove recalled items from their shelves, but others take a more consumercentric

CONTINUED

125. Donna Howell, *Products Recalled for Lead Still Being Sold on the Web*, Investor's Bus. Daily, Nov. 13, 2007; Annys Shin, *Groups Expose Hidden Toy Hazards; Products with Lead, Magnets Still for Sale*, Wash. Post, Nov. 21, 2007, at D3.

126. Patti Waldmeir, *Too Much Safety in America's Playrooms,* Fin. Times, Nov. 28, 2007, at 12; Consumer Product Safety Act Regulations, 16 C.F.R. § 1303.5 (2007) ("The adverse effects of this poisoning in children can cause a range of disorders such as hyperactivity, slowed learning ability, withdrawal, blindness, and even death.").

127. Louise Story & David Barboza, *Mattel Recalls 19 Million Toys Sent from China,* N.Y. Times, Aug. 15, 2007, at 1; Louise Story, *Mattel in Another Recall, Citing Lead in Toys from China,* N.Y. Times, Sept. 5, 2007, at 4.

128. *Senate Votes to Beef Up Consumer Protection Agency*, CNNPolitics.com, Mar. 7, 2008, http://www.cnn.com/2008/POLITICS/03/06/senate.products/index.html (last visited Apr. 27, 2008). Howell, *supra* note 125; Shin, *supra* note 125; *Sen. Casey Presses for Answers on Toy Safety*, U.S. Fed News, Nov. 15, 2007.

129. Nicholas Casey & Nicholas Zamiska, *Chinese Factory Is Identified in Tainted-Toy Recall—Mattel's Reluctance Was Seen by Critics as Regulatory Flaw*, Wall St. J., Aug. 8, 2007, at A4.

130. *Id.*

131. *Id.*

132. Jeannie Kever, *Excessive Lead, Other Risks Worry Toy Shoppers*, Houston Chron., Nov. 21, 2007.

approach. Following the rash of lead paint–related recalls, Toys "R" Us provided recall information on its website and adopted a "no quibble" return policy, agreeing to accept recalled items for refund regardless of where they were purchased or whether the consumer had a receipt.[133]

Once retailers have sold recalled items, it becomes harder for the CPSC to monitor the products. Consumers are often not aware of recalls. Secondhand and thrift shops, and even homeowners holding yard sales, may unknowingly sell recalled products.[134] For years, online marketplaces, such as eBay and Amazon, have been working with the CPSC to publicize recall information even though they are under no legal obligation to do so.[135] According to eBay's toy and gadget director Catherine Schwartz, "We see extra education as part of our responsibility in light of the recent toy recalls. Listing items on eBay which have been recalled is strictly prohibited, and if the CPSC asks eBay to remove an item, we will take it down."[136] Despite their efforts, however, recalled toys remained available through these sites.[137] Aside from withholding proceeds from prohibited sales, revoking "powerseller" status, or banning the seller altogether, online auction sites can do little to regulate postings.[138] For instance, more than 6 million items are listed for sale on eBay each day.[139] With no standard format for listings, the company cannot easily screen out banned items; reviewing each listing manually would be almost impossible.

Given that the CPSC has little punitive clout to wield against toy companies, their affiliates, and business partners in the toy industry, should other stakeholders take actions to protect consumers from recalled items? For example, should licensors, such as Nickelodeon and Disney, require their licensees to certify the safety of products carrying their brands?[140] Should they conduct their own inspections and product tests? Or should they simply require that licensees and subcontractors indemnify them against brand damage and costs associated with recalls?

Toys "R" Us is on record as supporting increased government involvement in overseeing the toy industry, including more funding for the CPSC and requiring production code stamps on products to make identifying recalled items easier. Hasbro has also called for tough global toy safety standards.[141] If you were a top manager at Mattel, would you oppose or support stronger regulation? Would your answer be the same if you were a manager at Lego or Playskool, two European firms that do not outsource production to China? To what extent is self-regulation a viable option? Should retailers follow the Toys "R" Us model, informing their customers about recalled items and compensating them through refunds or exchanges?

133. Press Release, Toys "R" Us, A Message from Gerald R. Storch, Chairman and CEO, *available at* http://www3.toysrus.com/safety/prodRecalls.cfm; M.P. McQueen, *Retailers Face the Test of Testing; Closer Oversight of Toys Is Designed to Head Off Costly Suits, New Laws,* WALL ST. J., Nov. 26, 2007, at A6.

134. David Migoya, *Recalls Reach Thrift Stores*, DENVER POST, Sept. 7, 2007, at C1.

135. OFFICE OF INFO. AND PUB. AFFAIRS, U.S. CONSUMER PROD. SAFETY COMM'N, CPSC ANNOUNCES INITIATIVE WITH EBAY INC. AND AMAZON.COM AUCTIONS TO PREVENT HAZARDOUS PRODUCTS FROM BEING SOLD ON AUCTION WEB SITES (2000).

136. *eBay Issues Recall Warning—Online Marketplace Will Remove Sellers from Its Web Site,* WALL ST. J. Oct. 3, 2007, at B10.

137. *Id.*

138. *Toxic Toys on the Web,* FORBES.COM, Nov. 12, 2007, http://www.forbes.com/home/technology/2007/11/09/banned-toys-china-technology-personaltech-cx_ag_1112toys.html (last visited Dec. 7, 2007).

139. *Id.*

140. Shin, *supra* note 125.

141. Tom Mitchell, *Hasbro Chairman Calls for Global Toy Rules*, FIN. TIMES, Jan. 10, 2008.

INSIDE STORY

MERCK AND VIOXX

In September 2004, pharmaceutical giant Merck & Co. voluntarily recalled one of its most profitable drugs, Vioxx, after finding that the anti-inflammatory drug, which was used to treat arthritis and other conditions, increased the risk of heart attacks and strokes in patients who took it for more than eighteen months. An estimated 20 million people in the United States took Vioxx during the five years it was on the market.[142] By November 2004, Merck was the defendant in about 375 Vioxx personal-injury lawsuits, involving roughly 1,000 plaintiff groups, and its stock had dropped from $45 to less than $26 per share.[143]

Despite the tidal wave of suits, Merck vowed to fight the cases one-by-one. It successfully resisted the plaintiffs' efforts to certify the cases as class actions, arguing that each plaintiff had

CONTINUED

142. Heather Won Tesoriero, Sarah Rubenstein, & Jamie Heller, *Merck's Tactics Largely Vindicated as It Reaches Big Vioxx Settlement*, WALL ST. J., Nov. 10, 2007, at A1.

143. Scott Hensley, *Merck Faces Twin Vioxx Inquiries,* WALL ST. J., Nov. 9, 2004, at A3.

to exclude other possible causes of heart attacks and strokes, such as smoking and taking illicit drugs, in order to establish that Vioxx was the primary cause.

Although Merck won eleven of sixteen trials over the ensuing three years, the pharmaceutical company opted to settle most of the remaining suits in November 2007.[144] Merck and a committee of plaintiffs' attorneys agreed that the company would pay a total of $4.85 billion into two funds to dispose of more than 48,500 lawsuits.[145] Plaintiffs who suffered heart attacks split $4 billion, while those who had strokes shared $850 million.[146] After legal fees and expenses, the average plaintiff received between $50,000 and $70,000.[147] Merck's stock jumped more than 5 percent the day after the settlement was announced.

The agreement stipulated that the deal would become effective only if at least 85 percent of the plaintiffs with the most serious claims agreed to its terms;[148] in fact, 97 percent of eligible claimants enrolled in the settlement program. To keep the plaintiffs' lawyers from cherry-picking their cases, that is, settling the weak cases and taking the stronger ones to trial, the settlement agreement provided that 100 percent of a lawyer's clients had to agree to the settlement before any of that lawyer's clients could participate. Mark Lanier, the plaintiffs' lawyer who won the first case against Merck, announced that he would recommend that his 1,000 Vioxx clients take the deal. Any clients electing not to settle had to find another attorney to represent them.[149] Experts questioned whether this would put undue pressure on the attorney–client relationship.[150]

Several factors likely motivated Merck to settle. First, Merck had already spent $1.2 billion in legal fees and yet had tried only 16 of the 27,000 lawsuits pending. Second, the judges responsible for hearing most of the Vioxx cases pressured Merck to settle. As Judge Carol E. Higbee, who was overseeing thousands of cases in New Jersey, remarked, "When you have four judges running 90% of the litigation asking you to sit down, I don't think you're going to say no."[151] Third, Merck's success at trial put it in a strong negotiating position and gave plaintiffs incentive to come to the bargaining table. Additionally, statutes of limitations were expiring in the vast majority of states, which allowed the parties to more accurately estimate Merck's exposure.[152]

Merck also faced serious risk to its reputation. A 2004 *Wall Street Journal* article's description of Merck documents and e-mails raised the possibility that Merck might have known more about the risks of Vioxx than it had previously acknowledged.[153] In April 2006, a jury in New Jersey—Merck's home state—found that Merck had not disclosed certain analyses of Vioxx-related health concerns to the FDA and assessed $4.5 million in compensatory and $9 million in punitive damages against the company.[154] Just days earlier, a jury had found Merck liable for the death of a Texas man.[155] Although the jury awarded the man's family $32 million, the state cap on punitive damages reduced the actual figure to $7.75 million.[156] The previous summer, another Texas jury had awarded $253 million in a suit over another death connected to Vioxx.[157] Even though that award was also reduced by law, Merck faced the possibility that plaintiffs in states without statutory limitations on punitive damages would prevail at trial by showing that the company had put consumers at risk by withholding negative research data.

In addition to the adverse jury verdicts in the Vioxx civil suits, the specter of indictments from onoing criminal investigations may have compelled Merck to rethink its aggressive litigation approach. As of early 2008, the U.S. Justice Department

CONTINUED

144. Tesoriero, Rubenstein, & Heller, *supra* note 142. Merck scored three victories on appeal in mid-2008: (1) a Texas appeals court overturned a $26 million jury verdict in favor of Carol Ernst after concluding that the plaintiffs had failed to prove that Vioxx caused her husband's death (Merck & Co. v. Ernst, 2008 Tex. App. LEXIS 3951 (Tex. App. May 29, 2008)); (2) a New Jersey appeals court reduced a jury verdict to $4.5 million after ruling that the jury should not have been allowed to award punitive damages or to find that Merck had committed consumer fraud (McDarby v. Merck & Col, 949 A.2d 223 (N.J. App. 2008)); and (3) the New Jersey Supreme Court ruled that Vioxx users involved in a class action suit seeking to recover the cost of medical monitoring were not eligible to recover those costs because they were not claiming injury and therefore were not harmed within the meaning of the New Jersey Product Liability Act (Sinclair v. Merck & Co., 948 A.2d 587 (N.J. 2008)).

145. Alex Berenson, *Merck Is Said to Agree to Pay $4.85 Billion for Vioxx Claims*, N.Y. TIMES, Nov. 9, 2007, at 1; *Merck to Pay $4.85 Billion in Vioxx Settlement*, CNN MONEY.COM (July 17, 2008).

146. Tesoriero, Rubenstein, & Heller, *supra* note 142.

147. *See* Berenson, *supra* note 145.

148. *Id.*

149. Nathan Koppel, *Vioxx Plaintiffs' Choice: Settle or Lose Their Lawyer*, WALL ST. J., Nov. 16, 2007, at B1.

150. Adam Liptak, *In Vioxx Settlement, Testing a Legal Ideal: A Lawyer's Loyalty*, N.Y. TIMES, Jan. 22, 2008.

151. Tesoriero, Rubenstein, & Heller, *supra* note 142.

152. *Id.*

153. Hensley, *supra* note 143.

154. Berenson, *supra* note 145. The punitive damages award was reversed on appeal. Mc Darby v. Merck & Co., 949 A.2d 223 (N.J. App. 2008).

155. *Latest Vioxx Loss Not Seen Pushing Merck to Jump Ship*, DOW JONES NEWSWIRES, Apr. 21, 2006.

156. *Id.*

157. Kris Axtman, *Jury's Vioxx Award: Not So Texas-Sized After All*, CHRISTIAN SCI. MONITOR, Aug. 25, 2005, at 3. That verdict was reversed on appeal. Merck & Co. v. Ernst, 2008 Tex. App. LEXIS 3951 (Tex. App. May 29, 2008).

was continuing its criminal probe into the manner in which the company marketed and sold the drug.[158]

Experts characterized the deal as a victory for Merck. As litigation efforts were gaining steam in 2005, experts estimated that Merck faced between $10 billion and $25 billion in liability exposure related to Vioxx.[159] Including the $1.2 billion expended in earlier litigation, the total cost of handling the Vioxx claims was roughly $6 billion.[160]

Even after the Vioxx settlement became effective in July 2008, Merck still faced a variety of other suits from users of other popular medications. As of mid-2008, more than 500 cases had been filed by people prescribed Fosamax, a drug designed to treat osteoporosis that may actually cause bone deterioration.[161] Merck's anticholesterol drug Vytorin became the subject of another batch of lawsuits in 2008, after Merck admitted that the drug was not more effective than the far cheaper generic drug Zocor.[162] A third Merck product, the cervical cancer vaccine Gardisil, may spawn future litigation as federal officials investigate reports of serious side effects.[163]

Even if the U.S. Supreme Court curtails state product liability claims related to FDA-approved drugs, this likely would not shield Merck and other pharmaceutical companies from claims of fraudulent misrepresentation or failure to disclose all relevant data to the FDA. In any event, the Vioxx experience has prompted calls in Congress for more onerous drug approval and postsale monitoring requirements and stalled a number of promising drugs in the FDA-approval pipeline.

158. Heather Won Tesoriero, *Trouble Brews over Merck Product*, WALL ST. J., Jan. 30, 2008, at A12.

159. *Id.*

160. *Id.*

161. Bloomberg, *Merck Faces 100 New Fosamax Lawsuits* (May 1, 2008), available at http://www.levinlaw.com/PracticeAreas/100NewFosamaxLawsuits.asp.

162. Karl Stark, *Lawsuits Target Vytorin's Makers*, PHILADELPHIA INQUIRER, Jan. 26, 2008, at D1.

163. Tesoriero, *supra* note 158.

KEY WORDS AND PHRASES

assumption of risk 350
comparative fault 350
continuity-of-enterprise approach 348
design defect 342
discovery-of-injury statute 363
failure to warn 342
government-contractor defense 352
indemnity 345
limited fund class action 349
manufacturing defect 342
market-share liability 348
obvious risk 350
preemption defense 353
premises liability 349
privity of contract 335
product 340
product liability 335
product-line theory 348
proximate cause 343
reasonable-alternative-design requirement 367
revival statute 363
sophisticated user defense 351
state-of-the-art defense 353
statute of limitations 363
statute of repose 363
subsequent remedial measures 337
unavoidably unsafe product 345
useful life statutes 364

QUESTIONS AND CASE PROBLEMS

1. Johnson was a trained and certified heating, ventilation, and air-conditioning (HVAC) technician with a "universal" certification, the highest obtainable from the Environmental Protection Agency. He purchased R-22 refrigerant manufactured by American Standard and used it in maintaining and repairing air-conditioning units. Johnson sued American Standard for negligence, failure to warn, and design defect, alleging that the R-22 refrigerant exposed him to phosgene gas, causing him to develop pulmonary fibrosis. He admitted receiving and reading the Material Safety Data Sheets (MSDS) with

each of his purchases of R-22 refrigerant, but claimed that he did not understand that heating the R-22 refrigerant could produce allegedly harmful phosgene exposures. Who should prevail? Should the result be the same if Johnson did not purchase the R-22 refrigerant himself but was an employee of a company that would qualify as a sophisticated user? What public policies are implicated in cases such as this? [*Johnson v. American Standard, Inc.*, 179 P.3d 904 (Cal. 2008).]

2. Roy Mercurio drove his Nissan Altima into a tree in the middle of the night at a speed of approximately thirty-five miles per hour. When the car struck the tree, the passenger compartment collapsed, and Mercurio was seriously injured. He was driving while intoxicated with a blood alcohol content of at least .18 percent. Mercurio brought a product liability action against Nissan on the grounds that the car was not crashworthy. Nissan argued that the claim should be dismissed, asserting as defenses assumption of risk and unforeseeable misuse of the car in that Mercurio was driving while intoxicated. Mercurio argued that evidence of his blood alcohol level at the time of the accident was irrelevant and should be excluded. How should the court rule? What public policies are at issue here? [*Mercurio v. Nissan Motor Corp.,* 81 F. Supp. 2d 859 (N.D. Ohio 2000).]

3. Federal Motor Vehicle Safety Standard (FMVSS) 208, promulgated by the U.S. Department of Transportation (DOT), required auto manufacturers to equip 10 percent of their 1987 vehicles with passive restraints, such as air bags. Through the standard, the DOT sought to encourage both the incorporation of passive restraint systems into automobiles and the passage of state mandatory seat belt laws, which was a factor in determing whether the passive restraint requirements became permanent. In 1992, despite wearing shoulder and lap belts, Alexis Geier was injured when she crashed her 1987 Honda Accord. Geier and her parents sued American Honda under a state common law negligence theory for failing to include a driver's side air bag. Should the Geiers' suit be allowed to move forward? [*Geier v. American Honda Motor Co.,* 529 U.S. 861 (2000).]

4. Terrell Redman, a senior vice president of Alligator Corporation, is evaluating a potential acquisition for the company. The entity he wishes to acquire has several divisions, two of which manufacture chemicals and industrial tools.
   a. What risks does the acquisition present to Alligator Corporation under product liability law?
   b. Are there ways to limit the company's exposure?
   c. To the extent that product liability law will expose Alligator to liability for the acquired company's prior conduct, what steps must be taken at the time of the acquisition to ensure Alligator's ability to defend potential claims? [*See, e.g., Tolo v. Wexco,* 993 F.2d 884 (9th Cir. 1993).]

5. Rochelle Black's husband worked as an auto mechanic in the Air Force from 1971 to 1986. When he died of lung cancer in 1991, Mrs. Black sued forty-eight asbestos manufacturers, alleging that her husband's death had been caused by his exposure to asbestos-containing products while working as an auto mechanic. She based her claims on market-share liability. Although she conceded that market-share liability would be inappropriate if she were alleging injury from exposure to many different types of asbestos products, she argued that she should be allowed to proceed in her market-share claims against four manufacturers of asbestos-containing "friction products," including brake and clutch products. These four companies produced friction products, which contained between 7 and 7.5 percent asbestos fibers. How should the court rule? What if the range of asbestos fibers in the products produced by the four companies was 40 to 60 percent? [*Black v. Abex Corp.,* 603 N.W.2d 182 (N.D. 1999).]

6. Laura Hollister was a business student at Northwestern University. She attended a business school party and then returned to her apartment with a friend. When Hollister left the party, she was intoxicated. She woke the next morning with no memory of subsequent events after she had returned to her apartment, but she had third-degree burns over 55 percent of her body. From the evidence, police determined that she had been cooking; when she reached for the cupboard over the stove, her shirt brushed against the hot burner and caught fire. Hollister brought an action against the department store where her mother purchased the shirt on the grounds that the shirt was defective because it lacked a warning regarding its extreme flammability. The department store argued that the danger inherent in having clothing come into contact with a hot stove is "open and obvious." How should the court rule? [*Hollister v. Dayton Hudson Corp.,* 201 F.3d 731 (6th Cir. 2000), *cert. denied,* 531 U.S. 819 (2000).]

7. Richard Welge loved to sprinkle peanuts on his ice cream sundaes. One day Karen Godfrey, with whom Welge boarded, bought a 24-ounce vacuum-sealed plastic-capped glass jar of peanuts at a convenience store in Chicago. To obtain a $2 rebate that the manufacturer was offering to anyone who bought a "party" item, such as peanuts, Godfrey needed proof of her purchase from the jar of peanuts. Using an Exacto knife, she removed the part of the label that contained the bar code. She then placed the jar on top of the refrigerator. About a week later, Welge removed

the plastic seal from the jar, uncapped it, took some peanuts, replaced the cap, and returned the jar to the top of the refrigerator, all without incident.

A week later, Welge took down the jar, removed the plastic cap, spilled some peanuts into his left hand to put on his sundae, and replaced the cap with his right hand. But as he pushed the cap down on the open jar, the jar shattered. His hand was severely cut and is now, he claims, permanently impaired.

Welge brought suit and named three defendants: the convenience store, the manufacturer of the peanuts, and the manufacturer of the jar itself. From whom will Welge be able to recover? On what theories? What defenses, if any, are available to the defendants? [*Welge v. Planters Lifesavers Co.,* 17 F.3d 209 (7th Cir. 1994).]

8. Darleen Johnson was driving her Ford car under rainy conditions on a two-lane highway through Missouri. The car's front tires had a reasonable amount of tread remaining on them, but the back tires were nearly bald. For an undetermined reason, Johnson lost control of the car, spun into the other lane, and collided with a pickup truck driven by Kathyleen Sammons. Johnson was killed instantly.

Johnson's father claimed that the inboard C.V. joint boot on the front axle was torn, which allowed debris to contaminate the joint. (The boot is a covering that contains the grease that lubricates the joint.) This contamination allegedly made the joint act like a brake on the left front wheel and caused Johnson's car to pivot around that wheel and into the path of the oncoming pickup truck. Ford admits that the joint boot can become torn, which will allow contamination of the joint. In its manuals, Ford recommends periodic inspection of the boots. However, Ford contends that the joint on Johnson's car was contaminated during or after the accident. Ford also contends that contamination of the joint could not result in the joint seizing and creating a loss of steering control, and that the worst that could result from contamination would be some vibration and noise. According to Ford, Johnson's accident was caused by road conditions and driving error. The case is submitted to the jury on theories of strict liability and negligent design and manufacture. Is Ford liable for Johnson's death? Are there any additional arguments that Ford can raise in its defense? [*Johnson v. Ford Motor Co.,* 988 F.2d 573 (9th Cir. 1993).]

11

INTELLECTUAL PROPERTY

INTRODUCTION

Strategic Importance of Intellectual Property

Today's legally astute managers recognize that intellectual property is an essential part of their business. *Intellectual property* is any product or result of a mental process that is given legal protection against unauthorized use. Although intellectual property represents somewhere in the range of 87 percent of an average firm's value (up from 62 percent in 1992 and 38 percent in 1982),[1] more than 60 percent of executives in a recent survey said that their companies could extract substantially more value from their intellectual property. Over two-thirds reported that intellectual property management was too frequently treated as only a legal issue, reflecting an outdated approach to IP management. As Horatio Gutierrez, vice president and deputy general counsel in Microsoft's intellectual property and licensing group, observed, "We're moving toward a global economy where the true strategic asset is IP."[2]

There are four basic types of intellectual property: patents, copyrights, trademarks, and trade secrets. The Semiconductor Chip Protection Act of 1984 created a fifth, highly specialized form of intellectual property, the registered mask work. Different types of intellectual property are protected in different ways, and the protections apply to different aspects of a product.

1. Richard Lee, *Don't Underestimate the Value of Intellectual Property, Expert Says,* GREENWICH TIME, June 24, 2004, *available at* http://www.usa-canada.les.org/chapters/connecticut/prior/6.24_newspaper_article.pdf.
2. PriceWaterhouseCoopers, *Exploiting Intellectual Property in a Complex World,* vol. 4 (2007), *available at* http://www.pwc.com/extweb/pwcpublications.nsf/docid/F5DBAFA7B3F4501D852570830007AD84/$File/tecv4ip.pdf.

A *patent* is a government-granted right to exclude others from making, using, or selling an invention. The patent holder is not required to personally make use of the invention. After a period of time (in the United States, twenty years from the application date for utility patents and fourteen years for design patents), the patent expires and the invention is dedicated to the public.

A *copyright* is the legal right to prevent others from copying an original expression embodied in any original work of authorship fixed in a tangible medium. Copyright protects the expression, not the underlying ideas in the work. The owner has exclusive rights to reproduce, distribute, display, and perform the work. The owner also has the exclusive right to create *derivative works*, that is, works based upon the copyrighted work. Copyright protection lasts for at least seventy years. The Semiconductor Chip Protection Act of 1984 provides copyright-like protection for the layout or topography of an integrated circuit, but the duration of protection is limited to ten years.

Trademarks—words or symbols (such as brand names) that identify the source of goods or services—are also legally protected. Because trademarks tend to embody or represent the goodwill of the business, they are not legally transferable without that goodwill. Trademarks are protected for an indefinite time and can be valuable marketing and business assets. The packaging or dressing of a product may also be protected under the trademark laws as *trade dress*.

A *trade secret* is information that gives a business an advantage over its competitors that do not know the information. The classic example of a trade secret is the formula for Coca-Cola. Trade secrets are protected for an indefinite time.

Know-how—detailed information on how to make or do something—can be a trade secret, or it can be show-how. *Show-how* is nonsecret information used to teach someone how to make or do something; it is generally not protectable.

International piracy, or the unauthorized reproduction and distribution of patented, copyrighted, or trademarked goods, is a major issue today. The U.S. Chamber of Commerce claims that illegal counterfeiting costs America's economy from $200 to $250 billion per year and has caused the loss of 750,000 jobs. According to industry executives, piracy not only depletes the profits of American companies but can also, in the case of fake drugs, threaten people's lives. As a result, leaders of industry associations like the U.S. Chamber of Commerce and the Motion Picture Association have urged the U.S. government to adopt tougher legal penalties against counterfeiters and to appoint an intellectual property enforcement czar to help wage the global fight against piracy.[3]

CHAPTER OVERVIEW

This chapter describes the law of patents, copyrights, mask work rights, trademarks, and trade secrets in detail. The chapter concludes with a discussion of international intellectual property protection and the growing trend toward harmonization of national laws.

3. Justin Code, *US Firms Urge Clampdown on Piracy "Epidemic,"* June 14, 2007, http://uk.biz.yahoo.com/14062007/323/firms-urge-clampdown-piracy-epidemic.html.

PATENTS

Patents are one of the oldest recognized forms of intellectual property. Their importance has increased as our society has become more technologically advanced. Patents have formed the basis for whole businesses, such as the production of instant cameras, high-engineering plastics, and biotechnology.

Article I of the U.S. Constitution specifically grants Congress the power "to promote the Progress of Science and useful Arts, by securing for limited times to . . . Inventors the exclusive Right to their . . . Discoveries." The Patent and Trademark Office (PTO), an agency of the U.S. Department of Commerce, is responsible for issuing patents.

The PTO issued its first patent in 1790. Since that time, the PTO has issued more than 7.5 million patents. It issued 199,885 patents in 2006 alone, a 60 percent increase from the number issued in 1996.[4] The types of patents issued by the PTO have varied dramatically over the years, particularly in the last century. The first patent issued in 1900 was for an early version of the washing machine. The first patent issued in 2000 was for a sun visor/eye shield for athletes participating in "extreme" sports.[5] The top ten private-sector patent recipients for the 2007 calendar year are identified in Exhibit 11.1.

4. U.S. Patent Activity—Calendar Years 1790 to the Present, Table of Annual U.S. Patent Activity Since 1790, *available at* http://www.uspto.gov/web/offices/ac/ido/oeip/taf/h_counts.htm.
5. Press Release, U.S. Patent & Trademark Office, PTO Announces First Patent and Trademark of New Millennium (Jan. 13, 2000), *available at* http://www.uspto.gov/web/offices/com/speeches/00-05.htm.

EXHIBIT 11.1

Top Ten Private-Sector Patent Recipients for the 2007 Calendar Year

Rank in 2007	Organization	Number of Patents in 2007
1	International Business Machines Corp.	3,125
2	Samsung Electronics Co., Ltd.	2,723
3	Canon Kabushiki Kaisha	1,983
4	Matsushita Electric Industrial Co., Ltd.	1,910
5	Intel Corp.	1,864
6	Microsoft Corp.	1,637
7	Toshiba Corp.	1,519
8	Micron Technology, Inc.	1,476
9	Hewlett-Packard Development Co., L.P.	1,466
10	Sony Corp.	1,454

Source: Patenting by Organizations 2007, *available at* http://www.uspto.gov/web/offices/ac/ido/oeip/taf/topo_07.htm.

TYPES OF PATENTS

U.S. patent law provides for three types of patents: utility, design, and plant patents.

Utility Patents

Utility patents, the most frequently issued type, protect any novel, useful, and nonobvious process, machine, manufacture, or composition of matter, or any novel, useful, and nonobvious improvement thereof. To be approved, an application for a utility patent must satisfy the *utility requirement;* that is, the invention must have a practical or real-world benefit. If the PTO issues a utility patent, the patent owner has the exclusive right to make, use, sell, and import for use the invention for a nonrenewable period of twenty years from the date on which the patent application was filed.

An invention is *novel* if it was not anticipated, that is, if it was not previously known or used by others in the United States and was not previously patented or described in a printed publication in any country. Even if the invention is novel, it will be denied patent protection if its novelty merely represents an obvious development over existing technology, also referred to as *prior art.* Two New Yorkers applying for a patent for their device to remove garbage bags blown into tree branches worried that it might not meet this novelty requirement. Although similar to the fruit picker, invented in 1869, their "bag-snagger" was found sufficiently different to warrant a separate patent.

The inventor must be diligent in filing for patent protection. A *statutory bar* precludes protection in the United States if, prior to one year before the inventor's filing, the invention was either described in a printed publication in the United States or a foreign country, or was publicly used or sold in the United States. In most other countries, a patent application must be filed *before* the invention is described in a publication, publicly used, or sold.

Even when the inventor files promptly for protection of a novel, useful, and nonobvious invention, he or she may still be denied a patent. There is no protection for nonstatutory subject matter, such as abstract ideas (rather than specific applications of ideas), mental processes, naturally occurring substances, arrangements of printed matter, scientific principles, or laws of nature.

Biotechnology In *Diamond v. Chakrabarty,*[6] a microbiologist sought patent protection for his invention of a live human-made, genetically engineered bacterium capable of breaking down crude oil. The patent examiner rejected the application. On appeal, the U.S. Supreme Court held that living organisms can be patented if they are human-made.

6. 447 U.S. 303 (1980).

"Yeah, yeah—and I invented the ticket."

Stating that the patent statute should include "anything under the sun that is *made* by man," the Supreme Court extended patent protection to the new organism.

The Supreme Court prophetically noted that its decision in *Chakrabarty* might determine whether research efforts would be accelerated by the hope of reward or slowed by the want of incentives. In fact, the *Chakrabarty* decision allowed small biotechnology firms to attract venture capitalists and other investors, and spawned a whole new industry.

In 1987, the PTO confirmed that nonnaturally occurring, nonhuman multicellular living organisms (including animals) are patentable subject matter. The PTO issued a patent in 1988 on a transgenic mouse that was engineered to be susceptible to cancer. It issued three more mouse patents in 1993.

More recently, patent laws have been applied even more broadly to include patents on human and other genes. According to the PTO, gene sequences are patentable subject matter. Specifically, a gene patent covers "the genetic composition isolated from its natural state and processed through purifying steps that separate the gene from other molecules naturally associated with it."[7] As of October 2005, over 4,000 genes, or 20 percent of the almost 24,000 human genes, had been claimed in U.S. patents.[8] More than twenty human pathogens are privately owned, including haemophilus influenza and Hepatitis C. Many gene patents have been associated with research leading to the treatment of the related disease.

Gene patenting (which has always been controversial) sparked new controversy when a patent was issued to Human Genome Sciences, Inc. for a gene found to serve

7. Notice, 66 Fed. Reg. 1097 (Jan. 5, 2001).

8. Stefan Lovgren, *One-Fifth of Human Genes Have Been Patented, Study Reveals,* NAT'L GEOGRAPHIC NEWS, Oct. 13, 2005, *available at* http://news.nationalgeographic.com/news/2005/10/1013_051013_gene_patent.html; *see also* DNA Patent Database, *available at* http://dnapatents.georgetown.edu/ (last visited Jan. 11, 2005).

> **ETHICAL CONSIDERATION**
>
> Children with Canavan disease, an inherited disorder, begin to display symptoms at three months of age. They never crawl or walk, suffer seizures, eventually become paralyzed, and die by adolescence. Canavan families around the world donated tissue and money to identify the gene that causes the disease so that a test could be developed to tell parents if they were at risk of producing a child with the disorder. When the gene was identified by a researcher at Miami Children's Hospital Research Institute, a New York hospital promised that it would offer the test, free of charge, to all who wanted it, but Miami Children's, which had patented the gene, refused to allow any health care provider to offer the test without paying a royalty. Is it ethical to require families at risk for Canavan disease (including those who had contributed money and tissue to Miami Children's research) to pay for the test? Is it ethical to require researchers to pay royalties if they wish to study this disease further?

as a platform from which the AIDS virus can infect cells of the body. Questions arose as to the legal and moral right to own a human gene. Perhaps more significantly, concerns arose over the effect of giving one company the ability to control medical research related to a life-threatening disease, especially when that company may not appreciate the medical value of the gene.[9] In response to these concerns, on January 5, 2001, the PTO issued guidelines for examination of gene applications for compliance with the utility requirement.[10] The PTO had been faulted for issuing patents on genes before the inventors had ascertained the gene's function. The new guidelines were designed to make it more difficult for genes to be patented by requiring a stronger showing of utility. These guidelines have had a great impact; by 2003, the explosive growth of the biotech industry had leveled off. The strategy of many U.S. biotech firms seems to have shifted from acquiring new patents to vigorously defending their existing patents.

Computer Software The law's embrace of software patents began in 1981, when the Supreme Court held, in *Diamond v. Diehr,* that if a "claim containing a mathematical formula implements or applies that formula in a structure or process, which when considered as a whole, is performing a function which the patent laws were designed to protect (e.g., transforming or reducing an article to a different state or thing), then the claim [may be patentable]."[11] After this decision, developers successfully acquired software patents at a quickening pace.

Most software code is not published, so much of the relevant prior art is not accessible to the PTO examiners. In addition, until recently, U.S. patent applications were not published until and unless a patent was issued. As a result, many experts believed that the PTO was issuing patents for computer programs that were not novel or were merely obvious improvements of existing programs.

In 1994, partly in response to charges from intellectual property lawyers that the patent was overly broad, the PTO took the unusual step of reversing a patent granted to Compton's New Media and Encyclopedia Britannica. The patent (which covered virtually all ways of storing and retrieving text, sound, and images stored on compact discs) appeared to give Compton's a dominant position in the fast-growing multimedia market. The fact that the patent was issued in the first place was cited by the Interactive Multimedia Association as evidence of the need to improve the training of the PTO's software examiners.

Business Method Patents In recent years, some of the most criticized patents have been patents on "business method" inventions, particularly in connection with the Internet and electronic commerce. Until 1998, the courts had held that business methods were not patentable, but in *State Street Bank & Trust Co. v. Signature Financial Group,*[12] the U.S. Court of Appeals for the Federal Circuit upheld the validity of a patent on a mutual fund investment method. The court determined that business methods, like all processes, are patentable if they meet all the usual requirements for patentability.

The case spurred a wave of patent applications; in 2000 alone, 8,058 inventors filed business method applications, and 845 business method patents were issued.[13] Some of the most "notorious" e-commerce business method patents are well known. Amazon.com's patent for the "one-click" shopping system, Priceline.com's patent for the online reverse auction, and Microsoft's patent on "e-commerce" all pushed the boundaries of the novelty requirement.

In response to criticism that these patents were granted too readily, with an inadequate review of prior art, the PTO announced in 2000 that it was adding a second layer of review for applications seeking protection for e-commerce-based business methods. These efforts initially had an impact: in 2002, 7,400 business method applications were filed, but only 493 patents were issued, and in 2003, 7,750 business method applications were filed, but only 486 patents were

9. For an excellent collection of articles on the pros and cons of gene patents, see MIT TECH. REV. (Sept.–Oct. 2000). *See also* Michael Crichton, *Patent Life*, N.Y. TIMES, Feb. 13, 2007, at A23, *available at* http://www.nytimes.com/2007/02/13/opinion/13crichton.html.

10. 66 Fed. Reg. 1097.

11. 450 U.S. 175, 176 (1981).

12. 149 F.3d 1368 (Fed. Cir. 1998).

13. U.S. Patent & Trademark Office, *available at* http://www.uspto.gov/web/menu/pbmethod/applicationfiling.htm (last visited Mar. 22, 2008).

issued. More recently, however, the number of issued business method patents has risen dramatically. In 2006, 10,108 business method applications were filed, and 1,191 patents were issued, and in 2007, 11,378 business method applications were filed, and 1,330 patents were issued.[14]

This growth in the issuance of business method patents may be slowed down by the U.S. Supreme Court's decision in *KSR International Co. v. Teleflex, Inc.*[15] In this case, Teleflex asserted that one of KSR's products infringed its patent on connecting an adjustable vehicle control pedal to an electronic throttle control. KSR moved for summary judgment, claiming that combining the pedal and the throttle control was not patentable because it was obvious. The U.S. Court of Appeals for the Federal Circuit granted summary judgment for Teleflex. The court applied the Teaching Suggestion Motivation (TSM) test, under which a patent claim is proved obvious only if "some motivation or suggestion to combine the prior art teachings" can be found in the prior art, the nature of the problem, or the knowledge of a person having ordinary skill in the art. The Supreme Court reversed, concluding that the Federal Circuit had applied the TSM test too narrowly and holding that "[t]he proper question to have asked was whether a pedal designer of ordinary skill, facing the wide range of needs created by developments in the field of endeavor, would have seen a benefit to upgrading [a prior art patent] with a sensor."

Soon thereafter, the PTO struck down twenty-one of the twenty-six claims in the Amazon one-click patent on the basis of obviousness in a reexamination decision that cited the *KSR* case.

Design Patents

A *design patent* protects any novel, original (rather than nonobvious), and ornamental (rather than useful) design for an article of manufacture. Design patents protect against copying the appearance or shape of an article such as a computer terminal cabinet, a perfume bottle, a typeface, or the icons and screen displays used in computer programs. A design dictated by function rather than aesthetic concerns cannot be protected by a design patent, but it may be protectable by a utility patent. A design patent has a duration of fourteen years from the date on which the patent application is filed, compared to twenty years for utility and plant patents.

Traditionally, design patents have rarely been used in the United States; other forms of protection, such as unfair competition law, have been relied on instead. Recently, however, the use of design patents has been increasing, in part because the application process is simpler and less expensive than for utility patents.

Plant Patents

Plant patents protect any distinct and new variety of plant that is asexually reproduced (that is, not reproduced by means of seeds). The variety must not exist naturally. Thus, a plant patent will not be issued to someone who merely discovers a wild plant not previously known to exist. Once a plant patent is granted, the patent owner has the exclusive right to exclude others from asexually reproducing, using, or selling the plant. In 2001, the U.S. Supreme Court affirmed that plant patents do not foreclose utility patent protection for the same plants.[16]

FILING FOR PATENT PROTECTION

To obtain patent protection in the United States, the inventor must file a patent application with the PTO. Each patent application contains four parts: the specifications, the claims, the drawings (except in chemical cases), and a declaration by the inventor.

The *specifications* must describe the invention (as defined by the claims) in its best mode and the manner and process of making and using the invention, in such a way that a person skilled in the relevant field could make and use it. The description of the *best mode* must be the best way the inventor knows to make the invention at the time of filing the application. All descriptions must be clear, concise, and exact.

The *claims* (the numbered paragraphs at the end of the patent) describe the elements of the invention that the patent will protect. Any element not specifically set forth in the claims is unprotected by the patent. Thus, drafting the claims is crucial to obtaining adequate protection.

The *drawings* must show the claimed invention. The *declaration by the inventor* must state that the inventor has reviewed the application and believes that he or she is the first inventor of the invention. The inventor must also make full disclosure of any known relevant prior art. Knowing the prior developments assists the patent attorney in drafting the claims to avoid the prior art; it also permits the patent examiner to determine whether the patent is novel or would have been obvious to those familiar with the relevant field.

The patent examiner may initially reject the application, as being precluded by prior inventions or otherwise failing to meet the statutory requirements (the PTO initially rejects 99 percent of all patent applications). The inventor may then either present arguments (and in extreme cases, evidence) to contest the rejection or seek to amend the application to overcome the examiner's objections. If the application is finally rejected, the inventor can either refile the application as a *continuation application* or appeal to the PTO's Board of Appeals and subsequently to either the U.S. District Court

14. *Id.*

15. 127 S. Ct. 1727 (2007).

16. J.E.M. AG Supply v. Pioneer Hi-Bred Int'l, 534 U.S. 124 (2001).

for the District of Columbia or the U.S. Court of Appeals for the Federal Circuit. Once the examiner agrees that a patent should be issued, and the examiner and applicant agree on the precise language of the claims, a patent will be issued.

Since 1995, inventors have been able to file provisional patent applications, which can be filed without formal patent claims; a provisional application must be followed by a nonprovisional application within twelve months. The provisional application provides a low-cost way to establish an early filing date for the later, nonprovisional patent application.

TYPES OF INFRINGEMENT

A patent may be infringed in three ways: directly, indirectly, or contributorily. *Direct patent infringement* is the making, use, or sale of any patented invention within the United States during the term of the U.S. patent. When an accused device or process does not have precisely each element of a particular claim of a patent (that is, the patent is not literally infringed), but the patented invention is replicated in a product or process that works in substantially the same way and accomplishes substantially the same result, a direct infringement can be found under the *doctrine of equivalents*. In 2002, the U.S. Supreme Court narrowed the reach of this doctrine so that it is now effectively available only to inventors who did not amend their patent applications in order to satisfy patentability requirements.[17] As the patent examiner asks the majority of patent applicants to amend their applications to satisfy these requirements, the doctrine of equivalents now provides patent owners with considerably less recourse against competitors who design around their patents.

Indirect patent infringement, also referred to as *inducement to infringe,* is a party's active inducement of another party to infringe a patent. *Contributory patent infringement* occurs when one party knowingly sells an item with one specific use that will result in the infringement of another's patent. For example, if a company sells a computer add-on card for a specific use that will infringe another's patent, the sale is a contributory infringement even though the add-on card itself does not infringe any patent. Direct infringement can be committed innocently and unintentionally; indirect and contributory infringement require some knowledge or intent that a patent will be infringed.

DEFENSES

A defendant to a patent-infringement action may claim a variety of defenses, including (1) noninfringement of the patent, (2) invalidity of the patent, (3) misuse of the patent, or (4) innocent infringement.

Noninfringement

The defense of *noninfringement* asserts that the allegedly infringing matter does not fall within the claims of the issued patent. Under this defense, the specific language of the patent claims is compared with the allegedly infringing matter. If the allegedly infringing matter is not described by the patent claims, the defense of noninfringement is successful. The doctrine of *file-wrapper estoppel* prevents a patent owner from asserting any claim interpretation at odds with the application on file with the PTO. Because the patent holder has previously negotiated the scope of his or her invention with the PTO, the patent holder may not renegotiate that scope in a subsequent court proceeding.

In 1996, the U.S. Supreme Court held that the construction of the words in patent claims is a matter of law for the court, not the jury, to decide.[18] The Court reasoned that "[t]he construction of written instruments is one of those things that judges often do and are likely to do better than jurors unburdened by training in exegesis."

Invalidity

A patent is presumed to be valid, but a court may find it invalid if (1) the invention was not novel, useful, or nonobvious when the patent was issued; (2) the patent covers nonstatutory subject matter such as an abstract idea, a scientific principle, or a mental process; (3) a statutory bar was created by a publication or sale of the invention more than one year prior to the filing of the patent application; or (4) any other requirement of the patent law was not met.

Patent Misuse

A *patent misuse* defense asserts that although the defendant has infringed a valid patent, the patent holder has abused its patent rights and therefore has lost, at least temporarily, its right to enforce them. Improperly expanding the physical or temporal scope of a patent constitutes patent misuse. For example, forcing a party to sign a license agreement that calls for royalty payments beyond the expiration of the patent would be a patent misuse. Seeking to enforce a patent obtained through inequitable conduct might also be a patent misuse.

The patent holder is barred from recovering for any infringement of its patent during the period of misuse. If the patent holder later "purges" itself of the misuse, it may

17. Festo Corp. v. Shoketsu Kinzoku Kogyo Kabushiki Co., 535 U.S. 722 (2002).

18. Markman v. Westview Instruments, Inc., 517 U.S. 370 (1996).

recover for any subsequent infringement. For example, if a provision in a patent license caused the patent misuse, eliminating the provision from all of the patent holder's patent licenses would enable the holder to once again enforce the patent, but the holder would not be entitled to judicial relief for conduct prior to the effective date of the purge.

Innocent Infringement

A defendant may claim innocent infringement if the patented item did not carry adequate notice of its patent status. Although this is not a complete defense to patent infringement, a patent owner cannot sue for damages arising out of infringement occurring before the defendant received actual notice of infringement. In the case of physical products, notice is normally given by putting the patent number on the product or its packaging. In the case of intangible patented items, such as business processes, the patent owner generally does not need to provide any patent marking to recover damages for the full period of infringement, although at least one case has held that marking is required for a method or system patent if the patent owner sold the patented system over the Internet.[19]

First Sale Doctrine

Under the *first sale doctrine,* an authorized sale of a patented article exhausts the patent holder's exclusive rights as to that article, to the extent that the article embodies the invention. As a result, the patent holder is precluded from obtaining any further royalties or imposing any further restrictions on the article or its subsequent sale or transfer.

19. IMX, Inc. v. Lendingtree, LLC, 2005 WL 3465555 (D. Del. 2005).

> **› ETHICAL CONSIDERATION**
>
> Some inventors have made fortunes by turning out a steady stream of blueprints and drawings for new or improved devices without bothering to develop them into commercial products or even to create prototypes. Instead, they design their claims on top of existing products in order to create infringements by current manufacturers; then they delay filing their applications as long as possible to maximize their patents' value and longevity.[a] Is it ethical to use the patent system simply to collect revenue rather than to spur innovation?
>
> **a.** For an example of such a controversy, see Bernard Wysocki, Jr., *How Patent Lawsuits Make a Quiet Engineer Rich and Controversial,* WALL ST. J., Apr. 9, 1997, at A1.

REMEDIES

If a valid patent has been infringed, the patent holder may seek preliminary and permanent injunctive relief and damages, as well as court costs and attorneys' fees.

Injunctive Relief

A patent holder may seek a preliminary injunction to prevent any further infringement of the patent pending the court's ultimate decision. Most courts, however, are reluctant to grant injunctive relief before they have determined that a valid patent has actually been infringed. For many years, U.S. courts granted permanent injunctive relief almost as a matter of right after a finding of infringement. In 2006, the U.S. Supreme Court examined whether a finding of patent infringement required the issuance of a permanent injunction in the following case.

A CASE IN POINT | **SUMMARY**

CASE 11.1

EBAY INC. V. MERCEXCHANGE, L.L.C.

UNITED STATES SUPREME COURT
547 U.S. 388 (2006).

FACTS The popular Internet website eBay allows private sellers to list goods that they want to sell at auction or at a fixed price. MercExchange, L.L.C. holds many patents, including a business method patent for an electronic market designed to facilitate the sale of goods between individuals by creating a central authority to promote trust among participants. MercExchange licenses this patent for use by other companies. After failing to reach a licensing agreement with eBay and eBay's subsidiary, Half.com, MercExchange filed a suit alleging patent infringement.

A jury found patent infringement and awarded $29.5 million in money damages. Later, the federal district court judge denied MercExchange's motion for permanent injunctive relief.[20] The U.S. Court

CONTINUED

20. eBay Inc. v. MercExchange, L.L.C., 275 F. Supp. 2d 695 (E.D.Va. 2003).

of Appeals for the Federal Circuit reversed, noting that U.S. courts have granted injunctive relief upon a finding of infringement in the vast majority of patent cases since the early nineteenth century and concluding that, as a general rule, "courts will issue permanent injunctions against patent infringement absent exceptional circumstances."[21] eBay appealed.

ISSUE PRESENTED Does a finding of patent infringement require the issuance of a permanent injunction absent exceptional circumstances?

SUMMARY OF OPINION Justice Thomas, writing for the majority, cited the Patent Act, which states that "patents shall have the attributes of personal property,"[22] such as "the right to exclude others from making, using, offering for sale, or selling the invention."[23] Disagreeing with the Federal Circuit, which had adopted the view that this statutory right to exclude justified a general rule in favor of permanent injunctive relief when patent infringement is found, the Court ruled that the right to exclude is separate from the provision of remedies under the Act. In fact, the Court pointed out that the Patent Act itself includes a provision that injunctive relief "may" issue only "in accordance with the principles of equity."[24]

Instead of applying the general rule requiring permanent injunctive relief in cases of patent infringement offered by the Federal Circuit, the Court presented the traditional four-factor test a plaintiff must satisfy in order to obtain a permanent injunction. These factors include demonstrating that (1) an irreparable injury exists; (2) the remedies available at law, such as monetary damages, are inadequate; (3) in balancing the hardships between the plaintiff and the defendant, an injunction is appropriate; and (4) the public interest would not be disserved by a permanent injunction. The Court held that this test applies to disputes arising under the Patent Act.

Thus, the Court found that both lower courts erred in their rulings. The district court incorrectly suggested that a permanent injunction would be barred even in cases where patent holders would be able to satisfy the traditional four-factor test. For example, the district court found that a "plaintiff's willingness to license its patents" and "its lack of commercial activity" in putting the patents into practice would be enough to establish that the patent holder would not suffer irreparable harm if an injunction was not issued. The Court noted, however, that those patent holders might intend to license patents rather than develop them for market and therefore could still face irreparable harm if an injunction was not granted. Conversely, the court of appeals incorrectly found categorical relief in the form of a permanent injunction where patent infringement existed. Thus, the Court found that the district court's treatment of injunctive relief was too narrow and that the court of appeals' treatment of injunctive relief was too broad. As a result, the Court held that the decision to grant or deny injunctive relief in patent cases lies within the equitable discretion of the district court and that this discretion must be exercised consistent with the traditional four-factor injunctive relief test.

RESULT The Court vacated the judgment of the Federal Circuit that permanent injunctions must always be granted in cases of patent infringement and remanded the case for further proceedings. In order to obtain a permanent injunction, MercExchange had the burden of establishing the traditional four factors for equitable relief.

COMMENTS In his concurring opinion, Justice Kennedy referred to the recent proliferation of firms that use patents primarily to obtain license fees and noted, "For these firms, an injunction, and the potentially serious sanctions arising from its violation, can be employed as a bargaining

CONTINUED

21. eBay Inc. v. MercExchange, L.L.C., 401 F.3d 1323, 1339 (Fed. Cir. 2005).
22. 35 U.S.C. § 261.
23. 35 U.S.C. § 154(a)(1).
24. 35 U.S.C. § 283.

tool to charge exorbitant fees to companies that seek to buy licenses to practice the patent." See the "Inside Story" for the story of one of these firms called NTP. NTP filed a lawsuit against Research in Motion (RIM), the Canadian manufacturer of the BlackBerry, a handheld device that provides wireless e-mail access and is used by over three million Americans, for infringing five NTP patents. In March 2006, RIM agreed to pay NTP $612.5 million, without any right to a refund even if the PTO eventually overturned NTP's patents. The RIM settlement was reached several months before the Supreme Court's decision in *eBay Inc. v. MercExchange, L.L.C.*

CRITICAL THINKING QUESTIONS

1. If the Supreme Court had rendered its decision in *eBay v. MercExchange* before RIM settled with NTP, how might it have affected the negotiations?
2. How might this decision affect the incentives of individuals and companies to create new inventions?

Damages

Damages may also be awarded, based on (1) the patent holder's lost profits (in the case of a patent holder practicing its invention), (2) the infringer's profits, or (3) a reasonable royalty for the infringer's use of the invention. To this, court costs, as fixed by the court, may be added. The court also has discretion to increase the damages award by up to three times for intentional or willful infringement and to award attorneys' fees in exceptional cases.

The instant-camera litigation between Polaroid Corporation and Eastman Kodak Company illustrates the potential for large damages awards for patent infringement. In the 1970s, Kodak sought a license from Polaroid to produce instant cameras and film, but the parties never reached an agreement. When Kodak nonetheless introduced an instant camera and film in 1976, Polaroid sued for patent infringement. A federal district court held that Kodak had infringed twenty claims of seven Polaroid patents and enjoined Kodak from any further infringements. The injunction terminated Kodak's instant-camera business, leaving it with $200 million worth of useless manufacturing equipment and $600 million in losses.[25] Kodak was later ordered to pay Polaroid $910 million for infringing its patents, including $454.2 million in lost profits and royalties and $455.3 million in interest.[26] The Kodak award remained the largest in a U.S. patent-infringement suit until February 2007, when a San Diego jury ordered Microsoft to pay Alcatel-Lucent $1.52 billion for using patented digital music technology without permission. The Microsoft verdict was later thrown out by a trial judge, however, and the decision was appealed.[27]

Patent litigation is a high stakes game for both established market participants and small companies. In 2005, Nokia, the world's largest mobile phone maker, and five other companies filed a complaint with the European Commission over the high royalty rate charged by Qualcomm, Inc., the largest chipmaker for mobile phones, for its patent portfolio. Nokia had entered into a license agreement with Qualcomm in 1992, pursuant to which Nokia is thought to be paying Qualcomm $500 million annually. Although Qualcomm had dominated the code division multiple access (CDMA) market, Nokia claimed that Qualcomm had contributed much less to its successor high-speed Wideband CDMA (WCDMA) handsets (which include many more features, such as cameras, music and video players, and Internet browsers), as well as to a variety of receivers and transmitters to connect different kinds of networks. As a result, Nokia sought a significant reduction in the royalties it pays. Litigation escalated after the licensing agreement expired in 2006, and as of 2008, patent infringement actions filed by Qualcomm or Nokia were pending in California, Wisconsin, Texas, Great Britain, Germany, the Netherlands, France, Italy, and China, as well as before the European Commission and the International Trade Commission. In February 2008, the parties agreed to a stand-down, pursuant to which most of this litigation was placed on hold until the Delaware lawsuit was resolved. On July 23, 2008, the German Federal Patent Court ruled that one of the Broadcom patents asserted against Nokia was invalid. The case

25. Polaroid Corp. v. Eastman Kodak Co., 789 F.2d 1556 (Fed. Cir. 1986).
26. Lawrence Ingrassia & James S. Hirsch, *Polaroid's Patent-Case Award, Smaller than Anticipated, Is a Relief for Kodak,* WALL ST. J., Oct. 15, 1990, at A3.
27. Stephen Larson, *Big Win for Microsoft in Alcatel-Lucent Patent Case*, PC WORLD, Aug. 7, 2007, *available at* http://www.pcworld.com/article/id,135598-c,%20legalissues/article.html.

followed similar decisions by the U.S. International Trade Commission and the United Kingdom's High Court. The Delaware court case was scheduled to begin trial on July 23, 2008, but the judge delayed the opening day of the trial to address the licensing fees and Nokia's complaint that Qualcomm has ignored its commitment to license its patents on fair terms. On July 24, 2008, the parties announced that they had brokered a final agreement to lay their long-running global patent dispute to rest.[28] The fifteen-year agreement covers various standards including CDMA and WCDMA. Nokia has been granted a license under all Qualcomm patents for use in Nokia mobile devices and Nokia-Siemens infrastructure equipment. Nokia also agreed not to use any of its patents directly against Qualcomm and to hand over several patents essential to WCDMA and certain other standards. Nokia will also make an upfront financial settlement and ongoing royalty payments, although the specifics of the financial arrangement were not disclosed.

The prohibitive cost of patent litigation can make it much more difficult for small companies to recover damages from larger firms. The median cost of litigation for patent matters involving over $25 million is $3.5 million.[29] Some corporations purposely lengthen and complicate the discovery process in order to strain the resources of their smaller challengers. Perhaps as a result, 86 percent of patent lawsuits in 2005 were settled.[30] Even when patent cases settle, however, each side will generally incur more than $1 million in direct legal fees and indirect expenses.[31] Nevertheless, patent rights can provide a David with an effective means to strike down a Goliath. For example, after Burst.com sued Microsoft for patent infringement relating to Media Player, it negotiated a $60 million settlement in 2005.[32] More recently, when Z4 sued Microsoft for patent infringement, a jury found willful infringement and awarded Z4 $115 million.[33]

COPYRIGHTS

Best-selling novels, award-winning films, off-the-shelf software packages, and compact discs are all copyrightable works. So are restaurant menus, digital videodiscs, designer linens, plush toy animals, and cereal boxes. The United States Copyright Act of 1976 requires that the material for which copyright protection is sought be original (not copied) and fall within one of the following categories: (1) literary works; (2) musical works; (3) dramatic works; (4) pantomimes and choreographic works; (5) pictorial, graphic, and sculptural works; (6) motion pictures and other audiovisual works; and (7) sound recordings.

The Act requires that the works be fixed in a tangible medium from which they can be perceived, reproduced, or communicated. For example, stories may be fixed in written manuscripts, computer software on floppy disks, recordings of songs on compact discs, and the staging of a play recorded on videotape. Copyright does not extend to names, familiar phrases, government publications, standardized information, or facts. Copyright protects expression; it does not protect the underlying ideas.

In addition to being fixed, the works must be sufficiently original—have some degree of creativity—to qualify for protection. As mentioned, facts are not copyrightable. A compilation of facts may be eligible for copyright protection, but only to the extent that the selection, coordination, or arrangement of the facts is original. As the U.S. Supreme Court explained in *Feist Publications v. Rural Telephone Co.*, "[t]he sine qua non of copyright is originality."[34] In that case, Feist, a publisher of a rural telephone directory, sued Rural Telephone for copying its listings in its rival telephone directory. Feist argued that because it had invested substantial time and effort in compiling and arranging the factual listings, the data were copyrightable. The Supreme Court rejected this "sweat of the brow" argument, holding that originality is the critical element of copyright protection and that the alphabetical arrangement of the phone listings was not sufficiently original to entitle Feist to copyright protection.

28. Tarmo Virki, *Qualcomm Patent Ruled Invalid in German Nokia Case,* YAHOO! NEWS, July 23, 2008, *available at* http://news.yahoo.com/s/nm/20080723/tc_nm/nokia_qualcomm_dc_4&printer=1;ylt=AllQnkqt59212NrerbUvMad U.3QA; *Nokia, Qualcomm Settle Licensing Dispute,* Assoc. PRESS, July 24, 2008, *available at* http://www.siliconvalley.com/news/ci_9980707?nclick_check=1; *Nokia and Qualcomm Declare a Ceasefire in Long-Running Patent War,* COMMUNICATIONSDIRECT, July 24, 2008, http://www.communicationsdirectnews.com/do.php/150/31784?199.

29. American Intellectual Property Law Ass'n, *AIPLA Report of the Economic Survey 2007,* July 2007, at 25.

30. http://www.patstats.org/HISTORICAL_DISPOSITION_MODES_FOR_PATENT_CASES.rev2.doc.

31. Kimberly Moore, *Judges, Juries, and Patent Cases—An Empirical Peek Inside the Black Box,* 99 MICH. L. REV. 365, 367 (2000).

32. Eriq Gardner, *First Bill, Now Steve*, IP L. & BUS., Apr. 2005, *available at* http://www.ipww.com/display.php/file=/texts/0406/burst.

33. Xenia P. Kobylarz, *Microsoft Wins Patent Case with "eBay" Argument,* RECORDER, June 16, 2006, *available at* http://www.law.com/jsp/article.jsp?id=1150362322460.

34. 499 U.S. 340, 345 (1991).

If an author can establish the fixity and originality of a work, copyright protection is automatic and entitles the author to the exclusive economic rights to (1) reproduce the copyrighted work, (2) prepare derivative works based on the copyrighted work, (3) distribute copies or phonorecords of the copyrighted work to the public, (4) perform the copyrighted work publicly, and (5) display the copyrighted work publicly.

OWNERSHIP AND SCOPE OF PROTECTION

The creator of the work or, in the case of a work made for hire, the party for whom the work was prepared, is the author of the copyrighted work. A *work made for hire* is either (1) a work created by an employee within the scope of his or her employment or (2) a work in one of nine listed categories that is specially commissioned through a signed writing that states that the work is a "work made for hire."

The author of a copyrighted work can transfer ownership by an assignment of copyright. Parties that commission independent contractors to produce works that fall outside the nine listed categories, such as computer programs, often seek copyright assignments.

The advent of nonprint media, such as CD-ROMs and electronic databases, has led to disputes between freelance writers and photographers on one side, and the newspapers and magazines that buy their work on the other, about who owns the electronic or digital rights. For example, a group of freelance writers sued the newspapers to which they sold their stories, alleging that the newspapers' publishing of their work in nonprint media exceeded the newspapers' rights to the material. The U.S. Court of Appeals for the Second Circuit agreed. Although the owner of a copyright for a collective work (in this case, the publisher of the newspaper or magazine) has the right to revise the individual works, it does not have the right to republish them in an electronic database.[35] The publishers appealed, but the U.S. Supreme Court affirmed the Second Circuit's ruling, underscoring the importance of negotiating an assignment of rights that clearly applies to any known or future media.[36]

Expression Versus Idea

The Copyright Act prohibits unauthorized copying of the *protected expression* of a work, but the underlying ideas embodied in the work remain freely usable by others. Section 102 of the Act excludes from copyright protection any "idea, procedure, process, system, method of operation, concept, principle or discovery, regardless of the form in which it is described, explained, illustrated, or embodied."

The U.S. Court of Appeals for the First Circuit held that the menu-command structure of the Lotus 1-2-3 computer spreadsheet program, taken as a whole—including the choice of command terms; the structure, sequence, and organization of these terms; their presentation on the screen; and the long prompts—was an unprotectable method of operation.[37] The court reasoned that Lotus 1-2-3's use of commands labeled "Print" and "Copy" was no different from buttons on a videocassette recorder (VCR) labeled "Play" and "Fast Forward." Labeling and arranging the VCR buttons does not make them an expression of the abstract method of operating a VCR. Rather, the buttons *are* the method of operating the VCR. To the extent there was expression in Lotus 1-2-3's choice of terms such as "Exit" or "Save," the court deemed it part of the method of operation and therefore not copyrightable. Quoting the U.S. Supreme Court's *Feist* decision,[38] the court noted that "copyright assures authors the right to their original expression, but encourages others to build freely upon the ideas and information conveyed by that work." An evenly divided U.S. Supreme Court affirmed.

When an idea and its expression are inseparable, the *merger doctrine* dictates that the expression is not copyrightable. If it were, the copyright would confer a monopoly over the idea. Thus, a manufacturer of a karate video game cannot keep a competitor from producing another video game based on standard karate moves and rules. The idea of a karate game (including game procedures, karate moves, background scenes, a referee, and the use of computer graphics) is not protected expression. The manufacturer can, however, keep a competitor from copying any original graphics it has used in the game, as long as they are inseparable from the idea of karate or of a karate video game.

Useful Article Doctrine

The *useful article doctrine* provides that copyright protection does not extend to the useful application of an idea. The Copyright Act defines pictorial, graphic, and sculptural works to include "works of artistic craftsmanship insofar as their form but not their mechanical or utilitarian aspects are concerned." For example, blank forms used to record, rather than convey, information are considered noncopyrightable useful articles.

35. Tasini v. New York Times, 206 F.3d 161 (2d Cir. 2000), *cert. granted,* 531 U.S. 978 (2000).

36. Tasini v. New York Times, 533 U.S. 483 (2001).

37. Lotus Dev. Corp. v. Borland Int'l, Inc., 49 F.3d 807 (1st Cir. 1995), *aff'd,* 516 U.S. 233 (1996).

38. 499 U.S. 340 (1991).

If the expression of a pictorial, graphic, or sculptural work cannot be identified separately from and exist independently of such utilitarian aspects, courts will deny copyright protection to the whole work. An example of an article whose expression is separable from its utilitarian aspects would be a lamp that incorporates a statue of a woman in its base. An example of an article whose expression is not separable from its utilitarian aspects is the layout of an integrated circuit. Although a drawing of the circuit is copyrightable, the actual circuitry is not copyrightable, because it is impossible to separate the utilitarian aspect of the circuit from its expression or layout. It is the layout of the circuit that enables the circuit to operate correctly. The circuit may be patentable, however. In addition, the layout or topography of the circuit may be protectable as a registered mask work under the Semiconductor Chip Protection Act of 1984.

PREEMPTION OF STATE LAW

Because the Copyright Act is a federal statute, it preempts any state law that enforces rights "equivalent" to one of the exclusive rights in federal copyright. Nonetheless, copyright law does not preempt a state law if the state-protected rights are qualitatively different from those protected under federal copyright.

For example, in *National Basketball Ass'n v. Motorola, Inc.,*[39] the National Basketball Association (NBA) sued Motorola and STATS for federal copyright infringement and for unfair competition under state law when Motorola began marketing the SportsTrax paging device, which displayed information on NBA games in progress with only a two- to three-minute lag time. STATS reporters, who watched the games on television or listened to them on the radio, provided the data feed for SportsTrax.

The U.S. Court of Appeals for the Second Circuit noted that although a live event itself is not an "original [work] of authorship," a simultaneously recorded broadcast of the event is entitled to protection under the Copyright Act.[40] The court recognized that the *hot-news exception* applies in cases where (1) the plaintiff generates or gathers the information at a cost, (2) the information is time-sensitive, (3) the defendant's use of the information amounts to free riding on the plaintiff's efforts, (4) the defendant is in direct competition with the plaintiff, and (5) the availability of other parties to free ride on the plaintiff's efforts would so reduce the plaintiff's incentive to provide the product or service that its existence or quality would be threatened. The court concluded, however, that the hot-news exception did not apply in this case, because the NBA failed to show that SportsTrax's free riding had any competitive effect on the NBA's incentive to provide a high-quality product; therefore, federal copyright law preempted the state misappropriation claim. Nonetheless, federal copyright law did not preclude STATS from collecting its data from television or radio broadcasts, and therefore the NBA's case was dismissed.

In contrast, in *Brown v. Ames,*[41] the U.S. Court of Appeals for the Fifth Circuit ruled that state tort claims for misappropriation of the names and likenesses of music artists were not preempted by federal copyright law. The defendants had allegedly marketed CDs and cassettes of musical performances by the plaintiff artists without obtaining copyright permission and had used the artists' names and likenesses to assist in the illegal marketing effort. The artists sued for copyright infringement and for misappropriation. In deciding that the misappropriation claim was not preempted, the court emphasized that names and likenesses are not copyrightable and therefore could not be the subject of a federal copyright claim.

TERM OF PROTECTION

The Sonny Bono Term Extension Act of 1998 extended the duration of U.S. copyrights by twenty years.[42] If the author is a known individual, the term is now the life of the author plus seventy years. For a work made for hire or for an anonymous or pseudonymous work, the term is the lesser of ninety-five years after first publication or one hundred and twenty years after creation of the work. Publishers and librarians, among others who opposed the Bono Act, brought an action to obtain an injunction on its enforcement, challenging the constitutionality of the Act on the basis that it was not "necessary and proper" to achieve the purpose of "promoting the progress of science and useful arts." In 2003, however, the Supreme Court upheld the extension, citing congressional authority to determine the scope and duration of copyright protection.[43]

COPYRIGHT FORMALITIES: REGISTRATION AND NOTICE

U.S. copyright law traditionally required authors to both register their works with the Copyright Office and affix a notice to the work itself. Although neither formality is now required, U.S. copyright law still encourages authors to comply by conferring substantial benefits on those who do.

39. 105 F.3d 841 (2d Cir. 1997).

40. 17 U.S.C. § 101.

41. 201 F.3d 654 (5th Cir. 2000).

42. Sonny Bono Term Extension Act of 1998, Pub. L. No. 105-298, 11 Stat. 2827 (1998).

43. Eldred v. Ashcroft, 537 U.S. 186 (2003).

Copyright Notice

Copyright notices are not mandatory for works first published after March 1, 1989, but use of a notice precludes an infringer from claiming innocent infringement in mitigation of actual or statutory damages.[44] Proper U.S. copyright notice for works distributed within the United States includes these elements: "Copyright" or "Copr." or "©," the year of first publication, and the name of the copyright owner.

Copyright Registration

For U.S. copyright owners, registration with the Copyright Office is a prerequisite to filing any infringement suit. Statutory damages and attorneys' fees are available only if either (1) the work was registered prior to the infringement at issue, or (2) the owner registered the work within ninety days after first publication. Availability of statutory damages (up to $30,000 per infringement or up to $150,000 per willful infringement) can be particularly important for a start-up—or a more established company selling a new product—because the absence of historical sales can make it very difficult to prove actual damages (discussed later under Remedies). Registration also creates a legal presumption of ownership and copyright validity, which can be extremely helpful to a plaintiff in a copyright-infringement suit.

COPYRIGHT INFRINGEMENT

Copyright infringement occurs when a party copies, modifies, displays, performs, or distributes a copyrighted work without the owner's permission. The plaintiff in a copyright-infringement suit must show (1) substantial similarity of the protected expression, not merely substantial similarity of the ideas contained in the work, and (2) that the alleged infringer had access to the plaintiff's work.

TYPES OF INFRINGEMENT

Copyright infringement may take three forms: direct, contributory, or vicarious.

Direct Infringement

Direct copyright infringement occurs when the copyright owner alleges that the defendant violated at least one of the five exclusive rights of the copyright holder. For example, the publishers in *Princeton University Press v. Michigan Document Service*[45] successfully sued a Michigan copy shop for direct infringement when the copy shop reproduced and sold excerpts of a variety of copyrighted works selected by professors without obtaining the publishers' permission to do so.

Contributory Infringement

A party may also be liable for *contributory copyright infringement*—inducing, causing, or materially contributing to the infringing conduct of another with knowledge of the infringing activity. Recent case law on contributory infringement is based on the seminal Supreme Court decision in *Sony Corp. of America v. Universal City Studios.*[46] In 1984, Universal City Studios alleged that Sony, by manufacturing and selling the Betamax videocassette recorder, contributed to the infringement of Universal's copyrights on programs broadcast over the public airwaves, which viewers could copy using their VCRs. The Court held that the sale of copying equipment does not constitute contributory infringement, if the product has substantial noninfringing uses. In Sony's case, the trial court had found that time-shifting of television programs by private, noncommercial viewers, so they could view the programs later, was such a substantial noninfringing use. As a result, the Court held that Sony's manufacture and sale of VCRs did not contributorily infringe on Universal's copyrights.[47]

Vicarious Infringement

A defendant may face *vicarious copyright liability* for a direct infringer's actions if the defendant (1) has the right and ability to control the infringer's acts and (2) receives a direct financial benefit from the infringement. Unlike contributory infringement, vicarious infringement does not require that the defendant know of the primary infringement. Although "direct financial benefit" certainly includes a percentage of the value of each illegal sale, it is not limited to such per-unit arrangements.

The *Napster* case illustrates how the Sony-Betamax principle of "substantial noninfringing use" and vicarious liability principles apply to peer-to-peer networks. In Napster's original system, users downloaded free file-sharing software from the Napster website that enabled them to (1) make

44. For works published before March 1, 1989, most copyright authorities agree that owners should continue to use a copyright notice to avoid the risk of releasing the work into the public domain.

45. 99 F.3d 1381 (6th Cir. 1996).

46. 464 U.S. 417 (1984).

47. Courts have also applied the concept of contributory infringement to trademark law. *See* Hard Rock Café Licensing Corp. v. Concession Serv., Inc., 955 F.2d 1143 (7th Cir. 1992).

MP3 files stored on their hard drives available to other Napster users, (2) search for MP3 files stored on other users' computers, and (3) transfer exact copies of those files from one computer to another. By uploading MP3 file names to Napster network servers, users added to the collective library of files available for transfer to any user logged into Napster. The music industry brought suit, claiming Napster had engaged in contributory and vicarious copyright infringement.

In 2001, the U.S. Court of Appeals for the Ninth Circuit reviewed the case.[48] Because there can be no contributory or vicarious liability without direct infringement by a third party, the court first considered whether Napster's users engaged in direct infringement. Napster argued that its users did not directly infringe because they were engaged in a fair use of the material ("fair use" is discussed in the next section). The Ninth Circuit disagreed, holding that the users were engaged in wholesale, commercial copying of copyright-protected works. The court then found Napster liable for both contributory and vicarious infringement. Napster contributorily infringed because it knowingly encouraged and assisted its users' direct infringement. Napster met the two-prong vicarious liability test as well; the availability of the infringing material attracted customers, thereby increasing the user base on which Napster's future revenues depended. Napster's ability to control access to its servers and its software was sufficient to give it the requisite right and ability to supervise the infringing activity.

This and subsequent court decisions contributed to Napster's demise and its resurrection as a paid subscription service, but the file-sharing seed had been planted. Grokster, StreamCast, and other systems arose to take Napster's place. Unlike Napster, these companies provided free software that allowed users to connect to a decentralized file-sharing network of computers. There was no centralized server, and any computer on the network could function as a server if it met the technical requirements. Neither Grokster nor StreamCast maintained control over entry to the network. In their continuing battle against peer-to-peer file-sharing software, a number of music publishers and motion picture studios (the copyright owners) sued Grokster and StreamCast (the software distributors) for contributory and vicarious liability. The copyright owners claimed that the software distributors enabled users of their software to illegally copy and transmit copyrighted materials.

The U.S. Court of Appeals for the Ninth Circuit distinguished the *Napster* decision. It found that the software distributors were not contributorily infringing because, unlike Napster, they did not provide the "site and facilities" for infringement or otherwise materially contribute to the users' direct infringement. Similarly, the software distributors were not vicariously liable because, unlike Napster, they did not operate an integrated service and therefore had no ability to block access to infringing users.[49]

The U.S. Supreme Court granted certiorari and invoked the theory of inducement to infringe from patent law to decide this case.

48. A & M Records, Inc. v. Napster, 239 F.3d 1004 (9th Cir. 2001).

49. Metro-Goldwyn-Mayer Studios v. Grokster, 380 F.3d 1154 (9th Cir. 2004).

A CASE IN POINT

CASE 11.2

MGM Studios v. Grokster, Ltd.

Supreme Court of the United States

545 U.S. 913 (2005).

SUMMARY

FACTS The defendants, Grokster, Ltd. and StreamCast Networks, both distributed electronic file-sharing software that implemented a peer-to-peer network sharing system, so called because it allowed users' computers to directly communicate and share files. This was in contrast to an earlier model, used by Napster, which had not only distributed file-sharing software, but had also operated network servers that maintained a centralized index of users and files. After Napster was sued for facilitating copyright infringement, the defendants marketed themselves as legal Napster alternatives. The defendants asserted that they were not liable for secondary infringement, because there were no centralized servers and they maintained no control over entry to the decentralized file-sharing network of computers operated solely by the users of their software.

MGM and a group of copyright owners, including motion picture studios, recording companies, songwriters, and music publishers (MGM), sued the defendants for copyright infringement based on either contributory or vicarious theories of secondary liability. The district court granted summary judgment for the defendants. The U.S. Court of Appeals for the Ninth Circuit affirmed. With respect to the claim of contributory infringement, the court noted that when a product is capable

CONTINUED

of substantial noninfringing uses, the decision in *Sony* requires "reasonable knowledge of specific infringement." The court found that MGM was unable to demonstrate that the defendants had such knowledge. The court also found that MGM was unable to prove that the defendants had the right and ability to supervise the direct infringers, one of the three elements required to prove vicarious infringement.

ISSUE PRESENTED When a product is capable of both lawful and unlawful use, under what circumstances is a distributor of that product liable for acts of copyright infringement by third parties who use the product?

SUMMARY OF OPINION In a unanimous decision, the Court observed that it had dealt with secondary copyright infringement in only one recent case, *Sony Corp. v. Universal City Studios*. The Court noted that there was no evidence in that case that Sony had expressed any intent to promote infringing uses of its VCRs, and the Court had held that Sony was not liable for contributory infringement, because the VCR was "capable of commercially significant noninfringing uses." The Court agreed with MGM that the Ninth Circuit had misapplied *Sony*, which the Ninth Circuit had read to mean that a producer can never be contributorily liable if its product is capable of substantial lawful use. The Court concluded that *Sony* was never meant to preclude other theories of secondary liability.

The Court then discussed the history of the active inducement theory of liability in patent cases and concluded that it should apply equally to copyright cases. The theory requires intent to promote infringement as shown by "clear expression or other affirmative steps taken to foster infringement," the distribution of a device suitable for infringing use, and evidence of actual direct infringement by a third party.

The Court then considered whether the evidence showed the requisite intent to promote infringement. Recognizing the classic instance of inducement, as either advertisement or solicitation intended to encourage someone to commit some violation, the Court emphasized three notable features of the evidence in finding that the intent element of the inducement test was satisfied. First, internal documents and advertisements aiming the software at former Napster users showed that each defendant was actively aiming its product toward a known source of demand for copyright infringement. Second, the lack of development of any filtering tools or other mechanisms to prevent users from engaging in infringing activity, "underscore[d] Grokster's and StreamCast's intentional facilitation of their users' infringement."[50] Third, the Court emphasized the defendants' business model, which relied on selling advertising space and turned on high-volume use, which the record showed was infringing. The Court concluded that the defendants were not passive recipients of information regarding the infringing use of their software, but rather that each defendant had as its objective that its software be used for infringing uses and clearly and actively encouraged such infringement.[51] Additionally, with both defendants clearly distributing a device suitable for infringing use, and with "evidence of infringement on a gigantic scale," the Court easily found that the other two elements of the inducement test were satisfied to the extent needed to survive summary judgment.

RESULT The Court rejected the Ninth Circuit's broad reading of *Sony*. Because it found that there was substantial evidence in MGM's favor on all elements of inducement to infringe, the Court reversed the summary judgment in favor of the defendants and remanded the case for further proceedings, including reconsideration of MGM's motion for summary judgment.

CONTINUED

50. The Court made clear, however, that in the absence of other evidence of intent, the failure to take affirmative steps to prevent infringement is not in and by itself enough to find infringement under the inducement theory, if the product is capable of substantial noninfringing uses as in *Sony*.

51. The Court noted that evidence supported the conclusion that the defendants' unlawful objective was "unmistakable."

COMMENTS The *Grokster* decision offers little guidance on whether a company can be liable for distributing file-sharing software if it is not actively inducing, encouraging, or promoting its use. Three Justices (Ginsburg, Rehnquist, and Kennedy) said yes, if the product is primarily used for infringement. However, three other Justices (Breyer, Stevens, and O'Connor) said no, as long as there is evidence that the product is capable of being used in a noninfringing way.

CRITICAL THINKING QUESTIONS

1. What does this decision mean for companies that distribute Internet browsers, CD burners, MP3 players, and other technologies that are frequently used by their customers to infringe? What does this decision mean for companies like YouTube?
2. Will this decision have a chilling effect on the development of new copying and sharing technologies?

DEFENSES TO COPYRIGHT INFRINGEMENT

Defenses to copyright-infringement claims include the doctrines of fair use, first sale, and copyright misuse.

Fair Use Doctrine

The *fair use doctrine,* embodied in Section 107 of the Copyright Act, provides that a person may infringe the copyright owner's exclusive rights without liability, if he or she engages in such activities as literary criticism, social comment, news reporting, education, scholarship, or research. To decide what constitutes fair use, courts balance the public benefit of the defendant's use against any detrimental effect on the copyright owner's interests. In doing so, they consider (1) the purpose and character of the use (including whether it was for profit), (2) the economic effect of the use on the copyright owner, (3) the nature of the work used, and (4) the amount of the work used.

Courts often find that all four factors in the fair use test tilt in favor of one party or of the other. In some cases, however, the court must weigh the various factors. For example, in *Perfect 10, Inc. v. Amazon.com,* the plaintiff operated an Internet website that marketed and sold copyrighted images of nude models. Some website publishers republished Perfect 10's images on the Internet without authorization. Google's search engine automatically indexed some of the webpages containing Perfect 10's images and provided reduced-size, "thumbnail" versions of them in response to user inquiries. From 2001 through 2004, Perfect 10 repeatedly notified Google that these thumbnail images infringed its copyright, and in 2004 it filed a lawsuit against Google. The trial court granted a preliminary injunction against Google's use of the images, but the U.S. Court of Appeals for the Ninth Circuit reversed the decision.[52] The court found that the nature of the copyrighted work weighed slightly in favor of Perfect 10; the economic effect of the use and the amount of the work used, however, weighed in neither party's favor because there was no proven adverse effect of Google's use on Perfect 10's market and Google's use was reasonable in relation to the purpose of the copying. Finally, citing the Supreme Court's decision in *Campbell v. Acuff* (discussed below), the court considered the purpose and character of the use. The court found that this factor weighed heavily in Google's favor because its use was transformative, in that Google used the work in a different context transforming it into a new creation, and this was more significant than any other incidental superseding use or the minor commercial aspects of Google's search engine.

Fair use arguments are common in the academic environment. As mentioned earlier, a publisher sued a Michigan copy shop that was in the business of preparing course readers for university professors.[53] The professors excerpted a variety of copyrighted works, which the copy shop then compiled and sold to students without the permission of the copyright owners. The U.S. Court of Appeals for the Sixth Circuit noted that the copy shop's motivation was commercial profit, not education; the "transformative value" was slight, at best; the excerpts were substantial; and the market value of the original works was indeed harmed. As a result, the court found that the copy shop was liable for copyright infringement and enjoined it from further infringement.

In *Campbell v. Acuff-Rose Music, Inc.*,[54] the U.S. Supreme Court held that a parody that uses no more than necessary

52. 487 F.3d 701 (9th Cir. 2007).
53. Princeton Univ. Press v. Michigan Document Serv., 99 F.3d 1381 (6th Cir. 1996).
54. 510 U.S. 569 (1994).

of the lyrics and music of the original work to make it recognizable constitutes a fair use, even if the copied part is the heart of the original work. Subsequently, the U.S. Court of Appeals for the Eleventh Circuit refused to enjoin the publication of a novel that was a parody of *Gone with the Wind*. The Court found that the plaintiff copyright owners of *Gone with the Wind* were unlikely to defeat the defendant's claim of fair use because of the transformative nature of the parodic novel, as well as the low risk that it would serve as a market substitute for the original work.[55]

First Sale Doctrine

Under the *first sale doctrine,* codified in Section 109(a) of the Copyright Act, a copyright owner has exhausted its statutory right to control distribution of a copyrighted item once the owner sells the item and thereby puts it in the stream of commerce. The U.S. Supreme Court has held that the first sale doctrine applies even when the product is sold outside the United States with the expectation that it will not be resold in the United States.[56] This decision dealt a blow to U.S. companies trying to combat the *gray market,* in which products are sold outside the normal channel of distribution, often at a discounted price.[57]

Copyright Misuse

Modeled after the patent misuse doctrine, copyright misuse exists when a copyright owner leverages his or her statutory copyright to gain control over areas outside the copyright's intended scope. For example, if a copyright owner licenses its software on the condition that the licensee may not use its competitors' products or develop complementary products, that action will constitute copyright misuse. If a court finds misuse, the copyright owner cannot enforce its copyright against infringers until the misuse has been purged.

PIRACY AND CURRENT RESPONSES

Piracy is a problem for many companies, but especially for software companies, which lose billions of dollars each year because of illegal copying or pirating of their software. The Business Software Alliance estimated that worldwide losses from all software piracy in 2006 amounted to nearly $40 billion.[58]

As discussed earlier, music publishers are being challenged by the file-sharing technologies that help evaders become ever more elusive. To identify illegal copying, the Recording Industry Association of America (RIAA) is using *web robots;* these programs search and index the Internet for specific content by visiting websites, requesting documents based on certain criteria, and following up with requests for documents referenced in the documents already retrieved. Companies are also using encryption, watermarking, and mandatory online activation. The RIAA focuses at least three-fourths of its antipiracy resources on the Internet and new technology.[59] Those resources include lawsuits against online music servers and against downloaders themselves, as in the RIAA's high-profile lawsuits against college students, elementary and high school students, and many other casual music downloaders since 2003. In 2007, the RIAA launched an education and deterrence program aimed at illegal file trafficking on college campuses and has sent approximately 2,926 pre-litigation settlement letters to universities nationwide. These letters are in addition to the lawsuits that the RIAA continues to file on a rolling basis against those engaging in music theft via commercial Internet accounts.[60]

REMEDIES

Under the Copyright Act, a plaintiff can recover both its actual damages and the defendant's profits attributable to the infringements, to the extent that these are not duplicative. Alternatively, if the copyright is registered within three months of first publication or prior to the alleged infringement, a plaintiff may elect to recover statutory damages (which can be up to $30,000 for infringement and up to $150,000 for willful infringement), as well as attorneys' fees under certain circumstances. Injunctive relief, the seizure of infringing copies, and exclusion of infringing copies from import into the United States may also be available.

Although the Copyright Act does not provide a statutory right to a jury trial, a defendant in a copyright-infringement suit in which the copyright owner seeks statutory damages

55. Suntrust Bank v. Houghton Mifflin Co., 268 F.3d 1257 (11th Cir. 2001).

56. Quality King Distrib., Inc. v. L'anza Research Int'l, Inc., 523 U.S. 135 (1998).

57. *See* Edward Felsenthal, *Copyright Scope Limited for Some Firms,* Wall St. J., Mar. 10, 1998, at B5.

58. Bus. Software Alliance, *Fourth Annual BSA and IDC Global Software 2006 Piracy Study,* 2007, at 12, *available at* http://w3.bsa.org/globalstudy//upload/2007-Global-Piracy-Study-EN.pdf.

59. *Copyright Owners Learning to Police Online Sales, Performance of Musical Works,* 66 U.S.L.W. 2483 (Feb. 17, 1998).

60. Recording Indus. Ass'n of Am., *RIAA Pre-Lawsuit Letters Go to 22 Campuses in New Wave of Deterrence Program,* Dec. 6, 2007, *available at* http://www.riaa.com/newsitem.php?id=8E8AE31D-2CD9-5E90-8892-5FEBD3A603B9.

is entitled to a jury trial under the Seventh Amendment to the U.S. Constitution.[61] The defendant also has the right to have the jury determine the amount of statutory damages.

The Digital Millennium Copyright Act (DMCA) may apply to copyright violations as well. In a civil action, a court may impose injunctions and award damages, costs, and attorneys' fees. It may also order impounding, modification, or destruction of any devices or products involved in the violation. The court may punish repeat offenders by awarding treble damages.

CRIMINAL LIABILITY

Willful infringers may face criminal penalties as well as civil remedies. The No Electronic Theft Act punishes with fines and prison time those who copy compact discs, videocassettes, or software worth more than $1,000 without permission of the copyright holder. The law requires no proof that the defendant commercially gained from the infringement.[62] It is also a crime to fraudulently use or remove a copyright notice or to make false representations in connection with a copyright application.

The DMCA also imposes criminal sanctions of up to $500,000 in fines and up to five years' imprisonment for violators a court finds to be willful or motivated by financial gain. Repeat offenders face increased fines (up to $1 million) and up to ten years in prison.

REGISTERED MASK WORK

The Semiconductor Chip Protection Act of 1984 created a highly specialized form of intellectual property, the *registered mask work*. Semiconductor masks are detailed transparencies representing the topological layout of semiconductor chips. The mask work was the first significant new intellectual property right introduced in the United States in nearly one hundred years. The Act gives the owner copyright-like exclusive rights in the registered mask work for a period of ten years and prohibits its copying or use by others, although reverse engineering is specifically allowed. The law was aimed primarily at counterfeiters who replicate semiconductor masks for a chip already on the market and produce the chips without having to expend their own resources on development. Remedies include injunctive relief, damages, and impoundment of the infringing mask and chips.

There have been very few reported cases involving the Act. One recent decision involved Altera, a manufacturer of programmable logic devices, which are semiconductor chips that can be programmed to perform various logic functions, and Clear Logic, a manufacturer of application specific integrated circuits (ASICs), which are designed to perform a single, specific function. When a customer programs an Altera device using Altera software, a bitstream file is generated with the specific program for the customer's purpose. Clear Logic asked its ASIC customers to send this bitstream file to it and used the file to create an ASIC for each customer's specific function and purpose. Altera sued Clear Logic, alleging that this use of the bitstream files, which provided the placement of groupings of various transistors on the chip, violated the Semiconductor Chip Protection Act. Clear Logic argued that the placement was a system or idea and therefore not entitled to protection. Analogizing the situation to copyright infringement, where the outline of an article or chapters in a book may not be protectable, but the content is, the U.S. Court of Appeals for the Ninth Circuit held that the Act protected the organization of the groupings of logic functions on Altera's mask works and the interconnectedness between them.[63]

TRADEMARKS

Most people associate a particular trademark with the product to which it is applied, without considering how this association has been generated. For example, when consumers purchase Apple computers, they usually do not think about how the word for a type of fruit has become representative of that particular brand of personal computer. Trademark law concerns itself with just such questions: how trademarks are created, how trademark rights arise, how such rights are preserved, and why certain marks are given greater protection than others.[64] The PTO registered more than 390,000 trademarks in 2007 alone.[65]

OWNERSHIP AND SCOPE OF PROTECTION

The federal trademark act, known as the Lanham Act, and the 1988 Trademark Law Revision Act[66] define a trademark as "any word, name, symbol, or device or any combination thereof adopted and used by a manufacturer or merchant

61. Feltner v. Columbia Pictures Television, Inc., 523 U.S. 340 (1998).
62. No Electronic Theft Act of 1997, Pub. L. No. 105-147, 111 Stat. 2687 (1997).
63. Altera Corp. v. Clear Logic, Inc., 424 F.3d 1079 (9th Cir. 2005).
64. Ron Zapata, *Patent Infringement Actions Declining: Study,* IP L. BULL., Feb. 27, 2007, *available at* http://ip.lawbulletin.com/secure/ViewArticle.aspx?id=19358.
65. U.S. Patent & Trademark Office Performance and Accountability Report Fiscal Year 2007, at 60, *available at* http://www.uspto.gov/web/offices/com/annual/2007/2007annualreport.pdf.
66. 15 U.S.C. §§ 1051–1072.

Economic PERSPECTIVE

Intellectual Property Rights and Incentives to Innovate

A basic tenet of neoclassical economic theory is that productive efficiency and allocative efficiency will be achieved through free competition by private parties interested in maximizing their own welfare. Productive efficiency exists when competition among individual producers drives all but the lowest-cost producers of goods or services out of the market. Allocative efficiency exists when scarce societal resources are allocated to the production of various goods and services up to the point at which the cost of producing each good or service equals the benefit society reaps from its use.

In general, U.S. economic policy is to foster the functioning of free markets in which individuals may compete. For example, the antitrust laws, discussed in Chapter 17, are designed to protect competition by prohibiting any individual entity or group of entities from monopolizing an industry.

The area of intellectual property is a seeming exception to the general free-market orientation of the U.S. economy. Patent laws provide inventors with the opportunity to gain a legally enforceable monopoly to prevent the manufacture, use, and sale of their inventions for a limited time.

The economic rationale for granting monopolies to inventors is based on the high value of innovation to society and the need to provide incentives to inventors. Without legal rules protecting the ownership of inventions, once a valuable new product or cost-saving technique is introduced, others could immediately copy and profit from it, even though they bore none of the cost of its creation. Technological advances are crucial to a growing economy. Development of new techniques increases productive efficiency, thereby expanding the quantity of goods and services that can be produced with a given level of societal resources. Development of new products meeting previously unfulfilled needs increases the welfare of society as a whole. Such innovation has taken on increasing importance for the United States in the international context. Although countries with lower-cost labor have a competitive advantage in the manufacture of goods with established production techniques, the United States' competitive advantage lies in its ability to develop new technologies.

Individuals will produce innovations only up to the point at which the rewards they reap equal their costs. To ensure that innovations are produced fully up to the point at which the social cost equals the social benefit (that is, to ensure allocative efficiency), the law must guarantee to innovators a significant part of the benefit from their innovations. The U.S. solution to this problem is to provide inventors, whose inventions meet the requirements for a patent, with a limited monopoly to exclude others from the manufacture, use, and sale of those inventions. This system ensures that inventors will be able to capture the full benefit of their inventions during the period of their monopoly and that the innovation will be freely available to others thereafter. The stringent requirements for patents are designed to prevent unnecessary restrictions on free competition. In fact, overly broad patents can actually hamper innovation.[a]

An important secondary objective is to give the scientific community access to state-of-the-art technology. Without a legal monopoly, innovators would keep their advances secret to prevent others from copying them. Such secrecy would result in waste of scarce societal resources, as other researchers would struggle to discover what is already known.

The World Bank has identified property rights, including intellectual property rights, as one of the keys to energizing countries in transition to market-based economies. Many developing and transitioning economies have already adopted intellectual property laws similar to those of the developed nations, but, as the World Bank acknowledges, these laws are difficult to enforce. Nevertheless, enforcement of these laws will encourage development of intellectual property and the foreign investment needed to spur growth.

---

a. Adam B. Jaffe & Josh Lerner, Innovation and Its Discontents: How Our Broken Patent System Is Endangering Innovation and Progress, and What to Do About It, 56–77 (2004).

to identify and distinguish his goods, including a unique product, from those manufactured or sold by others, and to indicate the source of the goods, even if that source is unknown."

This definition has been interpreted as recognizing four different purposes of a trademark: (1) to provide an identification symbol for a particular merchant's goods, (2) to indicate that the goods to which the trademark has been applied are from a single source, (3) to guarantee that all goods to which the trademark has been applied are of a constant quality, and (4) to advertise the goods.

A trademark tells a consumer where a product comes from and who is responsible for its creation. A trademark also implies that all goods sold under the mark are of a consistent level of quality. A consumer purchasing french fries at a McDonald's restaurant, for instance, can reasonably expect them to taste as good as those sold at any other McDonald's. The trademark does not necessarily reveal the product's manufacturer. For example, the trademark Sanka identifies a brand of decaffeinated coffee. We may not know whether the manufacturer is a company called Sanka, but we know that all coffee products bearing the Sanka mark are sponsored by a single company (or its licensees).

For producers, a trademark represents the goodwill of a business, that is, an accumulation of satisfied customers who will continue buying from that business. Trademark rights are largely determined by the perceptions and associations in the minds of the buying public, so maintaining a strong trademark is essential to preserving the success of a business. The top brand names for 2007 are listed in Exhibit 11.2.

Although most trademarks are verbal or graphic, trademark law also protects distinctive shapes, odors, packaging, and sounds. Apple, Inc. trademarked the three-dimensional shape of its iPod.[67] Both the unique shape of the Coca-Cola bottle and the sound of NBC's three chimes have trademark protection. Color may also qualify as a trademark. In *Qualitex Co. v. Jacobson Products Co.*,[68] the U.S. Supreme Court articulated two principal criteria for determining whether trademark protection is available for a color: (1) the color must have attained secondary meaning and thus identifies and distinguishes a particular brand, and (2) the color must not serve a useful function, because granting trademark protection in this circumstance would amount to the grant of monopoly control.

OTHER MARKS

Trademarks should not be confused with other forms of legally protected identifying marks, such as service marks, trade names, and certification marks.

Service Marks

A trademark is used in connection with a tangible product; a *service mark* is used in connection with services. The law concerning service marks is almost identical to that of trademarks.

Trade Names

Whereas a trademark is used to identify and distinguish products, a *trade name* identifies a company, partnership, or business. Trade names cannot be registered under federal law, unless they are also used as trademarks or service marks. The use of a trade name—evidenced by the filing of articles of incorporation or a fictitious business name

67. David Orozco & James Conley, *Innovation, Shape of Things to Come*, WALL ST. J., May 12, 2008, at R6.

68. 514 U.S. 159 (1995).

EXHIBIT 11.2 Most Valuable Brand Names in 2007

2007 Rank	2007 Brand Value (in millions)	2006 Brand Value (in millions)	Percentage Change (from prior year)
1. Coca-Cola	$65,324	$67,000	–3%
2. Microsoft	58,709	56,926	+3
3. IBM	57,091	56,201	+2
4. GE	51,569	48,907	+5
5. Nokia	33,696	30,131	+12
6. Toyota	32,070	27,941	+15
7. Intel	30,954	32,319	–4
8. McDonald's	29,398	27,501	+7
9. Disney	29,210	27,848	+5
10. Mercedes-Benz	23,568	21,795	+8

Source: *Top 100 Global Brands Scorecard,* BUS.WK. ONLINE, *available at* http://bwnt.businessweek.com/interactive_reports/top_brands/index.asp.

statement—gives the company using the name certain common law rights, however.

Certification Marks

A *certification mark* placed on a product indicates that the product has met the certifier's standards of safety or quality. An example is the "Good Housekeeping" seal of approval placed on certain consumer goods.

THE VARYING DISTINCTIVENESS OF TRADEMARKS

As shown on Exhibit 11.3, different types of marks fall on a distinctiveness continuum. The same word can be fanciful or arbitrary, suggestive, descriptive, or generic, depending on the product on which it is used.

Fanciful and Arbitrary Marks

Fanciful or arbitrary marks are often called strong marks because they are immediately protectable.

Fanciful Marks A *fanciful mark* is a coined term that has no prior meaning, until used as a trademark in connection with a particular product. Fanciful marks are usually made-up words, such as Kodak for camera products and Exxon for gasoline.

Arbitrary Marks *Arbitrary marks* are real words whose ordinary meaning has nothing to do with the trademarked product, for example, Camel for cigarettes and Shell for gasoline.

Suggestive Marks

A *suggestive mark* suggests something about the product without directly describing it. After seeing the mark, a consumer must use his or her imagination to determine the nature of the goods. For instance, Chicken of the Sea does not immediately create an association with tuna fish; it merely suggests some type of seafood.

Descriptive Marks

Descriptive marks specify certain characteristics of the goods, such as size or color, proposed uses, the intended consumers of the goods, or the effect of using the goods. Laudatory terms, such as First Rate or Gold Medal, are also considered descriptive marks.

Geographic Terms Geographic descriptive terms are usually considered nondistinctive unless a secondary meaning (discussed below) has been established. Geographic terms used in an arbitrary manner are distinctive, however, for example, Salem for cigarettes and North Pole for bananas.

Personal Names Personal first names and surnames are not distinctive. But an arbitrary use of a historical name, such as Lincoln for a savings bank, does not require secondary meaning to be protectable.

Even judges may not agree on whether a proposed trademark is distinctive. For example, in 1998, AOL Time Warner registered "Buddy List" as a trademark for its Buddy Chat function, which let Internet users know when friends and family were online, thereby permitting real-time instant exchange of e-mails. After AOL sued AT&T to prevent it

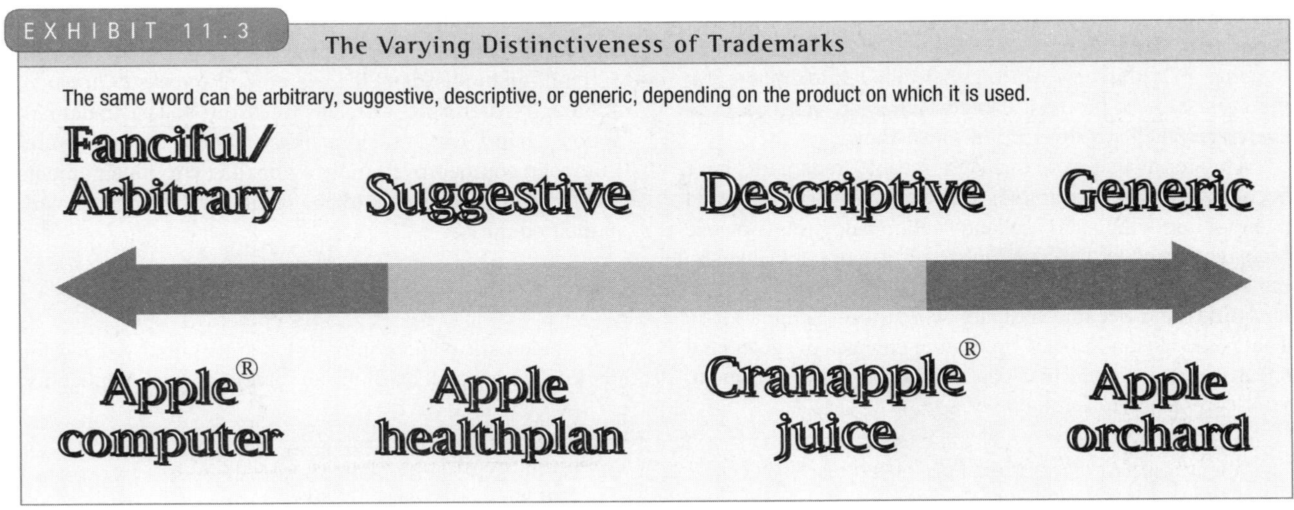

from using the term "Buddy List" on its WorldNet online service, the trial court held that the mark was not distinctive enough to warrant protection and dismissed the suit. The U.S. Court of Appeals for the Fourth Circuit reversed, concluding that the trial judge had failed to give proper weight to the PTO's finding that the "Buddy List" phrase was sufficiently distinctive.[69] It remanded the case for a trial to determine whether "Buddy List" was a protectable trademark.

Secondary Meaning Descriptive marks are initially unprotectable, but they can still become protectable if they acquire *secondary meaning*, that is, a mental association by the buyer that links the mark with a single source of the product. Through secondary meaning, a mark obtains distinctiveness. Once this occurs, the mark is granted trademark protection. Secondary meaning is necessary to establish trademark protection for descriptive marks, including geographic terms and personal names.

Establishment of secondary meaning depends on a number of factors, such as the amount of advertising, the type of market, the number of sales, and consumer recognition and response. The testimony of random buyers or of product dealers may be required to prove that a mark has acquired secondary meaning. For example, the term "Holiday Inn" has acquired secondary meaning because the public associates that term with a particular provider of hotel services, and not with hotel services in general.

GENERIC TERMS

Trademark law grants no protection to generic terms, such as "spoon" or "software," because doing so would permit a producer to monopolize a term that all producers should be able to use equally. It would be ridiculous to permit one manufacturer to obtain the exclusive right to use the word "computer," for example, and thereby force all competitors to come up with a new word, rather than a brand name, for the same type of product. Generic terms are not protected even when they acquire secondary meaning.

Many terms that were once enforceable trademarks have become generic. For example, "escalator" was once the brand name of a moving staircase, and "cellophane" was a plastic wrap developed by DuPont. Due to misuse or negligence by the owners, these marks lost their connection with particular brands and became ordinary words (see Exhibit 11.4). That is the reason Xerox Corporation engages in substantial advertising to explain that you don't "Xerox" a document, you "copy" it on a Xerox copier.

For terms that describe products made by only one company, the problem of *genericism*—the use of the product name as a generic name—is acute. Without competitive products, buyers may begin to think of the trademark as indicative of what the product is rather than where the product comes from. Manufacturers can try to avoid this problem by always using the trademark as an adjective in conjunction with a generic noun. It is all right to say "Kleenex tissue" or "I'm going to use the Google search engine for research," but not "a Kleenex" or "I'm going to Google that research topic." Once the buying public starts using the mark as a synonym for the product, rather than as a means of distinguishing its source, loss of the trademark is imminent.

Microsoft battled genericism in its suit against Lindows.com, in which it claimed that the "Lindows.com" name infringed its Windows trademark. Lindows.com argued that Windows was a generic term used to describe general user interfaces at the time Microsoft launched its product. In response, Microsoft presented studies demonstrating that users subsequently came to associate the Windows term with Microsoft's operating system. The district court rejected Microsoft's argument, stating:

> [T]he Court declares it will instruct the jury to consider whether the Windows mark was generic during the period before Microsoft Windows 1.0 entered the marketplace in November 1985. Furthermore, the Court will *not* instruct the jury that even if Windows were generic prior to November 1985, the trademark would nonetheless be valued today so long as the primary significance of the term today is not generic.[70]

The U.S. Court of Appeals for the Ninth Circuit denied Microsoft's appeal of the district court's decision. Subsequent to the Ninth Circuit's decision, Microsoft reached an unusual settlement in which it agreed to pay Lindows.com $20 million to phase out the use of the Lindows.com name. Although Microsoft was unsuccessful in its trademark action against Lindows.com in the United States, several European courts proved more sympathetic to its arguments and forced Lindows.com to change its name and trademark in their countries.

CREATING RIGHTS IN A TRADEMARK

U.S. trademark owners initially obtain rights by using the mark in commerce or filing an "intent to use" application

69. Am. Online, Inc. v. AT&T Corp., 243 F.3d 812 (4th Cir. 2001), *cert. dismissed,* 534 U.S. 946 (2001).

70. Microsoft Corp. v. Lindows.com, Inc., 2004 WL 329250 (W.D. Wash. Feb. 10, 2004), *appeal denied,* Microsoft Corp. v. Lindows.com, Inc., 2004 WL 1208044 (9th Cir. 2004).

EXHIBIT 11.4 Attempts to Preserve a Trademark

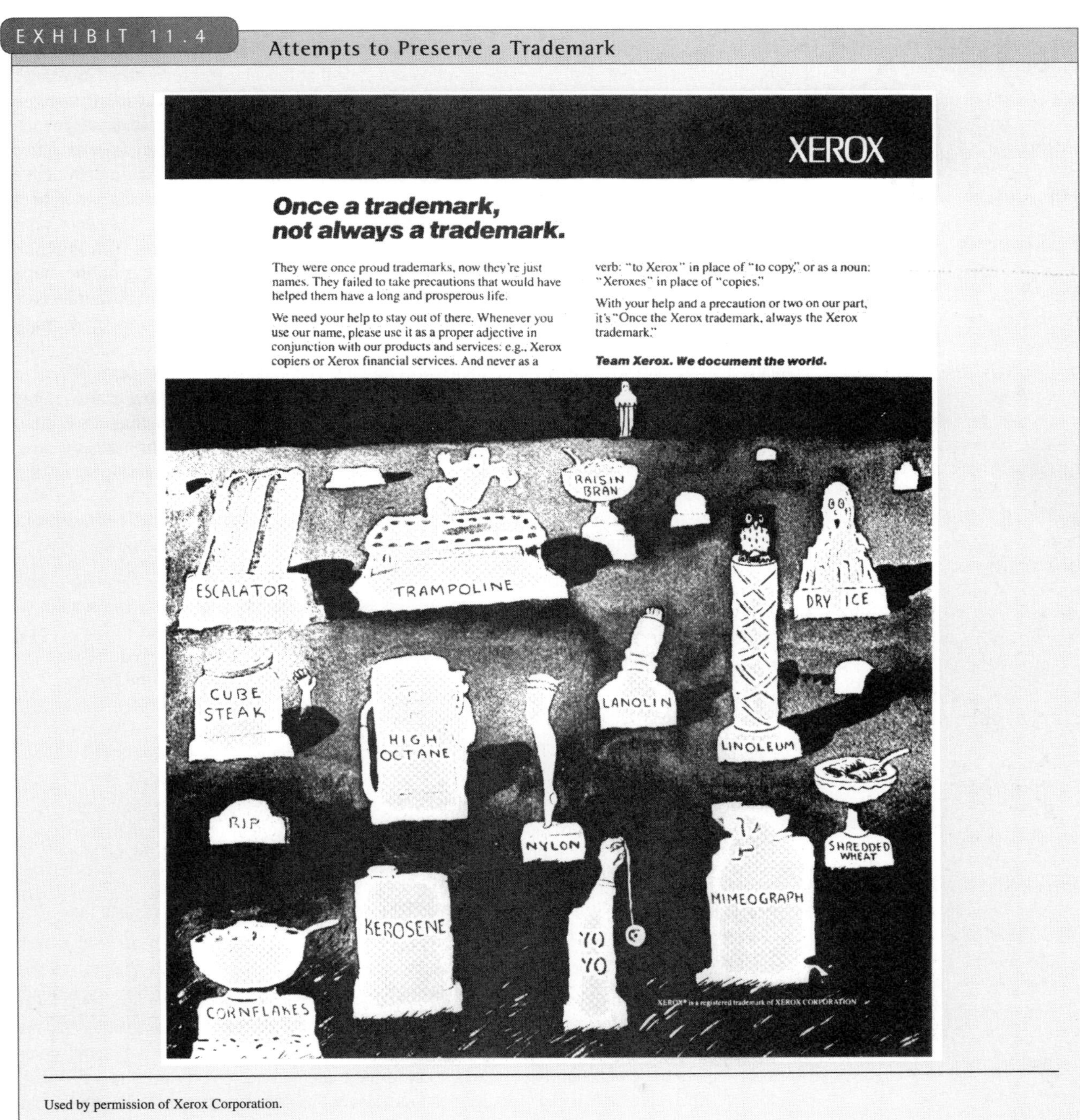

Used by permission of Xerox Corporation.

with the PTO. Following use in interstate commerce, owners may obtain additional rights by federal registration. State registration requires only intrastate use. 1-800 Contacts sued WhenU.com because WhenU delivered advertisements of 1-800's competitors to computer users who accessed 1-800's website. Before the court could consider infringement, it had to decide whether WhenU.com had "used" 1-800's trademarks.

A CASE IN POINT

CASE 11.3

1-800 Contacts, Inc. v. WhenU.com, Inc.

United States Court of Appeals for the Second Circuit
414 F.3d 400 (2d Cir. 2005), cert. denied, 546 U.S. 1033 (2005).

In the Language of the Court

FACTS WhenU.com is an Internet marketing company that provides its proprietary "SaveNow" software without charge to computer users, usually as part of a software bundle that the user voluntarily downloads from the Internet. Once installed, the SaveNow software requires no action by the user to activate its operations. Instead, the software responds to a user's Internet activities by generating pop-up advertisement windows that are relevant to the activities. To deliver this contextually relevant advertising, the SaveNow software employs an internal directory with about 32,000 website addresses and address fragments, 29,000 search terms, and 1,200 keyword algorithms that correlate with particular consumer interests. It screens the words that a user types into a web browser or search engine, or that appear within the Internet sites that a user visits. When the software recognizes a term, it randomly selects an advertisement from the corresponding product or service category to deliver to the user's computer screen at roughly the same time the website or search results sought by the user appear. Plaintiff 1-800 filed a complaint alleging, among other things, that WhenU was infringing its trademarks by causing pop-up ads of 1-800's competitors to appear on a user's screen when the user accessed 1-800's website. If a SaveNow user who has accessed the 1-800 website and has received a WhenU.com pop-up advertisement does not want to view the ad or the advertiser's website, the user can click on the visible part of the 1-800 window, which moves the 1-800 site to the front of the screen display, with the pop-up ad moving behind the website window. Alternatively, the user can close the pop-up website by clicking on its "X," or close, button. If the user clicks on the pop-up ad, the main browser window containing the 1-800 website will be navigated to the website of the advertiser that was featured inside the pop-up ad.

ISSUE PRESENTED Does WhenU "use" 1-800's trademarks within the meaning of the Lanham Act by delivering advertisements of 1-800's competitors to computer users who have intentionally accessed 1-800's website?

OPINION WALKER, C.J., writing for the U.S. Court of Appeals for the Second Circuit:

The Lanham Act defines "use in commerce," in relevant part, as follows:

> . . . For purposes of this Chapter, a mark shall be deemed to be in use in commerce—
>
> (1) on goods when—
> (A) it is placed in any manner on the goods or their containers or the displays associated therewith or on the tags or labels affixed thereto, or if the nature of the goods makes such placement impracticable, then on documents associated with the goods or the sale, and
> (B) the goods are sold or transported in commerce, and
>
> (2) on services when it is used or displayed in the sale or advertising of services and the services are rendered in commerce. . . .

. . . .

. . . [W]e note that WhenU does not "use" 1-800's trademark in the manner ordinarily at issue in an infringement claim: it does not "place" 1-800 trademarks on any goods or services in order to pass them off as emanating from or authorized by 1-800. The fact is that WhenU does not reproduce or display 1-800's trademarks at all, nor does it cause the trademarks to be displayed to a . . . user. Rather, WhenU reproduces 1-800's website address, www.1800contacts.com, which is similar, but not identical to, 1-800's 1-800CONTACTS trademark.

. . . .

. . . [I]t is plain that WhenU is using 1-800's website address precisely because it is a website address, rather than because it bears any resemblance to 1-800's trademark, because the only place WhenU reproduces the address is in the SaveNow directory. Although the directory resides in the . . .

CONTINUED

user's computer, it is inaccessible to both the . . . user and the general public. Thus, the appearance of 1-800's website address in the directory does not create a possibility of visual confusion with 1-800's mark. More important, a WhenU pop-up ad cannot be triggered by a . . . user's input of the 1-800 trademark or the appearance of that trademark on a webpage accessed by the . . . user.

. . . .

A company's internal utilization of a trademark in a way that does not communicate it to the public is analogous to an individual's private thoughts about a trademark. Such conduct simply does not violate the Lanham Act, which is concerned with the use of trademarks in connection with the sale of goods or services in a manner likely to lead to consumer confusion as to the source of such goods or services. . . .

. . . .

. . . Absent improper use of 1-800's trademark, . . . such conduct does not violate the Lanham Act. . . . Indeed it is routine for vendors to seek specific "product placement" in retail stores precisely to capitalize on their competitors' name recognition. For example, a drug store typically places its own store-brand generic products next to the trademarked products they emulate in order to induce a customer who has specifically sought out the trademarked product to consider the store's less-expensive alternative. WhenU employs this same marketing strategy by informing . . . users who have sought out a specific trademarked product about available coupons, discounts, or alternative products that may be of interest to them.

. . . .

. . . Not only are "use," "in commerce," and "likelihood of confusion" three distinct elements of a trademark infringement claim, but "use" must be decided as a threshold matter because, while any number of activities may be "in commerce" or create a likelihood of confusion, no such activity is actionable under the Lanham Act absent the "use" of a trademark. Because 1-800 has failed to establish such "use," its trademark infringement claims fail.

RESULT The court reversed the district court's entry of a preliminary injunction and remanded with instructions to dismiss with prejudice 1-800's trademark-infringement claims against WhenU.

CRITICAL THINKING QUESTIONS

1. Would the court have reached the same conclusion if WhenU's pop-up ads displayed the 1-800 trademark? If WhenU's activities altered or affected 1-800's website? If WhenU diverted or misdirected users away from 1-800's website, or altered the results a user obtained when searching with the 1-800 trademark or website address?
2. Through programs like Google's AdWare, advertisers can choose to have their ads triggered when an Internet user searches a keyword (which may include a third party's trademark) that the advertiser has "purchased" from Google. Is this a "use in interstate commerce"?

Trademark Searches

A company about to use a new trademark should first conduct a trademark search to determine whether use of the proposed mark will constitute an infringement. The time, money, and effort spent on promotion and advertising will be wasted if use of the mark is ultimately prohibited.

There are various ways to search a mark. The records of the PTO provide information on federally registered marks; the office of the secretary of state can usually provide relevant data for that state's registered marks. Both state and federal registrations describe the mark and the goods it identifies, the owners of the mark, the date of registration, and the date on which the mark was first used. Most of this registration material has been computerized and can be accessed online.

Searching for unregistered common law marks is more difficult. Trade and telephone directories are often a good source of common law marks. Some searches can be done by anyone using the Internet. There are also professional trademark search firms that search databases for customers. Although there is always the risk that a new mark or a common law user may be untraceable, any search is better than no search. Searching is evidence of a good faith effort to determine whether any other entity has preexisting rights in a mark.

Common Law Rights in a Trademark

A trademark is used in commerce if it is physically attached to goods that are then sold or distributed. Each subsequent use of a trademark creates greater rights, because increased sales and advertising generate greater customer awareness of the mark as representing the product. Use is also necessary to establish secondary meaning for descriptive marks.

In the United States, the first person to sell the goods under a mark becomes the owner and senior user of the mark. The mark is protected immediately, provided that it was adopted and used in good faith and without actual or constructive knowledge of any superior rights in the mark.

There is an exception to the rule of first use. If a subsequent, or junior, user establishes a strong consumer identification with its mark in a separate geographic area, the junior user may be granted superior rights for that area. By failing to expand its business to other parts of the country, the senior user takes the risk that a junior user may be permitted to use the same or a confusingly similar mark in a distant area. The junior user's use must be in good faith; that is, the junior user must take reasonable steps to determine whether any preexisting mark is confusingly similar to the one it plans to use.

This geographic rule is inapplicable, however, if the senior user has applied for or obtained federal registration (see the next section). Once the senior user has filed an application or has obtained federal registration, it is permitted to claim nationwide constructive notice of the mark. This precludes any use of the mark—even a good faith use—by a junior user. Even with an application pending or registration, however, the senior user may not take any action against the junior user in a geographically removed area until the senior user is likely to expand into that area.

Federal Registration

Although not a requirement for obtaining U.S. rights in a mark, registration on the federal Principal Register provides (1) constructive notice of a claim of ownership in all fifty states, which makes it easier to enjoin subsequent users; (2) *prima facie* evidence of ownership; (3) the "incontestable" right (subject to certain defenses) to use the mark, obtainable after five years of continuous use following registration; and (4) the right to prevent importation into the United States of articles bearing an infringing mark.

Trademarks are grouped into different classes, covering more than forty different industries and goods. When a trademark is registered, the holder of the mark must specify the particular class to which the mark belongs. Although a single trademark may be registered in more than one classification, it is also possible for the same mark to be registered by different holders for different types of products.

Certain marks that do not qualify for registration on the Principal Register may be registered on the Supplemental Register. Such registration does not afford the owner any of the above benefits, however, and should be pursued only upon the advice of counsel.

The PTO conducts federal registration of trademarks. An applicant may file either an "actual use" application or an "intent to use" application. For the latter, the applicant must state a bona fide intent to use the mark and must then commence use and provide the PTO with a statement of use within six months of receiving notice that its application is entitled to registration. The six-month period can be extended for up to thirty months, giving applicants a total of three years from the date of the notice of allowance in which to file the statement of use. Registration is postponed until the applicant actually uses the mark. The applicant has priority rights, however, against any party who did not use the same mark or file an application for it before the filing date of the intent to use application.

State Registration

Although state registration does not provide as much protection as federal registration, it does offer certain benefits. In most states, registration can be obtained within a few weeks of filing and is proof of ownership of the mark. For marks that are not eligible for federal registration, state registration usually provides at least some protection as long as there has been sufficient use of the mark.

State registration cannot preempt or narrow the rights granted by federal registration. For example, a junior user with a state registration predating a senior user's federal registration gains exclusive rights in the mark only in the geographic area of continuous usage preceding the federal registration, and not the entire state. A state trademark law that purported to reserve the entire state for the junior user would be preempted by the Lanham Act.

LOSS OF TRADEMARK RIGHTS

Failure to use one's mark—known as *abandonment*—may result in the loss of rights. A federally registered mark that has been abandoned can be used by a junior user. Trademark searches can reveal whether a previously registered trademark has lost its enforceability. There are two types of abandonment: actual and constructive.

Actual Abandonment

Actual abandonment occurs when an owner discontinues use of the mark with the intent not to resume use. Mere nonuse for a limited period does not result in loss of protection. After two years of nonuse, however, there is a presumption of abandonment. Because protection for federally registered marks is nationwide, the abandonment must be nationwide for loss of rights to result.

Constructive Abandonment

Constructive abandonment results when the owner does something, or fails to do something, that causes the mark to lose its distinctiveness. Constructive abandonment can result from a mark lapsing into genericism through improper use. It can also result from an owner's failure to adequately control companies licensed to use its mark. Thus, a licensor should carefully exercise quality controls and approval procedures for its licensees' products in order to ensure a consistent quality level.

TRADEMARK INFRINGEMENT

To establish direct trademark infringement, a trademark owner must prove (1) the validity of the mark (note that a federally registered mark is prima facie valid), (2) priority of usage of the mark, and (3) a likelihood of confusion in the minds of the purchasers of the products in question. A trademark owner may also allege vicarious and/or contributory infringement of his or her marks.

Proving validity and priority of usage is fairly straightforward if the mark is registered. If the mark is not registered, such proof is a factual matter. Establishing likelihood of confusion, on the other hand, involves subjectively weighing a variety of factors. These may include (1) the similarity of the two marks with respect to appearance, sound, connotation, and commercial impression; (2) the similarity of the goods; (3) the similarity of the channels of trade in which the goods are sold; (4) the strength of the marks, as evidenced by the amount of sales and advertising, and the length of use; (5) the use of similar marks by third parties with respect to related goods and services; (6) the length of time of concurrent use without actual confusion; and (7) the extent and nature of any actual confusion of the two marks in the marketplace.[71]

Taking advantage of trademark confusion does not necessarily amount to infringement. In 1996, the U.S. Court of Appeals for the Sixth Circuit ruled that a travel agency had not infringed Holiday Inns' trademark in its vanity toll-free telephone number by using a similar number.[72] To promote itself, Holiday Inns had widely publicized its toll-free reservation line as 1-800-HOLIDAY, which translates to 1-800-465-4329 on a numeric keypad. Perhaps anticipating that dialers would mistake Holiday Inns' letter "O" for the number zero, the travel agency reserved the toll-free number 1-800-405-4329 for its own use. Though acknowledging the potential for confusion, the court rejected Holiday Inns' claim of trademark infringement. The travel agency did not create the confusion; it merely took advantage of it.

The Federal Trademark Dilution Act[73] allows the owner of a famous mark to sue for injunctive relief from a party whose commercial use of a mark "begins after the mark has become famous and causes dilution of the distinctive quality of the mark." Dilution can result from "blurring" or "tarnishment." *Blurring* occurs when the nonfamous mark reduces the strong association between the owner of the famous mark and its products. *Tarnishment* occurs when use of the famous mark in connection with a particular category of goods or goods of an inferior quality reduces the positive image associated with the products bearing the famous mark.

In 2003, the U.S. Supreme Court held that a trademark owner must prove actual dilution, not just the potential for dilution, to prevail in an action under the Federal Trademark Dilution Act.[74] Congress responded to this decision by amending the statute to require only a showing of a likelihood of dilution.[75] Damages are available only if the defendant willfully intended to trade on the reputation of the famous mark's owner or to cause dilution of the famous mark; in this event, the trademark owner is entitled to recover its damages and costs, as well as the dilutor's profits. Unlike in an action for trademark infringement, relief is available even if the other mark does not cause consumer confusion as to the source of the product. In one dilution case, a court found that use of candyland.com for a child pornography website tarnished the value of Hasbro's popular trademarked "Candy Land" children's game.[76]

71. *See, e.g.,* Interstellar Starship Servs., Ltd. v. Epix, Inc., 304 F.3d 936 (9th Cir. 2002).

72. Holiday Inns, Inc. v. 800 Reservation, Inc., 86 F.3d 619 (6th Cir. 1996), *cert. denied,* 519 U.S. 1093 (1997).

73. 15 U.S.C. §§ 1125, 1127.

74. Moseley v. V. Secret Catalogue, Inc., 537 U.S. 418 (2003).

75. 15 U.S.C. § 1127.

76. Hasbro, Inc. v. Internet Entm't Group, Ltd., 1996 WL 84853 (W.D. Wash. Feb. 9, 1996).

DEFENSES

Possible defenses in trademark-infringement cases include the first sale and fair use doctrines, nominative use, genericity, and the First Amendment.

First Sale Doctrine

The first sale doctrine provides that a trademark owner cannot act against resellers of products after the first sale of the product. The idea behind the first sale doctrine is that the trademark owner had the chance to control the quality of the product and to make money on the first sale of the trademarked product. The first sale doctrine attempts to strike a balance among (1) trademark law's goal of allowing producers to reap the benefits of their reputation, (2) consumers' desire to receive what they bargain for, and (3) the public interest in maintaining competitive markets by limiting a producer's control of resale.

In 2003, Taylor Made Golf, a manufacturer of trademarked golf clubs, sued MJT Consulting, a company that sold Taylor Made clubs without authorization.[77] The court found that MJT had taken defective club heads that Taylor Made had rejected and discarded, affixed alternative shafts and grips, and sold the "new" clubs under the Taylor Made trademark. MJT's defense was that it had bought the club heads from a middleman (that represented that it had bought the club heads from another middleman), and that Taylor Made's infringement claim was therefore invalid under the first sale doctrine. Pointing to factual evidence that the club heads were originally Taylor Made club heads and that Taylor Made did not intend them to be sold, the court rejected MJT's defense on the basis that the first sale doctrine applies only where the seller is legally selling genuine trademarked goods.

Fair Use

The defense of fair use is available when a trademark user truthfully uses a competitor's mark to identify the competitor's product for the user's own purposes. To establish fair use, a defendant must show that its use is (1) other than as a mark, (2) in a descriptive sense, and (3) in good faith (the user must not intend to capitalize on the mark's goodwill or reputation). For example, International Stamp Art (ISA) produced note cards that incorporated a perforated design calling to mind a traditional postage stamp. When the U.S. Postal Service began selling its own line of stamp design cards including the perforated border, ISA sued for infringement of its perforated border trademark. Applying the foregoing test, the U.S. Court of Appeals for the Eleventh Circuit found no infringement, because ISA presented no evidence showing the Postal Service had the required intent to capitalize on ISA's mark.[78]

Nominative Use

A defendant is not liable for trademark infringement if its use is *nominative use,* where the defendant uses the mark to talk about the mark itself. For example, Century 21, Coldwell Banker, and ERA Franchise Systems sued Lending Tree, an Internet real estate referral service, for using their trademarks on its website. Lending Tree asserted a nominative use defense, but the district court rejected the defense and granted a preliminary injunction against Lending Tree on the basis that its use of the trademarks was likely to cause confusion. On appeal, the U.S. Court of Appeals for the Third Circuit noted that the U.S. Supreme Court has held that a defendant asserting a classic fair use defense does not have the burden of showing that there is no likelihood of consumer confusion.[79] Extending this holding to nominative fair use cases, the court took a bifurcated approach. It found the plaintiff must first demonstrate that the defendant's use of the plaintiff's mark is likely to create confusion. If the plaintiff meets this burden, the defendant must then prove the nominative fair use defense by showing that (1) the use of the plaintiff's mark is necessary to describe both the plaintiff's product or service and the defendant's product and service; (2) the defendant has used only so much of the plaintiff's mark as is necessary to describe the plaintiff's product; and (3) the defendant's conduct or language reflects the true and accurate relationship between the plaintiff and the defendant's product.[80] The court remanded the case to the trial court to determine if the defendant's use of the plaintiffs' trademarks was likely to cause consumer confusion and, if so, whether such use of the marks amounted to nominative fair use.

Genericity

As seen in the *Microsoft v. Lindows.com* litigation, genericity can be a defense when a trademark owner brings suit over a trademark that is arguably a generic term. Trademark owners must take appropriate measures to ensure that their marks are not, and do not become, generic.

77. Taylor Made Golf Co. v. MJT Consulting Group, LLC, 265 F. Supp. 2d 732 (N.D. Tex. 2003).

78. Int'l Stamp Art, Inc. v. U.S. Postal Serv., 456 F.3d 1270 (11th Cir. 2006).

79. KP Permanent Make-Up, Inc. v. Lasting Impressions, Inc., 543 U.S. 111 (2004).

80. Century 21 Real Estate Corp. v. Lending Tree, Inc., 425 F.3d 211 (3d Cir. 2005).

First Amendment

Defendants may claim a First Amendment defense when their use of another's trademark is part of their communicative or expressive message and thus is protected as free speech. For example, courts have upheld consumers' rights to criticize corporations or service providers through websites that use the corporation's trademarked name. Courts have protected these so-called gripe sites as protected speech, even though the corporations often allege that the sites confuse other consumers, hurt their business, and dilute their trademarks.[81]

REMEDIES FOR TRADEMARK INFRINGEMENT

One of the most common remedies for trademark infringement is injunctive relief. Courts may also award damages, measured either by the owner's lost sales and profits due to the infringement, or by economic injury to the owner's goodwill and reputation. To the extent they are not duplicative, courts may award the trademark owner the profits that the infringer earned through its use of the mark. In cases of flagrant infringement, a court may take the unusual step of awarding attorneys' fees to the trademark owner. Finally, in the particular case of trafficking in goods or services that knowingly use a *counterfeit mark,* the Lanham Act imposes substantial fines and/or imprisonment.[82]

81. Tresa Baldas, *The Cost of Griping on the Web: Lawsuits,* NAT'L L.J., Nov. 29, 2004, *available at* http://www.law.com/jsp/nlj/PubArticleNLJ.jsp?id=1101136524084.

82. The Lanham Act defines a "counterfeit mark" as "(a) a spurious mark (i) that is used in connection with trafficking in goods or services; (ii) that is identical with, or substantially indistinguishable from, a registered trademark; and (iii) the use of which is likely to cause confusion or mistake or to deceive; or (b) a spurious designation that is identical with, or substantially indistinguishable from, the holder of the right to use the designation." 18 U.S.C. § 2320(e).

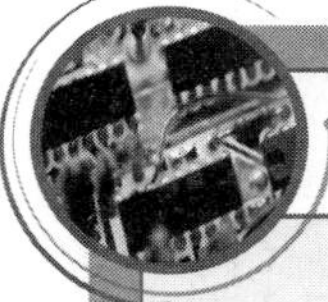

VIEW FROM CYBERSPACE

Domain Names and Cybersquatting

Internet addresses are called *domain names.* The top-level domain is the domain name's suffix, which characterizes the type of organization. For example, ".edu" is used by educational organizations, and ".com" is used by commercial organizations. Country codes, such as ".fr" for France, serve as top-level domain names. The secondary domain identifies the specific organization. For example, in the domain name "cnn.com," the "cnn" identifies Cable News Network. As the Internet increasingly is used to conduct business, companies seek domain names that easily identify their web locations. Disputes have arisen when entities have registered domain names that are confusingly similar to another business's trademark. Unlike the trademark system, where more than one company can register the same mark for noncompetitive products or services, only one entity can own the right to each domain name.

The Internet Corporation for Assigned Names and Numbers (ICANN) is the regulatory body that oversees the Internet's address system. Until 2000, only a limited number of general top-level domain (gTLD) names were available through ICANN, forcing companies to compete for the treasured .com address. In 2000, ICANN accepted applications for additional gTLDs and approved the use of the following seven new top-level domain names, thereby increasing the list of possible Internet addresses available: .aero, .biz, .coop, .info, .museum, .name, and .pro. In 2003 and 2004, ICANN once again accepted applications for additional gTLDs and approved three more: .mobi, for use in the cellphone industry; .jobs, for human resources; and .travel, for the travel industry. Since 2004, ICANN has been working on a policy to guide the introduction of new gTLDs, and it plans to announce a new gTLD application round after the policy is adopted.[a]

Domain names are registered on a first-come, first-served basis. Because the registrar does not check whether use of the name by the person seeking registration would violate someone else's trademark, the practice of *cybersquatting* developed: an individual would register famous trademarks as domain

CONTINUED

names and then offer to sell them to the trademark owner for a "ransom."[b]

To combat this practice, ICANN developed a worldwide, fast-track, online domain name dispute resolution policy (UDRP), which became effective in 1999; under the UDRP, a trademark owner who proves cybersquatting can receive an order from an arbitration panel that the domain name be canceled or transferred to the trademark owner. To prove cybersquatting under the UDRP, the complainant must prove that (1) the disputed domain name is identical or misleadingly similar to a trademark to which the complainant has rights, (2) the respondent has no legitimate rights in the domain name, and (3) the domain name is being held and used in bad faith. A successful complainant is not entitled to money damages under the UDRP. Supporters applauded the ICANN process, saying that it would "benefit small-business defendants who do not have the financial resources to battle major corporations in court."[c] From the institution of the ICANN arbitration system through April 2004, 7,790 arbitration decisions involving more than 13,311 domain names were issued. The 7,790 decisions resulted in 10,779 domain name transfers or cancellations.[d]

Even though the U.S. Department of Commerce had designated ICANN to set up a global system for Internet management, including trademark issues, Congress passed the Anticybersquatting Consumer Protection Act (ACPA), before it was clear whether ICANN's process would be able to solve the cybersquatting problem. The ACPA, which became effective on November 29, 1999, created a separate, federal remedy, applicable only to domestic name registrations. Under the ACPA, a complainant must prove that (1) the defendant has a bad faith intent to profit from a mark, including a defendant name that is protected as a mark; and (2) registers, traffics in, or uses a domain name that (a) in the case of a mark that is distinctive at the time of registration of the domain name, is identical or confusingly similar to that mark; or (b) in the case of a famous mark that is famous at the time of registration of the domain name, is identical or confusingly similar to or dilutive of that mark. The ACPA's definition of cybersquatting is broader than ICANN's definition in that it makes bad faith alone actionable, regardless of use. In addition to authorizing a court to order the forfeiture or cancellation of a domain name or the transfer of the domain name to the owner of the mark, the ACPA also authorizes the award of actual or statutory damages of not less than $1,000 and not more than $100,000 per domain name.

Critics of the ACPA expressed concern that Congress had undermined ICANN's worldwide dispute resolution process: "In acting unilaterally, Congress has set a bad precedent. It[s action] encourages every nation to pass its own laws, creating a fragmented approach to resolving cross-border disputes over domain names."[e] Opponents also claimed that the ACPA infringed free speech rights and overlooked small-business and individual interests. Calling the ACPA "massive overkill," Michael Froomkin, a law professor at the University of Miami, predicted that its $100,000 in statutory penalties would allow large companies, like the Hollywood studios that pushed for its passage, to threaten small businesses and individuals. The first lawsuits based on the ACPA were filed just weeks after it was enacted. Harvard University filed a complaint on December 6, 1999, seeking an injunction against a defendant who registered sixty-five domain names related to Harvard and Radcliffe. A consent judgment was issued in 2000 that required the defendant, among other things, to immediately cancel the registrations of all infringing and diluting names and to supply lists of the domain names containing Harvard's marks that he had registered.[f] More recently, Microsoft used the ACPA as the basis for a lawsuit against a defendant who had registered numerous Internet domain names similar to the names of Microsoft products and services, a practice referred to as "typo squatting." Microsoft sought $100,000 per domain name, or an aggregate of approximately $9.5 million. The defendant agreed to settle the case, and an order was entered prohibiting him from "registering, using, or trafficking in any domain name that is identical or confusingly similar to Microsoft's marks and domain names containing misspelling of Microsoft's marks."[g]

---

a. http://www.icann.org/topics/news-gtld-program-faq.htm.

b. *See, e.g.*, Panavision Int'l, L.P. v. Toeppen, 141 F.3d 1316 (9th Cir. 1998).

c. Aaron L. Melville, *New Cybersquatting Law Brings Mixed Reactions from Trademark Owners, available at* http://www.bu.edu/law/scitech/volume6/Melville.htm (last visited Jan. 14, 2005).

d. Statistical Summary of Proceedings Under Uniform Domain Name Dispute Resolution Policy, May 10, 2004, *available at* http://www.icann.org/udrp/proceedings-stat.htm.

e. Editorial, *What's in a (Domain) Name?*, San Jose Mercury News, Nov. 1, 1999, at 6B.

f. Alayne E. Manas, *Harvard as a Model in Trademark and Domain Name Protection*, Rutgers Computer & Tech. L.J., June 22, 2003, at 475.

g. Rebecca S. Green, *Local Resident, Microsoft Settle Web Name Suit*, J. Gazette, Feb. 23, 2008, *available at* http://www.journalgazette.net/apps/pbcs.dll/article?aid=/20080223/local03/802230327/1002/local.

TRADE DRESS

In addition to protecting registered marks, courts interpret the Lanham Act to include protection for trade dress, that is, the packaging or dressing of a product. Trade dress includes all elements making up the total visual image by which a product is presented to customers, as defined by its overall composition and design.

The elements of trade dress infringement parallel those of trademark infringement, with the likelihood of consumer confusion as the core issue. In one case, Best Cellars sued Grape Finds for copying the style and arrangement of its retail wine shops.[83] Best Cellars' business model was predicated on demystifying wine purchases for unsophisticated shoppers by using a "wall of wine" racking system and other distinctive visual displays. Grape Finds started using the same system. The court ruled that Best Cellars' store arrangements were arbitrary and therefore protectable, and granted a preliminary injunction to prevent Grape Finds from using the same system in its stores.

The U.S. Supreme Court has held that trade dress protection may not be claimed for functional product features.[84] In general, a product feature is functional if it is essential to the use or purpose of the article, or if it affects the cost or quality of the article.

TRADE SECRETS

In our free-market system, the demand for modern technologies and innovation may lead to unauthorized disclosure of sensitive information. Trade secret law is necessary to protect the owners of such information.

SCOPE OF PROTECTION

The growing value of trade secrets has been accompanied by increasingly high stakes litigation. In 2005, a jury found Toshiba Corporation and Toshiba America Electronic Components, Inc. liable for breach of fiduciary duty and theft of trade secrets. It awarded Lexar more than $380 million in compensatory damages and $84 million in punitive damages—at the time, the largest award involving intellectual property in California history and the third largest IP award in U.S. history.[85]

83. Best Cellars, Inc. v. Grape Finds at Dupont, Inc., 90 F. Supp. 2d 431 (S.D.N.Y. 2000).

84. Traffix Devices, Inc. v. Mktg. Displays, Inc., 532 U.S. 23 (2001).

85. *Lexar Wins $465.4 Million Against Toshiba,* DIGITAL PHOTOGRAPHY REV., Mar. 25, 2005, *available at* http://www.dpreview.com/news/0503/05032501lexarvstoshiba.asp.

Trade secret law is primarily the province of the states. Until 1996, courts developed the law of trade secrets on a case-by-case basis, applying the laws of the relevant state. Courts based their decisions on tort theories in cases involving theft or misappropriation of trade secrets and on contract theories when a special relationship or duty was present. Many trade secret cases involved a combination of the two theories. Now courts also consider the federal Economic Espionage Act that intersects with these traditional state law approaches.

COMMON LAW

The most widely accepted definition of "trade secret" is contained in the Restatement (Second) of Torts. Section 757(b) provides:

> A trade secret may consist of any formula, pattern, device, or compilation of information which is used in one's business, and which gives him an opportunity to obtain an advantage over competitors who do not know or use it. It may be a formula for a chemical compound, a process of manufacturing, treating or preserving materials, a pattern for a machine or other device, or a list of customers.

The courts have developed a number of factors to determine whether specific information qualifies as a trade secret. These factors include (1) the extent to which the information is known outside the business, (2) the extent to which measures are taken to protect the information, (3) the value of the information, (4) the amount of money or time spent to develop the information, and (5) the ease of duplicating the information.

Unfortunately, even with this formal definition and set of factors, a certain amount of guesswork is still required to determine whether a particular type of information qualifies as a trade secret under the common law. Faced with only slightly different factual settings, the courts have classified identical types of information differently.

THE UNIFORM TRADE SECRETS ACT

In 1979, the National Conference of Commissioners on Uniform State Laws (NCCUSL) promulgated the Uniform Trade Secrets Act (UTSA) in an attempt to provide a coherent framework for trade secret protection. NCCUSL hoped to eliminate the unpredictability of the common law by providing a more comprehensive definition of trade secrets. In particular, NCCUSL expanded the common law definition by adding the terms "method," "program," and "technique" to the Restatement's list of types of protected information. The intention was to specifically include know-how (technical knowledge, methods, and experience). In addition, NCCUSL broadened the common law definition by deleting the requirement that the secret be continuously used in a business. Accordingly, the UTSA defines a trade secret as:

> Information, including a formula, pattern, compilation, program, device, method, technique, or process, that (1) derives independent economic value, actual or potential, from not being generally known to, and not being readily ascertainable by proper means by, other persons who can obtain economic value from its disclosure or use; and (2) is the subject of efforts that are reasonable under the circumstances to maintain its secrecy.

Although the common law does not protect information unless it is in use, the UTSA definition is broad enough to include (1) information that has potential value from being secret, (2) information regarding one-time events, and (3) negative information, such as test results showing what will not work for a particular process or product.

The most significant difference between the UTSA and the common law definitions is in the overall approach to determining whether information is protectable as a trade secret. As discussed above, at common law a fairly objective five- or six-part test was developed. Although many courts adopted a reasonableness standard when interpreting the individual factors of the test, the focus was on objectivity, as delineated in this test. The UTSA uses a more flexible test, indicating that the steps taken to preserve the information as a trade secret must be reasonable and that the owner must derive independent economic value from secrecy. Although the "independent economic value" factor is subjective, a number of courts now use it as part of their trade secret test.

Adopted, at least in part, in forty-five states, the UTSA has only partially fulfilled its goal of standardizing trade secret law. States have tended to enact only those parts of the UTSA that embody the existing common law of the particular state. Consequently, in states that have adopted the UTSA, the courts rely on a combination of the common law and the UTSA. Although the UTSA seems to have fallen short of its goal of establishing consistent protection for trade secrets, it may provide broader protection to owners of trade secrets in states that have adopted it. Its definition of the term "trade secret" is broader than the common law definition, so the burden of proof on the owner is reduced. In addition, the UTSA provides more effective remedies.

CRIMINAL LIABILITY UNDER THE ECONOMIC ESPIONAGE ACT

The Federal Economic Espionage Act,[86] enacted in 1996, imposes criminal liability (including fines and prison sentences) on any person who intentionally or knowingly steals a trade secret or knowingly receives or purchases a wrongfully obtained trade secret. The Act's definition of trade secret is substantially similar to the definition in the Uniform Trade Secrets Act.

Although the Economic Espionage Act was prompted by a desire to remedy perceived problems created by foreign thefts of trade secrets from U.S. businesses, it applies to any trade secret related to or included in products placed in interstate commerce. Organizations (other than foreign instrumentalities) can be fined up to $5 million (or two times the greater of the defendant's gain or the trade secret owner's loss). Foreign instrumentalities, defined as entities substantially owned or controlled by a foreign government, can be fined up to $10 million; individuals knowingly benefiting a foreign instrumentality can be fined up to $500,000 and imprisoned up to fifteen years.

The Act has extraterritorial application: it applies to any violation outside the United States by a U.S. citizen, a resident alien, or an organization organized in the United States. It also applies to violations outside the United States, if any act in furtherance of the offense was committed in the United States.

The government has moved swiftly to add violations of the Economic Espionage Act to its arsenal of potential actions against white-collar criminals. A nineteen-year-old student in Los Angeles was sentenced to five years' probation, six months' home detention, and restitutionary fees when he stole trade secrets relating to smart card technology during his work as a contractor for a law firm defending a smart card client.[87] In *United States v. Lange,*[88] a disgruntled former employee of Replacement Aircraft Parts offered to sell secret manufacturing details to competitors. Even though he pleaded guilty to criminal violation of the Economic Espionage Act, Lange received a fairly substantial thirty-month prison sentence.

---

86. Economic Espionage Act of 1996, 18 U.S.C. §§ 1831–1839.

87. Press Release, U.S. Dept. of Justice, L.A. Man Sentenced for Stealing Trade Secrets Pertaining to "Smart Card" Technology (Sept. 8, 2003), *available at* http://www.usdoj.gov/criminal/cybercrime/serebryanySent.htm.

88. 312 F.2d 263 (7th Cir. 2002).

CREATING RIGHTS IN A TRADE SECRET

In contrast to the formal process required for patent and copyright protection, no lengthy application and filing procedures are needed for trade secret protection. No review or approval by a governmental agency is required. To create and protect a trade secret, one need only develop and maintain a trade secret protection program. When the information being protected has a short shelf life, trade secret protection may be a more practical solution than copyright or patent protection.

Trade secrets are immediately protectable and continue to be protectable as long as the information remains confidential and is not developed independently by someone else. Material that would not qualify for patent or copyright protection is often protectable as a trade secret. A trade secret need not be as unique as a patentable invention or as original as a copyrightable work. It only needs to provide a competitive advantage. It may be merely an idea that has been kept secret, such as a way to organize common machines in an efficient manner, a marketing plan, or a formula for mixing the ingredients of a product. Trade secrets can also consist of a compilation of information, even though each component part of the compilation is generally known.

In addition, obtaining patent and copyright protection usually requires the disclosure of valuable information. There is always a risk that after the sensitive information has been revealed, the reviewing agency will not grant the protection. To avoid this risk, trade secret protection may be the safest course of action.

There are two disadvantages to using trade secret protection, however. First, maintaining a full-fledged protection program can be expensive, because confidentiality procedures must be continuously and rigidly followed to preserve trade secret status. Second, trade secret protection provides no protection against reverse engineering or independent discovery, and the uncertainty of protection may limit the productive uses of the trade secret.

PROTECTING A TRADE SECRET

Misappropriation of trade secrets most commonly occurs as a result of inadvertent disclosures or employee disclosures. To properly protect trade secret information, the owner must develop a program to preserve its confidentiality. In almost every jurisdiction, the test of a trade secret program's adequacy may be reduced to the question of whether the owner has taken reasonable precautions to preserve the confidentiality of his or her trade secrets.

A trade secret program should cover four areas: (1) notification, (2) identification, (3) security, and (4) exit interviews.

Notification

The first critical element is a written notice, which should be posted, to confirm that all employees have been made aware of the trade secret program. Ideally, the company's trade secret policy should be explained to each new employee during orientation, and each new employee should sign a confidentiality agreement that specifies how long confidentiality will be required.[89]

Labeling, such as using a rubber stamp to denote confidential material and posting signs in areas containing sensitive materials, is another means of notification. Some authorities, however, believe that labeling may actually hurt the trade secret status of information, because in practice it can be difficult to ensure consistent and continuous labeling procedures. These authorities claim that failure to label some documents may be seen as evidence that the information in those documents should not be afforded trade secret status.

The company should also provide written notice to any consultant, vendor, joint venturer, or other party to whom a trade secret must be revealed. This notice should take the form of a confidentiality agreement that describes the protected information and limits the receiving party's rights to use it. Without such notice, the receiving party may be unaware of the nature of the information and unwittingly release it into the public domain.

A nondisclosure agreement (NDA) can serve as the basis for recovery, if a court later determines that the party who gained access to trade secrets used or disclosed them in violation of the agreement. For example, in *Celeritas Technologies, Ltd. v. Rockwell,*[90] the parties entered into negotiations for licensing Celeritas's "de-emphasis technology," a method for reducing high-frequency noise in cellular communications. Prior to allowing access to the information, Celeritas asked Rockwell to sign an NDA. The licensing negotiations ultimately failed, and Rockwell subsequently developed its own modem chips that incorporated de-emphasis technology. The same engineers who had access to Celeritas's technology under the NDA worked on Rockwell's de-emphasis technology project. Celeritas brought suit claiming, among other things, breach of the NDA. Because the technology was not readily ascertainable in the public domain and was found to have come directly from Celeritas, the court concluded that Rockwell had breached the NDA and that Celeritas was entitled to damages.

89. Many confidentiality agreements do not include a fixed term. Instead, they require an employee to maintain confidentiality as long as the information remains confidential and is not otherwise publicly released by the employer.

90. 150 F.3d 1354 (Fed. Cir. 1998).

Sometimes an NDA may contain a "residuals" provision, which permits either party to use and exploit any information that representatives of the nondisclosing party learned in the course of the subject negotiations or engagement and retained in their minds. This can create a very large loophole in the restrictions on nondisclosure.

Identification

There is some controversy about the appropriate method of identifying trade secrets. One view is that everything in the workplace, or pertaining to the business, is a trade secret, but a court will most likely deem this umbrella approach to be overly restrictive of commerce and therefore against public policy. Such a finding could undermine the company's trade secret program, exposing all of its trade secrets to unrecoverable misappropriation.

At the other extreme is a program that attempts to specify every one of the company's trade secrets. This approach may be too narrow because any legitimate trade secrets that are not specified will not be protected. Also, it is often difficult to pinpoint all of a company's potential trade secrets. For example, although it may be easy to designate all research and development projects as trade secrets, gray areas such as sales data, customer lists, or marketing surveys may cause problems. The best solution may be a program that specifies as much information as possible, while also including a limited number of catchall categories.

Security

Measures must be taken to ensure that trade secret information remains secret, at least from the public. The disclosure of a trade secret, whether intentional (for example, as part of a sale) or by mistake, destroys any legal protection. Access to trade secret information should therefore be limited to those who truly have a need to know. Hard copies of trade secret information should be locked in secure filing cabinets or a secure room. Photocopying machines should be placed as far as possible from trade secret files. Digital confidential information should be encrypted and password protected.

A company should also guard against unintentional disclosure of a trade secret during a public tour of the facility. An offhand remark in the hall overheard by a visitor, or a formula left written on a chalkboard in plain view of a tour group, is all that is needed. The best way to avoid this situation is to keep all trade secrets in areas restricted from public access. If such physical barriers are not possible, visitors' access should be controlled through a system that logs in all visitors, identifies them with badges, and keeps track of them while they are on the premises.

Employees may inadvertently disclose trade secrets when participating in trade groups, conferences, and conventions, and through publication of articles in trade journals and other periodicals. To avoid this problem, an employer should consistently remind its employees and contractors of when and how to talk about the company's business activities.

Exit Interviews

When an employee who has had access to trade secrets leaves the company, he or she should be given an exit interview. The exit interview provides an opportunity to reinforce the confidentiality agreement that the employee signed on joining the company. If no confidentiality agreement exists, the exit interview is even more important, because it provides the notice and possibly the identification necessary to legally protect the employer's trade secrets. The exit interview also lets the departing employee know that the company is serious about protecting its trade secrets and that any breach of confidentiality could result in legal proceedings against him or her. After such a warning, any misappropriation would be deliberate and could therefore result in punitive damages.

In some states, post-termination restrictions on competition imposed on a departing employee may be unenforceable. In California, for example, a provision in an employment contract that prohibits an employee based in California from later working for a competitor is void as an unlawful business restraint, except to the extent necessary to prevent the misappropriation of trade secrets. It is therefore important to consult with local counsel concerning the permissible scope of post-termination restrictions.

MISAPPROPRIATION OF TRADE SECRETS

An individual misappropriates a trade secret when he or she (1) uses or discloses the trade secret of another or (2) learns of a trade secret through improper means. The UTSA defines "improper means" by a list of deceitful actions. The list is not exclusive, however, and anything that strikes a court as improper would probably qualify as an improper means.

In one misappropriation case, Wyeth, a large pharmaceutical company, sued Natural Biologics for misappropriating its secret manufacturing process for Premarin, a highly profitable hormone replacement therapy drug.[91] Pretrial discovery uncovered a series of phone calls between Natural Biologics and a retired Wyeth scientist who had been instrumental in developing the Premarin manufacturing process. The court determined that these calls gave the fledgling company

91. Wyeth v. Natural Biologics, Inc., 2003 WL 22282371 (D. Minn. 2003), *aff'd*, 395 F.3d 897 (8th Cir. 2005).

all the knowledge it needed to copy the process. Because Natural Biologics had improperly obtained this information, the court issued a permanent injunction forbidding it from using the information or in any way engaging in drug development processes.

Inevitable Disclosure Doctrine

Some courts have recognized a form of employee misappropriation under the *inevitable disclosure doctrine,* which recognizes that former employees who go to work for a competitor in a similar capacity will inevitably rely on and disclose the trade secrets gained in their former employment.

The inevitable disclosure doctrine was first recognized by a federal appeals court in *PepsiCo, Inc. v. Redmond.*[92] William Redmond, Jr. worked as a senior marketing manager for PepsiCo in its Pepsi-Cola North America division. Redmond had just completed work on the strategic marketing plans for AllSport (a sports drink that competed against Gatorade) and PepsiCo's powdered teas (which competed against Snapple, among others). In November 1994, Redmond accepted an offer from Quaker Oats to work as the vice president of field operations in Quaker's combined Gatorade and Snapple drinks subsidiary. PepsiCo sued to enjoin Redmond from working at Quaker Oats on grounds of threatened misappropriation.

The U.S. Court of Appeals for the Seventh Circuit held that a company may prove trade secret misappropriation by demonstrating that the employee's new position will inevitably lead him to rely on his ex-employer's trade secrets. Because of the competition between AllSport and Gatorade, the court concluded that Redmond could not help but rely on PepsiCo's trade secrets as he planned Gatorade's future course. Specifically, Quaker Oats would have a substantial advantage by knowing how PepsiCo would price, distribute, and market its sports drinks. The court likened the situation to that faced by a football team whose key player leaves to play for another team and takes the play book with him.

By recognizing the notion of inevitable disclosure as being within the UTSA's provision of "threatened disclosure," the *PepsiCo* case gives employers greater leverage over departing employees and a powerful weapon against competitors who lure away valuable employees. Nevertheless, situations that spark the risk of inevitable disclosure have continued to arise. For example, after initiating a lawsuit, Campbell Soup Company entered into a settlement agreement with H.J. Heinz that allowed the former head of Campbell's U.S. soup business to join the Heinz tuna and pet-food businesses, on the condition that he stay out of the soup business for one year. When one of Intel's chief software architects left to work on a competing semiconductor chip at Intel's rival, Broadcom, Intel sued to block his move based on the inevitable disclosure doctrine. Ultimately, however, a court found little risk of trade secret disclosure.[93]

Although a number of courts have accepted the inevitable disclosure doctrine in some form, other courts have hesitated to apply the doctrine. For example, in *Earthweb, Inc. v. Schlack,*[94] the U.S. District Court for the Southern District of New York refused to apply the inevitable disclosure doctrine in circumstances where a noncompete agreement was considered overbroad and thus unenforceable. The court reasoned that the inevitable disclosure doctrine "treads an exceedingly narrow path through judicially disfavored territory. Absent evidence of actual misappropriation by an employee, the doctrine should be applied in only the rarest of cases." A California district court went further, holding that the inevitable disclosure doctrine created a "de facto covenant not to compete," which was contrary to California law and public policy.[95]

REMEDIES FOR TRADE SECRET MISAPPROPRIATION

Once a trade secret has been misappropriated, the law provides a choice of remedies, which are not mutually exclusive.

Injunctions

A court may issue an injunction ordering the misappropriator to refrain from disclosing or using the stolen trade secret. An injunction is available only to prevent irreparable harm, however. If the trade secret has already been disclosed, an injunction may no longer be appropriate to protect the trade secret. The court may, however, still enjoin the misappropriator from using the information, so that the misappropriator will not benefit from his or her wrongful act. In this situation, the injunction is often combined with an award of damages.

The owner may also be able to seek an injunction or damages from anyone receiving the misappropriated trade secret or anyone hiring the individual who misappropriated it. For example, as mentioned earlier, the court issued a permanent injunction against Natural Biologics forbidding it from any drug development, because its entire drug manufacturing business was based on information stolen from Wyeth.

92. 54 F.3d 1262 (7th Cir. 1995).

93. Intel Corp. v. Broadcom Corp., 2000 WL 33260713 (Cal. Super. Ct. June 20, 2000).

94. 71 F. Supp. 2d 299 (S.D.N.Y. 1999), *aff'd,* 205 F.3d 1322 (2d Cir. 2000).

95. Whyte v. Schlage Lock Co., 125 Cal. Rptr. 277 (Cal. App. Ct. 2002).

IN BRIEF

Advantages and Disadvantages of Different Types of Intellectual Property Protection

	Trade Secret	Copyright	Patent	Trademark
Benefits	Very broad protection for sensitive, competitive information; very inexpensive	Prevents copying of a wide array of artistic and literary expressions, including software; very inexpensive	Very strong protection; provides exclusive right to make, use, and sell an invention	Protects corporate image and identity by protecting marks that customers use to identify a business; prevents others from using confusingly similar identifying marks
Duration	For as long as the information remains valuable and is kept confidential	Life of author plus 70 years; for works made for hire, 95 years from year of first publication or 120 years from year of creation, whichever is shorter	20 years from date of filing the patent application	Indefinitely as long as the mark is not abandoned and steps are taken to police its use
Weaknesses	No protection from accidental disclosure, independent creation by a competitor, or disclosure by someone without a duty to maintain confidentiality	Protects only the particular way an idea is expressed, not the idea itself; apparent lessening of protection for software; hard to detect copying in digital age	High standards of patentability; often expensive and time-consuming to pursue (especially when overseas patents are needed); must disclose invention to the public	Can be lost or weakened if not appropriately used and enforced; can be costly if multiple overseas registrations are needed
Required Steps	Take reasonable steps to protect—generally, a trade secret protection program	None required,. though notice and registration can strengthen rights	Detailed filing with U.S. Patent and Trademark Office, which performs a search for prior art and can impose hefty fees	Only need to use mark in commerce, though filing with U.S. Patent and Trademark Office is usually desirable to gain stronger protections
U.S. Rights Valid Internationally?	No. Trade secret laws vary significantly by country, and some countries have no trade secret laws.	Generally, yes	No. Separate patent examinations and filings are required in each country; however, a single international patent application can be filed with the national patent office or the World International Property Organization, and a single filing in the European Patent Office can cover a number of European countries.	No. Separate filings are required in foreign jurisdictions, and a mark available in the U.S. may not be available overseas. A single CTM filing can cover a number of European countries, however.

Source: Adapted from Constance E. Bagley & Craig E. Dauchy, The Entrepreneur's Guide to Business Law 545–46 (2008).

Finally, an injunction may also be appropriate when an individual threatens to use or disclose a trade secret, although the real damage has not yet occurred. In the *PepsiCo* case, the former PepsiCo employee was not permitted to work for Quaker Oats, until the information he had in his head about PepsiCo's marketing strategy became stale and lacked competitive value.

Damages

When the owner of the trade secret has suffered financial harm, courts often award money damages, based on either a contract or a tort theory. Under the tort theory of trade secrets, the purpose of the damages is not only to make the owner whole, but also to disgorge any profits the misappropriator may have made due to his or her wrongful act. The key to the tort measure of damages is that there was either a harm or an unjust gain, or both. The contract theory of trade secrets, on the other hand, measures damages by the loss of value of the trade secret to the owner as a result of a breach of contract. Courts determine the loss of value by adding the general loss to any special losses resulting from the breach and subtracting any costs avoided by the owner as a result of the breach.

The technical differences between the two measures of damages make little practical difference. Most courts will attempt to fairly compensate the owner of a misappropriated trade secret regardless of how the case is characterized.

Punitive Damages

Punitive damages are available when the misappropriation was willful and wanton. Under the UTSA, the court may award double the ordinary damages if it finds willful and malicious misappropriation; in some states, courts may award attorneys' fees as well.

CRIMINAL LIABILITY

As described earlier, the Economic Espionage Act criminalizes the theft of trade secrets and imposes fines and imprisonment on those convicted under it. In addition, many state statutes also impose criminal liability for theft of trade secrets. Although criminal charges are less common than civil charges, in part due to the higher standard of proof for a criminal conviction, they still occur.

GLOBAL VIEW

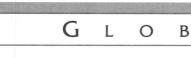

The Move Toward Harmonization of Intellectual Property Regimes

Several multinational treaties are attempting to harmonize the application of intellectual property laws across jurisdictions. Although they do not alter the substantive criteria that each jurisdiction applies to determine whether patent, trademark, or copyright protection is available, the treaties seek to coordinate the registration and recognition process among signatory countries.[96]

In most countries, if two entities file for protection of the same invention or trademark, the entity that filed first receives protection. This can be a problem for an inventor or trademark owner who files for protection in one country and later discovers that someone else has subsequently filed for protection of the same invention or trademark in another country. The International Convention for the Protection of Industrial Property Rights (known as the Paris Convention) addresses this problem by encouraging reciprocal recognition of patents, trademarks, service marks, and similar forms of

CONTINUED

96. "Not withstanding these harmonization efforts, countries—both developed and less developed—have become increasingly dissatisfied with the international intellectual property regime. . . . To protect themselves and to reclaim autonomy over their intellectual property policies, [they] have recently pushed for measures that frustrate the harmonization project." *See* Peter K. Yu, *Five Disharmonizing Trends in the International Intellectual Property Regime* (Michigan State Univ. Coll. of Law, Legal Studies Research Paper Series No. 03-28, 2006).

intellectual property rights among its eighty-plus signatory nations. Each signatory nation grants nationals of other signatory nations a grace period after filing in their home country, within which to file corresponding patent or trademark applications. Patent applicants have one year and trademark owners have six months.

The Paris Convention does not alter the substantive requirements of the laws of each nation, so patent or trademark protection in one country does not necessarily translate into protection in another country. Differing rules governing eligibility may mean that actions in one's home country that do not compromise protection there may forfeit protection abroad (for example, disclosure or sale of inventions prior to filing for a patent).

Patents

The Patent Cooperation Treaty (PCT) allows an inventor to file a single international patent application to preserve the right to seek patent protection in each contracting country, rather than having to initially apply for separate patents in many different countries. The inventor may file this application either with the national patent office (e.g., the PTO for U.S. inventors) or the International Bureau of the World Intellectual Property Organization (WIPO).

Every international patent application is subject to an "international search" by an International Searching Authority. The search results include a list of citations of prior art relevant to the international patent application claims and information regarding possible relevance of the citations to questions of novelty and inventiveness (nonobviousness). This information enables the applicant to evaluate its chances of obtaining patents in the countries designated. An applicant may also have an international preliminary examination of the patent, which provides even more information about the invention's patentability. This information helps an applicant decide whether to file applications in individually designated countries.

The patent practice of other countries is often different from that of the United States. For example, foreign laws regarding statutory bars are radically different from U.S. patent law. A rule of thumb is that any public disclosure of an invention prior to filing the patent application will prevent an inventor from obtaining foreign patent protection. Also, some jurisdictions are more receptive to certain types of patents than others. In Europe, there are significant obstacles to obtaining patents on certain types of software innovations, including business methods. Some countries do not permit composition patents for pharmaceuticals, although they may receive some protection under process patents. Given these differences, managers should discuss the rules that apply in foreign jurisdictions with an attorney prior to disclosure or sale of any patentable invention.

Copyrights

International copyright protection has also begun to harmonize. For decades, the United States was the lone holdout from the two key international copyright treaties: the Berne Convention and the Universal Copyright Convention. Realizing the importance of international standards, the United States slowly adjusted its copyright law to comply with treaty standards (e.g., removing formality requirements, extending the term of protection, and enacting the Digital Millennium Copyright Act). Under these treaties, American works receive the same protection that is afforded to the works of a national in foreign countries that are signatories of the same treaty.

In May 2001, the European Union approved a Copyright Directive that would update and harmonize member state copyright laws to bring them into conformity with the WIPO Treaty and the WIPO Performances and Phonograms Treaty. The Copyright Directive identified four areas that require legislative action if the European Union (EU) is to achieve harmony in its copyright laws: (1) a reproduction right, (2) a communication to the public right, (3) a distribution right, and (4) protection against circumvention of abuse and protection systems.

The directive outlaws the manufacture of devices that facilitate the circumvention of technology used for copyright protection. The directive also provides authors with the exclusive right to authorize or prohibit communication of their work to the public by wire or wireless means, including interactive Internet sites that offer such works without the author's permission. In contrast to the DMCA in the United States, however, the directive contains several different, yet still compliant, implementation methods regarding exceptions, penalties, and remedies that allow each country to modify the proposal as needed.

Although all EU member countries were required to ratify the directive by December 2002, implementing it proved difficult because of the controversies surrounding the balance between copyright owners' rights and the public's right of use. As of 2008, most EU countries had enacted the legislation required for compliance with the directive.

CONTINUED

Trademarks

Every country has its own methods for determining what is a protectable trademark, how to obtain and maintain trademarks, and the scope of protection available for trademarks. In contrast to the United States, in most countries use of a mark confers no rights; the first person to register the mark owns the rights to use it. In addition, registration of a trademark in the United States confers no rights in foreign countries, although a U.S. registration can provide an easy basis for registration of corresponding trademarks in countries that participate in multilateral trademark conventions with the United States.

Currently, several overlapping international regimes govern trademark applications, reflecting the trend toward increased global harmonization. As noted earlier, the Paris Convention provides a six-month grace period from the date an owner files a trademark registration application in his or her home country to file in other signatory countries. As long as the foreign filing is made within that grace period, it is treated as if it had been filed in the foreign jurisdiction on the date the home country filing occurred.

The Madrid Protocol allows for centralized international registration of trademarks. The United States joined the Madrid Protocol in 2003, and there were eighty-one signatory countries as of January 2008.[97] A U.S. trademark owner can register the trademark in all signatory countries by filing a single application at WIPO's International Bureau in Geneva or at the U.S. PTO. Many lawyers see this process as beneficial and believe that it will substantially reduce the time and expense associated with trademark application filings. Others, however, point to differences in protection between national trademark regimes that may prove disadvantageous to U.S. trademark holders who use the WIPO registration process. For example, the PTO application requires narrower descriptions of goods and services than are required in many countries. As a result, a U.S. trademark holder may be better off filing separate, broader applications in each relevant foreign country.

The Pan American Convention recognizes the right of a trademark owner in one signatory country to successfully challenge the registration or use of that same trademark in another country. The key issue is whether persons using or applying to register the mark had knowledge of the existence and continuous use of the mark in any of the member states on goods of the same category.

For EU members, the Community Trade Mark (CTM) can confer protection in the entire EU. The CTM does not replace national rights or Madrid Protocol rights but coexists with them. A CTM can only be registered, assigned, or canceled with respect to the entire EU.

In an effort to attract foreign investment and trade, several foreign nations have enacted laws to harmonize their trademark procedures with the international community. In 1997, Japan enacted a trademark law to address the accumulation of unused registered trademarks by allowing anyone to petition for the cancellation of a mark that has gone unused and by making it more difficult to defend against such petitions. The law also shortened the time required to approve trademark applications. Observers expected the new trademark regime would make it easier for non-Japanese businesses to register and protect their marks in Japan. Among its many provisions, the law allowed for the registration of three-dimensional marks for the first time.

As part of the normalization of trade relations with the United States in 1996, Cambodia signed a bilateral treaty with the United States. In exchange for formally receiving most favored nation status in the United States and the lower tariffs that accompany such status, Cambodia agreed to allow U.S. trademark holders to take legal action against companies using their already established and popular names. For instance, one company in Phnom Penh had been selling pizza under the name "Pizza Hot" and using the familiar red triangle roof of PepsiCo's Pizza Hut. The new law allowed PepsiCo to petition to have the imitator's mark canceled.

Trade Secrets

International trade secret protection is perhaps the least codified and harmonized aspect of intellectual property; thus, this area is the riskiest for U.S. companies doing business abroad. A primary concern is that countries differ in their interpretation of what constitutes a trade secret. For example, in the EU, trade secrets must be fixed in a tangible medium to be legally recognized. Japan does not recognize trade secrets as protectable property in and of themselves; instead, Japanese law forbids unfair acts of acquiring, disclosing, or using information in a manner that harms the trade secret

CONTINUED

97. Madrid System for the International Registration of Marks, Summary Report for the Year 2007, *available at* http://www.wipo.int/export/sites/www/madrid/en/statistics/pdf/summary2007.pdf.

owner. Other countries, like the Philippines, provide no legal protection at all for trade secrets.

Some countries recognize the importance of trade secrets, but have legislation that forces their exposure. For example, at one time, India required foreign companies to create joint venture arrangements that result in compulsory technology transfers to Indian companies. In 1977, Coca-Cola abandoned its Indian operations, rather than divulge the trade secret for its secret formula. And in China, government approval is required for any licensing agreement involving trade secrets; if the parties fail to comply, the trade secret owner forfeits the trade secret after ten years.

Most foreign countries will enforce reasonable nondisclosure restrictions in contracts, at least against parties to the contract; however, most countries do not recognize the tort law aspect of trade secrets that is recognized in the United States. In some countries, the judicial process itself may destroy the confidential character of the misappropriated information.

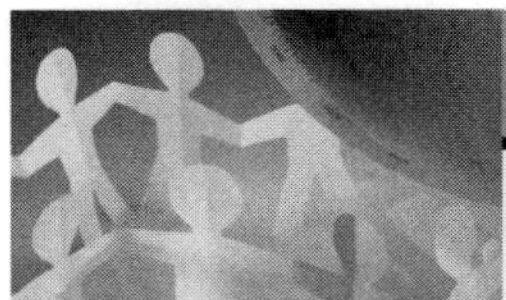

THE RESPONSIBLE MANAGER

PROTECTING INTELLECTUAL PROPERTY RIGHTS

Some of a company's most important assets may be intangible forms of intellectual property. Consider the formula for Coke, never registered as a patent, but kept as a trade secret by generations of executives at the Coca-Cola Company. An effective trade secret policy is essential to almost all forms of business today. This chapter has provided suggestions regarding the implementation of such a policy.

Problems can arise when a manager leaves the employment of one company to assume a position at another. During the exit interview, employees should be reminded of their obligations, and materials and computers being removed from the employer's premises should be inspected. It is critical that the manager and the new employer ensure that no confidential information, including trade secrets, is conveyed to the new employer, either in the form of documents or as information in the manager's head. At the time of hire, the employer should determine whether the potential employee is bound by a restrictive covenant. Moreover, a company should provide written notice to all employees that it has a policy against receiving, using, or purchasing any trade secrets belonging to third parties. Misappropriation of trade secrets is a civil and criminal offense.

If the manager cannot fulfill all the duties of his or her new job without using the prior employer's trade secrets, the new employer should scale back the manager's activities and responsibilities. This can be accomplished by having the former employer and the new employer agree that the manager will not assume responsibility for certain product lines that compete with his or her former employer's until a date when the strategic and other confidential information known by the manager is stale. If possible, the departing manager should negotiate this issue as part of his or her severance arrangement, rather than wait for a costly lawsuit to be brought by the former employer.

Because international trade secret protection is the least codified and least harmonized aspect of intellectual property, a manager should consult with local counsel before making trade secrets available, by license or otherwise, in a foreign country. Patents, copyrights, and trademarks also provide legal protection for different aspects of a company's intellectual property. Patents are extremely important to high-tech companies and some e-commerce firms. Royalties from patents can add tens or even hundreds of millions of dollars to a company's revenues.

Patents also have an important strategic use as a defensive measure in the event that another company claims patent infringement. In such a case, it is very helpful for a manager to have patents that can be used as bargaining chips to negotiate a settlement, which often takes the form of a cross-license.

A manager should develop a global patent strategy because 180 different jurisdictions grant patents, each of

CONTINUED

which gives the holder exclusive rights only in the granting jurisdiction. The United States is the only country that uses a "first-to-invent," instead of "first-to-file," approach in issuing patents.

Copyrights prevent others from copying literary works, musical works, sound recordings, computer software, and other forms of expression fixed in a tangible medium. A manager should consult with an experienced copyright attorney to ensure that his or her company obtains copyright ownership when it commissions, or contracts with, a third party to prepare a copyrighted work. A manager should also discuss with an attorney what, if any, copyright protection is available for a work in any foreign jurisdiction in which the company wants to distribute the work, and what steps are necessary to obtain such protection. A manager should be aware that copyright registration with the U.S. Copyright Office is a prerequisite for filing an infringement suit for a work of U.S. origin. Statutory damages and attorneys' fees are available only to owners who have registered the work within ninety days of first publication or prior to the infringement that forms the basis of the suit. Because the timing of the registration is critical, a manager should consult with a copyright attorney before publication of an important copyrighted work.

Trademarks that identify brands of goods or services are protected for an indefinite time. Managers must work to preserve trademarks, however. Once the buying public starts using the trademark as a synonym for the product, rather than as a means of distinguishing its source, loss of the trademark is imminent. The trademark registration process can be complex and confusing. It can also take up to eighteen months after an application is filed for a federal registration to be issued. Early consultation with legal counsel is therefore strongly advised.

In addition to protecting his or her company's own intellectual property, a manager should also ensure that the company does not infringe the intellectual property rights of others, whether they be patents, copyrights, trademarks, or trade secrets.

A company may benefit from technology licensing. The volume of such arrangements, which offer advantages and disadvantages for both the licensor and the licensee, has increased dramatically since World War II and is accelerating. Whereas revenues from patent licensing amounted to only about $15 billion in 1990, they exceeded $100 billion by 2000 and were predicted to top $500 billion by 2005.[98] In 2005, U.S. businesses earned $57.4 billion in revenues from global licensing of intellectual property.[99]

Finally, managers should evaluate the adequacy of the company's insurance coverage for losses and claims related to electronic commerce and intellectual property. In light of the importance of computers, it is crucial to ensure that policies for property damage and business interruption cover damage to hardware and software, loss of data, and business disruptions caused by a virus, hacker attack, or other electronic assault. Commercial general liability policies, which provide coverage for liability a company may face for harm to third parties, usually cover bodily injury, property damage, personal injury, and advertising injury. Emerging issues include whether data are tangible property, whether the insertion of a defective computer part or software into a larger system causes property damage, and whether any company with a website is in the business of advertising and therefore is not covered by the usual advertising injury provisions, which can cover intellectual property infringement and defamation claims.

Some insurance companies are attempting to eliminate coverage for cyberspace and e-commerce claims from traditional policies, often with the hope of selling specialty policies to cover cyber-risks. Although the new specialty policies are potentially valuable, policyholders must be careful to assess the gaps in coverage that can result if traditional "all-risk" liability coverage is replaced with a patchwork of specialty policies. Also, the language of the new policies can vary widely, so managers need to ensure that the coverage chosen matches the risks. Finally, managers should be aware that the new language used in these policies will inevitably result in disputes about its meaning.

98. Iain M. Cockburn, *Is the Market for Technology Working Well? Obstacles to Licensing and Ways to Overcome Them* (Conference Paper, Conference on Economics of Technology Policy, Monte Verità, Switzerland, June 2007).

99. *Chapter 6: Industry: Technology, and the Global Marketplace*, SCI. & ENGINEERING INDICATORS 2008, Jan. 2008, *available at* http://www.nsf.gov/statistics/seind08/c6/c6s4.htm.

A Manager's Dilemma

Putting It into Practice

A Patent for Your Thoughts

In the 1980s, three university doctors conducting research into vitamin deficiencies found a correlation between high levels of an amino acid called homocysteine in the blood and deficiencies of two essential vitamins, folate and cobalamin. The doctors also developed more accurate methods for testing body fluids for homocysteine by using gas chromatography and mass spectrometry. They obtained a patent that claims a process for helping to diagnose deficiencies of folate and cobalamin. The patent contained several claims that covered the researchers' new methods for testing homocysteine levels using gas chromatography and mass spectrometry. Competitive Technologies, Inc. (CTI) eventually acquired ownership of the patent, which it licensed to Metabolite Laboratories, Inc.

In 1991, Laboratory Corporation of America (LabCorp) entered into a license agreement with Metabolite pursuant to which Metabolite granted LabCorp the right to use the tests described in the patent in consideration of a royalty equal to 27.5 percent of LabCorp's related revenues. The agreement permitted LabCorp to terminate the arrangement if a more cost-effective commercial alternative became available that did not infringe a valid and enforceable claim of the CTI patent. By 1998, growing recognition that elevated homocysteine levels might predict risk of heart disease had led to increased testing demand, and other companies began to produce alternative testing procedures. LabCorp decided to use a test for elevated homocysteine levels that was developed by Abbott Laboratories. LabCorp continued to pay royalties to Metabolite when it used the patented Metabolite tests, but LabCorp did not pay Metabolite royalties when it used the Abbott test, which it had concluded did not fall within the patent's claims.

In response, CTI and Metabolite sued LabCorp for patent infringement and breach of the license agreement.[100] The plaintiffs did not claim that LabCorp's use of the Abbott test infringed the CTI patent's claims for testing homocysteine. Instead, they accused LabCorp of indirect infringement arguing that LabCorp induced its customers to infringe Claim 13 of the patent, a broader claim that was not limited to the tests. Claim 13 reads in full as follows:

> A method for detecting a deficiency of cobalamin or folate in warm-blooded animals comprising the steps of:
>
> assaying a body fluid for an elevated level of total homocysteine; and correlating an elevated level of total homocysteine in said body fluid with a deficiency of cobalamin or folate.

The plaintiffs argued that Claim 13 created a protected monopoly over the process of "correlating" test results and potential vitamin deficiencies. The parties agreed that the words "assaying a body fluid" refer to the use of any test, whether patented or unpatented, that determines whether a body fluid has an "elevated level of total homocysteine." At trial, the inventors testified that Claim 13's "correlating" step consists simply of a physician's recognition that a test showing an elevated homocysteine level—by that very fact—indicates that the patient is likely to have a cobalamin or folate deficiency. Because the natural relationship between homocysteine and vitamin deficiency was well known by then, the inventors acknowledged that the "correlating" step would automatically occur in the mind of any competent doctor. Therefore, the plaintiffs asserted, LabCorp was liable for inducing infringement of the patent when it conducted the Abbott test and reported homocysteine levels to its physician customers who, because of their training, would automatically reach a conclusion about whether the person tested was suffering from a vitamin deficiency.

Should Claim 13 be invalidated on the basis that it improperly seeks to claim a basic scientific relationship between homocysteine and vitamin deficiency? If not, will its enforcement "promote the Progress of Science and useful Arts," the constitutional objective of patent and copyright protection? Was it legal, and was it ethical, for CTI and Metabolite to acquire the CTI patent and to seek to enforce it in this way? Was it legal, and was it ethical, for LabCorp to encourage doctors to order diagnostic tests for measuring homocysteine levels?

100. Metabolite Labs., Inc. v. Lab. Corp. of Am. Holdings, 370 F.3d 1354 (Fed. Cir. 2004), *cert. granted in part,* 546 U.S. 999 (2005), *and cert. dismissed in part,* 548 U.S. 124 (2006).

INSIDE STORY

TROLLING FOR DOLLARS

The term "patent troll" is generally understood to refer to a party that purchases one or more patents with the intent to enforce the patents against infringers, rather than to manufacture a patented product or supply a patented service. It has also been used to refer to companies that file patent applications covering new technologies, wait for others to develop and create markets for these technologies, and then sue these newcomers for patent infringement after they are locked into using the patented technologies.

Patent trolls operate much like any other company that seeks to exploit its patent portfolio. However, a patent troll focuses on extracting money from existing users of the patent rather than seeking out new applications for the patented technology. The patent troll often starts by sending demand letters to smaller companies, hoping that early settlements with these companies will encourage others to agree to take licenses as well.

One well-known troll is NTP, a one-man Virginia firm that has no employees and makes no products. NTP was founded in 1991 by the late inventor Thomas Campana and his patent attorney David Stout.[101] In the early 1990s, NTP filed for, and ultimately obtained, a series of patents premised on wireless e-mail. Then NTP sat back and waited for others to develop the wireless e-mail market. By 2000, wireless e-mail devices were in widespread use among executives and professionals, who had come to rely on the virtually instant access to e-mail the devices offered. NTP decided the time was right to ask a number of companies, including Research in Motion, the maker of the BlackBerry device, to pay license fees for their use of patented technology.[102]

When RIM refused to pay NTP a royalty, NTP sued, and in 2002 the U.S. District Court for the Eastern District of Virginia entered a judgment against RIM for $53 million and issued an injunction ordering RIM to stop further use of the NTP patents. This would have shut down the BlackBerry systems in the United States, but the injunction was stayed pending RIM's appeal. Although the appellate court reversed on several counts, including the grant of injunctive relief to NTP, and remanded the case to the district court for additional proceedings, there was still a chance that the district court would enter another injunction against RIM. During the litigation, the U.S. Patent and Trademark Office reexamined all seven of NTP's patents and had issued notices rejecting all of them by the end of 2005. After the court refused to delay the litigation pending the final outcome of the reexamination process, and with the threat of another injunction looming over its head, RIM agreed to settle the case for a one-time payment of $612 million.[103]

Since the NTP settlement in 2006, the U.S. Supreme Court has issued a series of decisions that have diminished the leverage that trolls can exert on other companies. The most important case, *eBay, Inc. v. MercExchange, L.L.C.*,[104] limited the availability of an injunction against a defendant in a patent-infringement suit to circumstances in which the plaintiff can satisfy a four-factor test. Because *eBay* established that an injunction in a patent-infringement suit is no longer quasi-automatic, the threat of an injunction is no longer as imminent for defendants in these cases. Additionally, *KSR International Co. v. Teleflex, Inc.*[105] established that the test of whether a patent would have been an obvious innovation requires a flexible interpretation of preexisting patents and innovations. This change may create a more substantial burden for patent holders that are asserting their rights against others, because defendants invariably assert that the patent in question is invalid. Finally, in *Medimmune, Inc. v. Genentech, Inc.*,[106] the Supreme Court held that a patent licensing agreement is not equivalent to a settlement between the parties. This decision will permit a company to take a license from a troll to avoid later claims of willful infringement, while preserving the right to subsequently challenge the validity of the agreement and the underlying patent. Whether the Supreme Court decided these cases with trolls in mind is unclear, but as a result of these decisions, defendants

CONTINUED

101. Roger Parloff, *BlackBerry Held Hostage*, CNNMONEY.COM, Nov. 29, 2005, http://money.cnn.com/2005/11/28/technology/blackberry_fortune_121205/index.htm.

102. Teresa Riordan, *Patents; A Canadian Company Appeals in Court for the Right to Keep Selling BlackBerries in the U.S.*, N.Y. TIMES, June 7, 2004, *available at* http://www.nytimes.com/2004/06/07/technology/07patent.html.

103. Rob Kelley, *BlackBerry Maker, NTP Ink $612 Million Settlement*, CNNMONEY.COM, Mar. 2, 2006, http://money.cnn.com/2006/03/03/technology/rimm_ntp/index.htm.

104. 547 U.S. 388 (2006).

105. 127 S. Ct. 1727 (2007).

106. 127 S. Ct. 764 (2007).

in future patent-infringement cases will have more weapons in their arsenal.

Recently, Congress has considered a substantial overhaul of the patent system with the Patent Reform Act. The House of Representatives passed a version of this legislation in 2007, and the Act is currently pending in the Senate. The Act would make changes in several key areas, including damages and postgrant review of patents. The proposed legislation provides a clearer definition of willful infringement.[107] Additionally, the proposed legislation changes how damages are calculated, which would be beneficial to defendants in situations where the infringed patent constitutes only a minor portion of the defendant's product. In that situation, damages would be proportional to the value of the infringed patent within the larger product, rather than being based on the overall sales of the product.[108]

The proposed legislation also establishes a process for reviewing granted patents ("post-grant" review) that seeks to eradicate invalid patents and potentially reduce the amount of patent litigation by determining the validity of a patent in a nonjudicial forum. Many consider post-grant review very important because of concerns about the number of invalid patents that the PTO issues every year. Several provisions of the legislation remain highly controversial because of the disparate impact the changes could have on different industries, and the ultimate fate of the Act in its current form is still unclear.

107. Electronic Frontier Foundation, *Patent Reform Act Stalls in the Senate,* May 2, 2008, http://www.eff.org/deeplinks/2008/05/patent-reform-act-stalls-senate.

108. Ted Frank, *There Is a Role for Congress in Patent Litigation Reform,* AM. ENTERPRISE INST. FOR PUB. POL'Y RES., LIABILITY OUTLOOK, Feb. 21, 2008, *available at* http://www.aei.org/publications/pubID.27550/pub_detail.asp.

KEY WORDS AND PHRASES

abandonment 402
actual abandonment 403
arbitrary mark 397
best mode 381
blurring 403
certification mark 397
claims 381
constructive abandonment 403
continuation application 381
contributory copyright infringement 389
contributory patent infringement 382
copyright 377
counterfeit mark 405
cybersquatting 405
declaration by the inventor 381
derivative works 377
descriptive marks 397
design patent 381
direct copyright infringement 389
direct patent infringement 382
doctrine of equivalents 382
domain name 405
drawings 381
fair use doctrine 392
fanciful mark 397
file-wrapper estoppel 382
first sale doctrine (patents) 383
first sale doctrine (copyrights) 393
genericism 398
gray market 393
hot-news exception 388
indirect patent infringement 382
inducement to infringe 382
inevitable disclosure doctrine 411
intellectual property 377
know-how 378
merger doctrine 387
nominative use 404
noninfringement 382
novel 379
patent 377
patent misuse 382
plant patent 381
prior art 379
protected expression 387
registered mask work 394
secondary meaning 398
service mark 396
show-how 378
specifications 381
statutory bar 379
suggestive mark 397
tarnishment 403
trade dress 377
trade name 396
trade secret 377
trademark 377
useful article doctrine 387
utility patent 379
utility requirement 379
vicarious copyright liability 389
web robots 393
work made for hire 387

QUESTIONS AND CASE PROBLEMS

1. LG Electronics owns several patents related to systems and methods for receiving and transmitting data in computer systems. In 2000, LG granted Intel the right under these patents to make, use, and sell microprocessors and chipsets, pursuant to a license agreement that expressly disclaimed any express or implied license for acts of infringement that might occur when a subsequent purchaser of Intel microprocessors or chipsets combined these Intel components with non-Intel components or products. Although Intel notified its customer, Quanta Computer, Inc., that it could face an infringement lawsuit by LG for combining Intel products with non-Intel products, Quanta disregarded the notice. LG sued Quanta for patent infringement. What defenses can Quanta assert against LG? [*LG Electronics, Inc. v. Bizcom Electronics, Inc.,* 453 F.3d 1364 (Fed. Cir. 2006), *cert. granted,* 128 S. Ct. 28 (2007).]

2. Virgil Richards conceived a way to regulate the translation of heterologous DNA in bacteria. He worked on this invention with three other people. Richards conceived of the idea in May 2003, reduced it to practice on May 14, 2004, and filed a patent application on June 1, 2005. Richards was sued by the co-inventors for not including their names on the application. On May 3, 2004, Richards published an article in Japan that explained his idea in detail. Clyde Taylor reduced this idea to practice on May 14, 2004, making only minor changes to the procedure disclosed in the article. He applied for a patent on June 1, 2004. Can Richards or Taylor obtain a patent for the technology? The process includes some basic scientific principles. Does that mean that both patent applications will be rejected? [*In re O'Farrell,* 853 F.2d 894 (Fed. Cir. 1988).]

3. A hypothetical new communications product is described below. After reading the product description, think up three trademarks for this product: one that is fanciful, arbitrary, or suggestive; one that is geographic, descriptive, or a personal name; and one that is nondistinctive.

   New Product Description

   This new product incorporates global positioning technology into a multifunctional device that is worn like a watch. Not only does the device provide the time, but it also allows others to determine the location of the device and thus the location of the person. Moreover, the device is equipped to send and receive simple e-mail messages. The device may be especially suited for parents hoping to track remotely the whereabouts of their children. The location of the device can be determined through an online site that requires input of an identifying password.

4. Gerald Hsu, a vice president at Cadence Design Systems, a maker of integrated circuit design software, resigned to work for Avant!, a direct competitor. Cadence told Hsu that because of its concern that he would share proprietary information and trade secrets with Avant!, it was planning to sue him and Avant! for trade secret misappropriation. Hsu was able to negotiate a mutual general release with Cadence that released all parties from claims against each other concerning any trade secret misappropriation or other unfair competition at the time of the settlement. One year later, a Cadence engineer discovered line-by-line copying of Cadence code in an Avant! software product. It turned out the copying occurred four years earlier—three years before the general release—and was continuing through the present day. Cadence argued that it could still bring a trade secret misappropriation against Avant! because the misappropriation continued to occur after the general release. Hsu and Avant! argued that the general release precluded any suit for misappropriation occurring before the date of the release. Who should prevail? [*Cadence Design Systems v. Avant! Corp.,* 253 F.3d 1147 (9th Cir. 2001).]

5. McNeil Nutritionals sells Splenda, a highly successful national brand of sucralose, in yellow boxes and bags with blue lettering; the name "Splenda" is on the front in italicized blue lettering, surrounded by a white, oval-shaped cloud. The boxes and bags display photographs of different physical props, such as a white cup of coffee and saucer, a glass and pitcher of iced tea, and a bowl of cereal and a scoop of Splenda behind a piece of pie on a plate. The defendant's private label and store brands are also sold in yellow boxes and bags, with blue or black lettering (some outlined in white) and photographs of various items that can use the sweetener. Applying the following ten-factor test to determine whether there is a likelihood of confusion, does the defendant's packaging infringe McNeil's packaging? What other facts would you need to know? What steps could the defendant take to avoid a finding of infringement?

   The ten factors are (1) degree of similarity between the plaintiff's trade dress and the allegedly infringing trade dress; (2) strength of the plaintiff's trade dress; (3) price of the goods and other factors indicative of the care and attention expected of consumers when making a purchase; (4) length of time the defendant has used the trade dress without evidence of actual confusion arising; (5) intent of the defendant in adopting its trade dress; (6) evidence of actual confusion; (7) whether the goods, although not competing, are marketed through the same channels of trade and advertised through the same media; (8) extent to which the targets of the parties' sales efforts are the same; (9) relationship of the goods in the minds of consumers because of the similarity of function; and (10) other facts suggesting the consuming public might expect the plaintiff to manufacture a product in the defendant's market, or that the plaintiff is likely to expand into that market. [*McNeil Nutritionals, LLC v. Heartland Sweeteners, LLC,* 511 F.3d 350 (3d Cir. 2007).]

6. JCW Investments, Inc., doing business as Tekky Toys, manufactures "Meet Pull My Finger Fred," a plush doll. Fred is a white, middle-aged, overweight man with black hair and a receding hairline, sitting in an armchair wearing a white tank top and blue pants. When one squeezes Fred's extended finger on his right hand, he farts. He also makes crude funny statements about bodily noises, such as "Did somebody step on a duck?" or "Silent but deadly." JCW was not happy when Novelty, Inc. began producing Fartman, a plush doll of a white, middle-aged, overweight man with black hair and a receding hairline sitting in an armchair wearing a white tank top and blue pants. Fartman (as his name suggests) also farts when his finger is squeezed and cracks jokes about bodily functions. Can JCW sue Novelty? If so, on what basis? What defenses could Novelty assert on its behalf? [*JCW Investments, Inc. v. Novelty, Inc.,* 509 F.3d 339 (7th Cir. 2007).]

7. Martha Graham, one of the founders of modern dance, created the nonprofit Martha Graham Center of Contemporary Dance to support her work and the work of other artists. She was its artistic director and created much of her choreography while employed by the center; after 1966, her primary duty was to create new dances. At her death in 1991, Graham left her estate, including rights and interests in her work, to a friend, Ronald Portas, who opened a rival dance group, the Martha Graham School and Dance Foundation. Portas claimed the copyrights to all Graham's choreography. The Graham Center, however, claimed ownership under the "work for hire" doctrine. In arguments before the court, Portas claimed that the Center's lack of direct control over Graham's creative endeavors exempts Graham's choreography from the "work for hire" doctrine. Should the court accept this exemption? What result? [*Martha Graham School & Dance Foundation v. Martha Graham Center of Contemporary Dance,* 380 F.3d 624 (2d Cir. 2004).]

8. FairTest, a nonprofit organization dedicated to improving standardization tests, posted data on its website that demonstrated that minorities and low-income students score lower on the SAT and ACT than white and upper-class students. The College Board, the nonprofit that administers the SAT, demanded that FairTest remove the data, claiming that it was using College Board copyrighted data without permission. The College Board has a formal process by which it grants permission to organizations wishing to use its data; FairTest did not use this process. In reply, FairTest alleged that the data were not owned by the College Board and that even if they were, the data are widely available in the public domain, thus removing them from copyright protection. Does FairTest's defense have merit? [*See* http://www.fairtest.org/univ/FT_Response_to_CB.html.]

12

ENVIRONMENTAL LAW

INTRODUCTION

Role in Business Management

Environmental law consists of numerous federal, state, and local laws with the common objective of protecting human health and the environment. These laws are of great concern to a variety of firms, many of which may not have considered environmental liability when they first went into business.

Some industries (such as petroleum, mining, and chemical manufacturing) are well accustomed to intense government regulation of the environmental effects of their operations. In the last forty years, however, the scope and impact of environmental laws have grown steadily. Today, real estate owners and investors, developers, insurance companies, and financial institutions find that their operations, too, are often affected by laws and regulations intended to protect the environment. In addition, concerns about global warming have prompted virtually every company to consider ways to reduce its *carbon footprint*, the amount of carbon dioxide and other greenhouse gases it releases into the air.

Failure to comply with environmental laws can result in large judgments and punitive fines for companies, as well as criminal penalties (including imprisonment) for the corporate executives responsible for these violations. In 2004, an asbestos removal company executive was sentenced to twenty-five years in prison, the longest sentence ever issued under federal environmental laws, after being convicted of a decade's worth of Clean Air Act violations. The executive had repeatedly ordered workers to remove asbestos without wetting it first and falsified at least 1,500 air quality reports.[1]

1. Michelle York, *Father and Son Get Long Terms in Defective Asbestos Removal*, N.Y. TIMES, Dec. 24, 2004, at 5.

CHAPTER OVERVIEW

This chapter examines four federal environmental laws that illustrate the importance of environmental regulation for an expanding scope of business activities. The Clean Air Act, the Clean Water Act, and the Resource Conservation and Recovery Act are discussed as examples of environmental statutes that control the release of pollutants into the air, water, and land. The Comprehensive Environmental Response, Compensation, and Liability Act is discussed as an example of a remedial statute with broad application to all kinds of businesses and individuals. The chapter also addresses the potential liability under the environmental laws of shareholders, directors, officers, and managers, as well as affiliated companies and lenders. We outline the key elements of effective compliance programs and conclude with a discussion of international efforts, including the Kyoto Protocol, to stop global warming.

ENVIRONMENTAL LAWS

In recent decades, growing awareness of the environmental problems posed by an industrial society has led to an increase in the number and reach of environmental laws and regulations at both the federal and state levels.

COMMON LAW NUISANCE

Historically, public officials relied primarily on the common law tort theory of nuisance to control industrial and agricultural activities that interfered with the health or comfort of the community. Thus, industrial odors, noise, smoke, and pollutants of all kinds were the subjects of numerous lawsuits that attempted to balance the legitimate business interests of the polluter with the private interests of the surrounding community. But the need to file a lawsuit in each case and the complexity of the common law made nuisance a cumbersome way to control environmental pollution in an industrial society. Moreover, a lawsuit could not prevent pollution; it could only provide a remedy after the fact. Today, state and federal regulatory programs have largely replaced common law nuisance as a means of pollution control.

ENVIRONMENTAL STATUTES AND REGULATIONS

Environmental law consists of federal and state statutes, administrative regulations, and the administrative and judicial interpretations of their meaning. Environmental statutes establish policy, set goals, and authorize the executive branch or one of its administrative agencies to adopt regulations specifying how the law will be implemented. The statutes and regulations are interpreted and applied in administrative and judicial proceedings. In addition, administrative agencies, such as the Environmental Protection Agency, often issue policy statements and technical guidance, which do not have the force of law but guide enforcement efforts and provide assistance to the regulated community.

Three Categories

There are three broad categories of environmental law. The largest category consists of laws that regulate the release of pollutants into the air, water, or ground. These laws usually authorize the government to issue and enforce permits for release of pollutants. They may also authorize emergency responses and remedial action if, for example, improper waste disposal or accidental chemical spills threaten human health or the environment. Statutes in this category include the Clean Air Act; the Federal Water Pollution Control Act, as amended by the Clean Water Act; the Solid Waste Disposal Act, as amended by the Resource Conservation and Recovery Act (RCRA); the Comprehensive Environmental Response, Compensation, and Liability Act (CERCLA or Superfund);[2] and similar state laws. These four federal pollution-control laws are discussed in this chapter.

A second category governs the manufacture, sale, distribution, and use of chemical substances as commercial products. This category includes (1) the Federal Insecticide, Fungicide and Rodenticide Act, which applies to pesticide products; and (2) the Toxic Substances Control Act, which applies to all chemical substances either manufactured in or imported into the United States, excluding certain substances that are regulated under other federal laws. The Safe Drinking Water Act, which governs the quality of drinking water served by public drinking-water systems, can also be included in this category.

A third category includes laws that require government decision makers to take into account the effects of their decisions on the quality of the environment. These include the National Environmental Policy Act of 1969 (NEPA)[3] and similar laws adopted by most states. NEPA affects all business activities that require governmental authorizations, permits, or licenses.[4]

NATURAL RESOURCES LAWS

Although environmental law contributes to the protection of natural resources, it generally does not include

2. As amended by the Superfund Amendments and Reauthorization Act of 1986, the Superfund Recycling Equity Act of 1999, and the Small Business Liability Relief and Brownfields Revitalization Act of 2002. *See* the Superfund section on laws, policy, and guidance on the EPA's website, http://www.epa.gov/superfund/policy/index.htm.

3. Codified, as amended, at 42 U.S.C. §§ 4321–4370f.

4. The U.S. Supreme Court upheld the Federal Motor Carrier Safety Administration's proposed rules concerning Mexican motor carriers even though the agency did not consider the environmental impact of having more Mexican trucks after an executive order was issued allowing a larger number to cross the U.S. border. Dep't of Transp. v. Pub. Citizens, 541 U.S. 752 (2004). The Court reasoned that because the agency lacked discretion to prevent these cross-border operations, neither NEPA nor the Clear Air Act required an evaluation of their environmental effects.

INTERNATIONAL SNAPSHOT

Under the treaty between members of the European Union, "environmental protection is to be integrated into the definition and implementation of all Community activities and policies" and not just segregated to legislation enacted specifically to address broad environmental concerns. Central to environmental policy acts is the requirement that the government expressly consider environmental values in its decision making and that it document this consideration in written environmental impact reports that can be reviewed by the public. These requirements are especially important when the government itself is responsible for major development projects.

wilderness preservation, wildlife protection,[5] coastal zone management, energy conservation, national park designation, and the like. Those laws are commonly referred to as *natural resources laws*. Nor does environmental law cover land-use regulation and zoning. Such laws, which are generally administered by local governments, are commonly referred to as land-use laws and are discussed in Chapter 19.

Administration of Environmental Laws

The *Environmental Protection Agency (EPA)* administers all the federal laws that set national goals and policies for environmental protection, except the National Environmental Policy Act, which is administered by the Council on Environmental Quality. The EPA was created in 1970 by an executive order and operates under the supervision of the President. The EPA administrator and assistant administrators are appointed by the President with the advice and consent of the Senate. The EPA is, however, neither an independent agency nor a cabinet-level department.

Several of the assistant administrators are responsible for administering the agency's regulatory programs; others have internal administrative functions. These national program managers share responsibility with the ten regional administrators who head each of the ten EPA regional offices. The national managers at headquarters develop policy and set goals for the regional offices. The regional administrators take responsibility for day-to-day program operation.

State Programs

State agencies administer state laws and, with the authorization of the EPA, federal laws as well. State environmental laws and programs often predate the comparable federal programs. Moreover, many states have laws that are more stringent and more comprehensive than the federal laws. For example, California's hazardous-waste-management laws, water-quality-control laws, underground-tank regulations, and ban on the land disposal of certain hazardous wastes all predate and, in some cases, provided the model for subsequent federal legislation.

In light of these preexisting state environmental programs and the need to reduce the EPA's administrative burden, Congress gave the EPA the authority to authorize or approve a state program in lieu of the federal program in that state. The EPA does not delegate its federal authority; it merely approves a state program as "equivalent to or more stringent than" the federal program and then refrains from implementing the federal program in that state. The EPA generally does provide oversight, however. It retains its enforcement authority and may revoke its authorization if the state program fails to meet federal requirements. In addition, as discussed further below, in some instances the EPA invokes federal preemption (discussed in Chapter 4) to prevent the states from inposing stricter standards than the ones mandated by the EPA.

Industry Participation

Environmental laws and regulations are constantly changing as new threats to human health and the environment become apparent and new ways are discovered to manage such threats safely and economically. Congressional or administrative agency staff may be unaware of how a proposed law or regulation may affect a particular industry and usually welcome constructive industry participation in the law- and rule-making process. This is particularly the case when a company can propose alternative ways to accomplish the same legislative goals.

In the final months of the George W. Bush administration, a number of firms lobbied for a variety of so-called midnight regulations, including updating the air-monitoring rules for dry cleaners, simplifying the rules for recycling solid waste, and exempting feedlots from the requirement

> **› Ethical Consideration**
>
> Environmental laws establish minimum standards to which companies must adhere. Companies also have fiduciary duties to their shareholders, and many labor activists argue that companies have similar duties to their employees. Is it ethical for a manager to adhere to stricter standards than mandated by law when such adherence will raise costs, reduce shareholder returns, and possibly jeopardize existing jobs? Is it more ethical, or less, to do so when the standards are to be implemented in a developing country with no environmental laws?

5. The Ninth Circuit ruled that dolphins, whales, and other cetaceans did not have standing under the Endangered Species Act to sue to challenge the Navy's use of active sonar. Cetacean Cmty. v. Bush, 386 F.3d 1169 (9th Cir. 2004). The court dismissed as dicta its statement in *Palila v. Hawaii Department of Land & Natural Resources*, 852 F.2d 1106, 1107 (9th Cir. 1988), that the Hawaiian Palila bird "has legal status and wings its way into federal court as a plaintiff in its own right" to enforce the Endangered Species Act.

of obtaining a discharge permit under the Clean Water Act. Rick Melbert, director of regulatory policy at the nonpartisan group OMB Watch, remarked: "Whatever your political agenda, you're going to try to accomplish it through these regulations. . . . There's much less public scrutiny, and so much less transparency."[6]

The Clean Air Act

The Clean Air Act[7] sets four types of air quality goals. First, it requires the EPA to establish *national ambient air quality standards (NAAQS)*, which are the maximum levels of pollutants in the outdoor air that, with adequate margins of safety, are compatible with public health.[8] Standards must be set without regard for cost considerations.[9] The EPA has set standards for six pollutants: (1) particulate matter, (2) sulfur dioxide, (3) ozone, (4) nitrogen dioxide, (5) carbon monoxide, and (6) lead. Every state and locality must seek to achieve and maintain these national air quality standards, which are revised periodically. If a nonattainment area fails to develop an adequate plan to attain the national standard, the federal government is required to impose penalties, such as bans on construction of new sources of pollution, limits on drinking-water hookups, withholding of federal air-pollution funds, and limits on the use of federal highway funds. By affecting decisions concerning land use and transportation, as well as imposing emission controls, the law helps determine which areas of the country and which industrial sectors will be able to grow.

Second, the Clean Air Act requires that air quality in those areas that already meet the NAAQS not be allowed to deteriorate. Third, the Act requires the preservation of natural visibility within the major national parks and wilderness areas. Fourth, it requires the EPA to establish emission standards that protect public health, with an ample margin of safety, from hazardous air pollutants.[10]

The law also requires reductions in vehicle tail-pipe emissions of certain pollutants and the use of reformulated gasoline. It mandates that fleets use clean, low-emission fuels in some nonattainment areas. Major sources of some 200 hazardous air pollutants are required to meet emission limits based on best available control technology. Electric power plants must reduce emissions that lead to the formation of acid rain. Finally, the law phased out methylchloroform and chlorofluorocarbons and placed limitations on the production of certain substitute chemicals.

In the following case, the U.S. Court of Appeals for the District of Columbia Circuit invalidated a rule that would have relieved electric power plants from an obligation to use best available technology to reduce mercury emissions.

6. Elizabeth Williamson, *Rush Is On to Cement Regulations: Industries Bet They'll Fare Better with This White House Than the Next One*, Wall St. J., Mar. 11, 2008, at A6.
7. 42 U.S.C. § 7401 *et seq.* The Fifth Circuit held that the Clean Air Act was a valid exercise of Congress's power under the Commerce Clause in *United States v. Ho*, 311 F.3d 589 (5th Cir. 2002), *cert. denied*, 539 U.S. 914 (2003).
8. The U.S. Supreme Court rejected claims that the Act constituted an unconstitutional delegation of legislative power because it arguably left the EPA free to set the NAAQS at any point between zero and concentrations that would yield a "killer fog." Whitman v. Am. Trucking Ass'ns, 531 U.S. 457 (2001).
9. *Id.*
10. *See also* Massachusetts v. EPA, 549 U.S. 497 (2007) (rejecting the EPA's contention that the agency was not authorized to regulate vehicle emissions as a means of combating global warming and pointing out that the Clean Air Act granted the power to regulate emissions to the agency and that policy considerations were irrelevant to that mandate).

A CASE IN POINT

CASE 16.1

New Jersey v. EPA

United States Court of Appeals for the District of Columbia

517 F.3d 574 (D.C. Cir. 2008).

Summary

Facts In 2000, acting pursuant to Section 112 of the Clean Air Act, the EPA concluded that it was "appropriate and necessary" to regulate mercury emissions from coal- and oil-fired electric utility steam generating units (EGUs) because they could "cause, or contribute to, an increase in mortality or an increase in serious irreversible or incapacitating reversible illness."[11] When mercury drops out of the air, it accumulates in rivers and streams and is stored in the tissues of fish. If pregnant women or children eat the fish, the mercury can cause the child to suffer serious developmental problems. In 2005, the EPA issued a rule purporting to remove coal- and oil-fired EGUs from the Section 112 list (the Delisting Rule). A second rule adopted that same year (1) set

CONTINUED

11. 42 U.S.C. § 7412(a)(1).

performance standards pursuant to Section 111 for new coalfired EGUs; (2) established a national mercury emissions cap for new and existing EGUs, allocating each state and certain tribal areas a mercury emissions budget; and (3) created a voluntary market-based cap-and-trade program for new and existing coal-fired EGUs. In a *cap-and-trade system,* plants' allowable emissions would be capped, and plants that emitted more than their allotments could buy credits from plants with emissions below the specified levels. New Jersey and fourteen other states, the city of Baltimore, and various environmental organizations sued to invalidate both rules on the grounds that the EPA violated Section 112's plain text when it delisted the EGUs and acted in an arbitrary and capricious manner when it reversed its determination that regulation of the EGUs' release of mercury was appropriate and necessary.

ISSUE PRESENTED Did the EPA violate the Clean Air Act when it removed EGUs from the list of sources of mercury pollution listed in the Clean Air Act after having previously determined that the release of mercury from the plants was hazardous to human health?

SUMMARY OF OPINION The U.S. Court of Appeals for the District of Columbia Circuit began by noting that Congress's concern about the EPA's slow pace in regulating sources of hazardous air pollution resulted in amendments to the Clean Air Act in 1990 that eliminated much of the EPA's discretion to regulate sources of hazardous air pollution. In the eighteen years following passage of Section 112 in 1970, the EPA had listed only eight pollutants and established standards for only seven of these, which addressed only a limited selection of possible pollution sources. The court explained that the 1990 amendments required the EPA to regulate more than 100 specific pollutants, including mercury. Congress gave the EPA the power, pursuant to Section 112(c)(9), to remove sources of pollutants from the Section 112 list, but only after determining that "emissions from no source in the category or subcategory concerned . . . exceed a level which is adequate to protect public health with an ample margin of safety and no adverse environmental effect will result from emissions from any source." Because the EPA failed to make the requisite finding before adopting the Delisting Rule, the court invalidated that rule and the rule purporting to regulate EGUs under Section 111.

The court rejected the EPA's argument that it had the authority to remove coal- and oil-fired plants from the Section 112(c) list at any time it made a negative "appropriate and necessary" finding. It also rejected, as contrary to the EPA's 2000 determination, the EPA's assertion that the EGUs were not a source meeting the statutory criteria for listing under Section 112. Citing *Chevron, U.S.A., Inc. v. Natural Resources Defense Council, Inc.,*[12] the court ruled that Congress had directly spoken to the issue of delisting and that "the court, as well as the agency, must give effect to the unambiguously expressed intent of Congress."[13] The court characterized the EPA's reasoning as "the logic of the Queen of Hearts, substituting EPA's desires for the plain text of section 112(c)(9)." (In Lewis Carroll's *Alice in Wonderland,* the Queen of Hearts declares, "Sentence first—verdict afterwards.") Because the EPA failed to make the findings required by Section 112(c)(9) to delist the EGUs from the Section 112(c)(1) list, both EPA rules were invalid.

RESULT Both the Delisting Rule and the cap-and-trade rules were invalidated.

COMMENTS Environmentalists cautioned that the cap-and-trade system could result in "hot spots" of pollution if local plants could buy their way out of the obligation to use the best available technology to cut mercury emissions.[14] EPA spokesperson Jonathan Shrader criticized the court's ruling, saying, "We have now no control over existing power plants, which should be

CONTINUED

12. 467 U.S. 837 (1984).
13. Quoting *id.* at 843–44.
14. David A. Fahrenthold & Steven Mufson, *Court Rejects Emission "Trades,"* WASH. POST, Feb. 9, 2008.

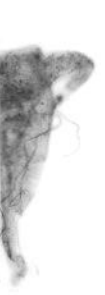

of concern to the American people," and asserting that the court's ruling invalidated a program that would have reduced mercury emissions by 70 percent.[15] Professor Robert Percival of the University of Maryland commented, "It's fairly clear that even judges that are, you know, not that fond of environmental regulation are kind of appalled at how willing the [administration] has been to try to bend the law."[16]

15. *Id.*

16. *Id.*

Federal and State Regulation of Greenhouse Gases

In *Masssachusetts v. EPA*,[17] the U.S. Supreme Court confirmed the EPA's authority to regulate carbon dioxide and other greenhouse gases in motor vehicles and directed the EPA to make a finding regarding its obligation to regulate such emissions. The Court also ordered the EPA to consider whether it should provide a waiver under the Clean Air Act to permit California to impose the tough fuel economy standards embodied in California Health and Safety Code Section 43018.5(b)(1). California's standards are stricter than those imposed under federal law. Stressing the need for a uniform set of national standards, the EPA denied California's waiver request on December 19, 2007.[18]

In June 2008, the U.S. District Court for the Eastern District of California refused to lift an injunction prohibiting California from enforcing its fuel economy standards until a waiver of federal preemption is granted or federal legislation permitting their enforcement is enacted.[19] The court did, however, decline to insulate automobile and truck manufacturers from a California provision that would give them only forty-five days to conform to the tougher California standards following the grant of a waiver of federal preemption by the EPA. After noting that "[e]nvironmental regulation is a constantly evolving part of the normal business landscape," the court stated:

> Plaintiffs' arguments suggest, without actually so stating, that at least some of the Plaintiff auto manufacturers made a conscious decision to proceed on the assumption that a waiver of federal preemption would never be granted by the EPA. If it turns out that the manufacturers that made that assumption are wrong, those Plaintiff auto manufacturers may well be at a significant disadvantage relative to auto manufacturers that are currently positioned more favorably with respect to compliance. But, so far as this court can discern, the choice to proceed as though California would never be granted waiver of federal preemption is fundamentally just a business decision that, like any other, may have negative consequences if wrongly made. It is not up to the courts to deflect the burden of such business decisions.

"I think we agree, gentlemen, that one can respect Mother Nature without coddling her."

A rider to the 2008 Consolidated Appropriations Act signed by President Bush on December 26, 2007, directed the EPA "to require mandatory reporting of greenhouse gases above appropriate thresholds."[20] Many see this as a

17. 549 U.S. 497 (2007) (Case 6.2).

18. *EPA Begins Rule on Greenhouse Gas Registry; Will Avoid Duplicative Reporting, Official Says,* 76 U.S.L.W. 2471 (2008).

19. Cent. Valley Chrysler-Jeep, Inc. v. Goldstene, 2008 U.S. Dist. LEXIS 50420 (June 24, 2008).

20. *EPA Begins Rule on Greenhouse Gas Registry, supra* note 18.

necessary first step in creating a national cap-and-trade program. The EPA announced that the new rule, which under the Act must be proposed before October 2008 and finalized before July 2009, will cover "basically all sectors of the economy."[21]

In June 2008, the EPA sent the Office of Management and Budget a draft proposal for regulating greenhouse gas emissions from vehicles under the Clean Air Act. In response, the Departments of Agriculture, Commerce, Energy, and Transportation declared that "the Clean Air Act is fundamentally ill-suited to the effective regulation of greenhouse gas emissions."[22] Edward Lazear, chair of the Council of Economic Advisers, and John H. Marburger, director of the Office of Science and Technology Policy, asserted that "acting in a globally uncoordinated fashion will put the United States at a competitive disadvantage. . . . If businesses in other countries do not suffer the penalty for emitting greenhouse gases, production has an incentive to move abroad."[23] One month later, EPA Administrator Stephen Johnson announced that the EPA had decided to defer making a regulatory determination of whether emissions of greenhouse gases endanger public health and welfare and should be regulated under the Clean Air Act.[24] Instead, the EPA issued an advanced notice of proposed rulemaking requesting public comment on the advantages and disadvantages of regulating emissions under the Clean Air Act, technologies for reducing emissions, and alternative regulatory approaches.[25]

The Clean Water Act

The Federal Water Pollution Control Act was adopted in 1972 and was substantially amended by the Clean Water Act of 1977 and by the Water Quality Act of 1987. The Act, as amended, is commonly referred to as the Clean Water Act.[26] The principal goal of the Clean Water Act is to eliminate the discharge of pollutants into the navigable waters of the United States.

Navigable waters are all "waters of the United States which are used in interstate commerce," including "all freshwater wetlands that are adjacent to all other covered waterways." In *Solid Waste Agency of Northern Cook County v. Army Corps of Engineers,*[27] the U.S. Supreme Court ruled that an abandoned sand and gravel pit in northern Illinois that provided habitat for migratory birds did not constitute "navigable waters" within the meaning of the Clean Water Act. The Court held that the Act does not apply to ponds that are not adjacent to open water, reasoning that the term "navigable" in the statute reflected Congress's intention to limit application of the Clean Water Act to waters that are or have been navigable in fact or that could reasonably be made so. Permitting federal jurisdiction over ponds and mudflats would impinge on the states' traditional power over land and water use. In *Rapanos v. United States,*[28] the Court further refined its interpretation of "waters of the United States" to include "those relatively permanent, standing or continuously flowing bodies of water 'forming geographic features'" such as streams, oceans, rivers, and lakes, but excluding "channels through which water flows intermittently or ephemerally, or channels that periodically provide drainage for rainfall."[29]

National Pollutant Discharge Elimination System

The principal regulatory program established by the Clean Water Act is the *National Pollutant Discharge Elimination System (NPDES),* which requires permits for the discharge of pollutants from any point source to navigable waters. EPA regulations establish *national effluent limitations,* which impose increasingly stringent restrictions on pollutant discharges, based on the availability of economically achievable treatment and recycling technologies. More stringent restrictions are imposed on new sources through the setting of national standards of performance. General and specific industry pretreatment standards are set for discharges to *publicly owned sewage treatment works (POTWs).* The pretreatment standards are designed to ensure the effective operation of the POTW and to avoid the pass-through of pollutants. The POTW, in turn, must comply with its own NPDES permit for the discharge of treated waters. The NPDES program is administered largely through approved state programs, although the EPA maintains NPDES authority in areas not within the jurisdictions of states having EPA-approved programs.

21. *Id.*
22. *EPA Proposal Lacks Agency Support, Is Not Administrative Policy, OMB Says,* 77 U.S.L.W. 2058 (2008).
23. *Id.*
24. *EPA Requests Comments, Defers Decision on Whether Warming Imperils Public Health,* 77 U.S.L.W. 2057 (2008).
25. 73 Fed. Reg. 44,354 (July 30, 2008).
26. 33 U.S.C. § 1251 *et seq.*
27. 531 U.S. 159 (2001).
28. 547 U.S. 715 (2006).
29. *Id* at 739.

INDIVIDUAL LIABILITY OF CORPORATE OFFICERS

A corporate officer can be held civilly liable under the Clean Water Act if he or she had the authority to exercise control over the activity that caused the unlawful discharge. A corporate officer can also be held criminally responsible if he or she knowingly violated the act.

In *United States v. Iverson,*[30] the U.S. Court of Appeals for the Ninth Circuit upheld a one-year prison sentence for the president and chairman of the board of CH20, Inc., a manufacturer of acid cleaners and alkaline compounds, after finding that he had actual authority to prevent the company's dumping of industrial waste into a sewer. The executive was also fined $75,000 and received an additional sentence of three years of supervised release.

Similarly, the owner of a steel drum recycling company was found to have directed employees to dispose of hazardous waste water in various clandestine ways, from dumping it directly into sewers to bribing a city worker to put drums of waste in the city incinerator. He even ordered the construction of a fake evaporation tank that deceived enforcement officials into believing that contaminated water was being properly handled. Calling the owner's actions "environmental homicide," the district court judge sentenced to him to thirteen years in prison and ordered him to pay $14,000 in restitution.[31]

THE RESOURCE CONSERVATION AND RECOVERY ACT

The Solid Waste Disposal Act, as amended by the Resource Conservation and Recovery Act of 1976 and the Hazardous and Solid Waste Amendments of 1984 (RCRA),[32] governs the management of hazardous wastes. The Act authorizes the EPA to identify and list hazardous wastes, to develop standards for the management of hazardous wastes by generators and transporters of wastes, and to set standards for the construction and operation of hazardous waste treatment, storage, and disposal facilities. RCRA covers current and future hazardous waste treatment facilities. Abandoned or historically polluted sites are governed by the Comprehensive Environmental Response, Compensation, and Liability Act (CERCLA), discussed later in this chapter. The Federal Facility Compliance Act of 1992 and the Land Disposal Program Flexibility Act of 1996 strengthened enforcement of RCRA at federal facilities and eased RCRA-based restricitions on the disposal of certain types of waste, respectively.[33]

CRADLE-TO-GRAVE RESPONSIBILITY

RCRA imposes "cradle-to-grave" responsibility on generators of hazardous waste. Each generator must obtain an EPA identification number and use a transportation manifest when transporting wastes for treatment or disposal. This allows the EPA to track the transportation, treatment, and disposal of hazardous wastes from the generator's facility to the final disposal site. A manifest is also required to transport hazardous wastes to an authorized storage facility.

RCRA bans the disposal of hazardous wastes onto land without treatment to render them less hazardous. To comply with the EPA's requirements for disposal on land, companies that generate hazardous waste may have to make substantial capital investments in treatment systems or incur increased costs for having wastes treated elsewhere prior to disposal.

Generators of hazardous waste must certify that they have a program in place to reduce the quantity and toxicity of their wastes. They must also certify that they are disposing of their wastes in a manner that, to the extent practicable, minimizes future threats to human health and the environment.

Owners and operators of hazardous waste facilities must obtain permits and comply with stringent standards for the construction and operation of their facilities. These standards include maintaining certain liability insurance coverage and providing financial assurances that show the owner/operator has the financial wherewithal to close the facility at the appropriate time and to maintain it properly after closure.

Even though hazardous waste transporters and treatment and storage facilities are closely regulated, companies that generate hazardous wastes must carefully select treatment, transportation, and disposal facilities. Liability may be imposed not only on the persons who "own or operate" the facility but also on those who have used the facility for the storage, treatment, or disposal of wastes. Persons who "contributed" to the improper waste disposal are also potentially liable. This includes individuals, such as officers who had no direct involvement in the disposal but had the authority to control the corporation's actions and failed to do so.

30. 162 F.3d 1015 (9th Cir. 1998).

31. Richard Danielson, *Lutz Man Gets 13 Years for Toxic Waste Dumping,* St. Petersburg Times, Aug. 17, 1999, at 1B.

32. 42 U.S.C. § 6901 *et seq.*

33. *See* the Wastes section on laws and regulations on the EPA's website, http://www.epa.gov/osw/laws-reg.htm.

Strategic Environmental Management

Although the use of laws, regulations, and standards, referred to as "command and control" policy, is still an important tool for ensuring that companies' operations do not pollute the environment, many corporations have gone beyond simply complying with the laws.[a] In response to the Union Carbide plant explosion in Bhopal, India, in 1984, which killed and injured thousands of people, the U.S. Chemical Manufacturers Association required its members to implement a program, called Responsible Care, to improve environmental performance.

Two years later, Congress enacted the Superfund Amendments and Reauthorization Act (SARA), which required companies to publish emission levels for hundreds of chemicals. This opened corporate books to public scrutiny and prompted many companies to try to reduce emissions. For example, in 1988, Monsanto announced a plan to reduce its emissions by 90 percent. Other companies, such as AT&T, made similar commitments to go beyond simply complying with the legal limits.

Corporations also broadened their focus to include the materials they used in production, as well as the pollutants they generated. After scrutinizing both their inputs and outputs, companies began to implement principles of "eco-efficiency" in their operations by using less energy, fewer new materials, and more reused and recycled materials. For example, Lockheed reduced the amount of energy it used in its 600,000-square-foot building by using sunlight rather than electrical lighting. This required an initial investment of $2 million, but saved the company $500,000 per year thereafter. Lockheed's use of sunlight also increased employee productivity.

During this period, corporations also began to look for pollution-prevention and eco-efficiency strategies that would produce economic savings, as well as environmental benefits. Michael E. Porter and Claas van der Linde maintained that firms could remain competitive and, in fact, gain competitive advantage through *innovation offsets,* technological advantages gained by companies that meet the challenge of environmental regulations and discover lower costs and better-quality products as a result.[b] Corporations started implementing the concept of *strategic environmental management,* which advocates placing environmental management on the profit side of the corporation rather than the cost side. This represented a profound shift in how companies viewed their relationship with the environment.

In the next era of corporate environmentalism that began in the 1990s and continues in the twenty-first century, companies are working not just to reduce waste but to eliminate it altogether. This process involves looking at whole systems, rather than the individual parts, to create designs that take advantage of feedback loops within the company's operations. Some companies have begun to sell services rather than products, for example, by providing a rug or copying machine to a corporation for a period of time and then recycling it for continued use.

Companies are also working with other firms for both economic and environmental benefit. For example, *industrial ecology* is an approach that advocates a systems approach to eco-efficiency and applies it to groups of corporations working together. The best-known application of this approach is in Kalundborg, Denmark, where a refinery, power plant, pharmaceutical company, and fish farm located next to each other reduce costs by using each other's waste as resource inputs. For example, heat generated from one operation is used in another company's manufacturing operations.

Finally, corporations have begun to exploit the opportunities created by environmental problems.[c] Honda and Toyota have introduced hybrid cars and SUVs with reduced emissions and increased gas mileage and are racing to develop vehicles powered by fuel cells. Energy companies are also investing in developing alternative sources of energy.

Forest Reinhardt has identified five approaches that companies can take to incorporate environmental issues into their business model: (1) differentiate their products by making them environmentally friendly and, as a result, command high prices; (2) "manage" competitors by imposing a set of private regulations or helping government write rules; (3) cut costs by implementing environmental practices; (4) manage risk and reduce lawsuits and accidents; and (5) make systemic changes concerning environmental issues that will redefine competition in their markets.[d]

---

a. This "Economic Perspective" is based in part on CARL FRANKEL, IN EARTH'S COMPANY: BUSINESS, ENVIRONMENT, AND THE CHALLENGE OF SUSTAINABILITY (1998).

b. Michael E. Porter & Claas van der Linde, *Green and Competitive: Ending the Stalemate, in* MICHAEL E. PORTER, ON COMPETITION 351–75 (1980).

c. *See* C. Nehrt, *Maintainability of First Mover Advantages When Environmental Regulations Differ Between Countries,* 23 ACAD. MGMT. REV. 77 (1998); J. Alberto Aragon-Correa & Sanjay Sharma, *A Contingent Resource-Based View of Proactive Corporate Environmental Strategy,* 28 ACAD. MGMT. REV. 71 (2003).

d. FOREST REINHARDT, DOWN TO EARTH: APPLYING BUSINESS PRINCIPLES TO ENVIRONMENTAL MANAGEMENT (2000).

CRIMINAL LIABILITY

Although RCRA imposes strict civil liability, a criminal violation requires some sort of knowledge. In particular, RCRA provides criminal sanctions for any person who "knowingly transports any hazardous waste identified or listed under this subchapter to a facility which does not have a permit."[34] As explained in Chapter 15, it is not always clear how far down the sentence the word "knowingly" travels.

In *United States v. Hayes International Corp.*,[35] the U.S. Court of Appeals for the Eleventh Circuit held that knowledge of the regulation banning transport of hazardous waste to an unlicensed facility is not an element of the offense. Furthermore, the defendants could be found guilty even if they did not know that the substance being disposed of was a hazardous waste within the meaning of the regulations. It was enough that they knew that they were disposing of a mixture of paint and solvents. The court distinguished *Liparota v. United States*,[36] which required knowledge that the purchase of food stamps was illegal, on the grounds that (1) the food stamp law required "knowing violation of a regulation" and (2) RCRA, unlike the food stamp law, was a public welfare statute involving a heavily regulated area with great ramifications for the public health and safety. The court concluded that it was fair to charge those who chose to operate in such an area with knowledge of the regulatory provisions.

The court held, however, that the government did have to prove that the defendants knew that the facility to which the waste was sent did not have a permit. Thus, even if the transporters did not know a permit was required, as long as they knew the facility did not have one or knew that they had not inquired, that would be sufficient knowledge for a conviction. Such knowledge could be shown circumstantially. For example, given that it is common knowledge that properly disposing of wastes is an expensive task, if someone is willing to take away wastes at an unusually low price or under unusual circumstances, then a juror could infer that the transporter knew that the wastes were not being taken to a licensed facility.

The court did acknowledge that mistake of fact would be a defense if the defendants had had a good faith belief that the materials were being recycled. The regulations applicable at the time provided an exemption from the permit requirement for waste that was recycled. The court distinguished a case in which the U.S. Supreme Court had held that a person who believed in good faith that he was shipping distilled water, when in fact he was shipping dangerous acid, did not "knowingly" ship dangerous chemicals in violation of applicable regulations.[37] Unlike the defendant in that case, the defendants in *Hayes* knew what was being shipped—a combination of waste and solvents—and they did not have a good faith belief that the materials were being recycled. Therefore, the convictions were upheld.

THE FEDERAL SUPERFUND LAW (CERCLA)

More than any other environmental law, the Comprehensive Environmental Response, Compensation, and Liability Act (CERCLA) of 1980, as amended,[38] has affected individuals and businesses that do not themselves produce environmental pollutants. CERCLA authorizes the federal government to investigate and take remedial action in response to a release or threatened release of hazardous substances to the environment. CERCLA established the *Hazardous Substance Superfund* to finance federal response activity. Through 2007, the Superfund has been replenished with tax revenue numerous times, for a total of more than $32 billion in appropriations.[39]

How federal Superfund money will be spent is determined in part by the EPA's National Priorities List, which identifies sites that may require remedial action. The EPA lists the sites in a rulemaking proceeding based on a *hazard ranking score*, which represents the degree of risk that the site presents to the environment and public health.

STRICT LIABILITY

The courts have interpreted the liability provisions of CERCLA broadly in order to effectuate the statute's remedial policies. With few exceptions, CERCLA imposes strict liability, meaning that the any of the potentially responsible parties are liable regardless of fault. It is now well established, for example, that the present owner of the land is liable for the cleanup of hazardous substances disposed of on the land by another person (usually a previous owner or tenant), unless it can establish the third-party defense (also called the innocent landowner defense), discussed later in this chapter.

34. 42 U.S.C. § 6928(d)(1).
35. 786 F.2d 1499 (11th Cir. 1986).
36. 471 U.S. 419 (1985).
37. United States v. Int'l Minerals, 402 U.S. 558 (1971).
38. 42 U.S.C. § 9601 *et seq.*
39. U.S. Gov't No. Accountability Office, *Superfund: Funding and Reported Costs of Enforcement and Administration Activities* (July 18, 2008), at 2.

POTENTIALLY RESPONSIBLE PARTIES

The EPA may undertake remedial action itself or require the potentially responsible parties to do so. The *potentially responsible parties (PRPs)* include (1) the present owner or operator of the facility, (2) the owner or operator at the time of disposal of the hazardous substance, (3) any person who arranged for treatment or disposal of hazardous substances at the facility, and (4) any person who transported hazardous substances to or selected the facility.[40] If the EPA performs the remedial work, it can recover its cleanup costs from the responsible parties. CERCLA does not permit punitive damages absent a showing of recklessness.

40. 42 U.S.C. § 9607.

INTERNATIONAL SNAPSHOT

A fundamental element of the U.S. environmental scheme is that the polluter pays. The European Union (EU) has also adopted this policy: "The cost of preventing and eliminating nuisances must, as a matter of principle, be borne by the polluter."[a] The EU's policy on the environment is designed to (1) preserve, protect, and improve the quality of the environment; (2) protect human health; (3) ensure prudent and rational utilization of natural resources; and (4) promote measures at the international level to deal with regional or worldwide environmental problems.

This concept has also been introduced in Asia. Taiwan, for example, enacted an environmental law modeled, in part, on CERCLA, with modifications to address the local culture, issues, and concerns. On a smaller scale, the government of Delhi, India, has begun enforcing local litter and recycling ordinances more stringently under the "polluter pays" principle.

When the laws of other nations are closely patterned on U.S. laws, compliance may be easier for U.S. companies operating in those countries; nonetheless, close attention should be paid to the differences between the U.S. laws and the laws of other countries. As other governments embrace U.S. pollution remediation principles, the United States may find itself in an awkward position. For example, Suresh Prabhu, India's former environment minister, remarked: "The polluters pay principle is internationally accepted today. So if the US and other rich countries are responsible for 70% of all the [greenhouse gases] in the atmosphere today, it's their responsibility to ensure the world doesn't hurtle towards an environmental crisis."[b]

a. Objective 17, Restatement of the Objectives and Principles of a Community Environment Policy, 1977 O.J. (C 139).

b. Nitin Sethi, *UN Report Tells India to Clean Up*, TIMES OF INDIA, Oct. 31, 2007.

Lessee as Owner

Certain courts have held lessees of contaminated property liable as "owners" under CERCLA, reasoning that site control is a sufficient indicator of ownership to impose owner liability on lessees or sublessors. The U.S. Court of Appeals for the Second Circuit rejected this approach, reasoning that site control confuses the two statutorily distinct categories of owner and operator under CERCLA.[41] Instead, the Second Circuit ruled, the critical question is whether the lessee's status is that of a de facto owner. In determining whether a lessee is an owner, important factors to consider are (1) the length of the lease and whether it allows the owner/lessor to determine how the property is used; (2) whether the owner has the power to terminate the lease before it expires; (3) whether the lessee can sublet the property without notifying the owner; (4) whether the lessee must pay taxes, insurance, assessments, and operation and maintenance costs; and (5) whether the lessee is responsible for making structural repairs.

JOINT AND SEVERAL LIABILITY

The law permits the imposition of joint and several liability, which means that any one responsible party can be held liable for the total amount of response (cleanup) costs and natural resource damage even though others may also be responsible for the release. A responsible party who incurs costs cleaning up a toxic-waste site can seek cost recovery or contribution from other responsible parties. In resolving contribution claims, the court may allocate response costs among liable parties using such equitable factors as the court determines are appropriate.[42] Of course, the right of contribution is of value only if the other parties are still in existence and able to pay. Many times, they are not. Thus, joint and several liability allows the government to select financially sound parties from whom to collect response costs and puts the burden of recovering these costs from other responsible parties on the selected defendants.

A party may escape joint and several liability if it can prove that it contributed to only a divisible portion of the harm or that it was the source of waste that, when mixed with

41. Commander Oil Corp. v. Barlo Equip. Corp., 215 F.3d 321 (2d Cir. 2000), *cert. denied,* 531 U.S. 979 (2000).

42. In *Browning-Ferris Industries of Illinois v. Ter Maat,* 195 F.3d 953 (7th Cir. 1999), the U.S. Court of Appeals for the Seventh Circuit held that if one party has been required to pay the entire cost of cleaning up a site to which several other parties also contributed hazardous waste, the other parties can be held jointly and severally liable for contribution.

other hazardous waste, did not contribute to the release and cleanup costs that followed. The party bears the burden of establishing a reasonable basis for apportioning liability.[43]

43. United States v. Alcan Aluminum Corp., 990 F.2d 711 (2d Cir. 1993).

In the following companion cases, the court considered what form of compensation CERCLA permits current landowners to seek from prior occupants for costs associated with voluntarily cleaning up contaminated soil and water.

A CASE IN POINT

IN THE LANGUAGE OF THE COURT

CASE 16.2

KOTROUS v. GOSS-JEWETT CO.

UNITED STATES COURT OF APPEALS FOR THE NINTH CIRCUIT
523 F.3D 924 (9TH CIR. 2008).

FACTS The U.S. Court of Appeals for the Ninth Circuit addressed the issue of recovering costs for CERCLA-related cleanup in two separate cases. As both turned on the same point of law, the court addressed them in one opinion. The first case involved Kotrous, a businessman, who in 1995 had purchased land that had housed a dry cleaning business for the preceding quarter century. After discovering that the soil and groundwater at the site were contaminated with chemicals used for dry cleaning, Kotrous undertook voluntary remediation efforts (that is, he cleaned up the hazardous waste without first being sued by the EPA or any other person) and then sued to recover the cost of those efforts from other potentially responsible parties, including the Goss-Jewett Company, which had operated the cleaning business, and Bayer, the company that had supplied the chemicals.

The second case was similar. Adobe Lumber had recently purchased a shopping center and then discovered that it had contaminated soil and water. The source of the contamination was also a dry cleaning business. Adobe took steps to rectify the contamination voluntarily and then brought suit against other potentially responsible parties to defray the cost of the cleanup.

The defendants in both cases argued that because the plaintiffs had not themselves been sued under CERCLA, they had no right to seek *contribution* (partial coverage of the cleanup costs under CERCLA Section 113) or to recover costs (complete coverage of the cleanup costs under Section 107) from other potentially responsible parties. Under Section 113, PRPs who are held jointly liable in a common suit under CERCLA have an explicit right to seek contribution, that is, partial repayment of the costs incurred, from the other PRPs. Section 107 gives a person who has cleaned up a site the right to recover its actual cleanup costs but is silent on the availability of contribution.

ISSUE PRESENTED May a landowner who has not been sued under CERCLA receive contribution or recover costs associated with the voluntary remediation of contaminants on its property?

OPINION TASHIMA, J., writing for the U.S. Court of Appeals for the Ninth Circuit:

In *Atlantic Research,*[44] the Supreme Court answered [a] question left open [by prior holdings]: "whether § 107(a) provides. . . [potentially responsible parties] . . . with a cause of action to recover costs from other PRPs." The Court held that it does.

. . . .

CERCLA § 113(f) grants an explicit right to contribution to PRPs "with common liability stemming from an action instituted under § 106 or § 107(a)." Section § 107(a), by contrast, "permits recovery of cleanup costs but does not create a right to contribution. A private party may recover under § 107(a) without any establishment of liability to a third party," but a PRP may recover only the costs it has incurred in cleaning a site, not the costs of a settlement agreement or a court judgment.

. . . .

Under *Atlantic Research*, a PRP such as Kotrous or Adobe that incurs costs voluntarily, without having been subject to an action under § 106 or § 107, may bring a suit for recovery of its costs

CONTINUED

44. United States v. Atl. Research Corp., 127 S. Ct. 2331 (2007).

under § 107(a); a party in such a position does not need a right to implied contribution under § 107. Any of the defendants sued by such a PRP may seek contribution under § 113(f) because they now will have been subject to an action under § 107.

RESULT Both cases were remanded for further proceedings. Kotrous and Adobe could sue the other potentially responsible parties under Section 107 of CERCLA to recover the response costs they voluntarily paid. They were not entitled to contribution under Section 113, however, because they had not themselves been sued under Section 106 or 107

CRITICAL THINKING QUESTIONS

1. What percentage of the cleanup costs, if any, should the current owners, Kotrous and Adobe, be required to pay?
2. If Kotrous or Adobe had refused to pay the cleanup costs and instead had sold the land to a third party without disclosing the contamination, could that party later bring a claim against the prior owner under CERCLA?

LIABILITY OF AFFILIATED COMPANIES AND PIERCING THE CORPORATE VEIL

Corporate relatives also face potential CERCLA liability under certain circumstances. In *United States v. Bestfoods,*[45] the U.S. Supreme Court outlined the responsibility a parent corporation has for the hazardous waste disposal activities of a subsidiary. There are two bases for imposing liability on parent corporations for facilities ostensibly operated by their subsidiaries: (1) as an owner of a subsidiary whose corporate veil has been pierced and (2) as an operator of the facility.

Derivative Liability as an Owner

A parent corporation will have derivative CERCLA liability as an owner for its subsidiary's actions when (but only when) there are grounds for piercing the subsidiary's corporate veil. As explained more fully in Chapter 20, such a collapsing of the legal distinction between parent and subsidiary is appropriate only if the corporation is just a sham or if the distinction is a fiction meant simply to protect shareholders from illegal activity.

In its initial ruling in *Bestfoods,* the U.S. Court of Appeals for the Sixth Circuit had turned to Michigan corporate law to decide whether to pierce the Michigan firm's corporate veil. Other courts have turned to federal common law, that is, the principles found in cases that the courts have developed for interpreting federal statutes like CERCLA. Under federal common law, courts may give less respect to the corporate form than under the common law of many states.

Direct Liability as an Operator of the Subsidiary's Facility

A parent corporation will have direct liability for its own actions if it operates a facility owned by its subsidiary. To be deemed an operator, the parent corporation "must manage, direct, or conduct operations specifically related to pollution, that is, operations having to do with the leakage or disposal of hazardous waste, or decisions about compliance with environmental regulations."[46] Thus, the question is not whether the parent operates the subsidiary, but rather whether it operates the facility.

The Supreme Court acknowledged in *Bestfoods* that it is common for directors of a parent corporation to serve as directors of its subsidiary. Directors and officers holding positions with both the parent and its subsidiary can and do legitimately "change hats" to represent the two corporations separately. Courts generally presume that the directors are wearing their "subsidiary hats," and not their "parent hats," when managing the subsidiary. As a result, the parent is not liable just because dual officers and directors made policy decisions and supervised activities at the subsidiary's facility. But if an agent of the parent who wears only the parent's hat manages or directs activities at the subsidiary's facility, then the parent company may be held directly liable as an operator.

45. 524 U.S. 51 (1998).

46. *Id.*

The parent company may also be directly liable if (1) the parent operates the facility in the stead of its subsidiary or alongside the subsidiary in some sort of joint venture; or (2) a dual officer or director departs so far from the norms of parental influence exercised through dual officeholding as to serve the parent in operating the facility, even when ostensibly acting on behalf of the subsidiary. Activities involving the facility that are consistent with the parent's investor status (such as monitoring the subsidiary's performance, supervising the subsidiary's finance and capital budget decisions, and articulating general policies and procedures) should not give rise to direct operator liability for the parent.

SUCCESSOR LIABILITY

Another important issue is *successor liability*, that is, the responsibility an acquirer of corporate assets has for the liabilities of the seller. Ordinarily, a purchaser of corporate assets—as opposed to a purchaser of all the stock of a corporation or a merger partner—does not automatically assume any of the seller's liabilities. The doctrine of successor liability arose out of attempts by companies to evade liability by selling the bulk of their business or assets to another firm and then distributing the proceeds to their shareholders, thereby leaving creditors with no assets to collect against. Although this aspect of corporate law is normally a province of state common law, several federal courts refer to a federal common law of successor liability for environmental cleanup under CERCLA.

The U.S. Courts of Appeals for the Third, Fourth, Seventh, and Eighth Circuits have taken the position that the doctrine of successor liability under CERCLA should be fashioned by reliance on federal common law. For example, the Seventh Circuit reasoned that resort to federal common law was warranted to achieve national uniformity in interpreting CERCLA and to prevent parties from frustrating the statute's aims by incorporating under the laws of states that restrict successor liability.[47]

In contrast, the Second Circuit read *Bestfoods*[48] to require reference to state corporate law to determine when there should be successor liability[49] and abandoned the substantial continuity test it had embraced in an earlier case.[50] The *substantial continuity test* (sometimes referred to as the *continuity of enterprise approach*) imposes successor liability when the purchaser of assets "maintains the same business, with the same employees doing the same jobs, under the same supervisors, working conditions, and production process, and produces the same products for the same customers" as the seller corporation.[51] Although several states employ this test, the majority of states impose successor liability only when there is a single corporation after the transfer of assets with the same shareholders and directors before and after the acquisition.[52] Because most states apply this more stringent *mere continuation (identity) test,* the Second Circuit concluded that the substantial continuity test should not be applied in this case. Instead, the Second Circuit applied the traditional common law rule, which states that a corporation acquiring the assets of another takes on its liabilities only when (1) the acquirer has expressly or implicitly agreed to assume them, (2) the transaction may be viewed as a de facto merger or consolidation,[53] (3) the successor is the mere continuation of the predecessor, or (4) the transaction is fraudulent. The First,[54] Sixth, and Eleventh Circuits have also relied on state common law to determine successor liability.

LIABILITY OF LENDERS AND FIDUCIARIES

Lenders face potential liability under CERCLA because foreclosure of a contaminated property potentially makes them an owner. The Asset Conservation, Lender Liability, and Deposit Insurance Protection Act of 1996[55] excluded from the definition of "owner or operator" a lender that did not participate in the management of a facility prior to foreclosure. Participation in management means "actually participating in the management or operational affairs" of the facility. Mere capacity to influence management is not a sufficient basis for imposing operator liability on a lender. Thus, a lender may hold "indicia of ownership," such as a deed of trust, to protect its security interest without facing liability as long as it does not actually manage or operate the facility.

47. North Shore Gas Co. v. Salomon, Inc., 152 F.3d 642 (7th Cir. 1998).

48. 524 U.S. 51 (1998).

49. New York v. Nat'l Servs. Indus., 352 F.3d 682 (2d Cir. 2003). *Accord* Ne. Conn. Econ. Alliance, Inc. v. ATC P'ship, 861 A.2d 473 (Conn. 2004).

50. B.F. Goodrich v. Betkoski, 99 F.3d 505 (2d Cir. 1996).

51. United States v. Caroling Transformer Co., 978 F.2d 832 (4th Cir. 1992).

52. *Id.*

53. *See* New York v. Nat'l Servs. Indus., 460 F.3d 201 (2d Cir. 2006) (holding de facto merger requires continuity of ownership).

54. Cyr v. B. Offen & Co., 501 F.2d 1145 (1st Cir. 1974); United States v. Davis, 261 F.3d 1, 54 (1st Cir. 2001) (noting that *Bestfoods* "left little room" for the creation of a special federal rule of liability under CERCLA).

55. 42 U.S.C. § 9601(20).

Although a lender may take steps to sell the property if the debtor defaults and may even buy it at the foreclosure sale, without automatically becoming a potentially responsible party, the lender must attempt to sell or re-lease the property as soon as practicable for a commercially reasonable price. Failure to do so will make the lender potentially liable as an owner.

The liability of a fiduciary, such as a trustee, is limited to the assets held in trust. There is also a safe harbor for fiduciaries that undertake lawful response actions, but the safe harbor does not protect against negligence that causes or contributes to the release or threatened release of hazardous substances.[56]

DEFENSES

There are five defenses to liability under CERCLA. The defendant can avoid liability by showing that the release of hazardous substances was caused solely by (1) an act of God (that is, an unavoidable natural disaster, such as an earthquake); (2) an act of war; or (3) the act or omission of a third party, provided that certain other requirements are met. A fourth defense for purchasers of *brownfields*, contaminated sites that are eligible for cleaning and reclaiming with assistance from the Superfund,[57] was added by the Brownfields Revitalization Act. A fifth defense is available for recyclers against claims brought by private parties but not against claims by the federal or state government.

Third-Party or Innocent Landowner Defense

To assert the *third-party defense* (also referred to as the *innocent landowner defense*), a defendant must show that the third party responsible for the release was not an employee and had no contractual relationship with the person asserting the defense. If the facility was acquired from the third party, the written instrument of transfer (usually a deed) is deemed to create a contractual relationship, unless the purchaser acquired the facility after the hazardous substances were disposed of and without any knowledge or reason to know that hazardous substances had previously been disposed of at the facility. To establish that the purchaser had no reason to know that hazardous substances were disposed of at the facility, the purchaser must show that, prior to the sale, it undertook "all appropriate inquiry into the previous ownership and uses of the property consistent with good commercial or customary practice in an effort to minimize liability."[58]

56. 42 U.S.C. § 9607(n).

57. For a more in-depth look at brownfields, see the "Inside Story" in Chapter 19.

58. 42 U.S.C. § 9601(35)(B).

The EPA initially declined to define what constituted "all appropriate inquiry," but was instructed to do so by the 2002 Small Business Liability Relief and Brownfields Revitalization Act. After forming a negotiated rulemaking committee comprising environmental engineers, representatives of industry, state and local government officials, and community activists, the EPA promulgated a final rule in 2007 that gave prospective purchasers definitive guidance on what is necessary to prove the appropriate inquiry required for the third-party defense.[59] The requirements are summarized in Exhibit 16.1.

Brownfields and Ready-for-Reuse Certificates

As discussed more fully in Chapter 19, the Brownfields Revitalization Act[60] makes it possible for acquirers of certain contaminated sites to avoid liability for legacy (that is, preexisting) contamination on the site. Landowners must comply with all institutional controls and guidelines issued by the EPA. For example, a landowner must take "reasonable steps" to prevent future or continuing releases of hazardous materials onto the land. Failure to comply with the guidelines exposes landowners to liability for the entire cleanup costs.[61] A full review of federal and state EPA guidelines is recommended to determine what constitutes "reasonable steps."

To offer more certainty to acquirers of contaminated sites, the EPA will, under certain circumstances, issue certificates of reuse under RCRA. The EPA issued its first certificate of reuse to a steel plant in Oklahoma in 2002. This certificate "verifies that environmental conditions on this property are protective of its current use and anticipated future uses."[62] These reuse certificates are incentives to clean up formerly contaminated land.

59. 70 Fed. Reg. 66,070 (Nov. 1, 2005); *see also* the section on Brownfields and Land Revitalization on the EPA's website, http://www.epa.gov/brownfields/regneg.htm.

60. Small Business Liability Relief and Brownfields Revitalization Act (2002); *see also* Robert Dahlquist & Tiffany Barzal, *Ah: Relief from CERCLA. But Where's the Relief?,* 12 Bus. Law. 39 (2003), for an excellent discussion of the relief from Superfund liability granted to some small businesses. The Economic Development Administration Reauthorization Act of 2003, Pub. L. No. 108-373, 118 Stat. 1756 (2004), provided for a demonstration program to encourage the use of solar energy technologies at brownfields sites. Up to $5 million for each fiscal year from 2004 through 2008 is authorized to develop "brightfield" sites.

61. These guidelines are available at http://www.cfpub.epa.gov/compliance/resource/policies/cleanup/brownfields/index.cfm. *See also EPA Guidance Issued on Avoiding Liability for Properties Tainted by Contiguous Sites,* 72 U.S.L.W. 2448 (2003).

62. *First-Ever Certificate of Reuse Awarded Under RCRA to Oklahoma Steelmaking Plant,* 71 U.S.L.W. 2061 (2002).

EXHIBIT 16.1

What Constitutes "All Appropriate Inquiry" Under CERCLA?

To avail itself of the third-party defense, the landowner or prospective purchaser must hire an environmental professional, as defined in the final rule, to conduct a site assessment. That assessment must include:

- Interviews with past and present owners, operators, and occupants.
- Reviews of historical sources of information.
- Reviews of federal, state, tribal, and local government records.
- Visual inspections of the facility and adjoining properties.
- Commonly known or reasonably ascertainable information.
- An assessment of the degree of obviousness of the presence or likely presence of contamination at the property and the ability to detect the contamination.

Additional inquiries that must be conducted by or for the prospective landowner include:

- Searches for environmental cleanup liens.
- Assessments of any specialized knowledge or experience of the prospective landowner.
- An assessment of the relationship of the purchase price to the fair market value of the property, if the property was not contaminated.
- Commonly known or reasonably ascertainable information.

The rule specifies that any assessment conducted in accordance with ASTM standard E1527-05 (Standard Practice for Environmental Site Assessments: Phase I Environmental Site Assessment Process) will comply with the rule and thereby satisfy the requirement of "all appropriate inquiry."

Source: Section on Brownfields and Land Revitalization, at the EPA's website, http://www.epa.gov/brownfields/aai/aai_final_factsheet.htm.

Recyclers

The Superfund Recycling Equity Act of 1999 exempts recyclers from liability in private-party actions under CERCLA. They remain liable in suits brought by the state or federal government, however. Under the statute, a person "who arranged for recycling of a recyclable material shall not be liable under [CERCLA's cost recovery and contribution sections] with respect to such material." The term "recyclable material" includes lead-acid and nickel-cadmium used in batteries. The Act applies retroactively to private actions that were pending on its date of enactment, November 29, 1999.[63]

RETROACTIVE APPLICATION

In *United States v. Olin Corp.*,[64] the U.S. Court of Appeals for the Eleventh Circuit ruled that owners can be held liable for hazardous waste disposed of before CERCLA became law. The court reasoned that "Congress's twin goals of cleaning up pollution that occurred prior to December 11, 1980, and of assigning responsibility to culpable parties can be achieved only through retroactive application of CERCLA's response cost liability provisions."

Subsequent to the Eleventh Circuit's decision in this case, the U.S. Supreme Court held in *Eastern Enterprises v. Apfel*[65] that retroactive application of the Coal Industry Retiree Health Benefit Act of 1992 to a company that had abandoned its coal business in 1965 violated the Takings Clause of the Fifth Amendment to the U.S. Constitution. Although defendant firms have argued in several cases that *Eastern Enterprises* overrules all previous decisions holding that CERCLA could be constitutionally applied retroactively, three federal circuit courts (the U.S. Courts of Appeals for the Second, Sixth, and Eighth Circuits), as well as several federal district courts (including the Eastern District of Virginia, the Northern District of New York, the Western District of Arkansas,

63. Gould Inc. v. A&M Battery & Tire Serv., 232 F.3d 162 (3d Cir. 2000).

64. 107 F.3d 1506 (11th Cir. 1997).

65. 524 U.S. 498 (1998).

and the District of New Jersey),[66] have rejected this argument and upheld the retroactive application of CERCLA.

66. United States v. Alcan Aluminum Corp., 315 F.3d 179, 189–90 (2d Cir. 2003) (listing post–*Eastern Enterprises* decisions finding retroactive application of CERCLA constitutional). *But see* Gen. Elec. Co. v. EPA, 360 F.3d 188 (D.C. Cir. 2004) (ordering district court to consider General Electric's preenforcement constitutional challenge).

EXTRATERRITORIAL APPLICATION

In what appears to be the first application of CERCLA to activity outside the United States, the court in the following case permitted an action to proceed against a Canadian smelter that dumped hazardous waste into a river that ran into Washington State.

A CASE IN POINT

IN THE LANGUAGE OF THE COURT

CASE 16.3

PAKOOTAS V. TECK COMINCO METALS, LTD.

UNITED STATES DISTRICT COURT FOR THE EASTERN DISTRICT OF WASHINGTON
2004 U.S. DIST. LEXIS 23041 (E.D. WASH. NOV. 8, 2004).

FACTS Plaintiffs Joseph A. Pakootas and Donald R. Michel, enrolled members of the Confederated Tribes of the Colville Reservation, sued to enforce a unilateral administration order (UAO) by the U.S. EPA requiring the defendant, Teck Cominco Metals, Ltd. (TCM), to investigate and determine the full nature of the contamination at the "Upper Columbia River Site" due to materials disposed of into the Columbia River from the defendant's smelter. TCM is a Canadian corporation that owned and operated a smelter in Trail, British Columbia, located approximately ten Columbia River miles north of the United States–Canada border. The State of Washington was also a plaintiff, having intervened in the litigation as a matter of right under CERCLA.

TCM moved to dismiss the action, contending that the U.S. court did not have subject matter or personal jurisdiction and that the plaintiffs' complaints failed to state claims upon which relief could be granted.

ISSUE PRESENTED Does a U.S. court have the power to enforce the provisions of CERCLA against a Canadian corporation for actions taken by that corporation in Canada?

OPINION MCDONALD, J., writing for the U.S. District Court for the Eastern District of Washington:

A. Subject Matter Jurisdiction

This case arises under CERCLA and, therefore, there is a federal question which confers subject matter jurisdiction on this court.

. . . .

B. Personal Jurisdiction

. . . .

Absent one of the traditional bases for personal jurisdiction—presence, domicile, or consent—due process requires a defendant have "certain minimum contracts with [the forum state] such that the maintenance of the suit does not offend traditional notions of fair play and substantial justice." *International Shoe Co. v. Washington.*[67] The forum state must have a sufficient relationship with the defendants and the litigation to make it reasonable to require them to defend the action in a federal court located in that state. . . .

The extent to which a federal court can exercise personal jurisdiction, absent the traditional bases of consent, domicile or physical presence, depends on the nature and quality of defendant's "contacts" with the forum state. . . .

If a non-resident, acting entirely outside of the forum state, intentionally causes injuries within the forum state, local jurisdiction is presumptively reasonable. Under such circumstances, the

CONTINUED

67. 326 U.S. 310 (1945).

defendant must "reasonably anticipate" being haled into court in the forum state. Personal jurisdiction can be established based on: (1) intentional actions; (2) expressly aimed at the forum state; (3) causing harm, the brunt of which is suffered, and which defendant knows is likely to be suffered, in the forum state. . . .

The facts alleged in the individual plaintiffs' complaint and the State of Washington's complaint-in-intervention satisfy this three-part test. The complaints allege that from approximately 1906 to mid-1995, defendant generated and disposed of hazardous substances directly into the Columbia River and that these substances were carried downstream into the waters of the United States where they have eventually accumulated and cause continuing impacts to the surface water and ground water, sediments, and biological resources which comprise the Upper Columbia River and Franklin D. Roosevelt Lake. . . . This disposal causes harm which defendant knows is likely to be suffered downstream by the State of Washington and those individuals, such as Pakootas and Michel, who fish and recreate in the Upper Columbia River and Lake Roosevelt.

The burden is on the defendant to prove the forum's exercise of jurisdiction would not comport with "fair play and substantial justice.". . .

. . . .

The exercise of jurisdiction over defendant TCM does not offend traditional notions of fair play and substantial justice. The burden on defendant in defending in this forum is not great. Trail, B.C. is located approximately 10 miles from the Eastern District of Washington. For reasons discussed below, the court finds the exercise of personal jurisdiction over defendant does not create any conflicts with Canadian sovereignty. It is obvious the State of Washington has a significant interest in adjudicating this dispute, as evidenced by its intervention as a plaintiff, and venue is proper here under CERCLA.

. . . .

C. Failure to State a Claim

A Rule 12(b)(6) dismissal is proper only where there is either a "lack of a cognizable legal theory" or "the absence of sufficient facts alleged under a cognizable legal theory.". . .

Defendant contends the UAO cannot be enforced against a Canadian corporation based on conduct which occurred in Canada. . . .

. . . CERCLA's definition of "environment" is limited to waters, land, and air under the management and authority of the United States, within the United States, or under the jurisdiction of the United States.

. . . The court . . . will assume this case involves an extraterritorial application of CERCLA to conduct occurring outside U.S. borders. In doing so, however, the court does not find that said application is an attempt to regulate the discharges at the Trail smelter, but rather simply to deal with the effects thereof in the United States.

Congress has the authority to enforce its laws beyond the territorial boundaries of the United States. It is, however, a longstanding principle of American law "that legislation of Congress, unless a contrary intent appears, is meant to apply only within the territorial jurisdiction of the United States.". . .

. . . .

"[I]f Congressional intent concerning extraterritorial application cannot be divined, then courts will examine additional factors to determine whether the traditional presumption against extraterritorial application should be disregarded in a particular case." First, "the presumption is generally

CONTINUED

not applied where the failure to extend the scope of the statute to a foreign setting will result in adverse effects within the United States."

. . . .

Here, defendant TCM contends the presumption against extraterritorial application is not defeated because CERCLA is "bare of any language affirmatively evidencing any intent to reach foreign sources." There is no dispute that CERCLA, its provisions and its "sparse" legislative history, do not clearly mention the liability of individuals and corporations located in foreign sovereign nations for contamination they cause within the U.S. At the same time, however, there is no doubt that CERCLA affirmatively expresses a clear intent by Congress to remedy "domestic conditions" within the territorial jurisdiction of the U.S. That clear intent, combined with the well established principle that the presumption is not applied where failure to extend the scope of the statute to a foreign setting will result in adverse effects within the United States, leads this court to conclude that extraterritorial application of CERCLA is appropriate in this case.

. . . .

There is no direct evidence that Congress intended extraterritorial application of CERCLA to conduct occurring outside the United States. There is also no direct evidence that Congress did not intend such application. There is, however, no doubt that Congress intended CERCLA to clean up hazardous substances at sites within the jurisdiction of the United States. That fact, combined with the well-established principle that the presumption against extraterritorial application generally does not apply where conduct in a foreign country produces adverse effects within the United States, leads the court to conclude that extraterritorial application of CERCLA is not precluded in this case. The Upper Columbia River Site is a "domestic condition" over which the United States has sovereignty and legislative control. Extraterritorial application of CERCLA in this case does not create a conflict between U.S. laws and Canadian laws.

. . . .

Because the fundamental purpose of CERCLA is to ensure the integrity of the domestic environment, we expect that Congress intended to proscribe conduct associated with the degradation of the environment, regardless of the location of the agents responsible for said conduct.

RESULT The motion to dismiss was denied so that the case could proceed.

CRITICAL THINKING QUESTIONS

1. Would the Canadian government be able to cite this case as precedent for holding U.S. companies liable under Canadian law for acid rain in Canada?[68]
2. What public policy considerations are involved when deciding whether to apply U.S. environmental laws to conduct occurring outside the United States? Are they the same as those implicated when deciding whether to apply U.S. antitrust,[69] employment discrimination,[70] securities,[71] or copyright and trademark law[72] to conduct occurring outside the United States?

---

68. *See* Shi-Ling Hsu & Austen L. Parrish, *Litigating Canada–U.S. Transboundary Harm: Intentional Environmental Lawmaking and the Threat of Territorial Reciprocity*, 48 VA. J. INT'L L. 1 (2007).
69. Envtl. Def. Fund v. Massey, 986 F.2d 528 (D.C. Cir. 1993).
70. Carnero v. Boston Scientific Corp., 433 F.3d 1 (1st Cir. 2006).
71. Tamari v. Bache & Co., 730 F.2d 1103 (7th Cir. 1984).
72. Suba Films v. MGM–Pathe Commc'ns Co., 24 F.3d 1088 (9th Cir. 1994).

Environmental Justice

In 1992, the EPA created the Office of Environmental Justice and began integrating environmental justice into the agency's policies, programs, and activities. *Environmental justice* refers to the belief that decisions with environmental consequences (such as where to locate incinerators, dumps, factories, and other sources of pollution) should not discriminate against poor and minority communities. Because such decisions usually require state or municipal permits, environmental justice concerns are often enforced by the federal government against states, cities, and counties.

Enforcement Activities and Sanctions for Noncompliance

Enforcement of environmental laws includes the monitoring of regulated companies' compliance with the laws, remediation of problems, and the punishment of violators.

AGENCY INSPECTIONS

The environmental laws give broad authority to the administering agencies to conduct on-site inspections of plant facilities and their records. Many laws authorize the collection of samples for analysis. Inspections may be conducted routinely or in response to reports or complaints from neighbors or employees. If criminal violations are suspected, the agency may be required to obtain a search warrant before conducting a nonroutine inspection. Violations observed during the inspection may result in civil or criminal enforcement actions.

ADMINISTRATIVE AND CIVIL ENFORCEMENT ACTIONS

Because the environmental laws are intended to accomplish such important societal goals and violations of the laws may cause serious harm or injury, environmental regulatory agencies generally are given strong enforcement powers. For a first violation, the agency might issue a warning and impose a schedule for compliance. If the schedule is not met or the violations are repeated, more aggressive enforcement action will likely follow. Such action may take the form of an administrative order to take specified steps to achieve compliance or a formal administrative complaint containing an assessment of administrative penalties. The penalties vary. Because they can be assessed for each day of each violation, they can be substantial for repeated, multiple, or long-standing violations.

CRIMINAL PROSECUTION

In more egregious cases, the enforcing agency may refer the case to the U.S. Attorney's office or its state counterpart for criminal prosecution. In most instances, courts are authorized to impose penalties of $25,000 to $100,000 per day of violation and to sentence individuals to prison terms of one year or more.[73] In some cases, the agency may have authority to close down the violator's operations.

73. *See, e.g.*, 33 U.S.C. § 1319 & 42 U.S.C. § 6928.

INTERNATIONAL SNAPSHOT

Although historically pollution laws were often not enforced in India, in November 1999, the Supreme Court of India ordered New Delhi authorities to comply with its 1996 order to close approximately 90,000 small factories that were polluting residential areas in the capital city or to relocate them to areas outside the city. The businesses at issue included leather, fertilizer, chemical, food processing, and paint plants that polluted the city's air and water sources. After the India Supreme Court issued the order, thousands of workers violently protested the closure of the factories by torching buses, blocking major roads, and throwing stones.[a] These protests essentially shut down the capital for a week. Opponents of the closures argued that shutting down the small factories, which provided employment to approximately one million people and generated business worth more than $1 billion annually, would cripple the city's economy.[b] The India Supreme Court argued that closure of the polluting factories was necessary for public health reasons and stated that it would not be influenced by the protests: "The court will not withdraw its orders just because hooligans have taken to the streets."[c] The governments of the rapidly industrializing states of Haryana and Uttar Pradesh, which are just north of New Delhi, ran advertisements encouraging factories to relocate there.[d]

a. Celia W. Dugger, *A Cruel Choice in New Delhi: Jobs vs. a Safer Environment*, N.Y. Times, Nov. 24, 2000.
b. Ranjit Devrai, *Development—India: Thousands of Jobless Question Green Concerns*, Inter Press Service, Dec. 29, 2000.
c. Dugger, *supra* note a.
d. Kartik Goyal, *India: Neighbouring States Gain As Delhi Shuts Polluting Units*, Reuters Eng. News Service, Dec. 29, 2000.

The EPA often recommends against criminal prosecution by the Department of Justice if the company self-reports and cooperates with the EPA. Any protection against criminal prosecution gained by voluntary disclosures under the audit policy applies only to the company, however. Officers and employees may still be subject to criminal liability based on information disclosed by the company.

The following case has been described as the most expansive application to date of the responsible corporate officer doctrine in a criminal case.

A CASE IN POINT

IN THE LANGUAGE OF THE COURT

CASE 16.4

UNITED STATES v. HANSEN

UNITED STATES COURT OF APPEALS FOR THE ELEVENTH CIRCUIT
262 F.3D 1217 (11TH CIR. 2001), *CERT. DENIED*, 535 U.S. 1111 (2002).

FACTS Christian Hansen founded the Hanlin Group in 1972 and served as its CEO until April 1993. The Hanlin Group operated a chemical plant in Brunswick, Georgia, through its subsidiary LCP Chemicals–Georgia (LCP). The plant employed about 150 workers. Before Hanlin acquired the Brunswick facility in 1979, the site had been occupied by other companies that had produced and dumped hazardous materials on the land and the surrounding area. LCP constructed a wastewater treatment system and obtained a permit in 1990 to dump "treated" water into Purvis Creek, a nearby waterway. Although LCP had represented that its treatment facilities could process seventy gallons of water per minute, in fact, the facility could process only thirty-five gallons per minute. In August 1992, the Occupational Safety and Health Administration cited the plant for safety hazards associated with contaminated water on the cell room floors.

Hanlin filed for bankruptcy in 1991. Soon thereafter, Christian asked his son Randall to join LCP as an executive vice president to help turn the facility around.

In February 1992, James Johns, the Brunswick plant manager, informed Randall that, without "extensive work" on the wastewater treatment system, the plant could not operate for more than a few days without willfully violating environmental regulations. Randall attempted to raise additional funds by selling excess equipment and reducing the payroll, but the funds available for maintenance, repair, and environmental compliance remained limited. All major projects and all capital and extraordinary expenditures required the approval of the Hanlin board, the Hanlin bankruptcy creditors' committee, and the bankruptcy court. Although Randall requested funds to address the wastewater problems, the funds were usually not released.

Later that year, Randall visited the plant again after meeting with representatives from the EPA and was told by Alfred Taylor, the new plant manager, that the water treatment problem was growing even more serious. Taylor testified at trial that Randall was "just as concerned as they were" about the problems and authorized him to hire a task force to help solve the problem.

After a year and a half of more violations, which were duly reported to the state and federal EPA by Randall and LCP, Randall and his managers considered shutting down the facility either permanently or temporarily. But Randall told his managers, "They won't let me do that." In April 1993, the board removed Christian as CEO and elected Randall in his place. Randall also served as plant manager of the Brunswick facility from July through September 1993.

Randall searched for a suitable buyer with the resources and capital to fix the plant's problems. During this time, he received reports of the continuing violations at the plant.

In June 1993, the Georgia Environmental Protection Division (EPD) proposed a revocation of LCP's license to dump wastewater into Purvis Creek. In July and August 1993, Christian told employees to pump wastewater into drums containing oil, even though he knew that wastewater mixed with oil could not be run through the wastewater treatment system. He also advised employees not to dump any more water into Purvis Creek. Employees repeatedly told Randall, Christian, and Taylor that water was running out of the treatment facility's doors due to breaks in the beams. These employees were told that conditions would change as soon as the plant had a cash infusion from a buyer, but that nothing more could be done at that time.

CONTINUED

During this period, Randall found a buyer that was willing to advance funds to help alleviate the releases of hazardous waste. Although conditions improved briefly, the deal fell through, and the Georgia EPD revoked LCP's license in September 1993, forcing LCP to close the plant entirely. Randall requested $1.5 million from the bankruptcy court to deal with the environmental impacts of a full plant closure, but his request was denied.

Following the closure, the facility was turned over to the U.S. EPA for cleanup, which cost approximately $50 million. Shortly thereafter, the U.S. Attorney's office indicted Christian and Randall Hansen and Taylor for violating numerous environmental laws from 1984 through the plant's final shutdown in 1994. The government also indicted Douglas Hanson, LCP's environmental and health and safety manager. Hanson pleaded guilty to violating CERCLA and the Endangered Species Act and testified against Christian, Randall, and Taylor.

Christian Hansen was convicted of violating the Clean Water Act (CWA), the Resource Conservation and Recovery Act (RCRA), and CERCLA, and he was sentenced to 108 months in prison. Randall was convicted of violating the CWA and RCRA and was sentenced to 46 months in prison. Taylor was convicted of violating the CWA, RCRA, and CERCLA and was sentenced to 78 months in prison. All three appealed their convictions.

Issue Presented When may corporate officers and plant managers be held individually guilty as operators of a hazardous waste facility under the CWA, RCRA, and CERCLA?

Opinion PER CURIAM, by the U.S. Court of Appeals for the Eleventh Circuit:

The indictment alleged that the defendants, "after learning that the Brunswick facility was disposing of hazardous wastes . . . without a RCRA permit, continued to operate the Brunswick facility in such a manner as to continue the disposal of these hazardous wastes without expending adequate funds . . . to prevent the disposal of such hazardous wastes into the environment." The jury was instructed that the defendants were responsible for the acts of others that they "willfully directed," "authorized," or aided and abetted by "willfully joining together with [another] person in the commission of a crime." . . .

a. Hansen

. . . .

The testimony at trial indicated that Christian Hansen was aware that wastewater was permitted to flow out the cell room back door in June 1993, and directed the use of the old Bunker C storage tanks for storage of wastewater, including the inadequately treated wastewater from the treatment system, from July through September 1993. Although the acts continued after Hansen left his decision-making position, the acts occurred at his direction. This evidence was sufficient for the jury to reasonably conclude beyond a reasonable doubt that his acts were in furtherance of the violations. . . .

b. Randall

Randall claims that the government presented no evidence that he personally treated, stored, or disposed of a hazardous waste, personally effected a CWA violation, or instructed an agent to do so. He maintains that, under the laws of bankruptcy and corporate governance, he lacked the authority to close the plant or to allocate the funds for the needed capital improvements. He contends that LCP needed the bankruptcy court's approval to use the bankruptcy estate's assets, or to obtain a new debt, to perform the needed repairs at the Brunswick plant.

In February 1994, LCP applied to the bankruptcy court for the funds "to shutdown" the plant and for new equipment, but the motion was denied. . . . LCP Board of Directors member James Mathis testified that Randall was responsible for "running the day-to-day operations of the company" once he became the interim CEO and COO. . . .

CONTINUED

LCP, as a debtor in possession, could use the property of the estate in the ordinary course of business, but needed court approval to use, sell, or lease, other than in the ordinary course of business, property of the estate. It could obtain secured credit . . . in the ordinary course of business, but needed court approval to obtain unsecured credit or to incur unsecured debt other than in the ordinary course of business. Bankruptcy does not insulate a debtor from environmental regulatory statutes. In reviewing an injunction to clean up a hazardous waste site, the U.S. Supreme Court commented:

> We do not suggest that [the debtor's] discharge [in bankruptcy] will shield him from prosecution for having violated the environmental laws . . . or for criminal contempt for not performing his obligations under the injunction prior to bankruptcy. . . . We do not hold that the injunction . . . against any conduct that will contribute to the pollution of the site or the State's wasters is dischargeable in bankruptcy. . . . Finally, we do not question that anyone in possession of the site . . . must comply with the environmental laws. . . . Plainly, that person or firm may not maintain a nuisance, pollute the waters of the State, or refuse to remove the source of such conditions.[74]

Although Randall claims that his role as Executive Vice-President and acting CEO was limited to financial matters, he also received daily reports about the plant's operations and environmental problems, wrote and received memos regarding specific plant operational problems, received monthly written environmental reports, and oral environmental reports. He admitted that Hanlin's bankruptcy was not an excuse for violating environmental laws. There is no indication that he asked the Hanlin Board or the bankruptcy court to close the plant. The evidence indicates that he apparently misled them into believing that environmental compliance was not a problem. After the Georgia EPD attempted to revoke the plant's [dumping] permit in June 1993, Randall contested the revocation, explaining that the plant's CWA violations were due to a lightning strike and equipment failures, and asserted that "LCP has already taken steps to improve the situation." This evidence was sufficient for the jury to conclude that Randall's actions were in furtherance of the violations.

c. Taylor

Taylor argues that he should not be held responsible for the environmental violations that occurred after he resigned as plant manager. Taylor resigned as plant manager on 16 July 1993, but returned shortly thereafter as a project engineer and continued in that position until the plant closed. . . .

Although Taylor left his managerial position, he continued to work in a position in which he directed or authorized acts of the employees on environmental and safety problems. . . . This evidence was sufficient for the jury to conclude beyond a reasonable doubt that these acts were in furtherance of the violations.

RESULT The defendants' convictions were supported by the evidence and were, accordingly, upheld.

COMMENTS The Justice Department has responded to criticism that environmental crime prosecutors are "overreaching by criminalizing what should be handled through the civil or regulatory process" with a resolute stance of continuing to criminally pursue those it considers violators.

CRITICAL THINKING QUESTIONS

1. Is it fair to hold an officer criminally liable for environmental problems when the officer lacks the funds to fix the problems or to shut the plant down properly to prevent further violations?
2. Is it fair to attribute corporate actions to the corporation's officers when they never instructed or encouraged their employees to violate the environmental laws?

---

74. Ohio v. Kovacs, 469 U.S. 274, 284–85 (1985).

SELF-REPORTING REQUIREMENTS

Many statutes and regulations require regulated companies to report certain facts to the EPA, such as the concentrations or the amounts of pollutants discharged from a facility or both. These reports may indicate a violation and may therefore prompt an enforcement action by the agency. There are severe penalties for filing false reports, including criminal sanctions for knowingly providing false information to a government agency.

EPA INCENTIVES FOR SELF-POLICING

The EPA's audit policy statement on self-policing is designed "to enhance protection of human health and the environment by encouraging regulated entities to voluntarily discover, promptly disclose and expeditiously correct violations of Federal environmental requirements."[75] If a company meets all nine conditions for leniency set forth in Exhibit 16.2 or all except the first one (that the discovery is made through systematic monitoring), then the EPA will generally opt not to pursue criminal proceedings.[76] Parties that meet these nine conditions for leniency are also eligible for a substantial reduction in civil penalties or the elimination of the gravity component of civil penalties.[77] Companies that fulfill all the conditions except the first can receive 75 percent mitigation of gravity-based civil penalties.[78] As an additional incentive, the EPA may "refrain from routine audits."[79]

A company may also qualify under the policy if, after having been found liable for violations at one facility, it discloses similar violations at others. The voluntary disclosure policy has been widely used. To date, more than

75. EPA, *Incentives for Self-Policing: Discovery, Disclosure, Correction and Prevention of Violations, Final Policy Statement* (May 11, 2000), at 16–28.

76. *Id.*

77. The gravity component is that portion of the penalty over and above the violator's economic gain from noncompliance.

78. *Id.*

79. *Id.*

EXHIBIT 16.2

Conditions for Leniency Under the EPA's Audit Policy Statement

1. *Systematic discovery of the violation through an environmental audit or a compliance management system:* The violation must have been discovered through either (a) an environmental audit or (b) a compliance management system that reflects due diligence in preventing, detecting, and correcting violations.
2. *Discovery and disclosure independent of government or third-party plaintiff:* The entity must discover the violation independently. That is, the violation must be discovered and identified before the EPA or another government agency likely would have identified the problem either through its own investigative work or from information received through a third party.
3. *Correction and remediation:* The entity must remedy any harm caused by the violation and expeditiously certify in writing to appropriate federal, state, and local authorities that it has corrected the violation.
4. *Preventing recurrence:* The regulated entity must agree to take steps to prevent a recurrence of the violation after it has been disclosed. Preventive steps may include, but are not limited to, improvements to the entity's environmental auditing efforts or compliance management system.
5. *No repeat violations:* Repeat offenders are not eligible to receive audit policy credit. Under the repeat violations exclusion, the same or a closely related violation must not have occurred at the same facility within the past three years.
6. *Other violations excluded:* Policy benefits are not available for violations that result in serious actual harm to the environment or that may have presented an imminent and substantial endangerment to public health or the environment. When events of such a consequential nature occur, violators are ineligible for penalty relief and other incentives under the audit policy.
7. *Cooperation:* The regulated entity must cooperate as required by the EPA and provide the EPA with the information it needs to determine policy applicability. The entity must not hide, destroy, or tamper with possible evidence following discovery of potential environmental violations.
8. *Voluntary disclosure:* The violation must have been identified voluntarily, and not through a monitoring, sampling, or auditing procedure that is required by statute, regulation, permit, judicial or administrative order, or consent agreement.
9. *Prompt disclosure:* The entity must disclose the violation in writing to the EPA within twenty-one calendar days after discovery.

Source: EPA, *Incentives for Self-Policing: Discovery, Disclosure, Correction and Prevention of Violations, Final Policy Statement* (May 11, 2000), at 16–28.

670 companies have made voluntary disclosures, resulting in the resolution of claims at more than 1,300 facilities.[80]

Management of Environmental Compliance

Legally astute managers recognize the need to adopt corporate policies and create management systems to ensure that company operations are protective of human health and the environment. These programs generally include several key elements.

CORPORATE POLICY

A strong corporate policy of environmental protection, adopted and supported at the highest levels of management, is usually the keystone of an effective program. Mere compliance with environmental laws may not be enough. A practice that is lawful today could nevertheless lead to environmental harm and future liability. For example, underground storage of flammable materials was once considered a sound practice and was actually required by many local fire codes. Little thought was given to the possibility of leaks or spillage around the tanks, with resulting harm to underground water supplies. If the risks had been perceived properly, double containment could have been provided when the tanks were first installed. This lack of foresight caused many companies to incur substantial costs for groundwater restoration.

The corporate policy should require every employee to comply with environmental laws. It should encourage management to consider more stringent measures than those required by law if such measures are necessary to protect human health and the environment. Finally, the policy should encourage a cooperative and constructive relationship with government agency personnel and should support active participation in legislative and administrative rule-making proceedings.[81]

WELL-DEFINED ORGANIZATIONAL STRUCTURE AND CRISIS-MANAGEMENT PLAN

Management of environmental compliance requires a well-defined organizational structure with clearly delineated responsibilities and reporting relationships. The complex and technical nature of environmental laws and regulations requires a highly trained professional staff with legal and technical expertise.

A company should have policies and procedures for reporting environmental law violations to corporate management and for managing the company's reporting obligations to government agencies. Top management also needs to ensure that whistleblowers are not subject to retaliation.

Environmental problems are what Max Bazerman and Michael Watkins call "predictable surprises."[82] Therefore, every company should have a crisis-management plan in place that designates someone other than the CEO to coordinate the response. That response, in turn, should include immediate stabilization of the situation, objective inquiry into it, and some immediate action to assure the company's constituencies that things are being put under control. For that reason, constituencies must receive information as the response continues. To the extent that crises are at least foreseeable, more detailed plans should be developed ahead of time.[83]

EDUCATION AND TRAINING

A corporation can be held liable for the malfeasance of its employees acting within the scope of employment, even if they acted contrary to company policies. At the same time, an employee involved in illegal conduct can be held personally criminally liable, even if he or she was just following orders from a supervisor. In addition, as explained in this chapter and in Chapter 15, under certain circumstances, the corporate executive officers responsible for operating or overseeing the operation of facilities or activities involving

80. Peyton Sturges, *Revisions to EPA Audit Policy Dovetail with Enforcement Initiatives, Official Says,* 68 U.S.L.W. 2576 (2000). In the spring of 2003, the EPA announced that it had waived $1.5 million in fines payable by East Coast–based companies after they self-reported violations occurring as far back as 1994 and as recently as 2001. The violations ranged from failing to file appropriate waste authorization forms to misreporting the qualities of dangerous chemicals being dumped by the companies. *EPA Waives $1.5 Million in Potential Fines Against Companies Reporting Own Violations,* 71 U.S.L.W. 2551 (2003).

81. *EPA May Recommend Not Prosecuting Companies That Uncover, Report Crimes,* 66 U.S.L.W. 2520 (1998). The official EPA statement of its policy is available at http://es.epa.gov/compliance/index.html.

82. Max H. Bazerman & Michael D. Watkins, Predictable Surprises (2004).

83. Stanley Sporkin, A Plan for Crisis Management and Avoidance, Address at the Nonprofit Risk Management Institute (Nov. 12, 1997).

hazardous waste can be civilly and criminally liable for illegal conduct by the employees under their supervision.

The most essential component of good environmental management is comprehensive education and training. Every employee must know about and understand the company's environmental policy and recognize his or her responsibilities in carrying it out.

RECORD KEEPING, ACCOUNTING, AND DISCLOSURE

Good record-keeping and cost-accounting systems are also essential. Many environmental laws require certain records to be developed and maintained for specified periods of time. These laws should be consulted when a company develops a record-retention policy. The company should also develop cost-accounting procedures that will allow it to forecast and report the costs of environmental compliance.

Publicly traded companies must carefully evaluate the costs of complying with environmental law and potential environmental liabilities in order to meet the disclosure and reporting requirements of the Securities and Exchange Commission (SEC). The SEC requires disclosure of environmental enforcement proceedings and litigation, as well as estimated costs of environmental compliance, including capital expenditures and any effects of compliance on earnings and competitive position that may be material. The SEC uses information provided by the EPA in enforcing these reporting requirements. In particular, FIN 47 requires companies to include any future environmental liabilities, particularly those related to closing a facility, in their financial statements. According American Bar Association estimates, FIN 47 reduced the 2005 after-tax earnings of Eli Lilly & Co. by $22 million, Commonwealth Edison by $42 million, Ford Motor Company by $251 million, and Citigroup by $49 million.[84]

PERIODIC ENVIRONMENTAL AUDITS

An important step in comprehensively managing environmental liability and reducing penalties for noncompliance is to conduct periodic environmental audits. Such candid, internal self-assessments document and measure (1) compliance with occupational health and safety requirements; (2) compliance with federal, state, and local emissions limits and other requirements of a company's licensing, if any; (3) current practices for the generation, storage, and disposal of hazardous wastes; and (4) potential liability for past disposal of hazardous substances. Audits should also test the effectiveness of the management system and ensure that all instances of noncompliance are corrected.

Although such programs can generate valuable information for management, they may also be self-incriminating. A thorough audit that reveals contaminated properties, shoddy disposal practices, and lax compliance with regulations will certainly aid a company seeking to improve its environmental compliance. If the results of such an audit were publicly available, however, plaintiffs in the discovery stage of litigation could use the audit results to further their case. For that reason, several states have enacted laws making such information privileged in order to encourage companies to produce and use it. At least one court has established a qualified privilege for certain self-critical analyses.[85]

The more stringent governmental financial reporting required by the Sarbanes–Oxley Act of 2002 has prompted auditors to take a closer look at the actual procedures used by in-house environmental managers. The requirement that the CEO and CFO of public companies certify the accuracy of their financial statements provides yet another reason for companies to perform in-house environmental evaluations with diligence and foresight.[86]

Many businesses are complying with standards established by nongovernmental certification programs.[87] Environmental certification programs verify that the activities of certified firms are environmentally appropriate. The International Organization for Standardization (ISO) environmental management program and the chemical industry's Responsible Care program are two of the most widely used programs. Complying with these standards offers a number of benefits. The EPA has enacted a number of policies that promote certification, including the "Performance Track" program that gives special treatment to businesses meeting certification-like requirements. Among the prerequisites for qualifying for both ISO and Performance Track are (1) the adoption of an in-house environmental management system, (2) a commitment to improve environmental performance and open reporting to the public, and (3) a record of compliance with environmental requirements. Companies that meet the requirements enjoy streamlined monitoring, record keeping, and reporting under the Clean Air Act and Clean Water Act and greater flexibility in installing "best available control technology" under the Clean Air Act.[88] Furthermore, a

84. Kaija Wilkinson, *SOX Offshoot: Poison the Land, Prepare to Pay,* Birmingham Bus. J., Feb. 17, 2006.

85. Reichhold Chems., Inc. v. Textron, Inc., 157 F.R.D. 522 (N.D. Fla. 1994).

86. Goodwin & Procter, *Environmental Law Advisory,* June 2004.

87. Errol E. Meidinger, Environmental Certification and U.S. Environmental Law: Closer Than You May Think (2001).

88. *Id.*

International Snapshot

Although internal environmental audits in the United States may be protected through the attorney–client privilege, that may not be the case in other countries where the attorney–client privilege is either not recognized or provides less protection than in U.S. courts. For example, in many countries in Latin America, the attorney–client privilege does not extend to attorney memos that a company may have in its files. Internal environmental audit documents, including attorney memos, may be obtained in most Latin American countries through a court order. As a result, foreign citizens can use these documents to file claims in U.S. courts against domestic companies for their actions outside the United States.[a]

The scope of the doctrine varies even within more developed areas. In the United Kingdom employees below a certain level fall outside the bounds of the privilege. In Italy, a conversation with a patent agent is granted the same protection as a meeting with a lawyer. Only thirteen of thirty-nine European countries extend the privilege to communications with in-house counsel, believing there is insufficient independence between the client and its lawyer.

a. *U.S. Business Documents Can Be Used in Suits by Foreign Citizens, Attorney Says,* 69 U.S.L.W. 2251 (2000).

number of major international banks have agreed to finance environmentally sensitive projects, such as power plants, dams, and pipelines, only if the projects also qualify under international environmental and social-impact standards.[89]

PROTOCOLS FOR AGENCY INSPECTIONS

Government agencies may undertake inspections with little or no advance notice. The company should be prepared in advance for such an event by having a protocol for handling the inspection. Individuals trained in the company protocol should accompany the inspector to ensure that the inspection is conducted properly and within the inspector's authority. The person who accompanies the inspector should prepare a report to management and make sure that any instances of noncompliance identified during the inspection are corrected.

PUBLIC AND COMMUNITY RELATIONS

As popular sentiment increasingly favors environmental sensitivity and protection, companies must pay attention to the public relations consequences of their environment-affecting actions. Dissatisfaction with a company's environmental record can lead to adverse publicity, activist protests, consumer boycotts, and more stringent regulation.

The manner in which a company handles an environmental problem can also have an important impact on its relationship with the community where it is located, as well as on the economic damages it will suffer. A company can gain credibility and respect by handling an environmental accident in a proactive and fair manner.

For example, Eastman Kodak's response to an environmental problem increased its standing in the city of Rochester, New York, where it is headquartered. When the local newspaper reported that toxic chemicals from Kodak had seeped into the bedrock beneath the soil and were moving underground toward homes, panic erupted and the prices of the homes plummeted. The company instituted a series of homeowner relief programs to assure homeowners that they would lose no money as a result of the decline in value of their homes. Kodak offered discounted refinanced mortgages and home improvement grants to encourage people to stay in their homes rather than sell them. For those who wanted to sell, the company agreed to pay the difference between the selling price and the home's market value before the environmental problem was discovered. If a house took longer than three months to sell, Kodak supplied interest-free bridge loans so that owners could move into their new homes before their old homes were sold. The president of the neighborhood association that represented 5,000 Rochester households commented, "The program was a perfect example of a company being proactive in their interactions with the community. Everyone I know [from the polluted area] felt they were given a good deal. I've not heard any objections."[90]

LONG-TERM STRATEGIES

The company should develop strategies for reducing the costs of compliance and the risk of liability over the long term. These might include minimizing the amounts and kinds of pollutants produced, developing ways to recycle waste products, and investing in new technologies to render wastes nonhazardous. If hazardous wastes are produced, the company should have procedures for evaluating and selecting well-managed and well-constructed treatment and disposal facilities.

Firms are also well advised to plan now for more stringent greenhouse gas limits in the future. In 2008, three leading U.S. banks (Citigroup, JP Morgan–Chase, and

89. Michael Phillips & Mitchell Pacelle, *Banks Accept Environmental Rules,* Wall St. J., June 4, 2003, at A2.

90. *Uncivil Action,* 9 Treasury & Risk Mgmt. 25 (Jan.–Feb. 1999).

Morgan Stanley) established a set of principles—*The Carbon Principles*—for evaluating requests to finance projects involving power plants. The principles include a requirement of Enhanced Diligence, whereby the banks will investigate their clients' commitment to cleaner power sources, and a commitment to encourage clients to lower carbon dioxide emissions and to support legislation and regulations designed to cut emissions and promote carbon capture and storage.[91]

91. *Three U.S. Banks Develop Guidelines to Protect Against Climate Change Risk,* 76 U.S.L.W. 2468 (2008).

IN BRIEF

Developing an Environmental Compliance Program

In evaluating or developing an environmental program, a manager should consider the following areas and ask the following questions:

1. *Achieving and maintaining compliance:*
   - What laws and regulations affect the company's facilities?
   - What procedures effectively balance compliance costs with liability?
   - How can those procedures be communicated to those responsible for their implementation?
   - How can employees be persuaded they have a stake in the program's success?
2. *Obtaining timely notice of new requirements:*
   - What is being done to keep abreast of new requirements?
   - Will management receive notice early enough to make necessary changes cost-effectively?
3. *Influencing future requirements:*
   - What environmental laws and regulations are on the horizon?
   - How are they being tracked?
   - What is being done to influence their wording and enactment?
4. *Monitoring compliance accurately:*
   - What kind of monitoring is required?
   - Who will perform that monitoring?
   - How will the results be assessed?
5. *Timely and accurate reporting:*
   - When must a manager report information to regulators?
   - What procedures ensure that reportable incidents are brought to management's attention?
   - Does the company have databases for tracking chemical use and other technical information?
6. *Responding to emergencies:*
   - What systems are in place to respond to emergencies?
   - Are responsible employees trained to respond appropriately?
7. *Maintaining community relations:*
   - How strong is the company's relationship with the surrounding community?
   - What kind of programs are in place to maintain and expand that relationship?
   - How would management expect the community to respond to emergencies?

Source: Based on Steven J. Koorse, *When Less Is More—Trouble,* Bus. L. Today, Sept.–Oct. 1997, at 24.

GLOBAL VIEW

Global Warming: Kyoto and Beyond

As the 2012 Kyoto Protocol deadline approaches, world leaders are left to wonder whether the first global effort to combat greenhouse gas emissions has had any substantial positive impact on this key world issue. The Kyoto Protocol is an amendment to the United Nations Framework Convention on Climate Change, which was ratified by thirty-seven industrialized countries (excluding the United States and Australia) that pledged to reduce harmful greenhouse gas emissions to an average of 5 percent below the levels emitted in 1990. Each country was assigned an allowed level of emissions of carbon dioxide gases it was allowed to emit, but was also allowed to trade or purchase emissions credits from other (often developing) countries in order to meet the assigned goals.[92]

Even though the United States produces nearly a quarter of the world's greenhouse gases each year, President George W. Bush opposed the ratification of Kyoto.[93] He cited the cost of reductions and the fact that Kyoto exempted developing countries, such as Indonesia and China (the world's current top carbon polluter[94]), from the emissions caps applicable to industrialized nations.[95] In 2006 alone, China built 114,000 megawatts of fossil-fuel-based generating capacity, almost all of it coal-fired.[96] Critics of Kyoto argued that dramatic, and very costly, reductions in U.S. emissions would not reduce global levels of greenhouse gases if these other countries were not subject to the same limits.[97]

The European Union (EU) adopted a cap-and-trade system in 2005 as a way to meet the requirements set forth in Kyoto. As mentioned earlier, a cap-and-trade system is a market-based system that caps the amount of carbon dioxide that companies, such as power generators, are allowed to output.[98] If a company emits more than the amount allotted, it must then cut its emissions levels, buy allowances from more efficient companies, or buy extra allowances at government auctions. Nonetheless, emissions in the EU still rose about 1 percent a year from 2005 to 2008.[99] The failure of Europe's system to reduce emissions has been blamed on the national governments' handing out too many carbon permits. When officials designed the system, they based the emissions caps on estimates provided by each country, which received their data from the companies emitting the harmful gases—meaning that companies had no incentive to overhaul their factories or to install emissions-reducing technology.[100]

In response to criticisms of Kyoto, legislators from the Group of Eight nations (G8), India, Mexico, Brazil, China, and South Africa met in Washington, D.C., in February 2007 in an attempt to reach a nonbinding agreement on climate change that would require developing countries to meet targets for cutting greenhouse emissions and institute a cap-and-trade system.[101] As of August 2008, these efforts had not borne fruit. The United Nations already administers a pollution-trading program whereby poorer countries can sell pollution credits to polluters in rich countries, which can use the credits to help satisfy Kyoto or EU limits. The program was designed to spur investment in pollution-control technology in poorer countries to enable them to cut emissions without curtailing economic growth. Yet French chemical maker Rhodia SA, which operates facilities in South Korea and Brazil that destroy nitrous oxide (a greenhouse gas), stands to generate more than $1 billion from sales of pollution credits. Rhodia's facility in South Korea is expected to generate more revenues than all the registered pullution-cutting projects in Africa.[102]

CONTINUED

92. United Nations Framework Convention on Climate Change, *Fact Sheet: The Kyoto Protocol*, *available at* http://unfccc.int/files/press/backgrounders/application/pdf/fact_sheet_the_kyoto_protocol.pdf.

93. Bryan Walsh, *How to Win the War on Global Warming*, TIME, Apr. 16, 2008.

94. Roger Harrabin, *China "Now Top Carbon Polluter*," BBC NEWS, Apr. 14, 2008.

95. Steven Lee Myers, *Bush to Skip U.N. Talks on Global Warming*, N.Y. TIMES, Sept. 24, 2007.

96. Keith Bradsher, *China's Green Energy Gap*, N.Y. TIMES, Oct. 24, 2007.

97. Walsh, *supra* note 93.

98. Leila Abboud & Stephen Power, *U.S. Aims to Skirt Flaws in Europe's Carbon Limits; Cap-and-Trade Bill to Stress Auctions, Balance for Permits*, WALL ST. J., May 30, 2008, at A4.

99. *Id.*

100. *Id.*

101. *Politicians Sign a New Climate Pact*, BBC NEWS, Feb. 16, 2007.

102. Charles Forelle, *French Firm Cashes in Under U.N. Warming Program*, WALL ST. J., July 23, 2008.

In theory, the United States would be able to cut emissions to 71 percent below their 2005 levels by 2050 if it adopted a cap-and-trade system.[103] A bill proposed by U.S. Senators John Warner of Virginia and Joe Lieberman of Connecticut called for a national cap-and-trade program that would cap U.S. emissions of greenhouse gases by 18 percent by 2020. It faced heavy opposition, however.[104] Critics asserted that a national cap-and-trade law would stifle the economy and result in the loss of up to four million U.S. jobs by 2030 as well as cost $660 billion per year to enforce.[105] As the Senate began debating the bill in June 2008, White House spokesperson Dana Perino warned that President Bush would veto the proposed cap-and-trade bill in the unlikely event it passed.[106]

Whether or not a cap-and-trade system is the answer, the need for a solution of some kind is becoming increasingly apparent. During the July 2008 G8 Summit, Japanese Prime Minister Yasuo Fukuda led a discussion designed to reach a consensus on the growing issue of global warming.[107] In hopes of leading this global initiative, Japan has proposed a "Cool Earth Promotion Programme," a three-part plan to expand upon the post-Kyoto framework, seek international cooperation, and look into other technologies and innovations that will foster economic growth while reducing greenhouse emissions.[108] But as David G. Victor, Adjunct Senior Fellow for Science and Technology for the Council on Foreign Relations, cautioned:

> With a growing consensus for action, the world now faces the challenge of designing an effective policy response. International cooperation will be required because greenhouse gases are long-lived in the atmosphere—emissions from every country spread worldwide to create a truly global problem. . . . Today, awareness abounds and the main impediment to action is the lack of a viable architecture for international cooperation.[109]

103. Steve Mufson, *Is This Green Enough? We Can Clean Up Our Act, but It'll Cost Us*, WASH. POST, Apr. 20, 2008, at B1.

104. H. Josef Hebert, *Senate Votes to Begin Global Warming Debate*, ASSOC. PRESS, June 2, 2008.

105. Walsh, *supra* note 93.

106. Hebert, *supra* note 104.

107. G8 Hokkaido Toyako Summit, *Summit Info, available at* http://www.g8summit.go.jp/eng/index.html.

108. *Id.*

109. DAVID G. VICTOR, THE COLLAPSE OF THE KYOTO PROTOCOL AND THE STRUGGLE TO SLOW GLOBAL WARMING vii–xi (2001).

THE RESPONSIBLE MANAGER

MANAGING ENVIRONMENTAL RISKS

Several sources of potential environmental liability present risks to the parties in business transactions. In evaluating a company for purposes of acquisition, investment, or financing, a manager must consider that the company's earnings may be affected by the costs of compliance with environmental laws. The value of its equipment assets may be affected by regulatory limitations that make the equipment obsolete. Its ability to expand in existing locations may be impaired as a result of limitations on new sources of air emissions or the lack of nearby waste treatment or disposal facilities. A company's cash flow may be affected by additional capital investments or by increased operating costs necessitated by environmental regulations. Failure to comply with existing regulations may lead to the imposition of substantial penalties, also affecting cash flow. Small companies or companies that are highly leveraged may not be able to meet these additional demands for cash.

Similarly, a small company may not be able to survive the imposition of liability for response costs under CERCLA or similar state laws. Potential liabilities may not be properly reflected in the company's financial statements. Finally, a company's operations or the condition of its properties may present risks of injury to other persons and their property, giving rise to possible tort claims.

The most important element in managing the risk of these potential liabilities is ***due diligence***, that is, a systematic

CONTINUED

and ongoing process for determining whether property contains or emits hazardous substances and whether the company is in compliance with environmental laws. The object of environmental due diligence investigations is to identify and characterize the risks associated with the properties and operations involved in the business transaction. Such investigations have become highly sophisticated undertakings, often requiring the use of technical consultants and legal counsel with special expertise. Although much of the effort focuses on the review of company documents and available public records, it may also involve physical inspections of the properties, including soil and groundwater sampling and analysis. Care should be taken to avoid negligent soil investigations, which can create liability for disposal of hazardous waste. Environmental due diligence may represent a significant cost of the transaction and may take much longer to complete than traditional due diligence efforts.

The scope of the due diligence effort will depend on the nature of the assets and the structure of the transaction. For example, if the transaction is a simple purchase and sale of real estate, then the due diligence can be limited to the property to be acquired and its surroundings. If the transaction involves the acquisition of a business with a long history of operations in many locations, however, then the due diligence investigation must cover not only the current operating locations but also prior operating locations and the sites used for off-site disposal of wastes. This is particularly true when a company is acquired by merger because the surviving company takes over all of the liabilities of the disappearing company.

Allocation of the risk of liability under CERCLA and other environmental laws has become a significant issue in the negotiation of business transactions. The parties can, by contract, allocate the identified risks of environmental liability by undertaking specified obligations, assuming and retaining contingent liabilities, adjusting the purchase price, making representations and warranties, giving indemnities, and the like. But care must be exercised when the identified risks are not yet quantifiable. For example, if liability for response costs is accepted in return for a reduction in the purchase price, it should be borne in mind that response costs often exceed by a wide margin the initial estimate provided by a consultant or government agency.

It is also important to remember that contractual arrangements to shift environmental liability are not binding on federal or state governments. Thus, even if the seller of a piece of property agrees to indemnify the purchaser for any environmental claims arising out of the seller's activities, the EPA can still recover response costs from the present owner. The present owner could sue the seller for indemnification and contribution, but the present owner will bear the entire cleanup cost if the previous owner is insolvent or has insufficient assets.

Under CERCLA, secured lenders, and in some cases equity investors, may be deemed liable for response costs as present operators if they participate in the day-to-day management of the borrower's facilities. If a lender takes title at foreclosure, it may also be deemed liable for response costs as a present owner unless it attempts to dispose of the property reasonably quickly. Thus, the risk of hazardous substance releases on the subject property should be carefully evaluated in connection with the loan application. The operations of the borrower should also be carefully reviewed to evaluate the risks they present during the life of the loan. If a release of hazardous substances occurs on the property, its value as collateral is impaired. Upon default, the lender may not be able to recover the outstanding amount of the debt.

In trying to protect against diminishment of the value of collateral, a lender must be careful not to participate in management, however. Overly strict loan covenants that involve the lender in making operational decisions (such as approval of major capital expenditures) may create operator liability for the lender.

In addition, some states have adopted *superlien* provisions, which secure recovery of response costs incurred by state agencies. Where a superlien exists, it may take priority over existing security interests.

When an owner leases property, it must take care to evaluate the environmental risks of the tenant's operations. Use of the property should be carefully limited to prevent any unauthorized activities. If the tenant's activities present significant risks, financial assurances in the form of parent corporation guarantees, letters of credit, or performance bonds might be obtained to ensure that any damage caused by the tenant will be remedied. Tenants also should be cautious in taking possession of property formerly occupied by others. Many tenants perform *baseline assessments* to establish the environmental condition of the property at both the commencement and the termination of the lease. These assessments may provide some protection from liability for conditions caused by prior or succeeding tenants.

A Manager's Dilemma

Putting It into Practice

Exporting Environmental Compliance

American Widgets is a manufacturing company that has gained a large share of the international widget market, largely because of its high quality and competitive pricing. The disposal of the company's wastes has become increasingly expensive, however. A new ban on land disposal will require the company to incinerate one of its largest waste streams. Plants of competitors located in Southeast Asia and South America are subject to increasing environmental regulation modeled after the laws in the United States, but they are not subject to a land-disposal ban and will have a significant competitive advantage over plants located in the United States. Jimmy Tsai, an American Widgets manager, is considering the possibility of locating a new plant in Southeast Asia. What factors should he take into account? What alternatives are there besides relocation?

Inside Story

GE: FROM PCBs IN THE HUDSON TO ECOMAGINATION

From 1947 to 1977, the General Electric Company (GE) dumped as much as 1.3 million pounds of polychlorinated biphenyls (PCBs) from its capacitor manufacturing plants at the Hudson Falls and Fort Edward facilities into the Hudson River in New York State. At that time, the dumping of PCBs was legal. In 1977, after PCBs were found to be a threat to the environment and to people who ate fish caught in the river, GE ended decades of river contamination.[110]

For years GE repeatedly pointed out that it did nothing illegal and ran a massive media campaign to convince the public that the best way to heal the Hudson was to take no action at all.[111] The company also claimed that PCBs had fallen to acceptable levels and that dredging up the settled soil would only lead to spikes in levels, impose an undue burden on its shareholders, and expose the people of the Hudson Valley to unnecessary health risks.[112]

After years of fighting the EPA and environmental activists, GE finally agreed in October 2005 to clean up forty-three miles of the river bottom stretching from Hudson Falls to Troy, New York.[113] Under the terms of the agreement, which was approved by the U.S. District Court for the Northern District of New York in 2006, GE agreed to dredge the heaviest deposits of PCBs, at a cost of $100 million to $150 million. The first phase of the job, scheduled to begin in 2009, will remove about 10 percent of the 2.65 million cubic yards of PCB-contaminated sediment. The second phase of cleanup, where the contamination is less concentrated but spread over a larger area, is expected to take several years and cost about $500 million.

Also in 2005, GE launched "Ecomagination," a business initiative designed to reduce GE's own emissions and to demonstrate GE's commitment to make environmentally friendly, but profitable products.[114] GE, in conjunction with GreenOrder, a sustainability strategy and marketing firm, created the Ecomagination Product Review (EPR) scorecard, which quantifies a product's environmental impacts and benefits relative to other products to determine whether it is worthy to bear the Ecomagination brand.

GE's results speak for themselves. As of early 2008, the firm had met its original four Ecomagination commitments: (1) increasing revenues from Ecomagination products to $20 billion a year by 2010, (2) doubling investments in the research and

CONTINUED

110. EPA, Hudson River PCBs, *available at* http://www.epa.gov/hudson.

111. Associated Press, *EPA Vows to Clean Up Hudson River; GE Opposes Plan*, Dec. 6, 2000.

112. Anthony DePalma, *G.E. Commits to Dredging 43 Miles of Hudson River*, N.Y. Times, Oct. 7, 2005.

113. *Id.*

114. Martin LaMonica, *Newsmaker: Stirring GE's Ecoimagination*, CNET News.com, Oct. 26, 2007.

development of environmentally friendly products to $10 billion a year by 2010, (3) reducing its own greenhouse gas emissions and improving the energy efficiency of its operations, and (4) keeping the public informed of its progress through audited reporting. GE sold $14 billion in Ecomagination products in 2007 alone. In the period from 2004 to 2006, GE reduced its own greenhouse gas emissions by 4 percent and saved more than $100 million a year in energy costs by utilizing solar panels, switching to natural gas, cutting emissions in the manufacture of locomotive engines, and adopting other conservation techniques.[115] In its 2007 annual report, GE added a fifth commitment: to decrease its water consumption by 20 percent by 2012 and to develop new water purification and conservation processes and products.[116] In his February 20, 2008 letter to investors, GE CEO Jeff Immelt called Ecomagination "a global brand, symbolic of innovation at GE" and stated that GE had raised its original Ecomagination revenue target to $25 billion by 2010.[117]

115. *Id.*

116. General Electric Co., Ecomagination Report 2007, *available at* http://ge.ecomagination.com/site/downloads/news/2007ecoreport.pdf.

117. General Electric Co., 2007 Annual Report, *available at* http://ge.com.

Key Words and Phrases

baseline assessments 637
brownfields 621
cap-and-trade system 611
carbon footprint 607
continuity of enterprise approach 620
contribution 618
due diligence 636
environmental justice 626
environmental law 607
Environmental Protection Agency (EPA) 609
hazard ranking score 616
Hazardous Substance Superfund 616
industrial ecology 615
innocent landowner defense 621
innovation offsets 615
mere continuation (identity) test 620
national ambient air quality standards (NAAQS) 610
national effluent limitations 613
National Pollutant Discharge Elimination System (NPDES) 613
natural resources laws 609
navigable waters 613
potentially responsible parties (PRPs) 617
publicly owned sewage treatment works (POTWs) 613
strategic environmental management 615
substantial continuity test 620
successor liability 620
superlien 637
third-party defense 621

Questions and Case Problems

1. Northeastern Pharmaceutical and Chemical Company (NEPACCO) had a manufacturing plant in Verona, Missouri, that produced various hazardous and toxic by-products. The company pumped the by-products into a holding tank, which a waste hauler periodically emptied. Michaels founded the company, was a major shareholder, and served as its president. In 1971, a waste hauler named Mills approached Ray, a chemical-plant manager employed by NEPACCO, and proposed disposing of some of the firm's wastes at a nearby farm. Ray visited the farm and, with the approval of Lee, the vice president and a shareholder of NEPACCO, arranged for disposal of wastes at the farm.

   Approximately eighty-five 55-gallon drums were dumped into a large trench on the farm. In 1976, NEPACCO was liquidated, and the assets remaining after payment to creditors were distributed to its shareholders. Three years later the EPA investigated the area and discovered dozens of badly deteriorated drums containing hazardous waste buried at the farm. The EPA took remedial action and then sought to recover its costs under RCRA and other statutes. From whom and on what basis can the government recover its costs? [*United States v. Northeastern Pharmaceutical and Chemical Co.,* 810 F.2d 726 (8th Cir. 1986), *cert. denied,* 484 U.S. 848 (1987).]

2. In 1968, Habco, Inc. purchased property on Armour Road in North Kansas City, Missouri, that had been contaminated by a series of firms—including U.S. Borax Inc.—that made and blended various herbicides on the premises. The contamination continued under Habco, which was principally owned by Donald Horne. Habco subsequently sold its operating assets—but not the Armour Road real property—to a new company called Habco-Loram Inc. Although Horne remained associated with Habco-Loram, he did not have a personal equitable interest in the firm. When Habco-Loram was unable to meet its obligations, it transferred its assets to Horne, who formed another new firm called Habco International, Inc. Habco International substantially carried on the herbicide operations begun by Habco and continued by Habco-Loram but at a different locale. Habco International never owned or leased the Armour Road site. The DeAngelo brothers purchased Habco International's stock in 1997 and merged Habco International into DeAngelo Brothers Inc. in 1998. The EPA declared the Armour Road site a Superfund site in the early 1990s, and a court ultimately ordered Horne to pay 40 percent of the $1.16 million in cleanup costs, Borax 10 percent, and DeAngelo 15 percent. Should each of these parties be responsible for paying part or all of the cleanup costs? If you conclude that more than one party has liability, what percentage of the total cleanup costs should each responsible party be required to pay? [*K.C. 1986 Limited Partnership v. Reade Manufacturing*, 472 F.3d 1009 (8th Cir. 2007).]

3. George Lu was named the executive director of the Cornell University Foundation, a nonprofit association organized to support the university. As part of its efforts, the foundation has begun a program to preserve open-space land and ecologically sensitive environments near the university's campus in upstate New York. The foundation plans to buy or receive gifts of land, especially from alumni, and then sell the land to public entities for permanent preservation. The difference between the purchase price and the sale price will be used to finance the association's efforts and to support Cornell generally. One of Lu's first tasks is to develop a protocol and prepare model agreements for making acquisitions.

   a. As a nonprofit, educational organization, does the association have potential liability under the environmental laws?

   b. What procedures should Lu establish to protect the association from potential environmental law liabilities in connection with its acquisitions?

   c. What kinds of contractual arrangements should be considered to protect the association from environmental law liabilities? [*See, e.g., United States v. Alcan Aluminum Corp.,* 34 E.R.C. 1744 (N.D.N.Y. 1991).]

4. RCRA regulations defining solid waste state that a "solid waste is any discarded material." The EPA issued a new regulation classifying reclaimed mineral-processing materials destined for recycling as regulated "solid waste." These reclaimed materials are stored in tanks and containers before they are recycled. Industry groups representing most U.S. producers of steel, metal, and coal and most industrial miners challenged the new regulations. They argued that by allowing the materials stored before recycling to be considered waste, the rule conflicts with RCRA's definition of waste as discarded materials. How should the court rule? [*Ass'n of Battery Recyclers v. EPA,* 208 F.3d 1047 (D.C. Cir. 2000).]

5. The City of Florence, a municipal corporation organized under the laws of Alabama, purchased property for the purpose of encouraging industrial development within the county where the city is located. Florence leased the property to Stylon, a corporation that planned to construct and operate a ceramic tile manufacturing factory on the property. Florence issued bonds to finance the purchase of the property and mortgaged the property to First National Bank of Florence, pledging that Stylon's rent payments for the property would be used to secure the repayment on the bonds held by the bank.

   Stylon operated a tile manufacturing facility on the property for approximately twenty years until it went bankrupt. During that time, it discharged hazardous substances, which contaminated the property. After Stylon went bankrupt, Monarch Tile, Inc. leased the property for fifteen years from the City of Florence, with the city retaining title. Subsequently, Monarch purchased the property from the city.

   After Monarch discovered the contamination, it notified the EPA and was directed to remediate pursuant to CERCLA. Monarch brought suit against the City of Florence for contribution under CERCLA. The City of Florence argued that it was not liable because it held ownership of the property primarily to protect its security interest. How should the court rule? Should the National Bank of Florence or the former Stylon shareholders be forced to contribute to the cost of remediation? [*Monarch Tile Inc. v. City of Florence,* 212 F.3d 1219 (11th Cir. 2000).]

6. Gregg Entrepreneur is organizing a small company to manufacture a new biotechnology product. Entrepreneur will be a principal shareholder and president of the company. What measures should Entrepreneur take to ensure that his company operates in compliance with environmental laws?

   Despite all the measures Entrepreneur has taken to ensure environmental law compliance, his vice president of operations reports that the production manager has been disposing of wastes into the sewer in violation of national pretreatment standards and that she has been submitting false reports to the publicly owned sewage treatment works (POTWs) to cover up the violations. All of the reports have been signed by the vice president of operations, who had no knowledge that they contained false statements. What steps should Entrepreneur take? Should he report the violations to the POTWs even if it could result in personal civil or criminal liability? What about the vice president? The production manager? What is Entrepreneur's ethical responsibility? [*United States v. Alley,* 755 F. Supp. 771 (N.D. Ill. 1990).]

7. A Colorado silver mine was owned by a company that went bankrupt. The three main creditors of the bankrupt firm formed the Raytheon Mine Company (RMI) as part of the plan of reorganization. RMI ran and operated the mine and gave each creditor a percentage of its stock commensurate with the original bankrupt company. Biller Company was one such minor creditor and never owned more than 20 percent of RMI. Years after the money owed Biller Company was repaid and Biller had sold its interest in the mine, the government assessed serious environmental cleanup costs under CERCLA. Biller's former partners in RMI brought a claim for contribution against Biller as a successor in interest to the tainted land to recover part of the cleanup costs. Will their claim be successful? [*Raytheon Construction Inc. v. Asarco Inc.,* 368 F.3d 1214 (10th Cir. 2003).]

8. After paying to clean the portion of the Mohawk River around its oil refinery and storage operation, Niagara Mohawk Power Corporation (NMPC) filed claims for contribution against several other companies that had maintained facilities in the area. One of the companies, Mohawk Valley Oil (MVO), had used a parcel to store oil as part of its own petroleum business. On one side of that parcel was the river and on the opposite side was land used by a tar manufacturing company, Tar Asphalt Services (TAS). Among other activities, TAS washed tar from its trucks using kerosene. TAS allowed the contaminated runoff to cross MVO's property into the river. MVO became aware of this TAS practice after it purchased the land and took steps to prevent the runoff from reaching its property as it developed the location. NMPC argued that while MVO's actions had prevented the flow of additional kerosene-tainted water across its property, it had done nothing to remediate the prior disposals and therefore remained liable under CERCLA. Does failing to prevent contaminated water from crossing one's property qualify as a "disposal" of hazardous waste under CERCLA? What liability would MVO have faced if it had failed to take steps to prevent the runoff from TAS's activities once it became aware of it? [*Niagara Mohawk Power Corp. v. Jones Chemical Inc.,* 315 F. 3d 171 (2d Cir. 2003).]

13

CONSUMER PROTECTION

INTRODUCTION

Role of Consumer Protection Law in Business

Historically, consumers had little recourse in the event of a dispute with a vendor, manufacturer, producer, service provider, or creditor. Consumer transactions were commonly governed by the concept of *caveat emptor* ("let the buyer beware"). Today, the standard has shifted closer to *venditur emptor* ("let the seller beware"). Federal and state laws protect consumers from unsafe or harmful consumer products, unfair and deceptive trade practices, fraud, and misleading or discriminatory credit requirements. Managers must, of course, comply with the law. In addition, by being proactive, working with administrative agencies, and promoting industry self-regulation, managers may be able to both protect brand equity and forestall burdensome new regulatory restrictions.

CHAPTER OVERVIEW

This chapter examines three primary areas of consumer protection law and the agencies, departments, and commissions that administer and enforce them: (1) consumer health and safety (including the regulation of food, drugs, medical devices, automobiles, broadcasting, and the Internet); (2) unfairness, deception, and fraud (including the regulation of advertising, packaging and labeling, pricing, warranties, and certain sales practices); and (3) consumer credit. The discussion focuses primarily on federal legislation, although numerous state law topics are also discussed. In general, consumer protection law at the state level is more stringent than federal law and, as discussed in the "Global View," product safety and environmental standards in the European Union are higher than those in the United States. We discussed privacy protection in Chapter 9 and will discuss consumer bankruptcy under Chapter 13 of the Bankruptcy Code in Chapter 24.

COMMISSIONS AND AGENCIES

Federal regulatory agencies involved in consumer protection are either independent commissions or executive branch agencies. Independent commissions include the Federal Trade Commission, the Federal Communications Commission, the Securities and Exchange Commission, the Federal Reserve Board, and the Consumer Product Safety Commission. The Federal Trade Commission, for example, has five commissioners appointed by the president and confirmed by the Senate for seven-year terms. No more than three of them can be from the same political party. The commissioners make decisions by majority vote and issue rules.

Executive branch regulatory agencies are located in cabinet departments. Examples include the Food and Drug Administration (located within the U.S. Department of Health and Human Services), the Office of Interstate Land Sales Registration (U.S. Department of Housing and Urban Development), and the National Highway Traffic Safety Administration (U.S. Department of Transportation).

CONSUMER HEALTH AND SAFETY

A number of federal, state, and local regulatory agencies protect consumers' health and safety, including the Food and Drug Administration (FDA), the Department of

Agriculture, the Department of Transportation's National Highway Traffic Safety Administration, and the Consumer Product Safety Commission. For example, under the Food, Drug and Cosmetic Act,[1] the FDA monitors the production and sale of more than $1 trillion of food and medical products each year. In addition to specifying the proper labeling of food, drugs, medical devices, and cosmetics to prevent *misbranding*, the FDA also regulates the new-drug approval process.

The Federal Trade Commission also regulates the packaging and labeling of certain products. Numerous state laws cover such items as food, drugs, medical devices, cosmetics, clothing, tobacco, and alcohol.

1. 21 U.S.C. § 321 *et seq.*

Consumer protection law should not be confused with product liability law, discussed in Chapter 10. Product liability law provides a common law remedy enforced by private action, whereas consumer protection law provides a statutory remedy enforced by the government (and, in some cases, also by private parties).

At the state level, consumer health and safety laws cover a wide variety of areas, such as the availability of alcohol, tobacco, and gambling. State and local laws also address prohibitions against smoking, restaurant inspections, and the competency of professional workers through the granting of various occupational licenses.

The "In Brief" identifies the key federal commissions and agencies charged with administering major consumer protection laws.

IN BRIEF

Consumer Protection Laws and Their Administration

Agency, Department, or Commission	Consumer Credit	Unfairness, Deception, and Fraud	Consumer Health and Safety
Federal Trade Commission Established: 1914 Commissioners: 5	Credit advertising; Fair Credit Reporting Act; Fair Debt Collection Practices Act	Advertising; sales practices	
Food and Drug Administration (U.S. Department of Health and Human Services) Established: 1930 Commissioner: 1			Labeling of food (except meat, poultry, and eggs), drugs, and cosmetics; adulterated food and cosmetics; approval of drugs and medical devices
U.S. Department of Agriculture Established: 1862			Labeling of meat, poultry, and eggs; inspection of meat, poultry, and egg processing facilities
National Highway Traffic Safety Administration (NHTSA) (U.S. Department of Transportation) Established: 1970 Administrator: 1			Automobile safety standards; driver safety
Consumer Product Safety Commission Established: 1972 Commissioners: 3			Consumer Product Safety Act (CPSA)
Federal Communications Commission Established: 1934 Commissioners: 5		Telemarketing	Broadcast standards

CONTINUED

Agency, Department, or Commission	Consumer Credit	Unfairness, Deception, and Fraud	Consumer Health and Safety
U.S. Postal Service Established: 1775 Reorganized: 1970		Sales practices	
Securities and Exchange Commission Established: 1934 Commissioners: 5		Securities fraud	
Federal Reserve Board Established: 1913 Governors: 7	Truth in Lending Act (Regulation Z); Consumer Leasing Act (Regulation M); Equal Credit Opportunity Act (Regulation B); Electronic Fund Transfer Act (Regulation E)		
U.S. Department of Labor Established: 1913	Garnishment of wages		
Office of Interstate Land Sales Registration (U.S. Department of Housing and Urban Development) Established: 1969		Interstate land sales	
Bankruptcy courts	Chapter 13 consumer bankruptcy		

FOOD SAFETY AND LABELING

The Food and Drug Administration and the Department of Agriculture have the primary responsibility for food safety and labeling.

PRODUCT DEFINITION: FOOD OR DRUG?

Because the distinction between drugs and food is important in the application of both the mislabeling and the adulteration provisions of the Food, Drug and Cosmetic Act, as well as in the drug-approval process, the FDA must categorize each product. *Drugs*, as defined by the Act, include (1) articles intended for use in the diagnosis, cure, mitigation, treatment, or prevention of disease; and (2) articles (other than food) intended to affect the structure or any function of the body. Thus, many things that are, in fact, food may fit this definition. For example, orange juice might be used to prevent disease. Under the Act, *food* is defined as (1) articles used for food or drink, (2) chewing gum, and (3) articles used for components of either.

In general, the FDA looks at the intended use of a product in determining how to categorize it. Intent may be apparent from the manufacturer's purpose or from consumers' reasons for using the product, or it may be inferred from labels, promotional material, or advertisements.

FDA STANDARDS FOR FOOD CONDEMNATION

The FDA protects consumer health and safety through the confiscation of contaminated or adulterated foods. Tainted food causes more than 5,000 deaths annually in the United States and millions of illnesses.[2]

The standards for condemnation differ depending on whether the product is a natural food or contains additives. An *additive* is anything not inherent in the food product, including pesticide residue, unintended environmental contaminants, and substances unavoidably added from packaging. If an additive (in the quantity present in the food product) is injurious to any group in the general population, then the product will be deemed adulterated. A natural food is *adulterated* if it "consist[s] in whole or in

2. Greg Winter, *Contaminated Food Makes Millions Ill Despite Advances*, N.Y. TIMES, Mar. 18, 2001, *available at* http://query.nytimes.com/gst/fullpage.html?res=9900E3D8123DF93BA25750C0A9679C8B63.

part of any filthy, putrid or decomposed substance, or if it is otherwise unfit for food." All foods contain some level of unavoidable natural defects, so the FDA sets minimum tolerance standards for defects that will be tolerated. Articles that exceed those minimum levels are deemed adulterated and seized by the FDA. In some cases, a seized product may be rehabilitated by a manufacturer and released by the FDA for sale.

In a hotly debated decision, the FDA allowed U.S. meat providers to sell "downed" cattle and other livestock.[3] Opponents claimed that these cattle, which were either too weak to walk or had collapsed entirely before slaughter, had a much greater chance of carrying a potentially fatal disease, known as mad cow disease. Nonetheless, the FDA concluded that as long as a postmortem inspection was performed by an official veterinarian, this food was safe for human consumption.

A chief executive officer of a food company was held vicariously and strictly criminally liable for introducing adulterated articles into interstate commerce.[4] A CEO should require top managers to have adequate policies and checks in place to ensure the proper handling and storage of food. If a problem is brought to a manager's attention, he or she should immediately report it to a supervisor and personally ensure that it is remedied.

INTERNATIONAL SNAPSHOT

Free trade treaties have made the U.S. food market one of the most open in the world. Yet problems with imported food, such as the salmonella outbreak in the summer of 2008 caused by tomatoes and peppers grown in Mexico, present challenges for regulators. Effective September 30, 2008, the U.S. Department of Agriculture requires all stores to label unprocessed beef, pork, lamb, veal, chicken and nuts with the country of origin.

The USDA estimates that labeling will cost $2.5 billion in the first year and $500 million annually thereafter; these costs will be borne mainly by supermarkets. Many retailers and meat producers see little benefit for the consumer, particularly because the law does not cover processed foods. Mark Dopp, a senior vice president for the American Meat Institute, asked, "What can they learn from seeing the country? This tells nothing about safety."[a] Ultimately, the burden of ensuring safe food may fall on the globalized food industry.

a. Bob Lamendola, *Do You Know Where Your Beef Comes From? New Labels Soon Will Tell You Nations of Origin of More Foods*, S. FL. SUN-SENTINEL, Sept. 23, 2008.

ROLE OF THE U.S. DEPARTMENT OF AGRICULTURE

The U.S. Department of Agriculture (USDA) also plays a major role in food safety. The USDA's primary consumer protection activities all involve food. They include inspecting facilities engaged in the slaughtering or processing of meat, poultry, and egg products; preventing the sale of mislabeled meat or poultry products; and offering producers a voluntary grading program for various agricultural products. In February 2008, the USDA ordered the largest meat recall in its history: 143 million pounds of beef produced by a California meatpacker that failed to prevent ailing animals from entering the U.S. food supply were recalled.[5]

PESTICIDES AND HUMAN-MADE BUGS

Under the Food, Drug and Cosmetic Act, the FDA shares with the Environmental Protection Agency (EPA) the responsibility for regulating pesticide residues on food. The EPA regulates pesticides and establishes tolerances under the Act. The FDA enforces the tolerance levels and deems a food to be adulterated if its residues exceed those levels.

Scientists are creating genetically engineered insects and microbes to fight pests, such as the glassy-winged sharpshooter, which has already destroyed $14 billion worth of grapes and other crops in California. In the absence of a clear framework for regulating bioengineered insects and pathogens, scientists are seeking approvals from the EPA. According to the executive director of the nonprofit Pew Initiative on Food and Biotechnology, "The regulatory system is lagging well behind the science."[6]

GENETICALLY MODIFIED FOOD AND CLONED MEAT AND MILK

The FDA authorized the sale of genetically modified food in 1992 but did not require that it be labeled as such. At the state level, Vermont requires the labeling of genetically modified seeds, and Alaska requires the labeling of transgenic fish.[7] In April 2000, the National Academy of Science issued a

3. Baur v. Veneman, 352 F.3d 625 (2d Cir. 2003) (Case 6.3).
4. United States v. Park, 421 U.S. 658 (1975).
5. *See* David Brown, *USDA Orders Largest Meat Recall in U.S. History*, WASH. POST, Feb. 18, 2008, at A1; Adam Cohen, *100 Years Later, the Food Industry Is Still "The Jungle,"* N.Y. TIMES, Jan. 2, 2007.
6. Catherine Arnst, *Panacea—Or Pandora's Box?*, BUS. WK., May 3, 2004, at 75.
7. Pallavi Gogoi, *States Move to Label Cloned Food*, BUS. WK., Mar. 4, 2008.

report advising the federal government to increase its regulation of genetically modified foods. Although the report did not find that genetically modified food was unsafe, it urged scientists to develop better methods for identifying potential allergens and called on regulatory agencies to monitor the environmental impact of genetically modified organisms (GMOs).[8] The report also concluded that the EPA, USDA, and FDA should do a better job of coordinating their work and informing the public about GMOs.[9]

European consumers have vehemently opposed the sale of genetically modified foods and launched a major campaign against efforts to market GMOs in Europe. In 2001, the European Parliament approved legislation that requires continuous monitoring of GMOs. The law calls for labeling and monitoring of genetically modified foods, seeds, feeds, and pharmaceuticals, and it requires governments to maintain a registry of where such plants are being grown.[10] Australia and New Zealand also require labeling of genetically modified food.

Opposition to GMOs has spread to the United States where consumers have protested GMOs because of both health safety and environmental concerns. In July 2003, the "Genetically Engineered Food Right to Know Act" was proposed in Congress.[11] As of 2008, it had not been enacted. Given the potentially enormous benefits of genetically modified foods, particularly for developing countries, the debate over regulating genetically engineered crops is far from over.

In 2008, the FDA authorized the sale of food from cloned animals and decided not to require labels for cloned food after concluding that meat and milk from cloned animals were "as safe to eat as food from conventionally bred animals."[12] In response, state legislators introduced mandatory labeling bills in thirteen states, including California, New Jersey and Kentucky.[13] The California House and Senate passed a mandatory labeling and tracking bill in 2007, but it was vetoed by Governor Arnold Schwarzenegger on the grounds that it was "unworkable, costly, and unenforceable."[14] The Cloned Food Labeling Act, which Senator Barbara Mikulski (D.-Md.) first introduced in 2007, would require that food from cloned animals bear the label: "This product is from a cloned animal or its progeny." Senator Mikulski explained the bill's rationale: "Labeling does two things. It gives consumers the right to know and allows scientists to monitor."[15]

IRRADIATED FOODS

In December 1997, the FDA authorized the irradiation of fresh and frozen red meat as a means of killing foodborne bacteria (including *E. coli*) and lengthening shelf life. During irradiation, food is passed through a sealed chamber, where it is exposed to gamma ray radiation from cobalt 60 or cesium 137 or to an electron beam. FDA regulations require irradiated foods to be prominently and conspicuously labeled with the radura symbol (a stylized green flower) and the words "Treated with Radiation" or "Treated by Irradiation."

For many consumers, irradiation conjures up images of mushroom clouds and the nuclear reactor meltdown in 1986 at Chernobyl in Ukraine.[16] Nonetheless, experts predicted that consumers will be won over by irradiation's safety and effectiveness in protecting consumers from bacteria and other microbes. Former FDA commissioner Dr. David Kessler drew parallels to the public's shunning of pasteurized milk in the early twentieth century and the initial distrust of microwave ovens in the 1970s.[17]

ORGANIC FOODS

Sales of organic products in the United States amounted to approximately $17 billion in 2006.[18] Uniform standards promulgated by the USDA for organic food ban the use of pesticides, genetic engineering, growth hormones, and irradiation. They also require dairy cattle to have access to pasture. Foods grown and processed according to the standards may bear the seal "USDA Organic."[19]

FOOD LABELING

The FDA has primary responsibility for regulating the packaging and labeling of food (except meat, poultry, and eggs, which are under the jurisdiction of the USDA), drugs, medical devices, and cosmetics. The Fair Packaging and

8. GMOs are discussed further in Chapter 25.
9. Scott Kilman, *Government Is Advised to Tighten Regulation of Bioengineered Crops,* WALL ST. J., Apr. 6, 2000, at B2.
10. *Genetic Engineering: Euro Parliament Approves Guidelines,* Feb. 14, 2001, *available at* http://www.eenews.net.
11. H.R. 2916, 108th Cong. (2003).
12. Gogoi, *supra* note 7.
13. *Id.*
14. *Id.*
15. *Id.*
16. Martha Groves, *Less-Than Glowing Image Hampers Food Irradiation,* L.A. TIMES, Mar. 15, 1998, at A1.
17. Joanna Ramey, *Food Industry Groups Near Start of Irradiation Campaign,* SUPERMARKET NEWS, Apr. 17, 1998, at 23.
18. Organic Consumers Ass'n, *U.S. Organic Food Sales Up 22%, Hit $17 Billion in 2006,* May 7, 2007.
19. Frederick J. Frommer, *Some Worry New USDA Label Will Change Organic Farming,* ASSOC. PRESS, Jan. 13, 2001.

Labeling Act[20] requires prepackaged foods to bear labels containing the name and address of the manufacturer, packer, or distributor; the net quantity, placed in a uniform location on the front panel; the quantity in servings, with the net quantity of each serving stated; and the quantity listed in certain other ways, depending on how the product is classified. This last provision requires dual declarations of sizes (for example, one quart and thirty-two ounces) and forbids the use of terms such as "jumbo quart" and "super ounce." Many supermarkets now provide unit-pricing information so that consumers can more easily compare the prices of competing products. Manufacturers of goods that are to be exported also need to consider foreign labeling requirements, such as language translations, country of origin disclosures, and weight conversions.

Nutrition Facts

The Nutrition Labeling and Education Act of 1990[21] (1) requires nutrition labeling of almost all foods through a nutrition panel entitled "Nutrition Facts," (2) requires expanded ingredient labeling, and (3) restricts nutrient content claims and health claims. The FDA has also issued regulations governing the use of nutrient claims, such as "light," "fat free," and "low calorie," and providing uniform definitions so that these terms mean the same for any product on which they appear.

Approximately 90 percent of processed food must carry nutrition information. Exceptions include plain coffee and tea, delicatessen items, and bulk food. The Nutrition Facts panel must include the amount per serving of saturated fat, cholesterol, dietary fiber, sodium, and other nutrients. These panels also provide information on how the food fits into an overall daily diet. Point-of-purchase nutrition information is voluntary under the Act for many raw foods, including meat, poultry, raw fish, and fresh produce. The information may be shown in a poster or chart at a butcher's counter or a produce stand.

Effective 2006, the FDA required labels to list "trans fat," a form of partially hydrogenated oil that improves the shelf life and taste of products but contributes to fatal and nonfatal coronary heart disease.[22] PepsiCo's Frito-Lay division was the first major food company to eliminate trans fats from its potato chips and other products. It then obtained approval from the FDA to label its products "0 trans fats" before the FDA labeling requirement went into effect, thereby gaining a marketing edge.

Public health officials have increasingly put pressure on chain restaurants to display the number of calories their offerings contain next to each item on the menu. In January 2008, New York City began to require chain restaurants to post calorie information on their menus. As of 2008, more than a dozen state and local governments were considering imposing a similar requirement. These initiatives have met strong opposition from the food industry, with organizations like the National Restaurant Association claiming that calorie counts would confuse consumers and lead patrons to base food choices on the number of calories alone.[23]

Health Claims

The Nutrition Labeling and Education Act of 1990 permits manufacturers to make health claims for foods on labels without FDA approval as a new drug, or the risk of sanctions for issuing a "misbranded" product, as long as the claim has been certified by the FDA as being supported by significant scientific agreement. The FDA has approved several health claims on foods, including the relationship between calcium and osteoporosis, fiber-containing products and cancer, fruits and vegetables and cancer, folate and neural tube defects, and soluble fiber and coronary heart disease.

Drugs and Medical Devices

Drugs and medical devices, as well as drug advertising, are regulated by the FDA.

FDA STANDARDS FOR DRUG APPROVAL

The FDA has the authority to require that certain drugs be available only by prescription. If a drug authorized only for prescription use is sold over-the-counter, then it is misbranded, and the FDA will halt its sale. In general, the FDA will require prescription use only when a drug is toxic, requires a physician's supervision for safe use, or is addictive.

The first step in the approval process for new drugs is their classification by the Drug Enforcement Administration (DEA) into one of five schedules based on potential for abuse and currently accepted medical use. Only Schedule I drugs, those with the highest potential for abuse and no currently accepted medical use, cannot be approved by the FDA.

The drug-approval process for non-Schedule I drugs begins with preclinical research (which includes animal testing) aimed at the discovery and identification of drugs

20. 15 U.S.C. § 1451 *et seq.*

21. 21 U.S.C. §§ 301, 321, 337, 343, 371.

22. 64 Fed. Reg. 62,772 (Nov. 17, 1999).

23. Michael Orey, *A Food Fight Over Calorie Counts: Public Health Officials Want Caloric Content Listed On Menus.*, Bus. Wk., Feb. 11, 2008.

that are sufficiently promising to study in humans. The drugmaker then submits this preclinical research, along with a document called "Claimed Exemption for Investigational New Drug," to the FDA. The FDA can then permit or deny continued research. If approved for investigational purposes, a drug will be tested in humans in three separate phases, with FDA review at the end of each phase. This framework is designed to protect the safety of the human subjects used in the study, to develop necessary data on the drug, and to ensure that all studies are done properly. Once all of the testing data are assembled, they are submitted to the FDA, which may approve or deny the application. Approval is based on a drug's safety and effectiveness. The approval may require marketing restrictions, and it can be contested by anyone. The FDA must also approve the description of a drug (for example, labels and package inserts).

Drugs with a high potential for therapeutic gain and no satisfactory alternative may be given priority (expedited) review by the FDA. In addition, through open protocols, such drugs may be available during the investigational stage to people not within the clinical test group. For example, people with AIDS may have access to new drugs under investigation if studies yield preliminary evidence of effectiveness.

Congress passed the Food and Drug Administration Modernization Act of 1997[24] to speed up the approval of new drugs and medical devices and to make it easier for seriously ill patients to obtain experimental drugs. The Act permits the FDA to use outside reviewers to evaluate certain drugs and medical devices. This Act also includes a safe harbor for the distribution by drug manufacturers of certain third-party materials concerning "off-label" uses of their drugs.[25] "Off-label" uses are uses of a drug other than those for which it was approved. A physician can prescribe a drug to serve any purpose that he or she thinks is appropriate regardless of whether the drug was initially approved for that use, but the FDA restricts companies' ability to promote off-label uses.[26]

24. 21 U.S.C. § 353a.

25. 21 U.S.C. § 360aaa *et seq.*

26. *See* 65 Fed. Reg. 14,286 (Mar. 16, 2000).

› Ethical Consideration

Drug companies provide financial support to academic researchers in the form of employment or consulting fees, research funds, money to attend symposiums, and speaking honoraria. Should scientists disclose their ties to drug companies when publishing articles about their research? Should drug companies disclose these financial ties?

In *Thompson v. Western States Medical Center*,[27] the U.S. Supreme Court struck down the provisions of the Food and Drug Administration Modernization Act that exempted compounded drugs from the FDA's approval requirements only if the compounding pharmacy refrained from advertising particular compounded drugs. Compounding is a process whereby a pharmacist, pursuant to a physician's prescription, mixes ingredients to create a medication for a particular patient, usually because the patient is allergic to an ingredient in a mass-produced product. The Court held that the ban violated the Free Speech Clause of the First Amendment, as construed by the U.S. Supreme Court in *Central Hudson Gas & Electric Corp. v. Public Service Commission*.[28] The Act prohibited commercial speech that was neither unlawful nor misleading. The Court recognized the importance of the government's interests in preserving the effectiveness and integrity of the FDA's new-drug approval process while also permitting compounding to create drugs produced on such a small scale that it would be prohibitively expensive to require them to undergo safety and efficiency testing. Nonetheless, the Court concluded that the speech restrictions were more extensive than necessary to serve these interests. The Court identified several non-speech-related means of drawing a line between compounding and large-scale manufacturing that the government never even considered. The Court admonished Congress that "[i]f the First Amendment means anything, it means that regulating speech must be a last—not first—resort."

As discussed in Chapter 10, Merck & Co issued a voluntary recall of the popular anti-inflammatory drug Vioxx in 2004 after finding that the drug increased the risk of heart attacks and strokes. The FDA had approved Vioxx in 1999 to treat pain and inflammation caused by osteoarthritis and rheumatoid arthritis. In June 2000, Merck submitted to the FDA a safety study that found an increased risk of heart attacks and strokes in patients taking the drug. Nearly two years later, the FDA implemented labeling changes to reflect the study's findings, but did not issue a public health advisory until the fall of 2004, *after* Merck had voluntarily withdrawn Vioxx from the market.

The FDA's failure to respond to evidence that Vioxx was a potentially dangerous substance sparked criticism of the agency, including allegations that the FDA is too closely aligned with the commercial interests of the pharmaceutical producers that it is tasked to regulate.[29] Hardly the agency's only misstep in recent years, the Vioxx scandal was one in

27. 535 U.S. 357 (2002).

28. 447 U.S. 557 (1980).

29. Alicia Mundy, *Congress Moves to Beef Up FDA as Crisis Mounts*, WALL ST. J., July 30, 2008, at A4.

a string of drug-safety controversies that spurred congressional hearings on FDA regulatory procedure.

In the summer of 2008, Representative John Dingell (D.-Mich.) and Senator Chuck Grassley (R.-Iowa) led the drive to remake the FDA by giving it broader powers while monitoring its relationship with the drug companies.[30] Although Congress was unable to pass legislation during the brief fall session before the November 2008 elections, experts predicted that 2009 might bring the most significant overhaul of the FDA in a generation. Advocates of reform asserted that the FDA should be restructured to give the agency the authority to recall drugs and to impose significant fines on drug companies for safety violations.[31] Having an independent and effective FDA is particularly important in light of the U.S. Supreme Court's decision holding that FDA approval of a medical device preempts state law product liability claims.[32]

LABELING OF MEDICAL DEVICES

The labeling of medical devices is also under the jurisdiction of the FDA. As noted in Chapter 10, if a medical device has undergone full premarket FDA review and the manufacturer provides the FDA-mandated warnings, then state law failure-to-warn-claims are preempted. If, however, the device was exempt from full review, then the manufacturer could still be found liable under state product liability law for failure to warn if reasonable manufacturers would have done more.[33] For example, the U.S. Court of Appeals for the Tenth Circuit upheld a $10 million punitive damages award against International Playtex for failure to adequately warn users about the risk of fatal toxic shock syndrome from use of high-absorbing tampons.[34] The court concluded that Playtex had shown reckless indifference to consumer safety by deliberately disregarding studies and medical reports linking high-absorbency tampon fibers with increased risk of toxic shock at a time when other tampon manufacturers were responding to this information by modifying or withdrawing their high-absorbency products.

DRUG ADVERTISING

In 1997, the FDA eased the restrictions on the advertising of prescription drugs on television and radio. Drug companies can tout a drug's benefits without listing all of the side effects and explaining how to properly use the drug. Television ads must, however, warn of major risks and provide a quick way (such as a toll-free telephone number, Web address, or magazine advertisement) for consumers to obtain full information about the drug. Merck's recall of its heavily advertised drug Vioxx in 2004 sparked further debate on the proper use of drug advertising.[35]

HEALTH CLAIMS AND LABELING OF DIETARY SUPPLEMENTS

Under the Dietary Supplement Health and Education Act of 1994,[36] the sale of dietary supplements is regulated only when the supplement contains a new dietary ingredient or poses a safety risk. Dietary supplements include products such as vitamins, minerals, herbs, and amino acids. As with foods, however, health claims on dietary supplements can cause them to be characterized as drugs. The Nutrition Labeling and Education Act created a safe harbor for health claims on dietary supplements akin to that provided for food but delegated to the FDA the task of establishing a procedure and standard governing the validity of health claims.

The FDA issued regulations providing that it would authorize a health claim only if there was substantial scientific agreement among experts that the claim was supported by the totality of publicly available scientific evidence.[37] In 1999, however, the U.S. Court of Appeals for the District of Columbia curtailed the FDA's right to ban health-related claims made by sellers of nutritional supplements.[38] The FDA published a final rule in 2000 clarifying the types of claims that manufacturers of dietary supplements may make without prior review by the FDA and identifying those that require prior authorization.[39]

In early 2003, the FDA came under heavy fire when Steve Bechler, a twenty-three-year-old pitcher for the Baltimore Orioles baseball team, died suddenly during spring training workouts in Florida. Initially, Bechler's death was attributed to heat stroke, but a further medical examination revealed that

30. *Id.*

31. *Id.*

32. Riegel v. Medtronic, Inc., 128 S. Ct. 999 (2008) (Case 10.).

33. Medtronic, Inc. v. Lohr, 514 U.S. 470 (1996).

34. Ogilvie v. Int'l Playtex, Inc., 821 F.2d 1438 (10th Cir. 1987), *cert. denied,* 486 U.S. 1032 (1988).

35. For an interesting article, coauthored by the Senior Corporate Counsel of Pfizer, Inc., promoting even less FDA regulation of drug advertising, see George W. Evans & Arnold I. Friede, *The Food and Drug Administration's Regulation of Prescription Drug Manufacturer Speech: A First Amendment Analysis,* 58 FOOD & DRUG L.J. 363 (2003).

36. 21 U.S.C. §§ 350b, 342(f).

37. 21 C.F.R. pt. 101.14(c) (1998).

38. Pearson v. Shalala, 164 F.3d 650 (D.C. Cir. 1999).

39. *FDA Regulates Statements Made on Effects of Dietary Supplements,* 68 U.S.L.W. 2392–93 (Jan. 11, 2000).

Bechler had been taking Xenadrine, a legal over-the-counter drug containing a weight-loss supplement known as ephedra. The drug, which its makers liken to caffeine, was said to have strongly contributed to Bechler's death. Shortly thereafter, a young football player's sudden death was also linked to ephedra. Its makers claimed that improper use of the drug may have contributed to the deaths, but the FDA was blasted for allowing the drug to be marketed over-the-counter without significant warnings. In response, the FDA banned the use of ephedra in any dietary supplements and advised consumers to stop using any products containing ephedra.[40]

Labeling of Other Products

The Federal Trade Commission (FTC) has the primary responsibility for regulating the packaging and labeling of commodities other than food, drugs, medical devices, and cosmetics.

CLOTHING

Numerous federal laws regulate the labeling of clothing. Among these are the Wool Products Labeling Act,[41] the Fur Products Labeling Act,[42] the Flammable Fabrics Act,[43] and the Textile Fiber Products Identification Act.[44] Each of these acts is intended to protect distributors and consumers against misbranding and false advertising.

ALCOHOL

The Bureau of Alcohol and Tobacco Tax and Trade, a branch of the Treasury Department, regulates everything that appears on packages of alcoholic beverages and bottles of wine. The Bureau's regulations attach legal meanings to various statements made on wine labels, including the vintage year, grape variety, producer, and alcohol content. Warnings are also required to alert those who are allergic to sulfites that wine contains trace amounts of the substances, which may be used as a preservative and are also produced naturally during fermentation. Bottles, cans, and packages of wine, beer, and spirits are required to carry a congressionally mandated warning label, which states that alcohol consumption increases the risks of birth defects, warns that consuming alcoholic beverages can impair one's ability to drive a car, and cautions against the use of alcohol when operating machinery.[45]

"MADE IN USA"

The FTC has adopted guidelines specifying when manufacturers and marketers can label their products "Made in USA." Under the FTC's Made in USA policy, "all or virtually all" of the product must be made in the fifty states, the District of Columbia, or the U.S. territories and possessions. "All or virtually all" means that all significant parts and processing that go into the product must be of U.S. origin. A manufacturer or marketer must have a reasonable basis, based on competent and reliable evidence, to support its claim that the product was made in the USA.[46]

STATE LABELING LAWS

Many states have enacted labeling laws aimed at protecting consumers from dangerous products. Historically, these laws have sought to protect consumers from risks that involved the danger of imminent bodily harm. Of particular note is California's Safe Drinking Water and Toxic Enforcement Act of 1986, better known as Proposition 65. Proposition 65 provides that "no person . . . shall knowingly and intentionally expose any individual to a chemical known to the state to cause cancer or reproductive toxicity without first giving clear and reasonable warning to such individual."[47] The law requires the governor to compile a list of the chemicals requiring warnings and to update the list annually. The current list includes ingredients such as alcohol and saccharin, as well as potential contaminants such as lead and mercury. The labeling requirements apply to manufacturers, producers, packagers, and retail sellers, and the warnings may be in the form of product labels, signs at retail outlets, or public advertising. An example of a Proposition 65 warning is: "Warning: This product contains a chemical known to the State of California to cause birth defects or other reproductive harm." The FDA has the authority to issue regulations that would preempt state labeling requirements, such as Proposition 65, but so far it has chosen not to do so.

40. Jennifer Warner, *FDA Issues Final Ban on Ephedra,* Feb. 6, 2004, *available at* http://my.webmd.com/content/article/81/97056.htm.

41. 15 U.S.C. § 68 *et seq.*

42. 15 U.S.C. § 69 *et seq.*

43. 15 U.S.C. § 1191 *et seq.*

44. 15 U.S.C. § 70 *et seq.*

45. Dan Berger, *Modern Wine Industry Still Fears the "Feds" but for Labeling Reasons,* L.A. Times, Nov. 24, 1989, at H2; *see generally* 27 C.F.R. pts. 4, 5 & 7 (Alcohol & Tobacco Tax & Trade Bureau, Department of the Treasury).

46. FTC Bureau of Consumer Protection, *Complying with the Made in the USA Standard, available at* http://www.ftc.gov/os/1997/12/madeusa.pdf.

47. Cal. Health & Safety Code § 25,249.6.

BROADCASTING AND THE INTERNET

The Federal Communications Commission (FCC) has the authority to regulate broadcasting and aspects of the Internet.

BROADCASTING

The FCC is charged with ensuring that broadcast media are competitive and operate for the public's benefit and use. During the 2004 Super Bowl half-time performance, a "wardrobe malfunction" caused Janet Jackson's breast to be exposed on national television for nine-sixteenths of a second. Many viewers were outraged, and the National Football League and MTV (the group that sponsored and prepared the show) were embarrassed. The incident prompted regulators to propose sharply higher penalties for indecent broadcasts. In response, the FCC assessed $550,000 in fines against twenty CBS affiliates for violating its indecency requirements. In 2008, the U.S. Court of Appeals for the Third Circuit overturned the FCC's fine, reasoning that it was arbitrary and capricious and in violation of the Administrative Procedure Act.[48]

As explained in Chapter 4, FCC regulation of the content of broadcast programming raises First Amendment issues. Controversial radio personalities like Howard Stern and Rush Limbaugh, called "shock jocks," have often been involved in First Amendment battles with the FCC over their right to say things that many Americans find offensive. In the following case, the U.S. Court of Appeals for the Second Circuit considered whether the FCC had the authority to ban broadcasts with "fleeting expletives."

48. CBS Corp. v. FCC, 535 F.3d 167 (3d Cir. 2008).

A CASE IN POINT

CASE 18.1

FEDERAL COMMUNICATIONS COMMISSION V. FOX TELEVISION STATIONS INC.

UNITED STATES COURT OF APPEALS FOR THE SECOND CIRCUIT
489 F.3D. 444 (2D CIR. 2007),
CERT. GRANTED,
128 S. CT. 1647 (2008).

IN THE LANGUAGE OF THE COURT

FACTS The Federal Communications Commission levied an indecency fine against Fox Television Stations, Inc. for the single use of expletives in two of its broadcasts. Fox protested the fine and filed a petition for review of the FCC's Remand Order.[49] The FCC had acted pursuant to its *Golden Globes* decision, in which it greatly expanded the scope of what constitutes indecency in response to Bono's use of the "F-Word" in his acceptance speech at the 2003 Golden Globes Awards.[50]

ISSUE PRESENTED Did the FCC correctly determine that the broadcast of vulgar expletives may violate federal restrictions on the broadcast of "any obscene, indecent, or profane language" when the expletives are used only once in a single broadcast?

OPINION POOLER, J., writing on behalf of the U.S. Court of Appeals for the Second Circuit:

The FCC's policy of "indecent" speech stems from 18 U.S.C. § 1464, which provides that "[w]hoever utters any obscene, indecent, or profane language by means of radio communication shall be fined under this title or imprisoned not more than two years, or both." The FCC's authority to regulate the broadcast medium is expressly limited by Section 326 of the Communications Act, which prohibits the FCC from engaging in censorship.

. . . .

. . . [The FCC] explained that an indecency finding involves the following two determinations: (1) whether the material falls within the "subject matter scope of [the] indecency definition—that is, the material must describe or depict sexual or excretory organs or activities"; and (2) whether the broadcast is "*patently offensive* as measured by contemporary community standards for the broadcast medium" . . . . The FCC considers the following three factors in determining whether the material is patently offensive: "(1) *the explicitness or graphic nature* of the description or depiction

CONTINUED

49. FCC 06-166 (Nov. 6, 2006).

50. *Complaints Against Various Broadcast Licenses Regarding the Airing of the "Golden Globes Awards" Program* (Memorandum Opinion & Order), 19 F.C.C.R. 4985 (Mar. 18, 2004).

of sexual or excretory organs or activities; (2) whether the material *dwells on or repeats at length* descriptions of sexual or excretory organs or activities; (3) *whether the material appears to pander or is used to titillate, or whether the material appears to have been presented for its shock value*."

. . . .

The factual situations at issue are as follows:

- **2002 Billboard Music Awards:** In her acceptance speech, Cher stated: "People have been telling me I'm on the way out every year, right? So fuck 'em."
- **2002 Billboard Music Awards:** Nicole Richie, a presenter on the show, stated: "Have you ever tried to get cow shit out of a Prada purse? It's not so fucking simple."

. . . .

. . . [T]here is no question that the FCC has changed its policy. . . . Prior to the *Golden Globes* decision the FCC has consistently taken the view that isolated, non-literal, fleeting expletives did not run afoul of its indecency regime. . . . The FCC now concedes that *Golden Globes* changed the landscape with regard to the treatment of fleeting expletives.

. . . .

. . . . [T]he Commission provides no reasonable explanation for why it has changed its perception that a fleeting expletive was not a harmful "first blow" for the nearly thirty years between *Pacifica*[51] and *Golden Globes*. More problematic, however, is that the "first blow" theory bears no rational connection to the Commission's actual policy regarding fleeting expletives. As the FCC itself stressed during oral argument in this case, the Commission does not take the position that *any* occurrence of an expletive is indecent or profane under its rules.

. . . .

The Remand Order makes passing reference to . . . reasons that purportedly support [the FCC's] change in policy, none of which we find sufficient. For instance, the Commission states that even non-literal uses of expletives fall within its indecency definition because it is "difficult" (if not impossible) to distinguish whether a word is being used as an expletive or as a literal description of sexual or excretory functions." This defies any commonsense understanding of these words, which, as the general public well knows, are often used in everyday conversation without any "sexual or excretory" meaning. Bono's explanation that his victory at the Golden Globe Awards was "really, really fucking brilliant" is a prime example of a non-literal use of the "F-Word" that has no sexual connotation. In recent times even the top leaders of our government have used variants of these expletives in a manner that no reasonable person would believe references "sexual or excretory organs or activities." See Brief of Intervenor NBC at 31–32 & n. 3 (citing President Bush's remarks to British Prime Minister Tony Blair that the United Nations needed to "get Syria to get Hezbollah to stop doing this shit" and Vice President Cheney's widely-reported "Fuck yourself" comment to Senator Patrick Leahy on the floor of the U.S. Senate).

. . . .

While the FCC is free to change its previously settled view on this issue, it must provide a reasoned basis for that change. . . . The FCC's decision, however, is devoid of any evidence that suggests a fleeting expletive is harmful, let alone establishes that this harm is serious enough to warrant government regulation. Such evidence would seem to be particularly relevant today when children likely hear this language far more often from other sources than they did in the 1970s when the Commission first began sanctioning indecent speech. Yet the Remand Order provides no reasoned

CONTINUED

51. *Citizen's Complaint Against Pacifica Foundation Station WBAI (FM), New York, N.Y.* (Declaratory Order), 56 F.C.C.2d 94 (Feb. 12, 1975).

analysis of the purported "problem" it is seeking to address with its new indecency policy from which this court can conclude that such regulation of speech is reasonable.

. . . .

Accordingly, we find that the FCC's new policy regarding "fleeting expletives" fails to provide a reasoned analysis justifying its departure from the agency's established practice. For this reason, Fox's petition for review is granted, the Remand Order is vacated, and the matter is remanded to the FCC for further proceedings consistent with this opinion. Because we have found that the FCC's new indecency regime, announced in *Golden Globes* and applied in the Remand Order, is invalid under the Administrative Procedure Act, the stay of enforcement previously granted by this court in our September 6th order is vacated as moot.

RESULT The court found in favor of Fox and invalidated the FCC's new policy on "fleeting expletives" as arbitrary and capricious under the Administrative Procedure Act. Fox was not required to pay a fine for either broadcast.

COMMENTS The FCC had issued the contested indecency fines against Fox after receiving tens of thousands of complaints from members of the Parents Television Council, a nonprofit organization founded by conservative activist L. Brent Bozell III in 1995 that has the stated goal to "promote and restore responsibility to the entertainment industry."

CRITICAL THINKING QUESTIONS

1. Is a court qualified to make inferences about how public attitudes toward indecent language have changed since the FCC began levying sanctions in the 1970s?
2. Would the court have reached the same decision if it had been unable to cite instances in which both the president and the vice president of the United States used "fleeting expletives"?

Licenses cannot be transferred or assigned without the permission of the FCC and a finding that such a transfer will serve the public interest. In 2003, Congress invalidated FCC regulations that would have relaxed the limits on concentrated media ownership in the United States.[52] Enforcement of many of the FCC's policies is achieved primarily through its ability to withhold license renewals.

INTERNET

The Internet also raises free speech issues, as discussed in Chapter 4. As explained in Chapters 9 and 23, the Internet has spawned new types of fraudulent schemes, such as online auction fraud, pyramid schemes, and securities fraud. The FTC, the U.S. Department of Justice, and the Securities and Exchange Commission are active in prosecuting offenders.

In August 2008, the FCC took action against Comcast, the country's second-largest Internet provider, after concluding that Comcast had violated the federal *net neutrality policy* by hindering transfers of large data files by customers who use peer-to-peer file-sharing programs, such as BitTorrent, to share music and video.[53] The FCC based its order on a 2005 policy statement outlining principles designed to ensure that broadband networks are open, affordable, and accessible to all consumers. The FCC found that Comcast had a convincing motive for interference: peer-to-peer applications are used to load video that could pose a competitive threat to Comcast's video-on-demand service.

The FCC ordered Comcast to disclose the details of its "unreasonable network management practices" within thirty days and to submit a compliance plan to implement protocol-agnostic network congestion management practices by the end of 2008.[54] Republican FCC Chair Kevin J. Martin wrote the enforcement decision with support from the FCC's two Democratic Commissioners. Martin was opposed by members of his own party in a divided three-to-two vote. Although Comcast stated that it would comply fully with the ruling, the cable giant filed a petition for

52. S.J. Res. 17, 108th Cong. (2003).

53. John Dunbar, *FCC Rules Against Comcast: Firm Ordered to End Delays on File-Sharing Traffic*, ASSOC. PRESS, Aug. 2, 2008.

54. Memorandum Opinion & Order, FCC 08-183 (Aug. 1, 2008).

> **Ethical Consideration**
>
> On average, an American child sees about 8,000 murders on television before reaching high school. How should programming managers respond to scientific evidence that television violence leads to more violent behavior by children? What additional precautions (such as time, place, and manner restrictions), if any, should they take to protect children?

review with the U.S. Court of Appeals for the D.C. Circuit in Washington.[55]

The Consumer Product Safety Commission

Congress created the Consumer Product Safety Commission (CPSC), an independent regulatory agency, in 1972. The Consumer Product Safety Act[56] and related legislation[57] gave the CPSC the authority to set consumer product safety standards, such as performance or product-labeling specifications. The CPSC is charged with protecting the public against unreasonable risks of injury associated with consumer products and assisting consumers in evaluating the comparative safety of such products. The CPSC has no jurisdiction over tobacco products, firearms, pesticides, motor vehicles, food, drugs, medical devices, or cosmetics. These matters are regulated by other entities, such as the FDA, or are unregulated.

Before implementing a mandatory safety standard, the CPSC must find that voluntary standards are inadequate. Any standards that the CPSC issues must also be reasonably necessary to eliminate an unreasonable risk of injury that the regulated product presents. To determine whether a standard is reasonably necessary, the Commission weighs the standard's effectiveness in preventing injury against its effect on the cost of the product. The CPSC maintains an Injury Information Clearinghouse to collect and analyze information relating to the causes and prevention of death, injury, and illness associated with consumer products.

The statute provides a detailed scheme governing the adoption of a mandatory standard. Any interested person may petition the CPSC to adopt a standard and may resort to judicial remedies if the CPSC denies the petition. One obvious concern for the Commission is that producers motivated solely by short-term profits may not be willing or able to self-regulate. The CPSC can itself begin a proceeding to develop a standard by publishing a notice in the *Federal Register* inviting any person to submit an offer to do the development. Within a specified time limit, the CPSC can then accept such an offer, evaluate the suggestions submitted, and publish a proposed rule. The issuance of the final standard is subject to notice and comment by interested persons.

The penalty provisions of the Act make it unlawful to manufacture for sale, offer for sale, distribute in commerce, or import into the United States a consumer product that does not conform to an applicable standard. Violators are subject to civil penalties, criminal penalties, injunctive enforcement and seizure, private suits for damages, and private suits for injunctive relief. This means that if a product cannot be made free of unreasonable risk of personal injury, the CPSC may ban its manufacture, sale, or importation altogether. The supplier of any already-distributed products that pose a substantial risk of injury may be compelled by the CPSC to repair, modify, or replace the products, or refund the purchase price.

In addition to the Federal Consumer Product Safety Act, several states have enacted laws to protect children from dangerous products. Two University of Chicago professors, whose son died when his Playskool Travel-Lite portable crib collapsed while he was napping, initiated Illinois's Children's Product Safety Act, which was signed into law in August 1999. Michigan followed suit and enacted the same law in June 2000.[58]

Consumer Product Safety Improvement Act of 2008

On August 14, 2008, President George W. Bush signed the Consumer Product Safety Improvement Act of 2008.[59] Characterized by *The Wall Street Journal* as "the biggest overhaul of U.S. product-safety rules in a generation,"[60] this Act sought to strengthen consumer product safety standards and modernize and re-energize the CPSC. Sponsored by U.S. Representative

55. *Comcast to Comply with, Appeal FCC's Network Management Order*, 77 U.S.L.W. 2143 (2008).

56. 15 U.S.C. § 2051 *et seq,*

57. *See, e.g.,* the Hazardous Substances Labeling Act, the Child Protection Act, and the Child Protection and Toy Safety Act. 15 U.S.C. § 2052.

58. E. Marla Felcher, *Children's Products and Risk,* Atlantic Monthly (Nov. 2000).

59. Pub. L. No. 110–314.

60. Melanie Trottman, *Lawmakers Clinch Deal to Overhaul Product Safety*, Wall St. J., July 29, 2008, at A1.

Bobby Rush (D.-Ill.), the bill was first introduced on the House floor on November 1, 2007, in the wake of a media onslaught that dubbed 2007 "The Year of the Recall."

In that year, there were 472 voluntary recalls involving nearly 110 million products. As discussed in this chapter's "Inside Story," most of the recalls involved lead paint and other hazards in imported children's toys. The scandals damaged the performance of major U.S. importers and retailers, including Mattel, Inc. and Wal-Mart Stores, Inc.

Mattel alone executed three major recalls in the summer of 2007 for products including the Barbie Living Room Play Set, Fisher-Price Bongo Band Toys, and "Sarge" toy cars from the Walt Disney movie *Cars*, all of which were believed to contain lead-contaminated paint. Four other items from the Barbie, Batman, Doggie Day Care, and Polly Pocket toy lines were also recalled when it was discovered that they included tiny magnets that could injure children if swallowed. Worldwide, Mattel recalled about 2.8 million toys due to lead paint and 18.2 million toys due to a design flaw. All of the recolled toys were made in China. In light of the summer recalls, Mattel's stock fell more than 25 percent from its fifty-two-week high in April 2007.[61] These recalls spurred public outrage and weakened consumer confidence in manufacturers and retailers selling products made outside the United States.

Although passage of the law was largely motivated by widespread concern over children's toys, the Act affects virtually all manufacturers, importers, distributors, and retailers of consumer products. Some of the most significant provisions of the Act include (1) widespread bans on lead and phthalates (a material used in some plastics), (2) new safety standards and test procedures, (3) mandatory third-party testing and certification for imported children's products, (4) mandatory product tracking labels and product registration, and (5) new warnings in advertising and on websites for toys and games. It also banned most shipments of faulty products to other nations, from which they had historically found their way back onto U.S. store shelves.

The Act placed more inspectors at U.S. ports to examine imported products. Before this law was passed, CPSC officials relied mostly on agents from Customs and Border Protection to investigate products at the borders. Hardly optimal partners, these agencies tended to look for counterfeit products, rather than goods that might not comply with safety standards.

Perhaps the most significant aspect of the Act is its effort to institutionally strengthen the CPSC, which was overwhelmed, underfunded, and ill-equipped to manage the recall crisis. The agency's budget in 2007 was only $62 million, one-seventh the size of the Food and Drug Administration's budget for food safety alone.[62] The CPSC, which once boasted 1,000 federal employees, had shrunk to a low of 420 employees under President George W. Bush and had the capability to investigate only 10 to 15 percent of the reported injuries or deaths linked to consumer goods.

The 2008 Act increased the CPSC staff to 500 and will increase its budget by more than 50 percent by 2013. To give the Commission real teeth, civil fines on violators were increased from $5,000 to $100,000 per offense, with each day of violation of the Act constituting a separate offense. The maximum civil penalty for a related series of violations was increased more than tenfold, from $1.25 million to $15 million. Additionally, employees who blow the whistle on manufacturers, private labelers, retailers, or distributors to expose violations of any CPSC-enforced product safety requirements will now be protected from retaliation under federal law.

The Act allows the CPSC to exempt state statutes from federal preemption if the state's standards or regulations provide more protection and do not unduly burden interstate commerce. Therefore, states can continue to enforce many of the safety requirements that were in effect before enactment of the Act. In the absence of comprehensive federal oversight and congressional action, at least sixteen states have adopted product-safety laws in recent years. The Act explicitly prohibits the CPSC from preempting any cause of action under state or local common law or state statutory law regarding damage claims, and it grants authority to state attorneys general to enforce CPSC regulations.

Although many manufacturers criticized the bill and warned that it will threaten their international competitiveness, for some the bill may offer a potential competitive advantage. For example, the bill sets tougher standards for makers of all-terrain vehicles, which could work to the advantage of U.S. producers hit hard by cheaper vehicles produced in China. Although imports currently account for 44 percent of consumer products sold in the United States, they account for more than 75 percent of CPSC product recalls, suggesting that the Act will affect foreign producers more than domestic manufacturers.[63]

61. Nicholas Casey, *Mattel Issues Third Major Recall: Top Toy Brands Barbie, Fisher-Price Are Latest Facing Lead-Paint Issues*, WALL ST. J., Sept. 5, 2008, at A3.

62. Tom Lowry & Lorraine Woellert, *More Paper Tiger Than Watchdog? The Consumer Product Safety Agency Is Overwhelmed and Underfunded*, BUS. WK., Sept. 3, 2007, at 45.

63. Christie L. Grymes, Kelley Drye & Warren LLP, *"The Year of the Recall": CPSC Lessons to Learn*, METROPOLITAN CORP. COUNS., July 22, 2008, *available at* http://www.metrocorpcounsel.com/current.php?artType=view&artMonth=June&artYear=2008&EntryNo=8363.

In the first four months of 2008 alone, the CPSC initiated 121 recalls of unsafe products, totaling nearly 10 million products. In August 2008, the CPSC initiated legal action against SFCA, Inc., a Pennsylvania-based designer, distributor, and importer of cribs, toddler beds, and bassinets. SFCA had acquired the assets of Simplicity, Inc., another bassinet manufacturer whose products were found to be responsible for two infant deaths by strangulation. The products in question had been on the market since 2001. The CPSC began investigating the products after learning about the first death in September 2007, but the Commission did not have the authority to bring legal action against Simplicity at that time. At the time of the second death, CPSC used its new authority under the 2008 Act to take action against SFCA. After the CPSC issued a public warning urging consumers to stop using certain Simplicity-brand bassinets, seven major retailers, including Toys "R" Us, J.C. Penney, and Wal-Mart, agreed to take back the hazardous products.[64]

Due to SFCA's lack of cooperation and claims that it was not liable for products sold by Simplicity before it acquired Simplicity's assets in May 2008, the CPSC stopped short of requiring a product recall. As discussed in Chapter 10, the purchaser of another firm's assets generally does not have liability for defective products sold before the date of purchase unless the acquirer agreed to assume those liabilities or effects a de facto merger. As of September 2008, the CPSC was seeking access to SFCA's financial records in order to determine the terms of the acquisition and thereby ascertain SFCA's potential liability. The Commission's decision to stop short of a full product recall suggests that even the CPSC's new powers may prove inadequate to protect consumers from unsafe products.[65]

AUTOMOBILES

Automobile safety has seen enormous gains since Ralph Nader first brought the issue to the nation's attention in the 1960s.[66] Air bags (for the driver and front passenger) and antilock brakes have become popular safety features.

The National Highway Traffic Safety Administration (NHTSA), created in 1970, is an agency of the U.S. Department of Transportation. By law, the NHTSA has the power to establish motor vehicle safety standards,[67] establish a National Motor Vehicle Safety Advisory Council, engage in testing and development of motor vehicle safety, prohibit manufacture or importation of substandard vehicles, and develop tire safety.[68] In addition, the NHTSA is charged with developing national standards for driver safety performance, accident reporting, and vehicle registration and inspection. States refusing to comply with established federal standards are denied federal highway funds.[69]

> **ETHICAL CONSIDERATION**
>
> Adding new safety requirements for automobiles can increase product cost and shut some consumers out of the market. Should governments coerce individuals into paying for unwanted safety features, or should individual consumers be allowed to choose which features they are willing to pay for?

PRIVACY PROTECTIONS

As discussed in Chapter 9, technological developments, especially the Internet, have made it possible to amass large amounts of detailed personal information, causing Scott McNealy, CEO of Sun Microsystems, to quip, "You have zero privacy. . . . Get over it."[70] In response to public concerns about identity theft and other violations of privacy, state and federal governments have enacted a variety of laws dealing with the collection and transmission of private data and the transmission of unsolicited e-mail (*spam*). These laws, which are discussed in detail in Chapter 9, include the Controlling the Assault of Non-Solicited Pornography Act of 2003 (the CAN-SPAM Act).[71] In 2008, "Spam King" Robert Soloway, the second person charged under CAN-SPAM, pleaded guilty to several charges, including e-mail fraud, and was sentenced to four years in prison.[72] Soloway used unprotected computer networks to send out millions of e-mails and employed misleading e-mail header information to evade e-mail filters. During

64. Melanie Trottman, *Firm Disputes Liability for Bassinet Recall,* WALL ST. J., Aug. 30–31, 2008.

65. *Id.*

66. RALPH NADER, UNSAFE AT ANY SPEED (1965) (criticizing in particular General Motors Corporation's Corvair model). For a critique of Ralph Nader's consumer activist activities, see DAN BURT, ABUSE OF TRUST (1982).

67. Boats are subject to safety regulation under the Federal Boat Safety Act of 1971 (46 U.S.C. § 4301 *et seq.*), and aircraft safety is regulated by the Federal Aviation Act of 1958 (49 U.S.C. § 1421 *et seq.*).

68. Motor Vehicle Safety Act of 1966, 15 U.S.C. § 1381 *et seq.*

69. Highway Safety Act of 1966, 23 U.S.C. § 401 *et seq.*

70. Adam Cohen, *Internet Insecurity,* TIME, July 2, 2001, at 47–51.

71. 17 U.S.C. §§ 7701–13.

72. Paul Shukovsky, *"Spam King" Gets Nearly 4 Years in Prison,* SEATTLE POST-INTELLIGENCER, July 23, 2008, at A1.

one three-month period, Soloway sent 90 million spam e-mails. The presiding judge compared Soloway's spam to pollution on the Internet.

UNFAIRNESS, DECEPTION, AND FRAUD

A number of regulatory agencies, both federal and state, are involved in the area of unfair and deceptive trade practices and consumer fraud. They include the Federal Trade Commission, the Food and Drug Administration, the Federal Communications Commission, the U.S. Postal Service, the U.S. Department of Housing and Urban Development, and the Securities and Exchange Commission. (Securities fraud is discussed in Chapter 23.) These federal agencies regulate advertising, packaging and labeling, pricing, warranties, and numerous sales practices. State attorneys general and state departments of consumer affairs are also involved on the state level in protecting consumers through their administration of various state labeling laws, state warranty provisions (such as "lemon laws"), state deceptive sales practices statutes, and state privacy laws.

DECEPTIVE ADVERTISING AND WARRANTIES

Consumers are bombarded daily with the competing claims of various advertisers trying to generate new sales. From billboards to television to banner ads on websites and even the back of grocery receipts, advertisers vie for the consumer's attention. In this competitive environment, companies sometimes make claims that are deceptive or false. Legal solutions to this problem have historically involved three separate approaches: the common law, statutory law, and regulatory law. Regulatory law, enacted and enforced through the Federal Trade Commission, has proved to be the most effective vehicle for combating false advertisements.

Common Law

A traditional common law approach provides two remedies for a consumer who has been misled by false advertising. First, a consumer can sue for breach of contract. In this instance, however, it may be difficult to prove the existence of a contract because the courts usually consider advertisements to be only an offer to deal. A consumer might also sue for the tort of deceit. *Deceit* requires the proof of several elements, including knowledge by the seller that the misrepresentation is false. In addition, the misrepresentation must be one of fact and not opinion, a difficult distinction to make in the context of advertising. (Deceit, also called fraudulent misrepresentation, is discussed in Chapter 9.)

Statutory Law

The Uniform Commercial Code (UCC) and the Lanham Trademark Act are two statutes that may protect consumers from false advertising. As noted in Chapter 8, under Section 2-313 of the UCC, any statement, sample, or model may constitute an *express warranty* if it is part of the basis of the bargain. Thus, an advertising term may be construed as an express warranty for a product. If the product does not conform to the representation made, the warranty is breached.

The Lanham Trademark Act forbids the use of any false "description or representation" in connection with any goods or services and provides a private cause of action for any competitor injured by any other competitor's false claims. The purpose of the Act is to ensure truthfulness in advertising and to eliminate misrepresentations of quality regarding one's own product or the product of a competitor. Neither consumers nor retailers have standing to sue for violations of the Lanham Act. Only direct commercial competitors or surrogates for direct commercial competitors have standing to pursue claims under the Lanham Act.[73]

> **ETHICAL CONSIDERATION**
>
> Procter & Gamble Company recruited 600,000 moms for Vocalpoint, a word-of-mouth marketing program it developed to pitch its own and other companies' products. P&G gives these moms talking points, samples, and coupons in an attempt to enhance its customer base through personal endorsements.[a] Is this an acceptable form of marketing or a dangerous commercialization of human relations? Should the person spreading the product message be required to disclose her affiliation with P&G?
>
> **a.** *I Sold It Through the Grapevine*, BUS. WK., May 29, 2006, *available at* http://www.businessweek.com/magazine/content/06_22/b3986060.htm.

73. Conte Bros. Auto., Inc. v. Quaker State, Inc., 165 F.3d 221 (3d Cir. 1998).

For example, the Coca-Cola Company, maker of Minute Maid orange juice, successfully sued Tropicana Products, Inc. in the early 1980s under the Lanham Trademark Act. At issue was a television commercial in which athlete Bruce Jenner squeezed an orange while saying, "It's pure, pasteurized juice as it comes from the orange," and then poured the juice into a Tropicana carton. Coca-Cola claimed that the commercial was false because it represented that Tropicana contains unprocessed, fresh-squeezed juice when in fact the juice is heated (pasteurized) and sometimes frozen before packaging. The court agreed that the representation was false because it suggested that pasteurized juice comes directly from oranges. The court enjoined Tropicana from continuing to use the advertisement.[74]

FTC Regulatory Law

The Federal Trade Commission is charged with preventing unfair and deceptive trade practices, including false advertising. Among the areas that the FTC has addressed under Section 5 of the Federal Trade Commission Act are deceptive price and quality claims and false testimonials and mock-ups.[75] If the FTC believes a violation of Section 5 exists, it will attempt to negotiate a consent order with the alleged violator. A *consent order* is an agreement to stop the activity that the FTC has found illegal. If an agreement cannot be reached, the matter will be heard by an administrative law judge. The judge's decision can be appealed to the full commission, and the full commission's decision can be appealed to a U.S. court of appeals. Exhibit 18.1 lists the top twenty consumer fraud complaints that the FTC received in 2007.

FTC remedies include civil damages, affirmative advertising (the advertiser is required to include specific information), counter or corrective advertising, and cease and desist orders. A *cease and desist order* instructs advertisers to stop using the methods deemed unfair or deceptive. In one case, the FTC required the maker of Listerine to cease and desist from making the claim that Listerine prevented colds and sore throats or lessened their severity. Tests performed by the FTC revealed that this claim, which the

74. Coca-Cola Co. v. Tropicana Prods., Inc., 690 F.2d 312 (2d Cir. 1982).

75. Other applications of Section 5 are discussed in Chapter 17. (*See* Appendix F on page A-16.)

EXHIBIT 18.1

FTC Top Consumer Fraud Complaints in 2007

Rank	Category	Complaints	Percent
1	Identity theft	258,427	32
2	Shop-at-home/catalog sales	62,811	8
3	Internet services	42,266	5
4	Foreign money offers	32,868	4
5	Prizes/sweepstakes and lotteries	32,162	4
6	Computer equipment and software	27,036	3
7	Internet auctions	24,376	3
8	Health-care claims	16,097	2
9	Travel, vacations, and timeshares	14,903	2
10	Advance-fee loans and credit protection/repair	14,342	2
11	Investments	13,705	2
12	Magazines and buyers clubs	12,970	2
13	Business opportunities and work-at-home plans	11,362	1
14	Real estate (not timeshares)	9,475	1
15	Office supplies and services	9,211	1
16	Telephone services	8,155	1
17	Employment agencies/job counseling/overseas work	5,932	1
18	Debt management/credit counseling	3,442	<1
19	Multilevel marketing/pyramids/chain letters	3,092	<1
20	Charitable solicitations	1,843	<1

Source: FTC, *FTC Releases List of Top Consumer Fraud Complaints in 2007,* Feb. 13, 2008, *available at* http://www.ftc.gov/opa/2008/02/fraud.shtm.

company had made for more than fifty years, was false. To counteract years of false claims, the FTC required the company to disclose in any future advertisements for Listerine that, contrary to prior advertising, Listerine did not help prevent colds or sore throats or lessen their severity. The order applied to the next $10 million of Listerine advertising.[76]

Deceptive Price One example of deceptive pricing practices involves the sale of advertised items at higher prices to customers unaware of the advertised price. In one case, a person purchased a blue 1986 Chevrolet Celebrity with 29,000 miles from an automobile dealer for $8,524.[77] The buyer did not know that the dealership was currently advertising a blue 1986 Celebrity with 29,000 miles for $6,995 in a local newspaper. When he returned home, the buyer saw the ad and telephoned the dealership to demand that the deal be renegotiated. The salesman refused, claiming that the advertised car had been sent to auction. The customer sued under the Illinois Consumer Fraud Act, which forbids false misrepresentations as well as omission of material facts. The trial court held that the dealership had a duty to inform the customer of the advertised price and awarded him the difference in prices, plus costs.

Deceptive pricing practices also include offers of free merchandise with a purchase and two-for-one deals when the advertiser recovers the cost of the free merchandise by charging more than the regular price for the merchandise bought. Another example of deceptive pricing is bait and switch advertising. An advertiser violates the FTC *bait and switch advertising* rules if it refuses to show an advertised item, fails to have a reasonable quantity of the item in stock, fails to promise to deliver the item within a reasonable time, or discourages employees from selling the advertised item.

76. Warner–Lambert Co. v. FTC, 562 F.2d 749 (D.C. Cir. 1977), *cert. denied,* 435 U.S. 950 (1978).

77. Affrunti v. Vill. Ford Sales, Inc., 597 N.E.2d 1242 (Ill. App. Ct. 1992).

› ETHICAL CONSIDERATION

A newspaper's publication of an article entitled "A Car Buyer's Guide to Sanity," which taught consumers how to negotiate lower prices, so angered car dealers that they pulled at least $1 million worth of advertising from the newspaper. The FTC challenged the dealers' actions under the antitrust laws, claiming that they had deprived consumers of essential price information in the form of newspaper advertising and had chilled the newspaper from publishing similar stories in the future.[a] Should the government become embroiled in an advertiser's decision to pull advertising from a news publication? Was the advertisers' conduct ethical?

a. Anthony Ramirez, *Car Dealers to Stop Ad Threat,* S.F. CHRON., Aug. 2, 1995, at B3.

› ETHICAL CONSIDERATION

Should free-market, competitive forces determine the price of "essential" goods such as pharmaceuticals, or should their prices be regulated? What constitutes "reasonable" profits on a product such as AZT and the cocktail of protease inhibitors recommended for people with HIV or AIDS?[a] Is the answer the same for drugs sold in Africa as for drugs sold in the United States?

a. For a complete discussion of the AZT controversy, see *Ethics, Pricing and the Pharmaceutical Industry,* J. BUS. ETHICS, Aug. 1992, at 617. See also Brian O'Reilly, *The Inside Story of the AIDS Drug,* FORTUNE, Nov. 5, 1990, at 112.

Quality Claims Advertisements often include quality claims. To determine whether an advertiser has made a deceptive quality claim, the FTC must first identify the claim and then determine whether the claim is substantiated. Quality claims made without any substantiation are considered deceptive. For example, the FTC concluded that the marketers of Doan's pills had disseminated false and deceptive statements when they claimed the pills were more effective at relieving back pain than other over-the-counter pain relievers without any reasonable basis for substantiating the representations.[78] In contrast, obvious exaggerations and vague generalities are considered *puffing* and are not deemed deceptive because they are unlikely to mislead consumers. (Puffing is also discussed in Chapter 8.)

In the following case, a purchaser of the over-the-counter painkiller Aleve sued its distributor for false advertising in violation of California's Unfair Competition Law (UCL), which has been interpreted in accordance with the FTC Act.

78. Novartis Corp. v. FTC, 223 F.3d 783 (D.C. Cir. 2000).

A CASE IN POINT

CASE 18.2

LAVIE V. PROCTER & GAMBLE CO.

CALIFORNIA COURT OF APPEAL
129 CAL. RPTR. 2D 486
(CAL. APP. 2003).

IN THE LANGUAGE OF THE COURT

FACTS Zion Lavie developed a stomach ulcer after using Aleve, an over-the-counter drug distributed by Procter & Gamble Company. He sued P&G, alleging that the company had engaged in false advertising. Aleve's advertising campaign explicitly claimed that Aleve was gentler on the stomach than aspirin. The plaintiff claimed that this implied that Aleve would not cause any stomach upset. The trial court granted summary judgment for P&G and dismissed all claims. Lavie appealed.

ISSUE PRESENTED Should false advertising claims be based on what a reasonable consumer would understand, or should they be based on what the "least sophisticated consumer" would think about a product and its corresponding advertising?

OPINION KLINE, J., writing on behalf of the California Court of Appeal:

The standard to be used in evaluating whether an advertisement is deceptive under the UCL is purely a question of law and certainly has important public policy implications for California consumers and businesses. Moreover, the Attorney General has a particular interest in the interpretation of [the provisions of the California Unfair Competition Law because they] are the basic tools of the Attorney General and the district attorneys in combating consumer fraud. . . . The Attorney General and district attorneys have an independent role in the enforcement of this state's false advertising laws. They are authorized to prosecute violations of the UCL criminally and may also seek redress through the bringing of civil law enforcement cases seeking equitable relief and civil penalties beyond those available to private parties. . . .

Asserting that an advertisement violates the law if it is false or if it has the capacity to mislead unwary, unsophisticated or the most gullible consumers, the Attorney General maintains, the "trial court's failure to apply the 'least sophisticated consumer' standard as the measure of deception and the court's imposition of responsibility on consumers to investigate the merits of advertising claims were error."

We disagree. California and federal courts applying the UCL have never applied a "least sophisticated consumer standard," absent evidence that the ad targeted particularly vulnerable customers. Rather, they have consistently applied a standard closer to an ordinary or "reasonable consumer" standard to evaluate unfair advertising claims. Nor do we view the court's application of the "reasonable consumer" standard as requiring consumers to investigate the merits of advertising claims.

. . . .

As a necessary corollary to his argument, the Attorney General urges that we reject *Freeman v. Time, Inc.*[79] and *Haskell v. Time, Inc.*[80] as well as other federal decisions which have concluded that California employs the reasonable person or reasonable consumer standard in evaluating deceptive advertising. In *Freeman,* the Ninth Circuit agreed with the district court in *Haskell* that the "reasonable consumer" standard was the appropriate test for a violation of the UCL.

. . . .

As *Haskell* observed, "[T]he reasonable person standard is well ensconced in the law in a variety of legal contexts in which a claim of deception is brought. It is the standard for false advertising and unfair competition under the Lanham Act; for securities fraud, for deceit and misrepresentation and for common law unfair competition."

CONTINUED

79. 68 F.3d 285 (9th Cir. 1995).

80. 857 F. Supp. 1392 (E.D. Cal. 1994).

. . . .

Haskell also relied upon the FTC's interpretation of the Federal Trade Commission Act because of the relationship between the UCL and the federal act. "[T]he Unfair Business Practices Act is one 'of the so-called "little FTC Acts" of the 1930's, enacted by many states in the wake of amendments to the Federal Trade Commission Act enlarging the commission's regulatory jurisdiction to include unfair business practices that harmed, not merely the interests of business competitors, but of the general public as well.' Because of this relationship between the [UCL] and the Federal Trade Commission Act, judicial interpretations of the federal act have persuasive force. Since 1982 the FTC has interpreted 'deception' in Section 5 of the Federal Trade Commission Act to require a showing of 'potential deception of "consumers acting reasonably in the circumstances," not just any consumers.' "

. . . .

Unless the advertisement targets a particular disadvantaged or vulnerable group, it is judged by the effect it would have on a reasonable consumer. As noted by the FTC many years ago: "Perhaps a few misguided souls believe, for example, that all 'Danish pastry' is made in Denmark. Is it, therefore, an actionable deception to advertise 'Danish pastry' when it is made in this country? Of course not. A representation does not become 'false and deceptive' merely because it will be unreasonably misunderstood by an insignificant and unrepresentative segment of the class of persons to whom the representation is addressed."

RESULT The appeals court affirmed the dismissal of the complaint. P&G's ads were not misleading.

CRITICAL THINKING QUESTIONS

1. Would you interpret the statement that Aleve is gentler on the stomach than aspirin to mean that it will not cause an ulcer?
2. Why shouldn't advertisers be required to ensure that their ads do not mislead the most gullible consumers?

Testimonials and Mock-ups Testimonials and endorsements in which the person endorsing a product does not, in fact, use or prefer it are considered to be deceptive and therefore in violation of the FTC Act. It is also deceptive for the endorser to imply falsely that he or she has superior knowledge or experience.

In the mid-1960s, the FTC successfully challenged a series of three television commercials for Colgate–Palmolive Company's Rapid Shave shaving cream. Each commercial featured a sandpaper test, in which Rapid Shave was applied to a substance that appeared to be sandpaper, and immediately thereafter a razor was shown shaving the substance clean. Meanwhile, an announcer informed the audience that "[t]o prove Rapid Shave's super-moisturizing power, we put it right from the can onto this tough, dry sandpaper. It was apply . . . soak . . . and off in a stroke." The FTC charged that the commercials were false and deceptive. Evidence disclosed that sandpaper of the type depicted in the commercials could not be shaved immediately following the application of Rapid Shave but required a soaking period of approximately eighty minutes. The evidence also showed that the substance resembling sandpaper was in fact a simulated prop, or "mock-up," made of plexiglass to which sand had been applied. Ultimately, the U.S. Supreme Court agreed with the FTC and decided that the commercials were unlawfully deceptive.[81]

Infomercials

Infomercials, also known as long-form marketing programs or direct response television, are advertisements generally presented in the format of half-hour television talk shows or news programs. Their very format, however, may present problems by blurring the line between advertising

81. FTC v. Colgate–Palmolive Co., 380 U.S. 374 (1965).

and regular television programming.[82] The next trend in infomercials was the "sitcommercial," a full-length show resembling a family sitcom. For example, Bell Atlantic filmed "The Ringers," a sitcom intended to show off and sell telephone equipment.

In response to numerous complaints alleging deceptive advertising in infomercials, the infomercial industry established an internal watchdog agency, the National Infomercial Merchandising Association, in 1990. The association offers guidelines to combat deceptive practices, endorses legitimate infomercial producers, and reports violations to the FTC.

Magnuson–Moss Warranty Act

As noted earlier, an advertisement may create an express warranty. Article 2 provides a buyer of goods with a remedy for a seller's breach of an express or implied warranty. UCC warranties are discussed in Chapter 8.

In addition to the statutory protections provided by the UCC, the federal government has passed a law that is designed to inform consumers about the products they buy. This law, which applies only when a seller offers a written warranty, is the Magnuson–Moss Warranty Act.[83] The Act does not require any seller to provide a written warranty, but if a seller does offer one, the Act requires certain disclosures. In addition, it restricts disclaimers for implied warranties and permits consumers to sue violators of the Act and to recover damages plus costs, including reasonable attorneys' fees.

A manufacturer or seller offering a written warranty on consumer goods costing more than $15 must "fully and conspicuously disclose in simple and understandable language the terms and conditions of the warranty." The FTC has issued various rules relating to this provision, including one that requires consumer notification that some states do not allow certain manufacturer exclusions or limitations. A manufacturer or seller that offers a written warranty on consumer goods costing more than $10 must also state whether the warranty is full or limited.

Under the Act, for a warranty to be "full," it must meet the following minimum federal standards. First, a full warranty must give the consumer the right to free repair of the product within a reasonable time or, after a reasonable number of failed attempts to fix the product, permit the customer to elect a full refund or replacement. Second, the warrantor may not impose any time limit on the warranty's duration. Lastly, the warrantor may not exclude or limit damages for breach of warranty unless such exclusions are conspicuous on the face of the warranty. Any warranty that does not meet these minimum federal standards must be designated as "limited."

The Act prohibits sellers offering a written warranty from disclaiming *implied warranties*, such as the implied warranty of merchantability. These implied warranties may be limited to the duration of the written warranty, but then the written warranty must be designated as "limited." A seller is permitted to disclaim all implied warranties but only if it does not offer any written warranty or service contract at all and sells a product "as is."

FTC rules allow a seller to establish an informal dispute resolution procedure and to require consumers to use this procedure before filing a lawsuit under the Act. Magnuson–Moss also requires that the warrantor be given an opportunity to remedy its noncompliance before a lawsuit is filed. In *Borowiec v. Gateway 2000, Inc.*, the Illinois Supreme Court held that the Magnuson–Moss Warranty Act does not invalidate arbitration provisions in a written warranty.[84] A Virginia federal court reached the opposite conclusion.[85]

State Lemon Laws

A majority of states have laws dealing with warranties on new cars and new mobile homes. These *lemon laws* are designed to protect consumers from defective products that cannot be adequately fixed. The statutes vary considerably from state to state, but there are several common features. In general, a new vehicle must conform to the warranty given by the manufacturer. This means that if, after a reasonable number of attempts (usually four), the manufacturer or dealer is unable to remedy a defect that substantially impairs the value of the vehicle, the vehicle must be replaced or the purchase price refunded. Lemon laws also typically require replacement or refund if a new vehicle has been out of service ("in the shop") for thirty days during the statutory warranty period.

In addition to permitting the revocation of a sales contract, state lemon laws are designed to encourage informal resolution of disputes concerning defective new vehicles. They do this by requiring that a consumer use a manufacturer's arbitration program before litigating, as long as the manufacturer has established an informal dispute resolution program that complies with FTC regulations. Some states,

82. Karen Zagor & Gary Mead, *Illumination from the Stars: A Look at the New-Found Respectability of So-Called "Infomercials,"* FIN. TIMES, Nov. 5, 1992, at 18.

83. 15 U.S.C. § 2301 *et seq.*

84. 209 Ill. 2d 376 (2004).

85. Browne v. Kline Tysons Imports, Inc., 190 F. Supp .2d 827 (E.D. Va. 2002).

including New York, have adopted their own standards for these dispute resolution programs.

SALES PRACTICES

A number of state and federal agencies currently regulate sales practices, including the FTC, the FCC, the Postal Service, and the Department of Housing and Urban Development. Their regulations may apply to all industries or be industry specific, such as the FTC's rules for sellers of used cars or state insurance regulations. For example, Prudential Insurance Company of America paid more than $2.7 billion to settle claims that its agents had engaged in illegal sales tactics, including tricking policyholders into cashing in old policies with accrued cash-surrender value to purchase new expensive ones with no surrender value, making false promises that dividends would build up quickly enough to pay for premiums, and disguising insurance policies as retirement programs.

Sometimes laws of general application can be invoked to protect consumers. For example, a lawyer in Washington, D.C., won two state court judgments totaling $11.6 million against affiliates of Tele-Communications, Inc. for charging excessive late fees on monthly cable television bills.[86] He successfully argued that the fees violated the general principle of contract law that damages assessed for breach of contract cannot be disproportionate to the actual harm caused by the breach.

State Deceptive Practices Statutes

Most state consumer protection laws are directed at deceptive trade practices and prohibit sellers from providing false or misleading information to consumers. Although there is considerable variation among state laws, they often provide more stringent protections than federal laws.

UCC Unconscionability Principle

Also on the state level, the Uniform Commercial Code protects consumers from unfair sales practices through the unconscionability principle contained in Section 2-302 of the UCC, as discussed in Chapter 8. This section prohibits the enforcement of any contracts, or contract provisions, for the sale of goods that are so unfair and one-sided that they shock the conscience of the court.

Door-to-Door Sales

Door-to-door sales are initiated and concluded at a buyer's home. They pose special risks because individuals may feel more pressure to buy something from someone standing at their door, or they may make a purchase just to get rid of a persistent salesperson. As a result, the FTC has mandated a three-day cooling-off period during which a consumer may rescind a door-to-door purchase. Under FTC rules, the seller must also notify a buyer of the right to cancel. Laws in some states provide longer periods during which consumers can cancel a sale.

Referral Sales and Pyramid Sales

A number of states have enacted legislation restricting referral and pyramid sales. In a *referral sale*, the seller offers the buyer a commission, rebate, or discount for furnishing the seller with a list of additional prospective customers. The discount, however, is usually contingent on the seller actually making later sales to the prospects provided by the original customer. In a *pyramid selling* scheme, a consumer is recruited as a product "distributor" and receives commissions based on the products he or she sells and on the recruitment of additional sellers (or even receives commissions on the sales of the recruits). The problem with both referral and pyramid sales is that unless the buyer or "distributor" becomes involved early in the chain, the supply of prospective recruits is quickly exhausted.

Telemarketing

As discussed in Chapter 9, aggressive telemarketing sales practices, particularly the use of autodialers and "900" telephone numbers, have prompted congressional intervention. In addition, state securities commissioners and the FTC continue to fight investment-related telemarketing fraud ranging from ostrich ranching in Idaho to digital fingerprint identification in Indiana and worthless oil and gas programs in Kentucky.

Mail-Order Sales

Unscrupulous mail-order sales practices have led to a high incidence of consumer complaints with resultant state and federal regulation. Sellers must respond to consumer mail orders by shipping merchandise or offering refunds within a reasonable time. Unsolicited or unordered merchandise sent by U.S. mail may be kept or disposed of by the recipient without incurring any obligation to the sender. Book and record clubs are generally legal as long as they comply with state law provisions requiring sellers to provide consumers with forms or announcement cards that the consumer may use to instruct the seller not to send the offered merchandise. The U.S. Postal Service has authority to assess criminal and civil penalties for fraudulent mail schemes that injure consumers.

86. Eben Shapiro, *Attorney Finds a Way to Battle Bills' Late Fees,* WALL ST. J., Oct. 6, 1997, at B1.

Industry-Specific Sales Practices

Since the early 1980s, the FTC has become more involved in regulating the sales practices of specific industries. For example, in 1985 the FTC began to require used-car sellers to affix a Buyer's Guide label to the cars that they sell.[87] The Buyer's Guide is intended to disclose to potential buyers information about the car's warranty and any service contract provided by the dealer. If the car is sold without a warranty, the label must state that the car is being sold "as is."

A related and well-developed area of state and federal consumer law concerns restrictions on tampering with car odometers. Consumers purchasing a motor vehicle rely heavily on odometer readings as an indication of a car's safety and reliability. The Motor Vehicle Information and Cost Savings Act[88] makes it a crime to change car odometers.

On the state level, industry-specific regulation covers the insurance industry. State insurance commissioners both establish regulations regarding the disclosure of information to prospective policyholders and set maximum rates within a state.

Real Estate Sales

A number of state and federal laws, including the Federal Real Estate Settlement Procedures Act[89] and the Interstate Land Sales Full Disclosure Act,[90] protect consumers in real estate transactions. Certain disclosure requirements of the Truth-in-Lending Act apply to real estate credit transactions as well. In some transactions, real estate buyers have the right to cancel the purchase contract if certain information is not disclosed to them or if other procedures are not properly followed.

The Real Estate Settlement Procedures Act and revisions made to it in 1976 are designed to assist home buyers by requiring disclosure of any requirements for settlement proceedings, which may include title insurance, taxes, and fees for attorneys, appraisers, and brokers. In general, lenders must give an estimate of settlement costs, identify service providers the applicant is required to use, and provide a statement showing the annual percentage rate for the mortgage.

In response to fraudulent practices used in the sale of subdivided land for investment purposes or for second or retirement homes, Congress passed the Interstate Land Sales Full Disclosure Act in 1968. It is administered by the secretary of the Department of Housing and Urban Development (HUD). Under the Act, the secretary created the Office of Interstate Land Sales Registration and imposed federal disclosure requirements on the sale of 100 or more lots of undeveloped subdivided land akin to those required for the offer of securities under the Securities Act of 1933. The Act gives the secretary of HUD the power to bring suit in federal district court to enjoin sales by developers who have not registered in accordance with the Act. Purchasers affected by a promoter's wrongdoing have a private cause of action and may cancel the purchase contract.

State Occupational Licensing

State departments of consumer affairs protect the public by examining and licensing firms and individuals who possess the necessary education and demonstrated skills to perform their services competently. Among the occupations generally regulated are accountants, architects, barbers, contractors, cosmetologists, dentists, dry cleaners, marriage counselors, nurses, pharmacists, physical therapists, physicians, and social workers. Attorneys are regulated by state bar associations and the courts. As noted in Chapter 7, any person required to be licensed who is in fact not licensed cannot enforce a promise to pay for unlicensed work. State departments of consumer affairs also investigate and resolve consumer complaints and hold public hearings involving consumer matters.

Consumer Credit and the Consumer Credit Protection Act

Because credit plays an important role in many consumer transactions, a number of consumer protection laws address this area. Federal consumer credit law can be confusing because many of the acts have similar names. These complex acts and regulations are all part of the lengthy Consumer Credit Protection Act (CCPA),[91] which was initially passed by Congress in 1968. Since 1968, several additional acts (or titles) have been added to the original legislation. Exhibit 18.2 provides an overview of the CCPA and indicates the provisions that are omitted from the discussion in this chapter.

87. 16 C.F.R. pt. 455 (Used Motor Vehicle Trade Regulation Rule).
88. 15 U.S.C. § 1901 *et seq.*
89. 12 U.S.C. § 2601 *et seq.*
90. 15 U.S.C. § 1701 *et seq.*
91. 15 U.S.C. § 1601 *et seq.*

EXHIBIT 18.2 Consumer Credit Protection Act (CCPA)

Title	Consumer Credit Protection Act
I.	Truth-in-Lending Act (TILA) Chapter 1: General Provisions [omitted] Chapter 2: Credit Transactions Chapter 3: Credit Advertising Chapter 4: Fair Credit Billing Act Chapter 5: Consumer Leasing Act [omitted]
II.	Extortionate Credit Transactions
III.	Restrictions on Garnishment
IV.	National Commission on Consumer Finance [omitted]
V.	General Provisions [omitted]
VI.	Fair Credit Reporting Act
VII.	Equal Credit Opportunity Act
VIII.	Fair Debt Collection Practices Act
IX.	Electronic Fund Transfer Act

TRUTH-IN-LENDING ACT

Title I, the Truth-in-Lending Act (TILA), is intended "to assure a meaningful disclosure of credit terms so that the consumer will be able to compare more readily the various credit terms available and avoid the uninformed use of credit, and to protect the consumer against inaccurate and unfair credit billing and credit card practices."[92] In particular, the Act makes uniform the actuarial method for determining the rate of charge for consumer credit and requires certain disclosures. It is not a *usury statute*, however, and does not set maximum interest rates. TILA applies only to credit transactions between creditors and individual consumers, not to credit transactions between two consumers. Typical transactions covered by TILA include car loans, student loans, and home improvement loans; credit cards (such as Visa and MasterCard), which permit deferred payment over a period of time; charge cards (such as American Express), which require payment of the full balance upon receipt of the bill; and certain real estate loans in which the amount financed is less than $25,000.

Congress directed the Federal Reserve Board to issue regulations for the enforcement and interpretation of TILA. To that end, the Federal Reserve has produced model disclosure forms for use with credit sales and loans. The two most important terms in a TILA disclosure statement are the *finance charge* (interest over the life of the loan expressed as a dollar amount) and the annual percentage rate (interest expressed as a percentage), which are both defined in the Federal Reserve Board's *Regulation Z*.[93] Regulation Z also contains provisions dealing with disclosure of the terms of any credit or mortgage insurance offered in connection with a loan.

Regulation Z requires marketing materials for credit cards to prominently display a table that clearly states the annual percentage rate and other critical information (including the annual fee). The annual percentage rate for purchases and the variable rate information, grace period, minimum finance charge, method of computing the balance, cash advance fees, and over-limit fees, as well as any other fees that vary by state, must be printed in a box in at least eighteen-point type to prevent information from being hidden in the "fine print." In addition, the overall disclosure statement must be printed in at least twelve-point type and be in a reasonably understandable form.[94]

TILA draws a distinction between open-end credit and closed-end credit. *Open-end credit* occurs when the parties intend the creditor to make repeated extensions of credit (for example, Visa or MasterCard); *closed-end credit* involves only one transaction (for example, a car or house loan). Open-end consumer credit plans must make certain disclosures at three separate times: (1) in an initial disclosure statement when the account is opened, (2) in subsequent periodic billing statements, and (3) annually when a consumer must be notified of his or her rights under the Fair Credit Billing Act. In general, the required information includes finance and other charges, security interests (collateral), previous balance and credits, identification of transactions, closing date and new balance, and annual percentage rates and period rates.

Closed-end credit plans require disclosure of at least the following for each transaction: identity of creditor, amount financed, finance charge, annual percentage rate, variable rate, payment schedule, total of payments, total sale price, prepayment provisions, late payment fee, security interest, credit insurance, loan assumption policy, and required deposit. Special rules apply for certain residential mortgages and adjustable rate transactions.

In 2000, the FTC settled a claim against providers of short-term, high-interest-rate "payday loans" for alleged violations of TILA and the FTC's Telemarketing Sales Rule.[95] Two companies used direct mail and telemarketing to market the MoneyMarketCard. They offered consumers,

92. 15 U.S.C. § 1601.

93. 12 C.F.R. pt. 226.

94. *Fed Issues Final Regulation Under TILA Requiring New Clarity for Card Disclosures,* 69 U.S.L.W. 2200 (2000).

95. FTC v. Consumer Money Mkts., Inc., No. CVS001071 (D. Nev. Sept. 6, 2000).

regardless of their credit history, a credit line of $5,500 at a 14.99 percent interest rate. After consumers paid $149 to $169 to receive the MoneyMarketCard, they discovered that they could use the credit only to buy items from one of the company's catalogs and that the cash advance privileges were short-term payday loans of $20 to $40 with annual interest rates of 360 percent or more. The FTC alleged that although the companies collected membership fees of more than $12 million between 1996 and 1999, less than 8 percent of the customers ever purchased even one catalog product or took out a cash loan. The settlement required the companies to stop their deceptive practices, disgorge $350,000 received from consumers, and forgive $1.6 million in outstanding consumer debts.

Consumers can be required to arbitrate their claims if they agreed to do so when applying for or procuring credit and are not forced to relinquish statutorily protected rights. For example, in 2000, a federal district court in Illinois ruled that a claim that a lender's consumer loan agreement violated TILA for failing to disclose the annual percentage rate, finance charge, and financing costs for rollover loans was subject to mandatory arbitration.[96] The loan agreement stated that any dispute regarding the loan was subject to arbitration. The court rejected the borrowers' argument that TILA gave them a statutory right to seek relief through a class action.[97]

TILA limits the liability of credit cardholders to $50 per card for unauthorized charges made before a card issuer is notified that the card has been lost or stolen. Once a card issuer has been notified, a cardholder incurs no liability from unauthorized use. In addition, a credit or charge card company cannot bill a consumer for unauthorized charges if the card was improperly issued by the card company.

Home Equity Lending Plans, Subprime Mortgages, and Predatory Lending

TILA provides specific protections for consumers who use their home as collateral for a second mortgage or an open-end line of credit. Because losing one's home has such significant consequences, Congress felt special disclosure requirements were in order. TILA provides consumers a *right of rescission* (that is, a right to cancel the contract) whenever their home is used as collateral except for original construction or acquisition. These cancellation rights are generally available for three days if all procedures are properly followed by the lender, three years if they are not. TILA also mandates disclosure of up-front costs, repayment schedules, and the annual percentage rate and its method of calculation.

Predatory lending involves mortgage loans secured by the borrower's house that are made at subprime interest rates to borrowers who often lack the ability to repay them. These loans tend to be concentrated in low-income communities and to be used for consumer debt rather than housing purposes. Because the loans are often based solely on the homeowner's equity in the home, without regard to the borrower's income and thus his or her ability to repay the loan, foreclosures are common. Although subprime lending has enabled many Americans with modest incomes and poor credit histories to buy homes, these loans have cost thousands of borrowers their homes and brought others near the brink of financial ruin. In 2004, the Federal Reserve Board fined Citigroup a record $75 million for violating regulations against predatory lending practices.

A 2007 study by researchers at New York University found that home buyers in predominantly black and Hispanic neighborhoods in New York City were more likely to get their mortgages from a subprime lender than home buyers in white neighborhoods. According to NYU's Furman Center for Real Estate and Urban Policy, this disparity held true even when median income levels were comparable.[98] This study confirmed the suspicion that certain mortgage brokers offering subprime mortgages worked only in certain neighborhoods or tended to offer white borrowers better rates than equally qualified African American or Hispanic customers.

The NAACP (National Association for the Advancement of Colored People) filed a lawsuit in federal court in Los Angeles in 2007 against twelve major mortgage lenders, accusing the companies of targeting African American

96. Thompson v. Ill. Title Loans, Inc., 2000 U.S. Dist. LEXIS 232 (N.D. Ill. Jan. 6, 2000).

97. *Contra* Lozada v. Dale Baker Oldsmobile, 91 F. Supp. 2d 1087 (W.D. Mich. 2000) (refusing to enforce a mandatory arbitration clause in a car purchasing agreement that required the purchaser to waive TILA's right to bring a class action).

98. Manny Fernandez, *Study Finds Disparities in Mortgages by Race*, N.Y. TIMES, Oct. 15, 2007.

> **› ETHICAL CONSIDERATION**
>
> **Should businesses serving communities with a large non-English-speaking population provide written translations of written documents? Should businesses provide oral translations, perhaps on voice recording cassettes, of important terms in consumer transactions, such as home equity loans and door-to-door sales, so that consumers who have difficulty reading English can understand what the transaction entails?**

borrowers for subprime loans. In July 2008, the Federal Reserve Board revised Regulation Z to add rules designed to protect mortgage customers from predatory lending practices and "higher-priced" mortgages and to discourage prepayment penalties. These rules were due to take effect on October 1, 2009.

Credit Advertising

TILA includes specific provisions that regulate credit advertising. The idea behind these provisions is that consumers equipped with complete and accurate credit information will be able to find the best terms. Regulation Z requires that any advertised specific credit terms actually be available and that any credit terms (for example, the finance charge or annual percentage rate) mentioned in the advertisement be explained fully. The FTC enforces the advertising provisions of Regulation Z. For example, all credit card advertising must have a "Schumer Box" (named after the New York Senator who championed the regulation) that contains all basic credit card information. Unlike the other sections of TILA, this provision does not give consumers a private cause of action to sue credit advertisers directly. On September 14, 2004, the Office of the Comptroller of the Currency issued an advisory letter to national banks, which warned against (1) increasing the cost of credit to the cardholder without disclosing fully and prominently in promotional materials the circumstances under which the credit card agreement permits the bank to increase the consumer's annual percentage rate (APR), increase fees, or otherwise increase the cost of credit; (2) failing to disclose fully and prominently the bank's unilateral right to change the APR, fees, or other terms; (3) promoting credit limits up to a maximum amount that is seldom extended; or (4) advertising possible uses of the card when the initial available credit line is unlikely to cover such purchases.[99]

Credit Billing

The Fair Credit Billing Act requires creditors, such as credit card companies, to respond to consumer complaints with an acknowledgment of the complaint, followed by a reasonable investigation to determine whether the complaint is justified. Companies cannot evade this requirement by canceling a cardholder's account.

For example, in 1982, American Express Company canceled a cardholder's account during a dispute about incorrect billings. American Express argued that its contract with the cardholder allowed it to revoke a credit card at any time for any reason, but the U.S. Court of Appeals for the District of Columbia ruled that the Fair Credit Billing Act's protections could not be waived.[100] As the court explained:

> The rationale of consumer protection legislation is to even out the inequalities that consumers normally bring to the bargain. To allow such protection to be waived by boiler plate language of the contract puts the legislative process to a foolish and unproductive task. A court ought not impute such nonsense to a Congress intent on correcting abuses in the market place.

Hence, the Fair Credit Billing Act protected the cardmember from the revocation of his account despite the provisions of the Cardmember Agreement purporting to permit American Express to cancel the account at any time.

EXTORTIONATE CREDIT TRANSACTIONS

The CCPA prohibits any *extortionate extension of credit*, that is, the extension of credit where the parties expect nonpayment to result in bodily harm.

RESTRICTIONS ON GARNISHMENT

Garnishment is the legal procedure by which a creditor may collect a debt by attaching a portion of the debtor's weekly wages. The CCPA restricts the amount of a debtor's wages that is available for garnishment to the lesser of (1) 25 percent of the "disposable earnings" for that week (defined by the Act as the amount remaining after deductions required by law) or (2) the amount by which "disposable earnings" for that week exceed thirty times the current federal minimum hourly wage. The secretary of labor enforces the provisions of this title. Some states prohibit garnishment of wages altogether.

FAIR CREDIT REPORTING ACT

Almost everyone over the age of eighteen has a credit report on file somewhere. Lenders look to these various reporting agencies for information on an individual's creditworthiness. Because negative information in a credit report can make obtaining credit considerably more difficult, it is important for consumers to be able to access these credit reports and to correct any false information before it is reported to lenders or shared with another reporting agency's computer.

Under the Fair Credit Reporting Act of 1970 (FCRA), as amended by the Fair and Accurate Credit Transactions Act of 2003 (FACT Act), consumers can request all information

99. The OCC Advisory Letter (AL 2004-10) is available at http://www.occ.treas.gov/ftp/advisory/2004-10.txt.

100. Gray v. Am. Express Co., 743 F.2d 10 (D.C. Cir. 1984).

(except medical information) on themselves, the source of the information, and any recent recipients of a report. The FCRA also gives consumers a right to have corrected copies of their credit reports sent to creditors. The FTC has the primary responsibility for the enforcement of the FCRA.

Credit bureaus must investigate disputed information in credit reports and resolve consumer complaints within thirty days. They must give consumers written notice of the results of the investigation within five days after it is completed. The credit-reporting agency must go beyond the original source of information to determine whether it is accurate. Thus, when a consumer notified the agency that she had never held the credit cards her report showed as being delinquent, the agency could not just rely on the credit card companies' statements that the applications for the cards had the correct information. Instead, the agency should have checked the handwriting on the credit applications and determined whether the applications were obtained by fraud.[101]

When a consumer tells a credit-reporting agency that he or she disputes a charge, the agency is required to notify the furnisher of the information that the information provided is in dispute. The creditor must then conduct a "reasonable" investigation and review all relevant information to determine whether it is accurate.[102] Any finding that information is inaccurate or incomplete must be reported to all national credit bureaus. Under certain circumstances, consumers can require the firm that furnished disputed information to the credit bureau to reinvestigate the accuracy of the information it passed on to the bureau. A furnisher is liable for providing inaccurate information if it "knows or has reasonable cause to believe that the information is inaccurate."[103]

As noted in Chapter 9, the FACT Act gave consumers new tools to fight identity theft and to correct erroneous information resulting from the fraudulent use of credit cards and accounts. The FACT Act does not, however, contain an express private cause of action for consumers harmed by erroneous credit reports.

The FCRA also contains restrictions on *investigative consumer reporting*, that is, reports that contain information on character and reputation, not just credit history. In most cases, a consumer must be notified in writing that such a report may be made. This requirement applies to potential or current employers as well.

Before asking a credit bureau or private investigator for a report on a credit applicant or employee, the lender or employer must notify the individual in writing that a report may be used and obtain the individual's consent. Neither a lender nor an employer may rely on a credit or investigative consumer report to take adverse action (including denying credit or denying a job applicant a position, reassigning or terminating an employee, or denying a promotion), unless it first provides the individual with a "pre-adverse action disclosure," which includes a copy of the report and the FTC's "A Summary of Your Rights Under the Fair Credit Reporting Act." Lenders and employers who fail to obtain permission before requesting a credit or investigative report or to provide the pre-adverse action disclosures are subject to suits for damages (including punitive damages for deliberate violations) by individuals and civil penalties by the FTC.

After a lender or an employer has taken adverse action, it must give the individual notice—orally, in writing, or electronically—that the action has been taken. The notice must include (1) the name, address, and phone number of the credit bureau or private investigator that supplied the report; (2) a statement that the credit bureau or investigator did not make the decision to take adverse action and cannot give specific reasons for it; and (3) a notice of the individual's right to dispute the accuracy or completeness of any information the bureau or investigator furnished and the individual's right upon request to an additional free report from the credit bureau or investigator within sixty days.

Lenders that use risk-based pricing must provide notices to consumers who receive loans on "material terms that are materially less favorable than the most favorable terms available to a substantial portion of consumers . . . based in whole or in part on a consumer report."[104]

EQUAL CREDIT OPPORTUNITY ACT

The Equal Credit Opportunity Act was originally intended to address the difficulty many women faced in obtaining credit, but it has since been expanded to prohibit discrimination against credit applicants on many other grounds. The current list of protected categories includes gender, marital status, race, color, religion, national origin, and age (except that older applicants may be given favorable treatment). The Act also prohibits discrimination against applicants who derive their income from public assistance or have exercised in good faith any right under the CCPA. The FACT Act generally prohibits lenders from using medical information about a consumer as a factor in decisions about credit eligibility.

Unlike most of the other lending acts discussed in this chapter, the Equal Credit Opportunity Act applies to business credit as well as consumer credit. In general, the rejection of

101. Cushman v. Trans Union Corp., 115 F.3d 220 (3d Cir. 1997).

102. Johnson v. MBNA Am. Bank NA, 357 F.3d 426 (4th Cir. 2004).

103. FACT Act § 312 (b).

104. FACT Act § 311.

> **ETHICAL CONSIDERATION**
>
> Is it ethical for a lender to call a friend in the police department to see whether a loan applicant has a criminal record? Should the applicant be notified of that investigation?

an application for credit triggers the Act and various compliance steps, which include written notification of the reasons for denial. The regulations also establish methods for evaluating the creditworthiness of an applicant.

FAIR DEBT COLLECTION PRACTICES ACT

The Fair Debt Collection Practices Act (FDCPA), which is enforced by the FTC, regulates debt collectors and debt collection practices and provides a civil remedy for anyone injured by a violation of the statute. In general, FTC guidelines require collectors to tell the truth and not to use any deceptive means to collect a debt or locate a debtor. For example, a collector sending a dunning letter must state very clearly and explicitly the amount owed.

The Act covers only third-party debt collectors (for example, collection agencies) or someone pretending to be a third-party collector. First-party debt collectors (for example, retail store collection departments) are not covered, although the FTC can reach these collectors under its duty to address "unfair and deceptive trade practices" under Section 5 of the Federal Trade Commission Act. The U.S. Court of Appeals for the Second Circuit held that a letter from an attorney for a landlord demanding that a tenant pay back rent within three days or face eviction was

> **ETHICAL CONSIDERATION**
>
> The FDCPA specifically forbids a debt collector to engage in certain practices, including contacting a debtor directly at any time if that debtor is represented by an attorney. What self-imposed limits, if any, might a debt collector adopt, and what role should a debtor's personal circumstances (for example, unemployment or terminal illness) play in how aggressive a debt collector chooses to be?

subject to the FDCPA.[105] The court held that past due rent is a debt and that the lawyer's letter was a debt collection "communication" within the meaning of the statute.

People who write bad checks for goods and services are also protected from abusive debt collection practices by the FDCPA. The U.S. Courts of Appeals for the Seventh,[106] Eighth,[107] and Ninth Circuits[108] have each held that the payment obligation that arises from a bounced check is a "debt" within the meaning of the Act even though the transaction did not involve an offer or extension of credit.

As the following case illustrates, debt collectors have serious obligations when attempting to collect a debt.

105. Romea v. Helberger & Assocs., 163 F.3d 111 (2d Cir. 1998).

106. Bass v. Stolper, Koritzinsky, Brewer & Neider, 111 F.3d 1322 (7th Cir. 1997).

107. Duffy v. Landberg, 133 F.3d 1120 (8th Cir. 1998), *cert. denied,* 525 U.S. 821 (1998).

108. Charles v. Lundgren & Assocs., P.C., 119 F.3d 739 (9th Cir. 1997), *cert. denied,* 522 U.S. 1028 (1997).

A CASE IN POINT

CASE 18.3

CHUWAY V. NATIONAL ACTION FINANCIAL SERVICES INC.

UNITED STATES COURT OF APPEALS FOR THE SEVENTH CIRCUIT
362 F.3D 944
(7TH CIR. 2004).

IN THE LANGUAGE OF THE COURT

FACTS Caldean Chuway received a letter from National Action Financial Services (NAFS), on behalf of a credit card company, stating that Chuway owed $367.42 to the card company. The letter notified Chuway that the account had been "assigned to our agency for collection." It went on to instruct the debtor, "Please remit the balance listed above in the return envelope provided." The letter further stated, "[T]o obtain your most current balance information, please call 1-800-916-9006. Our friendly and experienced representatives will be glad to assist you and answer any questions you may have." Chuway found the letter confusing. She was not sure whether the amount stated in the letter ($367.42) was the actual amount being sought or whether she needed to call NAFS for current balance information. She claimed that the letter violated the Fair Debt Collection Practices Act.

ISSUE PRESENTED Does a dunning letter violate the FDCPA by stating an exact amount of debt owed, when that statement is followed by a message calling into question the current debt owed?

CONTINUED

OPINION POSNER, C.J., writing for the U.S. Court of Appeals for the Seventh Circuit:

The Fair Debt Collection Practices Act requires that any dunning letter by a debt collector as defined by the Act state "the amount of the debt" that the debt collector is trying to collect.

. . . .

[I]f the letter had stopped after the "Please remit" sentence, the defendant would be in the clear. But the letter didn't stop there. It went on to instruct the recipient on how to obtain "your most current balance information." If this means that the defendant was dunning her for something more than $367.42, it's in trouble because the "something more" is not quantified.

. . . .

It is not enough that the dunning letter state the amount of the debt that is due. It must state it clearly enough that the recipient is likely to understand it. Otherwise the collection agency could write the letter in Hittite and have a secure defense. The defendant concedes the principle but insists that to withstand summary judgment the plaintiff must always submit a survey or some other form of systematic empirical evidence demonstrating the propensity of the letter to confuse. There is no basis for so flat a rule. If it is apparent just from reading the letter that it is unclear . . . . and the plaintiff testifies credibly that she was indeed confused and that . . . she is representative of the type of people who received that or a similar letter, no further evidence is necessary to create a triable issue.

. . . .

No survey was conducted here, but the entire bench was confused about the meaning of the letter until the defendant's lawyer explained it to us at the oral argument, and our confusion, coupled with the plaintiff's affidavit in which she plausibly attested that she had been confused by the letter, is enough to satisfy her burden of proof.

. . . .

Our conclusion does not place debt collectors on a razor's edge, where if they say too little they violate the Act by failing to disclose the amount of the debt they are trying to collect and if they say too much they violate the Act by confusing the consumer. If the debt collector is trying to collect only the amount due on the date the letter is sent, then he complies with the Act by stating the "balance" due, stating that the creditor "has assigned your delinquent account to our agency for collection," and asking the recipient to remit the balance listed—and stopping there, without talk of the "current" balance. If, instead, the debt collector is trying to collect the listed balance plus the interest running on it or other charges, he should use the safe-harbor language of *Miller*:[109] "As of the date of this letter, you owe $___ [the exact amount due]. Because of interest, late charges, and other charges that may vary from day to day, the amount due on the day you pay may be greater. Hence, if you pay the amount shown above, an adjustment may be necessary after we receive your check, in which event we will inform you before depositing the check for collection. For further information, write the undersigned or call 1-800-[phone number]."

RESULT The appeals court ordered judgment for the plaintiff and remanded the case to the trial court for the computation of statutory damages, costs, and attorneys' fees.

CRITICAL THINKING QUESTIONS

1. Would you have understood the meaning of the dunning letter?
2. Does Chief Judge Posner have the requisite knowledge to explain to NAFS, a business designed specifically to collect debts, how to do so?

---

109. Miller v. McCalla, Raymer, Padrick, Cobb, Nicholas & Clark, L.L.C., 214 F.3d 872, 875 (7th Cir. 2000).

ELECTRONIC FUND TRANSFER ACT: DEBIT CARDS AND PREAUTHORIZED FUND TRANSFERS

The Electronic Fund Transfer Act, passed by Congress in 1978, covers online debit cards issued by banks for use with automatic teller machines (ATMs) and point-of-sale transactions, as well as preauthorized electronic fund transfers or automatic payments from a consumer's account. As with credit cards, banks are prohibited from sending out debit cards except in response to a consumer's request.

The Federal Reserve Board has issued regulations and model forms for banks to use to satisfy disclosure requirements under the Act. In general, the Federal Reserve forms ensure disclosure of contract terms, potential customer liability for unauthorized use (as with credit cards, customer liability is usually limited to no more than $50), and consumer complaint procedures. Banks are also required to issue receipts with every ATM transaction and to mail periodic statements showing electronic fund transfer activity on a consumer's account during the period. For preauthorized transfers or automatic payments, banks are required to provide either (1) written or oral notice within two days of the scheduled transaction date that the transaction did or did not occur or (2) a telephone line for consumers to call and ascertain whether the transfer occurred. Most financial institutions have adopted the latter approach.

Online debit cards are usually PIN-protected; that is, cash cannot be withdrawn from an ATM and a deduction cannot be made at a point-of-sale terminal unless the holder uses a personal identification number (PIN). In contrast, off-line debit cards (which may bear the Visa or MasterCard logo) have the characteristics of both an ATM card and a credit card, and they can be used without a PIN. For example, the holder of an off-line debit card can authorize a deduction from his or her bank account by signing a charge slip at a restaurant. Visa and MasterCard voluntarily agreed to impose a $50 cap on liability for their off-line debit cards.

STATE LAWS REGULATING CONSUMER CREDIT

All states have statutes regulating consumer credit. Two types of consumer credit transactions are addressed primarily at the state level: installment sales and loans to consumers. State statutes vary widely, and an attempt to create uniform state laws on consumer credit through adoption of the Uniform Consumer Credit Code (UCCC, called the U–Triple C) has been largely unsuccessful. The UCCC is intended to replace a state's consumer credit laws, including those that regulate usury, installment sales, consumer loans, truth in lending, and garnishment. The UCCC has been adopted by only a handful of states, and in each of those it has been so significantly altered that little uniformity remains. Exhibit 18.3 summarizes common provisions in state credit laws.

Credit card companies have found a way around particularly stringent state credit card fee limits and usury laws by moving their operations to states with more lax laws. The Supreme Court ruled that the usury laws of the state in which the card company is located apply.[110] Thus, a bank with credit card operations in a state that permits high rates, such as South Dakota or Delaware, can charge a resident of Massachusetts the high rates of interest and fees permitted in the state of operation even though they are in excess of the Massachusetts limits.

110. Marquette Nat'l Bank of Minneapolis v. First of Omaha Serv. Corp., 439 U.S. 299 (1978).

EXHIBIT 18.3 State Credit Laws

Area Law Covers	Examples	Primary Goals
Installment sales	Legal interest rates, late charges, deferral charges, and other permissible charges	Place caps on late charges and limit remedies, attorney's fees, and rights to assign sales contract
Consumer loans	Mortgages and private loans	Set maximum permissible interest rate, with exceptions available for special license holders
Credit cards	Credit card repayment rates, credit card fees	Stop exploitation by credit card companies

GLOBAL VIEW

International Recycling and Chemical Safety Standards

Although the United States initially set the standard for consumer and environmental protection, the European Union (EU) is increasingly replacing America as the leader in environmental and chemical policy development.[111] Three recent environmental policies, including two directives and one regulation, are being implemented in the twenty-seven member states that comprise the European Union.

The first directive, WEEE,[112] is intended to increase the recovery and recycling of electrical and electronic equipment. The second, RoHS,[113] outlines restrictions on the use of certain hazardous substances in the production of such equipment. These measures, adopted in February 2003, require manufacturers to dispose of consumers' used electronic equipment free of charge and prohibit the export of hazardous waste to developing countries outside the EU for disposal.

Unlike American policy, these measures demand significant producer accountability, placing the burden of environmental responsibility entirely on the manufacturer. European producers are now required to finance the recycling, reprocessing, and safe disposal of regulated equipment and its components. Advocates of the policies hope that these requirements will provide substantial incentives for producers to design environmentally friendly electrical and electronic equipment and to consider waste management while designing new products. In the past, public authorities, not private manufacturers, were responsible for both waste management and the risk assessment of chemicals.

The WEEE directive regulates the production of products in ten different categories, including large household appliances, small household appliances, information technology and telecommunications equipment, consumer equipment, lighting equipment, electrical and electronic tools, toys and leisure and sports equipment, medical devices, monitoring and control instruments, and automatic dispensers. The RoHS directive overlaps and supplements the WEEE directive, limiting the use of six toxic substances in eight of the ten product categories addressed by WEEE. These substances include four heavy metals (lead, mercury, cadmium, and hexavalent chromium) and two chemicals (PBB and PBDE), all of which are common in electrical and electronic goods produced in Europe and around the world. Each EU state is expected to design its own implementation system to enforce these directives.

In January 2007, the European Union adopted a third chemical regulation, REACH (registration, evaluation, and authorization of chemicals). Perhaps the world's most strict and rigorous policy on potentially hazardous chemical substances, this initiative requires registration and evaluation of more than 30,000 existing chemical substances and of any new ones that may be developed. At present, there is little information available on most of the tens of thousands of chemicals used in existing products. REACH is designed to yield data on these chemicals, particularly in the areas of emissions, toxicity, the ecosystem, and effect on human health. For the first time, producers will be required to present risk assessment data for every new substance before introducing it to the market. The technical, scientific, and administrative aspects of REACH are to be managed by the recently established European Chemicals Agency located in Helsinki, Finland.[114]

Extensive negotiations among the European Commission, the European Council, and the European Parliament led to the development of these three policy initiatives. These governmental entities developed these policies with input from concerned lobbyists representing private-sector and civil society groups, and the EU adopted the three initiatives notwithstanding significant resistance from organized industry in Europe and abroad.

111. Henrik Selin & Stacy D. VanDeveer, *Raising Global Standards: Hazardous Substances and E-Waste Management in the European Union*, 48 ENV'T 6–17 (Dec. 2006).

112. Council directive 2002/96/EC on waste electrical and electronic equipment (WEEE); Council directive 2003/108/EC amending Council directive 2002/96/EC on waste electrical and electronic equipment (WEEE).

113. Council directive 2002/95/EC on the restriction of the use of certain hazardous substances (RoHS) in electrical and electronic equipment.

114. European Chemicals Agency, ECHA Mission, *available at* http://echa.europa.eu/about/mission_en.asp.

CONTINUED

Since the adoption of these regulations, the member states of the EU have attempted to translate the broad directives into concrete national legislation. A number of EU countries had adopted domestic electronics waste legislation before 2003 and needed only to make limited additions. Germany, the Netherlands, Denmark, and Sweden pioneered much of the EU's policy on substantial producer responsibility; officials in these countries labored to "trade up" their strict regulations to the EU level. For many other countries, however, the implementation of these directives required a massive overhaul of domestic legislation. Certain countries, including the United Kingdom, have been slower than others in translating the new EU legislation into domestic law.[115]

Opponents of the new legislation expressed concerns about the economic costs to individual firms and consumers as well as potentially adverse implications for international trade and jobs. The European Commission estimated that REACH alone would cost the chemical industry 2.1 billion euros over eleven years.[116] Industry-commissioned studies predicted more then two million lost jobs and a 6 percent reduction in German GDP alone.

Major chemical companies, including Bayer and Shell Chemicals, argued that the economic burden of enforcement would threaten their competitiveness. According to the Environmental Data Services (ENDS), REACH "attracted more hostility from industry than any other item of EU environmental legislation in 30 years."[117]

Roughly one in fourteen people in the world lives in the European Union, which boasts an economy of $11 trillion and a population of 485 million.[118] Given that almost all multinational companies operate or sell their products in the EU, these new regulatory standards will almost certainly have significant implications for international trade. Firms operating in the United States and in Asia must comply with EU product rules and standards in order to sell their products in Europe.

In recent years, Asian countries have responded favorably to the new European policies. China and South Korea are already developing legislation inspired by WEEE and RoHS. Japanese environmental legislation tends to follow Europe's lead, so Japan is also likely to look to the EU for further policy guidance on effective chemical waste management.

Substantial opposition to these regulations continues to come from the United States, however. Many American companies criticized the EU's invocation of the precautionary principle to justify its identification and assessment of risks. The *precautionary principle* provides guidance for protecting public health and the environment in the face of uncertain risks and stipulates that the absence of full scientific certainty shall not be used as a reason to postpone measures where there is a risk of serious or irreversible harm to public health or the environment.[119] Critics argue that the EU has stifled scientific and industrial innovation and ignored the basic reality that a certain amount of risk is unavoidable in industry and in everyday life. Many in the U.S. government and industry have also expressed concern about the potential costs (estimated to be in the billions of dollars) and jobs lost as a result of compliance with these strict regulations.

It is too early to tell whether the concept of extended producer responsibility will spread beyond the borders of the European Union. Nevertheless, these standards are certainly drawing attention from policymakers, regulators, industry leaders, and environmentalists around the globe. In an increasingly interdependent world, it is likely that the EU's new policies will push many global standards upward.

---

115. Editorial, *Wasting Time on Waste: The UK Trails in Carrying out EU Law on Electrical Recycling*, FIN. TIMES (LONDON), June 7, 2006.

116. *Commission White Paper on a Strategy for a Future Chemicals Policy* (Brussels: European Commission: 2001).

117. ENDS, *REACH Caught up in EU's Competitiveness Agenda*, ENDS REPORT 346, Nov. 2003, at 51–53.

118. Central Intelligence Agency, *The World Factbook* 2008 (2008), *available at* https://www.cia.gov/cia/publications/factbook/index.html.

119. *See generally* PROTECTING PUBLIC HEALTH AND THE ENVIRONMENT: IMPLEMENTING THE PRECAUTIONARY PRINCIPLE (Carolyn Raffensberger & Joel Tickner eds., 1999).

THE RESPONSIBLE MANAGER

COMPLYING WITH CONSUMER PROTECTION LAWS

Managers have a responsibility to make sure that current and potential customers are treated fairly and in a manner that will not subject them to economic or physical injury. Supervisors must take steps to ensure that employees are aware of, and in compliance with, various federal and state consumer protection regulations. Because both managers and employees can be held legally accountable for their actions (and criminally liable in some cases), specific procedures should be in place to educate employees about important consumer law topics.

In a competitive marketplace, managers often feel the need to be aggressive in their advertising of products or services. Nonetheless, managers must refrain from making claims that may be deceptive or false. The FTC and state attorneys general aggressively pursue companies that make false advertising claims. Remedies can include civil damages and corrective advertising campaigns, which can cost millions of dollars.

Consider Volvo's ill-fated "Bear Foot" advertising campaign in 1990, which almost destroyed thirty years of consistent brand messaging that equated Volvo with safety. The ad showed a Volvo suffering no damage after being driven over by a monster truck. The ad failed to disclose, however, that the internal structure of the Volvo had been reinforced and that the pillars in competing cars had been weakened for the commercial. According to five-time Clio award winner Mike Moser, "When people found out that the demonstration was rigged, the credibility of the brand was suddenly on shaky ground. People had bought into safety's being a core value of Volvo. . . . These same people didn't want to hear that Volvo didn't believe its own demonstration."[120]

The attorney general of Texas called the Volvo ads "a hoax and a sham"[121] and fined Volvo and its ad agency, Scali, McCabe, Sloves, $150,000 each for deceptive advertising. Volvo withdrew the spots and ran corrective ads in nineteen Texas newspapers, *USA Today,* and *The Wall Street Journal.* One month later, Scali, McCabe, Sloves resigned from the Volvo account. The incident cost the agency $40 million in annual revenues and the jobs of thirty-five to fifty staffers.[122]

Business leaders should not be satisfied merely to meet minimum government standards. Mere compliance may not be sufficient to release a manager or his or her company from liability when the manager has superior product information and should have taken additional precautions. Managers whose companies extend credit to customers need to be aware that many discriminatory practices in the extension of credit are illegal under the Equal Credit Opportunity Act. Some states also prohibit discrimination in credit based on sexual orientation.

Legally astute managers embrace the opportunity to self-regulate or, at least, work closely with a regulatory agency to establish industry standards that meet the concerns of both the agency and the company. A good example of a self-regulating industry is the infomercial industry. Faced with possible government regulation, the industry established its own watchdog agency. In doing so, it was able to avert government involvement and the possibility of more restrictive regulation. The Consumer Product Safety Improvement Act of 2008 and the new Federal Reserve rules governing "high-priced" mortgages are just two examples of the tougher regulation that results when firms fail to meet society's expectations of appropriate behavior.

120. MIKE MOSER, UNITED WE BRAND 16 (2001).

121. Bruce Horowitz, *Volvo, Agency Fined $150,000 Each for TV Ad Commercials,* L.A. TIMES, Aug. 22, 1991.

122. Joshua Levine, *Image Maker, Heal Thyself,* FORBES, May 27, 1991.

A Manager's Dilemma

Putting It into Practice

Downplaying Hazards and Keeping Product Liability Settlements Confidential

Frequently, companies are reluctant to generate negative publicity about their product, so they try to negotiate with the CPSC to issue a press release that uses language that minimizes the hazards. For example, the company may issue a press release announcing a "recall for repair" rather than a straight recall. Is this ethical? Good business practice?

Suppose that you are the product manager for your company's portable infant playpen. Two infants suffocate after their caregivers fail to properly latch the sides open, permitting the unit to collapse. The CPSC orders a recall of the playpens but requires only minimal publicity about the recall. Should you do more than the CPSC requires to publicize the recall? What would you do if you knew that another three infants would die the same way if you did not publicize the recall? Suppose the parents of the third infant to die sue your company. Is it ethical to settle the case on the condition that the settlement be kept confidential?[123] Is it good business practice?

123. Felcher, *supra* note 58.

Inside Story

TOXIC TOYS

In 2007, tests of a children's backpack made in China revealed lead levels as high as 4,600 parts per million, almost eight times the 600 parts per million standard for lead paint set by the CPSC.[124] Of the 40 million children's toys and accessories recalled for safety reasons in the United States in 2007, 30 million were manufactured in China. They included backpacks, vinyl baby bibs, pencil cases, an infant wrist rattle, and a toy bear.[125]

According to the Toy Industry Association, 70 to 80 percent of the toys sold in the United States are made in China,[126] earning China the nickname of the "world's toy chest." With increased production, however, have come increased recalls. China was responsible for 60 percent of all product recalls in 2007, compared with 36 percent in 2000.

Exposure to lead, by children chewing on lead toys or repeatedly playing with toys containing lead, has been proved to cause severe neurological and behavioral problems.[127] Toys and other products made for children containing lead paint were banned in the United States in the 1970s, but items made in China were not subject to the same regulations that applied to toys manufactured in the United States.

Children's products also often contain phthalates, a family of chemicals that make plastics softer. A study conducted by the Center for Reproductive Epidemiology at the University of Rochester Medical School found that infants exposed to phthalate levels were more likely to have liver and kidney cancer later in life.[128]

As the recalls mounted, the CPSC acknowledged that more needed to be done to protect U.S. consumers, but it lacked the resources to act.[129] For example, the CPSC stated in a 2007 budget report that "because of resource limitations," it would be curtailing efforts aimed at preventing children from drowning in swimming pools and bathtubs.[130]

In an attempt to cut the problem off at the source, Nancy A. Nord, the acting head of the CPSC, traveled to China in

CONTINUED

124. Jad Mouawad, *550,000 More Chinese Toys Recalled for Lead*, N.Y. Times, Sept. 27, 2007.

125. Kevin Diaz & H.J. Cummins, *House Bans Lead from Children's Toys; A Local Boy's Death from Lead Poisoning Sparked the Move for Product Safety*, Star Trib., July 31, 2008, *available at* http://www.startribune.com/politics/national/congress/26122814.html?page=1&c=y.

126. Eric S. Lipton & David Barboza, *As More Toys Are Recalled, Trail Ends in China*, N.Y. Times, June 19, 2007.

127. Mouawad, *supra* note 124.

128. Lyndsey Layton, *Lawmakers Agree to Ban Toxins in Children's Items*, Wash. Post, July 29, 2008, at A1.

129. Lipton & Barboza, *supra* note 126.

130. *Id.*

September 2007 to ask Chinese officials to stop using lead paint on export toys.[131] As a result of these talks, China agreed to stop the use of lead paint on toys exported to the United States, to hold regular product safety talks with American regulators, to help the United States trace products to their source when problems arise, and to cooperate on improving the overall safety of toy exports.

Although Chinese toys accounted for many of the toys recalled, Chinese manufacturing methods were not always at fault. In September 2007, after the largest single recall, involving 18 million toys, Mattel Inc. issued a public apology to China for causing damage to the country's reputation.[132] According to Mattel, the recall had nothing to do with Chinese manufacturing problems and actually resulted from Mattel's own "design flaw," namely, using tiny magnets that could fall off the toys and become deadly if swallowed.

In July 2007, U.S. lawmakers took matters into their own hands by passing the Consumer Product Safety Improvement Act of 2008, which, among other things, banned lead in children's products and gave consumers access to a new database of complaints or accident reports for goods. As noted earlier, the measure also provided stiffer fines for violations and enhanced enforcement of consumer safety laws.[133]

ExxonMobil, a manufacturer of phthalates used in children's toys, strongly opposed the measure, spending a large piece of its $22 million lobbying budget in an effort to prevent any ban on use of the chemical. Exxon argued that banning the compounds could force toymakers to use a substitute chemical that might pose an even greater health risk.[134] The United States is one of the last industrialized countries to outlaw phthalates in children's toys. The European Union banned them in 1999. Diana Zuckerman, president of the National Research Center for Women and Families, strongly supported a ban on phthalates for all product use: "Everybody in Congress is now well aware that phthalates are ubiquitous and exposure is coming from many different products . . . . And children's toys are probably not the main culprit. Clearly the next step is personal care products."[135]

131. Associated Press, *China Signs Pact to Ban Lead Paint in Export Toys*, N.Y. Times, Sept. 12, 2007, *available at* http://www.nytimes.com/2007/09/12/business/worldbusiness/12lead.html.

132. Nicholas Casey, *Mattel Seeks to Placate China with Apology*, Wall St. J., Sept. 22, 2007, at A1.

133. Layton, *supra* note 128.

134. Lyndsey Layton, *Despite Additive Ban, Some Parents Voice Worry; Congress Moves to Keep Phthalates Out of Toys, but Some Parents Have Questions*, Wash. Post, Aug. 2, 2008, at A5.

135. *Id.*

Key Words and Phrases

additive 691
adulterated 691
bait and switch advertising 706
caveat emptor 689
cease and desist orders 705
closed-end credit 712
consent order 705
deceit 704
drug 691
express warranty 704
extortionate extension of credit 714
finance charge 712
food 691
garnishment 714
implied warranties 709
infomercial 708
investigative consumer reporting 715
lemon laws 709
misbranding 690
net neutrality policy 700
open-end credit 712
precautionary principle 720
predatory lending 713
puffing 706
pyramid selling 710
referral sale 710
Regulation Z 712
right of rescission 713
spam 703
usury statute 712
venditur emptor 689

Questions and Case Problems

1. Ravlona, a cosmetic company, has developed an innovative makeup that holds fast on the skin for thirty-six hours. The makeup uses a new chemical dye recently developed by the in-house research team at Ravlona. The dye is manufactured from commonly used dyes that are converted to different forms with a platinum catalyst. The catalyst must be present in order to retard the natural fading of the dye, but when the makeup is applied, some of the catalyst leaches into the skin. Preliminary research has shown that this leaching may cause long-term damage but the effects would not be noticable for ten to twenty years. Assume that there are no federal rules regulating the presence of platinum in cosmetics. If you were the marketing director at Ravlona, would you feel comfortable introducing this product to the market even though problems may emerge ten or twenty years down the line? Is Ravlona obligated to disclose the findings of its study to the FDA?

2. Gulender Ozkaya wrote a check for $1,041.55 to pay an automobile dealership for repairs to her car. When she realized that her car had not been properly repaired, Ozkaya stopped payment on the check. The canceled check was then purchased by Telecheck Services, Inc., which sent Ozkaya a form dunning letter attempting to collect payment. In the letter, Telecheck said, "Until this is resolved, we may not approve your checks or the opening of a checking account at over 90,000 merchants and banks who use Telecheck nationally." It also warned, "We have assigned your file to our Recovery Department where it will be given to a professional collection agent. Please be aware that we may take reasonable steps to contact you and secure payment of the balance in full." To resolve the issue and update her record quickly, Ozkaya was instructed to send a cashier's check or money order for the amount due in a return envelope that was provided. Telecheck added a $25 service charge, listed as a "fee" at the top of the letter, to the amount of the original check. Finally, it cautioned that "[a]ny delay, or attempt to avoid this debt, may affect your ability to use checks."

   At the bottom of the page, the reader was referred to the back "for important legal notice and corporate address." The reverse side of the letter contained a standard debt validation notice, which indicated that if the consumer disputed the debt, she should contact Telecheck in writing within thirty days.

   Ozkaya filed suit against Telecheck. What claims could she make against the company? What are Telecheck's strongest defenses? [*Ozkaya v. Telecheck Services, Inc.,* 982 F. Supp. 578 (N.D. Ill. 1997).]

3. Virginia passed a statute that made it a crime to falsify the transmission information in any unsolicited e-mail message. The only way to send an anonymous e-mail message is to employ false routing information, such as the sender's domain name or Internet service provider address. Virginia construed the law as a prohibition on lying to commit trespass, that is, the unauthorized use of e-mail servers. Is the Virginia statute a valid exercise of state power? [*Jaynes v. Virginia*, 666 S.E.2d 303 (Va. 2008).]

4. In 1989, John M. Stevenson began receiving phone calls from bill collectors regarding overdue accounts that were not his. After Stevenson obtained a copy of his credit report from TRW, Inc., a credit-reporting agency, he discovered numerous errors in the report. The report included information on accounts that belonged to another John Stevenson; it also included accounts belonging to his estranged son, John Stevenson, Jr., who had fraudulently obtained some of the disputed accounts by using the senior Stevenson's Social Security number. In all, Stevenson disputed sixteen accounts, seven inquiries, and much of the identifying information.

   TRW investigated the complaint. On February 9, 1990, it told Stevenson that all disputed accounts containing negative credit information had been removed. Inaccurate information, however, either continued to appear on Stevenson's reports or was reentered after TRW had deleted it. Stevenson then filed suit, alleging both common law libel and violations of the Fair Credit Reporting Act. Did TRW violate the Fair Credit Reporting Act in its handling of Stevenson's dispute? [*Stevenson v. TRW, Inc.,* 987 F.2d 288 (5th Cir. 1993).]

5. Fleet Bank advertised a credit card with no annual fees. Within the Schumer Box for Fleet's card, the column entitled "Annual Fee" contained only the word "None." On Fleet's "Consumer Information" enclosure, but outside the Schumer Box, Fleet listed other fees. Also in that location was the statement, "We reserve the right to change the benefit features associated with your Card at any time." Paula Rossman obtained a Fleet credit card, but within a few months after issuing her the card, Fleet sent her a letter stating that the Federal Reserve had raised interest rates and that Fleet would begin charging a $35 annual fee. Did Fleet violate any laws? Did Fleet act ethically? Did it exercise sound business judgment? Would the answer be the same if Fleet had included an asterisk next to "none" in the Schumer box and added a note within the box stating, "Subject to change at Fleet's discretion"? [*Rossman v. Fleet Bank (R.I.) National Ass'n,* 280 F.3d 384 (3d Cir. 2002).]

6. From 1934 to 1939, Charles of the Ritz Distributors sold more than $1 million worth of its "Rejuvenescence Cream." Advertisements for the cosmetic product typically referred to "a vital organic ingredient" and certain "essences and compounds" that the cream allegedly contained. Users were promised that the cream would restore their youthful appearance, regardless of the condition of their skin. How might the FTC analyze the representations made by Charles of the Ritz? What evidence might the FTC consider to determine whether the advertisements are deceptive? Is it important that consumers actually believe that the product will make them look younger? How might the product's name affect the FTC's analysis? [*Charles of the Ritz Distributors Corp. v. FTC,* 143 F.2d 676 (2d Cir. 1944).]

7. In a 1991 attempt to persuade soft drink bottlers to switch from 7UP to Sprite, Coca-Cola Company, the distributor of Sprite, developed a promotional campaign entitled "The Future Belongs to Sprite." In its presentation, Coca-Cola used charts and graphs to compare the two drinks' relative sales and market share during the previous decade. The campaign was especially targeted at seventy-four "cross-franchise" bottlers, which distribute 7UP along with Coca-Cola products other than Sprite. After Coca-Cola made the presentation to eleven of these cross-franchise bottlers, five decided to switch from 7UP to Sprite. In response, Seven-Up Company filed suit against Coca-Cola, alleging that the presentation violated the Lanham Act's prohibition on misrepresentations "in commercial advertising or promotion." Coca-Cola argued that its presentation was not sufficiently disseminated to the public to constitute advertising under the statute. Was Coca-Cola's presentation "advertising" and therefore subject to the Lanham Act? [*Seven-Up Co. v. Coca-Cola Co.,* 86 F.3d 1379 (5th Cir. 1996).]

8. Mr. Begala obtained a sixty-month car loan from PNC Bank, which provided the disclosures required under the Truth-in-Lending Act. On nine occasions during the life of the loan, the bank sent him a letter offering him a payment holiday. During this holiday, he could pay a small fee, skip his monthly payment, and add that month onto the rest of the loan. The letters did not state that additional finance charges would be added to the loan as a result of his deferral of monthly payments. Begala took advantage of each of these payment holidays. When he made his final payment on the loan, PNC told him that he owed an additional $1,000 due to his deferrals of the monthly payments. He filed a class action, alleging that the bank violated its duty under TILA to disclose the additional finance charges assessed on his loan due to the payment holidays. How should the court rule? Did PNC act ethically? [*Begala v. PNC Bank,* 163 F.3d 948 (6th Cir. 1998), *cert. denied,* 528 U.S. 868 (1999).]

Directors, Officers, and Controlling Shareholders

INTRODUCTION

Fiduciary Duties

Directors and officers are agents of the corporation and owe a fiduciary duty to the corporation they serve. Under certain circumstances, a controlling shareholder owes a fiduciary duty to other shareholders as well.

These duties take two basic forms: a duty of care and a duty of loyalty. Generally, the *duty of care* requires fiduciaries to make informed and reasonable decisions and to exercise reasonable supervision of the business. The *duty of loyalty* mandates that fiduciaries act in good faith and in what they believe to be the best interest of the corporation, subordinating their personal interests to the welfare of the corporation. As then Judge Benjamin Cardozo stated, many forms of conduct permissible in the business world for those acting at arm's length are forbidden to those bound by fiduciary ties. A trustee, he said, is held to something stricter than the morals of the marketplace. Not mere honesty, but a "punctilio of honor the most sensitive" is the standard of behavior with which fiduciaries must comply.[1]

As discussed further below, in certain cases, the courts have tended to treat directors' duty to act in good faith as an independent duty, rather than subsuming it within the duties of care and loyalty. For example, in *McMullin v. Beran*,[2] the Delaware Supreme Court referred to the directors' "triad of fiduciary duties, loyalty, good faith, due care."[3] (As explained in Chapter 20, Delaware law is particularly important because so many large public companies are incorporated there.)

1. Meinhard v. Salmon, 164 N.E. 545, 546 (N.Y. 1928) (Case 5.1).
2. 765 A.2d 910, 917 (Del. 2000).
3. For a discussion of the fiduciary duties of directors of a corporation near insolvency or in bankruptcy, see Myron M. Sheinfeld & Judy Harris Pippitt, *Fiduciary Duties of Directors of a Corporation in the Vicinity of Insolvency and After Initiation of a Bankruptcy Case*, 60 Bus. Law. 79 (2004).

CHAPTER OVERVIEW

This chapter outlines the duties of directors, officers, and controlling shareholders. First, it analyzes the duty of care in terms of the most applicable judicial doctrine, the business judgment rule. Next, the chapter analyzes the duty of good faith and addresses issues arising under the duty of loyalty, including corporate opportunities. We then discuss the fiduciary duties of directors that arise when the directors must decide whether to sell the company or resist a corporate takeover bid. Legislative responses to these issues are also described. Finally, we address the duties of controlling shareholders in connection with sales of corporate control and squeeze-out mergers.

The Business Judgment Rule and the Duty of Care

In cases challenging board decisions for breach of the duty of care, the courts generally defer to the business judgment of the directors, acknowledging that courts are ill equipped to second-guess directors' decisions at a later date. Thus, under the *business judgment rule*, as long as certain standards are met, a court will presume that the directors have acted in good faith and in the honest belief that the action taken was in the best interest of the company. The court will not question whether the action was wise or whether the directors made an error of judgment or a business mistake.

To take advantage of the rule, the directors must have made an informed decision with no conflict between their personal interests and the interests of the corporation and its shareholders. Courts will not respect directors' business judgment if the directors (1) were interested in the transaction, (2) did not act in good faith, (3) acted in a manner that cannot be attributed to a rational purpose, or (4) reached their decision by a grossly negligent process.[4] If the business judgment rule does not apply to a transaction, courts generally shift to directors the burden of proving that their acts were not grossly negligent (or in cases involving transactions in which the directors are interested, that the transaction was fair and reasonable).

4. Brehm v. Eisner, 746 A.2d 244 (Del. 2000).

INFORMED DECISION

The business judgment rule is applicable only if the directors make an informed decision. The general corporation law of most jurisdictions authorizes directors to rely on the reports of officers and certain outside experts. However, passive reliance on such reports may result in an insufficiently informed decision, as in the following landmark case.

A CASE IN POINT

CASE 21.1

SMITH V. VAN GORKOM

SUPREME COURT OF DELAWARE
488 A.2D 858 (DEL. 1985).

SUMMARY

FACTS Trans Union Corporation was a publicly traded, diversified holding company engaged in the railcar-leasing business. Its stock was undervalued, largely due to accumulated investment tax credits. Jerome W. Van Gorkom, the chairman of the board of Trans Union, was reaching retirement age. He asked the chief financial officer, Donald Romans, to work out the per-share price at which a leveraged buyout could be done, given current cash flow. Romans came up with $55, based on debt-servicing requirements. He did not attempt to determine the intrinsic value of the company. Van Gorkom later met with Jay Pritzker and worked out a merger at $55 per share. Trans Union stock was then trading at about $37 per share.

Van Gorkom called a board meeting for September 20, 1980, on one day's notice, to approve the merger. All of the directors were familiar with the company's operations as a going concern, but they were not apprised of the merger negotiations before the board meeting on September 20. They were also familiar with the current financial status of the company; a month earlier they had discussed a Boston Consulting Group strategy study. The ten-member board included five outside directors who were CEOs or board members of publicly held companies, as well as a former dean of the University of Chicago Business School.

Copies of the merger agreement were delivered to the directors, but too late for study before or during the meeting. The meeting began with a twenty-minute oral presentation by chairman Van Gorkom. The chief financial officer then described how he had arrived at the $55 figure. He stated that it was only a workable number, not an indication of a fair price. Trans Union's president stated that he thought the proposed merger was a good deal.

The board approved the merger after a two-hour meeting. Board members later testified that they had insisted that the merger agreement be amended to ensure that the company was free to consider other bids before the closing; however, neither the board minutes nor the merger documents clearly reflected this.

Plaintiff Smith sued to challenge the board's action, arguing that the merger price was too low. The Delaware Court of Chancery held that, given the premium over the market value of Trans Union stock, the business acumen of the board members, and the effect on the merger price of the prospect of other bids, the board was adequately informed and did not act recklessly in approving the Pritzker deal. In making its findings, the court relied in part upon actions taken by the board after the meeting on September 20, 1980, that were intended to cure defects in the directors' initial level of knowledge. Smith appealed.

CONTINUED

ISSUE PRESENTED Were directors who accepted and submitted to the shareholders a proposed cash merger at a premium over market without determining the intrinsic value of the company grossly negligent in failing to inform themselves adequately before making their decision?

SUMMARY OF OPINION The Delaware Supreme Court reversed the lower court and held that the directors were grossly negligent in failing to reach a properly informed decision. They were not protected by the business judgment rule even though there were no allegations of bad faith, fraud, or conflict of interest. The court found that the directors could not reasonably base their decision on the inadequate information presented to the board. They should have independently valued the company.

The court found that the directors had inadequate information as to (1) the role of Van Gorkom, Trans Union's chairman and chief executive officer, in initiating the transaction; (2) the basis for the proposed purchase price of $55 per share; and, most important, (3) the intrinsic value of Trans Union, as opposed to its current and historical stock price. The court held that in the absence of any apparent crisis or emergency, it was grossly negligent for the directors to approve the merger after a two-hour meeting, with eight of the ten directors having received no prior notice of the proposed merger.

The court stated:

> None of the directors, management or outside, were investment bankers or financial analysts. Yet the board did not consider recessing the meeting until a later hour that day (or requesting an extension of Pritzker's Sunday evening deadline) to give it time to elicit more information as to the sufficiency of the offer, either from inside management (in particular Romans) or from Trans Union's own investment banker, Salomon Brothers, whose Chicago specialist in mergers and acquisitions was known to the Board and familiar with Trans Union's affairs. Thus, the record compels the conclusion that on September 20 the Board lacked valuation information adequate to reach an informed business judgment as to the fairness of $55 per share for sale of the Company.

The court additionally held that the directors' subsequent efforts to find a bidder willing to pay more than Pritzker were inadequate to cure the infirmities of their uninformed exercise of judgment.

The court rejected the directors' argument that they properly relied on the officers' reports presented at the board meeting. A pertinent report may be relied on in good faith, but not blindly. The directors were duty bound to make reasonable inquiry of Van Gorkom (the chief executive officer) and Romans (the chief financial officer). If they had done so, the inadequacy of those officers' reports would have been apparent. Van Gorkom's summary of the terms of the deal was inadequate because he had not reviewed the merger documents and was basically uninformed as to the essential terms. (Indeed, he had signed the merger agreement without reading it while at the opening of the Chicago Lyric Opera.) Romans's report on price was inadequate because it was just a cash flow feasibility study, not a valuation study.

The court also held that the mere fact that a substantial premium over the market price was being offered did not justify board approval of the merger. A premium may be one reason to approve a merger, but sound information as to the company's intrinsic value is required to assess the fairness of an offer. In this case, there was no attempt to determine the company's intrinsic value.

RESULT The Delaware Supreme Court held that the Trans Union directors were grossly negligent in making an uninformed decision regarding the proposed merger agreement. Their decision was not protected by the business judgment rule. The case was remanded to the Delaware Court of Chancery for an evidentiary hearing to determine the fair value of the shares based on Trans Union's intrinsic value on September 20, 1980, the day when the board met to consider Pritzker's

CONTINUED

offer. If the chancellor found that value to be higher than $55 per share, the directors would be liable for the difference.

COMMENTS The case was settled for $23.5 million—$13.5 million in excess of the directors' liability insurance coverage. Although the purchasers, the Pritzker family, ultimately paid the amount by which the settlement exceeded the directors' coverage, they were not legally obligated to do so.

Smith v. Van Gorkom is one of the most debated corporate law cases ever decided. Three years after the decision, one of the key defendants—Trans Union's CEO, Jerome W. Van Gorkom—wrote an article giving the defendants' side of the story. The article makes it clear that the defendants and the Delaware Supreme Court had very different views about what the directors actually did and what their options really were.

In his article, Van Gorkom stated that at the September 20 meeting:

> The directors, all broadly experienced executives, realized that an all-cash offer with a premium of almost 50 percent represented an unusual opportunity for the shareholders. They also knew, however, that $55 might not be the highest price obtainable. At the meeting, therefore, there was considerable discussion about seeking an outside "fairness opinion" that might shed further light on the ultimate value of the company.[5]

Furthermore, Van Gorkom explained:

> Acceptance of the offer was not a decision by the directors that the company should be sold for $55 a share. The acceptance was the only mechanism by which the offer could be preserved for the shareholders. *They* would make the ultimate decision as to the fairness of the price and they would do so only after the free market had had ample time in which to determine if $55 was the top value obtainable. The market's opinion would be definitive and worth infinitely more to the shareholders than any theoretical evaluation opinion that the directors could obtain in 39 hours or even longer. On this reasoning the offer was accepted.[6]

Following the meeting, the Trans Union directors hired Salomon Brothers to conduct an intensive search for a higher bidder. In addition, Van Gorkom stated that once the $55 offer became a matter of public knowledge, an auction occurred in the market with Trans Union's stock sometimes selling above $56 on the New York Stock Exchange. After three months of the intensive search and the public auction, no higher bid was ever received. "[T]he market had proven beyond a shadow of a doubt that $55 was the highest price obtainable."[7]

Van Gorkom believed that he and the other Trans Union directors wholeheartedly fulfilled their fiduciary obligations. He concluded that their actions clearly should have been protected under the business judgment rule.

5. J.W. Van Gorkom, *Van Gorkom's Response: The Defendant's Side of the Trans Union Case,* MERGERS & ACQUISITIONS, Jan.–Feb. 1988.

6. *Id.*

7. *Id.*

Reliability of Officers' Reports

As *Van Gorkom* underscores, not every statement of an officer can be relied on in good faith, and no statement is entitled to blind reliance. The passivity of the Trans Union directors in *Van Gorkom* unquestionably influenced the court's finding of gross negligence:

> When the chief financial officer, Romans, told the board that the $55 figure was within a "fair price range" for a

> leveraged buyout, no director sought any further information from Romans. No director asked him why he put $55 at the bottom of his range. No director asked Romans for any details as to his study, the reason why it had been undertaken or its depth. No director asked to see the study; and no director asked Romans whether Trans Union's finance department could do a fairness study within the remaining 36-hour period available under the Pritzker offer. . . . [If he had been asked,] Romans would have presumably . . . informed the Board of his view, and the widespread view of Senior Management, that the timing of the offer was wrong and the offer inadequate.[8]

When the CEO, Van Gorkom, told the board that $55 per share was fair, no questions were asked:

> The Board thereby failed to discover that Van Gorkom had suggested the $55 price to [the bidder] Pritzker and, most crucially, that Van Gorkom had arrived at the $55 figure based on calculations designed solely to determine the feasibility of a leveraged buy-out. No questions were raised either as to the tax implications of a cash-out merger or how the price for the one million share option granted Pritzker was calculated.[9]

Reliability of Experts' Reports

Two principles regarding the use of experts' reports emerge from the cases. First, a board should engage a reputable investment banking firm, aided if necessary by an outside appraiser, (1) to prepare a valuation study and (2) to give a written opinion as to the financial fairness of the transaction and of any related purchase of assets or options.

Second, directors have a duty to pursue reasonable inquiry and to exercise reasonable oversight in connection with their engagement of investment bankers and other advisers. A conclusory fairness opinion (that is, an opinion that merely states a conclusion without giving the factual grounds for that conclusion) of an investment banker, however expert, is not a sufficient basis for a board decision, particularly if the investment banker's conclusion is questionable in light of other information known to the directors. As the directors of SCM Corporation learned in *Hanson Trust PLC v. ML SCM Acquisition, Inc.*,[10] an expert's opinion must be in writing and be reasoned.

SCM was the target of a hostile tender offer by a British conglomerate, Hanson Trust PLC. SCM's board negotiated a friendly management leveraged buyout led by "white knight" Merrill Lynch. As part of this agreement, SCM granted Merrill Lynch an *asset lock-up option* to purchase two of SCM's divisions, considered to be SCM's key assets or *crown jewels*. The option was exercisable if Merrill Lynch was not successful in acquiring control of SCM. A lock-up option is a kind of consolation prize for the loser in a bidding war; depending on how it is priced, a lock-up option can have the effect of deterring other bids. Merrill Lynch represented in negotiations that it would not proceed with its leveraged buyout offer without the lock-up.

SCM's investment banker, Goldman Sachs, issued a written fairness opinion on the overall deal, stating that the sale of SCM to Merrill Lynch was fair to the shareholders of SCM from a financial point of view. A partner at Goldman Sachs also orally advised SCM's directors that the option prices were "within the range of fair value." However, the directors did not inquire what the range of fair value was or how it was calculated. Unfortunately for the directors, the banker had not in fact calculated the fair value of the two divisions. Although the directors knew that the two divisions generated more than two-thirds of SCM's earnings, they never asked the investment banker why the divisions were being sold for less than half the total purchase price. The U.S. Court of Appeals for the Second Circuit held that the SCM directors' "paucity of information" and "their swiftness of decision-making" strongly suggested a breach of the duty of care. The asset lock-up was struck down. As in the case of officers' reports, blind reliance on the reports of experts creates a risk that the directors will not receive the protection of the business judgment rule.

REASONABLE SUPERVISION

As fiduciaries, directors have a responsibility to exercise reasonable supervision over corporate operations. Because the prescribed role of the corporate directors is to establish broad policies and then rely on managers to implement them, the question of what constitutes reasonable supervision is necessarily one of degree. The outcome in reasonable supervision cases depends heavily on particular facts. The Delaware Court of Chancery refined and clarified the reasonable supervision doctrine in the following leading case.

8. Smith v. Van Gorkom, 488 A.2d 858, 876 (Del. 1985).

9. *Id.*

10. 781 F.2d 264 (2d Cir. 1986).

A CASE IN POINT

CASE 21.2

In re Caremark International Derivative Litigation

Court of Chancery of Delaware
698 A.2d 959 (Del. Ch. 1996).

Summary

Facts After the Department of Health and Human Services and the Department of Justice conducted an extensive four-year investigation of alleged violations by Caremark employees of federal and state laws and regulations applicable to health-care providers, Caremark was charged with multiple felonies. It thereafter entered into a number of plea agreements in which it agreed to pay civil and criminal fines and to make payments to various private and public parties. In all, Caremark agreed to pay approximately $250 million.

A shareholder derivative suit was filed in 1994, in which the plaintiff initially sought to recover these losses from the individual members of Caremark's board of directors. The complaint charged that the directors had allowed a situation to develop and continue that exposed the corporation to enormous legal liability and that, in so doing, they had violated a duty to be active monitors of corporate performance. The complaint did not charge the directors with either self-dealing or a breach of the duty of loyalty. The parties sought court approval of a proposed settlement that did not include any payment by individual board members; instead, it outlined a series of procedures the company would implement to promote future compliance with applicable laws and regulations.

Issue Presented What is the scope of a director's duty to exercise reasonable supervision over corporate operations?

Summary of Opinion The Delaware Chancery Court began by noting that director liability for a breach of the duty to exercise appropriate attention may, in theory, arise in two distinct contexts. First, such liability may follow from a board decision that results in a loss because that decision was ill advised or negligent. Second, liability may arise from an unconsidered failure of the board to act in circumstances in which due attention would, arguably, have prevented a loss to the corporation.

Most of the decisions that a corporation, acting through its human agents, makes are not the subject of director attention. Legally, the board itself will be required only to authorize the most significant corporate acts or transactions: mergers, changes in capital structure, fundamental changes in business, appointment and compensation of the CEO, and the like. However, ordinary business decisions that are made by officers and employees deeper in the interior of the organization can vitally affect the welfare of the corporation and its ability to achieve its various strategic and financial goals. This raises the question: What is the board's responsibility with respect to the organization and monitoring of the enterprise to ensure that the corporation functions within the law to achieve its purposes?

The court noted an increasing tendency, especially under federal law, to employ the criminal law to ensure corporate compliance with external legal requirements, including environmental, financial, employee, and product safety regulations, as well as assorted other health and safety regulations. The federal Organizational Sentencing Guidelines[11] offer powerful incentives for corporations to have in place compliance programs to detect violations of law, to promptly report violations to appropriate public officials when discovered, and to take prompt, voluntary remedial efforts.

In light of these developments, the court held that directors cannot satisfy their obligation to be reasonably informed concerning the corporation unless they assure themselves that appropriate information and reporting systems exist in the organization. These systems must be reasonably designed to provide senior management and the board itself with timely and accurate information sufficient to allow management and the board to reach informed judgments concerning both the corporation's compliance with the law and its business performance.

CONTINUED

11. These are discussed in Chapter 15.

The level of detail that is appropriate for such an information system is a question of business judgment. The court acknowledged that no rationally designed information and reporting system will eliminate the possibility that the corporation will violate laws or regulations. But the board is required to exercise a good faith judgment that the corporation's information and reporting system is in concept and design adequate to assure the board that appropriate information will come to its attention in a timely manner as a matter of ordinary operations, so that it may satisfy its responsibility.

Thus, the court ruled that a director's obligation includes a duty to attempt in good faith to ensure that there is a corporate information and reporting system that the board concludes is adequate. Failure to do so under certain circumstances may, in theory at least, render a director liable for losses caused by noncompliance with applicable legal standards.

RESULT The court concluded that the settlement was fair and reasonable and, therefore, approved it.

COMMENTS The court noted that if the shareholders are not satisfied with the informed good faith judgment of the directors, their recourse is to elect different directors.

In 1997, the Securities and Exchange Commission (SEC) issued a release emphasizing the affirmative responsibility of officers and directors under the federal securities laws to ensure the accuracy and completeness of public company filings with the SEC, such as annual and quarterly reports and proxy statements.[12] In addition, as discussed further in Chapter 22, the Sarbanes–Oxley Act of 2002 requires the chief executive officer and the chief financial officer to certify the accuracy of public companies' SEC filings.

Officers and directors are required to conduct a full and informed review of the information contained in the final draft of the filings. If an officer or director knows or should have known about an inaccuracy in a proposed filing, he or she has an obligation to correct it. An officer or director may rely on the company's procedures for determining what disclosure is required only if he or she has a reasonable basis for believing that those procedures are effective and have resulted in full consideration of those issues.

If a director or officer is aware of facts that might have to be disclosed, he or she must go beyond the established procedures to inquire into the reasons for nondisclosure. Officers and directors cannot blindly rely on legal counsel's conclusions about the need for disclosure if they are aware of facts that seem to suggest that disclosure is required. They must raise the issue specifically with disclosure counsel, telling counsel exactly what they know and asking specifically whether disclosure is required. If they are not satisfied with the answers provided, they should insist that the documents be revised before they are filed with the SEC.

12. Report of Investigation Pursuant to Section 21(a) of the Securities Exchange Act of 1934 Concerning the Conduct of Certain Former Officers and Directors of W.R. Grace & Co., Exchange Act Release No. 39, 157 (Sept. 30, 1997).

DISINTERESTED DECISION

Even when the board makes an informed decision, the business judgment rule is not applicable if the directors have a financial or other personal interest in the transaction at issue. For example, if a board dominated by *inside directors* (that is, directors who are also officers of the corporation) sets executive compensation, they can be required to prove to a court that the transaction was fair and reasonable. To be disinterested in the transaction normally means that the directors can neither have an interest on either side of the transaction nor expect to derive any personal financial benefit from the transaction (other than benefits that accrue to all shareholders of the corporation, which are not considered self-dealing).

Even if one or more individual directors have an interest in the transaction, the board's decision may still be entitled to the protection of the business judgment rule if the transaction is approved by a majority of the disinterested directors. If the board delegates too much of its authority or is too much influenced by an interested party, however, then the entire board may be tainted with that individual's personal motivations and lose the protection of the business judgment rule.

In some jurisdictions, a relevant factor in determining whether a board is disinterested is whether the majority of the board consists of outside directors. The fact that outside directors receive directors' fees but not salaries is viewed as heightening the likelihood that the directors were not

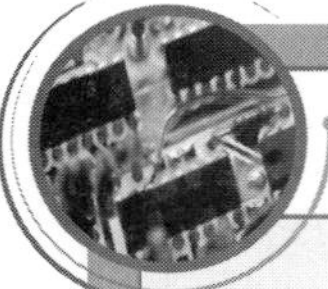

VIEW FROM CYBERSPACE

Shareholder Meetings in Cyberspace

Section 228(d) of the Delaware General Corporation Law permits a shareholder's written consent to be effected by electronic transmission (including e-mail), facsimile (fax), or other reliable methods of reproducing a consent. Section 212(c) authorizes electronic transmission of proxies and the use of copies and faxes. Section 232 permits the electronic delivery of notice to a shareholder if the shareholder has consented to delivery of notice in such form. Section 211(a) gives directors the power to authorize shareholders who are not physically present at a meeting to participate by means of remote communication, such as a conference call. Indeed, directors are given sole discretion to hold meetings either partially or totally by remote communication, without any physical location.

Section 141 permits director action by unanimous consent to be effected by electronic transmission. Although the drafters considered authorizing board meetings by remote communication, they determined that "considerations of collegiality precluded 'chat room' or similar formats, and that the current practice of holding meetings by telephone conference calls provided sufficient flexibility."[a]

a. Frederick H. Alexander, *Amendments to Delaware Corporation Law Allow for Evolving Technology*, 69 U.S.L.W. 2051, 2052 (2000).

motivated by personal interest. Application of these rules in the context of takeovers, mergers, and acquisitions is discussed later in this chapter.

STATUTORY LIMITATIONS ON DIRECTORS' LIABILITY FOR BREACH OF DUTY OF CARE

Cases such as *Van Gorkom* had a devastating impact on the market for directors' and officers' liability insurance and on the availability of qualified outside directors. In response, Delaware adopted legislation in 1986 to allow shareholders to limit the monetary liability of directors for breaches of the duty of care (but not the duty of loyalty or good faith) in any suit brought by the corporation or in a *shareholder derivative suit*, that is, a suit by a shareholder on behalf of the corporation. Most other states followed suit. Delaware and most other states require that the limitation be contained in the original certificate of incorporation or in an amendment approved by a majority of the shareholders. The statutes do not affect directors' liability for suits brought by third parties; they merely allow the shareholders to agree that, under certain circumstances, they will not seek monetary recovery against the directors. The directors' liability for breach of the duty of loyalty may not be limited. Also, most states do not allow officers to be exonerated from liability for breach of the duty of care or the duty of loyalty.

DELAWARE'S STATUTE

Section 102(b)(7) of the Delaware Corporation Code permits the certificate of incorporation to include a provision limiting or eliminating the personal liability of directors to the corporation or to its shareholders for monetary damages for breach of fiduciary duty. Such a provision cannot, however, eliminate or limit the liability of a director for (1) any breach of the director's duty of loyalty to the corporation or its shareholders, (2) acts or omissions that are not in good faith or that involve intentional misconduct or knowing violation of law, (3) unlawful payments of dividends or stock purchases, or (4) any transaction from which the director derived an improper personal benefit.

CALIFORNIA'S STATUTE

Section 204(a)(10) of the California Corporation Code, which applies to corporations organized under California law, is more restrictive. In addition to the four exceptions contained in the Delaware statute, California prohibits the elimination or limitation of director liability for (1) acts or omissions that show a reckless disregard for the director's duty to the corporation or its shareholders in circumstances in which the director was aware, or should have been aware, of a risk of serious injury to the corporation or its shareholders; and (2) an unexcused pattern of inattention that amounts to an abdication of the director's duties to the corporation or its shareholders.

Although other states apply their corporate governance rules only to corporations incorporated there, California imposes its pro-shareholder provisions on so-called privately held *quasi-foreign corporations*. Such corporations are incorporated elsewhere but (1) have more than 50 percent of their stock owned by California residents and (2) derive more than 50 percent of their sales, payroll, and property tax from activities in California. As a result, a privately held quasi-foreign corporation will be subject to California's more restrictive limits on monetary liability even though the state of incorporation (e.g., Delaware) is more permissive.

Duty of Good Faith

Allegations of failure to act in good faith take on special significance in cases involving corporations that have eliminated directors' personal liability for breaches of the duty of care. Because the statutes authorizing such limitations list failures to act in good faith separately from breaches of the duty of loyalty, courts have started to focus more directly on good faith, especially when the directors had no personal interest in the transaction at hand.

In certain cases, the duty of good faith may be subsumed within the duty of loyalty. As the Delaware Supreme Court explained, "'[a] director cannot act loyally towards the corporation unless she acts in the good faith belief that her actions are in the corporation's best interest.'"[13]

But, as Chancellor Chandler explained in the litigation discussed in Chapter 14 arising out of Walt Disney Company's termination payments to Michael Ovitz, in certain instances:

> The fiduciary duties of care and loyalty, as traditionally defined, may not be aggressive enough to protect shareholder interests when the board is well advised, is not legally beholden to the management or a controlling shareholder and when the board does not suffer from other disabling conflicts of interest, such as a patently self-dealing transaction. Good faith may serve to fill this gap and ensure that the persons entrusted *by shareholders* to govern Delaware corporations do so with an honesty of purpose and with an understanding of whose interests they are there to protect.[14]

On appeal, the Delaware Supreme Court stated:

> '[I]ssues of good faith are (to a certain degree) inseparably and necessarily intertwined with the duties of care and loyalty. . . .' But, in the pragmatic, conduct-regulating legal realm which calls for more precise conceptual line drawing, the answer is that grossly negligent conduct, without more, does not and cannot constitute a breach of the fiduciary duty to act in good faith. The conduct that is the subject of due care may overlap with the conduct that comes within the rubric of good faith in a psychological sense, but from a legal standpoint those duties are and must remain quite distinct. Both our legislative history and our common law jurisprudence distinguish sharply between the duties to exercise due care and to act in good faith, and highly significant consequences flow from that distinction.[15]

As a result, mere gross negligence was not enough to constitute the lack of good faith that would have subjected the disinterested directors to personal monetary liability. To invoke an exception to a Section 102(b)(7) exculpatory provision, the plaintiff must make "a strong showing of misconduct,"[16] such as "intentionally acting 'with a purpose other than that of advancing the best interests of the corporation,' acting 'with the intent to violate applicable positive law,' or 'intentionally failing to act in the face of a known duty to act.'"[17]

In *Stone v. Ritter*,[18] the Delaware Supreme Court recognized that "good faith may be described colloquially as part of a 'triad' of fiduciary duties," but ruled that the obligation to act in good faith does not establish an independent fiduciary duty that stands on the same footing as the duties of care and loyalty. Only the latter two duties, where violated, "may directly result in liability, whereas a failure to act in good faith may do so, but indirectly."[19] As a result, in Delaware, a failure to act in good faith, taken alone, does not appear to give rise to liability.

Nonetheless, as seen in the following case, directors who consciously ignore known risks of noncompliance risk losing the protection of both the business judgment rule and any exculpatory provisions in their corporate charter. As the Delaware Court of Chancery stated, the duty of loyalty is breached when the directors "utterly fail to exercise oversight of the corporation" or "were conscious of the fact that they were not doing their job [as monitors]."[20]

---

13. Stone v. Ritter, 911 A.2d 363 (Del. 2006), *quoting* Guttman v. Huang, 823 A.2d 492, 506 n.34 (Del. Ch. 2003).
14. *In re* Walt Disney Co. Derivative Litig., 907 A.2d 693, 761 (Del. Ch. 2005) (Case 14.1).
15. *In re* Walt Disney Co. Derivative Litig., 906 A.2d 27, 65 (Del. 2006).
16. *Id.*
17. *In re* Lear Corp. S'holder Litig., 2008 WL 4053221 (Del. Ch. Sept. 2, 2008).
18. 911 A.2d 362 (Del. 2006).
19. *Id.*
20. Ryan v. Lyondell Chem. Co., 2008 WL 4174038 (Del. Ch. Aug. 9, 2008) (denying directors' motion for summary judgment in a case in which the plaintiffs alleged that the directors breached their duty of good faith when they failed to act for two months after the filing of a Schedule 13D that clearly put the company in play and then agreed to a merger agreement with deal protection within one week of a hostile takeover offer).

A CASE IN POINT

IN THE LANGUAGE OF THE COURT

CASE 21.3

IN RE ABBOTT LABORATORIES DERIVATIVE SHAREHOLDERS LITIGATION

UNITED STATES COURT OF APPEALS FOR THE SEVENTH CIRCUIT
325 F.3D 795 (7TH CIR. 2003).

FACTS In 1999, Abbott Laboratories, an Illinois corporation, entered into a consent decree that required it to pay a $100 million fine, at the time the largest penalty ever imposed for a civil violation of Food and Drug Administration (FDA) regulations. The FDA also required Abbott to withdraw 125 types of medical diagnostic test kits, destroy certain inventory, and make a number of corrective changes in its manufacturing procedures after six years of quality control violations. Abbott shareholders brought a shareholder derivative suit alleging that the directors breached their fiduciary duties when they failed to take necessary action to correct repeated noncompliance problems brought to Abbott's attention by the FDA in the period from 1993 until 1999.

Not only had the FDA sent Abbott a Form 483 noting deviations from the requirements set forth in the FDA's "Current Good Manufacturing Practice" after each of its thirteen inspections of Abbott's Abbott Park and North Chicago facilities, but the FDA had also sent four formal certified Warning Letters to Abbott. The first was sent to David Thompson, president of Abbott's Diagnostics Division (ADD), on October 20, 1993. The letter stated that the FDA had found adulterated in vitro diagnostic products and warned: "Failure to correct these deviations may result in regulatory action being initiated by the Food and Drug Administration without further notice. These actions include, but are not limited to, seizure, injunction, and/or civil penalties." A second Warning Letter was sent to Thompson on March 28, 1994, with a copy to Duane Burnham, Abbott's CEO and board chair.

On January 11, 1995, the *Wall Street Journal* reported that the FDA had uncovered a wide range of flaws in Abbott's quality assurance procedures used in assembling its diagnostic products. In July 1995, the FDA and Abbott entered into a Voluntary Compliance Plan to work together to correct Abbott's deficiencies. In February 1998, after finding continued deviations from the regulations, the FDA sent Abbott the equivalent of a Warning Letter closing out the plan. In 1999, the FDA sent the fourth and final Warning Letter to Miles White, a member of Abbott's board and the current CEO. White had replaced Burnham as CEO in April 1999.

The plaintiffs did not demand that the members of Abbott's board institute an action against themselves for breach of their fiduciary duties, arguing that such a demand would be futile. Under applicable law, such a demand is not required if the plaintiffs plead facts showing that the directors faced a substantial likelihood of liability for their actions. In particular, "demand can only be excused where facts are alleged with particularity which create a reasonable doubt that the directors' action was entitled to the protections of the business judgment rule."[21] The district court dismissed the complaint, and the plaintiffs appealed.

ISSUE PRESENTED Is it a breach of directors' duty of good faith for them to fail to follow up on repeated notices of regulatory noncompliance?

OPINION WOOD, J., writing on behalf of the U.S. Court of Appeals for the Seventh Circuit:

Plaintiffs in *Abbott* allege facts that the directors were aware of known violations, providing evidence that there was direct knowledge through the Warning Letters and as members of the Audit Committee. Under proper corporate governance procedures—the existence of which is not contested by either party in *Abbott*—information of the violations would have been shared at the board meetings. In addition, plaintiffs have alleged that, as fiduciaries, the directors all signed the annual SEC forms which specifically addressed government regulation of Abbott's products. The *Abbott* case is clearly distinguished from the "unconsidered" inaction in *In re Caremark*.[22]

CONTINUED

21. Aronson v. Lewis, 473 A.2d 805 (Del. 1984), *overruled on other grounds by* Brehm v. Eisner, 746 A.2d 244 (Del. 2000).
22. 698 A.2d 959, 967 (Del. Ch. 1996) (Case 21.2).

. . . .

The district court noted, correctly, that the plaintiffs did not allege that Abbott's reporting system was inadequate. . . . Where there is a corporate governance structure in place, we must then assume the corporate governance procedures were followed and that the board knew of the problems and decided no action was required. . . .

. . . .

Delaware law states that director liability may arise from the breach of the duty to exercise appropriate attention to potentially illegal corporate activities or from "an *unconsidered failure of the board to act* in circumstances in which due attention would, arguably, have prevented the loss." *In re Caremark*. The court held that "a sustained or systematic failure of the board to exercise oversight . . . will establish the lack of good faith that is a necessary condition to [director] liability.". . .

Given the extensive paper trail in *Abbott* concerning the violations and the inferred awareness of the problems, the facts support a reasonable assumption that there was a "sustained and systematic failure of the board to exercise oversight," in this case intentional in that the directors knew of the violations of law, took no steps in an effort to prevent or remedy the situation, and that failure to take any action for such an inordinate amount of time resulted in substantial corporate losses, establishing a lack of good faith. We find that six years of noncompliance, inspections, 483s, Warning Letters, and notice in the press, all of which then resulted in the largest civil fine ever imposed by the FDA and the destruction and suspension of products which accounted for approximately $250 million in corporate assets, indicate that the directors' decision to not act was not made in good faith and was contrary to the best interests of the company.

With respect to demand futility based on the directors' conscious inaction, we find that the plaintiffs have sufficiently pleaded allegations, if true, of a breach of the duty of good faith to reasonably conclude that the directors' actions fell outside the protection of the business judgment rule. . . .

The directors contend that they are not liable under Abbott's certificate of incorporation provision which exempts the directors from liability [for breach of the duty of care]. Directors are not protected by that provision when a complaint alleges facts that infer a breach of loyalty or good faith. [*Eds.*: The court stated that the burden of establishing good faith rests with the director seeking protection under the exculpatory provision.]

Plaintiffs in Abbott accused the directors not only of gross negligence, but of intentional conduct in failing to address the federal violation problems, alleging "a conscious disregard of known risks, which conduct, if proven, cannot have been undertaken in good faith."

RESULT The plaintiffs pleaded sufficient facts to prove that the directors were not entitled to the protection of the business judgment rule. The plaintiffs' claims were also not precluded by Abbott's charter provision. The trial court's dismissal of the complaint was reversed. The plaintiffs could proceed with the derivative action.

COMMENTS The directors were potentially liable even though a majority of the board was independent and there were no allegations of self-dealing.

CRITICAL THINKING QUESTIONS

1. Would the independent directors have been liable if the CEO and board chair had not given them copies of the FDA Warning Letters?
2. If you had been an independent director on Abbott's board, how would you have responded upon receiving notice of the second FDA Warning Letter?

Duty of Loyalty

To comply with their duty of loyalty, directors and managers must act in good faith and subordinate their own interests to those of the corporation and its shareholders. As a result, when a shareholder attacks a transaction in which managers or directors are engaged in self-dealing or have a self-interest other than that of a corporate fiduciary, courts will closely review the merits of the deal. Traditionally, such a transaction has been voidable unless its proponents could show that it was fair and reasonable to the corporation.

CORPORATE OPPORTUNITIES

One central corollary of the fiduciary duty of loyalty is that officers and directors may not take personal advantage of a business opportunity that rightfully belongs to the corporation. This is known as the *corporate opportunity doctrine.* For example, suppose that a copper-mining corporation is actively looking for mining sites. If an officer of the corporation learns of an attractive site in the course of his or her business for the corporation, the officer may not buy it for himself or herself. If the officer attempts to do so, a shareholder can block the sale or impose a *constructive trust* on any profits the officer makes from the acquisition, that is, force the officer to hold such profits for the benefit of the corporation and pay them over to the corporation on request.

The courts have devised several tests for determining whether an opportunity belongs to a corporation. Perhaps the most widely used is the *line-of-business test.* Under this test, if an officer, director, or controlling shareholder learns of an opportunity in the course of his or her business for the corporation and the opportunity is in the corporation's line of business, a court will not permit the officer, director, or controlling shareholder to keep the opportunity for himself or herself.

For example, the Delaware Supreme Court ruled in a classic case that the president and director of Loft, Inc., a company engaged in the manufacturing of candies, syrups, beverages, and foodstuffs, could not set up a new corporation to acquire the secret formula and trademarks of Pepsi Cola.[23] He had unsuccessfully sought a volume discount for Loft's purchases of syrup from the Coca-Cola Company and was contemplating substituting Pepsi for Coke.

If an officer or director develops an idea on company time using company resources, a court will be more likely to find a breach of fiduciary duty if the officer or director then leaves to pursue the idea. If the officer or director has signed an assignment of inventions, then the idea will usually belong to the company under the terms of that agreement. Even without such an agreement, use of company time or resources may restrict the ability of the officer or director to define the line of business narrowly.

Other courts have considered whether (1) it would be fair for the fiduciary to keep the opportunity, (2) the corporation has an expectancy or interest growing out of an existing right in the opportunity, or (3) the interference by the fiduciary will hinder the corporation's purposes. Because different states apply different tests, a corporate fiduciary should always consult local counsel if there is any question of the fiduciary's usurpation of a corporate opportunity.

An officer or director presented with a corporate opportunity is required to disclose it to the disinterested directors, who may then accept or reject the opportunity. Disclosure is required even when the officers or directors taking advantage of the opportunity, acting in their capacity as controlling shareholders, could have prevented the corporation from pursuing it. For example, *Thorpe v. CERBCO Inc.*[24] involved two brothers who were officers, directors, and controlling shareholders of CERBCO. When a potential acquirer brought up the possibility of buying one of CERBCO's subsidiaries, the brothers instead proposed to sell their own shares to the acquirer. Because the brothers (in their capacity as shareholders) could have blocked every viable sale of the subsidiary, CERBCO was not in fact able to take advantage of the opportunity. Thus, CERBCO suffered no damages as a result of this lost opportunity because there was zero probability of the sale occurring (due to the brothers' lawful right to vote against it). Nevertheless, the brothers were fiduciaries of CERBCO and, as such, had the duty to present the sale opportunity to CERBCO. The court held that the brothers were not entitled to the profit gained by their breach of this duty. As a result, they were not entitled to keep the profit they had made on the sale of their stock to the potential acquirer of CERBCO's subsidiary and had to disgorge all of their gains to the corporation.

Duty of Candor

When requesting shareholder action, directors have a duty to disclose all material facts. In *Malone v. Brincat,*[25] the Delaware Supreme Court went a step further and held that

23. Guth v. Loft, Inc., 5 A.2d 503 (Del. 1939).

24. 703 A.2d 645 (Del. 1997).

25. 722 A.2d 5 (Del. 1998).

whenever directors disseminate information to shareholders, the fiduciary duties of care, loyalty, and good faith apply, even if no shareholder action is sought. As a result, the court held that "directors who knowingly disseminate false information that results in corporate injury or damage to an individual stockholder violate their fiduciary duty, and may be held accountable in a manner appropriate to the circumstances."

DUTIES IN THE CONTEXT OF TAKEOVERS, MERGERS, AND ACQUISITIONS

In deciding whether to sell a company, directors should consider seven key factors: (1) the company's intrinsic value, (2) the appropriateness of delegating negotiating authority to management, (3) nonprice considerations, (4) the reliability of officers' reports to the board, (5) the reliability of experts' reports, (6) the investment banker's fee structure, and (7) the reasonableness of any defensive tactics. As explained earlier, the directors must act in good faith and be adequately informed.

THE COMPANY'S INTRINSIC VALUE

The ability to make an informed decision as to the acceptability of a proposed buyout price requires knowledge of the company's intrinsic value. Determining intrinsic value entails more than an assessment of the premium of the offering price over the market price per share of the company's stock. When, as in *Van Gorkom,* it is believed that the market has consistently undervalued the company's stock, evaluating the offered price by comparing it with the market price is, according to the Delaware Supreme Court, "faulty, indeed fallacious."

Thus, the directors must do more than assess the adequacy of the premium and compare it with the premiums paid in other takeovers in the same or similar industries. They must also assess the intrinsic or fair value of the company (or division) as a going concern and on a liquidation basis.

Practitioners have read *Van Gorkom* as virtually mandating participation by an investment banker if directors are to avoid personal liability. However, the *Van Gorkom* court expressly disclaimed such an intention:

> We do not imply that an outside valuation study is essential to support an informed business judgment; nor do we state that fairness opinions by independent investment bankers are required as a matter of law. Often insiders familiar with the business of a going concern are in a better position than are outsiders to gather relevant information; and under appropriate circumstances, such directors may be fully protected in relying in good faith upon the valuation reports of their management.[26]

For all practical purposes, however, directors should look to both internal and external sources for guidance. The most reliable valuation information will consist of financial data supplied by management and evaluated by investment bankers knowledgeable about the industry and recent merger and acquisition activity.

The *Hanson Trust* decision makes it clear, however, that the mere presence of investment bankers in the target's boardroom will not shield its directors from personal liability. In that case, the Goldman Sachs partner's oral opinion that the option prices were "within the range of fair value" did not withstand the scrutiny of the Second Circuit on appeal.

DELEGATION OF NEGOTIATING AUTHORITY

If members of management are financial participants in the proposed transaction, the delegation of negotiation responsibilities to management or inside directors will expose the board to greater risks of liability. The Second Circuit observed in *Hanson Trust:*

> SCM's board delegated to management broad authority to work directly with Merrill to structure an LBO proposal, and then appears to have swiftly approved management's proposals. Such broad delegations of authority are not uncommon and generally are quite proper as conforming to the way that a Board acts in generating proposals for its own consideration. However, when management has a self-interest in consummating an LBO, standard post hoc review procedures may be insufficient. SCM's management and the Board's advisers presented the various agreements to the SCM directors more or less as faits accompli, which the Board quite hastily approved. In short, the Board appears to have failed to ensure that negotiations for alternative bids were conducted by those whose only loyalty was to the shareholders.[27]

26. Smith v. Van Gorkom, 488 A.2d 858, 876 (Del. 1985) (Case 21.1).

27. Hanson Trust PLC v. ML SCM Acquisition, Inc., 781 F.2d 264, 277 (2d Cir. 1986).

NONPRICE CONSIDERATIONS

In evaluating a buyout proposal, directors have a fiduciary duty to familiarize themselves with any material nonprice provisions of the proposed agreement. Directors are duty bound to consider separately whether such provisions are in the best interest of the company and its shareholders or, if not, whether the proposal as a whole, notwithstanding such provisions, is in the best interest of their constituencies.

In *Van Gorkom,* for example, several outside directors maintained that Pritzker's merger proposal was approved with the understanding that "if we got a better deal, we had a right to take it." The directors also asserted that they had "insisted" upon an amendment reserving to Trans Union the right to disclose proprietary information to competing bidders. However, the court found that the merger agreement reserved neither of these rights to Trans Union. In the court's view, the directors had "no rational basis" for asserting that their acceptance of Pritzker's offer was conditioned upon a market test of the offer or that Trans Union had a right to withdraw from the agreement in order to accept a higher bid.

Directors should therefore ensure not only that they correctly understand the nonprice provisions of a proposed merger agreement but also that the provisions find their way into the definitive agreement. They should verify this by reading the documents prior to execution.

TAKEOVER DEFENSES

The business judgment rule creates a powerful presumption in favor of actions taken by the directors of a corporation. As noted earlier, the business judgment rule does not apply if the directors have an interest in the transaction being acted upon. If a hostile raider is successful, it is probably going to replace the company's management and board of directors as its first step after assuming control. A successful defense against the takeover has the effect of preserving the positions of current management and directors. Thus, the directors arguably have a personal interest whenever a board opposes a hostile takeover.

Unocal Proportionality Test

Unocal Corp. v. Mesa Petroleum Co.[28] established the principle that the business judgment rule applies to takeover defenses, provided that the directors can show that they had reasonable grounds for believing that the unwelcome suitor posed a threat to corporate policy and effectiveness and that the defense was a reasonable response to that threat. This enhanced judicial scrutiny is designed to guard against "the omnipresent specter that a board may be acting primarily in its own interests, rather than those of the corporation and its shareholders."

The Delaware Supreme Court further explained:

> If a defensive measure is to come within the ambit of the business judgment rule, it must be reasonable in relation to the threat posed. This entails an analysis by the directors of the nature of the takeover bid and its effect on the corporate enterprise. Examples of such concerns may include: inadequacy of the price offered, nature and timing of the offer, questions of illegality, the impact on "constituencies" other than shareholders (that is, creditors, customers, employees, and perhaps even the community generally), the risk of nonconsummation, and the quality of securities being offered in the exchange. While not a controlling factor, it also seems to us that a board may reasonably consider the basic stockholder interests at stake, including those of short term speculators, whose actions may have fueled the coercive aspect of the offer at the expense of the long term investor.

If the directors succeed in making this initial showing, then they are entitled to the protection of the business judgment rule. Under those circumstances, the Delaware Supreme Court stated:

> [U]nless it is shown by a preponderance of the evidence that the directors' decisions were primarily based on perpetuating themselves in office, or some other breach of fiduciary duty such as fraud, overreaching, lack of good faith, or being uninformed, a court will not substitute its judgment for that of the board.

Applying these standards to the hostile bid for Unocal by Mesa Petroleum and its CEO, T. Boone Pickens, the court upheld a discriminatory *self-tender* by Unocal for its own stock, whereby all of the shareholders, except Mesa Petroleum, Pickens, and their affiliates, could exchange their Unocal stock for debt securities worth $18 more per share than the $54 per share offered by Pickens in the first stage of his two-tier front-loaded tender offer. Pickens's offer was deemed coercive because he was acquiring just enough shares in the first stage to get control. Hence, even if shareholders considered the price inadequate, they might well feel coerced into tendering in the first stage for fear of receiving securities of even less value in the second stage, when Unocal was merged with

28. 493 A.2d 946 (Del. 1985).

a Mesa-controlled corporation. The Unocal board viewed the threat as a grossly inadequate two-tier coercive tender offer coupled with the threat of greenmail. (*Greenmail* occurs when a raider acquires stock in a target company and then threatens to commence a hostile takeover unless its stock is repurchased by the target at a premium over the market price.)

The strategy used in *Unocal* is no longer available because of the SEC's "all holders rule." According to the rule, a selective stock repurchase plan is deemed a tender offer in which all holders of securities of the same class must be allowed to participate. Nonetheless, this case remains a key Delaware precedent for the analysis of defensive tactics, including shareholder rights plans (also called poison pills), which can have much the same effect as a discriminatory self-tender.

Duty to Maximize Shareholder Value Under *Revlon*

Once the judgment is made that a sale or breakup of the corporation is in the best interests of the shareholders or is inevitable, directors have a fiduciary duty to obtain the best available price for the shareholders. This rule was first articulated in a case involving a hostile takeover bid for Revlon, Inc. by Pantry Pride.[29]

After initially resisting the takeover attempt, the Revlon board elected to go forward with a friendly buyout from another company at a lower price than that offered by the hostile bidder. The Revlon board sought to justify the lower price by pointing out the benefits of the friendly buyout for other corporate constituencies, such as the Revlon noteholders. The hostile bidder sued to enjoin the friendly buyout.

The Delaware Supreme Court required the Revlon board to seek the highest price for the shareholders. The court defined the duty of the directors as follows:

> The Revlon board's authorization permitting management to negotiate a merger or buyout with a third party was a recognition that the company was for sale. The duty of the board had thus changed from the preservation of Revlon as a corporate entity to the maximization of the company's value at a sale for the stockholders' benefit. . . . The directors' role changed from defenders of the corporate bastion to auctioneers charged with getting the best price for the stockholders at a sale of the company.

29. Revlon, Inc. v. MacAndrews & Forbes Holdings, Inc., 506 A.2d 173 (Del. 1986).

In *Barkan v. Amsted Industries*,[30] the Delaware Supreme Court held that the basic teaching of cases such as *Revlon* is simply that directors of corporations must act in accordance with their fundamental duties of care and loyalty. The court ruled, however, that acting in accordance with these duties does not mean that every change of corporate control necessitates an auction. If fairness to shareholders and the minimizing of conflicts of interest can be demonstrated, the added burden of having an auction may not be necessary. The court in *Barkan* declined to make a specific rule for determining when a market test (or "market check") is required. The court simply stated: "[I]t must be clear that the board had sufficient knowledge of relevant markets to form the basis for its belief that it acted in the best interests of the shareholders."[31]

It is doubtful that a failure of directors to consider every conceivable alternative would in itself amount to a breach of fiduciary duty. Such a rule would be unduly harsh. In hindsight, a complaining shareholder could almost always conjure up at least one alternative that the directors failed to consider. On the other hand, the failure of a board to consider any alternatives at all, or the unwillingness of a board to negotiate with anyone other than its chosen white knight (or with the initial offeror), would be a breach of fiduciary duty unless there were special circumstances.

When Is a Company in* Revlon *Mode? The case of *Paramount Communications, Inc. v. Time Inc.*[32] examined the question of what constitutes an event triggering the *Revlon* duty to maximize shareholder value. (A company with such an obligation is deemed to be in *Revlon mode*.) Time had entered into a friendly stock-for-stock merger agreement with Warner Communications. Under that agreement, roughly 60 percent of the stock of the new combined entity Time–Warner would be held by former public shareholders of Warner. The merger agreement was subject to the approval of Time's shareholders.

Shortly before the Time shareholder vote was to take place, Paramount Communications made a hostile, unsolicited cash tender offer for all Time shares. In response, Time proceeded with its own highly leveraged cash tender offer to acquire 51 percent of Warner, to be followed by a back-end, second-step merger of the two companies. This tender offer, which would preclude acceptance of the Paramount tender offer, did not require approval by the Time

30. 567 A.2d 1279 (Del. 1989).

31. *Id.* at 1288.

32. 571 A.2d 1140 (Del. 1990).

shareholders. Paramount challenged the actions of Time's directors in opposing its offer, arguing that the Time board had put Time in the *Revlon* mode when it agreed to the stock merger with Warner.

The Delaware Supreme Court held that this transaction did not trigger *Revlon* duties because there was no change in control. Majority control shifted from one "fluid aggregation of unaffiliated shareholders" to another and remained in the hands of the public. As a result, the Time board could properly take into account such intangibles as the desire to preserve the Time culture and journalistic integrity in deciding to reject Paramount's hostile tender offer, which was arguably worth more to shareholders than the Time–Warner combination. The court considered this to be a strategic alliance, not a sale of Time to Warner, which would have triggered the *Revlon* duty to maximize shareholder value.

Relying heavily on the precedent established by the *Time–Warner* case, Paramount entered into a friendly merger agreement with Viacom, Inc. in September 1993. At the time Paramount agreed to merge with Viacom, control of Paramount was vested in the "fluid aggregation of unaffiliated stockholders," and not in a single person, entity, or group. Sumner Redstone was the CEO, chair, and majority shareholder of Viacom. After the proposed merger, he would be the controlling shareholder of the combined Paramount–Viacom entity. When QVC Network, Inc. made a hostile unsolicited offer for Paramount that was worth $1.3 billion more than Viacom's offer, the Paramount board refused to negotiate with QVC and instead stood by its merger agreement with Viacom.

QVC then sued the Paramount directors, arguing that the Paramount board had put Paramount in the *Revlon* mode when it committed to a transaction that would shift control of Paramount from the public shareholders to Redstone. The Paramount board argued that it had no duty to maximize shareholder value because it was pursuing a strategic alliance with Viacom, not a breakup of the company. The Delaware Supreme Court rejected this argument and ruled that the Paramount directors had an obligation to continue their search for the best value reasonably available to the stockholders.[33]

The court ruled:

> [W]hen a corporation undertakes a transaction which will cause: (a) a change in corporate control; or (b) a break-up of the corporate entity, the directors' obligation is to seek the best value reasonably available to the stockholders. This obligation arises because the effect of the Viacom–Paramount transaction, if consummated, is to shift control of Paramount from the public stockholders to a controlling stockholder, Viacom.

Regardless of the present Paramount board's vision of a long-term strategic alliance with Viacom, once the Paramount–Viacom deal was consummated, Redstone would have the power to alter that vision. Furthermore, once control shifted, the current Paramount stockholders would have no leverage to demand another control premium in the future.

The Delaware Supreme Court was highly critical of the process the Paramount board followed:

> The directors' initial hope and expectation for a strategic alliance with Viacom was allowed to dominate their decisionmaking process to the point where the arsenal of defensive measures established at the outset was perpetuated (not modified or eliminated) when the situation was dramatically altered. QVC's unsolicited bid presented the opportunity for significantly greater value for the stockholders and enhanced negotiating leverage for the directors. Rather than seizing those opportunities, the Paramount directors chose to wall themselves off from material information which was reasonably available and to hide behind the defensive measures as a rationalization for refusing to negotiate with QVC or seeking other alternatives.

In *In re Lukens Inc. Shareholders Litigation,*[34] the Delaware Court of Chancery concluded that a merger of Lukens with Bethlehem Steel triggered *Revlon* duties even though more than 30 percent of the merger consideration consisted of shares of common stock of Bethlehem, a widely held company with no controlling stockholder. Because 62 percent of the consideration was cash, the court concluded that "for a substantial majority of the then-current shareholders, 'there is no long run.'"

The "In Brief" provides a decision tree for analyzing when the business judgment rule will apply to board decisions.

DEAL PROTECTION DEVICES

Often the parties to a friendly merger will use *deal protection devices,* such as no-talk provisions, to dissuade other bidders and thereby protect the consummation of the friendly merger transaction. Defensive devices can be economic, structural, or both.

33. Paramount Commc'ns, Inc., v. QVC Network, Inc., 637 A.2d 34 (Del. 1994).

34. 757 A.2d 720 (Del. Ch. 1999), *aff'd,* 757 A.2d 1278 (Del. 2000).

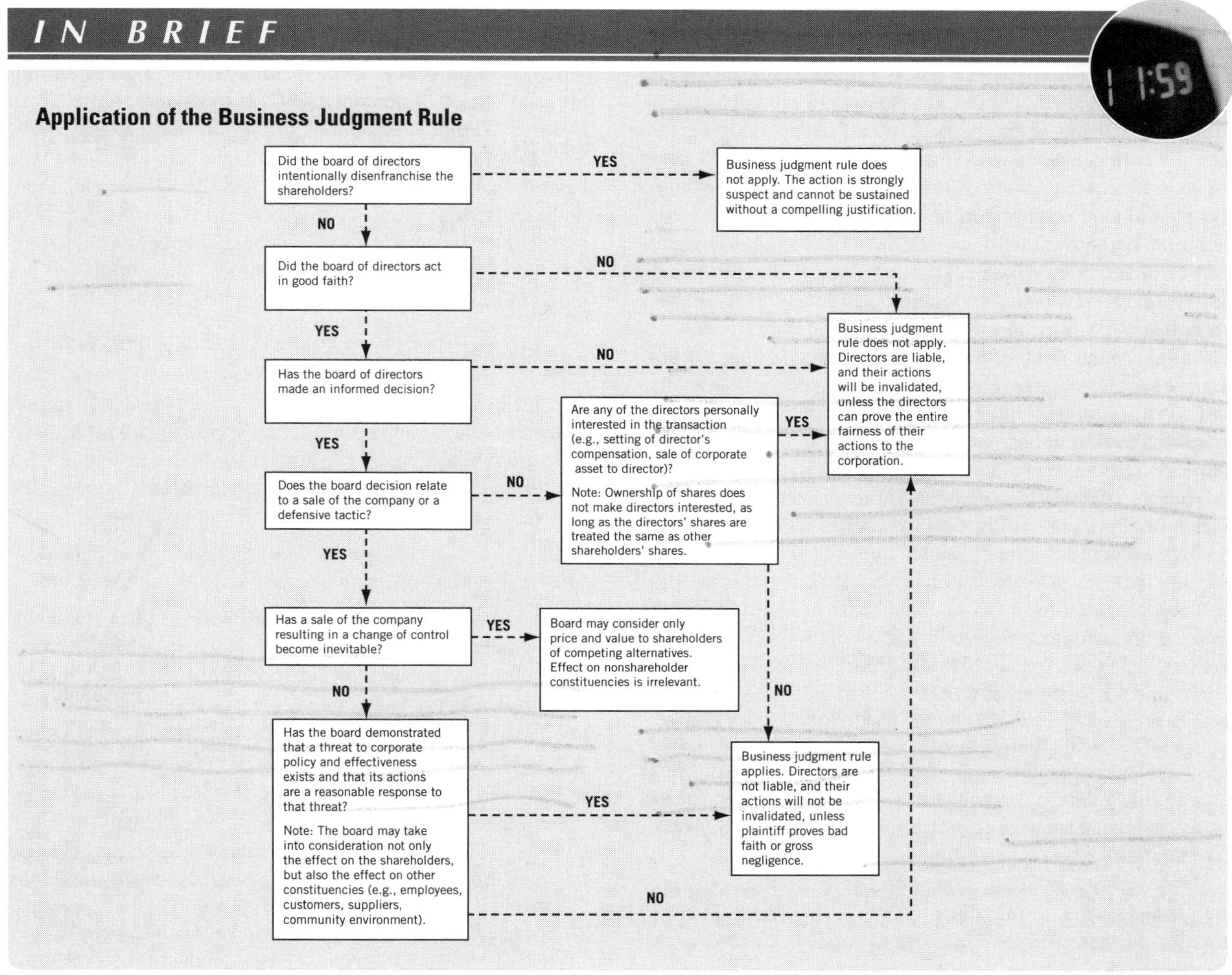

No-Talk Provisions

Delaware courts are highly skeptical of agreements that purport to limit directors' ability to fulfill what they in good faith perceive their fiduciary duties to be. For example, the Court of Chancery refused to enforce a no-talk clause in a stock-for-stock merger agreement between Capital Re Corporation and Ace Limited. The *no-talk clause* permitted Capital Re to engage in discussions with and provide information to other bidders only if the board concluded, based on the written opinion of outside legal counsel, that engaging in discussions or providing information was required to prevent the board from breaching its fiduciary duties to its stockholders.[35] Although Capital Re's counsel opined that negotiating with other bidders was consistent with the board's fiduciary duties, counsel did not state that the board was *required* to discuss an offer by another bidder. The court indicated that a provision that purports to prevent a board from talking with other bidders, even if the directors determine that they have a fiduciary duty to do so, is "particularly suspect when a failure to consider other offers guarantees the consummation of the original transaction, however more valuable an alternate transaction may be and however less valuable the original transaction might have become since the merger agreement was signed."

The court did suggest that a no-talk clause with no *fiduciary out* (a clause allowing the board of directors to negotiate with other bidders or to terminate a merger agreement) might be permissible if (1) the stockholders could

35. Ace Ltd. v. Capital Re Corp., 747 A.2d 95 (Del. Ch. 1999).

freely vote for or against the existing merger agreement and choose among the present merger, a subsequent merger, or no merger at all; or (2) the board agreed to the provision as a way to end an auction for sale of a company after a thorough canvass of the market. While acknowledging the tension between a vested contract right and the board's duty to determine what its own fiduciary duties require, the court concluded that a contract right must give way when (1) "the acquirer knew, or should have known, of the target board's breach of fiduciary duty"; (2) the "transaction remains pending"; and (3) "the board's violation of fiduciary duty relates to policy concerns that are especially significant."

On the other hand, courts are more likely to permit *no-shop agreements,* whereby the target agrees not to actively solicit other bidders but retains the right to negotiate with parties who submit unsolicited bids to the target. Once again, such devices are more likely to withstand attack when they are put into place after a canvass of the market and as a condition to a bidder's willingness to make a favorable bid.

Breakup Fees

In exchange for providing a fiduciary out, a bidder will usually demand that some predetermined amount of money be paid to it if the deal fails to close because the target terminates the agreement. *Termination* or *breakup fees* are sometimes characterized as liquidated damages provisions, and they are often 2 to 3 percent of the value of the deal. They are usually intended to help make the bidder whole for its out-of-pocket expenses (for attorneys, investment bankers, and the like) and lost opportunity costs.

For example, in 2000, American Home Products Corporation received a termination fee of $1.8 billion when its merger partner, Warner–Lambert Company, walked away from their $72 billion deal and agreed to be acquired by Pfizer Inc. In mergers of equals, where there is no clear buyer or seller, there are often reciprocal termination fee provisions. For example, the agreement for the $131.49 billion merger of America Online, Inc. and Time–Warner, Inc. provided that if AOL backed out of the deal under certain conditions, it would have to pay Time–Warner a $5.37 billion breakup fee (2.75 percent of AOL's market capitalization); if Time–Warner walked away, it would have to pay AOL $3.9 billion.[36] Although courts in Delaware and elsewhere have upheld termination fees in the 1 to 3 percent range under either the business judgment rule or the standard of reasonableness applied to liquidated damages provisions, fees that are so large as to constitute "showstoppers" are much more likely to be struck down.[37]

Options

The Delaware Supreme Court struck down a put option Paramount had granted to Viacom, which would have given Viacom an additional $1 billion if its deal with Paramount fell through.[38] The court upheld the 1.5 percent breakup fee as a valid liquidated damages provision, however.

Other Devices

In the following case, the Delaware Supreme Court considered whether the directors of an insolvent publicly traded corporation breached their fiduciary duty when they agreed to submit a merger agreement to a stockholder vote, knowing that the stockholders with a majority of the voting power had agreed unconditionally to vote all of their shares in favor of the inferior offer.

36. Nikhil Deogun & Nick Wingfield, *Stock Drops Spur Questions on AOL Deal,* WALL ST. J., Jan. 13, 2000, at A3.

37. For an interesting empirical analysis of deals involving breakup fees and other forms of lock-ups, see John C. Coates IV & Guhan Subramanian, *A Buy-Side Model of M&A Lockups: Theory and Evidence,* 53 STAN. L. REV. 307 (2000).

38. Paramount Commc'ns, Inc. v. QVC Network, Inc., 637 A.2d 34 (Del. 1994).

A CASE IN POINT

CASE 21.4

OMNICARE, INC. v. NCS HEALTHCARE, INC.

SUPREME COURT OF DELAWARE
818 A.2D 914 (DEL. 2003).

SUMMARY

FACTS NCS Healthcare, Inc., a leading independent provider of pharmacy services to skilled nursing facilities and other long-term care institutions, became insolvent after changes in the timing and level of reimbursements by government and third-party payors adversely affected market conditions in the health-care industry. The price of its common stock dropped from about $20 in January 1999 to a range of $0.09 to $0.50 per share by early 2002 when Omnicare, Inc. offered to pay $313,750,000 for NCS's assets in a proposed asset sale in bankruptcy. Omnicare's offer was less than the amount of NCS's outstanding debt and would have resulted in no recovery for NCS's stockholders.

CONTINUED

NCS's operating performance was improving by early 2002, when NCS contacted Genesis Health Ventures, Inc. in hopes of negotiating a transaction that would provide some recovery for NCS's stockholders. An independent committee of NCS board members, who were neither NCS employees nor major NCS stockholders, negotiated a transaction whereby Genesis agreed to repay the NCS senior debt in full, assume the trade debt, purchase the NCS notes or exchange them for cash and stock, and provide $24 million in value for the NCS common stock.

Genesis had previously lost a bidding war for another company when Omnicare made a last-minute overbid. Genesis told NCS that it was unwilling to be a stalking horse for a higher Omnicare bid and insisted on an exclusivity agreement that prevented NCS from negotiating with other bidders for a short period of time.

After NCS entered into the agreement, Omnicare concluded that NCS was negotiating a transaction with a competitor that would potentially present a competitive threat. In light of a run-up in the price of the NCS common stock, Omnicare also came to believe that whatever transaction NCS was negotiating probably included a payment for its stock. Omnicare then proposed a transaction that included $3 cash for the common shares but was conditioned on negotiating a merger agreement, obtaining certain third-party consents, and completing its due diligence. Although Omnicare's economic terms were attractive, the due diligence condition weakened its offer.

Genesis agreed to improve its offer by, among other things, increasing the payment to the stockholders by 80 percent but stipulated that the transaction had to be approved by midnight the next day or else it would terminate the discussions and withdraw its offer. After "balancing the potential loss of the Genesis deal against the uncertainty of Omnicare's letter," the NCS special committee and full board concluded that the only reasonable alternative was to approve the Genesis transaction. The NCS board authorized the voting agreements with the two majority stockholders, whereby they agreed to vote for the Genesis deal, and agreed to submit the merger agreement to the NCS stockholders regardless of whether the board continued to recommend the merger under Section 251(c) of the Delaware General Corporation Law.

Shortly thereafter Omnicare made an irrevocable offer to acquire the NCS stock for $3.50 per share in cash. The NCS board then withdrew its recommendation that the stockholders vote in favor of the NCS–Genesis merger agreement, and NCS's financial adviser withdrew its fairness opinion. Nonetheless, the stockholder agreement ensured NCS stockholder approval of the Genesis merger. Omnicare then sued to prevent the consummation of the inferior Genesis transaction.

Issue Presented Did the directors of an insolvent publicly traded company violate their fiduciary duty when they entered into an agreement for a "bullet-proof" sale of the company to the "only game in town"?

Summary of Opinion The Delaware Supreme Court began by explaining that a board's management decision to enter into and recommend a merger transaction can become final only when ownership action is taken by a vote of the stockholders. As a result, "a board of directors' decision to adopt defensive devices to protect a merger agreement may implicate the stockholders' right to effectively vote contrary to the initial recommendation of the board in favor of the transaction."

The court then reasoned that there is an "omnipresent specter" of conflicts of interest when a board of directors acts to prevent stockholders from effectively exercising their right to vote contrary to the will of the board. To be protected under the business judgment rule, defensive devices adopted by the board to protect the original merger transaction must withstand enhanced judicial scrutiny under the *Unocal* standard applied to antitakeover devices. The court explained that the board "does not have unbridled discretion to defeat perceived threats by any draconian means available." Defensive measures that are either preclusive or coercive are, by definition, considered draconian and invalid.

CONTINUED

Enhanced judicial scrutiny requires (1) a "judicial determination regarding the adequacy of the decisionmaking process employed by the directors, including the information on which the directors based their decision," and (2) "a judicial examination of the reasonableness of the directors' action in light of the circumstances then existing." The directors have the burden of proving that they were adequately informed and acted reasonably. As long as the deal protection devices are not draconian and are within a range of reasonableness, a court will not substitute its judgment for that of the board.

The court first considered whether the NCS directors had demonstrated that they had reasonable grounds for believing that a danger to corporate policy and effectiveness existed. The threat identified by the NCS board was the possibility of losing the Genesis offer and being left with no comparable alternative transaction.

The court then applied the second stage of the *Unocal* test, which required the NCS directors to demonstrate that their defensive response was reasonable in relation to the threat posed. The court explained that this inquiry involves a two-step analysis. First, the NCS directors were required to establish that the merger deal protection devices adopted in response to the threat were not "coercive" or "preclusive." Second, they had to demonstrate that their response was within a "range of reasonable responses" to the threat perceived.

In this case, the court concluded that the deal protection devices the NCS board agreed to were *both* preclusive and coercive. The tripartite defensive measures—the Section 251(c) provision, the voting agreements, and the absence of an effective fiduciary out clause—made it "mathematically impossible" and "realistically unattainable" for the Omnicare transaction or any other proposal to succeed, no matter how superior the proposal. Although the minority stockholders were not forced to vote for the Genesis merger, they were required to accept it because it was a *fait accompli*. The court concluded that the NCS directors' defensive devices were not within a reasonable range of responses to the perceived threat of losing the Genesis offer because they were preclusive and coercive. As a result, the devices were unenforceable.

The court went on to hold that the deal protection devices were unenforceable for a second independent reason. Taken together, they completely prevented the board from discharging its fiduciary responsibilities to the minority stockholders.

Although the NCS board was seeking to ensure that the NCS creditors were paid in full and that the NCS stockholders received the highest value available for their stock, the NCS board did not have authority to accede to the Genesis demand for an absolute "lock-up." Because the directors of a Delaware corporation have a continuing obligation to discharge their fiduciary responsibilities, as future circumstances develop, after approving the merger with Genesis, the NCS board was required to negotiate a fiduciary out clause to protect the NCS stockholders if the Genesis transaction became an inferior offer. "By acceding to Genesis' ultimatum for complete protection in futuro, the NCS board disabled itself from exercising its own fiduciary obligations at a time when the board's own judgment is most important, i.e., receipt of a subsequent superior offer." Although the stockholders with majority voting power "had an absolute right to sell or exchange their shares with a third party at any price," the NCS directors had a supervening responsibility to discharge their fiduciary duties on a continuing basis.

The court explained:

> Any board has authority to give the proponent of a recommended merger agreement reasonable structural and economic defenses, incentives, and fair compensation if the transaction is not completed. To the extent that defensive measures are economic and reasonable, they may have become an increased cost to the proponent of any subsequent transaction. Just as defensive measures cannot be draconian, however, they cannot limit or circumscribe the directors' fiduciary duties.

CONTINUED

RESULT The provisions in the merger agreement requiring a stockholder vote on the Genesis deal were invalid, so the NCS board was not required to put the Genesis deal to a stockholder vote.

COMMENTS This case resulted in a rare three–two split decision of the Delaware Supreme Court. The dissenting opinion by Chief Justice Veasey, with whom Justice Steele joined, pointed out that the merger agreement and the voting commitments of the majority stockholders concluded a lengthy search and intense negotiation process in the context of insolvency and creditor pressure where no other viable bid had emerged:

> Going into negotiations with Genesis, the NCS directors knew that, up until that time, NCS had found only one potential bidder, Omnicare. Omnicare had refused to buy NCS except at a fire sale price through an asset sale in bankruptcy. Omnicare's best proposal at that stage would not have paid off all creditors and would have provided nothing for stockholders. Genesis expressed interest that became increasingly attractive. Negotiations with Genesis led to an offer paying creditors off and conferring on NCS stockholders $24 million—an amount infinitely superior to the prior Omnicare proposals.
>
> But there was, understandably, a sine qua non. In exchange for offering the NCS stockholders a return on their equity and creditor payment, Genesis demanded certainty that the merger would close. If the NCS board would not have acceded to the Section 251(c) provision, if [the majority shareholders] had not agreed to voting agreements and if NCS had insisted on a fiduciary out, there would have been no Genesis deal! Thus, the only value-enhancing transaction available would have disappeared.
>
> The Majority invalidates the NCS board's action by announcing a new rule that represents an extension of our jurisprudence. That new rule can be narrowly stated as follows: A merger agreement entered into after a market search, before any prospect of a topping bid has emerged, which locks up stockholder approval and does not contain a "fiduciary out" provision, is per se invalid when a later significant topping bid emerges. As we have noted, this bright-line, per se rule would apply regardless of (1) the circumstances leading up to the agreement and (2) the fact that stockholders who control voting power had irrevocably committed themselves, *as stockholders*, to vote for the merger. Narrowly stated, this new rule is a judicially-created "third rail" that now becomes one of the given "rules of the game," to be taken into account by the negotiators and drafters of the given "rules of the game," to be taken into account by the negotiators and drafters of merger agreements. In our view, this new rule is an unwise extension of existing precedent.
>
> The NCS board's actions—as the Vice Chancellor correctly held—were reasonable in relation to the threat because the Genesis deal was the "only game in town," the NCS directors got the best deal they could from Genesis and—but for the emergence of Genesis on the scene—there would have been no viable deal.

Because the deal protection measures were not adopted unilaterally by the board to fend off an existing hostile offer, the dissent argued that the majority's reliance on the discussion in an earlier case of "draconian" antitakeover devices measures was misplaced.

In a second dissenting opinion, Justice Steele chided the majority:

> In effect, the majority has adopted the "duck" theory of contract interpretation. In my view, just as all ducks have their season and the wary hunter carefully scans the air to determine which duck may and which may not be shot at a given time on a certain day, the same holds true for distinguishing between contract provisions that could in another context be deemed truly defensive measures demanding enhanced scrutiny by a court. When certain, or when in doubt that the "duck" is not in season, courts, like prudent waterfowls, should defer.

Allocation of Power Between the Directors and the Shareholders

A key issue that emerges from cases involving hostile takeovers and defensive tactics is who gets to decide whether the corporation should be sold—the board of directors or the shareholders. Theoretically, the board of directors is the guardian of the shareholders' interests, but the interests and obligations of the two groups sometimes conflict.

Frequently, a hostile takeover attempt presents such a conflict. Sometimes the proposed terms are attractive to the shareholders because the acquiring corporation offers to pay a substantial premium for their stock. The board of directors, however, may believe that the acquiring company's plans for the corporation are ultimately destructive, as in the case of a *bust-up takeover,* in which the acquired corporation is taken apart and its assets sold piecemeal. The directors may have legitimate concerns about the effect of such a takeover on the company's employees or on the community where the corporation is located. Or the directors might believe that the long-term value of the company is greater than the price being offered. Of course, directors might oppose a transaction just so they can remain on the corporation's board in violation of their legal obligation to put the corporation's interests before their own.

POISON PILLS

In one of the first cases addressing the allocation of power between the directors and the shareholders in deciding whether the corporation should be sold, a board of directors, without shareholder approval, had adopted a *poison pill* or *shareholder rights plan,* that is, a plan that would make any takeover not approved by the directors prohibitively expensive.[39] In 1984, the directors of Household International, fearing that Household might be taken over and busted up, adopted a poison pill in the form of a Preferred Share Purchase Rights Plan. This plan provided that, under certain triggering circumstances, common shareholders would receive a "right" for every common share of Household. In the event of a merger in which Household was not the surviving corporation, the holder of each common share of Household would have the right to purchase $200 of the common stock of the acquiring company for only $100. If these rights were triggered and exercised, they would dilute the value of the stock of the acquiring company, making a takeover prohibitively expensive for the acquirer.

The Delaware Supreme Court upheld the board's power to adopt the plan. The court found that the plan did not usurp the shareholders' ability to receive tender offers and to sell their shares to a bidder without board approval of the sale. Household's poison pill left "numerous methods to successfully launch a takeover." For example, a bidder could make a tender offer on the condition that the board redeem the rights, that is, buy them back for a nominal sum before they were triggered. A bidder could set a high minimum of shares and rights to be tendered; it could solicit consents to remove the board and replace it with one that would redeem the rights; or it could acquire 50 percent of the shares and cause Household to self-tender for the rights. In a self-tender, the company would agree to buy back the shareholders' rights for a fair price.

The court also found that the plan did not fundamentally restrict the shareholders' right to conduct a proxy contest. In a *proxy contest,* someone wishing to replace the board with his or her own candidates must acquire a sufficient number of shareholder votes to do so. Such votes are usually represented by *proxies,* or limited written powers of attorney entitling the proxy holder to vote the shares owned by the person giving the proxy. The court found that a proxy contest could be won with an insurgent ownership of less than 20 percent (the threshold for triggering distribution of the rights) and that the key to success in a proxy contest is the merit of the insurgent's arguments, not the size of his or her holdings.

The court concluded that the decision to adopt the poison-pill plan was within the board's authority. Moreover, because the directors "reasonably believed Household was vulnerable to coercive acquisition techniques and adopted a reasonable defensive mechanism to protect itself," the court held that the board had discharged its fiduciary duty appropriately under the business judgment rule.

Although the Delaware Supreme Court upheld the adoption of a poison-pill plan in *Moran,* it reserved judgment on how such a plan would operate in practice. In particular, it left open the question of when directors must redeem the poison-pill rights to permit shareholders to tender their shares to a bidder.

The question of whether a board must redeem a pill is fact-specific—a court will look at all of the circumstances in making its decision. Certain factors will favor keeping the pill in place. These include (1) a tender offer that is only slightly above the market price of the stock; (2) a tender offer for less than all of the shares; (3) an active attempt by the board to solicit other offers; (4) a conscious effort by the board to allow its outside directors, deemed

39. Moran v. Household Int'l, Inc., 500 A.2d 1346 (Del. 1985).

more disinterested, to make the decisions in this area; and (5) the fact that the tender offer is only in its early stages. The *Time–Warner* case made it clear that, under certain circumstances, a board faced with a hostile takeover bid can "just say no." Yet, in recent years, shareholder activists have pressured companies to submit their poison pills to a shareholder vote. In addition, as happened when PeopleSoft rejected Oracle's hostile takeover offer and when Yahoo! rebuffed Microsoft's takeover bid, disgruntled shareholders may commence a proxy contest to try to replace directors who block an offer favored by a large number of shareholders.

The Delaware Court of Chancery struck down a so-called *dead-hand pill,* which could be redeemed only by the directors in office before the hostile bidder gained control or their designated successors.[40] The court held that the dead-hand provision violated the requirement under Section 141 of the Delaware General Corporation Law that the directors manage the business and affairs of the corporation because it gave one category of directors distinctive voting rights that were not shared by the other directors. Although the Delaware statute permits different directors to be given distinctive voting rights, those rights must be set forth in the certificate of incorporation, which was not the case here.

The court also held that the dead-hand feature violated the directors' duty of loyalty for two reasons. First, the provision failed to meet the more exacting *Blasius*[41] standard (after the case of the same name in which the Delaware Court of Chancery first articulated this standard) applicable to defensive tactics touching upon issues of control because it purposefully disenfranchised the company's shareholders without any compelling justification. In particular, "even in an election contest fought over the issue of the hostile bid, the shareholders will be powerless to elect a board that is both willing and able to accept the bid." Instead, the shareholders "may be forced to vote for [incumbent] directors whose policies they reject because only those directors have the power to change them." Second, the dead-hand provision failed to satisfy *Unocal*'s requirement that the defense be proportionate to the threat because it was preclusive: it eliminated the use of a proxy contest as a possible means to gain control.

The Delaware Supreme Court also struck down a so-called *no-hand pill,* which could not be redeemed for six months even if the insurgent's slate of directors was elected and wanted to redeem it.[42] The delayed redemption provision in the plan would have prevented a new board of directors from redeeming the plan in order to facilitate a transaction that would serve the stockholders' best interests, even under circumstances where the board would be required to do so because of its fiduciary duty to the stockholders. Because the delayed redemption provision impermissibly circumscribed the board's statutory power under Section 141(a) to manage the business and affairs of the company and the directors' ability to fulfill their concomitant fiduciary duties, the delayed redemption provision was invalid.

PROTECTING THE SHAREHOLDER FRANCHISE AND THE *BLASIUS* STANDARD OF REVIEW

A number of takeover cases have drawn a distinction between the exercise of two types of corporate power: (1) the power over the assets of the corporation, and (2) the power relationship between the board and the shareholders.[43] As explained earlier, directors have broad power over the assets of the corporation. Such decisions are generally protected by the business judgment rule or subjected to *Unocal*'s proportionality analysis if they relate to defensive tactics. As Delaware Chancellor William Allen explained in *Paramount Communications, Inc. v. Time Inc.*, "The corporation law does not operate on the theory that directors, in exercising their powers to manage the firm, are obligated to follow the wishes of a majority of shares."[44] Thus, the Time directors had the power to acquire Warner Communications even though the holders of a majority of Time's stock would have preferred to take Paramount's offer. Or, as the Delaware Court of Chancery put it, "Directors are not thermometers, existing to register the ever-changing sentiments of stockholders."[45]

If a board's unilateral decision to adopt a defensive measure touches on issues of voting control, however, then further judicial scrutiny is required to protect the shareholder franchise essential for corporate democracy. In particular, the court must decide whether the board purposefully disenfranchised its shareholders (that is, interfered with their right to elect the directors). If so, then under the *Blasius* standard, the action is strongly suspect and cannot be sustained without a compelling justification.[46]

40. Carmody v. Toll Bros., Inc., 723 A.2d 1180 (Del. Ch. 1998).

41. Blasius Indus. v. Atlas Corp., 564 A.2d 651 (Del. Ch. 1988).

42. Quickturn Design Sys., Inc. v. Shapiro, 721 A.2d 1281 (Del. 1998).

43. *See* Hilton Hotels Corp. v. ITT Corp., 978 F. Supp. 1342 (D. Nev. 1997).

44. Fed. Sec. L. Rep. (CCH) 94,514 (Del. Ch. July 14, 1989), *aff'd,* 571 A.2d 1140 (Del. 1990).

45. *In re* Lear Corp. S'holder Litig., 2008 WL 4053221 (Del. Ch. Sept. 2, 2008).

46. *See* Stroud v. Grace, 606 A.2d 75 (Del. 1992); Unitrin, Inc. v. Am. Gen. Corp., 651 A.2d 1361 (Del. 1995); Blasius Indus. v. Atlas Corp., 564 A.2d 651 (Del. Ch. 1988).

Protecting the shareholder franchise is critical because the business judgment rule provides the directors and officers with great latitude in managing the day-to-day affairs of the corporation. As a result, shareholders who are displeased with the business performance generally have only two options: sell their shares or vote to replace the incumbent board members. The corporate governance system loses a key control if unhappy shareholders cannot vote the directors out of office.

For example, in *Chesapeake Corp. v. Shore,*[47] the Delaware Court of Chancery held that a supermajority bylaw provision adopted by the board of Shorewood Packing Corporation to thwart a hostile bid by Chesapeake Corporation was "a preclusive, unjustified impairment of the Shorewood stockholders' right to influence their company's policies through the ballot box." The provision increased the number of Shorewood shares needed to amend the bylaws from a simple majority to 60 percent. Because Shorewood's management controlled almost 24 percent of its stock, the supermajority provision made it virtually impossible for Chesapeake to garner enough votes to amend the bylaws to eliminate the classified board so that it could unseat the current directors and install a new board amenable to its offer.

The Shorewood board claimed that Chesapeake's offer posed two threats: (1) the price was grossly inadequate, so Shorewood stockholders faced great harm if they sold their stock at that price; and (2) "there was a danger that Shorewood stockholders would be confused about the intrinsic value of the company, fail to understand management's explanation as to why the market was undervaluing their stock, and mistakenly tender consents to Chesapeake to facilitate its unfair offer." The court found the threat of confusion "at best quite a weak one" in light of (1) the fact that more than 80 percent of Shorewood's shares were held by management and institutional holders, (2) the ability of the board to engage in a more vigorous communications campaign, and (3) the fact that reputable analysts were already tracking the stock. Although the court acknowledged that the price offered might be inadequate, it held that the supermajority bylaw was "an extremely aggressive and overreaching response to a very mild threat." Instead, if the board truly believed that price inadequacy was the problem, it could have taken Chesapeake up on its offer to negotiate price and structure.

The court acknowledged that several cases have stated that a corporate board may consider a fully financed all-cash, all-shares, premium-to-market tender offer a threat to stockholders when "the board believes that the company's present strategic plan will deliver more value than the premium offer, the stock market has not yet bought that rationale, the board may be correct, and therefore there is a risk that 'stockholders might tender . . . in ignorance or based upon a mistaken belief.'" Yet the court noted that this threat of *substantive coercion*[48] can be invoked in almost every situation, seeing as how "[t]here is virtually no CEO in America who does not believe that the market is not valuing [his or] her company properly," so it called on courts to ensure that the threat is real and that the board is not imagining or exaggerating it.

The court also pointed out:

> [O]ne of corporate management's functions is to ensure that the market recognizes the value of the company and that the stockholders are apprised of relevant information about the company. This informational responsibility would include, one would think, the duty to communicate the company's strategic plans and prospects to stockholders as clearly and understandably as possible.

Duty of Directors to Disclose Preliminary Merger Negotiations

Directors can face a difficult decision when deciding whether they must disclose an offer to buy the company or the company's participation in merger negotiations. As is discussed more fully in Chapter 23, disclosure can be required even if the parties have not reached an agreement in principle on the price and structure of the transaction. The Supreme Court held in *Basic, Inc. v. Levinson*[49] that such "soft information" can be material.

Managers planning a management buyout (MBO) of a company face a real conflict of interest in deciding whether to disclose their offer to the public because disclosure will often bring forth competing bidders. Prudent directors, like the independent directors of RJR Nabisco when faced with CEO Ross Johnson's bid, will often require public announcement of the bid even if it puts the company "in play."

---

47. 771 A.2d 293 (Del. Ch. 2000).

48. *See* Ronald J. Gilson & Reiner Kraakman, *Delaware's Standard for Defensive Tactics: Is There Substance to Proportionality Review?,* 44 Bus. Law. 247, 267 (1989).

49. 485 U.S. 224 (1988).

Political PERSPECTIVE

The Pennsylvania Antitakeover Statute

The nation's toughest state antitakeover statute, Pennsylvania Senate bill 1310, also known as Act 36, was signed into law by Governor Bob Casey (a Democrat) on April 27, 1990.[a] An examination of the events surrounding the enactment of this controversial statute highlights the ever-changing battle over defining, shaping, and reshaping the law in this area, as well as the role that politics can play in that process.

Background

The impetus for drafting the statute came from the Belzberg family's hostile takeover bid for Armstrong World Industries, Inc., a *Fortune* 500 company specializing in flooring and furnishings, headquartered in Lancaster, Pennsylvania. After Armstrong's board rejected the Belzbergs' offer to buy the company, the Belzbergs' holding company, First City Financial Corporation, initiated a proxy fight for control of four directors' seats on the board. The shareholders' meeting, at which the results of the proxy fight were to be announced, was scheduled for April 30, 1990.

Noah W. Wenger (a Republican), the state senator from the Lancaster district, introduced a comprehensive antitakeover bill while the Belzbergs and Armstrong were in the midst of their conflict. The bill, drafted in part by the Pennsylvania Chamber of Business and Industry, was designed not only to throw a wrench into the plans of corporate raiders in general but perhaps also to impede the Belzberg bid in particular.

The Statute

Pennsylvania's antitakeover statute attacks hostile bids for corporate control on three major fronts. First, it requires controlling persons (defined as those who own, or control proxies for, 20 percent of a company's stock) to disgorge—that is, give back to the company—any profits they make by selling stock of the company within eighteen months after becoming a controlling person. Such disgorgement is required if stock acquired within twenty-four months before or within eighteen months after becoming a controlling person is sold by the controlling person within eighteen months after becoming a controlling person.

This provision is aimed at those who, after failed takeover attempts, try to reap short-term profits by selling acquired stock at a premium. Institutional investors and other shareholders who launch proxy fights for purposes other than gaining control of a majority of the board are exempted from the disgorgement provision.

Second, the statute expands the directors' ability to consider other constituencies when making change-of-control decisions. Subsection (d) of Section 511 provides an expansive list of constituencies that a director may consider when exercising his or her duty to the corporation:

> In discharging the duties of their respective positions . . . directors may, in considering the best interests of the corporation, consider to the extent they deem appropriate:
>
> **(1)** The effects of any action upon *any or all groups affected by such action,* including shareholders, employees, suppliers, customers and creditors of the corporation, and upon communities in which offices or other establishments of the corporation are located.
>
> **(2)** The short-term and long-term interests of the corporation, including benefits which may accrue to the corporation from its long-term plans and the *possibility that these interests may be best served by the continued independence of the corporation.*
>
> **(3)** The resources, intent and conduct (past, stated and potential) of the person seeking to acquire control of the corporation.
>
> **(4)** *All other pertinent factors.* (Emphasis added.)

In addition, the directors are not required to regard any particular corporate interest or the interest of any group as "a dominant or controlling interest or factor." The implication is clear. A director's duty when considering a proposal for a change of control is not simply to maximize shareholder value.

Third, like some other states' antitakeover statutes, the Pennsylvania law deprives a shareholder of its voting rights when it crosses certain ownership lines, placed at 20 percent, 33 percent, and 50 percent of the company's stock. The voting rights can be regained only if the holders of a majority of the shares—excluding holders of shares acquired in the previous twelve months—give their approval at a special shareholders' meeting.

CONTINUED

The statute also protects the employees of a company that is taken over. Existing labor contracts must be honored, and a successful bidder must pay severance benefits to employees who lose their jobs within two years of the takeover.

Corporations are allowed to opt out of various provisions of the antitakeover statute. As of 1992, more than 66 corporations (including Westinghouse Electric) of the estimated 200 corporations affected by the statute had opted out of at least one of its subchapters.[b]

In 1998, the Pennsylvania statute proved important in the successful effort by Mellon Bank (a Pennsylvania corporation) to thwart a hostile bid by the Bank of New York.[c] In rejecting Bank of New York's $23.6 billion offer (which represented a premium of 28 percent over Mellon's closing stock price the day before the offer was announced and a premium of 34 percent over Mellon's average closing stock price over the last thirty trading days), the chairman of Mellon's board seemed to be invoking the Pennsylvania statute when he criticized the proposed merger as not benefiting "our shareholders, employees, customers and—in particular—the communities we serve."[d]

a. The independent sections are codified as 15 Pa. Cons. Stat. Ann. §§ 511, 512, 1721, 2502 (1990); 15 Pa. Cons. Stat. Ann. §§ 2561–2567, 2571–2574, 2581–2583, 2585–2588 (1990).

b. Jeffrey L. Silberman, *How Do Pennsylvania Directors Spell Relief? Act 36,* 17 Del. J. Corp. L. 115 (1992).

c. *See* Bloomberg News, *In Pennsylvania, Watch Out What You Try to Take Over: Thanks to Tough Rules, Mellon Bank Is Able to Flatly Reject an Offer from Bank of New York,* L.A. Times, Apr. 23, 1998, at D7.

d. Associated Press, *Mellon Bank Sues Bank of New York to Avoid Takeover; $23 Billion Bid Was Rejected,* Star Trib. (Minneapolis), Apr. 24, 1998, at 1D.

Duties of Controlling Shareholders

A shareholder who owns sufficient shares to outvote the other shareholders, or to otherwise set corporate policy, and thus to control the corporation is known as a *controlling shareholder.* A person owning a majority of the outstanding shares is almost always a controlling shareholder, but persons owning a lower percentage (30 percent, for example) may still be deemed controlling if the shares are widely dispersed and there are no other large holders. In certain situations, controlling shareholders owe a fiduciary duty to the corporation and to its other shareholders. Generally, controlling shareholders have a responsibility to minority shareholders to control the corporation in a fair, just, and equitable manner. They may not engage in a bad faith scheme to drain off the corporation's earnings, thereby ensuring that minority shareholders are frozen out of all financial benefits.[50]

Sale of Control

The obligation not to exercise control in a manner that intentionally harms the corporation and minority shareholders spills over into a sale of control. For instance, if a controlling shareholder knows or has reason to believe that the purchaser of its shares intends to use controlling power to the detriment of the corporation, the controlling shareholder has a duty not to transfer the power of management to such a purchaser.

A controlling interest in a corporation usually commands a higher price per share than a minority interest. Does this control premium belong to the corporation or to the majority shareholder? The widely accepted rule is that controlling shareholders normally have a right to derive a premium from the sale of a controlling block of stock.[51] For instance, in *Zetlin v. Hanson Holdings, Inc.,*[52] the New York Court of Appeals commented:

> In this action plaintiff Zetlin contends that minority stockholders are entitled to an opportunity to share equally in any premium paid for a controlling interest in the corporation. This rule would profoundly affect the manner in which controlling stock interests are now transferred. It would require, essentially, that a controlling interest be transferred only by means of an offer to all stockholders, that is, a tender offer. This would be contrary to existing law and if so radical a change is to be effected it would be best done by the Legislature.

50. Sugarman v. Sugarman, 797 F.2d 3 (1st Cir. 1986).

51. *See, e.g.,* Essex Universal Corp. v. Yates, 305 F.2d 572 (2d Cir. 1962).

52. 397 N.E.2d 387 (N.Y. 1979).

In extreme circumstances, however, courts may be willing to characterize the control premium as a corporate asset, thus entitling minority shareholders to a portion. The U.S. Court of Appeals for the Second Circuit took such an approach in *Perlman v. Feldmann.*[53] *Perlman* involved Newport Steel Corporation, whose mills produced steel sheets for sale to manufacturers of steel products. C. Russell Feldmann was the chairman of the board of directors and president of the corporation; he was also the controlling shareholder. In August 1950, when the supply of steel was tight due to the Korean War, Feldmann and some other shareholders sold their stock to a syndicate of end users of steel who were interested in securing a source of supply.

Minority shareholders brought a shareholder derivative suit to compel the controlling shareholders to account for, and make restitution of, their gains from the sale. The court held that the consideration received by the defendants included compensation for the sale of a corporate asset, namely the ability of the board to control the allocation of the corporation's product in a time of short supply.

53. 219 F.2d 173 (2d Cir. 1955), *cert. denied,* 349 U.S. 952 (1955).

Note that the court did not seek to prohibit majority shareholders from ever selling their shares at a premium; it was careful to circumscribe its holding with an emphasis on the extreme market conditions:

> We do not mean to suggest that a majority stockholder cannot dispose of his controlling block of stock to outsiders without having to account to his corporation for profits or even never do this with impunity when the buyer is an interested customer, actual or potential, for the corporation's product. But when the sale necessarily results in a sacrifice of this element of corporate good will and consequent unusual profit to the fiduciary who has caused the sacrifice, he should account for his gains. So when in a time of market shortage, where a call on a corporation's product commands an unusually large premium, in one form or another, we think it sound law that a fiduciary may not appropriate to himself the value of this premium.

The following classic case involved elements of abuse of control and sale of control. The dominant shareholders took a series of steps to ensure that they would participate in the financial benefits of the company without letting the minority shareholders also participate.

A CASE IN POINT

CASE 21.5

JONES V. H.F. AHMANSON & CO.

SUPREME COURT OF CALIFORNIA
460 P.2D 464 (CAL. 1969).

SUMMARY

FACTS The shares of the United Savings and Loan Association were not actively traded due to their high book value, the closely held nature of the association, and the failure of its management to provide information to shareholders, brokers, or the public.

In 1958, investor interest in shares of savings and loan associations and holding companies increased. Savings and loan stocks that were publicly marketed enjoyed a steady increase in market price. The controlling shareholders of the United Savings and Loan Association decided to create a mechanism by which the association, too, could attract investor interest. They did not, however, attempt to render the association's shares more readily marketable.

Instead, a holding company, the United Financial Corporation of California, was incorporated in Delaware on May 8, 1959. On May 14, pursuant to a prior agreement, certain association shareholders owning a majority of the association's stock exchanged their shares for those of United Financial.

After the exchange, United Financial held 85 percent of the association's outstanding stock. The former majority shareholders of the association had become the majority shareholders of United Financial and continued to control the association through the holding company. They did not offer the minority shareholders of the association an opportunity to exchange their shares.

The first public offering of United Financial stock was made in June 1960. An additional public offering in February 1961 included a secondary offering (that is, an offering by selling shareholders) of 600,000 shares. There was active trading in the United Financial shares. Sales of the association shares, however, decreased from 170 shares per year before the formation of United Financial to half that number by 1961. United Financial acquired 90 percent of the association's shares that were sold.

CONTINUED

A shareholder of the association brought suit, on behalf of herself and all other similarly situated minority shareholders, against United Financial and the individuals and corporations that had set up the holding company. The plaintiff contended that the defendants' course of conduct constituted a breach of fiduciary duty owed by the majority shareholders to the minority. She alleged that they had used their control of the association for their own advantage and to the detriment of the minority when they created United Financial, made a public market for its shares that rendered the association's stock unmarketable except to United Financial, and then refused either to purchase the minority's association stock at a fair price or to exchange the stock on the same terms afforded to the majority. She further alleged that they had created a conflict of interest that might have been avoided had they offered all association shareholders the opportunity to participate in the initial exchange of shares.

ISSUE PRESENTED Did the majority shareholders who transferred their shares to a holding corporation, then took it public without allowing the minority to exchange their shares, breach their fiduciary duty to the minority shareholders?

SUMMARY OF OPINION The California Supreme Court began its analysis by stating that the majority shareholders, acting either singly or in concert, have a fiduciary responsibility to the minority and to the corporation. They must use their ability to control the corporation fairly. They may not use it to benefit themselves alone or in a manner detrimental to the minority. Any use to which they put their power to control the corporation must benefit all shareholders proportionately and must not conflict with the proper conduct of the corporation's business. The court summarized the rule as one of "inherent fairness from the viewpoint of the corporation or those interested therein."

The court noted that the controlling shareholders of the association could have taken advantage of the bull market in savings and loan stock in two other ways. They could have caused the association to effect a stock split, thereby increasing the number of outstanding shares, or they could have created a holding company and permitted all shareholders to exchange their shares before offering the holding company's shares to the public. Either course would have benefited all of the shareholders alike, although the majority shareholders would have had to relinquish some of their control shares. Instead, the defendants chose to set up a holding company that they controlled and did not allow the minority shareholders to exchange their association shares for shares of the holding company. Moreover, the market created by the defendants for United Financial shares would have been available for association shares had the defendants chosen a stock split of the association's shares.

The court stated that when a controlling shareholder sells or exchanges its shares, the transaction is subject to close scrutiny, particularly if the majority receives a premium over market value for its shares. If the premium constitutes payment for what is properly a corporate asset, all shareholders are entitled to a proportionate share of the premium (citing *Perlman v. Feldmann*). The defendants' exchange of association stock for United Financial stock was an integral part of a scheme that the defendants could have reasonably foreseen would destroy the potential public market for association stock. The remaining association shareholders would thus be deprived of the opportunity to realize a profit from those intangible characteristics that attach to publicly marketed stock.

RESULT The majority shareholders who transferred their shares to a holding corporation, then took it public without allowing the minority to exchange their shares, breached their fiduciary duty to the minority shareholders. The minority shareholders were awarded damages that would place them in a position at least as favorable as the majority shareholders had created for themselves.

FREEZE-OUTS

The Delaware Supreme Court has held that a majority shareholder may *freeze out* the minority, that is, force the minority shareholders to convert their shares into cash, as long as the transaction is fair.[54] Sometimes a freeze-out is effected by merging a subsidiary into its parent, as in *Rosenblatt v. Getty Oil Co.*[55] In this case, Skelly Oil Company and Mission Corporation merged into Getty Oil Company, which was indirectly the majority shareholder of both Skelly and Mission. All three corporations were in the oil business. At issue was the fairness of the exchange ratio in the merger, that is, the ratio that would be used to convert the minority shareholders' stock into cash.

The Delaware Supreme Court stated that the concept of fairness in parent–subsidiary mergers has two aspects: fair dealing and fair price. Both must be examined together in resolving the ultimate question of entire fairness.

As to fair dealing, a court will look at the timing of the transaction; how it was initiated, structured, negotiated, and disclosed to the board; and how director and shareholder approval was obtained. The court cited a number of factors leading to a conclusion of fair dealing by Getty, including the adversarial nature of the negotiations between the parties to the merger.

Regarding fair price, a court will look at such economic factors as asset value, market value, earnings, and future prospects, and at any other elements that affect the intrinsic value of a company's stock. Both Getty and Skelly believed that the real worth of an oil company is centered in its reserves. Therefore, the court was especially impressed with the fact that they had employed D & M, a petroleum consulting engineering firm with a worldwide reputation and with nearly thirty-seven years of experience, to estimate Getty's and Skelly's respective oil and natural gas reserves.

54. Weinberger v. UOP, Inc., 457 A.2d 701 (Del. 1983).

55. 493 A.2d 929 (Del. 1985).

The court concluded that Getty had dealt fairly with the Skelly minority shareholders in the merger.

Although the controlling shareholder may be permitted to negotiate a deal for the sale of the entire company, the board of directors of the target must still determine the intrinsic value of the company and the maximum shareholder value reasonably attainable so that it has an informed basis for recommending the proposed deal to the minority stockholders or for suggesting that the minority stockholders vote against the deal and exercise their appraisal rights.[56] The representatives of the controlling shareholder on the target board owe the target's minority shareholders "an uncompromising duty of loyalty."[57] This includes an obligation to provide the minority full and accurate information about the company even if the minority has no right to vote on the deal.

GREENMAIL

Delaware courts analyze the payment of greenmail in the same way they analyze other defensive tactics under *Unocal.* Greenmail is a purchase of a dissident shareholder's stock by the issuer at a premium over market, often in exchange for a *standstill agreement,* whereby the shareholder agrees not to commence a tender offer or proxy contest or to buy additional shares of the issuer for a period of time, often ten years. If the board demonstrates that the shareholder to be bought out poses a threat to corporate policy and effectiveness and the repurchase of shares at a premium is a reasonable response to that threat, then the payment will be protected by the business judgment rule.[58]

56. McMullin v. Beran, 765 A.2d 910 (Del. 2000).

57. *Id.* at 923.

58. *See also* Grobow v. Perot, 539 A.2d 180 (Del. 1988) (upholding repurchase by General Motors of GM stock and notes from H. Ross Perot at a "giant premium").

GLOBAL VIEW

Hostile Takeovers Come of Age in Germany

The laws of Germany and several Scandinavian countries require union and employee representation on the boards of directors of most public corporations. These representatives participate in all of the basic decisions related to investment policy, choice of product and technology, marketing, employee relations, and other matters of managerial concern. For example, when Germany's Daimler-Benz AG merged with Chrysler Corporation in 1998, the combined entity, DaimlerChrysler, was organized under German law. As required by Germany's codetermination laws, half of the members of the supervisory board were elected by the employees and union

CONTINUED

leaders; half were elected by the shareholders. (Chrysler was subsequently sold to a U.S. private equity firm.) Under Germany's two-tier board system, the supervisory board consists solely of nonemployee directors, and it is often chaired by a representative of the corporation's main bank. The supervisory board appoints the management board, which consists solely of inside directors and reports to the supervisory board.[59] French law gives firms the option of having a two-tiered board or a unitary board elected by shareholders.

Schaeffler's Hostile Takeover of Continental

Schaeffler's hostile takeover of German tire giant Continental AG in 2008 made it clear that codetermination and Germany's efforts to protect German firms from hostile takeovers are inadequate to immunize German corporations from corporate raiders. Although German law generally requires any person who acquires more than 5 percent of the voting securities of a target company to disclose its purchases and intentions to the target management and investors, Schaeffler eluded this requirement by entering into a series of cash-settled stock swap contracts with its ally Merrill Lynch that ultimately gave it control over more than one-third of Continental's stock. Continental cried foul, but the German Financial Supervisory Authority (BaFin) upheld the tactic after finding no side agreement that required Merrill Lynch to hold the shares on Schaeffler's behalf, to sell them to Schaeffler, or to jointly share voting rights.[60] Banks entering into stock swaps usually buy the underlying shares or find a third party to do so. When the contracts are unwound, the block becomes available for purchase. According to an unnamed senior German mergers and acquisitions lawyer, "There will always be vague agreements that are not legally binding and therefore there will always be sneak attacks by shareholders via swaps."[61] Porsche had used a similar sneak attack to acquire automaker Volkswagen, its much larger rival. When asked whether Daimler AG was vulnerable to a similar attack, CEO Dieter Zetsche stated, "If I would tell you that any activity of that kind is absolutely impossible, I would have to lie."[62] Reuters reported that Daimler was considering its defensive options.

A German statute that goes into effect on March 1, 2009, will require the disclosure of both shareholdings and options but not of swaps. Although the United Kingdom's Financial Services Authority has recommended rules that would require disclosure of contracts for difference, which give investors an economic interest in the underlying shares, it also does not require the disclosure of swaps. As explained in Chapter 22, a case on appeal to the U.S. Court of Appeals for the Second Circuit in 2008 turns on whether stock swaps must be disclosed under U.S. law on Schedule 13D.[63]

EU Takeover Directive

Takeovers in Germany and the rest of the European Union (EU) are governed by the European Union Directive on Takeover Bids (DTB), one of the most ambitious and highly contested pieces of legislation to pass the European Parliament. Adopted in April 2004, after thirty years of political wrangling among the EU member states, its aim was to open up European markets; harmonize the conflicting laws that regulate the economies of individual member states; and create clarity, transparency, and legal certainty through a set of common, universal rules governing shareholders' rights and defensive mechanisms in the event of takeover bids. Originally intended as a major step toward an integrated European capital market, the legislation foundered over sharp differences between the competitive, liberal, "Anglo-Saxon" version of shareholder rights and the coordinated, protectionist, "Rhenish" model.[64]

The United Kingdom and Ireland supported provisions that would ease takeover restrictions across Europe, arguing that takeovers would facilitate restructuring and prepare companies for tougher competition in the global market. Germany, Sweden, and Norway, however, pressed for the protection of their national antitakeover defenses. In an effort to reach a consensus, the European Parliament ultimately left adoption of the two key articles that would have sharply limited the ability of target firms to adopt takeover defenses (Articles 9 and 11) to the discretion of individual member states. The result

CONTINUED

59. Greg Steinmetz & Gregory L. White, *Chrysler Pay Draws Fire Overseas*, Wall St. J., May 26, 1998, at B1, B4.

60. Michael Shields & Patricia Uhlig, *German Sneak Takeover Tool Passes Continental Test*, Reuters, Aug. 26, 2008.

61. *Id.*

62. *Id.*

63. CSX Corp. v. Children's Inv. Fund Mgmt. (U.K.) LLP, 2008 U.S. Dist. LEXIS 46039 (S.D.N.Y. June 11, 2008) (Case 22.4).

64. Simon Hix, Abdoul G. Noury & Gerard Roland, Democratic Politics in the European Parliament 200 (2007).

was a gutted and largely symbolic bill that left national antitakeover statutes mostly intact.[65]

As passed, the DTB consists of twenty-three articles, which together stipulate greater transparency, a mandatory bid rule, and an optional British-style "neutrality rule." The Directive applies to takeover bids for securities of an EU company whose securities are admitted to trading on a regulated market in at least one member state, but it specifically excludes takeover bids for securities issued by member states' central banks.[66]

Article 9, the contentious *neutrality rule*, generally requires the target's board of directors to remain neutral when faced with a hostile takeover bid and stipulates that once a takeover bid has been launched, the target's board cannot adopt any antitakeover devices, such as poison pills, without first obtaining the specific approval of shareholders.[67] The *mandatory bid provision* prohibits coercive two-tier offers by requiring any person who acquires 30 percent or more of a target company's stock to offer to buy all remaining shares at the highest price paid to acquire the 30 percent block.[68]

The *breakthrough rule* in Article 11 was designed to weaken the differential voting structures common in German and Nordic companies. It enables the hostile bidder to break through prebid defenses, such as multiple voting rights and other measures that distribute control rights in a manner that is disproportionate to the cash flow rights, thereby ensuring that a bidder that acquires a majority of the equity can successfully mount a takeover. Germany, France, and the Scandinavian countries bitterly resisted the rule's adoption.[69]

To break the deadlock, the drafters added Article 12, which allows the member states to opt out of the neutrality rule and breakthrough rule altogether. As a result, firms in each member state can retain the antitakeover defenses legal under existing national laws. Fritz Bolkestein, the EU Commissioner responsible for the Directive, was so angry at the extent of the compromise that he threatened to withdraw the Directive entirely, but he could not gain sufficient support from the other Commissioners.[70] According to an EU Commission report, only 1 percent of listed companies in the EU will apply the breakthrough rule on a mandatory basis.[71]

The Future

Even through Germany succeeded in retaining its existing antitakeover legislation, the corporate culture in the EU is changing, and German companies are increasingly vulnerable to hostile takeovers. With decreased state ownership since the 1980s and 1990s, and an increasing number of European firms being managed by CEOs with American MBAs, firms are finding new ways around the laws. The hostile takeover of Continental by Schaeffler may spawn new German antitakeover legislation or the adoption of stronger takeover defenses or both.

65. Luca Enriques, *EC Company Law Directives and Regulations: How Trivial Are They?*, 27 U. PA. J. INT'L ECON. L. 1 (2006).
66. Directive 2004/25/EC of the European Parliament and of the Council of 21 April 2004 on Takeover Bids, OJ. (L 142), 12 (Sept. 18, 2008), *available at* http://eur-lex.europa.eu/LexUriServ/LexUriServ.do?uri=CELEX:32004L0025:EN:HTML.
67. Matteo Gatti, *Optionality Arrangements and Reciprocity in the European Takeover Directive*, 5 EUR. BUS. ORG. L. REV. 553 (2005).
68. Harald Baum, *Takeover Law in the EU and Germany: Comparative Analysis of a Regulatory Model*, 3 U. TOKYO J. L. & POL. 60 (2006).
69. HIX, NOURY & ROLAND, *supra* note 64, at 204.
70. *EU Approves New Takeover Rules*, BBC NEWS, Nov. 28, 2003.
71. Aoife White, *EU: Many European Governments Reluctant to Lift Takeover Barriers*, ASSOC. PRESS, Feb. 27, 2007.

THE RESPONSIBLE MANAGER

CARRYING OUT FIDUCIARY DUTIES

Officers, directors, and controlling shareholders are fiduciaries. They owe their principal (the corporation and its shareholders) undivided loyalty. They must act in good faith. They may not put their own interests before those of the corporation and its shareholders. They cannot, for example, fight off a hostile takeover just to keep their jobs. They cannot

CONTINUED

use the company's confidential information for their personal gain.

Officers and directors also owe the corporation and its shareholders a duty of care. They should act with the care reasonable persons would use in the management of their own property. They have a duty to make only informed decisions. They cannot rely blindly on the advice of other people, even experts.

The duty to make informed decisions, which is a part of the duty of care, takes various forms. In the context of takeovers, board members cannot reject an offer without taking sufficient time to analyze its merit. Managers must be able to demonstrate that they made their decisions only after sufficient deliberation and after review of all relevant information. They should consider the possible effects of both the monetary and the nonmonetary aspects of the transaction.

A manager should never sign a document without reading it first. Ideally, each director should read the document the board is asked to approve. If that is not practical, the directors should demand and read a written summary prepared by counsel. They should also make sure that the officers who are authorized to sign the agreement have read it before signing it.

A manager should be informed as to the rules regarding the duty of care in the company's state of incorporation. Some jurisdictions permit the shareholders to amend the articles of incorporation to relieve directors of any financial liability for violations of the duty of care. But even with such provisions in place, directors must still act in good faith and in what they honestly believe is the best interest of the corporation. Otherwise, they will breach their duty of loyalty. Such a breach can not only result in monetary liability but can also demoralize the shareholders and employees of the corporation, making it difficult to maintain a high level of ethical behavior among them.

In a situation involving a potential conflict of interest, a manager should excuse himself or herself and leave the decision to others who do not have a conflict. It is common, for example, to establish special independent committees of the board of directors, either to examine the fairness of a management offer to acquire the company or to review the merits of shareholder litigation against the directors or officers.

A repurchase of stock at a premium from a dissident (or unhappy) shareholder may violate both the directors' duty to the corporation and the shareholder's duty to the other shareholders. Different courts view such repurchases differently, and local counsel should always be consulted. It is often appropriate for the board not only to obtain a written opinion from counsel that such a repurchase is permissible but also to convene a special independent committee of directors to decide whether the consideration that will be paid for the stock is fair.

Any controlling shareholder engaging in a transaction such as a merger with the company it controls must be able to prove that the transaction is fair both procedurally and substantively. The use of independent committees, advised by independent financial consultants and counsel, helps show procedural fairness, as does a willingness to negotiate the proposed transaction with such a committee on an arm's length basis. Paying a fair price for corporate assets or for shares of a corporation shows substantive fairness. The fairness of a price can be demonstrated by evidence of competing offers or independent appraisals or evaluations. The form of compensation of the appraiser or investment banker should not give that person an interest in the outcome of the appraisal or of the transaction. It is often preferable to pay the appraiser or investment banker a flat fee regardless of whether the deal goes through, rather than an incentive fee based on the value of the deal struck.

Certain acts of directors, officers, and controlling shareholders are both illegal and unethical, such as the seizing of a corporate opportunity by an officer. Other conduct may be legal yet ethically questionable, such as the payment of greenmail.

Some situations present conflicting ethical concerns. The Delaware Supreme Court has held that the directors must maximize shareholder value, that is, get the best price available, if they decide to sell control of the corporation. Yet a sale to a bust-up artist who will sell the company's assets, or to a union buster, might adversely affect the corporation's other constituencies, such as employees, suppliers, and the community in which the corporation does business.[72] A manager should try to select a course of action that protects the corporation's constituencies without sacrificing the shareholders' right to the best price. If the management team itself bids for the company, the board may find itself forced to become an auctioneer whose sole goal is to get the best price for the shareholders.

A board of directors can use various defensive measures to prevent a hostile takeover, provided that the measures are reasonable in relation to the threat posed and that the board considers it in the best interests of the company and its

CONTINUED

72. See Constance E. Bagley & Karen Page, *The Devil Made Me Do It: Replacing Corporate Directors' Veil of Secrecy with the Mantle of Stewardship*, 36 San Diego L. Rev. 4 (1999), for a discussion of the legal, economic, and organizational behavioral aspects of directors' consideration of factors other than simply shareholder return when acting on behalf of the corporation.

constituencies for the company to remain independent. Any measures designed to interfere with the shareholder franchise require proof by the directors of a compelling justification.

Similarly, if the board adopts a strategy resulting in a change of control of a corporation, it cannot use defensive tactics such as no-shop provisions (whereby the board agrees not to consider other offers) or large asset or stock lock-ups to deter competing bidders. In short, if the board agrees to a change of control, it breaches its fiduciary duties if it makes competing offers impossible by adopting a scorched-earth policy that leaves the successful bidder with a depleted target. Although legal counsel will advise managers and directors in this area, a knowledge of the rules of the game is essential to good management.

A MANAGER'S DILEMMA

PUTTING IT INTO PRACTICE

Should Mickey Pay Greenmail?

In March 1984, a group headed by Saul Steinberg purchased more than two million shares of stock of Walt Disney Productions, the owner of Disneyland. Disney responded by announcing that it would acquire the Arvida Corporation for $200 million in newly issued Disney stock and would assume Arvida's $190 million debt. The Steinberg group countered with a shareholder derivative suit in federal court, seeking to block the Arvida transaction. A shareholder derivative suit is a suit brought on behalf of the corporation by one or more of its shareholders. All of the proceeds of such a suit (less expenses) go to the corporation for the benefit of all of its shareholders.

While the shareholder derivative suit was pending, the Steinberg group proceeded to acquire two million additional shares of Disney stock, increasing its ownership position to approximately 12 percent of the outstanding Disney shares. On June 8, 1984, the Steinberg group advised Disney's directors of its intention to make a tender offer for 49 percent of the outstanding shares at $67.50 a share and its intention to later tender for the balance at $72.50 a share.

Should the Disney directors offer to repurchase all the Disney stock held by the Steinberg group at a premium and to reimburse the estimated cost incurred in preparing the tender offer in return for the Steinberg group's agreement not to purchase any more Disney stock and to drop the Arvida litigation? Is it legal or ethical for the Steinberg group to agree not to oppose a motion to dismiss the Arvida litigation? To sell its shares at a premium not offered to other Disney shareholders?[73]

73. *See* Heckman v. Ahmanson, 214 Cal. Rptr. 177 (Cal. Ct. App. 1985).

INSIDE STORY

THE LONG TWILIGHT OF IMPERIAL CEOs

As a scandal involving the insurance industry unfolded in the fall of 2004, an article in the *Wall Street Journal* commented: "The long twilight of imperial CEOs—who run opaque giants that are granted unquestioning trust from shareholders—finally is coming to an end. True, the imperial CEO is harder to get rid of than Rasputin. But this seems to be it."[74]

On October 14, 2004, New York Attorney General Eliot Spitzer announced a civil suit against Marsh & McLennan Companies, the largest insurance brokerage firm in the United States. Spitzer charged the company with accepting kickbacks, price-fixing, and bid-rigging that forced corporate clients to pay higher prices for insurance coverage. The company practiced bid-rigging by prompting insurers to submit phony "B" quotes—bids that were too high to win but gave the appearance of competition.[75] In this way, executives at Marsh ensured that preferred insurers, the ones who paid the highest

CONTINUED

74. *See* Jesse Eisinger, *AIG's Chief Shows Signs of Humility as Spitzer Probe Rattles the Industry,* WALL ST. J., Oct. 20, 2004, at C1.

75. *See* Ianthe Jeanne Dugan & Monica Langley, *Marsh Suspends Four Employees amid Spitzer Probe,* WALL ST. J., Oct. 20, 2004, at A10.

commissions, would win lucrative bids from corporate clients. An e-mail written by a Marsh executive to Ace Ltd., an insurer, was indicative of the coercive bid-rigging practice: "I do not want to hear that you are not doing 'B' quotes or we will not bind anything."[76]

Brokers who met volume or profitability targets on business they brought to the insurer were rewarded with contingent commissions, giving the brokers a financial incentive to place a client's business with insurers paying the most generous bonuses.[77] American International Group (AIG) was one of several firms facing investigation into its potential collaboration with Marsh. Two AIG executives pleaded guilty to illegal activities and agreed to cooperate with investigators against Marsh.

As the charges became public, Marsh's stock price halved, and its directors hastened to respond.[78] Board directors cooperated fully with the investigation to avoid Spitzer's biggest threat: a criminal indictment against the corporation itself.[79] Five executives implicated in the wrongdoing, including the chairman and CEO Jeffrey Greenberg, were dismissed. Upon Greenberg's departure, Spitzer announced he would not indict the company but would seek criminal charges against individuals. Michael G. Cherkasky, Marsh's new CEO and Spitzer's former boss, moved to implement a compliance program at Marsh. As part of its compliance effort, the board agreed to waive attorney–client privilege and submit the results of internal investigations to investigators. Cherkasky also ended the practice of offering contingent commissions, which comprised $843 million or 12 percent of the company's revenue in 2003.[80]

Roughly one year before the Marsh investigation, in August 2003, former SEC Commissioner Richard C. Breeden, corporate monitor of WorldCom during its bankruptcy proceedings, had proposed a series of corporate governance measures designed to prevent a recurrence of the massive fraud that destroyed roughly $200 billion in shareholder value, put tens of thousands of employees out of work, and wiped out the entire value of stock held in employee retirement accounts as well as the value of accumulated equity-based compensation.[81] According to Breeden, WorldCom's CEO Bernard J. Ebbers "was allowed nearly imperial reign over the affairs of the Company, without the board of directors exercising any apparent restraint on his actions, even though he did not appear to possess the experience or training to be remotely qualified for his position."[82] The board allowed "lavish compensation," including more than $400 million in "loans" to Ebbers, which were unlikely ever to be repaid. It also approved a $238 million "compensation slush fund" that Ebbers could allocate to favored executives or employees with no standards or supervision. Citing Lord Acton's remark in 1887 that, "power tends to corrupt and absolute power corrupts absolutely," Breeden said that "'backbone' and 'fortitude' may be the most important qualities needed by a director of a public company."

As a condition to emerging from bankruptcy, WorldCom, which is now known as MCI, Inc., was required to convert its articles of incorporation into a governance constitution, which could be changed only with prior shareholder consent. MCI was required to:

- Give a group of shareholders the power to nominate their own candidates for inclusion in the management proxy statement if the group did not agree with the board's proposed candidates.
- Create the position of nonexecutive chair of the board.
- Ban the issuance of stock options without prior shareholder approval.
- Expense both stock options and restricted stock grants on its financial statements.
- Ban a staggered board, set ten-year term limits for directors, and restrict independent directors to a maximum of three boards, including the MCI board.
- Prohibit related-party transactions involving board members.
- Compensate directors solely with cash and require them to utilize not less than 25 percent of those fees to purchase MCI stock, which had to be held until they left the board.
- Have the board of directors meet at least eight times a year, hold an annual strategic review, and attend annual refresher training on topics relating to board responsibilities.
- Limit change-in-control devices, such as poison pills.

As the "Inside Story" in Chapter 14 concerning the lavish compensation given the former CEO of the failing subprime mortgage firm Countryside Mortgage makes clear, it appears that the reports of the demise of the imperial CEO were premature. Congressional Democrats pressed for caps on executive pay as a condition to voting in favor of the Bush administration's $700 billion bailout of the mortgage-backed securities market. (The bailout and associated regulatory reforms are discussed in more detail in the "Inside Story" in Chapter 22.)

76. *Id.*

77. Theo Francis & Vanessa Fuhrmans, *Class-Action Threat Added to Challenges Facing Insurers,* Wall St. J., Oct. 20, 2004, at C6.

78. *See* Alex Berenson, *To Survive the Dance, Marsh Must Follow Spitzer's Lead,* N.Y. Times, Oct. 25, 2004, at A1.

79. *Id.* at C8.

80. Joseph B. Treaster, *Insurance Chief Quits in Inquiry Led by Spitzer,* N.Y. Times, Oct. 26, 2004, at A1.

81. Richard C. Breeden, *Restoring Trust,* filed with the U.S. District Court for the Southern District of New York (2003).

82. *Id.*

Key Words and Phrases

asset lock-up option 803
breakthrough rule 829
breakup fee 816
business judgment rule 799
bust-up takeover 820
constructive trust 810
controlling shareholder 824
corporate opportunity doctrine 810
crown jewels 803
dead-hand pill 821
deal protection devices 814
duty of care 799
duty of loyalty 799
fiduciary out 815
freeze out 827
greenmail 813
inside directors 805
line-of-business test 810
mandatory bid provision 829
neutrality rule 829
no-hand pill 821
no-shop agreement 816
no-talk clause 815
poison pill 820
proxy 820
proxy contest 820
quasi-foreign corporation 807
Revlon mode 813
self-tender 812
shareholder derivative suit 806
shareholder rights plan 820
standstill agreement 827
substantive coercion 822
termination fee 816

Questions and Case Problems

1. On September 29, 2008, Citigroup entered into an agreement in principle whereby it agreed to acquire Wachovia's banking subsidiaries for $2 billion in a deal that would have netted Wachovia's shareholders $1 per share. The agreement provided that Wachovia's brokerage and asset management businesses would be sold separately and that the federal government would guarantee up to $35 billion in Wachovia losses. Although Wells Fargo had considered making a bid for Wachovia, it had walked away, leaving Citigroup as the sole bidder. According to Citigroup, "Had an agreement between Citigroup and Wachovia not been reached on September 29, Wachovia would have failed the following day and the debt issued by its holding company would have collapsed with potentially devastating implications for the stability and security of the financial markets." After Congress passed the $700 billion bailout bill and while Citigroup was finalizing the agreements required to consummate its government-brokered deal, Wachovia announced that it had agreed to sell all of its assets to Wells Fargo for $15 billion in Wells Fargo stock, netting the Wachovia shareholders $7 per share. The Wachovia-Wells Fargo deal included a share exchange agreement whereby Wachovia issued preferred stock to Wells Fargo that voted as a single class with Wachovia's common stock and represented 39.9 percent of total voting power. In response, Citigroup sued Wachovia and Wells Fargo for $20 billion in compensatory and $40 billion in punitive damages, alleging that Wachovia had breached the exclusivity provision in its agreement with Citigroup and that Wells Fargo had tortiously interfered with Citigroup's contract. Who should prevail? Did Wells Fargo and Wachovia act ethically? [*See* Steven M. Davidoff, *Wachovia and the Uncertainty Principle,* N. Y. Times, Oct. 3, 2008.]

2. Lee Gray was a director, president, and treasurer of HMG/Courtland Properties, Inc. (HMG), a publicly held real estate investment trust, and of its investment adviser Courtland Group, Inc. As such, he negotiated the terms of a joint venture with Norman Fieber, another HMG director, for the development of a portfolio of properties located in the northeastern United States. During the course of the negotiations, Gray told Fieber that Martine Avenue Associates, a general partnership controlled by Gray and his sister, would be interested in co-investing with Fieber as a buyer of an interest in the properties. Neither Gray nor Fieber disclosed that possibility to HMG, but all parties agreed that the negotiated price was fair and reasonable. Martine did ultimately join a group of investors on Fieber's side of the transaction in May 1986, but HMG did not learn of Gray's economic interest in Martine until October 1996. Did either Gray or Fieber violate their fiduciary duties to HMG? [*HMG/Courtland Properties, Inc. v. Gray,* 749 A.2d 94 (Del. Ch. 1999).]

3. In 1997, General Cigar Holdings Inc., a family-owned business since 1906, went public at an offering price of $18 per share of class A stock. The founding Cullman family retained control with super-voting class B shares that were entitled to ten votes per share. Share prices for the class A stock rose as high as $33, but by 1999, they had sunk to $5.

   In 1999, tobacco giant Swedish Match AB offered to discuss acquiring a "significant stake" in General Cigar but indicated that it wanted Edgar Cullman Sr. and Edgar Cullman Jr. to remain in charge. General Cigar's board of directors formed a special committee of independent directors, which hired legal counsel and an investment bank to conduct a fairness review of any resulting offer. Swedish Match proposed a transaction whereby the public shareholders would be cashed out at $15.25 per share, Swedish Match would buy one-third of the Cullman family's equity interest at $15 per share, and General Cigar would be merged into a Swedish Match subsidiary. As a condition to continuing negotiations, Swedish Match required the Cullmans to enter into a lock-up arrangement or stockholders' voting agreement providing that if the proposed merger of Swedish Match and General Cigar failed, the Cullmans would not sell their shares in any other merger and would vote against any other merger for the next eighteen months. What legal and ethical considerations should the Cullmans take into account when deciding whether to sign such an agreement? Would it be enforceable if a higher bidder surfaced later?

   If the Cullmans did sign such an agreement and the independent committee decided in good faith, after informing itself about the value of General Cigar and unsuccessfully seeking higher bidders, that it was in the best interests of the public shareholders to enter into a merger agreement with Swedish Match, what, if any, nonprice terms would you recommend the board insist on including in the merger agreement? Should the General Cigar board agree to recommend the Swedish Match deal, to put it to a vote of the shareholders, or to use best efforts to consummate it? [*Orman v. Cullman,* 2004 Del. Ch. LEXIS 150 (Del. Ch. Oct. 20, 2004).]

4. Missouri Fidelity Union Trust Life Insurance Company stock was trading at $2.63 per share. Eight directors sold their shares for $7.00 per share, conditioned on the resignation of eleven of the fifteen directors of the corporation and the provision that five nominees of the buyer be elected as a majority of the executive and investment committees. Did the directors violate their fiduciary duty? Would the answer be different if the directors had controlled a majority of the voting stock? [*Snyder v. Epstein,* 290 F. Supp. 652 (E.D. Wis. 1968).]

5. The After-School Care Corporation owned more than forty day-care centers specializing in providing care to elementary-school-aged children in the afternoons. The president of the company, Clark Holmes, received a phone call at work one day from Marney Stein, the owner and sole proprietor of Pro Providers, a firm that owned six nursery schools for children aged two to four. Stein indicated that she wanted to sell Pro Providers for $1 million and asked if After-School was interested. Holmes proposed the sale to the After-School board of directors. The directors were divided on the issue because they were not certain whether branching out into nursery care would be a smart move. As funds were not available, however, they saw no need to vote on the issue at that time.

   Holmes decided that he would try to purchase Pro Providers on his own. After securing a loan, Holmes entered into negotiations with Stein. They agreed on a price of $900,000, and the sale went through. Holmes did not inform the board of his activity until after the sale was completed.

   A shareholder is considering suing Holmes for breach of fiduciary duty. Does she have a valid claim? Should it matter whether Holmes plans to expand one of the Pro Provider nursery schools into a nursery/after-school center?

6. The Engulf Corporation is a large media and entertainment conglomerate with its stock trading on the New York Stock Exchange. Engulf is a major producer of films and videos and also publishes several magazines. The company has a shareholder rights plan (that is, a poison pill), which would make any hostile takeover financially prohibitive unless the pill is redeemed by Engulf's board of directors. On January 10, the Megaclout Corporation, in a move designed to gain control of Engulf, announced a tender offer for 51 percent of Engulf's shares at $140, an $11 premium over the market price.

   On January 14, in a meeting that lasted more than thirteen hours, the Engulf board of directors met to consider Megaclout's offer. Engulf's lawyers and investment bankers attended and made detailed presentations on the adequacy of the offer. The next day, the directors officially announced that they believed the Megaclout offer was unacceptable for two reasons: (1) the long-term value of the Engulf stock ranged from $160 to $170, so $140 was financially inadequate; and (2) Engulf had a distinct corporate culture that included special ways of doing business, an outstanding record of management–employee relations, and strong support of community projects in the towns in which Engulf businesses were located. Acceptance of Megaclout's tender offer would pose a direct threat to this corporate culture. For these reasons, the board refused to redeem the poison pill.

Megaclout brought suit as an Engulf shareholder against the Engulf board of directors, demanding that the board redeem the poison pill, which would allow all the shareholders to decide whether they wanted to accept the offer by tendering their shares.

a. Must the Engulf board of directors redeem the poison pill at this time?
b. The board argues that the offer, which is $11 over the market price of the stock, is financially inadequate. Is the argument convincing? Why or why not?
c. Should managers be concerned about corporate constituencies other than shareholders, such as employees or communities in which businesses are located? What if these different concerns conflict?

7. Shlensky was a minority shareholder of Chicago National League Ball Club, Inc., which owned and operated the Chicago Cubs baseball team. The defendants were directors of the club. Shlensky alleged that since night baseball was first played in 1935, every major league team except the Cubs has scheduled most of its home games at night. This has allegedly been done for the specific purpose of maximizing attendance, thereby maximizing revenue and income.

   The Cubs have sustained losses from their direct baseball operations. Shlensky attributed the losses to inadequate attendance at the Cubs' home games, which are played at Wrigley Field. He feels that if the directors continue to refuse to install lights at Wrigley Field and schedule night baseball games, the Cubs will continue to sustain similar losses.

   Shlensky further alleged that Philip Wrigley, the president of the corporation, refused to install lights not, as Wrigley claims, for the welfare of the corporation, but because of his personal opinion that "baseball is a daytime sport." Shlensky charged the other directors with acquiescing in Wrigley's policy.

   In his complaint, Shlensky claimed that the directors were acting for reasons contrary to the business interests of the corporation and wasting corporate assets. Have the directors failed to exercise reasonable care in the management of the corporation's affairs? Does the directors' decision fall within the scope of their business judgment? [*Shlensky v. Wrigley,* 237 N.E.2d 776 (Ill. App. Ct. 1968).]

8. McDonald, a potential buyer of financial institutions, visited Halbert at the Tulane Savings and Loan Association. Halbert was president, manager, and chairman of the board, and, along with his wife, the owner of 53 percent of the stock of the association. McDonald asked if the association was for sale. Halbert replied that it was not for sale but that he and his wife would sell their controlling stock for $1,548 per share. Halbert did not tell the association's board of directors or its shareholders about McDonald's interest in acquiring the association.

   In addition to agreeing to sell his stock, Halbert also agreed to cause the association to withhold the payment of dividends. After Halbert's shares were purchased, Halbert, who had not yet relinquished his corporate offices, helped McDonald solicit the minority shareholders' shares and even advised them that, because McDonald was going to withhold dividends for ten to twenty years, they ought to take his offer of $300 per share. McDonald bought some of the minority shares at $300 and others for between $611 and $650.

   Did Halbert owe the minority shareholders a fiduciary duty? If so, what was his duty in selling his minority stock position? Was his conduct ethical? [*Brown v. Halbert,* 76 Cal. Rptr. 781 (Cal. App. Ct. 1969).]

15

SECURITIES FRAUD AND INSIDER TRADING

INTRODUCTION

Maintaining the Integrity of the Securities Markets

Many attribute the size and success of the U.S. capital markets to the transparency and perceived fairness of the securities markets, which is a direct result of the registration requirements imposed by the Securities Act of 1933 (the 1933 Act), the periodic reporting requirements imposed by the Securities Exchange Act of 1934 (the 1934 Act), and the antifraud provisions in both acts. But as the market turbulence in 2008 demonstrated, investors will abandon the U.S. capital markets if they lose confidence in their fairness or integrity.[1] As the U.S. Supreme Court remarked in *Basic, Inc. v. Levinson*,[2] no one "would knowingly roll the dice in a crooked crap game."

The meltdown in the subprime-mortgage market in 2007 and 2008 (the subject of the "Inside Story" in Chapter 24) spawned numerous investigations by the Securities and Exchange Commission (SEC) and the Financial Industry Regulatory Authority to determine "who knew what when and what did they disclose to the marketplace along the way."[3] Linda Chatman Thomsen, head of the SEC's enforcement division, indicated that "'tone at the top,' ethical culture, call it whatever you want" would be an important factor in the ultimate outcome of the investigations including the decision whether to seek criminal sanctions.[4] Areas of investigation include possible manipulative rumormongering and short selling; insider trading; misrepresentations and omissions in offering circulars, prospectuses, SEC reports, and press releases; and conflicts of interest and breaches of fiduciary duty. Public company shareholders, including retirement funds and other institutional investors, have filed a raft of private suits alleging (1) securities fraud by issuers and their executives for allegedly misleading investors about the health of their firms; (2) misrepresentations by underwriters, including Deutsche Bank Securities and Bear Stearns, in offering documents; and (3) securities fraud and breach of fiduciary duty by credit rating agencies, including Standard & Poor's and Moody's, that allegedly failed to disclose that they had "assigned excessively high ratings to bonds backed by risky subprime mortgages—including bonds packaged as collateralized debt obligations—which was materially misleading to investors concerning the quality and relative risk of these investments."[5]

Each company that takes advantage of the capital markets has a legal and ethical duty to ensure the integrity of those markets. Securities fraud, in any form, erodes investor confidence and makes it more difficult and expensive for honest businesses to raise capital.

The principal antifraud provisions of the federal securities laws are Sections 11 and 12(a)(2) of the 1933 Act, discussed in Chapter 22, and Section 10(b) of the 1934 Act. As explained in Chapter 22, Section 11 applies only to registered offerings, and Section 12(a)(2) applies only to public offerings not exempt from the 1933 Act's registration

1. Joe Nocera, *A Day (Gasp) Like Any Other,* N.Y. TIMES, Oct. 6, 2008.
2. 485 U.S. 224 (1988).
3. Quoting Cheryl Scarboro, associate director of the SEC's division of enforcement. *SEC Pursuing Dozens of Investigations Regarding Subprime Mortgage Industry,* 76 U.S.L.W. 2484, 2485 (2008); *New FINRA Task Force Is Investigating Nine Regulated Firms for Subprime Misdeeds,* 76 U.S.L.W. 2727 (2008).
4. *SEC Pursuing Dozens of Investigations, supra* note 3.
5. *Subprime Mortgage Crisis Generating New Areas of Litigation,* CORP. COUNS. WKLY., Nov. 28, 2007, at 368.

requirements. In contrast, Section 10(b) of the 1934 Act applies to all purchases and sales of securities, regardless of whether they are registered or exempt from registration.

Under Section 10(b) and Rule 10b–5, promulgated by the SEC pursuant to the 1934 Act, it is unlawful for any person to use a fraudulent, manipulative, or deceptive device in connection with the purchase or sale of any security. Rule 10b–5 also prohibits *insider trading,* that is, trading securities based on material nonpublic information in violation of a duty to the corporation or its shareholders or the source of the information. SEC Rules 10b5–1 and 10b5–2, which are excerpted in Appendix I, clarify certain aspects of insider trading.

Section 16(b) of the 1934 Act regulates "short-swing" trading by insiders of publicly traded companies. In particular, it allows a public corporation to recover the profits earned by any officer or director of the corporation or any person who owns more than 10 percent of the corporation's securities as a result of purchases and sales, or sales and purchases, of the corporation's securities within a six-month period.

CHAPTER OVERVIEW

This chapter focuses on Section 10(b) and Rule 10b–5. It sets forth the seven elements necessary in a Rule 10b–5 securities fraud case and the fraud-on-the-market theory of liability. We discuss the safe harbor for certain forward-looking statements as well as Section 17(a) of the 1933 Act, under which the U.S. government can bring fraud claims, and the securities fraud offense added by the Sarbanes–Oxley Act of 2002. We then identify the legal elements of an insider trading case and SEC Regulation FD's ban on selective disclosure. Finally, we explain the rules for calculating the recoverable profits from short-swing trading and outline the requirements for reporting by insiders.

SECTIONS 10(B) AND 20 OF THE 1934 ACT AND RULE 10B–5

Section 10(b) gives the SEC power to prohibit individuals and companies from engaging in securities fraud by authorizing the SEC to prescribe specific rules for the protection of investors. The SEC promulgated Rule 10b–5 to encourage disclosure of information relevant to the investing public, to protect investors, and to deter fraud in the securities industry. *Rule 10b–5* states:

> It shall be unlawful for any person, directly or indirectly, by the use of any means or instrumentality of interstate commerce, or of the mails, or of any facility of any national securities exchange,
>
> (1) to employ any device, scheme, or artifice to defraud,
>
> (2) to make any untrue statement of a material fact or to omit to state a material fact necessary in order to make the statements made, in the light of the circumstances under which they were made, not misleading, or
>
> (3) to engage in any act, practice, or course of business which operates or would operate as a fraud or deceit upon any person, in connection with the purchase or sale of any security.

The SEC has broad power to investigate apparent violations of Rule 10b–5, to order the violator to stop its wrongful conduct, and to recommend criminal prosecution for willful violations.

More suits are brought under Rule 10b–5 than under any other provision of securities law, including those, such as Sections 11 and 12(a)(2) of the 1933 Act, that explicitly create private rights of action. Although there is some overlap, Rule 10b–5 extends to misconduct not covered by other securities laws. Under Rule 10b–5, managers could be liable for misleading statements contained in any document—such as a press release or a letter to shareholders or posting on a website—or even a speech to a trade association, as long as the statements were made in a manner reasonably calculated to influence the investing public.

Since 1946, courts have held that Rule 10b–5 also creates an implicit private right of action, giving individual investors the right to sue a violator for damages. Although the Supreme Court in recent decisions has shown increasing hostility toward implied rights of action under other provisions of the securities laws, Congress "ratified" the implied private right of action for violations of Section 10(b) and Rule 10b–5 in the Private Securities Litigation Reform Act.[6]

AIDING AND ABETTING

In *Central Bank of Denver, N.A. v. First Interstate Bank of Denver, N.A.,*[7] the Supreme Court ruled that a private plaintiff may not maintain an aiding and abetting suit under

6. Stoneridge Inv. Partners, LLC v. Scientific-Atlanta, Inc., 128 S. Ct. 761 (2008) (citing the reference in 15 U.S.C. § 78u-4(b) to "any private action" arising under the 1934 Act).

7. 511 U.S. 164 (1994).

Section 10(b). In that case, the plaintiff had attempted to hold the bank that was the indenture trustee for a municipal bond issue secondarily liable as an aider and abettor of the fraud perpetrated by the issuers of the bonds. In reaching its decision, the Supreme Court noted the vexatious nature of Rule 10b–5 suits and the fact that such suits require secondary actors to expend large sums for pretrial defense and the negotiation of settlements. The Court went on to state:

> This uncertainty and excessive litigation can have ripple effects. For example, newer and smaller companies may find it difficult to obtain advice from professionals. A professional may fear that a newer or smaller company may not survive and that business failure would generate securities litigation against the professional, among others. In addition, the increased costs incurred by professionals because of the litigation and settlement costs under 10b–5 may be passed on to their client companies, and in turn incurred by the company's investors, the intended beneficiaries of the statute.

The SEC can still bring aider-and-abettor cases seeking injunctive relief or damages under Section 10(b). To prove that a person is an *aider and abettor*, it is necessary to show (1) the existence of a primary violation of Section 10(b) or Rule 10b–5, (2) the defendant's knowledge of (or recklessness as to) that primary violation, and (3) substantial assistance of the violation by the defendant.

CONSPIRACY

In *Dinsmore v. Squadron, Ellenoff, Plesent, Sheinfeld & Sorkin*,[8] the U.S. Court of Appeals for the Second Circuit applied *Central Bank*'s reasoning to a claim of conspiracy to fraudulently buy or sell securities and held that there is no implied private cause of action for conspiracy under Section 10(b).

SCHEME LIABILITY

In the following case, the U.S. Supreme Court extended *Central Bank* to bar claims against third parties that engaged in fraudulent business transactions designed to enable the issuer to artificially inflate its earnings (so-called *scheme liability*).

8. 135 F.3d 837 (2d Cir. 1998).

A CASE IN POINT — **IN THE LANGUAGE OF THE COURT**

CASE 23.1

STONERIDGE INVESTMENT PARTNERS, LLC v. SCIENTIFIC-ATLANTA, INC.

SUPREME COURT OF THE UNITED STATES
128 S. CT. 761 (2008).

FACTS Charter Communications, Inc., a cable operator, allegedly engaged in a variety of fraudulent practices so that its quarterly reports would meet Wall Street expectations for cable subscriber growth and operating cash flow. The fraud included misclassification of its customer base, delayed reporting of terminated customers, improper capitalization of costs that should have been shown as expenses, and manipulation of the company's billing cutoff dates to inflate reported revenues. In late 2000, Charter executives realized that, despite these efforts, the company would miss projected operating cash-flow numbers by $15 to $20 million.

To help meet the shortfall, Charter decided to alter its existing arrangements with Scientific-Atlanta and Motorola, which supplied Charter with the digital cable converter (set top) boxes that Charter furnished to its customers. Charter arranged to overpay the two suppliers $20 for each set top box it purchased until the end of the year, with the understanding that they would return the overpayment by purchasing advertising time from Charter at inflated prices. Charter recorded the advertising purchases as revenue and capitalized its purchases of the set top boxes, thereby inflating revenue and operating cash flow by approximately $17 million. The transactions had no economic substance, and Charter's accounting treatment violated generally accepted accounting principles.

To keep Arthur Andersen, Charter's auditor, from discovering the link between Charter's increased payments for the boxes and the advertising purchases, the companies drafted documents to make it appear that the transactions were unrelated and were conducted in the ordinary course of business. In particular, following a request from Charter, Scientific-Atlanta sent documents to Charter stating—falsely—that it faced increased production costs and was increasing the price for set top boxes, by $20 per box, for the rest of 2000. As for Motorola, Charter entered into a written contract whereby it agreed to purchase from Motorola a specific number of set top boxes and to pay liquidated damages

CONTINUED

of $20 for each unit it did not take. The contract was made with the expectation that Charter would fail to purchase all the units and would pay Motorola the liquidated damages.

To return the additional money from the set top box sales, Scientific-Atlanta and Motorola signed contracts with Charter to purchase advertising time for a premium. The new set top box agreements were backdated to make it appear that they were negotiated a month before the adversting agreements. The backdating was important to convey the impression that the negotiations were unconnected, a point Arthur Andersen considered necessary for separate treatment of the transactions. The inflated number was shown on financial statements filed with the SEC and reported to the public.

Scientific-Atlanta and Motorola had no role in preparing or disseminating Charter's financial statements. They booked the transactions as a wash in their own financial statements, in accordance with generally accepted accounting principles. The plaintiff purchasers of Charter stock filed a securities fraud class action under Section 10(b) of the 1934 Act and SEC Rule 10b–5, alleging that the two suppliers knew or were in reckless disregard of Charter's intention to use the transactions to inflate its revenues and knew that the resulting financial statements issued by Charter would be relied upon by research analysts and investors.

The district court dismissed the complaint, for failure to state a claim on which relief could be granted, and the U.S. Court of Appeals for the Eighth Circuit affirmed.

ISSUE PRESENTED Are customer/supplier companies that agreed to arrangements that allowed an issuer to mislead its auditor liable in a private action under Section 10(b) of the 1934 Act?

OPINION KENNEDY, J., writing on behalf of the U.S. Supreme Court:

In this suit investors sought to impose liability on entities who, acting both as customers and suppliers, agreed to arrangements that allowed the investors' company to mislead its auditor and issue a misleading financial statement affecting the stock price. We conclude the implied right of action does not reach the customer/supplier companies because the investors did not rely upon their statements or representations. We affirm the judgment of the Court of Appeals.

I

In *Central Bank*, the Court determined that § 10(b) liability did not extend to aiders and abettors. The Court found the scope of § 10(b) to be delimited by the text, which makes no mention of aiding and abetting liability.

. . . .

The decision in *Central Bank* led to calls for Congress to create an express cause of action for aiding and abetting within the Securities Exchange Act. . . . Congress did not follow this course. Instead, in § 104 of the Private Securities Litigation Reform Act of 1995 (PSLRA)[9] it directed prosecution of aiders and abettors by the SEC.[10]

. . . .

II

. . . .

A

Reliance by the plaintiff upon the defendant's deceptive acts is an essential element of the § 10(b) private cause of action. It ensures that, for liability to arise, the "requisite causal connection between a defendant's misrepresentation and a plaintiff's injury" exists as a predicate for liability. We have found a rebuttable presumption of reliance in two different circumstances. First, if there is an omission of a material fact

CONTINUED

9. 109 Stat. 757.

10. 15 U.S.C. § 78t(e).

by one with a duty to disclose, the investor to whom the duty was owed need not provide specific proof of reliance. Second, under the fraud-on-the-market doctrine, reliance is presumed when the statements at issue become public. The public information is reflected in the market price of the security. Then it can be assumed that an investor who buys or sells stock at the market price relies upon the statement.

Neither presumption applies here. Respondents [Scientific-Atlanta and Motorola] had no duty to disclose; and their deceptive acts were not communicated to the public. No member of the investing public had knowledge, either actual or presumed, of respondents' deceptive acts during the relevant times. Petitioner [the plaintiff investors], as a result, cannot show reliance upon any of respondents' actions except in an indirect chain that we find too remote for liability.

Invoking what some courts call "scheme liability," petitioner nonetheless seeks to impose liability on respondents even absent a public statement. In our view this approach does not answer the objection that petitioner did not in fact rely upon respondents' own deceptive conduct. Liability is appropriate, petitioner contends, because respondents engaged in conduct with the purpose and effect of creating a false appearance of material fact to further a scheme to misrepresent Charter's revenue. The argument is that the financial statement Charter released to the public was a natural and expected consequence of respondents' deceptive acts; had respondents not assisted Charter, Charter's auditor would not have been fooled, and the financial statement would have been a more accurate reflection of Charter's financial condition. That causal link is sufficient, petitioner argues, to apply *Basic*'s presumption of reliance to respondents' acts. In effect petitioner contends that in an efficient market investors rely not only upon the public statements relating to a security but also upon the transactions those statements reflect. Were this concept of reliance to be adopted, the implied cause of action would reach the whole marketplace in which the issuing company does business; and there is no authority for this rule.

. . . .

[W]e conclude respondents' deceptive acts, which were not disclosed to the investing public, are too remote to satisfy the requirement of reliance. It was Charter, not respondents, that misled its auditor and filed fraudulent financial statements; nothing respondents did made it necessary or inevitable for Charter to record the transactions as it did.

The petitioner invokes the private cause of action under § 10(b) and seeks to apply it beyond the securities markets—the realm of financing business—to purchase and supply contracts—the realm of ordinary business operations. The latter realm is governed, for the most part, by state law. It is true that if business operations were used, as alleged here, to affect securities markets, the SEC enforcement power may reach the culpable actors. It is true as well that a dynamic, free economy presupposes a high degree of integrity in all of its parts, an integrity that must be underwritten by rules enforceable in fair, independent, accessible courts. Were the implied cause of action to be extended to the practices described here, however, there would be a risk that the federal power would be used to invite litigation beyond the immediate sphere of securities litigation and in areas already governed by functioning and effective state-law guarantees. Our precedents counsel against the extension.

. . . .

Petitioner's theory, moreover, would put an unsupportable interpretation on Congress' specific response to *Central Bank* in § 104 of the PSLRA. Congress amended the securities laws to provide for limited coverage of aiders and abettors. Aiding and abetting liability is authorized in actions brought by the SEC but not by private parties. See 15 U.S.C. § 78t(e). Petitioner's view of primary liability makes any aider and abettor liable under § 10(b) if he or she committed a deceptive act in the process of providing assistance. Were we to adopt this construction of § 10(b), it would revive in substance the implied cause of action against aiders and abettors except those who committed no deceptive act in the process of facilitating the fraud; and we would undermine Congress' determination that this class of defendants should be pursued by the SEC and not by private litigants.

. . . .

CONTINUED

III

Secondary actors are subject to criminal penalties, and civil enforcement by the SEC. The enforcement power is not toothless. Since September 20, 2002, SEC enforcement actions have collected over $10 billion in disgorgement and penalties, much of it for distribution to injured investors. In addition, some state securities laws permit state authorities to seek fines and restitution from aiders and abettors. See, *e.g.*, Del. Code Ann., Tit. 6, § 7325 (2005). All secondary actors, furthermore, are not necessarily immune from private suit. The securities statutes provide an express private right of action against accountants and underwriters in certain circumstances, and the implied right of action in § 10(b) continues to cover secondary actors who commit primary violations.

Here respondents were acting in concert with Charter in the ordinary course as suppliers and, as matters then evolved in the not so ordinary course, as customers. Unconventional as the arrangement was, it took place in the marketplace for goods and services, not in the investment sphere. Charter was free to do as it chose in preparing its books, conferring with its auditor, and preparing and then issuing its financial statements. In these circumstances the investors cannot be said to have relied upon any of the respondents' deceptive acts in the decision to purchase or sell securities; and as the requisite reliance cannot be shown, respondents have no liability to petitioner under the implied right of action. This conclusion is consistent with the narrow dimensions we must give to a right of action Congress did not authorize when it first enacted the statute and did not expand when it revisited the law.

RESULT The judgment of the court of appeals was affirmed. The Section 10(b) and Rule 10b–5 claims against Scientific-Atlanta and Motorola were subsequently dismissed.[11]

DISSENT STEVENS, J., with whom Souter and Ginsburg, J.J., joined:[12]

The Court's conclusion that no violation of § 10(b) giving rise to a private right of action has been alleged in this case rests on two faulty premises: (1) the Court's overly broad reading of *Central Bank*, and (2) the view that reliance requires a kind of super-causation—a view contrary to both the Securities and Exchange Commission's (SEC) position . . . and our holding in *Basic Inc. v. Levinson.*

I

. . . The Court correctly explains why the statute covers nonverbal as well as verbal deceptive conduct. The allegations in this case—that respondents produced documents falsely claiming costs had risen and signed contracts they knew to be backdated in order to disguise the connection between the increase in costs and the purchase of advertising—plainly describe "deceptive devices" under any standard reading of the phrase.

What the Court fails to recognize is that this case is critically different from *Central Bank* because the bank in that case did not engage in any deceptive act and, therefore, did not itself violate § 10(b). . . . The facts of this case would parallel those of *Central Bank* if respondents had, for example, merely delayed sending invoices for set-top boxes to Charter. Conversely, the facts in *Central Bank* would mirror those in the case before us today if the bank had knowingly purchased real estate in wash transactions at above-market prices in order to facilitate the appraiser's overvaluation of the security. *Central Bank*, thus, poses no obstacle to petitioner's argument that it has alleged a cause of action under § 10(b).

II

The Court's next faulty premise is that petitioner is required to allege that Scientific-Atlanta and Motorola made it "necessary or inevitable for Charter to record the transactions in the way it did" in order to demonstrate reliance. . . . In *Basic Inc.*, we stated that "[r]eliance provides the requisite causal connection between a defendant's misrepresentation and a plaintiff's injury." The Court's view of the causation required to demonstrate reliance is unwarranted and without precedent.

CONTINUED

11. Stoneridge Inv. Partners, LLC v. Scientific-Atlanta, Inc., 519 F.3d 730 (8th Cir. 2008).

12. Justice Breyer took no part in the consideration or decision of this case.

. . . The holding in *Basic* is surely a sufficient response to the argument that a complaint alleging that deceptive acts which had a material effect on the price of a listed stock should be dismissed because the plaintiffs were not subjectively aware of the deception at the time of the securities' purchase or sale.

. . . Reliance is often equated with "transaction causation." Transaction causation, in turn, is often defined as requiring an allegation that but for the deceptive act, the plaintiff would not have entered into the securities transaction. Even if but-for causation, standing alone, is too weak to establish reliance, petitioner has also alleged that respondents proximately caused Charter's misstatement of income; petitioner has alleged that respondents knew their deceptive acts would be the basis for statements that would influence the market price of Charter stock on which shareholders would rely. Thus, respondents' acts had the foreseeable effect of causing petitioner to engage in the relevant securities transactions. . . .

The Court's view of reliance is unduly stringent and unmoored from authority. The Court first says that if the petitioner's concept of reliance is adopted the implied cause of action "would reach the whole marketplace in which the issuing company does business." The answer to that objection is, of course, that liability only attaches when the company doing business with the issuing company has *itself* violated § 10(b). The Court next relies on what it views as a strict division between the "realm of financing business" and the "ordinary business operations." But petitoner's positon does not merge the two: A corporation engaging in a business transaction with a partner who transmits false information to the market is only liable where the corporation *itself* violates § 10(b). Such a rule does not invade the province of "ordinary" business transactions.

. . . .

Finally, the Court relies on the course of action Congress adopted after our decision in *Central Bank* to argue that siding with petitioner on reliance would run contrary to congressional intent. . . . Congress stopped short of undoing *Central Bank* entirely, instead adopting a compromise which restored the authority of the SEC to enforce aiding and abetting liability. . . . That Congress chose not to restore the aiding and abetting liability removed by *Central Bank* does not mean that Congress wanted to exempt from liability the broader range of conduct that today's opinion excludes.

The Court is concerned that such liability would deter overseas firms from doing business in the United States or "shift securities offerings away from domestic capital markets." But liability for those who violate § 10(b) "will not harm American competitiveness; in fact investor faith in the safety and integrity of our markets *is* their strength. The fact that our markets are the safest in the world has helped make them the strongest in the world."

. . . .

. . . Congress enacted § 10(b) with the understanding that federal courts respected the principle that every wrong would have a remedy. Today's decision simply cuts back further on Congress' intended remedy. I respectfully dissent.

Critical Thinking Questions

1. Are there any circumstances under which secondary actors who did not themselves make an actionable omission or representation could still be liable under Section 10(b)?[13]
2. Do strict securities antifraud rules make the U.S. capital markets more or less attractive to foreign investors?

13. *See* James Stengel, Steven Fink & Kristen Fournier, *Stoneridge Investment v. Scientific Atlanta, Inc.*, Lexis Nexis Expert Commentaries (Feb. 2008).

"I got eight to twelve years, which was in line with Wall Street expectations."

› ETHICAL CONSIDERATION

Accountants must sign a written consent before their audited report can be included in a registration statement. Before doing so, they generally conduct an *S–1 review,* which is a review of events subsequent to the date of the certified balance sheet in the registration statement to ascertain whether any material change has occurred in the company's financial position that should be disclosed to prevent the financial statements from being misleading. This review includes comparing recent financial statements to earlier ones, reading minutes of the shareholders' and directors' meetings, and investigating changes in material contracts, bad debts, and newly discovered liabilities.

Suppose that, in the course of the S–1 review, the accountants learn that the company's earnings have dropped dramatically from earnings for the comparable periods included in the registration statement. Should the accountants refuse to sign the consent for inclusion of their opinion on the financial statements for the previous period unless the adverse results are disclosed in the prospectus?

PRIMARY LIABILITY FOR SECONDARY ACTORS

Both the Supreme Court in *Stoneridge* and the Second Circuit in *Dinsmore* took pains to make it clear that secondary actors (such as an accountant, lawyer, or bank) can be liable in private suits if their conduct satisfies the requirements for primary liability. For example, the U.S. Court of Appeals for the Ninth Circuit ruled in *McGann v. Ernst & Young*[14] that an auditor that produced a fraudulent audit report knowing that its client would include the audit opinion in its annual report on Form 10–K filed with the SEC committed fraudulent acts "in connection with" the trading of securities and thus was subject to primary liability under Section 10(b) of the 1934 Act. The court reasoned that *Central Bank* did not undercut *SEC v. Texas Gulf Sulphur Co.*,[15] which stands for the proposition that any false and misleading assertions made "in a manner reasonably calculated to influence the investing public" are made "in connection with" the purchase or sale of securities within the meaning of Section 10(b). Section 10(b) does not limit liability to those who actually trade securities. One who "introduces fraudulent information into the securities market does no less damage to the public because that party did not trade stocks."[16] Therefore, Ernst & Young could be liable for a primary violation of Section 10(b) if the plaintiff could prove that Ernst & Young made a misleading statement in the audit opinion, knowing that the opinion would be included in its client's Form 10–K.

McGann involved an alleged failure to disclose that caused the audit opinion to be false and misleading. Accountants are generally not responsible for misrepresentations or omissions in other parts of a document that they did not certify.[17]

Similarly, the Second Circuit held that a securities broker could be held primarily liable for market manipulation in violation of Section 10(b) and Rule 10b–5 when he followed a stock promoter's directions to execute stock trades designed to create the appearance of an actual market for a company's shares and thereby artificially raise the stock price.[18] The court stated that the broker would be liable if he knew, or was reckless in not knowing, that the trades were manipulative, even if he did not share the promoter's specific overall purpose of manipulating the market for the stock.

LIABILITY OF CONTROLLING PERSONS

Section 20(a) imposes joint and several liability on every person who, directly or indirectly, controls any person liable under the 1934 Act, unless the controlling person acted in good faith and did not directly or indirectly induce the acts constituting the violation. This provision is generally interpreted in the same way as Section 15 of the 1933 Act, which was discussed in Chapter 22.

STATUTE OF LIMITATIONS

Suits under Section 10(b) must be brought within two years after the date the plaintiff discovered the facts constituting the violation or within five years after the violation

14. 102 F.3d 390 (9th Cir. 1996), *cert. denied,* 520 U.S. 1181 (1997).
15. 401 F.2d 833 (2d Cir. 1968) (Case 23.2).
16. *Id.*
17. *See* Shapiro v. Cantor, 123 F.3d 717 (2d Cir. 1997).
18. SEC v. U.S. Envtl., Inc., 155 F.3d 107 (2d Cir. 1998).

occurred, whichever is earlier.[19] The five-year limit has been construed as a statute of repose that "may expire before a plaintiff discovers he has been wronged or even before damages have been suffered at all."[20]

ELEMENTS OF A RULE 10B–5 CAUSE OF ACTION

To recover damages from a defendant under Rule 10b–5, a plaintiff must show each of the following elements:

1. The defendant used either an instrumentality of interstate commerce or the mails or a facility of a national securities exchange.
2. The defendant made a statement that either misrepresented or omitted a fact.
3. The fact was of material importance.
4. The misrepresentation or omission was made with *scienter* (culpable state of mind).
5. The statement or omission was made in connection with the purchase or sale of securities.
6. The plaintiff acted in reliance either on the defendant's misrepresentation or on the assumption that the market price of the stock accurately reflected its value.
7. The defendant's misrepresentation or omission caused the plaintiff to suffer losses.

Each of these seven elements is described in more detail next.

19. 28 U.S.C. § 1658(b).

20. *In re* Exxon Mobil Corp. Sec. Litig., 500 F.3d 189 (3d Cir. 2007).

INTERSTATE COMMERCE

The requirement that the defendant used interstate commerce, the mails, or a national securities exchange gives Congress the power to regulate the defendant's conduct under the Commerce Clause of the U.S. Constitution. The requirement is usually easy to satisfy. Use of interstate commerce includes use of a radio broadcast heard in more than one state; use of a newspaper advertisement in a newspaper delivered to more than one state; or use of a telephone wired for interstate calls, even if no interstate calls were actually made. Use of the mails includes sending a letter within a state because the mail is an instrumentality of interstate commerce. Use of a national securities exchange includes use of any facility of such an exchange.

MISSTATEMENT OR OMISSION

A *misstatement* is a misrepresentation of a fact; in other words, a lie. An *omission* is a fact left out of a statement, such that the statement becomes misleading.

Misstatement

In the following landmark case, a company's attempts to dispel rumors were found to misrepresent the facts.

A CASE IN POINT

CASE 23.2

SEC v. TEXAS GULF SULPHUR CO.

UNITED STATES DISTRICT COURT FOR THE SOUTHERN DISTRICT OF NEW YORK
312 F. SUPP. 77 (S.D.N.Y. 1970), *AFF'D*, 446 F.2D 1301 (2D CIR. 1971), *CERT. DENIED*, 404 U.S. 1005 (1971).

SUMMARY

FACTS Texas Gulf Sulphur Company (TGS) drilled a test hole on November 12, 1963, which indicated the possible presence of copper. TGS did not immediately disclose the results of its drill hole or undertake further drilling because it wanted to acquire property in the surrounding area and did not want to drive up the price of the property.

On April 12, 1964, in response to rumors about the copper discovery, TGS issued a press release. By this time, the company had confirmed the presence of copper. Preliminary tests indicated that the amount was significant. The press release, however, minimized the importance of the discovery. It said (in part):

> For Immediate Release
>
> TEXAS GULF SULPHUR COMMENT ON TIMMINS, ONTARIO, EXPLORATION NEW YORK, April 12—The following statement was made today by Dr. Charles F. Fogarty, executive vice president of Texas Gulf Sulphur Company, in regard to the company's drilling operations near Timmins, Ontario, Canada. Dr. Fogarty said:
>
> During the past few days, the exploration activities of Texas Gulf Sulphur in the area of Timmins, Ontario, have been widely reported in the press, coupled with rumors of a substantial copper

CONTINUED

> discovery there. These reports exaggerate the scale of operations, and mention plans and statistics of size and grade of ore that are without factual basis and have evidently originated by speculation of people not connected with TGS.
>
> The facts are as follows. TGS has been exploring in the Timmins area for six years as part of its overall search in Canada and elsewhere for various minerals—lead, copper, zinc, etc. During the course of this work, in Timmins as well as in Eastern Canada, TGS has conducted exploration entirely on its own, without the participation by others. Numerous prospects have been investigated by geophysical means and a large number of selected ones have been core-drilled. These cores are sent to the United States for assay and detailed examination as a matter of routine and on advice of expert Canadian legal counsel. No inferences as to grade can be drawn from this procedure.
>
> Most of the areas drilled in Eastern Canada have revealed either barren pyrite or graphite without value; a few have resulted in discoveries of small or marginal sulfide ore bodies. Recent drilling on one property near Timmins has led to preliminary indications that more drilling would be required for proper evaluation of this prospect. The drilling done to date has not been conclusive, but the statements made by many outside quarters are unreliable and include information and figures that are not available to TGS.
>
> The work done to date has not been sufficient to reach definite conclusions and any statement as to size and grade of ore would be premature and possibly misleading. When we have progressed to the point where reasonable and logical conclusions can be made, TGS will issue a definite statement to its stockholders and to the public in order to clarify the Timmins project.

The SEC contended that TGS's April 12 release was a misstatement because it left investors with an impression that was contrary to the known facts at the time.

ISSUE PRESENTED Does a press release giving a misleading impression about the results of a drilling operation violate Rule 10b–5?

SUMMARY OF OPINION The U.S. District Court for the Southern District of New York acknowledged that the timing of disclosure is a matter for the business judgment of the corporate officers. When a company chooses to issue a press release to respond to spreading rumors regarding its activities, it must, however, describe the true picture at the time of the press release. This should include the basic facts known, or which reasonably should be known, to the drafters of the press release. Such facts are necessary to enable the investing public to make a reasonable appraisal of the existing situation.

Because the press release misled reasonable investors to believe either that there was no ore discovery or that any discovery was not a significant one, TGS violated Section 10(b) and Rule 10b–5.

RESULT TGS violated Section 10(b) and Rule 10b–5.

COMMENTS A company may have excellent reasons to attempt to dispel rumors. TGS, for example, had an interest in keeping the find quiet in order to keep down the acquisition costs of land. Or consider a company involved in merger negotiations that is asked by the press whether there is any reason for unusual trading in its stock. The company may well want to keep the negotiations under wraps for a variety of legitimate reasons. Yet, if it says that it is unaware of any corporate developments, it runs the risk of Rule 10b–5 liability. The SEC has indicated that it considers such a statement in these circumstances to be a violation of Rule 10b–5. The Supreme Court addressed this issue in *Basic, Inc. v. Levinson,* discussed further below.

A prediction about the future can be a misstatement, but only if the person making the prediction does not believe it at the time. A prediction is not a guarantee, and it does not become a misstatement simply because the facts do not develop as predicted. If there is no reasonable basis for a prediction, however, then it is a misstatement because the person who made it could not honestly have believed it.[21] As discussed later in this chapter, the Private Securities Litigation Reform Act of 1995 (the Litigation Reform Act) contains a safe harbor for certain forward-looking statements.

INTERNATIONAL SNAPSHOT

Under the London Stock Exchange rules, if a listed company's share price moves significantly on the basis of rumor and the rumor is true, the company must disclose the existence of the rumored event. For example, in January 1998, drug powerhouse SmithKline Beecham PLC was required to disclose that it was engaged in merger negotiations with American Home Products after rumors of a deal sent shares of both companies rising.[a] Although there is no numerical threshold for disclosure, a rule of thumb is that a 10 percent move in the stock triggers the duty to disclose the accuracy of truthful rumors. On the other hand, if the rumors are not true, then the company can continue to say "no comment."

a. Steven Lipin & Sara Calian, *Did U.K.'s Strict Rules Spur Deal?*, WALL ST. J., Feb. 2, 1998, at C1.

Omission

It is clear that a company must be careful if it chooses to speak. What if it chooses not to speak?

The general rule is that a company has no general duty under Rule 10b–5 to reveal corporate developments unless the company or its insiders (1) trade in its securities, (2) recommend trading to someone else, or (3) disclose the information as a *tip*—that is, a disclosure made to an individual and withheld from the general public. The fact that information is material does not, in itself, give rise to a duty to disclose.[22]

But the securities laws do require that certain information be disclosed in registration statements; annual, quarterly, and special reports; and proxy solicitations. In particular, Management's Discussion and Analysis of Financial Condition and Results of Operations must disclose any known material event or uncertainty that would cause reported financial information not to be necessarily indicative of future operating results or financial condition.[23] Stock exchange rules require that issuers promptly reveal material developments unless there is a business reason not to do so.

Silence or a "no comment" statement in response to rumors will not lead to liability if the company has not previously spoken on the subject and insiders are not trading or tipping. There is a caveat, however: A policy of not commenting on rumors must be adhered to in the face of both true and untrue rumors. If the company always says "no comment" when the rumor is true but provides facts to dispel untrue rumors, then the "no comment" acts as an admission that the rumor is true.

Although keeping silent may be safer under Rule 10b–5, in many cases that will be hard to do. If a corporation's stock is traded on rumors of some major development, silence may contribute to disorderly market activity, distrust of company management, and possible abuse by those with access to inside information. Moreover, a blanket "no comment" policy makes it impossible to dispel false but damaging rumors.

Once the company has said something about a particular topic, it has a duty to disclose enough relevant facts so that the statement is not inaccurate, incomplete, or misleading.[24] The statement may be an obligatory one. Or the statement may be voluntary; for example, a company may choose to publicize information about favorable new developments or to respond to unfavorable rumors. Whether the statement is obligatory or voluntary, the company's officials must tell the whole truth with respect to that topic or risk being sued later for a misleading omission.

The following case addressed the issue of whether a company has a duty to update or correct statements that have become misleading in light of subsequent events.

21. *See* Va. Bankshares v. Sandberg, 501 U.S. 1083 (1991) (holding that a statement as to beliefs or opinions may be actionable if the opinion is known by the speaker at the time it is expressed to be untrue or to have no reasonable basis in fact).

22. Backman v. Polaroid Corp., 910 F.2d 10 (1st Cir. 1990).

23. *See* Item 303 of SEC Regulation S–K, Management's Discussion and Analysis of Financial Condition and Results of Operations, 17 C.F.R. § 229.303(a)(3)(ii).

24. *See* Dale E. Barnes, Jr. & Constance E. Bagley, *Great Expectations: Risk Management Through Risk Disclosure*, 1 Stan. J.L. Bus. & Fin. 155 (1994).

A CASE IN POINT

IN THE LANGUAGE OF THE COURT

CASE 23.3

WEINER V. QUAKER OATS CO.

UNITED STATES COURT OF APPEALS FOR THE THIRD CIRCUIT
129 F.3D 310 (3D CIR. 1997).

FACTS On November 2, 1994, the Quaker Oats Company and Snapple Beverage Corporation announced that Quaker would acquire Snapple in a tender offer and merger transaction for $1.7 billion in cash. The market disapproved of the deal. Subsequent to the announcement, Quaker's stock price fell $7.375 per share—approximately 10 percent of the stock's value.

To finance the acquisition, Quaker had obtained $2.4 billion of credit from a banking group led by NationsBank Corporation. The Snapple acquisition nearly tripled Quaker's debt, from approximately $1 billion to approximately $2.7 billion. The acquisition also increased Quaker's total debt-to-total capitalization ratio to approximately 80 percent.

Over the course of the year prior to its acquisition of Snapple, Quaker had announced in several public documents the company's guideline for debt-to-equity ratio and its expectations for earnings growth. The announcements formed the basis for the plaintiffs' action.

In its 1993 Annual Report (dated October 4, 1993), Quaker stated that "our debt-to-total capitalization ratio at June 30, 1993 was 59 percent, up from 49 percent in fiscal 1992. For the future, our guideline will be in the upper-60 percent range." Quaker's president reiterated this "guideline" in a letter contained in the same Annual Report. Quaker's Form 10–Q for the quarter ended September 30, 1993 (filed with the SEC in November 1993) repeated the total debt-to-total capitalization ratio guideline.

In its 1994 Annual Report (dated September 23, 1994), Quaker stated that "we are committed to achieving real earnings growth of at least 7 percent over time." In addition, the report noted that Quaker's total debt-to-total capitalization ratio was 68.8 percent, "in line with our guideline in the upper-60 percent range."

Negotiations between Quaker and Snapple apparently began in the spring of 1994. By early August 1994, Quaker had advised Snapple that it was interested in pursuing a merger of the two companies and had commenced a due diligence investigation. As noted, the merger was completed in November of that year.

The gist of the plaintiffs' complaint was that, even if Quaker's announcements about its total debt-to-total capitalization ratio and projected earnings growth were true at the time they were made, Quaker still had a duty to update or correct those statements if it knew they had become materially misleading in light of subsequent events. The plaintiffs alleged that (1) Quaker knew those statements were materially misleading as soon as it was reasonably certain the Snapple merger would be finalized, and (2) Quaker had such certainty at least sometime prior to its formal announcement of the merger on November 2, 1994.

The district court dismissed both portions of the plaintiffs' claim, on the basis that neither Quaker's statements relating to its total debt-to-total capitalization ratio nor its statements relating to its projected earnings growth were material. The plaintiffs appealed.

ISSUE PRESENTED Under what circumstances do a corporation and its officers have a duty to update, or at least not to repeat, particular projections regarding the corporation's financial condition (for example, total debt-to-total capitalization ratio or earnings growth projections)?

OPINION POLLAK, J., writing for the U.S. Court of Appeals for the Third Circuit:

Rule 10b–5, promulgated pursuant to § 10(b) of the [1934] Act, provides the framework for a private cause of action for violations involving false statements or omissions of material fact. To establish a valid claim of securities fraud under Rule 10b–5, plaintiffs must prove that the defendant: (1) made misstatements or omissions of material fact, (2) with *scienter*, (3) in connection with the purchase or sale of securities, (4) upon which plaintiffs relied, and (5) that plaintiffs' reliance was the proximate cause of their injury.

CONTINUED

In the present litigation, the plaintiffs allege that . . . they purchased shares in reliance on statements made by Quaker . . . about (1) Quaker's guideline for the ratio of total debt-to-total capitalization (in the upper 60 percent range) governing the company's financial planning and (2) Quaker's expected earnings growth in fiscal 1995.

The statements about expected earnings growth were made in August and September of 1994 . . . and it is plaintiffs' contention that, at a point when Quaker was in active pursuit of Snapple, Quaker and Smithburg [Quaker's CEO] must have known that the projections were illusory.

Plaintiffs' central complaint with respect to [the statements regarding the guideline for the ratio of total debt-to-total capitalization] is that, when the Snapple negotiations went into high gear, Quaker . . . had to have known that a . . . ratio in the high 60 percent range was no longer a realistic possibility. At that point, plaintiffs contend, defendants had a duty publicly to set the guidelines record straight.

. . . .

A. The Total Debt-to-Total Capitalization Ratio Guideline

. . . .

Plaintiffs' claims under this heading are claims of nondisclosure. "When an allegation of fraud under Section 10(b) is based upon a nondisclosure, there can be no fraud absent a duty to speak." In general, Section 10(b) and Rule 10b–5 do not impose a duty on defendants to correct prior statements—particularly statements of intent—so long as those statements were true when made. However, "[t]here can be no doubt that a duty exists to correct prior statements, if the prior statements were true when made but misleading if left unrevised." To avoid liability in such circumstances, "notice of a change of intent [must] be disseminated in a timely fashion." Whether an amendment is sufficiently prompt is a question that "must be determined in each case based upon the particular facts and circumstances."

. . . .

1. Materiality

. . . .

In *Basic,* the Court adopted in the context of § 10(b) and Rule 10b–5 the standard of materiality set forth in *TSC Industries v. Northway, Inc.,* 426 U.S. 438 (1976). The *Basic* Court approved . . . the principle that "[a]n omitted fact is material if there is a substantial likelihood that a reasonable shareholder would consider it important in deciding how to [proceed]."

. . . .

Therefore, "[o]nly if the alleged misrepresentations or omissions are so obviously unimportant to an investor that reasonable minds cannot differ on the question of materiality is it appropriate for the district court to rule that the allegations are inactionable as a matter of law."

. . . .

In sum, in the present case, we find that a trier of fact could conclude that a reasonable investor reading the 1993 Annual Report published on October 4, 1993, and then the 1994 Annual Report published on September 23, 1994, would have no ground for anticipating that the total debt-to-total capitalization ratio would rise as significantly as it did in fiscal 1995. There was after all no abjuration of the "upper 60-percent range" guideline. The company had predicted the rise from 59 percent to the "upper 60-percent range" in the 1993 report and that rise had occurred by and was confirmed in the 1994 report. Therefore, it was reasonable for an investor to expect that the company would make another such prediction if it expected the ratio to change markedly in the ensuing year.

. . . .

CONTINUED

B. Earnings Growth Projections

. . . .

Quaker's 1994 Annual Report—issued on September 23, 1994, more than five weeks prior to the November 2 merger announcement—contained the statement that "we are committed to achieving a real earnings growth of at least 7 percent over time." We conclude that the phrase "over time" in this second statement inoculates Quaker from any claims of fraud that point to a decline in earnings growth in the immediate aftermath of the Snapple acquisition. No reasonably careful investor would find material a prediction of seven-percent growth followed by the qualifier "over time." Therefore, we hold that no reasonable finder of fact could conclude that the projection influenced prudent investors.

RESULT The claim relating to Quaker's total debt-to-total capitalization ratio guideline was reinstated and remanded to the district court; the dismissal of the claim relating to Quaker's earnings growth projections was affirmed.

CRITICAL THINKING QUESTIONS

1. Given that a wealth of data compiled by market analysts demonstrates that, over the long run, stock prices follow corporate earnings, which piece of information would you find more important when deciding whether to buy or sell Quaker stock: (a) forecasts relating to the company's total debt-to-total capitalization ratio, or (b) forecasts relating to the company's real earnings growth?
2. Would an announcement by Quaker that it was contemplating increasing its total debt-to-total capitalization ratio have "tipped the market" to a pending acquisition?

An omission can occur when a company makes a statement that was true at the time it was made but becomes misleading in light of later events. There is a duty to correct when "a company makes a historical statement [of a material fact] that at the time made, the company believed to be true, but as revealed by subsequently discovered information actually was not."[25] In contrast, the duty to update—which may arise when a statement, reasonable at the time it is made, becomes misleading due to a subsequent event—is more limited.[26] There is no duty to update if the original statement was not material,[27] or "when the original statement was not forward looking and does not contain some factual representation that remains 'alive' in the minds of investors as a continuing representation."[28] On the other hand, if investors are reasonably relying on the previous statements, the company can be held liable for failing to disclose the new information. For example, a company incurs a duty to update its financial projections when a projection changes or the company discovers that the projection was incorrect from the outset.

There is a duty to disclose the results of product safety tests, if they make previously disclosed test results false. For example, A.H. Robins Company, a pharmaceutical manufacturer, reported in 1970 that its Dalkon Shield intrauterine contraceptive device was safe and effective. In 1972, internal studies indicated that the Dalkon Shield was not as safe or effective as originally reported.[29] The U.S. Court of Appeals for the Second Circuit held that Robins's omission of the new information rendered its earlier statements misleading. Because investors were still relying on the statement that the Dalkon Shield was safe, the company had a duty to correct that statement once it learned that it was inaccurate.

25. Stransby v. Cummins Engine Co., 51 F.3d 1329 (7th Cir. 1995).

26. *See, e.g., In re* Time Warner, Inc. Sec. Litig., 9 F.3d 259 (2d Cir. 1993).

27. Hillson Partners Ltd. P'ship v. Adage, Inc., 42 F.3d 204 (4th Cir. 1994).

28. *In re* Int'l Bus. Machs. Corp. Sec. Litig., 163 F.3d 102 (2d Cir. 1998). *See also In re* Burlington Coat Factory Sec. Litig., 114 F.3d 1410 (3d Cir. 1997).

29. Ross v. A.H. Robins Co., 607 F.2d 545 (2d Cir. 1979), *cert. denied,* 446 U.S. 946 (1980).

In contrast, in *Oran v. Stafford,*[30] the U.S. Court of Appeals for the Third Circuit held that reports that the diet pill combination fen-phen (made by American Home Products Corporation) caused heart-valve abnormalities were not material because they did not definitively establish a link between the two drugs and heart-valve disorders. As a result, AHP's failure to disclose this information did not render its statements about the inconclusiveness of the relationship materially misleading. The fact that there was no adverse effect on AHP's stock price when the data were eventually released was further evidence of nonmateriality.

In *Dura Pharmaceuticals, Inc. v. Broudo,*[31] the U.S. Supreme Court ruled that allegedly false and misleading statements about Dura Pharmaceuticals' Albuterol Spiros asthma medication delivery device could not have caused the plaintiff investor's loss because the market price of the stock did not decline after the corrective disclosure was made. As a result, the plaintiff failed to prove loss causation. The court rejected the Ninth Circuit's assertion that loss causation "merely requires pleading that the price at the time of purchase was overstated and sufficient identification of the cause."

Statements by Third Parties and Entanglement

Even if the company itself did not publish the misleading projection, make the statement, or start the rumor, it may nevertheless have a duty to reveal all of the facts regarding the issue. This is the case when the company is so entangled with the third party's statement that the statement can be attributed to the company. The company is then responsible for making sure that the statement is accurate. For example, if a company makes it a practice to review and correct drafts of analysts' forecasts, then the company implicitly represents that the corrected forecast is in accord with the company's view, and it has a duty to reveal all facts necessary to ensure that the analyst's report is not misleading.[32] Similarly, a company's distribution of copies of an analyst's report to investors or other members of the public or the posting of an analyst's report on the company's website may be construed as an implied representation that the information in the report is accurate or reflects the company's views.

30. 226 F.3d 275 (3d Cir. 2000).

31. 544 U.S. 336 (2005).

32. *See, e.g.,* Stack v. Lobo, 903 F. Supp. 1361 (N.D. Cal. 1995).

MATERIAL FACT

A buyer or seller of stock cannot recover damages just because an executive misrepresented or omitted a fact about the company. The fact must be material. As explained in Chapter 22, a fact is material if a reasonable investor would consider it important in deciding how to act. Materiality is judged at the time of the misstatement or omission. Materiality is not affected by the intent of the party making the statement. There can be liability even if the manager did not know that the omitted or misrepresented fact came within the legal definition of a material fact.

Although it is not always possible to predict which facts a court will consider material, certain matters are almost always considered material. For example, any statements about the earnings, distributions, or assets of a company (unless the misrepresentation is inadvertent and concerns a minor amount) are material. In August 1999, the SEC accounting staff cautioned companies and their auditors against using "rules of thumb" to determine whether errors in the financial statements are material.[33] Even if two errors net out to zero, they can still be material. For example, an overstatement of revenues can be material even if it is accompanied by an overstatement of cost of goods sold. The SEC staff also stated that any intentional misstatement of a number in the financial statements is, by definition, material.

Significant facts about a parent or a subsidiary are usually material. These include the discovery of embezzlement or falsification of financial statements, an impending tender offer, or the loss of a manufacturer's major customer. Other facts that are probably material include inability to obtain supplies, increased costs of supplies, a decision to close a plant, information regarding the outlook in the industry, an intention to market a new product or cease marketing an old one, potential liability for damages in a lawsuit, a major discovery or product development, cost overruns, a change in management or compensation of corporate officers, and an increase in real estate taxes. As this list illustrates, a material fact is any fact that is likely to affect the market value of the company's stock.

The Supreme Court has recognized that for contingent or speculative events, such as negotiations regarding a potential merger, it can be difficult to tell whether a reasonable investor would consider the omitted fact material at the time. The Court has declined to adopt a bright-line rule,

33. Staff Accounting Bulletin No. 99, 1999 WL 1123073 (SEC Aug. 12, 1999).

however; materiality is a fact-specific determination.[34] If a misstatement or omission concerns a future event, such as a potential merger, its materiality will depend upon a balancing of the probability that the event will occur and the anticipated magnitude of the event in light of the totality of the company's activity.

Thus, the materiality of preliminary merger discussions in any particular case depends on the facts. Generally, to assess the probability that the event will occur, a fact finder will look to indicia of interest in the transaction at the highest corporate levels. Without attempting to catalog all such possible factors, the Court has noted by way of example that board resolutions, instructions to investment bankers, and actual negotiations between principals or other intermediaries may serve as indicia of interest.[35] To assess the magnitude of the transaction to the issuer of the securities allegedly manipulated, a fact finder will consider such facts as the size of the two corporate entities and of the potential premiums over market value. No particular event or factor short of closing the transaction is either necessary or sufficient by itself to render merger discussions material.

Vague statements of corporate optimism that are not capable of objective verification and mere puffing are immaterial as a matter of law because reasonable investors would not rely on them in making investment decisions.[36] For example, the U.S. Court of Appeals for the Second Circuit characterized a statement made on October 15, 1992, by Jim Clippard, the director of investor relations of International Business Machines Corporation (IBM), that "we're not—despite your anxiety—concerned about being able to cover the dividend for quite a foreseeable time" as an immaterial expression of optimism, not a guarantee, because he qualified it by noting that "this is a relatively short-term period of economic difficulty we're going through. And we think that we can ride through this with no problem [whatsoever] as far as [the] dividend is concerned."[37] The court held that there was no duty to *correct* the statement when the CFO concluded in late November 1992 that the dividend was likely to be cut because, at the time the statement was made (October 15, 1992), IBM did not have a plan or need to alter the dividend. The court also held that "there is no duty to *update* vague statements of optimism or expressions of opinion." (Emphasis added.) In another case, however, a prediction that the company "expects . . . a net income of approximately $1.00 a share" for the fiscal year that would close in two months was held to be a material statement.[38]

> **ETHICAL CONSIDERATION**
>
> Managers of companies frequently act as promoters, describing the company's products to the press and the public in an aggressive, upbeat manner. It is reasonable to expect them to engage in a certain amount of puffing and exaggeration. Are these exaggerations ethically justifiable as long as they do not violate the securities laws?

Bespeaks Caution Doctrine

As explained in Chapter 22, under the judicially developed *bespeaks caution doctrine,* a court may determine that the inclusion of sufficient cautionary statements in a document renders immaterial any misrepresentation and omission contained therein. The doctrine applies only to projections, estimates, and other forward-looking statements that are accompanied by precise cautionary language that adequately discloses the risks involved. The cautionary language must relate to the specific information that the plaintiffs allege is misleading[39] and reflect what the speaker knows or strongly suspects. As one judge commented, "The doctrine of bespeaks caution provides no protection to someone who warns his hiking companion to walk slowly because there might be a ditch ahead when he knows with near certainty that the Grand Canyon lies one foot away."[40]

Unlike the safe harbor provided in the Litigation Reform Act, the bespeaks caution doctrine applies to forward-looking statements in any context, including initial public offerings. The legislative history of the Litigation Reform Act makes it clear that Congress did not intend its statutory safe-harbor provisions to replace the judicial bespeaks

34. Basic, Inc. v. Levinson, 485 U.S. 224 (1988).

35. *Id.*

36. *See, e.g.,* Raab v. Gen. Physics Corp., 4 F.3d 286 (4th Cir. 1993) (holding that statements in annual report that company expected 10 to 30 percent growth rate over the next several years and was "poised to carry the growth and success of 1991 well into the future" were immaterial puffing); San Leandro Emergency Med. Group Profit Sharing Plan v. Philip Morris Cos., 75 F.3d 801 (2d Cir. 1996) (holding that statement that company was "optimistic" about its earnings in 1993 and that it should deliver income growth consistent with its historically superior performance was mere puffery and lacked the sort of definite positive projections that might require later correction).

37. *In re* Int'l Bus. Machs. Corp. Sec. Litig., 163 F.3d 102 (2d Cir. 1998).

38. Marx v. Computer Scis. Corp., 507 F.2d 485 (9th Cir. 1974).

39. *See, e.g.,* Grossman v. Novell, Inc., 120 F.3d 1112 (10th Cir. 1997).

40. *In re* Prudential Sec., Inc. P'ships Litig., 930 F. Supp. 68, 72 (S.D.N.Y. 1996).

caution doctrine or to foreclose further development of that doctrine by the courts.

SCIENTER

Rule 10b–5 does not impose liability for innocent misstatements or omissions. The misstatements or omissions must be made with scienter, that is, a mental state embracing the intent to deceive, manipulate, or defraud. Intent to deceive means that the defendant says something he or she believes is untrue with the expectation that others will rely on the statement, or that the defendant omits a fact in the hope that the omission will cause others to misunderstand what he or she does say. Scienter is more than mere negligence or lack of care.

The Litigation Reform Act requires the plaintiff to plead with particularity specific facts giving rise to a "strong inference" that the defendant acted with scienter. The Supreme Court clarified this pleading requirement in the following case.

A CASE IN POINT

SUMMARY

CASE 23.4

Tellabs, Inc. v. Makor Issues & Rights

Supreme Court of the United States
127 S. Ct. 1511 (2007).

FACTS After Tellabs, Inc., a fiber optics equipment manufacturer, announced that demand for its TITAN 5500 and TITAN 6500 switching systems had declined and lowered its revenue forecasts, its stock price dropped sharply. The plaintiffs sued, alleging that Tellabs's CEO had misled investors when he misrepresented that demand for its products was strong. The CEO did not sell any Tellabs's securities during the period in question. The district court dismissed the complaint, which contained allegations from twenty-seven anonymous sources. The U.S. Court of Appeals for the Seventh Circuit reversed after concluding that the complaint was sufficient to create a strong inference of scienter because a reasonable person could infer scienter from the facts alleged. Tellabs appealed.

ISSUE PRESENTED What must a plaintiff allege to meet the heightened pleading standards for scienter under the Litigation Reform Act? Can fraud be pleaded with sufficient particularity if the plaintiff relies on unnamed confidential sources?

SUMMARY OF OPINION The U.S. Supreme Court acknowledged that Congress did not clearly define what was required to create a "strong inference" of scienter, but reasoned that the phrase should be interpreted in a workable manner that would promote the Reform Act's goal of deterring "frivolous, lawyer-driven litigation, while preserving investors' ability to recover on meritorious claims." After analyzing the ordinary meaning of the word "strong," the Court concluded that a strong inference must be more than merely "reasonable" or "permissible." It has to be "powerful," "cogent and compelling." Thus, a complaint will survive a motion to dismiss "only if a reasonable person would deem the inference of scienter cogent and at least as compelling as any opposing inference one could draw from the facts alleged." The Court made it clear that no single factor is determinative and rejected the defendant CEO's assertion that he could not have had scienter because he sold no stock during the period of alleged fraud. Instead, the significance to be ascribed to the lack of sales, or any other single fact, "depends on the entirety of the complaint."

RESULT The Seventh Circuit's ruling was vacated and the case remanded to the appeals court to determine whether the complaint satisfied the stricter pleading standards set forth by the Supreme Court. If it did not, then the case would be dismissed.

COMMENTS On remand, the Seventh Circuit adhered to its earlier finding that the plaintiffs had adequately pleaded a strong inference of scienter.[41] In an opinion by Judge Richard Posner, the court concluded that it is "conceivable, yes, but it is exceedingly unlikely" that the false statements "were the result of merely careless mistakes at the management level based

CONTINUED

41. Makor Issues & Rights Ltd. v. Tellabs Inc., 513 F.3d 702 (7th Cir. 2008).

on false information fed it from below, rather than of an intent to deceive or a reckless indifference to whether the statements were misleading." The court noted that the TITAN 5500 and 6500 were the company's key products, that they "were to Tellabs as Windows XP and Vista are to Microsoft." Moreover, almost all the false statements quoted in the complaint were made by the CEO, who sat at the "top of the corporate pyramid." The court found it "very hard to credit" the defendants' claim that no member of senior management involved in authorizing "the public statements knew they were false" and stated that the defendants had failed to tell a "plausible story" that might "dispel our incredulity."

In *Higginbotham v. Baxter International Inc.*,[42] the U.S. Court of Appeals for the Seventh Circuit ruled that information from anonymous sources must be discounted when considering whether there are plausible competing inferences: "Perhaps these confidential sources have axes to grind. Perhaps they are lying. Perhaps they don't even exist." Although such statements are not to be ignored, usually the discount will be "steep."[43] In *South Ferry LP #2 v. Killinger*,[44] the U.S. Court of Appeals for the Ninth Circuit held that an allegation that key officials know facts critical to the company's "core operations" is "usually," but not always, insufficient in and of itself to create a strong inference of scienter.

Recklessness

The U.S. Supreme Court acknowledged in *Tellabs* that there is a split in the circuits on whether recklessness is sufficient for a finding of scienter, but it declined to resolve the issue. On remand, the Seventh Circuit equated scienter with intent to deceive or recklessness. The U.S. Court of Appeals for the Second Circuit has also made clear its view that recklessness continues to be sufficient for a showing of scienter.[45] It defined reckless conduct as

> conduct which is "highly unreasonable" and which represents "an extreme departure from the standards of ordinary care . . . to the extent that the danger was either known to the defendant or so obvious that the defendant must have been aware of it." . . . "[A]n egregious refusal to see the obvious, or to investigate the doubtful, may in some cases give rise to an inference of . . . recklessness."
>
> . . . .
>
> . . . [S]ecurities fraud claims typically have sufficed to state a claim based on recklessness when they have specifically alleged defendants' knowledge of facts or access to information contradicting their public statements. . . .
>
> Under certain circumstances, we have found allegations of recklessness to be sufficient where plaintiffs alleged facts demonstrating that defendants failed to review or check information that they had a duty to monitor, or ignored obvious signs of fraud. . . .
>
> At the same time, however, we have identified several important limitations on the scope of liability for securities fraud based on reckless conduct. First, we have refused to allow plaintiffs to proceed with allegations of "fraud by hindsight." . . . Corporate officials need not be clairvoyant; they are only responsible for revealing those material facts reasonably available to them. . . .
>
> Second, as long as the public statements are consistent with reasonably available data, corporate officials need not present an overly gloomy or cautious picture of current performance and future prospects. . . .
>
> Third, there are limits to the scope of liability for failure adequately to monitor the allegedly fraudulent behavior of others.[46]

The U.S. Court of Appeals for the Ninth Circuit reached a contrary conclusion in a case involving Silicon Graphics[47] and held that the Litigation Reform Act precludes liability under Section 10(b) for mere recklessness. Instead, a "heightened form of recklessness, i.e., deliberate or conscious

42. 495 F.3d 753 (7th Cir. 2007).

43. *Id.*

44. 2008 WL 4138237 (9th Cir. Sept. 9, 2008).

45. Kasaks v. Novak, 216 F.3d 300 (2d Cir. 2000).

46. *Cf. In re* Comshare, Inc. Sec. Litig., 183 F.3d 542 (6th Cir. 1999) (holding that allegations giving rise to a strong inference of recklessness are sufficient to pass muster but that facts showing a mere motive and opportunity to commit fraud are not). *Accord* Greebel v. FTP Software, Inc., 194 F.3d 185 (1st Cir. 1999) (holding that the Litigation Reform Act did not alter preexisting scienter requirements for securities fraud cases).

47. *In re* Silicon Graphics, Inc. Sec. Litig., 183 F.3d 970 (9th Cir. 1999).

recklessness, at a minimum, is required to establish a strong inference of intent."

To avoid liability, officers should investigate what the facts are before making any statement. Managers should make no statement unless they in good faith believe it to be true. The investigation must be fairly thorough. At least in the Second Circuit, an officer may be liable for misrepresenting facts that he or she should have been aware of, even if the officer was not in fact aware of them. For example, directors may be deemed to have knowledge of facts in the corporate books regardless of whether they have actually examined the books.

These tough pleading requirements make it more important than ever for insiders to avoid trading while in possession of material nonpublic information. Plaintiffs can be expected to claim that insiders who sold before the announcement of bad news knew of the impending negative developments and sold their stock while the market price was artificially high, thereby "cashing in" on their alleged misrepresentations and omissions.[48] This arguably creates an inference of fraud.

For example, the U.S. Court of Appeals for the Ninth Circuit characterized Oracle CEO Larry Ellison's sale of $900,000 of Oracle stock approximately one month prior to the announcement of lower-than-expected sales as "suspicious" and ruled that the unusual stock sales supported a strong inference of scienter.[49] Ellison had not sold any Oracle stock in the previous five years. Although Ellison sold only 2.1 percent of his Oracle stock, the court reasoned that "where, as here, stock sales result in a truly astronomical figure, less weight should be given to the fact that they may represent a small portion of the defendant's holdings." Although the sales, taken alone, may not have created a strong inference of scienter, when they were coupled with (1) evidence that Oracle maintained an internal database of sales that was monitored by top executives, (2) Oracle customers' billing and payment histories that were corroborated by a former Oracle senior manager and showed improper revenue accounting, and (3) the Oracle executives' detail-oriented management style, the plaintiffs had made allegations that in their totality created a strong inference that Oracle and its top three executives acted with scienter. Characterizing this as "far from a cookie-cutter complaint," the court concluded by stating: "The PSLRA was designed to eliminate frivolous or sham actions, but not actions of substance."

48. *See* Dale E. Barnes, Jr. & Karen Kennard, *Greater Expectations: Risk Disclosure Under the Private Securities Litigation Reform Act of 1995—An Update,* 2 STAN. J.L. BUS. & FIN. 331, 347–48 (1996).

49. Nursing Home Pension Fund v. Oracle Corp., 380 F.3d 1226 (9th Cir. 2004).

It is not yet clear how the U.S. Supreme Court will rule on this issue. Until there is a definitive ruling, managers and companies are well advised to assume that insider trading shortly before the announcement of bad news can create an inference of fraud sufficient to satisfy the Litigation Reform Act's pleading requirements.

IN CONNECTION WITH THE PURCHASE OR SALE OF ANY SECURITY

Rule 10b–5 requires that the conduct occur "in connection with the purchase or sale of any security." This requirement defines both those who can sue and those who can be sued under Rule 10b–5.

The U.S. Supreme Court has made it clear that only persons who actually purchase or sell securities can sue under Rule 10b–5. Persons who have not purchased (or sold) cannot sue on the theory that they would have purchased (or sold) had they known the true facts. Thus, liability under Rule 10b–5 does not extend to the whole world of potential investors but only to those who actually buy or sell stock after a misstatement or omission.

Certain states permit suits under their blue sky laws by investors who allege that they did not sell their securities because of the defendants' fraud (*holder claims*). The Supreme Court, however, ruled that the Securities Litigation Uniform Standards Act of 1998 bars all state securities fraud class actions, including holder claims.[50] As a result, plaintiffs cannot bring holder claims as a class action in state court. They cannot be brought in federal court either because the plaintiffs did not purchase or sell securities based on the fraud.

Parties that can be sued under Rule 10b–5 are those that make or are responsible for misstatements or omissions in connection with the purchase or sale of securities. Statements are made "in connection with" the purchase or sale of securities if they were made in a manner reasonably calculated to influence the investing public or if they were of the sort upon which the investing public might reasonably rely.

For example, the U.S. Court of Appeals for the Third Circuit held that fraudulent financial statements issued by Cendant during the course of its tender offer for American Bankers Insurance Group (ABI) were misrepresentations made "in connection with" the plaintiffs' purchase of ABI shares during Cendant's tender offer even though the plaintiffs had neither purchased any Cendant shares nor tendered shares of ABI stock to Cendant.[51] The plaintiffs had alleged that Cendant's misrepresentations artificially inflated the

50. Merrill Lynch, Pierce, Fenner & Smith Inc. v. Dabit, 547 U.S. 71 (2006).

51. Semerenko v. Cendant Corp., 223 F.3d 165 (3d Cir. 2000).

price at which they purchased their ABI shares, and that they suffered a loss when those misrepresentations were disclosed to the public and the merger agreement between Cendant and ABI was terminated.

In summary, a company must be careful to monitor its public statements, such as those made in periodic reports, press releases, proxy solicitations, and annual reports, and on the company's website. Even when addressing non-investors, such as creditors or labor union representatives, a manager should exercise caution if the statements can reasonably be expected to reach investors.

RELIANCE

To establish liability under Rule 10b–5, investors must show that they relied either directly or indirectly on the misrepresentation or omission. If the investors did not rely on the misstatement or omission in deciding to buy or sell stock, then any loss they incurred cannot be blamed on the person that made the misrepresentation or omission.

Direct Reliance

A plaintiff may show reliance by showing that he or she actually read the document, such as a press release or prospectus, that contained the misstatement. In the case of an omission, the U.S. Supreme Court has ruled that the plaintiff will be presumed to have relied on the omission if it was material. That presumption of reliance can be rebutted—that is, shown to be not true—by a showing that the plaintiff would have bought (or sold) the stock even if the omitted fact had been included.

In the following case, the seller of stock in a private placement sought to avoid liability for allegedly deceptive oral statements and omissions based on a nonreliance clause in the stock purchase contract.

A CASE IN POINT

CASE 23.5

EMERGENT CAPITAL INVESTMENT MANAGEMENT, LLC v. STONEPATH GROUP, INC.

UNITED STATES COURT OF APPEALS FOR THE SECOND CIRCUIT
343 F.3D 189 (2D CIR. 2003).

SUMMARY

FACTS Emergent Capital Investment Management, LLC invested $2 million in Net Value Holdings, Inc. (NETV), now Stonepath Group, Inc. The investment arose out of a meeting set up by Lee Hansen, director and president of NETV and the former roommate and personal friend of Mark Waldron. Mark Waldron and Daniel Yun, the managing members of Emergent, owned 90 percent of Emergent's stock. Andrew Panzo, the chair and CEO of NETV, had a long history of collaborating with Howard Appel, who had been barred for life by the National Association of Securities Dealers from associating with any member of that organization in any capacity. In the negotiations leading up to the purchase, NETV executives represented, orally and in a brochure, that NETV's largest investment was a $14 million purchase of a 12 percent equity interest in Brightstreet.com. In fact, the Brightstreet.com investment amounted to only $4 million. NETV never mentioned any connection to Appel, who allegedly played a significant role in NETV's founding, financing, and control.

Emergent and NETV executed a stock purchase agreement, in which NETV made extensive warranties and representations regarding its capital structure, indebtedness, involvement in litigation, ownership and leases of real and personal property, and other matters connected with its business. Further, the agreement contained a passage stating that the agreement and accompanying documents "contained the entire understanding and agreement among the parties . . . and superseded any prior understandings or agreements" between or among any of them.

Appel and Panzo apparently engaged in a number of investment schemes whereby Appel would acquire control of a public shell corporation and subsequently install Panzo as a director or senior officer. The company would transfer substantial quantities of stock to affiliates of Appel and Panzo, and the two men would, "through extraordinarily complex corporate legal maneuvers," end up with large amounts of stock. They would then sell the stock at a high price, leaving behind a virtually worthless company.

Between January and March 2000, the price of NETV's stock hovered between $10 and $30 per share. The stock subsequently fell to less than $1 per share. As the stock fell, Emergent demanded

CONTINUED

rescission of the agreement. NETV refused, prompting Emergent to sue for securities fraud under Rule 10b–5. Emergent alleged that NETV had misrepresented the size of the Brightstreet.com investment and had failed to disclose the company's connection to Appel.

ISSUE PRESENTED Does a nonreliance clause in a stock purchase agreement preclude liability in cases of misrepresentations or omissions?

SUMMARY OF OPINION The U.S. Court of Appeals for the Second Circuit first laid out the substantive law, explaining that plaintiffs in such an action must establish reasonable reliance on the alleged misrepresentations or omissions. The reasonableness of the reliance is judged in light of the entire context of the transaction, including factors such as its complexity and magnitude, the sophistication of the parties, and the content of any agreements between them.

As for the misrepresentation of the Brightstreet.com investment, the court noted that the plaintiff had secured from the defendants extensive contractual representations concerning NETV's financial condition and operations. Because Emergent was a sophisticated investor, it should have protected itself by insisting that the representation regarding the Brightstreet.com investment be included in the stock-purchase agreement. The court ruled that Emergent's failure to require such a representation in the agreement precluded a finding of reasonable reliance on the misrepresentation.

Unlike the affirmative misrepresentation, the omission of Panzo's investment history and NETV's ties to Appel was not known by Emergent. As a result, Emergent could not have protected itself against them in the agreement. The court held that the plaintiff had sufficiently alleged that, but for the omission, the purchase would not have taken place. Further, the court found that the plaintiff had sufficiently asserted that Emergent's loss was a foreseeable consequence of the defendants' omissions, particularly in light of the drastic price declines that occurred in the shares of the other companies controlled by Panzo and Appel.

RESULT The dismissal of Emergent's claim regarding the misstatement of the value of the Brightstreet.com investment was affirmed, but the dismissal of Emergent's claim regarding Panzo's investment history and NETV's connection to Appel was vacated. Emergent could pursue the latter claim.

COMMENTS Given the "sophistication of the parties," the Second Circuit expected the buyer to include every material fact in the purchase agreement. In effect, the court reasoned that if a statement was important enough to be relied upon by a sophisticated investor, then it should have been included in the agreement.

The Seventh Circuit reached a similar result in *Rissman v. Rissman.*[52] As Judge Easterbrook noted, "Prudent people protect themselves against the limitations of memory (and the temptation to shade the truth) by limiting their dealings to those memorialized in writing, and promoting the primacy of the written word is a principal function of the federal securities laws." The court also rejected the argument that the no-reliance clause should be ignored as mere "boilerplate." Judge Easterbrook explained that "the fact that language has been used before does not make it less binding when used again. Phrases become boilerplate when many parties find that the language serves their ends. That's a reason to enforce the promises, not to disregard them."

---

52. 213 F.3d 381 (7th Cir. 2000).

Fraud on the Market

In the securities market, direct reliance is rare because transactions usually are not conducted on a face-to-face basis. The market is interposed between the parties, providing important information to them in the form of the market price. As the U.S. District Court for the Northern District of Texas said in the *LTV Securities Litigation*: "The market is acting as the unpaid agent of the investor, informing him that, given all the information available to it, the value of the stock is worth the market price."

The theory underlying this view is known to economists as the *efficient-market theory.* It holds that in an open and developed securities market, the price of a company's stock equals its true value. The market is said to evaluate information efficiently and to incorporate it into the price of a company's securities.

Against this background, the courts have approved the *fraud-on-the-market theory:* If the information available to the market is incorrect, then the market price will not reflect the true value of the stock. Under this theory, an investor who purchases or sells a security is presumed to have relied on the market, which has in turn relied on the misstatement or omission when it set the price of the security.

The Supreme Court affirmed this theory in *Basic, Inc. v. Levinson*: "It is hard to imagine that there ever is a buyer or seller who does not rely on market integrity. Who would knowingly roll the dice in a crooked crap game?"[53]

Thus, plaintiffs do not have to show that they read or heard a defendant's misstatement in order to recover damages from that defendant. Instead, reliance is presumed if the investor shows that (1) the defendant made a public material misrepresentation that would have caused reasonable investors to misjudge the value of the defendant's stock and (2) the investor traded shares of the defendant's stock in an open securities market after the misrepresentations were made and before the truth was revealed.

A defendant can rebut the fraud-on-the-market presumption by showing that the plaintiff traded or would have traded despite knowing the statement was false. For example, an insider who is aware of nonpublic information that results in the stock being undervalued, but who sells for other reasons, cannot be said to have relied on the integrity of the market price.

Lower courts have declined to apply the fraud-on-the-market presumption in cases that do not involve an efficient, open, and developed market. The courts have identified at least five factors to consider in identifying an efficient market: (1) sufficient weekly trading volume, (2) sufficient reports and analyses by investment professionals, (3) the presence of market makers and arbitrageurs, (4) the existence of issuers eligible to file Form S–3 short-form registration statements, and (5) a historical showing of immediate price response to unexpected events or financial releases. In short, for a market to be open and developed, it must have a large number of buyers and sellers and a relatively high level of trading activity and frequency. It also must be a market where prices rapidly reflect new information.

Truth on the Market Defendants have also used the efficient-market theory to their advantage. For example, even if the defendant makes overly optimistic sales projections for a product, there is no fraud on the market if the market makers were privy to the truth. In such a case, an investor who did not directly rely on the misrepresentation (for example, by actually reading a misleading press release) could not successfully assert a securities fraud claim based on fraud on the market.

As the U.S. Court of Appeals for the Ninth Circuit explained, in a fraud-on-the-market case, a defendant's failure to disclose material information may be excused if that information has been made credibly available to the market by other sources: "[I]ndividuals who hear [only good news or only bad news] may receive a distorted impression . . . , and thus may have an actionable claim. But the market, and any individual who relies only on the price established by the market, will not be misled."[54]

A defendant is not relieved of its duty to disclose material information unless that information has been transmitted to the public with a degree of intensity and credibility sufficient to counterbalance any misleading impression created by the defendant. A brief mention of the omitted fact in a few poorly circulated or lightly regarded publications would be insufficient.

CAUSATION

A plaintiff must prove that the defendant's misstatement or omission caused him or her to suffer losses. Increasingly, this is an economic question—what factors influence the price of a stock in the securities market?

In a securities case involving Nucorp Energy, for example, investors claimed that a misrepresentation by the company of the value of its oil reserves caused them to suffer losses. The claim was based on the contention that the stock price was maintained at an artificially high level as a result of the misrepresentation. The investors attributed

53. 485 U.S. at 246–47 (1988).

54. *In re* Apple Computer Sec. Litig., 886 F.2d 1109 (9th Cir. 1989), *cert. denied,* 496 U.S. 943 (1990).

the subsequent drop in the stock price to the revelation of the true facts. At trial, the defendants presented the testimony of an economist that the drop in the stock price was caused by a drop in the price of oil and was not attributable to any misrepresentation of the value of the oil reserves. The jury found that the plaintiffs had failed to prove their claim. Thus, proponents of the efficient-market theory may be right when they predict that an entire Rule 10b–5 case may boil down to one question: Did the misleading statement artificially affect the market price?

In early 2005, the U.S. Court of Appeals for the Second Circuit dismissed securities fraud claims against Merrill Lynch & Co., its star analyst Henry M. Blodget, and other research analysts for allegedly issuing false and misleading analyst reports on two Internet companies—24/7 Media and Interliant.[55] Merrill Lynch had acted as lead underwriter for two public offerings by 24/7 Media and as co-lead underwriter of Interliant's initial public offering. The plaintiffs alleged that Blodget and other research analysts issued knowingly or recklessly false bullish research reports to generate investment banking business for Merrill.

The plaintiffs suing Merrill did not claim to have read Merrill's reports or to have bought 24/7 Media or Interliant shares through the firm. Instead, they asserted fraud on the market. To prevail, the plaintiffs had to show *loss causation,* that is, that "the misstatement or omission concealed something from the market that, when disclosed, negatively affected the value of the security." The plaintiffs did not allege that Merrill "doctored" the facts or hid the risks, the price volatility of the stocks, the negative earnings-per-share ratios, or the consistent quarterly losses. There was also no allegation that the market reacted negatively to a corrective disclosure regarding the falsity of Merrill's positive recommendations. The Second Circuit declared this "fatal" to the plaintiffs' case. The court also rejected the plaintiffs' efforts to characterize Merrill's actions as market manipulation in violation of Rule 10b–5(a) and (c).

An earlier investigation of analyst conflicts of interest by New York Attorney General Eliot Spitzer had led to Merrill's agreement in 2002 to pay $100 million to settle New York's civil complaint and spawned more than 100 class-action complaints. Ultimately, ten investment banking firms paid more than $1 billion in a global settlement reached in 2003 to settle government investigations of the incestuous relationships between the firms' research groups—which purported to provide objective research reports—and their investment banking arms, which used favorable analyst coverage to garner more investment banking business.

55. Lentell v. Merrill Lynch & Co., 396 F.3d 161 (2d Cir. 2005).

The scandal resulted in a new SEC regulation—*Regulation Analyst Certification (Regulation AC)*[56]—that prohibits analysts from issuing reports that they do not personally believe to be true and requires the disclosure of any analyst compensation arrangements related to the specific recommendation or views contained in the research report.[57] The SEC has suggested that violation of Regulation AC may give rise to a private right of action under Section 10(b) and Rule 10b–5.[58] Moreover, the SEC stated, "even without Regulation AC, analysts may be found to have violated the anti-fraud provisions of the federal securities laws if they make baseless recommendations that they disbelieve."[59]

The Sarbanes–Oxley Act of 2002 created a new crime, securities fraud involving a publicly traded company.[60] The Act made it a felony to knowingly execute or attempt to execute a scheme or artifice (1) to defraud any person in connection with any security of a publicly traded company or (2) to obtain, by means of false or fraudulent pretenses, representations, or promises, any money or property in connection with the purchase or sale of any security of a publicly traded company. The provision applies to any security of an issuer that has a class of securities registered under Section 12 of the 1934 Act or that is required to file reports under Section 15(d) of the 1934 Act. Congress thereby made it clear that any fake or misleading statements reasonably calculated to affect the public securities markets—such as those made by Henry Blodget of Merrill Lynch, Jack Grubman of Citigroup, and other securities analysts who touted stocks they privately called "junk" or worse—constitute securities fraud.

CALCULATION OF DAMAGES

The measure of damages in a Rule 10b–5 case is typically the out-of-pocket loss, that is, the difference between what the investor paid (or received) and the fair value of the stock on the date of the transaction. Alternatively, investors can elect to rescind the transaction, returning what they received and getting back what they gave. In the court's discretion, ***prejudgment interest***—that is, interest on the amount of the award between the date the securities were purchased and

56. Regulation Analyst Certification, 17 C.F.R. §§ 242.500–242.505.

57. *See* Securities Exchange Act Release No. 47,384 (Feb. 20, 2003), 68 Fed. Reg. 9,482 (Feb. 27, 2003).

58. *Id. See also* Robert F. Serio & Matthew S. Kahn, *Private Rights of Action May Emerge from Sarbanes-Oxley Act,* CORP. COUNS. WKLY., Apr. 19, 2006, at 127.

59. Regulation Analyst Certification, *supra* note 56.

60. 18 U.S.C. § 1348.

the date of the judgment—may also be awarded. Punitive damages are not available.

In theory, damages must be proved with reasonable certainty. In practice, however, damages are awarded on the basis of expert testimony, which can be highly conjectural. For example, a claim that a company's failure to reveal negative information about its new product artificially inflated the price of its stock is quite difficult to evaluate with any scientific certainty because even the experts do not agree to what extent any particular piece of information affects the price of a company's securities.

In addition, the number of traders who can claim damage can only be estimated. For example, in-and-out traders' trades are included in the total volume of trading; but such traders who buy, then quickly sell, suffer no damage if they sell the securities before the price drop.

Evidence of damages is therefore often presented by comparing the stock's performance with the industry or market performance, on the assumption that the industry or the market was not subject to the same artificial inflation. This clearly remains a fertile field for argument and future litigation.

Litigation Reform Act Safe Harbor for Forward-Looking Statements

The Private Securities Litigation Reform Act provides issuers subject to the 1934 Act's reporting requirements and persons acting on their behalf a two-prong safe harbor for certain forward-looking statements.[61] *Forward-looking statements* include (1) a statement containing a projection of revenues, income, earnings per share, capital expenditures, dividends, capital structure, or other financial items; (2) a statement of the plans and objectives of management for future operations, including plans relating to the issuer's products and services; (3) a statement of future economic performance, including any such statement in Management's Discussion and Analysis of Financial Condition and Results of Operations (MD & A) required to be included by the SEC; and (4) any statement of the assumptions underlying or relating to any such statement.

The safe harbor does not apply to forward-looking statements in connection with (1) an initial public offering; (2) an offering of securities by a blank check company; (3) a rollup or going-private transaction; (4) a tender offer; or (5) an offering by a partnership, limited liability company, or direct participation investment program. The safe harbor also does not apply to any forward-looking statement included in (1) a financial statement prepared in accordance with generally accepted accounting principles or (2) a report of beneficial ownership on Schedule 13D.

As explained in Chapter 22, the statutory safe harbor for forward-looking statements was designed to promote market efficiency by encouraging companies to disclose projections and other information about their future prospects. Anecdotal evidence indicated that corporate counsel were advising their clients to say as little as possible due to fear that if the company failed to satisfy its announced earning projections—perhaps due to an industry downturn or the timing of a large order or release of a new product—the company would automatically be sued.

Under the first prong of the safe harbor, a person is protected from liability for a misrepresentation or omission based on a written forward-looking statement as long as the statement (1) is identified as forward-looking and (2) is accompanied by meaningful cautionary statements identifying important factors that could cause actual results to differ materially from those projected in the statement. The safe harbor also protects oral forward-looking statements if the person making the statement (1) identifies the statement as forward-looking, (2) states that results may differ materially from those projected in the statement, and (3) identifies a readily available written document (such as a document filed with the SEC) that contains factors that could cause results to differ materially.

The stated factors must be relevant to the projection and of a nature that could actually affect whether the forward-looking statement is realized. Boilerplate warnings will not suffice. Failure to include the particular factor that ultimately causes the forward-looking statement not to come true will not mean that the statement automatically is not protected by the safe harbor. The company must disclose all important factors, not all factors. In this respect, the safe harbor provides greater protection than the bespeaks caution doctrine.

For example, in *Harris v. Ivax Corp.*,[62] the U.S. Court of Appeals for the Eleventh Circuit held that a generic drug manufacturer was not liable for securities fraud despite its failure to disclose the possibility of a $104 million reduction in the carrying value of goodwill for several of its businesses. The company's cautionary language was adequate even though it did not explicitly mention the factor that ultimately belied the forward-looking statement. The court explained: "When an investor has been warned of risks of a significance similar to that actually realized, she

61. 15 U.S.C.S. § 77z-2.

62. 182 F.3d 799 (11th Cir. 1999).

is sufficiently on notice of the danger of the investment to make an intelligent decision about it according to her own preferences for risk and reward."

When a court is ruling on a motion to dismiss based on this prong of the safe harbor, the state of mind of the person making the statement is not relevant. The court looks only at the cautionary language accompanying the forward-looking statement.

Even if a person cannot rely on this first prong, there is an independent prong based on the state of mind of the person making the statement. A person or business entity will not be liable in a private lawsuit involving a forward-looking statement unless the plaintiff proves that the person or business entity made a false or misleading forward-looking statement with actual knowledge that it was false or misleading. A statement by a business entity will come within the safe harbor unless it was made by or with the approval of an executive officer of the entity with actual knowledge by that officer that the statement was false or misleading.

Section 17(a)

Section 17(a) of the 1933 Act prohibits fraud in connection with the sale of securities. It is similar in scope to Section 10(b) of the 1934 Act, which prohibits fraud in both the sale and the purchase of securities. Unlike Section 10(b), Section 17(a) does not require proof of scienter. The SEC and the U.S. Attorney's Office can use Section 17(a) to prosecute securities fraud, but private parties cannot sue based on it.

Responsibility of Auditors to Detect and Report Illegalities

The Litigation Reform Act added a new Section 10A to the 1934 Act to promote disclosure by independent public accountants of illegal acts committed by their publicly traded audit clients. Each audit must include, in accordance with generally accepted auditing standards, (1) procedures designed to provide reasonable assurance of detecting illegal acts that would have a direct and material effect on the determination of financial statement amounts, (2) procedures designed to identify material related-party transactions (such as those involving officers, directors, and controlling shareholders of the company being audited), and (3) an evaluation of whether there is substantial doubt about the ability of the company to continue as a going concern during the ensuing fiscal year. The Sarbanes–Oxley Act of 2002 also requires auditors to report on the adequacy of the company's internal controls (see Appendix N).

If, in the course of the audit, the independent public accountant detects or otherwise becomes aware of information indicating that an illegal act has or may have occurred (regardless of whether it is perceived to have a material effect on the financial statements), then the accountant must (1) determine whether it is likely that an illegal act has occurred and, if so, determine and consider the possible effect on the financial statements; and (2) inform the appropriate level of the management of the company. The accountant must ensure that the audit committee, or the board of directors in the absence of such a committee, is adequately informed with respect to the illegal acts, unless the illegal act is clearly inconsequential. If after informing the audit committee (or board in the absence of an audit committee), the accountant concludes that (1) the illegal act has a material effect on the financial statements of the company, (2) senior management has not taken timely and appropriate remedial actions with respect to the illegal act, and (3) the failure to take remedial action is reasonably expected to warrant departure from a standard audit report or resignation, then the accountant must, as soon as practicable, directly report its conclusions to the full board of directors. The board is then required to notify the SEC within one business day after its receipt of the report. If the board fails to do so, the accountant must furnish the SEC a copy of its report (or the documentation of any oral report given).

Definition of Insider Trading

Insider trading refers in general terms to trading by persons (often insiders, such as officers and directors) based on material nonpublic information. The U.S. Supreme Court has held, however, that not every trade while in possession of material nonpublic information violates Section 10(b). Because there is no statutory definition of insider trading, the law in this area has developed on a piecemeal basis. This lack of a clear definition has caused enforcement problems for the SEC and federal prosecutors. It can also make it difficult for investors to know whether their actions constitute prohibited insider trading.

The safest course is never to trade while in possession of material nonpublic information; however, such a premise is unduly restrictive. The nature of insider trading can best be understood by examining the purposes underlying the laws that prohibit it.

Two fundamental goals of the securities laws in general are to protect the investing public and to maintain fairness in the securities markets. Allowing a party who knows that the market is incorrectly pricing a security to exploit another party's ignorance of that fact is fundamentally unfair. Yet, if an efficient market is to be maintained, market professionals, such as securities analysts, must be given an incentive to ferret out the truth about companies and their prospects. There would be no incentive if the persons who expended the time and effort to piece together the truth were precluded from either trading on that information or selling it to others in the form of a tip or analyst report.

In light of this need to promote an efficient market and the language of Section 10(b), which refers to fraudulent and manipulative practices, the Supreme Court has held that a trade based on material nonpublic information is illegal only if there is a breach of duty by the person trading; or if the person trading is the recipient of a tip—a piece of inside information—there must be a breach of duty by the person who gave the tip. The person giving the tip is known as the *tipper;* the person receiving it is known as the *tippee*.

Insider trading cases focus specifically on the duty to disclose, before trading, material information that is not publicly known (that is, not commonly available to the investing public). An insider must either disclose material nonpublic information in his or her possession or refrain from trading. The fundamental question in an insider trading case is whether this obligation should be imposed on a particular trader.

For example, corporate officers and directors have specific legal duties to the corporation and the shareholders they serve, which prohibit them from engaging in insider trading. As corporate fiduciaries, these individuals are required to subordinate their self-interests to the interests of the shareholders, as discussed in Chapter 21.

In 2000, the SEC sought to clarify several aspects of insider trading by promulgating Rules 10b5–1 and 10b5–2 (which are set forth in Appendix I). Rule 10b5–1 provides that any person who purchases or sells securities of any issuer on the basis of material nonpublic information about the security or issuer violates Section 10(b) if the purchase or sale was in breach of a duty of trust or confidence owed directly, indirectly, or derivatively to (1) the issuer or its security holders or (2) any other person who is the source of the material nonpublic information. A trade is "on the basis of" material nonpublic information if the person trading was aware of the information at the time of the trade, unless the person can demonstrate that:

1. Before becoming aware of the information, he or she (a) entered into a binding contract to purchase or sell, (b) gave instructions for the trade, or (c) adopted a written plan to trade; *and*
2. The contract, instruction, or plan either (a) specified the amount of securities to be traded and the price, or (b) included a written formula or algorithm for determining the amount and price, or (c) did not permit the person to exercise any subsequent influence over how, when, and whether to trade; *and*
3. The trade was pursuant to the contract, instruction, or plan.

Thus, Rule 10b5–1 creates a presumption that persons who trade while in possession of material nonpublic information trade on the basis of that information unless the trade is pursuant to a preexisting *10b5–1 plan*.[63] The rule was adopted in response to several cases in which the court held that a person who trades while in possession of inside information violates Rule 10b–5 only if he or she decided to trade based on that information.[64]

The affirmative defense is designed to cover situations in which the person trading can demonstrate that the material nonpublic information was not a factor in the trading decision. It permits those who would like to plan securities transactions in advance, at a time when they are not aware of material nonpublic information, to carry out those preplanned transactions at a later time, even if they later become aware of material, nonpublic information. Rule 10b5–2, discussed further later, creates certain presumptions about the existence of a duty of trust or confidence in certain nonbusiness relationships, such as marriage.

CLASSICAL THEORY OF INSIDER TRADING

An *insider* is a person with access to confidential information and an obligation of disclosure to other traders in the marketplace. Insiders include not only traditional insiders—such as officers and directors—but also temporary insiders, such as outside counsel and financial consultants.

Traditional Insiders

Traditionally, only persons closely allied with the corporation itself were considered insiders. They are true insiders because they acquire information by performing duties within or on behalf of the issuer corporation. Persons or entities

63. Research suggests that some executives may be abusing 10b5–1 plans by canceling them when the stock price goes up and selling pursuant to them when the price drops. Barry G. Sher & Kenneth Breen, *Increased SEC Scrutiny of 10b5–1 Plans on Horizon?* N.Y. L.J. (Dec. 3, 2007).

64. *See, e.g.*, SEC v. Adler, 137 F.3d 1325 (11th Cir. 1998).

traditionally considered insiders include (1) officers and directors, (2) employees, (3) controlling shareholders, and (4) the corporation itself. Even if an insider resigns before trading, he or she will still be liable for trading on the basis of material inside information learned while on the job.

Officers and Directors Officers and directors have a fiduciary obligation of loyalty and care to the corporate shareholders. They also have the greatest access to sensitive information regarding corporate events.

Employees As agents or servants of a corporation, employees have a duty of loyalty. They may not personally profit from confidential information that they receive in the course of their employment.

Controlling Shareholders Because of their majority stock ownership, controlling shareholders are generally in a position to control the activities of the corporation. They are therefore likely to be aware of impending corporate events.

The Corporation Often a corporation (or other issuer) will engage in the purchase or sale of its own securities. Under these circumstances, the corporation and those acting on its behalf are insiders and must not trade while in possession of material nonpublic information.

Temporary Insiders

Outside attorneys, accountants, consultants, and investment bankers who are not directly employed by the corporation, but who acquire confidential information through the performance of professional services, are also considered insiders. The U.S. Supreme Court extended liability under Section 10(b) to such *temporary insiders* in footnote 14 to the *Dirks* case, which is presented as Case 23.6.

Tippees of Insiders

Tippees may also be subject to liability under Rule 10b–5, but only if they can be considered derivative insiders. In most cases, a tippee has no independent duty to the shareholders of the corporation, whose shares the tippee is buying or selling and with which he or she may have little or no connection. A tippee will not be held liable as a *derivative insider* unless the insider's duty of disclosure can somehow be imposed upon the tippee. This rule was established in the following landmark case.

A CASE IN POINT

SUMMARY

CASE 23.6

DIRKS V. SEC

SUPREME COURT OF THE UNITED STATES
463 U.S. 646 (1983).

FACTS Raymond Dirks, an officer of a New York broker–dealer firm, who specialized in providing investment analysis of insurance company securities to institutional investors, was contacted by Ronald Secrist, a former employee of Equity Funding of America. Secrist was seeking aid in exposing fraudulent activities that had resulted in an overvaluation of Equity Funding's assets. Dirks was thus the potential tippee, with Secrist the tipper. After corroborating Secrist's story, Dirks advised certain clients that they should sell their shares in the company. When the corporate fraud was later revealed, the price of Equity Funding's stock went down.

The SEC brought proceedings against Dirks on the theory that he had constructively breached a fiduciary duty. In effect, the SEC maintained that anyone receiving information from an insider stands in the insider's shoes and should be held to the same standards and be subject to the same duties as that insider.

ISSUE PRESENTED Is a tippee liable when the tipper has not violated a fiduciary duty?

SUMMARY OF OPINION The U.S. Supreme Court rejected the argument that anyone receiving information from an insider should be held to the same standards as the insider. The Court held instead that a tippee is not liable unless the tippee and the tipper join in a co-venture to exploit the information. Only in such a case will the fiduciary duty of the tipper be derivatively imposed on the tippee. For the tippee to be liable, therefore, the tipper must have a duty to the corporation not to disclose the information and must breach this duty by seeking to benefit personally from the disclosure of the information. The benefit sought by the tipper can be either tangible or intangible. Intangible benefits might include an enhanced reputation or the intangible benefit received through the giving of gifts.

CONTINUED

In this case, the insider was motivated solely by a desire to expose fraudulent conduct. He did not breach any fiduciary duties because it was in the interests of the corporation that this information be disclosed.

RESULT Without a breach of duty on the part of the insider/tipper, no derivative duty could be imposed on Dirks, the tippee. Dirks was not guilty of illegal insider trading.

The requirement that the tipper be seeking some benefit implies that the tipper must desire that the tippee trade on the information, but it is unclear whether such a showing is necessary. For example, the tipper could derive a benefit merely from impressing the tippee with his or her access to confidential information. Such a desire could stem from social or career aspirations of the tipper and could have nothing to do with the stock-trading ramifications of the information.

Breach of Fiduciary Duty In addition to seeking some benefit, the tipper must also be acting in breach of a fiduciary duty to the corporation (or to another under the misappropriation theory, discussed later in this chapter) by disclosing the information to the tippee. The information must be nonpublic at the time it is divulged, and it must be in the interests of the corporation (or the other party in a misappropriation case) to keep the information confidential.

In a classic case of illegal tipping, the former CEO of ImClone, Samuel D. Waksal, was convicted in 2003 of telling his daughter and father to sell their ImClone stock based on his nonpublic knowledge that the Food and Drug Administration (FDA) was denying approval of ImClone's anticancer drug Erbitex. In the course of sentencing Waksal to more than seven years in prison and ordering him to pay a $3 million fine, Judge William H. Pauley III stated:

> The harm that you wrought is truly incalculable. You abused your position of trust as chief executive officer of a major corporation and undermined the public's confidence in the integrity of the financial markets. Then you tried to lie your way out of it, showing a complete disregard for the firm administration of justice.[65]

Judge Pauley further rebuked Waksal, saying, "Your spectacular success in building ImClone into a company worthy of inclusion in the Nasdaq 100 led you to disconnect from reality and, most importantly, from the rule of law."[66]

The SEC sued Samuel Waksal's father in 2003 to recover the $7 million in profits he earned when he sold his ImClone shares before the public announcement of the FDA's rejection of the drug application. The complaint alleged that Samuel Waksal intended to bestow a gift of illegal profits or illegal loss avoidance on his father by telling him about the impending announcement of bad news and that his father knew that he should not have traded on that information.[67]

The tippee is liable only if he or she knew or should have known that the tipper's disclosure of the confidential information constituted a fiduciary breach. If the tippee has reason to know that the insider's disclosure was wrong or against the interest of the corporation, the tippee's actual knowledge will be irrelevant. For example, the U.S. Court of Appeals for the Sixth Circuit upheld the conviction of Kelly Hughes and her husband Kevin Stacy after they purchased thousands of shares of Worthington Foods, just days before its acquisiton by Kellogg Company. Hughes received material nonpublic information about the acquisition from Roger Blackwell, a director of Worthington, and Blackwell's wife then shared that information with Stacy.[68] They earned profits of $104,955. The court concluded that Hughes was a knowledgeable investor who would have known that Blackwell was breaching his duty to Worthington when he shared information about the acquisition. Hughes and Stacy were each sentenced to prison (thirty-three months for Hughes, twenty-seven for Stacy) and three years of supervised release, and each was fined $53,443. These fines were in addition to the $104,955 Hughes and Stacy were ordered to disgorge as a result of a civil case brought by the SEC.[69]

Remote Tippees

Remote tippees—that is, the tippees of tippees—may be found to have violated Section 10(b) and Rule 10b-5 even if they are completely unacquainted with and removed from

65. Constance L. Hays, *Former Chief of ImClone Is Given 7-Year Term,* N.Y. TIMES, June 11, 2003, at C1.

66. *Id.*

67. Constance L. Hays, *Waksal's Father Named in S.E.C. Suit,* N.Y. TIMES, Oct. 11, 2003, at C3.

68. United States v. Hughes, 505 F.3d 578 (6th Cir. 2007).

69. SEC v. Blackwell, 2007 WL 1169362 (S.D. Ohio Apr. 18, 2007).

the original insider tipper. However, remote tippees are not liable unless they knew or should have known that the first-tier tipper was breaching a fiduciary duty in passing on the nonpublic information.[70] The phrase "should have known" is key to this formulation. It means that tippees cannot insulate themselves from liability merely by failing to inquire as to the source of the information. If a tippee has reason to suspect that the information was wrongfully acquired, such conscious avoidance of knowledge will not prevent a finding of scienter.

MISAPPROPRIATION THEORY OF INSIDER TRADING

From time to time, the SEC has unsuccessfully attempted to impose liability on anyone who trades while in possession of material nonpublic information. In *Chiarella v. United States,*[71] the U.S. Supreme Court rejected the argument that every trade based on material nonpublic information should be held to violate the securities laws.

The Supreme Court expanded the class of possible defendants to include so-called outsiders when it embraced the misappropriation theory in *United States v. O'Hagan.*[72] Under the *misappropriation theory,* a Rule 10b–5 violation occurs when a person breaches a fiduciary duty to the source of the nonpublic information by trading on that information after misappropriating it for his or her own use. The trader can be held liable even if he or she is not an insider of the company whose securities are traded and has no independent duty of disclosure to the person from whom the securities were bought or sold.

The case involved James Herman O'Hagan, a partner of the law firm Dorsey & Whitney, who had purchased stock and options for stock in Pillsbury Company prior to the public announcement of a tender offer for Pillsbury's stock by Grand Met PLC. O'Hagan possessed material nonpublic information about Grand Met's intentions, which he had obtained as a partner of the law firm representing Grand Met in connection with its acquisition of Pillsbury. O'Hagan realized a profit in excess of $4 million on his Pillsbury-related transactions.

The U.S. Supreme Court upheld O'Hagan's criminal conviction of securities fraud under Rule 14e–3(a), Section 10(b), and Rule 10b–5. Rule 14e–3 prohibits a person with nonpublic information about a pending tender offer that he or she knows or has reason to know has been acquired directly or indirectly from the offeror or the target or someone working on their behalf from trading on that information. (See Appendix J for the full text of Rule 14e–3.) The Supreme Court ruled that the SEC had not exceeded its powers under Section 14(e) when it adopted Rule 14e–3, which does not require proof that the trader breached any fiduciary duty. With respect to the Section 10(b) and Rule 10b–5 counts, the Court concluded that "it makes scant sense to hold a lawyer like O'Hagan a § 10(b) violator if he works for a law firm representing the target of a tender offer, but not if he works for a law firm representing the bidder. The text of the statute requires no such result."

In the following case, the U.S. Court of Appeals for the Ninth Circuit applied *O'Hagan* to a director of a major shareholder of an acquisition target who traded the target's stock based on nonpublic information about the potential acquisition.

70. SEC v. Musella, 678 F. Supp. 1060 (S.D.N.Y. 1988).

71. 445 U.S. 222 (1980).

72. 521 U.S. 642 (1997).

A CASE IN POINT

IN THE LANGUAGE OF THE COURT

CASE 23.7

SEC v. Talbot

United States Court of Appeals for the Ninth Circuit

530 F.3d 1085 (9th Cir. 2008).

FACTS On April 18 or 19, 2003, LendingTree's CEO Doug Lebda told Fidelity Financial's Vice President Brent Bickett that LendingTree was negotiating a sale of the firm to a third party on terms that were favored by a majority of the LendingTree board. Fidelity owned approximately 10 percent of LendingTree's common stock. Lebda did not disclose the name of the potential acquirer, but he did tell Bickett that he "would need to keep this information confidential." Bickett then relayed that information to Fidelity's CEO William Foley.

On April 22, 2003, Fidelity held its quarterly board meeting, which J. Thomas Talbot, an attorney and Fidelity board member, attended. Foley told the board that negotiations were proceeding for a third party to acquire LendingTree. The board then discussed whether Fidelity should agree to refrain from selling its LendingTree stock during the pendency of the transaction and or to vote its shares in favor of the deal. According to Terry Christensen, another board member, Foley informed the board that Fidelity's stock in LendingTree "would be acquired at a very attractive

CONTINUED

price," between $16 and $18, which represented a 23–29 percent increase over LendingTree's closing price of $12.97 per share on April 22, 2003. Talbot remembered the meeting differently, declaring that, although he could "not recall the exact words spoken . . . some person or company might be interested in acquiring LendingTree, Inc. . . . and [Fidelity] would benefit if the transaction occurred."

Although Foley did not tell the board that the information was confidential, one board member, Cary Thompson, said "something to the effect that this is inside information, no one trade in the stock. Make sure you don't do anything with the stock." Thompson said this "plenty loud. It was loud enough to hear him." All board members present at the meeting, except for Talbot, considered the LendingTree information to be confidential.

Various directors testified as to their understanding of how far along the negotiations had proceeded between LendingTree and the unnamed acquirer, as conveyed by Foley: "far along, and it would be announced as a deal shortly thereafter" (Thompson); "advanced discussions" (Bickett); and that "it looked like there was going to be a transaction" (Christensen). Talbot interpreted Foley's words as far less definite, understanding the information about LendingTree to be a "rumor," not a "factual statement."

On April 24, 2003, two days after the meeting, Talbot purchased on margin 5,000 shares of LendingTree at approximately $13.50 per share for a total of $67,000. Talbot testified that Foley's comments at the April 22, 2003 board meeting regarding LendingTree "triggered [his] conduct on April 23rd to look into [LendingTree] more carefully." He claimed that a number of factors influenced his decision to purchase the stock: Fidelity had invested in it; it was a real estate company, which he considered to be a good buy; interest rates would likely remain low; the high-tech market was experiencing a resurgence; and, based on the "rumor" at the April 22 meeting, other people were clearly interested in it, so he should be as well. Talbot "wanted to buy before anything happened."

On April 25, 2003, LendingTree sent Fidelity a written letter agreement restricting the manner in which Fidelity could use any confidential information it received from LendingTree in connection with the proposed tender offer. The directors were not advised of the confidentiality agreement, and the court concluded that the SEC had failed to prove that Fidelity and, by extension, Talbot owed a fiduciary duty to LendingTree.

Talbot continued to monitor LendingTree's stock closely. After being satisfied that "the price was moving up . . . [a]nd the volume was solid," he purchased on margin an additional 5,000 shares at $14.50 per share for $72,500 on April 30, 2003.

On May 5, 2003, three major events occurred. First, Fidelity executed an agreement with the acquiring company, USA Interactive Corporation, and LendingTree to vote its shares in favor of the acquisition. Second, LendingTree and USA Interactive issued a press release announcing the acquisition. Third, LendingTree's stock rose roughly 41 percent on the news, immediately after which Talbot sold all of his LendingTree shares for a profit of $67,881.20. LendingTree stock closed on Monday, May 5, at $20.72, up $6.03 from its previous closing price of $14.69 on Friday, May 2. Talbot resigned from the Fidelity board on September 19, 2003.

On June 23, 2004, the SEC brought a civil action against Talbot alleging that he had traded on material, nonpublic information in violation of Section 10(b) of the 1934 Act and Rule 10b–5. The district court held that Talbot could not be liable under the misappropriation theory because there was no continuous chain of fiduciary relationship from LendingTree to Fidelity to Talbot. With respect to whether the information Talbot received at the Fidelity board meeing was material, the district court held that it could not make that determination one way or the other as a matter of law. There were genuine issues of material fact that a jury would have to consider to decide whether the information was material or not. The SEC appealed.

CONTINUED

ISSUE PRESENTED Did a director of a major shareholder of an acquisition target violate Rule 10b–5 when he traded in the stock of the target while in possession of nonpublic information concerning a possible acquisition of the target?

OPINION WARDLAW, J., writing on behalf of the U.S. Court of Appeals for the Ninth Circuit:

We must decide whether Talbot can be held liable under § 10(b) of the Securities Exchange Act of 1934 ("Exchange Act"), and Rule 10b–5, promulgated thereunder, for misappropriating information from Fidelity, in the absence of a fiduciary duty of confidentiality owed to LendingTree by Fidelity or Talbot when he executed the trades. We hold that Talbot can be held liable, under the circumstances here, but that a genuine issue of material fact exists as to the issue of materiality. We therefore reverse and remand the district court's grant of summary judgment in favor of Talbot.

A. The Misappropriation Theory

Traditionally, § 10(b) and Rule 10b–5 have reached only what is termed "classical" insider trading. "Under the 'traditional' or 'classical theory' of insider trading liability, § 10(b) and Rule 10b–5 are violated when a corporate insider trades in the securities of his corporation on the basis of material, nonpublic information." Such trading qualifies as a "deceptive device" under § 10(b) because a "relationship of trust and confidence [exists] between the shareholders of a corporation and those insiders who have obtained confidential information by reason of their position with that corporation." The relationship of trust and confidence between the trader and the shareholders of the corporation in which he trades "gives rise to a duty to disclose [or to abstain from trading] because of the 'necessity of preventing a corporate insider from . . . taking unfair advantage of . . . uninformed . . . stakeholders.'"

. . . .

. . . In 1997, the Supreme Court . . . recogniz[ed] a "complementary" theory of liability referred to as the "misappropriation" theory.[73] Under this theory, "a person commits fraud 'in connection with' a securities transaction, and thereby violates § 10(b) and Rule 10b–5, when he misappropriates confidential information."[74] The misappropriation theory reaches trading by corporate outsiders, not insiders; therefore, as a corporate outsider, the misappropriator owes no duty to the investor with whom he trades, a requirement for liability under the classical theory of insider trading. Rather, "[i]n lieu of premising liability on a fiduciary relationship between company insider and purchaser or seller of the company's stock, the misappropriation theory premises liability on a fiduciary-turned-trader's deception of those who entrusted him with access to confidential information. Under this theory, a fiduciary's undisclosed, self-serving use of a principal's information to purchase or sell securities, in breach of a duty of loyalty and confidentiality, defrauds the principal of the exclusive use of that information."[75] "Because the deception essential to the misappropriation theory involves feigning fidelity to the source of the information, if the fiduciary discloses to the source that he plans to trade on the nonpublic information, there is no 'deceptive device' and thus no § 10(b) violation. . . ."[76]

B. Talbot's Liability Under the Misappropriation Theory

Because Talbot traded in LendingTree securities—a corporation in which he was not an insider—liability can attach to his conduct only under the misappropriation theory. . . . [F]or the SEC to prevail on appeal, it must demonstrate that (1) Talbot breached a fiduciary duty arising from a relationship of trust and confidence owed to the source of the information on which he traded; and (2) the information on which Talbot traded was material.

CONTINUED

73. United States v. O'Hagan, 521 U.S. 642 (1997).

74. *Id.*

75. *Id.*

76. *Id.*

1. Breach of Duty

The SEC contends that because "Talbot had a duty to . . . Fidelity, to keep information about the LendingTree transaction confidential, and [because] he secretly breached that duty by trading securities for personal profit," he can be held liable under the misappropriation theory. We agree.

In *United States v. O'Hagan*, the leading Supreme Court decision addressing the misappropriation theory, . . . the Supreme Court . . . noted that "it [was O'Hagan's] failure to disclose his personal trading to Grand Met and Dorsey [his law firm], in breach of his duty to do so, that made his conduct 'deceptive' within the meaning of [§] 10(b)."

The district court interpreted the misappropriation theory as requiring that "the trader and the originating source of the nonpublic information [be] linked through a continuous chain of fiduciary relationships: The employee [must owe] a duty to his employer to refrain from exploiting the information, and the employer in turn [must owe] the same duty to the corporate client."

Although a continuous chain of duties existed in each of the cases relied upon by the district court, a continuous chain of duties is not a requirement for liability to attach under the misappropriation theory. In *O'Hagan*, the Supreme Court held that O'Hagan had breached two independent duties: (1) his duty to Dorsey & Whitney, his law firm; and (2) his duty to Grand Met, the corporation that his law firm represented. That a continuous chain of duties flowed from O'Hagan to Dorsey & Whitney to Grand Met is of no moment, as the Court never intimated that such a chain was necessary. Thus, O'Hagan's relationship with Dorsey & Whitney was sufficient to support liability under the misappropriation theory. The district court misinterpreted the misappropriation theory as requiring that the duty of confidentiality be owed to the "originating source" of the information. *O'Hagan* stated quite clearly that the duty must be owed only the "source"; we decline to read an "originating source" requirement into *O'Hagan*.

. . . Talbot traded on information he received from Fidelity, the immediate source and rightful owner of the information on which he traded. . . .

. . . Talbot, as a member of Fidelity's Board, owed a duty arising from a relationship of trust and confidence to Fidelity, the source of the information on which he traded. The information on which Talbot traded was confidential, as it was properly "entrusted" to him by Fidelity in his capacity as a Fidelity director. This is textbook misappropriation.

Talbot contends that "[n]o reasonable factfinder could conclude that Mr. Talbot was obligated to keep the LendingTree information confidential." We disagree. Although the Court did not define the precise contours of the fiduciary duty captured by the misappropriation theory, it is clear that Talbot falls within *O'Hagan*'s ambit. In *O'Hagan*, the Court found that a partner in a law firm is in a relationship of trust and confidence with his firm. It follows that Talbot, as a member of Fidelity's Board of Directors, was also in a relationship of trust and confidence with Fidelity. This conclusion is supported by nearly seven decades of Delaware law and common sense: Corporate officers and directors are not permitted to use their position of trust and confidence to further their private interests. While technically not trustees, they stand in a fiduciary relation to the corporation and its stockholders.

Talbot further contends that the information on which he traded was not confidential. He relies on his belief that the LendingTree information was a "rumor," and the fact that Foley did not indicate the information was confidential. We find these arguments to be unpersuasive. As a matter of law, the very nature of the information on which Talbot traded was confidential. As the SEC points out, "the information about the possible LendingTree acquisition went to the very heart of Talbot's duties to Fidelity." Talbot learned of the LendingTree information from Foley, the CEO of Fidelity, at a meeting of the Board of Directors. Foley announced it to the Board to get a reading on whether the Board would vote Fidelity's shares in favor of the transaction. Because Fidelity had a large stake in LendingTree's stock, this decision would have a big impact on Fidelity's financials, a point

CONTINUED

that Foley made explicit by informing the Board that Fidelity could potentially make $50 million if the deal went through. This was not a passing reference to a company in which Fidelity had no interest; rather, the weight of the evidence counsels that Foley's comments to the Board, and the Board's subsequent discussion of the transaction, would make clear to any Board member—especially an individual who has sat on boards of directors for over three decades—that the information was confidential and not to be used for personal gain. Indeed, every other director present at the meeting considered the information to be confidential.

Talbot's use of Fidelity's confidential information, in breach of his duty to disclose that he intended to use the information before doing so, was in direct contravention of the purposes of the Exchange Act. As the Court recognized in *O'Hagan*:

> An animating purpose of the Exchange Act . . . [is] to insure honest securities markets and thereby promote investor confidence. Although informational disparity is inevitable in the securities markets, investors likely would hesitate to venture their capital in a market where trading based on misappropriated nonpublic information is unchecked by law. An investor's informational disadvantage vis-à-vis a misappropriator with material, nonpublic information stems from contrivance, not luck; it is a disadvantage that cannot be overcome with research or skill.

Talbot contends that . . . the SEC cannot prevail because it cannot demonstrate that Fidelity was harmed by his conduct. We cannot determine from the record before us whether Talbot's trading injured Fidelity, but it most certainly injured the trading public. The failure to hold a person in Talbot's trusted position who traded on information acquired by him in that capacity would diminish the public perception of the markets as "honest," as investors would understand that board members—those who have superior access to information about the businesses in which their companies invest—are free to profit off the informational advantages they possess by virtue of their rank.

2. Materiality

The SEC also contends that the LendingTree information on which Talbot traded was material as a matter of law. The district court found that a genuine issue of material fact exists regarding materiality. We agree with the district court.

An omitted fact is material if there is a substantial likelihood that a reasonable investor would consider it important in deciding whether to buy or sell securities.[77] "[T]o fulfill the materiality requirement 'there must be a substantial likelihood that the disclosure of the omitted fact would have been viewed by the reasonable investor as having significantly altered the 'total mix' of information made available.'"

. . . .

The district court did not clearly err in determining that a genuine issue of material fact exists as to the materiality of the information on which Talbot traded. On the one hand, much of the deposition testimony would support a finding of materiality. Foley informed the Board that Fidelity stood to make a $50 million profit on the acquisition. Thompson and Bickett testified that, based on Foley's representations to the Board, they perceived the acquisition to be in the very advanced stages. Talbot purchased LendingTree stock just two days after hearing the information, and again six days later. The stock rose roughly 41 percent upon announcement of the acquisition, immediately after which Talbot sold all of his LendingTree stock. And, perhaps most tellingly, Talbot testified that he purchased the stock on margin because he "wanted to buy before anything happened."

On the other hand, there is also evidence to support a finding that the information was immaterial. Most notable, Talbot remembers what was said at the meeting differently than some of the

CONTINUED

77. Basic Inc. v. Levinson, 485 U.S. 224 (1988).

other directors. He recalled Foley saying, only generally, that "some person or company might be interested in acquiring LendingTree, Inc. . . . and that [Fidelity] would benefit if the transaction occurred." In contrast with those who believed that the transaction was in the advanced stages, Talbot understood the transaction to be just a "rumor," not a factual statement." Moreover, he asserted that no one discussed "when [the acquisition] would occur." This account is generally confirmed by Christensen, who testified that "Mr. Foley was indicating that it looked like [Fidelity's] stock would be sold. I mean, you know, one never knows for sure, but that's what it looked like." Both Talbot's and Christenson's deposition testimony refute the countervailing evidence that Foley communicated a detailed and definite description of the worth of the potential acquisition. Therefore, we cannot say that the district court clearly erred in determining that the information on which Talbot traded was not material as a matter of law, given the genuine issues of material fact, particularly as to what information was actually conveyed to the Fidelity Board.

For the foregoing reasons, we *reverse the district court* and hold that Talbot can be held liable under the misappropriation theory because he traded on confidential information received in his capacity as a member of Fidelity's Board, but that a genuine issue of material fact as to the materiality of the information precludes judgment as a matter of law.

RESULT The case was remanded to the district court for a determination by a jury of whether the information Talbot knew about the possible acquisition of LendingTree was material. If the jury found the information material, then Talbot engaged in illegal insider trading.

CRITICAL THINKING QUESTIONS

1. Would the misappropriation theory apply to a case in which a person defrauded a bank into giving him a loan, or embezzled cash from another, and then used the proceeds of the misdeed to purchase securities?
2. If the fiduciary disclosed to the source of the nonpublic information that she planned to trade on that information, would trading on that information constitute a Section 10(b) violation? Would it violate any other laws? Would it be ethical?

Duty of Trust or Confidence

Rule 10b5–2 sets forth a nonexclusive list of three situations in which a person has a duty of trust or confidence for purposes of the misappropriation theory of insider trading. A duty of trust or confidence exists (1) whenever a person agrees to maintain information in confidence; (2) when two people have a history, pattern, or practice of sharing confidences such that the recipient of the information knows or reasonably should know that the person communicating the material nonpublic information expects that the recipient will maintain its confidentiality; and (3) when a person receives or obtains material nonpublic information from a spouse, parent, child, or sibling unless the recipient of the information can demonstrate that, under the facts and circumstances of that family relationship, no duty of trust or confidence existed.

The misappropriation theory widens the class of persons who can be found liable for insider trading, but the requirement that there must be a duty of trust or confidence remains a limiting factor. For instance, an outsider who infers from the movements of corporate executives that an event will likely take place owes no duty to the corporation or its employees.

MAIL AND WIRE FRAUD

The U.S. Supreme Court upheld the conviction of R. Foster Winans, author of the *Wall Street Journal* column "Heard on the Street," under the Mail and Wire Fraud Acts, thereby providing an additional way to prosecute insider trading.[78] Winans had misappropriated the content of his soon-to-be-published columns and tipped the information to two stockbrokers, who used the information to make trades based on the anticipated positive market response to the column's publication. The Court held that if a business generates confidential information and has the right to control the use of that information prior to public disclosure, then use of that information to trade can be prohibited under the wire and mail fraud statutes.

78. Carpenter v. United States, 484 U.S. 19 (1987).

IN BRIEF

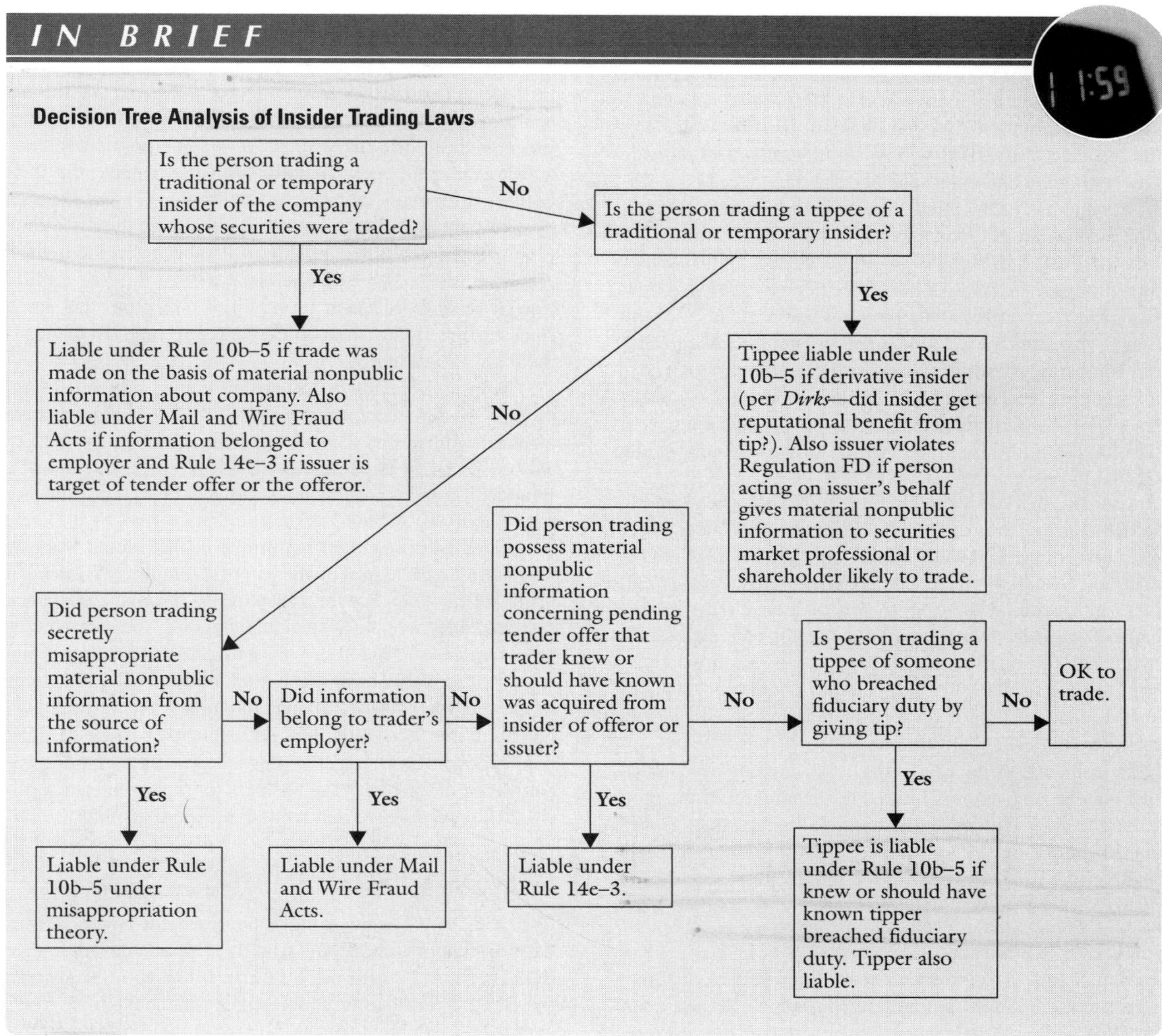

1:59
Decision Tree Analysis of Insider Trading Laws
Is the person trading a traditional or temporary insider of the company whose securities were traded?
No
Is the person trading a tippee of a traditional or temporary insider?
Yes
Liable under Rule 10b–5 if trade was made on the basis of material nonpublic information about company. Also liable under Mail and Wire Fraud Acts if information belonged to employer and Rule 14e–3 if issuer is target of tender offer or the offeror.
Yes
Tippee liable under Rule 10b–5 if derivative insider (per Dirks—did insider get reputational benefit from tip?). Also issuer violates Regulation FD if person acting on issuer's behalf gives material nonpublic information to securities market professional or shareholder likely to trade.
No
Did person trading secretly misappropriate material nonpublic information from the source of information?
No
Did information belong to trader's employer?
No
Did person trading possess material nonpublic information concerning pending tender offer that trader knew or should have known was acquired from insider of offeror or issuer?
No
Is person trading a tippee of someone who breached fiduciary duty by giving tip?
No
OK to trade.
Yes
Liable under Rule 10b–5 under misappropriation theory.
Yes
Liable under Mail and Wire Fraud Acts.
Yes
Liable under Rule 14e–3.
Yes
Tippee is liable under Rule 10b–5 if knew or should have known tipper breached fiduciary duty. Tipper also liable.

RICO

A securities fraud claim cannot be used as a predicate act in a civil case under the Racketeer Influenced and Corrupt Organizations Act (RICO) (discussed in Chapter 15) unless the defendant has been criminally convicted in connection with the fraud. However, a criminal conviction under the Wire and Mail Fraud Acts for misappropriation of an employer's confidential information may, assuming other requirements are met, be the basis for a civil RICO case.

ENFORCEMENT OF ANTIFRAUD PROHIBITIONS

Persons who violate the antifraud provisions of the federal securities laws are subject to private suits for damages, civil enforcement actions by the SEC, and criminal prosecution.

PRIVATE ACTIONS

In private actions, the plaintiff must be an actual purchaser or seller of securities, and the plaintiff's loss must have been proximately caused by the acts of the defendant. All contemporaneous traders, that is, persons who purchased or sold securities of the same class at the same time the fraud was ongoing or the insider was trading, have standing to sue. Any amounts disgorged pursuant to court order or at the instance of the SEC will offset the amount of damages recoverable by contemporaneous traders.

In what has been called "the largest settlement ever by a single corporate defendant in a securities class action," Tyco International Ltd. agreed in 2007 to pay approximately $3 billion to settle investor claims.[79] PricewaterhouseCoopers LLP, Tyco's auditors, agreed to pay an additional $225 million to investors.[80] In 2008, Ernst & Young LLP agreed to pay almost $300 million to its former audit client Cendant Corporation for negligently failing to discover massive fraud by senior managers of a Cendant subsidiary. This was in addition to the $335 million Ernst & Young paid to Cendant's shareholders in 2000.[81]

In 2008, the European Union responded to large auditor settlements and awards by authorizing member states to permit auditors to limit their liability to their audit clients by contract.[82] Auditors in the United States have renewed calls for limits, arguing that the growth of their clients' market capitalization and the concentration of public company audits by the Big Four accounting firms (PricewaterhouseCoopers, Ernst & Young, KPMG, and Deloitte) could leave the markets in chaos if one of the Big Four failed as a result of a massive judgment against it.[83]

In insider trading cases, the total amount of damages that may be recovered is limited to the amount of the profit gained or loss avoided in the unlawful transaction. Tippers and all direct and remote tippees are jointly and severally liable. That means that any individual in the chain of information can be found liable for all of the profits gained or losses avoided in every transaction within the chain.

79. *PWC to Pay $225M to Settle Claims Over Tyco Mismanagement,* Corp. Couns. Wkly., July 11, 2007, at 213.

80. *Id.*

81. David Reilly & Nathan Koppel, *Cendant Case Costs Ernst Almost $300 Million More,* Wall St. J., Feb. 16–17, 2008, at B3.

82. Jennifer Hughes, *FRC Gives Liability Reform Guidance,* Fin. Times, June 30, 2008. In May 2008, the European Commission stated that unlimited auditor liability was "no longer tenable," and the internal market and services commissioner recommended that the EU member states introduce legislation to limit auditor liability. *Id.* The U.K. Financial Reporting Council has authorized contractual limits on liability but requires them to be approved each year by the shareholders. *Id.*

83. Jennifer Hughes, *US Auditors Renew Calls for Liability Limits,* Fin. Times, Sept. 1, 2008.

SEC CIVIL ENFORCEMENT ACTIONS

In an SEC civil enforcement action, violators may be liable for damages and disgorgement of profits and may be subject to other penalties and injunctions prohibiting future violations. Both in deciding whether to seek corporate penalties and in determining the magnitude of the penalty, the SEC focuses principally on two considerations: (1) Did the corporation obtain a direct benefit as a result of the violation? (2) Will the penalty recompense or further harm the injured shareholders?[84] The SEC assessed a record $750 million fine against WorldCom, prompting complaints that large fines further injure shareholders already hurt by management's wrongdoing.

The Insider Trading and Securities Fraud Enforcement Act of 1988, passed in the wake of insider trading charges against Michael Milken and Drexel Burnham Lambert in the late 1980s (discussed more fully in this chapter's "Inside Story"), provided strong encouragement to the brokerage industry to police itself. A brokerage house can be fined if it "knew or recklessly disregarded" information that would indicate insider trading activities on the part of its employees. Intended to force firms to police their employees, institute compliance systems, and monitor suspicious activities, the Act specifically requires registered brokers and dealers to maintain and enforce reasonably designed written policies and procedures to prevent the misuse of material nonpublic information. Although this legislation does not explicitly require it, many commentators have suggested that it is prudent for other companies not in the brokerage business to implement such policies and procedures in light of their potential liability.

CRIMINAL PROSECUTIONS

The SEC itself has no criminal enforcement power. Criminal prosecutions are brought by the Department of Justice through the U.S. Attorney's Office, often on referral from the SEC. If criminally convicted, a defendant faces fines and/or imprisonment for willful violations. Willfulness has been interpreted as awareness by the defendant that he or she was committing a wrongful act; the defendant need not specifically know that he or she was violating a statute.

BOUNTY PAYMENTS

Individuals whose tips result in insider trading prosecutions are entitled to receive bounties, similar to the payments provided by the Internal Revenue Service in tax

84. SEC *Unveils Statement of Penalty Principles with Announcement of McAfee Settlement,* Corp. Couns. Wkly., Jan. 11, 2006, at 9.

cases. These bounties can be as high as 10 percent of any revenues recovered from a defendant through penalties or settlement.

Selective Disclosure and Regulation FD

Effective October 23, 2000, the SEC adopted a broad prohibition on the practice of *selective disclosure,* whereby issuers of publicly traded securities disclose material nonpublic information, such as advance warnings of earning results, to securities analysts or selected institutional investors before making full disclosure of the same information to the general public. Those privy to the information were able to make a profit or avoid a loss at the expense of those kept in the dark. According to the SEC, this led "to a loss of investor confidence in the integrity of our capital markets. Investors who see a security's price change dramatically and only later are given access to the information responsible for that move rightly question whether they are on a level playing field with market insiders."[85]

Selective disclosure also threatened the integrity of the securities markets by creating "the potential for corporate management to treat material information as a commodity to be used to gain or maintain favor with particular analysts or investors."[86] Analysts might feel pressure to report favorably about a company for fear of being excluded from calls and meetings to which other analysts are invited. Finally, the SEC reasoned, "Whereas issuers may once have had to rely on analysts to serve as information intermediaries, issuers now can use a variety of methods to communicate directly with the market." These include Internet webcasting and teleconferencing. Accordingly, the SEC concluded: "Technological limitations no longer provide an excuse for abiding the threats to market integrity that selective disclosure represents."[87]

Regulation FD (Fair Disclosure) provides that whenever an issuer, or a person acting on its behalf, discloses material nonpublic information to securities market professionals or holders of the issuer's securities who may well trade on the basis of the information, the issuer must publicly disclose that same information simultaneously (for intentional disclosures) or promptly (for nonintentional disclosures). Market professionals include broker–dealers, investment advisers and investment managers, investment companies and hedge funds, and official persons thereof. A disclosure is considered intentional only if the person knows, or is reckless in not knowing, that the information he or she is communicating is both material and nonpublic. In cases of nonintentional disclosure, the issuer must disclose the information to the public as soon as practical (but no later than twenty-four hours) after a senior official learns of the disclosure and knows (or is reckless in not knowing) that the information disclosed was both material and nonpublic. No public disclosure is required for communications (1) made to a person who owes the issuer a duty of trust or confidence (such as an investment banker, accountant, or attorney); (2) made to any person who expressly agrees to maintain the information in confidence; (3) with a credit-rating agency; or (4) made in connection with most offerings of securities registered under the 1933 Act.

Information is material if there is a substantial likelihood that a reasonable shareholder would consider it important in making an investment decision. Types of information or events likely to be considered material include (1) earnings information; (2) mergers, acquisitions, tender offers, or changes in assets; (3) new products or developments involving customers or suppliers; (4) changes in control or management; (5) changes in auditors; (6) defaults on senior securities, repurchase plans, or stock splits; and (7) bankruptcies. The SEC cautioned that an official who engages in a private discussion with an analyst seeking guidance about earnings estimates "takes on a high degree of risk under Regulation FD."[88] On the other hand, an issuer is not prohibited from disclosing nonmaterial information to an analyst even if, unbeknown to the issuer, that piece of information helps the analyst complete a "mosaic" of information that, taken together, is material.

To avoid creating a chilling effect on issuers' willingness to communicate with outsiders, the SEC expressly provided that private parties cannot sue issuers for violations of Regulation FD. It is not an antifraud rule, and failure to make a public disclosure required solely by Regulation FD is not in and of itself a violation of Rule 10b–5. If an issuer fails to comply with Regulation FD, the SEC is empowered to bring an enforcement action and can seek an injunction and/or civil monetary penalties.

85. Selective Disclosures and Insider Trading, SEC Release Nos. 33-7881, 34-43154, IC-24599, 17 C.F.R. pts. 240, 243, 249 (Aug. 15, 2000).

86. *Id.*

87. *Id.*

88. *Id.*

Other Restrictions on Trading by Officers, Directors, and Greater-Than-10 Percent Shareholders

In addition to the prohibition against trading based on material nonpublic information, Section 16 of the 1934 Act and Section 306 of the Sarbanes–Oxley Act impose several additional requirements on officers, directors, and greater-than-10 percent shareholders of publicly traded firms.

SHORT-SWING TRADING

Section 16(b) of the 1934 Act governs *short-swing trading*—the purchase and sale, or the sale and purchase, by officers, directors, and greater-than-10 percent shareholders of equity securities of a public company registered under the 1934 Act within a six-month period. Unlike Section 10(b), which requires scienter (that is, a showing of bad intent), liability is imposed under Section 16(b) regardless of the insider's state of mind.

Although the purpose of Section 16(b) is to prevent insiders of publicly held companies from exploiting information not generally available to the public in order to secure quick profits, it need not be proved that the insider actually possessed any material nonpublic information at the time the insider traded in the securities. To establish liability under Section 16(b), it is sufficient to prove that an insider purchased and then sold, or sold and then purchased, equity securities within a period of six months.

Definition of an Equity Security

An *equity security* includes (1) any stock or similar security; (2) any security that is convertible, with or without consideration, into such a security; (3) any security carrying any warrant or right to subscribe to or purchase such a security; (4) any such warrant or right; and (5) any other security that the SEC deems to be of a similar nature and that, for the protection of investors or in the public interest, the SEC considers appropriate to treat as an equity security. Thus, equity securities may include hybrids that ordinarily are not considered equity securities, such as convertible debt securities that have not been registered under the 1934 Act.

Special problems can arise in connection with the grant and exercise of stock options and other derivative securities. A set of complicated rules embodied largely in Rule 16b–3, adopted by the SEC under Section 16(b) of the 1934 Act, governs this area. Before becoming an officer or director, a person should consult counsel to avoid inadvertent Section 16(b) liability.

Persons Covered

Section 16(b) applies to officers, directors, and greater-than-10 percent shareholders.

Officer or Director A person may be liable under Section 16(b) if he or she was an officer or director at the time of either the purchase or the sale. It is not necessary that both transactions occur during the person's tenure.

For example, if an officer purchased 100 shares of XYZ Corporation common stock at $10 per share on January 1, resigned as an officer on February 1, then sold 100 shares of XYZ common stock at $20 per share on March 1, she would be liable for $1,000 of short-swing profits because she was an officer when she made the January 1 purchase. Similarly, if a person purchased 100 shares of XYZ Corporation at $10 per share on January 1, became an officer of XYZ Corporation on February 1, and sold the shares at $20 on March 1, that person would be liable for $1,000 of short-swing profits because he was an officer at the time of the sale. On the other hand, if an officer who had not traded for more than six months before March 1 resigned on March 1, bought 100 shares of XYZ Corporation at $10 on April 1, then sold them at $20 on April 2, she would not have recoverable profits because she was not an officer or director at the time of either the purchase or the sale.

Greater-than-10 Percent Shareholder The rule is different for persons who are not officers or directors but are beneficial owners of more than 10 percent of the issuer's equity securities. Such persons are liable under Section 16(b) only if they hold more than 10 percent of the securities both at the time of the purchase and at the time of the sale. The transaction whereby the person becomes a 10 percent shareholder does not count.

For example, if a person who previously owned less than 10 percent of the shares of XYZ Corporation's stock purchased 10.5 percent of XYZ Corporation's common stock at $10 on January 1, then sold those shares at $20 on March 1, he would have no recoverable short-swing profits. However, if the same person had purchased another 2 percent of XYZ common stock in February, then the February purchase could be matched against the March sale because he owned more than 10 percent of the stock at the time of the February purchase and also at the time of the March sale.

Beneficial Ownership of Shares

Officers, directors, and greater-than-10 percent shareholders can be liable for purchases and sales of shares they do not own of record but are deemed to own beneficially. Under Section 16(b), a person will be considered the *beneficial owner* of any securities held by his or her immediate family—his or her spouse, any minor children, or any other relative living in his or her household. There is a rebuttable presumption that a person is the beneficial owner of any securities over which he or she has the practical power to vest title in himself or herself, or from which he or she receives economic benefits (such as sales proceeds) substantially equal to those of ownership.

Purchases and sales of securities held beneficially by an officer, director, or greater-than-10 percent shareholder will be attributed to that person in determining his or her liability for short-swing trading. For example, the purchase of securities by an officer's husband could be matched under Section 16(b) with the sale of other securities by the officer herself within six months of her husband's purchase, thereby resulting in liability for short-swing profits. Thus, any officer, director, or greater-than-10 percent shareholder planning a purchase or sale must consider not only his or her own trading record but also the record of those persons whose securities he or she is deemed to own beneficially.

Purchase and Sale Within Six Months

To result in recoverable short-swing profits, the purchase and sale, or sale and purchase, must have occurred "within any period of less than six months." That period commences on the day on which the first purchase or sale occurred and ends at midnight two days before the corresponding date in the sixth succeeding month. For example, for a transaction on January 1, the six-month period ends at midnight on June 29, two days before July 1.

Profit Calculation

To calculate the profits recoverable under Section 16(b), the sale price is compared with the purchase price. If several purchases and sales occur within a six-month period, the lowest purchase price will be matched with the highest sale price; then the next lowest purchase price with the next highest sale price; and so on, regardless of the order in which the purchases and sales actually occurred. Matching purchases and sales in this manner maximizes the recoverable profit.

The shares that are sold need not be the same shares that were purchased. Any purchase and any sale will incur liability if they occur less than six months apart, regardless of whether the transactions involve the same shares. For example, if on January 1, an officer of XYZ Corporation sold 100 shares of XYZ common stock that he had held for ten years, then on February 1 purchased 200 shares of XYZ common stock at a lower price, he would be liable for the short-swing profits on 100 of the shares. The January 1 sale would be matched with the February 1 purchase, even though the officer had held the securities for ten years before he sold them.

Short-swing profits cannot be offset by trading losses that were incurred in the same period. Thus, there may be recoverable profits under Section 16(b) even though the officer or director suffered a net loss on the trading transactions.

The following example illustrates the "lowest-in, highest-out" matching principle just described. Assume that an officer made purchases and sales, each of 100 shares, as follows:

Date	Transaction	Price
Jan. 1	Purchase	$ 9
Jan. 30	Sale	10
Feb. 15	Sale	15
Feb. 28	Purchase	12
Mar. 15	Purchase	6
Mar. 30	Sale	4

These transactions will result in a recoverable short-swing profit of $1,000, calculated as follows. The February 15 sale is matched with the March 15 purchase, for a profit of $15 ⊠ $6 ⊠ $9 per share, or $900. Then the January 30 sale is matched with the January 1 purchase, for a profit of $10 ⊠ $9 ⊠ $1 per share, or $100. Even though the March 15 purchase at $6 per share and the subsequent sale at $4 per share resulted in a loss of $2 per share, or $200, that loss will not be taken into account. The officer will have to surrender $900 ⊠ $100 ⊠ $1,000, even though she actually realized only $200 of net profit in the trading transactions (total sales of $2,900 less purchases of $2,700).

Unorthodox Transactions

If a purchase or sale by an officer, director, or greater-than-10 percent shareholder that would otherwise result in recoverable short-swing profits was involuntary and did not involve the payment of cash, and if there was no possibility of speculative abuse of inside information, then a court may hold that it was an *unorthodox transaction* to which no liability will attach. These situations generally arise in the context of exchanges in mergers and other corporate reorganizations, stock conversions, stock reclassifications, and tender offers in which securities are sold or exchanged for consideration other than cash.[89]

Embracing the judicial doctrine, the SEC exempts certain mergers, reclassifications, and consolidations under amendments to Rule 16b–7 adopted in 2005. On the other hand, in a tender offer or acquisition, an exchange of securities for cash by an officer, director, or greater-than-10 percent shareholder would almost certainly be deemed a sale for which the person receiving the cash could be liable under Section 16(b).

FILING OF BENEFICIAL-OWNERSHIP REPORTS

Section 16(a) of the 1934 Act requires officers, directors, and greater-than-10 percent shareholders of companies that have registered any class of equity securities under the 1934 Act to file beneficial-ownership reports with the SEC and with any national securities exchange on which their company's equity securities are listed. Within ten days of becoming an officer or director, a person must file an initial ownership report on Form 3, even if the person does not beneficially own any securities of the company at that time. In the case of greater-than-10 percent shareholders, a Form 3 must be filed within ten days of the date they acquire a greater-than-10 percent interest. (In addition, as noted in Chapter 22, any person who acquires more than 5 percent of the voting securities of a public company must file a Schedule 13D within ten days after the date he or she acquired the more-than-5 percent stake. An amendment to the Schedule 13D must be filed promptly after any material change in beneficial ownership or investment purpose.)

Subsequently, an officer, director, or greater-than-10 percent shareholder must file a Form 4 within two business days after any transaction resulting in any change in beneficial ownership. For example, a transaction executed on Tuesday, September 3, would have to be reported to the SEC by the close of business (5:30 P.M. Eastern time) on Thursday, September 5. In the initial Form 4, an officer or director must report all purchases or sales that occurred within the previous six months, even if those transactions were effected before the person became an officer or director. A Form 5 showing changes in beneficial ownership during the preceding year must be filed annually within forty-five days after the issuer's fiscal year-end.

Acquisitions and dispositions of shares acquired by officers or directors pursuant to employee benefit plans must also be reported within two business days on Form 4 even if the transactions are exempt from short-swing recovery under Rule 16b-3. A person who ceases to be an officer or director must continue to report any changes in beneficial ownership that occur within six months of the last reportable transaction while he or she was an officer or director.

The SEC has brought enforcement actions to force executives to file these ownership reports within the required time frame. Publicly traded companies must disclose in their proxy statements and in their annual reports on Form 10–K whether their officers and directors have complied with their Section 16(a) reporting obligations.

PROHIBITION ON SELLING SHORT

Section 16(c) of the 1934 Act prohibits officers or directors from *selling* any of their company's equity *securities short,* that is, from selling a security that the seller does not own. If the officer or director owns the security being sold, he or she must deliver it within twenty days after the sale or deposit it in the mails or other usual channels of delivery within five days. If the officer or director fails to do this, he or she will be liable under Section 16(c) unless (1) he or she acted in good faith and was unable to make the delivery or deposit within the specified time, or (2) he or she acted in good faith and satisfying the time requirements would have caused undue inconvenience or expense.

SOX BAN ON TRADING DURING BLACKOUT PERIOD AND DISGORGEMENT AFTER RESTATEMENTS

Section 306[90] of the Sarbanes–Oxley Act (SOX)[91] prohibits officers and directors from trading equity securities acquired in connection with their services as officers or directors during any retirement plan blackout period. As explained in Chapter 14, a *blackout period* is any period longer than three business days during which 50 percent or more of the participants in a retirement plan are prevented from trading. Private actions to recover any profit realized by the offender may be brought by the issuer or

89. *See, e.g.,* At Home Corp. v. Cox Commc'ns Inc., 446 F.3d 403 (2d Cir. 2006) (finding no Section 16(b) "purchase" when insider acquired stock in At Home by acquisition of three third-party intermediaries that held warrants for At Home stock because the acquisition of the three cable systems holding At Home's stock "entail[ed] appreciable risks and opportunities independent of the risks and opportunities that inhere in the stock of the issuer," likening it to "speculating in tractors by buying a farm").

90. 15 U.S.C. § 7244.

91. Pub. L. No. 107-204, 116 Stat. 745 (2002).

derivatively on its behalf by a shareholder. As explained in Chapter 14, Section 304[92] provides that the CEO and CFO of an issuer required to restate its financial statements "as a result of misconduct" must disgorge all bonuses and incentive- and equity-based compensation received in the twelve months following the filing of the faulty document as well as all profits realized from the sale of the issuer's securities during that period.

92. 15 U.S.C. § 7243.

GLOBAL VIEW

Insider Trading in the European Union and China

The European Union (EU) Market Abuse Directive[93] requires member states to enact national legislation punishing primary and secondary insiders who trade publicly held securities on the basis of "inside information," which is defined as nonpublic information "a reasonable investor would be likely to use as part of the basis of his investment decisions."[94] Primary insiders include officers, directors, employees, and shareholders of the issuer as well as persons who have access to inside information by virtue of their professional duties. Secondary insiders are those who obtain inside information from primary insiders, that is, tippees.

Issuers are required to maintain lists of persons working for them with access to inside information, and senior managers must report changes in beneficial ownership to the appropriate national authority within five business days.[95] In addition, the principle of "equal treatment" prohibits the selective disclosure of inside information.

Although the EU Directive does not on its face embrace the misappropriation theory, persons who obtain information as a result of their professional duties are deemed primary insiders even if they have no fiduciary duty to the issuer. Thus, trading by a person like O'Hagan[96] would violate European law.

The legislation in China banning insider trading is based in substantial part on the U.S. regulatory approach[97] and is enforced by the China Securities Regulatory Commission (CSRC). Although there are very few reported cases, research suggests that insider trading in the Chinese markets is "widespread," "everyday," "extensive," and "ingrained."[98] One interviewee remarked, "Many people do not trade shares unless they have inside information. We simply have no choice in such an environment."[99]

93. European Parliament and Council Directive 2003/6/EC on Insider Dealing and Market Manipulation (Market Abuse), 2003 O.J. (L 96). This supersedes Commission Directive 89/592: Coordinating Regulations on Insider Dealing.

94. Commission Directive 2003/124/EC, 2003 O.J. (L 339).

95. Commission Directive 2004/72/EC, 2004 O.J. (L 162).

96. United States v. O'Hagan, 521 U.S. 642 (1997).

97. Hui Huang, International Securities Markets: Insider Trading Law in China 25–26 (2006).

98. *Id.* at 38.

99. Quoted in *id.*

THE RESPONSIBLE MANAGER

PREVENTING SECURITIES FRAUD AND INSIDER TRADING

Managers have an obligation not to mislead investors in company public announcements, periodic reports, or speeches. Although a company may remain silent about material developments if neither the company nor insiders are trading, early disclosure is often the better course. This gives all investors equal access to current information about the company. There is a trade-off here, however. Sometimes the company's business or transactions may be in a state of

CONTINUED

flux. For example, a party with no visible source of financing may have made an offer to buy the company's assets. In this case, it may be worse to disclose the offer and get the market's hopes up than to wait and see if the offer is real. Managers, together with their lawyers, must make these judgment calls.

Another reason for early disclosure is to avoid illegal insider trading. A company must make disclosure if it knows its insiders, such as officers or directors, are trading in the company's securities.

Any forward-looking statements should be identified as such and be accompanied by meaningful cautionary language identifying important factors that could cause actual results to differ materially from those in the forward-looking statement. It is often helpful to (1) prioritize the order of risk factors, (2) state the risk in the first sentence, (3) be specific, (4) convey the magnitude of the risk, and (5) focus risk factors on the negatives without softening them by including positives.

Trading by a manager based on material nonpublic information is illegal. It violates the manager's fiduciary duty to subordinate his or her personal interests to the interests of the corporation and shareholders he or she serves. A manager is given access to nonpublic information not for the manager's own personal gain but to better enable the manager to serve his or her principal—the corporation and its shareholders. Violation of those rules erodes both shareholder confidence and the confidence of investors generally in the capital markets. It is also unethical.

A manager cannot give tips to others in exchange for money or even just to enhance his or her reputation as "someone in the know." A manager should carefully guard the information given in confidence by his or her employer or client. Managers must also instill these values in their subordinates. Everyone, from the person who empties the trash or runs the copy machine to the person who occupies the largest office in the executive suite, must be told to follow these rules or risk dismissal. This edict should be made clear in the corporation's code of ethics and in its personnel manual. All corporations, and especially brokerage firms, without adequate procedures in place to prevent illegal insider trading face potential liability for their insiders' illegal trades.

Inquiries into insider trading tend to focus on high-volume trading that occurs before major corporate announcements. Enforcement agencies generally watch organized trading rings and well-known public figures because of their high profiles. However, ordinary investors and isolated violations are also detected and prosecuted. Surveillance groups monitor daily trading and investigate any suspicious activity.

A company cannot disclose material information only to certain favored analysts. This is unfair to the public investors and can result in liability for the company and for the manager who tips an analyst whose clients then trade based on the tip. It also violates Regulation FD.

A company's policy on insider trading[100] should prohibit any person associated with the company from trading in any security, regardless of whether it was issued by the company, based on material nonpublic information. The policy should also ban passing on material nonpublic information to outsiders who may trade (tipping). It should require persons who are likely to obtain material nonpublic information on a regular basis to pre-clear all purchases and sales of the company's securities. The policy should also (1) describe the legal penalties for insider trading and the company's potential liability for the insider trading violations of its employees and (2) provide that any employee who violates the policy may be terminated.

An officer or director of a public company who buys and sells securities within a six-month period has a legal and ethical responsibility to come forward and pay all profits over to the corporation. This is true even if the short-swing trade was inadvertent, as might happen if an officer sold securities not realizing that his or her spouse had bought securities less than six months before. A corporation that discovers a short-swing trade must try to persuade the insider to voluntarily turn the profits over to the corporation. If the insider refuses to do so, the corporation has an obligation to bring suit to recover the profits from the short-swing trading. If a corporation fails to bring suit, any shareholder has the right to sue on behalf of the corporation.

Officers and directors of public companies must report their security holdings and their trades in a timely manner. Disregard of these filing requirements breeds contempt for the law and encourages illegal or unethical behavior by others in the organization.

Each manager has a role to play in preventing securities fraud and insider trading. As with preventing the other types of criminal behavior described in Chapter 15, legally astute managers lead by example. If a manager permits

CONTINUED

100. Aspects of this discussion are drawn from *Effective Company Policy May Avoid Violations, ABA Told,* Corp. Couns. Wkly., Aug. 11, 1999, at 2.

his or her company to engage in unlawful or unethical conduct, the manager exposes himself or herself and the company to considerable risk of civil and criminal liability. Such a manager is also likely to encourage illegal behavior by subordinates. Although many executives complained mightily about the costs of Sarbanes-Oxley, especially the requirements in Section 404[101] that (1) management maintain a sound internal-control structure for financial reporting and assess its effectiveness and (2) the auditors attest to the soundness of management's assessment and report on the state of the overall financial control system, a number of firms ranging from PepsiCo and Iron Mountain (a $1.8 billion records and information company) to Yankee Candle and RSA Security "approached the new law with something like gratitude."[102]

Section 906 of SOX made "willful failure" to portray the true state of the company's operations and financial condition a crime, and Sections 302 and 404 require the CEO and CFO to attest personally to the effectiveness of the firm's internal control over financial reporting.[103] Compliance with these requirements led to (1) improved job-description documentation, training, oversight, and performance evaluation at BlackRock, an investment firm with more than $450 billion in assets under management, which survived the subprime-mortgage crisis unscathed; (2) fewer unenforceable contracts and miscalculated rent escalations at a Fortune 1000 real estate company; (3) significant gains in efficiency at Iron Mountain; and (4) standardized software at Manpower.[104] While acknowledging that "[f]ear can be a powerful generator of upstanding conduct," Deloitte & Touche partner Stephen Wagner and Deloitte Consulting partner Lee Dittmar point out that "business runs on discovering and creating value."[105] They go on to assert: "The procrastinators need to start viewing the Sarbanes-Oxley Act of 2002 as an ally in that effort."[106]

101. *See* Appendix K.

102. Stephen Wagner & Lee Dittmar, *The Unexpected Benefits of Sarbanes–Oxley*, Harv. Bus. Rev. (Apr. 2006), at 133.

103. False certifications may give rise to private actions under Section 10(b) and Rule 10b-5. Certification of Disclosure in Companies' Quarterly and Annual Reports, SEC Release No. 8124 (Aug. 28, 2002).

104. Wagner & Dittmar, *supra* note 102.

105. *Id.* at 140.

106. *Id.*

A Manager's Dilemma

Putting It into Practice

When May an Accountant Look the Other Way?

In 1984, several individuals (including David Greenberg) formed seven limited partnerships to develop and operate a chain of 100 "Video USA" video rental stores. One hundred and sixteen limited partners, who had invested $13 million in three private placements, sued accounting firm Touche Ross, among others, for securities fraud. They alleged that Touche Ross (1) had failed to disclose that David Greenberg was a convicted felon; that his twelve-year-old son was the sole officer, director, and shareholder of one of the corporations that served as a general partner; and that the principals used fraudulent invoices and made fraudulent claims against insurance companies; and (2) had prepared the materially misleading financial projections attached as exhibits to the offering memoranda. Touche Ross did not issue an opinion or certification as to any part of the offering documents. Attached to each of the projections that Touche Ross issued was a letter stating that the projection was based on management's "knowledge and belief" and cautioning that the projection "does not include an evaluation of the support for the assumptions underlying the projections." If you were the account manager at Touche Ross and learned about Greenberg's felony conviction and the existence of fraudulent invoices, what would you have done? Is Touche Ross liable under Section 10(b) to the limited partners?[107]

107. Shapiro v. Cantor, 123 F.3d 717 (2d Cir. 1997).

INSIDE STORY

MICHAEL MILKEN, DREXEL BURNHAM, AND THE INSIDER TRADING SCANDALS OF THE 1980s

The philosopher George Santayana once said, "Those who cannot remember the past are condemned to repeat it."[108] In October 2007, Linda Thomson, the SEC Enforcement Director, reported that insider trading among Wall Street professionals "appears to be rampant again."[109] She and others attributed the spike in cases to the fact that the younger professionals working in hedge funds and brokerage firms "were very young or not even born during the era of the high profile Dennis Levine prosecution in the 1980s."[110]

Dennis Levine and Ivan Boesky

In addition to information gained from monitoring trading, prosecutors and enforcement agencies investigating suspicious activity rely heavily on information gathered from informers and persons already under indictment. For example, the arrest and prosecution of Dennis Levine and Ivan Boesky in 1986 set off the most comprehensive investigation of securities trading practices in the history of federal regulation.

Levine, a former managing director of Drexel Burnham Lambert, was initially charged with illegal trading in approximately fifty-four stocks. An investment banker, Ira B. Sokolow, then pleaded guilty to passing stolen information to Levine. As a result of cooperation by Levine, the SEC was able to bring insider trading charges against one of Wall Street's richest and most active speculators, Ivan Boesky.

Boesky, the son of an immigrant restaurateur, made his career and fortune as a risk arbitrageur who concentrated on the purchase and sale of stock in target corporations that were the subject of tender offers. Generally, the acquiring corporation pays a premium for the stock of the target corporation; thus, people who invest prior to the announcement of the acquisition are in a position to make swift and substantial profits. The SEC alleged that Levine, who worked on mergers and acquisitions, passed on information to Boesky, who was able to purchase shares in the target prior to public announcement of the impending takeover. It is further believed that Boesky offered Levine a 5 percent commission for any information leading to an initial stock purchase and a 1 percent commission for information pertaining to stocks already owned by Boesky.

In 1985, Levine allegedly passed to Boesky information received from Sokolow regarding the merger of Nabisco and R.J. Reynolds. Use of this information resulted in approximately $4 million in profits for Boesky. In all, Boesky was alleged to have made approximately $50 million through these insider trading activities. Both Levine and Boesky pleaded guilty to criminal charges. Boesky settled the SEC's civil charges by agreeing to pay $100 million and to cooperate with the government in future prosecutions of others. Boesky was sentenced to three years in prison and ultimately served two years.

One commentator speculated on Boesky's motivation: "His need was not simply to be rich, but to be seen as richer and smarter than anyone else. He gambled less on stocks than on his ability to beat the cops."[111]

Drexel Burnham Lambert

Approximately two years later, with the cooperation of Ivan Boesky, the SEC brought dramatic charges against Drexel Burnham Lambert and four of its prominent employees, including the head of its junk-bond department, Michael Milken. According to the SEC, Drexel had entered into a secret agreement with Boesky to defraud its clients and drive up the price of target-company stocks. The complaint, filed in September 1988, alleged that Drexel utilized Boesky to engage in *stock parking*—the temporary sale of shares to another entity or individual so as to hide the true ownership of the shares in order to avoid tax-reporting requirements or the net-margin requirements of the securities laws applicable to brokerage firms. Drexel, which assisted companies interested in acquisitions, was also accused of advising Boesky to purchase massive amounts of shares in certain companies in order to give the appearance of active trading in them and to drive up the takeover price.

In December 1988, Drexel agreed to plead guilty to six felony counts and to pay $650 million in fines and restitution—"by far the largest penalty ever paid in a securities case."[112] It agreed

CONTINUED

108. E.D. Hirsch, Jr., Joseph F. Kett & James Trefil, The New Dictionary of Cultural Literacy, § Proverbs (3d ed. 2005).

109. *Insider Trading Appears to Be Rampant Again, Says Thomson,* Corp. Couns. Wkly., Oct. 31, 2007, at 332.

110. *Id.*

111. Robert J. Samuelson, *The Super Bowl of Scandal,* Newsweek, Dec. 1, 1986, at 64.

112. Larry Reibstein & Carolyn Friday, *Nailing the Junk Kings,* Newsweek, Jan. 2, 1989, at 44.

to pay an additional $30 million to settle civil charges in April 1989. As a condition to the settlement, Drexel was required to cooperate in the investigation of Milken and to fire him.

Michael Milken

In 1990, Milken pleaded guilty to six felony counts, ranging from securities and mail fraud to tax evasion and conspiracy.[113] He agreed to pay a fine of $200 million and to put $400 million into a fund for restitution to defrauded investors. The *Wall Street Journal* provided a vivid image of the courtroom scene when Milken pleaded guilty:

> He was almost at the end of a detailed confession when his voice faltered. Michael Milken bent forward, sobbing, as two of his lawyers rushed to support him. Suddenly, under the vast ceiling of Manhattan's largest federal courtroom, the world's once-most-powerful financier, the bigger-than-life commander of the X-shaped trading desk, seemed mortal, even frail.[114]

Milken was sentenced to ten years in prison but was released after serving only twenty-two months. He was also banned for life from acting as a securities broker or dealer.

U.S. Attorney General Richard Thornburgh characterized Milken's crimes as "some of the most serious efforts undertaken to manipulate and subvert Wall Street's securities markets."[115] But Thornburgh also observed that the case sends a strong message to those involved in "crime in the suites: those white-collar criminals are never so powerful or clever that they cannot be caught by diligent and persistent law enforcement efforts."[116] The convictions of Samuel Waksal (former CEO of ImClone), Bernie Ebbers (former CEO of WorldCom), John Rigas (former CEO of Adelphia Communications), and others convicted of securities fraud in the early twenty-first century suggest that they failed to take this message to heart.

113. Laurie P. Cohen, *Public Confession: Milken Pleads Guilty to Six Felony Counts and Issues an Apology*, WALL ST. J., Apr. 25, 1990, at A1.

114. *Id.*

115. *Id.*

116. *Id.* For an excellent detailed account of the insider trading scandals of the 1980s, see JAMES B. STEWART, DEN OF THIEVES (1991).

KEY WORDS AND PHRASES

aider and abettor 889
beneficial owner 925
bespeaks caution doctrine 902
blackout period 926
derivative insider 913
efficient-market theory 908
equity security 924
forward-looking statement 910
fraud-on-the-market theory 908
holder claims 905
insider 912
insider trading 888
loss causation 909
misappropriation theory 915
misstatement 895
omission 895
prejudgment interest 909
Regulation Analyst Certification (Regulation AC) 909
Regulation FD (Fair Disclosure) 923
remote tippees 914
Rule 10b–5 888
S–1 review 894
scheme liability 889
scienter 898
selective disclosure 923
selling securities short 926
short-swing trading 924
stock parking 930
temporary insiders 913
10b5–1 plan 912
tip 897
tippee 912
tipper 912
unorthodox transaction 925

QUESTIONS AND CASE PROBLEMS

1. During a session with her psychiatrist, Dr. Robert Willis, Joan Weill mentioned in confidence the imminent merger of the company headed by her husband, Sanford Weill, with another company. Willis, upon hearing of the merger, communicated the information to Martin Sloate, who traded in the company's securities for his own account and for his customers' accounts.

   Did Weill, Willis or Sloate engage in illegal insider trading? Was the conduct of the parties ethical? [*SEC v. Willis,* 777 F. Supp. 1165 (S.D.N.Y. 1991).]

2. The Todman & Co. accounting firm audited the financial statements of Direct Brokerage, Inc. (DBI) from 1999 through 2002. Each year Todman issued an unqualified opinion that DBI's financial statements accurately portrayed DBI's finances. In fact, DBI failed to pay its payroll taxes for 1999 or 2000, a fact that came to light in 2003. After DBI collapsed in 2004, investors sued Todman, alleging that Todman was aware of DBI's undisclosed liability and its need for an infusion of capital but failed to correct or withdraw its 2002 certified opinion or to advise DBI to withdraw its financial statements. The plaintiffs identified five red flags:

   - In 1998, a Todman auditor noted a "large payroll tax payable at the end of the year" necessitating further analysis, but no analysis was ever done.
   - Todman did not investigate DBI's failure to pay any payroll tax after June 1998.
   - Todman knew that DBI's payroll taxes dropped from $248,899 to zero between 1998 and 1999, but never investigated.
   - Todman knew that DBI's employee compensation rose significantly in 1999 while its payroll taxes plunged, but did not investigate.
   - That trend continued in 2000, and Todman knew it but did not investigate.

   Did Todman violate Section 10(b) or Rule 10b–5? [*Overton v. Todman & Co.,* 478 F.3d 479 (2d Cir. 2007).]

3. Gallop, Inc. is a toy manufacturer specializing in games for boys and girls aged eight to twelve. On March 30, Gallop had predicted first-quarter earnings of $.20 per share. On April 15, Gallop received a fax from its key distributor reporting a $10 million claim for personal injury of a nine-year-old child who was allegedly injured by a design defect in Gallop's most popular product line, the Spartan Warriors. Gallop's outside counsel was instructed to prepare a press release describing the claim. Before the press release was sent to the copy center at Gallop's executive office, the vice president of marketing, one director, and the outside counsel sold all of their Gallop shares at the prevailing market price of $25.25 per share.

   Collin Copier, who ran the photocopying machine at Gallop's executive office, saw the draft press release; called his broker, Barbara Broker; told her about the press release; and ordered her to sell the 500 shares of Gallop that Copier had acquired in Gallop's initial public offering. Broker then called her best client, Charleen Client, and suggested that she sell her 100,000 shares of Gallop stock but did not tell her why. Client agreed, and Broker sold Copier's and Client's stock at $25.25 a share right before the market closed on April 17.

   The press release was publicly announced and was reported on the Business Wire after the market closed on April 17. The next day, Gallop's stock dropped to $20.75 per share. A class-action suit has been brought, and the SEC has commenced enforcement proceedings. Criminal prosecution is threatened by the U.S. Attorney's Office.

   What are the bases on which each proceeding could be brought? Who is potentially liable? For how much?

4. Dow Chemical Company owned Destec Energy, Inc. (Destec), which owned Destec Engineering, Inc. (DEI). Dow decided to try to sell Destec. AES Corporation wanted to buy Destec's international assets, including DEI. DEI's sole asset was a contract to design and build a power plant in the Netherlands. Because Dow would not sell Destec's international assets alone, AES paired with NGC Corporation to make a joint bid. NGC bought all outstanding Destec stock from Dow through a merger agreement, and then AES bought all of Destec's international assets, including the DEI stock, from NGC under an asset purchase agreement. During the course of the negotiations, Dow and Destec orally represented what it would cost to build the power plant, but these representations were not reflected in the written documents.

   Most of the documents in the transaction contained nonreliance clauses, that is, clauses that attempted to limit the information on which the parties to the document could legally rely. For example, the merger agreement between NGC and Dow contained two pages of representations and warranties but stated that other than those, "neither Dow nor any other person makes any other express or implied representation or warranty on behalf of Dow." Unfortunately for AES, the Netherlands plant deal proved far more costly than represented, and AES lost $70 million on the plant.

   Section 29(a) of the 1934 Act provides that "any condition, stipulation or provision binding any person to waive compliance with any provision of this title or of any rule or regulation thereunder, or of any rule of an exchange required thereby shall be void." Does AES have a valid claim under Section 10(b) and Rule 10b–5? [*AES Corp. v. Dow Chemical Co.,* 325 F.3d 174 (3d Cir. 2003).]

5. American Banknote Corporation (ABN) spun off its wholly owned subsidiary American Bank Note Holographics (ABNH) in an initial public offering. Morris Weissman was the founder of ABN and also the chair and CEO of both ABN and ABNH. Plaintiff purchasers of ABNH's stock sued Weissman, among others, for securities fraud under Sections 11, 12(a)(2), and 10(b). In two press releases, Weissman stated:

> Our most important goal in 1998 is to enhance shareholder value. We hope to prove to the market that inherent values of our underlying operating subsidiaries, not apparent when evaluating American Banknote on the basis of traditionally consolidated earnings per share, are indeed significant.
>
> This IPO is a win-win for both companies. . . . ABNH can now concentrate on continuing the profitable growth of its core security holography business as well as explore business and market expansion opportunities.

In fact, ABNH was neither a valuable company nor profitable. Is Weissman liable under Section 10(b) and Rule 10b–5? What would be the best argument in his defense? [*In re American Bank Note Holographics, Inc. Securities Litigation,* 93 F. Supp. 2d 424 (S.D.N.Y. 2000).]

6. Texas International Speedway, Inc. (TIS) filed a registration statement for $4,398,900 in securities with the proceeds to be used to construct an automobile racetrack called the Texas International Speedway. The entire issue was sold on the offering date, October 30, 1969. On November 30, 1970, TIS filed for bankruptcy.

The prospectus stated that the speedway was under construction. It also included a pro forma balance sheet showing that, upon completion of the public offering and application of the proceeds to the construction costs of the speedway, TIS would have $93,870 in cash on hand on the speedway's opening date.

The TIS prospectus warned that "THESE SECURITIES INVOLVE A HIGH DEGREE OF RISK" and that the construction costs might be underestimated. If the plaintiff investors present evidence from which a jury could infer that, on the effective date of the registration statement, the two officers and directors of TIS and its accountant knew that the cost of construction was understated and that consequently TIS's working capital position would not be as favorable as the prospectus reflected, will the plaintiffs win a suit under Section 10(b) and Rule 10b–5? What would be the result if the Litigation Reform Act applied? [*Huddleston v. Herman & MacLean,* 640 F.2d 534 (5th Cir. 1981), *rev'd in part and aff'd in part,* 456 U.S. 914 (1982).]

7. In 1998, after working at two banks for about ten years, Bryan J. Mitchell helped found MCG Capital Corporation, a venture-capital firm that invested in the media, communications, and technology sectors. MCG went public in 2001, and Mitchell served as its CEO and chair of the board. Various documents filed with the SEC stated that Mitchell "earned a B.A. in economics from Syracuse University." In fact, he attended Syracuse for only three years and did not graduate. After being pressured by a journalist, Mitchell disclosed the misrepresentation to the MCG board. The same day, the company issued a press release correcting the statement. The board subsequently stripped Mitchell of his title as chair of the board and made him repay certain bonuses and loans.

The press responded negatively to "another CEO that lied about his résumé" and speculated about "what else might not be right." On the day the press release was issued, MCG's stock price dropped from $11.85 per share to $8.40 but fully recovered within a month.

Shareholders sued, alleging that the misrepresentation violated Section 11 of the 1933 Act, Section 10(b) of the 1934 Act, and Rule 10b–5. Was Mitchell's lie about having a college degree material? If you had been a member of the MCG board, would you have been comfortable keeping Mitchell as CEO? [*Greenhouse v. MCG Capital Corp.,* 392 F.3d 650 (4th Cir. 2004).]

8. EchoCath was a small New Jersey research and development company engaged in developing, manufacturing, and marketing medical devices to enhance and expand the use of ultrasound technology for medical applications and procedures. EchoCath consummated its initial public offering on January 17, 1996, and issued a lengthy prospectus, which cautioned that "an investment in the securities offered . . . is speculative in nature and involves a high degree of risk." It also set forth several pages of risk factors. In particular, EchoCath cautioned investors that the company "intended to pursue licensing, joint development and other collaborative arrangements with other strategic partners . . . but there can be no assurance . . . that the Company will be able to successfully reach agreements with any strategic partners, or that other strategic partners will ever devote sufficient resources to the Company's technologies."

More than six months after the public offering, MedSystems began to consider a sizable investment in EchoCath.

Frank DeBernardis, the CEO of EchoCath, orally represented to MedSystems that EchoCath had engaged in lengthy negotiations to license its products and was on the verge of signing contracts with a number of prominent medical companies, which he identified as including UroHealth, Johnson & Johnson, Medtronic, and C.R. Bard, Inc., to develop and market EchoCath's women's health products. Throughout the negotiations and until the closing in February 1997, EchoCath's CEO continued to represent to MedSystems officials that the contracts with these companies to develop these products were "imminent." In the fifteen months after MedSystems made its investment, EchoCath failed to enter into a single contract.

MedSystems filed suit under Section 10(b) and Rule 10b–5, alleging that EchoCath intentionally or recklessly made misrepresentations to MedSystems in connection with the sale of securities in an effort to induce MedSystems to purchase its securities. MedSystems alleged that EchoCath was not on the verge of signing contracts with any company to develop its line of women's health products in August 1996, or any other time up to the closing on February 27, 1997. EchoCath moved to dismiss the complaint on the grounds that the CEO's statements were not material. Result? [*ER MedSystems v. EchoCath, Inc.*, 235 F.3d 865 (3d Cir. 2000).]

APPENDICES

APPENDIX A: The Constitution of the United States of America

Preamble

We the People of the United States, in Order to form a more perfect Union, establish Justice, insure domestic Tranquility, provide for the common defence, promote the general Welfare, and secure the Blessings of Liberty to ourselves and our Posterity, do ordain and establish this Constitution for the United States of America.

Article I

Section 1. All legislative Powers herein granted shall be vested in a Congress of the United States, which shall consist of a Senate and House of Representatives.

Section 2. The House of Representatives shall be composed of Members chosen every second Year by the People of the several States, and the Electors in each State shall have the Qualifications requisite for Electors of the most numerous Branch of the State Legislature.

No Person shall be a Representative who shall not have attained to the Age of twenty five Years, and been seven Years a Citizen of the United States, and who shall not, when elected, be an Inhabitant of that State in which he shall be chosen.

Representatives and direct Taxes shall be apportioned among the several States which may be included within this Union, according to their respective Numbers, which shall be determined by adding to the whole Number of free Persons, including those bound to Service for a Term of Years, and excluding Indians not taxed, three fifths of all other Persons. The actual Enumeration shall be made within three Years after the first Meeting of the Congress of the United States, and within every subsequent Term of ten Years, in such Manner as they shall by Law direct. The Number of Representatives shall not exceed one for every thirty Thousand, but each State shall have at Least one Representative; and until such enumeration shall be made, the State of New Hampshire shall be entitled to chuse three, Massachusetts eight, Rhode Island and Providence Plantations one, Connecticut five, New York six, New Jersey four, Pennsylvania eight, Delaware one, Maryland six, Virginia ten, North Carolina five, South Carolina five, and Georgia three.

When vacancies happen in the Representation from any State, the Executive Authority thereof shall issue Writs of Election to fill such Vacancies.

The House of Representatives shall chuse their Speaker and other Officers; and shall have the sole Power of Impeachment.

Section 3. The Senate of the United States shall be composed of two Senators from each State, chosen by the Legislature thereof, for six Years; and each Senator shall have one Vote.

Immediately after they shall be assembled in Consequence of the first Election, they shall be divided as equally as may be into three Classes. The Seats of the Senators of the first Class shall be vacated at the Expiration of the second Year, of the second Class at the Expiration of the fourth Year, and of the third Class at the Expiration of the sixth Year, so that one third may be chosen every second Year; and if Vacancies happen by Resignation, or otherwise, during the Recess of the Legislature of any State, the Executive thereof may make temporary Appointments until the next Meeting of the Legislature, which shall then fill such Vacancies.

No Person shall be a Senator who shall not have attained to the Age of thirty Years, and been nine Years a Citizen of the United States, and who shall not, when elected, be an Inhabitant of that State for which he shall be chosen.

The Vice President of the United States shall be President of the Senate, but shall have no Vote, unless they be equally divided.

The Senate shall chuse their other Officers, and also a President pro tempore, in the Absence of the Vice President, or when he shall exercise the Office of President of the United States.

The Senate shall have the sole Power to try all Impeachments. When sitting for that Purpose, they shall be on Oath or Affirmation. When the President of the United States is tried, the Chief Justice shall preside: And no Person shall be convicted without the Concurrence of two thirds of the Members present.

Judgment in Cases of Impeachment shall not extend further than to removal from Office, and disqualification to hold and enjoy any Office of honor, Trust, or Profit under the United States: but the Party convicted shall nevertheless be liable and subject to Indictment, Trial, Judgment, and Punishment, according to Law.

Section 4. The Times, Places and Manner of holding Elections for Senators and Representatives, shall be prescribed in each State by the Legislature thereof; but the Congress may at any time by Law make or alter such Regulations, except as to the Places of chusing Senators.

The Congress shall assemble at least once in every Year, and such Meeting shall be on the first Monday in December, unless they shall by Law appoint a different Day.

Section 5. Each House shall be the Judge of the Elections, Returns, and Qualifications of its own Members, and a Majority of each shall constitute a Quorum to do Business; but a smaller Number may adjourn from day to day, and may be authorized to compel the Attendance of absent Members, in such Manner, and under such Penalties as each House may provide.

Each House may determine the Rules of its Proceedings, punish its Members for disorderly Behavior, and, with the Concurrence of two thirds, expel a Member.

Each House shall keep a Journal of its Proceedings, and from time to time publish the same, excepting such Parts as may in their Judgment require Secrecy; and the Yeas and Nays of the Members of either House on any question shall, at the Desire of one fifth of those Present, be entered on the Journal.

Neither House, during the Session of Congress, shall, without the Consent of the other, adjourn for more than three days, nor to any other Place than that in which the two Houses shall be sitting.

Section 6. The Senators and Representatives shall receive a Compensation for their Services, to be ascertained by Law, and paid out of the Treasury of the United States. They shall in all Cases, except Treason, Felony and Breach of the Peace, be privileged from Arrest during their Attendance at the Session of their respective Houses, and in going to and returning from the same; and for any Speech or Debate in either House, they shall not be questioned in any other Place.

No Senator or Representative shall, during the Time for which he was elected, be appointed to any civil Office under the Authority of the United States, which shall have been created, or the Emoluments whereof shall have been increased during such time; and no Person holding any Office under the United States, shall be a Member of either House during his Continuance in Office.

Section 7. All Bills for raising Revenue shall originate in the House of Representatives; but the Senate may propose or concur with Amendments as on other Bills.

Every Bill which shall have passed the House of Representatives and the Senate, shall, before it become a Law, be presented to the President of the United States; If he approve he shall sign it, but if not he shall return it, with his Objections to the House in which it shall have originated, who shall enter the Objections at large on their Journal, and proceed to reconsider it. If after such Reconsideration two thirds of that House shall agree to pass the Bill, it shall be sent together with the Objections, to the other House, by which it shall likewise be reconsidered, and if approved by two thirds of that House, it shall become a Law. But in all such Cases the Votes of both Houses shall be determined by Yeas and Nays, and the Names of the Persons voting for and against the Bill shall be entered on the Journal of each House respectively. If any Bill shall not be returned by the President within ten Days (Sundays excepted) after it shall have been presented to him, the Same shall be a Law, in like Manner as if he had signed it, unless the Congress by their Adjournment prevent its Return in which Case it shall not be a Law.

Every Order, Resolution, or Vote to which the Concurrence of the Senate and House of Representatives may be necessary (except on a question of Adjournment) shall be presented to the President of the United States; and before the Same shall take Effect, shall be approved by him, or being disapproved by him, shall be repassed by two thirds of the Senate and House of Representatives, according to the Rules and Limitations prescribed in the Case of a Bill.

Section 8. The Congress shall have Power To lay and collect Taxes, Duties, Imposts and Excises, to pay the Debts and provide for the common Defence and general Welfare of the United States; but all Duties, Imposts and Excises shall be uniform throughout the United States;

To borrow Money on the credit of the United States;

To regulate Commerce with foreign Nations, and among the several States, and with the Indian Tribes;

To establish an uniform Rule of Naturalization, and uniform Laws on the subject of Bankruptcies throughout the United States;

To coin Money, regulate the Value thereof, and of foreign Coin, and fix the Standard of Weights and Measures;

To provide for the Punishment of counterfeiting the Securities and current Coin of the United States;

To establish Post Offices and post Roads;

To promote the Progress of Science and useful Arts, by securing for limited Times to Authors and Inventors the exclusive Right to their respective Writings and Discoveries;

To constitute Tribunals inferior to the supreme Court;

To define and punish Piracies and Felonies committed on the high Seas, and Offenses against the Law of Nations;

To declare War, grant Letters of Marque and Reprisal, and make Rules concerning Captures on Land and Water;

To raise and support Armies, but no Appropriation of Money to that Use shall be for a longer Term than two Years;

To provide and maintain a Navy;

To make Rules for the Government and Regulation of the land and naval Forces;

To provide for calling forth the Militia to execute the Laws of the Union, suppress Insurrections and repel Invasions;

To provide for organizing, arming, and disciplining, the Militia, and for governing such Part of them as may be employed in the Service of the United States, reserving to the States respectively, the Appointment of the Officers, and the Authority of training the Militia according to the discipline prescribed by Congress;

To exercise exclusive Legislation in all Cases whatsoever, over such District (not exceeding ten Miles square) as may, by Cession of particular States, and the Acceptance of Congress, become the Seat of the Government of the United States, and to exercise like Authority over all Places purchased by the Consent of the Legislature of the State in which the Same shall be, for the Erection of Forts, Magazines, Arsenals, dock-Yards, and other needful Buildings;—And

To make all Laws which shall be necessary and proper for carrying into Execution the foregoing Powers, and all other Powers vested by this Constitution in the Government of the United States, or in any Department or Officer thereof.

Section 9. The Migration or Importation of such Persons as any of the States now existing shall think proper to admit, shall not be prohibited by the Congress prior to the Year one thousand eight hundred and eight, but a Tax or duty may be imposed on such Importation, not exceeding ten dollars for each Person.

The privilege of the Writ of Habeas Corpus shall not be suspended, unless when in Cases of Rebellion or Invasion the public Safety may require it.

No Bill of Attainder or ex post facto Law shall be passed.

No Capitation, or other direct, Tax shall be laid, unless in Proportion to the Census or Enumeration herein before directed to be taken.

No Tax or Duty shall be laid on Articles exported from any State.

No Preference shall be given by any Regulation of Commerce or Revenue to the Ports of one State over those of another: nor shall Vessels bound to, or from, one State be obliged to enter, clear, or pay Duties in another.

No Money shall be drawn from the Treasury, but in Consequence of Appropriations made by Law; and a regular Statement and Account of the Receipts and Expenditures of all public Money shall be published from time to time.

No Title of Nobility shall be granted by the United States: And no Person holding any Office of Profit or Trust under them, shall, without the Consent of the Congress, accept of any present, Emolument, Office, or Title, of any kind whatever, from any King, Prince, or foreign State.

Section 10. No State shall enter into any Treaty, Alliance, or Confederation; grant Letters of Marque and Reprisal; coin Money; emit Bills of Credit; make any Thing but gold and silver Coin a Tender in Payment of Debts; pass any Bill of Attainder, ex post facto Law, or Law impairing the Obligation of Contracts, or grant any Title of Nobility.

No State shall, without the Consent of the Congress, lay any Imposts or Duties on Imports or Exports, except what may be absolutely necessary for executing its inspection Laws: and the net Produce of all Duties and Imposts, laid by any State on Imports or Exports, shall be for the Use of the Treasury of the United States; and all such Laws shall be subject to the Revision and Controul of the Congress.

No State shall, without the Consent of Congress, lay any Duty of Tonnage, keep Troops, or Ships of War in time of Peace, enter into any Agreement or Compact with another State, or with a foreign Power, or engage in War, unless actually invaded, or in such imminent Danger as will not admit of delay.

Article II

Section 1. The executive Power shall be vested in a President of the United States of America. He shall hold his Office during the Term of four Years, and, together with the Vice President, chosen for the same Term, be elected, as follows:

Each State shall appoint, in such Manner as the Legislature thereof may direct, a Number of Electors, equal to the whole Number of Senators and Representatives to which the State may be entitled in the Congress; but no Senator or Representative, or Person holding an Office of Trust or Profit under the United States, shall be appointed an Elector.

The Electors shall meet in their respective States, and vote by Ballot for two Persons, of whom one at least shall not be an Inhabitant of the same State with themselves. And they shall make a List of all the Persons voted for, and of the Number of Votes for each; which List they shall sign and certify, and transmit sealed to the Seat of the Government of the United States, directed to the President of the Senate. The President of the Senate shall, in the Presence of the Senate and House of Representatives, open all the Certificates, and the Votes shall then be counted. The Person having the greatest Number of Votes shall be the President, if such Number be a Majority of the whole Number of Electors appointed; and if there be more than one who have such Majority, and have an equal Number of Votes, then the House of Representatives shall immediately chuse by Ballot one of them for President; and if no Person have a Majority, then from the five highest on the List the said House shall in like Manner chuse the President. But in chusing the President, the Votes shall be taken by States, the Representation from each State having one Vote; A quorum for this Purpose shall consist of a Member or Members from two thirds of the States, and a Majority of all the States shall be necessary to a Choice. In every Case, after the Choice of the President, the Person having the greater Number of Votes of the Electors shall be the Vice President. But if there should remain two or more who have equal Votes, the Senate shall chuse from them by Ballot the Vice President.

The Congress may determine the Time of chusing the Electors, and the Day on which they shall give their Votes; which Day shall be the same throughout the United States.

No person except a natural born Citizen, or a Citizen of the United States, at the time of the Adoption of this Constitution, shall be eligible to the Office of President; neither shall any Person be eligible to that Office who shall not have attained to the Age of thirty five Years, and been fourteen Years a Resident within the United States.

In Case of the Removal of the President from Office, or of his Death, Resignation or Inability to discharge the Powers and Duties of the said Office, the same shall devolve on the Vice President, and the Congress may by Law provide for the Case of Removal, Death, Resignation or Inability, both of the President and Vice President, declaring what Officer shall then act as President, and such Officer shall act accordingly, until the Disability be removed, or a President shall be elected.

The President shall, at stated Times, receive for his Services, a Compensation, which shall neither be increased nor diminished during the Period for which he shall have been elected, and he shall not receive within that Period any other Emolument from the United States, or any of them.

Before he enter on the Execution of his Office, he shall take the following Oath or Affirmation: "I do solemnly swear (or affirm) that I will faithfully execute the Office of President of the United States, and will to the best of my Ability, preserve, protect and defend the Constitution of the United States."

Section 2. The President shall be Commander in Chief of the Army and Navy of the United States, and of the Militia of the several States, when called into the actual Service of the United States; he may require the Opinion, in writing, of the principal Officer in each of the executive Departments, upon any Subject relating to the Duties of their respective Offices, and he shall have Power to grant Reprieves and Pardons for Offenses against the United States, except in Cases of Impeachment.

He shall have Power, by and with the Advice and Consent of the Senate to make Treaties, provided two thirds of the Senators present concur; and he shall nominate, and by and with the Advice and Consent of the Senate, shall appoint Ambassadors, other public Ministers and Consuls, Judges of the supreme Court, and all other Officers of the United States, whose Appointments are not herein otherwise provided for, and which shall be established by Law; but the Congress may by Law vest the Appointment of such inferior Officers, as they think proper, in the President alone, in the Courts of Law, or in the Heads of Departments.

The President shall have Power to fill up all Vacancies that may happen during the Recess of the Senate, by granting Commissions which shall expire at the End of their next Session.

Section 3. He shall from time to time give to the Congress Information of the State of the Union, and recommend to their Consideration such Measures as he shall judge necessary and expedient; he may, on extraordinary Occasions, convene both Houses, or either of them, and in Case of Disagreement between them, with Respect to the Time of Adjournment, he may adjourn them to such Time as he shall think proper; he shall receive Ambassadors and other public Ministers; he shall take Care that the Laws be faithfully executed, and shall Commission all the Officers of the United States.

Section 4. The President, Vice President and all civil Officers of the United States, shall be removed from Office on Impeachment for, and Conviction of, Treason, Bribery, or other high Crimes and Misdemeanors.

Article III

Section 1. The judicial Power of the United States, shall be vested in one supreme Court, and in such inferior Courts as the Congress may from time to time ordain and establish. The Judges, both of the supreme and inferior Courts, shall hold their Offices during good Behaviour, and shall, at stated Times, receive for their Services a Compensation, which shall not be diminished during their Continuance in Office.

Section 2. The judicial Power shall extend to all Cases, in Law and Equity, arising under this Constitution, the Laws of the United States, and Treaties made, or which shall be made, under their Authority;—to all Cases affecting Ambassadors, other public Ministers and Consuls;—to all Cases of admiralty and maritime Jurisdiction;—to Controversies to which the United States shall be a Party;—to Controversies between two or more States;—between a State and Citizens of another

State;—between Citizens of different States;—between Citizens of the same State claiming Lands under Grants of different States, and between a State, or the Citizens thereof, and foreign States, Citizens or Subjects.

In all Cases affecting Ambassadors, other public Ministers and Consuls, and those in which a State shall be a Party, the supreme Court shall have original Jurisdiction. In all the other Cases before mentioned, the supreme Court shall have appellate Jurisdiction, both as to Law and Fact, with such Exceptions, and under such Regulations as the Congress shall make.

The Trial of all Crimes, except in Cases of Impeachment, shall be by Jury; and such Trial shall be held in the State where the said Crimes shall have been committed; but when not committed within any State, the Trial shall be at such Place or Places as the Congress may by Law have directed.

Section 3. Treason against the United States, shall consist only in levying War against them, or, in adhering to their Enemies, giving them Aid and Comfort. No Person shall be convicted of Treason unless on the Testimony of two Witnesses to the same overt Act, or on Confession in open Court.

The Congress shall have Power to declare the Punishment of Treason, but no Attainder of Treason shall work Corruption of Blood, or Forfeiture except during the Life of the Person attainted.

Article IV

Section 1. Full Faith and Credit shall be given in each State to the public Acts, Records, and judicial Proceedings of every other State. And the Congress may by general Laws prescribe the Manner in which such Acts, Records and Proceedings shall be proved, and the Effect thereof.

Section 2. The Citizens of each State shall be entitled to all Privileges and Immunities of Citizens in the several States.

A Person charged in any State with Treason, Felony, or other Crime, who shall flee from Justice, and be found in another State, shall on Demand of the executive Authority of the State from which he fled, be delivered up, to be removed to the State having Jurisdiction of the Crime.

No Person held to Service or Labour in one State, under the Laws thereof, escaping into another, shall, in Consequence of any Law or Regulation therein, be discharged from such Service or Labour, but shall be delivered up on Claim of the Party to whom such Service or Labour may be due.

Section 3. New States may be admitted by the Congress into this Union; but no new State shall be formed or erected within the Jurisdiction of any other State; nor any State be formed by the Junction of two or more States, or Parts of States, without the Consent of the Legislatures of the States concerned as well as of the Congress.

The Congress shall have Power to dispose of and make all needful Rules and Regulations respecting the Territory or other Property belonging to the United States; and nothing in this Constitution shall be so construed as to Prejudice any Claims of the United States, or of any particular State.

Section 4. The United States shall guarantee to every State in this Union a Republican Form of Government, and shall protect each of them against Invasion; and on Application of the Legislature, or of the Executive (when the Legislature cannot be convened) against domestic Violence.

Article V

The Congress, whenever two thirds of both Houses shall deem it necessary, shall propose Amendments to this Constitution, or, on the Application of the Legislatures of two thirds of the several States, shall call a Convention for proposing Amendments, which, in either Case, shall be valid to all Intents and Purposes, as part of this Constitution, when ratified by the Legislatures of three fourths of the several States, or by Conventions in three fourths thereof, as the one or the other Mode of Ratification may be proposed by the Congress; Provided that no Amendment which may be made prior to the Year One thousand eight hundred and eight shall in any Manner affect the first and fourth Clauses in the Ninth Section of the first Article; and that no State, without its Consent, shall be deprived of its equal Suffrage in the Senate.

Article VI

All Debts contracted and Engagements entered into, before the Adoption of this Constitution shall be as valid against the United States under this Constitution, as under the Confederation.

This Constitution, and the Laws of the United States which shall be made in Pursuance thereof; and all Treaties made, or which shall be made, under the Authority of the United States, shall be the supreme Law of the Land; and the Judges in every State shall be bound thereby, any Thing in the Constitution or Laws of any State to the Contrary notwithstanding.

The Senators and Representatives before mentioned, and the Members of the several State Legislatures, and all executive and judicial Officers, both of the United States and of the several States, shall be bound by Oath or Affirmation, to support this Constitution; but no religious Test shall ever be required as a Qualification to any Office or public Trust under the United States.

Article VII

The Ratification of the Conventions of nine States shall be sufficient for the Establishment of this Constitution between the States so ratifying the Same.

Amendment I [1791]

Congress shall make no law respecting an establishment of religion, or prohibiting the free exercise thereof; or abridging the freedom of speech, or of the press; or the right of the people peaceably to assembly, and to petition the Government for a redress of grievances.

Amendment II [1791]

A well regulated Militia, being necessary to the security of a free State, the right of the people to keep and bear Arms, shall not be infringed.

Amendment III [1791]

No Soldier shall, in time of peace be quartered in any house, without the consent of the Owner, nor in time of war, but in a manner to be prescribed by law.

Amendment IV [1791]

The right of the people to be secure in their persons, houses, papers, and effects, against unreasonable searches and seizures, shall not be violated, and no Warrants shall issue, but upon probable cause, supported by Oath or affirmation, and particularly describing the place to be searched, and the persons or things to be seized.

Amendment V [1791]

No person shall be held to answer for a capital, or otherwise infamous crime, unless on a presentment or indictment of a Grand Jury, except in cases arising in the land or naval forces, or in the Militia, when in actual service in time of War or public danger; nor shall any person be subject for the same offence to be twice put in jeopardy of life or limb; nor shall be compelled in any criminal case to be a witness against himself, nor be deprived of life, liberty, or property, without due process of law; nor shall private property be taken for public use, without just compensation.

Amendment VI [1791]

In all criminal prosecutions, the accused shall enjoy the right to a speedy and public trial, by an impartial jury of the State and district wherein the crime shall have been committed, which district shall have been previously ascertained by law, and to be informed of the nature and cause of the accusation; to be confronted with the witnesses against him; to have compulsory process for obtaining witnesses in his favor, and to have the Assistance of Counsel for his defence.

Amendment VII [1791]

In Suits at common law, where the value in controversy shall exceed twenty dollars, the right of trial by jury shall be preserved, and no fact tried by jury, shall be otherwise re-examined in any Court of the United States, than according to the rules of the common law.

Amendment VIII [1791]

Excessive bail shall not be required, nor excessive fines imposed, nor cruel and unusual punishments inflicted.

Amendment IX [1791]

The enumeration in the Constitution, of certain rights, shall not be construed to deny or disparage others retained by the people.

Amendment X [1791]

The powers not delegated to the United States by the Constitution, nor prohibited by it to the States, are reserved to the States respectively, or to the people.

Amendment XI [1798]

The Judicial power of the United States shall not be construed to extend to any suit in law or equity, commenced or prosecuted against one of the United States by Citizens of another State, or by Citizens or Subjects of any Foreign State.

Amendment XII [1804]

The Electors shall meet in their respective states, and vote by ballot for President and Vice-President, one of whom, at least, shall not be an inhabitant of the same state with themselves; they shall name in their ballots the person voted for as President, and in distinct ballots the person voted for as Vice-President, and they shall make distinct lists of all persons voted for as President, and of all persons voted for as Vice-President, and of the number of votes for each, which lists they shall sign and certify, and transmit sealed to the seat of the government of the United States, directed to the President of the Senate;—The President of the Senate shall, in the presence of the Senate and House of Representatives, open all the certificates and the votes shall then be counted;— The person having the greatest number of votes for President, shall be the President, if such number be a majority of the whole number of Electors appointed; and if no person have such majority, then from the persons having the highest numbers not exceeding three on the list of those voted for as President, the House of Representatives shall choose immediately, by ballot, the President. But in choosing the President, the votes shall be taken by states, the representation from each state having one vote; a quorum for this purpose shall consist of a member or members from two-thirds of the states, and a majority of all states shall be necessary to a choice. And if the House of Representatives shall not choose a President whenever the right of choice shall devolve upon them, before the fourth day of March next following, then the Vice-President shall act as President, as in the case of the death or other constitutional disability of the President.—The person having the greatest number of votes as Vice-President, shall be the Vice-President, if such number be a majority of the whole number of Electors appointed, and if no person have a majority, then from the two highest numbers on the list, the Senate shall choose the Vice-President; a quorum for the purpose shall consist of two-thirds of the whole number of Senators, and a majority of the whole number shall be necessary to a choice. But no person constitutionally ineligible to the office of President shall be eligible to that of Vice-President of the United States.

Amendment XIII [1865]

Section 1. Neither slavery nor involuntary servitude, except as a punishment for crime whereof the party shall have been duly convicted, shall exist within the United States, or any place subject to their jurisdiction.

Section 2. Congress shall have power to enforce this article by appropriate legislation.

Amendment XIV [1868]

Section 1. All persons born or naturalized in the United States, and subject to the jurisdiction thereof, are citizens of the United States and of the State wherein they reside. No State shall make or enforce any law which shall abridge the privileges or immunities of citizens of the United States; nor shall any State deprive any person of life, liberty, or property, without due process of law; nor deny to any person within its jurisdiction the equal protection of the laws.

Section 2. Representatives shall be apportioned among the several States according to their respective numbers, counting the whole number of persons in each State, excluding Indians not taxed. But when the right to vote at any election for the choice of electors for President and Vice President of the United States, Representatives in Congress, the Executive and Judicial officers of a State, or the members of the Legislature thereof, is denied to any of the male inhabitants of such State, being twenty-one years of age, and citizens of the United States, or in any way abridged, except for participation in rebellion, or other crime, the basis of representation therein shall be reduced in the proportion which the number of such male citizens shall bear to the whole number of male citizens twenty-one years of age in such State.

Section 3. No person shall be a Senator or Representative in Congress, or elector of President and Vice President, or hold any office, civil or military, under the United States, or under any State, who having previously taken an oath, as a member of Congress, or as an officer of the United States, or as a member of any State legislature, or as an executive or judicial officer of any State, to support the Constitution of the United States, shall have engaged in insurrection or rebellion against the same, or given aid or comfort to the enemies thereof. But Congress may by a vote of two-thirds of each House, remove such disability.

Section 4. The validity of the public debt of the United States, authorized by law, including debts incurred for payment of pensions and bounties for services in suppressing insurrection or rebellion, shall not be questioned. But neither the United States nor any State shall assume or pay any debt or obligation incurred in aid of insurrection or rebellion against the United States, or any claim for the loss or emancipation of any slave; but all such debts, obligations and claims shall be held illegal and void.

Section 5. The Congress shall have power to enforce, by appropriate legislation, the provisions of this article.

Amendment XV [1870]

Section 1. The right of citizens of the United States to vote shall not be denied or abridged by the United States or by any State on account of race, color, or previous condition of servitude.

Section 2. The Congress shall have power to enforce this article by appropriate legislation.

Amendment XVI [1913]

The Congress shall have power to lay and collect taxes on incomes, from whatever source derived, without apportionment among the several States, and without regard to any census or enumeration.

Amendment XVII [1913]

Section 1. The Senate of the United States shall be composed of two Senators from each State, elected by the people thereof, for six years; and each Senator shall have one vote. The electors in each State shall have the qualifications requisite for electors of the most numerous branch of the State legislatures.

Section 2. When vacancies happen in the representation of any State in the Senate, the executive authority of such State shall issue writs of election to fill such vacancies: Provided, That the legislature of any State may empower the executive thereof to make temporary appointments until the people fill the vacancies by election as the legislature may direct.

Section 3. This amendment shall not be so construed as to affect the election or term of any Senator chosen before it becomes valid as part of the Constitution.

Amendment XVIII [1919]

Section 1. After one year from the ratification of this article the manufacture, sale, or transportation of intoxicating liquors within, the importation thereof into, or the exportation thereof from the United States and all territory subject to the jurisdiction thereof for beverage purposes is hereby prohibited.

Section 2. The Congress and the several States shall have concurrent power to enforce this article by appropriate legislation.

Section 3. This article shall be inoperative unless it shall have been ratified as an amendment to the Constitution by the legislatures of the several States, as provided in the Constitution, within seven years from the date of the submission hereof to the States by the Congress.

Amendment XIX [1920]

Section 1. The right of citizens of the United States to vote shall not be denied or abridged by the United States or by any State on account of sex.

Section 2. Congress shall have power to enforce this article by appropriate legislation.

Amendment XX [1933]

Section 1. The terms of the President and Vice President shall end at noon on the 20th day of January, and the terms of Senators and Representatives at noon on the 3d day of January, of the years in which such terms would have ended if this article had not been ratified; and the terms of their successors shall then begin.

Section 2. The Congress shall assemble at least once in every year, and such meeting shall begin at noon on the 3d day of January, unless they shall by law appoint a different day.

Section 3. If, at the time fixed for the beginning of the term of the President, the President elect shall have died, the Vice President elect shall become President. If the President shall not have been chosen before the time fixed for the beginning of his term, or if the President elect shall have failed to qualify, then the Vice President elect shall act as President until a President shall have qualified; and the Congress may by law provide for the case wherein neither a President elect nor a Vice President elect shall have qualified, declaring who shall then act as President, or the manner in which one who is to act shall be selected, and such person shall act accordingly until a President or Vice President shall have qualified.

Section 4. The Congress may by law provide for the case of the death of any of the persons from whom the House of Representatives may choose a President whenever the right of choice shall have devolved upon them, and for the case of the death of any of the persons from whom the Senate may choose a Vice President whenever the right of choice shall have devolved upon them.

Section 5. Sections 1 and 2 shall take effect on the 15th day of October following the ratification of this article.

Section 6. This article shall be inoperative unless it shall have been ratified as an amendment to the Constitution by the legislatures of three-fourths of the several States within seven years from the date of its submission.

Amendment XXI [1933]

Section 1. The eighteenth article of amendment to the Constitution of the United States is hereby repealed.

Section 2. The transportation or importation into any State, Territory, or possession of the United States for delivery or use therein of intoxicating liquors, in violation of the laws thereof, is hereby prohibited.

Section 3. This article shall be inoperative unless it shall have been ratified as an amendment to the Constitution by conventions in the several States, as provided in the Constitution, within seven years from the date of the submission hereof to the States by the Congress.

Amendment XXII [1951]

Section 1. No person shall be elected to the office of the President more than twice, and no person who has held the office of President, or acted as President, for more than two years of a term to which some other person was elected President shall be elected to the office of President more than once. But this Article shall not apply to any person holding the office of President when this Article was proposed by the Congress, and shall not prevent any person who may be holding the office of President, or acting as President, during the term within which this Article becomes operative from holding the office of President or acting as President during the remainder of such term.

Section 2. This article shall be inoperative unless it shall have been ratified as an amendment to the Constitution by the legislatures of three-fourths of the several States within seven years from the date of its submission to the States by the Congress.

Amendment XXIII [1961]

Section 1. The District constituting the seat of Government of the United States shall appoint in such manner as the Congress may direct:

A number of electors of President and Vice President equal to the whole number of Senators and Representatives in Congress to which the District would be entitled if it were a State, but in no event more than the least populous state; they shall be in addition to those appointed by the states, but they shall be considered, for the purposes of the election of President and Vice President, to be electors appointed by a state; and they shall meet in the District and perform such duties as provided by the twelfth article of amendment.

Section 2. The Congress shall have power to enforce this article by appropriate legislation.

Amendment XXIV [1964]

Section 1. The right of citizens of the United States to vote in any primary or other election for President or Vice President, for electors for President or Vice President, or for Senator or Representative in Congress, shall not be denied or abridged by the United States, or any State by reason of failure to pay any poll tax or other tax.

Section 2. The Congress shall have power to enforce this article by appropriate legislation.

Amendment XXV [1967]

Section 1. In case of the removal of the President from office or of his death or resignation, the Vice President shall become President.

Section 2. Whenever there is a vacancy in the office of the Vice President, the President shall nominate a Vice President who shall take office upon confirmation by a majority vote of both Houses of Congress.

Section 3. Whenever the President transmits to the President pro tempore of the Senate and the Speaker of the House of Representatives his written declaration that he is unable to discharge the powers and duties of his office, and until he transmits to them a written declaration to the contrary, such powers and duties shall be discharged by the Vice President as Acting President.

Section 4. Whenever the Vice President and a majority of either the principal officers of the executive departments or of such other body as Congress may by law provide, transmit to the President pro tempore of the Senate and the Speaker of the House of Representatives their written declaration that the President is unable to discharge the powers and duties of his office, the Vice President shall immediately assume the powers and duties of the office as Acting President.

Thereafter, when the President transmits to the President pro tempore of the Senate and the Speaker of the House of Representatives his written declaration that no inability exists, he shall resume the powers and duties of his office unless the Vice President and a majority of either the principal officers of the executive department or of such other body as Congress may by law provide, transmit within four days to the President pro tempore of the Senate and the Speaker of the House of Representatives their written declaration and the President is unable to discharge the powers and duties of his office. Thereupon Congress shall decide the issue, assembling within forty-eight hours for that purpose if not in session. If the Congress, within twenty-one days after receipt of the latter written declaration, or, if Congress is not in session, within twenty-one days after Congress is required to assemble, determines by two-thirds vote of both Houses that the President is unable to discharge the powers and duties of his office, the Vice President shall continue to discharge the same as Acting President; otherwise, the President shall resume the powers and duties of his office.

Amendment XXVI [1971]

Section 1. The right of citizens of the United States, who are eighteen years of age or older, to vote shall not be denied or abridged by the United States or by any State on account of age.

Section 2. The Congress shall have power to enforce this article by appropriate legislation.

Amendment XXVII [1992]

No law, varying the compensation for the services of the Senators and Representatives, shall take effect, until an election of Representatives shall have intervened.

APPENDIX B: Title VII of the Civil Rights Act of 1964 [Excerpts]

Title VII of the Civil Rights Act of 1964—The Employment Discrimination Section

Section 703. Unlawful Employment Practices. (a) It shall be an unlawful employment practice for an employer—

(1) to fail or refuse to hire or to discharge any individual, or otherwise to discriminate against any individual with respect to his compensation, terms, conditions, or privileges of employment, because of such individual's race, color, religion, sex, or national origin; or

(2) to limit, segregate, or classify his employees or applicants for employment in any way which would deprive or tend to deprive any individual of employment opportunities

or otherwise adversely affect his status as an employee, because of such individual's race, color, religion, sex, or national origin.

(b) It shall be an unlawful employment practice for an employment agency to fail or refuse to refer for employment, or otherwise to discriminate against, any individual because of his race, color, religion, sex, or national origin, or to classify or refer for employment any individual on the basis or his race, color, religion, sex, or national origin.

(c) It shall be an unlawful employment practice for a labor organization—

(1) to exclude or to expel from its membership, or otherwise to discriminate against, any individual because of his race, color, religion, sex, or national origin;

(2) to limit, segregate, or classify its membership or applicants for membership, or to classify or fail or refuse to refer for employment any individual, in any way which would deprive or tend to deprive any individual of employment opportunities, or would limit such employment opportunities or otherwise adversely affect his status as an employee or as an applicant for employment, because of such individual's race, color, religion, sex, or national origin; or

(3) to cause or attempt to cause an employer to discriminate against an individual in violation of this section.

(d) It shall be an unlawful employment practice for any employer, labor organization, or joint labor-management committee controlling apprenticeship or other training or retraining, including on-the-job training programs to discriminate against any individual because of his race, color, religion, sex, or national origin in admission to, or employment in, any program established to provide apprenticeship or other training.

(e) Notwithstanding any other provision of this subchapter—

(1) it shall not be an unlawful employment practice for an employer to hire and employ employees, for an employment agency to classify, or refer for employment any individual, for a labor organization to classify its membership or to classify or refer for employment any individual, or for an employer, labor organization, or joint labor-management committee controlling apprenticeship or other training or retraining programs to admit or employ any individual in any such program, on the basis of his religion, sex, or national origin in those certain instances where religion, sex, or national origin is a bona fide occupational qualification reasonably necessary to the normal operation of that particular business or enterprise, and

(2) it shall not be an unlawful employment practice for a school, college, university, or other educational institution or institution of learning to hire and employ employees of a particular religion if such school, college, university, or other educational institution or institution of learning is, in whole or in substantial part, owned, supported, controlled, or managed by a particular religion or by a particular religious corporation, association, or society, or if the curriculum of such school, college, university, or other educational institution or institution of learning is directed toward the propagation of a particular religion.

(f) As used in this subchapter, the phrase "unlawful employment practice" shall not be deemed to include any action or measure taken by an employer, labor organization, joint labor-management committee, or employment agency with respect to an individual who is a member of the Communist Party of the United States or of any other organization required to register as a Communist-action or Communist-front organization. . . .

(g) Notwithstanding any other provision of this subchapter, it shall not be an unlawful employment practice for an employer to fail or refuse to hire and employ any individual for any position, for an employer to discharge any individual from any position, or for an employment agency to fail or refuse to refer any individual for employment in any position, or for a labor organization to fail or refuse to refer any individual for employment in any position, if—

(1) the occupancy of such position, or access to the premises in or upon which any part of the duties of such position is performed or is to be performed, is subject to any requirement imposed in the interest of the national security of the United States . . . and

(2) such individual has not fulfilled or has ceased to fulfill that requirement.

(h) Notwithstanding any other provision of this subchapter, it shall not be an unlawful employment practice for an employer to apply different standards of compensation, or different terms, conditions, or privileges of employment pursuant to a bona fide seniority or merit system, or a system which measures earnings by quantity or quality of production or to employees who work in different locations, provided that such differences are not the result of an intention to discriminate because of race, color, religion, sex, or national origin, nor shall it be an unlawful employment practice for an employer to give and act upon the results of any professionally developed ability test provided that such test, its administration or action upon the results is not designed, intended or used to discriminate because of race, color, religion, sex, or national origin. . . .

(j) Nothing contained in this subchapter shall be interpreted to require any employer, employment agency, labor organization, or joint labor-management committee subject to this subchapter to grant preferential treatment to any individual or to any group because of the race, color, religion, sex, or national origin of such individual or group on account of an imbalance which may exist with respect to the total number or percentage of persons of any race, color, religion, sex, or national origin employed by any employer, referred or classified for employment by any employment agency or labor organization, or admitted to, or employed in, any apprenticeship or other training program, in comparison with the total number or percentage of persons of such race, color, religion, sex, or national origin in any community, State, section, or other area, or in the available work force in any community, State, section, or other area.

Section 704. Other Unlawful Employment Practices. (a) It shall be an unlawful employment practice for an employer to discriminate against any of his employees or applicants for employment, for an employment agency, or joint labor-management committee controlling apprenticeship or other training or retraining, including on-the-job training programs, to discriminate against any individual, or for a labor organization to discriminate against any member thereof or applicant for membership, because he has opposed any practice made an unlawful employment practice by this subchapter, or because he has made a charge, testified, assisted, or participated in any manner in an investigation, proceeding, or hearing under this subchapter.

(b) It shall be an unlawful employment practice for an employer, labor organization, employment agency, or joint labor-management committee controlling apprenticeship or other training or retraining, including on-the-job training programs, to print or publish or cause to be printed or published any notice or advertisement relating to employment by such an employer or membership or any classification or referral for employment by such a labor organization, or relating to any classification or referral for employment by such an employment agency, or relating to admission to, or employment in, any program established to provide apprenticeship or other training by such a joint-labor-management committee, indicating any preference, limitation, specification, or discrimination, based on race, color, religion, sex, or national origin, except that such a notice or advertisement may indicate a preference, limitation, specification, or discrimination based on religion, sex or national origin when religion, sex, or national origin is a bona fide occupational qualification for employment.

APPENDIX C: Americans with Disabilities Act of 1990 [Excerpts] and ADA Amendments Act of 2008 [Excerpts]

Americans with Disabilities Act of 1990 [Excerpts]

Title 1– Employment

Sec. 101. Definitions

As used in this title: . . .

(8) Qualified individual with a disability. The term "qualified individual with a disability" means an individual with a disability who, with or without reasonable accommodation, can perform the essential functions of the employment position that such individual holds or desires. For the purposes of this title, consideration shall be given to the employer's judgment as to what functions of a job are essential, and if an employer has prepared a written description before advertising or interviewing applicants for the job, this description shall be considered evidence of the essential functions of the job.

(9) Reasonable accommodation. The term "reasonable accommodation" may include

(A) making existing facilities used by employees readily accessible to and usable by individuals with disabilities; and (B) job restructuring, part-time or modified work schedules, reassignment to a vacant position, acquisition or modification of equipment or devices, appropriate adjustment or modifications of examinations, training materials or policies, the provision of qualified readers or interpreters, and other similar accommodations for individuals with disabilities.

(10) Undue Hardship.

(A) *In general.* The term "undue hardship" means an action requiring significant difficulty or expense, when considered in light of the factors set forth in subparagraph(B).

(B) *Factors to be considered.* In determining whether an accommodation would impose an undue hardship on a covered entity, factors to be considered include

(i) the nature and cost of accommodation needed under this Act;

(ii) the overall financial resources of the facility or facilities involved in the provision of the reasonable accommodation; the number of persons employed at such facility; the effect on expenses and resources, or the impact otherwise of such accommodation upon the operation of the facility;

(iii) the overall financial resources of the covered entity; the overall size of the business of a covered entity with respect to the number of its employees; the number, type, and location of its facilities; and

(iv) the type of operation or operations of the covered entity, including the composition, structure, and functions of the workforce of such entity; the geographic separateness, administrative, or fiscal relationship of the facility or facilities in question to the covered entity.

Sec. 102. Discrimination

(a) General Rule. No covered entity shall discriminate against a qualified individual with a disability because of the disability of such individual in regard to job application procedures, the hiring, advancement, or discharge of employees, employee compensation, job training, and other terms, conditions, and privileges of employment.

(b) Construction. As used in subsection (a), the term "discriminate" includes

(1) limiting, segregating, or classifying a job applicant or employee in a way that adversely affects the opportunities or status of such applicant or employee because of the disability of such applicant or employee;

(2) participating in a contractual or other arrangement or relationship that has the effect of subjecting a covered entity's qualified applicant or employee with a disability to the discrimination prohibited by this title (such relationship includes a relationship with an employment or referral agency, labor union, an organization providing fringe benefits to an employee of the covered entity, or an organization providing training and apprenticeship programs);

(3) utilizing standards, criteria, or methods of administration

(A) that have the effect of discrimination on the basis of disability; or

(B) that perpetuate the discrimination of others who are subject to common administrative control;

(4) excluding or otherwise denying equal jobs or benefits to a qualified individual because of the known disability of an individual with whom the qualified individual is known to have a relationship or association;

(5)(A) not making reasonable accommodations to the known physical or mental limitations of an otherwise qualified individual with a disability who is an applicant or employee, unless such covered entity can demonstrate that the accommodation would impose an undue hardship on the operation of the business of such covered entity; or

(B) denying employment opportunities to a job applicant or employee who is an otherwise qualified individual with a disability, if such denial is based on the need of such covered entity to make reasonable accommodation to the physical or mental impairments of the employee or applicant;

(6) using qualification standards, employment tests or other selection criteria that screen out or tend to screen out an individual with a disability or a class of individuals with disabilities unless the standard, test or other selection criteria, as used by the covered entity, is shown to be job-related for the position in question and is consistent with business necessity; and

(7) failing to select and administer tests concerning employment in the most effective manner to ensure that, when such test is administered to a job applicant or employee who has a disability that impairs sensory, manual, or speaking skills, such test results accurately reflect the skills, aptitude, or whatever other factor of such applicant or employee that such test purports to measure, rather than reflecting the impaired sensory, manual, or speaking skills of such employee or applicant (except where such skills are the factors that the test purports to measure). . . .

Sec. 104. Illegal Use of Drugs and Alcohol

(b) Rules of Construction. Nothing in subsection (a) shall be construed to exclude as a qualified individual with a disability an individual who

(1) has successfully completed a supervised drug rehabilitation program and is no longer engaging in the illegal use of drugs, or has otherwise been rehabilitated successfully and is no longer engaging in such use;

(2) is participating in a supervised rehabilitation program and is no longer engaging in such use; or

(3) is erroneously regarded as engaging in such use, but is not engaging in such use; except that it shall not be a violation of this Act for a covered entity to adopt or administer reasonable policies or procedures, including but not limited to drug testing, designed to ensure that an individual described in paragraph (1) or (2) is no longer engaging in the illegal use of drugs. . . .

Sec. 107. Enforcement.

(a) Powers, Remedies, and Procedures. The powers, remedies, and procedures set forth in sections 705, 706, 707, 709, and 710 of the Civil Rights Act of 1964 (42 U.S.C. 2000e-4, 2000e-5, 2000e-6, 2000e-8, and 2000e-9) shall be the powers, remedies, and procedures this title provides to the Commission, to the Attorney General, or to any person alleging discrimination on the basis of disability in violation of any provision of this Act, or regulations promulgated under section 106, concerning employment.

(b) Coordination. The agencies with enforcement authority for actions which allege employment discrimination under this title and under the Rehabilitation Act of 1973 shall develop procedures to ensure that administrative complaints filed under this title and under the Rehabilitation Act of 1973 are dealt with in a manner that avoids duplication of effort and prevents imposition of inconsistent or conflicting standards for the same requirements under this title and the Rehabilitation Act of 1973. The Commission, the Attorney General, and the Office of Federal Contract Compliance Programs shall establish such coordinating mechanisms (similar to provisions contained in the joint regulations promulgated by the Commission and the Attorney General at part 42 of title 28 and part 1691 of title 29, Code of Federal Regulations, and the Memorandum of Understanding between the Commission and the Office of Federal Contract Compliance Programs dated January 16, 1981 (46 Fed. Reg. 7435, January 23, 1981)) in regulations implementing this title and Rehabilitation Act of 1973 not later than 18 months after the date of enactment of this Act.

Sec. 108. Effective Date.

This title shall become effective 24 months after the date of enactment.

ADA Amendments Act of 2008 [Excerpts]

Sec. 2. Findings and Purposes

(a) Findings. Congress finds that

(1) in enacting the Americans with Disabilities Act of 1990 (ADA), Congress intended that the Act "provide a clear and comprehensive national mandate for the elimination of discrimination against individuals with disabilities" and provide broad coverage;

(2) in enacting the ADA, Congress recognized that physical and mental disabilities in no way diminish a person's right to fully participate in all aspects of society, but that people with physical or mental disabilities are frequently precluded from doing so because of prejudice, antiquated attitudes, or the failure to remove societal and institutional barriers;

(3) while Congress expected that the definition of disability under the ADA would be interpreted consistently with how courts had applied the definition of a handicapped individual under the Rehabilitation Act of 1973, that expectation has not been fulfilled;

(4) the holdings of the Supreme Court in Sutton v. United Air Lines, Inc., 527 U.S. 471 (1999) and its companion cases have narrowed the broad scope of protection intended to be afforded by the ADA, thus eliminating protection for many individuals whom Congress intended to protect;

(5) the holding of the Supreme Court in Toyota Motor Manufacturing, Kentucky, Inc., v. Williams, 534 U.S. 184 (2002) further narrowed the broad scope of protection intended to be afforded by the ADA;

(6) as a result of these Supreme Court cases, lower courts have incorrectly found in individual cases that people with a range of substantially limiting impairments are not people with disabilities;

(7) in particular, the Supreme Court, in the case of Toyota Motor Manufacturing, Kentucky, Inc., v. Williams, 534 U.S. 184 (2002), interpreted the term "substantially limits" to require a greater degree of limitation than was intended by Congress; and

(8) Congress finds that the current Equal Employment Opportunity Commission ADA regulations defining the term "substantially limits" as "significantly restricted" are inconsistent with congressional intent, by expressing too high a standard. . . .

Sec. 4 Disability Defined and Rules of Construction

(a) Definition of Disability. Section 3 of the Americans with Disabilities Act of 1990 (42 U.S.C. 12102) is amended to read as follows:

"Sec. 3. Definition of Disability.

"As used in this Act:

"Disability. The term 'disability' means, with respect to an individual

"(A) A physical or mental impairment that substantially limits one or more major life activities of an individual;

"(B) a record of such an impairment; or

"(C) being regarded as having such an impairment (as described in paragraph (3)).

"(2) Major Life Activities.

"**(A)** In *General.* For purposes of paragraph (1), major life activities include, but are not limited to, caring for oneself, performing manual tasks, seeing, hearing, eating, sleeping, walking, standing, lifting, bending, speaking, breathing, learning, reading, concentrating, thinking, communicating, and working.

"**(B)** *Major Bodily Functions.* For purposes of paragraph (1), a major life activity also includes the operation of a major bodily function, including but not limited to, functions of the immune system, normal cell growth, digestive, bowel, bladder, neurological, brain, respiratory, circulatory, endocrine, and reproductive functions.

"(3) Regarded As Having Such An Impairment. For purposes of paragraph (1)(C):

"**(A)** An individual meets the requirement of 'being regarded as having such an impairment' if the individual establishes that he or she has been subjected to an action prohibited under this Act because of an actual or perceived physical or mental impairment whether or not the impairment limits or is perceived to limit a major life activity.

"**(B)** Paragraph (1)(C) shall not apply to impairments that are transitory and minor. A transitory impairment is an impairment with an actual or expected duration of 6 months or less.

"(4) Rules Of Construction Regarding The Definition Of Disability. The definition of 'disability' in paragraph (1) shall be construed in accordance with the following:

"**(A)** The definition of disability in this Act shall be construed in favor of broad coverage of individuals under this Act, to the maximum extent permitted by the terms of this Act.

"**(B)** The term 'substantially limits' shall be interpreted consistently with the findings and purposes of the ADA Amendments Act of 2008.

"**(C)** An impairment that substantially limits one major life activity need not limit other major life activities in order to be considered a disability.

"**(D)** An impairment that is episodic or in remission is a disability if it would substantially limit a major life activity when active.

"**(E)** (i) The determination of whether an impairment substantially limits a major life activity shall be made without regard to the ameliorative effects of mitigating measures such as—

"(I) medication, medical supplies, equipment, or appliances, low-vision devices (which do not include ordinary eyeglasses or contact lenses), prosthetics including limbs and devices, hearing aids and cochlear implants or other implantable hearing devices, mobility devices, or oxygen therapy equipment and supplies;

"(II) use of assistive technology;

"(III) reasonable accommodations or auxiliary aids or services; or

"(IV) learned behavioral or adaptive neurological modifications.

"(ii) The ameliorative effects of the mitigating measures of ordinary eyeglasses or contact lenses shall be considered in determining whether an impairment substantially limits a major life activity.

"(iii) As used in this subparagraph

"(I) the term 'ordinary eyeglasses or contact lenses' means lenses that are intended to fully correct visual acuity or eliminate refractive error; and

"(II) the term 'low-vision devices' means devices that magnify, enhance, or otherwise augment a visual image. . . . "

APPENDIX D: Sherman Antitrust Act [Excerpts]

Section 1. Every contract, combination in the form of trust or otherwise, or conspiracy, in restraint of trade or commerce among the several States, or with foreign nations, is hereby declared to be illegal. Every person who shall make any contract or engage in any such combination or conspiracy shall be deemed guilty of a felony, and, on conviction thereof, shall be punished by fine not exceeding $10,000,000 if a corporation, or, if any other person, $350,000 or by imprisonment not exceeding three years, or by both said punishments in the discretion of the court.

Section 2. Every person who shall monopolize, or attempt to monopolize, or conspire with any other person or persons, to monopolize any part of the trade or commerce among the several States, or with foreign nations, shall be deemed guilty of a felony, and, on conviction thereof, shall be punished by fine not exceeding $10,000,000 if a corporation, or, if any other person, $350,000 or by imprisonment not exceeding three years, or by both said punishments, in the discretion of the court.

APPENDIX E: Clayton Act of 1914 [Excerpts]

Section 3. That it shall be unlawful for any person engaged in commerce, in the course of such commerce, to lease or make a sale or contract for sale of goods, wares, merchandise, machinery, supplies, or other commodities, whether patented or unpatented, for use, consumption, or resale within the United States or . . . other place under the jurisdiction of the United States, or fix a price charged therefor, or discount from, or rebate upon, such price, on the condition, agreement, or understanding that the lessee or purchaser thereof shall not use or deal in the goods, wares, merchandise, machinery, supplies, or other commodities of a competitor or competitors of the lessor or seller, where the effect of such lease, sale, or contract for sale or such condition, agreement, or understanding may be to substantially lessen competition to tend to create a monopoly in any line of commerce.

Section 4. That any person who shall be injured in his business or property by reason of anything forbidden in the antitrust laws may sue therefor in any district court of the United States in the district in which the defendant resides or is found, or has an agent, without respect to the amount in controversy, and shall recover threefold the damages by him sustained, and the cost of suit, including a reasonable attorney's fee.

Section 4A. Whenever the United States is hereafter injured in its business or property by reason of anything forbidden in the antitrust laws it may sue therefor in the United States district court for the district in which the defendant resides or is found or has an agent, without respect to the amount in controversy, and shall recover actual damages by it sustained and the cost of suit.

Section 4B. Any action to enforce any cause of action under sections 4 or 4A shall be forever barred unless commenced within four years after the cause of action accrued. No cause of action barred under existing law on the effective date of this act shall be revived by this Act.

Section 6. That the labor of a human being is not a commodity or article of commerce. Nothing contained in the antitrust laws shall be construed to forbid the existence and operation of labor, agricultural or horticultural organizations, instituted for the purposes of mutual help, and not having capital stock or conducted for profit, or to forbid or restrain individual members of such organizations from lawfully carrying out the legitimate objects thereof; nor shall such organizations or the members thereof, be held or construed to be illegal combinations or conspiracies in restraint of trade, under the antitrust laws.

Section 7. That no person engaged in commerce shall acquire, directly or indirectly, the whole or any part of the stock or other share capital and no corporation subject to the jurisdiction of the Federal Trade Commission shall acquire the whole or any part of the assets of another corporation engaged also in commerce, where in any line of commerce in any section of the country, the effect of such acquisition may be substantially to lessen competition, or to tend to create a monopoly.

No person shall acquire, directly or indirectly, the whole or any part of the stock or other share capital and no corporation subject to the jurisdiction of the Federal Trade Commission shall acquire the whole or any part of the assets of one or more corporations engaged in commerce, where in any line of commerce in any section of the country, the effect of such acquisition, of such stocks or assets, or of the use of such stock by the voting or granting of proxies or otherwise, may be substantially to lessen competition, or to tend to create a monopoly.

This section shall not apply to persons purchasing such stock solely for investment and not using the same by voting or otherwise to bring about, or in attempting to bring about, the substantial lessening of competition . . . .

Section 8. . . . No person shall, at the same time, serve as a director or officer in any two or more corporations (other than banks, banking associations, and trust companies) that are—

(A) engaged in whole or in part in commerce; and

(B) by virtue of their business and location of operation, competitors, so that the elimination of competition by agreement between them would constitute a violation of any of the antitrust laws; if each of the corporations has capital, surplus, and undivided profits aggregating more than $10,000,000 as adjusted pursuant to paragraph (5) of this subsection.

APPENDIX F: Federal Trade Commission Act of 1914 [Excerpts]

Unfair Methods of Competition Prohibited

Section 5. Unfair methods of competition unlawful; prevention by Commission—declaration. Declaration of unlawfulness; power to prohibit unfair practices.

(a) (1) Unfair methods of competition in or affecting commerce, and unfair or deceptive acts or practices in or affecting commerce, are declared unlawful.

. . .

(b) Any person, partnership, or corporation who violates an order of the Commission to cease and desist after it has become final, and while such order is in effect, shall forfeit and pay to the United States a civil penalty of not more than $10,000 for each violation, which shall accrue to the United States and may be recovered in a civil action brought by the Attorney General of the United States. Each separate violation of such an order shall be a separate offense, except that in the case of a violation through continuing failure or neglect to obey a final order of the Commission, each day of continuance of such failure or neglect shall be deemed a separate offense.

APPENDIX G: Securities Act of 1933 [Excerpts]

Prohibitions Relating to Interstate Commerce and the Mails

Sec. 5. (a) Unless a registration statement is in effect as to a security, it shall be unlawful for any person, directly or indirectly—

(1) to make use of any means or instruments of transportation or communication in interstate commerce or of the mails to sell such security through the use or medium of any prospectus or otherwise; or

(2) to carry or cause to be carried through the mails or in interstate commerce, by any means or instruments of transportation, any such security for the purpose of sale or for delivery after sale.

[Prospectus Requirements]

(b) It shall be unlawful for any person, directly or indirectly—

(1) to make use of any means or instruments of transportation or communication in interstate commerce or of the mails to carry or transmit any prospectus relating to any security with respect to which a registration statement has been filed under this title, unless such prospectus meets the requirements of section 10, or

(2) to carry or to cause to be carried through the mails or in interstate commerce any such security for the purpose of sale or for delivery after sale, unless accompanied or preceded by a prospectus that meets the requirements of subsection (a) of section 10.

[Prohibition Against Offers Prior to Registration]

(c) It shall be unlawful for any person, directly or indirectly, to make use of any means or instruments of transportation or communication in interstate commerce or of the mails to offer to sell or offer to buy through the use or medium of any prospectus or otherwise any security, unless a registration statement has been filed as to such security, or while the registration statement is the subject of a refusal order or stop order or (prior to the effective date of the registration statement) any public proceeding or examination under section 8.

Civil Liabilities on Account of False Registration Statement

Sec. 11. (a) In case any part of the registration statement, when such part became effective, contained an untrue statement of a material fact or omitted to state a material fact required to be stated therein or necessary to make the statements therein not misleading, any person acquiring such security (unless it is proved that at the time of such acquisition he knew of such untruth or omission) may, either at law or in equity, in any court of competent jurisdiction, sue—

[Signers of Registration Statement]

(1) every person who signed the registration statement;

[Directors and Partners]

(2) every person who was a director of (or person performing similar functions), or partner in, the issuer at the time of the filing of the part of the registration statement with respect to which his liability is asserted;

[Persons Named as Being, or About to Become, Directors or Partners]

(3) every person who, with his consent, is named in the registration statement as being or about to become a director, person performing similar functions, or partner;

[Accountants, Engineers, Appraisers, and Other Professional Persons]

(4) every accountant engineer, or appraiser, or any person whose profession gives authority to a statement made by him, who has with his consent been named as having prepared or certified any part of the registration statement, or as having prepared or certified any report or valuation which is used in connection with the registration statement, with respect to the statement in such registration statement, report, or valuation, which purports to have been prepared or certified by him;

[Underwriters]

(5) every underwriter with respect to such security.

[Purchase after Publication of Earning Statement]

If such person acquired the security after the issuer has made generally available to its security holders an earning statement covering a period of at least twelve months beginning after the effective date of the registration statement, then the right of recovery under this subsection shall be conditioned on proof that such person acquired the securities relying on such untrue statement in the registration statement or relying upon the registration statement and not knowing of such omission, but such reliance may be established without proof of the reading of the registration statement by such person.

[Defenses of Persons Other than Issuer]

(b) Notwithstanding the provisions of subsection (a) no person, other than the issuer, shall be liable as provided therein who shall sustain the burden of proof—

[Resignation before Effective Date]

(1) that before the effective date of the part of the registration statement with respect to which his liability is asserted (A) he had resigned from or had taken such steps as are permitted by law to resign from, or ceased or refused to act in, every office, capacity or relationship in which he was described in the registration statement as acting or agreeing to act, and (B) he had advised the Commission and the issuer in writing, that he had taken such action and that he would not be responsible for such part of the registration statement; or

[Statements Becoming Effective without Defendants Knowledge]

(2) that if such part of the registration statement became effective without his knowledge, upon becoming aware of such fact he forthwith acted and advised the Commission, in accordance with paragraph (1), and, in addition, gave reasonable public notice that such part of the registration statement had become effective without his knowledge; or

[Belief on Reasonable Grounds that Statements Were True]

(3) that (A) as regards any part of the registration statement not purporting to be made on the authority of an expert, and not purporting to be a copy of or extract from a report or valuation of an expert and not purporting to be made on the authority of a public official document or statement, he had, after reasonable investigation, reasonable ground to believe and did believe, at the time such part of the registration statement became effective, that the statements therein were true and that there was no omission to state a material fact required to be stated therein or necessary to make the statements therein not misleading; and

[Statement Made on Authority of Defendant as Expert]

(B) as regards any part of the registration statement purporting to be made upon his authority as an expert or purporting to be a copy of or extract from a report or valuation of himself as an expert, (i) he had, after reasonable investigation, reasonable ground to believe and did believe, at the time such part of the registration statement became effective, that the statements therein were true and that there was no omission to state a material fact required to be stated therein or necessary to make the statements therein not misleading, or (ii) such part of the registration statement did not fairly represent his statement as an expert or was not a fair copy of or extract from his report or valuation as an expert; and

[Statement Made on Authority of Expert Other than Defendant]

(C) as regards any part of the registration statement purporting to be made on the authority of an expert (other than himself) or purporting to be a copy of or extract from a report or valuation of an expert (other than himself), he had no reasonable ground to believe and did not believe, at the time such part of the registration statement became effective, that the statements therein were untrue or that there was an omission to state a material fact required to be stated therein or necessary to make the statements therein not misleading, or that such part of the registration statement did not fairly represent the statement of the expert or was not a fair copy of or extract from the report or valuation of the expert; and

[Statement Made by Official Person; Copy of Public Official Document]

(D) as regards any part of the registration statement purporting to be a statement made by an official person or purporting to be a copy of or extract from a public official document, he had no reasonable ground to believe and did not believe, at the time such part of the registration statement became effective, that the statements therein were untrue, or that there was an omission to state a material fact required to be stated therein or necessary to make the statements therein not misleading, or that such part of the registration statement did not fairly represent the statement made by the official person or was not a fair copy of or extract from the public official document.

["Reasonable" Investigation and "Reasonable" Grounds for Belief]

(c) In determining, for the purpose of paragraph (3) of subsection (b) of this section, what constitutes reasonable investigation and reasonable ground for belief, the standard of reasonableness shall be that required of a prudent man in the management of his own property.

[Person Becoming Underwriter after Effectiveness of Registration Statement]

(d) If any person becomes an underwriter with respect to the security after the part of the registration statement with respect to which his liability is asserted has become effective, then for the purposes of paragraph (3) of subsection (b) of this section such part of the registration statement shall be considered as having become effective with respect to such person as of the time when he became an underwriter.

[Amount of Damages; Bond for Costs of Suit]

(e) The suit authorized under subsection (a) may be to recover such damages as shall represent the difference between the amount paid for the security (not exceeding the price at which the security was offered to the public) and (1) the value thereof as of the time such suit was brought, or (2) the price at which such security shall have been disposed of in the market before suit, or (3) the price at which such security shall have been disposed of after suit but before judgment if such damages shall be less than the damages representing the difference between the amount paid for the security (not exceeding the price at which the security was offered to the public) and the value thereof as of the time such suit was brought: Provided, that if the defendant proves that any portion or all of such damages represents other than the depreciation in value of such security resulting from such part of the registration statement, with respect to which his liability is asserted, not being true or omitting to state a material fact required to be stated therein or necessary to make the statements therein not misleading, such portion of or all such damages shall not be recoverable. In no event shall any underwriter (unless such underwriter shall have knowingly received from the issuer for acting as an underwriter some benefit, directly or indirectly in which all other underwriters similarly situated did not share in proportion to their respective interests in the underwriting) be liable in any suit or as a consequence of suits authorized under subsection (a) of this section for damages in excess of the total price at which the securities underwritten by him and distributed to the public were offered to the public. In any suit under this or any other section of this title the court may, in its discretion, require an undertaking for the payment of the costs of such suit, including reasonable attorney's fees, and if judgment shall be rendered against a party litigant, upon the motion of the other party litigant, such costs may be assessed in favor of such party litigant (whether or not such undertaking has been required) if the court believes the suit or the defense to have been without merit, in an amount sufficient to reimburse him for the reasonable expenses incurred by him, in connection with such suit, such costs to be taxed in the manner usually provided for taxing of costs in the court in which the suit was heard.

[Joint and Several Liability]

(f) (1) Except as provided in paragraph (2), All or any one or more of the persons specified in subsection (a) shall be jointly and severally liable, and every person who becomes liable to make any payment under this section may recover contribution as in cases of contract from any person who, if sued separately, would have been liable to make the same payment, unless the person who had become liable was, and the other was not, guilty of fraudulent misrepresentation.

(2)(A) The liability of an outside director under subsection (e) shall be determined in accordance with Section 21D(f) of the Securities Exchange Act of 1934.

[*Ed.*: Section 21D(f) provides that any person found liable shall be jointly and severally liable for all damages awarded the plaintiff only if the trier of fact specifically determines that the person knowingly committed a violation of the securities laws. Otherwise (except for uncollectible amounts, as described below), a person is liable solely for the portion of the judgment that corresponds to that person's percentage of responsibility (such percentage to be determined by considering both the nature of the person's conduct and the nature and extent of the causal relationship between the person's conduct and the damages incurred by the plaintiff). If part of the judgment owed by all defendants remains uncollectible, then each defendant has joint and several liability for the uncollectible share if the plaintiff is an individual with a net worth less than $200,000 and the recoverable damages represent more than 10 percent of that net worth. Otherwise, each defendant is liable for the uncollectible share in proportion to his or her percentage of responsibility up to a maximum of 50 percent of that person's proportionate share of liability.]

(B) For purpose of this paragraph, the term "outside director" shall have the meaning given such term by rule or regulation of the commission.

[Limitation on Amount of Damages]

(g) In no case shall the amount recoverable under this section exceed the price at which the security was offered to the public.

Civil Liabilities Arising in Connection with Prospectuses and Communications

Sec. 12. (a) *In General*—Any person who—

(1) offers or sells a security in violation of section 5, or

Offers or Sells by Use of Interstate Communications or Transportation

(2) offers or sells a security (whether or not exempted by the provisions of section 3, other than paragraph (2) of subsection (a) thereof), by the use of any means or instruments of transportation or communication in interstate commerce or of the mails, by means of a prospectus or oral communication, which includes an untrue statement of a material fact or omits to state a material fact necessary in order to make the statements, in the light of the circumstances under

which they were made, not misleading (the purchaser not knowing of such untruth or omission), and who shall not sustain the burden of proof that he did not know, and in the exercise of reasonable care could not have known, of such untruth or omission, shall be liable, subject to subsection (b), to the person purchasing such security from him, who may sue either at law or in equity in any court of competent jurisdiction, to recover the consideration paid for such security with interest thereon, less the amount of any income received thereon, upon the tender of such security, or for damages if he no longer owns the security.

(b) *Loss Causation.*—In an action described in subsection (a)(2), if the person who offered or sold such security proves that any portion or all of the amount recoverable under subsection (a)(2) represents other than the depreciation in value of the subject security resulting from such part of the prospectus or oral communication, with respect to which the liability of that person is asserted, not being true or omitting to state a material fact required to be stated therein or necessary to make the statement not misleading, then such portion or amount, as the case may be, shall not be recoverable.

APPENDIX H: Securities Exchange Act of 1934 [Excerpts]

Regulation of the Use of Manipulative and Deceptive Devices

Sec. 10. It shall be unlawful for any person, directly or indirectly, by the use of any means or instrumentality of interstate commerce or of the mails, or of any facility of any national securities exchange—

. . .

[Use or Employment of Manipulative or Deceptive Devices]

(b) To use or employ, in connection with the purchase or sale of any security registered on a national securities exchange or any security not so registered, any manipulative or deceptive device or contrivance in contravention of such rules and regulations as the commission may prescribe as necessary or appropriate in the public interest or for the protection of investors.

. . .

[Directors, Officers, and Principal Stockholders]

Sec. 16. (a) Every person who is directly or indirectly the beneficial owner of more than 10 per centum of any class of any equity security (other than exempted security) which is registered pursuant to section 12 of this title, or who is a director or an officer of the issuer of such security, shall file, at the time of the registration of such security on a national securities exchange or by the effective date of a registration statement filed pursuant to section 12(g) of this title, or within ten days after he becomes such beneficial owner, director, or officer, a statement with the Commission (and, if such security is registered on a national securities exchange, also with the exchange) of the amount of all equity securities of such issuer of which he is the beneficial owner, and within ten days after the close of each calendar month thereafter, if there has been a change in such ownership during such month, shall file with the Commission (and if such security is registered on a national securities exchange, shall also file with the exchange), a statement indicating his ownership at the close of the calendar month and such changes in his ownership as have occurred during such calendar month.

[Profits Realized from Purchase and Sales within Period of Less than Six Months]

(b) For the purpose of preventing the unfair use of information which may have been obtained by such beneficial owner, director, or officer by reason of his relationship to the issuer, any profit realized by him from any purchase and sale, or any sale and purchase, of any equity security of such issuer (other than an exempted security) within any period of less than six months, unless such security was acquired in good faith in connection with a debt previously contracted, shall inure to and be recoverable by the issuer, irrespective of any intention on the part of such beneficial owner, director, or officer in entering into such transaction of holding the security purchased or of not repurchasing the security sold for a period exceeding six months. Suit to recover such profit may be instituted at law or in equity in any court of competent jurisdiction by the issuer, or by the owner of any security of the issuer in the name and in behalf of the issuer if the issuer shall fail or refuse to bring such suit within sixty days after request or shall fail diligently to prosecute the same thereafter; but no such suit shall be brought more than two years after the date such profit was realized. This subsection shall not be construed to cover any transaction where such beneficial owner was not such both at the time of the purchase and sale, or the sale and purchase, of the security involved, or any transaction or transactions which the Commission by rules and regulations may exempt as not comprehended within the purpose of this subsection.

APPENDIX I: Rules 10b-5, 10b5-1, and 10b5-2 from Code of Federal Regulations

Regulations adopted by the Securities and Exchange Commission Pursuant to Section 10(b) of the Securities Exchange Act of 1934

§ 240.10b-5 Employment of manipulative and deceptive devices.

It shall be unlawful for any person, directly or indirectly, by the use of any means or instrumentality of interstate commerce, or of the mails or of any facility of any national securities exchange,

(1) to employ any device, scheme, or artifice to defraud,

(2) to make any untrue statement of a material fact or to omit to state a material fact necessary in order to make the statements made, in light of the circumstances under which they were made, not misleading, or

(3) to engage in any act, practice, or course of business which operates or would operate as a fraud or deceit upon any person, in connection with the purchase or sale of any security.

[13 Fed. Reg. 8, 183 (Dec. 22, 1948), as amended at 16 Fed. Reg. 7,928 (Aug. 11, 1951)]

§ 240.10b5–1 Trading "on the basis of" material nonpublic information in insider trading cases.

Preliminary Note to § 240.10b5–1: This provision defines when a purchase or sale constitutes trading "on the basis of" material nonpublic information in insider trading cases brought under Section 10(b) of the Act and Rule 10b–5 thereunder. The law of insider trading is otherwise defined by judicial opinions construing Rule 10b–5, and Rule 10b5–1 does not modify the scope of insider trading law in any other respect.

(a) General. The "manipulative and deceptive devices" prohibited by Section 10(b) of the Act (15 U.S.C. 78j) and § 240.10b–5 thereunder include, among other things, the purchase or sale of a security of any issuer, on the basis of material nonpublic information about that security or issuer, in breach of a duty of trust or confidence that is owed directly, indirectly, or derivatively, to the issuer of that security or the shareholders of that issuer, or to any other person who is the source of the material nonpublic information.

(b) Definition of "on the basis of." Subject to the affirmative defenses in paragraph (c) of this section, a purchase or sale of a security of an issuer is "on the basis of" material nonpublic information about that security or issuer if the person making the purchase or sale was aware of the material nonpublic information when the person made the purchase or sale.

(c) Affirmative defenses. (1)(i) Subject to paragraph (c) (1) (ii) of this section, a person's purchase or sale is not "on the basis of" material nonpublic information if the person making the purchase or sale demonstrates that:

(A) Before becoming aware of the information, the person had:

(1) Entered into a binding contract to purchase or sell the security,

(2) Instructed another person to purchase or sell the security for the instructing person's account, or

(3) Adopted a written plan for trading securities;

(B) The contract, instruction, or plan described in paragraph (c) (1) (i) (A) of this Section:

(1) Specified the amount of securities to be purchased or sold and the price at which and the date on which the securities were to be purchased or sold;

(2) Included a written formula or algorithm, or computer program, for determining the amount of securities to be purchased or sold and the price at which and the date on which the securities were to be purchased or sold; or

(3) Did not permit the person to exercise any subsequent influence over how, when, or whether to effect purchases or sales; provided, in addition, that any other person who, pursuant to the contract, instruction, or plan, did exercise such influence must not have been aware of the material nonpublic information when doing so; and

(C) The purchase or sale that occurred was pursuant to the contract, instruction, or plan. A purchase or sale is not "pursuant to a contract, instruction, or plan" if, among other things, the person who entered into the contract, instruction, or plan altered or deviated from the contract, instruction, or plan to purchase or sell securities (whether by changing the amount, price, or timing of the purchase or sale), or entered into or altered a corresponding or hedging transaction or position with respect to those securities.

(ii) Paragraph (c) (1) (i) of this section is applicable only when the contract, instruction, or plan to purchase or sell securities was given or entered into in good faith and not as part of a plan or scheme to evade the prohibitions of this section.

(iii) This paragraph (c) (1) (iii) defines certain terms as used in paragraph (c) of this Section.

(A) Amount. "Amount" means either a specified number of shares or other securities or a specified dollar value of securities.

(B) Price. "Price" means the market price on a particular date or a limit price, or a particular dollar price.

(C) Date. "Date" means, in the case of a market order, the specific day of the year on which the order is to be executed (or as soon thereafter as is practicable under ordinary principles of best execution). "Date" means, in the case of a limit order, a day of the year on which the limit order is in force.

(2) A person other than a natural person also may demonstrate that a purchase or sale of securities is not "on the basis of" material nonpublic information if the person demonstrates that:

(i) The individual making the investment decision on behalf of the person to purchase or sell the securities was not aware of the information; and

(ii) The person had implemented reasonable policies and procedures, taking into consideration the nature of the person's business, to ensure that individuals making investment decisions would not violate the laws prohibiting trading on the basis of material nonpublic information. These policies and procedures may include those that restrict any purchase, sale, and causing any purchase or sale of any security as to which the person has material nonpublic information, or those that prevent such individuals from becoming aware of such information.

[65 Fed. Reg. 51,716, 51,737 (Aug. 24, 2000)]

§ 240.10b5–2 Duties of trust or confidence in misappropriation insider trading cases.

Preliminary Note to § 240.10b5–2: This section provides a non-exclusive definition of circumstances in which a person has a duty of trust or confidence for purposes of the "misappropriation" theory of insider trading under Section 10(b) of the Act and Rule 10b–5. The law of insider trading is otherwise defined by judicial opinions construing Rule 10b–5, and Rule 10b5–2 does not modify the scope of insider trading law in any other respect.

(a) Scope of Rule. This section shall apply to any violation of Section 10(b) of the Act (15 U.S.C. 78j(b)) and § 240.10b–5 thereunder that is based on the purchase or sale of securities on the basis of, or the communication of, material nonpublic information misappropriated in breach of a duty of trust or confidence.

(b) Enumerated "duties of trust or confidence." For purposes of this section, a "duty of trust or confidence" exists in the following circumstances, among others:

(1) Whenever a person agrees to maintain information in confidence;

(2) Whenever the person communicating the material nonpublic information and the person to whom it is communicated have a history, pattern, or practice of sharing confidences, such that the recipient of the information knows or reasonably should know that the person communicating the material nonpublic information expects that the recipient will maintain its confidentiality; or

(3) Whenever a person receives or obtains material nonpublic information from his or her spouse, parent, child, or sibling; provided, however, that the person receiving or obtaining the information may demonstrate that no duty of trust or confidence existed with respect to the information, by establishing that he or she neither knew nor reasonably should have known that the person who was the source of the information expected that the person whould keep the information confidential, because of the parties' history, pattern, or practice of sharing and maintaining confidences, and because there was no agreement or understanding to maintain the confidentiality of the information.

[65 Fed. Reg. 51,716, 51,738 (Aug. 24, 2000)]

APPENDIX J: Rule 14e–3 from Code of Federal Regulations

§ 240.14e-3 Transactions in securities on the basis of material, nonpublic information in the context of tender offers. (a) If any person has taken a substantial step or steps to commence, or has commenced, a tender offer (the "offering person"), it shall constitute a fraudulent, deceptive or manipulative act or practice within the meaning of section 14(e) of the Act for any other person who is in possession of material information relating to such tender offer which information he knows or has reason to know is nonpublic and which he knows or has reason to know has been acquired directly or indirectly from:

(1) The offering person,

(2) The issuer of the securities sought or to be sought by such tender offer, or

(3) Any officer, director, partner or employee or any other person acting on behalf of the offering person or such issuer, to purchase or sell or cause to be purchased or sold any of such securities or any securities convertible into or exchangeable for any such securities or any option or right to obtain or dispose of any of the foregoing securities, unless within a reasonable time prior to any purchase or sale such information and its source are publicly disclosed by press release or otherwise.

(b) A person other than a natural person shall not violate paragraph (a) of this section if such person shows that:

(1) The individual(s) making the investment decision on behalf of such person to purchase or sell any security described in paragraph (a) of this section or to cause any such security to be purchased or sold by or on behalf of others did not know the material, nonpublic information; and

(2) Such person had implemented one or a combination of policies and procedures, reasonable under the circumstances, taking into consideration the nature of the person's business, to ensure that individual(s) making investment decision(s) would not violate paragraph (a) of this section, which policies and procedures may include, but are not limited to, (i) those which restrict any purchase, sale and causing any purchase and sale of any such security or (ii) those which prevent such individual(s) from knowing such information.

(c) Notwithstanding anything in paragraph (a) of this section to contrary, the following transactions shall not be violations of paragraph (a) of this section:

(1) Purchase(s) of any security described in paragraph (a) of this section by a broker or by another agent on behalf of an offering person; or

(2) Sale(s) by any person of any security described in paragraph (a) of this section to the offering person.

(d)(1) As a means reasonably designed to prevent fraudulent, deceptive or manipulative acts or practices within the meaning of section 14(e) of the Act, it shall be unlawful for any person described in paragraph (d)(2)) of this section to communicate material, nonpublic information relating to a tender offer to any other person under circumstances in which it is reasonably foreseeable that such communication is likely to result in a violation of this section except that this paragraph shall not apply to a communication made in good faith:

(i) To the officers, directors, partners or employees of the offering person, to its advisors or to other persons, involved in the planning, financing, preparation or execution of such tender offer;

(ii) To the issuer whose securities are sought or to be sought by such tender offer, to its officers, directors, partners, employees or advisors or to other persons, involved in the planning, financing, preparation or execution of the activities of the issuer with respect to such tender offer; or

(iii) To any person pursuant to a requirement of any statute or rule or regulation promulgated thereunder.

(2) The persons referred to in paragraph (d)(1) of this section are:

(i) The offering person or its officers, directors, partners, employees or advisors;

(ii) The issuer of the securities sought or to be sought by such tender offer or its officers, directors, partners, employees or advisors;

(iii) Anyone acting on behalf of the persons in paragraph (d)(2)(i) of this section or the issuer or persons in paragraph (d)(2)(ii) of this section; and

(iv) Any person in possession of material information relating to a tender offer which information he knows or has reason to know is nonpublic and which he knows or has reason to know has been acquired directly or indirectly from any of the above.

[46 FR 60418 (Sept. 12, 1980)]

APPENDIX K: Sarbanes–Oxley Act of 2002 [Excerpts]

Sec. 201. Services Outside the Scope of Practice of Auditors.

(g) ***Prohibited Activities.*** Except as provided in subsection (h), it shall be unlawful for a registered public accounting firm (and any associated person of that firm, to the extent determined appropriate by the [Securities and Exchange] Commission) that performs for any issuer any audit required by this title or the rules of the Commission under this title or . . . Board, the rules of the Public Company Accounting Oversight Board, to provide to that issuer, contemporaneously with the audit, any non-audit service, including—

(1) bookkeeping or other services related to the accounting records or financial statements of the audit client;

(2) financial information systems design and implementation;

(3) appraisal or valuation services, fairness opinions, or contribution-in-kind reports;

(4) actuarial services;

(5) internal audit outsourcing services;

(6) management functions or human resources;

(7) broker or dealer, investment adviser, or investment banking services;

(8) legal services and expert services unrelated to the audit; and

(9) any other service that the Board determines, by regulation, is impermissible.

(h) ***Preapproval Required for Non-Audit Services.*** A registered public accounting firm may engage in any non-audit service, including tax services, that is not described in any of paragraphs (1) through (9) of subsection (g) for an audit client, only if the activity is approved in advance by the audit committee of the issuer, in accordance with subsection (i).

[Codified at 15 U.S.C. § 78j-1.]

Sec. 302. Corporate Responsibility for Financial Reports.

(a) ***Regulations Required.*** The Commission shall, by rule, require, for each company filing periodic reports under section 13(a) or 15(d) of the Securities Exchange Act of 1934, that the principal executive officer or officers and the principal financial officer or officers, or persons performing similar functions, certify in each annual or quarterly report filed or submitted under either such section of such Act that—

(1) the signing officer has reviewed the report;

(2) based on the officer's knowledge, the report does not contain any untrue statement of a material fact or omit to state a material fact necessary in order to make the statements made, in light of the circumstances under which such statements were made, not misleading;

(3) based on such officer's knowledge, the financial statements, and other financial information included in the report, fairly present in all material respects the financial condition and results of operations of the issuer as of, and for, the periods presented in the report;

(4) the signing officers—

(A) are responsible for establishing and maintaining internal controls;

(B) have designed such internal controls to ensure that material information relating to the issuer and its consolidated subsidiaries is made known to such officers by others within those entities, particularly during the period in which the periodic reports are being prepared;

(C) have evaluated the effectiveness of the issuer's internal controls as of a date within 90 days prior to the report; and

(D) have presented in the report their conclusions about the effectiveness of their internal controls based on their evaluation as of that date;

(5) the signing officers have disclosed to the issuer's auditors and the audit committee of the board of directors (or persons fulfilling the equivalent function)—

(A) all significant deficiencies in the design or operation of internal controls which could adversely affect the issuer's ability to record, process, summarize, and report financial data and have identified for the issuer's auditors any material weaknesses in internal controls; and

(B) any fraud, whether or not material, that involves management or other employees who have a significant role in the issuer's internal controls; and

(6) the signing officers have indicated in the report whether or not there were significant changes in internal controls or in other factors that could significantly affect internal controls subsequent to the date of their evaluation, including any corrective actions with regard to significant deficiencies and material weaknesses.

[Codified at 15 U.S.C. § 7241.]

Sec. 404. Management Assessment of Internal Controls.

(a) ***Rules Required.*** The Commission shall prescribe rules requiring each annual report required by section 13(a) or 15(d) of the Securities Exchange Act of 1934 to contain an internal control report, which shall—

(1) state the responsibility of management for establishing and maintaining an adequate internal control structure and procedures for financial reporting; and

(2) contain an assessment, as of the end of the most recent fiscal year of the issuer, of the effectiveness of the internal control structure and procedures of the issuer for financial reporting.

(b) ***Internal Control Evaluation and Reporting.*** With respect to the internal control assessment required by subsection (a), each registered public accounting firm that prepares or issues the audit report for the issuer shall attest to, and report on, the assessment made by the management of the issuer. An attestation made under this subsection shall be made in accordance with standards for attestation engagements issued or adopted by the Board. Any such attestation shall not be the subject of a separate engagement.

[Codified at 15 U.S.C. § 7262.]

Sec. 802. Criminal Penalties for Altering Documents.
Whoever knowingly alters, destroys, mutilates, conceals, covers up, falsifies, or makes a false entry in any record, document, or tangible object with the intent to impede, obstruct, or influence the investigation or proper administration of any matter within the jurisdiction of any department or agency of the United States or any [bankruptcy] case filed under title 11, or in relation to or contemplation of any such matter or case, shall be fined under this title, imprisoned not more than 20 years, or both.

[Codified at U.S.C. § 1519.]

GLOSSARY

A

abandonment (of a trademark) The failure to use a mark after acquiring legal protection may result in the loss of rights, and such loss is known as abandonment.

abrogate To annul the states' Eleventh Amendment immunity.

absolute privilege In defamation cases, the right of the defendant to publish with impunity a statement known by the defendant to be false.

acceptance An agreement to the amount offered for certain services or products. Acceptance may be verbal, written, or implied by action.

accession A process whereby a nation that was not an original party to a treaty can elect to participate in the treaty at a later time.

accord *See* Accord and Satisfaction.

accord and satisfaction An agreement to accept performance that is different from what is called for in the contract.

act-of-state doctrine The doctrine that states that the courts of one country will not sit in judgment on the acts of the government of another done within its own territory.

actual abandonment Loss of trademark rights that occurs when a trademark owner discontinues use of a mark with the intent not to resume use.

actual authority The express or implied power of an agent to act for and bind a principal to agreements entered into by an agent.

actual cause Proof that but for the defendant's negligent conduct the plaintiff would not have been harmed.

actual damages The amount required to repair or to replace an item or the decrease in market value caused by tortious conduct. Actual damages restore the injured party to the position it was in prior to the injury. Also called *compensatory damages*.

actual intent The subjective desire to cause the consequences of an act, or the belief that the consequences are substantially certain to result from it.

actual malice A statement made with the knowledge that it is false or with a reckless disregard for the truth.

***actus reus* (guilty deed)** A crime; a criminal act.

ad valorem A condition of a tariff whereby the importer must pay a percentage of the value of the imported merchandise.

ad valorem tariffs Tariffs for which the importer must pay a percentage of the value of the imported merchandise.

additive Anything not inherent in a food product—including pesticide residues, unintended environmental contaminants, and unavoidably added substances from packaging.

adhesion contract An unfair type of contract by which sellers offer goods or services on a take-it-or-leave-it basis, with no chance for consumers to negotiate for goods except by agreeing to the terms of said contract.

adjustable-rate loan Loans that allow lenders to avoid the risk of fluctuating interest rates. The rate of interest is often set at a fixed number of percentage points over a specified standard.

adjustable-rate mortgages (ARMs) Mortgages that start out with a low fixed rate and usually adjust upward within two to five years as the rate resets.

administrative employee An employee whose primary duty consists of nonmanual work directly related either to management policies or to the general business operations of the employer or the employer's customers.

administrative law judge (ALJ) The presiding official at an administrative proceeding who has the power to issue an order resolving the legal dispute.

adoption Process by which a securities issuer explicitly or implicitly endorses or approves third-party information.

adulterated Consisting in whole or in part of any filthy, putrid, or decomposed substance, or otherwise unfit for food.

adverse employment action Action by an employer that materially affects the terms and conditions of employment, such as employee compensation or job responsibilities.

adverse possession Ownership of property that is not occupied by its owner for a certain period of time may be transferred to those who have been unlawfully occupying it and openly exercising rights of ownership. Such a transfer is usually not reflected in the official land records. Also called *squatter's rights*.

affidavit A written or printed declaration or statement of facts, made voluntarily, and confirmed by the oath or affirmation of the party making it, taken before a person having authority to administer such oath or affirmation.

affiliate Any person who controls an issuer of securities, or is controlled by the issuer, or is under common control. Includes officers, directors, and major shareholders of a corporation.

affirmative covenant The borrower's promise to do certain things under the loan agreement.

affirmative defense The admission in an answer to a complaint that defendant has acted as plaintiff alleges, but denies that defendant's conduct was the real or legal cause of harm to plaintiff.

after-acquired property The property a debtor acquires after the execution of a security agreement.

after-acquired title If, at the date of execution of a grant deed, the grantor does not have title to the real property referred to in the grant deed but subsequently acquires it, such after-acquired title is deemed automatically transferred to the grantee.

agency A relationship in which one person (the agent) acts for or represents another person (the principal).

agency by estoppel When the principal leads a third party to believe that a person is his or her agent, the principal is estopped (prevented) from denying that the person is his or her agent.

agency by ratification An agency formed when a principal approves or accepts the benefits of the actions of an otherwise unauthorized agent.

agent A person who manages a task delegated by another (the principal) and exercises whatever discretion is given to the agent by the principal.

aided-in-the-agency doctrine *See* Aided-in-the-Agency-Relation Doctrine.

aided-in-the-agency-relation doctrine An agency principle whereby the principal may be held vicariously liable for the wrongful acts of an agent acting outside of the scope of authority because the principal provided the instrumentality or created the circumstances that made it possible for the agent to commit the wrongful act.

aided-in the agency relation theory An employee is aided in accomplishing a tort by the existence of the agency relationship.

aider and abettor A person with knowledge of (or recklessness as to) a primary criminal violation who provides substantial assistance to the primary violation.

allocative efficiency An equilibrium in which scarce societal resources are allocated to the production of various goods and services up to the point where the cost of the resources equals the benefit society reaps from their use.

alter ego theory When owners have so mingled their own affairs with those of a corporation that the corporation does not exist as a distinct entity, it is an alter ego (second self) of its owners, permitting the piercing of the corporate veil.

alternative dispute resolution (ADR) Alternative techniques, such as negotiation, mediation, arbitration, med-arb, arb-med, minitrials, and summary jury trials, to resolve disputes without litigation.

alternative minimum tax (AMT) A tax law that was passed to prevent higher income taxpayers from paying too little tax because they were able to take advantage of a variety of tax deductions or exclusions, including the spread on exercise of an incentive stock option. Taxpayers who may be subject to AMT must calculate their taxable income in two ways and pay whichever formula yields the higher tax.

***amici curiae* brief** An appellate brief filed by interested parties (literally, "friends of the court") who are not themselves parties to the case on appeal.

amortize To pay the principal of a loan over a period of time.

angels Wealthy individual investors to whom entrepreneurs often turn for equity capital after exhausting the funds available from family and friends.

answer The instrument by which defendant admits or denies the various allegations stated in the complaint against the defendant.

anticipatory repudiation If a party indicates before performance is due that it will breach the contract, there is an anticipatory repudiation of the contract.

antideficiency laws Statutes that restrict lenders seeking remedies against real property security from suing the borrower personally. If a lender has recourse to the borrower or to other property of the borrower, and exercises such rights, the lender may be precluded from foreclosing on real estate mortgaged by the borrower. Alternatively, if the holder of a mortgage or deed of trust secured by real property forecloses on the property, the lender may be precluded from suing the borrower personally to recover whatever is still owing after a foreclosure sale. Also called *one-form-of-action laws*.

antitrust injury The damages sustained by a plaintiff in an antitrust suit as a result of the defendant's anticompetitive conduct.

antitrust laws The laws that seek to identify and forbid business practices that are anticompetitive. Also called *competition laws*.

apartheid Prior to its abolition in the 1980s, an official policy of racial segregation in South Africa that relegated its black citizens to a second-class status in employment, housing, and opportunity.

apparent authority A principal, by words or actions, causes a third party to reasonably believe that an agent has authority to act for or bind the principal.

appellant The person who is appealing a judgment or seeking a writ of certiorari. Also called a *petitioner*.

appellate jurisdiction The power of the Supreme Court and other courts of appeal to decide cases that have been tried in a lower court and appealed.

appellee The party in a case against whom an appeal is taken; that is, the party who has an interest adverse to setting aside or reversing the judgment. Also called *respondent*.

applicant Person (the buyer in a sales transaction) requesting an issuing bank to provide a letter of credit in favor of another party called the beneficiary (the seller in a sales transaction).

appraisal rights In a merger or sale of assets, shareholders who voted against the transaction have appraisal rights, that is, the right to receive the fair cash value of the shares they were forced to give up as a result of the transaction.

appropriate collective bargaining unit A collective bargaining unit in which the employees share a community of interest; that is, they have similar compensation, working conditions, and supervision, and they work under the same general employer policies.

appropriation of a person's name or likeness Unauthorized use of a person's name or likeness for financial gain.

arbitrary and capricious standard If an agency has a choice between several courses of action, the court will presume that the chosen course is valid unless the person challenging it shows that it lacks any rational basis.

arbitrary marks A real word whose ordinary meaning has nothing to do with the trademarked product.

arbitration The resolution of a dispute by a neutral third party.

arbitration clause A clause that specifies that in the event of a dispute arising out of a contract, the parties will arbitrate specific issues in a stated manner.

arbitrator The neutral third party who conducts an arbitration to resolve a dispute.

arb-med A shortened form of arbitration/mediation, a procedure whereby parties present their case to an arbitrator who makes an award but keeps it secret while the parties try to resolve the dispute through mediation. If the mediation fails, then the arbitrator's award is unsealed and becomes binding on the parties.

area plan A planning document that usually encompasses just a portion of the city's geographic area.

arrest To deprive a person of his or her liberty by legal authority. Taking, under real or assumed authority, custody of another for the purpose of holding or detaining him or her to answer a criminal charge or civil demand.

articles of incorporation The basic document filed with the appropriate governmental agency upon the incorporation of a business. The contents are prescribed in the general corporation statutes but generally include the name, purpose, agent for service of process, authorized number of shares, and classes of stock of a corporation. It is executed by the incorporator(s). Also called the *charter* or the *certificate of incorporation*.

articles of organization The charter document for a limited liability company. Also called *certificate of formation*.

assault An intent to create a well-grounded apprehension of an immediate harmful or offensive contact. Generally, assault also requires some act (such as a threatening gesture) and the ability to follow through immediately with the battery.

asset lock-up option A lock-up option relating to assets of the target company.

assignment The transfer by a tenant of all or a portion of rented premises.

association claim A claim under the Americans with Disabilities Act that an employer discriminated against an employee because of his or her "association" with someone (such as a relative) with a disability.

assumption of risk The expressed or implied consent by plaintiff to defendant to take the chance of injury from a known and appreciated risk.

asymmetric information A problem that arises during discovery because each party has information not possessed by the other party.

at-will contract An employment relationship of indefinite duration.

attach If the three basic prerequisites of a security interest exist (agreement, value, and collateral), the security interest becomes enforceable between the parties and is said to attach. Also called *attachment*.

attorney-client privilege The common law rule that a court cannot force the disclosure of confidential communications between client and client's attorney.

attractive nuisance Artificial conditions on land for which an owner is liable for physical injury to child trespassers if (1) the owner knew or should have known that children were likely to trespass; (2) the condition is one the owner would reasonably know involved an unreasonable risk of injury to such children; (3) the children, because of their youth, did not discover the condition or realize the risk involved; (4) the utility to the owner of maintaining the condition is not great; (5) the burden of eliminating the risk is slight compared with the magnitude of the risk to the children; and (6) the owner fails to exercise reasonable care to protect the children.

authoritative decision A court decision that must be followed regardless of its persuasive power, by virtue of relationship between the court that made decision and the court to which decision is cited.

automatic shelf registration offerings Securities offerings by well-seasoned large publicly traded companies registered pursuant to short-form registration statements filed with the Securities and Exchange Commission.

automatic stay Feature of bankruptcy filing that instantly suspends most litigation and collection activities against the debtor, its property, or property of the bankruptcy estate.

avoiding powers The powers bankruptcy trustees can use to invalidate or reverse certain prebankruptcy transactions.

B

backdating The intentional setting of a grant date that precedes the actual date of the corporate action that effected the grant of a stock option, in order to achieve a lower option exercise price and hence a higher value to the recipient.

back pay A damage remedy in an employment discrimination case to compensate the plaintiff for lost salary and benefits.

bad faith A breach of the duty to act in good faith.

bail The amount of money a defendant must post as a bond to guarantee his or her appearance at trial.

bait and switch advertising An area of deceptive pricing in which an advertiser refuses to show an advertised item, fails to have a reasonable quantity of the item in stock, fails to promise to deliver the item within a reasonable time, or discourages employees from selling the item.

bankruptcy estate Virtually all of a debtor's existing assets, less exempt property.

barristers A type of lawyer in the British system who may argue in court.

base rate The lowest rate of interest publicly offered by major lending institutions to their most creditworthy customers. Also called *reference rate* or *prime rate*.

battle of the forms A conflict between an offer and acceptance for the purchase of goods. Occurs when the parties negotiate the essential terms of the contract (for example, quantity, quality, and delivery date) but exchange standard preprinted forms that contain conflicting terms instead of executing a single, fully integrated contract.

baseline assessment The appraisal performed by a tenant that establishes the environmental condition of leased property at the commencement and termination of the lease.

battery The intentional, non-consensual harmful or offensive contact with an individual's body or with those things in contact with or closely connected with it.

bench trial A trial in which a judge, not a jury, decides all issues.

beneficial owner A person is considered to be a beneficial owner of any securities held by his or her immediate family, spouse, any minor children, and any other relative living in his or her household.

beneficiary An individual who is benefited by a trust or a will.

bespeaks caution doctrine A doctrine whereby a court may determine that the inclusion of sufficient cautionary statements in a prospectus or other document renders immaterial any misrepresentations and omissions contained therein.

best-efforts underwriting A situation wherein the underwriters do not agree to purchase the securities being offered but instead agree to use their best efforts to find buyers at an agreed-on price. These underwritings are often used for initial public offerings or for companies that are unseasoned.

best interests of creditors test In a Chapter 11 bankruptcy case, dissenters must be given a bundle of rights the current value of which is at least as great as the distribution they would receive through a Chapter 7 liquidation.

best mode The best way the inventor knows of making an invention at the time of filing the patent application.

BFOQ defense An affirmative defense wherein an employer may lawfully hire an individual on the basis of religion, sex, or national origin if religion, sex, or national origin is a bona fide occupational qualification (BFOQ).

bicameralism The state of being composed of two legislative chambers; in the case of the United States, the Congress consists of the House of Representatives and the Senate.

bidder The party who makes a tender offer.

bilateral contract A promise given in exchange for another promise.

bills of attainder A law enacted to punish individuals or an easily ascertainable member of a group and prohibited by Article I, Section 9, of the U.S. Constitution.

Bill of Rights The first ten amendments to the Constitution.

binding arbitration When arbitration parties agree on a resolution and are bound by the arbitrator's decision.

blackout period Any period longer than three business days during which 50 percent or more of the participants in a retirement plan are prevented from trading the employer's securities.

blank check company A development-stage company that has no specific business plan or whose business plan is to acquire a presently unknown business.

blue sky laws A popular name for the state statutes that regulate and supervise offerings and sales of securities to persons in that state.

blurring Dilution of a famous trademark that occurs when a non-famous mark reduces the strong association between the owner of the famous mark and its products.

board of directors The individuals elected by the shareholders of a corporation who by law are responsible for the overall management of a corporation.

bona fide occupational qualification (BFOQ) A requirement that an employer places on certain jobs that actually requires that the person in that job has a certain gender, religion, or national origin.

bona fide prospective purchaser (BFPP) A buyer who must do the following: (1) conduct a diligent investigation of the property and report any contamination to the appropriate governmental authorities; (2) exercise appropriate care concerning the contamination to stop future or continuing release of contaminants; (3) cooperate with any authorized group, including the federal government, to conduct a cleanup of the property; and (4) obey any land-use restrictions on the property.

booked Having criminal charges against someone who has been arrested written in a register at a police station.

bound tariffs The WTO principle that holds that each time tariffs are reduced, they may not be raised again.

breakthrough rule A provision in Article 11 of the European Union Directive on Takeover Bids that permits a hostile bidder to weaken a target company's prebid differential voting structures to ensure that a bidder that acquires a majority of the target's equity can successfully mount a takeover.

break-up fee An amount agreed to in a merger agreement to be paid to a friendly suitor company if the agreement with the target company is not consummated through no fault of the friendly suitor company.

brownfields Property contaminated with hazardous waste that can be acquired and used without assumption of liability for the cleanup of all the legacy contamination.

browse-wrap license An online license agreement that appears on a website but does not require the user to take any action to express his or her consent to the agreement.

bullet dodging Occurs when employee stock options are issued after a negative public announcement that the issuing company believes may temporarily reduce the market value of the stock.

burden of proof The requirement of a prosecutor in a criminal case to establish a defendant's guilt beyond a reasonable doubt.

business judgment rule In a case challenging a board decision, this rule holds that as long as directors have made an informed decision and are not interested in the transaction being considered, a court will not question whether the directors' action was wise or whether they made an error of judgment or a business mistake.

bust-up takeover An acquisition in which the acquired corporation is taken apart and its assets are sold piecemeal.

bylaws The internal rules governing a corporation.

C corporation A business organization that is taxed at both the entity level and the owner level.

call To demand repayment of fixed-rate loans or securities after a specified period, often after five, ten, or fifteen years.

capacity The ability (requisite presence of mind) to enter into a binding contract.

cap-and-trade system A system whereby allowable emissions are capped by law, and facilities that emit more than their allotments are required to buy credits from plants with emissions below the specified levels.

carbon footprint The amount of carbon dioxide and other greenhouse gases released into the air by a person or facility.

card-check election A method of certifying a labor union whereby employers are required to recognize a union after being presented with union authorization cards signed by a majority of eligible workers on the payrolls as long as there is no evidence of illegal coercion.

cartel A group of competitors that agrees to set prices.

cash-settled SAR A stock appreciation right (SAR) payable in cash.

***caveat emptor* (let the buyer beware)** This maxim summarizes the rule that a purchaser must examine, judge, and test for himself or herself. It does not apply where strict liability, warranty, or other consumer protection laws protect consumer-buyers.

cease and desist order An order of an administrative agency or court prohibiting a person or business firm from continuing a particular course of conduct.

cert. denied Indicates that a writ of certiorari was sought but denied by the Supreme Court.

certificate of deposit (CD) rate The CD rate is based on the average of the bid rates quoted to the bank by dealers in the secondary market for the purchase at face value of certificates of deposit of the bank in a given amount and for a given term.

certificate of formation The charter document for a limited liability company. Also called *articles of organization.*

certificate of incorporation *See* Articles of Incorporation.

certification mark A mark placed on a product or used in connection with a service that indicates that the product or service in question has met the standards of safety or quality that have been created and advertised by the certifier.

charging period A specific period of time in which an employee challenging an employment practice must file a complaint with the Equal Employment Opportunity Commission (EEOC).

choice-of-forum clause or provision The clause in a contract wherein the parties agree in advance to the jurisdiction in which a dispute arising out of their agreement must be litigated.

choice-of-law provision A provision in a contract that specifies which state's or country's laws will govern matters such as contract interpretation, performance, and remedies. Can also include a statute or treaty specifying which jurisdiction's laws govern disputes involving parties from more than one state or country.

circumstantial evidence The indirect (not based on personal knowledge or observation) evidence of certain facts that, taken alone, do not prove a particular conclusion but, if taken as a whole, give a trier of fact a reasonable basis for asserting a certain conclusion is true.

cite The citation of the court's decision in a case.

civil law legal system Legal system based on the Roman law as consolidated by the Corpus Juris Civilis in A.D. 533 and 534.

civil procedure The methods, procedures, and practices that govern the processing of a civil lawsuit from start to finish.

claims (under patent law) The description of those elements of an invention that will be protected by the patent.

class action If the conduct of the defendant affected numerous persons in a common way, litigation or arbitration may be brought as a class action by a representative of the class of persons affected.

classified board A board on which directors serve for specified terms, usually three years, with only a fraction of them up for reelection at any one time. Also called *staggered board.*

clawback provision The right for an employer to recoup some or all of the employee's stock option gain if the employee goes to work for a competitor within a certain period of time following exercise of the option in violation of a covenant not to compete.

clear and present danger test A phrase used to describe the circumstances under which the government may restrict or prohibit the constitutional guarantees of free speech and free press.

click-wrap agreement A prominent feature of electronic commerce whereby users assent by clicking on an acceptance box.

click-wrap license An online license agreement that presents the user with a notice on his or her computer screen that requires the user to agree to the terms of the license by clicking on an icon.

cliff vesting A common vesting schedule that provides that if a person granted stock options leaves within a certain period of time after employment (usually six months or a year), he or she forfeits all rights to any stock.

close To consummate a transaction.

close corporation A corporation owned by a limited number of shareholders, usually thirty, most of whom are actively involved in the management of the corporation, that elects close corporation status in its charter.

closed-end credit Credit that involves only one transaction, such as a car or house loan.

closely held corporation A corporation characterized by the absence of a market for its stock, though it may have any number of shareholders.

closing package The set of lending documents (including electronic documents) necessary to consummate a financing.

Code of Federal Regulations (CFR) A multi-volume codification of federal regulations and rules.

codification The process by which existing common law principles are restated and laid down in a statute.

codified To collect and arrange items, such as statutes or regulations, systematically.

collaborative law A quickly expanding breed of law that attempts to combine mediation and negotiation into a more efficient, more satisfying, and ultimately more successful form of dispute resolution.

collateral The property belonging to a borrower that will become the lender's if the loan is not repaid.

collateralized debt obligations (CDOs) Mortgages packaged together and securitized into bonds and other debt securities. Often sold in tranches.

collective entity doctrine Under this doctrine, the custodian of records for a collective entity (such as a corporation) may not resist a subpoena for such records on the ground that the act of production will incriminate him or her.

comfort letter Letter that describes the review the accountant has conducted of unaudited interim financial statements and of certain numbers in the prospectus.

comity A situation whereby a court will enforce another country's judgments under certain conditions.

Commerce Clause The constitutional clause that gives Congress the power to regulate commerce with other nations, with Indian tribes, and between states.

commercial activity exception An exception to the blanket immunity from suits provided by the Foreign Sovereign Immunity Act for cases in which the foreign state was engaged in commercial activities.

commercial facilities (under Americans with Disabilities Act) All structures and facilities except those intended for residential use.

commercial impracticability Provision in Section 2-615 of the Uniform Commercial Code that excuses a failure to perform if performance is made impractical by an event unforeseen by the contract.

commercial lease A contract that conveys an interest in real property from the landlord to the tenant and governs the respective rights and obligations of the parties during the lease term.

commercial paper Short-term corporate indebtedness.

commitment fee The fee payable to a lender in connection with a revolving loan as consideration for its promise to keep the commitment available.

common customs tariff A single set of tariffs applied by all European Union (EU) member states on goods imported from outside the EU.

common law Also known as *case law,* or the legal rules made by judges when they decide a case where no constitution, statute, or regulation exists to resolve the dispute.

common law legal system A legal system that primarily relies on case law and precedents and is used in most countries that are or were British territories or colonies.

common market The customs union in which there are no tariffs on trade among its members, and a single set of tariffs applies to goods imported from outside the union.

community plan *See* Specific Plan.

community property The property acquired during marriage with assets earned by either spouse during the marriage.

comp (compensatory) time Extra paid vacation time granted instead of extra pay for overtime work.

comparative fault Reduced recovery for an injured party because of misuse or abuse of manufacturer's product.

comparative negligence The doctrine by which courts decide amount of award to be given a plaintiff based on the amount (percentage) of negligence plaintiff demonstrated when injured by defendant.

compensatory damages In an action for breach of contract, the amount necessary to make up for the economic loss caused by the breach.

compensatory justice Aims at compensating people for the harm done by another.

complaint The statement of plaintiff's grievance that makes allegations of the particular facts giving rise to dispute and states the legal reason why plaintiff is entitled to a remedy, the request for relief, the explanation why the court applied to has jurisdiction over the dispute, and whether plaintiff requests a jury trial.

composition A reduction in the amount payable to creditors pursuant to a composition plan.

composition plan A composition plan in a Chapter 13 proceeding is a plan in which creditors receive a percentage of the indebtedness, and the debtor is discharged of the remaining obligation.

computer employee A computer systems analyst, computer programmer, software engineer, and similarly skilled worker in the computer field.

computer fraud The unauthorized access of a computer used by the federal government, by various types of financial institutions, or in interstate commerce with the intent to alter, damage, or destroy information or to prevent authorized use of the such computers.

computer piracy The theft or misuse of computer software or hardware.

computer virus A computer program that can replicate itself into other programs without any subsequent instruction, human or mechanical.

concerted activity Under the National Labor Relations Act, the exercise by employees of their rights to band together for mutual aid and protection that is engaged in with or on the authority of other employees and not solely by and on behalf of one employee.

conciliation A more formalized method of dispute resolution that is similar to inquiry but adds the element of acceptance in advance of the result of the commission by the parties and a "cooling-off" period.

condition An event or state of facts.

condition precedent A condition that must be met before a party's obligations to perform arise under a contract.

condition subsequent In contracts, a provision giving one party the right to divest itself of liability and obligation to perform further if the other party fails to meet the condition.

conditional-use permit A method of relief from the strict terms of a zoning ordinance that provides for other uses of real property that are not permitted as a matter of right, but for which a use permit must be obtained.

conditions concurrent Conditions that are mutually dependent and are to be performed at the same time or simultaneously.

confidentiality agreement A way to avoid future claims by settling a case where the parties agree not to disclose the terms of the settlement.

confiscation The process of nationalization when the host country does not compensate the company for its lost assets.

conflict-of-laws rules When choice of law is disputed, the court in which the suit is filed will apply conflict of laws principles to determine which state's or country's laws should govern the dispute. They usually focus on the significance of each state's or country's relationship to the parties and the contract.

Confrontation Clause Clause in the U.S. Constitution that limits the prosecution's ability to introduce prior statements by witnesses not subject to cross-examination at trial.

conglomerate merger A combination of firms that were not competitors at the time of the acquisition, but that may, absent the merger, have become competitors.

congruence-and-proportionality test The federal laws enacted pursuant to Section 5 will be upheld only if they are congruent with the injury to be prevented or remedied by the Fourteenth Amendment and proportionate to the wrong they are intended to prevent or remedy.

conscious parallelism In business, the act of consistently setting prices at the same levels and changing prices at the same time as competitors.

consent decree A judgment entered by the consent of the parties whereby the defendant agrees to stop the alleged illegal activity without admitting guilt or wrongdoing. Also called *consent order.*

consent order An agreement to stop the activity that a regulatory agency has found unlawful.

consequential damages Compensation for losses that occur as a foreseeable result of a breach of contract. Actual damages represent the damage, loss, or injury that flows directly and immediately from the act of the other party; in contrast, consequential damages refer to damage, loss, or injury flowing from some of the consequences or results of such act.

consideration A thing of value (money, services, an object, a promise, forbearance, or giving up the right to do something) exchanged in a contract.

construction (of a statute) Interpretation of a statute within that agency's area of expertise.

constructive abandonment Loss of trademark rights that occurs when a trademark owner does something, or fails to do something, that causes the mark to lose its distinctiveness.

constructive notice Notice attributed by the existence of a properly recorded deed.

constructive trust A trust imposed on profits derived from an agent's breach of fiduciary duty.

contingency fee A fee that is a percentage of the judgment awarded to the party that is represented by the attorney.

continuation application A patent application filed after the final office action on an earlier filed application that consists of the same disclosure; the claims may be the same or there may be a new set of claims directed to the same invention claimed in the prior application. Continuation applications must be filed before the earlier application is abandoned and must contain no new matter. A continuation application has the same filing date as the earlier filed application.

continuing guaranty A guaranty that covers all future obligations of the primary debtor to the lender.

continuity of enterprise approach *See* Substantial Continuity Test.

contract A legally enforceable promise or set of promises.

contract of adhesion *See* adhesion contract.

contribution The doctrine that provides for the distribution of loss among several defendants by requiring each to pay its proportionate share to one who has discharged the joint liability of the group.

contributory copyright infringement Inducing, causing, or materially contributing to the infringing conduct of another with knowledge of the infringing activity.

contributory patent infringement One party knowingly sells an item that has one specific use that will result in the infringement of another's patent.

contributory negligence Plaintiff was negligent in some manner when injured by defendant.

control group test The privilege only to communications between counsel and upper-echelon employees who are in a position to control, or at least take a substantial role in making, the decision about the action the corporation might take based on the corporate attorney's advice.

control securities The sale of securities to the public by a controlling shareholder or other affiliate of the issuer is a transaction involving an underwriter.

controlling-person liability A person (or other entity), usually an officer or director of a company, responsible and liable for a securities violation.

controlling shareholder A shareholder who owns sufficient shares to outvote the other shareholders, and thus to control the corporation.

Convention on Cybercrime The first international treaty to address various types of criminal behavior directed against computer systems, networks, or data, including computer-related fraud and forgery.

conversion The exercise of dominion and control over the personal property, rather than the real property (land), of another. Term includes any unauthorized act that deprives an owner of his or her personal property permanently or for an indefinite time.

conveyance An instrument transferring an interest in real estate, such as a deed or lease.

cookies Bits of code sent by websites that identify the user to the site at a future visit.

copyright The legal right to prevent others from copying the expression embodied in a protected work.

core proceedings Proceedings of bankruptcy cases such as allowing creditor claims, deciding preferences, and confirming plans of reorganization.

corporate charter The document issued by a state agency or authority granting a corporation legal existence and the right to function as a corporation. Also called the *articles or certificate of incorporation*.

corporate domicile The state under whose laws a corporation is formed.

corporate opportunity doctrine The doctrine that holds that a business opportunity cannot legally be taken advantage of by an officer, director, or controlling shareholder if it is in the corporation's line of business.

corporation An organization authorized by state law to act as a legal entity distinct from its owners.

corporation by estoppel When a third party, in all its transactions with an enterprise, acts as if it were doing business with a corporation, the third party is prevented or estopped from claiming that the enterprise is not a corporation.

counterclaim A legal claim by defendant in opposition to or as a deduction from claim of plaintiff.

counterfeit mark A spurious trademark (1) that is used in combination with trafficking in goods or services, (2) that is identical to, or substantially indistinguishable from, a registered trademark, and (3) the use of which is likely to cause confusion or mistake or to deceive; or a spurious designation that is identical with, or substantially indistinguishable from, the holder of the right to use the designation.

counteroffer A new offer by the initial offeree that rejects and modifies the terms originally proposed by the offeror.

countertrade A foreign investor uses its local currency profits to purchase local products for sale abroad.

countervailing duty The law that provides that if a U.S. industry is materially injured by imports of a product benefiting from a foreign subsidy, an import duty that offsets the amount of the benefit must be imposed on those imports.

covenant The borrower's promise to the lender that it will or will not take specific actions as long as either a commitment or a loan is outstanding.

covenant not to compete An agreement, generally part of a contract of employment or a contract to sell a business, in which the covenantor agrees for a specific period of time and within a particular area to refrain from competition with the covenantee. Also called a *noncompete agreement*.

cover A buyer's obligation to buy substitute goods elsewhere after the seller has defaulted.

cramdown A bankruptcy relief plan confirmed over the objections of creditors.

creative professional Under the Fair Labor Standards Act, a professional employee whose primary duty of performance of work requires invention, imagination, originality, or talent in a recognized field of artistic or creative endeavor.

credit default swaps A financial derivative contract used by lenders to hedge against a default by the borrower. Also used by hedge funds and other traders betting on how close a firm is to insolvency.

creditor beneficiary Third party to a contract that the promisee enters into in order to discharge a duty to said third party.

crime An offense against the public at large; an act that violates the duties owed to the community, for which the offender must make satisfaction to the public.

criminal An individual or entity that has been convicted of a crime.

cross-collateralization A provision in a loan agreement whereby the collateral for one loan may be used to secure obligations under another loan.

cross-default Any breach by the borrower under any other loan agreement will constitute an event of default under the subject loan agreement.

crown jewels The most valuable assets or divisions of a target company in a takeover battle.

cumulative voting The process by which a shareholder can cast all its votes for one director nominee or allocate them among nominees as it sees fit.

customary authority The authority that agents of that type would normally have.

customary international law A form of international law analogous to established practice and commercial usage as they are known in the commercial laws of many nations.

customary practice A form of international law whereby treaties between nations can be compared to "established practice" or "commercial usage" as they are known in the commercial laws of many nations.

customer restrictions Restrictions that prevent a dealer or distributor from selling to a certain class of customer.

customs union A group of countries that reduce or eliminate tariffs between themselves, but establish a common tariff for trading with all other states.

customs valuation The value assigned to an imported article by the U.S. Customs Service.

cybersquatting The registration of a domain name that is confusingly similar or identical to a protected trademark, where the person registering the domain name has no legitimate interest in that particular domain name and registers and uses it in bad faith.

D

***D'Oench, Duhme* doctrine** A doctrine that bars many claims and defenses against conservators and receivers that might have been valid against the failed bank or savings and loan itself. It bars enforcement of agreements unless those agreements are in writing and have been approved contemporaneously by the bank's board or loan committee and recorded in the bank's written records.

deceit Requires the proof of several elements, including knowledge by the seller that the misrepresentation is false.

deepening insolvency The fraudulent continuation of a corporation's life resulting in damages inflicted by the diminution of its assets and income.

***de facto* (in fact) corporation** When incorporators cannot show substantial compliance with incorporation requirements, a court may find a corporation is a *de facto* corporation (corporation in fact), even though it is not technically a corporation by law, if the incorporators demonstrate that they were unaware of the defect and that they made a good faith effort to incorporate correctly.

***de jure* (by law) corporation** When incorporators have substantially complied with incorporation requirements, the entity is a *de jure* corporation (a corporation by right).

de novo Anew; a *de novo* proceeding takes place when a case has been successfully appealed and will be litigated again from the beginning.

***de novo* review** A review of a dispute by a court as if it had not been heard before and no prior decision had been rendered.

dead-hand pill A type of poison pill anti-takeover device that can be redeemed only by the directors of the target who initially adopted it. It violates the directors' duty of loyalty; applicable to defensive tactics touching upon issues of control because it purposefully disenfranchised the company's shareholders without any compelling justification.

deal protection devices These devices dissuade other bidders and thereby protect the consummation of the friendly merger transaction favored by the target.

dealer Under the Securities Act of 1933, any person who engages either for all or part of his or her time, directly or indirectly, as agent, broker, or principal, in the business of offering, buying, selling, or otherwise dealing or trading in securities issued by another person.

debt subordination An agreement whereby one or more creditors of a common debtor agree to defer payment of their claims until another creditor of the same debtor is fully paid.

debtor Under the Uniform Commercial Code, the person who owes payment or other performance of the obligation secured, whether or not that person owns or has rights in the collateral.

debtor-in-possession (DIP) In most Chapter 11 bankruptcy cases the debtor is left in place to operate the business and is referred to as the debtor-in- possession (DIP). The DIP has the same powers as a trustee in bankruptcy, but also has the power to operate the debtor's business during the bankruptcy proceeding.

deceit *See* Fraudulent Misrepresentation.

decision A form of European Union legislation in which an order is directed at a specific person or member state.

declaration by the inventor Part of a patent application, the declaration by the inventor states that the inventor has reviewed the application and that he or she believes that he or she is the first inventor of the invention.

deed A written document transferring an interest in real estate that is recorded at a public office where title documents are filed.

deed of trust A document evidencing a loan to buy real property secured by a lien on the real property. Also called a *mortgage*.

deepening insolvency The fraudulent continuation of a corporation's life after it has become unable to meet its obligations, resulting in damages inflicted by the diminution of its assets and income.

defamation The intentional communication to a third party of an untrue statement of fact that injures the plaintiff's reputation or good name by exposing the plaintiff to hatred, ridicule, or contempt.

default judgment A judgment that may be entered in favor of the plaintiff if the defendant does not file an answer within the time required.

defendant The person defending or denying; the party against whom relief or recovery is sought in an action or suit. The accused in a criminal case.

defined benefit pension plan A plan in which an employee's retirement benefit is expressed as a monthly annuity, the exact amount of which is calculated based on variables such as (1) number of years of service, (2) average compensation, (3) marital status, and (4) age at which benefits begin.

defined contribution pension plan A plan in which an employer agrees only to make specific contributions, usually a percentage of salary, so the payout is dependent on both the total contributions and the plan's investment performance.

Delaware carve-out Permits shareholders to bring a state law class-action suit against a corporation and its directors for breach of preexisting common law fiduciary disclosure obligations.

denial-of-service attacks Computer viruses that prevent user access to an Internet site.

deontological theory of ethics An ethical theory that focuses on the motivation behind an action rather than the consequences of an action.

depeçage A choice-of-law doctrine under which the court is permitted to apply the laws of different states to different issues when more than one state has an interest in the outcome of a case.

deposition The oral questioning of any person who may have helpful information about the facts of a case.

derivative insider A person, such as a tippee, upon whom the insider's duty of disclosure is imposed.

derivative works Works based upon a copyrighted work.

descriptive mark The identifying marks that directly describe (size, color, use of) the goods sold under the mark.

design defect A type of product defect that occurs when the product is manufactured according to specifications, but its inadequate design or poor choice of materials causes it to be defective.

design patent A patent that protects any novel, original, and ornamental design for an article of manufacture.

detrimental reliance Occurs when an offeree has changed his or her position because of justifiable reliance on an offer.

development loans Loans used for the acquisition, subdivision, improvement, and sale of residential properties.

diplomatic sanctions The removal or reduction of a diplomatic relationship.

direct copyright infringement Occurs when one party is alleged to have violated at least one of the five exclusive rights of the copyright holder by its own actions.

direct damages The difference between the market price at the time the buyer or seller learned of the other party's breach and the contract price for goods.

direct patent infringement The making, use, or sale of any patented invention in the jurisdiction where it is patented during the term of the patent.

direct representation Rules that apply for an agent acting in the name of a principal pursuant to express, implied, or apparent authority, whether or not the principal's identity is revealed at the time the agent acts or is to be revealed later.

directed verdict After the presentation of evidence in a trial before jury, either party may assert that other side has not produced enough evidence to support the legal claim or defense alleged. The moving party then requests that the judge take the case away from the jury and direct that a verdict be entered in favor of the moving party.

directive A form of European Union legislation that is a law directing member states to enact certain laws or regulations.

disappearing corporation In a merger of two corporations, the corporation that no longer maintains its separate corporate existence is the disappearing corporation.

discharge Relieve.

discovery The process through which parties to a lawsuit collect evidence to support their claims.

discovery-of-injury statutes Statutes that provide that the statute of limitations does not begin to run until the person discovers the injury.

discretionary review The Supreme Court can decide which cases within its jurisdiction it will adjudicate.

dismissed with prejudice The plaintiff is precluded from asserting the same claims in another case.

dismissed without prejudice The plaintiff is permitted to refile the complaint (or an amended version thereof) and recommence litigation of the same claims.

disparagement Untrue statements derogatory to the quality or ownership of a plaintiff's goods or services, that the defendant knows are false, or to the truth of which the defendant is consciously indifferent.

disparate impact The systematic exclusion of women, ethnic groups, or others in a protected class from employment through testing and other selection procedures.

disparate treatment Intentional discrimination against a person by employer by denying the person employment or a benefit or privilege of employment because of race, religion, sex, national origin, age, or disability.

Disposal Rule This regulation applies to individuals and organizations of any size that obtain information from consumer reporting agencies. These recipients are required to take reasonable measures to protect against unauthorized access to or use of sensitive consumer information (such as names, addresses, and Social Security numbers) in connection with its disposal.

dispute negotiation Backward-looking negotiation that addresses past events that have caused disagreement.

disqualified disposition A sale of stock originally acquired pursuant to an incentive stock option that causes the recipient of the option to lose tax-favored treatment.

dissenting shareholder A shareholder who voted against a merger, sale of assets, or other reorganization.

dissolution The designation of the point in time when partners no longer carry on their business together.

distributive justice A theory of justice that looks to how the burden and benefits of a particular situation of a system are distributed.

distributive negotiations Negotiations in which the only issue is the distribution of the fixed pie. Also called *zero-sum negotiations*.

diversity jurisdiction The power of U.S. district courts to decide lawsuits between citizens of two different states when amount in controversy, exclusive of interest and all costs, exceeds $75,000.

doctrine of equivalents The doctrine that holds that a direct infringement of a patent has occurred when a patent is not literally copied, but is replicated to the extent that the infringer has created a product or process that works in substantially the same way and accomplishes substantially the same result as the patented invention.

doctrine of first sale *See* First Sale Doctrine.

doctrine of self-publication A doctrine that provides that a defamatory communication by an employer to an employee may constitute publication if the employer could foresee that the employee would be required to repeat the communication, for instance, to a prospective employer.

documentary letter of credit (L/C) A letter of credit issued by a bank that provides for payment by the bank to the beneficiary upon tender by the beneficiary (or its agent or assignee) of specified documents; frequently used to secure payment for goods and repayment of loans in international transactions.

domain name The unique name that identifies an Internet site. Domain names always have two or more parts, separated by dots. The part on the left is the most specific, and the part on the right is the most general.

donee beneficiary Third party to a contract to whom promisee does not owe an obligation, but rather wishes to confer a gift or a right of performance.

dormant commerce clause An implied constitutional limitation on state action affecting interstate commerce even in the absence of preempting federal legislation.

double jeopardy A law that forbids being tried twice for the same crime.

Double Jeopardy Clause A clause of the Fifth Amendment of the U.S. Constitution that protects criminal defendants from multiple prosecutions for the same offense.

dragnet clause In a security agreement, a provision giving the secured party a security interest in all the debtor's property and in the proceeds from the sale of such property.

drawings The drawings (except in chemical cases) must show the claimed invention in a patent application in graphic form.

drug Defined by the Food, Drug and Cosmetic Act to include (1) articles intended for use in the diagnosis, cure, mitigation, treatment, or prevention of disease; and (2) articles (other than food) intended to affect the structure or any function of the body.

dual agency In a real estate transaction, a broker acts for both the buyer and the seller.

dual distributor A manufacturer that sells its goods both at wholesale and at retail.

dual use The state of goods and technologies that have both military and nonmilitary applications.

due diligence The identification and characterization of risks associated with property and operations involved in various business transactions. A defense available to a defendant (other than the issuer) in a securities violation case concerning a registration statement who (1) conducted a reasonable investigation, and (2) reasonably believed that (a) the statements made were true, and (b) that there were no omissions that made those statements misleading.

Due Process Clauses A clause in the Fifth and Fourteenth Amendments of the U.S. Constitution that provides that the government (federal or state) shall not "deprive any person of life, liberty, or property without due process of law." Among other things, it prohibits the government from using involuntary confessions, even if the *Miranda* warnings were given, when the conduct of the law enforcement officials in obtaining a confession is deemed outrageous or shocking, among other things.

dumping Sale of imported products in the United States below the current selling price in the exporter's home market or below the exporter's cost of production.

dumping margin The difference between the U.S. price for foreign goods and the price of those goods in their country of origin.

duress Coercion.

duty (1) The obligation to act as a reasonably prudent person would act under the circumstances to prevent an unreasonable risk of harm to others. (2) The required payment on imports.

duty of care The fiduciary duty of agents, officers, and directors to act with the same care that a reasonably prudent person would exercise under similar circumstances. Sometimes expressed as the duty to use the same level of care a reasonably prudent person would use in the conduct of his or her own affairs.

duty of loyalty The fiduciary duty of agents, officers, and directors to act in good faith and in what they believe to be the best interest of the principal or the corporation.

duty of obedience The fiduciary duty of agents, officers, and directors to obey all reasonable orders of his or her principal.

E

early termination clause An out clause or provision that would allow the lessor or lessee to cancel the lease without completing the full term or paying the complete value of the lease.

earmarking doctrine A bankruptcy doctrine whereby a payment to a preexisting creditor may not be recoverable as a preference if the funds for the repayment were provided by some other creditor and not by the debtor.

economic duress The coercion of the borrower, threatening to do an unlawful act that might injure the borrower's business or property.

economic loss rule A common law doctrine that bars a plaintiff who is in privity of contract with the defendant or who has entered into a commercial transaction involving the defendant from bringing a lawsuit for negligence based solely on economic losses.

economic sanction A sanction imposed by one country (or a group of countries) against the commerce of another country in an effort to influence that country's behavior.

economic strike A union strikes employers when they are unable to extract acceptable terms and conditions of employment through collective bargaining.

economic union A union within which internal trade barriers are abolished, restrictions on mobility of factors of production among members are eliminated, and the economic policies of the member states (monetary, fiscal, taxation, and social welfare programs) are fully integrated in order to blend the member state economics into a single entity.

efficient-market theory The theory that holds that in an open and developed securities market, the price of a company's stock equals its true value.

electronic agents Autonomous computer programs that can be dispatched by the user to execute certain tasks.

electronically supplied services The electronic supply of software, music, films, and games, as well as other electronic content, web-hosting, distance maintenance of software and equipment, distance teaching, and the like.

embargo A special kind of sanction against all commerce of one country that is declared by a country, or more frequently, a group of countries.

embezzlement The acquisition by an employee of money or property by reason of some office or position, which money or property the employee takes for personal use.

eminent domain The power of state and federal governments to take private property for government uses for which property owners are entitled to just compensation.

employee stock ownership plan (ESOP) A type of qualified retirement plan that is governed by the tax qualification requirements of Internal Revenue Code Sections 401(a), 408 and 4975(e)(7) and which is invested primarily in stock of the employer.

employee stock purchase plan (ESSP) A plan structured under Internal Revenue Code Section 423 under which a company allows its employees to purchase stock at up to a 15 percent discount, and the employee-purchasers receive a favorable tax treatment.

***en banc* hearing** A hearing at which all the judges of a court of appeals sit together to hear and decide a particularly important or close case.

encroachment Occurs when a franchisor sells a franchisee an outlet and later sells another outlet nearby to another franchisee.

encumbrance A claim against real property.

enterprise Any individual, partnership, corporation, association, or other legal entity, and any union or group of individuals associated in fact although not a legal entity.

environmental assessment (EA) A document that identifies any significant impact of a development on the environment.

environmental impact statement (EIS) A required document for any proposal for legislation or other major governmental action that may significantly affect the quality of the environment.

environmental justice The notion that decisions with environmental consequences (such as where to locate incinerators, dumps, factories, and other sources of pollution) should not discriminate against poor and minority communities.

environmental laws The numerous federal, state, and local laws with the common objective of protecting human health and the environment.

Environmental Protection Agency (EPA) Federal agency that administers all of the federal laws that set national goals and policies for environmental protection, except for the National Environmental Policy Act, which is administered by the Council on Environmental Quality.

equal dignities rule Under this rule if an agent acts on behalf of another (its principal) in signing an agreement of the type that must under the statute of frauds be in writing, the authority of the agent to act on behalf of the principal must also be in writing.

equitable relief An injunction issued by the court to prohibit a defendant from continuing in a certain course of activity or to require a defendant to perform a certain activity.

equitable subordination The doctrine that prevents one creditor, through fraud or other wrongful conduct, from increasing its recovery at the expense of other creditors of the same debtor.

equity The value of real property that exceeds the liens against it.

equity capital The cash or property contributed to an enterprise in exchange for an ownership interest.

equity security An equity security includes (1) any stock or similar security; (2) any security that is convertible, with or without consideration, into such a security; (3) any security carrying any warrant or right to purchase such a security; (4) any such warrant or right; and (5) any other security that the Securities and Exchange Commission (SEC) deems to be of a similar nature and that, for the protection of investors or in the public interest, the SEC considers appropriate to treat as an equity security.

***Erie* doctrine** In a diversity action in federal court, except as to matters governed by the U.S. Constitution and acts of Congress, the law to be applied in any case is the law of the state in which the federal court is situated.

escrow The system by which a neutral stakeholder (escrow agent) allows parties to a real property transaction to fulfill the various conditions of the closing of the transaction without the physical difficulties of passing instruments and funds between the parties.

escrow agent A neutral stakeholder who facilitates the transfer of real property between interested parties.

essential facility Under antitrust law, a resource necessary to a company's rivals' survival that they cannot economically or feasibly duplicate.

Establishment Clause A clause in the First Amendment that prohibits the establishment of a religion by the federal government.

estopped A defendant is legally barred from alleging or denying a certain fact when the defendant's words and/or actions have been to the contrary.

Ethical Business Leader's Decision Tree A guide for managers to use when deciding how to act.

euro The common currency used in those members of the European Union that have agreed to accept it in lieu of their former national currency. For example, France has abandoned use of the French franc in favor of the euro.

events of default The events contained in a loan agreement that will trigger the lender's right to terminate the loan, accelerate the repayment obligations, and, if the loan is secured, take possession of the property securing the loan.

***ex post facto* clause (after the fact)** Clause in the U.S. Constitution prohibiting laws that punish actions that were not illegal when performed.

***ex post facto* laws** Laws that punish actions that were not illegal when performed; prohibited by Article I, Section 9, and Article I, Section 10.

exclusionary rule The evidence obtained in an unlawful search or interrogation cannot be introduced into evidence at trial against a defendant.

exclusive distributorship An agreement in which a manufacturer limits itself to a single dealer or distributor in a given territory.

exclusive listing A listing that grants the real estate broker the right to sell the property; any sale of the property during the term of the listing will entitle the broker to a commission.

executive An employee whose primary duty consists of the management of the enterprise where he or she is employed or of a customarily recognized department or subdivision of the enterprise.

executive privilege The type of immunity granted the president against the forced disclosure of presidential communications made in the exercise of executive power.

executory contract Contracts that have not yet been performed and involve an exchange of promises.

exemplary damages Damages awarded to a plaintiff over and above what will fairly compensate it for its loss. They are intended to punish the defendant and deter others from engaging in similar conduct. Also called *punitive damages*.

exempt employee An employee who is exempt from the minimum-wage and overtime requirements of the Federal Labor Standards Act; such an employee is generally paid a salary instead of an hourly wage.

exempt securities Securities listed in Section 3 of the Securities Act of 1933, including any security (1) issued or guaranteed by the United States or any state of the United States, (2) issued or guaranteed by any national bank, (3) issued by a charitable organization, and (4) that is part of an issue offered and sold only to persons residing within a single state or territory, if the issuer is a resident of the same state or territory.

exempt transactions Transactions described in Section 4 of the 1933 Act that include those (1) by any person other than an issuer, underwriter or dealer and (2) by an issuer not involving any public offering.

exercise period The fixed period during which a stock option may be exercised by the optionee, which is usually no longer than ten years.

exercise price The price at which the recipient of an option (the optionee) can exercise the option by purchasing the underlying stock. It is usually the market price of the stock at the time the option was granted. Also called *strike price*.

exhaustion of administrative remedies A court will not entertain an appeal from the administrative process until an agency has had a chance to act and all possible avenues of relief before the agency have been fully pursued.

expectation damages In the case of breach of contract, refers to remuneration that puts a plaintiff into the cash position the plaintiff would have been in if the contract had been fulfilled.

export license The control of exports.

express authority The power of an agent to act for a principal based on that agent's justifiable belief that the principal has authorized him or her to do so; may be given by the principal's actual words or by an action that indicates the principal's consent.

express ratification Express ratification occurs when the principal, through words or behavior, manifests an intent to be bound by the agent's act.

express warranty An explicit guarantee by the seller that the goods purchased by a buyer will have certain qualities.

expropriation The process of nationalization when the host country compensates the company for its lost assets.

extension plan A plan in a Chapter 13 bankruptcy proceeding in which creditors receive the entire indebtedness, but the period for payment is extended beyond the original due date.

extortionate extension of credit Making a loan for which violence is understood by the parties as likely to occur in the event of nonpayment.

extraterritoriality A practice whereby countries assert the right to regulate activities that occur beyond their borders.

F

facilitating payments Under the Foreign Corrupt Payments Act, payments to low-ranking officials who merely expedite the nondiscretionary granting of a permit or license or performance of an administrative act.

failure to warn Failure of a product to carry adequate warnings of the risks involved in the normal use of the product.

fair lending laws Laws that prohibit discrimination in lending practices.

fair trade law A federal law providing for temporary relief to domestic industries seriously injured by increasing imports, regardless of whether unfair practices are involved.

fair use doctrine The doctrine that protects from liability a defendant who has infringed a copyright owner's exclusive rights when countervailing public policies predominate. Activities such as literary criticism, social comment, news reporting, educational activities, scholarship, or research are traditional fair use domains.

false imprisonment The confinement of an individual without that individual's consent and without lawful authority.

family resemblance test A test for determining whether an instrument is a security by asking whether it bears a family resemblance to any nonsecurity.

family responsibility discrimination (FRD) Employment discrimination based on stereotypes of parental roles and responsibilities. Also referred to as *maternal wall discrimination*.

fanciful mark A coined term having no prior meaning until used as a trademark in connection with a particular product.

fast-track negotiating authority Congressional legislation allowing the president to negotiate trade agreements and then submit them for an up or down vote by Congress with no amendments permitted.

Federal Arbitration Act (FAA) The federal law requiring courts to honor agreements to arbitrate and arbitration awards.

federal question When a dispute concerns federal law, namely, a legal right arising under the U.S. Constitution, a federal statute, an administrative regulation issued by a federal government agency, federal common law, or a treaty of the United States, it is said to raise a federal question.

Federal Rules of Civil Procedure (FRCP) The procedural rules that govern civil litigation.

Federal Rules of Evidence (FRE) Federal rules governing the admissibility of evidence in litigation in federal court.

fee simple Title to property that grants owner full right of disposition during his or her lifetime that may be passed on to owner's heirs and assigns forever.

felony An offense punishable by death or prison term exceeding one year.

fetal-protection policy A company policy that bars a woman from certain jobs unless her inability to bear children is medically documented.

fictitious business name The name of a business that is other than that of the owner.

fiduciary A person having a duty to act primarily for the benefit of another in matters connected with undertaking fiduciary responsibilities.

fiduciary duty The obligation of a trustee or other fiduciary to act for the benefit of the other party.

fiduciary out A clause allowing the board of directors to negotiate with other bidders or to terminate a merger agreement.

file-wrapper estoppel The doctrine that prevents a patent owner involved in infringement from introducing any evidence at odds with the information contained in the owner's application on file with the U.S. Patent and Trademark Office.

final-offer arbitration A form of arbitration used most notably in baseball salary disputes; each side submits its "best and final" offer to the arbitrator, who must choose one of the two proposals.

financing lease Under a financing lease (commonly used to finance the acquisition of expensive capital equipment and vehicles such as airplanes, locomotives, and ships), the parties expect the lessee to purchase the leased equipment at the end of the lease term at an agreed-upon residual value.

firm commitment underwriting The underwriters agree to purchase the entire offering, thus effectively shifting the risk of the offering from the issuer to the underwriters.

firm offer Under the Uniform Commercial Code, an offer signed by a merchant that indicates that the offer will be kept open and is not revocable, for lack of consideration, during the time stated, or for a reasonable period of time if none is stated, but in no event longer than three months.

first sale doctrine (copyrights and trademarks) A U.S. doctrine that states that once the copyright or trademark owner places a copyrighted or trademarked item in the stream of commerce by selling it, the owner has exhausted its exclusive statutory right to control its distribution.

five forces According to Professor Michael Porter, the following five forces determine the attractiveness of an industry: buyer power, supplier power, the competitive threat posed by current rivals, the availability of substitutes, and the threat of new entrants.

fixtures The items of personal property that are attached to real property and that cannot be removed without substantial damage to the item.

floating Interest rates that fluctuate throughout the life of the loan according to the interest rate that the lender would pay if it borrowed the funds in order to relend them.

floating lien In a security interest, if the collateral is sold, exchanged, collected, or otherwise disposed of, the security interest is equally effective against cash, account, or whatever else is received from the transaction.

food Defined by the Food, Drug and Cosmetic Act as (1) articles used for food or drink; (2) chewing gum; and (3) articles used for components of either.

forbears A lender does not exercise any of its remedies for the forbearance period.

foreclose To take constructive or actual possession of collateral or real property subject to a mortgage or deed of trust.

foreclosure The legal process by which a mortgagee may put up a piece of property for sale in the public arena to raise cash in order to pay off a debt owed by the mortgagor to the mortgagee.

foreign corporation A corporation doing business in one state though chartered or incorporated in another state is a foreign corporation as to the first state.

foreseeable A condition that a reasonable person could have anticipated would result from his or her actions.

forgotten founder A problem that can arise when several persons work together on an informal basis with a common business objective, and then one leaves. The person who left (the forgotten founder) may have ownership rights in the enterprise.

Form S–1 The registration statement used in an initial public offering of securities.

Form S–3 An abbreviated form of registration statement that is available to companies that have filed periodic reports under the Securities Exchange Act of 1934 for at least three years and have a widespread following in the marketplace.

Form S–4 A combined securities registration statement and proxy statement.

forum non conveniens A doctrine whereby a suit is dismissed because an alternate, more convenient forum is available.

forum shopping A party to a lawsuit attempts to have a case tried in a particular court or jurisdiction where the party believes the most favorable judgment or verdict will be received.

forward-looking statement A statement by a publicly traded company (1) containing a projection of revenues, income, earnings per share, capital expenditures, dividends, capital structure, or other financial items; (2) of management's plans and objectives for future operations, including plans relating to the issuer's products and services; (3) of future economic performance, including any such statement in management's discussion and analysis of financial condition or in the results of operations required to be included by the SEC; and (4) of the assumptions underlying or relating to any such statement.

401(k) plan A defined contribution pension plan funded with contributions by the participants or a combination of participant and employer contributions.

franchise A business relationship in which one party (the franchisor) grants to another party (the franchisee) the right to use the franchisor's name and logo and to distribute the franchisor's products from a specified locale.

franchising An arrangement whereby the franchisor receives cash up front, followed by monthly payments based on a reseller's gross receipts, in exchange for granting the franchisee the right to use the franchisor's trademarks and marketing plan.

fraud Any intentional deception that has the purpose of inducing another in reliance upon the deception to part with some property or money. Fraud may involve false representations of fact, whether by words or conduct; false allegations; omission (especially by fiduciary); or concealment of something that should have been disclosed.

fraud in the factum A type of fraud that occurs when a party is persuaded to sign one document thinking that it is another.

fraud in the inducement A type of fraud that occurs when a party makes a false statement to persuade the other party to enter into an agreement.

fraud-on-the-market theory The theory that holds that if the information about a company available to the market is incorrect, then the market price will not reflect the true value of the stock.

fraudulent conveyance The direct or indirect transfer of assets to a third party with actual intent to defraud or have inadequate consideration in circumstances when the transferor is insolvent.

fraudulent misrepresentation Deceit; intentionally misleading by making material misrepresentations of fact that the plaintiff relied on that cause injury to the plaintiff.

Free Exercise Clause A clause in the First Amendment that prohibits certain, but not all, restrictions on the practice of religion.

free trade area A free trade area is created when a group of countries reduce or eliminate tariffs among themselves, but maintain their own individual tariffs as to other states.

free writing prospectus Any written offer under Section 2(a)(10) of the 1933 Act and subject to liability under Section 12(a)(2).

freeze out The majority forces the minority shareholders to convert their shares into cash, as long as the transaction is fair.

freeze-out merger In a merger with a controlling shareholder, some shareholders (usually the public shareholders) are required to surrender their shares in the disappearing corporation for cash.

front pay A damage remedy in an employment discrimination case that is generally equal to the compensation the employee would have received had he or she not been unlawfully discharged.

fruit of the poisonous tree Evidence acquired directly or indirectly as a result of an illegal search or arrest is generally inadmissible.

frustration of purpose Frustration of purpose occurs when performance is possible, but changed circumstances have made the contract useless to one or both of the parties.

full-service lease A lease that requires the lessor to maintain the property that a company is occupying, which means, in turn, that the tenant's responsibilities may be limited to seeing that the services provided are adequate.

full warranty The warranty that gives the consumer the right to free repair or replacement of a defective product.

G

gap financing Financing that a developer obtains to pay off a construction loan when it becomes due before the permanent financing is available. Also called *interim financing*.

garnishment The legal procedure by which a creditor may collect a debt by attaching a portion of a debtor's weekly wages.

general partners Partners of a general or limited partnership responsible for managing the partnership. They are jointly and severally liable for partnership obligations.

general partnership A form of business organization between two or more persons in which the partners share in the profits or losses of a common business enterprise.

general plan A long-range planning document that addresses the physical development and redevelopment of a city.

general release An agreement by person engaging in a dangerous activity to assume all risks and hold the party offering access to said dangerous activity free of all liability.

Generalized System of Preferences (GSP) A tariff program developed by industrialized countries to assist developing nations by improving their ability to export.

genericism The use of a trademark as a generic name for the product, for example, "a Kleenex" for "tissue."

Gharar A tenet of Islamic trade and commerce that refers to an event where the outcomes are unknown.

going effective Culmination of the securities registration process with the Securities and Exchange Commission. Sales can be legally consummated as of this date and time.

going private A corporation that has fewer than 300 shareholders (or 500 if the corporation's assets total less than $10 million) and ceases to be required to file public periodic reports under the Securities Exchange Act of 1934.

good faith exception An exception to the exclusionary rule that provides that evidence obtained by police in good faith will not be excluded from trial, even if it was obtained in violation of the Fourth Amendment.

good faith subsequent purchaser A person who acquires real property for fair value without being aware of a disputed claim to the property.

good offices A process mainly used in the area of public international law, by which a third party (often a disinterested government) brings the parties together through establishing communication and providing a site where the parties can meet, often in secrecy.

goods As defined in Article 2 of the Uniform Commercial Code, all things (including specially manufactured goods) that are movable at the time of identification to the contract for sale.

government-contractor defense The limited immunity available for manufacturers that produce products to the specifications of government contracts.

grant deed A deed that contains implied warranties that the grantor has not previously conveyed the same property or any interest in it to another person and that the title is marketable.

grantee A person to whom real property is conveyed.

grantor A person conveying real property.

gray market A market where products are sold outside the normal channel of distribution, often at a discounted price.

greenmail Payment by a target company to buy back shares owned by a potential acquiror at a premium over market. The acquiror in exchange agrees not to pursue its hostile takeover bid.

gross-up clause The clause in foreign investment contracts by which local partner or licensee is obligated to pay all taxes other than those specifically allocated to the foreign partner.

ground lease A lease for land on which a building will be built.

group boycott An agreement among competitors to refuse to deal with another competitor.

guarantor The person who agrees to be liable for the obligation of another person.

guaranty An undertaking by one person to become liable for the obligation of another person.

guaranty of collection Under a guaranty of collection, the guarantor becomes obliged to pay only after the lender has attempted unsuccessfully to collect the amount due from the primary debtor.

guaranty of payment A provision that holds guarantor's obligation to pay the lender is triggered, immediately and automatically, if the primary debtor fails to make a payment when due.

guaranty of performance A guaranty that specified nonpayment obligations will be performed.

guardian *ad litem* (guardian for the suit) A person authorized to bring suit for a minor.

gun-jumping A violation of the securities laws that occurs when an issuer or underwriter conditions the market with a news article, press release, or speech about a company engaged in the registration of its securities.

H

H-1B visa A work authorization issued by the U.S. Citizenship and Immigration Services that is available only for foreign workers in professional and specialty occupations (generally those involving a bachelor's degree or its equivalent), such as computer programmers, engineers, doctors, or fashion models, where the employer can show an inability to recruit qualified workers in the United States.

Harmonized Tariff Schedule (HTS) A U.S. government document that lists the tariffs on goods imposed by Congress and by the president pursuant to the Trade Agreements Program, based on the country of origin.

hazard ranking score The Environmental Protection Agency ranking that represents the risks presented by certain sites to the environment and public health.

Hazardous Substance Superfund Finances federal activity to investigate and take remedial action in response to a release or threatened release of hazardous substances to the environment.

hearing The phase of arbitration that is similar to a trial.

Herfindahl-Hirschman Index (HHI) An aid to the interpretation of market data when determining the anticompetitive effect of a merger; the HHI of market concentration is calculated by summing the squares of the individual market shares of all the firms in the market.

holder claims Lawsuits pursuant to certain state blue sky laws by investors who allege that they did not sell their securities because of the defendants' fraud. Not available in federal court.

horizontal agreement A conspiracy agreement between firms that compete with each other on the same level of production or distribution.

horizontal market division An agreement among competitors to divide a market according to class of customer or geographic territory; it violates antitrust law.

horizontal merger A corporate combination of actual or prospective competitors.

horizontal price-fixing An agreement between competitors at the same level of distribution to set a common price for a product; it violates antitrust law.

hostile environment harassment The creation of a hostile working environment, such as continually subjecting an employee to ridicule and racial slurs, or unwanted sexual advances.

hot issues Shares of high-demand initial public offerings.

hot news exception A state law misappropriation claim that applies in cases where (a) the plaintiff generates or gathers information at its cost; (b) the information is time-sensitive; (c) the defendant's use of the information amounts to free-riding on the plaintiff's efforts; (d) the defendant is in direct competition with the plaintiff; and (e) the availability of other parties to free ride on the plaintiff's efforts would reduce the plaintiff's incentive to provide the product or service such that plaintiff's existence would be threatened.

I

I-9 The Employment Eligibility and Verification Form that the U.S. government requires all employers to complete and keep on file to identify the identity and employment eligibility of all persons they hire.

identification to the contract Setting aside or otherwise designating the particular goods for sale under a contract.

identity theft Taking an individual's information (such as Social Security number and mother's maiden name) and using that information to fraudulently obtain credit or commit other financial crimes.

illegal contract A contract is illegal if its formation or performance is expressly forbidden by a civil or criminal statute, or if a penalty is imposed for doing the act agreed upon.

illegal *per se* A practice that is illegal regardless of its impact on the market or its procompetitive justifications.

illusory promise A promise that either does not in fact confer any benefit on the promisee or subject the promisor to any detriment.

impaired A characteristic of a claim when the plan does not provide for full cash payment on its effective date and if it alters the creditors' legal, equitable, or contractual rights in any way.

implied authority The power of an agent to do whatever is reasonable to complete the task he or she has been instructed to undertake.

implied contract An employment agreement—implied from such facts as long-term employment; receipt of raises, bonuses and promotions; and assurance from management that the employee was doing a good job—that the employee would not be terminated except for good cause.

implied covenant of good faith and fair dealing An implied covenant in every contract that imposes on each party a duty not to do anything that will deprive the other party of the benefits of the agreement.

implied ratification Implied ratification occurs when the principal, by his or her silence or failure to repudiate the agent's act, acquiesces in it.

implied warranties Representations about the quality or suitability of a product that are implied, not explicitly stated. *See also* Implied Warranty of Fitness for a Particular Purpose and Implied Warranty of Merchantability.

implied warranty of fitness for a particular purpose The warranty whereby goods involving the following elements are judged satisfactory for the buyer's purpose: (1) the buyer must have a particular purpose for the goods; (2) the seller must have known or have had reason to know of that purpose; (3) the seller must have known or had reason to know that the buyer was relying on the seller's expertise; and (4) the buyer must have relied upon the seller.

implied warranty of habitability A warranty made by a commercial seller of houses in which the seller warrants that the house is in reasonable working order and is of reasonably sound construction.

implied warranty of merchantability The warranty by which all goods sold by merchants in the normal course of business must meet following criteria: (l) pass without objection in the trade under the contract description; (2) be fit for the ordinary purposes for which such goods are used; (3) be within the variations permitted by the agreement, of even kind, quality and quantity within each unit and among all units involved; (4) be adequately contained, packaged, and labeled as the agreement may require; and (5) conform to the promises or affirmations of fact made on the container or label, if any.

import relief laws A series of laws through which Congress has authorized the president to raise U.S. tariffs on specified products and to provide other forms of import protection to U.S. industries.

impossibility An excuse for nonperformance based on the destruction of something vital to the performance of the contract or another unforeseen event that makes performance of the contract impossible.

impossibility defense A defense to strict liability in which a corporate officer might not be held strictly (and vicariously) liable if he or she did everything possible to ensure legal compliance to applicable standards, even though the company was still unable to comply.

impracticability A situation in which performance of a contract is possible but commercially impractical.

improper means Deceitful actions through which party obtains trade secrets of another.

imputed liability The imposition of civil or criminal liability on one party for the wrongful acts of another. Also called *vicarious liability*.

in loco parentis (in place of the parent) Refers to actions of a custodian, guardian, or other person acting in the parent's place.

***in personam* jurisdiction** Personal jurisdiction based upon the residence or activities of the person being sued. It is the power that a court has over the defendant itself, in contrast to the court's power over the defendant's interest in property (*quasi in rem* jurisdiction) or power over the property itself (*in rem* jurisdiction).

***in rem* jurisdiction** Jurisdiction over property based upon the location of the property at issue in the lawsuit.

incentive stock option (ISO) A stock option that qualifies for favorable tax treatment Internal Revenue Code Section 422, granted to an employee of a corporation to buy stock at a specified price (at least 100% of fair market value on the date of grant) for a specified period of time (no more than ten years).

incidental damages In an action for breach of contract, the lesser and relatively minor damages that a nonbreaching party incurs in mitigating damages resulting from the breach, such as the charges, expenses, and commissions incurred in stopping delivery; the cost of the transportation, care, and custody of goods after a breach; and the expenses incurred in connection with the return or subsequent disposition of goods that are the subject of the contract.

incorporation The process by which a corporation is formed.

indemnification The doctrine that allows a defendant to recover its individual loss from a co-defendant whose relative blame is greater or who has contractually agreed to assume liability.

indemnity A right to reimbursement for loss.

independent contractor A person is deemed to be an independent contractor only if the employer neither exercises control over the means of performing the work nor the end result of that work.

indictment Formal charges filed by a grand jury.

indirect patent infringement One party's active inducement of another party to infringe a patent.

indirect representation Rules that apply when an intermediary acts on instructions and on behalf of, but not in the name of, a principal, or when the third party does not know or have reason to know that the intermediary is acting as an agent.

inducement to infringe A party's active encouragement of another party to infringe a patent or copyright. Applies to those who supply a product or service that has substantial non-infringing uses if the supplier also encourages that product or service to be used in an infringing fashion.

industrial ecology A concept that advocates a systems approach to ecoefficiency and applies it to groups of corporations working together.

inevitable disclosure doctrine A doctrine that permits a former employer to prevent an employee from working for a competitor when the new position will require the employee to disclose or use the trade secrets of the former employer.

inevitable discovery exception An exception to the exclusionary rule that provides that illegally obtained evidence can lawfully be introduced at trial if it can be shown that the evidence would inevitably have been found by other legal means.

infomercial An advertisement generally presented in the format of half-hour television talk shows or news programs.

informal discretionary action The administrative agencies' decision-making process for repetitive actions that are inappropriate to litigate in courts.

information The formal charges filed with the court in a criminal case.

injunction A remedy granted by the court that requires defendant to perform or cease from performing some activity.

injurious falsehood False statements knowingly made that lead to economic loss for a plaintiff.

in loco parentis *(in place of the parents)* Obligations to ensure the safety of children and to serve as role models.

innocent landowner defense In a case under the Comprehensive Environmental Responsibility, Contribution, and Liability Act, a potentially responsible current owner can assert this defense if the release or disposal of hazardous materials was by a third party who was not an employee and with whom the current owner had no contractual relationship. Also called the *third-party defense*.

innovation offsets Technological advantages gained by companies that met the challenge of environmental regulations and discovered lower costs and better quality products as a result.

inquiry Done by a commission of inquiry that is established ad hoc, often after a violation of international law, it consists of two contending governments reviewing the finding of the commission with the goal to come to an acceptable solution for the dispute at hand.

inside director A member of a board who is also an officer.

insider A person with access to confidential information and an obligation of disclosure to other traders in the marketplace.

insider trading Trading securities based on material nonpublic information, in violation of a duty to the corporation or its shareholders or others.

integrate When an issuer makes successive sales of securities within a limited period of time, the Securities and Exchange Commission may integrate the successive sales; that is, it may deem them to be part of a single sale for purposes of deciding whether there was an exemption from registration.

integrative negotiations Negotiations in which mutual gains are possible as parties trade lower valued resources for higher valued ones. Also called *variable-sum negotiations*.

intellectual property Any product or result of a mental process that is given legal protection against unauthorized use.

intent The actual, subjective desire to cause the consequences of an act, or the belief that the consequences are substantially certain to result from it.

intent to be bound An oral or written statement or an action signaling that a party intended to enter into a contract.

intention to do wrong Subjective intent or desire to do wrong or intent to take action substantially certain to cause a wrong to occur.

intentional infliction of emotional distress Outrageous conduct by the individual inflicting the distress; intention to cause, or reckless disregard of the probability of causing, emotional distress; severe emotional suffering; and actual and proximate (or legal) causation of the emotional distress.

interbrand competition The price competition between a company and its competitors that sell a different brand of the same product.

interference with contractual relations A defendant intentionally induces another to breach a contract with a plaintiff.

interference with prospective business advantage Intentional interference by the defendant with a business relationship the plaintiff seeks to develop, which interference causes loss to the plaintiff.

interim financing Financing that a developer obtains to pay off a construction loan when it becomes due before the permanent financing is available. Also called *gap financing*.

interrogatory Written question to a party to a lawsuit and its attorney.

intrabrand competition The price competition among the different dealers selling products produced by the same company.

intrusion Objectionable prying, such as eavesdropping or unauthorized rifling through files. It includes the act of wrongfully entering upon or taking possession of property of another.

invasion of privacy Prying or intrusion that would be objectionable or offensive to a reasonable person, including eavesdropping, rifling through files one has no authorization to see, public disclosure of private facts, or unauthorized use of an individual's picture in an advertisement or article with which that person has no connection.

inverse condemnation The taking of private real property for a public use; requires payment of just compensation.

investigative consumer reporting Report that contains information on character and reputation, not just credit history.

investment contract A type of security created by an investment of money in a common enterprise with profits to come solely from the efforts of others.

investors Persons putting up cash or property in exchange for an equity interest in an enterprise.

invitee A business visitor who enters premises for the purposes of the possessor's business.

involuntary proceeding An involuntary proceeding in bankruptcy that is initiated when one or more of the debtor's creditors files a bankruptcy petition with the bankruptcy court.

***ipso facto* clause** A clause in a contract that expressly permits termination of the contract in the event of a bankruptcy filing by one or both parties to the contract.

irrevocable letter of credit A letter of credit that cannot be amended or canceled without the consent of the beneficiary and the issuing bank.

irrevocable offer An offer that cannot be revoked. Arises (1) when an option contract has been entered into or (2) when an offeree has relied on an offer to its detriment.

issuer A company that offers or sells any security.

J

joint and several liability In a case in which the court determines that multiple defendants are at fault; the doctrine whereby a plaintiff may collect the entire judgment from any single defendant, regardless of the degree of that defendant's fault.

joint tenancy A specialized form of co-ownership involving real property owned in equal shares by two or more persons who have a right of survivorship if one joint tenant dies.

joint venture A one-time group of two or more persons in a single specific business enterprise or transaction.

judgment n.o.v. (*j.n.o.v.*) The attorney can make a motion to reverse the jury verdict on the grounds that the evidence of the prevailing party was so weak that no reasonable jury could have resolved the dispute in that party's favor.

judgment notwithstanding the verdict (judgment n.o.v.) Reverses the jury verdict on the grounds that the evidence of the prevailing party was so weak that no reasonable jury could have resolved the dispute in that party's favor. Also called *judgment n.o.v. (non obstante veredicto, notwithstanding the verdict).*

judicial review The power of federal courts to review acts of the legislative and executive branches of government to determine whether they violate the Constitution.

junior debt Indebtedness that is subordinated under a debt subordination agreement.

junk bond A form of high yield, high risk unsecured corporate indebtedness that is not investment grade.

K

Kantian theory An ethical theory that looks to the form of an action, rather than the intended result, in examining the ethical worth.

know-how Detailed information on how to make or do something.

knowingly Knowledge by a defendant of the facts that constitute an offense. Defendant is generally deemed to knowingly violate a statute even if he or she was not aware that the conduct at issue was unlawful, unless the text of the statute dictates a different result. Contrast with *willful*.

L

larceny Theft. The taking of property without the owner's consent.

learned professional A professional employee whose primary duty is the performance of work requiring advanced knowledge (defined as (1) work that is predominantly intellectual in character and

(2) that includes work requiring the consistent exercise of discretion and judgment) in a field of science or learning customarily acquired by a prolonged course of intellectual instruction.

legal astuteness The ability of a manager to communicate effectively with counsel and to work together to solve complex problems.

legal duty The requirement to act reasonably under the circumstances to avoid harming another person.

lemon laws Laws designed to protect consumers from defective products that cannot be adequately fixed, such as new cars and new mobile homes.

lessee A tenant or one to whom an interest in real property is conveyed.

lessor A landlord or one who conveys an interest in real property.

letter of credit (L/C) A payment mechanism for international sales transactions involving a bank in the buyer's jurisdiction that commits to pay the seller. Also called a *documentary credit*.

letter of intent An instrument entered into by the parties to a real estate or other transaction for the purpose of setting forth the general terms and conditions of a purchase and sale agreement until a formal legal commitment can be made through the execution of a formal acquisition agreement.

leveraged buyout (LBO) A takeover financed with loans secured by the acquired company's assets, in which groups of investors, often including management, use borrowed money along with some of their own money to buy back the company's stock from its current shareholders.

libel A written communication to a third party by a defendant of an untrue statement of fact that injures a plaintiff's reputation.

licensee Anyone who is privileged to enter upon land of another because the possessor has given expressed or implied consent.

lien A claim on a property that secures a debt owed by the owner of the property.

lien subordination An agreement between two secured creditors whose respective security interest, liens, or mortgages attach to the same property. The subordinating party agrees that the lien of the other creditor shall have priority notwithstanding the relative priorities that the parties' liens would otherwise have under applicable law.

limited fund class action A class action in which the total of the aggregated liquidated claims exceeds the fund available to satisfy them.

limited guaranty A guaranty in which the maximum amount of the guarantor's liability is expressly stated in the guaranty instrument.

limited liability company (LLC) A form of business entity authorized by state law that is taxed like a limited partnership and provides its members with limited liability, but like a corporation gives its members the right to participate in management without incurring unlimited liability.

limited liability partnership (LLP) A form of limited partnership designed primarily for professionals who typically do business as a partnership that insulates its partners from vicarious liability for certain partnership obligations.

limited partners The participants in a limited partnership whose liability for partnership business is limited to their capital contribution.

limited partnership A form of business organization in which limited partners must refrain from actively participating in the management of the partnership but are liable for the debts of the partnership only up to the amount they personally contributed to the partnership.

limited warranty The warranty that limits the remedies available to the consumer for a defective product.

line-item veto Allowed the president to sign a bill into law and then cancel any dollar amounts that he or she believed to be fiscally irresponsible. Declared unconstitutional by the U.S. Supreme Court.

line-of-business test If an officer, director, or controlling shareholder learns of an opportunity in the course of business for the corporation, and if the opportunity is in the corporation's line of business, a court will not permit that person to keep the opportunity for personal gain.

liquidated damages The amount of money stipulated in a contract to be paid to non-breaching party should one of the parties breach the agreement.

London Interbank Offered Rate (LIBOR) An interest rate based on the cost of borrowing offshore U.S. dollars in the global interbank market, centered in several locations in addition to London.

long-arm statute A state statute that subjects an out-of-state defendant to jurisdiction when the defendant is doing business or commits a civil wrong in the state.

loss causation The misstatement or omission concealed something from the market that, when disclosed, negatively affected the value of the security.

lost volume seller A seller that can be put in as good a position as performance would have only by permitting the seller to recover the profit (including reasonable overhead) that it would have made from full performance by the buyer.

M

mail fraud A scheme intended to defraud or to obtain money or property by fraudulent means through use of the mails.

major life activity Under the Americans with Disabilities Act, an activity that an average person can perform with little or no difficulty, such as walking, seeing, hearing, and speaking.

majority voting A requirement that a nominee for the board of directors of a corporation must receive a majority of the shares voted to be elected. Contrast with *plurality voting*.

malicious defense A tort committed when a defendant creates false material evidence and gives false testimony advancing the evidence.

malicious prosecution A plaintiff can successfully sue for the tort of malicious prosecution if he or she shows that a prior proceeding was instituted against him or her maliciously and without probable cause or factual basis.

malpractice A claim of professional negligence.

managers Persons elected by the members (owners) of a limited liability company who, like a board of directors in a corporation, are responsible for managing the business, property, and affairs of the company.

mandatory arbitration One party will not do business with the other unless it agrees to arbitrate any future claims.

mandatory bid provision Prohibits coercive two-tier hostile tender offers and market purchases by requiring any person who acquires 30 percent or more of a target company's stock to offer to buy all remaining shares at the highest price paid to acquire the 30 percent block.

manufacturing defect A flaw in a product that occurs during production, such as a failure to meet the design specifications.

mark-to-market accounting When a business books the entire value of a contract on the day it is signed, rather than as cash is collected.

market power The power to control market prices or exclude competition in the relevant market. Also called *monopoly power*.

market-share liability The liability for damages caused by a manufacturer's products assessed based on a manufacturer's national market share.

marketable title Title to property that is fee simple and is free of liens or encumbrances.

materially breach A failure to perform a significant obligation under a contract, such as by not performing a service after receiving payment. A material breach discharges the nonbreaching party from its obligations and provides grounds to sue for damages.

material fact A fact that a reasonable investor would most likely have considered important in deciding whether to buy or sell his or her stock.

maturity date The date a term loan becomes due and payable.

McNulty Memorandum Memorandum issued by U.S. Department of Justice setting forth the determinants to be used in deciding whether to prosecute a company. Superseded in 2008 by amendments to U.S. Attorney Handbook.

med-arb A form of dispute resolution whereby the parties to a dispute enter mediation with the commitment to submit the dispute to binding arbitration if mediation fails to resolve the conflict.

mediation A form of dispute resolution whereby the parties agree to try to reach a solution themselves with the assistance of a neutral third party who helps them find a mutually satisfactory solution.

mediator The third party who helps the parties in mediation find a mutually satisfactory solution.

members The owners of a limited liability company.

***mens rea* (guilty state of mind)** Criminal intent.

merchant As defined in Article 2 of the Uniform Commercial Code, a person who deals in goods of the kind or otherwise by its occupation holds itself out as having knowledge or skill peculiar to the practices or goods involved in the transaction.

mere continuation (identity) A doctrine of successor liability whereby a firm that acquires the assets of a target firm is liable for the debts of the target firm when, after the asset purchase, there is a single corporation with the same shareholders and directors as the target firm prior to the asset purchase.

merger The combination of two or more corporations into one.

merger agreement An agreement between two companies to combine those companies into one.

merger doctrine If an idea and its expression are inseparable, the merger doctrine dictates that the expression is not copyrightable.

merit review A review by a state securities commissioner to determine whether the issuer's plan of business and the proposed issuance of securities are fair, just, and equitable.

military sanctions Military blockades or interventions.

minimum contacts As long as the person has sufficient minimum contacts with a state, such that it is fair to require him or her to appear in a court of that state, the state has personal jurisdiction over that person.

minitrial A cross between arbitration and negotiation, truncated presentation of evidence conducted by lawyers, usually with business persons present.

***Miranda* warnings** Once a person is placed in custody, he or she cannot be questioned by the police unless first advised of his or her constitutional rights to remain silent and to have counsel present.

mirror image rule A common law contract rule that requires acceptance to contain the exact same terms as the offer.

misappropriation theory A basis for an insider trading claim under SEC Rule 10b-5 when a person breaches a fiduciary duty to the source of the nonpublic information by trading on that information after misappropriating it for his or her own use.

misbranding False or misleading labeling prohibited by federal and state statutes. Includes claiming unsubstantiated medicinal benefits for a food, inadequate labeling for a drug, or selling over-the-counter a drug for which a prescription is required.

misdemeanor An offense lower than a felony, punishable by fine or imprisonment for less than one year (not in a penitentiary).

misrepresentation A misleading or false representation of the facts intended to deceive another party.

misstatement (Rule 10b–5) A misrepresentation of a fact; a lie.

mistake of fact A mistake about an underlying fact that may make a contract voidable.

mistake of judgment A mistake of judgment occurs when the parties make an erroneous assessment about the value of what is bargained for.

mitigate Lessen.

Model Panel Code A set of criminal law statutes that were proposed by the National Conference of Commissioners on Uniform State Laws for adoption by the states.

money laundering The transfer of funds derived from unlawful activities with the intent of concealing or disguising the location, source, ownership, or control of said funds.

monopoly power The power to control market prices or exclude competition in the relevant market. Also called *market power*.

mortgage A loan to buy real property secured by a lien on the real property. Also called *deed of trust*.

mortgagee The recipient of a mortgage, usually the lender.

mortgagor The party granting a mortgage, usually the owner of the real property securing a loan.

most favored nation (MFN) The principle that holds that each member country of the World Trade Organization (WTO) must accord to all other WTO members tariff treatment no less favorable than it provides to any other country.

motion Formally requests the court to take some action.

motion for judgment on the pleadings A motion filed immediately after the complaint and answer have been filed. One party, usually the defendant, argues that the pleadings alone demonstrate that the action is futile.

motion for summary judgment A motion requesting the trial judge to decide a case as a matter of law, without a trial, when there are no material facts in dispute.

motion to dismiss The formal request that the court terminate lawsuit on the ground that plaintiff's claim is technically inadequate.

multiple-brand product market A market made up of product or service offerings by different manufacturers or sellers that are economically interchangeable and may therefore be said to compete.

mutual rescission An agreement by both parties to a contract to terminate the contract. A mutual rescission is itself a type of contract.

mutuality of obligation Both parties in a bilateral contract are obligated to perform their side of the bargain.

N

narrow restraint doctrine A doctrine that permits restrictions on post-employment competition as long as they are limited and leave a substantial portion of the market available to the former employee.

national ambient air quality standards (NAAQS) The permissible levels of pollutants in the ambient or outdoor air that, with adequate margins of safety, are required to protect public health; set forth in the Clean Air Act.

National Pollutant Discharge Elimination System (NPDES) The principal regulatory program established by the Clean Water Act; requires permits for the discharge of pollutants from any point source to navigable waters.

national treatment The World Trade Organization principle that holds that WTO members must not discriminate against imported products in favor of domestically produced products.

nationalization When a host country decides to assert ownership over some or all of a company's assets.

natural resource law The laws that govern wilderness protection, wildlife protection, coastal zone management, energy conservation, and national park designation.

navigable waters The waters of the United States and the territorial seas, as well as lakes and streams that are capable of being used for purposes of navigation.

negative amortization loans Under which the debtor pays only the interest every month but owes a huge balloon payment at the end of the term.

negative Commerce Clause *See* Dormant Commerce Clause.

negative convenant The borrower's promise of what it undertakes not to do under the loan agreement.

negative equity An outstanding mortgage balance in excess of the value of the house or other property securing the loan.

negligence A breach of the requirement that a person act with the care a reasonable person would use in the same circumstances.

negligence *per se* Violation of a statute that shifts the burden to the defendant to prove the defendant was not negligent once the plaintiff shows that the defendant violated a statute and the violation caused an injury.

negligent-hiring theory An employer is negligent if the employer hires an employee who endangers the health and safety of other employees.

negligent infliction of emotional distress A tort committed when the defendant negligently inflicts emotional distress that causes the plaintiff some form of physical injury.

negotiation The give and take people engage in when coming to terms with each other.

nerve center test One of three tests that the Federal courts usually apply to determine where a company engaged in multistate operations has its principal place of business. The courts consider where (1) the executive and administrative offices are located, (2) the income tax return is filed, and (3) the directors and shareholders meet.

net listing A real estate listing in which the broker receives any sales proceeds in excess of the net listing amount specified by the seller.

neutrality rule Requires the target's board of directors to remain neutral when faced with a hostile takeover bid and stipulates that once a takeover bid has been launched, the target's board cannot adopt any antitakeover devices, such as poison pills, without first obtaining the specific approval of shareholders. Applicable in certain member states of the European Union.

nexus The legally required relationship between a condition to a land-use approval and the impacts of the development being approved.

1933 Act (Securities Act of 1933) Principal federal act that regulates offerings and sales of securities by generally requiring the registration of securities with the SEC and the delivery of a prospectus.

1934 Act (Securities Exchange Act of 1934) Principal federal act that prohibits securities fraud and requires companies of a certain size and with a certain number of shareholders or whose stock is traded on a national securities exchange to file periodic reports with the SEC.

no-hand pill A poison pill antitakeover device that cannot be redeemed for six months even if the insurgent's slate of directors is elected and votes to redeem it. Contrast with *dead-hand pill.*

nolo contendere **(I will not contest it)** A plea that means the accused does not contest the charges.

nominative use A fair-use defense to a trademark infringement action that permits use of a trademark when necessary for purposes of identifying another producer's product, not the user's own product.

non obstante veredicto Latin for "notwithstanding the verdict."

nonbinding arbitration Arbitration in which the parties are not bound by the arbitrator's decision.

nonconforming use An existing land use that was lawful but that does not comply with a later-enacted zoning ordinance.

noncore proceedings In bankruptcy cases, noncore proceedings are related actions concerning the debtor, such as decisions on personal injury and other civil proceedings. Federal or state courts have the power to adjudicate noncore proceedings. Bankruptcy judges may also adjudicate noncore proceedings, subject to *de novo* review by the federal district courts.

nonexempt employee An employee that is not exempt from the minimum wage and overtime requirements of the Federal Labor Standards Act; such an employee is often paid an hourly wage.

noninfringement In a patent dispute, the defense of noninfringement asserts that the allegedly infringing matter does not fall within the claims of the issued patent.

nonqualified deferred compensation arrangements (NQDCs) Non-tax favored employee and other compensation arrangements, including elective income deferral arrangements, supplemental employee retirement plans, stock appreciation rights, discounted stock options, and severance and change-in-control plans ("golden parachutes").

nonqualified stock option (NSO) A stock option that does not qualify for favorable tax treatment under Internal Revenue Code sections 422 or 423.

nontariff barriers (NTBs) Barriers to trade other than tariffs that have in some cases replaced tariffs as a means of protecting domestic industries threatened by import competition.

no-shop agreement An agreement whereby the target agrees not to actively solicit other bidders but retains the right to negotiate with parties who submit unsolicited bids to the target.

no-talk clause A clause permitting a corporation to engage in discussions with and provide information to other bidders only if the board has concluded, based on the written opinion of outside legal counsel, that engaging in discussions or providing information was required to prevent the board from breaching its fiduciary duties to its stockholders.

not an underwriter Under Rule 144, an affiliate or a person selling restricted securities is not an underwriter if certain conditions (e.g., holding period, volume limitations, manner of sale, filing of Form 144, and available public information) are met.

novation The method of contract modification by which the original contract is canceled and a new one is written with perhaps only one change, such as substitution of a new party.

novel (patents) An invention is novel if it was not anticipated; i.e., if it was not previously known or used by others in the United States and was not previously patented or described in a printed publication in any country.

nuisance A thing or activity that unreasonably and substantially interferes with an owner's use and enjoyment of owner's property.

obvious risk If the use of a product carries an obvious risk, the manufacturer will not be held liable for injuries that result from ignoring the risk.

offer (contracts) A proposal to enter into a contract. Proposal may be verbal, written, or implied by action.

offer (securities) Every attempt or offer to dispose of, or solicitation of an offer to buy, a security or interest in a security, for value.

offeree A person to whom an offer is made.

offering circular Also known as a private placement memorandum, this circular is the private offering counterpart to the prospectus and is both a selling document and a disclosure document.

offeror A person making an offer.

offshore transaction A security transaction in which no offer is made to a person in the United States and either (1) at the time the buy order is originated, the buyer is outside the United States; or (2) the transaction is one executed in, on, or through the facilities of a designated offshore securities market.

ombudsperson A person who hears complaints, engages in fact finding, and generally promotes dispute resolution through information methods such as counseling or mediation.

omission (Rule 10b–5) A company or its managers fail to tell the whole truth about a material fact, causing reasonable investors to take away an impression contrary to the true facts.

one-form-of-action laws *See* Antideficiency Laws.

open-end credit Credit in which the creditor makes repeated extensions of credit (for example, Visa or MasterCard).

open listing A real estate listing in which the broker receives a commission only if he or she procures a ready, willing, and able buyer.

operating agreement A contract that sets forth the rights, obligations, and powers of the owners, managers, and officers of a limited liability company.

operating lease Typically a short-term lease that does not appear on the balance sheet.

oppression An inequality of bargaining power that results in no real negotiation and an absence of meaningful choice for one party to the contract.

option contract A contract in which the offeror promises to hold an offer open for a certain amount of time.

optionee The recipient of a stock option.

order for relief The filing of a bankruptcy petition constitutes an order for relief. If the debtor challenges an involuntary petition for bankruptcy, a trial is held to determine whether an order for relief should be granted.

ordinary comparative negligence In an ordinary comparative negligence jurisdiction, the plaintiff may recover only if it is less culpable than the defendant.

original jurisdiction The power of the U.S. Supreme Court to take cognizance of a case at its inception, try it, and pass judgment upon the law and facts. Distinguished from appellate jurisdiction.

out clause A provision that would allow the lessor or lessee to cancel the lease without completing the full term or paying the complete value of the lease.

output contract A contract under which a buyer promises to buy all the products that the seller produces.

outside director A member of a board who is not also an officer.

outside sales employee An employee that has the primary duty of either making sales or obtaining orders or contracts for services or for the use of facilities and who is customarily and regularly engaged away from the employer's place of business in performing such duty.

override (of a president's veto) The ability of Congress to annul a president's veto by a two-thirds vote of both the House of Representatives and the Senate.

P

***parens patriae* (parent of the country) action** Antitrust suits brought by state attorneys general for injuries sustained by residents of their respective states.

parol evidence rule If there is a written contract that the parties intended would encompass their entire agreement, oral evidence of prior or contemporaneous statements will not be permitted to vary or alter the terms of the contract.

partial summary judgment A summary judgment granted on some issues of a case while other issues proceed to trial.

participation in a breach of fiduciary duty A tort committed when the defendant induces another party to breach its fiduciary duty to the plaintiff.

participation loan A loan in which the original lender sells shares to other parties, called participants.

pass-through entity A business organization that is not a separate taxpayer; all its income and losses are passed through and taxed to its owner. S Corporations, partnerships, and limited liability companies are pass-through entities.

patent A government-granted right to exclude others for a stated period of time (usually 20 years) from making, using, or selling within the government's jurisdiction an invention that is the subject of the patent.

patent misuse In a patent dispute, a defense asserting that although the defendant has infringed a valid patent, the patent holder has abused its patent rights and therefore has lost, at least temporarily, its right to enforce them.

pattern An involvement in racketeering activity demonstrated by at least two predicate acts occurring within a ten-year period.

penumbra The peripheral rights that are implied by the specifically enumerated rights in the Bill of Rights.

pension plan An employee retirement benefit plan established, and usually funded at least in part, by an employer.

***per se* analysis** A form of antitrust analysis that condemns practices that are completely void of redeeming competitive rationales.

percentage rent clause A clause frequently contained in retail leases that requires the tenant to pay, in addition to a base monthly rent, a percentage of its gross sales to the landlord.

perfect tender rule A Uniform Commercial Code rule that gives the buyer an absolute right to reject any goods not meeting all the contract requirements, including time of delivery.

perfecting (under the UCC) In connection with security interests, perfection refers to making the security interest valid as against other creditors of the debtor.

perjury An act by a person who takes an oath to tell the truth yet willingly and contrary to such oath states a material matter that he or she does not believe to be true.

permanent loan Usually a long-term loan used to acquire property that is repaid over five, ten, or sometimes up to twenty years.

personal jurisdiction The power of state court to hear (decide) a civil case based upon residence or location of activities of the person being sued.

persuasive A legal rule that reasonably and fairly resolves the dispute.

persuasive decision A well-reasoned court decision that another court, not bound by the first decision, would, when confronted with a similar dispute, probably follow.

petitioner The person who is appealing a judgment or seeking a writ of certiorari. Also called *appellant.*

phantom stock Promise to pay a bonus in the form of the equivalent of the value of company shares or the increase in value of the company shares over a period of time.

phishing Process by which individuals attempt to obtain personal information, including credit card numbers, using fake e-mails or websites that appear to come from a legitimate company.

pierce the corporate veil When a court denies limited liability to a corporation and holds shareholders personally responsible for claims against the corporation, the court has pierced the corporate veil.

plaintiff A person who brings an action; the party who complains or sues in a civil action and is so named on the record. The prosecution in a criminal case (i.e., the state or the United States in a federal case).

planned unit development (PUD) The land use regulations for a given piece of property that reflect the proposed development plans for that property. PUD allows for mixture of uses for property not possible under traditional zoning regulations.

plant patent A patent issued for new strains of asexually reproducing plants.

plea The response by a defendant in criminal case of guilty, not guilty, or *nolo contendere.*

plea bargaining The process by which the prosecutor agrees to reduce the charges in exchange for a guilty plea from the accused.

pleadings The formal allegations by the parties to a lawsuit of their respective claims and defenses.

pledge A type of security interest whereby the creditor or secured party takes possession of the collateral owned by the debtor.

plenary Complete, sufficient, unqualified.

plurality standard A process whereby a nominee for the board of directors can be elected as long as he or she receives a plurality of the votes cast for any nominee, without regard to the number of votes withheld. Contrast with *majority voting.*

plus factors (antitrust) Parallel behavior that would appear to be contrary to the economic interests of the defendants, were they acting independently; supports an inference of conspiracy.

points A one-time charge to a borrower buying real property (in addition to interest) computed by a lender by multiplying the amount funded by a fixed percentage.

poison pill A plan that would make any takeover of a corporation prohibitively expensive. Also called *shareholder rights plan.*

police power The general power granted state and city governments to protect the health, safety, welfare, or morals of its residents.

political question A conflict that should be decided by one of the political branches of government or by the electorate. A court will refuse to decide questions of a purely political character.

political union A union that represents the complete political and economic integration of the member states.

posthearing The final phase of arbitration in which the arbitrator renders his or her award after considering all the evidence presented in the prehearing and the hearing.

potentially responsible parties (PRPs) Parties potentially responsible for damages that include the present owner or operator of a facility, the owner or operator at the time of disposal of a hazardous substance, any person who arranged for treatment or disposal of hazardous substances at a facility, and any person who transported hazardous substances to or selected the facility.

power of attorney A written instrument that authorizes a person, called an attorney-in-fact (who need not be a lawyer), to sign documents or perform certain specific acts on behalf of another person.

prayer The request for relief in a complaint.

precautionary principle Provides guidance for protecting public health and the environment in the face of uncertain risks and stipulates that the absence of full scientific certainty shall not be used as a reason to postpone measures where there is a risk of serious or irreversible harm to public health or the environment.

precedents General rules that are to be used as guidelines for similar cases in the future.

precontractual liability The claims by the disappointed party if contract negotiations fail before a contract has been finalized.

predatory lending Involves mortgage loans secured by the borrower's house that are made at subprime interest rates to borrowers who often lack the ability to repay them. Also includes certain payday loans at exorbitant but legal interest rates.

predatory pricing The act of pricing below the producer's actual cost with the intent of driving other competitors out of the market, thus enabling the person engaging in predatory pricing to raise prices later.

preempt A federal law takes precedence when state law conflicts with federal law.

preemption defense (product liability) The immunity granted manufacturers if they meet minimum standards of conduct under certain regulatory schemes.

preferences Transfers to (or for the benefit of) creditors on account of antecedent debts that are made from an insolvent debtor's property within ninety days before bankruptcy (one year if creditor is insider) and that enable the creditors to receive more than they would through a Chapter 7 liquidation.

prehearing The first stage in arbitration in which parties may submit trial-like briefs, supporting documents, and other written statements making their case.

prejudgment interest The interest on the amount of an award from the date of the injury to the date of judgment.

preliminary hearing A hearing in which the prosecutor presents evidence demonstrating probable cause that the defendant committed the crime.

premises liability A theory under which a building owner may be found liable for violating its general duty to manage the premises and warn of dangers, such as asbestos.

prenegotiated bankruptcy In a prenegotiated bankruptcy, the debtor files its Chapter 11 bankruptcy petition as soon as it can after it has reached agreement on the terms of the restructuring with its key creditors, but votes on the plan are not solicited until after the bankruptcy case is filed.

prenuptial agreement An agreement entered into before marriage that sets forth the manner in which the parties' assets will be distributed and the support to which each party will be entitled, in the event the parties get divorced.

prepackaged bankruptcy A workout plan approved by key creditors and the debtor before the debtor files bankruptcy; it becomes the plan of reorganization in a Chapter 11 bankruptcy.

prepayment penalty A clause whereby a lender imposes a penalty if the loan is paid off early.

preponderance of the evidence The evidence offered in a civil trial that is more convincing than the evidence presented in opposition to it.

price discrimination Sellers charge different prices to purchasers in interstate sales for commodities of like grade and quality.

primary debtor The person with an obligation for which the guarantor becomes liable.

primary line violation Under the Robinson-Patman Act, a primary line violation occurs where the discriminating seller's price impacts competition with the seller's competitors.

prime rate The lowest rate of interest publicly offered by major lending institutions to their most creditworthy customers. Better practice dictates using the terms "base rate" or "reference rate" because sometimes lenders offer a loan below prime.

priming lien A lien that is senior to a previously granted security interest.

principal A person who delegates a portion of his or her tasks to another person who represents the principal as an agent.

prior art Developments or pre-existing art that relates to a claimed invention.

prior restraints Prohibitions barring speech before it occurs.

private international law Law that governs the relationships between private parties engaged in transactions across national borders.

private law The area of the law in which the sole function of government is recognition and enforcement of private rights, e.g., civil and commercial codes.

private nuisance Interference with a person's use and enjoyment of his or her land and water.

private offering An offering to selected individuals or entities who have the ability to evaluate and bear the risk of the investment; that is, they have the ability to fend for themselves. Also called *private placement*.

private placement *See* Private Offering.

private-placement memorandum A booklet offered by entrepreneurs seeking financing from private individual investors that furnishes information about themselves and their enterprise.

privatization The transfer of property ownership from a nation to a private entity.

Privileges and Immunities Clause (Fourteen Amendment) Provides that no state "shall make or enforce any law which shall abridge the privileges or immunities of citizens of the United States."

privity of contract The relationship which exists between the parties to a contract.

probable cause As applied to an arrest or a search warrant, a reasonable belief that the suspect has committed a crime or is about to commit a crime. Mere suspicion or belief, unsupported by facts or circumstances, is insufficient.

procedural due process The parties whose rights are to be affected are entitled to be heard and, in order that they may enjoy that right, they must be notified before adverse action is taken.

product A tangible item, as opposed to a service.

product liability The liability of a manufacturer or seller of a product that because of a defect, causes injury to a purchaser, user, or bystander.

product line theory A theory of successor liability whereby a corporation purchasing the assets of another is liable for the target company's debts where the purchaser continues to manufacture the same product line as the target company, under the same name and with no outward indication of any change of ownership, even if the particular item was manufactured and sold by the target company prior to the acquisition. Usually applied only in product-liability cases.

productive efficiency An equilibrium in which only the lowest cost producers of goods and services survive.

professional employee Under Fair Labor Standards Act, an employee who holds a position requiring advanced knowledge in a field of science or learning customarily acquired by a prolonged course of specialized intellectual instruction and study.

promisee In contract law, the promisee is the person to whom the promise (contract) was made.

promisor In contract law, the promisor is the person who made the promise.

promissory estoppel A promise that the promisor should reasonably expect to induce action or forbearance on the part of the promisee or a third person and that does induce such action or forbearance can create liability for reliance damages if injustice can be avoided only by providing some relief when promise is broken.

promissory fraud A type of fraud that occurs when one party induces another to enter into a contract by promising to do something without having the intention to carry out the promise.

proof of claim A claim filed by creditors on uncontingent and undisputed debt.

prospectus Any document that is designed to produce orders for a security, whether or not the document purports on its face to offer the security for sale or otherwise to dispose of it for value. The descriptive document that an issuer of securities provides to prospective purchasers.

protected computer A computer used in interstate or foreign commerce.

protected expression The part of a work that is subject to copyright protection.

proximate cause A reasonably foreseeable consequence of the defendant's negligence, without which no injury would have occurred.

proxy A written authorization by a shareholder to another person to vote on the shareholder's behalf.

proxy contest A battle for corporate control whereby someone wishing to replace the board with its own candidates seeks to acquire a sufficient number of shareholder votes to do so.

public accommodation Under Americans with Disabilities Act, includes any place of public accommodation, such as a restaurant, place of lodging, place of entertainment, place of public gathering, and place of exercise or recreation.

public disclosure of private facts The publication of a private fact that is not newsworthy. The matter must be private, such that a reasonable person would find publication objectionable. Unlike in a defamation case, truth is not a defense.

public figures Individuals, who, by reason of their achievements or the vigor and success with which they seek the public's attention, are injected into the public eye.

public international law Law that governs the relationships between and the interactions of nations.

public law The area of the law that focuses on effectuation of the public interest by state action, e.g., constitutional law, administrative law, and criminal law.

public officials Include legislators, judges, and police officers.

public nuisance Unreasonable and substantial interference with the public health, safety, peace, comfort, convenience, or utilization of land.

public policy exception An exception to the general employment at will doctrine that prohibits an employer from discharging an employee for a reason that violates public policy.

publication Communication to a third party.

publicly owned sewage treatment works (POTWs) General and specific industry pretreatment standards are set for discharges to publicly owned sewage treatment works (POTWs).

puffing The expression of opinion by a seller regarding goods; not a warranty.

pump and dump A term used to refer to situations where executives fraudulently manipulate their company's earnings in an attempt to keep stock prices high while they exercise their options and sell their stock at inflated prices.

punitive damages Damages awarded to a plaintiff over and above what will fairly compensate it for its loss. They are intended to punish the defendant and deter others from engaging in similar conduct. Also called *exemplary damages.*

purchase-money security interest A security interest created when a seller lends the buyer the money to buy the seller's goods.

pure comparative negligence A tort system in which the plaintiff may recover for the part of the injury due to the defendant's negligence, even if the plaintiff was the more negligent party.

pure notice statutes Under these statutes, a person who has notice that someone else has already bought the real property cannot validate his or her deed by recording it first.

pyramid selling A scheme whereby a consumer is recruited as a product "distributor" and receives commissions based on the products he or she sells and on the recruitment of additional sellers.

qualified disposition The sale of stock that occurs more than two years after an incentive stock option was granted and more than one year after the stock was purchased.

qualified institutional buyer Institutional investors holding and managing $100 million or more of securities.

quantum meruit A basis for equitable relief by a court when there was no contract between the parties, but one party has received a benefit for which it has not paid.

quasi-foreign corporation A corporation incorporated outside of California, for example, but with more than 50 percent of its stock owned by California residents and with more than 50 percent of its sales, payroll, and property tax derived from activities in California.

***qui tam* plaintiff** A plaintiff suing on the government's behalf, often entitled to a share of the amount recovered.

"quick look" rule of reason The "quick look" rule of reason is used whenever the practice has obvious anticompetitive effects but is not illegal per se; it allows for immediate inquiry into procompetitive justifications.

***quid-pro-quo* (this for that) harassment** The specific, job-related adverse action, such as denial of a promotion, in retaliation for a worker's refusal to respond to a supervisor's sexual advances.

quiet period The time between filing of securities registration statement and the date the registration statement becomes effective. Also called the *waiting period.*

quitclaim deed A deed that contains no warranties; the grantor conveys only any right, title, and interest held by the grantor, if any, at the time of execution.

quorum The holders of more than 50 percent of the outstanding shares of a corporation.

quotas Tariffs and quantitative limitations that place restrictions on imports.

R

race statutes Under these statutes, recording is a race—the rule is "first in time is first in right." The first to record a deed has superior rights, regardless of whether he or she knew that someone else had already bought or claimed an interest in the real property.

race–notice statutes These statutes protect only a good faith subsequent purchaser who recorded its deed before the prior purchaser recorded its deed.

racketeering activity The state and federal offenses involving a pattern of illegal acts, including mail and wire fraud.

raider In a hostile takeover, a third party who seeks to obtain control of a corporation, called the target, over the objections of its management.

ratification A principal affirms through words or actions a prior act of an agent that did not bind the principal.

ratify An agreement by an individual, after the individual becomes competent or reaches the age of majority, to be bound by contracts entered into while the person was incompetent or a minor; a principal's agreement to be bound by the acts of an agent.

rational basis test A test under which a discriminatory classification will be held valid if there is any conceivable basis upon which the classification might relate to a legitimate governmental interest; applies to all classifications that relate to matters of economics or social welfare.

Rawlsian moral theory A deontological line of thought that aims to maximize the utility of the worst off person in society.

reaffirmation agreement A contract with a creditor whereby an individual who has filed bankruptcy under Chapter 7 agrees to repay a debt even though the debt would otherwise be discharged in the debtor's bankruptcy case.

real estate investment trust (REIT) A tax-advantaged pool of real property.

reasonable accommodation (employment) A requirement that an employer takes steps necessary to reasonably accommodate an employee's disability or religious practices.

reasonable–alternative-design-requirement A requirement in a product liability case that the plaintiff prove that defendant acted wrongly or negligently in choosing an unsafe design.

reasonable care under the circumstances A standard requiring landowners to act in a reasonable manner with respect to entrants on their land, with liability hinging on the foreseeability of harm.

reasonable factor other than age (RFOA) defense In an age discrimination case, an employer's affirmative defense that its actions were based on reasonable factors other than age. Contrast with *business necessity.*

recklessness In the criminal context, conscious disregard of a substantial risk that an individual's actions would result in the harm prohibited by a statute.

recognitional picketing Picketing that strives to force the employer to recognize a labor union as a collective bargaining agent for its employees.

recognized hazard Under the Occupational Safety and Health Act, a workplace condition that is obviously dangerous or is regarded by an employer or other employers in the industry as dangerous.

record The oral and written evidence presented at an administrative hearing.

recordable form The requirements established by the state regarding how title to real estate is filed and recorded. Requirements generally include legibility and notarization.

recording statutes Statutes that establish an orderly process by which claims to interests in real property can be recorded as part of the public record and resolved.

red-herring prospectus Preliminary prospectus; incomplete version of the final prospectus.

reference rate The lowest rate of interest publicly offered by major lending institutions to their most creditworthy customers.

referendum A vote by the electorate to approve or reject a treaty or other governmental action.

referral sale The seller offers the buyer a commission, rebate, or discount for furnishing the seller with a list of additional prospective customers.

registered mask work Highly detailed transparencies that represent the topological layout of semiconductor chips.

registration statement The registration statement consists of filing forms and the prospectus, the disclosure document that an issuer of securities provides to prospective purchasers.

Regulation A A regulation whereby $5 million of securities can be offered and sold in a twelve-month period, of which up to $1.5 million may be sold by the selling security holders.

Regulation Analyst Certification (Regulation AC) An SEC regulation that prohibits analysts from issuing reports that they do not personally believe to be true and requires the disclosure of any analyst compensation arrangements related to the specific recommendation or views contained in the research report.

Regulation D An SEC regulation that offers a safe harbor for those seeking exemption from securities registration under the Securities Act of 1933. An issuer that fails to comply with all of the requirements of the applicable rule may still be able to rely on the private-offering exemption in Section 4(2).

Regulation FD (Fair Disclosure) An SEC regulation that provides that whenever an issuer, or a person acting on its behalf, discloses material nonpublic information to securities market professionals or holders of the issuer's securities who may well trade on the basis of the information, the issuer must publicly disclose that same information simultaneously or promptly.

Regulation S An SEC regulation that has clarified the general rule that any offer or sale outside the United States is not subject to the federal registration requirements.

Regulation Z Regulations issued by the Federal Reserve Board to interpret and enforce the federal Truth-in-Lending Act.

regulations The rules of order prescribed by superior or competent authority relating to action of those under its control.

regulatory negotiations (reg-neg) A style of administrative rulemaking in which representatives of major groups convene with an administrative agency and work out a compromise through negotiation on the substance of new regulations.

regulatory taking The taking by the government of private real property for a public use; requires payment of just compensation.

reliance damages The awards made to a plaintiff for any expenditures made in reliance on a contract that was subsequently breached.

remand The power of a court of appeal to send a case back to a lower court for reconsideration.

remote tippee Recipient of a tip from another tippee other than the original tippee.

repatriate The act of a multinational business returning profits earned in a host country to its home country.

repatriation A constraint on foreign ownership to restrict the profits that can be returned by a multinational company to its home country.

reporter The published volumes of case decisions by a particular court or group of courts.

reporting company A company registered under Section 12 of the Securities Exchange Act of 1934 that subjects issuers to various reporting requirements and to certain rules and regulations concerning proxies, tender offers, and insider trading.

reporting issuer An issuer that has been subject to the reporting requirements of Section 13 or 15(d) of the 1934 Act for at least ninety days before a Rule 144 sale.

representation and warranties Highly negotiated provisions in a purchase-and-sale contract concerning the parties and the stock, goods, or other assets being sold.

representation election An election among employees to decide whether they want a union to represent them for collective bargaining.

requests for production of documents Requests for documents such as medical records and personal files to be produced as part of the discovery process before a trial.

requirements contract A contract under which the buyer agrees to buy all of a specified commodity the buyer needs from the seller and the seller agrees to provide that amount.

***res ipsa loquitur* (the thing speaks for itself)** The doctrine that allows a plaintiff to prove breach and causation indirectly.

resale price maintenance An agreement on minimum price between firms at different levels of production or distribution that violates antitrust law.

resource-based view (RBV) A firm's resources can be a source of sustained competitive advantage if they are valuable, rare, and imperfectly imitable by competitors and have no strategically equivalent substitutes.

***respondeat superior* (let the master answer)** The doctrine under which an employer may be held vicariously or secondarily liable for the negligent or intentional conduct of the employee that is committed in the scope of the employee's employment.

respondent The party in a case against whom an appeal is taken; the party who has an interest adverse to setting aside or reversing the judgment.

responsible corporate officer doctrine A criminal law doctrine that, under certain circumstances, imposes vicarious liability on an officer responsible for compliance based on the actions of subordinates.

restatement Former common law rules in a particular subject area (e.g., contracts, torts) integrated into formal collections that a judge or legislature is free to adopt.

restitution An award made to a plaintiff of a benefit improperly obtained by the defendant.

restricted guaranty A guaranty in which the guarantor's liability is enforceable only with respect to a specified transaction or series of transactions.

restricted securities Securities issued in a private placement; they cannot be resold or transferred unless they are either registered or exempt from registration. The most common exemption is pursuant to Securities and Exchange Commission Rule 144.

restricted stock A conditional grant of shares of a company's stock, with vesting contingent upon continued employment for a specified period of time.

restricted stock unit (RSU) A promise to pay a bonus in the future in the form of shares of a company's stock. An RSU is usually subject to vesting conditions so that it is not paid unless the vesting conditions are satisfied.

retributive justice A theory that states that every crime demands payment in the form of punishment.

reverse piercing A doctrine whereby a corporation (including a subsidiary) may be held liable for the debts of a shareholder (including a parent corporation).

reversibility An ethical theory that looks to whether one would want a rule applied to one's self.

revival statutes State and federal statutes that allow plaintiffs to file lawsuits that have been barred by the running of the statute of limitations.

***Revlon* mode** A company is said to be in *Revlon* mode when a change of control or breakup of the company has become inevitable.

revoke To annul an offer by rescission.

revolving line of credit A line of credit that allows a borrower to borrow whatever sums it requires up to a specified maximum amount and reborrow amounts it has repaid.

revolving loan A loan that allows a borrower to borrow whatever sums it requires up to a specified maximum amount and to reborrow amounts it has repaid.

Riba A tenet of Islamic trade and commerce that prohibits unearned or unjustified (illicit) profits and can therefore lead to problems in the area of interest on loans.

right of first negotiation Gives the holder the right to negotiate the purchase of the property before the seller enters negotiations with another party.

right of first refusal A contract that provides the holder with the right to purchase property on the same terms and conditions offered by or to a third party.

right of redemption Gives the mortgagor and certain other categories of interested persons the right to redeem or get back foreclosed property within a statutorily limited period.

right of rescission A right to cancel a contract.

right of setoff Permits Party A to deduct automatically from payments due Party B amounts that are due from Party B to Party A.

ripeness A court will not hear agency cases if they are not ripe for decision, for example, after a rule is adopted but before the agency seeks to apply it to a particular case.

roadshow Oral presentations to large institutional investors in key cities in the United States, Europe, and Asia.

rule of impossibility The rule under which claims of predation are rejected because the marketplace in question cannot be successfully monopolized.

rule of reason The rule that takes into account a defendant's actions as well as the structure of the market to determine whether an activity promotes or restrains competition.

Rule 10b-5 An SEC regulation adopted pursuant to Section 10(b) of the Securities Exchange Act of 1934 that prohibits individuals and companies from engaging in fraudulent, manipulative, or deceptive practices in connection with the offer or sale of securities.

Rule 144 A safe harbor designed to reduce the uncertainty associated with the definition of the term "underwriter," this SEC rule permits nonissuers to sell restricted and control securities publicly without registration as long as the Rule's requirements are met.

S

S–1 review A review by the auditor of events subsequent to the date of the certified financial statements included in the securities registration statement to ascertain whether any material change has occurred in the company's financial position that should be disclosed in the final prospectus to prevent the financial statements from being materially misleading.

S Corporation A corporation meeting certain requirements that is taxed only at the owner level.

Safeguard Rule Requires financial services firms to protect consumer privacy by (1) promulgating a written information security plan, (2) designating at least one employee to coordinate the plan, (3) identifying and assessing the risks to customer financial information, and (4) evaluating the safeguards for controlling these risks.

sale (securities) Includes "every contract of sale or disposition of a security or interest in a security, for value."

sale and leaseback A simultaneous two-step transaction, whereby an institutional lender purchases real property from a company, and the property is leased back to the company for its use.

sanctions Laws imposed by one country (or a group of countries) against the commerce of another country as an effort to influence that country's behavior, for example with regard to international law.

satisfaction *See* Accord and Satisfaction.

Say on Pay proposal Annual shareholder advisory votes on a company's executive pay policies and practices.

scheme liability Fraudulent business transactions designed to enable the issuer to artificially inflate its earnings.

scienter An intent to deceive.

second-step back-end merger The second step in a corporate takeover whereby the shareholders who did not tender their shares receive cash or securities in a subsequent merger.

secondary boycott A strike against an employer with whom a union has no quarrel in order to encourage it to stop doing business with an employer with whom it does have a dispute.

secondary line violation Typically involves a "disfavored" purchaser that brings a suit against a seller, or the seller's "favored" purchaser, for giving the favored purchaser better pricing.

secondary meaning A descriptive trademark becomes protectable by acquiring secondary meaning, or sufficient consumer recognition through sufficient use and/or advertising of the goods under the mark.

secondary offering A securities offering by a person other than the issuer.

Section 4(11/2) exemption An exemption for a private offering of securities by an affiliate that would qualify as a private placement under Section 4(2) of the Securities Act of 1933 if made by the issuer.

Section 83(b) election When filed, the employee elects to pay tax at the time restricted stock is purchased in an amount equal to what would be due if the stock were not subject to vesting.

Section 201 Provides for temporary relief to U.S. industries seriously injured by increasing imports, regardless of whether unfair practices are involved. It is sometimes called the fair trade law.

Section 301 Authorizes the U.S. Trade Representative to investigate alleged unfair practices of foreign governments that impede U.S. exports of both goods and services.

Section 337 Provides that if a U.S. industry is injured (or there is a restraint or monopolization of trade in the United States) by reason of unfair acts in the importation of articles into the United States, an order must be issued requiring the exporters and importers to cease the unfair acts or, if necessary, excluding imports of the offending articles from all sources.

Section 423 plan An employee stock purchase plan (ESPP) satisfying Internal Revenue Code Section 423, which permits an employee to defer paying tax on the discount from the fair market value of stock purchased via the plan until the employee sells the stock.

secured loan A loan backed up by collateral.

secured party The lender, seller, or other person in whose favor there is a security interest.

secured transaction A loan or other transaction secured by collateral put up by the borrower.

security Any note, stock, treasury stock, bond, debenture, evidence of indebtedness, certificate of interest or participation in any profit-sharing agreement, collateral trust certificate, pre-organization certificate or subscription, transferable share, investment contract, voting-trust certificate, certificate of deposit for a security, fractional undivided interest in oil, gas, or other mineral rights; any put, call, straddle, option, or privilege on any security, certificate of deposit, or group or index of securities (including any interest therein or based on the value thereof); or any put, call, straddle, option, or privilege entered into on a national securities exchange relating to foreign currency; or, in general, any interest or instrument commonly known as a "security," or any certificate of interest or participation in temporary or interim certificate for, receipt for, guarantee of, or warrant or right to subscribe to or purchase, any of the foregoing.

security agreement An agreement that creates or provides for a security interest.

security interest Any interest in personal property, fixtures or letters of credit and accounts that is used as collateral to secure payment or the performance of an obligation.

selective disclosure A practice whereby issuers of publicly traded securities disclose material nonpublic information, such as advance warnings of earnings results, to securities analysts or selected institutional investors before making full disclosure of the same information to the general public.

self-publication A doctrine giving an employee a claim for defamation when the employer makes a false assertion in firing an employee, which the employer could reasonably expect the employee to repeat to a prospective employer.

self-tender An offer by a corporation to buy back its stock or shareholder rights for a fair price.

selling securities short The sale of securities the seller does not own.

senior debt Indebtedness that benefits from a debt subordination agreement.

separate property Property that belongs solely to the spouse who acquired it before marriage or received it by gift or inheritance.

separation of powers The distinct authority of governance granted the three branches of U.S. government (executive, legislative, and judicial) by the U.S. Constitution.

sequestration order A governmental order that requires spending levels to be reduced below the levels provided in the budget.

service mark A legally protected identifying mark connected with services.

service of process Notifying a defendant of a claim.

settlement conference A conference a judge may hold to give each side a candid assessment of the strengths and weaknesses of its case and the likely outcome if the case goes to trial.

sexual stereotyping Discrimination against employees because they are not "manly" enough men or "womanly" enough women. Illegal under Title VII of Civil Rights Act.

share sterilization An order precluding the defendants from voting their shares.

shareholder A holder of equity securities of a corporation. Also called *stockholder*.

shareholder derivative suit A lawsuit brought against directors or officers of a corporation by a shareholder on behalf of the corporation.

shareholder of record The persons whose names appear on a corporation's shareholder list on a specified date who are entitled to vote.

shareholder primacy Maximization of shareholder wealth, not legally mandated.

shareholder rights plan *See* Poison Pill.

Sharia The traditional Islamic rules and body of laws that regulate Muslim life.

shelf registration The registration of a number of securities at one time for issuance later.

short-swing trading The purchase and sale or sale and purchase by an officer, director, or greater-than-10 percent shareholders of securities of a public company within a six-month period.

show-how Nonsecret information used to teach someone how to make or do something; generally not legally protectable.

shrink-wrap license A license that customers cannot read when they purchase software but are deemed to have accepted when they open the wrapping around the envelope containing the discs.

signing statement A document attached to a bill at its execution describing the president's interpretation of that law.

SIMPLE Plan Retirement plans for employers with fewer than one hundred employees that are similar to 401(k) plans, but have stricter rules and simpler administration, that allow employees to defer a portion of their salaries on a pretax basis into an investment fund set up by the employer.

slander A spoken communication to a third party by a defendant of an untrue statement of fact that injures a plaintiff's reputation.

slander *per se* Words that are slanderous in and of themselves. Only statements that a person has committed a serious crime, has a loathsome disease, is guilty of sexual misconduct, or is not fit to conduct business are slanderous *per se*.

sole proprietorship One person owns all the assets of the business, has complete control of the business, and is solely liable for all the debts of the business.

solicitor A type of lawyer in the British system who is allowed to perform legal services outside the court.

sophisticated user defense An affirmative defense in a product liability case based on failure to warn whereby a manufacturer is not liable to a sophisticated user of its product for failure to warn of a risk, harm, or danger, if the sophisticated user knew or should have known of that risk, harm, or danger.

sovereign acts doctrine The government cannot be held liable for breach of contract due to legislative or executive acts of general application.

sovereign immunity The doctrine that prevents the courts of one country from hearing a suit against the government of another country.

spam Unsolicited e-mails.

Special 301 Provisions Provisions in U.S. trade law under which the U.S. Trade Representative identifies countries that deny adequate and effective protection for intellectual property rights or deny fair and equitable market access for persons who rely on intellectual property protection.

special plan *See* Specific Plan.

specific performance A court order to a breaching party to complete the contract as promised.

specific plan A planning document in addition to a general plan that usually encompasses just a portion of a city's geographic area; typically more detailed than the general plan.

specifications The description of an invention in a patent application in its best mode and the manner and process of making and using the invention so that a person skilled in the relevant field may make and use the invention.

spinning The practice whereby underwriters would distribute IPO shares to a corporate executive in exchange for the investment banking business of the executive's corporation.

split in the circuits When different courts of appeals disagree on a legal issue.

spoliation inference Inference, as instructed to a jury, that missing or altered evidence should be presumed to have been unfavorable to the party causing its destruction or loss.

spread (1) A margin which is added to the cost that a bank incurs to obtain, for a given period of time, the funds it will lend, in order to arrive at the actual interest rate for a loan. (2) The difference between the strike price of a stock option and the fair market value of the stock at the time the optionee exercises the option.

spring-loading Issuing employee stock options in advance of a positive public announcement that the issuing company believes will drive up the market value of its stock.

squatter's rights *See* Adverse Possession.

staggered board A board on which directors serve for specified terms, usually three years, with only a fraction of them up for reelection at any one time. Also called *classified board*.

standby letter of credit A method of securing a party's performance, whereby an issuing bank undertakes to pay a sum of money to the person (the beneficiary) to which performance is due on presentation of certain documents specified in the letter of credit, usually a brief statement (in language agreed on by the two parties) that the other party is in default and the beneficiary is entitled to payment from the issuing bank.

standing A party to a lawsuit has standing if the person seeking relief is the proper party to advance the litigation, has a personal interest in the outcome of the suit, and will benefit from a favorable ruling.

standstill agreement An agreement whereby the shareholder agrees not to commence a tender offer or proxy contest or to buy additional shares of the issuer for a period of time, often ten years.

***stare decisis* (to abide by)** The doctrine that holds that once a court resolves a particular issue, other courts addressing a similar legal problem generally follow the initial court's decision.

state-of-the-art defense A defense against claims based on a manufacturer's compliance with the best available technology (that may or may not be synonymous with the custom and practice of the industry).

state secrets doctrine A doctrine that bars the discovery or admission of evidence that would expose confidential matters which, in the interest of national security, should not be divulged.

statute of frauds A statute that requires that certain contracts, such as contracts conveying an interest in real property, must be in a signed writing to be enforceable in a court.

statute of limitations A time limit, defined by the statute, within which a lawsuit must be brought.

statute of repose A time limit that cuts off the right to assert a cause of action after a specified period of time from the date the product is sold.

statutory bar An inventor is denied patent protection in the event that prior to one year before the inventor's filing, the invention was (1) patented; (2) publicly used or sold in the United States; or (3) described in a printed publication in the United States or a foreign country.

statutory law Law that is based on statutes, not on existing common law rules.

statutory prospectus A prospectus for a registered offering of securities meeting the requirements of Section 10 of the Securities Act of 1933.

statutory stock options Another term for incentive stock options (ISOs) and options granted pursuant to employee stock purchase plans (ESPPs).

stock appreciation right (SAR) A contractual right to receive an amount equal to the appreciation in stock price that occurs between the date the SAR is granted and the date of exercise. Payments of appreciation may be in the form of cash, stock, or both.

stock option A contract that allows an individual to buy a certain number of shares of a company's stock at a certain price (typically the fair market value of the stock at the time the option is granted) within a certain timeframe (typically five to ten years), but ending upon termination of employment.

stock parking The temporary sale of shares to another entity or individual to avoid tax reporting requirements or the net margin requirements of the securities laws applicable to brokerage firms.

stock-settled SAR A stock appreciation right (SAR) paid in company stock, not cash.

stockholder A holder of equity securities of a corporation. Also called *shareholder*.

straight bankruptcy A Chapter 7 bankruptcy in which the trustee liquidates the estate and distributes the proceeds first to secured creditors (to the extent of their collateral) and then in a prescribed order, pro rata within each level.

straight voting A voting process whereby a shareholder can cast one vote for each share the shareholder owns for each nominee.

strategic compliance management Term coined by Professor Constance E. Bagley to describe a legally astute top management team's ability to go beyond mere compliance with law to seek opportunities to increase a firm's realizable value. Includes ability to frame the cost of complying with government regulations as an investment, not an expense.

strategic environmental management A concept that advocates placing environmental management on the profit side of the corporation rather than on the cost side. An example of strategic compliance management.

strict liability Liability without fault. The concept that sellers are liable for all defective products. Also imposed for abnormally dangerous (or ultrahazardous) activities and toxic torts.

strict scrutiny test Under this test, a discriminatory classification will be held valid only if it is necessary to promote a compelling state interest and narrowly tailored; applies to classifications based on race or religion.

strike price The price (which is generally the market price of the stock at the time the stock option is granted) at which an optionee can exercise his or her stock option by purchasing the stock. Also referred to as the *grant price*.

subdivision A division of land into separate parcels for development purposes.

subject matter jurisdiction The specific types of cases enumerated under Article III of the U.S. Constitution to be decided by the Supreme Court and lower courts established by Congress.

subject matter test The privilege that protects the communications or discussions of any company employee with counsel as long as the subject matter of the communication relates to that employee's duties and the communication is made at the direction of a corporate superior.

sublease An act by a tenant of renting out all or a portion of property the tenant has rented from a landlord.

subordination Relegation to a lesser position, usually in respect to a right or security.

subprime Debt issued by a lender that (1) predominantly refinances rather than makes or purchases loans and (2) does not sell a significant portion of its portfolio to the two government sponsored housing financing agencies.

subprime mortgage loans Loans that carry above-market interest rates to compensate for the added risk of default, to borrowers with poor credit.

subsequent remedial measures A manufacturer's later fix of a dangerous condition or improvement of a design in a product that has been found to be inherently defective.

substantial continuity test A test that imposes successor liability when the purchaser of assets maintains the same business, with the same employees doing the same jobs, under the same supervisors, working conditions, and production process, and produces the same products for the same customers as the seller corporation. Also known as the *continuity of enterprise approach*.

substantial evidence standard Under this standard, the courts defer to an administrative agency's factual determinations in formal adjudications even if the record would support other factual conclusions.

substantial factor test An actual-cause test whereby the plaintiff or prosecutor seeks to hold liable multiple defendants, including any person who played a substantial role in causing the harm or violation.

substantial risk of forfeiture Stock is subject to a substantial risk of forfeiture if the recipient's right to full enjoyment of the stock is conditional upon the future performance of substantial service.

substantially related test A test under which a discriminatory classification will be held valid if it furthers a governmental interest that is "important" or "substantial" and it prevents real, not conjectural, harm "in a direct and material way"; applies to classifications such as gender and legitimacy of birth.

substantive coercion A threat that shareholders may agree to sell their shares in an otherwise noncoercive tender offer out of ignorance about the target company's true value. Also occurs when management structures a deal in such a way that deprives shareholders of a meaningful choice.

substantive due process The constitutional guarantee that no person shall be arbitrarily deprived of life, liberty, or property; the essence of substantive due process is protection from arbitrary and unreasonable action.

successor liability Individuals or entities who acquire an interest in a business or in real property may be held liable for personal injury and property or environmental damage resulting from acts (including sale of products) of the predecessor entity or previous owner.

suggestive mark A trademark that suggests something about a product without directly describing it.

summary judgment A procedural device available for disposition of a controversy without trial. A judge will grant summary judgment only if all of the written evidence before the court clearly establishes that there are no disputed issues of material fact and the party who requested the summary judgment is entitled to prevail as a matter of law.

summary jury trial (SJT) Parties to a dispute put their cases before a real jury, which renders a nonbinding decision.

summons The official notice to a defendant that a lawsuit is pending against the defendant in a particular court.

Super 301 A provision of the Omnibus Trade Act of 1988 that required the U.S. Trade Representative to draw up a list of the foreign governments whose practices pose the most significant barriers to U.S. exports, and to immediately commence Section 301 investigations with respect to these practices.

super discharge After completing all payments in accordance with a Chapter 13 bankruptcy plan, the debtor obtains a Chapter 13 discharge (sometimes called a super discharge), which extinguishes otherwise nondischargeable debts (such as claims for fraud, theft, willful and malicious injury, or drunk driving), but not spousal or child support.

superlien An instrument that secures recovery of environmental cleanup response costs incurred by state agencies.

supervisor Anyone possessing specified personnel functions if the exercise of that authority is not of a merely routine or clerical nature, but requires the use of independent judgment.

suppress To prevent the prosecution from introducing evidence.

supranational law A principle of international law, under which nations submit their decision-making authority to a common organization or institution.

surprise The extent to which the supposedly agreed on terms of the bargain are hidden in a densely printed form drafted by the party seeking to enforce the disputed terms.

surviving corporation In a merger of two corporations, the corporation that maintains its corporate existence is the surviving corporation.

syndicate An underwriting group in a public offering; each member agrees to purchase a certain number of the securities of the issuer once the offering is declared effective by the Securities and Exchange Commission.

syndicated loan In a syndicated loan, the lenders enter into concurrent direct obligations with the borrower to make a loan, typically on a pro rata basis. The loan is coordinated by a lead lender that serves as agent for all the lenders in disbursing the funds, collecting payments of interest and principal, and administering and enforcing the loan.

synthetic lease A lease that is treated as a conventional operating lease for accounting purposes (so does not appear on the lessee's balance sheet) but is treated as if the lessee had purchased the property and obtained a loan from the seller for tax purposes.

systems approach to business and society The descriptive framework that integrates legal and societal considerations with mainstream theories of competitive advantage and social responsibility.

T

take-out commitment An agreement by a lender to replace the construction loan with a permanent loan, usually after certain conditions, such as the timely completion of the project, have been met.

takeover A bidder acquires sufficient stock from a corporation's shareholders to obtain control of the corporation.

target The subject of a tender offer or hostile corporate takeover attempt. Also a company that another firm controls after acquiring it via merger, a sale of stock by the target's shareholders, or a sale of substantially all the assets of the target.

tariff classification The tariff on articles imported to the United States is determined by their description on the Harmonized Tariff Schedule.

tariffs The basic tool for limiting imports to protect domestic industries.

tarnishment Dilution of a famous trademark that occurs when use of the famous mark in connection with a particular category of goods or goods of an inferior quality reduces the positive image associated with the products bearing the famous mark.

tax-deferred exchange A transfer of real property for an alternative piece of real property meeting certain requirements.

tax evasion The illegal practice whereby a person intentionally does not pay his or her tax liability.

teleological theory of ethics An ethical theory concerned with the consequences of something. The good of an action is to be judged by the effect of the action on others.

10b5-1 plan A securities trading plan meeting the requirements of SEC Rule 10b5-1. There is a presumption that persons who trade while in possession of material nonpublic information trade on the basis of that information unless the trade is pursuant to a preexisting 10b5–1 plan.

tenancy by the entirety A special type of co-ownership of real property between husband and wife; like joint tenancy, it includes a right of survivorship.

tenants in common The individuals who own undivided interests in a parcel of real property.

tender of delivery Under Article 2 of the Uniform Commercial Code, when the seller notifies the buyer that it has the goods ready for delivery.

tender offer A public offer to all the shareholders of a corporation to buy their shares at a stated price, usually higher than the market price.

term loan A loan for a specified amount funded in a lump sum or in installments to be repaid on a specified maturity date or paid off over a period of time.

term sheet A letter that outlines the terms and conditions on which a lender will lend.

termination The point after the dissolution of a partnership when all the partnership affairs are wound up and partners' authority to act for the partnership is completely extinguished.

termination fee *See* Breakup Fee.

territorial restrictions Restrictions that prevent a dealer or distributor from selling outside a certain territory.

territoriality One of the two prevalent domestic models for addressing international insolvency problems, pursuant to which each nation conducts its own proceeding with respect to the assets located in its jurisdiction and ignores any parallel proceedings in a foreign country.

third-party beneficiary One who does not give consideration for a promise yet has legal rights to enforce the contract. A person is a third-party beneficiary with legal rights when the contracting parties intended to benefit that person.

third-party defense In a case under the Comprehensive Environmental Responsibility, Contribution, and Liability Act, a potentially responsible current owner can assert this defense if the release or disposal of hazardous materials was by a third party who was not an employee and with whom the current owner had no contractual relationship. Also called the *innocent landowner defense*.

Thompson Memorandum The revised "Principles of Federal Prosecution of Business Organizations" issued by Attorney General Larry D. Thompson to establish determinants of whether to prosecute a company. Superseded by principles codified in 2008 in the U.S. Attorney Manual.

360/360 method A method for calculating interest whereby it is assumed that all months have 30 days; thus the monthly interest amounts are always the same.

365/360 method A method for calculating interest whereby the nominal annual interest rate is divided by 360, and the resulting daily rate is then multiplied by the outstanding principal amount and the actual number of days in the payment period.

365/365 method A method for calculating interest whereby the daily rate is determined by dividing the nominal annual interest rate by 365 (or 366, in leap years), then this daily rate is multiplied by the outstanding principal amount and the actual number of days in the payment period.

tip Disclosure of a fact made to an individual and withheld from the general public.

tippee A person who receives inside information.

tipper A person who gives inside information.

tombstone ad A newspaper advertisement surrounded by bold black lines identifying the existence of a public offering and indicating where a prospectus may be obtained.

tort A civil wrong causing injury to a person, his or her property, or certain economic relationships.

total-activity test A combination of tests used to determine where a company engaged in multistate operations is domiciled; considers all aspects of the corporate entity, including the nature and scope of the company's activities.

total cost Variable cost plus fixed costs, such as rent and overhead.

total return equity swap A type of derivative security whereby two counterparties agree to exchange cash flows on two financial instruments over a specific period of time. One counterparty generally buys the equity securities underlying the swap.

trade dress A manifestation of trademark law, the concept of trade dress is to protect the overall look of a product as opposed to just a particular design.

trade name A trade name or a corporate name identifies and symbolizes a business as a whole, as opposed to a trademark, which is used to identify and distinguish the various products and services sold by the business.

Trade Promotion Authority A law that allows the president to negotiate trade agreements and then submit them for an up or down vote by Congress with no amendments permitted.

trade secret Information that derives independent economic value from not being generally known and that is subject to reasonable efforts to maintain its secrecy.

trademark A word or symbol used on goods or with services that indicates their origin.

traditional shelf offerings The registration of (1) securities offered pursuant to employee benefit plans; (2) securities offered or sold pursuant to dividend or interest reinvestment plans; (3) warrants, rights, or securities to be issued upon conversion of other outstanding securities; (4) mortgage-related securities; and (5) securities issued in connection with business combination transactions.

transaction value The price of an imported article indicated on a sales invoice.

transactional immunity The prohibition from prosecution granted a witness that relates to any matter discussed in that person's testimony.

transactional negotiation Negotiation that is forward looking with concern for desired relationships.

transnational insolvency In its simplest form, an insolvency proceeding in one country, with a creditor located in a second country. More complex cases may involve subsidiaries, assets, creditors, and operations in many countries.

treaty An international agreement concluded between states in written form and governed by international law.

trespass to chattels When personal property is interfered with but not taken, destroyed, or substantially altered (i.e., not converted), there is a trespass to chattels. Also called *trespass to personal property*.

trespass to land The intentional invasion of real property (below the surface or in the airspace above) without consent of the owner.

trespass to personal property When personal property is interfered with but not taken, destroyed, or substantially altered (i.e., not converted), there is said to be a trespass to personal property. Also called *trespass to chattels*.

triple net lease A type of industrial lease that requires the tenant to pay all taxes, insurance, and maintenance expenses.

trust (1) A combination of competitors who act together to fix prices, thereby stifling competition. (2) A manner of holding property that is controlled by a trustee for the benefit of a beneficiary.

trustee The legal representative of a bankrupt debtor's estate.

2-28 loans Loans with a low initial interest rate that stays fixed for two years, after which the loan resets to a higher adjustable rate for the remaining twenty-eight years of the loan.

tying arrangement A business arrangement whereby a seller will sell product A (the tying or desired product) to the customer only if the customer purchases product B (the tied product) from the seller.

U

UCC-1 Form In most states, this is the form a secured creditor uses for a financing statement under the Uniform Commercial Code.

ultrahazardous Under tort law, an activity of a defendant is deemed ultrahazardous when it (1) necessarily involves a risk of serious harm to persons or property that cannot be eliminated by the exercise of utmost care and (2) is not a matter of common usage. Also called *abnormally dangerous*.

unavoidably unsafe product A product, such as a vaccine, that is generally beneficial but is known to have harmful side effects in some cases.

unconscionable A contract term that is oppressive or fundamentally unfair.

unconscionability As under common law, unconscionability can be either procedural (relating to the bargaining process) or substantive (relating to the provisions of the contract).

undercapitalization theory A corporation is a separate entity, but its lack of adequate capital may constitute a fraud on the public. May be a basis for piercing corporate veil.

underwriter Any person who has purchased any security from an issuer with a view to, or offers or sells for an issuer in connection with, the distribution of any security.

undisclosed principal Use of an agent so that the third party to an agreement does not know or have reason to know of a principal's identity or existence.

undue hardship An affirmative defense under the Americans with Disabilities Act that relieves an employer of the obligation to make reasonable accommodations for an employee's disability because doing so would constitute an undue hardship for the employer.

undue influence Sufficient influence and power over another as to make genuine assent impossible.

unfair labor practice strike A union strikes an employer for the employer's failure to bargain in good faith.

unfair labor practices Unlawful misconduct by an employer to employees exercising union rights.

unilateral contract A promise given in exchange for an act. Offer can be accepted only by performing the act.

universality A domestic model for addressing international insolvency problems that tracks these proceedings as a single case and treats creditors equally, no matter where they are located.

universalizability An ethical theory that asks whether one would want everyone to perform in this manner.

unjust enrichment The unfair appropriation of the benefits of negotiation of contracts for the party's own use.

unorthodox transaction The purchase or sale by an officer, director, or greater-than-10 percent shareholder that would otherwise result in recoverable short-swing profits but is involuntary and does not involve the payment of cash, and there is no possibility of speculative abuse of insider information.

upstream guaranty A guaranty whereby subsidiaries guarantee the parent corporation's debt, or pledge their assets as security for the parent corporation's debt.

use immunity The prohibition on the use of the testimony of a witness against that witness in connection with the case in which that person is testifying or another case.

useful article doctrine The doctrine that holds that copyrightable pictorial, graphic, and sculptural works include works of artistic craftsmanship insofar as their form but not their mechanical or utilitarian aspects are concerned.

useful life statutes Statutes that provide manufacturers and sellers protection from product liability claims after a specified period of time has elapsed since the product was sold.

usual authority The authority that the agent has been allowed to exercise in the past.

usury Charging an amount of interest on a loan that is in excess of the maximum specified by applicable law.

usury laws State statutes that set legal caps on what interest rates lenders may charge.

usury statutes Laws that limit the interest rate on loans and usually provide that any loan agreement in violation of the statute is unenforceable.

utilitarianism A major teleological system of ethics that stands for the proposition that the ideal is to maximize the total benefit for everyone involved.

utility patent A patent that protects any novel, useful, and nonobvious process, machine, manufacture, or composition of matter; or any novel, useful, and nonobvious improvement of such process, machine, manufacture, or composition of matter.

utility requirement A requirement that an invention must have a practical or real-world benefit in order for a utility patent to be issued.

V

vacate The power of a court of appeal to nullify a previous court's ruling.

value Cash, property, or compensation for past services.

variable cost The cost of producing the next incremental unit.

variable-sum negotiations Negotiations in which mutual gains are possible as parties trade lower valued resources for higher valued ones. Also called *integrative negotiations*.

variance A method of relief from the strict terms of a zoning ordinance that allows a landowner to construct a structure or carry on an activity not otherwise permitted under zoning regulations.

venditur emptor A phrase commonly associated with consumer transactions that means "let the seller beware."

venture capital Money managed by professional investors for investment in new enterprises.

venue The particular county or geographical area in which a court with jurisdiction may hear and determine a case.

vertical agreement An agreement between firms that operate at different levels of production or distribution.

vertical market division An agreement between a company and a dealer or distributor that prevents the dealer or the distributor from selling outside a certain territory or to a certain class of customer.

vertical merger A combination between firms at different points along the chain of distribution.

vertical restraint Unlawful restraint between firms at different levels in the chain of distribution, including price-fixing, market division, tying arrangements, and some franchise agreements.

vested right The right of a developer to develop property sometimes, but not always, obtained when a building permit is issued, substantial work is done, and substantial liabilities are incurred in reliance of that permit.

vesting restrictions Restrictions set by the company that grants a stock option on when the option can be exercised.

veto power The power of the president to prevent permanently or temporarily the enactment of a law created by Congress that does not meet his or her approval.

vicarious copyright infringement A doctrine that imposes liability on a third party for a direct copyright infringer's actions if the third party (a) has the right and ability to control the infringer's acts and (b) receives a direct financial benefit from the infringement.

vicarious liability The imposition of civil or criminal liability on one party (e.g., an employer) for the wrongful acts of another (e.g., an employee). Also called *imputed liability*.

voidable Unenforceable at the option of one party.

voir dire Questioning of potential jurors to determine possible bias.

voluntary conversion The exchange by a holder of preferred stock for common stock on the occurrence of certain events.

voluntary proceeding A voluntary proceeding in bankruptcy filing begins when the debtor files a petition with the bankruptcy court.

W

waiting period The period between the filing of the registration statement and the date the registration statement becomes effective with the SEC. Also called the *quiet period*.

waive To refrain from exercising certain rights.

warranty deed A warranty deed is similar to a grant deed. In addition to the implied warranties contained in a grant deed, the grantor of a warranty deed also expressly warrants the title to and the quiet possession of the property to grantee.

web robots Software programs that search and index the Internet for specific content by visiting websites, requesting documents based on certain criteria, and following up with requests for documents referenced in the documents already retrieved to identify illegal copying.

welfare benefit plans Employee medical, dental, and disability plans that are subject to ERISA's rules on reporting, disclosure, and fiduciary responsibility.

well-known seasoned issuers Firms eligible to use Form S-3 with $700 million of public common equity float and permitted to make unrestricted oral and written offers before the registration statement is filed without violating the gun-jumping provisions.

whistleblowing When an employee reports an employer's unlawful or wrongful conduct to a supervisor, inside counsel or ombudsperson, the board of directors, the government, or the public.

white-collar crime Nonviolent violations of the law by companies or their managers.

willful A defendant acting with knowledge that his conduct is unlawful. Contrast with *knowingly*.

winding up The process of settling partnership affairs after dissolution.

wire fraud A scheme intended to defraud or to obtain money or property by fraudulent means through use of telephone systems.

work made for hire A copyrightable work created by an employee within the scope of his or her employment, or a work in one of nine listed categories that is specially commissioned through a signed writing that states that the work is a "work made for hire."

work-product doctrine Protects information, including the private memoranda and personal thoughts of the attorney, created by the attorney while preparing a case for trial.

workout An out-of-court settlement between debtors and creditors that restructures the debtor's financial affairs in much the same way that a confirmed bankruptcy plan would, but it only binds those who expressly consent.

wraparound financing The transaction in which a new lender lends the owner of mortgaged real property additional funds and agrees to take over the servicing of the first loan. In exchange, the owner executes a deed of trust or mortgage and an all-inclusive note, covering the combined amount of the first and new loans.

writ An order in writing issued under seal in the name of a court or judicial officer commanding the person to whom it is directed to perform or refrain from performing an act specified therein.

writ of certiorari An order written by the U.S. Supreme Court when it decides to hear a case, ordering the lower court to certify the record of proceedings below and send it up to the U.S. Supreme Court.

wrongful discharge An employee termination without good cause that (1) violates public policy; (2) breaches an implied contract; or (3) violates the implied covenant of good faith and fair dealing.

Z

Zakat A tenet of Islamic trade and commerce that allocates certain taxes to deprived and poor people as a welfare contribution.

zero-sum negotiations Negotiations in which the only issue is the distribution of the fixed pie. Also called *distributive negotiations*.

zone of danger The area in which an individual is physically close enough to a victim of an accident as to also be in personal danger.

zone of insolvency There is no test or definition. The law suggests that a company may enter the zone when there is a substantial risk that the company will be unable to pay its debts.

zoning The division of a city into districts and the application of specific land use regulations in each district.

B

E

G

H

J

K

L

M

O

P

S

T

V

W